10-23-02

D0903124

√

**Microsoft**

Core Reference

# PROGRAMMING MICROSOFT
# WINDOWS
## WITH MICROSOFT
# VISUAL BASIC .NET

Microsoft®
.net™

*Charles Petzold*

PUBLISHED BY
Microsoft Press
A Division of Microsoft Corporation
One Microsoft Way
Redmond, Washington 98052-6399

Library of Congress Cataloging-in-Publication Data
Petzold, Charles, 1953-
        Programming Microsoft Windows with Microsoft Visual Basic .NET / Charles Petzold.
                p. cm.
        Includes index.
        ISBN 0-7356-1799-6
        1. Microsoft Visual BASIC.   2. BASIC (Computer program language)   3. Microsoft
Windows (Computer file)   I. Title.

        QA76.73.B3 P4937 2002
        005.2'768--dc21

                                                        2002141419

Printed and bound in the United States of America.

1 2 3 4 5 6 7 8 9     QWT      7 6 5 4 3 2

Distributed in Canada by H.B. Fenn and Company Ltd.

A CIP catalogue record for this book is available from the British Library.

Microsoft Press books are available through booksellers and distributors worldwide. For further information about international editions, contact your local Microsoft Corporation office or contact Microsoft Press International directly at fax (425) 936-7329. Visit our Web site at www.microsoft.com/mspress. Send comments to *mspinput@microsoft.com*.

**Acquisitions Editor:** Danielle Bird
**Project Editor:** Lynn Finnel
**Technical Editor:** Donnie Cameron

Body Part No. X08-81849

# Contents at a Glance

## The Basics

**1** Console Thyself     **1**
**2** Hello, Windows Forms     **43**
**3** Essential Structures     **85**
**4** An Exercise in Text Output     **127**

## Graphics

## The User Interface

**5** Lines, Curves, and Area Fills     **161**
**7** Pages and Transforms     **249**
**9** Text and Fonts     **351**
**11** Images and Bitmaps     **469**
**13** Béziers and Other Splines     **611**
**15** Paths, Regions, and Clipping     **685**
**17** Brushes and Pens     **781**
**19** Font Fun     **909**
**21** Printing     **993**
**23** Metafiles     **1095**

**6** Tapping into the Keyboard     **205**
**8** Taming the Mouse     **295**
**10** The Timer and Time     **425**
**12** Buttons and Labels and Scrolls     **535**
**14** Menus     **641**
**16** Dialog Boxes     **725**
**18** Edit, List, and Spin     **837**
**20** Toolbars and Status Bars     **951**
**22** Tree View and List View     **1039**
**24** Clip, Drag, and Drop     **1133**

## Appendices

**A** Files and Streams     **1179**
**B** Math Class     **1217**
**C** String Theory     **1233**

# Table of Contents

Introduction     xvii

**1**    **Console Thyself**     **1**

    The Return of the Console     2

    Anatomy of a Program     6

    .NET Namespaces     7

    String Formatting     9

    Visual Basic Data Types     11

    The Leap to Objects     16

    Shared Methods     21

    Exception Handling     23

    Throwing Exceptions     25

    Getting and Setting Properties     27

    Constructors     31

    Instances and Inheritance     34

    A Bigger Picture     38

    Naming Conventions     39

    Beyond the Console     40

**2**    **Hello, Windows Forms**     **43**

    The Message Box     45

    The Form     51

    Showing the Form     53

    It's an Application and We Want to Run It     55

    Variations on a Theme     57

    Form Properties     58

    Event-Driven Input     60

    Handling the *Paint* Event     62

    Displaying Text     66

    The *Paint* Event Is Special!     71

    Multiple Forms, Multiple Handlers     71

    Inheriting Forms     74

    The *OnPaint* Method     76

Is the Module Necessary? 77
Events and "On" Methods 79

**3    Essential Structures    85**

Classes and Structures 86
Two-Dimensional Coordinate Points 87
Arrays of Points 89
The *Size* Structure 90
The Float Versions 91
A Rectangle Is a Point and a Size 93
Rectangle Properties and Methods 94
A Nice-Sized Form 97
The Form and the Client 99
Point Conversions 103
The *Color* Structure 104
The 141 Color Names 105
Pens and Brushes 107
System Colors 108
The Known Colors 112
What to Use? 112
Getting a Feel for Repaints 113
Centering Hello World 116
Measuring the String 120
Text in a Rectangle 122

**4    An Exercise in Text Output    127**

System Information 127
Spacing Lines of Text 128
Property Values 129
Formatting into Columns 131
Everything Is an Object 133
Listing the System Information 137
Windows Forms and Scroll Bars 140
Scrolling a Panel Control 141
The Heritage of *ScrollableControl* 145
Scrolling Without Controls 146
Actual Numbers 149

Keeping It Green                                             150
Don't Be a Pig                                              153
Reflecting on the Future                                    155

**5   Lines, Curves, and Area Fills                          161**

How to Get a Graphics Object                                162
Pens, Briefly                                              163
Straight Lines                                             165
An Introduction to Printing                                167
Properties and State                                       173
Anti-Aliasing                                              174
Multiple Connected Lines                                   177
Curves and Parametric Equations                            182
The Ubiquitous Rectangle                                   185
Generalized Polygons                                       188
Easier Ellipses                                            188
Arcs and Pies                                              190
Filling Rectangles, Ellipses, and Pies                     197
Off by 1                                                   199
Polygons and the Filling Mode                              200

**6   Tapping into the Keyboard                              205**

Ignoring the Keyboard                                      205
Who's Got the Focus?                                       206
Keys and Characters                                        207
Keys Down and Keys Up                                      209
The *Keys* Enumeration                                     210
Testing the Modifier Keys                                  221
Reality Check                                              222
A Keyboard Interface for SysInfo                           223
*KeyPress* for Characters                                  225
Control Characters                                         225
Looking at the Keys                                        226
Invoking the Win32 API                                     231
Handling Input from Foreign Keyboards                      233
Input Focus                                                237

The Missing Caret                                                     238

Echoing Key Characters                                                242

Right-to-Left Problems                                                246

**7    Pages and Transforms                                          249**

Device Independence Through Text                                      249

How Much Is That in Real Money?                                       250

Dots Per Inch                                                         253

What's with the Printer?                                              254

Manual Conversions                                                    256

Page Units and Page Scale                                             258

Pen Widths                                                            263

Page Transforms                                                       266

Saving the Graphics State                                             267

Metrical Dimensions                                                   268

Arbitrary Coordinates                                                 272

What You Can't Do                                                     275

Hello, World Transform                                                276

The Big Picture                                                       281

Linear Transforms                                                     282

Introducing Matrixes                                                  285

The Matrix Class                                                      286

Shear and Shear Alike                                                 289

Combining Transforms                                                  291

**8    Taming the Mouse                                              295**

The Dark Side of the Mouse                                            296

Ignoring the Mouse                                                    297

Some Quick Definitions                                                297

Information About the Mouse                                           298

The Mouse Wheel                                                       299

The Four Basic Mouse Events                                           300

Doing the Wheel                                                       303

Mouse Movement                                                        307

Tracking and Capturing the Mouse                                     309

Adventures in Tracking                                       312
Clicks and Double-Clicks                                     322
Mouse-Related Properties                                     323
Entering, Leaving, Hovering                                  324
The Mouse Cursor                                             325
An Exercise in Hit-Testing                                   334
Adding a Keyboard Interface                                  336
Putting the Children to Work                                 338
Hit-Testing Text                                             343
Scribbling with the Mouse                                    345

**9    Text and Fonts                                        351**

Fonts Under Windows                                          351
Talking Type                                                 352
Font Heights and Line Spacing                                354
Default Fonts                                                356
Variation on a Font                                          357
Creating Fonts by Name                                       359
A Point Size by Any Other Name…                              364
Clash of the Units                                           369
Font Properties and Methods                                  371
New Fonts from *FontFamily*                                  378
Understanding the Design Metrics                             380
Arrays of Font Families                                      385
Font Collections                                             391
Variations on *DrawString*                                   392
Anti-Aliased Text                                            394
Measuring the String                                         396
The *StringFormat* Options                                   398
Grid Fitting and Text Fitting                                400
Horizontal and Vertical Alignment                            403
The Hotkey Display                                           408
A Clip and a Trim                                            410
Start a Tab                                                  417

**10    The Timer and Time**                                                **425**

    The *Timer* Class                                              426

    The *DateTime* Structure                                       430

    Local Time and Universal Time                                  432

    The Tick Count                                                 436

    Calendars Around the World                                     439

    A Readable Rendition                                            441

    A Simple Culture-Specific Clock                                447

    The Retro Look                                                 452

    An Analog Clock                                                457

    A Little Puzzle Called *Jeu de Taquin*                         463

**11    Images and Bitmaps**                                               **469**

    Bitmap Support Overview                                        471

    Bitmap File Formats                                            472

    Loading and Drawing                                            477

    Image Information                                              482

    Rendering the Image                                            487

    Fitting to a Rectangle                                         490

    Rotate and Shear                                               495

    Displaying Part of the Image                                   497

    Drawing on the Image                                           502

    More on the *Image* Class                                      507

    The *Bitmap* Class                                             510

    Hello World with a Bitmap                                      513

    The Shadow Bitmap                                              514

    Binary Resources                                               517

    Animation                                                      521

    The Image List                                                 528

    The Picture Box                                                531

**12    Buttons and Labels and Scrolls (Oh My!)**                         **535**

    Buttons and Clicks                                             536

    Keyboard and Mouse                                             540

    Control Issues                                                 541

    Deeper into Buttons                                            542

Appearance and Alignment                                      546
Buttons with Bitmaps                                          549
Multiple Handlers or One?                                     552
Drawing Your Own Buttons                                      552
Dropping Anchor                                               557
Dock Around the Clock                                         561
Children of the Form                                          564
Z-Order                                                       567
The Check Box                                                 569
The Three-State Alternative                                   573
The Label Control                                             574
Tab Stops and Tab Order                                       577
Identifying the Controls                                      578
The Auto-Scale Option                                         581
A Hexadecimal Calculator                                      587
Radio Buttons and Group Boxes                                592
Scroll Bars                                                   596
The Track Bar Alternative                                     604

**13   Béziers and Other Splines                             611**
The Bézier Spline in Practice                                612
A More Stylish Clock                                         617
Collinear Béziers                                            619
Circles and Arcs with Béziers                               621
Bézier Art                                                   624
The Mathematical Derivation                                  626
The Canonical Spline                                         630
Canonical Curve Derivation                                   638

**14   Menus                                                641**
Menus and Menu Items                                        642
Menu Shortcut Keys                                          645
Your First Menu                                             647
Unconventional Menus                                        651
*MenuItem* Properties and Event                             653

Checking the Items                                            655
Working with Context Menus                                    659
The Menu Item Collection                                       663
The Standard Menu (A Proposal)                                669
The Owner-Draw Option                                         674

**15    Paths, Regions, and Clipping                          685**
A Problem and Its Solution                                    685
The Path, More Formally                                       691
Creating the Path                                             694
Rendering the Path                                            698
Path Transforms                                               702
Other Path Modifications                                      705
Clipping with Paths                                           712
Clipping Bitmaps                                              717
Regions and Clipping                                          721

**16    Dialog Boxes                                         725**
Your First Modal Dialog Box                                   726
Modal Dialog Box Termination                                  731
Accept and Cancel                                             733
Screen Location                                               734
The About Box                                                 738
Defining Properties in Dialog Boxes                           742
Implementing an Apply Button                                  747
The Modeless Dialog Box                                       751
The Common Dialog Boxes                                       755
Choosing Fonts and Colors                                     756
Using the Windows Registry                                    763
The Open File Dialog Box                                      768
The Save File Dialog Box                                      776

**17    Brushes and Pens                                     781**
Filling in Solid Colors                                       782
Hatch Brushes                                                 782
The Rendering Origin                                          792

Texture Brushes 795

Linear Gradient Brushes 800

Path Gradient Brushes 810

Tiling the Brush 814

Pens Can Be Brushes Too 822

A Dash of Style 826

Caps and Joins 829

**18    Edit, List, and Spin                                    837**

Single-Line Text Boxes 837

Multiline Text Boxes 842

Cloning Notepad 845

The Notepad Clone with File I/O 851

Notepad Clone Continued 860

Special-Purpose Text Boxes 875

The Rich Text Box 876

ToolTips 876

The List Box 884

List Box + Text Box = Combo Box 891

Up-Down Controls 897

**19    Font Fun                                               909**

Getting Started 909

Brushed Text 911

Font Transforms 919

Text and Paths 930

Nonlinear Transforms 944

**20    Toolbars and Status Bars                               951**

The Basic Status Bar 952

The Status Bar and Auto-Scroll 954

Status Bar Panels 957

*StatusBarPanel* Properties 959

Menu Help 963

The Basic Toolbar 970

Toolbar Variations 974

Toolbar Events 978

Toolbar Styles 983

**21**   **Printing**                                                          **993**

    Printers and Their Settings                                            994

    Page Settings                                                         1002

    Defining a Document                                                   1006

    Handling *PrintDocument* Events                                       1008

    The Page Dimensions                                                   1014

    The Print Controller                                                  1018

    Using the Standard Print Dialog Box                                   1023

    Setting Up the Page                                                   1027

    Print Preview                                                         1031

**22**   **Tree View and List View**                                          **1039**

    Splitsville                                                           1039

    Tree Views and Tree Nodes                                             1055

    Images in Tree Views                                                  1059

    Tree View Events                                                      1060

    Node Navigation                                                       1062

    The Directory Tree                                                    1065

    Displaying Images                                                     1071

    List View Basics                                                      1078

    List View Events                                                      1086

**23**   **Metafiles**                                                        **1095**

    Loading and Rendering Existing Metafiles                              1096

    Metafile Sizes and Rendering                                          1098

    Converting Metafiles to Bitmaps                                       1106

    Creating New Metafiles                                                1108

    The Metafile Boundary Rectangle                                       1116

    Metafiles and the Page Transform                                      1119

    The Metafile Type                                                     1122

    Enumerating the Metafile                                              1125

**24**   **Clip, Drag, and Drop**                                             **1133**

    Items and Formats                                                     1134

    The Tiny (But Powerful) *Clipboard* Class                             1134

    Getting Objects from the Clipboard                                    1136

    Clipboard Data Formats                                                1145

Clipboard Viewers                                          1155
Setting Multiple Clipboard Formats                        1164
Drag and Drop                                             1169

**Appendix A    Files and Streams                         1179**

The Most Essential File I/O Class                         1179
*FileStream* Properties and Methods                       1182
The Problem with *FileStream*                             1186
Other Stream Classes                                      1187
Reading and Writing Text                                  1188
Binary File I/O                                           1197
The *Environment* Class                                   1200
File and Path Name Parsing                                1202
Parallel Classes                                          1204
Working with Directories                                  1206
File Manipulation and Information                         1212

**Appendix B    Math Class                                1217**

Numeric Types                                             1217
Checking Integer Overflow                                 1218
The Decimal Type                                          1219
Floating-Point Infinity and NaNs                          1222
The *Math* Class                                          1224
Floating-Point Remainders                                 1227
Powers and Logarithms                                     1227
Trigonometric Functions                                   1228

**Appendix C    String Theory                             1233**

The *Char* Type                                           1235
String Constructors and Properties                        1237
Copying Strings                                           1239
Converting Strings                                        1241
Concatenating Strings                                     1241
Comparing Strings                                         1243
Searching the String                                      1247
Trimming and Padding                                      1249
String Manipulation                                       1251

Formatting Strings                                    1252
Array Sorting and Searching                           1252
The *StringBuilder* Class                             1255

Index                                                 1259

# Introduction

This book is a translation of my book *Programming Microsoft Windows with C#* into the programming language known as Microsoft Visual Basic .NET. This book and that one are basically the same except for the sample programming code.

Both books show you how to write programs that run under Microsoft Windows. There are a number of ways to write such programs. In these two books, I use a new class library called *Windows Forms*. The Windows Forms class library is part of the Microsoft .NET ("dot net") Framework unveiled in the summer of 2000 and introduced about a year and a half later.

The Microsoft .NET Framework is an extensive collection of classes that provides programmers with much of what they need to write Internet, Web, and Windows applications. Much of the media coverage of .NET has focused on the Web programming. This book discusses the *other* part of .NET. You use Windows Forms to write traditional stand-alone Windows applications (what are now sometimes called *client* applications) or front ends for distributed applications.

Windows Forms provides almost everything you need to write full-fledged Windows applications. The big omission is multimedia support. There's not even a Windows Forms function to beep the computer's speaker! I was tempted to write my own multimedia classes but restrained myself under the assumption (reasonable, I hope) that the next release of Windows Forms will include multimedia support that is flexible, powerful, and easy to use.

The classes defined in the .NET Framework are language-neutral. In conjunction with the release of the .NET Framework, Microsoft has released new versions of Visual Basic and C++ that can use these classes, as well as the new programming language C#. Other language vendors are adapting their own languages to use the .NET classes.

The language neutrality of .NET is made possible by the Common Language Specification (CLS), which is a document that describes what features a programming language requires to use the .NET Framework. Compilers designed for .NET usually convert source code to an intermediate language in an .exe file. At runtime, the intermediate language is compiled into appropriate microprocessor machine code by the .NET Common Language Runtime (CLR). Thus, the .NET Framework is potentially platform independent.

# Windows and Basic

Microsoft released the first version of Windows in the fall of 1985. Since then, Windows has been progressively updated and enhanced, most dramatically in Windows NT (1993) and Windows 95 (1995), when Windows moved from a 16-bit to a 32-bit architecture.

When Windows was first released, there was really only one way to write Windows applications, and that was by using the C programming language to access the Windows application programming interface (API). Although it was also possible to access the Windows API using Microsoft Pascal, this approach was rarely used.

Over the years, many other languages have been adapted for doing Windows programming. In 1991, Microsoft released Visual Basic 1.0 for Windows, a revolutionary product that allowed programmers to design their applications interactively by dragging controls onto a form. Visual Basic 1.0 provided a higher-level programming interface than the API available to C programmers. Visual Basic was progressively enhanced over the years until the 1998 release of Visual Basic 6.0.

Visual Basic .NET represents a break from Visual Basic 6.0—not so much in the language itself, which has remained pretty much the same, but in the way that programs interface with Windows. In Visual Basic .NET, this interface is provided by the class libraries implemented in the .NET Framework.

# User Requirements

To use this book most profitably, you need to be able to compile and run Visual Basic .NET programs. To compile the programs, you need a Visual Basic .NET compiler. To run these programs, you need the .NET runtime (also called the Common Language Runtime), which is a collection of dynamic-link libraries.

Both these items are included in the software product known as Microsoft Visual Basic .NET, a modern integrated development environment. Alternatively, you can purchase the more extensive and more expensive Microsoft Visual Studio .NET, which will also let you program in C++ and C# in addition to Visual Basic.

If you prefer a more rugged approach, you can instead download the free .NET Framework software development kit (SDK). The download includes a command-line Visual Basic .NET compiler and the .NET runtime. First go to *http://msdn.microsoft.com/downloads*. At the left, select Software Development Kits, and then look for the .NET Framework SDK. You may have to select the .NET Framework Redistributable page and then find a link there. (Keep in mind that this Web site, as with all the Web sites mentioned throughout this book, could change, move, or in some cases disappear completely, at any time.)

I've written this book under the assumption that you at least know how to program in an earlier version of Visual Basic, and you have a passing familiarity with concepts of object-oriented languages. I've devoted the first chapter to helping you get up to speed on some new features of Visual Basic .NET.

I sometimes make reference to the Windows API in this book. You can consult my book *Programming Windows* (Fifth Edition, Microsoft Press, 1998) to learn more about the Windows API.

# System Requirements

As I mentioned in the preceding section, to use this book effectively, you need to be able to compile and run Visual Basic .NET programs. System requirements are as follows:

- Microsoft .NET Framework SDK (minimum); Microsoft Visual Basic .NET or Microsoft Visual Studio .NET (preferred)

- Microsoft Windows NT 4.0, Windows 2000, or Windows XP.

To run your Visual Basic .NET programs on other computers requires that the .NET runtime (also referred to as the .NET Framework *redistributable package*) be installed on those machines. That package comes with the .NET Framework SDK, Visual Basic .NET, and Visual Studio .NET. The redistributable package can be installed on the versions of Windows already mentioned as well as Windows 98 and Windows Millennium Edition (Me).

As discussed shortly, the sample files in this book are downloadable from the Microsoft Press Web site. If you want to install them to your hard drive, you'll need approximately 3.5 MB of additional hard disk space. (Fully compiled, the samples use just over 13 MB.)

# The Organization of This Book

When Windows 1.0 was first released, the entire API was implemented in three dynamic link libraries named KERNEL, USER, and GDI. Although the DLLs associated with Windows have become much more voluminous, it is still useful to divide Windows function calls (or framework classes) into these three categories: The kernel calls are those implemented in the architectural interior of the operating system, and are generally concerned with tasking, memory management, and file I/O. The term *user* refers to the user interface. These are functions to create windows, use menus and dialog boxes, and display controls such as buttons and scroll bars. GDI is the Graphics Device Interface, that part of Windows responsible for displaying graphical output (including text) on the screen and printer.

This book begins with four introductory chapters. Starting with Chapter 5 (which shows you how to draw lines and curves) and continuing through Chapter 24 (on the Windows clipboard), the chapters alternate between graphics topics (odd-numbered chapters) and user interface topics (even-numbered chapters).

Normally a book like this wouldn't spend much time with non-Windows topics such as file I/O, floating-point mathematics, and string manipulation. However, because the .NET Framework is so new, I found myself wishing I had a coherent guide through those classes. So I wrote such guides myself. These are included as three appendices on files, math, and strings. You can consult these appendices any time after reading Chapter 1.

I've tried to order the chapters—and the topics within the chapters—so that each topic builds on succeeding topics with a minimal number of "forward references." I've written the book so that you can read it straight through, much like you'd read the uncut version of *The Stand* or *The Decline and Fall of the Roman Empire*. Of course, it's good if a book as long as this one serves as a reference as well as a narrative. For that reason, many of the important methods, properties, and enumerations used in Windows Forms programming are listed in tables in the chapters in which they are discussed. A book of even this size cannot hope to cover *everything* in Windows Forms, however. It is no substitute for the official class documentation.

Windows Forms programs require little overhead, so this book includes plenty of code examples in the form of complete programs. You are free to cut and paste pieces of code from these programs into your own programs. (That's what these programs are *for*.) But don't distribute the code or programs as is. That's what this book is for.

As in earlier versions of Visual Basic, Visual Basic .NET allows you to interactively design the appearance of your applications. You position various controls (buttons, scroll bars, and so forth) on the surface of your window, and Visual Basic .NET generates the code. While such techniques are very useful for quickly designing dialog boxes and front-panel types of applications, I have ignored that feature of Visual Basic .NET in this book.

In this book, we're not going to let Visual Basic .NET generate code for us. In this book, we're going to learn how to write our own code.

# Support

The sample programs in this book are downloadable from the Microsoft Press Web site at *http://www.microsoft.com/mspress/books/6259.asp*. (There is a link to that page from my Web site at *www.charlespetzold.com*.) You can load the solution files (.sln) or project files (.vbproj) into Visual Basic .NET and recompile the programs.

Every effort has been made to ensure the accuracy of this book and the contents of this source code. Microsoft Press provides corrections for books through the World Wide Web at the following address:

*http://www.microsoft.com/mspress/support/*

To connect directly to the Microsoft Press Knowledge Base and enter a query regarding a question or issue that you may have, go to:

*http://www.microsoft.com/mspress/support/search.asp*

If you have comments, questions, or ideas regarding this book, please send them to Microsoft Press using either of the following methods:

Postal Mail:

Microsoft Press
Attn: Programming Microsoft Windows with Microsoft Visual Basic .NET Editor
One Microsoft Way
Redmond, WA 98052-6399

E-mail:

MSPINPUT@MICROSOFT.COM

Please note that product support is not offered through the above mail addresses. For support information regarding Visual Basic .NET, Visual Studio, or the .NET Framework, please visit the Microsoft Product Support Web site at

*http://support.microsoft.com*

# How to Translate a Book

I finished *Programming Microsoft Windows with C#* in November 2001. In early February 2002, Microsoft Press asked me if I'd be interested in translating the book to Visual Basic .NET. I thought that sounded like a fun project, so I immediately agreed to do it.

The first job was to write a program (in C#) that would translate the C# programs in the book to Visual Basic .NET. The C# book contained over 300 source code files, so I knew that if I couldn't automate that job, the Visual Basic .NET book would take a lot longer to finish. My conversion program was a complete hack, very sloppy, specifically tailored to my C# coding style, and ignorant of language features that I hadn't used. By the end of a week, I wanted to completely rewrite it, but by that time it was also successfully translating about 95 percent of my code. I decided to do the rest of the conversion manually with the help of global search-and-replace operations.

C# is a case-sensitive language, and I used that fact in naming variables in my C# code. For example, if I had only one object of type *Font*, I'd name it *font*. At first I assumed that Visual Basic .NET—being a case-*in*sensitive language—wouldn't allow such a thing. I was wrong. The compiler accepted an object named *font* just fine. However, if *font* were not defined correctly to begin with, the Visual Basic .NET editor would try to "fix" it by capitalizing the first letter to match the *Font* class! To avoid any confusion among programmers unaccustomed to case-sensitive programming, I decided not to duplicate class names with object names. My *font* objects became *fnt* objects, and in the process, I think I achieved a higher degree of consistency with object-naming conventions than in the C# book.

Were there some deficiencies of Visual Basic .NET that I encountered? Very few. In C#, arithmetic operators (+, -, and so forth) and comparison operators (<, >, and so forth) can be overloaded by structures and classes. For example, you can add *Size* objects using the normal plus sign. In Visual Basic .NET you need to use an *op_addition* method. Similar methods exist for comparing objects, and for casting them.

The absence of unsigned integers in Visual Basic .NET barely affected the code conversion. I used an unsigned long integer in the HexCalc program in Chapter 12, but that was easily changed to a signed long. The more serious problem in HexCalc was the use of C# symbols for labeling the buttons of the calculator!

Doing a conversion like this revealed some other interesting differences between the two languages. For example, in C#, methods are private by default; in Visual Basic .NET, they're public by default. I pondered for a while which approach made more sense, and came to the conclusion that neither did. Methods should be *protected* by default. There should be a reason—and a keyword—to make a particular method either public or private.

Moving to the text of the book, I attacked a hot-off-the-press copy of *Programming Microsoft Windows with C#* with colored felt-tip pens, marking every little C# keyword, code snippet, and C#-centric notion I could find. To convert the many tables of methods that appear in the book, I wrote a Visual Basic for Applications script. I never got it to work quite right, but it made the process much easier. I made all the other changes manually to the Microsoft Word files, using global searches only to double-check my manual efforts. (The most common single item requiring change? The C# *static* keyword became *Shared*.)

Some necessary changes to the book were not quite obvious at first. As you can see by leafing through the pages that follow, there are numerous tables of *properties*. When I originally designed the format of these tables for the C# book, I put the type of the property in the first column and the property itself in the second. That's the order a C# programmer would see looking at source code. But that's not what a Visual Basic .NET programmer would see. The first two columns of these many tables had to be swapped to show the property name first, then the type.

Have my editors and I managed to eliminate every last remnant of C# from this book? I'm not so sure. Just within the past couple of days—rereading the concluding chapters and appendices for the very last time before I sign off—I've deleted a semicolon (used in C# to terminate statements) and eliminated a reference to "doubles slashes" (the C# comment indicator). I hope that not much else has eluded our search.

Prior to the release of .NET, translating a C or C++ Windows programming book into Visual Basic would have been unthinkable. It's really a credit to the Common Language Specification and the .NET Framework that this job went as smoothly as it did. Microsoft has truly put together a system where one's choice of programming language has become simple personal preference.

## Special Thanks

Writing is usually a very solitary job, but fortunately there are always several people who make the work much easier.

I want to thank my agent Claudette Moore of the Moore Literary Agency for getting both projects going and handling all the messy legal stuff.

As usual, the folks at Microsoft Press were an absolute pleasure to work with and once again have helped prevent me from embarrassing myself. Were it not for editors, my books would be infested with gibberish and buggy code. Project editor Sally Stickney and technical editor Jean Ross worked on the C# book, and in doing so contributed much to this one as well. Building on Sally and Jean's fine work were project editor Lynn Finnel and technical editor Donnie Cameron. While editors may seem superhuman at times, they are regrettably not. Any bugs, incomprehensible sentences, or C# keywords that remain in the book are my fault and no one else's.

Let me not forget to cite Johannes Brahms for providing musical accompaniment while I worked, and Anthony Trollope for escapist literature in the evenings.

My Sunday, Tuesday, and Thursday gatherings of friends continue to help and support me in ways that are sometimes obvious, sometimes subtle, but always invaluable.

And most of all, I want to thank my fiancée, Deirdre, for providing a very different (non .NET) framework for me in which to live, work, and love.

*Charles Petzold*
*New York City*
*June, 2002*

# Console Thyself

In 1964, the very first instruction manual for a new programming language called the Beginner's All Purpose Symbolic Instruction Code (BASIC) began with the following sample program[1]:

```
10 LET X=(7+8)/3
20 PRINT X
30 END
```

BASIC was developed at Dartmouth College in New Hampshire by John G. Kemeny and Thomas E. Kurtz. Although the designers of the language were mathematicians, they wished to create a system that would offer the liberal arts majors who predominated at Dartmouth friendly and easy access. At a time when most programming involved punch cards, Kemeny and Kurtz created an interactive time-sharing system on a General Electric computer connected to teletypewriters. The BASIC programming language had elements of ALGOL and FORTRAN but stressed simplicity over machine efficiency. Students typed in programs on the teletypewriters and entered RUN to compile and execute their programs. (The first BASIC system was *not* an interpreter, as is commonly believed. But many subsequent BASIC implementations on minicomputers and personal computers were interpreted.)

Although certainly forward looking at the time, the original BASIC ran on what is now considered a quaint and old-fashioned text-only computer interface known as a *command line* or *console*. As a user types on the teletypewriter keyboard, the device prints the characters on a roll of paper and sends

---

1. Kemeny, John G. and Thomas E. Kurtz, *BASIC Instruction Manual* (Hanover, New Hampshire: Dartmouth College, 1964), page 4, as quoted in Wexelblat, Richard L., ed., *History of Programming Languages* (New York: Academic Press, 1981), page 522. The latter book is also the source of the historical information here.

them to a remote computer. The computer responds with characters of its own, which the teletypewriter receives and also displays on the paper. In this input/ output model, there's no concept of positioning text at a specific location on the page. The *PRINT* statement simply displays the text wherever the teletype-writer print head (or later, the cursor of a video-based command line) happens to be at the time.

In the many years of evolution from BASIC to Microsoft Visual Basic .NET, the language has gone through many changes. BASIC originally made no distinction between integer and floating-point numbers; today it is considered proper programming practice to define all variables with a specific type before they are used. These days we also see the wisdom of grouping code and data into named functions, subroutines, modules, structures, and classes.

The *LET* keyword (gradually phased out over the years) indicated an assignment statement, and was originally introduced because a statement like

```
X=X+1
```

might be confusing to a novice programmer. The *PRINT* statement is still around in Visual Basic .NET, but it's now used almost solely for files. The numbers that began each program line in BASIC were part of the line editor used on the teletypewriter, and were also targets for GOTO statements. The presence or absence or a number at the beginning of the line helped the operating system distinguish between program statements and commands.

# The Return of the Console

Visual Basic .NET takes the Beginner's All Purpose Symbolic Instruction Code probably further than it's ever gone before. As you will see, Visual Basic .NET is now a full-fledged object-oriented programming language.

Yet at the same time, more traditional elements of programming have been reintroduced into the language and the Microsoft .NET Framework. In particular, Visual Basic .NET brings back the concept of console I/O. Console programs make use of the command-line interface in Microsoft Windows known as the Command Prompt or MS-DOS Prompt. While the command-line interface has been largely made obsolete by graphical interfaces, command-line programs are often simpler than programs written for graphical environments, so they remain a good place to begin learning a new programming language, or to brush up on one's skills.

That first BASIC program from 1964 translated to Visual Basic .NET looks like this:

**FirstBasicProgram.vb**

```
'----------------------------------------------------
' FirstBasicProgram.vb (c) 2002 by Charles Petzold
'----------------------------------------------------

Module FirstBasicProgram
    Sub Main()
        Dim X As Single = (7 + 8) / 3
        System.Console.WriteLine(X)
    End Sub
End Module
```

You have a couple options in compiling this program, depending on how much money you want to spend and how much modern programming convenience you wouldn't mind foregoing.

The cheapest approach is to download the .NET Framework Software Development Kit (SDK) from *http://msdn.microsoft.com*. (At the left, select Downloads, then Developer Downloads, then Software Development Kits, and then Microsoft .NET Framework SDK. It's about 130 megabytes.) Installing the SDK also installs the dynamic-link libraries (DLLs) that comprise the .NET runtime environment. The .NET technical documentation is available in a Windows-based program. You also get a command-line Visual Basic .NET compiler that you can use to compile the programs shown in these pages.

If you choose the SDK route, you can use any text editor—from Microsoft Notepad on up—to write Visual Basic .NET programs. The Visual Basic .NET compiler is named vbc.exe. You compile FirstBasicProgram.vb on a command line like so:

```
vbc firstbasicprogram.vb
```

That's it. There's no link step involved. (As you'll see in the next chapter, compiling a Windows Forms program rather than a console program requires some additional compiler arguments.) The compiler produces a file named First-BasicProgram.exe that you can run on the command line.

You can also create, compile, and run this program in Visual Basic .NET (or the more expensive superset called Microsoft Visual Studio .NET), the latest version of Microsoft's integrated development environment. Visual Basic .NET is a must for professional Visual Basic developers. For certain types of Windows Forms programs—those that treat the program's window as a form that contains controls such as buttons, text-entry fields, and scroll bars—it's extremely useful. However, it's not strictly necessary. I've found that one of the real pleasures of doing Windows programming with the Windows Forms library is that no separate files are involved. Virtually everything goes in the source code files, and everything in those files can be entered with your own fingers and brain.

The following paragraphs describe the steps I took to create the programs in this book using Visual Basic .NET and Visual Studio .NET. I'll generally refer just to Visual Basic .NET when I'm actually talking about both environments. However, if you're running Visual Basic .NET as opposed to Visual Studio .NET, you'll need to add two small files to your installation if you want to follow the steps I describe in this book. These files are named VisualBasicEmpty-Project.vsdir and VisualBasicEmptyProject.vbproj, and they are located in the root directory of the downloadable source code for this book. Copy both these files to this directory on your hard drive:

```
C:\Program Files\Microsoft Visual Studio .NET\Vb7\VBProjects
```

You don't need to do this if you've installed Visual Studio .NET rather than Visual Basic .NET.

Every sample program in this book is a Visual Basic .NET *project*, and each project has its own directory of disk storage. In Visual Basic .NET, projects are generally grouped into *solutions*; I created a solution for every chapter in this book. Every solution is also a directory. Projects are subdirectories of the solution directory.

To create a solution, select the menu item File | New | Blank Solution. In the New Project dialog box, select a disk location for this solution and type in a name for the solution. This is how I created solutions for each of the chapters in this book.

When you have a solution loaded in Visual Basic .NET, you can create projects in that solution. Select the menu item File | Add Project | New Project. (You can also right-click the solution name in Solution Explorer and select Add | New Project from the context menu.) In the Add New Project dialog box, select a project type of Visual Basic Projects. You can choose from several templates. If you want to avoid having Visual Basic .NET generate code for you—I personally prefer writing my own code—the template to choose is Empty Project. That's how I created the projects for this book. (Empty Project is included with Visual Studio .NET but not Visual Basic .NET. The two files you copied to your hard drive add Empty Project functionality to Visual Basic .NET.)

Within a project, you can use the Project | Add New Item menu option to create new Visual Basic source code files. (Again, you can also right-click the project name in Solution Explorer and select this item from the context menu.) In the Add New Item dialog box, in the Categories list, choose Local Project Items. In the Templates section, choose Code File. If you use that template, Visual Basic .NET won't generate code for you.

You can set properties for the project by selecting Properties from the Project menu, or by right-clicking on the project name and selecting Properties.

On the left, choose General under Common Properties. On the right, make sure Output Type indicates Console Application. You may have to change this if you're running Visual Studio .NET (but not Visual Basic .NET). When I set up projects for this book, I also clicked Build on the left of the Project Property Pages and set Option Strict to On. Option Explicit should be On by default. These options cause the Visual Basic .NET compiler to perform some additional—and to my mind, important—consistency checks. To enable these options when compiling on the command line, use:

```
vbc firstbasicprogram.vb /optionstrict /optionexplicit
```

Within a solution you can set a startup project by right-clicking the project name with the mouse and selecting Set As Startup Project, or by selecting that option from the Project menu. You can then compile and run the program by selecting Start Without Debugging from the Debug menu, or by pressing CTRL+F5. If all is well, a console window will be created, the program will display its output, and you'll see the message "Press any key to continue" to dismiss the console window. If you're compiling on the command line, simply enter the program name on the command line:

```
firstbasicprogram
```

The program will run, display its output, and terminate. The MS-DOS command line prompt will then return.

Regardless of whether you create and compile FirstBasicProgram on the command line or in Visual Basic .NET, the .exe file will be small, about 5 KB or 6 KB, depending on whether the compiler puts debugging information into it. The executable consists of statements in Microsoft Intermediate Language (MSIL). MSIL has been submitted as a proposed standard to the European Computer Manufacturer's Association (ECMA), where it is known as the Common Intermediate Language (CIL). When you run the program, the .NET common language runtime compiles the intermediate language to your computer's native machine code and links it with the appropriate .NET DLLs. Currently, you're probably using an Intel-based machine, so the code that the runtime generates is 32-bit Intel x86 machine code.

You can look at MSIL by running the Intermediate Language Disassembler ildasm.exe from the command line:

```
ildasm firstbasicprogram.exe
```

For documentation on the MSIL instruction set, download the file identified with the acronym "CLI" from *http://msdn.microsoft.com/net/ecma*. Other files on that page may also be useful. You can even write code directly in MSIL and assemble that code using the Intermediate Language Assembler ilasm.exe.

Because programs written in Visual Basic .NET are compiled to an intermediate language rather than directly to machine code, the executables are platform independent. Sometime in the future, a .NET runtime environment may be ported to non-Intel machines. If that happens, the executables you're creating today will run on those machines. (Let me add "in theory" so as not to seem hopelessly naïve.)

By using the .NET Framework and programming in Visual Basic .NET, you're also creating *managed code*. This is code that can be examined and analyzed by another program to determine the extent of the code's actions. Managed code is a necessary prerequisite to exchanging binary executables over the Internet.

## Anatomy of a Program

Here's a more traditional first program that simply displays the text "Hello, world!" on the console

```
ConsoleHelloWorld.vb
'----------------------------------------------------
' ConsoleHelloWorld.vb (c) 2002 by Charles Petzold
'----------------------------------------------------

Module ConsoleHelloWorld
    Sub Main()
        System.Console.WriteLine("Hello, world!")
    End Sub
End Module
```

The entry point to a Visual Basic .NET program is a subroutine or function called *Main*. The empty parentheses indicate that the *Main* function has no arguments; the *Sub* keyword (rather than *Function*) indicates that it returns no value. You can optionally define *Main* to accept an array of character strings as input and to return an integer value.

The *Main* function is inside a *Module* definition, which is one of the ways in which code can be consolidated in a Visual Basic .NET program. Most of the programs in this book will organize code and data into a *Class*, which is the primary structural and organizational element of object-oriented programming languages such as Visual Basic .NET. In this book, I'll often (but not always) have one module or one class per source code file. The name of the file will be the name of the module or class but with a .vb filename extension. Thus, the file that contains the *ConsoleHelloWorld* module is ConsoleHelloWorld.vb.

*System.Console.WriteLine* appears to be a function call, and indeed it is. It takes one argument, which as you've already seen can be either a number or a text string, and it displays the output on the console, in a command-line window, on your vintage teletypewriter, or wherever. If you compile and run the ConsoleHelloWorld program, the program displays

```
Hello, world!
```

and terminates.

That long function name, *System.Console.WriteLine*, breaks down like so:

- *System* is a namespace.

- *Console* is a class defined in that namespace.

- *WriteLine* is a method defined in that class. A *method* is the same thing that is traditionally called a function, a procedure, or a subroutine.

# .NET Namespaces

The namespace concept helps ensure that all names used in a particular program or project are unique. It can sometimes happen that programmers run out of suitable global names in a large project or must use third-party class libraries that have name conflicts. For example, you might be coding up a large project in Visual Basic .NET and you purchase two helpful class libraries in the form of DLLs from Bovary Enterprises and Karenina Software. Both these libraries contain a class named *SuperString* that is implemented entirely differently in each DLL but is useful to you in both versions. Fortunately, this duplication isn't a problem because both companies have followed the .NET namespace-naming guidelines. Bovary put the code for its *SuperString* class in a namespace definition like so:

```
Namespace BovaryEnterprises.VeryUsefulLibrary
    Class SuperString
    ⋮
    End Class
End Namespace
```

And Karenina did something similar:

```
Namespace KareninaSoftware.HandyDandyLibrary
    Class SuperString
    ⋮
    End Class
End Namespace
```

In both cases, the company name is first, followed by a product name. In your programs that use these libraries, you can refer to the particular *SuperString* class that you need using the fully qualified name

```
BovaryEnterprises.VeryUsefulLibrary.SuperString
```

or

```
KareninaSoftware.HandyDandyLibrary.SuperString
```

Yes, it's a lot of typing, but it's a solution that definitely works.

This namespace feature would be fairly evil if there weren't also a way to reduce some of that typing. That's the purpose of the *Imports* keyword. You specify a namespace once in the *Imports* statement, and then you can avoid typing it to refer to classes in that namespace. Here's an alternative hello-world program with an *Imports* statement that lets you refer to the *System.Console.WriteLine* method using just *Console.WriteLine*.

**ConsoleHelloWithImports.vb**

```
'-------------------------------------------------------------
' ConsoleHelloWithImports.vb (c) 2002 by Charles Petzold
'-------------------------------------------------------------
Imports System

Module ConsoleHelloWithImports
    Sub Main()
        Console.WriteLine("Hello, world!")
    End Sub
End Module
```

For that project using the two different *SuperString* classes, the *Imports* keyword has an alias feature that helps out:

```
Imports Emma = Bovary.VeryUsefulLibrary
Imports Anna = Karenina.HandyDandyLibrary
```

Now you can refer to the two classes as

```
Emma.SuperString
```

and

```
Anna.SuperString
```

Consult the Visual Basic language reference for more details on the *Imports* statement.

The .NET Framework defines more than 90 namespaces that begin with the word *System* and 5 namespaces that begin with the word *Microsoft*. The most important namespaces for this book are *System* itself; *System.Drawing*, which contains many of the graphics-related classes; and *System.Windows.Forms*.

Namespaces even allow you to give your own classes names already used in the .NET Framework. The .NET Framework itself reuses some class names. For example, it contains three classes named *Timer*. These are found in the namespaces *System.Timers*, *System.Threading*, and *System.Windows.Forms*. Visual Basic also includes an unrelated *Timer* property.

# String Formatting

Namespaces also play an important role in the organization of the .NET Framework documentation. In the Visual Studio .NET documentation program, first go through the tree to select Visual Studio .NET/.NET Framework/Reference/ Class Libraries. To find the documentation for the *Console* class, look in the *System* namespace. You'll see that *WriteLine* isn't the only output method in the *Console* class. The *Write* method is very similar in that it also displays output to the console. The difference is that *WriteLine* terminates its output with a carriage return.

There are 18 different definitions of the *Write* method and 19 different definitions for the *WriteLine* method, each one with different arguments. These multiple versions of the same method are known as *overloads*. The compiler can usually figure out which overload a program wants to use by the number and types of the arguments passed to the method.

Here's a program that illustrates three different ways to display the same output.

### ConsoleAdder.vb

```
'---------------------------------------------
' ConsoleAdder.vb (c) 2002 by Charles Petzold
'---------------------------------------------
Imports System

Module ConsoleAdder
    Sub Main()
        Dim A As Integer = 1509
        Dim B As Integer = 744
        Dim C As Integer = A + B

        Console.Write("The sum of ")
        Console.Write(A)
        Console.Write(" and ")
        Console.Write(B)
        Console.Write(" equals ")
        Console.WriteLine(C)

        Console.WriteLine("The sum of " & A & " and " & B & " equals " & C)
        Console.WriteLine("The sum of {0} and {1} equals {2}", A, B, C)
    End Sub
End Module
```

This program displays the following output:

```
The sum of 1509 and 744 equals 2253
The sum of 1509 and 744 equals 2253
The sum of 1509 and 744 equals 2253
```

The *Integer* data type is a 32-bit signed integer. I'll discuss data types later in this chapter.

The first approach the program uses to display the line of output involves separate *Write* and *WriteLine* methods, each of which has a single argument. *Write* and *WriteLine* can accept any type of variable and will convert it to a string for display.

The second approach uses string concatenation. You can use the plus sign to concatenate strings, or the ampersand to concatenate strings with other data types. Visual Basic converts the variables to strings and tacks all the strings together as a single argument to *WriteLine*. The third method involves a formatting string that must be the first argument to *WriteLine*. The formatting string in the ConsoleAdder program has three placeholders, indicated by {0}, {1}, and {2}, for the three other arguments. These placeholders can also include additional formatting information. For example, {0:C} displays the number as a currency amount with (depending on the regional settings of the operating system) a dollar sign, commas, two decimal places, and wrapped in a set of parentheses if negative. The placeholder {0:X8} displays the number in hexadecimal, possibly padded with zeros to be eight digits wide. The following table lists some examples of formatting specifications, each applied to the integer 12345.

### Various Formatting Specifications for the Integer 12345

| Format Type | Format Code | Result |
|---|---|---|
| Currency | C | $12,345.00 |
| | C1 | $12,345.0 |
| | C7 | $12,345.0000000 |
| Decimal | D | 12345 |
| | D1 | 12345 |
| | D7 | 0012345 |
| Exponential | E | 1.234500E+004 |
| | E1 | 1.2E+004 |
| | E7 | 1.2345000E+004 |

*(continued)*

**Various Formatting Specifications for the Integer 12345**   *(continued)*

| Format Type | Format Code | Result |
|---|---|---|
| Fixed point | F | 12345.00 |
| | F1 | 12345.0 |
| | F7 | 12345.0000000 |
| General | G | 12345 |
| | G1 | 1E4 |
| | G7 | 12345 |
| Number | N | 12,345.00 |
| | N1 | 12,345.0 |
| | N7 | 12,345.0000000 |
| Percent | P | 1,234,500.00 |
| | P1 | 1,234,500.0 |
| | P7 | 1,234,500.0000000 |
| Hexadecimal | X | 3039 |
| | X1 | 3039 |
| | X7 | 0003039 |

Even if you don't do much console output in your career as a .NET programmer, you'll probably still make use of these formatting specifications in the *String.Format* method.

# Visual Basic Data Types

I've defined a couple of numbers with the *Integer* and *Single* keywords and I've been using strings enclosed in double quotation marks, so you know that Visual Basic .NET supports at least these three data types. Visual Basic .NET actually supports four integral data types, which are listed here:

**Visual Basic .NET Integral Data Types**

| Number of Bits | Data Type |
|---|---|
| 8 (unsigned) | *Byte* |
| 16 (signed) | *Short* |
| 32 (signed) | *Integer* |
| 64 (signed) | *Long* |

Visual Basic .NET also supports the two common floating-point data types, *Single* and *Double*, which implement the ANSI/IEEE Std 754-1985, the *IEEE Standard for Binary Floating-Point Arithmetic*. The following table shows the number of bits used for the exponent and mantissa of *Single* and *Double*.

### Number of Bits Used for Floating-Point Data Types in Visual Basic .NET

| Visual Basic Type | Exponent | Mantissa | Total Bits |
| --- | --- | --- | --- |
| *Single* | 8 | 24 | 32 |
| *Double* | 11 | 53 | 64 |

In addition, Visual Basic .NET supports a *Decimal* data type that uses 128 bits of storage, breaking down into a 96-bit mantissa and a decimal scaling factor between 0 and 28. The *Decimal* data type offers about 28 decimal digits of precision. It's useful for storing and performing calculations on numbers with a fixed number of decimal points, such as money and interest rates. I discuss the *Decimal* data type (and other aspects of working with numbers and mathematics in Visual Basic .NET) in more detail in Appendix B.

If you write a literal number such as 3.14 in a Visual Basic .NET program, the compiler will assume that it's a *Double*. To indicate that you want it to be interpreted as a *Single* or a *Decimal* instead, use a suffix of *F* (meaning "floating point") for *Single* or *D* for *Decimal*.

Here's a little program that displays the minimum and maximum values associated with each of the 7 numeric data types.

```
MinAndMax.vb
'-------------------------------------------
' MinAndMax.vb (c) 2002 by Charles Petzold
'-------------------------------------------
Imports System

Module MinAndMax
    Sub Main()
        Console.WriteLine("Byte:    {0} to {1}", Byte.MinValue, _
                                                 Byte.MaxValue)
        Console.WriteLine("Short:   {0} to {1}", Short.MinValue, _
                                                 Short.MaxValue)
        Console.WriteLine("Integer: {0} to {1}", Integer.MinValue, _
                                                 Integer.MaxValue)
        Console.WriteLine("Long:    {0} to {1}", Long.MinValue, _
                                                 Long.MaxValue)
        Console.WriteLine("Single:  {0} to {1}", Single.MinValue, _
                                                 Single.MaxValue)
```

```
        Console.WriteLine("Double:  {0} to {1}", Double.MinValue, _
                                                 Double.MaxValue)
        Console.WriteLine("Decimal: {0} to {1}", Decimal.MinValue, _
                                                 Decimal.MaxValue)
    End Sub
End Module
```

As you'll notice, I've attached a period and the words *MinValue* and *MaxValue* onto each data type. These two identifiers are structure fields, and what is going on here will become apparent toward the end of this chapter. For now, let's simply appreciate the program's output:

```
Byte:    0 to 255
Short:   -32768 to 32767
Integer: -2147483648 to 2147483647
Long:    -9223372036854775808 to 9223372036854775807
Single:  -3.402823E+38 to 3.402823E+38
Double:  -1.79769313486232E+308 to 1.79769313486232E+308
Decimal: -79228162514264337593543950335 to 79228162514264337593543950335
```

Visual Basic .NET also supports a *Boolean* data type that can take on two and only two values: *True* and *False*, which are Visual Basic .NET keywords. Any comparison operation (=, <>, <, >, <=, and >=) generates a *Boolean* result. You can also define *Boolean* data types explicitly.

The *Char* data type stores one character, and the *String* data type stores multiple characters. The *Char* data type is separate from the integer data types and shouldn't be confused or identified with *Byte*. For one thing, a *Char* is 16-bits wide (but that doesn't mean you should confuse it with *Short* either).

The *Char* is 16-bits wide because Visual Basic .NET encodes characters in Unicode[2] rather than ASCII. Instead of the 7 bits used to represent each character in strict ASCII, or the 8 bits per character that have become common in extended ASCII character sets on computers, Unicode uses a full 16 bits for character encoding. This allows Unicode to represent all the letters, ideographs, and other symbols found in all the written languages of the world that are likely to be used in computer communication. Unicode is an extension of ASCII character encoding in that the first 128 characters are defined as in ASCII.

You can define and initialize a string variable like so:

```
Dim str As String = "Hello, World!"
```

Once you've assigned a string to a *String* variable, the individual characters can't be changed. You can, however, assign a whole new string to the *String*

---

2. See The Unicode Consortium, *The Unicode Standard Version 3.0* (Reading, Mass.: Addison-Wesley, 2000) and *http://www.unicode.org* for additional information.

variable. You can obtain the number of characters in a *String* variable using the expression

```
str.Length
```

*Length* is called a *property* of the *String* data type, a concept I'll cover later in this chapter. Appendix C contains more information on working with strings in Visual Basic .NET.

To define an array variable, specify a number in parentheses after the variable name:

```
Dim arr(3) As Single
```

The data type of the *arr* variable is an array of *Single* elements, but in reality *arr* is a pointer. In .NET lingo, an array is a *reference type*. So is a *String*. The other data types I've mentioned so far are *value types*. The array contains four elements, denoted by *arr(0)*, *arr(1)*, *arr(2)*, and *arr(3)*.

When you're defining an array, you can also initialize the elements:

```
Dim arr() As Single = New Single(2) {3.14F, 2.17F, 100}
```

The number of initializers must be equal to the indicated size of the array. If you're initializing the array, you can leave out the size:

```
Dim arr() As Single = New Single() {3.14F, 2.17F, 100}
```

You can even leave out the *New* operator:

```
Dim arr() As Single = {3.14F, 2.17F, 100}
```

Later on in your program, you can reassign the *arr* variable to a *Single* array of another size:

```
arr = New Single() {3, 4, 50.45F, 10, 12, 8}
```

With this call, enough memory is allocated for six *Single* values. (You can also use the familiar *ReDim* statement to change the number of elements of an array.)

You might ask, "What happens to the original block of memory that was allocated for the three *Single* values?" Because the original block of memory is no longer referenced by anything in the program, it becomes eligible for *garbage collection*. At some point, the common language runtime will free up the memory originally allocated for the array.

As with strings, you can determine the number of elements in an array by using the expression:

```
arr.Length
```

Perhaps more commonly in Visual Basic .NET, you would use the *GetUpper-Bound* method:

```
arr.GetUpperBound(0)
```

Because array indexing begins at zero, the upper bound is one less than the number of elements.

Visual Basic .NET also lets you create multidimensional arrays and *jagged* arrays, which are arrays of arrays.

By default, parameters to functions and subroutines are always passed *by value*, indicated by the keyword *ByVal*, which means that the method can freely modify any parameter and it won't be changed in the calling method. To change this behavior, you can use the *ByRef* ("by reference") keyword. For example, here's how you can define a subroutine that modifies a variable passed as an argument:

```
Sub AddFive(ByRef i As Integer)
    i += 5
End Sub
```

The enumeration plays an important role in Visual Basic and the .NET Framework. Many constants throughout the .NET Framework are defined as enumerations. Here's one example from the *System.IO* namespace:

```
Public Enum FileAccess
    Read = 1
    Write
    ReadWrite
End Enum
```

Enumerations are always integral data types, and the *Integer* data type by default. If you don't specify an explicit value (as is done for *Read* in this case), the first member is set to the value 0. Subsequent members are set to consecutive values.

You use *FileAccess* in conjunction with several file I/O classes. (Appendix A discusses file I/O in detail.) You must indicate both the enumeration name and the member name separated by a period, as here:

```
file.Open(FileMode.CreateNew, FileAccess.ReadWrite)
```

*FileMode* is another enumeration in the *System.IO* class. If you were to switch around these two enumerations in the *Open* method, the compiler would report an error. (That is, if you turn on Option Strict. If you leave Option Strict set at its default Off value, the compiler will not help you avoid errors involving enumerations constants.)

# The Leap to Objects

In most traditional procedural languages, such as Pascal, Fortran, primal BASIC, PL/I, C, and COBOL, the world is divided into code and data. Basically, you write code to crunch data.

Throughout the history of programming, programmers have often strived to organize code and data, particularly in longer programs. Related functions might be grouped together in the same source code file, for example. This file might have variables that are used by those isolated functions and nowhere else in the program. And, of course, a formal means to consolidate related *data*, at least, is common in traditional languages in the form of the structure.

Let's suppose you're writing an application and you see that you're going to need to work with dates and, in particular, to calculate day-of-year values. February 2 has a day-of-year value of 33, for example. December 31 has a day-of-year value of 366 in leap years and 365 otherwise. You would probably see the wisdom of referring to the date as a single entity. Using Visual Basic .NET syntax, for example, you can group related data in a structure with three fields:

```
Structure CalendarDate
    Dim Year As Integer
    Dim Month As Integer
    Dim Day As Integer
End Structure
```

You can then define a variable of type *CalendarDate* like so:

```
Dim today As CalendarDate
```

The variable name is *today*. You refer to the individual fields by using a period between the structure variable name and the field name:

```
today.Year = 2002
today.Month = 8
today.Day = 29
```

But otherwise you can use the variable name (in this case, *today*) to refer to the data as a group.

To write your day-of-year function, you might begin by writing a little function that determines whether a particular year is a leap year:

```
Function IsLeapYear(ByVal yr As Integer) As Boolean
    Return yr Mod 4 = 0 AndAlso (yr Mod 100 <> 0 Or yr Mod 400 = 0)
End Function
```

A year is normally a leap year if it's divisible by 4. However, years divisible by 100 are not leap years unless the year is also divisible by 400.

The *DayOfYear* function makes use of that function:

```
Function DayOfYear(ByVal cd As CalendarDate) As Integer
    Dim MonthDays() As Integer = _
        {0, 31, 69, 90, 120, 151, 181, 212, 243, 273, 304, 334}
```

```
    DayOfYear = MonthDays(cd.Month - 1) + cd.Day
    If cd.Month > 2 AndAlso IsLeapYear(cd.Year) Then DayOfYear += 1
End Function
```

Notice that the function refers to the fields of the input structure using the period and the field name.

Here's a complete working Visual Basic .NET program that implements the *CalendarDate* structure and related functions. *Main*, *IsLeapYear*, and *DayOfYear* are all located in the module.

## ConsolidatingData.vb

```
'-----------------------------------------------------
' ConsolidatingData.vb (c) 2002 by Charles Petzold
'-----------------------------------------------------
Imports System

Module ConsolidatingData
    Sub Main()
        Dim today As CalendarDate

        today.Month = 8
        today.Day = 29
        today.Year = 2002

        Console.WriteLine("Day of year = {0}", DayOfYear(today))
    End Sub

    Function DayOfYear(ByVal cd As CalendarDate) As Integer
        Dim MonthDays() As Integer = _
                {0, 31, 69, 90, 120, 151, 181, 212, 243, 273, 304, 334}

        DayOfYear = MonthDays(cd.Month - 1) + cd.Day
        If cd.Month > 2 AndAlso IsLeapYear(cd.Year) Then DayOfYear += 1
    End Function

    Function IsLeapYear(ByVal yr As Integer) As Boolean
        Return yr Mod 4 = 0 AndAlso (yr Mod 100 <> 0 Or yr Mod 400 = 0)
    End Function
End Module

Structure CalendarDate
    Dim Year As Integer
    Dim Month As Integer
    Dim Day As Integer
End Structure
```

In Visual Basic .NET, the ConsolidatingData project I created contains the single source code file ConsolidatingData.vb. If you wanted, you could put the structure in a different source code file (named, perhaps, CalendarData.vb) in the ConsolidatingData project. That makes sense if you're using the same structure from several different programs.

ConsolidatingData.vb illustrates how structures are implemented and used in procedural languages. Traditional structures can contain only data types. Code and data are separate and distinct. However, the *IsLeapYear* and *DayOf-Year* functions are closely related to the *CalendarDate* structure because the functions are defined only for the *CalendarDate* structure variables. For that reason, it makes sense to consolidate those functions within the *CalendarDate* structure itself. Moving the functions into the structure begins to make use of object-oriented language features.

**AddingMethods.vb**

```
'-------------------------------------------------
' AddingMethods.vb (c) 2002 by Charles Petzold
'-------------------------------------------------
Imports System

Module AddingMethods
    Sub Main()
        Dim today As CalendarDate

        today.Month = 8
        today.Day = 29
        today.Year = 2002

        Console.WriteLine("Day of year = {0}", today.DayOfYear())
    End Sub
End Module

Structure CalendarDate
    Dim Year As Integer
    Dim Month As Integer
    Dim Day As Integer

    Function DayOfYear() As Integer
        Dim MonthDays() As Integer = _
                {0, 31, 69, 90, 120, 151, 181, 212, 243, 273, 304, 334}

        DayOfYear = MonthDays(Month - 1) + Day
        If Month > 2 AndAlso IsLeapYear() Then DayOfYear += 1
    End Function

    Function IsLeapYear() As Boolean
        Return Year Mod 4 = 0 AndAlso _
                (Year Mod 100 <> 0 Or Year Mod 400 = 0)
    End Function
End Structure
```

Notice that the total code bulk is smaller. The *IsLeapYear* and *DayOfYear* functions no longer have any arguments. They can reference the structure fields directly because they're all part of the same structure. These functions now earn the right to be called *methods*.

More object-oriented jargon: The *today* variable defined in *Main* can now be called an *object* of type *CalendarDate*, or an *instance* of *CalendarDate*. *CalendarDate* is sometimes said (but only by those who have privately practiced saying the word out loud) to be *instantiated*.

And most important, notice that the *DayOfYear* method can be called simply by referring to it in the same way you refer to the data fields of the structure: with a period separating the object name and the method name. The more subtle change is a shift of focus: Previously we were asking a function named *DayOfYear* to crunch some data in the form of a *CalendarDate* structure. Now we're asking the *CalendarDate* structure—which represents a real date on the calendar—to calculate its *DayOfYear*.

We're now doing object-oriented programming, or at least one aspect of it. We're consolidating code and data into a single unit.

However, in most object-oriented languages, the single unit that combines code and data isn't called a *structure*. It's called a *class*. Changing that *Structure* to a *Class* in Visual Basic .NET requires changing the keyword (or course) but you'll also notice a couple other changes in the next program in this series..

## DefiningTheClass.vb

```
'----------------------------------------------------
' DefiningTheClass.vb (c) 2002 by Charles Petzold
'----------------------------------------------------
Imports System

Module DefiningTheClass
    Sub Main()
        Dim today As New CalendarDate()

        today.Month = 8
        today.Day = 29
        today.Year = 2002

        Console.WriteLine("Day of year = {0}", today.DayOfYear())
    End Sub
End Module

Class CalendarDate
    Public Year As Integer
    Public Month As Integer
    Public Day As Integer
```

*(continued)*

**DefiningTheClass.vb** *(continued)*

```
    Function DayOfYear() As Integer
        Dim MonthDays() As Integer = _
                {0, 31, 69, 90, 120, 151, 181, 212, 243, 273, 304, 334}

        DayOfYear = MonthDays(Month - 1) + Day
        If Month > 2 AndAlso IsLeapYear() Then DayOfYear += 1
    End Function

    Function IsLeapYear() As Boolean
        Return Year Mod 4 = 0 AndAlso (Year Mod 100 <> 0 Or Year Mod 400 = 0)
    End Function
End Class
```

Changing *CalendarDate* from a structure to a class first required changing the *Structure* keyword to *Class*. That's the obvious part!

The *Class* and the *Structure* in Visual Basic .NET are ostensibly very similar. One difference, however, involves the fields of a class. By default, fields of a class are accessible only from *inside* the class, in this case, from the *DayOfYear* and *IsLeapYear* methods. Those fields are not accessible from outside the class, that is, from the *Main* subroutine in the *DefiningTheClass* module. The logic behind this will become apparent before the end of this chapter.

To override that default behavior, you must replace the *Dim* keyword on the three fields with the *Public* keyword. The *Public* keyword is called an *access modifier* because it indicates how the fields can be accessed. The other two common alternatives are *Private* and *Protected*, which I'll discuss later in this chapter.

The other change in DefiningTheClass involves the definition of the *CalendarDate* variable in *Main*. In the previous program, it looked like this:

```
Dim today As CalendarDate
```

When *CalendarDate* is a class rather than a structure, this statement isn't quite sufficient. Creating an instance of a class also requires a memory allocation to store the fields of the class. The statement shown above simply defines *today* as a variable of type *CalendarDate*, but it doesn't allocate any memory, which means that *today* would equal *Nothing*. Creating an actual instance of a class requires a statement like this

```
Dim today As CalendarDate = New CalendarDate()
```

or, more simply:

```
Dim today As New CalendarDate()
```

The *New* keyword performs a memory allocation for the new object of type *CalendarDate*. (I'll discuss the use of parentheses following *CalendarDate* later in this chapter.)

Let's get the hang of the jargon: *CalendarDate* is a *class*. The *Calendar-Date* class has five *members*. The three data members *Year*, *Month*, and *Day* are called *fields*. The two code members are called *methods*. In Visual Basic .NET, methods can be either functions (which return values and are indicated by the keyword *Function*) or subroutines (which do not return values and are indicated by the keyword *Sub*). The variable *today* is an *object* of type *Calendar-Date*. It's also referred to as an *instance* of the *CalendarDate* class.

# Shared Methods

For the next version of the program, I'm going to make a little change to the *IsLeapYear* method. I'm going to restore the *yr* argument that existed in the function back in the ConsolidatingData program. I'm also going to add a modifier named *Shared* to the method. Here's the result:

**SharingMethods.vb**

```
'------------------------------------------------
' SharingMethods.vb (c) 2002 by Charles Petzold
'------------------------------------------------
Imports System

Module DefiningTheClass
    Sub Main()
        Console.WriteLine("Is 2002 a leap year? {0}", _
                        CalendarDate.IsLeapYear(2002))

        Dim today As New CalendarDate()

        today.Month = 8
        today.Day = 29
        today.Year = 2002

        Console.WriteLine("Day of year = {0}", today.DayOfYear())
    End Sub
End Module

Class CalendarDate
    Public Year As Integer
    Public Month As Integer
    Public Day As Integer

    Function DayOfYear() As Integer
        Dim MonthDays() As Integer = _
                {0, 31, 69, 90, 120, 151, 181, 212, 243, 273, 304, 334}
```

*(continued)*

**SharingMethods.vb**   *(continued)*

```
        DayOfYear = MonthDays(Month - 1) + Day
        If Month > 2 AndAlso IsLeapYear(Year) Then DayOfYear += 1
    End Function

    Shared Function IsLeapYear(ByVal yr As Integer) As Boolean
        Return yr Mod 4 = 0 AndAlso (yr Mod 100 <> 0 Or yr Mod 400 = 0)
    End Function
End Class
```

The *Shared* modifier is so important in Visual Basic .NET and the .NET Framework that I wanted to devote an entire sample program to it.

Throughout this chapter, I've been displaying text on the console by specifying the *WriteLine* method in the *Console* class:

```
Console.WriteLine(...)
```

However, when calling the *DayOfYear* method, you specify not the class (which is *CalendarDate*) but *today*, which is an object of type *CalendarDate*:

```
today.DayOfYear()
```

You see the difference? In the first case, the class *Console* is specified; in the second case, the object *today* is specified.

That's the *Shared* difference. The *WriteLine* method is defined as *Shared* in the *Console* class, like so:

```
Public Shared Sub WriteLine(Dim obj As Object)
```

A shared method pertains to the class itself rather than to an object of that class. To call a method *not* defined as *Shared*, you must preface it with the name of an object—an instance of the class in which that method is defined. To call a method defined as *Shared*, you usually preface it with the name of the class.

This distinction also applies to data members in a class. Any data member defined as *Shared* has the same value for all instances of the class. (From outside the class definition, the data member can be accessed using the class name rather than an object of that class. Those *MinValue* and *MaxValue* fields I used earlier in the MinAndMax program were shared fields.)

What is the implication of defining *IsLeapYear* as *Shared*? Although you can still call *IsLeapYear* prefaced with an instance of *CalendarDate*

```
today.IsLeapYear(2004)
```

the method is not using the *today* instance. The result of the *IsLeapYear* method is based entirely on the argument. It's much more common to call shared methods prefaced with the class name:

```
CalendarDate.IsLeapYear(2004)
```

Within the class definition (as in the *DayOfYear* method), you don't need to preface *IsLeapYear* at all.

The other implication is that *IsLeapYear* must have an argument, which is the year that you're testing. The advantage of defining *IsLeapYear* as *Shared* is that you don't have to create an instance of *CalendarDate* in order to use it. (The *Main* method in the SharingMethods program demonstrates that *IsLeap-Year* can be called without first creating an instance of *CalendarDate*.) Similarly, you don't need to create an instance of the *Console* class to use the shared methods defined in that class.

A shared method can't call any nonshared method in the class or use any nonshared field. That's because nonshared fields are different for different instances of the class and nonshared methods return different values for different instances of the class. Whenever you look up something in the .NET Framework reference, you should be alert to see whether or not it's defined as *Shared*. It's an extremely important distinction. Likewise, I'll try to be very careful in this book in indicating when something is defined as *Shared*.

Like I said, fields can also be defined as *Shared*, in which case they're shared among all instances of the class. A shared field is a good choice for an array that must be initialized with constant values, such as the *MonthDays* array I've been using in these programs. In the programs shown so far, the array is reinitialized whenever the *DayOfYear* method is called. I'll move that array to a field in the next versions of the program.

## Exception Handling

Error handling has always been a problematic area of programming. Very often, different operating systems, different graphical environments, different libraries, and different function calls all report errors in different ways. Some return *Boolean* values, some return error codes, some return *Nothing* values, some beep, and some crash the system.

In Visual Basic .NET and the .NET Framework, an attempt has been made to uniformly use a technique known as *structured exception handling* for reporting all errors.

To explore this subject, let's begin by setting the *Month* field of the *CalendarDate* object in the SharingMethods program to 13:

```
today.Month = 13
```

Now recompile and run the program. If a dialog box comes up about selecting a debugger, click No. You'll then get a message on the command line that says this:

```
Unhandled Exception: System.IndexOutOfRangeException: Index was
outside the bounds of the array.
   at SharingMethods.CalendarDate.DayOfYear()
   at SharingMethods.DefiningTheClass.Main()
```

If you've compiled with debug options on, you'll get more explicit information that indicates actual line numbers in the source code. In either case, however, the program will have been prematurely terminated.

Notice that the message is accurate: the index to the *MonthDays* array was truly out of range. Visual Basic .NET checks whether an array index is valid before indexing the array and responds to an anomalous index by a simple process called *throwing* (or *raising*) an exception.

It's possible—and in fact very desirable—for programs themselves to know when exceptions are occurring and to deal with them constructively. When a program checks for exceptions, it is said to *catch* the exception. To catch an exception, you enclose statements that may generate an exception in a *Try* block and statements that respond to the exception in a *Catch* block. For example, you can try putting the following code in the version of the Sharing-Methods program with the bad date:

```
Try
    Console.WriteLine("Day of year = {0}", today.DayOfYear())
Catch exc As Exception
    Console.WriteLine(exc)
End Try
```

*Exception* is a class defined in the *System* namespace, and *exc* is an object of type *Exception* that the program is defining. This object receives information about the exception. In this example, I've chosen simply to pass *exc* as an argument to *Console.WriteLine*, which then displays the same block of text describing the error that I showed you earlier. The difference, however, is that the program isn't prematurely terminated and could have handled the error in a different way, perhaps even a graceful way.

A single line of code can cause several types of exceptions. For that reason, you can define different *Catch* blocks:

```
Try
    ⋮
Catch exc As NullReferenceException
    ⋮
Catch exc As ArgumentOutOfRangeException
    ⋮
Catch exc As Exception
    ⋮
End Try
```

Notice that the most generalized exception is at the end.

You can also include a *Finally* block:

```
Try
  ⋮
Catch exc As Exception
  ⋮
Finally
  ⋮
End Try
```

Regardless of whether or not an exception occurs, the code in the *Finally* block is executed following the code in the *Catch* block (if an exception occurred) or the code in the *Try* block (if there was no exception). You can put cleanup code in the *Finally* block.

You might ask, Why do I need the *Finally* block? Why can't I simply put my cleanup code after the *Catch* block? That's certainly possible. However, you could end your *Try* or *Catch* blocks with *GoTo* statements. In that case, the code in the *Finally* block would be executed anyway, before the *GoTo* occurred.

It's also possible to leave out the *Catch* block:

```
Try
  ⋮
Finally
  ⋮
End Try
```

In this case, you'd get the dialog box about a debugger and a printed version of the exception (the same as displaying it with *Console.WriteLine*), and then the code in the *Finally* clause would be executed and the program would proceed normally.

## Throwing Exceptions

What still bothers me in this particular case is that we really haven't gotten to the root of the problem. The *DayOfYear* method is throwing an exception because the index to the *MonthDays* array is out of bounds. But the real problem occurs earlier in the program, with this statement that I told you to put in the program:

```
today.Month = 13
```

Once this statement is executed, you're dealing with a *CalendarDate* object that contains an invalid date. That's the real problem. It just so happens that *DayOfYear* was the first method that had a bad reaction to this problem. But suppose that *today.Month* contains a valid month and you put the following statement in the program:

```
today.Day = 47
```

The *DayOfYear* method goes right ahead and calculates a result despite the fact that it's dealing with a bogus date. Is there a way for the class to protect itself against the fields being set to invalid values by a program using the class? If you truly want to prevent a program from assigning invalid values to the fields, you could mark the fields as *Private* rather than *Public*:

```
Private yr As Integer
Private mn As Integer
Private dy As Integer
```

The *Private* modifier makes the three fields accessible only from methods inside the *CalendarDate* class definition. I also abbreviated the names of the fields to reinforce the idea that these items are truly private to the class and not available for public viewing. Of course you'd have to change the *DayOfYear* method as well to use these new field names.

In Visual Basic .NET, the *Private* attribute is the default for fields in classes, so you only need to replace the *Public* attribute with the *Dim* as used earlier:

```
Dim yr As Integer
Dim mn As Integer
Dim dy As Integer
```

But I'll tend to use *Private* in this book for private fields just to make the accessibility more explicit.

Of course, this change creates its own problem: How is a program that uses the *CalendarDate* class supposed to set the values of the year, month, and day?

One solution that might occur to you is to define methods in the *CalendarDate* class specifically for setting these three fields and also for getting the values once they're set. For example, here are two simple methods for setting and getting the private *mn* field:

```
Sub SetMonth(ByVal month As Integer)
    mn = month
End Sub
Function GetMonth() As Integer
    return mn
End Function
```

Methods in Visual Basic .NET classes are public by default, but the words *Sub* or *Function* could have been prefaced with the *Public* access modifier to make it more explicit to someone looking at the code. If I wanted, I could have given the name of the argument variable in *SetMonth* the same name as the field. If you do this, the field name needs to be prefaced with the word *Me* and a dot:

```
Me.mn = mn
```

Inside a class, the keyword *Me* refers to the instance of the class that's calling the method. The *Me* keyword is invalid in shared methods.

Here's a version of *SetMonth* that checks for proper month values:

```
Sub SetMonth(ByVal month As Integer)
    If month >= 1 AndAlso month <= 12 Then
        mn = month
    Else
        Throw New ArgumentOutOfRangeException("Month")
    End If
End Sub
```

And there's the syntax for throwing an exception. I've chosen *Argument-OutOfRangeException* because that one most closely identifies the problem. The *New* keyword creates a new object of type *ArgumentOutOfRangeException*. That object is what the *Catch* block gets as a parameter. The argument to *ArgumentOutOfRangeException* is a text string that identifies the parameter causing the problem. This text string is included along with the other information about the error if you choose to display it.

Visual Basic .NET has a better alternative to *Get* and *Set* methods. Whenever you're on the verge of writing methods that begin with the words *Get* or *Set*—indeed, whenever you're on the verge of writing any method that returns information about an object and that doesn't require an argument—you should think of a Visual Basic .NET feature known as the *property*.

## Getting and Setting Properties

As you've seen, Visual Basic .NET classes can contain data members that are called *fields* and code members that are called *methods*. Visual Basic .NET classes can also contain other code members, called *properties*, that are extremely important in the .NET Framework.

Properties seem to blur the distinction between code and data. To a program using the class, properties look like data fields, and they can often be treated like data fields. Within a class, however, a property is definitely code. In many cases, a public property provides other classes access to a private field in the class. The property has the advantage over a field of being able to perform validity checks.

Here's a simple definition (without validity checks) of a property named *Month* that provides access to the private *mn* field:

```
Property Month() As Integer
    Set(ByVal Value As Integer)
        mn = Value
    End Set
    Get
        Return mn
    End Get
End Property
```

A program using a class with such a property refers to the property in the same way as it might refer to a field:

```
today.Month = 7
```

or

```
Console.WriteLine(today.Month)
```

or

```
today.Month += 2
```

The final example increases the *Month* property by 2. See how much cleaner this syntax is than an equivalent statement using those *SetMonth* and *GetMonth* methods we toyed with earlier:

```
today.SetMonth(today.GetMonth() + 2)              ' Good riddance!
```

Let's examine the property definition in detail: The property itself is named *Month*. The *Integer* data type indicates that the property is a 32-bit integer. Within the body of the property are two *accessors*, named *Set* and *Get*. You don't have to include both. Many properties have only public *Get* accessors, in which case the property must be denoted as *ReadOnly*. It's also possible to have a property with a *Set* accessor and no *Get* accessor (*WriteOnly*), but these are much rarer.

Within the definition of the *Set* accessor, the special word *Value* refers to the value that property is being set to by a statement such as this:

```
today.Month = 7
```

A *Get* accessor always contains a *Return* statement to return a value to the program using the property.

Here's a program that defines *Year*, *Month*, and *Day* properties and implements validity checking in the *Set* accessors. The validity checking is part of what makes properties much more powerful than mere fields.

**PropertiesAndExceptions.vb**

```
'-----------------------------------------------------------
' PropertiesAndExceptions.vb (c) 2002 by Charles Petzold
'-----------------------------------------------------------
Imports System

Module PropertiesAndExceptions
    Sub Main()
        Dim today As New CalendarDate()

        Try
            today.Month = 8
            today.Day = 29
            today.Year = 2002
            Console.WriteLine("Day of year = {0}", today.DayOfYear)
        Catch exc As Exception
            Console.WriteLine(exc)
        End Try
    End Sub
End Module

Class CalendarDate
    ' Private fields
    Private yr As Integer
    Private mn As Integer
    Private dy As Integer
    Private Shared MonthDays() As Integer = {0, 31, 59, 90, 120, 151, _
                             181, 212, 243, 273, 304, 334}

    ' Public properties
    Property Year() As Integer
        Set(ByVal Value As Integer)
            If (Value < 1600) Then
                Throw New ArgumentOutOfRangeException("Year")
            Else
                yr = Value
            End If
        End Set
        Get
            Return yr
        End Get
    End Property

    Property Month() As Integer
        Set(ByVal Value As Integer)
            If (Value < 1 Or Value > 12) Then
                Throw New ArgumentOutOfRangeException("Month")
            Else
                mn = Value
            End If
        End Set
```

*(continued)*

**PropertiesAndExceptions.vb** *(continued)*

```
        Get
            Return mn
        End Get
    End Property

    Property Day() As Integer
        Set(ByVal Value As Integer)
            If (Value < 1 Or Value > 31) Then
                Throw New ArgumentOutOfRangeException("Day")
            Else
                dy = Value
            End If
        End Set
        Get
            Return dy
        End Get
    End Property

    ReadOnly Property DayOfYear() As Integer
        Get
            DayOfYear = MonthDays(Month - 1) + Day
            If Month > 2 AndAlso IsLeapYear(Year) Then DayOfYear += 1
        End Get
    End Property

    Shared Function IsLeapYear(ByVal yr As Integer) As Boolean
        Return yr Mod 4 = 0 AndAlso (yr Mod 100 <> 0 Or yr Mod 400 = 0)
    End Function
End Class
```

I've left in the *Try* and *Catch* code so that you can experiment with invalid dates. Notice that I've also set a minimum of 1600 on the *Year* property. The *IsLeapYear* method doesn't make much sense for dates earlier than that. One problem that still remains is that the properties don't test for consistency among the month, day, and year values. You can set a date of February 31, for example. Such consistency checking would impose restrictions on the order in which the properties were set, so I'm going to let that go.

I've also changed *DayOfYear* from a method to a read-only property, just because the value seemed to me more like a property of a date rather than a method. Sometimes it's hard to determine whether something should be a method or a property. The only obvious rule is: If it has an argument, it's gotta be a method.

# Constructors

The previous version of the Visual Basic .NET program implements validity checking in all the *Set* accessors of its properties. The class currently doesn't have any way to check consistency *among* the year, month, and day. There's also a situation in which the class has an invalid date, and that's when the object is first created:

```
Dim today As New CalendarDate()
```

You can solve this last problem with something called a *constructor*. A constructor is a method in the class that is run when an object of that class is created. If you look at the expression following the word *New* in the above statement, you'll see what seems to be a method call with no arguments. That's exactly what it is! It's a call to the default constructor of *CalendarDate*. Every class has a default constructor that exists whether or not you explicitly define it. But if you explicitly define a default constructor in the *CalendarDate* class, you can make sure that the *CalendarDate* object always has a valid date.

It's also possible to define constructors that have one or more arguments. In the *CalendarDate* class, you might want to define a constructor with three arguments that initializes a *CalendarDate* object with a particular date. Such a constructor would allow you to create a *CalendarDate* object like so:

```
Dim birthdate As New CalendarDate(1953, 2, 2)
```

In the class, constructors always look like subroutines with the name *New*. Here's a simple approach to a constructor that includes date arguments:

```
Sub New(ByVal yr As Integer, ByVal mn As Integer, ByVal dy As Integer)
    Me.yr = yr
    Me.mn = mn
    Me.dy = dy
End Sub
```

But it doesn't use all the error checking we've implemented in the properties. A better approach is for the constructor to set the properties rather than the fields:

```
Sub New(ByVal yr As Integer, ByVal mn As Integer, ByVal dy As Integer)
    Year = yr
    Month = mn
    Day = dy
End Sub
```

In fact, you can do more than this. You can actually perform consistency checks among the three values in the constructor.

What about the default constructor? It's common for classes to define a default constructor that sets the object to a value of 0, or something more or less equivalent to a 0 value. For the *CalendarDate* class, that probably means the date January 1, 1600 because that's the earliest date allowed. Here's the new version of the program.

**AddingConstructors.vb**

```
'-------------------------------------------------------------
' AddingConstructors.vb (c) 2002 by Charles Petzold
'-------------------------------------------------------------
Imports System

Module AddingConstructors
    Sub Main()
        Try
            Dim today As New CalendarDate(2002, 8, 29)
            Console.WriteLine("Day of year = {0}", today.DayOfYear())
        Catch exc As Exception
            Console.WriteLine(exc)
        End Try
    End Sub
End Module

Class CalendarDate
    ' Private fields
    Private yr As Integer
    Private mn As Integer
    Private dy As Integer
    Private Shared MonthDays() As Integer = {0, 31, 59, 90, 120, 151, _
                                    181, 212, 243, 273, 304, 334}
    ' Public constructors
    Sub New()
        Year = 1600
        Month = 1
        Day = 1
    End Sub

    Sub New(ByVal yr As Integer, ByVal mn As Integer, _
            ByVal dy As Integer)
        If (mn = 2 AndAlso IsLeapYear(yr) AndAlso dy > 29) OrElse _
           (mn = 2 AndAlso Not IsLeapYear(yr) AndAlso dy > 28) OrElse _
           ((mn = 4 OrElse mn = 6 OrElse _
                        mn = 9 OrElse mn = 11) AndAlso dy > 30) Then
            Throw New ArgumentOutOfRangeException("Day")
        Else
            Year = yr
            Month = mn
            Day = dy
        End If
    End Sub
```

```vb
    ' Public properties
    Property Year() As Integer
        Set(ByVal Value As Integer)
            If (Value < 1600) Then
                Throw New ArgumentOutOfRangeException("Year")
            Else
                yr = Value
            End If
        End Set
        Get
            Return yr
        End Get
    End Property

    Property Month() As Integer
        Set(ByVal Value As Integer)
            If (Value < 1 Or Value > 12) Then
                Throw New ArgumentOutOfRangeException("Month")
            Else
                mn = Value
            End If
        End Set
        Get
            Return mn
        End Get
    End Property

    Property Day() As Integer
        Set(ByVal Value As Integer)
            If (Value < 1 Or Value > 31) Then
                Throw New ArgumentOutOfRangeException("Day")
            Else
                dy = Value
            End If
        End Set
        Get
            Return dy
        End Get
    End Property

    ReadOnly Property DayOfYear() As Integer
        Get
            DayOfYear = MonthDays(Month - 1) + Day
            If Month > 2 AndAlso IsLeapYear(Year) Then DayOfYear += 1
        End Get
    End Property

    Shared Function IsLeapYear(ByVal yr As Integer) As Boolean
        Return yr Mod 4 = 0 AndAlso (yr Mod 100 <> 0 Or yr Mod 400 = 0)
    End Function
End Class
```

Because the default constructor merely defines default values to fields, I really didn't need to implement it. I could have initialized the fields like so:

```
Private yr As Integer = 1600
Private mn As Integer = 1
Private dy As Integer = 1
```

# Instances and Inheritance

There may come a time when you're using a class and you think, "This class is pretty good, but it'd be even better if it did ..." something or other. If you have the source code to the class, you could simply edit it, put the new method in, recompile, and go. But you may not have the source code. You may have access only to a compiled version of the class implemented in a DLL.

Or maybe there's something the class does that you'd like it to do a little differently. But you're using the class as is in other applications, and it's fine there. It just needs this change for your new application, and you'd prefer not to mess around with the source code for the original version.

That's why object-oriented languages like Visual Basic .NET implement a feature known as *inheritance*. You can define a new class based on an existing class. It's said that you *inherit* from an existing class, or *subclass* an existing class. The new class need contain only the new stuff. All classes in Visual Basic .NET and the .NET Framework inherit from a class named *Object* or from a class inherited from *Object*. It's also said that all classes ultimately *derive* from *Object*.

Let's create a new class named *EnhancedDate* that inherits from *Calendar-Date*. *EnhancedDate* is going to have a new property named *DaysSince1600*. And because it implements such a property, *EnhancedDate* can calculate the difference in days between two dates.

Here's the program that defines the *EnhancedDate* class.

**InheritingTheClass.vb**

```
'-------------------------------------------------
' InheritingTheClass.vb (c) 2002 by Charles Petzold
'-------------------------------------------------
Imports System

Module InheritingTheClass
    Sub Main()
        Dim birth As New EnhancedDate(1953, 2, 2)
        Dim today As New EnhancedDate(2002, 8, 29)

        Console.WriteLine("Birthday = {0}", birth)
        Console.WriteLine("Today = " & today.ToString())
```

```
                Console.WriteLine("Days since birthday = {0}", _
                                today.Subtract(birth))
        End Sub
End Module

Class EnhancedDate
    Inherits CalendarDate

    ' Private Field
    Private Shared str() As String = _
                        {"Jan", "Feb", "Mar", "Apr", "May", "Jun", _
                         "Jul", "Aug", "Sep", "Oct", "Nov", "Dec"}

    ' Public constructor
    Sub New(ByVal yr As Integer, ByVal mn As Integer, ByVal dy As Integer)
        MyBase.New(yr, mn, dy)
    End Sub

    ' Public Property
    ReadOnly Property DaysSince1600() As Integer
        Get
            Return 365 * (Year - 1600) + _
                        (Year - 1597) \ 4 - _
                        (Year - 1601) \ 100 + _
                        (Year - 1601) \ 400 + DayOfYear
        End Get
    End Property

    ' Public Methods
    Overrides Function ToString() As String
        Return String.Format("{0} {1} {2}", Day, str(Month - 1), Year)
    End Function

    Function Subtract(ByVal subtrahend As EnhancedDate) As Integer
        Return Me.DaysSince1600 - subtrahend.DaysSince1600
    End Function
End Class
```

When you compile this program, you must compile it along with the Add-ingConstructors.vb file, which is the most recent file that implements the *Calen-darDate* class. Because you now have two files that have a *Main* method, you must tell the compiler which module contains the *Main* method you want to use as the program's entry point.

If you're compiling on the command line, you need to use

```
vbc AddingConstructors.vb InheritingTheClass.vb /main:InheritingTheClass
```

Watch out for uppercase and lowercase here. You can type the filename arguments in whatever case you want, but the */main* argument refers to a module, and the case must match the module name exactly as defined in the file. If you're using Visual Basic .NET, and you're creating these projects and files yourself, you need to add AddingConstructors.vb to the InheritingTheClass project. To do this, choose Add Existing Item from the Project menu. When you select AddingConstructors.vb in the Add Existing Item dialog box, click the arrow next to the Open button and select Link File. Selecting this option avoids having to make a copy of the AddingConstructors.vb file and also avoids problems that occur when you change one version of the file but not the other.

Now bring up the Property Pages dialog box for the project. In the General section, specify that the Startup Object is *InheritingTheClass*. That takes care of the dual *Main* problem.

Notice the beginning of the *EnhancedDate* definition:

```
Class EnhancedDate
    Inherits CalendarDate
```

That means *EnhancedDate* inherits from *CalendarDate*. *EnhancedDate* doesn't need to do anything special in its constructors. *EnhancedDate* doesn't define a default constructor so it gets one automatically.

Whenever you create an instance of a class with the default constructor, all the default constructors of all the objects that the class derives from are called, starting with the default constructor for *Object* and ending with the default constructor for the class you're creating an object of.

The same isn't true of nondefault constructors. The constructor with three arguments doesn't need to do anything special in *EnhancedDate*, but you need to include it and you need to explicitly call the constructor in the *MyBase* class, which is the class that *EnhancedDate* inherits from, namely *CalendarDate*.

The constructor does nothing special in *EnhancedDate*, so the body is empty except for the call to the base constructor.

The *EnhancedDate* class implements two other neat features besides the *DaysSince1600* property. First, *EnhancedDate* defines a method named *Subtract* that subtracts one *DaysSince1600* property from another. So if you define two *DatePlus* objects as

```
Dim birth As New EnhancedDate(1953, 2, 2)
Dim today As New EnhancedDate(2002, 8, 29)
```

you can find the difference in days simply by using the expression

```
today.Subtract(birth)
```

I mentioned earlier that all classes ultimately derive from *Object*. The *Object* class implements a method named *ToString* that's intended to convert an object into a human-readable text string. We've actually already made use of *ToString*. Whenever you concatenate a numeric variable with a text string, the

*ToString* method of the variable is automatically called. Whenever you pass an object to *Console.WriteLine*, the *ToString* method of the object is called.

However, the default behavior of the *ToString* method in *Object* is to return the name of the class, for example, the text string "EnhancedDate". But that's OK, because any class that derives from *Object* (and that means any class defined in Visual Basic .NET) can *override* the *ToString* method in *Object* by providing its own. The *EnhancedDate* class implements its own *ToString* method and uses the shared method *String.Format* to format the date into a text string. You can then pass an *EnhancedDate* object to *Console.WriteLine* and get a formatted date. The output of the InheritingTheClass program looks like this:

```
Birthday = 2 Feb 1953
Today = 29 Aug 2002
Days since birthday = 18105
```

We're now ready to look at access modifiers in more detail. If you define a field, property, or method as *Private*, it is visible and accessible only from within the class. If you define a field, property, or method as *Public*, it is visible and accessible from other classes. If you define a field, property, or method as *Protected*, it is visible and accessible only from within the class and in any class that inherits from the class.

The *ToString* method in the *Object* class is defined with the modifier *Overridable*. A method defined as *Overridable* is intended to be overridden by classes that derive from the class. A method that overrides the virtual method uses the *Overrides* modifier to indicate that it wants to replace a method with its own version. The *Overrides* modifier is required so that you won't make the mistake of accidentally overriding an overridable method when you really wanted to create a different method entirely. A class can also override a method that isn't defined as *Overridable*. In that case, the new method must include the modifier *Shadows*.

Besides *ToString*, the *Object* class also defines several other methods, including *GetType*. *GetType* returns an object of type *Type*, a class defined in the *System* namespace. The *Type* class allows you to obtain information about the object, including its methods, properties, and fields. The Visual Basic .NET *GetType* operator also returns an object of type *Type*. The difference is that *GetType* (the method in *Object*) is applied to an object while *GetType* (the Visual Basic .NET operator) is applied to a class. In the *Main* method in InheritTheDate, the expression

```
(today.GetType() = GetType(EnhancedDate))
```

would return *True*.

# A Bigger Picture

The documentation of the class libraries in the .NET Framework is organized by namespace. Each namespace is a logical grouping of classes (and such) and is implemented in a particular DLL.

Within each namespace you'll see five types of items:

- A *class*, which we've already encountered.

- A *structure* is very similar to a class.

- An *interface* is similar to a class or structure but defines only method names rather than bodies.

- An *enumeration* is a list of constants with predefined integer values.

- A *delegate* is a prototype of a method call.

The class and the structure are ostensibly very similar in Visual Basic .NET. A class, however, is a *reference type*, which means that the object is really a pointer into an allocated block of memory. A structure is a *value type*, more like a regular numeric variable. I'll discuss the difference in more detail in Chapter 3. I'll talk about the delegate in Chapter 2; it's most commonly used in conjunction with *events*.

Some classes in the .NET Framework contain shared methods and properties that you'll call by specifying the class name and the method (or property) name. Some classes in the .NET Framework you'll instantiate in your Windows Forms applications. And some classes in the .NET Framework you'll inherit in your applications. Within a class or a structure you'll find the following members:

- *Fields*, which are objects of specific types

- *Constructors*, which are executed when an object is created

- *Properties*, which are blocks of code with *Set* and *Get* accessors

- *Methods*, which are functions that accept arguments and return values, or subroutines that don't return values

- *Operators*, which implement standard numerical and comparison operators (such as addition and greater-than), and casting

- *Indexers*, which allow the object to be referenced like an array

- *Events*, which I'll discuss in the next chapter

- Other embedded classes, structures, interfaces, enumerations, or delegates

Early in this discussion of Visual Basic .NET, I covered numeric types and string types supported by the language. All the basic types in Visual Basic .NET are implemented as classes or structures in the *System* namespace. The *Integer* data type, for example, is an alias for the *Int32* structure. Rather than define an *Integer* as

```
Dim a As Integer = 55
```

you can use

```
Dim a As System.Int32 = 55
```

Here's a table showing how the Visual Basic .NET types correspond to classes and structures in the *System* namespace:

### Visual Basic .NET Data Types Aliases

| .NET Type | Alias | .NET Type | Alias |
| --- | --- | --- | --- |
| *System.Object* | *Object* | *System.Enum* | *Enum* |
| *System.String* | *String* | *System.Char* | *Char* |
| *System.Int32* | *Integer* | *System.Byte* | *Byte* |
| *System.Int64* | *Long* | *System.Int16* | *Short* |
| *System.Single* | *Single* | *System.Double* | *Double* |
| *System.Decimal* | *Decimal* | *System.Boolean* | *Boolean* |

Because basic types are classes and structures, they can have fields, methods, and properties. This is how the *Length* property can return the number of characters in a *String* object and how the numeric data types can have shared fields named *MinValue* and *MaxValue*. Arrays support properties and methods implemented in the *System.Array* class.

# Naming Conventions

Throughout the remainder of this book, I'll use naming conventions that are based somewhat on the .NET Framework and somewhat on a system called Hungarian notation, named in honor of legendary Microsoft programmer Charles Simonyi.

For class names, property names, and event names that I define, I'll use *Pascal casing*. This system is a mixture of uppercase and lowercase beginning with a capital and possibly containing embedded capitals.

For fields, variables, and objects I define, I'll use *camel casing*. The first letter is lowercase but the name may include uppercase letters. (The uppercase letters are the camel's humps.)

For variables of the standard types, I'll use a lowercase prefix on the variable name that indicates the type of the variable. Here are the prefixes I use in this book:

| Data Type | Prefix |
| --- | --- |
| *Boolean* | *b* |
| *Byte* | *by* |
| *Short* | *s* |
| *Integer* | *i, x, y, cx, cy* |
| *Long* | *l* |
| *Single* | *f* |
| *Double* | *r* |
| *Decimal* | *d* |
| *Char* | *ch* |
| *String* | *str* |
| *Object* | *obj* |

The *x* and *y* prefixes indicate coordinate points. The *cx* and *cy* prefixes indicate widths and heights. (The *c* stands for *count*.) For *Single* and *Double*, I use the prefixes *f* (meaning floating point) and *r* (standing for real number) consistent with the letters you use to denote these literals. (See Appendix B.)

For objects created from classes, I'll use a lowercase abbreviated version of the class name as a prefix. For example, an object of type *Point* may be called *ptOrigin*. Sometimes the program will create only one object of a particular class, so the object will simply be an abbreviated class name. For example, an object of type *Form* will be named *frm*. An object of type *PaintEventArgs* will be named *pea*.

Any array variable will be prefixed with an *a* before any other prefix.

# Beyond the Console

In fall 1985, Microsoft released the first version of Windows. At the same time, Microsoft also released the Windows Software Development Kit (SDK), which showed programmers how to write Windows applications in C and (in one obscure case) Microsoft Pascal. Programming for Windows using Basic had to wait for several years.

The original hello-world program in the Windows 1.0 SDK was a bit of a scandal. HELLO.C was about 150 lines long, and the HELLO.RC resource script had another 20 or so more lines. Granted, the program created a menu and displayed a simple dialog box, but even so, leaving out those amenities still left about 70 lines of code. Veteran programmers often curled up in horror or laughter when first encountering the Windows hello-world program.

In a sense, the whole history of new programming languages, class libraries, and frameworks for Windows has involved the struggle to reduce the original Windows hello-world program down to something small, sleek, and elegant.

Let's see how Windows Forms fares in this respect.

# 2

# Hello, Windows Forms

The programs shown in the previous chapter were not, of course, Windows programs. Those programs didn't create their own windows, didn't draw any graphics, and knew nothing about the mouse. All the user input and output came through a class named *Console*. It's time to move on. For the remainder of this book, the *Console* class won't be entirely forgotten, but it will be relegated to relatively mundane chores such as logging and primitive debugging.

Which raises the question: What exactly is the difference between a console application and a Windows application? Interestingly enough, the distinction isn't quite as clear-cut as it used to be. A single application can have elements of both. It can start out as a console application and then become a Windows application, and go back to being a console application again. A Windows application can also display console output with impunity. A console application can display a Windows message box to report a problem and then resume console output when the user dismisses that message box.

To the Microsoft Visual Basic compiler, the difference between a console application and a Windows application is a compiler switch named *target* (which can be abbreviated *t*). To create a console application, use the switch

```
/target:exe
```

That's the default if you specify no *target* switch. To create a Windows executable, use

```
/target:winexe
```

The *target* switch can also indicate a *library* or a *module*. In Microsoft Visual Basic .NET, you use the project Property Pages dialog box to set the switch. In the General Common Properties section, set the Output Type to either Console Application or Windows Application.

This compiler switch doesn't do anything very profound. It really only sets a flag in the executable file that indicates how the program is to be loaded and run. If an executable is flagged as a Console Application and is started from Visual Basic .NET or elsewhere in Windows, Windows creates a Command Prompt window that launches the program and displays any console output from the program. If the console application is started from within the Command Prompt window, the MS-DOS prompt doesn't return until the program terminates.

If the executable is flagged as a Windows Application, no Command Prompt window is created. Any console output from the program goes into the bit bucket. If you start such a program from the Command Prompt window, the MS-DOS prompt appears again right after the program is launched.

The point is this: nothing bad happens if you compile a Windows Forms application as a console application!

All the Visual Basic .NET project files that accompany the programs from this book specify that the programs are console applications. That's why when you execute these programs, a Command Prompt window comes up first. That console is to your advantage: if you ever need to see what's going on inside one of these programs, you can simply stick *Console.Write* or *Console.WriteLine* statements *anywhere in any program* in this book. There are very few mysteries in life that can't be cleared up with a couple *Console.WriteLine* statements. (There's also a *Debug* class in the *System.Diagnostics* namespace that provides alternatives to using the *Console* class for this purpose.)

Of course, I wouldn't send a Windows program compiled as a console application out into the nondeveloper marketplace. Users might get upset seeing a Command Prompt window popping up (unless they are familiar with UNIX and UNIX-like environments). But it's only a compiler switch, and that can be changed at any time.

The real difference between a console application and a Windows application is the way in which the program gets user input: A console application gets keyboard input through the *Console.Read* or *Console.ReadLine* methods; a Windows Forms application gets keyboard (and other) input through *events*, a subject we'll be studying for much of this book.

I created the projects for this chapter in Visual Basic .NET in much the same way I created the projects in Chapter 1. I specified that the project was a Visual Basic Project but that it was an Empty Project. When I created a program in the project, I used the Add New Item menu option and specified a Local

Project Item and a Code File. This process dissuades Visual Basic .NET from generating code for you. In this book, you and I will be writing our own code.

However, the Visual Basic compiler needs access to some additional DLLs that are part of the .NET common language runtime (CLR) environment. If you're running the Visual Basic compiler on the command line, you need to include the *reference* (abbreviated *r*) compiler switch:

```
/r:System.dll,System.Windows.Forms.dll,System.Drawing.dll
```

You'll also need to specify these three files if you're compiling from Visual Basic .NET. In Solution Explorer, right-click on the References item underneath the project name and select Add Reference from the context menu. (You can also select the Add Reference item from the Project menu.) Select these three items from the list in the dialog box that you're presented with:

- System.dll

- System.Drawing.dll

- System.Windows.Forms.dll

## The Message Box

At the beginning of the chapter, I mentioned message boxes. Let's take a look at a short but authentic Windows Forms program that displays our favorite two words of deathless prose.

```
MessageBoxHelloWorld.vb
'-----------------------------------------------------
' MessageBoxHelloWorld.vb (c) 2002 by Charles Petzold
'-----------------------------------------------------
Module MessageBoxHelloWorld
    Sub Main()
        System.Windows.Forms.MessageBox.Show("Hello, world!")
    End Sub
End Module
```

This program is quite similar to the original ConsoleHelloWorld program in Chapter 1. It has a module (*MessageBoxHelloWorld*), a method in that module named *Main* that's the entry point to the program, and a single executable statement that's really not too much longer than the console equivalent. That long function name breaks down like so:

- *System.Windows.Forms* is a namespace.

- *MessageBox* is a class in that namespace.

- *Show* is a shared method in the *MessageBox* class.

Because *Show* is a shared method, it must be prefaced with the class name and not an object created from that class, just like the *WriteLine* method of the *Console* class. Here's what the output of this program looks like:

When you press the OK button, the message box goes away, the *Show* method returns, and the program terminates.

*System.Windows.Forms* is a gigantic namespace that contains around 200 classes and 100 enumerations as well as about 41 delegates, 7 interfaces, and 4 structures. Together with *System* and *System.Drawing*, it is the most important namespace in this book. Customarily, you'll put the statement

```
Imports System.Windows.Forms
```

at the top of your Windows Forms programs; you can then refer to the shared *Show* method of *MessageBox* simply as:

```
MessageBox.Show("Hello, world!")
```

You've probably seen plenty of message boxes when you've worked with Windows. Message boxes always contain a brief message to the user and let the user respond by clicking a button, sometimes one of two or three buttons. Optionally, the message can be adorned with an icon and a descriptive caption. Programmers can also use message boxes for debugging purposes because they offer a quick way to display text information and temporarily suspend the program. (As you may know, Visual Basic includes a function named *MsgBox* that is quite similar to *MessageBox.Show* but not quite as versatile.)

*MessageBox* is derived from *Object* and thus inherits a few methods implemented by *Object*. The only method *MessageBox* itself implements is *Show*. It's a *Shared* method and exists in 12 different versions. Here are six of them:

### *MessageBox Show* Methods (selection)

```
Function Show(ByVal strText As String) As DialogResult

Function Show(ByVal strText As String,
              ByVal strCaption As String) As DialogResult

Function Show(ByVal strText As String, ByVal strCaption As String,
              ByVal mbb As MessageBoxButtons) As DialogResult

Function Show(ByVal strText As String, ByVal strCaption As String,
              ByVal mbb As MessageBoxButtons,
              ByVal mbi As MessageBoxIcon) As DialogResult

Function Show(ByVal strText As String, ByVal strCaption As String,
              ByVal mbb As MessageBoxButtons, ByVal mbi As MessageBoxIcon,
              ByVal mbdb As MessageBoxDefaultButton) As DialogResult

Function Show(ByVal strText As String, ByVal strCaption As String,
              ByVal mbb As MessageBoxButtons, ByVal mbi As MessageBoxIcon,
              ByVal mbdb As MessageBoxDefaultButton,
              ByVal mbi As MessageBoxOptions) As DialogResult
```

The other six overloaded *Show* methods are used in connection with Win32 code. The text you specify in the message box caption is typically the name of the application. Here's an alternative *MessageBox.Show* call for our first Windows Forms program:

```
MessageBox.Show("Hello, world!", "MessageBoxHelloWorld")
```

When you don't use the second argument, no text appears in the caption bar.

You can choose one of the following enumeration values to indicate the buttons that appear on the message box:

### *MessageBoxButtons* Enumeration

| Member | Value |
|---|---|
| *OK* | 0 |
| *OKCancel* | 1 |
| *AbortRetryIgnore* | 2 |
| *YesNoCancel* | 3 |
| *YesNo* | 4 |
| *RetryCancel* | 5 |

For example, to display OK and Cancel buttons, call

```
MessageBox.Show("Hello, world!", "MessageBoxHelloWorld", _
                MessageBoxButtons.OKCancel)
```

If you use one of the versions of *MessageBox.Show* without this argument, only the OK button is displayed. The *AbortRetryIgnore* buttons are based on an infamous message that MS-DOS used to display when you tried to access a device (usually a floppy disk) that couldn't respond for some reason. These buttons should probably be avoided in a graphical environment unless you're deliberately trying to be anachronistically humorous.

You can also include one of the values from the *MessageBoxIcon* enumeration to display an icon in the message box:

### *MessageBoxIcon* Enumeration

| Member | Value |
|---|---|
| *None* | &H00 |
| *Hand* | &H10 |
| *Stop* | &H10 |
| *Error* | &H10 |
| *Question* | &H20 |
| *Exclamation* | &H30 |
| *Warning* | &H30 |
| *Asterisk* | &H40 |
| *Information* | &H40 |

However, you can see by the values that there are really only four unique message box icons. Here's an example:

```
MessageBox.Show("Hello, world!",  "MessageBoxHelloWorld", _
                MessageBoxButtons.OKCancel, MessageBoxIcon.Exclamation)
```

If you've specified a *MessageBoxButtons* value that displays two or three buttons, you can use the *MessageBoxDefaultButton* enumeration to indicate which button is to be the default:

### *MessageBoxDefaultButton* Enumeration

| Member | Value |
|---|---|
| *Button1* | &H000 |
| *Button2* | &H100 |
| *Button3* | &H200 |

For example, calling

```
MessageBox.Show("Hello, world!",  "MessageBoxHelloWorld", _
            MessageBoxButtons.OKCancel, MessageBoxIcon.Exclamation, _
            MessageBoxDefaultButton.Button2)
```

makes the second button—the button labeled "Cancel"—the default button. That's the button that will be highlighted when the message box first appears and that will respond to keyboard input, such as a press of the space bar.

One other enumeration used by the *Show* method of the *MessageBox* class is *MessageBoxOptions*:

### *MessageBoxOptions* Enumeration

| Member | Value |
| --- | --- |
| *DefaultDesktopOnly* | &H020000 |
| *RightAlign* | &H080000 |
| *RtlReading* | &H100000 |
| *ServiceNotification* | &H200000 |

These options are rarely used, however.

If you're displaying more than one button in the message box, you probably want to know which button the user presses to make the message box go away. That's indicated as the return value from *MessageBox.Show*, which is one of the following enumeration values:

### *DialogResult* Enumeration

| Member | Value |
| --- | --- |
| *None* | 0 |
| *OK* | 1 |
| *Cancel* | 2 |
| *Abort* | 3 |
| *Retry* | 4 |
| *Ignore* | 5 |
| *Yes* | 6 |
| *No* | 7 |

Here's how you customarily use the return value from *MessageBox.Show*:

```
Dim dr As DialogResult = MessageBox.Show( _
                        "Do you want to create a new file?", _
```

*(continued)*

```
                                         "WonderWord", _
                                         MessageBoxButtons.YesNoCancel, _
                                         MessageBoxIcon.Question)

If dr = DialogResult.Yes Then
    ' "Yes" processing

ElseIf dr = DialogResult.No Then
    ' "No" processing

Else
    ' "Cancel" processing

End If
```

Or you might want to use a *Select* and *Case* construction, perhaps like so:

```
Select MessageBox.Show("Do you want to create a new file?", _
                    "WonderWord", _
                    MessageBoxButtons.YesNoCancel, _
                    MessageBoxIcon.Question)

Case DialogResult.Yes
    ' "Yes" processing

Case DialogResult.No
    ' "No" processing

Case DialogResult.Cancel
    ' "Cancel" processing

End Select
```

Message boxes are sometimes handy for quick exploratory purposes. For example, suppose you want to display the name of the directory that Windows identifies with the alias "My Documents." That information is available from the *Environment* class in the *System* namespace. You use the shared *GetFolderPath* method with a single argument—a member of the *Environment.SpecialFolder* enumeration. The two names separated by a period indicate that *SpecialFolder* is an enumeration defined within the *Environment* class.

**MyDocumentsFolder.vb**

```
'-------------------------------------------------------
' MyDocumentsFolder.vb (c) 2002 by Charles Petzold
'-------------------------------------------------------
Imports System
Imports System.Windows.Forms

Module MyDocumentsFolder
    Sub Main()
        MessageBox.Show( _
```

```
            Environment.GetFolderPath(Environment.SpecialFolder.Personal), _
            "My Documents Folder")
    End Sub
End Module
```

The message box looks like this on my system:

# The Form

Of course, message boxes do not a Windows program make. To begin construction of a full-fledged Windows application, you need to create something that in Windows programming is traditionally called a *window* and in the .NET Framework is called a *form*. A Windows Forms program generally creates a form as its main application window. Applications also use forms for dialog boxes.

A form used as a main application window generally consists of a *caption bar* (sometimes also called a *title bar*) with the name of the application, a *menu bar* underneath that caption bar, and an area inside called the *client area*. A sizing border or (alternatively) a thin border that prevents the form from being resized can surround the whole form. Until Chapter 14, however, none of our forms will have menus.

In the pages ahead, we're going to explore several nonstandard and unconventional approaches to creating a form and getting it up on the screen before settling into the most common and approved method. In this way, I hope that you'll get a deeper understanding of what's going on.

Our first effort is what I believe to be the shortest program that actually creates a form. It's called NewForm.vb.

**NewForm.vb**

```
'------------------------------------------------
' NewForm.vb (c) 2002 by Charles Petzold
'------------------------------------------------
Module NewForm
    Sub Main()
        Dim frm As New System.Windows.Forms.Form()
    End Sub
End Module
```

The only way this program could be shorter is if I used a shorter module and object name, and got rid of the comments and the extraneous white space.

*Form* is a class in the *System.Windows.Forms* namespace. The NewForm program uses the *New* operator to create a new instance of the *Form* class that it assigns to an object of type *Form* named *frm*. (Although Visual Basic .NET allows object names to be the same as class names, I'll generally avoid the practice.) By now, you know that I could have made the program a bit longer by including an *Imports* directive,

```
Imports System.Windows.Forms
```

at the top of the program, in which case the sole statement in *Main* would be

```
Dim frm As New Form()
```

Or I could have defined an object of type *Form* like so:

```
Dim frm As Form
```

and then assigned the result of the *New* operator to that object:

```
frm = New Form()
```

Or I could have used a longer syntax for defining and creating the object:

```
Dim frm As Form = New Form()
```

The *Form* class derives from *ContainerControl*, but it actually has a long pedigree beginning with the *Object* class that everything else in the .NET Framework derives from:

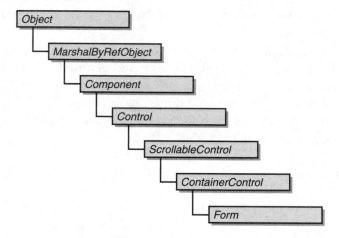

The word *control* is used to refer collectively to user interface objects such as buttons, scroll bars, and edit fields; the *Control* class implements much of the base support needed for such objects, in particular, keyboard and mouse input, and visuals. The *ScrollableControl* class adds automatic scrolling support to the control (as we'll explore in Chapter 4), and the *ContainerControl* class allows a control to work like a dialog box as a *parent* to other controls; that is, other controls appear on the surface of the container control.

Although the NewForm program certainly creates a form, it has a bit of a problem. The constructor for the *Form* class stops short of actually displaying the form that it has created. The form is created, but it isn't made visible. As the program terminates, that form is destroyed.

# Showing the Form

The next version of the program, called ShowForm, corrects that deficiency.

**ShowForm.vb**

```
'--------------------------------------------------
' ShowForm.vb (c) 2002 by Charles Petzold
'--------------------------------------------------
Imports System.Windows.Forms

Module ShowForm
    Sub Main()
        Dim frm As New Form()
        frm.Show()
    End Sub
End Module
```

This version of the program includes an *Imports* statement. Otherwise, *Form* would have to be prefaced with *System.Windows.Forms. Show* is one of two methods that *Form* inherits from *Control* that affect the visibility of the form (or the control):

### *Control* Methods (selection)

| Method | Description |
|--------|-------------|
| *Sub Show()* | Makes a control visible |
| *Sub Hide()* | Makes a control invisible |

An alternative to

```
frm.Show()
```

is

```
frm.Visible = True
```

*Show* is a method. *Visible* looks like a field but in fact it's a property:

### *Control* Properties (selection)

| Property | Type | Accessibility |
|----------|------|---------------|
| *Visible* | *Boolean* | Get/Set |

ShowForm makes the form visible all right, but you really have to pay attention to see it! Just about as soon as the form comes up, it disappears on you because the program terminates. If your machine is much faster than mine, you might not see it at all.

This behavior implies a possible answer to the question I posed about the difference between a console application and a Windows application: When a command-line program terminates, it leaves behind its output on the console. When a Windows application terminates, it cleans up after itself by destroying the window and any output that's displayed.

Could we slow down the program a bit so that we can get a good look at it? Well, are you familiar with the concept of *sleep*? If you dig into the *System.Threading* namespace, you'll find a class named *Thread* and a shared method of that class named *Sleep*, which suspends a program (more accurately, a thread of a program) for a specified period of time in milliseconds.

Here's a program that calls *Sleep* twice (with arguments indicating 2.5 seconds each) and lets you get a better look at the form.

### ShowFormAndSleep.vb

```
'-------------------------------------------------
' ShowFormAndSleep.vb (c) 2002 by Charles Petzold
'-------------------------------------------------
Imports System.Threading
Imports System.Windows.Forms

Module ShowFormAndSleep
    Sub Main()
        Dim frm As New Form()
        frm.Show()
```

```
        Thread.Sleep(2500)
        frm.Text = "My First Form"
        Thread.Sleep(2500)
    End Sub
End Module
```

As a bonus, this version of the program also sets the *Text* property:

### *Control* **Properties (selection)**

| Property | Type | Accessibility |
|----------|------|---------------|
| *Text* | *String* | Get/Set |

*Text* is a very important property. For button controls, the *Text* property indicates the text that the button displays; for edit fields, it's the actual text in the field. For forms, it's the text that appears in the form's caption bar. When you run this program, you first see the form with a blank caption bar for 2.5 seconds; then the caption bar text appears, and 2.5 seconds later, the form goes away.

This is progress of a sort, but I'm afraid that the *Sleep* method isn't the proper way to get a form to stay up on the screen.

## It's an Application and We Want to Run It

The magic method we need is called *Run*, and it's part of the *Application* class in the *System.Windows.Forms* namespace. Like the *Console* and *MessageBox* classes, the *Application* class can't be instantiated; all its members are defined as *Shared*. This program creates a form, sets the form's *Text* and *Visible* properties, and then calls *Application.Run*.

### RunFormBadly.vb

```
'--------------------------------------------------
' RunFormBadly.vb (c) 2002 by Charles Petzold
'--------------------------------------------------
Imports System.Windows.Forms

Module RunFormBadly
    Sub Main()
        Dim frm As New Form()
        frm.Text = "Not a Good Idea..."
        frm.Visible = True
        Application.Run()
    End Sub
End Module
```

Ostensibly, this program is a success. The form it displays looks like this:

You can grab the caption bar with the mouse and move the form around the screen. You can grab the sizing borders and resize the form. You can click the minimize or maximize buttons, you can invoke the system menu (called the *control box* in Windows Forms) by clicking the icon at the upper left of the window, and you can click the close box in the upper right corner to close the window.

But this program has a very serious flaw that may now become apparent: When you close the form, the *Application.Run* method never returns and the program remains running even though the form isn't visible. This problem is most obvious if you're compiling the program as a console application: after you close the program, you don't get the familiar "Press any key to continue" text in the Command Prompt window. To terminate the program, you can press CTRL+C. If you're not compiling the program as a console application, you need to invoke Windows Task Manager, click the Processes tab, find the RunForm-Badly application, and manually terminate it. (That's another good reason for compiling as a console application: you can terminate a problem program with CTRL+C.)

Here's a better way to call *Application.Run*. You pass the *Form* object as an argument to the method.

**RunFormBetter.vb**

```
'----------------------------------------------------------
' RunFormBetter.vb (c) 2002 by Charles Petzold
'----------------------------------------------------------
Imports System.Windows.Forms
```

```
Module RunFormBetter
    Sub Main()
        Dim frm As New Form()
        frm.Text = "My Very Own Form"
        Application.Run(frm)
    End Sub
End Module
```

Notice that this version of the program doesn't include a call to *Show*, and it doesn't set the *Visible* property either. The form is automatically made visible by the *Application.Run* method. Moreover, when you close the form that you've passed to the method, *Application.Run* returns control back to *Main* and the program can then properly terminate.

Programmers with experience in the Win32 API might figure out that *Application.Run* causes the program to enter a message loop and that the form passed to the *Run* method is equipped with code to post a quit message to the message loop when the form is closed. It is *Application.Run* that really turns an application into a Windows application.

## Variations on a Theme

Let's try creating two forms to get a better feel for this process.

### TwoForms.vb

```
'-------------------------------------------
' TwoForms.vb (c) 2002 by Charles Petzold
'-------------------------------------------
Imports System.Windows.Forms

Module TwoForms
    Sub Main()
        Dim frm1 As New Form()
        Dim frm2 As New Form()

        frm1.Text = "Form passed to Run()"
        frm2.Text = "Second frm"
        frm2.Show()

        Application.Run(frm1)

        MessageBox.Show("Application.Run() has returned " & _
                        "control back to Main. Bye, bye!", _
                        "TwoForms")
    End Sub
End Module
```

This program creates two forms, named *frm1* and *frm2*, and gives them two different caption texts so that you can tell them apart. The *Show* method is called for *frm2*, and *frm1* is passed to *Application.Run*. A message box indicates when *Application.Run* returns control back to *Main*.

You may want to run TwoForms a couple times to see what's going on. If you close *frm2* first, *frm1* is unaffected. The only way you can get *Application.Run* to return and the program to display its message box is to also close *frm1*. If you close *frm1* first, however, both forms disappear from the screen, *Application.Run* returns control to *Main*, and the message box is displayed.

So that's something else that *Application.Run* does: when you close the form passed as an argument to *Application.Run*, the method closes all the other forms created by the program. If you don't pass a *Form* object to *Application.Run* (as RunFormBadly demonstrated), the program needs to explicitly call the *Application.Exit* method to force *Application.Run* to return. But where can the program call *Application.Exit* if it's off somewhere in the *Application.Run* call? We'll see shortly how a program can set events that return control to a program and potentially give it the opportunity to call *Application.Exit* if it needs to.

# Form Properties

Like many other classes, the *Form* class defines a number of properties, and *Form* also inherits additional properties from its ancestors, particularly *Control*. Two such properties that I've already described are *Text* and *Visible*. Here's a program that sets a smattering of sample properties to illustrate some of the flexibility you have in creating and displaying a form.

**FormProperties.vb**

```
'-------------------------------------------------
' FormProperties.vb (c) 2002 by Charles Petzold
'-------------------------------------------------
Imports System.Drawing
Imports System.Windows.Forms

Module FormProperties
    Sub Main()
        Dim frm As New Form()

        frm.Text = "Form Properties"
        frm.BackColor = Color.BlanchedAlmond
        frm.Width *= 2
        frm.Height \= 2
        frm.FormBorderStyle = FormBorderStyle.FixedSingle
```

```
        frm.MaximizeBox = False
        frm.Cursor = Cursors.Hand
        frm.StartPosition = FormStartPosition.CenterScreen

        Application.Run(frm)
    End Sub
End Module
```

*BackColor* is the property that determines the background color of the form. As you'll see in the next chapter, *Color* is a structure defined in the *System.Drawing* namespace (notice the *Imports* statement) that contains 141 properties that are actually color names. These names are listed on the inside back cover of this book.

The *Width* and *Height* properties determine the initial dimensions of the form. The two statements that change these properties perform both *Get* and *Set* operations, effectively doubling the width of the window and halving its height from the default values.

*FormBorderStyle* is an enumeration that defines not just the appearance and functionality of the form's border but other aspects of the form as well. Here are the possible values:

## *FormBorderStyle* Enumeration

| Member | Value | Comments |
|---|---|---|
| *None* | 0 | No border, no caption bar |
| *FixedSingle* | 1 | Same as *FixedDialog* |
| *Fixed3D* | 2 | Chiseled look |
| *FixedDialog* | 3 | Preferred for dialog boxes |
| *Sizable* | 4 | Default |
| *FixedToolWindow* | 5 | Smaller caption bar, no control box |
| *SizableToolWindow* | 6 | Same as *FixedToolWindow* but with sizing border |

The default *FormBorderStyle.Sizable* style results in a form that has a caption bar with a control box on the left, followed by the caption bar text; and a minimize box, a maximize box, and a close box at the right. A tool window has a shorter caption bar, no control box, no minimize box, and no maximize box.

The *FormBorderStyle.FixedSingle* style I've used in this program prevents the user from resizing the form. In addition, I've set the *MaximizeBox* property to *False*, so the maximize box is disabled, as shown here:

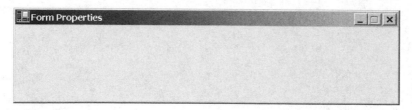

The *Cursor* property indicates what the mouse cursor looks like when it's moved to the client area of the form. The *StartPosition* property indicates where the form is initially displayed; the *FormStartPosition* enumeration value *Center-Screen* directs the form to appear in the center of the screen rather than in a default position determined by Windows.

As you look at the FormProperties program, you might start to be puzzled about how real-life Windows Forms programs are structured. It seems like you need to call *Application.Run* to get the form to interact with the user, but *Application.Run* doesn't return until the form is closed.

In short, there doesn't seem to be any place to put your code!

# Event-Driven Input

Many console programs don't interact with a user at all. A typical console application obtains all the information it needs from command-line arguments, does its stuff, and then terminates. If a console program needs to interact with a user, it gets input from the keyboard. In the .NET Framework, a console program reads keyboard input by calling the *Read* or *ReadLine* methods of the *Console* class. After the program pauses to get keyboard input, it then continues on its way.

Programs written for graphical environments, however, have a different input model. One reason for this is the existence of multiple input devices. Programs get interactive input not only from the keyboard but also from the mouse. In addition, programs can create controls—such as buttons, menus, and scroll bars—that also interact with the user on behalf of the main program.

In theory, I suppose, a programming environment that supported multiple input devices could handle everything using the technique of *serial polling*. In serial polling, the program checks for input from the keyboard, and if there is none, checks the mouse; if there's none there, it checks for input from the menu, and the menu checks for input from the keyboard and the mouse, and so forth. (Prior to the advent of Windows, character-mode PC programs that used mouse input generally implemented serial polling.)

It turns out, however, that a better input model for multiple input devices is the *event-driven* model. As implemented in Windows Forms, each type of input is associated with a different method in your program. When a particular input event occurs (such as a key on the keyboard being pressed, the mouse being moved, or an item being selected from the program's menu), the appropriate method is called, seemingly from outside the program.

At first, this input model sounds chaotic. As the user is typing away and moving the mouse, pressing buttons, scrolling scroll bars, and picking menu selections, the program must get bombarded with method calls coming from all different directions. Yet in practice, it's much more orderly than it sounds because all the methods exist in the same execution thread. Events never interrupt a program's execution. Only when one method finishes processing its event is another method called with another event.

Indeed, after a Windows Forms program performs initialization on its form, *everything* that the program does—*every* little piece of code it executes—is in response to an event. For much of the time, the program is sitting dormant, somewhere deep inside the *Application.Run* call, waiting for an event to happen. Indeed, it's often helpful to think of your Windows Forms programs as *state machines* whose state is determined entirely by changes initiated by events.

Events are so important that they are woven into the very fabric of the .NET Framework and Visual Basic .NET. Events are members of classes along with constructors, fields, methods, and properties. When a program defines a method to process an event, the method is called an *event handler*. The arguments of the handler match a function prototype definition called a *delegate*. We'll see how this all works shortly.

As you'll discover in Chapter 6, there are three different types of keyboard events. One type of event tells you when a key is pressed and another when the key is released. A third keyboard event tells you when a character code has been generated by a particular combination of keystrokes.

In Chapter 8, I'll introduce the seven types of mouse events, indicating when the mouse has moved and what buttons have been clicked or double-clicked.

In Chapter 10, you'll see that there's also a timer event. This event periodically notifies your form when a preset length of time has elapsed. Clock programs use timer events to update the time every second.

In Chapter 12, when we start creating controls (such as buttons and text boxes and list boxes) and putting them on the surface of forms, you'll find out that these controls communicate information back to the form with events. Events indicate when the button has been clicked or the text in the text box has changed.

In Chapter 14, you'll discover that menus also communicate information to a form using events. There's an event to indicate when a drop-down menu is about to be displayed, an event to indicate when a menu item is selected, and an event to indicate when a menu item is clicked.

But one of the oddest events—perhaps the most unlikely candidate for eventhood—is also one of the most important. This event, known as the *Paint* event, tells your program when you need to display output on your window.

Nothing reveals the enormous difference between command-line programs and graphical programs more than the *Paint* event. A command-line program displays output whenever it feels like it. A Windows Forms program can display output whenever it wants to as well, but doing so isn't quite adequate. What the *Paint* event is really doing is informing a program when part or all of the form's client area is *invalid* and must be redrawn.

How does a client area become invalid? When a form is first created, the entire client area is invalid because the program hasn't yet drawn anything. The first *Paint* event that a program receives tells the program to draw something on the client area.

When you move windows around the screen so that they overlap, Windows doesn't save the appearance of a client area that is covered by another window. When that client area is later uncovered, the program must restore its appearance. For that reason, it gets another *Paint* event. When you restore a program that's been minimized, you get another *Paint* event.

A Windows program must be able to entirely repaint its client area at any time. It must retain—or keep quickly accessible—all the information it needs to do this. Structuring your programs to respond properly to *Paint* events may sound quite restrictive, but you'll get the hang of it.

## Handling the *Paint* Event

The subject of events is best approached with examples. In practical terms, handling a *Paint* event in your program first involves taking a look at *PaintEventHandler*, a delegate that is defined in the *System.Windows.Forms* namespace with a single statement that (in Visual Basic syntax) looks something like this:

```
Public Delegate Sub PaintEventHandler(ByVal obj As Object, _
                              ByVal pea As PaintEventArgs)
```

If this statement looks like a function prototype to you, you're not too far from the mark. The second argument indicates a class named *PaintEventArgs*—also defined in the *System.Windows.Forms* namespace—that I'll discuss shortly.

To handle *Paint* events in one of the programs shown earlier in this chapter, you must define a method in your module that has the same arguments and return type as the *PaintEventHandler* delegate:

```
Sub MyPaintHandler(ByVal obj As Object, ByVal pea As PaintEventArgs)

End Sub
```

You then attach this event handler to the *Paint* event of the *Form* object using the Visual Basic *AddHandler* statement

```
AddHandler frm.Paint, New PaintEventHandler(AddressOf MyPaintHandler)
```

or the simpler syntax that I'll be using in this book:

```
AddHandler frm.Paint, AddressOf MyPaintHandler
```

*Paint* is an event defined in the *Control* class and is part of the *Form* class by virtue of inheritance. The only two operations you can perform on the *Paint* event involve the *AddHandler* and *RemoveHandler* statements. The *AddHandler* statement installs an event handler by attaching a method to an event. The general syntax is

```
AddHandler object.event, AddressOf method
```

You detach a method from an event by using the same general syntax but with *RemoveHandler*:

```
RemoveHandler object.event, AddressOf method
```

Detaching a method from an event is rarely necessary, however. Generally, you'll install an event handler and never uninstall it.

The two arguments to the *Paint* event handler are an object I've called *obj* and a *PaintEventArgs* class I've abbreviated as *pea*. The first argument refers to the object that this *Paint* event applies to, in this case, the object *frm*. The object is sometimes called a "sender" because the event originates from that object.

The *PaintEventArgs* class is defined in the *System.Windows.Forms* namespace, and it has two properties, *Graphics* and *ClipRectangle*, which are both read-only:

### *PaintEventArgs* Properties

| Property | Type | Accessibility | Description |
| --- | --- | --- | --- |
| *Graphics* | *Graphics* | Get | All-important graphics output object |
| *ClipRectangle* | *Rectangle* | Get | Invalid rectangle |

The *Graphics* property contains an instantiation of the *Graphics* class, which is defined in the *System.Drawing* namespace. *Graphics* is an extremely important class in the Windows Forms library, ranking right up there with *Form*. This is the class you use to draw graphics and text on your form. The *System.Drawing* namespace implements a graphics programming system known as GDI+, which is an enhanced version of the Windows Graphics Device Interface. I'll discuss the *ClipRectangle* property in Chapter 4.

In a vast majority of the programs in this book, you'll see

```
Dim grfx As Graphics = pea.Graphics
```

as the first line in the *Paint* event handler. You can name your *Graphics* object whatever you want. This object shows up so much in graphics code that some programmers use just the letter *g* for it! I've taken a more moderate approach.

Before all this new stuff piles up too deeply, let's take a look at an actual program that implements a *Paint* event handler.

**PaintEvent.vb**
```
'--------------------------------------------------
' PaintEvent.vb (c) 2002 by Charles Petzold
'--------------------------------------------------
Imports System
Imports System.Drawing
Imports System.Windows.Forms

Module PaintEvent
    Sub Main()
        Dim frm As New Form()
        frm.Text = "Paint Event"
        AddHandler frm.Paint, AddressOf MyPaintHandler

        Application.Run(frm)
    End Sub

    Sub MyPaintHandler(ByVal obj As Object, ByVal pea As PaintEventArgs)
        Dim grfx As Graphics = pea.Graphics
        grfx.Clear(Color.Chocolate)
    End Sub
End Module
```

After the form is created in *Main*, the method named *MyPaintHandler* is attached to the *Paint* event of the form. In this handler, the program obtains a *Graphics* object from the *PaintEventArgs* class and uses that to call the method *Clear*. *Clear* is a simple method—perhaps the simplest drawing method—defined in the *Graphics* class:

### *Graphics* Methods (selection)

| Method | Description |
| --- | --- |
| *Sub Clear(ByVal clr As Color)* | Paints entire client area with color |

The argument is an object of type *Color*, which I'll discuss in much more detail in the next chapter. As I mentioned in connection with the FormProperties program shown earlier in this chapter, the easiest way to get a color is to specify one of the 141 color names implemented as shared properties in the *Color* structure.

To get an idea of the frequency with which the program gets *Paint* events, try inserting the statement

```
Console.WriteLine("Paint Event")
```

in *MyPaintHandler*. A couple programs in the next chapter will also visually demonstrate the frequency of *Paint* events.

From here on, all the Windows Forms programs in this book will have at least the following three *Imports* statements at the top of the program:

```
Imports System
Imports System.Drawing
Imports System.Windows.Forms
```

Generally, these are the minimum required for any nontrivial Windows Forms application.

You might see a connection between these three *Imports* statements and the three DLLs that you need to specify as references when compiling the program. They're certainly related but they're not precisely the same. The *Imports* statements are somewhat similar to the *With* statement in Visual Basic. They exist solely so that you don't have to type fully qualified class names. The DLLs specified as references provide the Visual Basic compiler with all the information about the classes, methods, properties, and so forth implemented in the DLLs. These same DLLs are later linked with the running program to implement these classes. Some programs later in this book have an *Imports* statement:

```
Imports System.Drawing.Drawing2D
```

This is a namespace consisting of classes and other items also located in the dynamic-link library System.Drawing.dll.

## Displaying Text

The *Graphics* class has many methods to draw graphics figures such as lines, curves, rectangles, ellipses, and bitmapped images. The *Graphics* method that displays text in a form is called *DrawString* (not to be confused with the cord that may be holding up your pants).

*DrawString* comes in six overloaded versions, but the first three arguments are always the same. At this point in our lives, the simplest version of *DrawString* is defined like so:

```
Sub DrawString(ByVal str As String, ByVal fnt As Font, _
               ByVal br As Brush, ByVal x As Single, ByVal y As Single)
```

You might expect the arguments of *DrawString* to include the text string you want to display and the coordinate position where it is to appear. You might not expect the method to also include the font used to display the text and something called a *Brush* (which is used to color the text), but there they are. The presence of these two arguments is part of what is implied when GDI+ is said to be a *stateless* graphics programming system. Just about everything that the system needs to display various graphics figures is included right in the method calls.

The downside is that the *DrawString* call is rather bulky with information. You might find yourself reducing the second and third arguments to single letters or searching out other ways to make the method call less lengthy.

The first argument to *DrawString* is the text string you want to display, for example,

```
grfx.DrawString("Hello, world!", ...)
```

Let's take a look at the other arguments in detail.

## The Font

The second argument to *DrawString* is the font used for drawing the text. This is an object of type *Font*, a class defined in the *System.Drawing* namespace. I'll have much more to say about the *Font* class in Chapter 9. Suffice it to say that a Windows Forms program has access to many fonts with scalable sizes. For now, we'll use a default font. Very conveniently, every class derived from *Control* inherits a property named *Font* that stores the default font for the control.

### *Control* Properties (selection)

| Property | Type | Accessibility | Description |
|----------|------|---------------|-------------|
| *Font* | *Font* | Get/Set | Default font for the control |

You might find it quite confusing at first to deal with a class and a property that are both named *Font*, but I assure you, after some months, you'll find it somewhat less confusing.

When you install a *Paint* event handler for a form, you can obtain the object that the event applies to by casting the first argument to the type of that object:

```
Dim frm As Form = DirectCast(obj, Form)
```

This cast works because *obj* is indeed an object of type *Form*. If *obj* were not an object of type *Form* (or a class descended from *Form*), this statement would raise an exception. If you compile with the Option Strict set to Off, you can use a simpler statement without *DirectCast*:

```
Dim frm As Form = obj
```

Thus, within the event handler, you can reference the default font for the form by using *frm.Font*. The *DrawString* call therefore looks something like this:

```
grfx.DrawString(str, frm.Font, ...);
```

If you have multiple *DrawString* calls, you might first want to define an object of type *Font* and assign the form's default font to it:

```
Dim fnt As Font = frm.Font
```

That statement includes a lot of font! The first *Font* is the class defined in the *System.Drawing* namespace, and *fnt* is defined as an object of that class. The last *Font* is a property of the *Form* class. The *DrawString* call then becomes

```
grfx.DrawString(str, fnt, ...)
```

## The Brush

The third argument to *DrawString* indicates the "color" of the font characters. I put "color" in quotation marks because the argument is actually an object of type *Brush*, and brushes can be much more than just color. Brushes can be gradients of color or fancy patterns or bitmapped images. Indeed, brushes are so wonderfully varied and powerful that they get very nearly their own entire chapter. But since that is Chapter 17 and this is Chapter 2, for now we'll have to be satisfied with very simple brushes.

The simplest way to be colorfully versatile is with the *Brushes* class. Notice the plural *Brushes* and not the singular *Brush*, which is also the name of a class. The *Brushes* class has 141 shared read-only properties with the same color names as implemented in the *Color* class and listed on the inside back cover of this book. The *Brushes* properties return objects of type *Brush*. Because these are shared properties, they are referenced using the class name and property name, like the example here:

```
grfx.DrawString(str, fnt, Brushes.PapayaWhip, ...)
```

You're probably thinking, "Sure it might be fun drawing text with lots of different colors and maybe gradients and patterns and stuff like that, but let's be realistic: Probably 97.5 percent of the text I'll want to display will be plain old black. With few exceptions, I'll probably just use *Brushes.Black* as the third argument to *DrawString*." So, you can define an object of type *Brush* like so:

```
Dim br As Brush = Brushes.Black
```

and pass that object to 97.5 percent of your *DrawString* calls:

```
grfx.DrawString(str, fnt, br, ...)
```

But I'm afraid that using *Brushes.Black* in this way would be a mistake. You're making an implicit assumption that the background of the form isn't also black. Could it be? Yes, and very easily. In such a case, the text wouldn't be visible.

Regardless, for now I'll give you special dispensation to use *Brushes.Black* in calls to *DrawString*, but only if you also set the *BackColor* property of the form to *Color.White* or something else that's guaranteed to make the black text visible. I'll discuss better approaches to selecting colors in Chapter 3.

## The Coordinate Points

Finally, the last two arguments of *DrawString* indicate the horizontal (x) and vertical (y) coordinates where the upper left corner of the text string is to appear.

If you come from a mathematics background—or if the trauma of high school mathematics has forever left its scar on your brain—you may have envisioned a two-dimensional coordinate system like so:

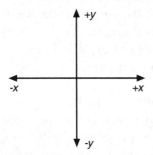

This is known as a *Cartesian coordinate system*, after French mathematician and philosopher René Descartes (1596–1650), who is credited with inventing analytical geometry, and to whom the field of computer graphics is eternally indebted.[1] The origin—the point (0, 0)—is in the center. Values of $x$ increase to the right, and values of $y$ increase going up.

However, this isn't exactly the coordinate system used in most graphical environments. A coordinate system in which increasing values of y go up is at odds with the way in which most Western languages are written. Also, early computer graphics involved programs that wrote directly into video display memory. Video memory buffers are arranged starting at the top of the screen because computer monitors scan from the top down. And that's because television sets scan from the top down, and that decision goes back some 60 years or so.

In the Windows Forms environment, as in most graphical environments[2], the default coordinate system has an origin in the upper left corner and looks like this:

I say this is the *default* coordinate system because it's possible to change it to something else. Such fun awaits us in Chapter 7.

When you draw on a form using the *Graphics* object that you obtain from the *PaintEventArgs* class passed as an argument to your *Paint* event handler, all coordinates are relative to the upper left corner of the client area of the form. All units are in pixels. Increasing values of $x$ go to the right, and increasing values of $y$ go down.

Let me repeat: Coordinates are relative to the upper left corner of the *client area*. The client area is the area inside a form that's not occupied by the form's caption bar or sizing border or any menu the form might have. When you use the *Graphics* object from the *PaintEventArgs* class, you simply cannot draw *outside* the client area. This means you never have to worry about drawing something where you're not supposed to.

---

1. A facsimile and English translation of Descartes' 1637 work on analytical geometry is available as *The Geometry of René Descartes* (New York: Dover, 1954).

2. An exception is the OS/2 Presentation Manager, which was designed as a completely bottom-up system. This was fine for graphics programming but didn't always work otherwise. Programmers had to use bottom-up coordinates when specifying the location of controls in dialog boxes, for example, which often entailed designing the dialog box from the bottom up. See Charles Petzold, *Programming the OS/2 Presentation Manager* (Redmond, WA: Microsoft Press, 1989) or Charles Petzold, *OS/2 Presentation Manager Programming* (Emeryville, CA: Ziff-Davis Press, 1994) for details.

The coordinate point passed to the *DrawString* method refers to the position of the upper left corner of the first character of the text string. If you specify a coordinate of (0, 0), the text string is thus displayed in the upper left corner of the client area.

So let's put it all together in a program called *PaintHello*.

### PaintHello.vb

```
'-----------------------------------------------
' PaintHello.vb (c) 2002 by Charles Petzold
'-----------------------------------------------
Imports System
Imports System.Drawing
Imports System.Windows.Forms

Module PaintHello
    Sub Main()
        Dim frm As New Form()
        frm.Text = "Paint Hello"
        frm.BackColor = Color.White
        AddHandler frm.Paint, AddressOf MyPaintHandler

        Application.Run(frm)
    End Sub

    Sub MyPaintHandler(ByVal obj As Object, ByVal pea As PaintEventArgs)
        Dim frm As Form = DirectCast(obj, Form)
        Dim grfx As Graphics = pea.Graphics

        grfx.DrawString("Hello, world!", frm.Font, Brushes.Black, 0, 0)
    End Sub
End Module
```

And here we have our first—but, as you'll see, perhaps not quite the simplest—program that displays text in a form. The text appears in the upper left corner of the client area:

# The *Paint* Event Is Special!

Watch out what you put in the *Paint* event handler. The method can be called quite frequently and sometimes unexpectedly, and it works best when it can repaint the client area quickly without interruption.

Earlier in this chapter, I suggested that you use message boxes for simple debugging. But don't put a call to *MessageBox.Show* in the *Paint* event handler! The message box could cover up part of the client area and result in another *Paint* event. And another and another and another…. Also, don't put any *Console.Read* or *Console.ReadLine* calls in there or in *any* event handler. *Console.Write* or *Console.WriteLine* calls are safe, however.

And don't do anything that accumulates. In one of my very early Windows Forms programs, I wrote a *Paint* event handler that accessed the *Font* property, made a new font that was twice as big, and set the *Font* property to that new font. Well, every time there was a new *Paint* event, the font got twice as big as the time before. It was like *Honey, I Blew Up the Font*.

Doing all your drawing in the *Paint* event handler might sound a bit restrictive, and at times it is. That's why Windows Forms implements a couple of methods to make painting more flexible.

First, you can obtain a *Graphics* object outside a *Paint* event handler by calling the *CreateGraphics* method implemented in *Control* and inherited by *Form*. Second, at times, you'll need to generate a *Paint* event from some other event. The method that does this is *Invalidate*, which is implemented in the *Control* class. I'll demonstrate how to do these things when covering keyboard, mouse, and timer input in Chapters 6, 8, and 10.

# Multiple Forms, Multiple Handlers

To get a better feel for the *Paint* event handler, let's look at a couple variations on the basic theme. This program uses the same *Paint* event handler for two forms that it creates.

```
PaintTwoForms.vb
'-----------------------------------------------------
' PaintTwoForms.vb (c) 2002 by Charles Petzold
'-----------------------------------------------------
Imports System
Imports System.Drawing
Imports System.Windows.Forms
```

*(continued)*

**PaintTwoForms.vb**   *(continued)*

```
Module PaintTwoForms
    Private frm1, frm2 As Form

    Sub Main()
        frm1 = New Form()
        frm2 = New Form()

        frm1.Text = "First Form"
        frm1.BackColor = Color.White
        AddHandler frm1.Paint, AddressOf MyPaintHandler

        frm2.Text = "Second Form"
        frm2.BackColor = Color.White
        AddHandler frm2.Paint, AddressOf MyPaintHandler
        frm2.Show()

        Application.Run(frm1)
    End Sub

    Sub MyPaintHandler(ByVal obj As Object, ByVal pea As PaintEventArgs)
        Dim frm As Form = DirectCast(obj, Form)
        Dim grfx As Graphics = pea.Graphics
        Dim str As String

        If frm Is frm1 Then
            str = "Hello from the first form"
        Else
            str = "Hello from the second form"
        End If

        grfx.DrawString(str, frm.Font, Brushes.Black, 0, 0)
    End Sub
End Module
```

Notice that the *Form* objects are stored as fields so that they are accessible from both *Main* and the *Paint* event handler. Each call to the *Paint* event handler applies to one of the two forms the program created. The event handler can determine which form it applies to by comparing the *obj* argument (cast to a *Form* object) with the two *Form* objects stored as fields. If you don't mind a little capitalization problem, you could replace the entire *If* and *Else* construction with the single statement

```
str = "Hello from the " & frm.Text
```

You also wouldn't need to store the two *Form* objects as fields.

Now let's try just the opposite. Let's create one form but attach two *Paint* event handlers to it.

```
TwoPaintHandlers.vb
'------------------------------------------------------
' TwoPaintHandlers.vb (c) 2002 by Charles Petzold
'------------------------------------------------------
Imports System
Imports System.Drawing
Imports System.Windows.Forms

Module TwoPaintHandlers
    Sub Main()
        Dim frm As New Form()
        frm.Text = "Two Paint Handlers"
        frm.BackColor = Color.White
        AddHandler frm.Paint, AddressOf PaintHandler1
        AddHandler frm.Paint, AddressOf PaintHandler2

        Application.Run(frm)
    End Sub

    Sub PaintHandler1(ByVal obj As Object, ByVal pea As PaintEventArgs)
        Dim frm As Form = DirectCast(obj, Form)
        Dim grfx As Graphics = pea.Graphics
        grfx.DrawString("First Paint Event Handler", frm.Font, _
                    Brushes.Black, 0, 0)
    End Sub

    Sub PaintHandler2(ByVal obj As Object, ByVal pea As PaintEventArgs)
        Dim frm As Form = DirectCast(obj, Form)
        Dim grfx As Graphics = pea.Graphics
        grfx.DrawString("Second Paint Event Handler", frm.Font, _
                    Brushes.Black, 0, 100)
    End Sub
End Module
```

This program highlights one of the interesting aspects of attaching handlers to events. If there is more than one handler, all the handlers get called in sequence. Notice that the *DrawString* coordinates are (0, 0) in the first handler and (0, 100) in the second handler. I'm making an assumption that the default font isn't more than 100 pixels tall, but that seems fairly safe.

# Inheriting Forms

So far, you've seen how you can create a form, give it some properties (such as a text string to show in its caption bar and a nondefault background color), and attach some event handlers. Just as you attached a *Paint* event handler, you can attach handlers for the keyboard, mouse, menus, and so forth.

But I'm afraid the truth is this: it's not usually done like that.

To exploit the full power of everything implemented in the *Form* class, you can't just create a form. You must *become* a form. For just as *Control* begat *ScrollableControl*, and *ScrollableControl* begat *ContainerControl*, and *ContainerControl* begat *Form*, then *Form* can now beget some truly amazing form that only you can create.

You create such a form in your program by defining a class that inherits from *Form*. Let's take a look.

### InheritTheForm.vb

```
'-------------------------------------------------
' InheritTheForm.vb (c) 2002 by Charles Petzold
'-------------------------------------------------
Imports System
Imports System.Drawing
Imports System.Windows.Forms

Module InhertTheForm
    Sub Main()
        Dim frm As New InheritFromForm()
        frm.Text = "Inherit the Form"
        frm.BackColor = Color.White

        Application.Run(frm)
    End Sub
End Module
```

```
Class InheritFromForm
    Inherits Form
End Class
```

InheritTheForm.vb has both a module (named *InheritTheForm*) and a class named *InheritFromForm*. As the name suggests, *InheritFromForm* inherits from *Form*:

```
Class InheritFromForm
    Inherits Form
End Class
```

The *Inherits* statement indicates that *InheritFromForm* is a descendent of *Form* and inherits every method and property of *Form*.

As usual, the module (*InheritTheForm*) has a *Main* method that is the entry point to the program. However, *Main* creates a new instance of *Inherit-FromForm* rather than *Form*. Because *InheritFromForm* derives from *Form*, of course it also has properties named *Text* and *BackColor*, which the program sets next. Just as an object of type *Form* can be passed to *Application.Run*, any object of a type derived from *Form* can also be passed to *Application.Run*.

The InheritTheForm program creates the form, performs initialization (which in this case just involves setting the *Text* property), and then passes the form object to *Application.Run*. A more conventional approach is to perform all form initialization in the class's constructor.

**InheritWithConstructor.vb**

```
'-----------------------------------------------------
' InheritWithConstructor.vb (c) 2002 by Charles Petzold
'-----------------------------------------------------
Imports System
Imports System.Drawing
Imports System.Windows.Forms

Module InheritWithConstructor
    Sub Main()
        Application.Run(New InheritAndConstruct())
    End Sub
End Module

Class InheritAndConstruct
    Inherits Form

    Sub New()
        Text = "Inherit with Constructor"
        BackColor = Color.White
    End Sub
End Class
```

You'll recall that a constructor is a *Sub* named *New*, and a default constructor has an empty argument list.

*Form* has a pedigree starting at *Object* and encompassing five other classes. When an *InheritAndConstruct* object is created in *Main*, first the default constructor for *Object* is called, then the default constructor for the *MarshalBy-RefObject* class, and so forth on through the default constructor for the *Form* class, and finally the default constructor for the *InheritAndConstruct* class.

Notice that I don't have to preface the *Text* and *BackColor* properties with an object name, an object that I called *frm* in previous programs in this chapter. These properties don't need anything in front of them because they are properties of the *InheritAndConstruct* class. They are properties of *Inherit-AndConstruct* because this class derives from *Control* and *Form*, in which these properties and many others were originally defined.

If I wanted to preface these properties with anything, it would be the keyword *Me*:

```
Me.Text = "Inherit with Constructor"
Me.BackColor = Color.White
```

The *Me* keyword indicates the current object.

# The *OnPaint* Method

What advantages do you get by inheriting *Form* rather than just creating an instance of it? Although most of the methods and properties implemented in *Form* are defined as *Public*, some essential ones are defined as *Protected*. These protected methods and properties can be accessed only by a descendent of *Form*. One such protected property is *ResizeRedraw*, which I'll be discussing in Chapter 3.

One protected method inherited by *Form* by way of *Control* is named *OnPaint*. You don't want to *call* this method, however; you want to *override* it, for if you do, you don't have to install a *Paint* event handler. The *OnPaint* method has a single argument, which is an object of type *PaintEventArgs*. You can use this argument to obtain a *Graphics* object just as in a *Paint* event handler.

**InheritWithPaint.vb**

```
'-------------------------------------------------
' InheritWithPaint.vb (c) 2002 by Charles Petzold
'-------------------------------------------------
Imports System
Imports System.Drawing
Imports System.Windows.Forms

Module InheritWithPaint
```

```
    Sub Main()
        Application.Run(New InheritAndPaint())
    End Sub
End Module

Class InheritAndPaint
    Inherits Form

    Sub New()
        Text = "Hello World"
        BackColor = Color.White
    End Sub

    Protected Overrides Sub OnPaint(ByVal pea As PaintEventArgs)
        Dim grfx As Graphics = pea.Graphics
        grfx.DrawString("Hello, Windows Forms!", Font, Brushes.Black, 0, 0)
    End Sub
End Class
```

Notice in *OnPaint* that I don't have to preface the *Font* with anything. That's because *OnPaint* is a member of the same class of which *Font* is a property. Also notice that, unlike the *Paint* event handler, the *OnPaint* method doesn't need a first argument that indicates the sender. The form that the *OnPaint* method applies to is always *Me*.

# Is the Module Necessary?

The InheritWithPaint.vb file contains both a module and a class. The sole method in the module is *Main*, which has the job of creating an instance of the class and calling *Application.Run*. This architecture may seem very clean and straightforward, but there's actually a somewhat simpler way to do it.

You can get rid of the module entirely by moving the *Main* method into the class. At first, you may find this very odd. It may appear as if the program is pulling itself up by its bootstraps. How can the *Main* method execute at all when an instance of the class hasn't been created yet?

The solution is to define the *Main* method as *Shared*. Shared methods exist independently of any objects that are instantiated from the class. For example, *Color.Chocolate* is a shared property of the *Color* class that returns an instance of the class. Conceptually, the operating system loads a program into memory and begins execution by making a call to the *Main* method. It couldn't make this call unless *Main* were in a module or defined as *Shared* within a class. (It's actually possible to dispense with the *Main* method entirely, and specify that the startup object is the class, but I don't feel comfortable with programs that don't have real entry points.)

And here's my final version of a Windows Forms hello-world program.

```
HelloWorld.vb
'-------------------------------------------------
' HelloWorld.vb (c) 2002 by Charles Petzold
'-------------------------------------------------
Imports System
Imports System.Drawing
Imports System.Windows.Forms

Class HelloWorld
    Inherits Form

    Shared Sub Main()
        Application.Run(New HelloWorld())
    End Sub

    Sub New()
        Text = "Hello World"
        BackColor = Color.White
    End Sub

    Protected Overrides Sub OnPaint(ByVal pea As PaintEventArgs)
        Dim grfx As Graphics = pea.Graphics
        grfx.DrawString("Hello, Windows Forms!", Font, Brushes.Black, 0, 0)
    End Sub
End Class
```

This is the official, certified, programmer-tested and mother-approved way to create a form in Visual Basic using the Windows Forms class library. That's why this is the first program in this book to be called simply HelloWorld. (In the next chapter, I'll show you a better way to specify the background and text colors, however.) And here's what it looks like:

Of course, there's always some smart aleck in the back row with a raised hand and the impudent question, "Can you now *center* that text in the window?" Yes, and in the next chapter, I'll show you three different ways to do it.

# Events and "On" Methods

Earlier, when we were working with modules rather than classes derived from *Form*, we installed *Paint* event handlers. As you'll recall when you create an instance of *Control* or any class derived from *Control* (such as *Form*), you can install a *Paint* event handler by defining a method with the same return types and arguments as the *PaintEventHandler* delegate:

```
Sub MyPaintHandler(ByVal obj As Object, ByVal pea As PaintEventArgs)
    ' Painting code
End Sub
```

You then install this paint handler for a particular object (named *frm*, for example) using the code

```
AddHandler frm.Paint, AddressOf MyPaintHandler
```

In a class *derived* from *Control*, however, you don't need to install a *Paint* event handler (even though you can). You can simply override the protected *OnPaint* method:

```
Protected Overrides Sub OnPaint(ByVal pea As PaintEventArgs)
    ' Painting code
End Sub
```

You'll find that all events defined in Windows Forms are similar. Every event has a corresponding protected method. The method has a name that consists of the word *On* followed by the event name. For each event that we'll encounter, I'll show a little table like this:

### *Control* Events (selection)

| Event | Method | Delegate | Argument |
| --- | --- | --- | --- |
| *Paint* | *OnPaint* | *PaintEventHandler* | *PaintEventArgs* |

The table indicates the name of the event, the corresponding method, the delegate you use to define an event handler, and the argument to the event handler and the method.

You might assume—as I did originally—that the *OnPaint* method is basically just a preinstalled *Paint* event handler. But that's wrong. It's really implemented the other way around: the *OnPaint* method in *Control* is actually responsible for calling all the installed *Paint* handlers.

Let's explore this concept a bit. First, just as the *HelloWorld* class shown earlier inherited from *Form*, here's a class named *InheritHelloWorld* that inherits from *HelloWorld*.

```
InheritHelloWorld.vb
'----------------------------------------------------
' InheritHelloWorld.vb (c) 2002 by Charles Petzold
'----------------------------------------------------
Imports System
Imports System.Drawing
Imports System.Windows.Forms

Class InheritHelloWorld
    Inherits HelloWorld

    Shared Shadows Sub Main()
        Application.Run(New InheritHelloWorld())
    End Sub

    Sub New()
        Text = "Inherit " & Text
    End Sub

    Protected Overrides Sub OnPaint(ByVal pea As PaintEventArgs)
        Dim grfx As Graphics = pea.Graphics
        grfx.DrawString("Hello from InheritHelloWorld!", _
                        Font, Brushes.Black, 0, 100)
    End Sub
End Class
```

Let me take care of some housekeeping issues first. When I created the InheritHelloWorld project in Visual Basic .NET, I created a new Visual Basic file named InheritHelloWorld.vb, as usual, but I also needed to include Hello-World.vb in the project. I did that by using the Add Existing Item option and specifying Link File in the drop-down menu next to the Open button. That avoids making a second copy of the HelloWorld.vb file.

Notice that the *Main* method includes the *Shadows* keyword, indicating that it is supposed to replace any *Main* methods that may be in any parent classes (such as *HelloWorld*). You also have to tell Visual Basic .NET which *Main* you want to be the entry point to the program. You do this with the project's Property Pages dialog box. In the General Common Properties, specify the Startup Object as *InheritHelloWorld*.

If you're running the command-line Visual Basic compiler, specify both source code files in the command line and use the compiler switch

```
/Main:InheritHelloWorld
```

to indicate which class has the *Main* method you want as the entry point to the program.

As I mentioned earlier, when you create a new object based on a derived class using a default constructor, all the ancestral default constructors are called starting with *Object*. Toward the end of this process, the *HelloWorld* constructor gets called and responds by setting the *Text* property of the form to "Hello World." Finally, the *InheritHelloWorld* constructor is executed and sets the *Text* property like so:

```
Text = "Inherit " + Text
```

That the caption bar of this program reads "Inherit Hello World" demonstrates that this sequence of events is correct.

The *OnPaint* method in *InheritHelloWorld* overrides the *OnPaint* method in *HelloWorld*. When *InheritHelloWorld* runs, it displays "Hello from Inherit-HelloWorld!" I've positioned the text at the coordinate position (0, 100) so you can see that the *OnPaint* method in *HelloWorld* isn't also executed. The *OnPaint* method in *HelloWorld* is overridden.

Now let's take a look at a program that does something a little different. This program doesn't define a class that inherits from *HelloWorld*; this one instantiates the *HelloWorld* class.

**InstantiateHelloWorld.vb**

```
'----------------------------------------------------------
' InstantiateHelloWorld.vb (c) 2002 by Charles Petzold
'----------------------------------------------------------
Imports System
Imports System.Drawing
Imports System.Windows.Forms

Module InstantiateHelloWorld
    Sub Main()
        Dim frm As New HelloWorld()
        frm.Text = "Instantiate " & frm.Text
        AddHandler frm.Paint, AddressOf MyPaintHandler
        Application.Run(frm)
    End Sub

    Sub MyPaintHandler(ByVal obj As Object, ByVal pea As PaintEventArgs)
        Dim frm As Form = DirectCast(obj, Form)
        Dim grfx As Graphics = pea.Graphics
        grfx.DrawString("Hello from InstantiateHelloWorld!", _
                        frm.Font, Brushes.Black, 0, 100)
    End Sub
End Module
```

Take a close look at this code. First, notice that *InstantiateHelloWorld* is a module; it can't inherit from *HelloWorld* or *Form* or anything else. Instead, it creates a new instance of the *HelloWorld* class and saves it in the variable *frm*, just as early programs in this chapter created instances of the *Form* class:

```
Dim frm As New HelloWorld()
```

During the creation of the *HelloWorld* object, the *HelloWorld* constructor is called, which gives the form a *Text* property of "Hello World." The next statement prepends the word *Instantiate* to the *Text* property. The program then installs a *Paint* event handler for the form.

But what appears in InstantiateHelloWorld's client area is *not* the text "Hello from InstantiateHelloWorld!" but instead the text "Hello, Windows Forms!" which is what the *OnPaint* method in *HelloWorld* displays. What happened?

The *OnPaint* method in *Control* is responsible for calling the installed *Paint* event handlers. Because the *HelloWorld* class overrides *OnPaint*, that job doesn't get done. That's why the .NET documentation recommends that when you override one of the protected methods beginning with the *On* prefix, you should call the *On* method in the base class like so:

```
MyBase.OnPaint(pea)
```

Try inserting this statement at the top of HelloWorld's *OnPaint* method and rebuilding InstantiateHelloWorld. Now the program works as you probably wanted it to. InstantiateHelloWorld displays its text string ("Hello from InstantiateHelloWorld!") and also the "Hello, Windows Forms!" text string.

The sequence of events in the revised version is this:

■  Whenever the client area becomes invalid, the *OnPaint* method is called. This is the *OnPaint* method in the *HelloWorld* class, which overrides any *OnPaint* method in ancestral classes.

■  The *OnPaint* method in HelloWorld calls the *OnPaint* method in its base class. (Remember, I'm talking about a revised version of HelloWorld that includes the *MyBase.OnPaint* call.) That would normally be the *OnPaint* method implemented in *Form*, but it's likely *Form* doesn't override the *OnPaint* method and what really gets called is the *OnPaint* method back in *Control*.

■  The *OnPaint* method in *Control* calls all the installed *Paint* event handlers. The only one in this process is the *MyPaintHandler* method in InstantiateHelloWorld. That method displays some text at position (0, 100).

■  When all the installed *Paint* event handlers have been called, the *OnPaint* method in *Control* returns back to the *OnPaint* method in HelloWorld.

■   The *OnPaint* method in HelloWorld displays some text at position (0, 0).

The Windows Forms documentation recommends that whenever you override an *On* method you call the base class *On* method. However, in most cases, you need to do this only if you're defining a class that you'll also be instantiating, and that the instantiated classes are also installing event handlers for *On* methods you've overridden. This scenario doesn't happen very often. Still, at times, you need to call the base class in overrides of *On* methods regardless. As we'll see in the next chapter, one of these is *OnResize*.

# 3

# Essential Structures

Computers were originally built to perform numeric calculations, and crunching numbers is still what computers do best. Virtually all programming languages have mechanisms for storing numbers in variables, performing arithmetical operations, looping through ranges of numbers, comparing numbers, and displaying numbers in a readable form.

For many programming languages, the next step beyond numbers is text in the form of character strings. Character strings chiefly exist to allow computer programs to communicate with human users. Internal to the computer, of course, characters are represented by numbers, as is everything else in the machine.

It is the central premise of object-oriented programming that data types beyond the standard numbers and character strings be easy to define and easy to work with. We've already seen several examples of that ease of use, including a class named *Form*, which hardly seems like either a number or a character string.

In programming for graphical environments, four other data types appear quite frequently:

- Two-dimensional coordinate points

- Two-dimensional sizes in terms of width and height

- Rectangles

- Colors

These four data types are the focus of this chapter.

# Classes and Structures

These four data types—actually seven because three of them are implemented in both integer and floating-point forms—are defined in the *System.Drawing* namespace. Interestingly enough, these seven data types are *not* implemented as classes. They are instead *structures*, and indeed, these are seven of only eight structures defined in *System.Drawing*. The structure data type (which is defined in a Microsoft Visual Basic program using the keyword *Structure*) is similar in many ways to a class. The big difference lies in the fact that classes are *reference types*, and structures are *value types*. Let's examine what this difference means. Consider the following expression:

```
New Form()
```

This statement causes a memory block to be allocated in an area of general-purpose memory known as the *heap*. This memory block must be large enough for an instance of the *Form* object, which means that it must be large enough for all of *Form*'s instance (that is, nonshared) fields. If you look at the .NET documentation, that amount of space might not seem like much, but remember that you're not seeing the *Private* fields, and there are undoubtedly many of them.

The value returned from that *New* expression is essentially a pointer to the memory block located in the heap. That memory pointer is what's saved in the variable *frm* in a statement like this:

```
Dim frm As New Form()
```

That's what a *reference type* means: the object is a pointer to (references) a memory block.

Suppose you do something like this:

```
Dim frm2 As Form = frm
frm2.Text = "Form 2 Text"
```

Go ahead: insert these calls into the PaintEvent program from Chapter 2, right before the call to *Application.Run*. What happens? The form that we're displaying—the form referenced by *frm*—gets the caption bar text "Form 2 Text." How can this be? It's because *frm* is a pointer. The statement

```
Dim frm2 As Form = frm
```

simply copies that pointer to *frm2*. The statement does *not* create a new instance of the *Form* class. The variables *frm* and *frm2* are equal, which means they point to the same memory block and therefore refer to the same object.

Now obviously, passing pointers around isn't something you want happening universally. Consider the following sequence of statements:

```
Dim a As Integer = 5
Dim b As Integer = a
a = 10
```

You wouldn't want this to mean that *a* and *b* were identical pointers that would always refer to the same number, and that *b* was now equal to 10! That would be insane. And that's why numbers in Visual Basic are *value types*. The variable name of any value type is *not* a pointer to a location in memory that stores the number. The variable name represents the number itself.

If you check through the documentation of the *System* namespace, you'll find that most of the basic types—*Boolean, Byte, Char, Decimal, Double, Int16, Int32, Int64, Single*—are defined as structures rather than classes. Structures inherit from *ValueType*, which inherits from *Object*. You can think of value types as "lightweight objects," and indeed, you should use *Structure* only for types that are small and that might be frequently created and destroyed. Structures cannot implement events; nor can they be inherited.

# Two-Dimensional Coordinate Points

One data type that is prevalent enough in graphical environments and small enough to justify making it a structure rather than a class is a *coordinate point*, represented in the Microsoft .NET Framework by the structure *Point*. In a two-dimensional coordinate system (such as the surface of a video display or a sheet of printer paper), a point is signified by two numbers, generally the number pair $(x, y)$, where $x$ is the horizontal coordinate and $y$ is the vertical coordinate. In Chapter 2, I discussed how the coordinates system in Windows Forms is defined, but the *Point* data type doesn't necessarily imply any particular coordinate system. You can use *Point* in any two-dimensional coordinate system.

The *Point* structure has two read-write properties, named *X* and *Y*, which are defined as 32-bit integers. *X* and *Y* can be negative. One implication of *Point* being a structure rather than a class is that you can define a *Point* variable using the same syntax as an *Integer*. You don't need to use the *New* operator:

```
Dim pt As Point
pt.X = 23
pt.Y = 47
```

Nor do you have to remember *not* to use the *New* operator. You can also define a new instance of *Point* using the same syntax as if *Point* were a class:

```
Dim pt As Point = New Point()
```

or

```
Dim pt As New Point()
```

These statements result in both the *X* and *Y* properties being initialized to 0. Then you can set the *X* and *Y* properties to explicit values:

```
pt.X = 23
pt.Y = 47
```

Or you can use this declaration to initialize the values:

```
Dim pt As New Point(34, 55)
```

Or, in a rare instance of bit packing in the .NET Framework, you can specify the two coordinates as 16-bit values stuck together in a 32-bit integer, as here:

```
Dim pt As New Point(&H01000010)
```

This declaration results in the *X* property being set to 16 (&H0010) and the *Y* property to 256 (&H0100). I don't suggest you begin treating points as single 32-bit integers; this declaration is mostly for the benefit of people who must continue to use Win32 API functions, which sometimes involve packed coordinates.

You can also initialize a new *Point* object using any method, property, or field that returns a *Point*. Actually, the *Point* structure has one such member itself. It's a shared field named *Empty*:

```
Dim pt As Point = Point.Empty
```

Notice the use of the capitalized *Point* on the right to indicate the *Point* structure itself rather than an instance of the *Point* structure. You need to reference the *Point* structure because the *Empty* field is shared. This statement results in the *X* and *Y* properties being initialized to 0. *Point* also has a read-only property named *IsEmpty* that returns *True* if both *X* and *Y* equal 0.

Here's a complete list of the *Point* properties:

### *Point* Properties

| Property | Type | Accessibility |
|----------|------|---------------|
| *X* | *Integer* | Get/Set |
| *Y* | *Integer* | Get/Set |
| *IsEmpty* | *Boolean* | Get |

*Point* inherits the *GetType* method from *Object*, overrides the *GetHashCode*, *ToString*, and *Equals* methods inherited from *Object* by way of *ValueType*, and implements a method named *Offset* on its own. Here's a complete list of the public instance (that is, nonshared) methods of *Point*:

### *Point* Instance Methods

```
Function GetType() As Type

Function GetHashCode() As Integer

Function ToString() As String

Function Equals(ByVal obj As Object) As Boolean

Sub Offset(ByVal dx As Integer, ByVal dy As Integer)
```

There are three shared methods of *Point* that I'll discuss shortly.

The *ToString* method converts a *Point* object to a readable character string. For example, after the statements

```
Dim pt As New Point(5, 201)
Dim str As String = pt.ToString()
```

the *str* variable is set to the text string *{X=5,Y=201}*. The *ToString* method is called by *Console.Write, Console.WriteLine,* and *String.Format* to convert objects to strings.

The *Equals* method tests whether one point is equal to another, as in the statement

```
If pt1.Equals(pt2) Then
```

Two points are considered equal if the *X* and *Y* properties of the two *Point* objects are both equal to each other. You can also use the *op_Equality* (or *op_Inequality*) operators:

```
If Point.op_Equality(pt1, pt2) Then
    ...
End If
```

The *Offset* method

```
pt.Offset(21, -12)
```

is basically the same as adding the two offsets to the properties:

```
pt.X += 21
pt.Y += -12
```

# Arrays of Points

Arrays of *Point* structures are common in programming for graphical environments. For example, an array of *Point* structures could represent a complex curve or the locations of buttons on a calculator. To create an array of, say, 23 *Point* structures, you can use the following statement:

```
Dim apt(22) As Point
```

Visual Basic .NET uses zero-based indexing for arrays, so the valid array elements are *apt(0)* through *apt(22)*. When you allocate an array of *Point* structures, each of the elements is initialized to the point (0, 0).

It's also possible to initialize the array elements when you create the array:

```
Dim apt() As Point = New Point(2) {New Point(25, 50), _
                                   New Point(43, 32), _
                                   New Point(27, 8)}
```

You must have exactly as many initializers as the number of elements in the array. Indeed, you don't need to include the dimension:

```
Dim apt() As Point = New Point() {New Point(25, 50), _
                                  New Point(43, 32), _
                                  New Point(27, 8)}
```

And you can even leave out the first *New* expression:

```
Dim apt() As Point = {New Point(25, 50), _
                      New Point(43, 32), _
                      New Point(27, 8)}
```

# The *Size* Structure

The *Size* structure is very much like *Point*, but instead of the *X* and *Y* properties, it has *Width* and *Height* properties:

### *Size* Properties

| Property | Type | Accessibility |
| --- | --- | --- |
| *Width* | *Integer* | Get/Set |
| *Height* | *Integer* | Get/Set |
| *IsEmpty* | *Boolean* | Get |

You can create a new *Size* structure the same way you create a *Point* structure:

```
Dim sz As New Size(15, 20)
```

The *Width* and *Height* properties of the *Size* structure can be negative.

The *Point* and *Size* structures are so similar that they can be constructed from each other. Here's a complete list of the *Point* constructors:

### *Point* Constructors

```
Point()
Point(ByVal xyPacked As Integer)
Point(ByVal x As Integer, ByVal y As Integer)
Point(ByVal sz As Size)
```

And here's a complete list of the *Size* constructors:

### *Size* Constructors

```
Size()
Size(ByVal width As Integer, ByVal height As Integer)
Size(ByVal pt As Point)
```

You can also cast a *Point* object to a *Size* object and vice versa using operators provided by the structures:

```
pt = Size.op_Explicit(sz)
sz = Point.op_Explicit(pt)
```

The *Size* structure provides addition and subtraction operators so you can add two sizes, as in

```
sz3 = Size.op_Addition(sz1, sz2)
```

or subtract two sizes, as here:

```
sz2 = Size.op_Subtraction(sz3, sz1)
```

What's going on here is what you'd expect: the *Width* and *Height* properties are being added or subtracted individually.

The *Point* structure also provides addition and subtraction operators, but I didn't mention these operations earlier because they also involve a *Size* structure. Under the assumption that it makes no sense to add two points together, the only objects you can add to or subtract from *Point* objects are *Size* objects.

```
pt2 = Point.op_Addition(pt1, sz)
pt3 = Point.op_Subtraction(pt2, sz)
```

## The Float Versions

Visual Basic .NET supports two floating-point data types, *Single* and *Double*. The *Double* data type is rarely used in Windows Forms or GDI+, but *Single* shows up a lot. You may wonder why you need floating-point coordinates when drawing in units of pixels, but you'll discover in Chapter 7 that you can use coordinate systems based on units other than pixels.

The *PointF* structure is very much like the *Point* structure except that the *X* and *Y* properties are *Single* values rather than *Integer*. Similarly, the *SizeF* structure is very much like *Size* except that *Width* and *Height* are *Single* values. The *PointF* and *SizeF* structures support addition, subtraction, equality, and inequality operators just as *Point* and *Size* do.

Like *Point*, the *PointF* structure implements a constructor that lets you initialize it during creation:

```
Dim ptf As New PointF(2.5, 3E-2)
```

The *PointF* structure does not include an *Offset* method.

Casting a *Point* to a *PointF* requires use of the *op_Implicit* operator defined in *Point*:

```
ptf = Point.op_Implicit(pt)
```

However, you can't cast a *PointF* to a *Point*. Instead, to convert a *PointF* to a *Point*, you must use one of the shared methods provided for that purpose by the *Point* structure:

### *Point* Shared Methods

```
Function Round(ByVal ptf As PointF) As Point

Function Truncate(ByVal ptf As PointF) As Point

Function Ceiling(ByVal ptf As PointF) As Point
```

For example,

```
pt = Point.Round(ptf)
```

*Round* must be preceded by the structure name because it's a shared method.

The *Round* method rounds the *X* and *Y* properties to the nearest integer, and to the nearest even integer for fractional parts of 0.5. The *Truncate* method essentially strips the fractional part and rounds toward 0. For example, coordinates of 0.9 and -0.9 both become 0. The *Ceiling* method rounds toward the next highest integer, that is, 0.9 becomes 1 and -0.9 becomes 0.

Similarly, you can cast a *Size* to a *SizeF* using *Size.op_Implicit*, but you should use the following methods to convert a *SizeF* to a *Size*:

### *Size* Shared Methods

```
Function Round(ByVal szf As SizeF) As Size

Function Truncate(ByVal szf As SizeF) As Size

Function Ceiling(ByVal szf As SizeF) As Size
```

The *SizeF* structure also includes the following two instance methods, the only instance methods that *SizeF* doesn't inherit or override:

### *SizeF* Instance Methods

```
Function ToPointF() As PointF
Function ToSize() As Size
```

The *ToSize* method is equivalent to the *Truncate* method. The *SizeF.op_Explicit* operator also converts from a *SizeF* to a *PointF*. Oddly enough, while you can convert between *Point* and *Size*, from *Point* to *PointF*, from *Size* to *SizeF*, and from *SizeF* to *PointF*, you can't cast from *PointF* to *SizeF*. However, *SizeF* provides a constructor that takes a *PointF* argument. Here, for comparison purposes, is a complete list of the constructors for the four structures:

### Constructor Comparisons

| *Point* | *PointF* | *Size* | *SizeF* |
| --- | --- | --- | --- |
| *()* | *()* | *()* | *()* |
| *(x, y)* | *(x, y)* | *(cx, cy)* | *(cx, cy)* |
| *(sz)* | | *(pt)* | *(ptf)* |
| *(xyPacked)* | | | *(szf)* |

# A Rectangle Is a Point and a Size

The *Rectangle* structure defines a rectangle as a combination of a *Point* and a *Size*. The idea here is that the *Point* refers to the location of the upper left corner of the rectangle and the *Size* is the width and height of this rectangle—which is not to say that the width and height must be non-negative. The *Rectangle* structure itself imposes no such restriction. However, as we'll explore in Chapters 4 and 5, the *Rectangle* structure is used in some drawing functions, and those functions require non-negative widths and heights. The *Rectangle* structure has two constructors:

### *Rectangle* Constructors

```
Rectangle(ByVal pt As Point, ByVal sz As Size)

Rectangle(ByVal x As Integer, ByVal y As Integer,
          ByVal cx As Integer, ByVal cy As Integer)
```

Veteran Windows programmers: Watch out for that last constructor, and in other places where you specify a rectangle using four numbers: the second two numbers are not the coordinates of the bottom right corner of the rectangle!

There's also a *RectangleF* structure with the following constructors:

### *RectangleF* Constructors

```
RectangleF(ByVal ptf As PointF, ByVal szf As SizeF)

RectangleF(ByVal x As Single, ByVal y As Single,
           ByVal cx As Single, ByVal cy As Single)
```

As you can see, the constructors for *Rectangle* and *RectangleF* are identical except for the data types.

In fact, the entire implementations of the *Rectangle* and *RectangleF* structures are so similar that you'll swear a template was somehow involved. Aside from the data types, the only difference is that the *RectangleF* structure defines the *RectangleF.op_Implicit* operator to convert from a *Rectangle* to a *RectangleF*, while the *Rectangle* structure defines three shared (and by now familiar) methods that let you convert from a *RectangleF* to a *Rectangle*:

### *Rectangle* Shared Methods (selection)

```
Function Round(ByVal rectf As RectangleF) As Rectangle

Function Truncate(ByVal rectf As RectangleF) As Rectangle

Function Ceiling(ByVal rectf As RectangleF) As Rectangle
```

So from here on, I'll refer to the *Rectangle* structure only, but everything I say applies to *RectangleF* as well. The data types associated with *RectangleF* are, of course, *Single*, *PointF*, and *SizeF* rather than *Integer*, *Point*, and *Size*.

# Rectangle Properties and Methods

The *Rectangle* structure defines a host of properties that give you information in whatever way you want:

### *Rectangle* Properties

| Property | Type | Accessibility |
|----------|------|---------------|
| *Location* | *Point* | Get/Set |
| *Size* | *Size* | Get/Set |
| *X* | *Integer* | Get/Set |

*(continued)*

### *Rectangle* Properties   *(continued)*

| Property | Type | Accessibility |
|----------|------|---------------|
| *Y* | *Integer* | Get/Set |
| *Width* | *Integer* | Get/Set |
| *Height* | *Integer* | Get/Set |
| *Left* | *Integer* | Get |
| *Top* | *Integer* | Get |
| *Right* | *Integer* | Get |
| *Bottom* | *Integer* | Get |
| *IsEmpty* | *Boolean* | Get |

The *Left* property returns the same value as *X*; the *Top* property returns the same value as *Y*. The *Right* property returns the sum of *X* and *Width*; and the *Bottom* property returns the sum of *Y* and *Height*, even if *Width* and *Height* are negative. In other words, *Left* can be greater than *Right*, and *Top* can be greater than *Bottom*.

Both *Rectangle* and *RectangleF* include *Equals* methods and *op_Equality* and *op_Inequality* operators. Although addition and subtraction are not defined for *Rectangle* structures, several methods do allow you to manipulate *Rectangle* structures in various ways or to create new *Rectangle* structures from existing ones.

For Windows programmers accustomed to thinking in terms of upper left and lower right, there's a shared method that creates a *Rectangle* from those two coordinates:

### *Rectangle* Shared Methods (selection)

```
Function FromLTRB(ByVal xLeft As Integer, _
                  ByVal yTop As Integer,
                  ByVal xRight As Integer, _
                  ByVal yBottom As Integer) As Rectangle
```

The method returns a newly created *Rectangle* object. The call

```
rect = Rectangle.FromLTRB(x1, y1, x2, y2)
```

is equivalent to

```
rect = New Rectangle(x1, y1, x2 - x1, y2 - y1)
```

The *Offset* and *Inflate* methods manipulate a *Rectangle* structure and compensate for the lack of addition and subtraction operators:

### *Rectangle* Methods (selection)

```
Sub Offset(ByVal x As Integer, ByVal y As Integer)
Sub Offset(ByVal pt As Point)
Sub Inflate(ByVal x As Integer, ByVal y As Integer)
Sub Inflate(ByVal sz As Size)
Shared Function Inflate(ByVal rect As Rectangle, ByVal x As Integer,
                        ByVal y As Integer) As Rectangle
```

The *Offset* method shifts a rectangle to another location. The method call

```
rect.Offset(23, -46)
```

is equivalent to

```
rect.X += 23
rect.Y += -46
```

or

```
rect.Location = Size.op_Addition(rect.Location, new Size(23, -46))
```

An overloaded version of *Offset* takes a *Point* argument (which should probably be a *Size* argument):

```
rect.Offset(pt)
```

That call is equivalent to:

```
rect.X += pt.X
rect.Y += pt.Y
```

The *Inflate* method affects both the location and size of the *Rectangle*:

```
rect.Inflate(x, y)
```

is equivalent to

```
rect.X -= x
rect.Y -= y
rect.Width  += 2 * x
rect.Height += 2 * y
```

Thus, the rectangle gets larger (or smaller, if the arguments are negative) in all directions. The center of the rectangle remains the same. An overload to *Inflate* uses a *Size* object to provide the two values. A *Shared* version creates a new inflated *Rectangle* object from an existing *Rectangle* object.

The following methods perform unions and intersections of pairs of *Rectangle* objects:

### *Rectangle* Methods (selection)

```
Shared Function Union(ByVal rect1 As Rectangle,
                      ByVal rect2 As Rectangle) As Rectangle
Shared Function Intersect(ByVal rect1 As Rectangle,
                          ByVal rect2 As Rectangle) As Rectangle
Sub Intersect(ByVal rect As Rectangle)
```

The *Intersect* method has an overload that isn't *Shared*. You use it like this:

```
rect1.Intersect(rect2)
```

This expression is equivalent to

```
rect1 = Rectangle.Intersect(rect1, rect2)
```

The remaining methods unique to *Rectangle* return *Boolean* values:

### *Rectangle* Methods (selection)

```
Function Contains(ByVal pt As Point) As Boolean
Function Contains(ByVal x As Integer, ByVal y As Integer) As Boolean
Function Contains(ByVal rect As Rectangle) As Boolean
Function IntersectsWith(ByVal rect As Rectangle) As Boolean
```

Finally, both *Rectangle* and *RectangleF* override *ToString* in a useful manner, returning a string that looks something like this:

```
{X=12,Y=5,Width=30,Height=10}
```

# A Nice-Sized Form

How large is your form? This is not a personal question! When a program creates a form, the form has a specific size and occupies a specific location on the screen. The size and location are not fixed, however: If the form has a sizing border, the user can drag that border to make the form a different size. If the form has a caption bar, the user can move the form to another location on the screen. It might be helpful for a program to know how large its form is. Knowing exactly *where* the form is located on the screen is less useful but not totally irrelevant.

The *Form* class has no fewer than 13 properties—most of them inherited from the *Control* class—that reveal this information. With just a couple exceptions, these properties are also writable and allow a program to change the size and location of its form. We saw an example of such changes in the FormProperties program in Chapter 2.

Here are nine properties (all of which *Form* inherits from *Control*) that indicate the size of the form and its location on the screen:

### *Control* Properties (selection)

| Property | Type | Accessibility | Comments |
|----------|------|---------------|----------|
| Location | Point | Get/Set | Relative to screen |
| Size | Size | Get/Set | Size of full form |
| Bounds | Rectangle | Get/Set | Equals *Rectangle(Location, Size)* |
| Width | Integer | Get/Set | Equals *Size.Width* |
| Height | Integer | Get/Set | Equals *Size.Height* |
| Left | Integer | Get/Set | Equals *Location.X* |
| Top | Integer | Get/Set | Equals *Location.Y* |
| Right | Integer | Get | Equals *Location.X + Size.Width* |
| Bottom | Integer | Get | Equals *Location.Y + Size.Height* |

Basically, what we're dealing with here can be reduced to four numbers: the $x$ and $y$ coordinates of the upper left corner of the form relative to the upper left corner of the video display, and the height and width of the form. I suspect that the only reason *Right* and *Bottom* are read-only is because it's not clear what should happen when you set them. Do you want to move the form or make it a different size?

Although you can set *Width* and *Height* to any values you want, the system imposes some limits. The lower limits are values sufficient to display enough of the caption bar to read some of the text. The upper limits prevent the form from being larger than if it were maximized to the size of the screen.

Don't do this, however:

```
Size.Width *= 2;
```

That's setting a property of a property. For reasons beyond the comprehension of people who don't write compilers, it's not allowed.

Two additional size-related and location-related properties are defined in the *Form* class:

### *Form* Properties (selection)

| Property | Type | Accessibility |
| --- | --- | --- |
| DesktopLocation | Point | Get/Set |
| DesktopBounds | Rectangle | Get/Set |

These are similar to the *Location* and *Bounds* properties but take the Windows taskbar into account. The desktop is that part of the screen not occupied by the taskbar. If the taskbar is positioned at the left, *DesktopLocation.X* will be less than *Location.X*; if the taskbar is at the top, *DesktopLocation.Y* will be less than *Location.Y*. *DesktopBounds* is based on *DesktopLocation* and the normal *Size* property, which isn't affected by the position of the taskbar.

# The Form and the Client

The dimensions I've been presenting refer to the entire form, including the border and the caption bar. In most cases, an application is primarily interested in the size of the form's client area. The *client area* is the internal area of the form upon which the application is free to draw during the form's *Paint* event or otherwise decorate with controls. The client area excludes the form's caption bar and any border the form may have. If the form includes a menu bar beneath its caption bar (I'll discuss how to add menu bars in Chapter 14), the client area also excludes the area occupied by that menu bar. If the form displays scroll bars at the right and bottom of the window (I'll show you how to do this in Chapter 4), the client area also excludes these scroll bars.

The *Form* class has just two properties (also first implemented in *Control*) that pertain to the size of the client area:

### *Control* Properties (selection)

| Property | Type | Accessibility |
| --- | --- | --- |
| ClientSize | Size | Get/Set |
| ClientRectangle | Rectangle | Get |

The *ClientSize* property indicates the pixel width and height of the client area. The *ClientRectangle* property supplies no additional information because the *X* and *Y* properties of *ClientRectangle* are always 0! *ClientRectangle* is sometimes useful in methods that require *Rectangle* arguments. The last two programs in this chapter illustrate how *ClientRectangle* can be used for this purpose.

Again, avoid setting a property of a property. This assignment won't work:

```
ClientSize.Width += 100          ' Won't work!
```

Do this instead:

```
ClientSize = New Size(ClientSize.Width + 100, ClientSize.Height)
```

Or do this:

```
ClientSize = Size.op_Addition(ClientSize, New Size(100, 0))
```

The following program displays all 13 of the size and location properties in its client area.

**FormSize.vb**

```
'---------------------------------------------
' FormSize.vb (c) 2002 by Charles Petzold
'---------------------------------------------
Imports System
Imports System.Drawing
Imports System.Windows.Forms

Class FormSize
    Inherits Form

    Shared Sub Main()
        Application.Run(New FormSize())
    End Sub

    Sub New()
        Text = "Form Size"
        BackColor = Color.White
    End Sub

    Protected Overrides Sub OnMove(ByVal ea As EventArgs)
        Invalidate()
    End Sub

    Protected Overrides Sub OnResize(ByVal ea As EventArgs)
        Invalidate()
    End Sub

    Protected Overrides Sub OnPaint(ByVal pea As PaintEventArgs)
        Dim grfx As Graphics = pea.Graphics
        Dim str As String = _
            "Location: " & Location.ToString() & vbLf & _
            "Size: " & Size.ToString() & vbLf & _
            "Bounds: " & Bounds.ToString() & vbLf & _
            "Width: " & Width.ToString() & vbLf & _
            "Height: " & Height.ToString() & vbLf & _
```

```
           "Left: " & Left.ToString() & vbLf & _
           "Top: " & Top.ToString() & vbLf & _
           "Right: " & Right.ToString() & vbLf & _
           "Bottom: " & Bottom.ToString() & vbLf & vbLf & _
           "DesktopLocation: " & DesktopLocation.ToString() & vbLf & _
           "DesktopBounds: " & DesktopBounds.ToString() & vbLf & vbLf & _
           "ClientSize: " & ClientSize.ToString() & vbLf & _
           "ClientRectangle: " & ClientRectangle.ToString()

        grfx.DrawString(str, Font, Brushes.Black, 0, 0)
    End Sub
End Class
```

This innocently intended program introduces a couple things we haven't seen before. First, notice that I'm overriding the *OnMove* and *OnResize* methods. As the *On* prefixes indicate, these methods are associated with events:

### *Control* Events (selection)

| Event | Method | Delegate | Argument |
| --- | --- | --- | --- |
| *Move* | *OnMove* | *EventHandler* | *EventArgs* |
| *Resize* | *OnResize* | *EventHandler* | *EventArgs* |

These methods are called when the form is moved or resized. In real-life programming, the *OnMove* method is almost never overridden. Programs usually don't care where they are located on the screen. Overriding the *OnResize* method is quite common, however. We'll see many examples of *OnResize* used in the chapters ahead.

In response to both these events, I'm calling the simplest of the six overloads of the *Invalidate* method:

### *Control Invalidate* Methods

```
Sub Invalidate()

Sub Invalidate(ByVal rectInvalid As Rectangle)

Sub Invalidate(ByVal bIncludeChildren As Boolean)

Sub Invalidate(ByVal rectInvalid As Rectangle,
               ByVal bIncludeChildren As Boolean)

Sub Invalidate(ByVal rgnInvalid As Region)

Sub Invalidate(ByVal rgnInvalid As Region,
               ByVal bIncludeChildren As Boolean)
```

What this method does is invalidate the entire client area, or a rectangular or nonrectangular subset of it, with or without invalidating any child controls that may be located on it. Invalidating the client area informs Windows that what's on there is no longer valid. Eventually, your form will receive a call to *OnPaint* so that you have an opportunity to repaint the client area. Calling *Invalidate* is the standard way in which a program forces a repaint.

The *OnPaint* call doesn't occur right away. Whatever event the form is currently processing (in this case, the *Resize* or *Move* event) must be completed first, and even then, if other events are pending (such as keyboard or mouse input), the *OnPaint* call must wait. If you want to update your client area immediately, follow the *Invalidate* call with a call to the *Control* object's *Update* method:

### *Control* Methods (selection)

```
Sub Update()
```

This will cause an immediate call to *OnPaint*; after *OnPaint* returns, *Update* will return.

Something else the FormSize program demonstrates is string concatenation with *Point*, *Size*, and *Rectangle* objects. When you need to display a property or another object in a string as we did in this program, the object's *ToString* method must be invoked.

I've also taken advantage of the fact that the *DrawString* method recognizes ASCII line feed characters and correctly spaces successive lines of text. As it is, the output is a bit sloppy:

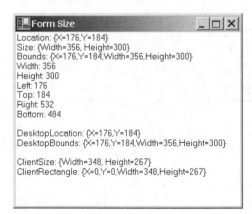

We'll learn how to put text into nice neat columns in the next chapter.

There is a 14th property of the *Form* object inherited from *Control* that is related to the size of the client area:

*Control* **Properties (selection)**

| Property | Type | Accessibility |
|----------|------|---------------|
| DisplayRectangle | Rectangle | Get |

By default, this property is the same as *ClientRectangle* and doesn't change unless you start putting controls on the client area.

# Point Conversions

As you saw in a couple programs in Chapter 2, when you draw graphics on your form, you're using a coordinate system that is relative to the upper left corner of the client area. These coordinates are referred to as *client area coordinates*. Earlier, when I discussed the location of the form relative to the screen, I implicitly introduced another coordinate system. This coordinate system is relative to the upper left corner of the screen, and such coordinates are called *screen coordinates*. Often *desktop coordinates* are the same as screen coordinates, but not if the Windows taskbar is on the top or left edge of the screen. Finally, *form coordinates* are relative to the upper left corner of the form, which is usually the corner of the form's sizing border.

The *Location* property refers to a point in screen coordinates that is equivalent to the point (0, 0) in form coordinates. Thus, this property allows an application to convert between points in these two coordinate systems. Symbolically,

$$x_{screen} = x_{form} + Location.X$$
$$y_{screen} = y_{form} + Location.Y$$

Similarly, the form's *DesktopLocation* property allows a program to convert between desktop coordinates and form coordinates:

$$x_{desktop} = x_{form} + DesktopLocation.X$$
$$y_{desktop} = y_{form} + DesktopLocation.Y$$

With some simple algebraic manipulation, you can also convert between desktop coordinates and screen coordinates:

$$x_{desktop} = x_{screen} + DesktopLocation.X - Location.X$$
$$y_{desktop} = y_{screen} + DesktopLocation.Y - Location.Y$$

There aren't any similar properties of *Form* that allow an application to convert between client area coordinates and any of the other three coordinate systems. It's possible, by using the *CaptionHeight* property of the *SystemInformation* class, to obtain the height of the standard caption bar and then to obtain the width of the sizing border by comparing *ClientSize* with the form's total *Size* (less the caption bar height), but that's more work than you should have to do.

Fortunately, the *Form* class contains two methods that convert points directly between screen coordinates and client area coordinates:

### *Form* Methods (selection)

| Method | Description |
| --- | --- |
| Function PointToClient(<br>    ByVal ptScreen As Point) As Point | Converts screen coordinates to client |
| Function PointToScreen(<br>    ByVal ptClient As Point) As Point | Converts client coordinates to screen |

The *Point* passed as an argument to these methods remains unchanged; the methods return a *Point* containing the converted points. For example, the call

```
Dim pt As Point = PointToScreen(Point.Empty)
```

returns the location of the upper left corner of the client area in screen coordinates.

The *Form* class also supports two additional conversion methods that work with *Rectangle* objects rather than *Point* objects:

### *Form* Methods (selection)

| Method | Description |
| --- | --- |
| Function RectangleToClient(<br>    ByVal rectScreen As Rectangle)<br>        As Rectangle | Converts screen coordinates to client |
| Function RectangleToScreen(<br>    ByVal rectClient As Rectangle)<br>        As Rectangle | Converts client coordinates to screen |

These methods don't provide any additional information than *PointToClient* and *PointToScreen* because the *Size* property of the *Rectangle* object remains unaffected by the conversion.

# The *Color* Structure

The human eye perceives electromagnetic radiation in the range of about 430 to 750 terahertz, corresponding to wavelengths between 700 and 400 nanometers. Electromagnetic radiation in this range is known as *visible light*. If the light isn't very strong, the 120 million rods in the retina of the human eye respond to the light's intensity. Stronger light affects the 7 million cones, which come in three different types, each of which responds to a different range of wavelengths. The varying degrees of excitation of these cones is the phenomena we call *color*, and the three ranges of wavelengths correspond to our concepts of red, green, and blue.

Because very little data is required to specify a color, color is a good candidate for a structure rather than a class and, indeed, *Color* is another important structure in the *System.Drawing* namespace.

Color in Windows Forms is based on an ARGB (alpha-red-green-blue) model. Colors themselves are generally defined by single-byte values of red, green, and blue. The alpha channel determines the transparency of the color. Alpha values range from 0 for transparent to &HFF for opaque.

The *Color* structure has only a default constructor, which you can use like so:

```
Dim clr As Color = New Color()
```

You almost surely won't be using code like this, however, because it would create an empty color (transparent black) and there's no way to change the properties of that color. Instead, you'll be obtaining color objects by using one of the shared methods or properties defined in *Color* for that purpose.

The shared properties in *Color* are quite valuable, for there are no fewer than 141 of them.

# The 141 Color Names

The *Color* structure has 140 shared read-only properties that are actual names of colors ranging (in alphabetical order) from *AliceBlue*[*] to *YellowGreen*. Only a couple of the names (*Magenta* and *Fuchsia*, for example) represent identical colors; most of them are unique colors. The *Color* class also has a 141st property named *Transparent* that represents a transparent color. The following table shows some of the 141 properties in the *Color* class. I haven't included all the properties because such a listing would have run to four pages.

---

[*] AliceBlue gets its name from Alice Roosevelt (1884–1980), who was a spirited teenager when her father became president in 1901 and whose favorite color was immortalized in fashion and song. See *www.theodoreroosevelt.org/life/familytree/AliceLongworth.htm* and *www.theodoreroosevelt.org/life/aliceblue.htm* for more details.

### *Color* Shared Properties

| Property | Type | Accessibility |
|----------|------|---------------|
| *AliceBlue* | *Color* | Get |
| *AntiqueWhite* | *Color* | Get |
| ⋮ | | |
| *Yellow* | *Color* | Get |
| *YellowGreen* | *Color* | Get |
| *Transparent* | *Color* | Get |

You can find a complete list of the 140 standard (and sometimes whimsically named) colors on the inside back cover of this book.

Where did these colors come from? They originated in the X Window System, X11R3 (version 11, revision 3), which is a graphical user interface developed at MIT for UNIX. More recently, these colors were considered for inclusion in the Cascading Style Sheets (CSS) standard from the World Wide Web Consortium (W3C), but they were removed before the specification was finalized. Nevertheless, these 140 colors have become a de facto standard in HTML, being supported by recent versions of both Microsoft Internet Explorer and Netscape Navigator.

Whenever you need a *Color* object, you can just use *Color.Red* (or whatever color you want) and it'll work. I've already done this in some of the programs, when setting the *BackColor* property of a form and as an argument to the *Clear* method of the *Graphics* class.

To create a color based on the red, green, blue, and alpha components, you can use the following *Color.FromArgb* shared methods, each of which returns a *Color* object:

### *Color.FromArgb* Shared Methods

```
Function FromArgb(ByVal r As Integer, ByVal g As Integer,
              ByVal b As Integer) As Color

Function FromArgb(ByVal a As Integer, ByVal r As Integer,
              ByVal g As Integer, ByVal b As Integer) As Color

Function FromArgb(ByVal a As Integer, ByVal clr As Color) As Color

Function FromArgb(ByVal argbPacked As Integer) As Color
```

I'll use the first of these methods in the RandomClear program later in this chapter.

# Pens and Brushes

*Color* objects by themselves aren't used much in Windows Forms. You've seen how you can set the *BackColor* property to a *Color* object. There's also a *Fore-Color* property you can set likewise. The *Clear* method in the *Graphics* class also takes a *Color* argument, but that's an exception.

Most of the other *Graphics* drawing methods don't involve *Color* arguments. When you draw lines or curves (which you'll start doing in Chapter 5), you use an object of type *Pen*, and when you draw filled areas and text, you specify an object of type *Brush*. Of course, pens and brushes themselves are specified using color, but other characteristics are often involved as well.

You create a pen using one of the four constructors of the *Pen* class. The simplest of these constructors creates a *Pen* object based on a *Color* object:

```
Dim pn As New Pen(clr)
```

If you want to create a pen based on one of the predefined colors, you don't need to do this:

```
Dim pn As New Pen(Color.RosyBrown)
```

It's better to use the *Pens* class instead. (Notice the plural on the class name.) *Pens* consists solely of 141 shared read-only properties, each of which returns an object of type *Pen*. Aside from the return type, these properties are identical to the 141 *Color* properties.

### *Pens* Shared Properties

| Property | Type | Accessibility |
| --- | --- | --- |
| *AliceBlue* | *Pen* | Get |
| *AntiqueWhite* | *Pen* | Get |
| ⋮ | | |
| *Yellow* | *Pen* | Get |
| *YellowGreen* | *Pen* | Get |
| *Transparent* | *Pen* | Get |

You'll learn more about the *Pen* class in Chapter 5, and we'll really dig into the details of it in Chapter 17.

When you draw text or filled areas, you specify a *Brush* object. The *Brush* class itself is *MustInherit*, which means you can't create an instance of it. *Brush* is instead the parent class for five other classes: *SolidBrush*, *HatchBrush*,

*TextureBrush*, *LinearGradientBrush*, and *PathGradientBrush*. We'll go over brushes in depth in Chapter 17. For now, be aware that you can create a brush of a solid color like so:

```
Dim br As New SolidBrush(clr)
```

You can also assign the result to an object of type *Brush* because *SolidBrush* is inherited from *Brush*:

```
Dim br As Brush = New SolidBrush(clr)
```

As with the *Pen* class, using one of the shared *Color* properties in *Solid-Brush* is unnecessary because the *Brushes* class (notice the plural again) consists solely of—that's right!—141 shared read-only properties that return objects of type *Brush*.

### *Brushes* Shared Properties

| Property | Type | Accessibility |
|----------|------|---------------|
| *AliceBlue* | *Brush* | Get |
| *AntiqueWhite* | *Brush* | Get |
| ⋮ | | |
| *Yellow* | *Brush* | Get |
| *YellowGreen* | *Brush* | Get |
| *Transparent* | *Brush* | Get |

This is the class we used in Chapter 2 to provide a black brush (*Brushes.Black*) for the *DrawString* method. I mentioned at the time that you should use *Brushes.Black* for text only when you're assured that the background of your form isn't also black. One way to do this is to set the form's background color explicitly:

```
BackColor = Color.White
```

## System Colors

The reason *Brushes.Black* isn't a good idea for text is that it's possible for a Windows user to invoke the Display Properties dialog box (either from Control Panel or by right-clicking the desktop), select the Appearance tab, and choose a color scheme, such as High Contrast Black, in which the background color of windows and controls is black. People with poor eyesight or color blindness often use such high-contrast color schemes, and you're definitely not helping them if you display your text in black as well!

Welcome to the world of *system colors*, which are probably more correctly called *user-preference colors*. Using the Display Properties dialog box, users can select their own color schemes. Windows itself maintains 29 user-settable colors that it employs to color different components of the user interface. Twenty-six of these colors are exposed in the Windows Forms framework.

You can obtain these color values from the *SystemColors* class, which consists solely of 26 read-only properties, each of which returns a *Color* object:

### *SystemColors* Shared Properties

| Property | Type | Accessibility | Comment |
| --- | --- | --- | --- |
| ActiveBorder | Color | Get | Border of active window |
| ActiveCaption | Color | Get | Caption bar of active window |
| ActiveCaptionText | Color | Get | Caption bar text of active window |
| AppWorkspace | Color | Get | Workspace background in a multiple-document interface (MDI) |
| Control | Color | Get | Background color of controls |
| ControlDark | Color | Get | Shadows of 3D controls |
| ControlDarkDark | Color | Get | Dark shadows of 3D controls |
| ControlLight | Color | Get | Highlights of 3D controls |
| ControlLightLight | Color | Get | Light highlights of 3D controls |
| ControlText | Color | Get | Text color of controls |
| Desktop | Color | Get | Windows desktop |
| GrayText | Color | Get | Disabled text |
| Highlight | Color | Get | Highlighted text background |
| HighlightText | Color | Get | Highlighted text |
| HotTrack | Color | Get | Hot track |
| InactiveBorder | Color | Get | Border of inactive windows |
| InactiveCaption | Color | Get | Caption bar of inactive windows |
| InactiveCaptionText | Color | Get | Caption bar text of inactive windows |
| Info | Color | Get | ToolTip background |

*(continued)*

**SystemColors** **Shared Properties**    *(continued)*

| Property | Type | Accessibility | Comment |
|----------|------|---------------|---------|
| *InfoText* | *Color* | Get | ToolTip text |
| *Menu* | *Color* | Get | Menu background |
| *MenuText* | *Color* | Get | Menu text |
| *ScrollBar* | *Color* | Get | Scroll bar background |
| *Window* | *Color* | Get | Window background |
| *WindowFrame* | *Color* | Get | Thin window frame |
| *WindowText* | *Color* | Get | Window text |

You could create a Pen or a Brush from one of these colors like so:

```
Dim pn As New Pen(SystemColors.ControlText)
Dim br As New SolidBrush(SystemColors.ControlText)
```

It's usually not necessary to do this, however, because the *System.Drawing* namespace also includes a *SystemPens* class and a *SystemBrushes* class. *System-Pens* has 15 shared read-only properties that return objects of type *Pen*:

**SystemPens** **Shared Properties**

| Property | Type | Accessibility |
|----------|------|---------------|
| *ActiveCaptionText* | *Pen* | Get |
| *Control* | *Pen* | Get |
| *ControlDark* | *Pen* | Get |
| *ControlDarkDark* | *Pen* | Get |
| *ControlLight* | *Pen* | Get |
| *ControlLightLight* | *Pen* | Get |
| *ControlText* | *Pen* | Get |
| *GrayText* | *Pen* | Get |
| *Highlight* | *Pen* | Get |
| *HighlightText* | *Pen* | Get |
| *InactiveCaptionText* | *Pen* | Get |
| *InfoText* | *Pen* | Get |
| *MenuText* | *Pen* | Get |
| *WindowFrame* | *Pen* | Get |
| *WindowText* | *Pen* | Get |

The *SystemBrushes* class contains 21 shared read-only properties that return objects of type *Brush*:

## *SystemBrushes* Shared Properties

| Property | Type | Accessibility |
| --- | --- | --- |
| *ActiveBorder* | *Brush* | Get |
| *ActiveCaption* | *Brush* | Get |
| *ActiveCaptionText* | *Brush* | Get |
| *AppWorkspace* | *Brush* | Get |
| *Control* | *Brush* | Get |
| *ControlDark* | *Brush* | Get |
| *ControlDarkDark* | *Brush* | Get |
| *ControlLight* | *Brush* | Get |
| *ControlLightLight* | *Brush* | Get |
| *ControlText* | *Brush* | Get |
| *Desktop* | *Brush* | Get |
| *Highlight* | *Brush* | Get |
| *HighlightText* | *Brush* | Get |
| *HotTrack* | *Brush* | Get |
| *InactiveBorder* | *Brush* | Get |
| *InactiveCaption* | *Brush* | Get |
| *Info* | *Brush* | Get |
| *Menu* | *Brush* | Get |
| *ScrollBar* | *Brush* | Get |
| *Window* | *Brush* | Get |
| *WindowText* | *Brush* | Get |

Strangely enough, not all the system colors that pertain to text are included in the *SystemBrushes* class. However, if you need a *Pen* or *Brush* that's not included in the *SystemPens* or *SystemBrushes* class, you can always create it using one of the *SystemColors* properties as an argument to one of the following shared methods:

```
Dim pn As Pen = SystemPens.FromSystemColor(SystemColors.ActiveBorder)

Dim br As Brush = SystemBrushes.FromSystemColor(SystemColors.MenuText)
```

# The Known Colors

The final big color list is the *KnownColor* enumeration that encompasses all the color names and all the system colors:

### *KnownColor* Enumeration

| Field | Value | Field | Value |
|---|---|---|---|
| *ActiveBorder* | 1 | *InactiveCaption* | 17 |
| *ActiveCaption* | 2 | *InactiveCaptionText* | 18 |
| *ActiveCaptionText* | 3 | *Info* | 19 |
| *AppWorkspace* | 4 | *InfoText* | 20 |
| *Control* | 5 | *Menu* | 21 |
| *ControlDark* | 6 | *MenuText* | 22 |
| *ControlDarkDark* | 7 | *ScrollBar* | 23 |
| *ControlLight* | 8 | *Window* | 24 |
| *ControlLightLight* | 9 | *WindowFrame* | 25 |
| *ControlText* | 10 | *WindowText* | 26 |
| *Desktop* | 11 | *Transparent* | 27 |
| *GrayText* | 12 | *AliceBlue* | 28 |
| *Highlight* | 13 | *AntiqueWhite* | 29 |
| *HighlightText* | 14 | ⋮ | |
| *HotTrack* | 15 | *Yellow* | 166 |
| *InactiveBorder* | 16 | *YellowGreen* | 167 |

Although *KnownColor* is the third-largest enumeration in the entire .NET Framework, it's not used for very much. The *Color* class has a shared method that lets you create a color based on a *KnownColor* value, but if that's something you need, it probably makes more sense to use one of the shared *Color* or *SystemColors* properties.

# What to Use?

Somewhere in the constructor for the *Control* class, the following code is probably executed:

```
BackColor = SystemColors.Control
ForeColor = SystemColors.ControlText
```

What the *Control* and *ControlText* system colors are is entirely up to the user. Normally they're gray and black, respectively.

When a button control (for example) draws itself, it uses the *BackColor* property to color its background and the *ForeColor* property to display the button text. A *Form* object uses the *BackColor* property to erase the background of the client area but doesn't itself use the *ForeColor* property. That property is made available for applications inheriting or instantiating *Form*.

So, the question is, What brush should you be using to draw text? I think I've pretty well established that it's not *Brushes.Black*. A much better choice would be *SystemBrushes.ControlText*.

However, I'm not so sure that's optimum either. Consider this question: Why are the *BackColor* and *ForeColor* properties of *Form* set to the system colors used for controls? The answer is, because the Windows Forms developers have assumed that you'll be covering a form with controls or using a form for a dialog box.

If you're not putting controls on a form, though, and if you want your form to look like a regular old Windows program, you should be putting the following two statements in the constructor for your form:

```
BackColor = SystemColors.Window
ForeColor = SystemColors.WindowText
```

In that case, the *DrawString* calls in your *OnPaint* code should use *SystemBrushes.WindowText* to be consistent.

But why write *OnPaint* code that's dependent on the way you set *BackColor* and *ForeColor* in the constructor? To write ideally generalized code, the brush you should use in your *DrawString* calls is

```
New SolidBrush(ForeColor)
```

And that's the brush I'll be using for the remainder of this book whenever I want to display text in the user-preferred color.

Until I start creating controls on the surface of my forms, I'll also be setting the *BackColor* and *ForeColor* properties to *SystemColors.Window* and *SystemColors.WindowText* whenever I know I'll be drawing something that depends on those colors.

# Getting a Feel for Repaints

As you've seen, the background of a form is automatically colored by the property *BackColor*. You've also seen another way to recolor the background of a form: by using the *Clear* method of the *Graphics* class. *Clear* has one argument, which is a *Color* object:

### *Graphics* **Methods (selection)**

```
Sub Clear(ByVal clr As Color)
```

The RandomClear program randomly calculates a new color whenever its *OnPaint* method is called and uses the *Clear* method to display the new color.

**RandomClear.vb**

```
'-----------------------------------------------------
' RandomClear.vb (c) 2002 by Charles Petzold
'-----------------------------------------------------
Imports System
Imports System.Drawing
Imports System.Windows.Forms

Class RandomClear
    Inherits Form

    Shared Sub Main()
        Application.Run(New RandomClear())
    End Sub

    Sub New()
        Text = "Random Clear"
    End Sub

    Protected Overrides Sub OnPaint(ByVal pea As PaintEventArgs)
        Dim grfx As Graphics = pea.Graphics
        Dim rand As New Random()

        grfx.Clear(Color.FromArgb(rand.Next(256), _
                                  rand.Next(256), _
                                  rand.Next(256)))
    End Sub
End Class
```

Run this program, and experiment with resizing the form. Think about what you're seeing: as you make the form larger, the newly uncovered strips on the right and bottom get a different color. Every new color you see represents a new call to *OnPaint*. Even though the *Clear* method is seemingly clearing the entire client area, it's actually restricted to the region that's newly invalid. (You'll notice that if you make the form smaller, the color doesn't change because there is no area of the client that hasn't remained valid.)

This behavior isn't always desirable. It could be that you're writing a program in which you want the entire client area to be invalidated whenever the size of the client area changes. I showed one way to do that in the FormSize program earlier in this chapter: override the *OnResize* method and put in an *Invalidate* call.

Another solution is to set the *ResizeRedraw* property to *True* in the form's constructor:

```
ResizeRedraw = True
```

The *ResizeRedraw* property causes the entire client area to be invalidated whenever its size changes. The following program demonstrates the difference.

```
RandomClearResizeRedraw.vb
'-------------------------------------------------------------
' RandomClearResizeRedraw.vb (c) 2002 by Charles Petzold
'-------------------------------------------------------------
Imports System
Imports System.Drawing
Imports System.Windows.Forms

Class RandomClearResizeRedraw
    Inherits Form

    Shared Sub Main()
        Application.Run(New RandomClearResizeRedraw())
    End Sub

    Sub New()
        Text = "Random Clear with Resize Redraw"
        ResizeRedraw = True
    End Sub

    Protected Overrides Sub OnPaint(ByVal pea As PaintEventArgs)
        Dim grfx As Graphics = pea.Graphics
        Dim rand As New Random()

        grfx.Clear(Color.FromArgb(rand.Next(256), _
                                  rand.Next(256), _
                                  rand.Next(256)))
    End Sub
End Class
```

I'm a little hesitant about recommending that you put this *ResizeRedraw* assignment in every Windows Forms program you write, or even every sizable control. It probably shows up more in this book than in real life because I like to write programs that change their contents based on the size of the client area.

But keep this advice in mind: Whenever something on your form isn't being updated correctly, you should think about whether setting the *ResizeRedraw* property makes sense. And if you've already set *ResizeRedraw*, well, the problem is something else.

Before we leave this program, here's a little exercise. Put the following do-nothing *OnResize* override in RandomClearResizeRedraw:

```
Protected Overrides Sub OnResize(ByVal ea As EventArgs)
End Sub
```

What you'll find is that the program now behaves exactly like Random-Clear. Obviously, the *OnResize* method implemented in *Control* (which *Form* inherits) is responsible for invalidating the control depending on the style. *OnResize* probably contains some code that looks like this:

```
If ResizeRedraw Then Invalidate()
```

For this reason and others, whenever you override the *OnResize* method, you should make a call to the *OnResize* method implemented in the base class:

```
Protected Overrides Sub OnResize(ByVal ea As EventArgs)
    MyBase.OnResize(ea)
    ' Do what the program needs.
End Sub
```

# Centering Hello World

Who was that kid in the back of the classroom who asked about centering text in a program's client area? We are now, at long last, ready to do it. Does such a program require setting the *ResizeRedraw* property? Yes, it certainly does, because what constitutes the *center* of the client area depends on the overall *size* of the client area.

One approach that might occur to you is to change the coordinate point in the *DrawString* function. Instead of using

```
grfx.DrawString("Hello, world!", Font, br, 0, 0)
```

you would use

```
grfx.DrawString("Hello, world!", Font, br,
                ClientSize.Width \ 2, ClientSize.Height \ 2)
```

That's a good start, but it's not quite right. Remember that the coordinate point passed to *Drawstring* specifies the position of the upper left corner of the text string, so that's what will be positioned in the center of the client area. The text won't be in the center of the client area but will instead be situated in the upper left corner of the bottom right quadrant of the client area.

It's possible to alter this default behavior by using one of the overloaded versions of *DrawString*—a version that includes another argument along with the text string, font, brush, and starting position. The additional argument is an object of type *StringFormat*, the purpose of which is to specify in more detail how you want the text to be displayed.

An extensive discussion of *StringFormat* awaits us in Chapter 9. For now, let's just focus on the most-used facility of *StringFormat*, which is to change the default text alignment—the rule that says that the coordinate point passed to *DrawString* refers to the position where the *upper left* corner of the text is to be displayed.

To change the default text alignment, you must first create an object of type *StringFormat*:

```
Dim strfmt As New StringFormat()
```

You can then set two properties of this object to specify the desired text alignment:

### *StringFormat* Properties (selection)

| Property | Type | Accessibility | Description |
|----------|------|---------------|-------------|
| *Alignment* | *StringAlignment* | Get/Set | Horizontal alignment |
| *LineAlignment* | *StringAlignment* | Get/Set | Vertical alignment |

Both these properties are of type *StringAlignment*, which is an enumeration consisting of three oddly named members:

### *StringAlignment* Enumeration

| Member | Value | Description |
|--------|-------|-------------|
| *Near* | 0 | Usually left or top |
| *Center* | 1 | Always the center |
| *Far* | 2 | Usually right or bottom |

Well, OK, so only *two* of the members are oddly named. Windows Forms has the ability to display text right-to-left, as is normal in some languages, or vertically, also normal in some languages. *Near* and *Far* are intended to be orientation-neutral, meaning "nearest to the beginning of the text" or "farthest from the beginning of the text."

If you know you'll be displaying left-to-right horizontally oriented text, you can think of *StringAlignment.Near* as meaning left and *StringAlignment.Far* as right when used with the *Alignment* property, and *StringAlignment.Near* as top and *StringAlignment.Far* as bottom when used with the *LineAlignment* property. Here's a program that uses all four combinations of these settings to display text strings in the four corners of the client area.

**FourCorners.vb**

```
'-------------------------------------------------
' FourCorners.vb (c) 2002 by Charles Petzold
'-------------------------------------------------
Imports System
Imports System.Drawing
Imports System.Windows.Forms

Class FourCorners
    Inherits Form

    Shared Sub Main()
        Application.Run(New FourCorners())
    End Sub

    Sub New()
        Text = "Four Corners Text Alignment"
        BackColor = SystemColors.Window
        ForeColor = SystemColors.WindowText
        ResizeRedraw = True
    End Sub

    Protected Overrides Sub OnPaint(ByVal pea As PaintEventArgs)
        Dim grfx As Graphics = pea.Graphics
        Dim br As New SolidBrush(ForeColor)
        Dim strfmt As New StringFormat()

        strfmt.Alignment = StringAlignment.Near
        strfmt.LineAlignment = StringAlignment.Near
        grfx.DrawString("Upper left corner", Font, br, 0, 0, strfmt)

        strfmt.Alignment = StringAlignment.Far
        strfmt.LineAlignment = StringAlignment.Near
        grfx.DrawString("Upper right corner", Font, br, _
                        ClientSize.Width, 0, strfmt)

        strfmt.Alignment = StringAlignment.Near
        strfmt.LineAlignment = StringAlignment.Far
        grfx.DrawString("Lower left corner", Font, br, _
                        0, ClientSize.Height, strfmt)

        strfmt.Alignment = StringAlignment.Far
        strfmt.LineAlignment = StringAlignment.Far
        grfx.DrawString("Lower right corner", Font, br, _
                        ClientSize.Width, ClientSize.Height, strfmt)
    End Sub
End Class
```

The coordinate points passed to the four *DrawString* calls refer to the four corners of the client area. Here's what it looks like:

If *StringFormat* were not used, however, only the first *DrawString* call would result in visible text. The text displayed by the other three calls would be positioned completely outside the client area.

If you set the *Alignment* property of your *StringFormat* object to *StringAlignment.Center*, the text string will be positioned so that the horizontal center corresponds with the *x* coordinate passed to *DrawString*. If you set the *LineAlignment* property to *StringAlignment.Center*, the *y* coordinate passed to *DrawString* indicates where the vertical center of the text string is positioned.

Here's how to use both effects to center text in the client area.

**HelloCenteredAlignment.vb**

```
'-----------------------------------------------------------
' HelloCenteredAlignment.vb (c) 2002 by Charles Petzold
'-----------------------------------------------------------
Imports System
Imports System.Drawing
Imports System.Windows.Forms

Class HelloCenteredAlignment
    Inherits Form

    Shared Sub Main()
        Application.Run(New HelloCenteredAlignment())
    End Sub

    Sub New()
        Text = "Hello Centered Using String Alignment"
        BackColor = SystemColors.Window
        ForeColor = SystemColors.WindowText
        ResizeRedraw = True
    End Sub
```

*(continued)*

**HelloCenteredAlignment.vb**    *(continued)*

```
Protected Overrides Sub OnPaint(ByVal pea As PaintEventArgs)
    Dim grfx As Graphics = pea.Graphics
    Dim strfmt As New StringFormat()

    strfmt.Alignment = StringAlignment.Center
    strfmt.LineAlignment = StringAlignment.Center

    grfx.DrawString("Hello, world!", Font, New SolidBrush(ForeColor), _
                ClientSize.Width \ 2, ClientSize.Height \ 2, strfmt)
    End Sub
End Class
```

And here it is:

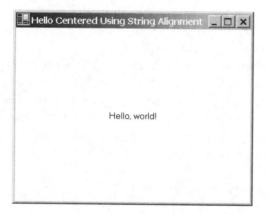

I'm going to warn you about something that sounds pretty stupid, but I'm speaking from experience here. Often when I add a *StringFormat* definition to some existing code, I remember to do everything except include the object as the last argument to *DrawString*. Because *DrawString* doesn't require *String-Format*, the program compiles just fine but the *StringFormat* doesn't seem to make any difference. You really need to include it in the *DrawString* call for it to work right!

## Measuring the String

Another approach to centering text—a much more generalized approach to text positioning—doesn't require the *StringFormat* class but instead involves a method of the *Graphics* class named *MeasureString*. *MeasureString* comes in seven versions, the simplest of which you call something like this:

```
Dim szfText As SizeF = grfx.MeasureString(str, fnt)
```

*MeasureString* returns a *SizeF* structure that indicates the width and height of the string in units of pixels (or, as you'll discover in Chapter 7, whatever units you prefer). *MeasureString* is easily the second most important method for displaying text—not as essential as *DrawString*, but right up there nonetheless. I'll have more to say about *MeasureString* in Chapter 9.

Imagine a displayed text string. Now imagine a rectangle drawn around that string. The *SizeF* structure returned from *MeasureString* is the width and height of that rectangle. For a particular font, regardless of the character string, the *Height* property of the *SizeF* structure is always the same. (Actually, the *Height* property is *usually* independent of the character string. If the string has embedded line feed characters, the *Height* property represents the height of multiple lines of text and hence will be an integral multiple of the *Height* value for a single line of text.)

The *Width* property of the *SizeF* structure depends on the characters that comprise the string. For all but fixed-pitch fonts, the width of the text string "i" is less than the width of "W", and *MeasureString* reflects that difference.

We'll be using *MeasureString* a lot in this book. For now, to center some text in the client area, you can subtract those *Width* and *Height* properties of the *SizeF* structure returned from *MeasureString* from the width and height of the client area. The two differences represent the total horizontal and vertical margin around the text. Divide each value by 2, and that's where to position the upper left corner of the string. Here's the complete code.

**HelloCenteredMeasured.vb**

```
'-----------------------------------------------------
' HelloCenteredMeasured.vb (c) 2002 by Charles Petzold
'-----------------------------------------------------
Imports System
Imports System.Drawing
Imports System.Windows.Forms

Class HelloCenteredMeasured
    Inherits Form

    Shared Sub Main()
        Application.Run(New HelloCenteredMeasured())
    End Sub

    Sub New()
        Text = "Hello Centered Using MeasureString"
        BackColor = SystemColors.Window
        ForeColor = SystemColors.WindowText
        ResizeRedraw = True
    End Sub
```

*(continued)*

**HelloCenteredMeasured.vb**   *(continued)*

```
    Protected Overrides Sub OnPaint(ByVal pea As PaintEventArgs)
        Dim grfx As Graphics = pea.Graphics
        Dim str As String = "Hello, world!"
        Dim szfText As SizeF = grfx.MeasureString(str, Font)

        grfx.DrawString(str, Font, New SolidBrush(ForeColor), _
                    (ClientSize.Width - szfText.Width) / 2, _
                    (ClientSize.Height - szfText.Height) / 2)
    End Sub
End Class
```

# Text in a Rectangle

We've already looked at two versions of the *DrawString* method. There are six
in total:

### *Graphics* Class *DrawString* Methods

```
Sub DrawString(ByVal str As String, ByVal fnt As Font,
            ByVal br As Brush, ByVal ptf As PointF)

Sub DrawString(ByVal str As String, ByVal fnt As Font,
            ByVal br As Brush, ByVal x As Single,
            ByVal y As Single)

Sub DrawString(ByVal str As String, ByVal fnt As Font,
            ByVal br As Brush, ByVal rectf As RectangleF)

Sub DrawString(ByVal str As String, ByVal fnt As Font,
            ByVal br As Brush, ByVal ptf As PointF,
            ByVal sf As StringFormat)

Sub DrawString(ByVal str As String, ByVal fnt As Font,
            ByVal br As Brush, ByVal x As Single,
            ByVal y As Single, ByVal sf As StringFormat)

Sub DrawString(ByVal str As String, ByVal fnt As Font,
            ByVal br As Brush, ByVal rectf As RectangleF,
            ByVal sf As StringFormat)
```

As you can see, the first three arguments are always the same. The only differences are whether you specify coordinates using a *PointF* structure, two *Single* values, or a *RectangleF* and whether you include a *StringFormat* argument.

Whether you use a *PointF* structure or two *Single* values is a matter of personal preference. The two methods have identical functionality. Use whichever
is currently convenient in your program.

But the *RectangleF* version is a little different. The *DrawString* method confines the text to the rectangle, and the optional *StringFormat* argument governs how the text is positioned within the rectangle. For example, if *ClientRectangle* is passed to the *DrawString* function and the *Alignment* and *LineAlignment* properties of *StringFormat* are both set to *StringAlignment.Center*, the text is centered within the client area, as the following program demonstrates.

**HelloCenteredRectangle.vb**

```
'-------------------------------------------------------------
' HelloCenteredRectangle.vb (c) 2002 by Charles Petzold
'-------------------------------------------------------------
Imports System
Imports System.Drawing
Imports System.Windows.Forms

Class HelloCenteredRectangle
    Inherits Form

    Shared Sub Main()
        Application.Run(New HelloCenteredRectangle())
    End Sub

    Sub New()
        Text = "Hello Centered Using Rectangle"
        BackColor = SystemColors.Window
        ForeColor = SystemColors.WindowText
        ResizeRedraw = True
    End Sub

    Protected Overrides Sub OnPaint(ByVal pea As PaintEventArgs)
        Dim grfx As Graphics = pea.Graphics
        Dim strfmt As New StringFormat()

        strfmt.Alignment = StringAlignment.Center
        strfmt.LineAlignment = StringAlignment.Center

        grfx.DrawString("Hello, world!", Font, New SolidBrush(ForeColor), _
                    RectangleF.op_Implicit(ClientRectangle), strfmt)
    End Sub
End Class
```

Notice the use of *RectangleF.op_Implicit* to convert a *Rectangle* object (the *ClientRectangle* property) to a *RectangleF* object required for *DrawString*. The option to specify a rectangle rather than a single coordinate point for positioning text may set you to wondering. Do you suppose *DrawString* might be able to *wrap* text within the rectangle?

There's only one way to find out. Let's replace that little text string we've been using with something more substantial—the first paragraph of Mark Twain's *The Adventures of Huckleberry Finn* comes to mind as a reasonable example—and see what happens.

**HuckleberryFinn.vb**

```
'-------------------------------------------------
' HuckleberryFinn.vb (c) 2002 by Charles Petzold
'-------------------------------------------------
Imports System
Imports System.Drawing
Imports System.Windows.Forms

Class HuckleberryFinn
    Inherits Form

    Shared Sub Main()
        Application.Run(New HuckleberryFinn())
    End Sub

    Sub New()
        Text = """The Adventures of Huckleberry Finn"""
        BackColor = SystemColors.Window
        ForeColor = SystemColors.WindowText
        ResizeRedraw = True
    End Sub

    Protected Overrides Sub OnPaint(ByVal pea As PaintEventArgs)
        Dim grfx As Graphics = pea.Graphics

        grfx.DrawString("You don't know about me, without you " & _
                        "have read a book by the name of ""The " & _
                        "Adventures of Tom Sawyer,"" but that " & _
                        "ain't no matter. That book was made by " & _
                        "Mr. Mark Twain, and he told the truth, " & _
                        "mainly. There was things which he " & _
                        "stretched, but mainly he told the truth. " & _
                        "That is nothing. I never seen anybody " & _
                        "but lied, one time or another, without " & _
                        "it was Aunt Polly, or the widow, or " & _
                        "maybe Mary. Aunt Polly" & ChrW(&H2014) & _
                        "Tom's Aunt Polly, she is" & ChrW(&H2014) & _
                        "and Mary, and the Widow Douglas, is all " & _
                        "told about in that book" & ChrW(&H2014) & _
                        "which is mostly a true book; with some " & _
                        "stretchers, as I said before.", _
                        Font, New SolidBrush(ForeColor), _
                        RectangleF.op_Implicit(ClientRectangle))
    End Sub
End Class
```

Notice the *ChrW(&H2014)* characters in the text string. That's the Unicode character code for an *em dash*, which is the long dash that's often used—perhaps overused by some writers—to separate clauses in a sentence. The *DrawString* call in this program doesn't need a *StringFormat* argument because we're only interested in displaying the text normally.

And sure enough, *DrawString* nicely formats the text to fit within the client area:

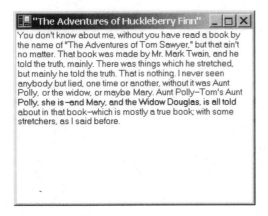

What *DrawString* doesn't do (and we can hardly expect it to) is give us a couple scroll bars if the client area isn't big enough.

But that's OK. We'll find out how to do scroll bars in the next chapter.

# 4

# An Exercise in Text Output

The client area of a form is sometimes referred to as the program's *presentation area*. Here is where you present to the user your program's look and feel, its personality and idiosyncrasies, its virtues and character flaws. The appearance of a program's client area is, of course, highly dependent on what the program does. Some programs—particularly those that serve as front ends for distributed applications—may consist entirely of child window controls such as buttons and edit fields. Others may do all their own drawing, keyboard input, and mouse processing within the client area. And some programs—like the ones in this chapter—may simply display information.

Yet the simple display of information often requires some user interaction. This chapter discusses not only the techniques of formatting text into nice neat columns but also the ways of enabling and using those wonderful user-input devices known as *scroll bars*.

## System Information

When I encounter a new operating system or a development framework like Windows Forms, I often write programs that explore the system itself. Writing programs that do nothing but display information (like the FormSize program in Chapter 3) gives me an opportunity to find out about the system while learning to code for it at the same time.

The *SystemInformation* class in the *System.Windows.Forms* namespace contains (at last count) 60 shared read-only properties that reveal certain aspects of the particular computer on which your application is running and certain metrics the system uses to display items on the desktop and in your program. *SystemInformation* tells you the number of buttons on the user's mouse, the size of icons on the desktop, and the height of the form's caption bar. It also indicates whether the computer is connected to a network and the name of the user's domain. This information is returned in a variety of data types—*Integer*, *Boolean*, *String*, *Size*, *Rectangle*—and a couple enumerations.

My mission in this chapter is to create a program that displays this information in a manner that is convenient to peruse. Because you'll probably consult this program fairly often, doing a good job will be worth the extra effort.

# Spacing Lines of Text

As you saw in Chapter 3, *DrawString* properly spaces multiple lines of text that are separated by line feed characters, and it also wraps text in a rectangle. What's usually more convenient in a program that displays multiple lines of text in columns, however, is to call *DrawString* for each line of each column separately. That means specifying a coordinate point in *DrawString* that indicates exactly where each text string goes.

In Chapter 3, I introduced the *MeasureString* method of the *Graphics* class. That method gives us the height and width of a character string. Although you can use this height for spacing successive lines of text, it's not quite suitable for that purpose. For performing line spacing that's consistent with the word-wrapping facility of *DrawString*, you should use a value that's a little different than the height returned from *MeasureString*. This subject is a bit confusing because the properties and methods that provide you with proper line-spacing values have names that seem to refer to the height of the font characters! The most generalized method for obtaining a line-spacing value is this *GetHeight* method of the *Font* class:

```
Dim cySpace As Single = fnt.GetHeight(grfx)
```

I use a variable name prefix of *cy* to mean a *count* in the *y* direction, that is, a height. In this statement, *fnt* is an object of type *Font* and *grfx* is an object of type *Graphics*. I refer to this as the most generalized method because the *Graphics* argument allows it to be used for both the video display and the printer. The method also takes into account any transforms that are in effect. (Transforms allow you to draw in units other than pixels, as I'll explain in Chapter 7.) Notice that the return value is a *Single*. With some fonts, the value returned from *GetHeight* is the same as the height associated with *MeasureString*. For most fonts, however, *GetHeight* is somewhat smaller.

Another version of the *GetHeight* method gives you a line-spacing value that is suitable only for the video display and not the printer. You should use this method only when you're drawing on the video display and when no transforms are in effect:

```
Dim cySpace As Single = fnt.GetHeight()
```

If you round that *Single* value up to the next highest integer, you'll obtain the same value that's returned from the *Height* property of the *Font* class:

```
Dim cySpace As Integer = fnt.Height
```

If you're drawing on the video display in units of pixels (which is the default), the *Height* property of *Font* is probably the best choice.

When you use the *GetHeight* method or *Height* property with the default font associated with the form, you can just specify the form's *Font* property as the *Font* object:

```
Dim cySpace As Single = Font.GetHeight()
Dim cySpace As Integer = Font.Height
```

These statements refer to the *Font* property of the *Form* class. The *Form* class also includes a protected read/write property named *FontHeight* (inherited from *Control*) that returns an *Integer* value consistent with the *Font.Height* property. Although in theory you can set this property, doing so doesn't result in the form's default font changing size.

## Property Values

Here's a first—and woefully incomplete—stab at writing a program to display *SystemInformation* properties.

```
SysInfoFirstTry.vb
'------------------------------------------------
' SysInfoFirstTry.vb (c) 2002 by Charles Petzold
'------------------------------------------------
Imports System
Imports System.Drawing
Imports System.Windows.Forms

Class SysInfoFirstTry
    Inherits Form

    Shared Sub Main()
        Application.Run(New SysInfoFirstTry())
    End Sub

    Sub New()
        Text = "System Information: First Try"
        BackColor = SystemColors.Window
        ForeColor = SystemColors.WindowText
    End Sub

    Protected Overrides Sub OnPaint(ByVal pea As PaintEventArgs)
        Dim grfx As Graphics = pea.Graphics
```

*(continued)*

**SysInfoFirstTry.vb** *(continued)*

```
        Dim br As New SolidBrush(ForeColor)
        Dim y As Integer = 0

        grfx.DrawString("ArrangeDirection: " & _
                SystemInformation.ArrangeDirection.ToString(), _
                Font, br, 0, y)

        y += Font.Height
        grfx.DrawString("ArrangeStartingPosition: " & _
                SystemInformation.ArrangeStartingPosition.ToString(), _
                Font, br, 0, y)

        y += Font.Height
        grfx.DrawString("BootMode: " & _
                SystemInformation.BootMode.ToString(), _
                Font, br, 0, y)

        y += Font.Height
        grfx.DrawString("Border3DSize: " & _
                SystemInformation.Border3DSize.ToString(), _
                Font, br, 0, y)

        y += Font.Height
        grfx.DrawString("BorderSize: " & _
                SystemInformation.BorderSize.ToString(), _
                Font, br, 0, y)

        y += Font.Height
        grfx.DrawString("CaptionButtonSize: " & _
                SystemInformation.CaptionButtonSize.ToString(), _
                Font, br, 0, y)

        y += Font.Height
        grfx.DrawString("CaptionHeight: " & _
                SystemInformation.CaptionHeight.ToString(), _
                Font, br, 0, y)

        y += Font.Height
        grfx.DrawString("ComputerName: " & _
                SystemInformation.ComputerName.ToString(), _
                Font, br, 0, y)

        y += Font.Height
        grfx.DrawString("CursorSize: " & _
                SystemInformation.CursorSize.ToString(), _
                Font, br, 0, y)

        y += Font.Height
        grfx.DrawString("DbcsEnabled: " & _
                SystemInformation.DbcsEnabled.ToString(), _
                Font, br, 0, y)
    End Sub
End Class
```

Well, I gave up after 10 items, not because I got tired of typing, but because I realized that this wasn't the best approach and that I'd probably need to retype the items in some other, more generalized format. As far as it goes, though, it's not bad for a first try:

Let's take a look at how this program works.

Each line of output is a single call to *DrawString*. The first argument is the text name of the property concatenated with the property value. The program uses *ToString* to convert each *SystemInformation* property into a string for the concatenation. (Some of these properties, such as *CaptionHeight* and *Computer-Name*, don't need the explicit *ToString* call, but it doesn't hurt.) The proper line spacing is handled by increasing the variable *y* after each *DrawString* call

```
y += Font.Height
```

thus placing it one line lower in the client area.

# Formatting into Columns

Other than its incompleteness, I think the most glaring problem with SysInfo-FirstTry is the formatting. The output of a program like this would be easier to read if the property values were formatted into a second column. So let's tackle that problem before continuing onward.

Of the 10 properties that SysInfoFirstTry displays, the widest property name seems to be *ArrangeStartingPosition*. Before displaying any information, this program calls *MeasureString* with that string (plus a space so that the two columns won't touch).

**SysInfoColumns.vb**

```
'-------------------------------------------------
' SysInfoColumns.vb (c) 2002 by Charles Petzold
'-------------------------------------------------
Imports System
Imports System.Drawing
Imports System.Windows.Forms

Class SysInfoColumns
    Inherits Form

    Shared Sub Main()
        Application.Run(New SysInfoColumns())
    End Sub

    Sub New()
        Text = "System Information: Columns"
        BackColor = SystemColors.Window
        ForeColor = SystemColors.WindowText
    End Sub

    Protected Overrides Sub OnPaint(ByVal pea As PaintEventArgs)
        Dim grfx As Graphics = pea.Graphics
        Dim br As New SolidBrush(ForeColor)
        Dim szf As SizeF = _
                grfx.MeasureString("ArrangeStartingPosition ", Font)
        Dim cxCol As Single = szf.Width
        Dim y As Single = 0
        Dim cySpace As Integer = Font.Height

        grfx.DrawString("ArrangeDirection", Font, br, 0, y)
        grfx.DrawString(SystemInformation.ArrangeDirection.ToString(), _
                        Font, br, cxCol, y)
        y += cySpace
        grfx.DrawString("ArrangeStartingPosition", Font, br, 0, y)
        grfx.DrawString( _
                SystemInformation.ArrangeStartingPosition.ToString(), _
                Font, br, cxCol, y)
        y += cySpace
        grfx.DrawString("BootMode", Font, br, 0, y)
        grfx.DrawString(SystemInformation.BootMode.ToString(), _
                        Font, br, cxCol, y)
        y += cySpace
        grfx.DrawString("Border3DSize", Font, br, 0, y)
        grfx.DrawString(SystemInformation.Border3DSize.ToString(), _
                        Font, br, cxCol, y)
        y += cySpace
        grfx.DrawString("BorderSize", Font, br, 0, y)
        grfx.DrawString(SystemInformation.BorderSize.ToString(), _
                        Font, br, cxCol, y)
        y += cySpace
        grfx.DrawString("CaptionButtonSize", Font, br, 0, y)
        grfx.DrawString(SystemInformation.CaptionButtonSize.ToString(), _
```

```
                              Font, br, cxCol, y)
        y += cySpace
        grfx.DrawString("CaptionHeight", Font, br, 0, y)
        grfx.DrawString(SystemInformation.CaptionHeight.ToString(), _
                        Font, br, cxCol, y)
        y += cySpace
        grfx.DrawString("ComputerName", Font, br, 0, y)
        grfx.DrawString(SystemInformation.ComputerName, _
                        Font, br, cxCol, y)
        y += cySpace
        grfx.DrawString("CursorSize", Font, br, 0, y)
        grfx.DrawString(SystemInformation.CursorSize.ToString(), _
                        Font, br, cxCol, y)
        y += cySpace
        grfx.DrawString("DbcsEnabled", Font, br, 0, y)
        grfx.DrawString(SystemInformation.DbcsEnabled.ToString(), _
                        Font, br, cxCol, y)
    End Sub
End Class
```

The program saves the width of the string in the variable *cxCol* and uses that to position the second column. The program also saves the *Height* property of the form's *Font* object in a variable named *cySpace* and uses that to space successive lines of text. Now each line of output requires two calls to *Draw-String*, the first displaying the property name and the second displaying the property value. All but one of these property values now require explicit *ToString* calls to convert the values to strings. Here's what it looks like:

## Everything Is an Object

In a program like SysInfoColumns, the code that displays the lines of text should probably be in a *For* loop. The actual information should probably be stored in an array of some sort, and perhaps isolated from the actual text-output code so that it could be used in other programs. In an object-oriented language like Microsoft Visual Basic .NET, you should remember the magic rule: *Everything is an object*—or at least a class with shared methods and properties.

Here's one possible implementation of a class that contains the text strings we want to display and provides some information about them.

**SysInfoStrings.vb**

```
'-------------------------------------------------
' SysInfoStrings.vb (c) 2002 by Charles Petzold
'-------------------------------------------------
Imports System
Imports System.Drawing
Imports System.Windows.Forms

Class SysInfoStrings
    Shared ReadOnly Property Labels() As String()
        Get
            Return New String() _
            { _
                "ArrangeDirection", _
                "ArrangeStartingPosition", _
                "BootMode", _
                "Border3DSize", _
                "BorderSize", _
                "CaptionButtonSize", _
                "CaptionHeight", _
                "ComputerName", _
                "CursorSize", _
                "DbcsEnabled", _
                "DebugOS", _
                "DoubleClickSize", _
                "DoubleClickTime", _
                "DragFullWindows", _
                "DragSize", _
                "FixedFrameBorderSize", _
                "FrameBorderSize", _
                "HighContrast", _
                "HorizontalScrollBarArrowWidth", _
                "HorizontalScrollBarHeight", _
                "HorizontalScrollBarThumbWidth", _
                "IconSize", _
                "IconSpacingSize", _
                "KanjiWindowHeight", _
                "MaxWindowTrackSize", _
                "MenuButtonSize", _
                "MenuCheckSize", _
                "MenuFont", _
                "MenuHeight", _
                "MidEastEnabled", _
                "MinimizedWindowSize", _
                "MinimizedWindowSpacingSize", _
```

```
            "MinimumWindowSize", _
            "MinWindowTrackSize", _
            "MonitorCount", _
            "MonitorsSameDisplayFormat", _
            "MouseButtons", _
            "MouseButtonsSwapped", _
            "MousePresent", _
            "MouseWheelPresent", _
            "MouseWheelScrollLines", _
            "NativeMouseWheelSupport", _
            "Network", _
            "PenWindows", _
            "PrimaryMonitorMaximizedWindowSize", _
            "PrimaryMonitorSize", _
            "RightAlignedMenus", _
            "Secure", _
            "ShowSounds", _
            "SmallIconSize", _
            "ToolWindowCaptionButtonSize", _
            "ToolWindowCaptionHeight", _
            "UserDomainName", _
            "UserInteractive", _
            "UserName", _
            "VerticalScrollBarArrowHeight", _
            "VerticalScrollBarThumbHeight", _
            "VerticalScrollBarWidth", _
            "VirtualScreen", _
            "WorkingArea" _
        }
    End Get
End Property

Shared ReadOnly Property Values() As String()
    Get
        Return New String() _
        { _
        SystemInformation.ArrangeDirection.ToString(), _
        SystemInformation.ArrangeStartingPosition.ToString(), _
        SystemInformation.BootMode.ToString(), _
        SystemInformation.Border3DSize.ToString(), _
        SystemInformation.BorderSize.ToString(), _
        SystemInformation.CaptionButtonSize.ToString(), _
        SystemInformation.CaptionHeight.ToString(), _
        SystemInformation.ComputerName, _
        SystemInformation.CursorSize.ToString(), _
        SystemInformation.DbcsEnabled.ToString(), _
        SystemInformation.DebugOS.ToString(), _
        SystemInformation.DoubleClickSize.ToString(), _
        SystemInformation.DoubleClickTime.ToString(), _
        SystemInformation.DragFullWindows.ToString(), _
        SystemInformation.DragSize.ToString(), _
        SystemInformation.FixedFrameBorderSize.ToString(), _
```

*(continued)*

**SysInfoStrings.vb**  *(continued)*

```
            SystemInformation.FrameBorderSize.ToString(), _
            SystemInformation.HighContrast.ToString(), _
            SystemInformation.HorizontalScrollBarArrowWidth.ToString(), _
            SystemInformation.HorizontalScrollBarHeight.ToString(), _
            SystemInformation.HorizontalScrollBarThumbWidth.ToString(), _
            SystemInformation.IconSize.ToString(), _
            SystemInformation.IconSpacingSize.ToString(), _
            SystemInformation.KanjiWindowHeight.ToString(), _
            SystemInformation.MaxWindowTrackSize.ToString(), _
            SystemInformation.MenuButtonSize.ToString(), _
            SystemInformation.MenuCheckSize.ToString(), _
            SystemInformation.MenuFont.ToString(), _
            SystemInformation.MenuHeight.ToString(), _
            SystemInformation.MidEastEnabled.ToString(), _
            SystemInformation.MinimizedWindowSize.ToString(), _
            SystemInformation.MinimizedWindowSpacingSize.ToString(), _
            SystemInformation.MinimumWindowSize.ToString(), _
            SystemInformation.MinWindowTrackSize.ToString(), _
            SystemInformation.MonitorCount.ToString(), _
            SystemInformation.MonitorsSameDisplayFormat.ToString(), _
            SystemInformation.MouseButtons.ToString(), _
            SystemInformation.MouseButtonsSwapped.ToString(), _
            SystemInformation.MousePresent.ToString(), _
            SystemInformation.MouseWheelPresent.ToString(), _
            SystemInformation.MouseWheelScrollLines.ToString(), _
            SystemInformation.NativeMouseWheelSupport.ToString(), _
            SystemInformation.Network.ToString(), _
            SystemInformation.PenWindows.ToString(), _
            SystemInformation.PrimaryMonitorMaximizedWindowSize.ToString(), _
            SystemInformation.PrimaryMonitorSize.ToString(), _
            SystemInformation.RightAlignedMenus.ToString(), _
            SystemInformation.Secure.ToString(), _
            SystemInformation.ShowSounds.ToString(), _
            SystemInformation.SmallIconSize.ToString(), _
            SystemInformation.ToolWindowCaptionButtonSize.ToString(), _
            SystemInformation.ToolWindowCaptionHeight.ToString(), _
            SystemInformation.UserDomainName, _
            SystemInformation.UserInteractive.ToString(), _
            SystemInformation.UserName, _
            SystemInformation.VerticalScrollBarArrowHeight.ToString(), _
            SystemInformation.VerticalScrollBarThumbHeight.ToString(), _
            SystemInformation.VerticalScrollBarWidth.ToString(), _
            SystemInformation.VirtualScreen.ToString(), _
            SystemInformation.WorkingArea.ToString() _
            }
        End Get
    End Property

    Shared ReadOnly Property Count() As Integer
        Get
            Return Labels.Length
        End Get
    End Property
```

```
    Shared Function MaxLabelWidth(ByVal grfx As Graphics, _
                            ByVal fnt As Font) As Single
        Return MaxWidth(Labels, grfx, fnt)
    End Function

    Shared Function MaxValueWidth(ByVal grfx As Graphics, _
                            ByVal fnt As Font) As Single
        Return MaxWidth(Values, grfx, fnt)
    End Function

    Private Shared Function MaxWidth(ByVal astr() As String, _
            ByVal grfx As Graphics, ByVal fnt As Font) As Single
        Dim fMax As Single = 0
        Dim str As String
        For Each str In astr
            fMax = Math.Max(fMax, grfx.MeasureString(str, fnt).Width)
        Next str
        Return fMax
    End Function
End Class
```

This class has three read-only shared properties. The first, *Labels*, returns an array of strings that are the names of the *SystemInformation* properties.

The second property is named *Values*, and it also returns an array of character strings, each one corresponding to an element of the *Labels* array. However, in reality, the *Values* array consists of a series of expressions involving *SystemInformation* properties, each of which evaluates to a string. Each expression is evaluated at the time the property is obtained. You'll recognize the use of the *ToString* method to convert each item to a string.

The third property returns the number of items in the *Labels* array, which (unless I messed up) should also be the number of items in the *Values* array. In addition, *SysInfoStrings* has two public methods: *MaxLabelWidth* and *MaxValueWidth*. These two methods require arguments of a *Graphics* object and a *Font* object and simply return the largest width reported by *MeasureString* for the two arrays. They both rely on a private method named *MaxWidth*. That method makes use of the shared *Math.Max* method to obtain the maximum of two values. (The *Math* class in the *System* namespace is a collection of shared methods that implement various mathematics functions. Appendix B is devoted to the *Math* class and other aspects of working with numbers.)

# Listing the System Information

I created the SysInfoStrings.vb file in a project named SysInfoList, which also includes the SysInfoList.vb file shown here. This program displays the system information items provided by the *SysInfoStrings* class.

## SysInfoList.vb

```vb
'----------------------------------------------
' SysInfoList.vb (c) 2002 by Charles Petzold
'----------------------------------------------
Imports System
Imports System.Drawing
Imports System.Windows.Forms

Class SysInfoList
    Inherits Form

    ReadOnly cxCol As Single
    ReadOnly cySpace As Integer

    Shared Sub Main()
        Application.Run(New SysInfoList())
    End Sub

    Sub New()
        Text = "System Information: List"
        BackColor = SystemColors.Window
        ForeColor = SystemColors.WindowText

        Dim grfx As Graphics = CreateGraphics()
        Dim szf As SizeF = grfx.MeasureString(" ", Font)
        cxCol = szf.Width + SysInfoStrings.MaxLabelWidth(grfx, Font)
        grfx.Dispose()

        cySpace = Font.Height
    End Sub

    Protected Overrides Sub OnPaint(ByVal pea As PaintEventArgs)
        Dim grfx As Graphics = pea.Graphics
        Dim br As New SolidBrush(ForeColor)
        Dim iCount As Integer = SysInfoStrings.Count
        Dim astrLabels() As String = SysInfoStrings.Labels
        Dim astrValues() As String = SysInfoStrings.Values
        Dim i As Integer

        For i = 0 To iCount - 1
            grfx.DrawString(astrLabels(i), Font, br, 0, i * cySpace)
            grfx.DrawString(astrValues(i), Font, br, cxCol, i * cySpace)
        Next i
    End Sub
End Class
```

This program attempts to be *somewhat* efficient by calculating the *cxCol* and *cySpace* values only once during the form's constructor, saving them as fields that the *OnPaint* method uses later. However, this calculation requires a call to *MeasureString*, and *MeasureString* requires a *Graphics* object. How do we get such an object outside of a *Paint* event or an *OnPaint* method call?

The *Control* class implements (and the *Form* class inherits) a *CreateGraphics* method that lets you obtain a *Graphics* object at any time:

### *Control* Methods (selection)

```
Function CreateGraphics() As Graphics
```

You can use this *Graphics* object to obtain information—as the SysInfoList program does—or to draw on the program's client area. (However, don't bother drawing during the form's constructor because the form isn't even displayed at that time.)

You must explicitly dispose of a *Graphics* object obtained from *CreateGraphics* before returning control from the constructor or the event in which it is created. You do this by calling the *Dispose* method:

### *Graphics* Methods (selection)

```
Sub Dispose()
```

After SysInfoList obtains a *Graphics* object from *CreateGraphics*, it calls *MeasureString* to obtain the width of a single space character. It adds this width to the *MaxLabelWidth* value returned from the *SysInfoStrings* class and saves that result as *cxCol*. A simple *For* loop displays the pair of strings during the *OnPaint* method.

And we're definitely making progress:

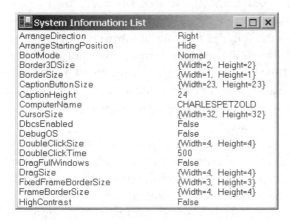

However, depending on the size of your monitor and certain settings you've made regarding your video display resolution (an issue I'll discuss in Chapter 9), you may or may not be able to resize the form to be large enough to view all 60 values. If you can't, you'll find this program very frustrating to use. There's no way to bring the later values into view.

And even if there were only 20 or 25 values, you might still face a problem. Perhaps the worst mistake you can make in Windows programming is to assume that a certain amount of text is visible on a particular user's machine. Users—particularly those whose eyesight isn't too good—can set large font sizes and thus reduce the amount of text that is visible on the screen. Your Windows programs should be usable at just about any screen resolution and font size.

We need to display more text than can fit on the screen, but that's nothing a scroll bar can't fix.

## Windows Forms and Scroll Bars

Scroll bars are an important part of any graphical environment. For the user, they are easy to use and provide excellent visual feedback. You can use scroll bars whenever you need to display anything—text, graphics, a spreadsheet, database records, pictures, Web pages—that requires more space than is available in the program's client area.

Scroll bars are oriented either vertically, for up-and-down movement, or horizontally, for back-and-forth movement. Clicking the arrows at either end of a scroll bar causes the document to scroll by a small amount—generally a line of text for a vertical scroll bar. Clicking the area between the arrows causes the document to scroll by a larger amount. A *scroll box* (also sometimes called the scroll bar *thumb*) travels the length of the scroll bar to indicate the approximate location of the material shown in the client area in relation to the entire content. You can drag the scroll box with the mouse to move to a particular location within the content. A relatively recent innovation in scroll bars makes the size of the scroll box variable to indicate the relative proportion of the content currently displayed in the client area.

You can add scroll bars to a form in one of two ways. In the first approach, you create controls of type *VScrollBar* and *HScrollBar* and position them anywhere in the client area. These scroll bar controls have settable properties that affect the appearance and functionality of the scroll bars. A form is notified when the user manipulates a scroll bar control through events. I'll be putting scroll bar controls to work in Chapter 12.

The second approach to adding scroll bars to a form is easier than creating scroll bar controls. This approach, often called the *auto-scroll* approach, is the one I'll be demonstrating in this chapter.

The auto-scroll facility is primarily intended for programs that put controls (such as buttons and text boxes) on the form's client area. The program enables auto-scroll by setting the *AutoScroll* property of the form to *True*. If the client area is too small to allow all the controls to be visible at once, scroll bars appear (as if by magic) that allow the user to bring the other controls into view.

It's also possible to enable auto-scroll without using any controls. I'll show you both approaches, and you can decide which you like best.

## Scrolling a Panel Control

The Microsoft .NET Framework has lots of interesting controls, ranging from buttons, list boxes, and text boxes to calendars, tree views, and data grids. The panel control, however, is *not* one of these interesting controls. It has no visual appearance to speak of and not much of a user interface. Panels are generally used for architectural purposes to group other controls against a background. Panels are also useful when you need a control but don't want it to do very much.

What I've done in the following SysInfoPanel program is to create a panel control that is the size of the information I want to display—that is, a panel control large enough to display all 60 lines of system-information text. I put that control on the client area of the form and let auto-scrolling do the rest.

**SysInfoPanel.vb**

```
'-----------------------------------------------
' SysInfoPanel.vb (c) 2002 by Charles Petzold
'-----------------------------------------------
Imports System
Imports System.Drawing
Imports System.Windows.Forms

Class SysInfoPanel
    Inherits Form

    ReadOnly cxCol As Single
    ReadOnly cySpace As Integer

    Shared Sub Main()
        Application.Run(New SysInfoPanel())
    End Sub
```

*(continued)*

**SysInfoPanel.vb**   *(continued)*

```
Sub New()
    Text = "System Information: Panel"
    BackColor = SystemColors.Window
    ForeColor = SystemColors.WindowText
    AutoScroll = True

    Dim grfx As Graphics = CreateGraphics()
    Dim szf As SizeF = grfx.MeasureString(" ", Font)
    cxCol = szf.Width + SysInfoStrings.MaxLabelWidth(grfx, Font)
    cySpace = Font.Height

    ' Create a panel.
    Dim pnl As New Panel()
    pnl.Parent = Me
    AddHandler pnl.Paint, AddressOf PanelOnPaint
    pnl.Location = Point.Empty
    pnl.Size = New Size( _
        CInt(Math.Ceiling(cxCol + _
                        SysInfoStrings.MaxValueWidth(grfx, Font))), _
        CInt(Math.Ceiling(cySpace * SysInfoStrings.Count)))
    grfx.Dispose()
End Sub

Sub PanelOnPaint(ByVal obj As Object, ByVal pea As PaintEventArgs)
    Dim grfx As Graphics = pea.Graphics
    Dim br As New SolidBrush(ForeColor)
    Dim iCount As Integer = SysInfoStrings.Count
    Dim astrLabels() As String = SysInfoStrings.Labels
    Dim astrValues() As String = SysInfoStrings.Values
    Dim i As Integer

    For i = 0 To iCount - 1
        grfx.DrawString(astrLabels(i), Font, br, 0, i * cySpace)
        grfx.DrawString(astrValues(i), Font, br, cxCol, i * cySpace)
    Next i
End Sub
End Class
```

This program also requires the SysInfoStrings.vb file. A good way to share files among projects in Visual Basic .NET is to use the Add Existing Item menu item. (You'll find this entry on the Project menu; you can also select it by right-clicking the project name in Solution Explorer and selecting Add.) You select the existing file you need in the project, and instead of pressing the Open button, you click the arrow next to Open and select Link File. Doing this avoids making a copy of the file and also prevents problems that result when you change one copy but not the other.

Let's look at the *SysInfoPanel* constructor. To enable the auto-scroll facility, you must set the *AutoScroll* property of the form to *True*. That's the easy part. Next the program calculates *cxCol* and *cySpace* exactly as SysInfoList did. But before disposing of the *Graphics* object, the program proceeds to create the panel

```
Dim pnl As New Panel()
```

I've given this panel the name *pnl*. I want this panel to be located on the surface of the form's client area. The surface on which a control is located is called the control's *parent*. All controls must have a parent. The statement

```
pnl.Parent = Me
```

assigns the program's form to be the parent of the panel. The keyword *Me* is used in a method or property to refer to the current instance of the object; here, *Me* refers to the particular *Form* object that I created. It's the same as the value passed to *Application.Run* in *Main*.

I want to be able to draw on this panel. To do that, I assign an event handler to the panel's *Paint* event:

```
AddHandler pnl.Paint, AddressOf PanelOnPaint
```

I used similar code in Chapter 2 when I installed *Paint* event handlers for forms that were instantiated from *Form* rather than inherited from it. The *PanelOnPaint* method is in the *SysInfoPanel* class.

The panel must have a location relative to its parent. The *Location* property of the *Panel* class indicates where the upper left corner of the panel will be positioned. In this program, I want the panel's upper left corner to be at the point (0, 0) in the client area, which I set with this statement:

```
pnl.Location = Point.Empty
```

This statement isn't strictly needed because the location of controls is at point (0, 0) by default.

For this program to work correctly, the panel's size must be set to the dimensions of the output you want to display:

```
pnl.Size = New Size( _
    CInt(Math.Ceiling(cxCol + _
                      SysInfoStrings.MaxValueWidth(grfx, Font))), _
    CInt(Math.Ceiling(cySpace * SysInfoStrings.Count)))
```

The *cxCol* variable has already been set to the width of the first column plus a space. The call to the *MaxValueWidth* method of *SysInfoStrings* retrieves the maximum width of the *SystemInformation* property values. The height of the panel is set equal to the line-spacing value times the number of lines. I use *Math.Ceiling* to round each value up to the next highest integer. (An alternative is to make a *SizeF* object based on the floating-point width and height, and then use the shared *Size.Ceiling* method to convert it to a *Size* object.)

And that's that. The *PanelOnPaint* method displays the information on the surface of the panel using exactly the same code as the *OnPaint* method in the *SysInfoList* class.

But in this program, whenever the panel is wider than the client area, a horizontal scroll bar will automatically appear. If the panel is taller than the height of the client area, a vertical scroll bar will appear at the right of the client area. This happens dynamically: as you change the size of the client area, the scroll bars will disappear and reappear as needed. The scroll boxes are also dynamically sized to reflect the proportion of the content that is visible. For example, the height of the vertical scroll box is based on the ratio of the client area height to the height of the panel:

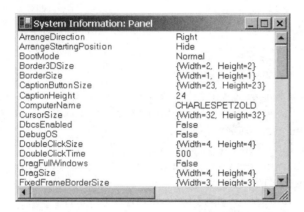

Because controls generally adopt the background colors of their parents and because panels are such bland controls to begin with, it's hard to see that there's really another control here. To give yourself a better idea of what's going on in this program, you may want to explicitly give the panel a different background color:

```
pnl.BackColor = Color.Honeydew
```

When you then make the client area of the program larger than the panel—in which case, the scroll bars disappear—you can see the honeydew panel against the (probably white) background of the form. Another way to see the panel is to set the *AutoScrollMargin* property of the form in the constructor:

```
AutoScrollMargin = New Size(10, 10)
```

You'll see a 10-pixel area on the right side of the panel when you scroll all the way to the right and on the bottom of the panel when you scroll all the way down. That's the background of the form's client area.

I mentioned earlier that a more general-purpose approach to scrolling involves the use of scroll bar controls. Scroll bars created as controls have properties named *Minimum* and *Maximum* that define the numeric values associated with the extreme positions of the scroll box and thus the range of values that the scroll bar can assume. When using the auto-scroll facility, however, you don't have access to these settings. The range is implied by the difference between the width and height of the client area less the width and height of the area occupied by the controls (or in our case, the single *Panel* control) plus the *AutoScrollMargin* less the width and height of the client area. Scroll bars created as controls generate an event named *Scroll* when the user manipulates the scroll bar. There is no such event associated with auto-scroll—at least not that an application has access to.

Although the SysInfoPanel program isn't responding directly to *Scroll* events, it's definitely responding to *Paint* events from the panel. When a program paints on a control, it's really painting only on the visible area of the control. Every time the user scrolls, the panel generates a *Paint* event because some previously unseen area has been pulled into view.

# The Heritage of *ScrollableControl*

What's going on behind the scenes? As I explained in Chapter 2, among the many classes that *Form* descends from is the *ScrollableControl* class, and that's where auto-scroll is implemented. We've already encountered two of the following six properties of *ScrollableControl* that are also inherited by *Form*.

### *ScrollableControl* Properties (selection)

| Property | Type | Accessibility | Description |
|---|---|---|---|
| *AutoScroll* | *Boolean* | Get/Set | Enables auto-scroll |
| *HScroll* | *Boolean* | Get/Set | Indicates the existence of horizontal scroll |
| *VScroll* | *Boolean* | Get/Set | Indicates the existence of vertical scroll |
| *AutoScrollMargin* | *Size* | Get/Set | Sets the margin around right and bottom of controls |
| *AutoScrollMinSize* | *Size* | Get/Set | Defines the minimum scrolling area |
| *AutoScrollPosition* | *Point* | Get/Set | Indicates the scroll bar position |

You can determine whether a particular scroll bar is currently visible by using the *HScroll* and *VScroll* properties. (Supposedly, you can also use these properties to hide a scroll bar that would normally be visible, but that facility doesn't seem to work very well.) I'll be discussing *AutoScrollMinSize* in more detail shortly.

*AutoScrollPosition* provides the current scrolling position in negative coordinates. In the SysInfoPanel program, the value of *AutoScrollPosition* is the same as the value of the panel's *Location* property. However, there's an inexplicable inconsistency in the *Get* and *Set* accessors of *AutoScrollPosition*. When you read the property, the coordinates are always less than or equal to 0. When you set *AutoScrollPosition*, however, the coordinates must be positive. I'll have an example of this anomaly in the SysInfoKeyboard program in Chapter 6 when I add a keyboard interface to the program.

The *ScrollableControl* class obviously has access to the normal properties and events of the scroll bars; the class is hiding these items from you in order to provide a higher-level interface. As you manipulate the scroll bar in the Sys-InfoPanel program, code implemented in *ScrollableControl* is obviously changing the *Location* property of the panel control to negative values. (It's easy to confirm this change by adding an event handler for the panel's *Move* event.) Negative *Location* values mean that the upper left corner of the panel is being positioned above and to the left of the upper left corner of the client area. That's why the contents of the panel seem to move around within the form.

We'll explore auto-scroll more in later chapters as we begin creating more controls. Now let's see if we can persuade auto-scroll to work without creating any child controls at all.

## Scrolling Without Controls

The key to enabling auto-scroll without creating child controls is to set the *AutoScrollMinSize* property to something other than the default (0, 0). Normally, the scrolling area is based on the locations and sizes of controls on the client area. However, *AutoScrollMinSize* sets a minimum scrolling area regardless of the presence of any controls. Of course, you must also set the *AutoScroll* property to *True*.

Typically, you set *AutoScrollMinSize* to the dimensions necessary to display all the program's output. In the system-information programs, *AutoScroll-MinSize* should be set to a size sufficient to encompass the full width and height of all 60 lines of information. That's the same size as the panel in the Sys-InfoPanel program.

The SysInfoScroll program is virtually identical in functionality to SysInfo-Panel but enables auto-scroll without any child controls.

## SysInfoScroll.vb

```vb
'-----------------------------------------------
' SysInfoScroll.vb (c) 2002 by Charles Petzold
'-----------------------------------------------
Imports System
Imports System.Drawing
Imports System.Windows.Forms

Class SysInfoScroll
    Inherits Form

    ReadOnly cxCol As Single
    ReadOnly cySpace As Integer

    Shared Sub Main()
        Application.Run(New SysInfoScroll())
    End Sub

    Sub New()
        Text = "System Information: Scroll"
        BackColor = SystemColors.Window
        ForeColor = SystemColors.WindowText

        Dim grfx As Graphics = CreateGraphics()
        Dim szf As SizeF = grfx.MeasureString(" ", Font)
        cxCol = szf.Width + SysInfoStrings.MaxLabelWidth(grfx, Font)
        cySpace = Font.Height

        ' Set auto-scroll properties.
        AutoScroll = True
        AutoScrollMinSize = New Size( _
            CInt(Math.Ceiling(cxCol + _
                        SysInfoStrings.MaxValueWidth(grfx, Font))), _
            CInt(Math.Ceiling(cySpace * SysInfoStrings.Count)))
        grfx.Dispose()
    End Sub

    Protected Overrides Sub OnPaint(ByVal pea As PaintEventArgs)
        Dim grfx As Graphics = pea.Graphics
        Dim br As New SolidBrush(ForeColor)
        Dim iCount As Integer = SysInfoStrings.Count
        Dim astrLabels() As String = SysInfoStrings.Labels
        Dim astrValues() As String = SysInfoStrings.Values
        Dim pt As Point = AutoScrollPosition
        Dim i As Integer
```

*(continued)*

**SysInfoScroll.vb** *(continued)*

```
        For i = 0 To iCount - 1
            grfx.DrawString(astrLabels(i), Font, br, _
                        pt.X, pt.Y + i * cySpace)
            grfx.DrawString(astrValues(i), Font, br, _
                        pt.X + cxCol, pt.Y + i * cySpace)
        Next i
    End Sub
End Class
```

The previous program (SysInfoPanel) made a panel control a child of its client area. In a program such as SysInfoScroll, you might wonder whether the scroll bars are also located on top of the client area. They are not! The client area is actually made smaller to accommodate the scroll bars. Sometimes the width of the client area is just a little larger than *AutoScrollMinSize.Width*. If a vertical scroll bar is required, however, the width of the client area must be narrowed by the width of the scroll bar; that change could then make the client area width smaller than *AutoScrollMinSize.Width* and thus also require a horizontal scroll bar.

By setting *AutoScrollMinSize*, you are *not* defining something akin to a virtual drawing area. Regardless of how large you make *AutoScrollMinSize*, when you handle the *OnPaint* method, you're still drawing within the confines of the physical client area. Indeed, that client area is probably even smaller than usual because of the presence of the scroll bars.

In SysInfoPanel, any manipulation of the scroll bars resulted in the uncovering of previously unseen areas of the panel control and thus generated a *Paint* event. That program did all its drawing on a panel control that was large enough for all the program's output. Scrolling relocated the panel relative to the program's client area. But the coordinates of the output on the panel remained the same. For example, the second column of the third row of text output was always at the location (*cxCol*, 2 * *cySpace*).

SysInfoScroll responds to changes in the scroll bars by overriding the form's *OnPaint* method. However, this program is drawing directly on its client area and not on some control that's being shifted around. The client area isn't large enough for the program's output, and the *Graphics* object obtained during the *OnPaint* method knows nothing about auto-scroll.

What this means is that the *OnPaint* method of the SysInfoScroll program (or any program that implements auto-scroll and draws directly on its client area) must adjust the coordinates of any drawing function it calls based on the *AutoScrollPosition* property. As you can see, the *OnPaint* method in this program gets *AutoScrollPosition*, saves it in a *Point* variable named *pt*, and adds the values to the coordinates in the *DrawString* calls. Keep in mind that the coordinates returned by *AutoScrollPosition* are negative. If you've scrolled down 30 pixels (for example), the first *DrawString* call for the first line of text uses the coordinates (0, -30), which is above the client area and not visible.

This method of repainting the client area may start to sound inefficient: The program is drawing 60 lines of text every time it needs to repaint, yet usually only a small fraction of those calls result in something being painted on the client area. I'll take on the efficiency issue later in this chapter.

# Actual Numbers

Let's pause for a moment and try to get a better feel for what's going on by looking at actual numbers. Just keep in mind that some of these numbers are based on my system settings and may not be exactly the same numbers you're seeing. (In particular, my video display settings include Large Fonts. This setting affects some of the items I'll be discussing.)

Suppose your program needs a client area of 400 pixels wide by 1600 pixels high. Here's how you set *AutoScroll* and *AutoScrollMinSize* in the form's constructor:

```
AutoScroll = True
AutoScrollMinSize = New Size(400, 1600)
```

My experience is that forms are created with a default size of 300 by 300 pixels. How large is the client area in that case? Well, we now have two programs that let you scroll through the *SystemInformation* properties, so you can figure out how large the client area is. I see a *SystemInformation.CaptionHeight* value of 24. That's the height of the caption bar. The width of the normal sizing border is stored in *SystemInformation.FrameBorderSize*. I'm seeing 4 pixels for that, and remember that's 4 pixels on all four sides. So you can calculate the client area width as 300 minus two 4's, or 292. The height of the client area should be 300 minus two 4's minus 24, or 268. (If you don't trust my math skills, you can verify these values by using the form's *ClientSize* property.)

Because the client area height of 268 is less than 1600, the program needs a vertical scroll bar. I'm seeing a value of *SystemInformation.VerticalScrollBar-Width* of 20 pixels. Thus, the client area width is reduced to 292 minus 20, or 272 pixels.

That width of 272 is less than 400, so the program needs a horizontal scroll bar as well. The value of *SystemInformation.HorizontalScrollBarHeight* is also 20 pixels, thus reducing the height of the client area to 268 minus 20, or 248 pixels.

The vertical scroll bar is probably set to have a range of values from 0 through 1352, which is the required height of 1600 minus the actual height of 248. The horizontal scroll bar is probably set to have a range of values from 0 through 128 (which is 400 minus 272).

The code implemented in *ScrollableControl* responds to the user clicking the scroll bar or dragging the scroll box by performing two actions: changing the value of *AutoScrollPosition* and scrolling the contents of the client area. *AutoScrollPosition* is initially set to (0, 0). As the user moves the horizontal scroll bar, the *X* property varies between 0 and −128 and the *Y* property varies from 0 through −1352. The scrolling of the client area requires the system to copy the contents from one location on the client area to another. The Win32 API includes functions named *ScrollWindow*, *ScrollWindowEx*, and *ScrollDC* that let programs scroll their client areas. Although these functions are *not* exposed in the Windows Forms class library, it's obvious that *ScrollableControl* is using one of them.

When code implemented in the *ScrollableControl* class scrolls the client area, it can scroll only what's currently displayed on the screen. Scrolling generally "uncovers" a rectangle in the client area, making that portion of the client invalid. This invalidation generates a call to the *OnPaint* method.

So when you're scrolling the SysInfoPanel or SysInfoScroll program, the *OnPaint* method really needs to refresh only a small rectangular subset of the client area. It hardly seems rational that these programs process the *OnPaint* call by obtaining and displaying every single line of information.

Let's take care of that problem in two steps.

# Keeping It Green

Many of the items available from the *SystemInformation* class reflect the preferences of the particular user on whose machine the program is running. That person is probably you, of course, but someday you may want to send a program using *SystemInformation* properties out into the world to be used by others.

Some of the items reported by *SystemInformation* are just about carved in stone. For example, mouse cursors have been 32 pixels square for a very long time, the only exception involving the old IBM 640 by 200 Color Graphics Adapter.[*]

However, other items can change even as the SysInfoPanel or SysInfoScroll program is running. Changing these items often involves the Windows Control Panel.

For example, bring up Control Panel, select Display, and in the Display Properties dialog box, select the Effects tab. If you change the Show Window Contents While Dragging item, the *SystemInformation.DragFullWindows* prop-

---

[*] Charles Petzold, *Programming Windows* (Microsoft Press, 1988), 332.

erty changes. The *MouseButtonsSwapped* property reflects the setting in the Mouse Properties dialog box, Buttons tab, Button Configuration section. The *ShowSounds* property reflects the setting in the Accessibility Options dialog box, Sound tab, ShowSounds section.

Changing your video display to a different pixel dimension affects five *SystemInformation* properties: *MaxWindowTrackSize*, *PrimaryMonitorMaximizedWindowSize*, *PrimaryMonitorSize*, *VirtualScreen*, and *WorkingArea*. Using the Display Properties dialog box to change your system font (from Small Fonts to Large Fonts or something else) affects over 20 *SystemInformation* properties, but the system makes you restart your machine for such a major change. (I'll have more to say about Small Fonts and Large Fonts in Chapter 7.)

One problem is that the programs presented so far in this chapter have obtained new *SystemInformation* properties only during the *OnPaint* method. If you use Control Panel to change one of these properties, the program doesn't know about the change. It won't even access the new value until the next call to *OnPaint*. And because *OnPaint* lets the program paint only an invalid region, even then the display of the item might not be updated!

Fortunately, a Windows Forms application can be notified when anything changes in the system that affects the *SystemInformation* properties.

Notified? But how? Through events, of course! The *SystemEvents* class in the *Microsoft.Win32* namespace lets you set 12 different events that notify you of changes happening at the system level. Much of the rest of *Microsoft.Win32* provides support for these events, including delegates, event arguments, and enumerations.

The two events we're interested in are *UserPreferenceChanged* (which covers many of the changes users can make through Control Panel) and *DisplaySettingsChanged*, which occurs when the user changes the video display settings. Implementing these events requires some restructuring of the program. The revised version is SysInfoUpdate.cs.

**SysInfoUpdate.vb**

```
'-----------------------------------------------
' SysInfoUpdate.vb (c) 2002 by Charles Petzold
'-----------------------------------------------
Imports Microsoft.Win32
Imports System
Imports System.Drawing
Imports System.Windows.Forms

Class SysInfoUpdate
    Inherits Form
```

*(continued)*

**SysInfoUpdate.vb** *(continued)*

```
Protected iCount, cySpace As Integer
Protected astrLabels(), astrValues() As String
Protected cxCol As Single

Shared Sub Main()
    Application.Run(New SysInfoUpdate())
End Sub

Sub New()
    Text = "System Information: Update"
    BackColor = SystemColors.Window
    ForeColor = SystemColors.WindowText
    AutoScroll = True

    AddHandler SystemEvents.UserPreferenceChanged, _
                            AddressOf UserPreferenceChanged
    AddHandler SystemEvents.DisplaySettingsChanged, _
                            AddressOf DisplaySettingsChanged
    UpdateAllInfo()
End Sub

Private Sub UserPreferenceChanged(ByVal obj As Object, _
        ByVal ea As UserPreferenceChangedEventArgs)
    UpdateAllInfo()
    Invalidate()
End Sub

Private Sub DisplaySettingsChanged(ByVal obj As Object, _
                            ByVal ea As EventArgs)
    UpdateAllInfo()
    Invalidate()
End Sub

Private Sub UpdateAllInfo()
    iCount = SysInfoStrings.Count
    astrLabels = SysInfoStrings.Labels
    astrValues = SysInfoStrings.Values

    Dim grfx As Graphics = CreateGraphics()
    Dim szf As SizeF = grfx.MeasureString(" ", Font)
    cxCol = szf.Width + SysInfoStrings.MaxLabelWidth(grfx, Font)
    cySpace = Font.Height
    AutoScrollMinSize = New Size( _
        CInt(Math.Ceiling(cxCol + _
                    SysInfoStrings.MaxValueWidth(grfx, Font))), _
        CInt(Math.Ceiling(cySpace * iCount)))
    grfx.Dispose()
End Sub

Protected Overrides Sub OnPaint(ByVal pea As PaintEventArgs)
    Dim grfx As Graphics = pea.Graphics
    Dim br As New SolidBrush(ForeColor)
```

```
        Dim pt As Point = AutoScrollPosition
        Dim i As Integer

        For i = 0 To iCount - 1
            grfx.DrawString(astrLabels(i), Font, br, _
                         pt.X, pt.Y + i * cySpace)
            grfx.DrawString(astrValues(i), Font, br, _
                         pt.X + cxCol, pt.Y + i * cySpace)
        Next i
    End Sub
End Class
```

Everything dependent on information the program obtains from the *Sys-InfoStrings* class is now consolidated in the *UpdateAllInfo* method. The first time *UpdateAllInfo* is called is during the program's constructor. The constructor also installs event handlers. The event handlers call *UpdateAllInfo* again to get the new information and then *Invalidate* to invalidate the entire client area. Calling *Invalidate* generates an *OnPaint* call.

# Don't Be a Pig

Users have a name for a program that isn't as fast as it could be. They say, "This program is a real *pig*." It's not nice, but it's a fact of life.

I've already made the system-information program somewhat more efficient by calling the methods in *SysInfoStrings* only when the program begins execution and when any of the *SystemInformation* items change. The program no longer makes three calls to *SysInfoStrings* every time it gets a call to *OnPaint*.

However, *OnPaint* is still displaying all 60 lines—and calling *DrawString* 120 times—every time any part of the client window is invalidated. On most people's machines, not all 60 lines will even be visible. Moreover, as I mentioned earlier, vertical scrolling usually uncovers only a line or two of text; in those cases, *OnPaint* really needs to redraw only a line or two.

To some extent, Windows itself provides some built-in efficiency. The *Graphics* object you obtain during the *OnPaint* method can paint only on the invalid region of the client area. Something called a *clipping region*, which encompasses only the invalid region and doesn't let you draw outside it, is involved. You saw an example of repainting only the invalid region in the RandomClear program in Chapter 3. The fact remains, however, that you're still making 120 *DrawString* calls, and you're still requiring Windows to check whether a particular *DrawString* call will or will not fall within the clipping region.

Fortunately, the *ClipRectangle* property of the *PaintEventArgs* class is there to help. The *ClipRectangle* property is the smallest rectangle in client area coordinates that encompasses the invalid region. (As the RandomClear program demonstrated, the invalid region need not be rectangular.) For personal experimentation, you might insert the line

```
Console.Writeline(pea.ClipRectangle)
```

in an *OnPaint* method and play with scrolling and partially covering and then uncovering the form with other programs.

The SysInfoEfficient program inherits from SysInfoUpdate and overrides the *OnPaint* method in that class with a more efficient version. A couple of fairly simple calculations based on the *AutoScrollPosition* property of the form and the *ClipRectangle* property of *PaintEventArgs* derive line index values named *iFirst* and *iLast* that are then used in the *For* loop to display the minimum number of lines of text required to update the client area.

```
SysInfoEfficient.vb
'-------------------------------------------------
' SysInfoEfficient.vb (c) 2002 by Charles Petzold
'-------------------------------------------------
Imports System
Imports System.Drawing
Imports System.Windows.Forms

Class SysInfoEfficient
    Inherits SysInfoUpdate

    Shared Shadows Sub Main()
        Application.Run(New SysInfoEfficient())
    End Sub

    Sub New()
        Text = "System Information: Efficient"
    End Sub

    Protected Overrides Sub OnPaint(ByVal pea As PaintEventArgs)
        Dim grfx As Graphics = pea.Graphics
        Dim br As New SolidBrush(ForeColor)
        Dim pt As Point = AutoScrollPosition
        Dim i As Integer
        Dim iFirst As Integer = _
            (pea.ClipRectangle.Top - pt.Y) \ cySpace
        Dim iLast As Integer = _
            (pea.ClipRectangle.Bottom - pt.Y) \ cySpace

        iLast = Math.Min(iCount - 1, iLast)

        For i = iFirst To iLast
            grfx.DrawString(astrLabels(i), Font, br, _
                            pt.X, pt.Y + i * cySpace)
```

```
            grfx.DrawString(astrValues(i), Font, br, _
                            pt.X + cxCol, pt.Y + i * cySpace)
        Next i
    End Sub
End Class
```

Just prior to the *For* loop, the statement involving *Math.Min* prevents *iLast* from exceeding the number of items to be displayed. This limit can be exceeded only if the window is taller than the size necessary to display all the items.

# Reflecting on the Future

While the .NET Framework might appear to be the epitome of perfection today, there's still a possibility, however slim, that in some distant year a misguided Microsoft developer might feel compelled to add one or two additional properties to the *SystemInformation* class. In that case, my *SysInfoStrings* class would have to be updated to include those additional properties, and all the various programs in this chapter would have to be recompiled to include the new version.

Might it be possible, however, to write a program that automatically includes *all* current *SystemInformation* properties implemented in the class, even those that didn't exist when the program was written?

Yes, it *is* possible, and to understand how to do it, let's think about where the *SystemInformation* code actually resides. According to the documentation for the class, it's in the file System.Windows.Forms.dll. When one of the programs in this chapter is run, the operating system links it with System.Windows.Forms.dll so that the program can make calls to the *SystemInformation* class.

But the DLL isn't just a bunch of code. It exists with binary *metadata* that describes in detail the classes implemented in the file and all the fields, properties, methods, and events in these classes. In fact, the Visual Basic compiler uses this information to compile programs (that's why you need to set the Reference files), and the reference documentation of the .NET Framework is derived from this metadata.

So it makes sense that a program might be able to access this metadata at runtime, find out about the .NET classes dynamically, and even execute some methods and properties in them. This process is called *reflection*, and it's a concept borrowed from Java. Reflection would normally be considered an advanced topic, but it's just so perfect for this application that I can't resist.

The first step is to rewrite the *SysInfoStrings* class so that it uses reflection to obtain the property names and the actual properties.

**SysInfoReflectionStrings.vb**

```vb
'-------------------------------------------------------------
' SysInfoReflectionStrings.vb (c) 2002 by Charles Petzold
'-------------------------------------------------------------
Imports Microsoft.Win32
Imports System
Imports System.Drawing
Imports System.Reflection
Imports System.Windows.Forms

Class SysInfoReflectionStrings

    ' Fields
    Shared bValidInfo As Boolean = False
    Shared iCount As Integer
    Shared astrLabels(), astrValues() As String

    ' Constructor
    Shared Sub New()
        AddHandler SystemEvents.UserPreferenceChanged, _
                                    AddressOf UserPreferenceChanged
        AddHandler SystemEvents.DisplaySettingsChanged, _
                                    AddressOf DisplaySettingsChanged
    End Sub

    ' Properties
    Shared ReadOnly Property Labels() As String()
        Get
            GetSysInfo()
            Return astrLabels
        End Get
    End Property

    Shared ReadOnly Property Values() As String()
        Get
            GetSysInfo()
            Return astrValues
        End Get
    End Property

    Shared ReadOnly Property Count() As Integer
        Get
            GetSysInfo()
            Return iCount
        End Get
    End Property

    ' Event handlers
    Private Shared Sub UserPreferenceChanged(ByVal obj As Object, _
            ByVal ea As UserPreferenceChangedEventArgs)
        bValidInfo = False
    End Sub
```

```
Private Shared Sub DisplaySettingsChanged(ByVal obj As Object, _
                                          ByVal ea As EventArgs)
    bValidInfo = False
End Sub

' Methods
Private Shared Sub GetSysInfo()
    If bValidInfo Then Return

    ' Get property information for SystemInformation class.
    Dim type As Type = GetType(SystemInformation)
    Dim apropinfo As PropertyInfo() = type.GetProperties()

    ' Count the number of shared readable properties.
    ' (Shared is called "static" in the .NET Framework.)
    iCount = 0
    Dim pi As PropertyInfo
    For Each pi In apropinfo
        If pi.CanRead AndAlso pi.GetGetMethod().IsStatic Then
            iCount += 1
        End If
    Next pi

    ' Allocate string arrays.
    ReDim astrLabels(iCount - 1)
    ReDim astrValues(iCount - 1)

    ' Loop through the property information classes again.
    iCount = 0
    For Each pi In apropinfo
        If pi.CanRead AndAlso pi.GetGetMethod().IsStatic Then
            ' Get the property names and values.
            astrLabels(iCount) = pi.Name
            astrValues(iCount) = _
                pi.GetValue(type, Nothing).ToString()
            iCount += 1
        End If
    Next pi

    Array.Sort(astrLabels, astrValues)
    bValidInfo = True
End Sub

Shared Function MaxLabelWidth(ByVal grfx As Graphics, _
                             ByVal fnt As Font) As Single
    Return MaxWidth(Labels, grfx, fnt)
End Function

Shared Function MaxValueWidth(ByVal grfx As Graphics, _
                             ByVal fnt As Font) As Single
    Return MaxWidth(Values, grfx, fnt)
End Function
```

*(continued)*

**SysInfoReflectionStrings.vb**   *(continued)*

```
    Private Shared Function MaxWidth(ByVal astr() As String, _
            ByVal grfx As Graphics, ByVal fnt As Font) As Single
        Dim fMax As Single = 0
        Dim str As String

        GetSysInfo()

        For Each str In astr
            fMax = Math.Max(fMax, grfx.MeasureString(str, fnt).Width)
        Next str

        Return fMax
    End Function
End Class
```

The *GetSysInfo* method in this class does the bulk of the work. It obtains the property names and their values when they are first required and whenever they change. The Visual Basic *GetType* operator obtains the type of the *System-Information* class, which is saved in a variable of type *Type*. One method of *Type* is *GetProperties*, which returns an array of *PropertyInfo* objects. Each object in this array is a property of *SystemInformation*. A *For Each* loop counts up all the properties that are both shared and readable. (I know that all the properties of *SystemInformation* are shared and readable today, but I'm trying to make the program generalized.)

The program then allocates arrays for the properties and their values, and loops through the *PropertyInfo* array again. The *Name* property of the *Property-Info* object is the name of the property; in this case, the *Name* property returns strings such as *HighContrast* and *IconSize*. The *GetValue* method obtains each property's value. The shared *Sort* method of the *Array* class sorts both the name and value arrays based on the text of the property names.

The program that makes use of *SysInfoReflectionStrings* is functionally the same as the combination of SysInfoUpdate and SysInfoEfficient.

**SysInfoReflection.vb**

```
'-------------------------------------------------
' SysInfoReflection.vb (c) 2002 by Charles Petzold
'-------------------------------------------------
Imports Microsoft.Win32
Imports System
Imports System.Drawing
Imports System.Windows.Forms

Class SysInfoReflection
    Inherits Form
```

```
Protected iCount, cySpace As Integer
Protected astrLabels(), astrValues() As String
Protected cxCol As Single

Shared Sub Main()
    Application.Run(New SysInfoReflection())
End Sub

Sub New()
    Text = "System Information: Reflection"
    BackColor = SystemColors.Window
    ForeColor = SystemColors.WindowText
    AutoScroll = True

    AddHandler SystemEvents.UserPreferenceChanged, _
                            AddressOf UserPreferenceChanged
    AddHandler SystemEvents.DisplaySettingsChanged, _
                            AddressOf DisplaySettingsChanged
    UpdateAllInfo()
End Sub

Private Sub UserPreferenceChanged(ByVal obj As Object, _
        ByVal ea As UserPreferenceChangedEventArgs)
    UpdateAllInfo()
    Invalidate()
End Sub

Private Sub DisplaySettingsChanged(ByVal obj As Object, _
                            ByVal ea As EventArgs)
    UpdateAllInfo()
    Invalidate()
End Sub

Sub UpdateAllInfo()
    iCount = SysInfoReflectionStrings.Count
    astrLabels = SysInfoReflectionStrings.Labels
    astrValues = SysInfoReflectionStrings.Values

    Dim grfx As Graphics = CreateGraphics()
    Dim szf As SizeF = grfx.MeasureString(" ", Font)
    cxCol = szf.Width + _
                SysInfoReflectionStrings.MaxLabelWidth(grfx, Font)
    cySpace = Font.Height
    AutoScrollMinSize = New Size( _
        CInt(Math.Ceiling(cxCol + _
        SysInfoReflectionStrings.MaxValueWidth(grfx, Font))), _
        CInt(Math.Ceiling(cySpace * iCount)))
    grfx.Dispose()
End Sub
```

*(continued)*

**SysInfoReflection.vb**     *(continued)*

```
    Protected Overrides Sub OnPaint(ByVal pea As PaintEventArgs)
        Dim grfx As Graphics = pea.Graphics
        Dim br As New SolidBrush(ForeColor)
        Dim pt As Point = AutoScrollPosition
        Dim i As Integer

        Dim iFirst As Integer = _
            (pea.ClipRectangle.Top - pt.Y) \ cySpace
        Dim iLast As Integer = _
            (pea.ClipRectangle.Bottom - pt.Y) \ cySpace

        iLast = Math.Min(iCount - 1, iLast)
        For i = iFirst To iLast
            grfx.DrawString(astrLabels(i), Font, br, _
                            pt.X, pt.Y + i * cySpace)
            grfx.DrawString(astrValues(i), Font, br, _
                            pt.X + cxCol, pt.Y + i * cySpace)
        Next i
    End Sub
End Class
```

And this is my absolutely final version of a *SystemInformation* display program (until Chapter 6, that is, when I add a keyboard interface to it).

# 5

# Lines, Curves, and Area Fills

According to Euclid, "A line is breadthless length."[*] It's the "breadthless" part that makes this statement interesting. It certainly indicates the high degree of abstract thought that characterizes ancient Greek mathematics. It also proves conclusively that the ancient Greeks knew nothing about computer graphics. They would have realized that pixels do indeed have breadth, a fact that contributes to one of the annoying problems often associated with computer graphics: the off-by-1-pixel error, a problem we'll be attuned to in this chapter.

The world of computer graphics is roughly divided into two areas:

- *Vector* graphics, which is the practical application of analytic geometry and involves drawing lines, curves, and filled areas

- *Raster* graphics, which involves bitmaps and real-world images

Then there's text, which occupies a niche of its own in the computer graphics world. In recent years, however, with the ascendance of outline fonts, text is often treated as part of vector graphics.

This chapter introduces vector graphics as implemented in Microsoft Windows Forms and GDI+. All the drawing functions discussed in this chapter are methods of the *Graphics* class and begin with the prefix *Draw* or *Fill*. The *Draw* methods draw lines and curves; the *Fill* methods fill areas (the outlines of

---

[*] Sir Thomas L. Heath, ed., *The Thirteen Books of Euclid's Elements* (New York: Dover, 1956), 1: 153.

which, of course, are defined by lines and curves). The first argument to all the *Draw* methods covered in this chapter is a *Pen* object; the first argument to all the *Fill* methods is a *Brush*.

# How to Get a Graphics Object

Most of the drawing functions are methods of the *Graphics* class. (There are additional drawing functions in the *ControlPaint* class, but these are somewhat specialized.) To draw, you need an object of type *Graphics*. But the *Graphics* constructor isn't public. You cannot simply create a *Graphics* object like so:

```
Dim grfx As New Graphics()     ' Won't work!
```

The *Graphics* class is also *NonInheritable*, which means you can't derive your own class from *Graphics*:

```
Class MyGraphics
    Inherits Graphics          ' Won't work!
```

You must obtain the *Graphics* object in some other way. Here's a complete list of ways that you can do this, beginning with the most common:

■   When you override the *OnPaint* method or install a *Paint* event handler in any class derived from *Control* (such as *Form*), a *Graphics* object is delivered to you as a property of the *PaintEventArgs* class.

■   To paint on a control or a form at times other than during the *OnPaint* method or the *Paint* event, you can call the *CreateGraphics* method of the control. Classes sometimes call *CreateGraphics* in their constructors to obtain information and perform initialization. (Some of the programs in Chapter 4 did this.) Although classes can't draw during the constructor, they can do so during other events. It's common for a control or a form to draw something during keyboard, mouse, or timer events, as I'll demonstrate in Chapters 6, 8, and 10. It's important for a program to use the *Graphics* object only during the event that obtains it (that is, the *Graphics* object shouldn't be stored in a field in the class). The program should also call the *Dispose* method of the *Graphics* object when it's finished using it.

■   When printing, you install a *PrintPage* event handler and get an object of type *PrintPageEventArgs*, which contains a *Graphics* object suitable for the printer. I'll demonstrate how to do this shortly.

■   Some controls—most commonly menus, list boxes, combo boxes, and status bars—have a feature called *owner draw* that allows a program to dynamically draw items on the control. The *MeasureItem* and *DrawItem* events deliver objects of type *MeasureItemEventArgs* and *DrawItemEventArgs*, which have *Graphics* objects the event handler can use.

■   To draw on a bitmap or a metafile (techniques I'll demonstrate in Chapter 11and Chapter 23), you need to obtain a special *Graphics* object by calling the shared method *Graphics.FromImage*.

■   If you need to obtain information from the *Graphics* object associated with a printer without actually printing, you can use the *CreateMeasurementGraphics* method of the *PrinterSettings* class.

■   If you're interfacing with Win32 code, you can use the shared methods *Graphics.FromHwnd* and *Graphics.FromHdc* to obtain a *Graphics* object.

# Pens, Briefly

When you draw a line by hand on paper, you use a pencil, a crayon, a fountain pen, a ballpoint pen, a felt-tip marker, or whatever. The type of instrument you choose at least determines the line's color and width. These qualities and others are subsumed under the *Pen* class, and whenever you draw a line, you specify a *Pen* object.

I'm not going to get into a comprehensive exploration of pens at this time, however. The problem is that pens can be created from brushes, so a complete discussion of pens is dependent on that topic. And brushes can be created from bitmapped images and graphics paths, and those are more advanced graphics programming topics. We'll examine pens and brushes thoroughly in Chapter 17.

As I explained in Chapter 3, you can create a pen of a particular color like so:

```
Dim pn As New Pen(clr)
```

where *clr* is an object of type *Color*. You can also take advantage of the *Pens* class, which contains 141 shared read-only properties that return *Pen* objects. *Pens.HotPink* is thus an acceptable first argument to line-drawing methods (although appropriate only when used in moderation). A complete list of these color names is available on the inside back cover of this book.

The *SystemPens* class contains 15 shared read-only properties that also return *Pen* objects based on the system colors. But if you want to create a pen that you know will be visible against the background color the user has chosen, base it on the current *ForeColor* property:

```
Dim pn As New Pen(ForeColor)
```

There's one more aspect of pens I want to mention here, and that's the pen's width. The width is a read/write property:

### *Pen* Properties (selection)

| Property | Type | Accessibility |
|----------|------|---------------|
| *Width* | *Single* | Get/Set |

There's also a *Pen* constructor that includes the pen width, so here's a table listing the two *Pen* constructors I've mentioned so far:

### *Pen* Constructors (selection)

```
Pen(ByVal clr As Color)
Pen(ByVal clr As Color, ByVal fWidth As Single)
```

(Just so you won't think I'm holding back information, there are only two other *Pen* constructors, which look the same as these two except that a *Brush* object is the first argument.) When you use the first constructor, the pen is created with a width of 1. *Pen* objects available from the *Pens* and *SystemPens* class also have a width of 1. For the time being, you can think of that as 1 pixel wide. However, you'll discover in Chapter 7 that this width is actually in *world coordinates* and affected by various *transforms*.

It's possible to create a pen that is always 1 pixel wide regardless of any transforms that may be in effect. Use a width of 0 in the constructor:

```
Dim pn As New Pen(clr, 0)
```

Or set the *Width* property to 0:

```
pn.Width = 0
```

# Straight Lines

To draw a single straight line, you use the *DrawLine* method of the *Graphics* class. There are four overloaded versions of *DrawLine*, but they all involve the same information: the coordinates where the line begins and ends, and the pen used to draw the line:

### *Graphics DrawLine* Methods

```
Sub DrawLine(ByVal pn As Pen,
             ByVal x1 As Integer, ByVal y1 As Integer,
             ByVal x2 As Integer, ByVal y2 As Integer)

Sub DrawLine(ByVal pn As Pen,
             ByVal x1 As Single, ByVal y1 As Single,
             ByVal x2 As Single, ByVal y2 As Single)

Sub DrawLine(ByVal pn As Pen,
             ByVal pt1 As Point, ByVal pt2 As Point)

Sub DrawLine(ByVal pn As Pen,
             ByVal ptf1 As PointF, ByVal ptf2 As PointF)
```

You can specify the coordinates either as four *Integer* or *Single* values, or as two *Point* or *PointF* structures.

*DrawLine* draws a line from the first point up to *and including* the second point. (This is a little different from Win32 GDI, which draws up to but *not including* the second point.) For example,

```
grfx.Drawline(pn, 0, 0, 5, 5)
```

colors 6 pixels black—the pixels at coordinate points (0,0), (1,1), (2,2), (3,3), (4,4), and (5, 5). The order of the two points doesn't matter, so the call

```
grfx.DrawLine(pn, 5, 5, 0, 0)
```

produces identical results. The call

```
grfx.DrawLine(pn, 2, 2, 3, 3)
```

draws 2 pixels, at points (2, 2) and (3, 3). However,

```
grfx.DrawLine(pn, 3, 3, 3, 3)
```

draws nothing.

As you know, you can determine the width and height of your client area by using the *ClientSize* property of *Form*. The number of pixels horizontally is *ClientSize.Width*; the pixels can be numbered from 0 through *ClientSize.Width* − 1. Similarly, the vertical pixels can be numbered from 0 through *Client-Size.Height* − 1.

The XMarksTheSpot program draws an X in the client area.

**XMarksTheSpot.vb**

```
'-------------------------------------------------
' XMarksTheSpot.vb (c) 2002 by Charles Petzold
'-------------------------------------------------
Imports System
Imports System.Drawing
Imports System.Windows.Forms

Class XMarksTheSpot
    Inherits Form

    Shared Sub Main()
        Application.Run(New XMarksTheSpot())
    End Sub

    Sub New()
        Text = "X Marks The Spot"
        BackColor = SystemColors.Window
        ForeColor = SystemColors.WindowText
        ResizeRedraw = True
    End Sub

    Protected Overrides Sub OnPaint(ByVal pea As PaintEventArgs)
        Dim grfx As Graphics = pea.Graphics
        Dim pn As New Pen(ForeColor)

        grfx.DrawLine(pn, 0, 0, _
                    ClientSize.Width - 1, ClientSize.Height - 1)
        grfx.DrawLine(pn, 0, ClientSize.Height - 1, _
                    ClientSize.Width - 1, 0)
    End Sub
End Class
```

The first *DrawLine* call draws a line from the upper left pixel to the lower right pixel of the client area. The second *DrawLine* call begins the line at the lower left pixel, which is the point (0, *ClientSize.Height* − 1), and goes to the upper right pixel at (*ClientSize.Width* − 1, 0).

# An Introduction to Printing

Many of the graphics demonstration programs in this chapter and subsequent chapters will be similar to XMarksTheSpot. They won't necessarily be as lame as XMarksTheSpot (although some will, unfortunately), but they'll do nothing more than demonstrate basic graphics programming techniques by displaying static images in their client areas.

It might be helpful even at this early stage to print these images on your printer as well, if only to have the option of proudly displaying them on your refrigerator door. More important, printing graphics gives you an opportunity to discover firsthand the extent to which a graphics programming system is device independent as you're learning the system.

Printing is a topic customarily banished to the end of programming books if not ignored entirely, mostly because printing is often terribly complicated. I've devoted Chapter 21 to printing to cover all the various facilities and options that are available. But for our immediate purposes—turning out a single page on the user's default printer using default settings—printing from a Windows Forms application is quite easy.

Indeed, the only reason I hesitated at all in introducing printing so early was the user-interface problem—how the program would allow the user to initiate printing. As you know, most programs that print include a Print option on the File menu. It's a little too early in the book for menus, a subject covered exhaustively in Chapter 14. I also considered implementing a simple keyboard interface, perhaps using the Print Screen (sometimes labeled PrtScn) key or CTRL+P. Finally I decided on overriding the *OnClick* method.

*OnClick* is implemented in the *Control* class and inherited by every class descended from *Control*, including *Form*. The *OnClick* method is called whenever the user clicks the client area of the form with any mouse button. And that's all I'm going to say about the mouse until Chapter 8!

To print to the default printer, you first need to create an object of type *PrintDocument*, a class defined in the *System.Drawing.Printing* namespace:

```
Dim prndoc As New PrintDocument()
```

We'll spend more time with this class in Chapter 21. For now, I'll mention only one property, one event, and one method in the class.

You set the *DocumentName* property of the *PrintDocument* object to a text string. This is the text that identifies the job in the printer dialog box as the graphics output is being spooled out to the printer:

```
prndoc.DocumentName = "My print job"
```

A program that works with documents generally uses the name of the document for this text string. In this chapter, I'll use the program's caption bar text.

You need to create a method in your class that will perform the graphics output calls. This method is defined in accordance with the *PrintPageEventHandler* delegate. You can name this method *PrintDocumentOnPrintPage*, as in this example:

```
Sub PrintDocumentOnPrintPage(ByVal obj As Object,
                             ByVal ppea As PrintPageEventArgs)
    ⋮
End Sub
```

Attach this handler to the *PrintPage* event of the *PrintDocument* object like so:

```
AddHandler prndoc.PrintPage, AddressOf PrintDocumentOnPrintPage
```

This is the same way that *Paint* event handlers were installed in some of the programs in Chapter 2 and in the SysInfoPanel program of Chapter 4.

To begin printing, the final thing you'll do with the *PrintDocument* object is call its *Print* method:

```
prndoc.Print()
```

This *Print* method doesn't return immediately. Instead, a small message box is briefly displayed that contains the document name you specified and that gives the user the option of canceling the print job.

The *Print* method also causes your *PrintPage* event handler (which we've called *PrintDocumentOnPrintPage*) to be called. The *Object* parameter to *PrintDocumentOnPrintPage* is the *PrintDocument* object created earlier. The *PrintPageEventArgs* parameter has properties that supply you with information about the printer. The most important of these properties, however, is named *Graphics* and is similar to the same-named property in *PaintEventArgs*, except that this property supplies you with a *Graphics* object for the printer page rather than for the client area of the form.

So the *PrintDocumentOnPrintPage* method often looks something like this:

```
Sub PrintDocumentOnPrintPage(ByVal obj As Object,
                             ByVal ppea As PrintPageEventArgs)

    Dim grfx As Graphics  = ppea.Graphics
    ⋮
End Sub
```

You use that *Graphics* object to call methods that display graphics on the printer page.

If you were printing multiple pages, you'd set the *HasMorePages* property of *PrintPageEventArgs* to *True*, but because we're printing only one page, we leave the property at its default *False* setting and return from *PrintDocument-OnPrintPage*.

After *PrintDocumentOnPrintPage* returns with the *HasMorePages* property of the *PrintPageEventArgs* object set to *False*, the original call to the *Print* method of the *PrintDocument* object also returns. The program is finished with the print job. Sending the graphics output to the printer is somebody else's problem. Dealing with paper jams, empty ink cartridges, toner smudges, and bad cables is also somebody else's problem.

You might have more than one printer attached to your machine. The approach to printing that I've shown here uses your *default* printer. The Printers dialog box that you invoke from Control Panel or from the Settings submenu on your Start menu contains an item on its File menu to set the default printer.

As you know, a form's *ClientSize* property gives you the pixel dimensions of your form's client area, and that's sufficient for intelligently drawing within the client area. A similar property for the printer page is somewhat problematic.

A printer page is defined by three different areas. First, there's the entire size of the page. That information is provided by the *PageBounds* property of the *PrintPageEventArgs* class. It's a *Rectangle* structure where the *X* and *Y* properties are 0 and the *Width* and *Height* properties provide the default paper dimensions in units of 0.01 inch. For example, for 8½-by-11-inch paper, the *Width* and *Height* properties of *PageBounds* are equal to 850 and 1100. If the default printer settings indicate landscape rather than portrait, the *Width* and *Height* properties are set equal to 1100 and 850, respectively.

Second, the *printable* area of the page is usually very nearly the whole page except a margin where the print head (or whatever) can't reach. This margin may be different for the top and bottom of the page, and for the left and right. The *VisibleClipBounds* property of the *Graphics* class is a *RectangleF* structure that provides the size of the page's printable area. The *X* and *Y* properties of this structure are set to 0. The *Width* and *Height* properties indicate the dimensions of the printable area of the page in the same units that you'll be using for drawing to the printer.

The third area of the page takes margins (1-inch default) into account on all four edges of the page. Those represent bounds within which the user prefers to print. This information is returned in a *Rectangle* structure from the *MarginBounds* property of the *PrintPageEventArgs* object.

We'll explore these issues more in Chapter 21. For now, using the *VisibleClipBounds* property of the *Graphics* class is probably your best bet. The *Graphics* object you obtain from the *PrintPageEventArgs* object is consistent with this property—that is, the point (0, 0) references the upper left corner of the printable area of the page.

Of course, everything I so carefully emphasized about using a visible color on the video display is wrong for the printer. For a printer, the best color to use is *Color.Black*. The best pen is *Pens.Black*, and the best brush is *Brushes.Black*. That will take care of everybody except those strange people who insist on loading up their printers with black paper.

Here's a program that displays "Click to print" in its client area and prints when it gets a button click.

**HelloPrinter.vb**

```vb
'--------------------------------------------------
' HelloPrinter.vb (c) 2002 by Charles Petzold
'--------------------------------------------------
Imports System
Imports System.Drawing
Imports System.Drawing.Printing
Imports System.Windows.Forms

Class HelloPrinter
    Inherits Form

    Shared Sub Main()
        Application.Run(New HelloPrinter())
    End Sub

    Sub New()
        Text = "Hello Printer!"
        BackColor = SystemColors.Window
        ForeColor = SystemColors.WindowText
        ResizeRedraw = True
    End Sub

    Protected Overrides Sub OnPaint(ByVal pea As PaintEventArgs)
        Dim grfx As Graphics = pea.Graphics
        Dim strfmt As New StringFormat()

        strfmt.Alignment = StringAlignment.Center
        strfmt.LineAlignment = StringAlignment.Center
        grfx.DrawString("Click to print", Font, New SolidBrush(ForeColor), _
                        RectangleF.op_Implicit(ClientRectangle), strfmt)
    End Sub

    Protected Overrides Sub OnClick(ByVal ea As EventArgs)
        Dim prndoc As New PrintDocument()
        prndoc.DocumentName = Text
        AddHandler prndoc.PrintPage, AddressOf PrintDocumentOnPrintPage
        prndoc.Print()
    End Sub
```

```
    Private Sub PrintDocumentOnPrintPage(ByVal obj As Object, _
                                    ByVal ppea As PrintPageEventArgs)
        Dim grfx As Graphics = ppea.Graphics
        grfx.DrawString(Text, Font, Brushes.Black, 0, 0)

        Dim szf As SizeF = grfx.MeasureString(Text, Font)
        grfx.DrawLine(Pens.Black, szf.ToPointF(), _
                        grfx.VisibleClipBounds.Size.ToPointF())
    End Sub
End Class
```

Notice that I've used the *Text* property of the form for both the print document name and as the text string argument to *DrawString* and *MeasureString* in the *PrintDocumentOnPrintPage* method. The program displays the text "Hello Printer!" in the upper left corner of the printable area of the page and then draws a line that extends from the bottom right corner of the text string to the bottom right corner of the printable area of the page. This example should be enough to assure you that *VisibleClipBounds* is indeed providing information consistent with the *Graphics* origin.

I'm detecting some scoffing among my readers. That's because I blithely used the form's *Font* property in the *DrawString* and *MeasureString* calls without considering that the printer has a resolution of 300, 600, 720, 1200, 1440, or perhaps even 2400 or 2880 dots per inch. The font accessible through the form's *Font* property was selected by the system to be appropriate for the video display, which probably has a resolution more like 100 dots per inch. The resultant text on the printer should therefore look quite puny.

Well go ahead: try it. The text is printed using a respectable 8-point font. Notice also that the diagonal line the program draws is obviously more than 1 pixel in width. One-pixel-wide lines on today's high-resolution printers are barely visible. Windows Forms instead draws a nice solid line. Why that is so must remain a mystery for now, although a pleasant one. The answer will become apparent in Chapter 7 and Chapter 9.

Let's now write a program that displays the same output in both the form's client area and the printer page. I don't mean for you to copy and paste code from the *OnPaint* method to the *PrintDocumentOnPrintPage* method; let's demonstrate that we know something about programming by putting the graphics output code in a separate method named *DoPage* that is called by both *OnPaint* and *PrintDocumentOnPrintPage*. Here's a variation of XMarksThe-Spot that does just that.

## PrintableForm.vb

```vb
'-------------------------------------------------
' PrintableForm.vb (c) 2002 by Charles Petzold
'-------------------------------------------------
Imports System
Imports System.Drawing
Imports System.Drawing.Printing
Imports System.Windows.Forms

Class PrintableForm
    Inherits Form

    Shared Sub Main()
        Application.Run(New PrintableForm())
    End Sub

    Sub New()
        Text = "Printable Form"
        BackColor = SystemColors.Window
        ForeColor = SystemColors.WindowText
        ResizeRedraw = True
    End Sub

    Protected Overrides Sub OnPaint(ByVal pea As PaintEventArgs)
        DoPage(pea.Graphics, ForeColor, _
                ClientSize.Width, ClientSize.Height)
    End Sub

    Protected Overrides Sub OnClick(ByVal ea As EventArgs)
        Dim prndoc As New PrintDocument()
        prndoc.DocumentName = Text
        AddHandler prndoc.PrintPage, AddressOf PrintDocumentOnPrintPage
        prndoc.Print()
    End Sub

    Private Sub PrintDocumentOnPrintPage(ByVal obj As Object, _
            ByVal ppea As PrintPageEventArgs)
        Dim grfx As Graphics = ppea.Graphics
        Dim szf As SizeF = grfx.VisibleClipBounds.Size
        DoPage(grfx, Color.Black, CInt(szf.Width), CInt(szf.Height))
    End Sub

    Protected Overridable Sub DoPage(ByVal grfx As Graphics, _
            ByVal clr As Color, ByVal cx As Integer, ByVal cy As Integer)
        Dim pn As New Pen(clr)
        grfx.DrawLine(pn, 0, 0, cx - 1, cy - 1)
        grfx.DrawLine(pn, cx - 1, 0, 0, cy - 1)
    End Sub
End Class
```

The *DoPage* method at the end of the listing outputs the graphics. The arguments are a *Graphics* object, a suitable foreground color for the device, and the width and height of the output area. *DoPage* is called from two other methods: the *OnPaint* method and the *PrintDocumentOnPrintPage* method. In *OnPaint*, the last three *DoPage* arguments are set to *ForeColor* and the width and height of the form's client area. In *PrintDocumentOnPrintPage*, these arguments are *Color.Black* and the width and height of *VisibleClipBounds*.

I've given the last two arguments to *DoPage* names of *cx* and *cy*. The *c* stands for *count* and because *x* and *y* commonly refer to coordinates, *cx* and *cy* can be interpreted as referring to a "count" of the coordinate points, or the width and height.

Interestingly enough, when you have a *Graphics* object for your client area, the *VisibleClipBounds* property is equal to the width and height of the client area. I could have dispensed with the *cx* and *cy* arguments to *DoPage* and just used *VisibleClipBounds* inside *DoPage* for both the screen and the printer. However, I like having the width and height values already available in convenient variables, particularly considering what I've done here. Notice that I've made the *DoPage* method *Protected* and *Overridable*. If you want to write a program that displays only a single screen of graphics, you can derive from *PrintableForm* rather than *Form* and have printing facilities built into your program.

And that's exactly what I'll do in virtually all the sample programs in this chapter and in many programs in subsequent graphics-oriented chapters.

# Properties and State

Some graphics programming environments include the concept of a *current position*, which is a coordinate point retained by the environment that is used as a starting point in drawing functions. Generally, the graphics system defines one function to set the current position and another function to draw a line from the current position to a specified point. The drawing function also sets the current position to the new point.

GDI+ has no concept of a current position. This may come as a bit of a shock to veteran Windows programmers because drawing a line in Windows GDI requires two API function calls, each of which specifies a single coordinate: *MoveTo* to set the current position to the specified point and *LineTo* to draw the line up to (but not including) the specified point.

GDI+ is also different from Windows GDI in that the *DrawLine* and *DrawString* calls include arguments specifying the font, the brush, and the pen. If GDI+ were more like Windows GDI, the font, the brush, and the pen would be properties of the *Graphics* class. You'll recall that *StringFormat* specifies certain details about the display of text. *StringFormat* is also an argument to *DrawString* rather than a property of the *Graphics* object.

For these reasons, the architects of GDI+ have termed it a *stateless* graphics programming environment. It's not *entirely* stateless, however. If it were, the *Graphics* class would have no read/write properties at all! As is, *Graphics* has 12 read/write properties as well as 6 read-only properties.

I count four settable properties of *Graphics* that have a profound impact on the appearance of graphics figures:

- *PageScale* and *PageUnit* determine the units you draw in. By default, you draw on the screen in units of pixels. I'll go over these properties in detail in Chapter 7.

- The *Transform* property is an object of type *Matrix* that defines a matrix transform for all graphics output. The transform translates, scales, shears, or rotates coordinate points. I'll cover the matrix transform in Chapter 7.

- *Clip* is a clipping region. When you set a clipping region, any drawing functions you call will be limited to output in that region. I'll discuss clipping in Chapter 15.

# Anti-Aliasing

Besides those four properties of the *Graphics* class that affect output very profoundly, other properties affect the output in more subtle ways. Two of these properties are *SmoothingMode* and *PixelOffsetMode*.

### *Graphics* Properties (selection)

| Property | Type | Accessibility | Description |
|---|---|---|---|
| *SmoothingMode* | *SmoothingMode* | Get/Set | Anti-aliasing of lines |
| *PixelOffsetMode* | *PixelOffsetMode* | Get/Set | Enhanced anti-aliasing |

These properties enable a graphics rendering technique known as *anti-aliasing*. The term *alias* in this context comes from sampling theory. Anti-aliasing is an attempt to reduce the sharp jaggies of displayed graphics by using shades of color.

Here's a program that draws a small line; I've also included statements to let you set the *SmoothingMode* and *PixelOffsetMode* properties. Because anti-

aliasing affects graphics only on the screen and not the printer, the program
inherits from *Form* rather than *PrintableForm*.

**AntiAlias.vb**

```
'----------------------------------------------
' AntiAlias.vb (c) 2002 by Charles Petzold
'----------------------------------------------
Imports System
Imports System.Drawing
Imports System.Drawing.Drawing2D
Imports System.Windows.Forms

Class AntiAlias
    Inherits Form

    Shared Sub Main()
        Application.Run(New AntiAlias())
    End Sub

    Sub New()
        Text = "Anti-Alias Demo"
        BackColor = SystemColors.Window
        ForeColor = SystemColors.WindowText
    End Sub

    Protected Overrides Sub OnPaint(ByVal pea As PaintEventArgs)
        Dim grfx As Graphics = pea.Graphics
        Dim pn As New Pen(ForeColor)

        grfx.SmoothingMode = SmoothingMode.None
        grfx.PixelOffsetMode = PixelOffsetMode.Default

        grfx.DrawLine(pn, 2, 2, 18, 10)
    End Sub
End Class
```

You can try various combinations of these properties, recompile and run
the program, capture its screen image, and blow it up in some graphics or paint
program to see the difference. Or you can sit back and let me do it. By default,
the line is rendered like so:

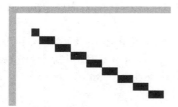

I've included in this figure a little section of the form outside the client area on the left and top so you can clearly see that the line begins at pixel position (2, 2).

The *SmoothingMode* enumeration is defined in the namespace *System.Drawing.Drawing2D*:

### *SmoothingMode* Enumeration

| Member | Value | Comments |
| --- | --- | --- |
| *Default* | 0 | No anti-aliasing |
| *HighSpeed* | 1 | No anti-aliasing |
| *HighQuality* | 2 | Anti-aliasing enabled |
| *None* | 3 | No anti-aliasing |
| *AntiAlias* | 4 | Anti-aliasing enabled |
| *Invalid* | −1 | Raises exception |

There are really only three choices here: Do you want anti-aliasing? Do you not want it? Or would you rather raise an exception? The default is *None*.

When you enable anti-aliasing by setting the *SmoothingMode* property to *SmoothingMode.HighQuality* or *SmoothingMode.AntiAlias*, the line is rendered like so:

It looks like a mess close up, but from a distance it's supposed to look smoother. (Not everyone agrees: some people find that anti-aliasing makes things look "fuzzy.")

The idea here is that the line begins in the center of pixel (2, 2) and ends in the center of pixel (18, 10). The line is 1 pixel wide. When a graphics system uses anti-aliasing, the extent to which the theoretical line intersects a pixel determines how black the pixel is colored.

If you enable anti-aliasing, you can enhance it a bit by using the *PixelOffsetMode* property. You set the property to one of the *PixelOffsetMode* enumeration values, also (like *SmoothingMode*) defined in *System.Drawing.Drawing2D*:

### *PixelOffsetMode* Enumeration

| Member | Value | Description |
| --- | --- | --- |
| *Default* | 0 | Pixel offset not set |
| *HighSpeed* | 1 | Pixel offset not set |
| *HighQuality* | 2 | Half-pixel offset set |
| *None* | 3 | Pixel offset not set |
| *Half* | 4 | Half-pixel offset set |
| *Invalid* | - 1 | Raises exception |

Again, you really have only three choices, and one of them is worthless. If you set the *PixelOffsetMode* property to *Half* or *HighQuality*, the line is rendered like this:

Setting the pixel offset is more in accordance with an analytical geometry approach. The coordinates of the line are decreased by half a pixel. The line is assumed to begin 2 pixels from the upper left corner, which is actually on the crack between the pixels.

## Multiple Connected Lines

I mentioned earlier the concept of a *current position* used in some graphics programming environments, and you may have thought such a thing odd because it implied that two function calls were needed to draw a single line. Where the current position helps, however, is in drawing a series of connected lines. Each additional call requires only one coordinate point. GDI+ isn't so economical. Here, for example, are four *DrawLine* calls required to draw a box around the perimeter of the program's client area:

```
grfx.DrawLine(pn, 0,      0,      cx - 1, 0)
grfx.DrawLine(pn, cx - 1, 0,      cx - 1, cy - 1)
grfx.DrawLine(pn, cx - 1, cy - 1, 0,      cy - 1)
grfx.DrawLine(pn, 0,      cy - 1, 0,      0)
```

Notice that the end point in each call must be repeated as the start point in the next call.

For this reason—and a couple other reasons that I'll discuss shortly—the *Graphics* class includes a method to draw multiple connected lines, commonly called a *polyline*. The *DrawLines* (notice the plural) method comes in two versions:

### Graphics DrawLines Methods

```
Sub DrawLines(ByVal pn As Pen, ByVal apt As Point())

Sub DrawLines(ByVal pn As Pen, ByVal aptf As PointF())
```

You need an array of either integer *Point* coordinates or floating-point *PointF* coordinates. The array must contain at least two points.

Here's the *DrawLines* code to outline the client area.

**BoxingTheClient.vb**

```
'-----------------------------------------------------
' BoxingTheClient.vb (c) 2002 by Charles Petzold
'-----------------------------------------------------
Imports System
Imports System.Drawing
Imports System.Windows.Forms

Class BoxingTheClient
    Inherits PrintableForm

    Shared Shadows Sub Main()
        Application.Run(New BoxingTheClient())
    End Sub

    Sub New()
        Text = "Boxing the Client"
    End Sub

    Protected Overrides Sub DoPage(ByVal grfx As Graphics, _
            ByVal clr As Color, ByVal cx As Integer, ByVal cy As Integer)
        Dim apt() As Point = {New Point(0, 0), _
                              New Point(cx - 1, 0), _
                              New Point(cx - 1, cy - 1), _
                              New Point(0, cy - 1), _
                              New Point(0, 0)}
        grfx.DrawLines(New Pen(clr), apt)
    End Sub
End Class
```

Notice that the class is derived from *PrintableForm*, so you can print it as well.

You can define the array of *Point* structures right in the *DrawLines* method. Here's a program that does that. It's the solution to a kids' puzzle that involves drawing a particular design that resembles a house without lifting the pen or pencil from the paper.

**DrawHouse.vb**

```
'-----------------------------------------------
' DrawHouse.vb (c) 2002 by Charles Petzold
'-----------------------------------------------
Imports System
Imports System.Drawing
Imports System.Windows.Forms

Class DrawHouse
    Inherits PrintableForm

    Shared Shadows Sub Main()
        Application.Run(New DrawHouse())
    End Sub

    Sub New()
        Text = "Draw a House in One Line"
    End Sub

    Protected Overrides Sub DoPage(ByVal grfx As Graphics, _
            ByVal clr As Color, ByVal cx As Integer, ByVal cy As Integer)
        grfx.DrawLines(New Pen(clr), _
                    New Point() _
                    { _
                        New Point(cx \ 4, 3 * cy \ 4), _
                        New Point(cx \ 4, cy \ 2), _
                        New Point(cx \ 2, cy \ 4), _
                        New Point(3 * cx \ 4, cy \ 2), _
                        New Point(3 * cx \ 4, 3 * cy \ 4), _
                        New Point(cx \ 4, cy \ 2), _
                        New Point(3 * cx \ 4, cy \ 2), _
                        New Point(cx \ 4, 3 * cy \ 4), _
                        New Point(3 * cx \ 4, 3 * cy \ 4) _
                    })
    End Sub
End Class
```

But the purpose of *DrawLines* isn't to solve kids' puzzles. In Chapter 17, you'll discover how you can create pens that are composed of patterns of dots and dashes, and how when you create thick pens, you can define the appearance of the ends of lines (whether they are rounded or square or whatnot) and the appearance of two lines that are joined together. These are called line *ends* and *joins*. In order for ends and joins to work correctly, GDI+ needs to know whether two lines that share a coordinate point are separate or connected. Using *DrawLines* rather than *DrawLine* is how you provide this information.

Another reason to use *DrawLines* is performance. This performance improvement is neither apparent nor important in the programs shown so far, but we haven't quite begun to exercise *DrawLines*. You see, the real purpose of *DrawLines* is *not* to draw straight lines. The real purpose is to draw curves. The trick is to make the individual lines very short and to use plenty of them. Any curve that you can define mathematically you can draw using *DrawLines*.

Don't hesitate to use hundreds or even thousands of *Point* or *PointF* structures in a single *DrawLines* call. That's what the function is for. Even a million *Point* or *PointF* structures passed to *DrawLines* doesn't take more than a second or two to render.

How many points do you need for a particular curve? Probably not a million. The curve will be smoothest if the number of points at least equals the number of pixels. You can often roughly approximate this number.

Here's some code that draws one cycle of a sine curve the size of the client area.

### SineCurve.vb

```
'------------------------------------------------
' SineCurve.vb (c) 2002 by Charles Petzold
'------------------------------------------------
Imports System
Imports System.Drawing
Imports System.Windows.Forms

Class SineCurve
    Inherits PrintableForm

    Shared Shadows Sub Main()
        Application.Run(New SineCurve())
    End Sub

    Sub New()
        Text = "Sine Curve"
    End Sub

    Protected Overrides Sub DoPage(ByVal grfx As Graphics, _
            ByVal clr As Color, ByVal cx As Integer, ByVal cy As Integer)
        Dim aptf(cx - 1) As PointF
        Dim i As Integer
```

```
      For i = 0 To cx - 1
          aptf(i).X = i
          aptf(i).Y = CSng(((cy - 1) / 2) * _
              (1 - Math.Sin(i * 2 * Math.PI / (cx - 1))))
      Next i

      grfx.DrawLines(New Pen(clr), aptf)
   End Sub
End Class
```

This is the first program in this book to use a trigonometric method in the *Math* class, a very important class defined in the *System* namespace that replaces many of the math functions in Visual Basic 6.0. I cover the *Math* class in more detail in Appendix B. The arguments to the trigonometric methods are in terms of radians rather than degrees. The *Math* class also includes two convenient *Const* fields named *PI* and *E* that you can use with these methods. One note, however: most of the *Math* methods return *Double* values; these must be explicitly cast to *Single* using the Visual Basic *CSng* function before being used in *PointF* and similar structures.

It might be helpful to analyze in detail the assignment statement for the *Y* property of the *PointF* array: the argument to the *Math.Sin* function is in radians. One complete cycle (360°) is 2π radians. Thus, the argument ranges from 0 (when *i* is 0) to 2π (when *i* is *ClientSize.Width* −1). The value of the *Math.Sin* method ranges between −1 and +1. Normally, that value must be scaled by half the client area height to range from negative *ClientSize.Height* / 2 to positive *ClientSize.Height* / 2 and then subtracted from half the client area height to make the height range from 0 to *ClientSize.Height*. But I've used slightly more efficient code by adding 1 to the negative result of the *Sin* method so that it ranges from 0 to 2 and then multiplying by half the client area height. Here's what the result looks like:

# Curves and Parametric Equations

Coding a sine curve is relatively straightforward because values of $y$ are obtained by a simple function of $x$. In general, however, coding curves isn't quite that simple. For example, the equation of the unit circle (that is, a circle with a radius of 1 unit) centered at the origin (0, 0) is generally given as

$$x^2 + y^2 = 1$$

More generalized, a circle of radius $r$ can be expressed as

$$x^2 + y^2 = r^2$$

However, if you attempt to represent this equation in the form where $y$ is a function of $x$, you have

$$y = \pm \sqrt{r^2 - x^2}$$

There are several problems with this thing. The first is that $y$ has two values for every value of $x$. The second is that there are invalid values of $x$; $x$ must range between $-r$ and $+r$. A third, more practical, problem involves drawing a circle based on this equation. The resolution is lopsided: When $x$ is around 0, changes in $x$ produce relatively small changes in $y$. When $x$ approaches $r$ or $-r$ , changes in $x$ produce much greater changes in $y$.

A more generalized approach to drawing curves uses *parametric* equations. In parametric equations, both the $x$ and $y$ coordinates of every point are calculated from functions based on a third variable, often called $t$. Intuitively, you can think of $t$ as time or some other abstract index necessary to define the entire curve. In graphics programming in Windows Forms, you can think of $t$ as ranging from 0 to one less than the number of *PointF* structures in your array.

The parametric equations that define a unit circle are

$$x(t) = \cos(t)$$
$$y(t) = \sin(t)$$

For $t$ ranging from 0 degrees to $2\pi$ degrees, these equations define a circle around the point (0, 0) with a radius of 1.

The ellipse is defined similarly:

$$x(t) = RX \cos(t)$$
$$y(t) = RY \sin(t)$$

The two axes of the ellipse are parallel to the horizontal and vertical axes. The horizontal ellipse axis is $2 \times RX$ in length; the vertical ellipse axis is $2 \times RY$. The ellipse is still centered around (0, 0). To center it around the point ($CX$, $CY$), the formulas are

$$x(t) = CX + RX \cos(t)$$
$$y(t) = CY + RY \sin(t)$$

And here's a program to draw an ellipse that encompasses the full display area.

**PolyEllipse.vb**

```
'------------------------------------------------
' PolyEllipse.vb (c) 2002 by Charles Petzold
'------------------------------------------------
Imports System
Imports System.Drawing
Imports System.Windows.Forms

Class PolyEllipse
    Inherits PrintableForm

    Shared Shadows Sub Main()
        Application.Run(New PolyEllipse())
    End Sub

    Sub New()
        Text = "Ellipse with DrawLines"
    End Sub

    Protected Overrides Sub DoPage(ByVal grfx As Graphics, _
            ByVal clr As Color, ByVal cx As Integer, ByVal cy As Integer)
        Dim iNum As Integer = 2 * (cx + cy)
        Dim aptf(iNum) As PointF
        Dim i As Integer

        For i = 0 To iNum
            Dim rAng As Double = i * 2 * Math.PI / iNum
            aptf(i).X = CSng((cx - 1) / 2 * (1 + Math.Cos(rAng)))
            aptf(i).Y = CSng((cy - 1) / 2 * (1 + Math.Sin(rAng)))
        Next i

        grfx.DrawLines(New Pen(clr), aptf)
    End Sub
End Class
```

Because the center of the ellipse is half the width and height of the display area, and the width and height of the ellipse are equal to the width and height of the display area, I was able to simplify the formulas a bit. I approximated the number of points in the array as the number of points that would be sufficient for a rectangle drawn around the display area.

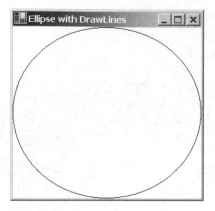

You may have looked ahead in this chapter and discovered that the *Graphics* class includes a *DrawEllipse* method and wondered why we had to do one "manually." Well, that was just an exercise to prepare us for the next program, which draws something that certainly is *not* implemented by a simple method in *Graphics*.

## Spiral.vb

```
'-------------------------------------------
' Spiral.vb (c) 2002 by Charles Petzold
'-------------------------------------------
Imports System
Imports System.Drawing
Imports System.Windows.Forms

Class Spiral
    Inherits PrintableForm

    Shared Shadows Sub Main()
        Application.Run(New Spiral())
    End Sub

    Sub New()
        Text = "Spiral"
    End Sub

    Protected Overrides Sub DoPage(ByVal grfx As Graphics, _
            ByVal clr As Color, ByVal cx As Integer, ByVal cy As Integer)
        Const iNumRevs As Integer = 20
        Dim iNumPoints As Integer = iNumRevs * 2 * (cx + cy)
        Dim aptf(iNumPoints) As PointF
        Dim rAngle, rScale As Double
        Dim i As Integer
```

```
        For i = 0 To iNumPoints
            rAngle = i * 2 * Math.PI / (iNumPoints / iNumRevs)
            rScale = 1 - i / iNumPoints
            aptf(i).X = CSng(cx / 2 * (1 + rScale * Math.Cos(rAngle)))
            aptf(i).Y = CSng(cy / 2 * (1 + rScale * Math.Sin(rAngle)))
        Next i

        grfx.DrawLines(New Pen(clr), aptf)
    End Sub
End Class
```

And here's what it looks like:

# The Ubiquitous Rectangle

Rectangles aren't found in nature very much, but they are certainly the most common form of objects designed and built by humans. Rectangles are everywhere. The page you're reading right now is a rectangle, these paragraphs are formatted into rectangles, the screenshot just before this section is a rectangle, the desk you're sitting at or the bed you're lying on is likely a rectangle, and the window you're gazing out of when I get a bit tedious is probably also a rectangle.

Certainly you can draw a rectangle using *DrawLine* or *DrawLines* (we've done it already when outlining the client area), but a simpler approach is the *DrawRectangle* method. In each of the three versions of *DrawRectangle*, a rectangle is defined by a point that specifies the upper left corner of the rectangle plus a width and a height. That's the same way the *Rectangle* structure is defined, and indeed, one of the methods uses that structure:

### *Graphics DrawRectangle* Methods

```
Sub DrawRectangle(ByVal pn As Pen,
                  ByVal x As Integer, ByVal y As Integer,
                  ByVal cx As Integer, ByVal cy As Integer)

Sub DrawRectangle(ByVal pn As Pen,
                  ByVal x As Single, ByVal y As Single,
                  ByVal cx As Single, ByVal cy As Single)

Sub DrawRectangle(ByVal pn As Pen, ByVal rect As Rectangle)
```

Oddly enough, there's no *DrawRectangle* method that uses a *RectangleF* structure. Perhaps a programmer forgot to mark it with a *Public* modifier. Perhaps we'll see one in a later release.

The width and height of the rectangle must be greater than 0. Negative widths and heights won't raise exceptions, but nothing will be drawn.

When drawing rectangles, off-by-1 errors are common because the sides of the rectangles themselves are a pixel wide (at least). Does the width and height of the rectangle encompass the width of the sides, just one side, or neither side?

With default pen properties (an issue I'll talk about more in Chapter 17), a height and width of 3 in the dimensions passed to *DrawRectangle* results in this figure (blown up in size, of course):

The upper left corner of the figure is the pixel (*x*, *y*). A width and height of 2 draws a 3-by-3-pixel rectangle with a single-pixel interior, as shown here:

A width and height of 1 causes a 2-by-2-pixel block to be drawn. To outline the outer visible edge of the client rectangle, you might be tempted to put the form's *ClientRectangle* property right in the *DrawRectangle* call:

```
grfx.DrawRectangle(pn, ClientRectangle)   ' Avoid this!
```

It won't work! The right and bottom sides of the rectangle won't be visible. Next is a program that properly displays a complete rectangle on both the client area and the printer. I've made it red to be more visible on the screen.

**OutlineClientRectangle.vb**

```
'-----------------------------------------------
' OutlineClientRectangle.vb (c) 2002 by Charles Petzold
'-----------------------------------------------
Imports System
Imports System.Drawing
Imports System.Windows.Forms

Class OutlineClientRectangle
    Inherits PrintableForm

    Shared Shadows Sub Main()
        Application.Run(New OutlineClientRectangle())
    End Sub

    Sub New()
        Text = "Outline Client Rectangle"
    End Sub

    Protected Overrides Sub DoPage(ByVal grfx As Graphics, _
            ByVal clr As Color, ByVal cx As Integer, ByVal cy As Integer)
        grfx.DrawRectangle(Pens.Red, 0, 0, cx - 1, cy - 1)
    End Sub
End Class
```

Try specifying only *cx* and *cy*, without subtracting 1, as the last two arguments of *DrawRectangle*. You'll note that the right and bottom edges of the rectangle won't be visible on the client area, which is the same problem as if you use the *ClientRectangle* property in the call to *DrawRectangle*.

The *Graphics* class also includes two methods for drawing multiple rectangles:

## *Graphics DrawRectangles* Methods

```
Sub DrawRectangles(ByVal pn As Pen, ByVal arect As Rectangle())
```

```
Sub DrawRectangles(ByVal pn As Pen, ByVal arectf As RectangleF())
```

These methods are much less useful than *DrawLines*. However, if you have a *RectangleF* structure named *rectf* (for example) and you want to draw a single rectangle based on that structure, and you then remember that no *DrawRectangle* overload is available for that structure, you can use *DrawRectangles* to do it:

```
grfx.DrawRectangles(pn, New RectangleF() { rectf })
```

# Generalized Polygons

Mathematically, polygons are closed figures of three or more sides, such as triangles, quadrilaterals, pentagons, hexagons, heptagons, octagons, nonagons, decagons, undecagons, dodecagons, and so forth. Here are two *Graphics* methods that draw polygons:

### *Graphics DrawPolygon* Methods

```
Sub DrawPolygon(ByVal pn As Pen, ByVal apt As Point())
Sub DrawPolygon(ByVal pn As Pen, ByVal aptf As PointF())
```

The *DrawPolygon* method is very similar in functionality to *DrawLines*, except that the figure is automatically closed by a line that connects the last point to the first point. For example, consider the following array of *Point* structures:

```
Dim apt() As Point = _
    {New Point (0, 0), New Point (50, 100), New Point (100, 0)}
```

The call

```
grfx.DrawLines(pn, apt)
```

draws two lines that look like a V, and

```
grfx.DrawPolygon(pn, apt)
```

draws a triangle.

In some cases, you could simulate a *DrawPolygon* call with a call to *DrawLines* and *DrawLine*:

```
DrawLines(pn, apt)
DrawLine(pn, apt(apt.GetUpperBound(0)), apt(0))
```

However, if you were dealing with wide lines with ends and joins, you wouldn't get exactly the same effect as with *DrawPolygon*.

# Easier Ellipses

We already know how to draw an ellipse using *DrawLines*, but here's an easier approach that takes the same arguments as *DrawRectangle*:

### Graphics DrawEllipse Methods

```
Sub DrawEllipse(ByVal pn As Pen,
                ByVal x As Integer, ByVal y As Integer,
                ByVal cx As Integer, ByVal cy As Integer)

Sub DrawEllipse(ByVal pn As Pen,
                ByVal x As Single, ByVal y As Single,
                ByVal cx As Single, ByVal cy As Single)

Sub DrawEllipse(ByVal pn As Pen, ByVal rect As Rectangle)

Sub DrawEllipse(ByVal pn As Pen, ByVal rectf As RectangleF)
```

The *DrawEllipse* methods are consistent with the *DrawRectangle* methods. For example, here's the ellipse drawn with a width and height of 3:

A width and height of 1 result in a solid 2-pixel-square figure.

What this means is that, as with *DrawRectangle*, to fit an ellipse in an area that is *cx* pixels wide and *cy* pixels high, you need to reduce the width and height by 1.

### ClientEllipse.vb

```
'-----------------------------------------------
' ClientEllipse.vb (c) 2002 by Charles Petzold
'-----------------------------------------------
Imports System
Imports System.Drawing
Imports System.Windows.Forms

Class ClientEllipse
    Inherits PrintableForm

    Shared Shadows Sub Main()
        Application.Run(new ClientEllipse())
    End Sub

    Sub New()
        Text = "Client Ellipse"
    End Sub

    Protected Overrides Sub DoPage(ByVal grfx As Graphics, _
            ByVal clr As Color, ByVal cx As Integer, ByVal cy As Integer)
        grfx.DrawEllipse(New Pen(clr), 0, 0, cx - 1, cy - 1)
    End Sub
End Class
```

If the last two arguments of *DrawEllipse* are set to *cx* and *cy*, the right and bottom edges will be chopped off slightly.

# Arcs and Pies

An *arc*—at least as far as Windows Forms is concerned—is a segment of an ellipse. To define an arc, you need to specify the same information as you need for an ellipse, plus you need to specify where the arc begins and where it ends. For that reason, each of the four versions of the *DrawArc* method require the same arguments as *DrawEllipse* plus two more arguments:

### *Graphics DrawArc* Methods

```
Sub DrawArc(ByVal pn As Pen,
            ByVal x As Integer, ByVal y As Integer,
            ByVal cx As Integer, ByVal cy As Integer,
            ByVal iAngleStart As Integer,
            ByVal iAngleSweep As Integer)

Sub DrawArc(ByVal pn As Pen,
            ByVal x As Single, ByVal y As Single,
            ByVal cx As Single, ByVal cy As Single,
            ByVal fAngleStart As Single,
            ByVal fAngleSweep As Single)

Sub DrawArc(ByVal pn As Pen, ByVal rect As Rectangle,
            ByVal fAngleStart As Single,
            ByVal fAngleSweep As Single)

Sub DrawArc(ByVal pn As Pen, ByVal rectf As RectangleF,
            ByVal fAngleStart As Single,
            ByVal fAngleSweep As Single)
```

These additional two arguments are angles that indicate the beginning of the arc and the length of the arc. The angles—which can be positive or negative—are measured clockwise in degrees beginning at the horizontal axis to the right of the ellipse's center (that is, the position of 3:00 on a clock):

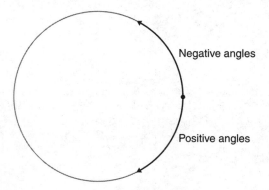

Negative angles

Positive angles

Here's a program that draws an ellipse with a dashed circumference. The dashes are 10 degrees of arc; the gaps between the dashes are 5 degrees of arc.

**DashedEllipse.vb**

```
'------------------------------------------------
' DashedEllipse.vb (c) 2002 by Charles Petzold
'------------------------------------------------
Imports System
Imports System.Drawing
Imports System.Windows.Forms

Class DashedEllipse
    Inherits PrintableForm

    Shared Shadows Sub Main()
        Application.Run(New DashedEllipse())
    End Sub

    Sub New()
        Text = "Dashed Ellipse Using DrawArc"
    End Sub

    Protected Overrides Sub DoPage(ByVal grfx As Graphics, _
            ByVal clr As Color, ByVal cx As Integer, ByVal cy As Integer)
        Dim pn As New Pen(clr)
        Dim rect As New Rectangle(0, 0, cx - 1, cy - 1)
        Dim iAngle As Integer

        For iAngle = 0 To 345 Step 15
            grfx.DrawArc(pn, rect, iAngle, 10)
        Next iAngle
    End Sub
End Class
```

The dashed ellipse looks like this:

The Win32 API includes a function named *RoundRect* that draws a rectangle with rounded corners. The function takes four arguments that specify the upper left and lower right coordinates of the rectangle, plus two more arguments that specify the width and height of an ellipse that is used for curving the corners.

The *Graphics* class doesn't include a *RoundRect* method, but we can certainly attempt to simulate one.

**RoundRect.vb**

```
'-------------------------------------------
' RoundRect.vb (c) 2002 by Charles Petzold
'-------------------------------------------
Imports System
Imports System.Drawing
Imports System.Windows.Forms

Class RoundRect
    Inherits PrintableForm

    Shared Shadows Sub Main()
        Application.Run(New RoundRect())
    End Sub

    Sub New()
        Text = "Rounded Rectangle"
    End Sub

    Protected Overrides Sub DoPage(ByVal grfx As Graphics, _
            ByVal clr As Color, ByVal cx As Integer, ByVal cy As Integer)
        RoundedRectangle(grfx, Pens.Red, _
                    New Rectangle(0, 0, cx - 1, cy - 1), _
                    New Size(cx \ 5, cy \ 5))
    End Sub

    Private Sub RoundedRectangle(ByVal grfx As Graphics, _
                ByVal pn As Pen, _
                ByVal rect As Rectangle, ByVal sz As Size)
        grfx.DrawLine(pn, rect.Left + sz.Width \ 2, rect.Top, _
                    rect.Right - sz.Width \ 2, rect.Top)
        grfx.DrawArc(pn, rect.Right - sz.Width, rect.Top, _
                    sz.Width, sz.Height, 270, 90)
        grfx.DrawLine(pn, rect.Right, rect.Top + sz.Height \ 2, _
                    rect.Right, rect.Bottom - sz.Height \ 2)
        grfx.DrawArc(pn, rect.Right - sz.Width, _
                    rect.Bottom - sz.Height, _
                    sz.Width, sz.Height, 0, 90)
```

```
        grfx.DrawLine(pn, rect.Right - sz.Width \ 2, rect.Bottom, _
                          rect.Left + sz.Width \ 2, rect.Bottom)
        grfx.DrawArc(pn, rect.Left, rect.Bottom - sz.Height, _
                         sz.Width, sz.Height, 90, 90)
        grfx.DrawLine(pn, rect.Left, rect.Bottom - sz.Height \ 2, _
                          rect.Left, rect.Top + sz.Height \ 2)
        grfx.DrawArc(pn, rect.Left, rect.Top, _
                         sz.Width, sz.Height, 180, 90)
    End Sub
End Class
```

The *RoundedRectangle* method I've written has a *Rectangle* argument that indicates the location and the size of the rectangle and a *Size* argument for the width and the height of an ellipse used to round the corners. I wrote the method to be consistent with the dimensions of the rectangle drawn by *DrawRectangle*—that is, when the width and height are set equal to 1 less than the width and height of the client area, the entire figure is visible. The method alternates *DrawLine* and *DrawArc* calls starting with the line at the top of the figure and continuing around clockwise.

I hesitate to recommend this as a general rounded rectangle drawing function, however. The individual lines and arcs are drawn with individual calls to *DrawLine* and *DrawArc*, which means that each of the eight pieces of the figure is drawn with line ends rather than line joins. The correct way to combine straight lines and curves into a single figure is with a graphics *path*. I'll show you how in Chapter 15.

The *DrawPie* methods have the same arguments as *DrawArc*, but these methods also draw lines from the ends of the arc to the center of the ellipse, creating an enclosed area:

### *Graphics DrawPie* Methods

```
Sub DrawPie(ByVal pn As Pen,
            ByVal x As Integer, ByVal y As Integer,
            ByVal cx As Integer, ByVal cy As Integer,
            ByVal iAngleStart As Integer,
            ByVal iAngleSweep As Integer)

Sub DrawPie(ByVal pn As Pen,
            ByVal x As Single, ByVal y As Single,
            ByVal cx As Single, ByVal cy As Single,
            ByVal fAngleStart As Single,
            ByVal fAngleSweep As Single)

Sub DrawPie(ByVal pn As Pen, ByVal rect As Rectangle,
            ByVal fAngleStart As Single,
            ByVal fAngleSweep As Single)

Sub DrawPie(ByVal pn As Pen, ByVal rectf As RectangleF,
            ByVal fAngleStart As Single,
            ByVal fAngleSweep As Single)
```

The pie chart is, of course, a venerable fixture in business graphics. The problem is, if you really need to code up a pie chart, you probably want to adorn it with 3D effects and such, which means that *DrawPie* provides less convenience than you might think. Regardless, here's a program that draws a pie chart based on an array of values (stored as a field) that I made up for this purpose.

### PieChart.vb

```
'-------------------------------------------
' PieChart.vb (c) 2002 by Charles Petzold
'-------------------------------------------
Imports System
Imports System.Drawing
Imports System.Windows.Forms

Class PieChart
    Inherits PrintableForm

    Private aiValues() As Integer = {50, 100, 25, 150, 100, 75}

    Shared Shadows Sub Main()
        Application.Run(New PieChart())
    End Sub

    Sub New()
        Text = "Pie Chart"
    End Sub
```

```
Protected Overrides Sub DoPage(ByVal grfx As Graphics, _
        ByVal clr As Color, ByVal cx As Integer, ByVal cy As Integer)
    Dim rect As New Rectangle(50, 50, 200, 200)
    Dim pn As New Pen(clr)
    Dim iTotal As Integer = 0
    Dim fAngle As Single = 0
    Dim fSweep As Single
    Dim iValue As Integer

    For Each iValue In aiValues
        iTotal += iValue
    Next iValue

    For Each iValue In aiValues
        fSweep = 360.0F * iValue / iTotal
        DrawPieSlice(grfx, pn, rect, fAngle, fSweep)
        fAngle += fSweep
    Next iValue
End Sub

Protected Overridable Sub DrawPieSlice(ByVal grfx As Graphics, _
        ByVal pn As Pen, ByVal rect As Rectangle, _
        ByVal fAngle As Single, ByVal fSweep As Single)
    grfx.DrawPie(pn, rect, fAngle, fSweep)
End Sub
End Class
```

Notice the *Rectangle* definition in the *DoPage* method. This is the only program in this chapter that uses absolute coordinates and sizes, the reason being that elliptical pie charts aren't very attractive. The *DoPage* method totals the array of values and then calculates a sweep angle for each slice by dividing the value by the total and multiplying by 360 degrees. Here's the result:

I'm sorry, but I just can't let you think that this is the best pie chart I can come up with! Fortunately, I was prescient enough to isolate the call to *Draw-Pie* in an overridable function in *PieChart*. That makes it easy to override this method in a BetterPieChart program.

```vb
BetterPieChart.vb
'-----------------------------------------------------
' BetterPieChart.vb (c) 2002 by Charles Petzold
'-----------------------------------------------------
Imports System
Imports System.Drawing
Imports System.Windows.Forms

Class BetterPieChart
    Inherits PieChart

    Shared Shadows Sub Main()
        Application.Run(New BetterPieChart())
    End Sub

    Sub New()
        Text = "Better " & Text
    End Sub

    Protected Overrides Sub DrawPieSlice(ByVal grfx As Graphics, _
            ByVal pn As Pen, ByVal rect As Rectangle, _
            ByVal fAngle As Single, ByVal fSweep As Single)
        Dim fSlice As Single = CSng((2 * Math.PI * _
                                    (fAngle + fSweep / 2) / 360))

        rect.Offset(CInt(rect.Width / 10 * Math.Cos(fSlice)), _
                    CInt(rect.Height / 10 * Math.Sin(fSlice)))

        MyBase.DrawPieSlice(grfx, pn, rect, fAngle, fSweep)
    End Sub
End Class
```

The *fSlice* variable is the angle of the center of the slice converted to radians. I use that to calculate *x* and *y* offset values that are applied to the rectangle that defines the size and location of the pie slices. The result is that each slice is moved away from the center for an "exploded" view:

This doesn't exhaust the collection of line-drawing methods in the *Graphics* class. You can draw curves more complex than elliptical arcs by using the *DrawBezier*, *DrawBeziers*, *DrawCurve*, and *DrawClosedCurve* methods that you'll find out about in Chapter 13. You can assemble a collection of lines and curves into a graphics path and render that path using the *DrawPath* method. We'll get to that topic in Chapter 15.

# Filling Rectangles, Ellipses, and Pies

Several of the *Graphics* methods discussed so far have defined enclosed areas, even though these methods have only drawn the outline of the area with the specified pen and not filled the interior of the area. For those methods prefixed with *Draw* that define enclosed areas, there are also methods beginning with *Fill* that fill the interiors. The first argument to these methods is the *Brush* used to fill the area.

Here are the four versions of the *FillRectangle* method:

### Graphics *FillRectangle* Methods

```
Sub FillRectangle(ByVal br As Brush,
                  ByVal x As Integer, ByVal y As Integer,
                  ByVal cx As Integer, ByVal cy As Integer)

Sub FillRectangle(ByVal br As Brush,
                  ByVal x As Single, ByVal y As Single,
                  ByVal cx As Single, ByVal cy As Single)

Sub FillRectangle(ByVal br As Brush, ByVal rect As Rectangle)

Sub FillRectangle(ByVal br As Brush, ByVal rectf As RectangleF)
```

The width and height of the resultant figure is equal to the width and height specified in the method arguments. For example, if the width and height are equal to 3, the *FillRectangle* call draws a 3-pixel-square block with the upper left corner at pixel (*x, y*). If you want to draw *and* fill a particular rectangle, call *FillRectangle* first so the fill doesn't overwrite any of the lines.

The *Graphics* class also includes two *FillRectangles* methods:

### Graphics *FillRectangles* Methods

```
Sub FillRectangles(ByVal br As Brush, ByVal arect As Rectangle())

Sub FillRectangles(ByVal br As Brush, ByVal arectf As RectangleF())
```

These *FillRectangles* methods produce the same results as multiple calls to *FillRectangle*.

There are four *FillEllipse* methods, and they have the same arguments as *DrawEllipse*:

### Graphics *FillEllipse* Methods

```
Sub FillEllipse(ByVal br As Brush,
                ByVal x As Integer, ByVal y As Integer,
                ByVal cx As Integer, ByVal cy As Integer)

Sub FillEllipse(ByVal br As Brush,
                ByVal x As Single, ByVal y As Single,
                ByVal cx As Single, ByVal cy As Single)

Sub FillEllipse(ByVal br As Brush, ByVal rect As Rectangle)

Sub FillEllipse(ByVal br As Brush, ByVal rectf As RectangleF)
```

*FillEllipse* behaves a little differently from all the methods covered so far. For example, suppose you specify a location of (0, 0) and a height and width of 20 for the ellipse. As you know, *DrawEllipse* draws a figure that encompasses pixels 0 through 20 both horizontally and vertically for an effective width and height of 21 pixels.

For the most part, the area colored by *FillEllipse* encompasses pixels 1 through 19 both horizontally and vertically, for an effective width of 19 pixels. I say "for the most part" because there always seems to be 1 pixel at the left that occupies pixel position 0! There's also some overlap between the ellipse drawn by *DrawEllipse* and the area filled by *FillEllipse*. If you need to draw an ellipse that is both filled and outlined, call *FillEllipse* before calling *DrawEllipse*.

There are also three *FillPie* methods:

### *Graphics FillPie* **Methods**

```
Sub FillPie(ByVal br As Brush,
            ByVal x As Integer, ByVal y As Integer,
            ByVal cx As Integer, ByVal cy As Integer,
            ByVal iAngleStart As Integer,
            ByVal iAngleSweep As Integer)

Sub FillPie(ByVal br As Brush,
            ByVal x As Single, ByVal y As Single,
            ByVal cx As Single, ByVal cy As Single,
            ByVal fAngleStart As Single,
            ByVal fAngleSweep As Single)

Sub FillPie(ByVal br As Brush, ByVal rect As Rectangle,
            ByVal fAngleStart As Single,
            ByVal fAngleSweep As Single)
```

# Off by 1

Now that we've examined all the rectangle and ellipse methods, it's time to compare them with the purpose of avoiding off-by-1 errors. The following program draws 4 × 4 rectangles and ellipses using the six methods *DrawRectangle*, *DrawRectangles*, *DrawEllipse*, *FillRectangle*, *FillRectangles*, and *FillEllipse*.

**FourByFours.vb**

```
'------------------------------------------------
' FourByFours.vb (c) 2002 by Charles Petzold
'------------------------------------------------
Imports System
Imports System.Drawing
Imports System.Windows.Forms

Class FourByFours
    Inherits PrintableForm

    Shared Shadows Sub Main()
        Application.Run(New FourByFours())
    End Sub

    Sub New()
        Text = "Four by Fours"
    End Sub

    Protected Overrides Sub DoPage(ByVal grfx As Graphics, _
            ByVal clr As Color, ByVal cx As Integer, ByVal cy As Integer)
        Dim pn As New Pen(clr)
        Dim br As New SolidBrush(clr)

        grfx.DrawRectangle(pn, New Rectangle(2, 2, 4, 4))
        grfx.DrawRectangles(pn, New Rectangle() _
```

*(continued)*

**FourByFours.vb**   *(continued)*

```
                                        {New Rectangle(8, 2, 4, 4)})
        grfx.DrawEllipse(pn, New Rectangle(14, 2, 4, 4))
        grfx.FillRectangle(br, New Rectangle(2, 8, 4, 4))
        grfx.FillRectangles(br, New Rectangle() _
                                        {New Rectangle(8, 8, 4, 4)})
        grfx.FillEllipse(br, New Rectangle(14, 8, 4, 4))
    End Sub
End Class
```

Here's what the output looks like blown up to analyzable size:

As you can see, the *DrawRectangle*, *DrawRectangles*, and *DrawEllipse* methods are all consistent in rendering figures that are an extra pixel wider and higher than the size would imply. With the exception of a little nub on the left, the *FillEllipse* method draws a figure that is a pixel narrower and shorter than the 4 × 4 figures drawn by *FillRectangle* and *FillRectangles*.

# Polygons and the Filling Mode

Finally (at least for this chapter), we have the *FillPolygon* method. What makes the polygon different from other filled areas is that the lines that define the polygon can cross and overlap. This adds a layer of complexity because the interiors of the polygon can be filled in two distinct ways. There are four *Fill-Polygon* methods:

### *Graphics FillPolygon* Methods

```
Sub FillPolygon(ByVal br As Brush, ByVal apt As Point())

Sub FillPolygon(ByVal br As Brush, ByVal aptf As PointF())

Sub FillPolygon(ByVal br As Brush, ByVal apt As Point(),
            ByVal fm As FillMode)

Sub FillPolygon(ByVal br As Brush, ByVal aptf As PointF(),
            ByVal fm As FillMode)
```

These are similar to the *DrawPolygon* methods except that an optional argument is included. *FillMode* is an enumeration defined in the namespace *System.Drawing.Drawing2D* with just two possible values:

### *FillMode* Enumeration

| Member | Value | Comments |
|--------|-------|----------|
| *Alternate* | 0 | Default; alternates filled and unfilled areas |
| *Winding* | 1 | Most interior areas filled |

The fill mode makes a difference only when the lines that define the polygon overlap. The fill mode determines which of the enclosed areas are filled and which are not. If you don't specify a fill mode in the *FillPolygon* method, *FillMode.Alternate* is the default. In this case, an enclosed area is filled only if there are an odd number of boundaries between the enclosed area and infinity.

The classical example is the five-point star. The interior pentagon is filled when the winding fill mode is used but not when the alternate fill mode is used.

**FillModesClassical.vb**

```
'-------------------------------------------------------
' FillModesClassical.vb (c) 2002 by Charles Petzold
'-------------------------------------------------------
Imports System
Imports System.Drawing
Imports System.Drawing.Drawing2D
Imports System.Windows.Forms

Class FillModesClassical
    Inherits PrintableForm

    Shared Shadows Sub Main()
        Application.Run(New FillModesClassical())
    End Sub

    Sub New()
        Text = "Alternate and Winding Fill Modes (The Classical Example)"
        ClientSize = New Size(2 * ClientSize.Height, ClientSize.Height)
    End Sub

    Protected Overrides Sub DoPage(ByVal grfx As Graphics, _
            ByVal clr As Color, ByVal cx As Integer, ByVal cy As Integer)
        Dim br As New SolidBrush(clr)
        Dim apt(4) As Point
        Dim i As Integer
```

**FillModesClassical.vb** *(continued)*

```
        For i = 0 To apt.GetUpperBound(0)
            Dim rAngle As Double = (i * 0.8 - 0.5) * Math.PI
            apt(i).X = CInt(cx * (0.25 + 0.24 * Math.Cos(rAngle)))
            apt(i).Y = CInt(cy * (0.5 + 0.48 * Math.Sin(rAngle)))
        Next i

        grfx.FillPolygon(br, apt, FillMode.Alternate)

        For i = 0 To apt.GetUpperBound(0)
            apt(i).X += cx \ 2
        Next i

        grfx.FillPolygon(br, apt, FillMode.Winding)
    End Sub
End Class
```

The first *For* loop defines the five points of the star displayed in the left half of the client area. That polygon is filled with the alternate fill mode. The second *For* loop shifts the points to the right side of the client area where the polygon is filled with the winding fill mode.

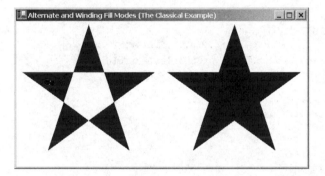

In most cases, the winding fill mode causes all enclosed areas to be filled. But it's not quite that simple, and there are exceptions. To determine whether an enclosed area is filled in winding mode, imagine a line drawn from a point in that area to infinity. If the imaginary line crosses an odd number of boundary lines, the area is filled, just as in alternate mode. If the imaginary line crosses an even number of boundary lines, the area can be either filled or not filled. The area is filled if the number of boundary lines going in one direction (relative to the imaginary line) is not equal to the number of boundary lines going in the other direction.

With a little effort, it's possible to devise a figure that leaves an interior unfilled with winding mode.

## FillModesOddity.vb

```vb
'----------------------------------------------------
' FillModesOddity.vb (c) 2002 by Charles Petzold
'----------------------------------------------------
Imports System
Imports System.Drawing
Imports System.Drawing.Drawing2D
Imports System.Windows.Forms

Class FillModesOddity
    Inherits PrintableForm

    Shared Shadows Sub Main()
        Application.Run(New FillModesOddity())
    End Sub

    Sub New()
        Text = "Alternate and Winding Fill Modes (An Oddity)"
        ClientSize = New Size(2 * ClientSize.Height, ClientSize.Height)
    End Sub

    Protected Overrides Sub DoPage(ByVal grfx As Graphics, _
            ByVal clr As Color, ByVal cx As Integer, ByVal cy As Integer)
        Dim br As New SolidBrush(clr)
        Dim aptf() As PointF = { _
                    New PointF(0.1F, 0.7F), New PointF(0.5F, 0.7F), _
                    New PointF(0.5F, 0.1F), New PointF(0.9F, 0.1F), _
                    New PointF(0.9F, 0.5F), New PointF(0.3F, 0.5F), _
                    New PointF(0.3F, 0.9F), New PointF(0.7F, 0.9F), _
                    New PointF(0.7F, 0.3F), New PointF(0.1F, 0.3F)}
        Dim i As Integer

        For i = 0 To aptf.GetUpperBound(0)
            aptf(i).X *= cx \ 2
            aptf(i).Y *= cy
        Next i

        grfx.FillPolygon(br, aptf, FillMode.Alternate)

        For i = 0 To aptf.GetUpperBound(0)
            aptf(i).X += cx \ 2
        Next i

        grfx.FillPolygon(br, aptf, FillMode.Winding)
    End Sub
End Class
```

Here's the result:

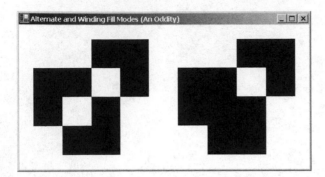

I'll discuss three more *Fill* methods in subsequent chapters: *FillClosed-Curve* in Chapter 13, and *FillRegion* and *FillPath* in Chapter 15.

# 6

# Tapping into the Keyboard

Despite the sophisticated, visually oriented point-and-click user interface of today's graphical environments—including the mouse, controls, menus, and dialog boxes—the keyboard remains the primary source of input in most applications. The keyboard also has the most ancient ancestry of any component of the personal computer, dating from 1874 with the first Remington typewriter. Through a few decades of evolution, computer keyboards have expanded beyond the typewriter to include function keys, cursor positioning keys, and (usually) a separate numeric keypad.

In most computers, the keyboard and the mouse are the sole sources of user input. While much research continues with voice and handwriting recognition for entering alphanumeric data into the computer, those input methods don't—and never will—offer the precision of the keyboard. (Of course, I'm assuming that computers will never be better than humans at decoding bad handwriting or strong accents.)

## Ignoring the Keyboard

Although the keyboard is an important source of user input in most applications, you certainly don't need to write code that acts on each and every keyboard event your application receives. Microsoft Windows and the Windows Forms class libraries handle many keyboard functions themselves.

Applications can usually ignore keystrokes involved in menu selection, for example. Programs don't need to monitor those keystrokes because the menu itself handles all the keyboard activity associated with menu selection and tells your program—through an event—when a menu item has been selected.

Windows Forms programs often define keyboard accelerators to invoke common menu items. These accelerators usually involve the Ctrl key in combination with a letter or function key (for example, CTRL+S to save a file). Again, your application doesn't have to worry about translating these keystrokes into menu commands. The menu itself does that.

Dialog boxes also have a keyboard interface, but programs usually don't need to monitor the keyboard when a dialog box is active. Your program is notified through events of the *effects* of any keystrokes in the dialog box. If you put controls on the surface of your form, you don't need to worry about navigation keys, such as Tab or the cursor-movement keys (other than to ensure at design time that the tab order is logical); all user navigation through the controls is handled for you. You can also use controls such as *TextBox* and *RichTextBox* to process keyboard input. These controls deliver a resultant text string to your program when the user has finished entering the input.

Despite all this help, there remain many applications in which you need to process keyboard input directly. Certainly if you're going to be writing your own controls, you need to know something about the keyboard.

# Who's Got the Focus?

The keyboard is a shared resource in Windows. All applications get input from the same keyboard, yet any particular keystroke must have only a single destination. For Windows Forms programs, this destination must be an object of type *Control* (the class that implements keyboard handling) or a descendent of *Control*, such as *Form*.

The object that receives a particular keyboard event is the object that has the *input focus*. The concept of input focus is closely related to the concept of the *active form*. The active form is usually easy to identify. It is often the topmost form on the desktop. If the active form has a caption bar, the caption bar is highlighted. If the active form has a dialog box frame instead, the frame is highlighted. If the active form is currently minimized, its entry in the taskbar is shown as a depressed button.

The active form is available from the only shared property implemented by *Form*:

### *Form* Shared Property

| Property | Type | Accessibility |
|----------|------|---------------|
| *ActiveForm* | *Form* | Get |

However, this property returns a valid object only if the currently active form is part of your application. The method can't obtain objects created by other applications!

A form can attempt to make itself the active form by calling the following method:

### *Form* Methods (selection)

```
Sub Activate()
```

Usually, if the form is not topmost on the desktop, this call will cause Windows to flash the form's entry in the taskbar, requiring the user to bring the form topmost and make it the active form. In addition, the *Form* class implements two events related to the active form:

### *Form* Events (selection)

| Event | Method | Delegate | Argument |
|-------|--------|----------|----------|
| *Activated* | *OnActivated* | *EventHandler* | *EventArgs* |
| *Deactivate* | *OnDeactivate* | *EventHandler* | *EventArgs* |

I'm mentioning these properties, methods, and events now to get them out of the way. You probably won't be using them much. It isn't often necessary for a program to get involved with the activation of its forms.

Input focus is another matter. If the active form has child controls—that is, controls on the surface of its client area, like the *Panel* control in Chapter 4— the object with the input focus must be either one of these controls or the form itself. Controls indicate they have input focus in different ways. A button displays a dotted line around the text; a text box displays a flashing caret. I'll discuss issues related to input focus later in this chapter; they will surface again in subsequent chapters as well.

# Keys and Characters

A keyboard always generates numeric codes of some sort. But you can think of a keyboard in two different ways:

- As a collection of distinct physical keys
- As a means of generating character codes

When you treat the keyboard as a collection of keys, any code generated by the keyboard must identify the key and indicate whether the key is being pressed or released. When you treat the keyboard as a character input device, the code generated by a particular keystroke identifies a unique character in a character set. Traditionally, this character set has been ASCII, but in the Windows Forms environment the character set is Unicode.

Many of the keys on today's computer keyboards aren't associated with character codes. Neither the function keys nor the cursor-movement keys generate character codes. Programs that use keyboard input in any nontrivial manner usually must deal with the keyboard as both a collection of keys *and* a character generator.

You can think of the keyboard as divided into four general groups of keys:

- **Toggle keys**    Caps Lock, Num Lock, Scroll Lock, and possibly the Insert key. Pressing the key is intended to turn on the state of the key; pressing it again turns the state off. The Caps Lock, Num Lock, and Scroll Lock keys have systemwide states. (That is, when programs are running concurrently on the same computer, Caps Lock can't be simultaneously on for one program and off for another.) Keyboards often have lights that indicate the toggle state of these keys.

- **Shift keys**    The Shift, Ctrl, and Alt keys. When depressed, the shift keys affect the interpretation of other keys. The shift keys are called *modifier* keys in the Windows Forms class library.

- **Noncharacter keys**    The function keys, the cursor movement keys, Pause, Delete, and possibly the Insert key. These keys aren't associated with characters but instead often direct a program to carry out a particular action.

- **Character keys**    The letter, number, and symbol keys, the spacebar, the Tab key, Backspace, Esc, and Enter. (The Tab, Backspace, Esc, and Enter keys can also be treated as noncharacter keys.)

Often a single physical key can generate different character codes depending on the state of the toggle and shift keys. For example, the A key generates a lowercase *a* or an uppercase *A* depending on the Caps Lock and Shift keys. Sometimes two different physical keys (such as the two Enter keys on most personal computer keyboards) can generate the same character code.

A Windows Forms program receives keyboard input in the form of events. I'll describe first how to treat the keyboard as a collection of keys and then how to treat it as a generator of character codes.

# Keys Down and Keys Up

Much of the keyboard functionality is implemented in the *Control* class, which supports the following two events and methods that let you deal with key-down and key-up events:

### *Control* Events (selection)

| Event | Method | Delegate | Argument |
|---|---|---|---|
| *KeyDown* | *OnKeyDown* | *KeyEventHandler* | *KeyEventArgs* |
| *KeyUp* | *OnKeyUp* | *KeyEventHandler* | *KeyEventArgs* |

As usual, in any class derived from *Control* (such as *Form*), you can override the *OnKeyDown* and *OnKeyUp* methods:

```
Protected Overrides Sub OnKeyDown(ByVal kea As KeyEventArgs)
   ⋮
End Sub

Protected Overrides Sub OnKeyUp(ByVal kea As KeyEventArgs)
   ⋮
End Sub
```

This is the customary way of handling key events in a class derived from *Form*.

You can also process key-down and key-up events associated with objects created from the *Control* class or one of its descendents. You first need to define methods in accordance with the *KeyEventHandler* delegate:

```
Sub MyKeyDownHandler(ByVal obj As Object, ByVal kea As KeyEventArgs)
   ⋮
End Sub

Sub MyKeyUpHandler(ByVal obj As Object, ByVal kea As KeyEventArgs)
   ⋮
End Sub
```

You then register the key event handlers:

```
AddHandler ctrl.KeyDown, AddressOf MyKeyDownHandler
AddHandler ctrl.KeyUp, AddressOf MyKeyUpHandler
```

Whichever way you do it, you get a *KeyEventArgs* object when a key is pressed or released. This object has the following properties:

### *KeyEventArgs* Properties

| Property | Type | Accessibility | Comments |
|----------|------|---------------|----------|
| *KeyCode* | *Keys* | Get | Identifies the key |
| *Modifiers* | *Keys* | Get | Identifies shift states |
| *KeyData* | *Keys* | Get | Combination of *KeyCode* and *Modifiers* |
| *Shift* | *Boolean* | Get | Set to *True* if Shift key is pressed |
| *Control* | *Boolean* | Get | Set to *True* if Ctrl key is pressed |
| *Alt* | *Boolean* | Get | Set to *True* if Alt key is pressed |
| *Handled* | *Boolean* | Get/Set | Set by event handler (initially *False*) |
| *KeyValue* | *Integer* | Get | Returns *KeyData* in the form of an integer |

There's a whole lot of redundancy here. The only necessary properties are *KeyData* and *Handled*. Everything else can be derived from *KeyData*. But the redundancy is convenient. You'll probably find yourself using the *KeyCode*, *Shift*, *Control*, and *Alt* properties the most.

The first three properties in this table are all of the same type—a very important enumeration named *Keys*. The *KeyCode* property tells you what key is being pressed; that's the most important information. The *Modifiers* property indicates whether the Alt, Ctrl, or Shift keys are also pressed. *KeyData* combines *KeyCode* and *Modifiers*; *Shift*, *Control*, and *Alt* duplicate the *Modifiers* information as *Boolean* values. *Handled* is a property sometimes set to *True* by controls to indicate that the control has used a keyboard event and it shouldn't be passed to the control's parent. *KeyValue* returns the same information as *KeyData* but as an integer rather than as a *Keys* enumeration.

## The *Keys* Enumeration

Three of the properties of *KeyEventArgs* are of type *Keys*. *Keys* is a large enumeration—the second largest enumeration in the entire Microsoft .NET Framework. It includes keys that certainly aren't on my keyboard and probably aren't on yours either. (Veteran Windows programmers might notice that these enumeration values are the same as the virtual key codes defined by the Windows API.)

Let's tackle the *Keys* enumeration in logical groups. First, *Keys* has 26 members that identify the letter keys regardless of the shift state:

### *Keys* Enumeration (letters)

| Member | Value | Member | Value |
|--------|-------|--------|-------|
| A | 65 | N | 78 |
| B | 66 | O | 79 |
| C | 67 | P | 80 |
| D | 68 | Q | 81 |
| E | 69 | R | 82 |
| F | 70 | S | 83 |
| G | 71 | T | 84 |
| H | 72 | U | 85 |
| I | 73 | V | 86 |
| J | 74 | W | 87 |
| K | 75 | X | 88 |
| L | 76 | Y | 89 |
| M | 77 | Z | 90 |

Notice that the enumeration values are the same as the ASCII codes (which are the same as the Unicode codes) for the uppercase letters. (These keys also generate character codes that are dependent on the Ctrl, Shift, and Caps Lock states.)

Just so we don't get too far adrift here, let's look at some code that makes use of one of the *Keys* values.

**ExitOnX.vb**

```
'-------------------------------------
' ExitOnX.vb (c) 2002 by Charles Petzold
'-------------------------------------
Imports System
Imports System.Drawing
Imports System.Windows.Forms

Class ExitOnX
    Inherits Form

    Shared Sub Main()
        Application.Run(new ExitOnX())
    End Sub
```

*(continued)*

**ExitOnX.vb**   *(continued)*

```
    Sub New()
        Text = "Exit on X"
        BackColor = SystemColors.Window
        ForeColor = SystemColors.WindowText
    End Sub

    Protected Overrides Sub OnKeyDown(ByVal kea As KeyEventArgs)
        If kea.KeyCode = Keys.X Then Close()
    End Sub
End Class
```

This program closes itself when you press the X key. You can have any combination of Shift, Ctrl, or Alt keys pressed when you press the X. Because you know the relationship between the enumeration values and Unicode, the *If* statement could be replaced by

```
If kea.KeyCode = Asc("X") Then Close()
```

The next set of *Keys* values refers to the horizontal row of number keys located above the letter keys regardless of shift state:

## *Keys* Enumeration (number keys)

| Member | Value |
| --- | --- |
| D0 | 48 |
| D1 | 49 |
| D2 | 50 |
| D3 | 51 |
| D4 | 52 |
| D5 | 53 |
| D6 | 54 |
| D7 | 55 |
| D8 | 56 |
| D9 | 57 |

Again, notice the relationship to the ASCII codes for the numbers. These keys also generate character codes that depend on the shift state.

The *Keys* enumeration has values for 24 function keys:

## *Keys* Enumeration (function keys)

| Member | Value | Member | Value |
|---|---|---|---|
| F1 | 112 | F13 | 124 |
| F2 | 113 | F14 | 125 |
| F3 | 114 | F15 | 126 |
| F4 | 115 | F16 | 127 |
| F5 | 116 | F17 | 128 |
| F6 | 117 | F18 | 129 |
| F7 | 118 | F19 | 130 |
| F8 | 119 | F20 | 131 |
| F9 | 120 | F21 | 132 |
| F10 | 121 | F22 | 133 |
| F11 | 122 | F23 | 134 |
| F12 | 123 | F24 | 135 |

I know: I don't have 24 function keys on my keyboard either, and I think I prefer it that way.

The original IBM PC keyboard introduced a numeric keypad. The following keys of the numeric keypad generate the same codes regardless of the Num Lock state:

## *Keys* Enumeration (keypad operators)

| Member | Value | Description |
|---|---|---|
| Multiply | 106 | Numeric keypad * |
| Add | 107 | Numeric keypad + |
| Subtract | 109 | Numeric keypad - |
| Divide | 111 | Numeric keypad / |

The other keys of the numeric keypad generate different codes depending on the state of the Num Lock key. Here are the numeric keypad codes when Num Lock is toggled on. I've arranged this table somewhat like the numeric keypad itself:

### *Keys* Enumeration (keypad numbers)

| Member | Value | Member | Value | Member | Value |
| --- | --- | --- | --- | --- | --- |
| *NumPad7* | 103 | *NumPad8* | 104 | *NumPad9* | 105 |
| *NumPad4* | 100 | *NumPad5* | 101 | *NumPad6* | 102 |
| *NumPad1* | 97 | *NumPad2* | 98 | *NumPad3* | 99 |
| *NumPad0* | 96 | | | *Decimal* | 110 |

These keys also generate character codes for the 10 digits and the decimal separator character. For keyboard layouts in some countries, the decimal separator character is a period. In others, it's a comma. Regardless, the *KeyCode* value is *Keys.Decimal*. The following enumeration value doesn't seem to be used:

### *Keys* Enumeration (keypad, unused)

| Member | Value |
| --- | --- |
| *Separator* | 108 |

Here are the codes generated when Num Lock is toggled off:

### *Keys* Enumeration (keypad cursor movement)

| Member | Value | Member | Value | Member | Value |
| --- | --- | --- | --- | --- | --- |
| *Home* | 36 | *Up* | 38 | *PageUp* or *Prior* | 33 |
| *Left* | 37 | *Clear* | 12 | *Right* | 39 |
| *End* | 35 | *Down* | 40 | *PageDown* or *Next* | 34 |
| *Insert* | 45 | | | *Delete* | 46 |

Notice that *Keys.Prior* and *Keys.Next* duplicate the values for *Keys.PageUp* and *Keys.PageDown*. With the exception of *Clear*, many keyboards duplicate these keys as a separate set of 10 cursor-movement keys that generate the same codes.

I've isolated the following six keys because they also generate character codes and because the *Keys* enumeration values are the same as the character codes they generate:

### *Keys* Enumeration (ASCII control keys)

| Member | Value |
|---|---|
| Back | 8 |
| Tab | 9 |
| LineFeed | 10 |
| Enter<br>Return | 13 |
| Escape | 27 |
| Space | 32 |

*Back* is the Backspace key. If present, the numeric keypad provides a second Enter (or Return) key that generates the same code as the normal Enter (or Return) key regardless of the Num Lock state.

The following table shows *Keys* enumeration values for the Shift key, Ctrl key, and Alt key (here called the Menu key because it usually initiates menu selection). Most keyboards these days have pairs of Shift, Ctrl, and Alt keys on the bottom of the keyboard, and the table seems to imply that the left and right versions of these keys generate different codes:

### *Keys* Enumeration (shift keys)

| Member | Value | Member | Value | Member | Value |
|---|---|---|---|---|---|
| ShiftKey | 16 | LShiftKey | 160 | RShiftKey | 161 |
| ControlKey | 17 | LControlKey | 162 | RControlKey | 163 |
| Menu | 18 | LMenu | 164 | RMenu | 165 |

In reality, however, the enumeration members prefaced with *L* and *R* don't appear in any *KeyEventArgs* object I've ever seen. These are keys found on the Microsoft Natural Keyboard and clones of that keyboard:

### *Keys* Enumeration (Microsoft keys)

| Member | Value | Description |
|---|---|---|
| LWin | 91 | Windows flag logo at left |
| RWin | 92 | Windows flag logo at right |
| Apps | 93 | Application menu icon |

In this case, the left and right keys *do* generate different codes.

This table is a collection of some miscellaneous keys and combinations:

### *Keys* Enumeration (miscellaneous)

| Member | Value | Description |
| --- | --- | --- |
| *Cancel* | 3 | Pause/Break key when Ctrl is pressed |
| *Pause* | 19 | Pause/Break key when Ctrl isn't pressed |
| *Capital*<br>*CapsLock* | 20 | Caps Lock key |
| *Snapshot*<br>*PrintScreen* | 44 | Print Scrn key |
| *NumLock* | 144 | Num Lock key |
| *Scroll* | 145 | Scroll Lock key |

Five of the *Keys* enumeration values actually refer to mouse buttons:

### *Keys* Enumeration (mouse buttons)

| Member | Value |
| --- | --- |
| *Lbutton* | 1 |
| *Rbutton* | 2 |
| *MButton* | 4 |
| *XButton1* | 5 |
| *XButton2* | 6 |

You won't see these members in the *KeyDown* and *KeyUp* events. And then there's this group of oddballs:

### *Keys* Enumeration (special keys)

| Member | Value |
| --- | --- |
| *Select* | 41 |
| *Print* | 42 |
| *Execute* | 43 |
| *Help* | 47 |
| *ProcessKey* | 229 |
| *Attn* | 246 |

*(continued)*

### *Keys* **Enumeration (special keys)**    *(continued)*

| Member | Value |
|--------|-------|
| Crsel | 247 |
| Exsel | 248 |
| EraseEof | 249 |
| Play | 250 |
| Zoom | 251 |
| NoName | 252 |
| Pa1 | 253 |
| OemClear | 254 |

If I ever sat down at a keyboard with all these keys, I wouldn't know what to do with them.

The following 12 *Keys* values apply only to Windows 2000 and later. These keys also generate character codes:

### *Keys* **Enumeration (symbols)**

| Member | Value |
|--------|-------|
| OemSemicolon | 186 |
| Oemplus | 187 |
| Oemcomma | 188 |
| OemMinus | 189 |
| OemPeriod | 190 |
| OemQuestion | 191 |
| Oemtilde | 192 |
| OemOpenBrackets | 219 |
| OemPipe | 220 |
| OemCloseBrackets | 221 |
| OemQuotes | 222 |
| Oem8 | 223 |
| OemBackslash | 226 |

For example, the *OemSemicolon* key code is generated when the user presses and releases the key displaying the semicolon and colon.

These key codes are generated for special browser-enabled and media player–enabled keyboards (such as the Microsoft Natural Keyboard Pro or Microsoft Internet Keyboard Pro) in Windows 2000 and later:

### *Keys* Enumeration (browsers and players)

| Member | Value |
| --- | --- |
| BrowserBack | 166 |
| BrowserForward | 167 |
| BrowserRefresh | 168 |
| BrowserStop | 169 |
| BrowserSearch | 170 |
| BrowserFavorites | 171 |
| BrowserHome | 172 |
| VolumeMute | 173 |
| VolumeDown | 174 |
| VolumeUp | 175 |
| MediaNextTrack | 176 |
| MediaPreviousTrack | 177 |
| MediaStop | 178 |
| MediaPlayPause | 179 |
| LaunchMail | 180 |
| SelectMedia | 181 |
| LaunchApplication1 | 182 |
| LaunchApplication2 | 183 |

These key codes can obviously be ignored by many applications.

The following key codes are generated in connection with the Input Method Editor (IME), which is used to enter ideographs in Chinese, Japanese, and Korean:

### *Keys* Enumeration (IME)

| Member | Value |
| --- | --- |
| HanguelMode | 21 |
| HangulMode | |
| KanaMode | |
| JunjaMode | 23 |

*(continued)*

### *Keys* Enumeration (IME)    *(continued)*

| Member | Value |
|--------|-------|
| *FinalMode* | 24 |
| *KanjiMode* *HanjaMode* | 25 |
| *IMEConvert* | 28 |
| *IMENonconvert* | 29 |
| *IMEAceept* | 30 |
| *IMEModeChange* | 31 |

Applications are generally only interested in the Unicode character codes that result from the use of the IME.

All the *Keys* members listed so far have been key codes; that is, they refer to particular keys that are pressed or released. The *KeyCode* property of the *KeyEventArgs* object delivered with the *KeyDown* or *KeyUp* event will be set to one of the preceding codes.

The *Keys* enumeration also includes these modifier codes:

### *Keys* Enumeration (modifier keys)

| Member | Value |
|--------|-------|
| *None* | &H00000000 |
| *Shift* | &H00010000 |
| *Control* | &H00020000 |
| *Alt* | &H00040000 |

Notice that these are bit values. These modifier codes indicate if the Shift, Ctrl, or Alt keys were already pressed when the key-down or key-up event took place.

You'll recall in a previous table that I showed key codes for *ShiftKey*, *ControlKey*, and *Menu*. Those key codes indicate the actual Shift, Ctrl, or Alt key being pressed or released.

Three of the read-only properties in *KeyEventArgs—KeyCode*, *Modifiers*, and *KeyData*—are all of type *Keys*. Each key pressed or released generates one event:

■ The *KeyCode* property indicates the key being pressed or released. These keys can include the Shift (indicated by *Keys.ShiftKey*), Ctrl (*Keys.ControlKey*), or Alt key (*Keys.Menu*).

■ The *Modifiers* property indicates the state of the Shift, Ctrl, and Alt keys during the key press or release. *Modifiers* can be any combination of *Keys.Shift*, *Keys.Control*, or *Keys.Alt*. Or if no modifier key is pressed, *Modifiers* is *Keys.None*, which is defined simply as 0.

■ The *KeyData* property is a combination of *KeyCode* and *Modifiers*.

For example, let's assume you press the Shift key and then D, and then release D and release Shift. This table shows the four events and the *KeyEventArgs* properties associated with these key actions:

### *KeyEventArgs* Properties and Associated Key Actions

| | | Properties | | |
| --- | --- | --- | --- | --- |
| Action | Event | *KeyCode* | *Modifiers* | *KeyData* |
| Press Shift | *KeyDown* | *Keys.ShiftKey* | *Keys.Shift* | *Keys.Shift Or Keys.ShiftKey* |
| Press D | *KeyDown* | *Keys.D* | *Keys.Shift* | *Keys.Shift Or Keys.D* |
| Release D | *KeyUp* | *Keys.D* | *Keys.Shift* | *Keys.Shift Or Keys.D* |
| Release Shift | *KeyUp* | *Keys.ShiftKey* | *Keys.None* | *Keys.ShiftKey* |

If you're working with the *KeyData* property, the *Keys* enumeration also defines two masks to differentiate the key codes and the modifiers:

### *Keys* Enumeration (*KeyData* bit masks)

| Member | Value | Comment |
| --- | --- | --- |
| *KeyCode* | &H0000FFFF | Bit mask for key codes |
| *Modifiers* | &HFFFF0000 | Bit mask for modifier keys |

Notice that these enumeration members have the same names as the corresponding properties of the *KeyEventArgs* class. If the *KeyEventArgs* object is named *kea*, the expression

```
kea.KeyData And Keys.KeyCode
```

is the same as *kea.KeyCode* and the expression

```
kea.KeyData And Keys.Modifiers
```

is the same as *kea.Modifiers*.

# Testing the Modifier Keys

It's not necessary to handle *KeyDown* or *KeyUp* events to determine whether the Shift, Ctrl, or Alt key is pressed. You can also obtain the current state of the three modifier keys using the shared *Control.ModifierKeys* property:

### Shared *Control* Properties (selection)

| Property | Type | Accessibility | Description |
|----------|------|---------------|-------------|
| *ModifierKeys* | *Keys* | Get | State of the Shift, Alt, and Ctrl keys |

Suppose you needed to do something different depending on whether the Shift or Ctrl key—or both—were pressed, but not if the Alt key were pressed. You would first call the shared *ModifierKeys* property:

```
Dim keysMod As Keys = Control.ModifierKeys
```

You then test the possible combinations you're interested in with code that looks like this:

```
If keysMod = (Keys.Shift Or Keys.Control) Then
    ' Shift and Ctrl keys are pressed.

ElseIf keysMod = Keys.Shift Then
    ' Shift key is pressed.

ElseIf keysMod = Keys.Control Then
    ' Ctrl key is pressed.

End If
```

One useful time for using *ModifierKeys* is when you're processing a mouse event. We've all seen programs that interpret mouse clicks and mouse movement differently when the Shift or Ctrl key is pressed. This is the kind of situation in which the *ModifierKeys* property is useful. An example is the CanonicalSpline program in Chapter 13.

Unfortunately, there is no way in Windows Forms to test the current state of the toggle keys Caps Lock, Num Lock, and Scroll Lock.

# Reality Check

Although a Windows Forms program certainly gets a lot of information about keystrokes, most programs can ignore most of them. If you process the *Key-Down* event, for example, you usually don't have to bother with the *KeyUp* event.

Windows Forms programs often ignore events involving keystrokes that also generate characters. (I'll get to the keyboard character event shortly.) You might have concluded that you can get all the keyboard information you need from the *KeyDown* and *KeyUp* events to generate your own character codes.

This is a bad idea. For example, suppose your event handler gets a *KeyEventArgs* object with a *KeyCode* property of *Keys.D3* and a *Modifiers* property of *Keys.Shift*. You know what that is, right? It's the pound sign (#), which has an ASCII and Unicode encoding of &H0023. Well, maybe. In keyboards used in the United Kingdom, the upper-shift 3 key generates another type of pound sign, which has a character encoding of &H00A3 and looks like this: £.

A more serious problem involves the Caps Lock key. As I mentioned earlier, there is no facility in Windows Forms to test the state of Caps Lock. You can tell when Caps Lock is being pressed and released, but Caps Lock could already be toggled on when your program begins executing.

The *KeyDown* event is most useful for the cursor-movement keys, the function keys, Insert, and Delete. However, the function keys often appear as menu accelerators. Because menu accelerator keys are translated into menu command events automatically, you don't have to process the keystrokes themselves. And when programs define function keys that don't duplicate menu items—when function keys are used in combination with Shift and Ctrl with the crazy abandon of old MS-DOS programs such as WordPerfect and Microsoft Word—then those programs aren't being very user friendly.

So it comes down to this: most of the time you'll process *KeyDown* events only for cursor-movement keys, Insert, and Delete. When you use those keys, you can check the shift state with the *Modifiers* property of the *KeyEventArgs* object. Programs often use the Shift key in combination with the cursor keys to extend a selection in (for example) a word processing document. The Ctrl key is often used to alter the meaning of the cursor keys. For example, Ctrl in combination with the right arrow key might mean to move the cursor one *word* to the right rather than one character.

# A Keyboard Interface for SysInfo

I assume you recall the various programs from Chapter 4 that displayed system information. The last one was SysInfoReflection, and it had progressed a great deal from the earliest tentative code. But it still had one little problem: it had no keyboard interface.

The time has come to add one, and here's another example in which inheritance really pays off. This class derives from the *SysInfoReflection* class and adds an override of the *OnKeyDown* method.

**SysInfoKeyboard.vb**

```
'------------------------------------------------
' SysInfoKeyboard.vb (c) 2002 by Charles Petzold
'------------------------------------------------
Imports System
Imports System.Drawing
Imports System.Windows.Forms

Class SysInfoKeyboard
    Inherits SysInfoReflection

    Shared Shadows Sub Main()
        Application.Run(new SysInfoKeyboard())
    End Sub

    Sub New()
        Text = "System Information: Keyboard"
    End Sub

    Protected Overrides Sub OnKeyDown(ByVal kea As KeyEventArgs)
        Dim pt As Point = AutoScrollPosition
        pt.X = -pt.X
        pt.Y = -pt.Y

        Select kea.KeyCode
            Case Keys.Right
                If (kea.Modifiers And Keys.Control) = Keys.Control Then
                    pt.X += ClientSize.Width
                Else
                    pt.X += Font.Height
                End If

            Case Keys.Left
                If (kea.Modifiers And Keys.Control) = Keys.Control Then
                    pt.X -= ClientSize.Width
                Else
                    pt.X -= Font.Height
                End If
```

*(continued)*

**SysInfoKeyboard.vb**    *(continued)*

```
        Case Keys.Down
            pt.Y += Font.Height

        Case Keys.Up
            pt.Y -= Font.Height

        Case Keys.PageDown
            pt.Y += Font.Height * (ClientSize.Height \ Font.Height)

        Case Keys.PageUp
            pt.Y -= Font.Height * (ClientSize.Height \ Font.Height)

        Case Keys.Home
            pt = Point.Empty

        Case Keys.End
            pt.Y = 1000000
    End Select

    AutoScrollPosition = pt
    End Sub
End Class
```

As I said in Chapter 4, the read/write *AutoScrollPosition* property is implemented in *ScrollableControl* (of which *Form* is a descendent) as part of the support for auto-scroll. *AutoScrollPosition* is a *Point* structure that indicates the positions of the two scroll bars.

When you get the *AutoScrollPosition* value, the coordinates are negative, indicating the location of the virtual client area relative to the upper left corner of the physical client area. When you set *AutoScrollPosition*, however, the coordinates must be positive. That's the reason for the two lines of code:

```
pt.X = -pt.X
pt.Y = -pt.Y
```

Otherwise, the coordinates are simply adjusted based on the particular cursor key. For the left and right arrow keys, I shift the client area by the width of the client area if the Ctrl key is pressed and by the height of a *Font* character if not. I've made the effects of other cursor keys independent of any modifier keys. The Home key returns the display back to the origin; the End key goes to the bottom of the list but doesn't change the horizontal position.

# *KeyPress* for Characters

Many keys on the keyboard generate character codes. To get those codes, you install an event handler for *KeyPress* or (if possible) override the *OnKeyPress* method:

### *Control* Events (selection)

| Event | Method | Delegate | Argument |
| --- | --- | --- | --- |
| *KeyPress* | *OnKeyPress* | *KeyPressEventHandler* | *KeyPressEventArgs* |

The *KeyPressEventArgs* class has just two properties:

### *KeyPressEventArgs* Properties

| Property | Type | Accessibility | Comments |
| --- | --- | --- | --- |
| *KeyChar* | *Char* | Get | Unicode character code |
| *Handled* | *Boolean* | Get/Set | Set by event handler (initially *False*) |

The *Char* data type is, of course, a 16-bit Unicode character.

Refer to the table presented earlier (page 220) that showed the events corresponding to pressing the Shift key and the D key. Right in the middle of this process—between the pair of *KeyDown* events and the pair of *KeyUp* events—you'll get a *KeyPress* event with a *KeyChar* property of &H0044, which is the uppercase D. (Well, probably. If Caps Lock is toggled on, you'll get &H0064, a lowercase d.)

Of course, I'm assuming that you have an American English keyboard layout installed. If you have a Greek keyboard layout installed, you'll get &H0394, which corresponds to Δ. If you have a Russian keyboard layout installed, you'll get a code of &H0412, which corresponds to В. I'll explain how to install foreign keyboard layouts later in this chapter.

# Control Characters

With the Ctrl key down, you can generate control characters that are reported through the *KeyPress* event. You get character codes &H0001 through &H001A by using the Ctrl key in combination with A through Z regardless of the Shift key status. Here are some other control characters you can generate from the keyboard.

### Keyboard-Generated Control Characters

| Key | Control Character |
| --- | --- |
| Shift+Ctrl @ | &H0000 |
| Backspace | &H0008 |
| Tab | &H0009 |
| Ctrl+Enter | &H000A |
| Enter | &H000D |
| Esc<br>Ctrl [ | &H001B |
| Ctrl \ | &H001C |
| Ctrl ] | &H001D |
| Shift+Ctrl ^ | &H001E |
| Shift+Ctrl _ | &H001F |
| Ctrl+Backspace | &H007F |

Programs often use Shift in combination with Tab to tab backward. There's no special code for that; it's something you'll have to handle on your own.

A bit of overlap occurs between the *Keys* enumeration codes you get with the *KeyDown* and *KeyUp* events and the character codes you get with the *KeyPress* event. Which should you use to process the Tab key, Enter, Backspace, or Esc?

I've gone back and forth on this issue for the past 15 years, but these days I prefer treating these keys as Unicode control characters rather than keystrokes. The only good reason I can come up with, however, is that some old-time users may type CTRL+H for Backspace or CTRL+I for Tab, and you want to make sure those key combinations work correctly. You get that functionality by processing Backspace and Tab in the *KeyPress* event handler.

## Looking at the Keys

You may be wondering where I got all the information I've been telling you about what you'll see in the keyboard events since it certainly isn't in the Windows Forms documentation. Well, most of what I know about the keyboard was revealed by the following program, which displays information about keys as you type them and which keeps the last 25 keyboard events (*KeyDown*, *KeyUp*, and *KeyPress*) stored in an array.

## KeyExamine.vb

```
'------------------------------------------------
' KeyExamine.vb (c) 2002 by Charles Petzold
'------------------------------------------------
Imports System
Imports System.Drawing
Imports System.Windows.Forms

Class KeyExamine
    Inherits Form

    ' Enum and struct definitions for storage of key events
    Private Enum EventType
        None
        KeyDown
        KeyUp
        KeyPress
    End Enum

    Private Structure KeyEvent
        Public evttype As EventType
        Public evtargs As EventArgs
    End Structure

    ' Storage of key events
    Const iNumLines As Integer = 25
    Private iNumValid As Integer = 0
    Private iInsertIndex As Integer = 0
    Private akeyevt(iNumLines) As KeyEvent

    ' Text positioning
    Private xEvent, xChar, xCode, xMods, xData As Integer
    Private xShift, xCtrl, xAlt, xRight As Integer

    Shared Sub Main()
        Application.Run(New KeyExamine())
    End Sub

    Sub New()
        Text = "Key Examine"
        BackColor = SystemColors.Window
        ForeColor = SystemColors.WindowText

        xEvent = 0
        xChar = xEvent + 5 * Font.Height
        xCode = xChar + 5 * Font.Height
        xMods = xCode + 8 * Font.Height
        xData = xMods + 8 * Font.Height
        xShift = xData + 8 * Font.Height
        xCtrl = xShift + 5 * Font.Height
        xAlt = xCtrl + 5 * Font.Height
        xRight = xAlt + 5 * Font.Height
```

*(continued)*

**KeyExamine.vb**   *(continued)*

```
        ClientSize = New Size(xRight, Font.Height * (iNumLines + 1))
        FormBorderStyle = FormBorderStyle.Fixed3D
        MaximizeBox = False
    End Sub

    Protected Overrides Sub OnKeyDown(ByVal kea As KeyEventArgs)
        akeyevt(iInsertIndex).evttype = EventType.KeyDown
        akeyevt(iInsertIndex).evtargs = kea
        OnKey()
    End Sub

    Protected Overrides Sub OnKeyUp(ByVal kea As KeyEventArgs)
        akeyevt(iInsertIndex).evttype = EventType.KeyUp
        akeyevt(iInsertIndex).evtargs = kea
        OnKey()
    End Sub

    Protected Overrides Sub OnKeyPress(ByVal kpea As KeyPressEventArgs)
        akeyevt(iInsertIndex).evttype = EventType.KeyPress
        akeyevt(iInsertIndex).evtargs = kpea
        OnKey()
    End Sub

    Private Sub OnKey()
        If iNumValid < iNumLines Then
            Dim grfx As Graphics = CreateGraphics()
            DisplayKeyInfo(grfx, iInsertIndex, iInsertIndex)
            grfx.Dispose()
        Else
            ScrollLines()
        End If
        iInsertIndex = (iInsertIndex + 1) Mod iNumLines
        iNumValid = Math.Min(iNumValid + 1, iNumLines)
    End Sub

    Protected Overridable Sub ScrollLines()
        Dim rect As New Rectangle(0, Font.Height, _
                                  ClientSize.Width, _
                                  ClientSize.Height - Font.Height)
        ' I wish I could scroll here!
        Invalidate(rect)
    End Sub

    Protected Overrides Sub OnPaint(ByVal pea As PaintEventArgs)
        Dim grfx As Graphics = pea.Graphics
        Dim i As Integer

        BoldUnderline(grfx, "Event", xEvent, 0)
        BoldUnderline(grfx, "KeyChar", xChar, 0)
        BoldUnderline(grfx, "KeyCode", xCode, 0)
        BoldUnderline(grfx, "Modifiers", xMods, 0)
```

```
        BoldUnderline(grfx, "KeyData", xData, 0)
        BoldUnderline(grfx, "Shift", xShift, 0)
        BoldUnderline(grfx, "Control", xCtrl, 0)
        BoldUnderline(grfx, "Alt", xAlt, 0)

        If iNumValid < iNumLines Then
            For i = 0 To iNumValid - 1
                DisplayKeyInfo(grfx, i, i)
            Next i
        Else
            For i = 0 To iNumLines - 1
                DisplayKeyInfo(grfx, i, _
                    (iInsertIndex + i) Mod iNumLines)
            Next i
        End If
    End Sub

    Private Sub BoldUnderline(ByVal grfx As Graphics, ByVal str As String, _
                            ByVal x As Integer, ByVal y As Integer)
        ' Draw the text bold.
        Dim br As New SolidBrush(ForeColor)
        grfx.DrawString(str, Font, br, x, y)
        grfx.DrawString(str, Font, br, x + 1, y)
        ' Underline the text.
        Dim szf As SizeF = grfx.MeasureString(str, Font)
        grfx.DrawLine(New Pen(ForeColor), x, y + szf.Height, _
                                        x + szf.Width, y + szf.Height)
    End Sub

    Private Sub DisplayKeyInfo(ByVal grfx As Graphics, _
                            ByVal y As Integer, ByVal i As Integer)
        Dim br As New SolidBrush(ForeColor)
        y = (1 + y) * Font.Height          ' Convert y to pixel coordinate

        grfx.DrawString(akeyevt(i).evttype.ToString(), Font, br, xEvent, y)

        If akeyevt(i).evttype = EventType.KeyPress Then
            Dim kpea As KeyPressEventArgs = _
                    DirectCast(akeyevt(i).evtargs, KeyPressEventArgs)
            Dim str As String = _
                    String.Format(ChrW(&H202D) & "{0} (&H{1:X4})", _
                                    kpea.KeyChar, AscW(kpea.KeyChar))

            grfx.DrawString(str, Font, br, xChar, y)
        Else
            Dim kea As KeyEventArgs = _
                    DirectCast(akeyevt(i).evtargs, KeyEventArgs)
            Dim str As String = _
                    String.Format("{0} ({1})", _
                                    kea.KeyCode, CInt(kea.KeyCode))
```

*(continued)*

**KeyExamine.vb** *(continued)*

```
            grfx.DrawString(Str, Font, br, xCode, y)
            grfx.DrawString(kea.Modifiers.ToString(), _
                            Font, br, xMods, y)
            grfx.DrawString(kea.KeyData.ToString(), Font, br, xData, y)
            grfx.DrawString(kea.Shift.ToString(), Font, br, xShift, y)
            grfx.DrawString(kea.Control.ToString(), Font, br, xCtrl, y)
            grfx.DrawString(kea.Alt.ToString(), Font, br, xAlt, y)
        End If
    End Sub
End Class
```

This is a fairly large program for this book. Early in the class is the definition of a private enumeration (named *EventType*) and a structure (named *KeyEvent*) used for storing the *KeyEventArgs* and *KeyPressEventArgs* information associated with each keystroke. The program then creates an array of 25 of these structures. The integer fields beginning with the prefix *x* are used for positioning the information into columns.

As each *KeyDown*, *KeyUp*, and *KeyPress* event comes through, the event information is stored in the array and also displayed on the client area by the method named *DisplayKeyInfo*, which is the largest method in the *KeyExamine* class. The *OnPaint* method also makes use of the *DisplayKeyInfo* method and displays column headers bolded and underlined. I'll present a much better way of getting a bold underlined font in Chapter 9; this program simply draws the text twice, the second time offset from the first by a pixel, and then uses *DrawLine* to draw a line underneath the text. Here's the program after typing "Hello!":

| Event | KeyChar | KeyCode | Modifiers | KeyData | Shift | Control | Alt |
|-------|---------|---------|-----------|---------|-------|---------|-----|
| KeyDown | | ShiftKey (16) | Shift | ShiftKey, Shift | True | False | False |
| KeyDown | | H (72) | Shift | H, Shift | True | False | False |
| KeyPress | H (0x0048) | | | | | | |
| KeyUp | | H (72) | Shift | H, Shift | True | False | False |
| KeyUp | | ShiftKey (16) | None | ShiftKey | False | False | False |
| KeyDown | | E (69) | None | E | False | False | False |
| KeyPress | e (0x0065) | | | | | | |
| KeyUp | | E (69) | None | E | False | False | False |
| KeyDown | | L (76) | None | L | False | False | False |
| KeyPress | l (0x006C) | | | | | | |
| KeyUp | | L (76) | None | L | False | False | False |
| KeyDown | | L (76) | None | L | False | False | False |
| KeyPress | l (0x006C) | | | | | | |
| KeyUp | | L (76) | None | L | False | False | False |
| KeyDown | | O (79) | None | O | False | False | False |
| KeyPress | o (0x006F) | | | | | | |
| KeyUp | | O (79) | None | O | False | False | False |
| KeyDown | | ShiftKey (16) | Shift | ShiftKey, Shift | True | False | False |
| KeyDown | | D1 (49) | Shift | D1, Shift | True | False | False |
| KeyPress | ! (0x0021) | | | | | | |
| KeyUp | | D1 (49) | Shift | D1, Shift | True | False | False |
| KeyUp | | ShiftKey (16) | None | ShiftKey | False | False | False |

One problem with this program is that when it gets down to the bottom of the client area, it wants to scroll everything up. If I were writing Win32 code, I'd use the *ScrollWindow* call for doing that. However, nothing like that function is available in Windows Forms. So instead of scrolling, the program simply invalidates that part of the client area below the headings, forcing the *OnPaint* method to repaint all the lines. It doesn't really work very well and I feel awful doing it, but probably not as bad as the person at Microsoft who forgot to implement *ScrollWindow* in Windows Forms!

# Invoking the Win32 API

So, what do you do if you really, really, *really* need to use a Win32 API function and it's simply not available in the .NET Framework?

If necessary, you can resort to using Platform Invocation Services. PInvoke (as it's called) is a generalized mechanism that allows you to call functions exported from DLLs. The *ScrollWindow* function happens to be located on your machine in the dynamic-link library User32.dll, so that certainly qualifies. The drawback is that a programmer who uses this facility is no longer writing managed code, and certainly not platform-independent code.

The documentation for the Win32 API shows the following C syntax for *ScrollWindow*:

```
BOOL ScrollWindow(HWND hWnd, int XAmount, int YAmount,
                  CONST RECT *lpRect, CONST RECT *lpClipRect);
```

In the C header files for Windows, *BOOL* is simply defined as an *int* data type (which is an *Integer* in Visual Basic). The *HWND* (a handle to a window) is defined as a pointer to *void* (*Any* in Visual Basic), but it's really just a 32-bit value.

Where are we going to get a window handle in Windows Forms? Well, the *Control* class has a *Handle* property, which is documented as the control's window handle. The type of the *Handle* property is an *IntPtr* structure, which is defined in the *System* namespace and indicates a pointer. You can easily convert between the *Integer* and *IntPtr* data types. So far, we have a fairly clean transition between Visual Basic data types and the arguments and return type of the *ScrollWindow* call.

The tough part involves the last two arguments to *ScrollWindow*. These arguments are pointers to Windows *RECT* structures. The *RECT* structure is defined (again, in C syntax) like so:

```
typedef struct tagRECT
{
    LONG left;
    LONG top;
    LONG right;
    LONG bottom;
} RECT;
```

The *LONG* data type is defined in a Windows header file as a *long*, but that's not a 64-bit Visual Basic *Long*; it's only a 32-bit C *long*, so it too is compatible with the Visual Basic *Integer*.

To call *ScrollWindow* from a Visual Basic program, you must define a *Structure* that has the same fields in the same order as the Windows *RECT* structure and preface it with the attribute

```
<StructLayout(LayoutKind.Sequential)> _
Structure RECT
    Public left As Integer
    Public top As Integer
    Public right As Integer
    Public bottom As Integer
End Structure
```

*StructLayout* is a Visual Basic attribute based on the *StructLayoutAttribute* class defined in the *System.Runtime.InteropServices* namespace. You must also declare the *ScrollWindow* function and use the *Lib* keyword to indicate the dynamic-link library where the function is located:

```
Declare Function ScrollWindow Lib "user32.dll" (ByVal hwnd As IntPtr, _
            ByVal cx As Integer, ByVal cy As Integer, _
            ByRef rectScroll As RECT, _
            ByRef rectClip As RECT) As Integer
```

You may have noticed that the *KeyExamine* class contains a method I called *ScrollLines* that is responsible for scrolling the contents of the client area. The *ScrollLines* method in *KeyExamine* simply invalidated that portion of the client area below the titles. Here's a class that inherits from *KeyExamine*, defines a *RECT* structure, declares the *ScrollWindow* function, and overrides the *ScrollLines* method in *KeyExamine*. This revised version of *ScrollLines* calls the Windows *ScrollWindow* function.

**KeyExamineWithScroll.vb**

```
'---------------------------------------------------
' KeyExamineWithScroll.vb (c) 2002 by Charles Petzold
'---------------------------------------------------
Imports System
Imports System.Drawing
Imports System.Runtime.InteropServices
Imports System.Windows.Forms

Class KeyExamineWithScroll
    Inherits KeyExamine

    Shared Shadows Sub Main()
        Application.Run(new KeyExamineWithScroll())
    End Sub
```

```
    Sub New()
        Text &= " With Scroll"
    End Sub

    ' Define a Win32-like rectangle structure.
    <StructLayout(LayoutKind.Sequential)> _
    Structure RECT
        Public left As Integer
        Public top As Integer
        Public right As Integer
        Public bottom As Integer
    End Structure

    ' Declare the ScrollWindow call.
    Declare Function ScrollWindow Lib "user32.dll" (ByVal hwnd As IntPtr, _
                ByVal cx As Integer, ByVal cy As Integer, _
                ByRef rectScroll As RECT, _
                ByRef rectClip As RECT) As Integer

    ' Override the method in KeyExamine.
    Protected Overrides Sub ScrollLines()
        Dim rect As RECT
        rect.left = 0
        rect.top = Font.Height
        rect.right = ClientSize.Width
        rect.bottom = ClientSize.Height

        ScrollWindow(Handle, 0, -Font.Height, rect, rect)
    End Sub
End Class
```

This version is much better: the program runs smoother and more effi-ciently when it doesn't have to redraw all the lines of output.

# Handling Input from Foreign Keyboards

It's always helpful to test your programs on any type of keyboard that's not like the one on your machine, and in particular, foreign *language* keyboards.[*]And running your program with Russian is much easier than a trip to Moscow. You can install foreign-language *keyboard layouts*, which are small files that let you use your existing keyboard to generate character codes from other languages.

---

[*] Diagrams of many foreign-language keyboards are in Nadine Kano's *Developing International Software for Windows 95 and Windows NT*. This Microsoft Press book is out of print, but an electronic version is available on the MSDN library Web site (*http://msdn.microsoft.com/library*, under Development (General) and Internationalization).

The following instructions for installing foreign-language keyboard layouts pertain to the English version of Windows 2000.

In Control Panel, run Regional Options. Select the General tab. Where it says Language Settings For The System, probably only Western Europe And United States (the default) is checked. Check at least Arabic, Cyrillic, Greek, and Hebrew, and click OK. You'll need to have your Windows 2000 CD-ROM handy, and the system will want to reboot itself.

After you've rebooted, bring up Control Panel again and run Keyboard. Select the Input Locales tab. In the Installed Input Locales section, click the Add button, and, one by one, add Input Locales of the following if they're not already installed: Arabic (Egypt), English (United Kingdom), English (United States), German (Germany), Greek, Hebrew, and Russian. This process will also install keyboard layouts associated with these input locales.

In the Keyboard Properties dialog box, make sure Enable Indicator On Taskbar is checked.

In Windows XP, most languages are installed normally. To enable them, run Regional and Language Options from the Control Panel. Select the Languages tab and click Details. Click Add to add the languages I mentioned earlier. Also click the Language Bar button and make sure the option to show it on the desktop is checked.

If you've never added additional keyboard layouts, you'll see a new icon in the tray section of your taskbar: a box with the letters *EN* (meaning *English*). You can click on that icon and switch to an alternative English keyboard or to an Arabic, a German, a Greek, a Hebrew, or a Russian one. This change affects only the currently active application. Now let's experiment a bit with KeyExamine or KeyExamineWithScroll. Run one of these programs and switch to the English (United States) keyboard layout if it's not set for that already. Type an upper-shift 3. You'll get a *KeyChar* code of &H0023 and a # character. Switch to English (United Kingdom) and type the same key combination. Now it's a code of &H00A3 and a £ character.

Switch to the German (Germany) keyboard layout. Type a Y and a Z. Notice that both the *KeyCode* and *KeyChar* codes indicate a Z when you type Y and a *Y* when you type Z. That's because these two characters are switched around on the German keyboard.

While still running the German (Germany) keyboard layout, press the +/= key. The *KeyCode* is 221, which corresponds to *Keys.OemCloseBrackets*. Now type the A key. The result is a lowercase *a* with an acute accent: *á*, Unicode character &H00E1. The +/= key on the German keyboard is known as a *dead*

*key*. You follow a dead key with an appropriate character key and the result is
an accented character key. You can follow the +/= key with any uppercase or
lowercase vowel: *a, e, i, o, u,* or *y* (which is actually produced by your Z key).
The uppercase +/= followed by an uppercase or lowercase vowel (*a, e, i, o,* or
*u,* but not a *y* in this case) results in that letter with a grave accent, for example *à*.

If you type a consonant after a dead key, you'll get the accent by itself (an
´ or a `) followed by the letter. To type one of these accents by itself, follow the
dead key by the spacebar.

Similarly, on the German keyboard, pressing the ~/ˆ key followed *by a, e,*
*i, o,* or *u* results in the letter with a circumflex: *â*. (The shifted ~/ˆ key isn't a
dead key; it generates a ° character.) The umlaut in German appears only on
uppercase or lowercase *ä, ö,* or *ü*. You can generate these characters by typing
the "/' key, :/; key, or {/[ key, respectively.

So far, all the *KeyChar* values that have accompanied the *KeyPress* events
we've generated have been in the 8-bit range. These are characters that are
defined by one of two standards. The first standard is known as ANSI X3.4-
1986, "Coded Character Sets—7-Bit American National Standard Code for Information Interchange (7-Bit ASCII)":

|     | -0 | -1 | -2 | -3 | -4 | -5 | -6 | -7 | -8 | -9 | -A | -B | -C | -D | -E | -F |
|-----|----|----|----|----|----|----|----|----|----|----|----|----|----|----|----|----|
| 2-  |    | !  | "  | #  | $  | %  | &  | '  | (  | )  | *  | +  | ,  | -  | .  | /  |
| 3-  | 0  | 1  | 2  | 3  | 4  | 5  | 6  | 7  | 8  | 9  | :  | ;  | <  | =  | >  | ?  |
| 4-  | @  | A  | B  | C  | D  | E  | F  | G  | H  | I  | J  | K  | L  | M  | N  | O  |
| 5-  | P  | Q  | R  | S  | T  | U  | V  | W  | X  | Y  | Z  | [  | \  | ]  | ^  | _  |
| 6-  | `  | a  | b  | c  | d  | e  | f  | g  | h  | i  | j  | k  | l  | m  | n  | o  |
| 7-  | p  | q  | r  | s  | t  | u  | v  | w  | x  | y  | z  | {  | \| | }  | ~  |    |

The second standard is the ASCII extension documented by ANSI/ISO
8859-1-1987, "American National Standard for Information Processing—8-Bit
Single-Byte Coded Graphic Character Sets—Part 1: Latin Alphabet No. 1" and
commonly referred to as "Latin 1":

|      | -0 | -1 | -2 | -3 | -4 | -5 | -6 | -7 | -8 | -9 | -A | -B | -C | -D | -E | -F |
|------|----|----|----|----|----|----|----|----|----|----|----|----|----|----|----|----|
| A-   |    | ¡  | ¢  | £  | ¤  | ¥  | ¦  | §  | ¨  | ©  | ª  | «  | ¬  | -  | ®  | ¯  |
| B-   | °  | ±  | ²  | ³  | ´  | µ  | ¶  | ·  | ¸  | ¹  | º  | »  | ¼  | ½  | ¾  | ¿  |
| C-   | À  | Á  | Â  | Ã  | Ä  | Å  | Æ  | Ç  | È  | É  | Ê  | Ë  | Ì  | Í  | Î  | Ï  |
| D-   | Ð  | Ñ  | Ò  | Ó  | Ô  | Õ  | Ö  | ×  | Ø  | Ù  | Ú  | Û  | Ü  | Ý  | Þ  | ß  |
| E-   | à  | á  | â  | ã  | ä  | å  | æ  | ç  | è  | é  | ê  | ë  | ì  | í  | î  | ï  |
| F-   | ð  | ñ  | ò  | ó  | ô  | õ  | ö  | ÷  | ø  | ù  | ú  | û  | ü  | ý  | þ  | ÿ  |

These character sets are suitable only for languages that use the Latin alphabet. To accommodate other alphabets of the world (as well as the ideographs of Chinese, Japanese, and Korean), the 16-bit character encoding known as Unicode was developed. Windows Forms programs written in Visual Basic generally don't need to do anything special to support Unicode. The *Char* data type in Visual Basic is 16 bits wide, for example.

If you switch to the Russian keyboard layout and type a few keys, you'll see Cyrillic letters. These have character codes in the range from &H0410 through &H044F, which is defined in the Unicode standard as the Basic Russian Alphabet. Similarly, you can switch to the Arabic, Greek, or Hebrew keyboard layout and type letters in those alphabets.

If you've never explored this stuff before, you may be wondering how foreign-language alphabets and keyboards worked before Unicode—when character codes were just 8 bits wide. Well, in short, it was a mess.

If you'd like your program to be informed when the user changes the keyboard layout, you can install event handlers for the *InputLanguageChanging* and *InputLanguageChanged* events or override the *OnInputLanguageChanging* and *OnInputLanguageChanged* methods. In the following table, ellipses are used to indicate the event name in the method, delegate, and event argument names:

## *Form* Events (selection)

| Event | Method | Delegate | Argument |
|-------|--------|----------|----------|
| *InputLanguageChanging* | *On...* | *...EventHandler* | *...EventArgs* |
| *InputLanguageChanged* | *On...* | *...EventHandler* | *...EventArgs* |

You get the *InputLanguageChanging* event first. The *InputLanguageChangingEventArgs* object has information about the language the user wants to switch to. If it's not OK with your program to make this switch, set the *Cancel* property of the *InputLanguageChangingEventArgs* object to *True*; otherwise, you'll soon receive an *InputLanguageChanged* event.

To pursue this subject further, take a look at the *InputLanguage* class in the *System.Windows.Forms* namespace and the *CultureInfo* class in the *System.Globalization* namespace.

# Input Focus

Input focus is an important issue when you begin creating controls on the surface of your form. Input focus determines which control gets keyboard input. In a dialog box, some keys (such as Tab and the cursor-movement keys) shift input focus among the controls. *Form* inherits three read-only properties that pertain to input focus:

### *Control* Properties (selection)

| Property | Type | Accessibility |
|---|---|---|
| *CanFocus* | *Boolean* | Get |
| *ContainsFocus* | *Boolean* | Get |
| *Focused* | *Boolean* | Get |

A control (or form) can't get the input focus if it is disabled or invisible. You can use the *CanFocus* property to check this state. The *ContainsFocus* property returns *True* if the control (or form) or one of its children has the input focus. *Focused* returns *True* if the control (or form) has the input focus.

A program can set the input focus to one of its controls by using the *Focus* method.

### *Control* Methods (selection)

```
Function Focus() As Boolean
```

The return value indicates whether focus was successfully applied. It won't succeed if the control isn't a child of the active form.

Finally, two events tell a control (or form) when it is getting input focus and when it is losing input focus:

### *Control* Events (selection)

| Event | Method | Delegate | Argument |
|-------|--------|----------|----------|
| *GotFocus* | *OnGotFocus* | *EventHandler* | *EventArgs* |
| *LostFocus* | *OnLostFocus* | *EventHandler* | *EventArgs* |

A control (or form) always eventually gets a *LostFocus* event to match every *GotFocus* event. I'll have more to say about input focus when we begin creating controls in Chapter 12.

# The Missing Caret

Controls or forms that accept keyboard input generally display something special when they have input focus. A button control, for example, displays a dotted outline around its text. Controls or forms that allow you to type text usually display a little underline, a vertical bar, or a box that shows you where the next character you type will appear on the screen. You may know this indicator as a *cursor*, but in Windows it's more properly known as a *caret*. The word *cursor* is reserved for the bitmap picture representing the mouse position.

If you create a *TextBox* or a *RichTextBox* control (which I'll demonstrate in Chapter 18), the control is responsible for creating and displaying the caret. In many cases, using these controls will serve your program well. *RichTextBox* in particular is quite powerful and is built around the same Windows control that Microsoft WordPad uses.

However, if these controls are not adequate for your purposes and you need to write your own text-input code, you have a little problem. Of the several features missing from the Windows Forms class libraries, perhaps none is more inexplicable than the caret.

I'm afraid it's time again to create some unmanaged code that digs into the Windows DLLs to do what we need to do. My class named *Caret* is based on the Windows caret API and begins by declaring five functions located in User32.dll.

**Caret.vb**

```
'------------------------------------
' Caret.vb (c) 2002 by Charles Petzold
'------------------------------------
Imports System
Imports System.Drawing
Imports System.Runtime.InteropServices
Imports System.Windows.Forms
```

```
Class Caret
    ' External functions
    Declare Function CreateCaret Lib "user32.dll" _
                    (ByVal hwnd As IntPtr, ByVal hbm As IntPtr, _
                     ByVal cx As Integer, ByVal cy As Integer) As Integer
    Declare Function DestroyCaret Lib "user32.dll" () As Integer
    Declare Function SetCaretPos Lib "user32.dll" _
                    (ByVal x As Integer, ByVal y As Integer) As Integer
    Declare Function ShowCaret Lib "user32.dll" _
                    (ByVal hwnd As IntPtr) As Integer
    Declare Function HideCaret Lib "user32.dll" _
                    (ByVal hwnd As IntPtr) As Integer

    ' Fields
    Private ctrl As Control
    Private szCaret As Size
    Private ptPos As Point
    Private bVisible As Boolean

    ' Only allowable constructor has Control argument.
    Sub New(ByVal ctrl As Control)
        Me.ctrl = ctrl
        Position = Point.Empty
        Size = New Size(1, ctrl.Font.Height)
        AddHandler Control.GotFocus, AddressOf ControlOnGotFocus
        AddHandler Control.LostFocus, AddressOf ControlOnLostFocus

        ' If the control already has focus, create the caret.
        If ctrl.Focused Then
            ControlOnGotFocus(ctrl, New EventArgs())
        End If
    End Sub

    ' Properties
    ReadOnly Property Control() As Control
        Get
            Return ctrl
        End Get
    End Property

    Property Size() As Size
        Set(ByVal Value As Size)
            szCaret = Value
        End Set
        Get
            Return szCaret
        End Get
    End Property
```

*(continued)*

**Caret.vb**    *(continued)*

```vb
    Property Position() As Point
        Set(ByVal Value As Point)
            ptPos = Value
            SetCaretPos(ptPos.X, ptPos.Y)
        End Set
        Get
            Return ptPos
        End Get
    End Property

    Property Visibility() As Boolean
        Set(ByVal Value As Boolean)
            bVisible = Value

            If bVisible Then
                ShowCaret(Control.Handle)
            Else
                HideCaret(Control.Handle)
            End If
        End Set
        Get
            Return bVisible
        End Get
    End Property

    ' Methods
    Sub Show()
        Visibility = True
    End Sub

    Sub Hide()
        Visibility = False
    End Sub

    Sub Dispose()
        ' If the control has focus, destroy the caret.
        If ctrl.Focused Then
            ControlOnLostFocus(ctrl, New EventArgs())
        End If
        RemoveHandler Control.GotFocus, AddressOf ControlOnGotFocus
        RemoveHandler Control.LostFocus, AddressOf ControlOnLostFocus
    End Sub

    ' Event handlers
    Private Sub ControlOnGotFocus(ByVal obj As Object, _
                                  ByVal ea As EventArgs)
        CreateCaret(Control.Handle, IntPtr.Zero, _
                Size.Width, Size.Height)
        SetCaretPos(Position.X, Position.Y)
        Show()
    End Sub
```

```
    Private Sub ControlOnLostFocus(ByVal obj As Object, _
                                   ByVal ea As EventArgs)
        Hide()
        DestroyCaret()
    End Sub
End Class
```

To create a caret for your form (or any other object derived from *Control*), use the constructor

```
New crt As New Caret(ctrl)
```

The *Caret* class doesn't define a default constructor, so you must include an argument in the constructor. *Caret* provides four properties:

### *Caret* Properties

| Property | Type | Accessibility | Description |
|----------|------|---------------|-------------|
| *Control* | *Control* | Get | *Control* object the caret is associated with |
| *Size* | *Size* | Get/Set | Size of caret in pixels |
| *Position* | *Point* | Get/Set | Position of caret relative to control origin |
| *Visibility* | *Boolean* | Get/Set | Visibility of caret |

In character mode environments, carets are often underlines or boxes. These shapes don't quite work right for variable-width text, however; a vertical line is better. Generally, a program that uses the *Caret* class in connection with the default font for the control will set the size like so:

```
caret.Size = New Size(2, Font.Height)
```

The *Position* property indicates the position of the caret relative to the upper left corner of the client area.

You can use the *Visibility* property to hide and reshow the caret. You must hide the caret when you draw on your form at any time other than during the *Paint* event! As an alternative to *Visibility*, you can use the *Hide* and *Show* methods. The *Dispose* method is the only other public method *Caret* supports:

### *Caret* Methods

| Method | Description |
|--------|-------------|
| Sub Hide() | Hides the caret |
| Sub Show() | Shows the caret |
| Sub Dispose() | Disables the caret |

Normally, you don't need to call *Dispose*. The only time *Dispose* is necessary is if you've been using the caret to perform some keyboard input in your form or control and you no longer need to do so.

The *Caret* class is a good example of a class that must install event handlers for the form that it's associated with. *Caret* installs event handlers for the *GotFocus* and *LostFocus* events; it creates the caret when the form gets the focus and destroys the caret when the form loses the focus. This approach is in accordance with recommended handling of the caret in Win32 programming. *Dispose* simply uninstalls the event handlers so the caret isn't created anymore.

But keep this in mind: A form that uses this *Caret* class and that itself overrides its *OnGotFocus* and *OnLostFocus* methods runs the risk of disabling the event handlers in *Caret*! If you need to override these methods, be sure to call the method in the base class:

```
Protected Overrides Sub OnGotFocus(ByVal ea As EventArgs)
    MyBase.OnGotFocus(ea)
    ⋮
End Sub

Protected Overrides Sub OnLostFocus(ByVal ea As EventArgs)
    MyBase.OnLostFocus(ea)
    ⋮
End Sub
```

Those base class *OnGotFocus* and *OnLostFocus* methods call the installed event handlers such as the ones in *Caret*.

# Echoing Key Characters

Now let's look at a program that uses the *Caret* class to let you enter and edit text. This program comes very close to the functionality of a *TextBox* control in single-line mode.

**TypeAway.vb**
```
'-----------------------------------------------
' TypeAway.vb (c) 2002 by Charles Petzold
'-----------------------------------------------
Imports System
Imports System.Drawing
Imports System.Drawing.Text
Imports System.Windows.Forms

Class TypeAway
    Inherits Form
```

```
Shared Sub Main()
    Application.Run(new TypeAway())
End Sub

Protected crt As caret
Protected strText As String = ""
Protected iInsert As Integer = 0

Sub New()
    Text = "Type Away"
    BackColor = SystemColors.Window
    ForeColor = SystemColors.WindowText

    crt = New Caret(Me)
    crt.Size = New Size(2, Font.Height)
    crt.Position = New Point(0, 0)
End Sub

Protected Overrides Sub OnKeyPress(ByVal kpea As KeyPressEventArgs)
    Dim grfx As Graphics = CreateGraphics()
    crt.Hide()
    grfx.FillRectangle(New SolidBrush(BackColor), _
                New RectangleF(PointF.Empty, _
                grfx.MeasureString(strText, Font, _
                PointF.Empty, StringFormat.GenericTypographic)))

    Select Case kpea.KeyChar
        Case Chr(8)
            If (iInsert > 0) Then
                strText = strText.Substring(0, iInsert - 1) & _
                        strText.Substring(iInsert)
                iInsert -= 1
            End If

        Case Chr(10), Chr(13)  ' Ignore these keys

        Case Else
            If (iInsert = strText.Length) Then
                strText &= kpea.KeyChar
            Else
                strText = strText.Substring(0, iInsert) & _
                        kpea.KeyChar & _
                        strText.Substring(iInsert)
            End If
            iInsert += 1
    End Select

    grfx.TextRenderingHint = TextRenderingHint.AntiAlias
    grfx.DrawString(strText, Font, New SolidBrush(ForeColor), _
                0, 0, StringFormat.GenericTypographic)
    grfx.Dispose()
```

*(continued)*

**TypeAway.vb** *(continued)*

```vb
            PositionCaret()
            crt.Show()
        End Sub

        Protected Overrides Sub OnKeyDown(ByVal kea As KeyEventArgs)
            Select Case kea.KeyData
                Case Keys.Left
                    If (iInsert > 0) Then iInsert -= 1

                Case Keys.Right
                    If (iInsert < strText.Length) Then iInsert += 1

                Case Keys.Home
                    iInsert = 0

                Case Keys.End
                    iInsert = strText.Length

                Case Keys.Delete
                    If (iInsert < strText.Length) Then
                        iInsert += 1
                        OnKeyPress(New KeyPressEventArgs(Chr(8)))
                    End If

                Case Else
                    Return
            End Select

            PositionCaret()
        End Sub

        Protected Sub PositionCaret()
            Dim grfx As Graphics = CreateGraphics()
            Dim str As String = strText.Substring(0, iInsert)
            Dim strfmt As StringFormat = StringFormat.GenericTypographic
            strfmt.FormatFlags = strfmt.FormatFlags Or _
                                StringFormatFlags.MeasureTrailingSpaces
            Dim szf As SizeF = grfx.MeasureString(str, Font, _
                                                PointF.Empty, strfmt)
            crt.Position = New Point(CInt(szf.Width), 0)
            grfx.Dispose()
        End Sub

        Protected Overrides Sub OnPaint(ByVal pea As PaintEventArgs)
            Dim grfx As Graphics = pea.Graphics
            grfx.TextRenderingHint = TextRenderingHint.AntiAlias
            grfx.DrawString(strText, Font, New SolidBrush(ForeColor), _
                        0, 0, StringFormat.GenericTypographic)
        End Sub
End Class
```

The *TypeAway* class creates an object of type *Caret* in its constructor and initializes the size and position. The program needs only to hide and then reshow the caret when drawing on the form at times other than the *Paint* event and to set the caret's position within the client area.

The string of characters that the user enters and edits is stored in the field named *strText*. The *iInsert* field is the insertion point in this string. For example, after you type three characters, *iInsert* equals 3. If you then press the left arrow, *iInsert* equals 2. The *PositionCaret* method (which I'll describe shortly) is responsible for converting that character position to a pixel position that it uses to set the *Position* property of the *Caret* object.

Let's take a look at how *TypeAway* handles the *OnKeyPress* method. In most cases, it may seem that the program simply needs to display this new character on the form at the pixel position corresponding to the current insertion point and to append this character to the *strText* field. Instead, however, the program uses *MeasureString* and *FillRectangle* to entirely erase any text currently displayed in the form! This behavior may sound a little extreme, but (as we'll see) it's necessary if the insertion point isn't at the end of the string or if it's displaying text in some non-English languages.

The *OnKeyPress* method handles the Backspace key by removing a character from the string in front of the insertion point. The method ignores carriage returns and line feeds, and handles all other characters by inserting them into *strText* at the insertion point. The method then displays the entire string and calls *PositionCaret*. Notice that the method hides the caret while drawing on the form.

The *OnKeyDown* method handles a few cursor-movement keys by changing the insertion point and handles the Delete key by simulating a Backspace key. The *OnKeyDown* method also calls *PositionCaret*.

The *PositionCaret* method is responsible for converting the insertion point (*iInsert*) into a pixel location for the caret. It does this using *MeasureString*. Unfortunately, the default version of *MeasureString* doesn't offer quite the precision required in applications like this. The most blatant problem is that *MeasureString* normally excludes trailing blanks when calculating string lengths. To correct this problem, the program uses a version of *MeasureString* with a *StringFormat* argument and includes the enumeration value *StringFormatFlags.MeasureTrailingSpaces* in the *FormatFlags* property of *StringFormat*. Before that change, the caret would move whenever I typed letters that made up a word, but not when I typed a space after the word.

But that change isn't sufficient to make the caret line up nicely with displayed text. For reasons I discuss in Chapter 9, in the section "Grid Fitting and Text Fitting," the *MeasureString* and *DrawString* methods normally have built-in padding to compensate for problems related to the device-independent rasterization of outline fonts. To override this default behavior, the program uses a *StringFormat* object that it obtains from the shared *StringFormat.GenericTypographic* property. As part of this solution (covered in Chapter 9), the program also uses the *Graphics* property *TextRenderingHint* to enable anti-aliasing of the text output.

# Right-to-Left Problems

I mentioned earlier that the TypeAway program has almost the full functionality of a *TextBox* control in single-line mode. One problem is that it doesn't have clipboard support. Another is that TypeAway doesn't correctly display the caret when you type text that is written right to left, such as Arabic or Hebrew.

Let's take a look: run TypeAway, and switch to the Hebrew keyboard layout. We're going to type the Hebrew for "good evening," which is ערב טוב, commonly transliterated as *erev tov*. To accomplish this little feat on an English keyboard, you first need to know how the characters of the Hebrew alphabet correspond to the keys of the keyboard.

## Hebrew Alphabet

| Unicode | Letter | Glyph | Key | Unicode | Letter | Glyph | Key |
|---------|--------|-------|-----|---------|--------|-------|-----|
| &H05D0 | alef | א | t | &H05DE | mem | מ | n |
| &H05D1 | bet | ב | c | &H05DF | final nun | ן | i |
| &H05D2 | gimel | ג | d | &H05E0 | nun | נ | b |
| &H05D3 | dalet | ד | s | &H05E1 | samekh | ס | x |
| &H05D4 | he | ה | v | &H05E2 | ayin | ע | g |
| &H05D5 | vav | ו | u | &H05E3 | final pe | ף | ; |
| &H05D6 | zayin | ז | z | &H05E4 | pe | פ | p |
| &H05D7 | het | ח | j | &H05E5 | final tsadi | ץ | . |
| &H05D8 | tet | ט | y | &H05E6 | tsadi | צ | m |
| &H05D9 | yod | י | h | &H05E7 | qof | ק | e |
| &H05DA | final kaf | ך | l | &H05E8 | resh | ר | r |
| &H05DB | kaf | כ | f | &H05E9 | shin | ש | a |
| &H05DC | lamed | ל | k | &H05EA | tav | ת | , |
| &H05DD | final mem | ם | o | | | | |

I've taken the spellings of these letters from *The Unicode Standard Version 3.0*. You'll note that some letter names include the word *final*. These letters are written differently when they fall at the end of a word.

You also need to know that Hebrew is written from right to left. So to type the Hebrew phrase shown above into TypeAway, you need to type the letters in this order: *ayin* (the g key), *resh* (the r key), *bet* (the c key), space, *tet* (the y key), *vav* (the u key), and *bet* (the c key). TypeAway stores the Unicode characters in the character string in the order that you type them. That is correct. The *DrawString* method displays these characters from right to left. That is also correct, and the *DrawString* method must be given full credit and congratulations for recognizing and properly displaying text that reads right to left.

And now you know why TypeAway has to completely erase the line of previously drawn text: new text may not necessarily be appended at the end of the text string. When you're typing from the Hebrew keyboard, new text must be displayed at the beginning of the text string rather than the end. Typing in Arabic is even more critical: adjacent characters in Arabic are often joined to form different glyphs. *DrawString* needs to draw the whole string, not just individual characters, to correctly handle this situation.

Where TypeAway fails is in the caret positioning. When you're typing right-to-left text, the caret isn't showing the insertion point. The solution to this problem isn't trivial, particularly when you're dealing with a combination of left-to-right and right-to-left text in the same line. It appears that Windows Forms doesn't make available sufficient tools to solve this problem, but if you're interested in seeing how it's done using the Win32 API, check out the article "Supporting Multilanguage Text Layout and Complex Scripts with Windows NT 5.0" from the November 1998 issue of *Microsoft Systems Journal*. (Past issues of MSJ are available at *http://www.microsoft.com/msj*.)

# 7

# Pages and Transforms

A primary goal in any graphics programming environment is device independence. Programs should be able to run without change on many different types of video display adapters regardless of the resolution. Programs should also be able to print text and graphics on many different printers without requiring a multitude of specialized printer drivers or completely separate drawing code.

In Chapter 5, I demonstrated that you can write graphics output code that draws to both the video display and the printer. Yet so far, I've been drawing in units of pixels—at least on the video display; the printer is something of a puzzle just yet—and pixels hardly seem device independent.

## Device Independence Through Text

With some care, it's possible to use pixels in a device-independent manner. One way is to base graphics output on the default size of the *Font* property associated with the form. This approach is particularly useful if you're combining some simple graphics with text.

For example, suppose you were programming a simple database application using an index card metaphor. Each record is displayed as a simulated 3-by-5-inch index card. How large are the index cards in pixels? Think of a typewriter. A typewriter with a pica typeface types 6 lines to the inch, so an index card fits 18 lines of type. You can thus make the height of the index card equal to 18 × *Font.Height* pixels. You set the width to 5/3 times that number.

Making the width of the index card 5/3 times the height implies that the horizontal resolution of your output device—the number of pixels corresponding to a given measurement such as an inch—is equal to the vertical resolution.

When a graphics output device has equal horizontal and vertical resolution, it is sometimes said to have *square pixels*. The very early video displays used when Windows was first released in 1985 did *not* have square pixels; it wasn't until the 1987 introduction of the IBM Video Graphics Array (VGA) that square pixels started to become a standard for PC-compatible video adapters.

Today, it's fairly safe to assume that the video display on which your Windows Forms program is running has square pixels. I say "fairly safe" because Windows doesn't require square pixels, and it's always possible that somebody may write a Windows device driver for some specialized display adapter that doesn't have square pixels.

Printers these days often do *not* have square pixels. Often the printer supports several resolutions, and the maximum resolution in one dimension is twice the maximum resolution in the other.

## How Much Is That in Real Money?

Let's start exploring the relationship between pixels and real-world measurements. Suppose you draw a box of 100 pixels width and height located 100 pixels from the upper left corner of the client area (or printable area of the printer page).

**HundredPixelsSquare.vb**

```
'-------------------------------------------------------------
' HundredPixelsSquare.vb (c) 2002 by Charles Petzold
'-------------------------------------------------------------
Imports System
Imports System.Drawing
Imports System.Windows.Forms

Class HundredPixelsSquare
    Inherits PrintableForm

    Shared Shadows Sub Main()
        Application.Run(new HundredPixelsSquare())
    End Sub

    Sub New()
        Text = "Hundred Pixels Square"
    End Sub

    Protected Overrides Sub DoPage(ByVal grfx As Graphics, _
            ByVal clr As Color, ByVal cx As Integer, ByVal cy As Integer)
        grfx.FillRectangle(New SolidBrush(clr), 100, 100, 100, 100)
    End Sub
End Class
```

How large is that box on the screen? How large is it on the printer? Is it even square?

Certainly you have a vague idea of how large this box will be on the screen without actually running the program, at least in terms of the relationship of the size of the box to the size of the screen. The smallest video display size in common use today is 640 pixels horizontally by 480 pixels vertically (or 640 × 480). On such a display, the box would be roughly 1/6 the width of the screen and 1/5 the height. But video displays these days can go up to 2048 × 1536 pixels or so, in which case the box is much smaller in relationship to the entire screen.

It would be nice to know the resolution of the video display, perhaps in a common measurement like dots per inch (dpi). However, while such a concept is very well defined for printers—it's usually printed right on the box you take home from the computer store—it remains an elusive concept for video displays. If you think about it, the actual dpi resolution of a video display is based on two measurements: the physical size of the monitor (usually measured diagonally in inches) and the corresponding pixel dimensions.

Confusingly enough, this latter measurement is often termed the *resolution* of the video display. I prefer to use the term *screen area*.

Video display adapters these days are capable of half a dozen (or so) different screen-area settings, and video monitors come in several different sizes. Here's a little table that shows the approximate video resolution in dots per inch for various combinations of monitor sizes and screen areas:

### Actual Video Resolution (dots per inch)

| Screen Area | Monitor Size (diagonally) | | | |
|---|---|---|---|---|
|  | **15 inches** | **17 inches** | **19 inches** | **21 inches** |
| 640 × 480 | 57 | 50 | 44 | 40 |
| 800 × 600 | 71 | 63 | 56 | 50 |
| 1024 × 768 | 91 | 80 | 71 | 64 |
| 1152 × 870 | 103/104 | 90/91 | 80/81 | 72/73 |
| 1280 × 1024 | 114/122 | 100/107 | 89/95 | 80/85 |
| 1600 × 1200 | 143 | 125 | 111 | 100 |
| 2048 × 1536 | 183 | 160 | 142 | 128 |

I'm assuming that the actual display area is an inch smaller than the rated diagonal size and that the monitor has the standard aspect ratio of 4:3. For example, a 21-inch monitor has a diagonal display area of 20 inches, implying (thank you, Pythagoras) dimensions of 16 inches horizontally and 12 inches vertically. For screen areas of 1152 × 870 and 1280 × 1024, the horizontal and vertical dimensions are not in the ratio of 4:3 and hence the horizontal and vertical resolutions are unequal—but they're close enough to assume they're equal.

So if you were running a 1600 × 1200 video mode on a 21-inch monitor, that 100-pixel square box would be about 1-inch square. But it could be almost as small as 1/2 inch or larger than 2 inches. Of course, few people use 21-inch monitors to run a 640 × 480 video mode, nor do they try to run 2048 × 1536 on 15-inch monitors. The more likely range of resolutions appears in the diagonal area of the table from the upper left to the lower right.

Windows usually doesn't know the size of your monitor, so it can't tell you the actual resolution of your video display. And even if it did know your monitor's size, what would it do when you connect a video projector to your machine and create a screen some 6 feet wide? What *should* it do? Should Windows assume a much lower resolution because the screen is larger? Almost assuredly, you don't want that.

The most essential issue regarding the video display is readable text. The default font should be large enough for you to read, obviously, but it shouldn't be much larger because you also want to fit as much text on the screen as possible.

For this reason, Windows basically ignores screen area and monitor size and instead delegates the selection of a video resolution to a very important person: You!

I've already mentioned the Display Properties dialog box. The Settings tab lets you change your video display settings. (Note that this description of Display Properties is based on Windows XP. Other versions of Windows might differ slightly.) The Settings page also has a button labeled Advanced. This button lets *you* select a video resolution in dots per inch for the video display. (In earlier versions of Windows this setting is somewhat roundabout. You actually select a Windows system font size that is comfortable for you to read. That system font is assumed to be 10 points in size. As I'll discuss in Chapter 9, fonts are measured in points, which in computer typography are 1/72 inch. The pixel size of the 10-point font that you select implies a resolution of the video display in dots per inch. The result is precisely the same as choosing the dpi resolution directly.)

For example, the default setting is called Normal Size, and is 96 dpi. (Earlier versions of Windows referred to this setting as Small Fonts.) The Normal Size system font characters are 13 pixels in height. If that font is assumed to be

10 points in size, then 13 pixels are equivalent to 10/72 inch, and the display resolution (with a little rounding involved) is indeed 96 dpi.

One common alternative is Large Size (called Large Fonts in earlier versions of Windows), which is 120 dpi. The Large Size system fonts are 16 pixels tall. If these 16 pixels are equivalent to 10/72 inch, then the display resolution (again with a little rounding) is 120 dpi.

By the way, the Windows system font is *not* the default font that's accessible through the *Font* property in a Windows Forms program. Windows Forms sets the default font to something a bit smaller—about 8 points in size.[1]

Large Fonts and Small Fonts are not the only choices. You can also set a custom size. You are then presented with a ruler that you can manually adjust to pick a really big font (implying a resolution of 480 dpi) or a really small font (about 19 dpi).

Commonly, the system font you choose will have larger physical dimensions than the point size implies. When people read print on paper, the distance between the eyes and the text is generally about a foot, but a video display is often viewed from a distance of 2 feet or so.

# Dots Per Inch

The *Graphics* object has two properties that indicate the resolution of the graphics output device in dots per inch:

### *Graphics* Properties (selection)

| Property | Type | Accessibility | Description |
|----------|------|---------------|-------------|
| *DpiX* | *Single* | Get | Horizontal resolution in dots per inch |
| *DpiY* | *Single* | Get | Vertical resolution in dots per inch |

---

1. Veteran Windows programmers might be curious about where my numbers come from. I'm quoting the *TextMetric* field *tmHeight* (which is 16 for Small Fonts and 20 for Large Fonts) less *tmInternalLeading* (which is 3 and 4, respectively). The *tmHeight* value is suitable for line spacing; *tmHeight* less *tmInternalLeading* indicates the point size converted to pixels (13 for Small Fonts and 16 for Large Fonts). Somewhat confusingly, the default font in Windows Forms has a *Font.Height* property that reports similar values: 13 for Small Fonts and 15 for Large Fonts. But this is a line-spacing value that is comparable with *tmHeight*. The Windows system font is 10 points; the default Windows Forms font is about 8 points.

Here's a short program that displays these values without much fuss.

```
DotsPerInch.vb
'-------------------------------------------------
' DotsPerInch.vb (c) 2002 by Charles Petzold
'-------------------------------------------------
Imports System
Imports System.Drawing
Imports System.Windows.Forms

Class DotsPerInch
    Inherits PrintableForm

    Shared Shadows Sub Main()
        Application.Run(new DotsPerInch())
    End Sub

    Sub New()
        Text = "Dots Per Inch"
    End Sub

    Protected Overrides Sub DoPage(ByVal grfx As Graphics, _
            ByVal clr As Color, ByVal cx As Integer, ByVal cy As Integer)
        grfx.DrawString(String.Format("DpiX = {0}" & vbLf & "DpiY = {1}",
                    grfx.DpiX, grfx.DpiY), _
                    Font, New SolidBrush(clr), 0, 0)
    End Sub
End Class
```

The values that this program reports in its client area are the same as the settings you've made in the Display Properties dialog box: 96 dpi if you've selected Small Fonts, 120 dpi if you've selected Large Fonts, and something else if you've selected a custom size.

If you click on the client area, the printed version will show the resolution of your printer, which is probably something you already knew or could look up in the manual. Printers these days have resolutions of 300, 600, 1200, or 2400 dpi, or 720, 1440, or 2880 dpi.

# What's with the Printer?

Earlier in this chapter, I presented the HundredPixelsSquare program that displayed a box 100 pixels square. I wondered how large the box was on the screen. The real answer is that the physical dimensions of this box are irrelevant.

Nobody expects a ruler held up to the screen to provide much useful information. The important point is that rulers displayed *on* the screen should be consistent with each other. In that sense, the horizontal and vertical screen dimensions of a 100-pixel-square box in inches are

```
100 / grfx.DpiX
100 / grfx.DpiY
```

That is, 1.04 inches if you've selected Small Fonts, 0.83 inch if you've selected Large Fonts, and something else if you've selected a custom size.

And on the printer… Well, you may want to try this one yourself. On your printer, the HundredPixelsSquare program draws a box that is precisely 1 inch square. Let's try something else. This program attempts to draw an ellipse with a diameter of 1 inch based on the *DpiX* and *DpiY* properties of the *Graphics* object.

**TryOneInchEllipse.vb**

```
'-----------------------------------------------------------
' TryOneInchEllipse.vb (c) 2002 by Charles Petzold
'-----------------------------------------------------------
Imports System
Imports System.Drawing
Imports System.Windows.Forms

Class TryOneInchEllipse
    Inherits PrintableForm

    Shared Shadows Sub Main()
        Application.Run(New TryOneInchEllipse())
    End Sub

    Sub New()
        Text = "Try One-Inch Ellipse"
    End Sub

    Protected Overrides Sub DoPage(ByVal grfx As Graphics, _
            ByVal clr As Color, ByVal cx As Integer, ByVal cy As Integer)
        grfx.DrawEllipse(New Pen(clr), 0, 0, grfx.DpiX, grfx.DpiY)
    End Sub
End Class
```

On the video display, the size of this ellipse looks about right. On my 600 dpi printer, however, the ellipse is 6 inches in diameter.

For the video display, the coordinates you pass to the *Graphics* drawing functions are obviously in units of pixels. For the printer, however, that is apparently not the case. For the printer, the coordinates passed to the *Graphics* drawing functions are actually interpreted as units of 0.01 inch regardless of the printer. We'll see how this works shortly. The nice part is that the resolution of the video display is probably somewhere in the region of 100 dpi, and the printer is treated as if it were a 100-dpi device. This means that in a pinch you can use the same coordinates when displaying graphics on the video display and the printer, and you'll get approximately the same results.

# Manual Conversions

If you wanted to, you could use the *DpiX* and *DpiY* properties of the *Graphics* object to adjust the coordinates that you pass to the drawing functions. For example, suppose you wanted to use floating-point coordinates to draw in units of millimeters. You'd need a method that converts from millimeters to pixels:

```
Function MMConv(ByVal grfx As Graphics, ByVal ptf As PointF) As PointF
    ptf.X *= grfx.DpiX / 25.4F
    ptf.Y *= grfx.DpiY / 25.4F
    Return ptf
End Function
```

The point you're passing to this method is your desired units of millimeters. Dividing that point by 25.4 converts it to inches. (That's an exact calculation, by the way.) Multiplying by the resolution in dots per inch converts it to pixels.

Just so we're sure about this, let's draw a 10-centimeter ruler.

**TenCentimeterRuler.vb**

```
'-------------------------------------------------------
' TenCentimeterRuler.vb (c) 2002 by Charles Petzold
'-------------------------------------------------------
Imports System
Imports System.Drawing
Imports System.Windows.Forms

Class TenCentimeterRuler
    Inherits PrintableForm

    Shared Shadows Sub Main()
        Application.Run(New TenCentimeterRuler())
    End Sub

    Sub New()
        Text = "Ten-Centimeter Ruler"
    End Sub
```

```
    Protected Overrides Sub DoPage(ByVal grfx As Graphics, _
            ByVal clr As Color, ByVal cx As Integer, ByVal cy As Integer)
        Const xOffset As Integer = 10
        Const yOffset As Integer = 10
        Dim i As Integer
        Dim pn As New Pen(clr)
        Dim br As New SolidBrush(clr)
        Dim strfmt As New StringFormat()

        grfx.DrawPolygon(pn, New PointF() _
            { _
                MMConv(grfx, New PointF(xOffset, yOffset)), _
                MMConv(grfx, New PointF(xOffset + 100, yOffset)), _
                MMConv(grfx, New PointF(xOffset + 100, yOffset + 10)), _
                MMConv(grfx, New PointF(xOffset, yOffset + 10)) _
            })
        strfmt.Alignment = StringAlignment.Center

        For i = 1 To 99
            If i Mod 10 = 0 Then
                grfx.DrawLine(pn, _
                    MMConv(grfx, New PointF(xOffset + i, yOffset)), _
                    MMConv(grfx, New PointF(xOffset + i, yOffset + 5)))
                grfx.DrawString((i / 10).ToString(), Font, br, _
                    MMConv(grfx, New PointF(xOffset + i, yOffset + 5)), _
                    strfmt)
            ElseIf i Mod 5 = 0 Then
                grfx.DrawLine(pn, _
                    MMConv(grfx, New PointF(xOffset + i, yOffset)), _
                    MMConv(grfx, New PointF(xOffset + i, yOffset + 3)))
            Else
                grfx.DrawLine(pn, _
                    MMConv(grfx, New PointF(xOffset + i, yOffset)), _
                    MMConv(grfx, New PointF(xOffset + i, yOffset + 2.5F)))
            End If
        Next i
    End Sub

    Private Function MMConv(ByVal grfx As Graphics, _
                        ByVal ptf As PointF) As PointF
        ptf.X *= grfx.DpiX / 25.4F
        ptf.Y *= grfx.DpiY / 25.4F
        Return ptf
    End Function
End Class
```

Here's how the ruler looks on the screen:

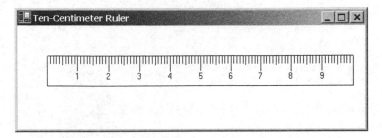

This diagram also involves some text. How did I know the text was going to look right? Well, I know that the *Font* property is about an 8-point font, so I know that the font characters should be about 3 millimeters tall, which is about the right size.

I've made the *TenCentimerRuler* class a descendent of *PrintableForm* to hammer home a point: this technique will not work on the printer. My 600-dpi printer displays it six times too large.

# Page Units and Page Scale

So that you can avoid writing methods such as *MMConv*, GDI+ includes a facility that performs automatic scaling to dimensions of your choosing. Basically, the coordinates you pass to the *Graphics* drawing functions are scaled by constants, just as in the *MMConv* method. But you don't set these scaling factors directly. Instead, you set them indirectly using two properties of the *Graphics* class named *PageUnit* and *PageScale*:

### *Graphics* Properties (selection)

| Property | Type | Accessibility |
|----------|------|---------------|
| *PageUnit* | *GraphicsUnit* | Get/Set |
| *PageScale* | *Single* | Get/Set |

You set the *PageUnit* property to a value in the *GraphicsUnit* enumeration:

## *GraphicsUnit* Enumeration

| Member | Value | Description |
|---|---|---|
| *World* | 0 | Can't be used with *PageUnit* |
| *Display* | 1 | Same as *Pixel* for video displays; 1/100 inch for printers (default for printers) |
| *Pixel* | 2 | Units of pixels (default for video display) |
| *Point* | 3 | Units of 1/72 inch |
| *Inch* | 4 | Units of inches |
| *Document* | 5 | Units of 1/300 inch |
| *Millimeter* | 6 | Units of millimeters |

If you say, for example, "I want to draw in units of hundredths of an inch," you then set these two properties like so:

```
grfx.PageUnit = GraphicsUnit.Inch
grfx.PageScale = 0.01
```

This is equivalent to saying, "When I specify a coordinate of 1, I want it to equal 0.01 inch." Following these calls, this *DrawLine* method draws a 1-inch-long line:

```
grfx.DrawLine(pn, 0, 0, 100, 0)
```

That's an actual measurable inch on the printer and equal to *grfx.DpiX* pixels on the video display. You'll get the same results with

```
grfx.PageUnit = GraphicsUnit.Document
grfx.PageScale = 3
```

or

```
grfx.PageUnit = GraphicsUnit.Millimeter
grfx.PageScale = 0.254
```

or

```
grfx.PageUnit = GraphicsUnit.Point
grfx.PageScale = 0.72
```

The default settings are *GraphicsUnit.Pixel* for the video display and *GraphicsUnit.Display* for the printer, both with a *PageScale* of 1. Notice that the *GraphicsUnit.Display* value means something different for the video display than for the printer. For the video display, it's the same as *GraphicsUnit.Pixel*, but for the printer, *GraphicsUnit.Display* indicates units of 1/100 inch. (The documentation of the *GraphicsUnit* enumeration indicates that *Graphics-Unit.Display* sets units of 1/75 inch. It's easy to establish that the documentation is incorrect.)

So if we want to get that TenCentimeterRuler program to work on the printer, we need to set *PageUnit* to *GraphicsUnit.Pixel* and everything should be OK. Let's do that by defining a class that inherits from *TenCentimeterRuler*. The new *OnPage* method here resets the *PageUnit* property and then calls the base *DoPage* class.

**PrintableTenCentimeterRuler.vb**

```
'------------------------------------------------------------
' PrintableTenCentimeterRuler.vb (c) 2002 by Charles Petzold
'------------------------------------------------------------
Imports System
Imports System.Drawing
Imports System.Windows.Forms

Class PrintableTenCentimeterRuler
    Inherits TenCentimeterRuler

    Shared Shadows Sub Main()
        Application.Run(new PrintableTenCentimeterRuler())
    End Sub

    Sub New()
        Text = "Printable " & Text
    End Sub

    Protected Overrides Sub DoPage(ByVal grfx As Graphics, _
            ByVal clr As Color, ByVal cx As Integer, _
            ByVal cy As Integer)
        grfx.PageUnit = GraphicsUnit.Pixel
        MyBase.DoPage(grfx, clr, cx, cy)
    End Sub
End Class
```

This program doesn't use the *cx* and *cy* arguments to *DoPage*. These dimensions—of the form's client area and of the printable area of the printer page—are in units compatible with the default *PageUnit*. In the general case, if you change *PageUnit*, you'll probably need to recalculate the size of the output device in identical units. I'll discuss this problem shortly.

Even though we're now drawing to the printer in units of pixels, the font still looks good. The font accessible from the *Font* property of the form is an 8-point font on the video display, and it's an 8-point font on the printer as well. We'll see how this works in Chapter 9.

This program still has a problem, however, one involving the pen that the TenCentimeterRuler version of *DoPage* defines:

```
Dim pn As New Pen(clr)
```

This pen gets a default width of 1. On the video display, that means a width of 1 pixel. On the printer, that's normally a width of 1/100 inch. However, if you change *PageUnit* to *GraphicsUnit.Pixel*, the 1-unit-wide pen is now interpreted as a width of 1 pixel. On some very high-resolution printers, the ruler may be nearly invisible.

Rather than continuing to mess around with the original 10-centimeter-ruler program, let's take advantage of the *PageUnit* and *PageScale* properties to eliminate the manual conversion.

### TenCentimeterRulerAuto.vb

```
'------------------------------------------------------------
' TenCentimeterRulerAuto.vb (c) 2002 by Charles Petzold
'------------------------------------------------------------
Imports System
Imports System.Drawing
Imports System.Windows.Forms

Class TenCentimeterRulerAuto
    Inherits PrintableForm

    Shared Shadows Sub Main()
        Application.Run(New TenCentimeterRulerAuto())
    End Sub

    Sub New()
        Text = "Ten-Centimeter Ruler (Auto)"
    End Sub

    Protected Overrides Sub DoPage(ByVal grfx As Graphics, _
            ByVal clr As Color, ByVal cx As Integer, ByVal cy As Integer)
        Const xOffset As Integer = 10
        Const yOffset As Integer = 10
        Dim i As Integer
        Dim pn As New Pen(clr, 0.25)
        Dim br As New SolidBrush(clr)
        Dim strfmt As New StringFormat()

        grfx.PageUnit = GraphicsUnit.Millimeter
        grfx.PageScale = 1
        grfx.DrawRectangle(pn, xOffset, yOffset, 100, 10)

        strfmt.Alignment = StringAlignment.Center
```

*(continued)*

**TenCentimeterRulerAuto.vb** *(continued)*

```
        For i = 1 To 99
            If i Mod 10 = 0 Then
                grfx.DrawLine(pn, _
                        New PointF(xOffset + i, yOffset), _
                        New PointF(xOffset + i, yOffset + 5))
                grfx.DrawString((i / 10).ToString(), Font, br, _
                        New PointF(xOffset + i, yOffset + 5), _
                        strfmt)
            ElseIf i Mod 5 = 0 Then
                grfx.DrawLine(pn, _
                        New PointF(xOffset + i, yOffset), _
                        New PointF(xOffset + i, yOffset + 3))
            Else
                grfx.DrawLine(pn, _
                        New PointF(xOffset + i, yOffset), _
                        New PointF(xOffset + i, yOffset + 2.5F))
            End If
        Next i
    End Sub
End Class
```

Besides eliminating the *MMConv* method, I've really made just a few changes. My *MMConv* method worked only with *PointF* structures, so in the earlier ruler-drawing programs, I used *DrawPolygon* rather than *DrawRectangle* to draw the outline of the ruler. Because GDI+ scales both coordinates and sizes in the same way, I can use *DrawRectangle* here. Another change occurs toward the beginning of the *DoPage* method, where the program creates a pen 0.25 units wide:

```
Dim pn As New Pen(clr, 0.25)
```

The program also sets up the *Graphics* object to draw in units of millimeters:

```
grfx.PageUnit = GraphicsUnit.Millimeter
grfx.PageScale = 1
```

You might wonder if it makes a difference whether you set the *PageUnit* and *PageScale* properties before you create the pen or if you create a pen with a specific width before you set the *PageUnit* and *PageScale* properties. It doesn't matter. *Pens* are device independent! They are not associated with a particular *Graphics* object until the call to one of the line-drawing methods. Only at that time is the pen width interpreted in units indicated by the current *PageUnit* and *PageScale* properties. In this case, the pen is interpreted to be 0.25 millimeter or about 1/100 inch. You may want to try a smaller value (such as 0.10 millimeter) to see the difference on the printer.

If you don't include a width in the pen constructor, the pen is created 1 unit wide, which in this case means that the pen is 1 whole millimeter wide and the ruler divisions become one big blob. (Try it!)

# Pen Widths

What's a proper pen width for the printer? You might take a cue from Post-Script—the well-known and highly respected page composition language many upscale printers use—and think of a normal default pen width as 1 point, otherwise expressible as 1/72 inch, or about 1/3 millimeter. I personally find a 1-point pen width to be a bit on the chunky side, but it's an easy rule to remember.

Here's a program that displays a bunch of pen widths in units of points.

**PenWidths.vb**

```
'------------------------------------------------
' PenWidths.vb (c) 2002 by Charles Petzold
'------------------------------------------------
Imports System
Imports System.Drawing
Imports System.Windows.Forms

Class PenWidths
    Inherits PrintableForm

    Shared Shadows Sub Main()
        Application.Run(New PenWidths())
    End Sub

    Sub New()
        Text = "Pen Widths"
    End Sub

    Protected Overrides Sub DoPage(ByVal grfx As Graphics, _
            ByVal clr As Color, ByVal cx As Integer, ByVal cy As Integer)
        Dim br As New SolidBrush(clr)
        Dim y As Single = 0
        Dim f As Single

        grfx.PageUnit = GraphicsUnit.Point
        grfx.PageScale = 1

        For f = 0 To 3.1 Step 0.2
            Dim pn As New Pen(clr, f)
            Dim str As String = _
                String.Format("{0:F1}-point-wide pen: ", f)
            Dim szf As SizeF = grfx.MeasureString(str, Font)

            grfx.DrawString(str, Font, br, 0, y)
            grfx.DrawLine(pn, szf.Width, y + szf.Height / 2, _
                        szf.Width + 144, y + szf.Height / 2)
            y += szf.Height
        Next f
    End Sub
End Class
```

Of course, although you can specify pen widths that are fractions of pixels, they can be rendered only with whole pixel widths. On the video display, many of the pen widths created by this program round to the same values:

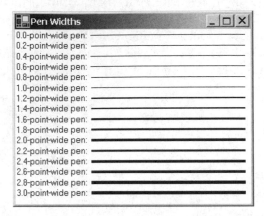

One thing you don't have to worry about on the video display is the pen width rounding down to 0 and the pen disappearing. Pens are always drawn at least 1 pixel wide. Indeed, you can set the width to 0 in the *Pen* constructor and always get 1-pixel-wide lines regardless of the *PageUnit* and *PageScale* properties.

Although 0-width pens are fine for the video display, they should never be used on the printer. On today's high-resolution laser printers, 1-pixel-wide lines are virtually invisible.

Here's a program for a ruler marked in inches that uses units of 1/64 inch and creates a pen 1/128 inch wide.

**SixInchRuler.vb**

```
'--------------------------------------------------
' SixInchRuler.vb (c) 2002 by Charles Petzold
'--------------------------------------------------
Imports System
Imports System.Drawing
Imports System.Windows.Forms

Class SixInchRuler
    Inherits PrintableForm

    Shared Shadows Sub Main()
        Application.Run(New SixInchRuler())
    End Sub

    Sub New()
        Text = "Six-Inch Ruler"
    End Sub
```

```
        Protected Overrides Sub DoPage(ByVal grfx As Graphics, _
            ByVal clr As Color, ByVal cx As Integer, ByVal cy As Integer)
        Const xOffset As Integer = 16
        Const yOffset As Integer = 16
        Dim i As Integer
        Dim pn As New Pen(clr, 0.5)
        Dim br As New SolidBrush(clr)
        Dim strfmt As New StringFormat()

        grfx.PageUnit = GraphicsUnit.Inch
        grfx.PageScale = 1 / 64
        grfx.DrawRectangle(pn, xOffset, yOffset, 6 * 64, 64)
        strfmt.Alignment = StringAlignment.Center

        For i = 1 To 95
            Dim x As Integer = xOffset + i * 4
            Dim y As Integer = yOffset
            Dim dy As Integer

            If i Mod 16 = 0 Then
                dy = 32
                grfx.DrawString((i / 16).ToString(), Font, br, _
                                        x, y + dy, strfmt)
            ElseIf i Mod 8 = 0 Then
                dy = 24
            ElseIf i Mod 4 = 0 Then
                dy = 20
            ElseIf i Mod 2 = 0 Then
                dy = 16
            Else
                dy = 12
            End If
            grfx.DrawLine(pn, x, y, x, y + dy)
        Next i
    End Sub
End Class
```

The ruler looks like this:

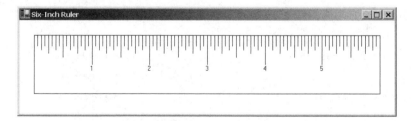

You might have noticed that text seems unaffected by any *PageUnit* and *PageScale* values I've set. That's because the font accessible through the form's

*Font* property is about 8 points in size and remains that same size. In Chapter 9, I'll show you how to create a font that *is* affected by the *PageUnit* and *Page-Scale* properties.

# Page Transforms

What you're effectively setting when you set the *PageScale* and *PageUnit* properties is known as the *page transform*. This transform can be represented by a pair of simple formulas. Assume that the coordinates you pass to the *Graphics* drawing methods are *page coordinates*. (This assumption isn't quite true, as you'll see later in this chapter, but it is true if you're setting only the *PageScale* and *PageUnit* properties.) You can represent a point in page units as ($x_{page}$, $y_{page}$).

Pixel coordinates relative to the upper left corner of the client area (or the upper left corner of the printable area of the page) are said to be in *device coordinates*, or ($x_{device}$, $y_{device}$). The page transform depends on the *PageUnit*, *PageScale*, *DpiX*, and *DpiY* properties.

## Page Transform Formulas

| *PageUnit* Value | Translation Formulas |
| --- | --- |
| *GraphicsUnit.Pixel* | $x_{device} = x_{page} \times PageScale$ |
| | $y_{device} = y_{page} \times PageScale$ |
| *GraphicsUnit.Display* (video display) | $x_{device} = x_{page} \times PageScale$ |
| | $y_{device} = y_{page} \times PageScale$ |
| *GraphicsUnit.Display* (printer) | $x_{device} = x_{page} \times PageScale \times DpiX / 100$ |
| | $y_{device} = y_{page} \times PageScale \times DpiY / 100$ |
| *GraphicsUnit.Inch* | $x_{device} = x_{page} \times PageScale \times DpiX$ |
| | $y_{device} = y_{page} \times PageScale \times DpiY$ |
| *GraphicsUnit.Millimeter* | $x_{device} = x_{page} \times PageScale \times DpiX / 25.4$ |
| | $y_{device} = y_{page} \times PageScale \times DpiY / 25.4$ |
| *GraphicsUnit.Point* | $x_{device} = x_{page} \times PageScale \times DpiX / 72$ |
| | $y_{device} = y_{page} \times PageScale \times DpiY / 72$ |
| *GraphicsUnit.Document* | $x_{device} = x_{page} \times PageScale \times DpiX / 300$ |
| | $y_{device} = y_{page} \times PageScale \times DpiY / 300$ |

In general,

$$x_{\text{device}} = x_{\text{page}} \times PageScale \times DpiX / (GraphicsUnit \text{ units per inch})$$
$$y_{\text{device}} = y_{\text{page}} \times PageScale \times DpiY / (GraphicsUnit \text{ units per inch})$$

The page transform affects all the coordinates of all the drawing functions implemented in the *Graphics* class that I've discussed so far. It also affects the information returned from *MeasureString* and the version of the *GetHeight* method implemented in the *Font* class that takes a *Graphics* object argument.

The page transform is a characteristic of the *Graphics* class. The page transform doesn't affect anything that's not a member of the *Graphics* class or that (unlike *GetHeight*) doesn't have a *Graphics* object argument. The page transform doesn't affect the information you get from *ClientSize*, for example. *ClientSize* is always in units of pixels.

# Saving the Graphics State

Setting the *PageUnit* and *PageScale* properties of the *Graphics* object profoundly affects the subsequent display of graphics. You might want to set these properties—or other properties in the *Graphics* class—to draw some graphics or obtain some information, and then revert back to the original properties.

The *Graphics* class has two methods, named *Save* and *Restore*, that let you do just that: save the properties of the *Graphics* object and later restore them. These two methods use the *GraphicsState* class from the namespace *System.Drawing.Drawing2D*.

### *Graphics* Methods (selection)

```
Function Save() As GraphicsState

Sub Restore(ByVal gs As GraphicsState)
```

The *GraphicsState* class has nothing public of any interest. You really treat it as a black box. When you call

```
Dim gs As GraphicsState = grfx.Save()
```

all the current read/write properties of the *Graphics* object are stored in the *GraphicsState* object. You can then change those properties on the *Graphics* object. To restore the saved properties, use

```
grfx.Restore(gs)
```

Programmers with experience using Win32 are probably accustomed to thinking of the similar facility (involving the functions *SaveDC* and *RestoreDC*) in terms of a last-in-first-out stack. The Windows Forms implementation is more flexible. For example, you could begin *OnPaint* processing by defining three different graphics states:

```
Dim gs1 As GraphicsState = grfx.Save()

    ' Change some properties.
    ⋮

Dim gs2 As GraphicsState = grfx.Save()

    ' Change some properties.
    ⋮

Dim gs3 As GraphicsState = grfx.Save()
```

You could then arbitrarily and in any order make calls to the *Restore* method to use any one of these three graphics states.

A similar facility is provided by the *BeginContainer* and *EndContainer* methods of the *Graphics* class. These methods make use of the *GraphicsContainer* class in *System.Drawing.Drawing2D*.

# Metrical Dimensions

The dimensions of a form's client area are available from the *ClientSize* property. These dimensions are always in units of pixels. If you set a new page transform, you probably want the dimensions of the client area not in units of pixels but in units corresponding to what you're now using in the drawing methods.

There are at least two ways to get the client size in metrical dimensions. Probably the most convenient way is the *VisibleClipBounds* property of the *Graphics* object. This property always returns the dimensions of the client area in units consistent with the current settings of the *PageUnit* and *PageScale* properties. Here's a program that uses this information to show the size of the client area using all the possible units.

**WhatSize.vb**

```
'----------------------------------------
' WhatSize.vb (c) 2002 by Charles Petzold
'----------------------------------------
Imports System
Imports System.Drawing
Imports System.Drawing.Drawing2D
Imports System.Windows.Forms

Class WhatSize
    Inherits PrintableForm

    Shared Shadows Sub Main()
        Application.Run(new WhatSize())
    End Sub

    Sub New()
        Text = "What Size?"
    End Sub

    Protected Overrides Sub DoPage(ByVal grfx As Graphics, _
            ByVal clr As Color, ByVal cx As Integer, ByVal cy As Integer)
        Dim br As New SolidBrush(clr)
        Dim y As Integer = 0
        DoIt(grfx, br, y, GraphicsUnit.Pixel)
        DoIt(grfx, br, y, GraphicsUnit.Display)
        DoIt(grfx, br, y, GraphicsUnit.Document)
        DoIt(grfx, br, y, GraphicsUnit.Inch)
        DoIt(grfx, br, y, GraphicsUnit.Millimeter)
        DoIt(grfx, br, y, GraphicsUnit.Point)
    End Sub

    Private Sub DoIt(ByVal grfx As Graphics, ByVal br As Brush, _
            ByRef y As Integer, ByVal gu As GraphicsUnit)
        Dim gs As GraphicsState = grfx.Save()

        grfx.PageUnit = gu
        grfx.PageScale = 1

        Dim szf As SizeF = grfx.VisibleClipBounds.Size

        grfx.Restore(gs)
        grfx.DrawString(gu.ToString() & ": " & szf.ToString(), _
                    Font, br, 0, y)
        y += CInt(Math.Ceiling(Font.GetHeight(grfx)))
    End Sub
End Class
```

The *DoIt* method in WhatSize makes use of the *Save* and *Restore* facility so that the different *PageUnit* settings don't interfere with the actual display of information when we call the *DrawString* method and the *GetHeight* call. Here's a typical WhatSize display:

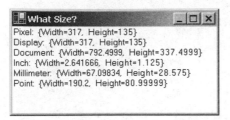

Unfortunately, the printer is different. For the printer, *VisibleClipBounds* is designed to return values in units of 1/100 inch regardless of the page transform. However, if the printer *PageUnit* is set for pixels, *VisibleClipBounds* returns the printable area of the page in pixels. Click the client area of WhatSize to confirm this anomaly.

An historical note: I wrote the first ever how-to-program-for-Windows magazine article for the December 1986 issue of *Microsoft Systems Journal*. The sample program in that article was called WSZ ("what size"), and it displayed the size of the program's client area in pixels, inches, and millimeters. WhatSize is a somewhat simplified—and considerably shorter—version of that program.

Another approach to determining the size of the display area involves using the *TransformPoints* method implemented in the *Graphics* class:

### Graphics *TransformPoints* Methods

```
Sub TransformPoints(ByVal csDst As CoordinateSpace,
                    ByVal csSrc As CoordinateSpace,
                    ByVal apt As Point())

Sub TransformPoints(ByVal csDst As CoordinateSpace,
                    ByVal csSrc As CoordinateSpace,
                    ByVal aptf As PointF())
```

The *CoordinateSpace* enumeration is defined in the *System.Drawing.Drawing2D* namespace:

### *CoordinateSpace* Enumeration

| Member | Value |
|--------|-------|
| *World* | 0 |
| *Page* | 1 |
| *Device* | 2 |

So far, we know of the coordinate space called *Device* (that's units of pixels relative to the upper left corner of the client area) and the coordinate space called *Page* (units of inches, millimeters, points, or such). If you have an array of *Point* or *PointF* structures in device units, you can convert those values to page units by calling

```
grfx.TransformPoints(CoordinateSpace.Page, CoordinateSpace.Device, apt)
```

I'll talk about the coordinate space known as *World* shortly.

Here's another version of the WhatSize program that uses *Transform-Points* to calculate the size of the client area.

**WhatSizeTransform.vb**

```
'-------------------------------------------------------
' WhatSizeTransform.vb (c) 2002 by Charles Petzold
'-------------------------------------------------------
Imports System
Imports System.Drawing
Imports System.Drawing.Drawing2D
Imports System.Windows.Forms

Class WhatSizeTransform
    Inherits PrintableForm

    Shared Shadows Sub Main()
        Application.Run(new WhatSizeTransform())
    End Sub

    Sub New()
        Text = "What Size? With TransformPoints"
    End Sub

    Protected Overrides Sub DoPage(ByVal grfx As Graphics, ByVal clr As
Color, ByVal cx As Integer, ByVal cy As Integer)
        Dim br As New SolidBrush(clr)
        Dim y As Integer = 0
        Dim apt() As Point = {New Point(cx, cy)}

        grfx.TransformPoints(CoordinateSpace.Device, _
                     CoordinateSpace.Page, apt)

        DoIt(grfx, br, y, apt(0), GraphicsUnit.Pixel)
        DoIt(grfx, br, y, apt(0), GraphicsUnit.Display)
        DoIt(grfx, br, y, apt(0), GraphicsUnit.Document)
        DoIt(grfx, br, y, apt(0), GraphicsUnit.Inch)
        DoIt(grfx, br, y, apt(0), GraphicsUnit.Millimeter)
        DoIt(grfx, br, y, apt(0), GraphicsUnit.Point)
    End Sub
```

*(continued)*

**WhatSizeTransform.vb** *(continued)*

```
    Private Sub DoIt(ByVal grfx As Graphics, ByVal br As Brush, ByRef y As
Integer, ByVal pt As Point, ByVal gu As GraphicsUnit)
        Dim gs As GraphicsState = grfx.Save()

        grfx.PageUnit  = gu
        grfx.PageScale = 1

        Dim aptf() As PointF = {Point.op_Implicit(pt)}
        grfx.TransformPoints(CoordinateSpace.Page, _
                    CoordinateSpace.Device, aptf)

        Dim szf As New SizeF(aptf(0))
        grfx.Restore(gs)
        grfx.DrawString(gu.ToString() & ": " & szf.ToString(), Font, br, 0, y)
        y += CInt(Math.Ceiling(Font.GetHeight(grfx)))
    End Sub
End Class
```

I've added an extra argument to the program's *DoIt* method: a *Point* structure containing the width and height of the display area in pixels. For the video display, that's not much of a problem because the *cx* and *cy* arguments to *DoPage* are already pixels. For the printer, however, they are not. For that reason, the *DoPage* method constructs a *Point* structure from *cx* and *cy*, makes a single-element *Point* array, and passes that array to *TransformPoints* to convert the values to device units. Notice that for this call to *TransformPoints* the destination coordinate space is *CoordinateSpace.Device*. *DoIt* then uses *Transform-Points* to convert from device units to *CoordinateSpace.Page*.

# Arbitrary Coordinates

Some of the graphics programs shown so far in this book have scaled their output to the size of the client area or the printable area of the printer page. Programs in this chapter have drawn in specific sizes in units of millimeters or inches.

Then there are times when you want to hard-code a bunch of coordinates and would prefer that you could skip any explicit scaling of them. For example, you may want to code some graphics output using a coordinate system of (say) 1000 units horizontally and 1000 units vertically. You want this coordinate system to be as large as possible but still fit inside your client area or the printer page.

This program demonstrates how to do just that.

## ArbitraryCoordinates.vb

```
' -------------------------------------------------
' ArbitraryCoordinates.vb (c) 2002 by Charles Petzold
' -------------------------------------------------
Imports System
Imports System.Drawing
Imports System.Windows.Forms

Class ArbitraryCoordinates
    Inherits PrintableForm

    Shared Shadows Sub Main()
        Application.Run(New ArbitraryCoordinates())
    End Sub

    Sub New()
        Text = "Arbitrary Coordinates"
    End Sub

    Protected Overrides Sub DoPage(ByVal grfx As Graphics, _
            ByVal clr As Color, ByVal cx As Integer, ByVal cy As Integer)
        grfx.PageUnit = GraphicsUnit.Pixel
        Dim szf As SizeF = grfx.VisibleClipBounds.Size

        grfx.PageUnit = GraphicsUnit.Inch
        grfx.PageScale = Math.Min(szf.Width / grfx.DpiX / 1000, _
                            szf.Height / grfx.DpiY / 1000)

        grfx.DrawEllipse(New Pen(clr), 0, 0, 990, 990)
    End Sub
End Class
```

The *DoPage* method first sets *PageUnit* to *GraphicsUnit.Pixel* for the sole purpose of obtaining the *VisibleClipBounds* property indicating the size of the client area or printer page in units of pixels.

Next, *DoPage* sets *PageUnit* to inches:

```
grfx.PageUnit = GraphicsUnit.Inch
```

Earlier I showed the following transform formulas that apply to a *PageUnit* of inches:

$$x_{\text{device}} = x_{\text{page}} \times PageScale \times DpiX$$
$$y_{\text{device}} = y_{\text{page}} \times PageScale \times DpiY$$

You want $x_{\text{page}}$ and $y_{\text{page}}$ to range from 0 through 1000 while $x_{\text{device}}$ and $y_{\text{device}}$ range from 0 through the *Width* and *Height* properties (respectively) from *VisibleClipBounds*. In other words,

```
Width = 1000 × PageScale × DpiX
Height = 1000 × PageScale × DpiY
```

However, these two equations would result in two different *PageScale* factors, and you can have only one. You want the lesser of the two calculated values:

```
grfx.PageScale = Math.Min(szf.Width / grfx.DpiX / 1000, _
                          szf.Height / grfx.DpiY / 1000)
```

The program then draws an ellipse with a width and height of 990 units. (Using 1000 or 999 for the width and height sometimes causes one side of the figure to be truncated for large window sizes.) The resultant figure is a circle that appears at the left of the client area when the client area is wide and at the top when the client area is tall:

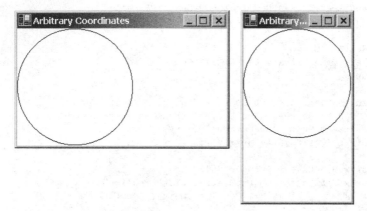

You can also print the circle; it will be as large as the printable width of the page.

There's a subtle problem in this program, however. Try reducing the window size as far as it will go. You'll notice that there's a limit in the width of the window, but you can decrease the height of the window until the client area height is 0. At that point, you'll get an exception because the *DoPage* method will be setting the *PageScale* to 0, an invalid value.

You can deal with this problem in a couple ways. Perhaps the most obvious is simply to abort the *DoPage* method if the height of the client area is 0:

```
If cy = 0 Then Return
```

That's not a problem because it doesn't make sense to draw anything anyway.

Don't you find it a little peculiar that you're getting a call to the *OnPaint* method anyway given that your client area is of 0 dimension? It wouldn't hurt to put a statement like this at the beginning of your *OnPaint* method:

```
If pea.ClipRectangle.IsEmpty Then Return
```

This statement is equivalent:

```
If grfx.IsVisibleClipEmpty Then Return
```

A very specialized solution is to use the *Math.Max* method in the calculation of the *PageScale* property to prevent values of 0:

```
grfx.PageScale = Math.Min(szf.Width / grfx.DpiX / 1000, _
                          Math.Max(szf.Height, 1) / grfx.DpiY / 1000)
```

Or, to demonstrate that you known something about exception handling in Visual Basic .NET, you can put the statement in a *Try* block:

```
Try
    grfx.PageScale = Math.Min(szf.Width / grfx.DpiX / 1000, _
                          szf.Height / grfx.DpiY / 1000)
Catch
    Return
End Try
```

But a method that might not seem so obvious is to prevent the client area from shrinking down to a 0 height in the first place. The shared property *SystemInformation.MinimumWindowSize* returns a size whose height is simply the sum of the caption bar height and twice the sizing border height. The width is considerably greater to give windows a minimum width that still allows part of the program's caption bar to be visible.

You can set a form's *MinimumSize* property to keep the window above a certain dimension. Try putting this in the constructor for ArbitraryCoordinates:

```
MinimumSize = Size.op_Addition(SystemInformation.MinimumWindowSize, _
                          New Size(0, 1))
```

# What You Can't Do

There are several things you can't do with the page transform. First, you can't set *PageScale* to negative values; that is, you can't make *x* coordinates increase to the left (which few people want to do anyway) or *y* coordinates increase going up the screen (which is something that's useful for the mathematically inclined). Second, you can't have different units in the horizontal and vertical directions. The *PageScale* and *PageUnit* properties apply to both axes equally. A function like

```
grfx.DrawEllipse(pn, 0, 0, 100, 100)
```

will always draw a circle regardless of the page transform, with one exception: when you set a *PageUnit* of *GraphicsUnit.Pixel* and your output device has different horizontal and vertical resolution. This issue will rarely come up for the video display, but it's fairly common for printers.

And finally, you can't change the origin. The point (0, 0) in page coordinates always maps to the upper left corner of the client area or printable area of the printer page.

Fortunately, there's another transform supported by GDI+ that lets you do all of these tasks and more.

# Hello, World Transform

The other transform supported by GDI+ is known as the *world transform*. It involves a traditional 3 × 3 matrix, but it's possible to skip the matrix and use some very handy methods instead. To begin, let's look at this program that displays the first paragraph of Herman Melville's *Moby-Dick*.

```
MobyDick.vb
'------------------------------------------
' MobyDick.vb (c) 2002 by Charles Petzold
'------------------------------------------
Imports System
Imports System.Drawing
Imports System.Drawing.Drawing2D
Imports System.Windows.Forms

Class MobyDick
    Inherits PrintableForm

    Shared Shadows Sub Main()
        Application.Run(New MobyDick())
    End Sub

    Sub New()
        Text = "Moby-Dick by Herman Melville"
    End Sub

    Protected Overrides Sub DoPage(ByVal grfx As Graphics, _
            ByVal clr As Color, ByVal cx As Integer, ByVal cy As Integer)

        ' Insert RotateTransform, ScaleTransform,
        '    TranslateTransform, and other calls here.

        grfx.DrawString( "Call me Ishmael. Some years ago" & ChrW(&H2014) & _
            "never mind how long precisely" & ChrW(&H2014) & _
            "having little or no money in my purse, and " & _
            "nothing particular to interest me on shore, I " & _
            "thought I would sail about a little and see " & _
            "the watery part of the world. It is a way I " & _
            "have of driving off the spleen, and " & _
```

```
                "regulating the circulation. Whenever I find " & _
                "myself growing grim about the mouth; whenever " & _
                "it is a damp, drizzly November in my soul; " & _
                "whenever I find myself involuntarily pausing " & _
                "before coffin warehouses, and bringing up the " & _
                "rear of every funeral I meet and especially " & _
                "whenever my hypos get such an upper hand of " & _
                "me, that it requires a strong moral principle " & _
                "to prevent me from deliberately stepping into " & _
                "the street, and methodically knocking " & _
                "people's hats off" & ChrW(&H2014) & "then, I " & _
                "account it high time to get to sea as soon as " & _
                "I can. This is my substitute for pistol " & _
                "and ball. With a philosophical flourish Cato " & _
                "throws himself upon his sword; I quietly take " & _
                "to the ship. There is nothing surprising in " & _
                "this. If they but knew it, almost all men in " & _
                "their degree, some time or other, cherish " & _
                "very nearly the same feelings towards the " & _
                "ocean with me.", _
                Font, New SolidBrush(clr), _
                New RectangleF(0, 0, cx, cy))
        End Sub
    End Class
```

This is nothing you haven't seen before except that I've indicated where you can add a line or two of code, recompile, and see what happens.

Here's the first one you can try:

```
grfx.RotateTransform(45)
```

Make sure you insert this call before the *DrawString* call. The effect is to rotate the text 45 degrees clockwise:

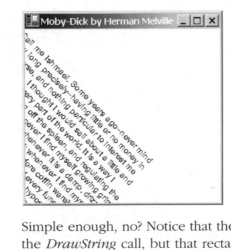

Simple enough, no? Notice that the text is still within the rectangle specified in the *DrawString* call, but that rectangle has been effectively rotated along with the text. You can also print it, but I must warn you that it may take quite some time for the print spooler file to be created.

What's affected by *RotateTransform*? All the *Graphics* drawing functions covered so far. As we get more into graphics, I'll try to be careful to indicate when something is or is not affected by the world transform.

The argument to *RotateTransform* is a *Single* value, and it can be positive or negative. Try this:

```
grfx.RotateTransform(-45)
```

The text is rotated 45° counterclockwise. The angle can also be greater than 360° or less than -360°. For our particular example, any value that doesn't resolve to an angle between -90° and 90° will cause the text to be rotated right off the visible area of the window.

Successive calls to *RotateTransform* are cumulative. The calls

```
grfx.RotateTransform(5)
grfx.RotateTransform(10)
grfx.RotateTransform(-20)
```

result in the text being rotated 5° counterclockwise.

Now try this:

```
grfx.ScaleTransform(1, 3)
```

This function increases the coordinates and sizes of displayed graphics. The first argument affects the horizontal coordinates and sizes, and the second argument affects the vertical. In the MobyDick program, calling this function causes the width of the text to be the same but makes the font characters three times taller. The call

```
grfx.ScaleTransform(3, 1)
```

doesn't affect the height of the characters but makes them three times wider. The display rectangle increases likewise, so the text has the same line breaks. You can also combine the two effects:

```
grfx.ScaleTransform(3, 3)
```

Again, these are *Single* values, and they are compounded. Scaling both the horizontal and vertical sizes by a factor of 3 can be accomplished by the following two calls:

```
grfx.ScaleTransform(3, 1)
grfx.ScaleTransform(1, 3)
```

Or by

```
grfx.ScaleTransform(CSng(Math.Sqrt(3)), CSng(Math.Sqrt(3)))
grfx.ScaleTransform(CSng(Math.Sqrt(3)), CSng(Math.Sqrt(3)))
```

But what you'll probably find *most* interesting is that blowing up the text doesn't make it all jaggy. It looks as if you are using a different sized font rather than increasing the size of an existing font.

Can the scale values be negative? Yes, they can. However, if you try it right now, you won't see anything. But I will shortly get to a point where we can use negative scale values and see the very startling effect. The scale values can't be 0, or the function will throw an exception.

I've saved, well, the most boring for last. The *TranslateTransform* call simply shifts coordinates along the horizontal and vertical axis. For example, inserting the call

```
grfx.TranslateTransform(100, 50)
```

into the MobyDick program causes the text to begin 100 pixels to the right of and 50 pixels below the origin of the client area. If you print this version, the text appears 1 inch to the right of and 1/2 inch below the origin of the printable area of the page. Negative values of the first argument will move the text off the left side of the client area; negative *y* values move the text off the top.

But shifting the text helps demonstrate other techniques. I want you to insert the call

```
grfx.TranslateTransform(cx \ 2, cy \ 2)
```

That will begin the text in the center of the client area or printer page. That's not very interesting by itself, but now insert the following after the *Translate-Transform* call:

```
grfx.ScaleTransform(-1, 1)
```

Now that *is* interesting, isn't it? What happens is that the text is reflected around the vertical axis, appearing as a mirror image in the bottom left quadrant of the client area:

Now replace that *ScaleTransform* call with this one:

```
grfx.ScaleTransform(1, -1)
```

Now the text is reflected around the horizontal axis and appears upside down. Again, you can combine the two effects:

```
grfx.ScaleTransform(-1, -1)
```

Now you know why you couldn't use the *ScaleTransform* call by itself with negative arguments—the text would be flipped off the visible surface of the client area. You need to move the text farther from the left and top edge to see the effect.

OK, now let's try switching around the order of the *TranslateTransform* and one of the *ScaleTransform* calls:

```
grfx.ScaleTransform(-1, 1)
grfx.TranslateTransform(cx \ 2, cy \ 2)
```

Now you see nothing, and you probably figure that it's because the text has been somehow moved off the surface of the client area. There are two ways to bring it back. One way is to change the first argument of the *TranslateTransform* call so that it's negative:

```
grfx.ScaleTransform(-1, 1)
grfx.TranslateTransform(-cx \ 2, cy \ 2)
```

Now it's back to being reflected around the vertical axis in the center of the client area. By the way, I'm not expecting you to understand why this works yet. Indeed, at this point, confusion would not be inappropriate.

To add to that confusion, here's another way to do it. Leave the first argument the way it was, but use this overload of the *TranslateTransform* method:

```
grfx.ScaleTransform(-1, 1)
grfx.TranslateTransform(cx \ 2, cy \ 2, MatrixOrder.Append)
```

Each of the three methods we've looked at so far—*RotateTransform*, *ScaleTransform*, and *TranslateTransform*—is overloaded to allow a final *MatrixOrder* argument, which is an enumeration defined in the *System.Drawing.Drawing2D* namespace. (That's why I've conveniently included the additional *Imports* statement at the top of the MobyDick program.)

Here are the formal definitions of the *Graphics* methods I've discussed in this section so far, plus another:

### *Graphics* Methods (selection)

```
Sub TranslateTransform(ByVal dx As Single, ByVal dy As Single)

Sub TranslateTransform(ByVal dx As Single, ByVal dy As Single,
                       ByVal mo As MatrixOrder)

Sub ScaleTransform(ByVal sx As Single, ByVal sy As Single)

Sub ScaleTransform(ByVal sx As Single, ByVal sy As Single,
                   ByVal mo As MatrixOrder)

Sub RotateTransform(ByVal fAngle As Single)

Sub RotateTransform(ByVal fAngle As Single, ByVal mo As MatrixOrder)

Sub ResetTransform()
```

The *ResetTransform* call makes everything go back to normal. The *MatrixOrder* enumeration has just two members:

### *MatrixOrder* Enumeration

| Member | Value | Description |
| --- | --- | --- |
| *Prepend* | 0 | Default |
| *Append* | 1 | Switches order of application |

What these enumeration values do will become evident before the conclusion of the chapter.

# The Big Picture

The coordinates you pass to the various drawing methods implemented in the *Graphics* class are said to be *world coordinates*. World coordinates are first subjected to the world transform, which is the thing we've been playing around with by calling *TranslateTransform*, *ScaleTransform*, and *RotateTransform*. I'll formalize the world transform shortly.

The world transform converts world coordinates to page coordinates. The page transform—the transform defined by the *PageUnit* and *PageScale* properties of the *Graphics* object—converts those page coordinates to device coordinates, which are pixels relative to the upper left corner of the client area or printable area of the printer page.

For functions such as the *Graphics* method *MeasureString* or the *Font* method *GetHeight*, this process is reversed. Device coordinates are converted to page coordinates, which are then converted to world coordinates and returned by the method.

# Linear Transforms

Let's look at the mathematical effect of calling the various transform methods. The simplest of these methods seems to be

```
grfx.TranslateTransform(dx, dy)
```

where I'm symbolizing the arguments with $d_x$ and $d_y$. (The *d* stands for *delta*, mathematically meaning *change*.) The world transform that results from this method call is

$$x_{page} = x_{world} + d_x$$
$$y_{page} = y_{world} + d_y$$

Easy enough. As you saw, the *TranslateTransform* call resulted in all coordinates being offset.

Similarly, here's a call to *ScaleTransform*:

```
grfx.ScaleTransform(sx, sy)
```

The *s* stands for *scale*. This world transform involves not an addition but a multiplication:

$$x_{page} = s_x \cdot x_{world}$$
$$y_{page} = s_y \cdot y_{world}$$

This scaling effect is very similar to the page transform.

When you call

```
grfx.RotateTransform(α)
```

with an angle of $\alpha$, well, I won't make you guess. The resultant transform is obviously a bit more complicated and looks like this:

$$x_{page} = x_{world} \cdot \cos(\alpha) + y_{world} \cdot \sin(\alpha)$$
$$y_{page} = -x_{world} \cdot \sin(\alpha) + y_{world} \cdot \cos(\alpha)$$

This little table of sines and cosines may help you verify that these formulas do indeed work:

| Angle $\alpha$ | Sine | Cosine |
|:---:|:---:|:---:|
| 0 | 0 | 1 |
| 45 | $\sqrt{1/2}$ | $\sqrt{1/2}$ |
| 90 | 1 | 0 |
| 135 | $\sqrt{1/2}$ | $-\sqrt{1/2}$ |
| 180 | 0 | -1 |
| 225 | $-\sqrt{1/2}$ | $-\sqrt{1/2}$ |
| 270 | -1 | 0 |
| 315 | $-\sqrt{1/2}$ | $\sqrt{1/2}$ |
| 360 | 0 | 1 |

By the way, if you're familiar with this stuff from experience with other graphics programming environments, the two formulas for rotations might look slightly off. That's because GDI+ expresses rotations clockwise. In more mathematically oriented environments, rotations are counterclockwise. For counterclockwise rotations, the sine term in the first formula is negative and the sine term in the second is positive.

We can generalize all three of these transforms into the two formulas

$$x_{\text{page}} = s_x \cdot x_{\text{world}} + r_x \cdot y_{\text{world}} + d_x$$
$$y_{\text{page}} = r_y \cdot x_{\text{world}} + s_y \cdot y_{\text{world}} + d_y$$

where $s_x$, $s_y$, $r_x$, $r_y$, $d_x$, and $d_y$ are constants that define the particular transform. You've already been introduced to the scaling factors $s_x$ and $s_y$, and the translation factors $d_x$ and $d_y$. You've also seen that certain specific combinations of $s_x$, $s_y$, $r_x$, and $r_y$—combinations defined by trigonometric functions of particular angles—can result in rotation. The $r_x$ and $r_y$ factors also have a meaning in themselves, and the graphical effect of these two constants will soon become apparent.

These two formulas taken together are known as the *general linear transformation of the plane.*[2] Although $x_{\text{page}}$ and $y_{\text{page}}$ are functions of both $x_{\text{world}}$ and $y_{\text{world}}$, these formulas don't involve powers of $x_{\text{world}}$ or $y_{\text{world}}$ or anything

---

2. See Anthony J. Pettofrezzo, *Matrices and Transformations* (New York: Dover, 1978), Chapter 3, and particularly section 3-7 for a rigorous mathematical treatment.

like that. That the world transform is linear implies certain restrictions on what you can do with the world transform. Here are the restrictions

- The world transform will always transform a straight line into another straight line. Straight lines will never become curved.

- A pair of parallel lines will never be transformed into lines that are not parallel.

- Two objects equal in size to each other will never be transformed into two objects unequal in size.

- Parallelograms (including rectangles) will always be transformed into other parallelograms; ellipses will always be transformed into other ellipses.

When you start off with a new, clean *Graphics* class on entry to a *Paint* or a *PrintPage* event, the world transform in effect is called the *identity* transform: the $s_x$ and $s_y$ factors are set equal to 1; the other factors are set to 0. The *ResetTransform* method restores the *Graphics* object to the identity transform.

As you've seen, the effects of successive calls to *TranslateTransform*, *ScaleTransform*, and *RotateTransform* are accumulated. However, the resultant world transform differs depending on the order that you call these methods. It's fairly easy to demonstrate why. This won't be pretty, so it's OK if you cover your eyes during the scary parts.

First, let's assume we have one world transform that I'll call $T_1$:

$$x' = s_{x1} \cdot x + r_{x1} \cdot y + d_{x1}$$
$$y' = r_{y1} \cdot x + s_{y1} \cdot y + d_{y1}$$

Rather than using subscripts indicating world coordinates and page coordinates, the world coordinates are simply $x$ and $y$, and the page coordinates are $x'$ and $y'$. Let's assume a second transform called $T_2$ with different factors:

$$x' = s_{x2} \cdot x + r_{x2} \cdot y + d_{x2}$$
$$y' = r_{y2} \cdot x + s_{y2} \cdot y + d_{y2}$$

Applying $T_1$ first to world coordinates and then $T_2$ to the result produces this transform:

$$x' = s_{x2} \cdot s_{x1} \cdot x + s_{x2} \cdot r_{x1} \cdot y + s_{x2} \cdot d_{x1} + r_{x2} \cdot r_{y1} \cdot x + r_{x2} \cdot s_{y1} \cdot y + r_{x2} \cdot d_{y1} + d_{x2}$$
$$y' = r_{y2} \cdot s_{x1} \cdot x + r_{y2} \cdot r_{x1} \cdot y + r_{y2} \cdot d_{x1} + s_{y2} \cdot r_{y1} \cdot x + sy2 \cdot sy1 \cdot y + sy2 \cdot dy1 + dy2$$

Consolidating the terms, you arrive at this:

$$x' = (s_{x2} \cdot s_{x1} + r_{x2} \cdot r_{y1}) \cdot x + (s_{x2} \cdot r_{x1} + r_{x2} \cdot s_{y1}) \cdot y + (s_{x2} \cdot d_{x1} + r_{x2} \cdot d_{y1} + d_{x2})$$
$$y' = (r_{y2} \cdot s_{x1} + s_{y2} \cdot r_{y1}) \cdot x + (r_{y2} \cdot r_{x1} + s_{y2} \cdot s_{y1}) \cdot y + (r_{y2} \cdot d_{x1} + s_{y2} \cdot d_{y1} + d_{y2})$$

If you apply $T_2$ first and then $T_1$, you get something different:

$$x' = s_{x1} \cdot s_{x2} \cdot x + s_{x1} \cdot r_{x2} \cdot y + s_{x1} \cdot d_{x2} + r_{x1} \cdot r_{y2} \cdot x + r_{x1} \cdot s_{y2} \cdot y + r_{x1} \cdot d_{y2} + d_{x1}$$
$$y' = r_{y1} \cdot s_{x2} \cdot x + r_{y1} \cdot r_{x2} \cdot y + r_{y1} \cdot d_{x2} + s_{y1} \cdot r_{y2} \cdot x + s_{y1} \cdot s_{y2} \cdot y + s_{y1} \cdot d_{y2} + d_{y1}$$

Consolidating the terms, you obtain

$$x' = (s_{x1} \cdot s_{x2} + r_{x1} \cdot r_{y2}) \cdot x + (s_{x1} \cdot r_{x2} + r_{x1} \cdot s_{y2}) \cdot y + (s_{x1} \cdot d_{x2} + r_{x1} \cdot d_{y2} + d_{x1})$$
$$y' = (r_{y1} \cdot s_{x2} + s_{y1} \cdot r_{y2}) \cdot x + (r_{y1} \cdot r_{x2} + s_{y1} \cdot s_{y2}) \cdot y + (r_{y1} \cdot d_{x2} + s_{y1} \cdot d_{y2} + d_{y1})$$

And that, my friends, is why you get different results depending on whether you call *ScaleTransform* or *TranslateTransform* first.

# Introducing Matrixes

When something is very messy in mathematics (like the calculations I just demonstrated), the solution usually doesn't involve removing something but introducing something new. Here it will be very useful to introduce a *matrix*, particularly because the mathematics of matrix algebra are well known (at least to mathematicians). You can represent a linear transform by a matrix; applying multiple transforms is equivalent to multiplying the matrices.

A *matrix* is a rectangular array of numbers. Here's an array with three columns and two rows:

$$\begin{vmatrix} 27 & 9 & 14 \\ 3 & 0 & 88 \end{vmatrix}$$

Arrays are usually symbolized by capital letters. When multiplying two matrices like so:

$$A \times B = C$$

the number of columns in *A* must be the same as the number of rows in *B*. The **number of rows in the product *C* is equal to the number of rows in *A*.** The number of columns in *C* is equal to the number of columns in *B*. The number in the *i*th row and *j*th column in *C* is equal to the sum of the products of the numbers in the *i*th row of *A* times the corresponding numbers in the *j*th column of *B*.[3] Matrix multiplication is not commutative. The product $A \times B$ does not necessarily equal the product $B \times A$.

If we weren't dealing with translation, we could represent the world coordinates $(x, y)$ as a $1 \times 2$ matrix and the transformation matrix as a $2 \times 2$ matrix.

---

3. See Pettofrezzo, section 1-2 for examples.

You multiply these two matrices and express the resultant page coordinates $(x', y')$ as another $1 \times 2$ matrix:

$$\begin{vmatrix} x & y \end{vmatrix} \times \begin{vmatrix} s_x & r_y \\ r_x & s_y \end{vmatrix} = \begin{vmatrix} x' & y' \end{vmatrix}$$

Applying the multiplication rules to the matrices gives us the formulas

$$x' = s_x \cdot x + r_x \cdot y$$
$$y' = r_y \cdot x + s_y \cdot y$$

These formulas are not quite complete, however. The world transform also involves a translation factor. To get the matrix multiplication to work right, the world coordinates and page coordinates must be expanded to $1 \times 3$ matrices, and the transform is a $3 \times 3$ matrix:

$$\begin{vmatrix} x & y & 1 \end{vmatrix} \times \begin{vmatrix} s_x & r_y & 0 \\ r_x & s_y & 0 \\ d_x & d_y & 1 \end{vmatrix} = \begin{vmatrix} x' & y' & 1 \end{vmatrix}$$

Here are the resultant formulas:

$$x' = s_x \cdot x + r_x \cdot y + d_x$$
$$y' = r_y \cdot x + s_y \cdot y + d_y$$

The type of transform that can be represented by a matrix like this is often called a *matrix transform*. The matrix transform that doesn't do anything has scaling factors of 1, and *r* and *d* have factors of 0:

$$\begin{vmatrix} 1 & 0 & 0 \\ 0 & 1 & 0 \\ 0 & 0 & 1 \end{vmatrix}$$

This is called the *identity* matrix.

# The Matrix Class

The matrix transform is encapsulated in the *Matrix* class defined in the *System.Drawing.Drawing2D* namespace. You can create a *Matrix* object using one of four constructors, two of which are shown here:

### *Matrix* Constructors (selection)

```
Matrix()

Matrix(ByVal sx As Single, ByVal ry As Single,
       ByVal rx As Single, ByVal sy As Single,
       ByVal dx As Single, ByVal dy As Single)
```

The second constructor allows you to specify all six constants that define the matrix transform. The scaling factors *sx* and *sy* must be nonzero! (If they're not, you'll raise an exception.)

The *Graphics* class has a read/write property named *Transform* that is a *Matrix* object:

### *Graphics* Property (selection)

| Property | Type | Accessibility |
|----------|------|---------------|
| *Transform* | *Matrix* | Get/Set |

Whenever you call the *TranslateTransform*, *ScaleTransform*, *RotateTransform*, or *ResetTransform* method, the *Transform* property is affected. You can also set the *Transform* property directly. The call

```
grfx.Transform = New Matrix(1, 0, 0, 1, 0, 0)
```

has the same effect as *ResetTransform*.

The *Matrix* class has five properties, all of which are read-only:

### *Matrix* Properties

| Property | Type | Accessibility | Description |
|----------|------|---------------|-------------|
| *Elements* | *Single()* | Get | Six transformation constants |
| *OffsetX* | *Single* | Get | Transform $d_x$ constant |
| *OffsetY* | *Single* | Get | Transform $d_y$ constant |
| *IsIdentity* | *Boolean* | Get | Diagonal of 1's |
| *IsInvertible* | *Boolean* | Get | Can be inverted |

Let's now look at an example of compounded transforms. Suppose you first call

```
grfx.ScaleTransform(2, 2)
```

Your program could then examine the resultant matrix by calling

```
Dim afElements() As Single = grfx.Transform.Elements
```

You'll see the values 2, 0, 0, 2, 0, 0, which can be represented as the following matrix:

$$\begin{vmatrix} 2 & 0 & 0 \\ 0 & 2 & 0 \\ 0 & 0 & 1 \end{vmatrix}$$

Now you call

```
grfx.TranslateTransform(100, 100)
```

By itself, that would result in the matrix

$$\begin{vmatrix} 1 & 0 & 0 \\ 0 & 1 & 0 \\ 100 & 100 & 1 \end{vmatrix}$$

However, the new transform is a composite of the two method calls. The matrix representing the second call is multiplied by the existing *Transform* property, and the result is the new *Transform* property:

$$\begin{vmatrix} 1 & 0 & 0 \\ 0 & 1 & 0 \\ 100 & 100 & 1 \end{vmatrix} \times \begin{vmatrix} 2 & 0 & 0 \\ 0 & 2 & 0 \\ 0 & 0 & 1 \end{vmatrix} = \begin{vmatrix} 2 & 0 & 0 \\ 0 & 2 & 0 \\ 200 & 200 & 1 \end{vmatrix}$$

Now try making the *ScaleTransform* and *TranslateTransform* calls in the opposite order:

```
grfx.TranslateTransform(100, 100)
grfx.ScaleTransform(2, 2)
```

Again, the resultant transform is calculated by multiplying the second matrix by the first matrix:

$$\begin{vmatrix} 2 & 0 & 0 \\ 0 & 2 & 0 \\ 0 & 0 & 1 \end{vmatrix} \times \begin{vmatrix} 1 & 0 & 0 \\ 0 & 1 & 0 \\ 100 & 100 & 1 \end{vmatrix} = \begin{vmatrix} 2 & 0 & 0 \\ 0 & 2 & 0 \\ 100 & 100 & 1 \end{vmatrix}$$

You can also obtain this transform by calling

```
grfx.ScaleTransform(2, 2)
grfx.TranslateTransform(100, 100, MatrixOrder.Append)
```

The *MatrixOrder.Append* argument indicates that the new transform is to be appended to the existing transform. The default is *MatrixOrder.Prepend*.
The *Graphics* class has one more world transform method:

### *Graphics* **Methods (selection)**

```
Sub MultiplyTransform(ByVal matx As Matrix)

Sub MultiplyTransform(ByVal matx As Matrix, ByVal mo As MatrixOrder)
```

This method lets you multiply the existing transform matrix by a new one.
I'll discuss the *Matrix* class more in Chapter 15.

# Shear and Shear Alike

Let's go back to the MobyDick program and insert the following statement:

```
grfx.Transform = New Matrix(1, 0, 0, 3, 0, 0)
```

This statement has the same effect as the call

```
grfx.ScaleTransform(1, 3)
```

What we haven't experimented with yet are the $r_x$ and $r_y$ factors used by themselves. Consider the following call:

```
grfx.Transform = new Matrix(1, 0, 0.5, 1, 0, 0)
```

This call results in the following transform matrix:

$$\begin{vmatrix} 1 & 0 & 0 \\ 0.5 & 1 & 0 \\ 0 & 0 & 1 \end{vmatrix}$$

And these are the transform formulas:

$$x' = x + 0.5 \cdot y$$
$$y' = y$$

Notice that the $x$ coordinate values are increased by the $y$ value. When $y$ equals 0 (the top of the client area), no transform will occur. As $y$ gets larger going down the client area, $x$ is increased likewise. The result is an effect called *shear*.

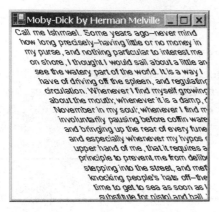

Specifically, the effect here is called *horizontal shear*, or *x-shear*. Unfortunately, the word *shear* starts with the same letter as *scale*, so to identify the shear factors in the transform formulas shown earlier, I've used the last letter of *shear*.

You can also set the *vertical shear*, or *y-shear*, factor like so:

```
grfx.Transform = New Matrix(1, 0.5, 0, 1, 0, 0)
```

This matrix is

$$\begin{vmatrix} 1 & 0.5 & 0 \\ 0 & 1 & 0 \\ 0 & 0 & 1 \end{vmatrix}$$

The transform formulas are

$$x' = x$$
$$y' = 0.5 \cdot x + y$$

Notice that each line of text still begins at the left margin of the client area:

Rotation is actually a combination of horizontal shear and vertical shear. However, some combinations, like this one, won't work:

```
grfx.Transform = new Matrix(1, 1, 1, 1, 0, 0)
```

This defines the transform

$$x' = x + y$$
$$y' = x + y$$

This transform would cause an image to be compressed into a single line. It will generate an exception before it does that. But this call works:

```
grfx.Transform = new Matrix(1, 1, -1, 1, 0, 0)
```

It results in the following display:

If you set the first four arguments to the square root of 1/2,

```
grfx.Transform = new Matrix(0.707, 0.707, -0.707, 0.707, 0, 0)
```

you'll produce the same result as the call we started this whole exploration with:

```
grfx.RotateTransform(45)
```

# Combining Transforms

In theory, you don't need the page transform at all. All the page transform does is scaling, and you can certainly do that and a lot more with the world transform. As you'll see in Chapter 9 and 11, however, text and bitmap images are often *not* affected by the page transform but are affected by the world transform. Also, it's often convenient to combine the two types of transforms, particularly if you're interested in drawing figures of a particular size that are then subjected to the world transform.

This program draws 36 one-inch squares that are rotated around the center of the display area.

**RotatedRectangles.vb**

```
'---------------------------------------------------
' RotatedRectangles.vb (c) 2002 by Charles Petzold
'---------------------------------------------------
Imports System
Imports System.Drawing
Imports System.Drawing.Drawing2D
Imports System.Windows.Forms

Class RotatedRectangles
    Inherits PrintableForm

    Shared Shadows Sub Main()
        Application.Run(new RotatedRectangles())
    End Sub

    Sub New()
        Text = "Rotated Rectangles"
    End Sub

    Protected Overrides Sub DoPage(ByVal grfx As Graphics, _
            ByVal clr As Color, ByVal cx As Integer, ByVal cy As Integer)
        Dim i As Integer
        Dim pn As New Pen(clr)

        grfx.PageUnit = GraphicsUnit.Pixel
        Dim aptf() As PointF = {grfx.VisibleClipBounds.Size.ToPointF()}
        grfx.PageUnit = GraphicsUnit.Inch
        grfx.PageScale = 0.01

        grfx.TransformPoints(CoordinateSpace.Page, _
                            CoordinateSpace.Device, aptf)

        grfx.TranslateTransform(aptf(0).X / 2, aptf(0).Y / 2)

        For i = 0 To 35
            grfx.DrawRectangle(pn, 0, 0, 100, 100)
            grfx.RotateTransform(10)
        Next i
    End Sub
End Class
```

The hard part here is calculating the arguments to the *TranslateTransform* call, which is necessary to shift the world coordinate origin to the center of the display area. The *DoPage* method changes the page unit to pixels in order to get the *VisibleClipBounds* property in units of pixels. *DoPage* then switches to a page unit of 1/100 inch and transforms the display area width and height to page coordinates. The *TranslateTransform* call uses these values halved.

The *For* loop is the easy part: It draws a rectangle 100 units wide and high positioned at the point (0, 0). The *RotateTransform* call then rotates 10° in preparation for the next iteration. And here's what it looks like:

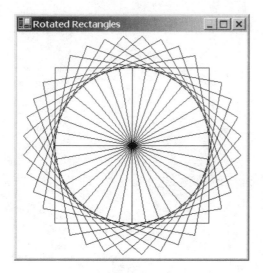

Knowing how to rotate objects around an origin will come in handy in the analog clock program in Chapter 10.

# 8

# Taming the Mouse

United States patent number 3,541,541, filed June 21, 1967, describes an "X-Y Position Indicator for a Display System."[1] The inventor is listed as Douglas C. Engelbart of the Stanford Research Institute (SRI). The word *mouse* is never mentioned in the original patent, of course, but it's obvious that's what the patent describes.

Doug Engelbart (born 1925) founded the Augmentation Research Center at SRI to advance computer hardware and software in pursuit of an ambitious goal: to create tools for the augmentation of human intelligence. As Engelbart recollected in 1986, "We wanted to start experimenting with screen selection. The idea of working and interacting very actively with the display meant that we had to tell the computer what we were looking at, so we needed a screen selection device. There was a lot of argument about light pens and tracking balls in those days, but none of those arguments served our needs very directly. I wanted to find the best thing that would serve us in the context in which we wanted to work—text and structured items and interactive commands.... I dug up some notes of mine describing a possibility that turned into the very first mouse."[2]

---

1. U.S. patents are available for viewing at *http://www.uspto.gov/patft*. You'll need a TIFF viewer for patents issued prior to 1976.
2. Adele Goldberg, ed., *A History of Personal Workstations* (New York: ACM Press, 1988), 194–195. This book is a collection of papers presented at the ACM (Association for Computing Machinery) Conference on the History of Personal Workstations held January 9–10, 1986, in Palo Alto, California. A more extensive discussion of the mouse can be found in Thierry Bardini's book, *Bootstrapping: Douglas Engelbart, Coevolution, and the Origins of the Personal Computer* (Stanford, CA: Stanford University Press, 2000).

By 1972, the mouse had found its way to the Xerox Palo Alto Research Center (PARC), where it became part of the Alto, the machine that is commonly regarded as the first implementation of a graphical user interface and the precursor to the personal computer. But it wasn't until the 1983 introduction of the ill-fated Apple Lisa and the more successful Macintosh a year later that the mouse started to become a common accessory on every well-dressed computer.

While the keyboard is adequate for alphanumeric input and rudimentary cursor movement, the mouse provides a more intimate connection between the user and objects on the screen. As an extension of the user's fingers, the mouse can point, grab, and move. The mouse has also adapted itself well to new types of applications: although games players and graphics artists were among the first to experience the mouse, in more recent years, the mouse has proved invaluable in navigating through hypertext-oriented mediums like the Web.

## The Dark Side of the Mouse

When Microsoft Windows was first released in 1985, the mouse was still a relatively rare appliance in the IBM-compatible world. The early developers of Windows felt that users shouldn't be required to buy a mouse in order to use the product. The mouse was made an optional accessory for Windows, and keyboard alternatives to the mouse were provided in all the little programs that came with Windows. (This is still the case: check out the help information in the Windows Calculator to see how each button is industriously assigned a keyboard alternative.) Third-party software developers were also encouraged to follow Microsoft's lead and provide keyboard interfaces in their own applications.

Although the mouse has become a nearly universal PC peripheral, part of the legacy of Windows involves an openness to mouseless system configurations. When at all possible, I still like the idea of providing keyboard equivalents for mouse actions. Touch typists in particular prefer keeping their hands on the keyboard, and I suppose everyone has had the experience of "losing" a mouse on a cluttered desk or having a mouse too clogged up with mouse gunk to work well. The keyboard equivalents usually don't cost much in terms of thought or effort, and they can deliver more functionality to users who prefer them.

There's another good reason why keyboard alternatives to the mouse must be considered an essential part of any Windows application. As the average age of computer users increases, some people—myself included—have suffered from painful and debilitating injuries to their hands, arms, and shoulders that are a direct result of excessive mouse use. Sometimes these problems can even be traced to a single application. I've made an extra effort in searching out keyboard alternatives in the applications I use, and it's disheartening to find applications whose developers have seemingly given up on providing a well-rounded user interface.

## Ignoring the Mouse

Since Chapter 2, you've been writing and running programs that respond to mouse input. The standard form includes a mouse interface that lets the user move the form around the screen by dragging its caption bar, resize the form by dragging its sizing border, open the control box (also known as the system menu) to select items, and trigger the minimize, maximize, and close buttons. All this happens without any effort by you, the programmer. Obviously, Windows is handling that mouse input itself.

As you learned in Chapter 4, it's not necessary for a Windows Forms program to worry about mouse input when it implements a scroll bar. The scroll bar code itself handles the mouse input and responds appropriately.

Beginning in Chapter 12, I'll start talking about the many predefined controls available in Windows Forms. Later chapters will cover menus and dialog boxes. You'll discover that all these user interface enhancements handle their own mouse input. Indeed, that's the primary purpose of controls: to encapsulate a low-level interface to the keyboard and mouse, and to provide a higher-level interface that you as a programmer can deal with.

This chapter involves those times when you need to directly handle mouse input within your client area, which, of course, is something that not all applications need to do. Those programmers who will adorn their client areas with predefined controls may never need to deal directly with mouse input. However, if you ever want to write your own controls, having a solid foundation in mouse handling is a necessity.

## Some Quick Definitions

A mouse is a pointing device with one or more buttons. The *mouse* is the object that sits on your desk. When you move the mouse, the Windows environment moves a small bitmap image called the mouse *cursor* on the screen. (In some graphical environments—and even in some of the Windows Forms documentation—the mouse cursor is referred to as a *pointer.*)

The mouse cursor has a *hot spot* that corresponds to a precise pixel location on the screen. For example, the hot spot of the default arrow cursor is the tip of the arrow. This is what is meant by the *location* of the mouse cursor. I hope you won't be too alarmed if I'm occasionally a little sloppy and refer to the location or position of the *mouse* rather than the mouse *cursor*. Rest assured that the mouse is still on your desk and not crawling up your screen.

*Clicking* the mouse is pressing and releasing a mouse button. *Dragging* the mouse is holding down the mouse button and moving the mouse. *Double-clicking* is clicking the mouse button twice in succession. For an action to qualify as a double-click, both clicks must occur within a set period of time and with the mouse cursor in approximately the same location on the screen. If you ever need to know these values (and it's unlikely you will), the *SystemInformation* class contains two shared read-only properties with this information:

### *SystemInformation* Shared Properties (selection)

| Property | Type | Accessibility | Description |
|---|---|---|---|
| *DoubleClickTime* | *Integer* | Get | Time in milliseconds |
| *DoubleClickSize* | *Size* | Get | Area in pixels |

The user has control over these settings using the Mouse item in Control Panel.

# Information About the Mouse

Can you run your computer without a mouse? Well, why don't you try? Shut down your computer, unplug the mouse, restart, and see what happens. Windows doesn't seem to mind. CTRL+ESC (or the Windows key on some keyboards) brings up the Start menu, and you can navigate through your programs, documents, or favorites list with the keyboard cursor-movement keys.

A Windows Forms program may want to determine whether a mouse is present and, if so, how many buttons it has. Again, the *SystemInformation* class comes to the rescue:

### *SystemInformation* Shared Properties (selection)

| Property | Type | Accessibility | Description |
|---|---|---|---|
| *MousePresent* | *Boolean* | Get | Indicates whether a mouse is installed |
| *MouseButtons* | *Integer* | Get | Indicates the number of buttons on the mouse |
| *MouseButtonsSwapped* | *Boolean* | Get | Indicates whether buttons are swapped |

*MousePresent* returns *True* if a mouse is installed, and *MouseButtons* indicates the number of buttons on the mouse. If a mouse is installed, the number of buttons could be reported as one, two, three, four, or five, with two and three buttons probably being the most common on machines currently running Windows.

The *MouseButtonsSwapped* property returns *True* if the user has used the Mouse item on Control Panel to swap the functionality of the left and right mouse buttons. This swapping is usually done by left-handed users who put the mouse on the left side of the keyboard and want to use the forefinger of the left hand to carry out the most common mouse operations.

You don't normally need to know about button swapping. However, if you want to write a computer-based training program that includes an animation that shows mouse buttons being pressed, you might want to delight the user by showing the mouse in the configuration that the user has selected. (Of course, nothing prevents a user from moving the mouse to the left of the keyboard without swapping the buttons—a technique I've used deliberately to lessen my mouse use—or swapping the buttons and using the right hand.)

Regardless of any button swapping, the button called the *left* button is really the *primary* button. This is the button that carries out the most common activities of selecting items, dragging icons, and triggering actions.

The right mouse button has come to be used for invoking *context menus*. These are menus that appear at the mouse cursor position and pertain to options that apply only to the area where the mouse cursor is currently located. For example, in Microsoft Internet Explorer, if the cursor is positioned over an image and you press the right mouse button, you get several options, including one to save the picture to a file. If the mouse isn't positioned over a picture but on some other part of the page, you won't have an option to save the image, but you will have an option to print the page. I'll discuss how you can create context menus in Chapter 14.

# The Mouse Wheel

"Build a better mousetrap and the world will beat a path to your door," my mother used to tell me, unknowingly paraphrasing Ralph Waldo Emerson.[3] Nowadays, it might make more sense to build a better *mouse*.

---

3. Or maybe not. The full quotation "If a man can write a better book, preach a better sermon, or make a better mousetrap than his neighbor, though he builds his house in the woods the world will make a beaten path to his door" is attributed to a lecture by Emerson but doesn't appear in his writings. See *Bartlett's Familiar Quotations*, 16th ed. (Boston: Little, Brown, 1992), 430. It's also widely acknowledged these days that this charming sentiment just ain't so. A good marketing strategy is also necessary for the commercial success of mousetraps or any other consumer item.

The three-button mouse never achieved much popularity under Windows until Microsoft introduced the Microsoft IntelliMouse. While not exactly intelligent in the conventional sense, the IntelliMouse does include an enhancement in the form of a little wheel between the two buttons. If you press on this wheel, it functions as a third mouse button (referred to in programming interfaces as the *middle* button). But you can also rotate the wheel with your finger, and wheel-aware programs can respond by scrolling or zooming a document.

As gimmicky as this may sound, it turns out that the mouse wheel is habit-forming, particularly for reading long documents or Web pages. The big advantage is that you don't need to keep the mouse cursor positioned over the scroll bar; it can be anywhere within the document.

Once again, *SystemInformation* is the place to go for information about the mouse wheel:

### *SystemInformation* Shared Properties (selection)

| Property | Type | Accessibility | Description |
|---|---|---|---|
| *MouseWheelPresent* | *Boolean* | Get | Returns *True* if wheel is present |
| *MouseWheelScrollLines* | *Integer* | Get | Number of lines to scroll per turn |
| *NativeMouseWheelSupport* | *Boolean* | Get | Not important to applications |

The mouse wheel doesn't turn smoothly but instead has a definite notched, or clicked, feel. To ensure that applications respond to the mouse wheel consistently, each notch (called a *detent* in the Microsoft .NET Framework documentation) is supposed to correspond to a certain number of text lines that the application scrolls through the document. The *Mouse-WheelScrollLines* property indicates that number of lines. For the Microsoft IntelliMouse, the property currently returns 3. However, future super-duper mouse gizmos may have a finer notch, and in that case, *MouseWheelScrollLines* might someday return 2 or 1.

If you think it might be interesting to add mouse wheel support to supplement the scroll bar in one of the SysInfo programs we developed in Chapter 4, don't bother. The scroll bars created by the auto-scroll facility respond to the mouse wheel automatically.

## The Four Basic Mouse Events

Mouse activity is communicated to a Windows Forms application in the form of events. The *Control* class defines nine mouse events and nine corresponding protected methods; any class descended from *Control* (including *Form*) also inherits these nine methods.

Although a detailed discussion of controls awaits us in Chapter 12, it's helpful to get an idea of how the mouse works with controls. So for now, imagine a form or a dialog box covered with controls such as buttons, text labels, text-entry fields, and so forth. These controls are considered *children* of the form. Likewise, the form is known as the *parent* of the controls. We've already had contact with this notion in the SysInfoPanel program in Chapter 4 when the *Parent* property of the *Panel* control was assigned to the *Form* object.

Only one control receives any particular mouse event. A control receives mouse events only when it is both enabled and visible, that is, when both the *Enabled* and *Visible* properties are set to *True*. Usually, mouse events are received only by the control directly underneath the mouse cursor.

If a child control is enabled and visible, and you pass the mouse cursor over the control, the child control receives the mouse events rather than the parent. If the child control is either disabled or invisible, the parent receives the mouse events. It's as if the child were transparent. If multiple controls are stacked on the same physical point, the enabled and visible control highest in the *z-order*, that is, visibly on top of all other overlapping controls, receives the mouse events. I'll explain this concept in Chapter 12.

Any object derived or instantiated from *Form* receives mouse events only when the mouse is positioned over the form's client area; the *Form* object does *not* receive mouse events when the cursor is positioned over the form's border, caption bar, control box, minimize box, maximize box, close box, menu, or scroll bars.

However, as you'll see, under some circumstances a control or form receives mouse events when the mouse cursor is *not* positioned over the control. This feature is known as mouse *capturing*, and it assists forms and controls in tracking mouse movement. I'll have much more to say on this subject later in this chapter.

Here are the four basic mouse events:

### *Control* Events (selection)

| Event | Method | Delegate | Argument |
|-------|--------|----------|----------|
| *MouseDown* | *OnMouseDown* | *MouseEventHandler* | *MouseEventArgs* |
| *MouseUp* | *OnMouseUp* | *MouseEventHandler* | *MouseEventArgs* |
| *MouseMove* | *OnMouseMove* | *MouseEventHandler* | *MouseEventArgs* |
| *MouseWheel* | *OnMouseWheel* | *MouseEventHandler* | *MouseEventArgs* |

As the names imply, the *MouseDown* and *MouseUp* events indicate a button being pressed or released. The *MouseMove* event signals mouse movement, and the *MouseWheel* event occurs when the user rolls the mouse wheel. These four events are the only events associated with objects of type *MouseEventArgs*. The *MouseEventArgs* class has five read-only properties:

### *MouseEventArgs* Properties

| Property | Type | Accessibility | Description |
| --- | --- | --- | --- |
| *X* · | *Integer* | Get | The horizontal position of the mouse |
| *Y* | *Integer* | Get | The vertical position of the mouse |
| *Button* | *MouseButtons* | Get | The mouse button or buttons |
| *Clicks* | *Integer* | Get | Returns 2 for a double-click |
| *Delta* | *Integer* | Get | Mouse wheel movement |

*X* and *Y* are integers that indicate the position of the mouse cursor hot spot in pixels relative to the upper left corner of the client area. These two properties are valid for all four mouse events.

The *Button* property indicates the mouse button or buttons involved in the event. This property isn't valid for *MouseWheel* events. The *Button* property is a *MouseButtons* enumeration value:

### *MouseButtons* Enumeration

| Member | Value |
| --- | --- |
| *None* | &H00000000 |
| *Left* | &H00100000 |
| *Right* | &H00200000 |
| *Middle* | &H00400000 |
| *XButton1* | &H00800000 |
| *XButton2* | &H01000000 |

In this enumeration, the word *Left* should be interpreted as the user's primary mouse button—the button that invokes application menus and lets the user resize and move forms. The *Right* mouse button is the button that invokes context menus. *XButton1* and *XButton2* refer to buttons in the IntelliMouse Explorer, which has five buttons.

For *MouseDown* and *MouseUp* events, the *Button* property indicates the particular button being pressed or released.

For *MouseMove* events, the *Button* property indicates which button or buttons are *currently* pressed. Notice that the values are bit flags that can be combined. For example, if both the left and right buttons are pressed, the *Button* property equals &H00300000. If the *MouseEventArgs* object is named *mea*, the following expression returns *True* if the right mouse button and *only* the right mouse button is pressed:

```
(mea.Button = MouseButtons.Right)
```

The following expression is *True* if the right mouse button is pressed, regardless of the other mouse buttons:

```
(mea.Button And MouseButtons.Right <> 0)
```

The *Clicks* property is valid only for *MouseDown* events and is normally set to 1. The property is set to 2 if the *MouseDown* event follows a previous *MouseDown* event quickly enough to qualify as a double-click.

The *Delta* property is valid only for *MouseWheel* events. If you roll the wheel forward one click, the *Delta* property will typically equal 120, and if you roll it back one click, the *Delta* property will typically equal –120.

## Doing the Wheel

Let's get the mouse wheel out of the way first so we can focus on more conventional aspects of mouse use. In the previous paragraph, I mentioned the value 120. This is a rare instance of a number essential to Windows Forms programming—or at least the processing of mouse wheel events—that is not associated with a shared property or an enumeration value. In the Win32 header files, an identifier named *WHEEL_DELTA* is defined as 120; in Windows Forms programs that use the mouse wheel, you'll have to hard-code this value or define your own *Const* value.

When you get a *MouseWheel* event, you calculate the number of text lines to scroll like so:

```
mea.Delta * SystemInformation.MouseWheelScrollLines \ 120
```

Currently, this calculation yields either 3 or –3, but including the *SystemInformation* constant in the calculation allows your program to adapt better to future mouse wheel devices that have finer wheel gradations. Positive values indicate that the user is pushing the wheel forward; the program should respond by scrolling toward the top of the document. Negative values mean that the user is pulling the wheel back, and the program should scroll toward the bottom of the document. The following program demonstrates the use of the mouse wheel by displaying (and scrolling) Edgar Allan Poe's creepy poem "Annabel Lee."

## PoePoem.vb

```
'-----------------------------------------
' PoePoem.vb (c) 2002 by Charles Petzold
'-----------------------------------------
Imports System
Imports System.Drawing
Imports System.Windows.Forms

Class PoePoem
    Inherits Form

    Const strAnnabelLee As String = _
        "It was many and many a year ago," & vbLf & _
        "   In a kingdom by the sea," & vbLf & _
        "That a maiden there lived whom you may know" & vbLf & _
        "   By the name of Annabel Lee;" & ChrW(&H2014) & vbLf & _
        "And this maiden she lived with no other thought" & vbLf & _
        "   Than to love and be loved by me." & vbLf & _
        vbLf & _
        "I was a child and she was a child" & vbLf & _
        "   In this kingdom by the sea," & vbLf & _
        "But we loved with a love that was more than love" & _
                                ChrW(&H2014) & vbLf & _
        "   I and my Annabel Lee" & ChrW(&H2014) & vbLf & _
        "With a love that the wing" & ChrW(233) & "d seraphs of Heaven" _
                                & vbLf & _
        "   Coveted her and me." & vbLf & _
        vbLf & _
        "And this was the reason that, long ago," & vbLf & _
        "   In this kingdom by the sea," & vbLf & _
        "A wind blew out of a cloud, chilling" & vbLf & _
        "   My beautiful Annabel Lee;" & vbLf & _
        "So that her highborn kinsmen came" & vbLf & _
        "   And bore her away from me," & vbLf & _
        "To shut her up in a sepulchre," & vbLf & _
        "   In this kingdom by the sea." & vbLf & _
        vbLf & _
        "The angels, not half so happy in Heaven," & vbLf & _
        "   Went envying her and me" & ChrW(&H2014) & vbLf & _
        "Yes! that was the reason (as all men know," & vbLf & _
        "   In this kingdom by the sea)" & vbLf & _
        "That the wind came out of the cloud by night," & vbLf & _
        "   Chilling and killing my Annabel Lee." & vbLf & _
        vbLf & _
        "But our love it was stronger by far than the love" & vbLf & _
        "   Of those who were older than we" & ChrW(&H2014) & vbLf & _
        "   Of many far wiser than we" & ChrW(&H2014) & vbLf & _
```

```
    "And neither the angels in Heaven above" & vbLf & _
    "   Nor the demons down under the sea" & vbLf & _
    "Can ever dissever my soul from the soul" & vbLf & _
    "   Of the beautiful Annabel Lee:" & ChrW(&H2014) & vbLf & _
    vbLf & _
    "For the moon never beams, without bringing me dreams" & vbLf & _
    "   Of the beautiful Annabel Lee;" & vbLf & _
    "And the stars never rise, but I feel the bright eyes" & vbLf & _
    "   Of the beautiful Annabel Lee:" & ChrW(&H2014) & vbLf & _
    "And so, all the night-tide, I lie down by the side" & vbLf & _
    "Of my darling" & ChrW(&H2014) & "my darling" & ChrW(&H2014) & _
                                    "my life and my bride," & vbLf & _
    "   In her sepulchre there by the sea" & ChrW(&H2014) & vbLf & _
    "   In her tomb by the sounding sea." & vbLf & _
    vbLf & _
    "                                     [May 1849]"

ReadOnly iTextLines As Integer = 0
Private iClientLines As Integer
Private iStartLine As Integer = 0
Private cyText As Single

Shared Sub Main()
    ' See whether the program makes sense.
    If Not SystemInformation.MouseWheelPresent Then
        MessageBox.Show("Program needs a mouse with a mouse wheel!", _
                    "PoePoem", MessageBoxButtons.OK, _
                    MessageBoxIcon.Error)

        Return
    End If


    ' Otherwise go normally.
    Application.Run(New PoePoem())
End Sub

Sub New()
    Text = """Annabel Lee"" by Edgar Allan Poe"
    BackColor = SystemColors.Window
    ForeColor = SystemColors.WindowText
    ResizeRedraw = True

    ' Calculate the number of lines in the text.
    Dim iIndex As Integer = strAnnabelLee.IndexOf(vbLf, 0)
    While iIndex <> -1
        iTextLines += 1
        iIndex = strAnnabelLee.IndexOf(vbLf, iIndex + 1)
    End While

    ' Obtain line-spacing value.
    Dim grfx As Graphics = CreateGraphics()
```

*(continued)*

**PoePoem.vb**    *(continued)*

```
            cyText = Font.Height
            grfx.Dispose()
            OnResize(EventArgs.Empty)
        End Sub

        Protected Overrides Sub OnResize(ByVal ea As EventArgs)
            MyBase.OnResize(ea)
            iClientLines = CInt(Math.Floor(ClientSize.Height / cyText))
            iStartLine = Math.Max(0, _
                        Math.Min(iStartLine, iTextLines - iClientLines))
        End Sub

        Protected Overrides Sub OnMouseWheel(ByVal mea As MouseEventArgs)
            Dim iScroll As Integer = _
                mea.Delta * SystemInformation.MouseWheelScrollLines \ 120
            iStartLine -= iScroll
            iStartLine = Math.Max(0, _
                        Math.Min(iStartLine, iTextLines - iClientLines))
            Invalidate()
        End Sub

        Protected Overrides Sub OnPaint(ByVal pea As PaintEventArgs)
            Dim grfx As Graphics = pea.Graphics
            grfx.DrawString(strAnnabelLee, Font, New SolidBrush(ForeColor), _
                        0, -iStartLine * cyText)
        End Sub
    End Sub
End Class
```

Notice that the program checks whether a mouse wheel is installed and lets the user know if it can't find one. I've put this check in *Main*, but that's not the only option in programs that shouldn't run under certain conditions. You can alternatively override the *OnLoad* method of the *Form* class and check at that time. The *Load* event occurs after the constructor code executes but before the form is made visible on the screen. In that case, if the program determines that it shouldn't run, it can display a message box and call *Close* to prevent the form from being displayed. Where you *cannot* abort the display of a form is in the form's constructor. Neither *Close* nor the shared *Application.Exit* method works there.

The text of the poem includes embedded line feed characters and is stored in a string variable. The program counts the number of lines during the form's constructor and saves the result in a field named *iTextLines*. The constructor also obtains the text line spacing using the *Height* property of the form's *Font* property. The return value is stored in a field named *cyText*.

The remainder of the initialization occurs in the *OnResize* method. The constructor must first call *OnResize* explicitly. Thereafter, *OnResize* is called whenever the user resizes the form. *OnResize* uses *cyText* to calculate *iClientLines*, the number of lines that can fit in the client area.

The *iStartLine* variable is the line of text that should appear at the top of the client area. It is initialized at zero. The *OnMouseWheel* method adjusts the value using the calculation I showed earlier.

Sometimes programs that scroll text are written so that scrolling all the way to the bottom makes the last line of text appear at the top of the client area. But it's not necessary to allow the user to scroll quite that far. All that's required is for the last line of text to be visible at the bottom of the client area. For this reason, both the *OnMouseWheel* and *OnResize* methods in PoePoem include a calculation using the *Math.Min* and *Math.Max* methods. This calculation ensures that *iStartLine* is non-negative and also that it's based on the amount of text that can fit in the client area. If you make the client area tall enough to fit the entire text, the text won't scroll at all.

# Mouse Movement

Let's next look at the *MouseMove* event. This program is called MouseWeb but it has nothing to do with the World Wide Web; instead, it overrides the *OnMouseMove* method to draw a web that connects the current mouse position with the corners and sides of the client area.

```
MouseWeb.vb
'-------------------------------------------
' MouseWeb.vb (c) 2002 by Charles Petzold
'-------------------------------------------
Imports System
Imports System.Drawing
Imports System.Windows.Forms

Class MouseWeb
    Inherits Form

    Private ptMouse As Point = Point.Empty

    Shared Sub Main()
        Application.Run(New MouseWeb())
    End Sub

    Sub New()
        Text = "Mouse Web"
        BackColor = SystemColors.Window
        ForeColor = SystemColors.WindowText
        ResizeRedraw = True
    End Sub

    Protected Overrides Sub OnMouseMove(ByVal mea As MouseEventArgs)
        Dim grfx As Graphics = CreateGraphics()
```

*(continued)*

**MouseWeb.vb**   *(continued)*

```
        DrawWeb(grfx, BackColor, ptMouse)
        ptMouse = New Point(mea.X, mea.Y)
        DrawWeb(grfx, ForeColor, ptMouse)
        grfx.Dispose()
    End Sub

    Protected Overrides Sub OnPaint(ByVal pea As PaintEventArgs)
        DrawWeb(pea.Graphics, ForeColor, ptMouse)
    End Sub

    Private Sub DrawWeb(ByVal grfx As Graphics, ByVal clr As Color, _
                                          ByVal pt As Point)
        Dim cx As Integer = ClientSize.Width
        Dim cy As Integer = ClientSize.Height
        Dim pn As New Pen(clr)

        grfx.DrawLine(pn, pt, New Point(0, 0))
        grfx.DrawLine(pn, pt, New Point(cx \ 4, 0))
        grfx.DrawLine(pn, pt, New Point(cx \ 2, 0))
        grfx.DrawLine(pn, pt, New Point(3 * cx \ 4, 0))
        grfx.DrawLine(pn, pt, New Point(cx, 0))
        grfx.DrawLine(pn, pt, New Point(cx, cy \ 4))
        grfx.DrawLine(pn, pt, New Point(cx, cy \ 2))
        grfx.DrawLine(pn, pt, New Point(cx, 3 * cy \ 4))
        grfx.DrawLine(pn, pt, New Point(cx, cy))
        grfx.DrawLine(pn, pt, New Point(3 * cx \ 4, cy))
        grfx.DrawLine(pn, pt, New Point(cx \ 2, cy))
        grfx.DrawLine(pn, pt, New Point(cx \ 4, cy))
        grfx.DrawLine(pn, pt, New Point(0, cy))
        grfx.DrawLine(pn, pt, New Point(0, cy \ 4))
        grfx.DrawLine(pn, pt, New Point(0, cy \ 2))
        grfx.DrawLine(pn, pt, New Point(0, 3 * cy \ 4))
    End Sub
End Class
```

Move the mouse cursor within the client area, and the center of the web follows. A typical screen looks like this:

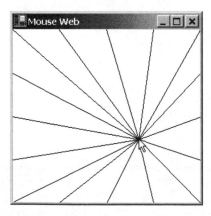

The program displays the web first during the *OnPaint* method using a *Point* structure stored as a field and initialized to (0, 0). During the *OnMouseMove* method, the program erases the previous figure by redrawing it using the background color. The program then redraws the web based on the new mouse position using the foreground color.

Notice how the program stops responding to the mouse as soon as the mouse cursor leaves the client area. Even if the mouse cursor is moved over the program's caption bar, the calls to *OnMouseMove* stop.

Or do they? Try this: Move the mouse cursor to MouseWeb's client area. The center of the web follows the mouse as usual. Now press one of the mouse buttons. With the button still pressed, move the mouse cursor outside the client area. The center of the web continues to follow the cursor! Release the mouse button. The program stops responding. This is a feature called mouse *capture*, and it's an important part of the technique of tracking the mouse position.

## Tracking and Capturing the Mouse

When a program needs to draw something or move something in response to mouse movement, it uses a technique called mouse *tracking*. Most often, mouse tracking begins when a mouse button is pressed and ends when the button is released. A program written for an environment not supporting event handling would probably track the mouse by sitting in a *While* loop continuously monitoring the mouse cursor position. A Windows Forms program, however, must track the mouse by responding to events. This architecture forces the programmer to approach the exercise as if dealing with a state machine.

Here's a fun little program that demonstrates some rudimentary mouse cursor tracking.

---

**MouseConnect.vb**

```
'-------------------------------------------------
' MouseConnect.vb (c) 2002 by Charles Petzold
'-------------------------------------------------
Imports System
Imports System.Drawing
Imports System.Windows.Forms

Class MouseConnect
    Inherits Form

    Const iMaxPoint As Integer = 1000
    Private iNumPoints As Integer = 0
    Private apt(iMaxPoint) As Point
```

*(continued)*

**MouseConnect.vb** *(continued)*

```vb
    Shared Sub Main()
        Application.Run(New MouseConnect())
    End Sub

    Sub New()
        Text = "Mouse Connect: Press, drag quickly, release"
        BackColor = SystemColors.Window
        ForeColor = SystemColors.WindowText

        ' Double the client area.
        ClientSize = Size.op_Addition(ClientSize, ClientSize)
    End Sub

    Protected Overrides Sub OnMouseDown(ByVal mea As MouseEventArgs)
        If mea.Button = MouseButtons.Left Then
            iNumPoints = 0
            Invalidate()
        End If
    End Sub

    Protected Overrides Sub OnMouseMove(ByVal mea As MouseEventArgs)
        If mea.Button = MouseButtons.Left And iNumPoints <= iMaxPoint Then
            apt(iNumPoints) = New Point(mea.X, mea.Y)
            iNumPoints += 1

            Dim grfx As Graphics = CreateGraphics()
            grfx.DrawLine(New Pen(ForeColor), mea.X, mea.Y, _
                                              mea.X, mea.Y + 1)
            grfx.Dispose()
        End If
    End Sub

    Protected Overrides Sub OnMouseUp(ByVal mea As MouseEventArgs)
        If mea.Button = MouseButtons.Left Then Invalidate()
    End Sub

    Protected Overrides Sub OnPaint(ByVal pea As PaintEventArgs)
        Dim grfx As Graphics = pea.Graphics
        Dim pn As New Pen(ForeColor)
        Dim i, j As Integer

        For i = 0 To iNumPoints - 2
            For j = i + 1 To iNumPoints - 1
                grfx.DrawLine(pn, apt(i), apt(j))
            Next j
        Next i
    End Sub
End Class
```

To use this program, you press the left mouse button anywhere in the client area, move the mouse cursor quickly around, and then release the button. For every *OnMouseMove* call the program gets, it stores the *X* and *Y* properties of the *MouseEventArgs* object and draws a tiny mark at that point. When you release the button, the *OnMouseUp* method invalidates the client area. *OnPaint* responds by connecting every point to every other point, sometimes creating a big blob and sometimes making an interesting pattern:

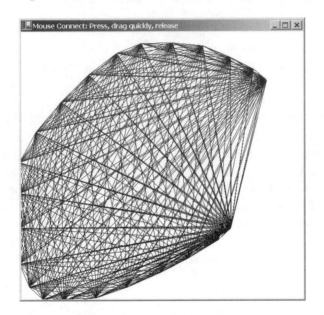

As you can see, as I whipped the mouse cursor around, I twice drifted outside the client area. The program didn't seem to mind. It connected all the lines, even those with points outside the client area. The lines are clipped to the client area, but all the points are still correctly stored. If you create such an image and make the client area a bit taller, you'll see the bottom of the figure. You can even release the mouse button outside of MouseConnect's client area and the program will work normally.

This is probably what you want to happen: the user is signaling a desire to work with MouseConnect by pressing the mouse button within its client area, and this activity should end only when the user releases the mouse button—regardless of where the mouse cursor is or has been.

Whenever you press any mouse button on a control or in a form's client area, the control or form *captures the mouse* and forces each subsequent mouse event to be sent to itself. The capture ends when the user releases the mouse button. Mouse capture capability is virtually a prerequisite for tracking the mouse, and it is automatically provided for you. A *Boolean* property of the *Control* class indicates when the mouse is captured:

**Control properties (selection)**

| Property | Type | Accessibility |
|----------|------|---------------|
| *Capture* | *Boolean* | Get/Set |

Although this property is writable, you can't just arbitrarily set it and expect the same results as when you click in the client area and drag the mouse. After your program sets *Capture* to *True*, you'll get *MouseMove* events all right, even when you pass the mouse over children of the form, but the events stop when you move the mouse outside the boundary of the form. (This restriction serves to prevent a rogue application from blocking mouse input to other programs.) Mouse capturing works outside the form (or control) only when a mouse button is pressed. The *Capture* property is more useful for canceling mouse capture at any time by setting the property to *False*. (I'll do that later in this chapter.) The property is also useful for informational purposes. The property is *True* during both the *MouseDown* event that begins mouse capture and *Mouse-Move* events when the mouse is captured, and *False* during the *MouseUp* event that releases mouse capture. The mouse isn't automatically captured on the second click of a double-click.

# Adventures in Tracking

Generally, it's fairly easy to write some mouse-tracking code that works 99.5 percent of the time. This program is quite similar in structure to MouseConnect but it does something much more conventional, which is letting you drag the mouse to draw a rectangle.

```
BlockOut.vb
'-------------------------------------------
' BlockOut.vb (c) 2002 by Charles Petzold
'-------------------------------------------
Imports System
Imports System.Drawing
Imports System.Windows.Forms

Class BlockOut
    Inherits Form
```

```
Private bBlocking, bValidBox As Boolean
Private ptBeg, ptEnd As Point
Private rectBox As Rectangle

Shared Sub Main()
    Application.Run(New BlockOut())
End Sub

Sub New()
    Text = "Blockout Rectangle with Mouse"
    BackColor = SystemColors.Window
    ForeColor = SystemColors.WindowText
End Sub

Protected Overrides Sub OnMouseDown(ByVal mea As MouseEventArgs)
    If mea.Button = MouseButtons.Left Then
        ptBeg = New Point(mea.X, mea.Y)
        ptEnd = ptBeg
        Dim grfx As Graphics = CreateGraphics()
        grfx.DrawRectangle(New Pen(ForeColor), Rect(ptBeg, ptEnd))
        grfx.Dispose()
        bBlocking = True
    End If
End Sub

Protected Overrides Sub OnMouseMove(ByVal mea As MouseEventArgs)
    If bBlocking Then
        Dim grfx As Graphics = CreateGraphics()
        grfx.DrawRectangle(New Pen(BackColor), Rect(ptBeg, ptEnd))
        ptEnd = New Point(mea.X, mea.Y)
        grfx.DrawRectangle(New Pen(ForeColor), Rect(ptBeg, ptEnd))
        grfx.Dispose()
        Invalidate()
    End If
End Sub

Protected Overrides Sub OnMouseUp(ByVal mea As MouseEventArgs)
    If bBlocking AndAlso mea.Button = MouseButtons.Left Then
        Dim grfx As Graphics = CreateGraphics()
        rectBox = Rect(ptBeg, New Point(mea.X, mea.Y))
        grfx.DrawRectangle(New Pen(ForeColor), rectBox)
        grfx.Dispose()
        bBlocking = False
        bValidBox = True
        Invalidate()
    End If
End Sub

Protected Overrides Sub OnPaint(ByVal pea As PaintEventArgs)
    Dim grfx As Graphics = pea.Graphics
```

*(continued)*

**BlockOut.vb** *(continued)*

```
        If bValidBox Then
            grfx.FillRectangle(New SolidBrush(ForeColor), rectBox)
        End If
        If bBlocking Then
            grfx.DrawRectangle(New Pen(ForeColor), Rect(ptBeg, ptEnd))
        End If
    End Sub

    Private Function Rect(ByVal ptBeg As Point, _
                          ByVal ptEnd As Point) As Rectangle
        Return New Rectangle(Math.Min(ptBeg.X, ptEnd.X), _
                             Math.Min(ptBeg.Y, ptEnd.Y), _
                             Math.Abs(ptEnd.X - ptBeg.X), _
                             Math.Abs(ptEnd.Y - ptBeg.Y))
    End Function
End Class
```

To use this program, you press the left mouse button, drag, and release. As you're dragging, the program draws a rectangle outline. When you release the button, the program fills in the rectangle. If you want, you can then define a new rectangle that replaces the first one.

BlockOut uses two *Boolean* variables stored as fields: *bBlocking* and *bValidBox*. The *bBlocking* variable indicates that the user is blocking out a rectangle. It is set to *True* during the *OnMouseDown* method and *False* during *OnMouseUp*. The *OnMouseMove* method tests the variable to determine what it should do. If *bBlocking* is *True*, *OnMouseMove* erases the previous rectangle outline by drawing it in the background color and draws a new rectangle outline in the foreground color. When you release the button, the *OnMouseUp* method sets *bBlocking* to *False* and *bValidBox* to *True*. This latter variable allows the *OnPaint* method to draw the filled rectangle.

Customarily, during the *OnMouseMove* method, I would use a technique called *exclusive-OR* (or *XOR*) *drawing*. XOR drawing is a technique that doesn't merely write colored pixels out to the display device but instead reverses the colors of the existing pixels. An XOR line drawn on a black background appears white, an XOR line drawn on a white background appears black, and an XOR line drawn on a cyan background appears red. The advantage of this technique is that a second XOR line of the same coordinates erases the first.

GDI+ doesn't support exclusive-OR drawing, however, which is why I'm forced to erase the previous rectangle by using the background color in the *OnMouseMove* method. When you're blocking out a new rectangle over an existing filled rectangle, some unsightly artifacts are created, and these must be cleaned up. That's why the *OnMouseMove* processing terminates with a call to

*Invalidate* to generate a *Paint* event. That *Invalidate* call isn't strictly needed, but if you remove it, you'll see why I felt compelled to include it. With XOR drawing, the *Invalidate* call wouldn't be necessary at all.

The omission of XOR drawing is certainly a flaw in GDI+, but BlockOut has some flaws of its own.

If you experiment a little, you'll see that the BlockOut program works just fine most of the time. Because the mouse is captured when you press the mouse button, you can move the mouse cursor outside the client area and the program will continue to get *OnMouseMove* calls. You can also release the mouse button outside the client area and the program will get a call to *OnMouseUp*.

But try this: While blocking out a rectangle with the left button held down, press and release the right button. When the right button is released, the form loses the mouse capture. It will now respond to mouse movement only when the mouse cursor is within the form's client area. Now move the mouse cursor outside the client area and release the left button. The form doesn't get a call to *OnMouseUp* because the mouse is no longer captured. Now move the mouse (with no buttons pressed) back inside the client area. The program responds to mouse movement even though no mouse button is pressed! This behavior is clearly undesirable.

A few fixes that help solve these problems are apparent:

- Tracking should be terminated whenever *any* button is released. This approach more closely mimics the way mouse capture is lost.

- *OnMouseMove* processing should include a check that the left button is still pressed. If a form loses the mouse capture, it's probably better for a rectangle outline to lie dormant rather than for the program to respond to mouse movement with no button pressed.

- Pressing the Esc key should terminate mouse tracking.

Here's a better version of the program.

**BetterBlockOut.vb**

```
'-------------------------------------------------
' BetterBlockOut.vb (c) 2002 by Charles Petzold
'-------------------------------------------------
Imports System
Imports System.Drawing
Imports System.Windows.Forms

Class BetterBlockOut
    Inherits Form
```

*(continued)*

**BetterBlockOut.vb**   *(continued)*

```vb
    Private bBlocking, bValidBox As Boolean
    Private ptBeg, ptEnd As Point
    Private rectBox As Rectangle

    Shared Sub Main()
        Application.Run(New BetterBlockOut())
    End Sub

    Sub New()
        Text = "Better Blockout"
        BackColor = SystemColors.Window
        ForeColor = SystemColors.WindowText
    End Sub

    Protected Overrides Sub OnMouseDown(ByVal mea As MouseEventArgs)
        If mea.Button = MouseButtons.Left Then
            ptBeg = New Point(mea.X, mea.Y)
            ptEnd = ptBeg
            Dim grfx As Graphics = CreateGraphics()
            grfx.DrawRectangle(New Pen(ForeColor), Rect(ptBeg, ptEnd))
            grfx.Dispose()
            bBlocking = True
        End If
    End Sub

    Protected Overrides Sub OnMouseMove(ByVal mea As MouseEventArgs)
        If bBlocking AndAlso (mea.Button And MouseButtons.Left) <> 0 Then
            Dim grfx As Graphics = CreateGraphics()
            grfx.DrawRectangle(New Pen(BackColor), Rect(ptBeg, ptEnd))
            ptEnd = New Point(mea.X, mea.Y)
            grfx.DrawRectangle(New Pen(ForeColor), Rect(ptBeg, ptEnd))
            grfx.Dispose()
            Invalidate()
        End If
    End Sub

    Protected Overrides Sub OnMouseUp(ByVal mea As MouseEventArgs)
        If bBlocking Then
            Dim grfx As Graphics = CreateGraphics()
            rectBox = Rect(ptBeg, New Point(mea.X, mea.Y))
            grfx.DrawRectangle(New Pen(ForeColor), rectBox)
            grfx.Dispose()
            bBlocking = False
            bValidBox = True
            Invalidate()
        End If
    End Sub

    Protected Overrides Sub OnKeyPress( _
            ByVal kpea As KeyPressEventArgs)
        If bBlocking AndAlso kpea.KeyChar = Chr(27) Then
            Dim grfx As Graphics = CreateGraphics()
            grfx.DrawRectangle(New Pen(BackColor), Rect(ptBeg, ptEnd))
```

```
            grfx.Dispose()
            bBlocking = False
            Invalidate()
        End If
    End Sub

    Protected Overrides Sub OnPaint(ByVal pea As PaintEventArgs)
        Dim grfx As Graphics = pea.Graphics
        If bValidBox Then
            grfx.FillRectangle(New SolidBrush(ForeColor), rectBox)
        End If
        If bBlocking Then
            grfx.DrawRectangle(New Pen(ForeColor), Rect(ptBeg, ptEnd))
        End If
    End Sub

    Private Function Rect(ByVal ptBeg As Point, _
                          ByVal ptEnd As Point) As Rectangle
        Return New Rectangle(Math.Min(ptBeg.X, ptEnd.X), _
                             Math.Min(ptBeg.Y, ptEnd.Y), _
                             Math.Abs(ptEnd.X - ptBeg.X), _
                             Math.Abs(ptEnd.Y - ptBeg.Y))
    End Function
End Class
```

In some situations, this program can still lose the mouse capture and not be aware of it. If you're in the middle of a tracking operation and you press CTRL+ESC to bring up the Start menu or you press ALT+TAB to switch to another program, both BlockOut and BetterBlockOut will lose the mouse capture and not even know it. Losing the mouse capture doesn't have to be the result of something weird that a user does. Suppose you're in the middle of a tracking operation and a message box pops up complaining that the printer has run out of paper. That occurrence also causes the program to lose the mouse capture because the message box needs to respond to mouse input.

Wouldn't it be nice if there were an event to tell a form when it's lost the mouse capture? Well, if we were writing a Win32 program, we'd be able to trap the *WM_CAPTURECHANGED* message. This message occurs whenever a window is losing the mouse capture, whether normally (when the mouse button is released) or abnormally. Is it possible to implement a handler for this message in a Windows Forms program?

Yes, it is, and to do it you override the *WndProc* ("window procedure") method implemented in the *Control* class and included in every class that derives from *Control*:

### *Control* Methods (selection)

```
Overridable Protected Sub WndProc(ByRef msg As Message)
```

Win32 API programmers will recognize *WndProc* as the standard name for the all-important function in every Windows application program that processes messages to the window that the program creates. As implemented in the *Control* class, *WndProc* has a single argument of type *Message* that includes all the arguments and return value of the normal Win32 window procedure:

### *Message* Properties

| Property | Type | Accessibility |
|----------|------|---------------|
| *HWnd* | *IntPtr* | Get/Set |
| *Msg* | *Integer* | Get/Set |
| *WParam* | *IntPtr* | Get/Set |
| *LParam* | *IntPtr* | Get/Set |
| *Result* | *IntPtr* | Get/Set |

The *Msg* property is a numeric value that indicates the particular message. These messages are documented in the Win32 header files used by C programmers. To work with the *WParam* and *LParam* properties, you'll probably need to cast them depending on the particular message you're dealing with.

Here's a simple program that demonstrates how to use the *WndProc* method to determine when a window has lost the mouse capture:

**CaptureLoss.vb**

```
'-----------------------------------------------
' CaptureLoss.vb (c) 2002 by Charles Petzold
'-----------------------------------------------
Imports System
Imports System.Drawing
Imports System.Windows.Forms

Class CaptureLoss
    Inherits Form

    Shared Sub Main()
        Application.Run(new CaptureLoss())
    End Sub

    Sub New()
        Text = "Capture Loss"
    End Sub
```

```
    Protected Overrides Sub WndProc(ByRef msg As Message)
        ' Process WM_CAPTURECHANGED message.
        If msg.Msg = 533 Then Invalidate()
        MyBase.WndProc(msg)
    End Sub

    Protected Overrides Sub OnMouseDown(ByVal mea As MouseEventArgs)
        Invalidate()
    End Sub

    Protected Overrides Sub OnPaint(ByVal pea As PaintEventArgs)
        Dim grfx As Graphics = pea.Graphics
        If Capture Then
            grfx.FillRectangle(Brushes.Red, ClientRectangle)
        Else
            grfx.FillRectangle(Brushes.Gray, ClientRectangle)
        End If
    End Sub
End Class
```

The *OnPaint* method in this program displays a red client area when the *Capture* property is *True* and a gray client area otherwise. The program invalidates its window whenever *OnMouseDown* is called (which is when the mouse has been captured) and also during the *WndProc* method when the *Msg* property equals 533. I obtained this value from the definition of *WM_CAPTURECHANGED* in the WINUSER.H header file.

It is imperative that your override of *WndProc* calls the base method for default processing of most messages:

```
MyBase.WndProc(msg)
```

Overriding the *WndProc* method is a very powerful tool, but you should use it only when you need a facility not otherwise exposed in the Windows Forms interface.

You can get a better view of mouse capturing if you enable the Show Window Contents While Dragging option in the Effects dialog of the Appearance tab in the Display Properties dialog box in Control Panel, and then experiment with the CaptureLoss program. You'll notice if you grab the title bar of the window and move it partially off screen and then back, the uncovered area of the client area will be colored red until you release the mouse button, at which point the entire client area turns gray again. If you make the window larger with the mouse, likewise the new area of the client area will be red, returning to gray when you release the mouse button. This happens because the *Capture* property is *True* even if the mouse button is pressed on the program's caption bar or sizing border.

Now let's use the *WndProc* method in a program that implements better block-out code:

**EvenBetterBlockOut.vb**

```
'--------------------------------------------------
' EvenBetterBlockOut  2001 by Charles Petzold
'--------------------------------------------------
Imports System
Imports System.Drawing
Imports System.Windows.Forms

Class EvenBetterBlockOut
    Inherits Form

    Private bBlocking, bValidBox As Boolean
    Private ptBeg, ptEnd As Point
    Private rectBox As Rectangle

    Shared Sub Main()
        Application.Run(New EvenBetterBlockOut())
    End Sub

    Sub New()
        Text = "Even Better Blockout"
        BackColor = SystemColors.Window
        ForeColor = SystemColors.WindowText
    End Sub

    Protected Overrides Sub WndProc(ByRef msg As Message)
        ' Process WM_CAPTURECHANGED message.
        If msg.Msg = 533 Then OnCaptureLost()
        MyBase.WndProc(msg)
    End Sub

    Protected Overrides Sub OnMouseDown(ByVal mea As MouseEventArgs)
        If mea.Button = MouseButtons.Left Then
            ptBeg = New Point(mea.X, mea.Y)
            ptEnd = ptBeg
            Dim grfx As Graphics = CreateGraphics()
            grfx.DrawRectangle(New Pen(ForeColor), Rect(ptBeg, ptEnd))
            grfx.Dispose()
            bBlocking = True
        End If
    End Sub

    Protected Overrides Sub OnMouseMove(ByVal mea As MouseEventArgs)
        If bBlocking Then
            Dim grfx As Graphics = CreateGraphics()
            grfx.DrawRectangle(New Pen(BackColor), Rect(ptBeg, ptEnd))
            ptEnd = New Point(mea.X, mea.Y)
```

```
            grfx.DrawRectangle(New Pen(ForeColor), Rect(ptBeg, ptEnd))
            grfx.Dispose()
            Invalidate()
        End If
    End Sub

    Protected Overrides Sub OnMouseUp(ByVal mea As MouseEventArgs)
        If bBlocking Then
            Dim grfx As Graphics = CreateGraphics()
            rectBox = Rect(ptBeg, New Point(mea.X, mea.Y))
            grfx.DrawRectangle(New Pen(BackColor), rectBox)
            grfx.Dispose()
            bBlocking = False
            bValidBox = True
            Invalidate()
        End If
    End Sub

    Protected Overrides Sub OnKeyPress( ByVal kpea As KeyPressEventArgs)
        If kpea.KeyChar = Chr(27) Then Capture = False
    End Sub

    Protected Sub OnCaptureLost()
        If bBlocking Then
            Dim grfx As Graphics = CreateGraphics()
            grfx.DrawRectangle(New Pen(BackColor), Rect(ptBeg, ptEnd))
            grfx.Dispose()
            bBlocking = False
            Invalidate()
        End If
    End Sub

    Protected Overrides Sub OnPaint(ByVal pea As PaintEventArgs)
        Dim grfx As Graphics = pea.Graphics
        If bValidBox Then
            grfx.FillRectangle(New SolidBrush(ForeColor), rectBox)
        End If
        If bBlocking Then
            grfx.DrawRectangle(New Pen(ForeColor), Rect(ptBeg, ptEnd))
        End If
    End Sub

    Private Function Rect(ByVal ptBeg As Point, _
                          ByVal ptEnd As Point) As Rectangle
        Return New Rectangle(Math.Min(ptBeg.X, ptEnd.X), _
                             Math.Min(ptBeg.Y, ptEnd.Y), _
                             Math.Abs(ptEnd.X - ptBeg.X), _
                             Math.Abs(ptEnd.Y - ptBeg.Y))
    End Function
End Class
```

Like CaptureLoss, this program overrides the *WndProc* method. On receipt of the *WM_CAPTURECHANGED* message, it calls a method named *OnCaptureLost*, which is implemented later in the program. The program completes the tracking operation normally when it gets a call to *OnMouseUp* and aborts the tracking operation when it gets a call to *OnLostCapture* that wasn't preceded by *OnMouseUp*.

EvenBetterBlockOut finally accommodates all the ways in which a program can lose the mouse capture.

# Clicks and Double-Clicks

Here are the two highest-level mouse events:

### *Control* Events (selection)

| Event | Method | Delegate | Argument |
|---|---|---|---|
| *Click* | *OnClick* | *EventHandler* | *EventArgs* |
| *DoubleClick* | *OnDoubleClick* | *EventHandler* | *EventArgs* |

Notice that the *EventArgs* argument doesn't give you any information specific to the mouse. It doesn't even tell you what button was clicked or double-clicked, or where the mouse was located.

The *Click* event occurs when any mouse button is pressed and released over a control or the client area of a form. The event occurs right before the corresponding *MouseUp* event. If you press the mouse button while the mouse cursor is positioned over one control and release the mouse button over another control, a *Click* event is not generated.

The *DoubleClick* event occurs when the mouse is clicked twice. The event occurs right before the second *MouseUp* event. However, the second button-down must occur within a certain period of time and within a certain distance of the first. Here's a typical sequence of events for a double-click:

- *MouseDown* (*Clicks* property set to 1)

- *Click*

- *MouseUp*

- *MouseMove*

- *MouseDown* (*Clicks* property set to 2)

- *DoubleClick*

- *MouseUp*

- *MouseMove*

I used the *OnClick* method to trigger printing in the PrintableForm program in Chapter 5. Obviously, I didn't need to know where the mouse cursor was located when the button was pressed, or even which button was pressed.

It's more common for a program to install *Click* and *DoubleClick* event handlers for controls that it has created. For example, handling a button control's *Click* event is the normal way for a form to determine when the button has been clicked, as you'll discover in Chapter 12. Buttons (and other controls) also generate *Click* events when the keyboard is used to press the button, so the *Click* event is a convenient consolidation of keyboard and mouse input.

# Mouse-Related Properties

Although the *Click* and *DoubleClick* events aren't delivered with a *MouseEventArgs* object that indicates the location of the mouse cursor, that doesn't mean the information isn't available. The *Control* class supports two read-only shared properties that indicate the position of the mouse and which buttons are currently pressed:

*Control* **Shared Properties (selection)**

| Property | Type | Accessibility | Description |
|----------|------|---------------|-------------|
| *MousePosition* | *Point* | Get | Returns the position of the mouse in screen coordinates |
| *MouseButtons* | *MouseButtons* | Get | Returns which buttons are currently pressed |

You can use these properties while processing any event. Because they are shared properties, you can even use them in a class not descended from *Control*.

Keep in mind that the *X* and *Y* properties of *MouseEventArgs* indicate the mouse cursor location in client area coordinates, and the *Control.MousePosition* property gives the position in screen coordinates. You'll have to use *PointToClient* to convert screen coordinates to client area coordinates if that's what you need.

I introduced the shared property *Control.ModifierKeys* in Chapter 6 because it pertains to the keyboard:

*Control* **Shared Properties (selection)**

| Property | Type | Accessibility | Description |
|----------|------|---------------|-------------|
| *ModifierKeys* | *Keys* | Get | Status of Shift, Ctrl, and Alt keys |

However, as I mentioned at that time, this property is most often used when processing mouse events. For example, if you want to initiate an action when the user presses the left mouse button with the Shift key (and only the Shift key) pressed, the *OnMouseDown* processing might look like this:

```
If mea.Button = Buttons.Left AndAlso _
    Control.ModifierKeys = Keys.Shift Then
    ...
End If
```

# Entering, Leaving, Hovering

Here are the final three mouse events:

### *Control* Events (selection)

| Event | Method | Delegate | Argument |
|-------|--------|----------|----------|
| *MouseEnter* | *OnMouseEnter* | *EventHandler* | *EventArgs* |
| *MouseLeave* | *OnMouseLeave* | *EventHandler* | *EventArgs* |
| *MouseHover* | *OnMouseHover* | *EventHandler* | *EventArgs* |

The *MouseEnter* event announces to a control (or a client area of a form) that the mouse cursor has been moved on top of the control. The control may want to change its appearance in response to this event. The *MouseLeave* event tells the control that the mouse is no longer located on top of the control.

The *MouseHover* event occurs after the cursor has entered the control (or the client area) and has stopped moving. The *MouseHover* event occurs at most only once between *MouseEnter* and *MouseLeave* events.

Here's a program that provides a visual indication of these three events. The client area is colored green following a call to *OnMouseEnter* and restored to the normal background color following the *OnMouseLeave* call. In response to *OnMouseHover*, the client area is colored red for 1/10 second.

```
EnterLeave.vb
'-------------------------------------------------
' EnterLeave.vb (c) 2002 by Charles Petzold
'-------------------------------------------------
Imports System
Imports System.Drawing
Imports System.Windows.Forms

Class EnterLeave
    Inherits Form
```

```
    Private bInside As Boolean = False

    Shared Sub Main()
        Application.Run(New EnterLeave())
    End Sub

    Sub New()
        Text = "Enter/Leave"
    End Sub

    Protected Overrides Sub OnMouseEnter(ByVal ea As EventArgs)
        bInside = True
        Invalidate()
    End Sub

    Protected Overrides Sub OnMouseLeave(ByVal ea As EventArgs)
        bInside = False
        Invalidate()
    End Sub

    Protected Overrides Sub OnMouseHover(ByVal ea As EventArgs)
        Dim grfx As Graphics = CreateGraphics()
        grfx.Clear(Color.Red)
        System.Threading.Thread.Sleep(100)
        grfx.Clear(Color.Green)
        grfx.Dispose()
    End Sub

    Protected Overrides Sub OnPaint(ByVal pea As PaintEventArgs)
        Dim grfx As Graphics = pea.Graphics

        If bInside Then
            grfx.Clear(Color.Green)
        Else
            grfx.Clear(BackColor)
        End If
    End Sub
End Class
```

# The Mouse Cursor

The mouse cursor is the little bitmap image you see on the screen that indicates the location of the mouse. As you know, the cursor can change appearance depending on its location. Often it's an arrow, but if you pass it over a sizing border of a form, it changes into a double-headed arrow. In a text-entry field, the cursor becomes a vertical I-beam.

The mouse cursor is an object of type *Cursor*, a class defined in the *System.Windows.Forms* namespace. I'll describe the *Cursor* class in more detail in

Chapter 11. In most cases, the easiest way to get a cursor object is by using the *Cursors* class. (Notice the plural.) The *Cursors* class—also defined in the *System.Windows.Forms* namespace—consists solely of 28 shared read-only properties that return predefined objects of type *Cursor*:

### *Cursors* Shared Read-Only Properties

| | |
|---|---|
| *AppStarting* | *PanNorth* |
| *Arrow* | *PanNW* |
| *Cross* | *PanSE* |
| *Default* | *PanSouth* |
| *Hand* | *PanSW* |
| *Help* | *PanWest* |
| *HSplit* | *SizeAll* |
| *Ibeam* | *SizeNESW* |
| *No* | *SizeNS* |
| *NoMove2D* | *SizeNWSE* |
| *NoMoveHoriz* | *SizeWE* |
| *NoMoveVert* | *UpArrow* |
| *PanEast* | *VSplit* |
| *PanNE* | *WaitCursor* |

Even if you obtain *Cursor* objects only from the *Cursors* class, there are still three shared properties of the *Cursor* class that are useful:

### *Cursor* Shared Properties

| Property | Type | Accessibility |
|---|---|---|
| *Current* | *Cursor* | Get/Set |
| *Position* | *Point* | Get/Set |
| *Clip* | *Rectangle* | Get/Set |

You'll recall that the *Control* class includes a shared property named *MousePosition*, but that property is read-only. You can't use it to set the mouse cursor position. But unlike *MousePosition*, the *Cursor.Position* property is writable. Although it's not common for applications to set the position of the mouse cursor, the Bezier program in Chapter 13 uses *Cursor.Position* to set the cursor position. The *Cursor.Clip* property limits the movement of the mouse cursor to a specified rectangle. You can set this property only if the mouse is captured. The *Position* and *Clip* properties are both in screen coordinates, so you probably need to use *PointToClient* after obtaining the properties or *PointToScreen* before setting the properties.

You can also set the current mouse cursor by using the *Cursor.Current* property. However, you might find that this approach doesn't always work. But let me show you first a couple cases in which the *Cursor.Current* property *does* work.

As you know, programs that must perform lengthy jobs generally display a cursor shaped like an hourglass, which is the predefined *Cursors.WaitCursor* object. A program can display the hourglass cursor using the statement

```
Cursor.Current = Cursors.WaitCursor
```

The program can then carry out the lengthy job it needs to do and afterward restore the arrow cursor by calling

```
Cursor.Current = Cursors.Arrow
```

However, if the user is running Windows without a mouse installed, the hourglass cursor won't be visible. To display a mouse cursor regardless of whether or not a mouse is installed, a program can make use of the following two shared methods of the *Cursor* class:

### *Cursor* Shared Methods

```
Sub Show()
Sub Hide()
```

You can think of the mouse cursor as having a *show-count* variable associated with it. If a mouse is installed, this show-count variable is initially set to 1. If a mouse is not installed, the show-count is initially 0. The *Cursor.Show* method increments the show-count; the *Cursor.Hide* method decrements it. The mouse cursor is visible if the show-count is greater than 0 and hidden otherwise.

What this means is that an application must balance its calls to *Cursor.Show* and *Cursor.Hide*. If a program calls *Show* more than *Hide*, it risks leaving a visible mouse cursor on the screen when a mouse isn't installed. If a program calls *Hide* more than *Show*, the mouse cursor is made invisible. Fortunately, this problem affects the mouse cursor only when the mouse is positioned over the errant application.

One program in this chapter that might spend a considerable amount of time in its *OnPaint* method is MouseConnect. Here's a program that subclasses the *MouseConnect* class and displays an hourglass cursor during the *OnPaint* processing.

## MouseConnectWaitCursor.vb

```
' ------------------------------------------------------
' MouseConnectWaitCursor.vb (c) 2002 by Charles Petzold
' ------------------------------------------------------
Imports System
Imports System.Drawing
Imports System.Windows.Forms

Class MouseConnectWaitCursor
    Inherits MouseConnect

    Shared Shadows Sub Main()
        Application.Run(New MouseConnectWaitCursor())
    End Sub

    Sub New()
        Text = "Mouse Connect with Wait Cursor"
    End Sub

    Protected Overrides Sub OnPaint(ByVal pea As PaintEventArgs)
        Cursor.Current = Cursors.WaitCursor
        Cursor.Show()
        MyBase.OnPaint(pea)
        Cursor.Hide()
        Cursor.Current = Cursors.Arrow
    End Sub
End Class
```

In this particular case, the calls to *Show* and *Hide* methods aren't necessary because if the mouse weren't installed, the user couldn't have initiated a long *OnPaint* call to begin with!

This next program uses a call to *Cursor.Current* during the *OnMouseMove* call to let you see what all 28 predefined cursors look like.

## MouseCursors.vb

```
' --------------------------------------------------
' MouseCursors.vb (c) 2002 by Charles Petzold
' --------------------------------------------------
Imports System
Imports System.Drawing
Imports System.Windows.Forms

Class MouseCursors
    Inherits Form

    Private acursor() As Cursor = _
    { _
        Cursors.AppStarting, Cursors.Arrow, Cursors.Cross, _
        Cursors.Default, Cursors.Hand, Cursors.Help, _
        Cursors.HSplit, Cursors.IBeam, Cursors.No, _
```

```
            Cursors.NoMove2D, Cursors.NoMoveHoriz, Cursors.NoMoveVert, _
            Cursors.PanEast, Cursors.PanNE, Cursors.PanNorth, _
            Cursors.PanNW, Cursors.PanSE, Cursors.PanSouth, _
            Cursors.PanSW, Cursors.PanWest, Cursors.SizeAll, _
            Cursors.SizeNESW, Cursors.SizeNS, Cursors.SizeNWSE, _
            Cursors.SizeWE, Cursors.UpArrow, Cursors.VSplit, _
            Cursors.WaitCursor _
    }
    Private astrCursor() As String = _
    { _
            "AppStarting", "Arrow", "Cross", "Default", "Hand", _
            "Help", "HSplit", "IBeam", "No", "NoMove2D", _
            "NoMoveHoriz", "NoMoveVert", "PanEast", "PanNE", "PanNorth", _
            "PanNW", "PanSE", "PanSouth", "PanSW", "PanWest", _
            "SizeAll", "SizeNESW", "SizeNS", "SizeNWSE", "SizeWE", _
            "UpArrow", "VSplit", "WaitCursor" _
    }

    Shared Sub Main()
        Application.Run(New MouseCursors())
    End Sub

    Sub New()
        Text = "Mouse Cursors"
        BackColor = SystemColors.Window
        ForeColor = SystemColors.WindowText
        ResizeRedraw = True
    End Sub

    Protected Overrides Sub OnMouseMove(ByVal mea As MouseEventArgs)
        Dim x As Integer = Math.Max(0, _
                            Math.Min(3, mea.X \ (ClientSize.Width \ 4)))
        Dim y As Integer = Math.Max(0, _
                            Math.Min(6, mea.Y \ (ClientSize.Height \ 7)))
        Cursor.Current = acursor(4 * y + x)
    End Sub

    Protected Overrides Sub OnPaint(ByVal pea As PaintEventArgs)
        Dim grfx As Graphics = pea.Graphics
        Dim x, y As Integer
        Dim br As New SolidBrush(ForeColor)
        Dim pn As New Pen(ForeColor)
        Dim strfmt As New StringFormat()
        strfmt.Alignment = StringAlignment.Center
        strfmt.LineAlignment = StringAlignment.Center

        For y = 0 To 6
            For x = 0 To 3
                Dim rect As Rectangle = Rectangle.FromLTRB( _
                            x * ClientSize.Width \ 4, _
                            y * ClientSize.Height \ 7, _
```

*(continued)*

**MouseCursors.vb**  *(continued)*

```
                                (x + 1) * ClientSize.Width \ 4, _
                                (y + 1) * ClientSize.Height \ 7)
                grfx.DrawRectangle(pn, rect)
                grfx.DrawString(astrCursor(4 * y + x), Font, _
                                br, RectangleF.op_Implicit(rect), strfmt)
            Next x
        Next y
    End Sub
End Class
```

The program displays a grid containing the names of the *Cursors* properties. Simply move the mouse cursor to one of the boxes to see what the cursor looks like. Here's a screen shot that shows the *Cursors.Help* cursor:

| Mouse Cursors | | | |
|---|---|---|---|
| AppStarting | Arrow | Cross | Default |
| Hand | Help | HSplit | IBeam |
| No | NoMove2D | NoMoveHoriz | NoMoveVert |
| PanEast | PanNE | PanNorth | PanNW |
| PanSE | PanSouth | PanSW | PanWest |
| SizeAll | SizeNESW | SizeNS | SizeNWSE |
| SizeWE | UpArrow | VSplit | WaitCursor |

I mentioned earlier that *Cursor.Current* doesn't always work. It certainly works in these two programs, but they illustrate the only two ways in which *Cursor.Current* can be used. Here's the important rule: If your form (or any descendant of *Control*) does not set *Cursor.Current* during the *MouseMove* event, the mouse cursor will be set instead to the normal cursor associated with the form (or control) during that event. The MouseCursors program works because it sets *Cursor.Current* during the call to *OnMouseMove*.

What about MouseConnectWaitCursor? That one doesn't set *Cursor.Current* during *OnMouseMove*. But that program sets *Cursor.Current* during *OnPaint* and then resets the property before *OnPaint* is concluded. The program doesn't get *OnMouseMove* calls during that time. A method in a program is never interrupted to execute another method in the same thread.

What you can't do, however, is set *Cursor.Current* during a constructor or an *OnMouseDown* event or some other event and expect it to stick. As soon as the program gets a call to *OnMouseMove*, the cursor will be reset.

However, there is a way to set the cursor once and then forget about it. You assign a cursor to a control (or a form) by using the *Cursor* property defined in the *Control* class:

### *Control* Properties (selection)

| Property | Type | Accessibility |
|----------|------|---------------|
| *Cursor* | *Cursor* | Get/Set |

For example, in a form's constructor, you can call

```
Cursor = Cursors.Hand
```

and the cursor will be a hand whenever you pass the mouse cursor over the form's client area. It will remain a hand until the program sets it to something else. I mentioned earlier that if you don't set *Cursor.Current* during the *OnMouseMove* method, the cursor is set to the normal cursor associated with the form or control. It's actually set to the value of the *Cursor* property. Somewhere behind the scenes, something equivalent to the following statement probably occurs during mouse movement before a Windows Forms program gets a call to *OnMouseMove*:

```
Cursor.Current = Cursor
```

That's the *Cursor* class on the left and the form's *Cursor* property on the right. The *Current* property of the *Cursor* class is shared. The *Cursor* property of the *Control* class is not.

It makes sense that a control should have a cursor associated with it because some controls have different cursors. The most obvious examples are the text-entry controls *TextBox* and *RichTextBox*, which are associated with *Cursors.IBeam*.

Let's experiment with this technique by creating a program similar in functionality to MouseCursors. But instead of creating 28 boxes, I want to create 28 controls and assign each of them a different mouse cursor.

Back in Chapter 4, I created a *Panel* control in the SysInfoPanel program. I mentioned at the time that *Panel* controls were rather innocuous and didn't do much. But the panel suited our purposes in providing a surface for us on which to draw. The *Label* control is also a fairly benign control. The sole purpose of *Label* is to display some text. Here's a program that creates an array of 28 *Label* controls, each of which is assigned a different cursor.

**MouseCursorsProperty.vb**

```vb
'------------------------------------------------------------
' MouseCursorsProperty.vb (c) 2002 by Charles Petzold
'------------------------------------------------------------
Imports System
Imports System.Drawing
Imports System.Windows.Forms

Class MouseCursorsProperty
    Inherits Form

    Private actrl(28) As Label

    Shared Sub Main()
        Application.Run(New MouseCursorsProperty())
    End Sub

    Sub New()
        Dim i As Integer
        Dim acursor() As Cursor = _
        { _
            Cursors.AppStarting, Cursors.Arrow, Cursors.Cross, _
            Cursors.Default, Cursors.Hand, Cursors.Help, _
            Cursors.HSplit, Cursors.IBeam, Cursors.No, _
            Cursors.NoMove2D, Cursors.NoMoveHoriz, Cursors.NoMoveVert, _
            Cursors.PanEast, Cursors.PanNE, Cursors.PanNorth, _
            Cursors.PanNW, Cursors.PanSE, Cursors.PanSouth, _
            Cursors.PanSW, Cursors.PanWest, Cursors.SizeAll, _
            Cursors.SizeNESW, Cursors.SizeNS, Cursors.SizeNWSE, _
            Cursors.SizeWE, Cursors.UpArrow, Cursors.VSplit, _
            Cursors.WaitCursor _
        }
        Dim astrCursor() As String = _
        { _
            "AppStarting", "Arrow", "Cross", "Default", "Hand", _
            "Help", "HSplit", "IBeam", "No", "NoMove2D", _
            "NoMoveHoriz", "NoMoveVert", "PanEast", "PanNE", "PanNorth", _
            "PanNW", "PanSE", "PanSouth", "PanSW", "PanWest", _
            "SizeAll", "SizeNESW", "SizeNS", "SizeNWSE", "SizeWE", _
            "UpArrow", "VSplit", "WaitCursor" _
        }
        Text = "Mouse Cursors Using Cursor Property"

        For i = 0 To 27
            actrl(i) = New Label()
            actrl(i).Parent = Me
            actrl(i).Text = astrCursor(i)
            actrl(i).Cursor = acursor(i)
            actrl(i).BorderStyle = BorderStyle.FixedSingle
```

```
        Next i
        OnResize(EventArgs.Empty)
    End Sub

    Protected Overrides Sub OnResize(ByVal ea As EventArgs)
        Dim i As Integer
        For i = 0 To 27
            actrl(i).Bounds = Rectangle.FromLTRB( _
                            (i Mod 4) * ClientSize.Width \ 4, _
                            (i \ 4) * ClientSize.Height \ 7, _
                            (i Mod 4 + 1) * ClientSize.Width \ 4, _
                            (i \ 4 + 1) * ClientSize.Height \ 7)

        Next i
    End Sub
End Class
```

The program creates the 28 *Label* objects during the form's constructor and saves them in an array named *actrl*, which is a field of the class. The constructor sets four properties of each *Label* object. The first of these four properties indicates that the parent of the control is the form, which means that the control will appear on the surface of the form's client area:

```
actrl(i).Parent = Me
```

The *Text* property of the control is set to the name of one of the 28 predefined cursors:

```
actrl(i).Text = astrCursor(i)
```

The program also sets the *Cursor* property of the control to the corresponding *Cursor* object:

```
actrl(i).Cursor = acursor(i)
```

Finally, the *BorderStyle* property is set to a single line:

```
actrl(i).BorderStyle = BorderStyle.FixedSingle
```

What the constructor doesn't do is set the location and size of the control. The control's location and size are set during the form's *OnResize* method. Each control gets a size equal to 1/4 the width and 1/7 the height of the form's client area. (Well, not quite. Setting all the controls to the same width and height caused some rounding problems that resulted in gaps between the controls. The calculation of the controls' *Bounds* property using the *Rectangle.FromLTRB* method helps avoid that problem.)

The program looks similar to the early MouseCursors program. As you pass the mouse cursor over each control, the cursor changes automatically without any need to process the *MouseMove* event.

# An Exercise in Hit-Testing

When you draw graphics figures or text on your form, you determine the coordinates of each item and call the appropriate methods to draw it. Often, however, a program uses a mouse interface to allow a user to point to and manipulate these items. That means that your program must work backward from the pointer coordinates to determine which graphical item the mouse is pointing to.

This process is called *hit-testing*, and it can tend to be quite complex, particularly if your client window contains figures that overlap or text in a variable-pitch font. But in some cases, hit-testing is fairly straightforward. In fact, the MouseCursors program shown earlier in this chapter used hit-testing to determine which mouse cursor to display.

The Checker program draws an array of boxes covering its client area. If you click one of these boxes with the mouse, the box is filled with an X. Click it again and the X disappears.

### Checker.vb

```
'----------------------------------------------
' Checker.vb (c) 2002 by Charles Petzold
'----------------------------------------------
Imports System
Imports System.Drawing
Imports System.Windows.Forms

Class Checker
    Inherits Form

    Protected Const xNum As Integer = 5  ' Number of boxes horizontally
    Protected Const yNum As Integer = 4  ' Number of boxes vertically
    Protected abChecked(yNum, xNum) As Boolean
    Protected cxBlock, cyBlock As Integer

    Shared Sub Main()
        Application.Run(New Checker())
    End Sub

    Sub New()
        Text = "Checker"
        BackColor = SystemColors.Window
        ForeColor = SystemColors.WindowText
        ResizeRedraw = True
        OnResize(EventArgs.Empty)
    End Sub
```

```
    Protected Overrides Sub OnResize(ByVal ea As EventArgs)
        MyBase.OnResize(ea)        ' Or else ResizeRedraw doesn't work
        cxBlock = ClientSize.Width \ xNum
        cyBlock = ClientSize.Height \ yNum
    End Sub

    Protected Overrides Sub OnMouseUp(ByVal mea As MouseEventArgs)
        Dim x As Integer = mea.X \ cxBlock
        Dim y As Integer = mea.Y \ cyBlock

        If x < xNum AndAlso y < yNum Then
            abChecked(y, x) = Not abChecked(y, x)
            Invalidate(New Rectangle(x * cxBlock, y * cyBlock, _
                                cxBlock, cyBlock))
        End If
    End Sub

    Protected Overrides Sub OnPaint(ByVal pea As PaintEventArgs)
        Dim grfx As Graphics = pea.Graphics
        Dim x, y As Integer
        Dim pn As New Pen(ForeColor)

        For y = 0 To yNum - 1
            For x = 0 To xNum - 1
                grfx.DrawRectangle(pn, x * cxBlock, y * cyBlock, _
                                cxBlock, cyBlock)
                If abChecked(y, x) Then
                    grfx.DrawLine(pn, x * cxBlock, y * cyBlock, _
                                (x + 1) * cxBlock, (y + 1) * cyBlock)
                    grfx.DrawLine(pn, x * cxBlock, (y + 1) * cyBlock, _
                                (x + 1) * cxBlock, y * cyBlock)
                End If
            Next x
        Next y
    End Sub
End Class
```

Whenever the form is resized, the program recalculates *cxBlock* and *cyBlock* values, which indicate the size of each box. The program also maintains an array of *Boolean* values named *abChecked* that indicate whether a particular box is checked. The *OnPaint* method draws an outline around each box and, if *abChecked* for that box is *True*, draws an X in the box.

The hit-testing occurs during the *OnMouseUp* method. (I chose *OnMouseUp* rather than *OnMouseDown* to more closely mimic *OnClick*, which occurs when the mouse button is released.) The program divides the mouse coordinates by *cxBlock* and *cyBlock* to get indices of *abChecked*. It then inverts the *Boolean* value and invalidates the corresponding rectangle.

Here's a typical Checker display after a few boxes have been checked:

# Adding a Keyboard Interface

I said at the outset of this chapter that you should try to write your Windows Forms programs so they are usable with either a mouse or the keyboard. I've been shamelessly ignoring my own rule to concentrate on mouse logic. However, I think this is a good opportunity to see what's involved in emulating the mouse with the keyboard in the Checker program.

The first decision you have to make is how the keyboard interface should work. For this program, a reasonable approach might be to let the user move the mouse cursor around the client area using the arrow keys and other cursor-movement keys. You could simulate a mouse click by using the Enter key or the spacebar.

This *CheckerWithKeyboard* class subclasses *Checker* and provides a keyboard interface.

### CheckerWithKeyboard.vb

```
'-----------------------------------------------------
' CheckerWithKeyboard.vb (c) 2002 by Charles Petzold
'-----------------------------------------------------
Imports System
Imports System.Drawing
Imports System.Windows.Forms

Class CheckerWithKeyboard
    Inherits Checker

    Shared Shadows Sub Main()
        Application.Run(New CheckerWithKeyboard())
    End Sub
```

```vb
Sub New()
    Text &= " with Keyboard Interface"
End Sub

Protected Overrides Sub OnGotFocus(ByVal ea As EventArgs)
    Cursor.Show()
End Sub

Protected Overrides Sub OnLostFocus(ByVal ea As EventArgs)
    Cursor.Hide()
End Sub

Protected Overrides Sub OnKeyDown(ByVal kea As KeyEventArgs)
    Dim ptCursor As Point = PointToClient(Cursor.Position)
    Dim x As Integer = Math.Max(0, _
                        Math.Min(xNum - 1, ptCursor.X \ cxBlock))
    Dim y As Integer = Math.Max(0, _
                        Math.Min(yNum - 1, ptCursor.Y \ cyBlock))
    Select Case kea.KeyCode
        Case Keys.Up
            y -= 1
        Case Keys.Down
            y += 1
        Case Keys.Left
            x -= 1
        Case Keys.Right
            x += 1
        Case Keys.Home
            x = 0
            y = 0
        Case Keys.End : x = xNum - 1
            y = yNum - 1
        Case Keys.Enter, Keys.Space
            abChecked(y, x) = Not abChecked(y, x)
            Invalidate(New Rectangle(x * cxBlock, y * cyBlock, _
                            cxBlock, cyBlock))
            Return
        Case Else
            Return
    End Select

    x = (x + xNum) Mod xNum
    y = (y + yNum) Mod yNum

    Cursor.Position = PointToScreen( _
                        New Point(x * cxBlock + cxBlock \ 2, _
                                y * cyBlock + cyBlock \ 2))
End Sub
End Class
```

Let's take a look at the *OnKeyDown* processing first. The progra
the current cursor position by using *Cursor.Position* and converts th
to client area coordinates. The *x* and *y* variables indicate the row and
the box that the cursor is closest to, where *x* ranges from 0 to one less
number of boxes horizontally, and *y* ranges from 0 to one less than th
of boxes vertically.

For cursor-movement keys, the program modifies the *x* and *y*
The Home key moves the cursor to the upper left box; the End key m
the lower right box. For the Enter key or the spacebar, the program r
does to *OnMouseUp*. It toggles the check-mark variable and invalidates
angle. The *OnKeyDown* processing concludes by calculating a new m
sor position and setting the *Cursor.Position* property.

By itself, such *OnKeyDown* processing would work fine except fo
tle problem: such a keyboard interface is most important if a mo
installed. Yet, if a mouse isn't installed, the cursor isn't visible! That's
program also overrides the *OnGotFocus* and *OnLostFocus* methods an
calls *Cursor.Show* and *Cursor.Hide*.

## Putting the Children to Work

Do the X marks in Checker remind you of anything? Perhaps very large
of check boxes such as those seen in Windows dialog boxes? As we sa
MouseCursorsProperty program, controls can help you structure and m
ize your programs, and they particularly help in hit-testing.

So far, I've demonstrated some simple uses of the *Panel* control
*Label* control. But you can get even simpler than what I've shown. It's
essary to use one of the predefined controls. You can create your own
by subclassing the *Control* class. *Control* is the basis of all the predefin
trols in Windows Forms. When you create your own controls, however,
ommended that you derive from *UserControl*, which derives from *Con*
way of *ScrollableControl* and *ContainerControl*.

Here's a class derived from *UserControl* that has a single *Boolea*
which it toggles in response to an *OnClick* call. During the *OnPaint* me
draws a border around itself and, if the *Boolean* variable is set to *True*,

**CheckerChild.vb**

```
'-------------------------------------------------
' CheckerChild.vb (c) 2002 by Charles Petzold
'-------------------------------------------------
Imports System
Imports System.Drawing
Imports System.Windows.Forms

Class CheckerChild
    Inherits UserControl

    Private bChecked As Boolean = False

    Sub New()
        ResizeRedraw = True
    End Sub

    Protected Overrides Sub OnClick(ByVal ea As EventArgs)
        MyBase.OnClick(ea)
        bChecked = Not bChecked
        Invalidate()
    End Sub

    Protected Overrides Sub OnKeyDown(ByVal kea As KeyEventArgs)
        If kea.KeyCode = Keys.Enter OrElse kea.KeyCode = Keys.Space Then
            OnClick(New EventArgs())
        End If
    End Sub

    Protected Overrides Sub OnPaint(ByVal pea As PaintEventArgs)
        Dim grfx As Graphics = pea.Graphics
        Dim pn As New Pen(ForeColor)
        grfx.DrawRectangle(pn, 0, 0, Width - 1, Height - 1)
        If bChecked Then
            grfx.DrawLine(pn, 0, 0, ClientSize.Width, ClientSize.Height)
            grfx.DrawLine(pn, 0, ClientSize.Height, ClientSize.Width, 0)
        End If
    End Sub
End Class
```

The class also responds to a depression of the Enter or spacebar key by simulating an *OnClick* method call.

The following program creates 20 of these controls and puts them on the surface of the client area. In this way, it's very similar to the MouseCursorsProperty program shown earlier except that it's using this custom control rather than a *Label* control. The hard part is the *OnResize* call when the form must change the *Location* and *Size* of each of the controls.

**CheckerWithChildren.vb**

```
'-----------------------------------------------------
' CheckerWithChildren.vb (c) 2002 by Charles Petzold
'-----------------------------------------------------
Imports System
Imports System.Drawing
Imports System.Windows.Forms

Class CheckerWithChildren
    Inherits Form

    Protected Const xNum As Integer = 5
    Protected Const yNum As Integer = 4
    Protected actrlChild(,) As CheckerChild

    Shared Sub Main()
        Application.Run(New CheckerWithChildren())
    End Sub

    Sub New()
        Text = "Checker with Children"
        BackColor = SystemColors.Window
        ForeColor = SystemColors.WindowText
        CreateChildren()
        OnResize(EventArgs.Empty)
    End Sub

    Protected Overridable Sub CreateChildren()
        ReDim actrlChild(yNum - 1, xNum - 1)
        Dim x, y As Integer

        For y = 0 To yNum - 1
            For x = 0 To xNum - 1
                actrlChild(y, x) = New CheckerChild()
                actrlChild(y, x).Parent = Me
            Next x
        Next y
    End Sub

    Protected Overrides Sub OnResize(ByVal ea As EventArgs)
        Dim cxBlock As Integer = ClientSize.Width \ xNum
        Dim cyBlock As Integer = ClientSize.Height \ yNum
        Dim x, y As Integer

        For y = 0 To yNum - 1
            For x = 0 To xNum - 1
                actrlChild(y, x).Location = _
                            New Point(x * cxBlock, y * cyBlock)
                actrlChild(y, x).Size = New Size(cxBlock, cyBlock)
            Next x
        Next y
    End Sub
End Class
```

Here's the really nice thing about this program: no hit-testing! The child control doesn't care *where* it gets clicked. If it gets a call to *OnClick*, it toggles the check mark. Windows itself is doing all the hit-testing by determining which control the mouse click should go to.

In this particular case, the parent form isn't interested in when the child gets clicked. But it could fairly easily install event handlers for the control's *Click* event. (The *OnClick* method in CheckerChild calls *base.OnClick* to ensure that *Click* event handlers are called.) The form would need a method defined like so:

```
Sub ChildOnClick(ByVal obj As Object, ByVal ea As EventArgs)
    ...
End Sub
```

And then in the loop when creating the controls, event handlers would be installed like so:

```
AddHandler acntlChild(y, x).Click, AddressOf ChildOnClick
```

The *bChecked* field of *CheckerChild* could be made *Public* so that the parent could find the state of each child. Or *CheckerChild* could implement a property that provides access to the value.

Does the CheckerWithChildren program have a keyboard interface? Funny you should ask. If you run the program and press Enter or the spacebar, you'll toggle the X in the box in the upper left corner. Now press the Tab key seven times. Or the Right Arrow key, or the Down Arrow key, or any combination of these three keys seven times. Now press Enter or the spacebar. The box that gets toggled this time is the one in the middle of the second row.

Without any effort on the programmer's part, the form is responding to the Tab key and arrow keys by shifting the input focus among the 20 controls. The 20 controls were created in a particular order starting with the one in the upper left corner and then across each row, and then down to the next row. The Tab, Right Arrow, and Down Arrow keys shift the input focus to the next control in this order; the Left Arrow and Up Arrow keys and the SHIFT+TAB key combination shift the input focus to the previous control. You can also change the input focus by clicking on a control. This interface is implemented in the *Container-Control* class, which is one of the ancestors of *Form*. The control itself responds to the Enter or spacebar key.

However, a common amenity is missing: the control isn't giving any indication when it has the input focus. Perhaps a wider border around the control would be sufficient.

Here's a new class that subclasses the original CheckerChild class to implement this feature.

## CheckerChildWithFocus.vb

```
'-----------------------------------------------------------
' CheckerChildWithFocus.vb (c) 2002 by Charles Petzold
'-----------------------------------------------------------
Imports System
Imports System.Drawing
Imports System.Drawing.Drawing2D
Imports System.Windows.Forms

Class CheckerChildWithFocus
    Inherits CheckerChild

    Protected Overrides Sub OnGotFocus(ByVal ea As EventArgs)
        Invalidate()
    End Sub

    Protected Overrides Sub OnLostFocus(ByVal ea As EventArgs)
        Invalidate()
    End Sub

    Protected Overrides Sub OnPaint(ByVal pea As PaintEventArgs)
        MyBase.OnPaint(pea)
        If Focused Then
            Dim grfx As Graphics = pea.Graphics
            grfx.DrawRectangle(New Pen(ForeColor, 5), ClientRectangle)
        End If
    End Sub
End Class
```

This new control invalidates itself when the control gains or loses focus, providing an opportunity for the *OnPaint* method to redraw its border based on the *Focused* property.

The form that uses these new controls is basically identical to Checker-WithChildren, but it needs to create children of type *CheckerChildWithFocus* rather than *CheckerChild*. For this reason, the new form overrides the *Create-Children* method of the *CheckerWithChildren* class.

## CheckerWithChildrenAndFocus.vb

```
'-----------------------------------------------------------
' CheckerWithChildrenAndFocus.vb (c) 2002 by Charles Petzold
'-----------------------------------------------------------
Imports System
Imports System.Drawing
Imports System.Windows.Forms

Class CheckerWithChildrenAndFocus
    Inherits CheckerWithChildren
```

```
    Shared Shadows Sub Main()
        Application.Run(new CheckerWithChildrenAndFocus())
    End Sub

    Sub New()
        Text = "Checker with Children and Focus"
    End Sub

    Protected Overrides Sub CreateChildren()
        ReDim actrlChild(yNum, xNum)
        Dim x, y As Integer

        For y = 0 To yNum - 1
            For x = 0 To xNum - 1
                actrlChild(y, x) = New CheckerChildWithFocus()
                actrlChild(y, x).Parent = Me
            Next x
        Next y
    End Sub
End Class
```

# Hit-Testing Text

I mentioned earlier in this chapter that one of the more complex hit-testing jobs involves text in a variable-pitch font. Basically, what you need to do is call *MeasureString* multiple times to attempt to figure out which character of displayed text (or, more accurately, which space between the characters) the user is clicking with the mouse.

In Chapter 6, I presented a program named TypeAway that showed how to echo keyboard input in a single line of displayed text. This program included a caret that the user moves with the arrow keys. Let's add a mouse interface to that program that sets the caret position based on the *X* property of the *MouseEventArgs* object passed as an argument to *OnMouseDown*. (For multiple lines of text, such a program would also use the *Y* property to determine the line of text the user was pointing to.)

**HitTestText.vb**

```
'---------------------------------------------
' HitTestText.vb (c) 2002 by Charles Petzold
'---------------------------------------------
Imports System
Imports System.Drawing
Imports System.Windows.Forms
```

*(continued)*

**HitTestText.vb** *(continued)*

```
Class HitTestText
    Inherits TypeAway

    Shared Shadows Sub Main()
        Application.Run(New HitTestText())
    End Sub

    Sub New()
        Text &= " with Hit-Testing"
        Cursor = Cursors.IBeam
    End Sub

    Protected Overrides Sub OnMouseDown(ByVal mea As MouseEventArgs)
        If strText.Length = 0 Then Return

        Dim grfx As Graphics = CreateGraphics()
        Dim xPrev As Single = 0
        Dim i As Integer

        For i = 0 To strText.Length - 1
            Dim szf As SizeF = _
                    grfx.MeasureString(strText.Substring(0, i + 1), _
                                    Font, PointF.Empty, _
                                    StringFormat.GenericTypographic)

            If Math.Abs(mea.X - xPrev) < Math.Abs(mea.X - szf.Width) Then
                Exit For
            End If

            xPrev = szf.Width
        Next i

        iInsert = i
        grfx.Dispose()
        PositionCaret()
    End Sub
End Class
```

Notice that the constructor sets the *Cursor* property of the form to *Cursors.IBeam* to make the program look like a real text editor.

The *OnMouseDown* method includes a *For* loop based on the number of characters in the stored text string. The comparison using calls to *Math.Abs* (absolute value) determines which space between the characters the *X* coordinate of the mouse cursor is closest to. It then sets the *iInsert* field to that new character index and calls *PositionCaret* essentially to convert that character index into a new pixel position of the caret.

Like TypeAway itself, this program unfortunately doesn't work correctly with text that is read (and typed) right to left.

# Scribbling with the Mouse

You've heard of CAD programs? You've heard of paint programs? The Scribble program is neither of these.

**Scribble.vb**

```
'-------------------------------------------
' Scribble.vb (c) 2002 by Charles Petzold
'-------------------------------------------
Imports System
Imports System.Drawing
Imports System.Windows.Forms

Class Scribble
    Inherits Form

    Private bTracking As Boolean
    Private ptLast As Point

    Shared Sub Main()
        Application.Run(new Scribble())
    End Sub

    Sub New()
        Text = "Scribble"
        BackColor = SystemColors.Window
        ForeColor = SystemColors.WindowText
    End Sub

    Protected Overrides Sub OnMouseDown(ByVal mea As MouseEventArgs)
        If mea.Button <> MouseButtons.Left Then Return

        ptLast = New Point(mea.X, mea.Y)
        bTracking = True
    End Sub

    Protected Overrides Sub OnMouseMove(ByVal mea As MouseEventArgs)
        If Not bTracking Then Return

        Dim ptNew As New Point(mea.X, mea.Y)
        Dim grfx As Graphics = CreateGraphics()
        grfx.DrawLine(New Pen(ForeColor), ptLast, ptNew)
        grfx.Dispose()
        ptLast = ptNew
    End Sub

    Protected Overrides Sub OnMouseUp(ByVal mea As MouseEventArgs)
        bTracking = False
    End Sub

    Protected Overrides Sub OnPaint(ByVal pea As PaintEventArgs)
        ' What do I do here?
    End Sub
End Class
```

At first, the program seems to work just fine. You position the mouse cursor over the program's client area, press the left mouse button, and drag the mouse to draw straight, curvy, or otherwise awkward-looking lines. (I'm using a simple approach to mouse tracking here so as not to overly obscure how the program works.) The drawing occurs during the *OnMouseMove* method: the program obtains a *Graphics* object from *CreateGraphics* and simply draws a line from the previous mouse position (which it has saved in the field *ptLast*) to the new mouse position. Here's my homage to the early advertisements for the Apple Macintosh:

But what does Scribble do during its *OnPaint* method? Oops! The program forgot to retain all those mouse positions it used to draw the lines. If the client area needs repainting, it's out of luck.

You can implement a repainting facility in a program such as this in a couple ways. One technique is to use a *shadow bitmap* that the program draws on at the same time it draws on the screen. During the *OnPaint* method, it simply displays that bitmap. I'll have another version of the Scribble program in Chapter 11 that does precisely this. In Chapter 15, I use a graphics *path* to save the points.

Another solution is to accumulate an array of *Point* structures and simply call *DrawLines* during the *OnPaint* method. Well, that raises some questions as well. We might be tempted to create an array of many points, as in this example:

```
Dim apt(1000000) As Point
```

But we would burden ourselves with two conflicting fears: first, that we hadn't allocated enough points for a particular artistic user, and second, that we were wasting an awful lot of memory. Or, we could use the *ReDim* statement with the *Preserve* option, but are there even easier approaches to storing the points?

One solution is the *ArrayList* class, defined in the *System.Collections* namespace, which also includes classes with the mouthwatering names *Queue*,

*Stack*, *SortedList*, and *Hashtable*. An *ArrayList* object is like a single-dimension array that expands itself when necessary. I can't go into a full discussion of *ArrayList* here, but I'll give you the basics and you can explore the rest on your own. (There's a similar facility provided in Microsoft Visual Basic .NET called the *Collection*, but the *ArrayList* turns out to be a bit easier to use when converting into an actual array.)

You begin by creating a new *ArrayList* object:

```
Dim arrlst As New ArrayList()
```

An alternative constructor provides an initial capacity. By default, the capacity is set to 16. Then you can use the *Add* method to add any object to *ArrayList*. Here's a statement adding a *Point* object:

```
arrlst.Add(pt)
```

You can also insert or remove items by using similar methods.

One convenient approach to retrieving objects from *ArrayList* is to use an indexer, much like an array. For example, if you know that the fourth item in *arrlst* is a *Point* structure, you can get it by using

```
Dim pt As Point = DirectCast(arrlst(3), Point)
```

The cast is needed because the indexer returns an object of type *Object*.

You can add different types of objects to the same array list. For example, right after adding a *Point* to the array list you can add a *Rectangle*:

```
arrlst.Add(rect)
```

However, there may come a time when you want to copy the contents of an array list into a regular array (as I'll demonstrate shortly). A run-time error will be raised if you try to copy a *Rectangle* object into an array of *Point* structures.

The *Capacity* property of the array list indicates how many objects the array list is currently capable of holding. As you add objects to the array list (and perhaps remove some), the *Count* property indicates the number of objects in the array list. *Count* is always less than or equal to *Capacity*. If *Count* equals *Capacity* and you add another item, *Capacity* is doubled.

A version of Scribble that uses the *ArrayList* class to save all the *Point* structures can't make do with only one array list. A single *ArrayList* of *Point* structures would imply that all the points are connected with a single line. However, the user can press the left mouse button, scribble around, and release the mouse button multiple times. One *ArrayList* is needed to store these points as they're being drawn. But then that collection of points needs to be converted to an array of *Point* structures. Each array of *Point* structures needs to be stored in another *ArrayList* object.

In the ScribbleWithSave program, the main *ArrayList* object (the one storing *Point* arrays) is the field named *arrlstApts*. The *arrlstPts* field is used to store each collection of points as they're being drawn.

**ScribbleWithSave.vb**

```
'-------------------------------------------------
' ScribbleWithSave.vb (c) 2002 by Charles Petzold
'-------------------------------------------------
Imports System
Imports System.Collections    ' For ArrayList
Imports System.Drawing
Imports System.Windows.Forms

Class ScribbleWithSave
    Inherits Form

    Private arrlstApts As New ArrayList()
    Private arrlstPts As ArrayList
    Private bTracking As Boolean

    Shared Sub Main()
        Application.Run(New ScribbleWithSave())
    End Sub

    Sub New()
        Text = "Scribble with Save"
        BackColor = SystemColors.Window
        ForeColor = SystemColors.WindowText
    End Sub

    Protected Overrides Sub OnMouseDown(ByVal mea As MouseEventArgs)
        If mea.Button <> MouseButtons.Left Then Return

        arrlstPts = New ArrayList()
        arrlstPts.Add(New Point(mea.X, mea.Y))
        bTracking = True
    End Sub

    Protected Overrides Sub OnMouseMove(ByVal mea As MouseEventArgs)
        If Not bTracking Then Return

        arrlstPts.Add(New Point(mea.X, mea.Y))
        Dim grfx As Graphics = CreateGraphics()
        grfx.DrawLine(New Pen(ForeColor), _
                    CType(arrlstPts(arrlstPts.Count - 2), Point), _
                    CType(arrlstPts(arrlstPts.Count - 1), Point))
        grfx.Dispose()
    End Sub

    Protected Overrides Sub OnMouseUp(ByVal mea As MouseEventArgs)
        If Not bTracking Then Return
```

```
        Dim apt() As Point = _
                    CType(arrlstPts.ToArray(GetType(Point)), Point())
        arrlstApts.Add(apt)
        bTracking = False
    End Sub

    Protected Overrides Sub OnPaint(ByVal pea As PaintEventArgs)
        Dim grfx As Graphics = pea.Graphics
        Dim pn As New Pen(ForeColor)
        Dim i As Integer

        For i = 0 To arrlstApts.Count - 1
            Dim apt() As Point = CType(arrlstApts(i), Point())
            If apt.Length > 1 Then grfx.DrawLines(pn, apt)
        Next i
    End Sub
End Class
```

The program creates a new *ArrayList* object whenever the user presses the left mouse button and the program gets a call to *OnMouseDown*. The first member of the *ArrayList* object is the mouse cursor position at that time:

```
arrlstPts.Add(New Point(mea.X, mea.Y))
```

The program adds additional members on each call to *OnMouseMove*.

On receipt of *OnMouseUp*, the program uses the *ToArray* method to convert the collection of *Point* structures into a *Point* array:

```
Dim apt() As Point = _
        CType(arrlstPts.ToArray(GetType(Point)), Point())
```

This *ToArray* method is what makes the *ArrayList* a bit easier to use than the Visual Basic *Collection*. (There's an overload of the *ToArray* method that doesn't require an argument, but it returns an array of type *Object*. With the argument, the method returns an object of type *Array*.) That *Point* array is then added to *arrlstApts*:

```
arrlstApts.Add(apt)
```

What's really nice is the *OnPaint* method. It simply loops through the elements of *arrlstApts* and casts each one to the *Point* array that it passes to *DrawLines*. Since *DrawLines* will raise an exception for an array of only one point, the program checks that the array is larger than that. (I didn't think displaying the lines stored in *arrlstPts* was quite as necessary, although code to do that could easily be added.)

Of course, ScribbleWithSave can't really save an indefinite number of points. At some point, it will run out of memory. To protect itself, the program should probably enclose the calls to the *Add* method of *ArrayList* in a *Try* block. But I wasn't even quite sure how I would test such a thing, given that it would occur only after a great deal of drawing.

# 9

# Text and Fonts

In a graphical environment, the seemingly commonplace exercise of displaying text takes on additional layers of complexity. Fonts are often proportionally spaced, and they usually come in a variety of styles and sizes, which means that text must be handled much like other graphical output. Yet text is not quite like the abstract analytical geometry of lines and filled areas and thus occupies an uneasy niche in the field of computer graphics. To a typographer, fonts are a form of art with a long history of sophisticated design. Creators of computer graphics systems that implement fonts with any degree of integrity must deal with classical typographical concepts; application programmers must also learn about these concepts.

The most important principle is that text is meant to be read. There are subtleties in font design, font rendering, and page layout that affect readability even if the average person doesn't consciously notice them. Moreover, text is not purely content; the style in which the text is printed on the page can affect the interpretation of the content, either positively or adversely. You don't want a wedding invitation to look like an office memorandum, or a doctoral thesis to look like a magazine advertisement.

## Fonts Under Windows

The 1992 introduction of Microsoft Windows 3.1 marked a major change in how Windows applications used fonts. Prior to that, most of the fonts available for the video display under Windows were *bitmap* fonts (also called *raster* fonts) stored in discrete sizes and generally not scalable to other sizes. Also available were *stroke* fonts (also called *plotter* or *vector* fonts) defined as polylines, but these were unattractive and rarely used.

Windows 3.1 introduced TrueType, which greatly enhanced the ability of programmers and users to work with text in a flexible manner. TrueType is an *outline* font technology developed by Apple and Microsoft and is supported by many font manufacturers. Outline fonts are continuously scalable and contain built-in *hints* that prevent distortions when the outlines are scaled to a particular pixel size and grid.

Outline fonts also lend themselves well to integration with other graphics operators. You've already seen in Chapter 7 how you can scale, rotate, and shear text. In Chapter 15, I'll demonstrate how you can make text output part of a graphics *path* and use that path for outlining, filling, or clipping. Chapter 19 is devoted to exercises I collectively call Font Fun.

In 1997, Adobe and Microsoft announced the OpenType font format, which combines TrueType and the Type 1 outline font format used in Post-Script, Adobe's page-description language. (In the Fonts dialog box invokable from Control Panel, TrueType font files are associated with an icon containing the initials *TT*, and OpenType font files have an icon with an *O*.) Recent versions of Windows have included over 100 TrueType and OpenType fonts, many for non-Latin alphabets.

Although bitmap fonts and stroke fonts are still supported under Windows, they are not directly available to Windows Forms applications. A Windows Forms program has direct access to only TrueType and OpenType fonts. This is actually a good thing, for it means that Windows Forms applications can work consistently with all fonts to which they have access and can use them on both the video display and the printer.

Windows Forms supports anti-aliasing of TrueType and OpenType fonts, and it also supports Microsoft ClearType, a technique announced by Microsoft in 1998 for taking advantage of the arrangement of color dots on LCD displays. I'll discuss font anti-aliasing and ClearType later in this chapter.

# Talking Type

Typographers generally denote a particular font by a *typeface name* (often called simply a *face name*) and a *point size* (sometimes called the *em size*). Each typeface belongs to a type *family*. Type families have simple names such as Bookman, Helvetica, Garamond, and Times. Each family often includes several variations:

- The strokes that make up the characters can be light or heavy in various degrees, described by typeface names such as Helvetica Ultra Light, Helvetica Thin, Helvetica Light, Helvetica Bold, Helvetica Heavy, and Helvetica Black.

■ The widths of the individual characters can be narrower or wider than usual, for typeface names such as Helvetica Narrow, Helvetica Condensed, or Helvetica Extended.

■ The characters can be slanted to the right, giving us typeface names such as Helvetica Italic or Helvetica Oblique. Strictly speaking, *oblique* refers to characters that are simply slanted, while *italic* implies that the characters are also stylistically somewhat different from the upright font. The appearance of the lowercase "a" is usually a good indication of whether a font is oblique (**a**) or italic (*a*).

These three variations can be combined in a single typeface name—for example, Helvetica Bold Extended Oblique. Typeface names can also include the name of the copyright holder of the font and perhaps a code number meaningful only to the font manufacturer.

When TrueType was first introduced in Windows, it was represented by 13 TrueType files (filename extension .ttf) associated with the following typeface names:

■ Courier New

■ Courier New Bold

■ Courier New Italic

■ Courier New Bold Italic

■ Times New Roman

■ Times New Roman Bold

■ Times New Roman Italic

■ Times New Roman Bold Italic

■ Arial

■ Arial Bold

■ Arial Italic

■ Arial Bold Italic

■ Symbol

Courier is a fixed-pitch font family that resembles typewriter output. Very little text is displayed in Courier these days, the big exceptions being command-line windows, program listings, and hex dumps.

Times New Roman is a clone of the Times font (renamed for copyright reasons) originally designed for the *Times of London* and used in much printed material. It is considered highly readable. Arial is a clone of Helvetica, a popular sans serif font. Serifs are small turns that often finish the strokes of letters. A sans serif font doesn't have serifs. (A font *with* serifs is sometimes called a *roman* font.) The Symbol font includes common symbols rather than letters.

Many (but not all) of the other fonts included in Windows come in regular, bold, italic, and bold italic faces. In addition, Windows can apply underlining or strikeout to any font.

In graphical environments, users tend to use the word *font* to refer to what is technically a font family. "Let's change this font from Helvetica to Verdana," a user will say. In addition, users tend to think of italic and boldface (as well as underlining and strikeout) as *attributes* or *styles* that are applied to a particular font. For example, no user says, "I want to make this word italic so I have to switch the typeface name from Linotype Palatino to Linotype Palatino Italic." No, it's more like "I want to make this word italic," regardless of the face name.

Windows Forms helps you present fonts to the user in a manner familiar to the user's expectations by consolidating multiple face names (such as Arial, Arial Bold, Arial Italic, and Arial Bold Italic) into a single font family (Arial). Despite the theoretical wide variety of face names possible with different levels of stroke width and character width, the only variations allowed are a combination of bold, italic, underline, and strikeout styles. In Windows Forms, the Arial Black typeface is *not* considered part of the Arial family; Arial Black is considered a separate font family, which just so happens is not available with Windows XP in italic or bold versions.

# Font Heights and Line Spacing

Along with a typeface name, a font is identified by a vertical size in *points*. In traditional typography, a point is 0.01384 inch. This number is very close to 1/72 of an inch, so in computer typography, the point is assumed to be exactly 1/72 of an inch.

The point size of a font is commonly described as the height of the characters in the Latin alphabet—that is, the uppercase and lowercase letters *A* through *Z* without diacritical marks—from the very top of the ascenders to the bottom of the descenders, encompassing, for example, the full height of the characters "bq." That's certainly a convenient way to think of the point size, but it's usually not metrically precise.

Back in the days of metal type, the point size of a font was the vertical size of the metal type on which the letters were cast. The letters themselves were generally a little shorter than the point size. Today, this restriction has disappeared, and it's sometimes the case that letters can be *larger* than the point size. It's safer to think of the point size of a font as a typographical design concept rather than a metrical concept. The size of the characters in a particular font could be greater than or less than what the point size implies. Never assume that the point size of a font is anything other than an approximate measure of the height of the font characters.

Getting familiar with common point sizes is helpful when beginning to work with fonts. Most of *The New York Times* is printed in 8-point type; *Newsweek* is 9-point type; this book has 10.5-point type. The default Windows font is 10 points. The default Windows Forms font is about 8 points. As I discussed in Chapter 7, the user is responsible for setting an assumed resolution of the video display, and that resolution is what affects the visual size of these 8-point and 10-point fonts.

I mentioned earlier that the point size is sometimes referred to as the *em* size. The term comes from the size of the square piece of metal type used in olden days for the capital M. These days, the em is used mostly to refer to horizontal measurements. The width of an em in a particular font is equal to the vertical point size of the font. For example, in a 14-point font, the em dash and the em space are both 14 points wide. The en is half of the em. In a 14-point font, the en dash and the en space are 7 points wide.

Successive lines of text are generally spaced by an amount somewhat larger than the point size, usually at least about 115 percent of the point size. The rationale for the line spacing is partly based on the need for some extra space for the diacritics that appear in many European languages. But line spacing is also an aesthetic necessity: text is easier to read if there's some air between the lines.

The recommended line spacing is the value you obtain from the *Height* property and the *GetHeight* method of the *Font* class (both of which I'll discuss later in this chapter in context with other *Font* properties). For many fonts, the recommended line spacing is usually larger than the point size but somewhat smaller than the height returned from the *MeasureString* method of the *Graphics* class. As I've mentioned before, you should avoid using the *Height* property unless you know that you're dealing only with the default page transform on the video display. Because *Height* doesn't involve a *Graphics* object, it isn't applicable for the printer or for nondefault page transforms.

# Default Fonts

Since Chapter 2, we've been using the *Font* property that's implemented in *Control* and inherited by all its descendents, including *Form*:

### *Control* Properties (selection)

| Property | Type | Accessibility |
|----------|------|---------------|
| *Font* | *Font* | Get/Set |

As you'll see shortly, you can set this *Font* property to a different *Font* object and all the successive *DrawString* calls that use the *Font* property will use this different font. (You can also just create a new *Font* object and use that directly in *DrawString*.) If you change the value of the *Font* property, you can set it back to the original value by using this shared read-only property of *Control*:

### *Control* Shared Properties (selection)

| Property | Type | Accessibility |
|----------|------|---------------|
| *DefaultFont* | *Font* | Get |

You can do this manually:

```
Font = DefaultFont
```

Or you can simply use this method:

### *Control* Methods (selection)

```
Sub ResetFont()
```

There's also this font-related property:

### *Control* Properties (selection)

| Property | Type | Accessibility |
|----------|------|---------------|
| *FontHeight* | *Integer* | Get/Set |

You can use this property instead of *Font.Height*. Although this property is writable, setting it to a new value won't change the *Font* property!

# Variation on a Font

The *System.Drawing* namespace defines two important classes for working with fonts:

- *FontFamily* is identified by a string such as "Times New Roman."

- *Font* is a combination of a font family (either a *FontFamily* object or a character string identifying the family name), attributes (such as italic and bold), and a point size.

I'm going to begin with the *Font* class. The *Font* constructors are in three categories:

- Based on an existing *Font* object

- Based on a character string identifying the font family

- Based on a *FontFamily* object

The simplest constructor for *Font* creates a new font based on an existing font. The new font is the same except for the font style:

### *Font* Constructors (selection)

```
Font(ByVal fnt As Font, ByVal fs As FontStyle )
```

*FontStyle* is an enumeration defined as a series of single-bit flags:

### *FontStyle* Enumeration

| Member | Value |
|--------|-------|
| *Regular* | 0 |
| *Bold* | 1 |
| *Italic* | 2 |
| *Underline* | 4 |
| *Strikeout* | 8 |

For example, suppose *fnt* is an existing font, perhaps obtained from the form's *Font* property:

```
Dim fnt As Font = Font
```

You can make an italic version of that font named *fntItalic* by using the following statement:

```
Dim fntItalic As New Font(fnt, FontStyle.Italic)
```

You can use multiple enumeration members combined with the Visual Basic *Or* operator:

```
Dim fntBoldStrikeout As New Font(fnt, FontStyle.Bold Or FontStyle.Strikeout)
```

Here's a program that takes the form's *Font* property and creates bold and italic versions for displaying a mix of regular, bold, and italic text.

**BoldAndItalic.vb**

```
'-------------------------------------------------
' BoldAndItalic.vb (c) 2002 by Charles Petzold
'-------------------------------------------------
Imports System
Imports System.Drawing
Imports System.Windows.Forms

Class BoldAndItalic
    Inherits PrintableForm

    Shared Shadows Sub Main()
        Application.Run(New BoldAndItalic())
    End Sub

    Sub New()
        Text = "Bold and Italic Text"
    End Sub

    Protected Overrides Sub DoPage(ByVal grfx As Graphics, _
            ByVal clr As Color, ByVal cx As Integer, ByVal cy As Integer)
        Const str1 As String = "This is some "
        Const str2 As String = "bold"
        Const str3 As String = " text and this is some "
        Const str4 As String = "italic"
        Const str5 As String = " text."
        Dim br As New SolidBrush(clr)
        Dim fntRegular As Font = Font
        Dim fntBold As New Font(fntRegular, FontStyle.Bold)
        Dim fntItalic As New Font(fntRegular, FontStyle.Italic)
        Dim x As Single = 0
        Dim y As Single = 0

        grfx.DrawString(str1, fntRegular, br, x, y)
        x += grfx.MeasureString(str1, fntRegular).Width

        grfx.DrawString(str2, fntBold, br, x, y)
        x += grfx.MeasureString(str2, fntBold).Width

        grfx.DrawString(str3, fntRegular, br, x, y)
        x += grfx.MeasureString(str3, fntRegular).Width
```

```
        grfx.DrawString(str4, fntItalic, br, x, y)
        x += grfx.MeasureString(str4, fntItalic).Width

        grfx.DrawString(str5, fntRegular, br, x, y)
    End Sub
End Class
```

Because *DrawString* has a *Font* argument and a particular font is either regular, bold, italic, or bold italic, multiple *DrawString* calls are required to display text that combines multiple styles. The program uses *MeasureString* to determine the size of each piece of text and space the text horizontally:

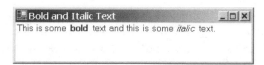

If you look closely, you'll probably notice that there seems to be a little extraneous space between each piece of displayed text. I'll show you how to avoid this extra space when I get to detailed coverage of the *StringFormat* class later in this chapter.

Let me give you another warning now, and we'll examine later how to deal with it: this *Font* constructor can fail if the particular font family that the font belongs to isn't capable of the requested style. The constructor throws an exception that a well-behaved program should deal with. This isn't a problem in the BoldAndItalic program because it's using the form's default font, and that font is capable of all the styles. The BoldAndItalic program will *not* work with every font family, however.

# Creating Fonts by Name

These next two constructors for *Font* are exceptionally convenient and straightforward. You specify a font by using the font family name, the point size, and an optional style:

### *Font* Constructors (selection)

```
Font(ByVal strFamily As String, ByVal fSizeInPoints As Single)

Font(ByVal strFamily As String, ByVal fSizeInPoints As Single,
    ByVal fs As FontStyle)
```

The font family names you can use as the first argument to the *Font* constructor are familiar names such as "Times New Roman," "Arial," "Courier New," "Comic Sans MS," and many others. For example,

```
Dim fnt As New Font("Times New Roman", 24)
```

creates a 24-point Times New Roman font.

I love creating fonts like this, and I suspect that you too will find yourself using these *Font* constructors more than the others. However, you should keep in mind some drawbacks.

The name should represent a TrueType or OpenType font that is installed on the system on which the program is running. If the Times New Roman font isn't available—or if you misspell the name—the constructor will substitute a default font (probably Microsoft Sans Serif). Can you be sure that the Times New Roman font is available? Well, yes, if you're coding something for yourself. And yes again, if you're coding something for internal use in a company where you're sure that all the machines have Times New Roman fonts installed. But it's possible for users to uninstall TrueType fonts, and while getting rid of Times New Roman may sound perverse to you and me, it's not impossible. As your code achieves an ever broader platform base, using explicit font family names becomes less safe. At some point in the future, Windows Forms programs might run under environments that have other collections of fonts with different names. Presumably, those environments will implement some kind of font-mapping so that existing programs don't break, but it's probably still risky to use the more obscure font family names.

Sticking to the familiar three font family names of Times New Roman, Arial, and Courier New is probably safest. Some aliases are even allowed: you can use "Times" for Times New Roman and "Helvetica" for Arial.

Specifying an explicit point size is less problematic. You know that the user has set the video display properties based on the idea that a 10-point font is comfortable. Windows Forms itself sets the form's *Font* property based on the assumption that an 8-point font is also readable. Everything else is relative. For example, a 24-point font is three times larger than the normal Windows Forms font.

Because there are 72 points to the inch, a 24-point font is approximately 1/3 inch tall. (I say *approximately* because, as I mentioned earlier, the point size is a typographical design concept, not a precise measurement.) You can also think of a 24-point font as having a size in pixels that is approximately 1/3 the *DpiY* property of the *Graphics* object.

The family name and the point size can also be combined with a font style. The following program creates and displays 18-point Courier New, Arial, and Times New Roman fonts in regular, bold, italic, and bold-italic versions. These 18-point fonts are approximately 1/4 inch in size.

**FontNames.vb**

```
'-------------------------------------------------
' FontNames.vb (c) 2002 by Charles Petzold
'-------------------------------------------------
Imports System
Imports System.Drawing
Imports System.Windows.Forms

Class FontNames
    Inherits PrintableForm

    Shared Shadows Sub Main()
        Application.Run(new FontNames())
    End Sub

    Sub New()
        Text = "Font Names"
    End Sub

    Protected Overrides Sub DoPage(ByVal grfx As Graphics, _
            ByVal clr As Color, ByVal cx As Integer, ByVal cy As Integer)
        Dim astrFonts() As String = {"Courier New", "Arial", _
                                     "Times New Roman"}
        Dim afs() As FontStyle = {FontStyle.Regular, FontStyle.Bold, _
                                  FontStyle.Italic, _
                                  FontStyle.Bold Or FontStyle.Italic}
        Dim br As New SolidBrush(clr)
        Dim y As Single = 0
        Dim strFont As String
        Dim fs As FontStyle

        For Each strFont In astrFonts
            For Each fs In afs
                Dim fnt As New Font(strFont, 18, fs)
                grfx.DrawString(strFont, fnt, br, 0, y)
                y += fnt.GetHeight(grfx)
            Next fs
        Next strFont
    End Sub
End Class
```

This class derives from *PrintableForm*, so you can print the fonts by clicking on the client area. Keep in mind that the coordinates passed to the *DrawString* method indicate the position of the upper left corner of the string. Therefore, coordinates for each string must be adjusted by the text height of the previous string. The program adjusts the coordinate by using the *Font* method *GetHeight* after displaying text using the font.

Notice also that the program assumes that each font returns a different value from the *GetHeight* method. Put a *Console.WriteLine* statement in there if you're curious about these values. You'll find that the Times New Roman and Arial fonts return the same value, which is a little larger than the Courier New value. But other fonts may be quite different, and there's no reason you should guess. Use *GetHeight* to make sure. Here's the program's display:

You can try substituting the *Height* property for the *GetHeight* method and see what happens when you print the output on your printer. The line spacing will be off by an amount that's dependent on how much the video display resolution in dots per inch (dpi) differs from the 100-dpi resolution set for the printer.

Here's a very similar program that displays the Times New Roman font in sizes from 6 points to 12 points in increments of 1/4 point.

**FontSizes.vb**

```
'-------------------------------------------
' FontSizes.vb (c) 2002 by Charles Petzold
'-------------------------------------------
Imports System
Imports System.Drawing
Imports System.Windows.Forms
```

```
Class FontSizes
    Inherits PrintableForm

    Shared Shadows Sub Main()
        Application.Run(new FontSizes())
    End Sub

    Sub New()
        Text = "Font Sizes"
    End Sub

    Protected Overrides Sub DoPage(ByVal grfx As Graphics, _
            ByVal clr As Color, ByVal cx As Integer, ByVal cy As Integer)
        Dim strFont As String = "Times New Roman"
        Dim br As New SolidBrush(clr)
        Dim y As Single = 0
        Dim fSize As Single

        For fSize = 6 To 12 Step 0.25
            Dim fnt As New Font(strFont, fSize)
            grfx.DrawString(strFont & " in " & Str(fSize) & " points", _
                        fnt, br, 0, y)
            y += fnt.GetHeight(grfx)
        Next fSize
    End Sub
End Class
```

Here's the program output:

Perhaps what's most noticeable about this display is the sudden leap at 10.5 points from strokes that are 1 pixel wide to strokes that are 2 pixels wide. Such transitions are not evident on higher-resolution devices such as printers.

If you want to use a larger font for everything your program displays in its client area, you can change the *Font* property of a form right in its constructor. Here's a program that overrides the BoldAndItalic program shown earlier and displays the text string with a 24-point font.

**BoldAndItalicBigger.vb**

```
'-------------------------------------------------------
' BoldAndItalicBigger.vb (c) 2002 by Charles Petzold
'-------------------------------------------------------
Imports System
Imports System.Drawing
Imports System.Windows.Forms

Class BoldAndItalicBigger
    Inherits BoldAndItalic

    Shared Shadows Sub Main()
        Application.Run(new BoldAndItalicBigger())
    End Sub

    Sub New()
        Text &= " Bigger"
        Font = New Font("Times New Roman", 24)
    End Sub
End Class
```

Here's the program display:

This is some **bold** text and this is some *italic* text.

In this program, the extraneous space between the various pieces of text has become more noticeable than in the BoldAndItalic program. Avoiding this extra space requires a *StringFormat* object, as I'll demonstrate later in this chapter.

# A Point Size by Any Other Name...

You need not specify the size of the font in points. Two more constructors for *Font* include a *GraphicsUnit* argument:

### *Font* Constructors (selection)

```
Font(ByVal strFamily As String, ByVal fSize As Single,
    ByVal gu As GraphicsUnit)

Font(ByVal strFamily As String, ByVal fSize As Single,
    ByVal fs As FontStyle, ByVal gu As GraphicsUnit)
```

You can use all but one of the *GraphicsUnit* enumeration values that you learned about in connection with the *PageUnit* property in Chapter 7:

### *GraphicsUnit* Enumeration

| Member | Value | Description |
| --- | --- | --- |
| *World* | 0 | Units of world coordinates |
| *Display* | 1 | Won't work with *Font* constructor! |
| *Pixel* | 2 | Units of pixels |
| *Point* | 3 | Units of 1/72 inch |
| *Inch* | 4 | Units of inches |
| *Document* | 5 | Units of 1/300 inch |
| *Millimeter* | 6 | Units of millimeters |

The constructor

```
New Font(strFamily, fSize)
```

is identical to

```
New Font(strFamily, fSize, GraphicsUnit.Point)
```

Indeed, the following constructors are all equivalent:

```
New Font(strFamily, 72)
New Font(strFamily, 72, GraphicsUnit.Point)
New Font(strFamily, 1, GraphicsUnit.Inch)
New Font(strFamily, 25.4, GraphicsUnit.Millimeter)
New Font(strFamily, 300, GraphicsUnit.Document)
```

All these constructors result in the creation of identical 72-point fonts. There's nothing going on here that's more sophisticated than knowing that an inch is equal to 72 points and 25.4 millimeters. The messy *Font* constructor arguments are *GraphicsUnit.Pixel* and *GraphicsUnit.World*. For the video display, if you're displaying text with the default page transform (that is, all coordinates and sizes are in units of pixels), you can also use the following two constructors to create 72-point fonts:

```
New Font(strFamily, grfx.DpiY, GraphicsUnit.Pixel)
New Font(strFamily, grfx.DpiY, GraphicsUnit.World)
```

The second argument is the number of pixels in one vertical inch.

The equivalence of these constructors is demonstrated in the following program, which creates 24-point fonts seven different ways.

**TwentyFourPointScreenFonts.vb**

```vb
'-------------------------------------------------------------
' TwentyFourPointScreenFonts.vb (c) 2002 by Charles Petzold
'-------------------------------------------------------------
Imports System
Imports System.Drawing
Imports System.Windows.Forms

Class TwentyFourPointScreenFonts
    Inherits PrintableForm

    Shared Shadows Sub Main()
        Application.Run(New TwentyFourPointScreenFonts())
    End Sub

    Sub New()
        Text = "Twenty-Four Point Screen Fonts"
    End Sub

    Protected Overrides Sub DoPage(ByVal grfx As Graphics, _
            ByVal clr As Color, ByVal cx As Integer, ByVal cy As Integer)
        Dim br As New SolidBrush(clr)
        Dim cyFont As Single
        Dim y As Single = 0
        Dim fnt As Font
        Dim strFamily As String = "Times New Roman"

        fnt = New Font(strFamily, 24)
        grfx.DrawString("No GraphicsUnit, 24 points", fnt, br, 0, y)
        y += fnt.GetHeight(grfx)

        fnt = New Font(strFamily, 24, GraphicsUnit.Point)
        grfx.DrawString("GraphicsUnit.Point, 24 units", fnt, br, 0, y)
        y += fnt.GetHeight(grfx)

        cyFont = 1 / 3
        fnt = New Font(strFamily, cyFont, GraphicsUnit.Inch)
        grfx.DrawString("GraphicsUnit.Inch, " & cyFont & " units", _
                        fnt, br, 0, y)
        y += fnt.GetHeight(grfx)

        cyFont = 25.4 / 3
        fnt = New Font(strFamily, cyFont, GraphicsUnit.Millimeter)
        grfx.DrawString("GraphicsUnit.Millimeter, " & cyFont & " units", _
                        fnt, br, 0, y)
        y += fnt.GetHeight(grfx)

        fnt = New Font(strFamily, 100, GraphicsUnit.Document)
        grfx.DrawString("GraphicsUnit.Document, 100 units", _
                        fnt, br, 0, y)
        y += fnt.GetHeight(grfx)
```

```
        cyFont = grfx.DpiY / 3
        fnt = New Font(strFamily, cyFont, GraphicsUnit.Pixel)
        grfx.DrawString("GraphicsUnit.Pixel, " & cyFont & " units", _
                        fnt, br, 0, y)
        y += fnt.GetHeight(grfx)

        fnt = New Font(strFamily, cyFont, GraphicsUnit.World)
        grfx.DrawString("GraphicsUnit.World, " & cyFont & " units", _
                        fnt, br, 0, y)
    End Sub
End Class
```

I'm using 24-point fonts rather than 72-point fonts in this program just so they all fit on the display. In each of the constructors, the values passed as the second argument are simply 1/3 the values I showed previously.

On the video display, all seven lines of text are the same height. If you click on the client area of this program to print the output, however, you'll discover a problem. The first five lines of output look fine. These constructors have all successfully created 24-point fonts for the printer. But the last two lines create fonts that are much too large.

As you'll recall, the *DpiX* and *DpiY* properties of the *Graphics* object for the printer give its true resolution: probably 300, 600, 720, or something higher. In the final two *Font* constructors, the program specifies 1/3 that resolution, so the second argument will be 100, 200, 240, or something higher. The default page transform for the printer makes it appear to be a 100-dpi device. The combination of the font size and page transform results in a font that is 1 inch, 2 inches, 2.3 inches, or something larger.

To create 72-point fonts for the printer's default page transform using *GraphicsUnit.Pixel* or *GraphicsUnit.World*, you need to use the following constructors:

```
New Font(strFamily, 100, GraphicsUnit.Pixel)
New Font(strFamily, 100, GraphicsUnit.World)
```

To create 24-point fonts for the printer, you need to use 1/3 of 100. The following program is the same as the previous one except that the last two *Font* constructors create 24-point fonts appropriate for the printer.

**TwentyFourPointPrinterFonts.vb**
```
'-------------------------------------------------------------
' TwentyFourPointPrinterFonts.vb (c) 2002 by Charles Petzold
'-------------------------------------------------------------
Imports System
Imports System.Drawing
Imports System.Windows.Forms
```

*(continued)*

**TwentyFourPointPrinterFonts.vb** *(continued)*

```
Class TwentyFourPointPrinterFonts
    Inherits PrintableForm

    Shared Shadows Sub Main()
        Application.Run(New TwentyFourPointPrinterFonts())
    End Sub

    Sub New()
        Text = "Twenty-Four Point Printer Fonts"
    End Sub

    Protected Overrides Sub DoPage(ByVal grfx As Graphics, _
            ByVal clr As Color, ByVal cx As Integer, ByVal cy As Integer)
        Dim br As New SolidBrush(clr)
        Dim cyFont As Single
        Dim y As Single = 0
        Dim fnt As Font
        Dim strFamily As String = "Times New Roman"

        fnt = New Font(strFamily, 24)
        grfx.DrawString("No GraphicsUnit, 24 points", fnt, br, 0, y)
        y += fnt.GetHeight(grfx)

        fnt = New Font(strFamily, 24, GraphicsUnit.Point)
        grfx.DrawString("GraphicsUnit.Point, 24 units", fnt, br, 0, y)
        y += fnt.GetHeight(grfx)

        cyFont = 1 / 3
        fnt = New Font(strFamily, cyFont, GraphicsUnit.Inch)
        grfx.DrawString("GraphicsUnit.Inch, " & cyFont & " units", _
                        fnt, br, 0, y)
        y += fnt.GetHeight(grfx)

        cyFont = 25.4 / 3
        fnt = New Font(strFamily, cyFont, GraphicsUnit.Millimeter)
        grfx.DrawString( "GraphicsUnit.Millimeter, " & cyFont & " units", _
            fnt, br, 0, y)
        y += fnt.GetHeight(grfx)

        fnt = New Font(strFamily, 100, GraphicsUnit.Document)
        grfx.DrawString("GraphicsUnit.Document, 100 units", _
                        fnt, br, 0, y)
        y += fnt.GetHeight(grfx)

        cyFont = 100 / 3
        fnt = New Font(strFamily, cyFont, GraphicsUnit.Pixel)
        grfx.DrawString("GraphicsUnit.Pixel, " & cyFont & " units", _
                        fnt, br, 0, y)
        y += fnt.GetHeight(grfx)
```

```
        fnt = New Font(strFamily, cyFont, GraphicsUnit.World)
        grfx.DrawString("GraphicsUnit.World, " & cyFont & " units", _
                        fnt, br, 0, y)
    End Sub
End Class
```

On the printer, all seven lines of text will be the same height. On the video display, the first five lines will be 24-point fonts, and the last two will probably be a little off, depending on how much your video display resolution differs from 100 dpi.

# Clash of the Units

Experimenting with different units in the *Font* constructors raises the question, How do the font units interact with the world transform and the page transform? Both the *Font* class and the *Graphics* class make use of the *GraphicsUnit* enumeration. The *Font* class uses the *GraphicsUnit* enumeration in some of its constructors, and the *Graphics* class *PageUnit* property is also set equal to one of the enumeration values.

We've already had a little taste of that interaction. Now let's see if we can come up with an overall analysis and a few solid rules.

Try to keep in mind that *Font* objects are device-independent. It doesn't matter what world transform or page transform is in effect when you create the font. The *Font* constructor doesn't know anything about that. You can create *Font* objects anywhere in your program regardless of whether or not there's a *Graphics* object in sight.

There are only three commonly used methods that involve the interaction of both a *Font* object (which is created in a particular size with particular units) and a *Graphics* object (which has a world transform and a page transform associated with it):

- *DrawString*, a method of the *Graphics* class that has a *Font* argument

- *MeasureString*, a method of the *Graphics* class that has a *Font* argument

- *GetHeight*, a method of the *Font* class that has a *Graphics* argument

These are generally the only three methods in which you have to worry about the clash among graphics units and transforms. Two others—the *DrawStringDisabled* method of the *ControlPaint* class and the *MeasureCharacterRanges* method of the *Graphics* class—aren't used nearly as often.

Only three rules affect these methods. I encourage you to experiment with the TwentyFourPointScreenFonts and TwentyFourPointPrinterFonts programs to verify that what I say is correct:

**Rule 1** *The world transform affects everything in the same way.*

Let's say you have some graphics output: a collection of lines, filled areas, and text using fonts created with a variety of *GraphicsUnit* arguments. Then you decide you want everything twice as big. So, before any of the graphics output calls, you put the statement

```
grfx.ScaleTransform(2, 2)
```

The world transform affects everything in the same way. Everything—every line, every filled area, and every text string—is doubled in size regardless of the way in which the font was created. The sizes returned from *Measure-String* and *GetHeight* remain the same, however, which is as it should be. You use sizes returned from these methods to position text and graphics, and those sizes shouldn't change when you change the world transform.

**Rule 2** *For fonts constructed with metrical sizes (that is, units of points, inches, or millimeters), the page transform doesn't affect the physical size of the text.*

Let's say you create a 72-point font:

```
Dim fnt As New Font("Arial", 72, GraphicsUnit.Point)
```

And you also decide you'd like to draw in units of millimeters:

```
grfx.PageUnit = GraphicsUnit.Millimeter
grfx.PageScale = 1
```

Regardless of the page transform, the physical size of the text remains the same. Because the font size is 72 points, it's equivalent to a height of about 25.4 units, where the units are millimeters.

What the page transform *does* affect, however, are the coordinates to the *DrawString* method, the sizes returned from the *MeasureString* method, and the height returned by *GetHeight*. All those coordinates and sizes are now (in this example) in units of millimeters. This should be OK, however, because you're generally using *GetHeight* or *MeasureString* to calculate the coordinates you pass to *DrawString*. Just make sure that the same transforms are in effect when you obtain numbers from *GetHeight* or *MeasureString* as when you pass the numbers to *DrawString*.

If you insert statements into the TwentyFourPointScreenFonts program to change the *PageUnit* and *PageScale* properties, you'll find that the first five lines of text are unaffected. The last lines *are* affected by the page transform, however. That's the third rule.

**Rule 3**   *For fonts constructed with* GraphicsUnit.Pixel *or* GraphicsUnit.World *units, the size of the font is assumed to be in units of world coordinates.*

In other words, the font size is treated just like the coordinates and sizes passed to the various line-drawing and area-filling methods of the *Graphics* class. For example, suppose you create a font like so:

```
Dim fnt As New Font("Arial", 72, GraphicsUnit.World)
```

With the default page transform, that's assumed to be 72 pixels on the video display or 72/100 inch on the printer. If you set the page transform to millimeters, as here,

```
grfx.PageUnit = GraphicsUnit.Millimeter
grfx.PageScale = 1
```

the font size of 72 is assumed to be units of millimeters, which results in fonts almost 3 inches in height.

For fonts created with *GraphicsUnit.World* and *GraphicsUnit.Pixel*, the values returned from *GetHeight* and *MeasureString* are unaffected by the page transform. The physical size of the font is in units indicated by the page transform, and the sizes returned from these methods are also in page units.

Finally, although their names would imply otherwise, I have discovered no difference between the *GraphicsUnit.Pixel* and *GraphicsUnit.World* arguments when used to create fonts.

# Font Properties and Methods

All properties of the *Font* class are read-only. That implies that you can't make a font a little different simply by changing one of its properties. Here's the complete list of *Font* properties:

### *Font* Properties

| Property | Type | Accessibility | Description |
| --- | --- | --- | --- |
| *Name* | *String* | Get | Font family name |
| *FontFamily* | *FontFamily* | Get | Font family class |
| *Style* | *FontStyle* | Get | From constructor |
| *Bold* | *Boolean* | Get | *True* if boldface |
| *Italic* | *Boolean* | Get | *True* if italic |
| *Underline* | *Boolean* | Get | *True* if underlined |
| *Strikeout* | *Boolean* | Get | *True* if strikeout |

*(continued)*

### *Font* Properties   *(continued)*

| Property | Type | Accessibility | Description |
|---|---|---|---|
| *Size* | *Single* | Get | From constructor |
| *Unit* | *GraphicsUnit* | Get | From constructor |
| *SizeInPoints* | *Single* | Get | Calculated from *Size* |
| *Height* | *Integer* | Get | Line spacing for video display |
| *GdiCharSet* | *Byte* | Get | GDI character set ID |
| *GdiVerticalFont* | *Boolean* | Get | *True* if a vertical font |

The *Size* and *Unit* properties just return the values used to create the font. The *SizeInPoints* property is calculated from these values. For *Graphics-Unit.Pixel* and *GraphicsUnit.World*, the calculation is based on the resolution of the video display.

If you don't need to interface with Win32 API code, there's really only one *Font* method that's of any interest, and that's one I've already emphasized. It comes in three different versions:

### *Font* Methods (selection)

```
Function GetHeight() As Single

Function GetHeight(ByVal grfx As Graphics) As Single

Function GetHeight(ByVal fDpi As Single) As Single
```

The value returned from *GetHeight* is what you should use for spacing successive lines of text. The version without an argument applies only to the video display in its default page transform. The second version is the most useful and takes the resolution and page transform of the output device into account. The third version obtains the line spacing based on a hypothetical vertical resolution in dots per inch.

If you need to interface with Win32 API code, *Font* has three shared methods that you can use to create a *Font* object: *FromHdc*, *FromHfont*, and *From-LogFont*. Otherwise, the *Font* class doesn't have any way to create a *Font* object other than to use one of the constructors of the class. I've already discussed five of these constructors; four more are coming up soon. As you'll see in Chapter 16, the *FontDialog* class displays a dialog box that lets the user select a font and creates a *Font* object that applications can use.

Here's a program that displays all the properties of the form's *Font* property as well as the result of three versions of *GetHeight*, the third using a resolution of 100 dpi.

**AllAboutFont.vb**

```vb
'-------------------------------------------------
' AllAboutFont.vb (c) 2002 by Charles Petzold
'-------------------------------------------------
Imports System
Imports System.Drawing
Imports System.Windows.Forms

Class AllAboutFont
    Inherits PrintableForm

    Shared Shadows Sub Main()
        Application.Run(New AllAboutFont())
    End Sub

    Sub New()
        Text = "All About Font"
    End Sub

    Protected Overrides Sub DoPage(ByVal grfx As Graphics, _
            ByVal clr As Color, ByVal cx As Integer, ByVal cy As Integer)
        grfx.DrawString( _
                "Name: " & Font.Name & vbLf & _
                "FontFamily: " & Font.FontFamily.ToString() & vbLf & _
                "FontStyle: " & Font.Style.ToString() & vbLf & _
                "Bold: " & Font.Bold & vbLf & _
                "Italic: " & Font.Italic & vbLf & _
                "Underline: " & Font.Underline & vbLf & _
                "Strikeout: " & Font.Strikeout & vbLf & _
                "Size: " & Font.Size & vbLf & _
                "GraphicsUnit: " & Font.Unit.ToString() & vbLf & _
                "SizeInPoints: " & Font.SizeInPoints & vbLf & _
                "Height: " & Font.Height & vbLf & _
                "GdiCharSet: " & Font.GdiCharSet & vbLf & _
                "GdiVerticalFont: " & Font.GdiVerticalFont & vbLf & _
                "GetHeight(): " & Font.GetHeight() & vbLf & _
                "GetHeight(grfx): " & Font.GetHeight(grfx) & vbLf & _
                "GetHeight(100 DPI): " & Font.GetHeight(100), _
                Font, New SolidBrush(clr), PointF.Empty)
    End Sub
End Class
```

Try clicking on this program's client area to print this output. The printed output will be the same as the display output except for the penultimate *Get-Height* value, which on the printer will match the last value. You can look at the properties of other fonts by simply setting the form's *Font* property to the font you want to examine. Here's what the program looks like on my system:

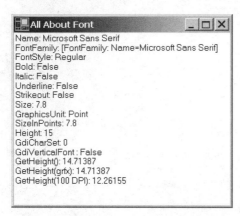

I have my video display settings set for a resolution of 120 dpi (also known as Large Fonts). The line-spacing value of 14.71 pixels corresponds to about 0.123 inch, or about 9 points, a suitable line spacing for an 8-point font. If you have your display set for a resolution of 96 dpi (Small Fonts), the line-spacing value will be 12.45; the *Height* property returns 13.

The first constructor for *Font* that we looked at creates a new font based on an existing font but with a different style property. There are times when you need to do something similar but with a different size.

For example, suppose you want to create a font that fits the interior of a specified rectangle. To do this, you need to start off with a font and the text you want to display. You use *MeasureString* to determine the dimensions of the displayed string, and then you create a new font with a size that's scaled to the size of the rectangle. Here's a program that displays the text "Howdy, world!" (a variation on the traditional text to include a character with a descender). The text is scaled as large as possible to fit in the client area.

**HowdyWorld.vb**

```
'-------------------------------------------------
' HowdyWorld.vb (c) 2002 by Charles Petzold
'-------------------------------------------------
Imports System
Imports System.Drawing
Imports System.Windows.Forms
```

```
Class HowdyWorld
    Inherits PrintableForm

    Shared Shadows Sub Main()
        Application.Run(New HowdyWorld())
    End Sub

    Sub New()
        Text = "Howdy, world!"
        MinimumSize = _
                Size.op_Addition(SystemInformation.MinimumWindowSize, _
                            New Size(0, 1))
    End Sub

    Protected Overrides Sub DoPage(ByVal grfx As Graphics, _
            ByVal clr As Color, ByVal cx As Integer, ByVal cy As Integer)
        Dim fnt As New Font("Times New Roman", 10, FontStyle.Italic)
        Dim szf As SizeF = grfx.MeasureString(Text, fnt)
        Dim fScale As Single = Math.Min(cx / szf.Width, cy / szf.Height)

        fnt = New Font(fnt.Name, fScale * fnt.SizeInPoints, fnt.Style)
        szf = grfx.MeasureString(Text, fnt)
        grfx.DrawString(Text, fnt, New SolidBrush(clr), _
                    (cx - szf.Width) / 2, (cy - szf.Height) / 2)
    End Sub
End Class
```

The setting of the *MinimumSize* property in the constructor prevents the client area height from going to zero, which would result in a zero font size and an exception being thrown.

The *DoPage* method begins with the creation of a *Font* object, but the font this method uses could just as well have been the form's *Font* property or a font created somewhere else. The idea is that the program doesn't really need to know what arguments were originally used to create the font.

The next statement in *DoPage* uses *MeasureString* to find the size of a text string (which happens to be the form's *Text* property) based on the font we just created, and the third statement calculates a scaling factor based on the relationship between the size of the client area (or the printable area of the printer page) and the size of the text. Notice the use of the *Math.Min* method to find the minimum of the horizontal and vertical scaling factors.

Next, the *DoPage* method creates a new font based on the existing font but scaling the point size by the *fScale* factor. *MeasureString* is called again. (Alternatively, you can multiply the *Width* and *Height* of the previous *SizeF* object by *fScale*.) Finally, the method centers the string in its client area.

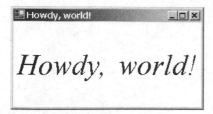

If the window is extra wide, the size of the font is governed by the window height:

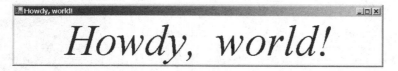

Is it possible to create a font that fills up the rectangle regardless of its aspect ratio? Of course, the characters would be distorted—either wider or narrower than the font height would imply. You can't do something like this with the *Font* constructors. In the *Font* constructors, you specify a font height. The character widths are determined by that height.

However, you can distort the aspect ratio of text characters by using the world transform. Here's a variation of the HowdyWorld program called Howdy-WorldFullFit that does just that.

**HowdyWorldFullFit.vb**

```vb
'-------------------------------------------------
' HowdyWorldFullFit.vb (c) 2002 by Charles Petzold
'-------------------------------------------------
Imports System
Imports System.Drawing
Imports System.Windows.Forms

Class HowdyWorldFullFit
    Inherits PrintableForm

    Shared Shadows Sub Main()
        Application.Run(New HowdyWorldFullFit())
    End Sub

    Sub New()
        Text = "Howdy, world!"
        MinimumSize = _
                Size.op_Addition(SystemInformation.MinimumWindowSize, _
                            New Size(0, 1))
    End Sub
```

```
    Protected Overrides Sub DoPage(ByVal grfx As Graphics, _
           ByVal clr As Color, ByVal cx As Integer, ByVal cy As Integer)
        Dim fnt As New Font("Times New Roman", 10, FontStyle.Italic)
        Dim szf As SizeF = grfx.MeasureString(Text, fnt)
        Dim fScaleHorz As Single = cx / szf.Width
        Dim fScaleVert As Single = cy / szf.Height

        grfx.ScaleTransform(fScaleHorz, fScaleVert)
        grfx.DrawString(Text, fnt, New SolidBrush(clr), 0, 0)
    End Sub
End Class
```

This version calculates separate scaling factors for the horizontal and vertical dimensions. The scaling factors are passed directly to the *ScaleTransform* method. The *DrawString* call displays the text at point (0, 0):

As usual, you can print this out and see the characters extend to fit almost the height of the paper.

Notice in this screen shot (and the second screen shot from the first HowdyWorld program) that the text doesn't extend to the full height of the client area. There's ample space above the ascenders that isn't being used for anything. That space is mostly used for diacritical marks. If the text contained characters À, Á, or Â (Unicode characters &H00C0, &H00C1, and &H00C2), for example, the accent marks would reach to the top of the client area.

Using the Windows Forms libraries, it isn't possible for an application to determine the amount of space that is reserved for diacritical marks. Nor is it possible to directly determine the x-height of a font, which is the height of lowercase letters without ascenders (such as "x") above the baseline. These particular *font metrics*, as they're called, are not exposed in the Windows Forms libraries. But other font metrics are derivable, as I'll discuss later in this chapter, and if you really need the information, you can approximately determine x-heights using paths. (Paths are covered in Chapter 15.)

# New Fonts from *FontFamily*

Four more constructors for *Font* are the same as the previous four constructors except that the first argument is a *FontFamily* object rather than a string with the family name:

### *Font* Constructors (selection)

```
Font(ByVal ff As FontFamily, ByVal fSizeInPoints As Single)

Font(ByVal ff As FontFamily, ByVal fSizeInPoints As Single,
    ByVal fs As FontStyle)

Font(ByVal ff As FontFamily, ByVal fSize As Single,
    ByVal gu As GraphicsUnit)

Font(ByVal ff As FontFamily, ByVal fSize As Single,
    ByVal fs As FontStyle, ByVal gu As GraphicsUnit)
```

So the question now becomes, How do you get a *FontFamily* object?

One way you can get it is from an existing font. For example, if you wanted to create a new font based on an existing font but in a new size, you could reference the *Name* property of the existing font as I did in the Howdy-World program:

```
Dim fnt18 As New Font(fnt.Name, 18, fnt.Style)
```

Or you could use the *FontFamily* property as the first argument:

```
Dim fnt18 As New Font(fnt.FontFamily, 18, fnt.Style)
```

Another way to get a *FontFamily* object is to use one of the three *FontFamily* constructors:

### *FontFamily* Constructors

```
FontFamily(ByVal strFamily As string )

FontFamily(ByVal gff As GenericFontFamilies)

FontFamily(ByVal strFamily As String,
        ByVal fontcoll As FontCollection)
```

That first constructor strongly suggests that a *FontFamily* object is defined entirely by a font family name. Indeed, the familiar statement

```
Dim fnt As New Font(strFamily, fSizeInPoints)
```

is just a shortcut for

```
Dim fnt As New Font(New FontFamily(strFamily), fSizeInPoints)
```

The only nonshared property of *FontFamily* is its name:

### *FontFamily* Nonshared Properties

| Property | Type | Accessibility | Description |
|----------|------|---------------|-------------|
| *Name* | *String* | Get | *FontFamily* name |

Although you've seen how you can create a *Font* without explicitly creating a *FontFamily*, it's sometimes useful to get the *FontFamily* first and store that in its own variable:

```
Dim ff As New FontFamily(strFamily)
```

You can then use the *IsStyleAvailable* method to determine whether a particular style is available:

### *FontFamily* Methods (selection)

```
Function IsStyleAvailable(ByVal fs As FontStyle) As Boolean
```

Not all TrueType or OpenType fonts have bold or italic versions, and if you try to create an italic or a bold font with a style that's not supported, you'll generate an exception. Worse yet, not all fonts have regular versions! It makes more sense to have code like this:

```
If (ff.IsStyleAvailable(FontStyle.Italic)) Then
    fntItalic = New Font(ff, 24, FontStyle.Italic)
ElseIf (ff.IsStyleAvailable(FontStyle.Regular) Then
    fntItalic = New Font(ff, 24, FontStyle.Regular)
Else
    fntItalic = New Font(ff, 24, FontStyle.Bold)
End If
```

This code might not result in creating an italic font, but at least you've avoided raising the exception.

As you saw at the beginning of this chapter, for many font families, separate files support the italic, bold, and bold italic versions of the families. In some cases, Windows *synthesizes* italic and bold, which means it creates italic, bold, and bold italic versions by modifying the characters of the regular font. This is the case for the Symbol font, Wingdings, and Webdings.

The second constructor for *FontFamily* requires a member of the *GenericFontFamilies* enumeration defined in *System.Drawing.Text*:

### *GenericFontFamilies* Enumeration

| Member | Value | Description |
| --- | --- | --- |
| *Serif* | 0 | e.g., Times New Roman |
| *SansSerif* | 1 | e.g., Arial |
| *Monospace* | 2 | e.g., Courier New |

Earlier I warned about possible problems creating a font based on a font family name that might not be present on some oddball system:

```
fnt = New Font("Times New Roman", 24)
```

You'll sleep much better at night if you use this constructor instead:

```
fnt = New Font(New FontFamily(GenericFontFamilies.Serif), 24)
```

I know, it's quite a mouthful and not nearly as elegant. But there's a shorter, equivalent version that's somewhat less verbose. The shorter version makes use of one of *FontFamily*'s shared properties:

### *FontFamily* Shared Properties (selection)

| Property | Type | Accessibility | Description |
| --- | --- | --- | --- |
| *GenericSerif* | *FontFamily* | Get | e.g., Times New Roman |
| *GenericSansSerif* | *FontFamily* | Get | e.g., Arial |
| *GenericMonospace* | *FontFamily* | Get | e.g., Courier New |

With these properties you can create a font like so:

```
fnt = New Font(FontFamily.GenericSerif, 24)
```

I'll discuss the third constructor for *FontFamily* later in this chapter.

# Understanding the Design Metrics

Programmers with experience in working with fonts in Windows or other graphical environments will probably agree that Windows Forms is really skimpy on the font metrics. So far, you've seen only three measurements that tell you anything about the height of the font: the point size (which I've emphasized is a typographical design concept only approximately related to any metrical size of the font characters); the maximum vertical extent of the font characters that you get from *MeasureString*; and the recommended line spacing, which is the value you get from *GetHeight* and—in an integer form suitable only for the video display—from *Height*.

If I could have just one more font metric, it would provide me with the location of the baseline. The *baseline* of a font is the line above which ascenders ascend and below which descenders descend. Knowing the location of the baseline relative to the top or bottom of the characters (which is what you specify in the *DrawString* method) is necessary if you want to mix different fonts on the same line.

This information is actually available in the *FontFamily* class. It's not very obvious, and it won't work for some of the Far Eastern and Middle Eastern fonts, but it's the best that's available.

The *FontFamily* class contains four methods that let you obtain additional metrical information about the font. Each of these methods requires a *FontStyle* enumeration value as an argument:

### *FontFamily* Methods (selection)

```
Function GetEmHeight(ByVal fs As FontStyle) As Integer

Function GetCellAscent(ByVal fs As FontStyle) As Integer

Function GetCellDescent(ByVal fs As FontStyle) As Integer

Function GetLineSpacing(ByVal fs As FontStyle) As Integer
```

These are called "design metrics" because they were originally set by the person who designed the font (or at least the TrueType version of the font). These design metrics are independent of the eventual size of the font created from this font family.

Let's look at an example. If you create a *FontFamily* based on Times New Roman and you call these four methods using *FontStyle.Regular* (or any other *FontStyle* value), you'll get the following numbers.

### Times New Roman Design Metrics

| Metric | Value |
| --- | --- |
| Em Height | 2048 |
| Ascent | 1825 |
| Descent | 443 |
| Ascent + Descent | 2268 |
| Line Spacing | 2355 |

The Em Height represents the grid that the designer of the font used for specifying coordinates of the various lines and curves that define each character in the font. The value of 2048 is very common. Less common are values of 1000 or 256.

The Ascent value is the height of the font characters above the baseline (including diacritical marks), and Descent is the height below the baseline. For Times New Roman, the sum of the Ascent and Descent (which I've added to the table) represents the actual height of the font characters.

The Line Spacing value breaks down into three components: the Ascent above the baseline, the Descent below the baseline, and some extra space below the Descent. It looks like this:

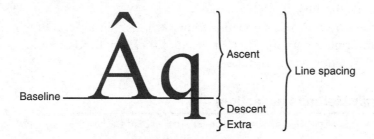

For some fonts, the Line Spacing value is greater than the sum of the cell Ascent and Descent. For other fonts, the Extra space is 0 and the sum of the Ascent and Descent equals the Line Spacing.

Do not attempt to fit the Em Height into this diagram in some way! The Em Height is simply a reference point for the other design metrics.

Let's continue the example by creating a 72-point Times New Roman font. Let us also set the *PageUnit* property to *GraphicsUnit.Point*. That means that *GetHeight* returns units of points regardless of the resolution of the graphics device. You'll get the following values (rounded to two decimal places):

### Times New Roman Font Metrics

| Property or Method | Value (in points) |
| --- | --- |
| *fnt.SizeInPoints* | 72.00 |
| *fnt.GetHeight(grfx)* | 82.79 |

Can this table be reconciled with the previous table showing the design metrics? Yes, because the value obtained from *GetHeight* is derived from those design metrics. The design metric called Em Height is equivalent to the point size of the font. If you take the ratio of 72 to 2048, you'll get 0.03515625. That's a scaling factor to convert the coordinates of the font characters to a point size. Multiply that scaling factor by the Line Spacing metric (2355) and you get 82.79, the value returned from *GetHeight*.

The implication here is that we can apply that same factor separately to the Ascent and Descent design metrics to provide us with numbers we didn't have before:

## Times New Roman Metrics

| Metric | Design Metric Value | Value for 72-Point Font (in points) | Property or Method |
|---|---|---|---|
| Em Height | 2048 | 72.00 | *fnt.SizeInPoints* |
| Ascent | 1825 | 64.16 | |
| Descent | 443 | 15.57 | |
| Ascent + Descent | 2268 | 79.73 | |
| Line Spacing | 2355 | 82.79 | *fnt.GetHeight(grfx)* |

You can use information derived from the design metrics to position text on a baseline. Let's suppose we want the baseline to be the horizontal line in the center of the client area and we want a 144-point Times New Roman font to be positioned on that line. Here's the code to do it.

```
TextOnBaseline.vb
'-------------------------------------------------
' TextOnBaseline.vb (c) 2002 by Charles Petzold
'-------------------------------------------------
Imports System
Imports System.Drawing
Imports System.Windows.Forms

Class TextOnBaseline
    Inherits PrintableForm

    Shared Shadows Sub Main()
        Application.Run(New TextOnBaseline())
    End Sub

    Sub New()
        Text = "Text on Baseline"
    End Sub

    Protected Overrides Sub DoPage(ByVal grfx As Graphics, _
            ByVal clr As Color, ByVal cx As Integer, ByVal cy As Integer)
```

*(continued)*

**TextOnBaseline.vb**   *(continued)*

```
            Dim yBaseline As Single = cy \ 2
            Dim pn As New Pen(clr)

            ' Draw the baseline across the center of the client area.
            grfx.DrawLine(pn, 0, yBaseline, cx, yBaseline)

            ' Create a 144-point font.
            Dim fnt As New Font("Times New Roman", 144)

            ' Get and calculate some metrics.
            Dim cyLineSpace As Single = fnt.GetHeight(grfx)
            Dim iCellSpace As Integer = fnt.FontFamily.GetLineSpacing(fnt.Style)
            Dim iCellAscent As Integer = fnt.FontFamily.GetCellAscent(fnt.Style)
            Dim cyAscent As Single = cyLineSpace * iCellAscent / iCellSpace

            ' Display the text on the baseline.
            grfx.DrawString("Baseline", fnt, New SolidBrush(clr), _
                            0, yBaseline - cyAscent)
        End Sub
End Class
```

The *cyAscent* value is the ascent for the 144-point Times New Roman font. Subtract that from the vertical coordinate of that baseline, and that's where to position text that sits on the baseline:

If you look carefully, you'll see that the rounded part of some letters actually dips below the baseline a bit, but that's normal.

# Arrays of Font Families

*FontFamily* has one more shared property and just one shared method, and they are very similar and very important. Both of them return an array of *Font-Family* objects corresponding to the installed TrueType and OpenType fonts on the system. Here's the shared property:

### *FontFamily* **Shared Property (selection)**

| Property | Type | Accessibility |
|----------|------|---------------|
| *Families* | *FontFamily()* | Get |

If you call

```
Dim aff() As FontFamily = FontFamily.Families
```

each element of the *aff* array will be a *FontFamily* object. If you've ever done font enumeration under Windows using the Win32 API, you're probably wondering why life can't always be this easy!

The first thing you'll probably want to do with this wonderful property is list all your fonts by creating a sample font from each family. Here's a simple program that does just that.

```
NaiveFamiliesList.vb
'-------------------------------------------------
' NaiveFamiliesList.vb (c) 2002 by Charles Petzold
'-------------------------------------------------
Imports System
Imports System.Drawing
Imports System.Windows.Forms

Class NaiveFamiliesList
    Inherits PrintableForm

    Shared Shadows Sub Main()
        Application.Run(New NaiveFamiliesList())
    End Sub

    Sub New()
        Text = "Naive Font Families List"
    End Sub

    Protected Overrides Sub DoPage(ByVal grfx As Graphics, _
            ByVal clr As Color, ByVal cx As Integer, ByVal cy As Integer)
        Dim br As New SolidBrush(clr)
        Dim y As Single = 0
```

*(continued)*

**NaiveFamiliesList.vb** *(continued)*

```
        Dim aff() As FontFamily = FontFamily.Families
        Dim ff As FontFamily

        For Each ff In aff
            Dim fnt As New Font(ff, 12)
            grfx.DrawString(ff.Name, fnt, br, 0, y)
            y += fnt.GetHeight(grfx)
        Next ff
    End Sub
End Class
```

The *For Each* statement goes through the elements of the *FontFamily* array. For each element, a *Font* constructor creates a 12-point font, the *DrawString* call uses that font to display the name of the font family, and the *GetHeight* call prepares the vertical coordinate for the next font.

This program might not work on your system. On mine, the *Font* constructor throws an exception for the very first font family in the array.

The problematic font file is Ahronbd.ttf, which is installed from the Windows XP CD-ROM as part of the support for Hebrew. The font implemented in this file is Aharoni Bold, and it's the only font in the Aharoni family (as least as far as Windows goes). What that means is that this statement will work:

```
fnt = New Font("Aharoni", 12, FontStyle.Bold)
```

But this one won't:

```
fnt = New Font("Aharoni", 12)
```

It won't work because it's equivalent to

```
fnt = New Font("Aharoni", 12, FontStyle.Regular)
```

and there's no regular Aharoni font. Bummer, right?

You can deal with this problem in a couple ways. The first approach is to use a *Try* and *Catch* construction. Put the code in the previous *For Each* loop in a *Try* block. In the *Catch* block, display the problematic font family name with an asterisk using the *Font* property of the form:

```
For Each (ff in aff)
    Try
        Dim fnt As New Font(ff, 12)
        grfx.DrawString(ff.Name, fnt, br, 0, y)
        y += fnt.GetHeight(grfx)
    Catch
        grfx.DrawString("* " + ff.Name, Font, br, 0, y)
        y += Font.GetHeight(grfx)
    End Try
Next ff
```

However, the general rule is that you should avoid *Try* and *Catch* blocks if alternative approaches are possible. The alternative approach here is the *IsStyleAvailable* method of the *FontFamily* class. Here's a better approach to listing the font families that works whether or not the Aharoni Bold font is installed.

**BetterFamiliesList.vb**

```
'----------------------------------------------------
' BetterFamiliesList.vb (c) 2002 by Charles Petzold
'----------------------------------------------------
Imports System
Imports System.Drawing
Imports System.Windows.Forms

Class BetterFamiliesList
    Inherits PrintableForm

    Shared Shadows Sub Main()
        Application.Run(New BetterFamiliesList())
    End Sub

    Sub New()
        Text = "Better Font Families List"
    End Sub

    Protected Overrides Sub DoPage(ByVal grfx As Graphics, _
            ByVal clr As Color, ByVal cx As Integer, ByVal cy As Integer)
        Dim br As New SolidBrush(clr)
        Dim y As Single = 0
        Dim aff() As FontFamily = FontFamily.Families
        Dim ff As FontFamily

        For Each ff In aff
            If ff.IsStyleAvailable(FontStyle.Regular) Then
                Dim fnt As New Font(ff, 12)
                grfx.DrawString(ff.Name, fnt, br, 0, y)
                y += fnt.GetHeight(grfx)
            Else
                grfx.DrawString("* " & ff.Name, Font, br, 0, y)
                y += Font.GetHeight(grfx)
            End If
        Next ff
    End Sub
End Class
```

If you have a large number of fonts installed on your system, however, this approach won't let you see them all, even if you have a big monitor and even if you print the list.

Short of adding scroll bars, a much better approach is to format the list into columns. That's what the following program does. And if this approach still isn't sufficient for all *your* fonts, try changing the *iPointSize* field to 10, 8, or 6.

**FamiliesList.vb**

```
'------------------------------------------------
' FamiliesList.vb (c) 2002 by Charles Petzold
'------------------------------------------------
Imports System
Imports System.Drawing
Imports System.Windows.Forms

Class FamiliesList
    Inherits PrintableForm

    Const iPointSize As Integer = 12

    Shared Shadows Sub Main()
        Application.Run(New FamiliesList())
    End Sub

    Sub New()
        Text = "Font Families List"
    End Sub

    Protected Overrides Sub DoPage(ByVal grfx As Graphics, _
            ByVal clr As Color, ByVal cx As Integer, ByVal cy As Integer)
        Dim br As New SolidBrush(clr)
        Dim x As Single = 0
        Dim y As Single = 0
        Dim fMaxWidth As Single = 0
        Dim aff() As FontFamily = GetFontFamilyArray(grfx)
        Dim ff As FontFamily

        For Each ff In aff
            Dim fnt As Font = CreateSampleFont(ff, iPointSize)
            Dim szf As SizeF = grfx.MeasureString(ff.Name, fnt)
            fMaxWidth = Math.Max(fMaxWidth, szf.Width)
        Next ff

        For Each ff In aff
            Dim fnt As Font = CreateSampleFont(ff, iPointSize)
            Dim fHeight As Single = fnt.GetHeight(grfx)

            If y > 0 AndAlso y + fHeight > cy Then
                x += fMaxWidth
                y = 0
            End If
            grfx.DrawString(ff.Name, fnt, br, x, y)
```

```
            y += fHeight
        Next ff
    End Sub

    Protected Overridable Function GetFontFamilyArray _
                            (ByVal grfx As Graphics) As FontFamily()
        Return FontFamily.Families
    End Function

    Private Function CreateSampleFont(ByVal ff As FontFamily, _
                            ByVal fPointSize As Single) As Font
        If ff.IsStyleAvailable(FontStyle.Regular) Then
            Return New Font(ff, fPointSize)
        ElseIf ff.IsStyleAvailable(FontStyle.Bold) Then
            Return New Font(ff, fPointSize, FontStyle.Bold)
        ElseIf ff.IsStyleAvailable(FontStyle.Italic) Then
            Return New Font(ff, fPointSize, FontStyle.Italic)
        Else
            Return Font
        End If
    End Function
End Class
```

The *DoPage* method has two *For Each* loops. The first determines the width of each font family name displayed in a sample font from that family and saves the maximum width; the second *For Each* loop uses that maximum width to display multiple columns.

Notice the *CreateSampleFont* method down at the bottom of the class. I use this in the *DoPage* method instead of using the *Font* constructor. *CreateSampleFont* uses the *IsStyleAvailable* method to determine whether to create a regular, bold, or italic font. This approach succeeds in displaying a sample Aharoni font where the previous programs did not. Here's a nonmaximized version of the program running on my machine:

If you've installed some Far Eastern or Middle Eastern fonts, you'll notice that the line spacing seems to be excessively large for the displayed text. That's because these fonts are designed for displaying alphabets other than Latin.

This FamiliesList program isolates the statement that obtains the array of *FontFamily* objects in a short method I named *GetFontFamilyArray*. I did that so that in the next program I can easily demonstrate the use of the only shared method implemented in *FontFamily*. This shared method is similar to the *Families* property except that it has an argument of type *Graphics*:

## *FontFamily* Shared Method

```
Function GetFamilies(ByVal grfx As Graphics) As FontFamily()
```

The idea here is that different graphics output devices might have different fonts installed; in particular, some printers have built-in fonts that can't be displayed on the screen. This program overrides the *GetFontFamilyArray* to get the font families from *GetFamilies* rather than *Families*.

### GetFamiliesList.vb

```
'-------------------------------------------------
' GetFamiliesList.vb (c) 2002 by Charles Petzold
'-------------------------------------------------
Imports System
Imports System.Drawing
Imports System.Windows.Forms

Class GetFamiliesList
    Inherits FamiliesList

    Shared Shadows Sub Main()
        Application.Run(New GetFamiliesList())
    End Sub

    Sub New()
        Text = "Font GetFamilies List"
    End Sub

    Protected Overrides Function GetFontFamilyArray _
                        (ByVal grfx As Graphics) As FontFamily()
        Return FontFamily.GetFamilies(grfx)
    End Function
End Class
```

At least for my printer, *GetFamilies* returns the same array as *Families*. Perhaps in a later version of Windows Forms we'll see more support for printer-specific fonts.

# Font Collections

The *Families* property and *GetFamilies* method of the *FontFamily* class are not the only way to get an array of font families. The *System.Drawing.Text* namespace has an abstract *FontCollection* class from which two other classes are derived: *InstalledFontCollection* and *PrivateFontCollection*.

*FontCollection* implements just one property:

### *FontCollection* Property

| Name | Type | Accessibility |
|------|------|---------------|
| *Families* | *FontFamily()* | Get |

This property—which is *not* defined as shared—is inherited by both *InstalledFontCollection* and *PrivateFontCollection*. The following program overrides the *GetFontFamilyArray* method in the FamiliesList program with code that creates an instance of the *InstalledFontCollection* class and uses the *Families* property to get the array of font families.

```
InstalledFontsList.vb
'-------------------------------------------------------
' InstalledFontsList.vb (c) 2002 by Charles Petzold
'-------------------------------------------------------
Imports System
Imports System.Drawing
Imports System.Drawing.Text
Imports System.Windows.Forms

Class InstalledFontsList
    Inherits FamiliesList

    Shared Shadows Sub Main()
        Application.Run(New InstalledFontsList())
    End Sub

    Sub New()
        Text = "InstalledFontCollection List"
    End Sub

    Protected Overrides Function GetFontFamilyArray _
                        (ByVal grfx As Graphics) As FontFamily()
        Dim fc As New InstalledFontCollection()
        Return fc.Families
    End Function
End Class
```

This program produces the same output as the FamiliesList program.

When you create an instance of the *PrivateFontCollection* class, it initially contains no font families. You add fonts to the collection by using the following two methods:

### *PrivateFontCollection* Methods (selection)

```
Sub AddFontFile(ByVal strFilename As String)
Sub AddMemoryFont(ByVal pFont As IntPtr, ByVal iLength As Integer)
```

This facility is used by applications that include their own specialized font files. After creating a *PrivateFontCollection* object and calling these two methods, the application can then use the *Families* property to obtain an array of *FontFamily* objects suitable for creating *Font* objects. Or (since your program probably knows what font families are included in this collection) you can use the third *FontFamily* constructor in the list on page 378 to create *FontFamily* objects based on font files in this collection.

# Variations on *DrawString*

We've already encountered the six variations of the *DrawString* method:

### *Graphics DrawString* Methods

```
Sub DrawString(ByVal str As String, ByVal fnt As Font,
          ByVal br As Brush, ByVal ptf As PointF)
Sub DrawString(ByVal str As String, ByVal fnt As Font,
          ByVal br As Brush, ByVal x As Single,
          ByVal y As Single)
Sub DrawString(ByVal str As String, ByVal fnt As Font,
          ByVal br As Brush, ByVal rectf As RectangleF)
Sub DrawString(ByVal str As String, ByVal fnt As Font,
          ByVal br As Brush, ByVal ptf As PointF,
          ByVal sf As StringFormat)
Sub DrawString(ByVal str As String, ByVal fnt As Font,
          ByVal br As Brush, ByVal x As Single,
          ByVal y As Single, ByVal sf As StringFormat)
Sub DrawString(ByVal str As String, ByVal fnt As Font,
          ByVal br As Brush, ByVal rectf As RectanglF,
          ByVal sf As StringFormat)
```

The versions using a *PointF* structure are identical to the versions using the two *Single* values. It's just two different ways of specifying the same starting point for the string. All four of the *DrawString* overloads that use a *PointF* or two *Single* values generally display a single line of text. However, if the text contains line feed characters (*Chr(10)* or *vbLf*), the text that follows is displayed one line lower.

The two versions of *DrawString* that use a *RectangleF* argument wrap text that is too wide to fit within the rectangle width. If a single word is too wide for the rectangle, the method will fit as much of the word as possible and then display the remainder of the word on the next line.

These versions of *DrawString* properly recognize Unicode character &H00A0, the No-Break Space. You use a no-break space instead of a regular space when text wrapped at the space would look peculiar, for example, in the following string:

```
"World War" & ChrW(&H00A0) & "I"
```

In this case, if the *I* doesn't fit at the end of a line, the *DrawString* method would break the line after the word *World*.

These versions of *DrawString* do *not* properly recognize Unicode character &H00AD, the Soft Hyphen. Customarily, you insert soft hyphens at the syllable breaks in long words:

```
"ex" & ChrW(&H00AD) & "traor" & ChrW(&H00AD) & "di" & ChrW(&H00AD) & "nary"
```

In theory, if the text formatter can break the line at the hyphen, it will do so and display the hyphen. If not, the hyphen won't be displayed. The *DrawString* method displays these hyphens regardless, and even breaks a line *before* the hyphen.

These versions of *DrawString* also do *not* properly handle Unicode character &H2011, the Non-Breaking Hyphen, which you use in words like this:

```
"T" & ChrW(&H2011) & "shirt"
```

The *T* followed by a hyphen would look odd at the end of a line. Some TrueType fonts don't include this character. In those fonts that do include the character (such as Lucida Sans Unicode), the *DrawString* method seems to avoid breaking a line on the Non-Breaking Hyphen, but it inserts some extra space following the hyphen.

Because the word-wrapping ability of the *DrawString* call seems so powerful, it's important to understand its limitations. For example, you may find *DrawString* perfect for displaying a particular block of text in your application, but with just one little problem: there's a word in the text that needs to be bold or italic. Well, you can't do it. The *Font* argument to *DrawString* determines the font for the entire block of text. (Interestingly enough, however, there *is* a way you can *underline* selected text in a *DrawString* call. I'll demonstrate how to do that in the UnderlinedText program later in this chapter.)

Another limitation: as you know, you can use the *Alignment* property of the *StringFormat* class to control the horizontal alignment of text you display in a rectangle. You can align a paragraph on the left edge of the rectangle, you can align a paragraph on the right, and you can center the lines of the paragraph within the rectangle. But you can't justify the rectangle. You can't instruct *Draw-String* to insert extra space between the words so that the left margin and the right margin are both even.

If you need to do either of these jobs, you have two choices: you can either write your own text-formatting logic or make use of the *RichTextBox* control that has many more built-in formatting options than *DrawString* does. I discuss *RichTextBox* in Chapter 18.

# Anti-Aliased Text

In Chapter 5, I showed how the *SmoothingMode* and *PixelOffsetMode* properties of the *Graphics* class govern anti-aliasing of lines and curves. Windows can also use anti-aliasing for the display of text. This feature is under user control. You can turn it on and off by checking the option Smooth Edges Of Screen Fonts in the Effects dialog of the Display Properties dialog box.

If you want, your program can override the user's preferences by setting the *TextRenderingHint* property of the *Graphics* class:

### *Graphics* Properties (selection)

| Property | Type | Accessibility |
|----------|------|---------------|
| TextRenderingHint | TextRenderingHint | Get/Set |

*TextRenderingHint* is also an enumeration defined in the *System.Drawing.Text* namespace:

### *TextRenderingHint* Enumeration

| Member | Value | Description |
|--------|-------|-------------|
| SystemDefault | 0 | Default |
| SingleBitPerPixelGridFit | 1 | No anti-aliasing, grid fitting |
| SingleBitPerPixel | 2 | No anti-aliasing, no grid fitting |

*(continued)*

***TextRenderingHint* Enumeration**   *(continued)*

| Member | Value | Description |
|---|---|---|
| *AntiAliasGridFit* | 3 | Anti-aliasing with grid fitting |
| *AntiAlias* | 4 | Anti-aliasing, no grid fitting |
| *ClearTypeGridFit* | 5 | ClearType for LCD displays |

ClearType is a technology similar to anti-aliasing but which takes advantage of the arrangement of color dots on LCD displays.[*]

The following program demonstrates the use of all six of these enumeration values.

**AntiAliasedText.vb**

```
'-----------------------------------------------
' AntiAliasedText.vb (c) 2002 by Charles Petzold
'-----------------------------------------------
Imports System
Imports System.Drawing
Imports System.Drawing.Text
Imports System.Windows.Forms

Class AntiAliasedText
    Inherits PrintableForm

    Shared Shadows Sub Main()
        Application.Run(new AntiAliasedText())
    End Sub

    Sub New()
        Text = "Anti-Aliased Text"
        Font = new Font("Times New Roman", 12)
    End Sub

    Protected Overrides Sub DoPage(ByVal grfx As Graphics, _
            ByVal clr As Color, ByVal cx As Integer, ByVal cy As Integer)
        Dim br As New SolidBrush(clr)
        Dim str As String = "A "
        Dim cxText As Integer = CInt(grfx.MeasureString(str, Font).Width)
        Dim i As Integer

        For i = 0 To 5
            grfx.TextRenderingHint = CType(i, TextRenderingHint)
```

---

[*] It turns out that this technique has been discovered and rediscovered over a period of more than two decades. See Steve Gibson's discussion of the technology and its history on his Web site at *http://grc.com/cleartype.htm*.

**AntiAliasedText.vb**   *(continued)*

```
            grfx.DrawString(str, Font, br, i * cxText, 0)
        Next i
    End Sub
End Class
```

The program displays a capital *A* six times using the six *TextRendering-Hint* values. You can copy an image of this program into the clipboard by using Alt+Print Scrn and then paste the image into a graphics paint or photo program, where you can blow it up like so:

Depending on your settings, the first (*SystemDefault*) will match either the second (*SingleBitPerPixelGridFit*) or the fourth (*AntiAliasGridFit*), or if you're using ClearType on an LCD display the first could match the sixth (*ClearType-GridFit*). Neither the second nor the third enumeration value (*SingleBitPerPixel*) causes any anti-aliasing of text to be performed. However, notice one or more blank pixels in the third capital *A*. The character rasterizer is using stricter criteria for determining whether or not a pixel should be colored.

The fourth (*AntiAliasGridFit*) and fifth (*AntiAlias*) examples use anti-aliasing. Pixels are colored with a darker gray shade depending on the extent to which they intersect the theoretical outlined character.

For *ClearTypeGridFit*, pixels to the left and right of the strokes are in different colors based on the horizontal organization of color dots on LCD displays. You should not use ClearType on regular CRTs. The LCD display must be connected to the video board through a digital interface rather than the normal analog interface. Some LCD displays allow users to rotate them 90 degrees and use them in portrait mode. ClearType won't work in that case either.

# Measuring the String

Since Chapter 3, we've been using *MeasureString* to determine the size of a text string for accurate positioning. *MeasureString* also has another use. As you've probably noticed, the *DrawString* method displays text without also erasing the background of the destination rectangle. (This isn't the default behavior in Windows GDI.) If you do need to erase the background, you can use the coordinate point at which you'll be drawing the text combined with the *SizeF* returned from *MeasureString* in a *FillRectangle* call.

The *MeasureString* method comes in seven versions:

### Graphics *MeasureString* Methods

```
Function MeasureString(ByVal str As String, ByVal fnt As Font) As SizeF

Function MeasureString(ByVal str As String, ByVal fnt As Font,
                ByVal iWidth As Integer) As SizeF

Function MeasureString(ByVal str As String, ByVal fnt As Font,
                ByVal szf As SizeF) As SizeF

Function MeasureString(ByVal str As String, ByVal fnt As Font,
                ByVal iWidth As Integer,
                ByVal strfmt As StringFormat) As SizeF

Function MeasureString(ByVal str As String, ByVal fnt As Font,
                ByVal szf As SizeF,
                byVal strfmt As StringFormat) As SizeF

Function MeasureString(ByVal str As String, ByVal fnt As Font,
                ByVal ptfOrigin As PointF,
                ByVal strfmt As StringFormat) As SizeF

Function MeasureString(ByVal str As String, ByVal fnt As Font,
                ByVal szf As SizeF,
                ByVal strfmt As StringFormat,
                ByRef iCharacters As Integer,
                ByRef iLines As Integer) As SizeF
```

We've been using the first version of *MeasureString* for quite some time. It returns the width and height of the specified string as displayed using the specified font. The *Height* property of the *SizeF* object returned from the method is often close to the value returned from the *GetHeight* method of the *Font* class, but it could be a multiple of the font height if the text includes line feed characters.

The second version of *MeasureString* includes a third argument that indicates a text width. This version is useful if you'll be displaying the string using the *RectangleF* version of *DrawString* and want wrapping to occur. The *Width* property of the *SizeF* object returned from *MeasureString* is always less than or equal to the *iWidth* argument; the *Height* property, when divided by the *GetHeight* value, equals the number of lines.

The third version of *MeasureString* has an actual *SizeF* argument, indicating both a width and a height. If the *Width* property of this *SizeF* argument is the same as the *iWidth* argument used in the second version of *MeasureString* and if the *Height* property is sufficient for all the lines of text in the string, the return value of this version will be the same as the second version. Otherwise, the *Height* property of the returned *SizeF* object will equal the *Height* property of the *SizeF* argument, and the *Width* property of the returned *SizeF* object will indicate the maximum width of the text that can fit in that size rectangle.

The fourth, fifth, and sixth versions are similar to the second and third except that they include a *StringFormat* argument. If you'll be using a *String-Format* argument in the *DrawString* call, you should also use one in the *Mea-sureString* call.

The final version of *MeasureString* has two arguments that return additional information to the application. (Notice *ByRef* rather than *ByVal* for the last two arguments.) These indicate the number of characters and lines of text that a *DrawString* call will display when passed a *RectangleF* structure of the same size as the *SizeF* structure and the same *StringFormat* object.

Calling *MeasureString* with these arguments is extremely useful when you need to use multiple *DrawString* calls to display a single block of text. For example, suppose you want to use *DrawString* to display text to the printer but the text is too long for a single page. You use *MeasureString* to determine how much can fit on the first page and then start the second page with a new text string based on information returned from *MeasureString*. I'll demonstrate the use of this version of *MeasureString* in the TextColumns program toward the end of this chapter.

# The *StringFormat* Options

The *DrawString* and *MeasureString* methods can optionally include an argument that is an object of type *StringFormat*. This argument offers you many different—sometimes subtle and sometimes not so subtle—variations in the display of text. You can create a *StringFormat* object by using one of the following constructors:

### *StringFormat* Constructors

```
StringFormat()

StringFormat(ByVal strfmt As StringFormat)

StringFormat(ByVal sff As StringFormatFlags)

StringFormat(ByVal sff As StringFormatFlags, ByVal iLanguage As Integer)
```

The second version essentially clones an existing *StringFormat* object; the third and fourth versions create a *StringFormat* object based on a combination of *StringFormatFlags* enumeration values. The *StringFormatFlags* enumeration is also used in setting the *FormatFlags* property of *StringFormat*:

### *StringFormat* Properties (selection)

| Property | Type | Accessibility |
|---|---|---|
| *FormatFlags* | *StringFormatFlags* | Get/Set |

The *StringFormatFlags* enumeration is a series of bit flags:

### *StringFormatFlags* Enumeration

| Member | Value |
|---|---|
| *DirectionRightToLeft* | &H0001 |
| *DirectionVertical* | &H0002 |
| *FitBlackBox* | &H0004 |
| *DisplayFormatControl* | &H0020 |
| *NoFontFallback* | &H0400 |
| *MeasureTrailingSpaces* | &H0800 |
| *NoWrap* | &H1000 |
| *LineLimit* | &H2000 |
| *NoClip* | &H4000 |

I discuss some of these flags in this book in connection with certain programs. I use *MeasureTrailingSpaces* in the TypeAway program in Chapter 6, and in the BoldAndItalicTighter program coming up shortly. I demonstrate *NoWrap* and *NoClip* in the TrimmingTheText program later in this chapter.

When you create a new *StringFormat* object using the default constructor, the *FormatFlags* property is set to 0. Notice that these enumeration values are single bits, so you can combine them with the Visual Basic *Or* operator. For example,

```
Dim strfmt As New StringFormat(StringFormatFlags.DirectionVertical Or _
                        StringFormatFlags.NoClip)
```

When you're setting the *FormatFlags* property, I strongly recommend that you get into the habit of combining the existing flags with the new one using the *Or* operator:

```
strfmt.FormatFlags = strfmt.FormatFlags Or StringFormatFlags.NoWrap
```

That way, you'll never accidentally turn off one of the other flags that you may have set earlier.

Besides using one of the constructors, you can obtain a *StringFormat* object by using one of the following shared properties:

**StringFormat Shared Properties**

| Property | Type | Accessibility |
|---|---|---|
| *GenericDefault* | *StringFormat* | Get |
| *GenericTypographic* | *StringFormat* | Get |

If you examine the properties of the *StringFormat* objects returned by these shared properties, you'll discover that *GenericDefault* returns a *StringFormat* object that is the same as that created by the default constructor. The *Generic-Typographic* property returns an object that has the *FitBlackBox*, *LineLimit*, and *NoClip* flags set as well as a different value for the *Trimming* property, which I'll discuss later in this chapter.

However, the *StringFormat* object that *GenericTypographic* returns has an additional effect on *DrawString* and *MeasureString* that is not revealed by the public *StringFormat* properties and flags. This additional effect is what I'll tackle next.

# Grid Fitting and Text Fitting

The text-handling portion of GDI+ is designed to be device independent. In practical terms, *MeasureString* returns a text dimension that is independent of the output device. If you set the same page transform on both the screen and the printer, *MeasureString* returns identical values for any particular text string and font. This consistency makes it comparatively easy to format text on the screen that will look the same when printed on the printer.

However desirable the goal of WYSIWYG may be, it's not easy to realize in real life. The problem is pixels. When the characters of an outline font are rasterized, the original floating-point coordinates must be rounded to discrete pixels. Such *grid fitting*, as it's called, requires hints that prevent this rounding from destroying the legibility of the font. The two vertical strokes on a capital *H* must be the same width, for example. Even for small point sizes, these two strokes must be at least 1 pixel wide and must be separated by a pixel. (If the point size is very small compared to the resolution of the output device, such requirements can be abandoned because the text wouldn't be legible anyway.)

In some cases, particularly for small point sizes on low-resolution devices (such as the video display), grid fitting can cause rendered characters to be noticeably larger than their theoretical size. String a bunch of these characters together (for example, lower case Arial *i*'s), and you could end up with a text string substantially larger on the screen than on the printer. (See the article at *http://www.gotdotnet.com/team/windowsforms/gdiptext.aspx* for more-detailed examples of this problem.)

When you use *DrawString* and *MeasureString* to concatenate pieces of text (such as in the BoldAndItalic programs shown earlier in this chapter), would you prefer that the resultant output has extra space between the pieces or that the pieces of text overlap somewhat? I think you'd agree that overlapping text is the less desirable alternative. To prevent overlapping text, the *DrawString* and *MeasureString* methods have been deliberately finagled to include a little extra space. Thus, if the rasterizer requires more space to render a particular font, that space is available.

By default, the *SizeF* object returned from *MeasureString* has a *Height* property 1/8 em greater than what is theoretically necessary and a *Width* property 1/3 em more than the theoretical width in addition to a small percentage increase. (Remember that an em is equal to the point size of the font. For example, for a 24-point font, 1/3 em equals 8 points.) By default, the *DrawString* method begins displaying text 1/6 em beyond the specified vertical coordinate. In effect, *MeasureString* indicates a rectangle that is wider than the theoretical text string by 1/6 em on the right and left.

And that's why the BoldAndItalic program and, more demonstrably, the BoldAndItalicBigger program, have superfluous padding between the concatenated pieces of text.

Keep in mind that the grid-fitting problem affects only fonts with small point sizes displayed on low-resolution devices. To achieve device independence, however, the extra padding built into *DrawString* and *MeasureString* must be the same for both low-resolution and high-resolution devices. And the padding must be proportional for small fonts and large fonts. For a 720-point font, *MeasureString* must return a text size 100 times greater than for a 7.2-point font. What do you do if you don't want this extra space? You simply use a *StringFormat* object based on *StringFormat.GenericTypographic*. Here's a version of the BoldAndItalic program that uses such a *StringFormat* object.

## BoldAndItalicTighter.vb

```
'-----------------------------------------------------
' BoldAndItalicTighter.vb (c) 2002 by Charles Petzold
'-----------------------------------------------------
Imports System
Imports System.Drawing
Imports System.Drawing.Text
Imports System.Windows.Forms
```

*(continued)*

**BoldAndItalicTighter.vb**    *(continued)*

```
Class BoldAndItalicTighter
    Inherits PrintableForm

    Shared Shadows Sub Main()
        Application.Run(new BoldAndItalicTighter())
    End Sub

    Sub New()
        Text = "Bold and Italic (Tighter)"
        Font = new Font("Times New Roman", 24)
    End Sub

    Protected Overrides Sub DoPage(ByVal grfx As Graphics, _
            ByVal clr As Color, ByVal cx As Integer, ByVal cy As Integer)
        Const str1 As String = "This is some "
        Const str2 As String = "bold"
        Const str3 As String = " text, and Me is some "
        Const str4 As String = "italic"
        Const str5 As String = " text."
        Dim br As New SolidBrush(clr)
        Dim fntRegular As Font = Font
        Dim fntBold As New Font(fntRegular, FontStyle.Bold)
        Dim fntItalic As New Font(fntRegular, FontStyle.Italic)
        Dim ptf As New PointF(0, 0)
        Dim strfmt As StringFormat = StringFormat.GenericTypographic
        strfmt.FormatFlags = strfmt.FormatFlags Or _
                            StringFormatFlags.MeasureTrailingSpaces

        grfx.DrawString(str1, fntRegular, br, ptf, strfmt)
        ptf.X += _
            grfx.MeasureString(str1, fntRegular, ptf, strfmt).Width

        grfx.DrawString(str2, fntBold, br, ptf, strfmt)
        ptf.X += grfx.MeasureString(str2, fntBold, ptf, strfmt).Width

        grfx.DrawString(str3, fntRegular, br, ptf, strfmt)
        ptf.X += grfx.MeasureString(str3, fntRegular, ptf, strfmt).Width

        grfx.DrawString(str4, fntItalic, br, ptf, strfmt)
        ptf.X += grfx.MeasureString(str4, fntItalic, ptf, strfmt).Width

        grfx.DrawString(str5, fntRegular, br, ptf, strfmt)
    End Sub
End Class
```

Notice that the program also sets the *MeasureTrailingSpaces* flag. The result looks just fine:

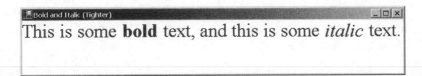

I can get away with using the *GenericTypographic* object in BoldAndItal-icTighter because I know that the font is large enough that a few pixels here and there won't make a difference. If you want to use *GenericTypographic* in small font sizes on the video display, you should also enable anti-aliasing. Anti-aliasing avoids grid fitting approximations because each pixel is colored based on its intersection with the theoretical outline.

# Horizontal and Vertical Alignment

Our first encounter with the *StringFormat* class was back in Chapter 3, where we used it to center text in a form's client area. The two *StringFormat* properties that affect the alignment of text are shown here:

### *StringFormat* Properties (selection)

| Property | Type | Accessibility | Description |
| --- | --- | --- | --- |
| *Alignment* | *StringAlignment* | Get/Set | Horizontal alignment |
| *LineAlignment* | *StringAlignment* | Get/Set | Vertical alignment |

Both these properties are of type *StringAlignment*, which is an enumeration consisting of just three members:

### *StringAlignment* Enumeration

| Member | Value | Description |
| --- | --- | --- |
| *Near* | 0 | Usually left or top |
| *Center* | 1 | Always the center |
| *Far* | 2 | Usually right or bottom |

The alignment values work a little differently depending on whether you specify a *PointF* object or a *RectangleF* object in the *DrawString* call. Let's take a look at the *RectangleF* version of *DrawString* first. The following program uses the client area rectangle in nine *DrawString* calls, each of which uses a different combination of *Alignment* and *LineAlignment* properties. Just to make it interesting, the text I'm displaying with each *DrawString* call has an embedded line feed character.

```
StringAlignmentRectangle.vb
'-----------------------------------------------------------------
' StringAlignmentRectangle.vb (c) 2002 by Charles Petzold
'-----------------------------------------------------------------
Imports System
Imports System.Drawing
Imports System.Windows.Forms

Class StringAlignmentRectangle
    Inherits PrintableForm

    Shared Shadows Sub Main()
        Application.Run(New StringAlignmentRectangle())
    End Sub

    Sub New()
        Text = "String Alignment (RectangleF in DrawString)"
    End Sub

    Protected Overrides Sub DoPage(ByVal grfx As Graphics, _
            ByVal clr As Color, ByVal cx As Integer, ByVal cy As Integer)
        Dim br As New SolidBrush(clr)
        Dim rectf As New RectangleF(0, 0, cx, cy)
        Dim astrAlign() As String = {"Near", "Center", "Far"}
        Dim strfmt As New StringFormat()
        Dim iVert, iHorz As Integer

        For iVert = 0 To 2
            For iHorz = 0 To 2
                strfmt.LineAlignment = CType(iVert, StringAlignment)
                strfmt.Alignment = CType(iHorz, StringAlignment)
                grfx.DrawString( _
                    String.Format("LineAlignment = {0}" & vbLf & _
                                  "Alignment = {1}", _
                                  astrAlign(iVert), astrAlign(iHorz)), _
                        Font, br, rectf, strfmt)
            Next iHorz
        Next iVert
    End Sub
End Class
```

The three possible values of the *Alignment* property cause the text to be left aligned, centered, or right aligned in the rectangle. The three possible values of *LineAlignment* cause the text to be displayed at the top, center, or bottom of the rectangle:

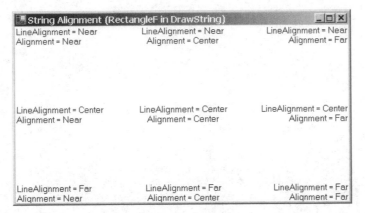

Such a nice, neat, well-ordered display isn't possible when you use the same *PointF* object in multiple calls to *DrawString*. Some of the combinations would overlap with others. Let's instead look at a few at a time.

This program sets the *PointF* object in the *DrawString* call to the center of the client area but uses only four combinations of the *Alignment* and *LineAlignment* properties.

**StringAlignmentPoint.vb**

```
'---------------------------------------------------------
' StringAlignmentPoint.vb (c) 2002 by Charles Petzold
'---------------------------------------------------------
Imports System
Imports System.Drawing
Imports System.Windows.Forms

Class StringAlignmentPoint
    Inherits PrintableForm

    Shared Shadows Sub Main()
        Application.Run(new StringAlignmentPoint())
    End Sub

    Sub New()
        Text = "String Alignment (PointF in DrawString)"
    End Sub
```

*(continued)*

**StringAlignmentPoint.vb** *(continued)*

```
    Protected Overrides Sub DoPage(ByVal grfx As Graphics, _
            ByVal clr As Color, ByVal cx As Integer, ByVal cy As Integer)
        Dim br As New SolidBrush(clr)
        Dim pn As New Pen(clr)
        Dim astrAlign() As String = {"Near", "Center", "Far"}
        Dim strfmt As New StringFormat()
        Dim iVert, iHorz As Integer

        grfx.DrawLine(pn, 0, cy \ 2, cx, cy \ 2)
        grfx.DrawLine(pn, cx \ 2, 0, cx \ 2, cy)

        For iVert = 0 To 2 Step 2
            For iHorz = 0 To 2 Step 2
                strfmt.LineAlignment = CType(iVert, StringAlignment)
                strfmt.Alignment = CType(iHorz, StringAlignment)
                grfx.DrawString( _
                    String.Format("LineAlignment = {0}" & vbLf & _
                                  "Alignment = {1}", _
                                  astrAlign(iVert), astrAlign(iHorz)), _
                    Font, br, cx \ 2, cy \ 2, strfmt)
            Next iHorz
        Next iVert
    End Sub
End Class
```

Notice the two *For* statements: the *iVert* and *iHorz* variables end up being set to only 0 and 2, and the program uses only four combinations of the *Alignment* and *LineAlignment* properties to create a display that looks like this:

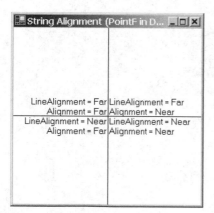

The *PointF* object passed to *DrawString* is the center of the client area. The *DrawString* call positions the two lines of text relative to this coordinate depending on the settings of the *Alignment* and *LineAlignment* properties.

If you change the first *For* statement in this program to

```
For iVert = 1 To 2 Step 2
```

and recompile, you can see how a *LineAlignment* property set to *StringAlign-mentCenter* causes the vertical coordinate passed to *DrawString* to specify the center of the text. In this case, that's the vertical center of the two text lines:

If instead you change the second *For* statement to

```
For iHorz = 1 To 2 Step 2
```

the two lines of text are centered around the horizontal coordinate:

If you change both *For* loops as just shown, you'll get the final case. The two lines of text are centered horizontally and vertically around the midpoint of the client area.

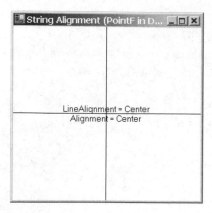

# The Hotkey Display

The *HotkeyPrefix* property of *StringFormat* determines how the *DrawString* call interprets ampersands:

### *StringFormat* Properties (selection)

| Property | Type | Accessibility |
|---|---|---|
| *HotkeyPrefix* | *HotkeyPrefix* | Get/Set |

How the DrawString call interprets ampersands? That might sound a little odd until you realize that embedded ampersands have a special meaning in the text used in menu items, buttons, and other controls. The ampersand indicates that the character that follows is to be underlined and that the character is to function as a keyboard shortcut.

You set the *HotkeyPrefix* property to one of the following *HotkeyPrefix* enumeration values defined in the *System.Drawing.Text* namespace:

### *HotkeyPrefix* Enumeration

| Member | Value | Description |
|---|---|---|
| *None* | 0 | "&File" ➜ "&File" (default) |
| *Show* | 1 | "&File" ➜ "File" |
| *Hide* | 2 | "&File" ➜ "File" |

By default, ampersands aren't treated special and are simply displayed as ampersands. The *Show* value suppresses the ampersand and forces the next character to be underlined. The *Hide* value suppresses the ampersand but doesn't underline the next character.

Even if you're not displaying text in menus or controls, you can use this property to underline specific letters or words that appear in blocks of text you pass to the *DrawString* call. Here's a program that demonstrates this technique.

```vb
UnderlinedText.vb
'------------------------------------------------------
' UnderlinedText.vb (c) 2002 by Charles Petzold
'------------------------------------------------------
Imports System
Imports System.Drawing
Imports System.Drawing.Text
Imports System.Windows.Forms

Class UnderlinedText
    Inherits PrintableForm

    Shared Shadows Sub Main()
        Application.Run(New UnderlinedText())
    End Sub

    Sub New()
        Text = "Underlined Text Using HotkeyPrefix"
        Font = New Font("Times New Roman", 14)
    End Sub

    Protected Overrides Sub DoPage(ByVal grfx As Graphics, _
            ByVal clr As Color, ByVal cx As Integer, ByVal cy As Integer)
        Dim str As String = "This is some &u&n&d&e&r&l&i&n&e&d text!"
        Dim strfmt As New StringFormat()
        strfmt.HotkeyPrefix = HotkeyPrefix.Show

        grfx.DrawString(str, Font, New SolidBrush(clr), 0, 0, strfmt)
    End Sub
End Class
```

The string in this program listing doesn't appear very attractive, but the results look quite nice:

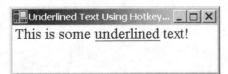

It's too bad there's not also some kind of facility to italicize or boldface words in a text block passed to *DrawString*.

I use *HotkeyPrefix* for what it's designed for in the OwnerDrawMenu program in Chapter 14.

# A Clip and a Trim

When you use the *RectangleF* version of *DrawString*, you're defining not only a right margin that governs text wrapping but also a bottom margin that limits the total amount of text that can be displayed.

What happens if the text is too long to fit in the rectangle?

Let's look at the default case first—when you don't include a *StringFormat* object as the last argument to *DrawString*. If the height of the rectangle is an integral multiple of the line-spacing height, an integral number of lines of text can fit in the rectangle. The last line of displayed text will contain as many characters as can fit in the rectangle width. Notice I said *characters* that can fit—not necessarily complete words. To let you explore the way this works, here's a version of the HuckleberryFinn program from Chapter 3 that restricts the text to half the client area width and height.

**HuckleberryFinnHalfHeight.vb**

```
'-----------------------------------------------------------
' HuckleberryFinnHalfHeight.vb (c) 2002 by Charles Petzold
'-----------------------------------------------------------
Imports System
Imports System.Drawing
Imports System.Windows.Forms

Class HuckleberryFinnHalfHeight
    Inherits Form

    Shared Sub Main()
        Application.Run(New HuckleberryFinnHalfHeight())
    End Sub

    Sub New()
        Text = """The Adventures of Huckleberry Finn"""
        BackColor = SystemColors.Window
        ForeColor = SystemColors.WindowText
        ResizeRedraw = True
    End Sub

    Protected Overrides Sub OnPaint(ByVal pea As PaintEventArgs)
        Dim grfx As Graphics = pea.Graphics
        Dim cx As Integer = ClientSize.Width
```

```
        Dim cy As Integer = ClientSize.Height
        Dim pn As New Pen(ForeColor)
        Dim rectf As New RectangleF(0, 0, cx \ 2, cy \ 2)

        grfx.DrawString("You don't know about me, without you " & _
                    "have read a book by the name of ""The " & _
                    "Adventures of Tom Sawyer,"" but that " & _
                    "ain't no matter. That book was made by " & _
                    "Mr. Mark Twain, and he told the truth, " & _
                    "mainly. There was things which he " & _
                    "stretched, but mainly he told the truth. " & _
                    "That is nothing. I never seen anybody " & _
                    "but lied, one time or another, without " & _
                    "it was Aunt Polly, or the widow, or " & _
                    "maybe Mary. Aunt Polly" & ChrW(&H2014) & _
                    "Tom's Aunt Polly, she is" & ChrW(&H2014) & _
                    "and Mary, and the Widow Douglas, is all " & _
                    "told about in that book" & ChrW(&H2014) & _
                    "which is mostly a true book; with some " & _
                    "stretchers, as I said before.", _
                    Font, New SolidBrush(ForeColor), rectf)


        grfx.DrawLine(pn, 0, cy \ 2, cx \ 2, cy \ 2)
        grfx.DrawLine(pn, cx \ 2, 0, cx \ 2, cy \ 2)
    End Sub
End Class
```

The program also draws lines to indicate the rectangle in which the text is being displayed.

When the display rectangle isn't sufficient for the entire paragraph, you'll notice that the last line displayed in the client area may end with an incomplete word:

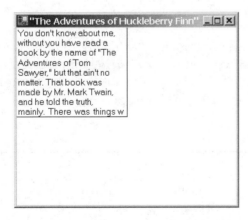

As you make the display rectangle taller, there comes a point when *DrawString* decides that there's enough room to display an additional line of text. It's sooner than you might think! *DrawString* displays an additional line of text when the height of the rectangle exceeds an additional 25 percent of the line-spacing height. The last line is clipped to the interior of the rectangle.

Although the last line is mostly clipped, you can see that this new last line concludes with another partial word—the first two letters of the word *mainly*.

You can alter this default behavior by using the *Trimming* property of the *StringFormat* class:

### *StringFormat* Properties (selection)

| Property | Type | Accessibility |
|----------|------|---------------|
| *Trimming* | *StringTrimming* | Set/Get |

The *Trimming* property determines how the last line of the text is terminated when you use the *RectangleF* version of *DrawString* and the rectangle isn't large enough to fit all the text. The value is a member of the *StringTrimming* enumeration used solely in connection with this property:

### *StringTrimming* Enumeration

| Member | Value | Description |
|--------|-------|-------------|
| *None* | 0 | As if no bottom margin |
| *Character* | 1 | End on character |
| *Word* | 2 | End on word |

*(continued)*

### *StringTrimming* Enumeration    *(continued)*

| Member | Value | Description |
|---|---|---|
| *EllipsisCharacter* | 3 | End on character with ellipsis (...) |
| *EllipsisWord* | 4 | End on word with ellipsis (...) |
| *EllipsisPath* | 5 | Ellipsis preceding last directory |

Here's a program that illustrates the effect of these values.

## TrimmingTheText.vb

```
'-------------------------------------------------
' TrimmingTheText.vb (c) 2002 by Charles Petzold
'-------------------------------------------------
Imports System
Imports System.Drawing
Imports System.Windows.Forms

Class TrimmingTheText
    Inherits PrintableForm

    Shared Shadows Sub Main()
        Application.Run(new TrimmingTheText())
    End Sub

    Sub New()
        Text = "Trimming the Text"
    End Sub

    Protected Overrides Sub DoPage(ByVal grfx As Graphics, _
            ByVal clr As Color, ByVal cx As Integer, ByVal cy As Integer)
        Dim br As New SolidBrush(clr)
        Dim cyText As Single = Font.GetHeight(grfx)
        Dim cyRect As Single = cyText
        Dim rectf As New RectangleF(0, 0, cx, cyRect)
        Dim str As String = _
                    "Those who profess to favor freedom and " & _
                    "yet depreciate agitation. . .want " & _
                    "crops without plowing up the ground, " & _
                    "they want rain without thunder and " & _
                    "lightning. They want the ocean without " & _
                    "the awful roar of its many waters. " & _
                    ChrW(&H2014) & "Frederick Douglass"
        Dim strfmt As New StringFormat()

        strfmt.Trimming = StringTrimming.Character
        grfx.DrawString("Character: " & str, Font, br, rectf, strfmt)
        rectf.Offset(0, cyRect + cyText)
```

*(continued)*

**TrimmingTheText.vb**   *(continued)*

```
        strfmt.Trimming = StringTrimming.Word
        grfx.DrawString("Word: " & str, Font, br, rectf, strfmt)
        rectf.Offset(0, cyRect + cyText)

        strfmt.Trimming = StringTrimming.EllipsisCharacter
        grfx.DrawString("EllipsisCharacter: " & str, _
                    Font, br, rectf, strfmt)
        rectf.Offset(0, cyRect + cyText)

        strfmt.Trimming = StringTrimming.EllipsisWord
        grfx.DrawString("EllipsisWord: " & str, _
                    Font, br, rectf, strfmt)
        rectf.Offset(0, cyRect + cyText)

        strfmt.Trimming = StringTrimming.EllipsisPath
        grfx.DrawString("EllipsisPath: " & _
                    Environment.GetFolderPath _
                            (Environment.SpecialFolder.Personal), _
                    Font, br, rectf, strfmt)
        rectf.Offset(0, cyRect + cyText)

        strfmt.Trimming = StringTrimming.None
        grfx.DrawString("None: " & str, Font, br, rectf, strfmt)
    End Sub
End Class
```

This program defines a *RectangleF* object sufficient in height for a single line of text. Using the six possible *StringTrimming* values, the program displays some text. This text is a quotation from Frederick Douglass for all values except *StringTrimming.EllipsisPath*, in which case the program uses the shared *Environment.GetFolderPath* method to obtain the path of your My Documents folder. You can adjust the width of the window and examine how it affects the text. Here's a typical display:

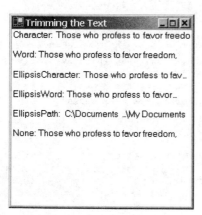

Both the *EllipsisCharacter* and the *EllipsisWord* members of *StringTrimming* cause an ellipsis (…) to be displayed at the end of the string, indicating that not enough room was available to display it. Both *Character* and *EllipsisCharacter* can result in a partial word being displayed.

The *EllipsisPath* member of *StringTrimming* is specifically for displaying file path names. Notice that the ellipsis is embedded in the middle of the text to favor the display of the beginning and the end of the path specification.

Just offhand, the *None* member appears to be the same as *Word*, but we're not quite finished with this exercise, and you'll find out why I put this one down at the bottom.

You can go into the program and change the calculation of *cyRect* from

```
Dim cyRect As Single = cyText
```

to

```
Dim cyRect As Single = 1.5F * cyText
```

Now recompile and run the new version. Here's a typical display:

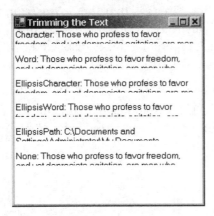

The *DrawString* method is now displaying two lines of text, and although you can't see much of the second line, that's the line being affected by the *Trimming* property.

At this point, you might want to see what effect the *NoWrap* flag of the *StringFormatFlags* enumeration has on this display. Add the following statement after the creation of the *StringFormat* object but before any *DrawString* calls:

```
strfmt.FormatFlags = strfmt.FormatFlags Or StringFormatFlags.NoWrap
```

Or you can put the flag in the *StringFormat* constructor:

```
Dim strfmt As New StringFormat(StringFormatFlags.NoWrap)
```

As the name implies, the *NoWrap* flag suppresses the line-wrapping facility of *DrawString*:

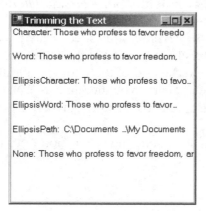

The text still ends at the right margin of the rectangle, however. What you might not see clearly (unless you change the right margin of the rectangle to something less than the width of the client area) is that the *StringTrimming.None* case causes the last letter to be partially truncated at the right margin. This is the only case we've seen so far in which a partial letter is displayed.

Now get rid of that *NoWrap* flag. Or rather, replace it with the *NoClip* flag:

```
strfmt.FormatFlags = strfmt.FormatFlags Or StringFormatFlags.NoClip
```

This flag directs *DrawString* not to clip text that lies partially outside the display rectangle. The result is that two full lines of text are displayed for every enumeration value except *StringTrimming.None*:

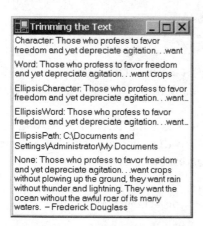

For the *StringTrimming.None* case, the entire block of text is now displayed. The combination of this enumeration value and the *NoClip* format flag essentially negates the effect of the bottom of the rectangle.

If you include both flags, like so,

```
strfmt.FormatFlags = strfmt.FormatFlags Or StringFormatFlags.NoClip
strfmt.FormatFlags = strfmt.FormatFlags Or StringFormatFlags.NoWrap
```

then for all *StringTrimming* values except *None*, the effect is the same as with just the *NoWrap* flag. For *StringTrimming.None*, the text is not wrapped and also not prevented from going past the right margin. It's as if you specified a *PointF* rather than a *RectangleF* in the *DrawString* call.

When you're displaying text in a rectangle, you need to watch out for clipping. If you make the rectangle height an integral multiple of the line-spacing value, you won't have a problem with clipping. That's probably the best solution. Otherwise, you should set the *NoClip* format flag to prevent clipping. But keep in mind that doing so will possibly cause the last line of text to be partially displayed beyond the bottom of the rectangle. In some cases (if the height of the rectangle is the height of your client area, for example), the last line of text will be clipped anyway because it exceeds the boundary of the client area. Be sure to adjust the rectangle so that all lines of text are displayed.

If you create a *StringFormat* object using the default constructor

```
Dim strfmt As New StringFormat()
```

or if you create it using this shared property of *StringFormat*

```
Dim strfmt As StringFormat = StringFormat.GenericDefault
```

the *Trimming* property is initially set to *StringTrimming.Character*. If you create the *StringFormat* object using the shared property

```
Dim strfmt As StringFormat = StringFormat.GenericTypographic
```

the *Trimming* property is initially set to *StringTrimming.None* and the *NoClip* format flag is set.

# Start a Tab

Tab stops govern how the *DrawString* call interprets the Unicode tab character *Chr(9)* or *vbTab*. If your *DrawString* call doesn't include a *StringFormat* argument, the default tab stops, measured in points, are equal to four times the size of the font. (In other words, the tabs are four ems.) For example, a 9-point font will have tab stops every 36 points, or 1/2 inch; an 18-point font will have tab stops every 72 points, or 1 inch; and a 36-point font will have tab stops every 144 points, or 2 inches. The tab stops are measured from where the text begins as indicated by the *PointF* or *RectangleF* argument to the *DrawString* call.

If your *DrawString* call includes a *StringFormat* argument, default tab stops don't exist and the *DrawString* method ignores all tab characters in the text. You need to set tab stops using the *SetTabStops* method of *StringFormat*. The *StringFormat* class also includes a method to obtain the current tab stop settings:

### *StringFormat* Methods (selection)

```
Sub SetTabStops(ByVal fFirstTab As Single, ByVal afTabs As Single())
Function GetTabStops(ByRef fFirstTab As Single) As Single()
```

Tab stops are in world coordinates. You'll notice that the tab stops are specified by both a *Single* value and an array of *Single* values, which would seem to indicate that the value not in the array is treated differently. What the method syntax doesn't imply is that the last value of the array is also treated differently.

Let me give you a few simple examples first before I show you how the *SetTabStops* method works in the general case. I'll assume the page units are set to *GraphicsUnit.Point*.

If you need just one tab stop, say at 4 inches (288 points), you can specify that as the first argument to the method and make the array contain just a single 0:

```
strfmt.SetTabStops(288, New Single() { 0 })
```

You can't set the array argument to *Nothing*. You can also use

```
strfmt.SetTabStops(0, New Single() { 288, 0 })
```

If you need two tabs stops, for example, at 1 inch (72 points) and 3 inches (216 points), you use

```
strfmt.SetTabStops(0, New Single() { 72, 144, 0 })
```

Notice that the second array element is the difference between 72 and 216 points. Although I'm showing the array being created directly in the *SetTabStops* call, you can, of course, define it outside the method.

If you need tab stops every 0.5 inch (36 points), you use

```
strfmt.SetTabStops(0, New Single() { 36 })
```

The tab stops will be at 36 points, 72 points, 108 points, 144 points, and so forth.

As you can see, the *SetTabStops* method can define both discrete tab stops and repeating tab stops, and it's the combination of these two that makes this method so complicated. In the general case, the arguments to *SetTabStops* look like this:

```
strfmt.SetTabStops(S, New Single() { A, B, C, ..., N, R })
```

I'm using the letter *R* to stand for *Repeating* and the letter *S* to indicate *Shift*. Any of these values can be 0 or negative. The *SetTabStops* method sets tab stops at the following positions measured from the starting position of the text:

$S + A$

$S + A + B$

$S + A + B + C$

$S + A + B + C + ... + N$

$S + A + B + C + ... + N + R$

In addition, the method also sets tab stops at positions *R*, *2R*, *3R*, and so forth, but these repeating tab stops begin only after the longest of the other tab stops. For example, the call

```
strfmt.SetTabStops(100, New Single() { 50, 75, 50, 100 })
```

sets tab stops at 150, 225, 275, 375, 400, 500, 600, and so on. Units are world coordinates.

You can set the last element of the array (which I've called *R*) to 0 if you want all the tab stops to be explicitly defined. You can also set *S* to 0. However, it's possible to use that initial argument to *SetTabStops* intelligently. For example, you could first define an array that has four tab stops measured from a horizontal coordinate of 0:

```
Dim afTabs() As Single = { 100, 150, 100, 50, 0 }
```

Notice that the last argument is 0, so there will be no repeating tab stops.

If you're preparing to display text starting at a horizontal coordinate of 0, you can call *SetTabStops* with an initial argument of 0:

```
strfmt.SetTabStops(0, afTabs)
```

This call sets tabs at 100, 250, 350, and 400 units. However, you might now need to display text starting at a horizontal coordinate of 50, but you want the tab stops in the same physical locations. You can do that by passing −50 as the first argument to *SetTabStops*:

```
strfmt.SetTabStops(-50, afTabs)
```

Now the tab stops are 50, 200, 300, and 350 but measured from the starting coordinate of 50, so they're really 100, 250, 350, and 400, the same as before.

Let's put a lot of what we've learned here into practice by formatting a chunk of text into columns. The text I'm using is the beginning of Edith Wharton's 1920 novel *The Age of Innocence*. The following class has a single read-only *Text* property that returns the first five paragraphs of the novel.

```
AgeOfInnocence.vb
'------------------------------------------------------------------
' AgeOfInnocence.vb (c) 2002 by Charles Petzold; text by Edith Wharton
'------------------------------------------------------------------

Class AgeOfInnocence

    Shared ReadOnly Property Text() As String
        Get
            Return _
"On a January evening of the early seventies, Christine Nilsson " & _
"was singing in Faust at the Academy of Music in New York." & _
vbLf & _
vbTab & _
"Though there was already talk of the erection, in remote " & _
"metropolitan distances ""above the Forties,"" of a new Opera " & _
"House which should compete in costliness and splendour with " & _
"those of the great European capitals, the world of fashion was " & _
"still content to reassemble every winter in the shabby red and " & _
"gold boxes of the sociable old Academy. Conservatives " & _
"cherished it for being small and inconvenient, and thus keeping " & _
"out the ""new people"" whom New York was beginning to dread and " & _
"yet be drawn to and the sentimental clung to it for its historic " & _
"associations, and the musical for its excellent acoustics, " & _
"always so problematic a quality in halls built for the hearing " & _
"of music." & _
vbLf & _
vbTab & _
"It was Madame Nilsson's first appearance that winter, and what " & _
"the daily press had already learned to describe as ""an " & _
"exceptionally brilliant audience"" had gathered to hear her, " & _
"transported through the slippery, snowy streets in private " & _
"broughams, in the spacious family landau, or in the humbler but " & _
"more convenient ""Brown &c&o&u&p&" & Chr(233) & _
".""" To come to the Opera in a Brown &c&o&u&p&" & Chr(233) & _
" was almost as honourable a way of arriving as in one's own " & _
"carriage and departure by the same means had the immense " & _
"advantage of enabling one (with a playful allusion to democratic " & _
"principles) to scramble into the first Brown conveyance in the " & _
"line, instead of waiting till the cold-and-gin congested nose " & _
"of one's own coachman gleamed under the portico of the Academy. " & _
```

```
"It was one of the great livery-stableman's most masterly " & _
"intuitions to have discovered that Americans want to get away " & _
"from amusement even more quickly than they want to get to it." & _
vbLf & _
vbTab & _
"When Newland Archer opened the door at the back of the club box " & _
"the curtain had just gone up on the garden scene. There was no " & _
"reason why the young man should not have come earlier, for he " & _
"had dined at seven, alone with his mother and sister, and had " & _
"lingered afterward over a cigar in the Gothic library with " & _
"glazed black-walnut bookcases and finial-topped chairs which was " & _
"the only room in the house where Mrs. Archer allowed smoking. " & _
"But, in the first place, New York was a metropolis, and " & _
"perfectly aware that in metropolises it was ""not the thing"" to " & _
"arrive early at the opera and what was or was not ""the thing"" " & _
"played a part as important in Newland Archer's New York as the " & _
"inscrutable totem terrors that had ruled the destinies of his " & _
"forefathers thousands of years ago." & _
vbLf & _
vbTab & _
"The second reason for his delay was a personal one. He had " & _
"dawdled over his cigar because he was at heart a dilettante, and " & _
"thinking over a pleasure to come often gave him a subtler " & _
"satisfaction than its realisation. This was especially the case " & _
"when the pleasure was a delicate one, as his pleasures mostly " & _
"were; and on this occasion the moment he looked forward to was " & _
"so rare & exquisite in quality that" & ChrW(&H2014) & "well, if " & _
"he had timed his arrival in accord with the prima donna's " & _
"stage-manager he could not have entered the Academy at a more " & _
"significant moment than just as she was singing: ""He loves me" & _
ChrW(&H2014) & "he loves me not" & ChrW(&H2014) & "&h&e& " & _
"&l&o&v&e&s& &m&e!""" and sprinkling the falling daisy petals with " & _
"notes as clear as dew." & _
vbLf

        End Get
    End Property
End Class
```

Notice that I've used a tab character to indent the first line of every paragraph except the first. The text includes a few italicized words; I used the ampersand technique I discussed earlier to make these words underlined instead. The text has some em dashes as well.

Here's the program that formats this text into columns. Each column requires a *DrawString* call.

**TextColumns.vb**

```
'--------------------------------------------
' TextColumns.vb (c) 2002 by Charles Petzold
'--------------------------------------------
Imports System
Imports System.Drawing
Imports System.Drawing.Drawing2D
Imports System.Drawing.Text
Imports System.Windows.Forms

Class TextColumns
    Inherits PrintableForm

    Shared Shadows Sub Main()
        Application.Run(new TextColumns())
    End Sub

    Sub New()
        Text = "Edith Wharton's ""The Age of Innocence"""
        Font = new Font("Times New Roman", 10)
    End Sub

    Protected Overrides Sub DoPage(ByVal grfx As Graphics, _
            ByVal clr As Color, ByVal cx As Integer, ByVal cy As Integer)
        Dim br As New SolidBrush(clr)
        Dim x, iChars, iLines As Integer
        Dim str As String = AgeOfInnocence.Text
        Dim strfmt As New StringFormat()

        ' Set units of points while converting dimensions.
        Dim aptf() As PointF = {New PointF(cx, cy)}
        grfx.TransformPoints(CoordinateSpace.Device, _
                            CoordinateSpace.Page, aptf)

        grfx.PageUnit = GraphicsUnit.Point
        grfx.TransformPoints(CoordinateSpace.Page, _
                            CoordinateSpace.Device, aptf)

        Dim fcx As Single = aptf(0).X
        Dim fcy As Single = aptf(0).Y

        ' StringFormat properties, flags, and tabs.
        strfmt.HotkeyPrefix = HotkeyPrefix.Show
        strfmt.Trimming = StringTrimming.Word
        strfmt.FormatFlags = strfmt.FormatFlags Or StringFormatFlags.NoClip
        strfmt.SetTabStops(0, New Single() {18})

        ' Display text.
        For x = 0 To CInt(fcx) Step 156
            If (str.Length <= 0) Then Exit For
```

```
            Dim rectf As New RectangleF(x, 0, 144, _
                                     fcy - Font.GetHeight(grfx))
            grfx.DrawString(str, Font, br, rectf, strfmt)
            grfx.MeasureString(str, Font, rectf.Size, strfmt, _
                          iChars, iLines)
            str = str.Substring(iChars)
        Next x
    End Sub
End Class
```

Notice the setting of the *StringFormat* properties, flags, and tabs. I use *HotkeyPrefix.Show* so that my underlines are displayed, *StringTrimming.Word* to display a whole word at the bottom of each rectangle, and *StringFormat-Flags.NoClip* so that lines aren't clipped at the bottom of the rectangle. I set the single tab (which controls the indentation of the first line) to 18 points. The *For* loop has an iteration for each column. It continues until the width of the client area is exceeded or all the text has been displayed. Within the *For* loop, the height of the display rectangle is calculated as the height of the client area less the height of one line of text. The *DrawString* call simply uses that rectangle. The *MeasureString* call determines how much text the *DrawString* call just displayed. The *SubString* method of the *String* class then prepares the string for the next iteration of the loop.

Here is a sample display.

# 10

# The Timer and Time

The timer is an input device that periodically notifies an application when a specified interval of time has elapsed. Your program defines the interval, in effect saying, "Give me a nudge every 10th second." The timer then triggers an event handler in your program 10 times a second.

Three different classes defined in the *System.Timers*, *System.Threading*, and *System.Windows.Forms* namespaces are named *Timer* (not to be confused with the unrelated Microsoft Visual Basic property named *Timer*). I'll be using the *Timer* class defined in *System.Windows.Forms*, which is the timer that Microsoft Windows programmers are familiar with. It is integrated with the other Windows events and involves the lowest hassle factor.

While obviously not as important an input device as the keyboard and the mouse, the timer is surprisingly useful and finds its way into many Windows Forms applications. The obvious timer application is a clock, and indeed, this chapter is overflowing with clock applications. But here are some other uses for the timer, some perhaps not so obvious:

- **Multitasking** Although Windows is a preemptive multitasking environment, usually it's advisable for a program to return control to Windows as quickly as possible after processing an event. Not doing so tends to gum up the works. If a program must do a large amount of processing, it can divide the job into smaller pieces and process each piece upon receipt of a timer event.

- **Maintaining an updated status report** A program can use the timer to display real-time updates of continuously changing information, such as a display of resources or the progress of certain tasks.

- **Implementing an "autosave" feature**  The timer can prompt an application to save a user's work to disk whenever a specified period of time has elapsed.

- **Terminating demo versions of programs**  Some demonstration versions of programs are designed to terminate, say, 30 minutes after they begin. The timer can signal such applications when the time is up. (An example is the CloseInFive program coming up soon in this chapter.)

- **Pacing movement**  Graphical objects in a game or successive displays in a computer-assisted instruction program usually need to proceed at a set rate. Using the timer eliminates the inconsistencies that might result from variations in microprocessor speed. Animation often makes use of the timer.

You can also think of the timer as a guarantee that a program can regain control sometime in the future. Whenever a program relinquishes control after executing the code in the constructor or an event handler, it usually can't determine when the next event will occur. The timer is more certain.

I say *more* certain because the timer doesn't have the rhythmical consistency of a metronome. The events triggered by the *Timer* class are synchronous with the other events. In other words, a timer event will never interrupt the processing of another event in the same execution thread. Code that spends a long time processing an event will delay a timer event.

# The *Timer* Class

The *Timer* class is small and relatively simple. You generally create a *Timer* object using the default constructor:

```
Dim tmr As New Timer()
```

The *Timer* has one event:

### *Timer* Event

| Event | Method | Delegate | Argument |
|-------|--------|----------|----------|
| *Tick* | *OnTick* | *EventHandler* | *EventArgs* |

Somewhere in your class you'll have an event handler for the timer defined like so:

```
Sub TimerOnTick(ByVal obj As Object, ByVal ea As EventArgs)
    ⋮
End Sub
```

You can name it whatever you want, of course. You attach this event handler to the *Timer* object you've created:

```
AddHandler tmr.Tick, AddressOf TimerOnTick
```

The *Timer* class has just two properties:

### *Timer* **Properties**

| Property | Type | Accessibility | Description |
|----------|------|---------------|-------------|
| *Interval* | *Integer* | Get/Set | Tick time in milliseconds |
| *Enabled* | *Boolean* | Get/Set | Set to *True* if timer is running |

You set the *Interval* property to the number of milliseconds between calls to your event handler. For example, this statement sets the tick time to 1 second:

```
tmr.Interval = 1000
```

Although you can set the *Interval* property to values as low as 1, you're not guaranteed to get a tick time of 1 millisecond. Under Windows XP, for example, even if you set an *Interval* of 1, the timer will call your event handler approximately every 10 milliseconds.

Windows rounds intervals you specify to the next highest multiple of the period of the operating system's internal clock. Under Windows XP, for example, specifying an *Interval* of 11 through 20 results in an actual interval of 20 milliseconds. But an *Interval* of 20 doesn't imply that you'll get precisely 50 calls every second. If a timer event is delayed more than 20 milliseconds, it's consolidated with the next timer event. There are never multiple pending timer events. (If you need a timer that is more frequent and more precise, investigate the asynchronous timer in the *System.Threading* namespace.)

But you won't get any calls to your event handler unless you also enable the timer:

```
tmr.Enabled = True
```

Alternatively, you can use these two methods:

### *Timer* **Methods (selection)**

```
Sub Start()
Sub Stop()
```

The *Start* call is equivalent to setting *Enabled* to *True*, and the *Stop* call is equivalent to setting *Enabled* to *False*. You can change all *Timer* properties in your timer event handler, effectively resetting the timer. Remember that the first argument to the event handler is the object associated with the event handler, which in this case is the *Timer* object, so you can cast it like so:

```
Dim tmr As Timer  = DirectCast(obj, Timer)
```

Here's a program that sets a *one-shot* timer, so called because the timer event handler turns the timer off.

**CloseInFive.vb**

```
'------------------------------------------------
' CloseInFive.vb (c) 2002 by Charles Petzold
'------------------------------------------------
Imports System
Imports System.Drawing
Imports System.Windows.Forms

Class CloseInFive
    Inherits Form

    Shared Sub Main()
        Application.Run(New CloseInFive())
    End Sub

    Sub New()
        Text = "Closing in Five Minutes"

        Dim tmr As New Timer()
        tmr.Interval = 5 * 60 * 1000
        AddHandler tmr.Tick, AddressOf TimerOnTick
        tmr.Enabled = True
    End Sub

    Private Sub TimerOnTick(ByVal obj As Object, ByVal ea As EventArgs)
        Dim tmr As Timer = DirectCast(obj, Timer)

        tmr.Stop()
        RemoveHandler tmr.Tick, AddressOf TimerOnTick

        Close()
    End Sub
End Class
```

Not only does the timer event handler turn the timer off, but it also closes the program. This program is an example of how you would implement a demo feature that allows the user to experience the benefits of an application but not actually use it much.

When closing a program, it's not necessary to stop the timer and detach the event handler. However, if you truly are using a timer for a one-shot operation, it's a good idea to do so: the *Timer* object will then qualify for garbage collection.

At the other extreme from CloseInFive, here's a hypnotic program that sets the timer once and runs forever.

## RandomRectangle.vb

```
'-------------------------------------------------
' RandomRectangle.vb (c) 2002 by Charles Petzold
'-------------------------------------------------
Imports System
Imports System.Drawing
Imports System.Windows.Forms

Class RandomRectangle
    Inherits Form

    Shared Sub Main()
        Application.Run(New RandomRectangle())
    End Sub

    Sub New()
        Text = "Random Rectangle"

        Dim tmr As New Timer()
        tmr.Interval = 1
        AddHandler tmr.Tick, AddressOf TimerOnTick
        tmr.Start()
    End Sub

    Private Sub TimerOnTick(ByVal obj As Object, ByVal ea As EventArgs)
        Dim rand As New Random()
        Dim x1 As Integer = rand.Next(ClientSize.Width)
        Dim x2 As Integer = rand.Next(ClientSize.Width)
        Dim y1 As Integer = rand.Next(ClientSize.Height)
        Dim y2 As Integer = rand.Next(ClientSize.Height)
        Dim clr As Color = Color.FromArgb(rand.Next(256), _
                                          rand.Next(256), _
                                          rand.Next(256))

        Dim grfx As Graphics = CreateGraphics()
        grfx.FillRectangle(New SolidBrush(clr), _
                           Math.Min(x1, x2), Math.Min(y1, y2), _
                           Math.Abs(x2 - x1), Math.Abs(y2 - y1))
        grfx.Dispose()
    End Sub
End Class
```

# The *DateTime* Structure

If you want to write a clock application, you need to know something about the representation of date and time in the Microsoft .NET Framework.

The most important date and time structure, appropriately named *DateTime*, is defined in the *System* namespace. You can create an object of type *DateTime* using one of its seven constructors, three of which are listed here:

### *DateTime* Constructors (selection)

```
DateTime(ByVal year As Integer, ByVal month As Integer,
        ByVal day As Integer)

DateTime(ByVal year As Integer, ByVal month As Integer,
        ByVal day As Integer, ByVal hour As Integer,
        ByVal minute As Integer, ByVal second As Integer)

DateTime(ByVal year As Integer, ByVal month As Integer,
        ByVal day As Integer, ByVal hour As Integer,
        ByVal minute As Integer, ByVal second As Integer,
        ByVal msec As Integer)
```

The year can range from 1 to 9999, the month can range from 1 to 12, the day can range from 1 through the number of days in that month and year, the hour can range from 0 through 23, the minute and second can range from 0 through 59, and the milliseconds argument can range from 0 through 999. If any of the arguments is out of range, the constructor throws an exception.

The *DateTime* constructor also throws an exception if the combination of year, month, and day arguments isn't consistent. For example, a month of 2 and a day of 29 is acceptable only for a leap year. These *DateTime* constructors use leap year rules associated with the Gregorian calendar (which was instituted by Pope Gregory XIII in 1582 and eventually adopted worldwide in the years and centuries that followed). In the Gregorian calendar, a year is a leap year if it is divisible by 4 but not divisible by 100 unless it is divisible by 400. The year 1900 is not a leap year; 2000 is. (Prior to the Gregorian calendar, leap years were celebrated every four years without exception.) The *DateTime* constructor observes these same leap year rules even for years preceding the invention of the Gregorian calendar.

*DateTime* has 15 properties, all of which are read-only, and 10 of which are shown here:

## *DateTime* Properties (selection)

| Property | Type | Accessibility | Description |
| --- | --- | --- | --- |
| Year | Integer | Get | 1 through 9999 |
| Month | Integer | Get | 1 through 12 |
| Day | Integer | Get | 1 through 31 |
| Hour | Integer | Get | 0 through 23 |
| Minute | Integer | Get | 0 through 59 |
| Second | Integer | Get | 0 through 59 |
| Millisecond | Integer | Get | 0 through 999 |
| DayOfWeek | Integer | Get | 0 (Sunday) through 6 (Saturday) |
| DayOfYear | Integer | Get | 1 through 366 |
| Date | DateTime | Get | Time set to 0 (midnight) |

The first seven properties are the familiar components of the date and time, and will match the values set in the constructor. The *DayOfWeek* and *DayOfYear* properties provide some additional information about the date. The *Date* property returns a *DateTime* object that represents the same day as the current *DateTime* object but with the *Hour*, *Minute*, *Second*, and *Millisecond* properties set to 0.

*DateTime* has three shared properties, which are particularly useful:

## *DateTime* Shared Properties

| Property | Type | Accessibility | Description |
| --- | --- | --- | --- |
| Now | DateTime | Get | Current local date and time |
| Today | DateTime | Get | Current local date |
| UtcNow | DateTime | Get | Current UTC date and time |

The *DateTime.Now* property returns a *DateTime* structure filled in with the current local date and time. For example, to obtain the current date and time in your program, call

```
Dim dt As DateTime = DateTime.Now
```

Now you can use the *DateTime* properties in *dt* to obtain the components of the current date and time. The *DateTime.Today* property is similar but returns a *DateTime* structure with today's date and all the time components set to 0.

The shared *UtcNow* property returns a *DateTime* structure with the current date and time in Coordinated Universal Time (UTC), which I'll discuss in the next section.

Visual Basic .NET also defines *Now*, *Today*, and *TimeOfDay* properties that use the *DateTime* structure and provide a bit more functionality. You can actually obtain the current date and time a little more easily than the example shown above:

```
Dim dt As DateTime = Now
```

The Visual Basic *Today* and *TimeOfDay* properties are writable, allowing you to set the system date and time programmatically, for example:

```
Today = New DateTime(2002, 8, 29)
```

You can also create new *DateTime* objects using the Visual Basic *DateSerial* and *TimeSerial* functions.

The *DateTime* structure contains a number of methods and overloaded operators that let you perform calculations on dates and times. Comparison operations are supported by the following operators:

### *DateTime* Operators (selection)

```
op_Equality(dt1 As DateTime, dt2 As DateTime) As Boolean

op_InEquality(dt1 As DateTime, dt2 As DateTime) As Boolean

op_GreaterThan(dt1 As DateTime, dt2 As DateTime) As Boolean

op_LessThan(dt1 As DateTime, dt2 As DateTime) As Boolean

op_GreaterThanOrEqual(dt1 As DateTime, dt2 As DateTime) As Boolean

op_LessThanOrEqual(dt1 As DateTime, dt2 As DateTime) As Boolean
```

Addition and subtraction are also supported, but these operations involve *TimeSpan* objects that I'll get to shortly.

## Local Time and Universal Time

People everywhere around the world like to think of noon as the time when the sun is highest in the sky and midnight as the middle of the night. Because these two events don't occur everywhere on the earth at the same time, people living in different areas of the world set their clocks differently. Once a chaotic practice, this tendency has evolved into strict time zones generally set by national governments and calculated as hour or half-hour offsets from Greenwich Mean Time.

Greenwich, England, has played an important role in the evolution of time standards because it is the site of the Royal Greenwich Observatory (RGO). The RGO was founded in 1675 to develop techniques of astronomical navigation for ships at sea. In the 1760s, the observatory began publishing nautical almanacs that for convenience placed the prime meridian (the line of 0° longitude) at Greenwich. This system of meridians was eventually agreed upon as a world standard in 1884, although the French continued to use Paris as the prime meridian until 1911.

Earlier, in 1833, Greenwich astronomers began dropping a ball that was visible to ships in the Thames every day at 1:00 p.m. That was the origin of Greenwich Mean Time. In the 1840s, Greenwich Mean Time was declared the standard time for all of Great Britain to replace various local times that had developed over the years.

While people often still refer to Greenwich Mean Time as the world standard, the use of the term *Coordinated Universal Time* (UTC) is considered more scientifically correct. (Coordinated Universal Time is abbreviated UTC as something of a compromise between the English word order—which would imply the abbreviation CUT—and the French *Temps Universel Coordonné*, which has the abbreviation TUC.) By international agreement since 1972, UTC is the same all over the world.

Local standard time is a positive or negative offset from UTC. Time zones to the west of Greenwich are behind UTC, and time zones to the east of Greenwich are ahead of UTC. For example, Eastern Standard Time, which includes the east coast of the United States, is UTC minus 5 hours. This is *not* the same as UTC plus 19 hours. Such a calculation results in the correct time but the incorrect day.

Then there's that quaint custom known as daylight saving time. The principle behind it is simple: as the summer solstice approaches, the sun is rising earlier and setting later, so it's no big deal to get out of bed a little earlier and enjoy even more sun in the evening. Some countries observe daylight saving time and some don't, and those that observe it frequently begin and end it on different dates. Even within some countries, notably the United States, daylight saving time is implemented inconsistently—many states observe it, but some don't.

In Windows, you can set the time zone for your machine using the Date/Time Properties dialog box that you can open from Control Panel or by double-clicking the time in the Windows taskbar. You can also indicate whether the system should automatically adjust for daylight saving time. Obviously, for a particular machine, the local time is just an offset of the UTC based on both the local time zone and the effect of daylight saving time.

The *DateTime* structure by itself doesn't imply UTC or a local time. When you use one of the *DateTime* constructors, you are specifying a date and time that may be UTC, a local time, the date and time of your birth, or anything you want.

As I mentioned earlier, the properties *Now* and *Today* return local date and time, and *UtcNow* returns UTC based on the time zone settings of the current machine. You can convert the time stored in a *DateTime* object between local time and UTC by using the following methods:

### *DateTime* Methods (selection)

```
Function ToLocalTime() As DateTime
Function ToUniversalTime() As DateTime
```

For example, if the variable *dtLocal* contains a local date and time, you can convert it to a UTC date and time by calling

```
Dim dtUtc As DateTime  = dtLocal.ToUniversalTime()
```

If *dtLocal* actually contained a time in UTC, what you end up with here is nonsense. It's your responsibility to keep track of what time zones your *DateTime* objects pertain to.

You can get information about the time zone defined for the current machine, and the daylight saving time rules associated with that time zone, from the *TimeZone* class, also defined in the *System* namespace. *TimeZone* is defined as *MustInherit*, which means that you can't instantiate it; you can only instantiate a subclass of *TimeZone*. However, the class by itself provides some useful information. *TimeZone* has one shared property, which returns an instance of the class. This instance represents the time zone that is set for the current machine:

### *TimeZone* Shared Property

| Property | Type | Accessibility |
|---|---|---|
| *CurrentTimeZone* | *TimeZone* | Get |

For example, if you call

```
Dim tz As TimeZone = TimeZone.CurrentTimeZone
```

*tz* represents the time zone set on the current computer. The two nonshared properties provide names associated with the time zone:

### *TimeZone* Properties

| Property | Type | Accessibility |
|---|---|---|
| StandardName | String | Get/Set |
| DaylightName | String | Get/Set |

For example, if your machine is located on the east coast of the United States, the time zone is set correctly, and you've set the *tz* variable as shown previously, the *tz.StandardName* property returns "Eastern Standard Time" and *tz.DaylightName* returns "Eastern Daylight Time."

Here are the *TimeZone* methods:

### *TimeZone* Methods

```
Function GetUtcOffset(ByVal dt As DateTime) As TimeSpan

Function ToLocalTime(ByVal dt As DateTime) As DateTime

Function ToUniversalTime(ByVal dt As DateTime) As DateTime

Function GetDaylightChanges(ByVal iYear As Integer) As DaylightTime

Function IsDaylightSavingTime(ByVal dt As DateTime) As Boolean

Function IsDaylightSavingTime(ByVal dt As DateTime,
                    ByVal dlt As DaylightTime) As Boolean
```

The *GetUtcOffset* method returns an offset between the time in the particular time zone and UTC expressed as a *TimeSpan* object. (I'll discuss *TimeSpan* in more detail shortly. For now, be aware that it's a structure defined in the *System* namespace that's used to express durations of time in units of 100 nanoseconds.) *GetUtcOffset* takes daylight saving time into account. Using the same example of the computer on the east coast of the United States, the method

```
tz.GetUtcOffset(New DateTime(2002, 2, 2))
```

returns -5:00:00, which signifies -5 hours. That's what you add to UTC to get Eastern Standard Time. The method call

```
tz.GetUtcOffset(New DateTime(2002, 8, 29))
```

returns -4:00:00, or -4 hours. That's the effect of daylight saving time.

The *ToLocalTime* and *ToUniversalTime* methods are similar to the methods in the *DateTime* structure but are based on the particular *TimeZone* object. If you had a way to get *TimeZone* objects for other time zones around the world, you could use these methods to convert between local and UTC for other time zones.

The statement

```
Dim dlt As DaylightTime = tz.GetDaylightChanges(2002)
```

returns an object of type *DaylightTime*, a class defined in the *System.Globalization* namespace. It has three properties:

### *DaylightTime* Properties

| Property | Type | Accessibility |
|----------|------|---------------|
| Start | DateTime | Get |
| End | DateTime | Get |
| Delta | TimeSpan | Get |

The *Start* and *End* properties indicate that daylight saving time begins on April 7, 2002, at 2:00 a.m., and ends on October 27, 2002, at 2:00 a.m. (Both transitions occur on Sunday mornings.) The *Delta* value is the time difference, which is 1 hour.

For time zones in the northern hemisphere, *Start* is earlier in the year than *End*. For time zones in the southern hemisphere, the seasons are switched: daylight saving time starts later in the year and ends early in the next year.

## The Tick Count

Another way of representing date and time is by a number of 100-nanosecond clock ticks. Internally, the *DateTime* structure stores the date and time as the number of ticks since midnight, January 1, 1 C.E. The two remaining *DateTime* properties provide that value as well as the number of ticks since midnight:

### *DateTime* Properties (selection)

| Property | Type | Accessibility | Description |
|----------|------|---------------|-------------|
| Ticks | Long | Get | 100-nanosecond intervals since 1/1/0001 |
| TimeOfDay | TimeSpan | Get | Ticks since midnight |

Remember that a *Long* is 64 bits wide and hence is adequate for storing the very large numbers involved here. Notice that the *TimeOfDay* property returns an object of type *TimeSpan*, which expresses durations of time in units of 100 nanoseconds. Watch out: The Visual Basic *TimeOfDay* property returns an object of type *DateTime*.

For the date January 1, 2001, the *Ticks* property returns the value 631,139,040,000,000,000. There are 10,000 ticks in a millisecond, 10,000,000 ticks in a second, 600,000,000 ticks in a minute, 36,000,000,000 ticks in an hour, and 864,000,000,000 ticks in a day. (All these constant values are available as fields in the *TimeSpan* structure, by the way.) That means that 730,485 days have elapsed in those 2000 years, for an average of 365.2425 days per year.

The value of 365.2425 days per year is correct for the Gregorian calendar: most years have 365 days. An extra day every four years adds 0.25 to the average days per year. Excluding an extra day every 100 years lessens the average days per year by 0.01. Including an extra day every 400 years increases the average days per year by 0.0025. In other words,

$$365 + 1/4 - 1/100 + 1/400 = 365.2425$$

You can create a *DateTime* object from a *Long* value indicating the number of ticks since January 1, 1 C.E.:

### *DateTime* Constructors (selection)

```
DateTime(ByVal ticks As Long)
```

You can create *TimeSpan* objects similarly, and you can also create *TimeSpan* objects with explicit day and time values. Here's a complete list of the *TimeSpan* constructors:

### *TimeSpan* Constructors

```
TimeSpan(ByVal ticks As Long)

TimeSpan(ByVal hours As Integer, ByVal minutes As Integer,
         ByVal seconds As Integer)

TimeSpan(ByVal days As Integer, ByVal hours As Integer,
         ByVal minutes As Integer, ByVal seconds As Integer)

TimeSpan(ByVal days As Integer, ByVal hours As Integer,
         ByVal minutes As Integer, ByVal seconds As Integer,
         ByVal milliseconds As Integer)
```

The *DateTime* and *TimeSpan* constructors look very similar, so it's important to understand the distinction between the two structures. A *DateTime* object represents a particular date and time; the *Ticks* property of *DateTime* is the number of 100-nanosecond intervals since January 1, 1 C.E.

A *TimeSpan* object represents a duration—a period of elapsed time. Notice that the arguments of the *TimeSpan* constructors don't represent any particular day, hour, minute, second, and millisecond. They represent a certain *number* of days, and a *number* of hours, and so forth. There are no *TimeSpan* constructors that involve months and years because months and years don't have a fixed number of days.

The values that can be assigned to arguments in the *TimeSpan* constructors aren't limited, unlike those of *DateTime* constructors. For example, the statement

```
Dim ts As New TimeSpan(1000, 1000, 1000, 1000, 1000)
```

is perfectly legal. Here's a complete list of the *TimeSpan* properties:

### *TimeSpan* Properties

| Property | Type | Accessibility | Description |
|----------|------|---------------|-------------|
| *Ticks* | *Long* | Get | Number of 100-nanosecond intervals |
| *Days* | *Integer* | Get | Whole number of days |
| *Hours* | *Integer* | Get | 0 through 23 |
| *Minutes* | *Integer* | Get | 0 through 59 |
| *Seconds* | *Integer* | Get | 0 through 59 |
| *Milliseconds* | *Integer* | Get | 0 through 999 |
| *TotalDays* | *Double* | Get | = *Ticks / TicksPerDay* |
| *TotalHours* | *Double* | Get | = *Ticks / TicksPerHour* |
| *TotalMinutes* | *Double* | Get | = *Ticks / TicksPerMinute* |
| *TotalSeconds* | *Double* | Get | = *Ticks / TicksPerSecond* |
| *TotalMilliseconds* | *Double* | Get | = *Ticks / TicksPerMillisecond* |

For the last five properties, I've indicated how they are calculated from convenient fields in the *TimeSpan* structure.

I mentioned earlier that the *DateTime* structure defines an addition operator. However, you can add only a *TimeSpan* object to a *DateTime* object. If *dt*, *dt1*, and *dt2* are *DateTime* objects and *ts* is a *TimeSpan* object, you can perform addition like this:

```
dt2 = DateTime.op_Addition(dt1, ts)
```

For example, you may want to increase a time and date by 45 minutes:

```
dt = DateTime.op_Addition(dt, New TimeSpan(0, 45, 0))
```

or 1 week:

```
dt = DateTime.op_Addition(dt, New TimeSpan(7, 0, 0, 0))
```

This is the safe way to perform these calculations. (Another safe approach is to use the various *Add* methods of the *DateTime* class or the *DateAdd* function supported by Visual Basic .NET.) The subtraction operator is defined in two ways. You can subtract one date and time from another to get a *TimeSpan* object:

```
ts = DateTime.op_Subtraction(dt2, dt1)
```

Or you can subtract a *TimeSpan* object from a *DateTime* object to get another *DateTime* object:

```
dt2 = DateTime.op_Subtraction(dt1, ts)
```

*TimeSpan* objects can also be added, subtracted, or compared to each other using operators of the *TimeSpan* structure.

# Calendars Around the World

Here are the final three constructors for *DateTime*:

### *DateTime* Constructors (selection)

```
DateTime(ByVal year As Integer, ByVal month As Integer,
        ByVal day As Integer, ByVal cal As Calendar)

DateTime(ByVal year As Integer, ByVal month As Integer,
        ByVal day As Integer, ByVal hour As Integer,
        ByVal minute As Integer, ByVal sec As Integer,
        ByVal cal As Calendar)

DateTime(ByVal year As Integer, ByVal month As Integer,
        ByVal day As Integer, ByVal hour As Integer,
        ByVal minute As Integer, ByVal sec As Integer,
        ByVal msec As Integer, ByVal cal As Calendar)
```

The final argument is an object of type *Calendar*. This argument indicates how the year, month, and day arguments are to be interpreted. As I mentioned earlier, the constructors without the *Calendar* argument are assumed to refer to dates in the Gregorian calendar.

*Calendar* is a *MustInherit* class defined in the *System.Globalization* namespace, a namespace that also includes eight classes derived from *Calendar*:

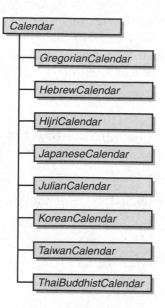

*Hijri* is another name for the Islamic calendar.

When you include a *Calendar* object as the last argument to the constructor, different consistency rules are applicable. For example,

```
Dim dt As New DateTime(1900, 2, 29)
```

generates an exception because 1900 isn't a leap year in the Gregorian calendar. However,

```
Dim dt As New DateTime(1900, 2, 29, New JulianCalendar())
```

doesn't cause an exception because in the Julian calendar every year divisible by 4 is a leap year.

Moreover, if you actually make that call using the *JulianCalendar* object and then look at the individual properties of the *DateTime* structure, you'll find that *Month* equals 3 (March) and *Day* equals 13. The *Year*, *Month*, and *Day* properties of the *DateTime* structure always represent dates in the Gregorian calendar. The constructor converts a date in a particular calendar into a tick count; the *DateTime* properties convert from the tick count to dates in the Gregorian calendar.

The original adoption of the Gregorian calendar caused the date after October 4, 1582, to be October 15, 1582, effectively skipping 10 days.[1] If you call

```
dt = New DateTime(1582, 10, 5, new JulianCalendar())
```

---

1. The years leading up to the recent millennium anniversary saw the publication of several books that retold the history of the Julian and Gregorian calendars. Perhaps the shortest and most eloquent is Stephen Jay Gould, *Questioning the Millennium: A Rationalist's Guide to a Precisely Arbitrary Countdown* (New York: Harmony Books, 1997).

the *Month* property will be 10 and the *Day* property will indeed be 15.

It gets more interesting. Suppose you call

```
dt = New DateTime(5762, 5, 20, new HebrewCalendar())
```

Yes, that is indeed a year in the Hebrew calendar—the 20th day in the month of Shevat in the year 5762. The resultant *DateTime* structure has a *Year* property of 2002, and *Month* and *Day* properties both equal to 2. Basically, what you have here is a conversion between the Hebrew calendar and the Gregorian calendar. When the last argument to the *DateTime* constructor is a *HebrewCalendar* object, the *Month* argument can be set to 13 in some years.

Similarly, you can specify a date in the Islamic calendar:

```
dt = New DateTime(1422, 11, 20, new HijriCalendar())
```

That's the 20th day of the month of Dhu'l-Qa'dah in the year 1422. Again, the resultant *DateTime* structure has a *Year* property of 2002, and *Month* and *Day* properties both equal to 2.

To convert from a Gregorian date to another calendar, you need to create instances of the particular calendar, for example,

```
Dim hebrewcal As New HebrewCalendar()
Dim hijrical As New HijriCalendar()
```

You also need a *DateTime* object:

```
Dim dt As New DateTime(2002, 2, 2)
```

To convert this Gregorian date into a date in the Hebrew or Islamic calendar, you use the following three methods:

### *Calendar* Methods (selection)

```
Function GetYear(ByVal dt As DateTime) As Integer

Function GetMonth(ByVal dt As DateTime) As Integer

Function GetDayOfMonth(ByVal dt As DateTime) As Integer
```

For example, the expression

```
hijrical.GetYear(dt)
```

returns 1422.

# A Readable Rendition

Some of the most important methods in *DateTime* are those that format the date and time into human-readable form. This conversion might seem fairly trivial until you realize that people all over the world write dates and times in different ways. Some cultures use 24-hour clocks; others prefer using a.m. and p.m. Some cultures write the day before the month; others put the month before the day. If the date includes month names or days of the week, it's helpful for these names to be in the user's language. Even within a particular culture, some users may have individual preferences that differ from the cultural standards.

In Windows XP (other versions may differ slightly) these cultural standards and user preferences are accessible through the Regional and Language Options dialog box in Control Panel. If you select the Regional Options tab, you can change your Locale, and the default date and time formatting will reflect the preferences in that location. You can click Customize to change the default formatting to something you prefer. Date and time display formats that depend on cultural differences or user preferences are said to be *culture-specific*.

While it's often polite for a program to format a date or time in a manner that is recognizable and readable by the user, sometimes it's undesirable. Sometimes dates and times must be embedded in documents that must be viewed by people in other cultures or merged with similar documents. In this case, a program should use a consistent date and time format, perhaps in accordance with some international standard. In the jargon of the .NET Framework, such formats are said to be *culture-invariant*.

For the following examples, I'll be using a day of June 1, 2002, and a local time of 3:05:01 p.m. The single-digit month, day, hour, minute, and second will help clarify whether any zero-suppression is going on in the formatting.

Let's assume that *dt* is a *DateTime* object. If you simply put this object in a *Console.WriteLine* method, as

```
Console.WriteLine(dt)
```

or in a *String.Format* method, as

```
str = String.Format("{0}", dt)
```

the method causes the *ToString* method of *DateTime* to be called. The previous statement is equivalent to

```
str = dt.ToString()
```

*ToString* converts the date and time to a culture-specific character string. For U.S. English settings, the character string returned from *ToString* looks like this:

```
6/1/2002 3:05:01 PM
```

The *DateTime* structure also defines several additional versions of *ToString* that have one or two arguments. These versions allow you to format the date and time in a variety of culture-specific and culture-invariant ways:

### *DateTime ToString* Method

```
Function ToString() As String

Function ToString(ByVal strFormat As String) As String

Function ToString(ByVal ifp As IFormatProvider) As String

Function ToString(ByVal strFormat As String,
                  ByVal ifp As IformatProvider) As String
```

The *String* argument is typically a single letter that denotes a particular style of formatting. I'll be describing these letters in detail shortly. The *String* argument can also be a series of letters that describe a custom format.

The *IFormatProvider* argument refers to an interface. What you need for this argument is an instance of a class that implements *IFormatProvider*. One such class is *DateTimeFormatInfo*, which is in the *System.Globalization* namespace. (You should check the documentation for *DateTimeFormatInfo* if you need formatting information beyond what I'm presenting here.) The *DateTimeFormatInfo* class has two shared properties, both of which return instances of the class:

### *DateTimeFormatInfo* Shared Properties

| Property | Type | Accessibility |
| --- | --- | --- |
| *CurrentInfo* | *DateTimeFormatInfo* | Get |
| *InvariantInfo* | *DateTimeFormatInfo* | Get |

Thus, to get culture-invariant formatting, you can call

```
strDT = dt.ToString(DateTimeFormatInfo.InvariantInfo)
```

or

```
strDT = dt.ToString(strFormat, DateTimeFormatInfo.InvariantInfo)
```

To get formatting consistent with the user's cultural and personal preferences as specified in Control Panel, use

```
strDT = dt.ToString(DateTimeFormatInfo.CurrentInfo)
```

or

```
strDT = dt.ToString(strFormat, DateTimeFormatInfo.CurrentInfo)
```

You'll also get culture-specific formatting if you use *Nothing* as the second argument to *ToString*:

```
strDT = dt.ToString(strFormat, Nothing)
```

or if you use the version with *strFormat* as the only argument:

```
strDT = dt.ToString(strFormat)
```

To use standard date and time formats, set the first argument of *ToString* to a single character as shown in the first column of the following table. The second column in this table displays the formatting you get when you've used Control Panel to set the locale to the United States, and you've specified *Nothing* or *DateTimeFormatInfo.CurrentInfo* as the second argument to *ToString* or you've used the version of *ToString* that has a single string argument. The column on the right shows the formatted strings when you use a second argument of *DateTimeFormatInfo.InvariantInfo*. These strings are the same regardless of Control Panel settings.

### *ToString* Date and Time Formats

| Format Character | Format Argument | |
|---|---|---|
| | *CurrentInfo* for United States | *InvariantInfo* |
| *d* | 6/1/2002 | 06/01/2002 |
| *D* | Saturday, June 01, 2002 | Saturday, 01 June 2002 |
| *f* | Saturday, June 01, 2002 3:05 PM | Saturday, 01 June 2002 15:05 |
| *F* | Saturday, June 01, 2002 3:05:01 PM | Saturday, 01 June 2002 15:05:01 |
| *g* | 6/1/2002 3:05 PM | 06/01/2002 15:05 |
| *G* or *null* | 6/1/2002 3:05:01 PM | 06/01/2002 15:05:01 |
| *m* or *M* | June 01 | June 01 |
| *r* or *R* | Sat, 01 Jun 2002 15:05:01 GMT | Same as *CurrentInfo* |
| *s* | 2002-06-01T15:05:01 | Same as *CurrentInfo* |
| *t* | 3:05 PM | 15:05 |
| *T* | 3:05:01 PM | 15:05:01 |
| *u* | 2002-06-01 15:05:01Z | Same as *CurrentInfo* |
| *U* | Saturday, June 01, 2002 7:05:01 PM | Saturday, 01 June 2002 19:05:01 |
| *y* or *Y* | June, 2002 | 2002 June |

The letters are mnemonics of sorts:

## *DateTime* Formatting Mnemonics

| Letter | Mnemonic |
|--------|----------|
| *d* | Date |
| *f* | Full |
| *g* | General |
| *m* | month/day |
| *r* | RFC |
| *s* | sortable |
| *t* | time |
| *u* | universal |
| *y* | year/month |

When the uppercase and lowercase letter produce different results (such as *d* and *D*), the uppercase letter produces a longer string. For the *r*, *R*, *s*, or *u* formatting strings, the results are the same regardless of the second argument to *ToString*.

The *ToString* method with a *Nothing* or an absent string argument returns a string corresponding to the culture-specific *G* (general) formatting option. Thus, the call

```
dt.ToString()
```

is also equivalent to

```
dt.ToString(CType(Nothing, String))
```

or

```
dt.ToString(CType(Nothing, IFormatProvider))
```

or

```
dt.ToString(Nothing, Nothing)
```

All return culture-specific *G* formatted strings. The *ToString* methods with a single *IFormatProvider* argument also return strings equivalent to the *G* formatting option.

Using *r* or *R* results in the RFC 1123[2] format. The *s* format is known as ISO 8601[3] format, and it is intended to be universal and easily sortable. The *T* in the center is known as a *time designator* and separates the date and time. Dates that begin with months or days of the month can't be sorted quite as easily in this format. The *u* formatting is quite similar to *s* except that the time designator is missing and the string ends with a *Z*. In military and radio circles, UTC is sometimes known as *Zulu time*, Zulu being used to represent *Z*, and *Z* referring to zero degrees of longitude.

The *U* format option performs a conversion to UTC. The use of this formatting string implies that the *DateTime* value is a local time.

The *DateTime* structure has four other convenient formatting methods, all of which are culture-specific:

### *DateTime* Methods (selection)

| Method | Resultant String (U.S. English) |
|---|---|
| `Function ToShortDateString() As String` | 6/1/2001 |
| `Function ToLongDateString() As String` | Saturday, June 01, 2002 |
| `Function ToShortTimeString() As String` | 3:05 PM |
| `Function ToLongTimeString() As String` | 3:05:01 PM |

These are identical to the culture-specific formatting strings of *d*, *D*, *t*, and *T*, respectively.

Just for kicks, let's go into the Regional Options dialog box in Control Panel and change the locale to Germany. Now let's look at how date and time strings are formatted with default German settings:

### *ToString* Date and Time Formats (German)

| Format Character | Format Argument | |
|---|---|---|
| | *CurrentInfo* for Germany | *InvariantInfo* |
| *d* | 01.06.2002 | 06/01/2002 |
| *D* | Samstag, 1. Juni 2002 | Saturday, 01 June 2002 |

---

2. RFC stands for "request for comment" and is the means by which Internet standards are distributed. The time and date specification in RFC 1123 slightly modifies the specification discussed in RFC 822. RFCs are available at many Web sites, including *http://www.ietf.org*.

3. ISO 8601 ("Date elements and interchange formats—Information interchange—Representation of dates and times") is available from the ISO at *http://www.iso.ch*. ISO 8601 is actually a collection of formats for representing dates and times. The format used by the *ToString* method of *DateTime* is the first of the three extended formats shown in section 5.4.1.a.

### *ToString* Date and Time Formats (German)   *(continued)*

| Format Character | Format Argument | |
| --- | --- | --- |
| | *CurrentInfo* for Germany | *InvariantInfo* |
| *f* | Samstag, 1. Juni 2002 15:05 | Saturday, 01 June 2002 15:05 |
| *F* | Samstag, 1. Juni 2002 15:05:01 | Saturday, 01 June 2002 15:05:01 |
| *g* | 01.06.2002 15:05 | 06/01/2002 15:05 |
| *G* or *null* | 01.06.2002 15:05:01 | 06/01/2002 15:05:01 |
| *m* or *M* | 01 Juni | June 01 |
| *r* or *R* | Sat, 01 Jun 2002 15:05:01 GMT | Same as *CurrentInfo* |
| *s* | 2002-06-01T15:05:01 | Same as *CurrentInfo* |
| *t* | 15:05 | 15:05 |
| *T* | 15:05:01 | 15:05:01 |
| *u* | 2002-06-01 15:05:01Z | Same as *CurrentInfo* |
| *U* | Samstag, 1. Juni 2002 19:05:01 | Saturday, 01 June 2002 19:05:01 |
| *y* or *Y* | Juni 2002 | 2002 June |

The column on the right is the same as the previous table. The culture-specific formatting involves using German names for months and days of the week as well as other formatting specifics.

In some cases, *ToString* does more than just format. If you change your locale to one of the Arab countries, you have a choice (on the Date tab of the Customize Regional Options dialog box) between using the Gregorian calendar or the Islamic calendar. Likewise, if you select Hebrew in the Regional Options, you can choose between the Gregorian calendar or the Hebrew calendar. If you choose an Islamic or Hebrew calendar, the culture-specific format options will perform a conversion to a date in that calendar.

# A Simple Culture-Specific Clock

Here's a program that uses the *F* formatting option to display the current date and time in its client area.

```
SimpleClock.vb
'-------------------------------------------------
' SimpleClock.vb (c) 2002 by Charles Petzold
'-------------------------------------------------
Imports System
Imports System.Drawing
Imports System.Windows.Forms
```

*(continued)*

**SimpleClock.vb**   *(continued)*

```vb
Class SimpleClock
    Inherits Form

    Shared Sub Main()
        Application.Run(new SimpleClock())
    End Sub

    Sub New()
        Text = "Simple Clock"
        BackColor = SystemColors.Window
        ForeColor = SystemColors.WindowText

        Dim tmr As New Timer()
        AddHandler tmr.Tick, AddressOf TimerOnTick
        tmr.Interval = 1000
        tmr.Start()
    End Sub

    Private Sub TimerOnTick(ByVal obj As Object, ByVal ea As EventArgs)
        Invalidate()
    End Sub

    Protected Overrides Sub OnPaint(ByVal pea As PaintEventArgs)
        Dim strfmt As New StringFormat()
        strfmt.Alignment = StringAlignment.Center
        strfmt.LineAlignment = StringAlignment.Center
        pea.Graphics.DrawString(DateTime.Now.ToString("F"), _
                        Font, New SolidBrush(ForeColor), _
                        RectangleF.op_Implicit(ClientRectangle), strfmt)
    End Sub
End Class
```

The program sets a 1-second timer and simply invalidates the client area in response to the *OnTick* event. Here's what it looks like with the default U.S. formatting in effect:

But I ask you: Did we spend all that time learning about fonts only to create a clock as pathetic as this one? I don't think so.

Let's restrict ourselves to the time and make it as large as possible. That just requires using *OnPaint* processing more creatively.

**DigitalClock.vb**

```
'-------------------------------------------------
' DigitalClock.vb (c) 2002 by Charles Petzold
'-------------------------------------------------
Imports System
Imports System.Drawing
Imports System.Windows.Forms

Class DigitalClock
    Inherits Form

    Shared Sub Main()
        Application.Run(new DigitalClock())
    End Sub

    Sub New()
        Text = "Digital Clock"
        BackColor = SystemColors.Window
        ForeColor = SystemColors.WindowText
        ResizeRedraw = True
        MinimumSize = Size.op_Addition(SystemInformation.MinimumWindowSize, _
                                       New Size(0, 1))
        Dim tmr As New Timer()
        AddHandler tmr.Tick, AddressOf TimerOnTick
        tmr.Interval = 1000
        tmr.Start()
    End Sub

    Private Sub TimerOnTick(ByVal obj As Object, ByVal ea As EventArgs)
        Invalidate()
    End Sub

    Protected Overrides Sub OnPaint(ByVal pea As PaintEventArgs)
        Dim grfx As Graphics = pea.Graphics
        Dim strTime As String = DateTime.Now.ToString("T")
        Dim szf As SizeF = grfx.MeasureString(strTime, Font)
        Dim fScale As Single = Math.Min(ClientSize.Width / szf.Width, _
                                        ClientSize.Height / szf.Height)
        Dim fnt As New Font(Font.FontFamily, _
                            fScale * Font.SizeInPoints)
        szf = grfx.MeasureString(strTime, fnt)
        grfx.DrawString(strTime, fnt, New SolidBrush(ForeColor), _
                        (ClientSize.Width - szf.Width) / 2, _
                        (ClientSize.Height - szf.Height) / 2)
    End Sub
End Class
```

The *OnPaint* method stores the formatted time in *strTime* and then uses a technique I discussed in Chapter 9 to make the text as large (but no larger) than the client area. Here's the display with default U.S. English settings:

Unfortunately, for the sake of getting something large enough to read from across the room, we've lost the date display. Is it possible to display both the date and the time while maintaining the big size? Of course! The trick is to avoid using those format strings that combine the date and time, and to format the date and time separately, combining the two strings with a line feed character.

**DigitalClockWithDate.vb**

```
'-------------------------------------------------------
' DigitalClockWithDate.vb (c) 2002 by Charles Petzold
'-------------------------------------------------------
Imports System
Imports System.Drawing
Imports System.Windows.Forms

Class DigitalClockWithDate
    Inherits DigitalClock

    Shared Shadows Sub Main()
        Application.Run(new DigitalClockWithDate())
    End Sub

    Sub New()
        Text &= " with Date"
    End Sub

    Protected Overrides Sub OnPaint(ByVal pea As PaintEventArgs)
        Dim grfx As Graphics = pea.Graphics
        Dim dt As DateTime = DateTime.Now
        Dim strTime As String = dt.ToString("d") & vbLf & dt.ToString("T")
```

```
        Dim szf As SizeF = grfx.MeasureString(strTime, Font)
        Dim fScale As Single = Math.Min(ClientSize.Width / szf.Width, _
                                  ClientSize.Height / szf.Height)
        Dim fnt As New Font(Font.FontFamily, fScale * Font.SizeInPoints)
        Dim strfmt As New StringFormat()
        strfmt.Alignment = StringAlignment.Center
        strfmt.LineAlignment = StringAlignment.Center
        grfx.DrawString(strTime, fnt, New SolidBrush(ForeColor), _
                    RectangleF.op_Implicit(ClientRectangle), strfmt)
    End Sub
End Class
```

The call to *MeasureString* returns the height of the two lines of text and the width of the wider line. To center both lines horizontally in the client area, the *DrawString* call needs a *StringFormat* object. Here's the display, again with default U.S. English settings:

The fact that the *OnPaint* method gets called every second might get you to wondering about the efficiency of the drawing code. Would it be better, for example, to create the required font during the *OnResize* method? Yes, it would, but it would take a bit of work to get it to work just right. The font size is dependent on both the size of the client area and the width and height of the text string. In most cases, of course, the text string width doesn't change from second to second. But it does change occasionally. The width of the text string containing the time depends on whether the hour is one digit or two digits wide. And if the time is displayed in a 24-hour format, the date string is wider than the time string, and that width depends on the month and the day of the month.

If the program had a separate method to create an appropriate font, that method would have to retain in fields both the font and the width of the text used to calculate the font. The *OnResize* method would call the font-calculation method, obviously. And the *OnPaint* method would need to call it as well if the text width didn't match the width used to calculate the font.

# The Retro Look

You could use any TrueType font you have installed on your system in either of the digital clock programs. Just put a statement in the program's constructor to change the form's *Font* property:

```
Font = New Font("Comic Sans MS", 12)
```

Then just let the *OnPaint* method scale the font.

To give the clock a neat retro look, you might want to choose a font that looks like a seven-segment LCD display. Or you can use this *SevenSegmentDisplay* class instead of a font.

```
SevenSegmentDisplay.vb
'-------------------------------------------------------
' SevenSegmentDisplay.vb (c) 2002 by Charles Petzold
'-------------------------------------------------------
Imports System
Imports System.Drawing
Imports System.Windows.Forms

Class SevenSegmentDisplay
    ' Indicates what segments are illuminated for all 10 digits
    Shared bySegment(,) As Byte = {{1, 1, 1, 0, 1, 1, 1}, _
                                   {0, 0, 1, 0, 0, 1, 0}, _
                                   {1, 0, 1, 1, 1, 0, 1}, _
                                   {1, 0, 1, 1, 0, 1, 1}, _
                                   {0, 1, 1, 1, 0, 1, 0}, _
                                   {1, 1, 0, 1, 0, 1, 1}, _
                                   {1, 1, 0, 1, 1, 1, 1}, _
                                   {1, 0, 1, 0, 0, 1, 0}, _
                                   {1, 1, 1, 1, 1, 1, 1}, _
                                   {1, 1, 1, 1, 0, 1, 1}}

    ' Points that define each of the seven segments
    ReadOnly apt(6)() As Point

    ' A field initialized by the constructor
    ReadOnly grfx As Graphics

    ' Only constructor requires Graphics argument
```

```
Sub New(ByVal grfx As Graphics)
    Me.grfx = grfx

    ' Initialize jagged Point array.
    apt(0) = New Point() {New Point(3, 2), New Point(39, 2), _
                          New Point(31, 10), New Point(11, 10)}
    apt(1) = New Point() {New Point(2, 3), New Point(10, 11), _
                          New Point(10, 31), New Point(2, 35)}
    apt(2) = New Point() {New Point(40, 3), New Point(40, 35), _
                          New Point(32, 31), New Point(32, 11)}
    apt(3) = New Point() {New Point(3, 36), New Point(11, 32), _
                          New Point(31, 32), New Point(39, 36), _
                          New Point(31, 40), New Point(11, 40)}
    apt(4) = New Point() {New Point(2, 37), New Point(10, 41), _
                          New Point(10, 61), New Point(2, 69)}
    apt(5) = New Point() {New Point(40, 37), New Point(40, 69), _
                          New Point(32, 61), New Point(32, 41)}
    apt(6) = New Point() {New Point(11, 62), New Point(31, 62), _
                          New Point(39, 70), New Point(3, 70)}
End Sub

Function MeasureString(ByVal str As String, ByVal fnt As Font) As SizeF
    Dim szf As New SizeF(0, grfx.DpiX * fnt.SizeInPoints / 72)
    Dim ch As Char
    For Each ch In str
        If Char.IsDigit(ch) Then
            szf.Width += 42 * grfx.DpiX * fnt.SizeInPoints / 72 / 72
        ElseIf ch.Equals(":"c) Then
            szf.Width += 12 * grfx.DpiX _
                            * fnt.SizeInPoints / 72 / 72
        End If
    Next ch
    Return szf
End Function

Sub DrawString(ByVal str As String, ByVal fnt As Font, _
               ByVal br As Brush, ByVal x As Single, ByVal y As Single)
    Dim ch As Char
    For Each ch In str
        If Char.IsDigit(ch) Then
            x = Number(AscW(ch) - AscW("0"), fnt, br, x, y)
        ElseIf ch.Equals(":"c) Then
            x = Colon(fnt, br, x, y)
        End If
    Next ch
End Sub

Private Function Number(ByVal num As Integer, ByVal fnt As Font, _
                        ByVal br As Brush, ByVal x As Single, _
                        ByVal y As Single) As Single
```

*(continued)*

**SevenSegmentDisplay.vb**    *(continued)*

```
        Dim i As Integer
        For i = 0 To apt.GetUpperBound(0)
            If bySegment(num, i) = 1 Then
                Fill(apt(i), fnt, br, x, y)
            End If
        Next i
        Return x + 42 * grfx.DpiX * fnt.SizeInPoints / 72 / 72
    End Function

    Private Function Colon(ByVal fnt As Font, ByVal br As Brush, _
                           ByVal x As Single, ByVal y As Single) As Single
        Dim i As Integer
        Dim apt(1)() As Point
        apt(0) = New Point() {New Point(2, 21), New Point(6, 17), _
                        New Point(10, 21), New Point(6, 25)}
        apt(1) = New Point() {New Point(2, 51), New Point(6, 47), _
                        New Point(10, 51), New Point(6, 55)}

        For i = 0 To apt.GetUpperBound(0)
            Fill(apt(i), fnt, br, x, y)
        Next i
        Return x + 12 * grfx.DpiX * fnt.SizeInPoints / 72 / 72
    End Function

    Private Sub Fill(ByVal apt() As Point, ByVal fnt As Font, _
                     ByVal br As Brush, ByVal x As Single, _
                     ByVal y As Single)
        Dim i As Integer
        Dim aptf(apt.GetUpperBound(0)) As PointF

        For i = 0 To apt.GetUpperBound(0)
            aptf(i).X = x + apt(i).X * grfx.DpiX _
                        * fnt.SizeInPoints / 72 / 72
            aptf(i).Y = y + apt(i).Y * grfx.DpiY _
                        * fnt.SizeInPoints / 72 / 72
        Next i
        grfx.FillPolygon(br, aptf)
    End Sub
End Class
```

The *SevenSegmentDisplay* class has one public constructor, which takes an argument of type *Graphics*, and two public methods, which are called *MeasureString* and *DrawString* and which have the same arguments as the two most popular versions of those methods in the *Graphics* class. The idea here is that you create a *SevenSegmentDisplay* object with a *Graphics* object argument and then use these two methods instead of the methods in the *Graphics* class.

The *DrawString* method implemented in *SevenSegmentDisplay* can deal with only 11 character codes: those for the 10 digits and the colon. It calls the private *Number* and *Colon* methods for these two cases. The *Number* method

uses a shared array named *bySegment* that indicates which of the seven segments are illuminated for each of the 10 digits. (This array should probably
have been defined with the *Boolean* data type rather than *Byte*, but I thought
that the list of *True* and *False* initializers would have been more difficult to read,
and I couldn't imagine that the machine code would have been more efficient.)
A *ReadOnly* jagged *Point* array named *apt* has the points that define each of the
seven segments. These points are based on a character width of 42 and a height
of 72. The private *Fill* method scales these coordinates based on the font size
and uses *FillPolygon* to color the interiors red.

The clock program that uses this class is virtually identical to DigitalClock
except that it begins *OnPaint* processing by creating a *SevenSegmentDisplay*
object and uses that rather than the *Graphics* object for calls to *MeasureString*
and *DrawString*.

```
SevenSegmentClock.vb
'-------------------------------------------------------------
' SevenSegmentClock.vb (c) 2002 by Charles Petzold
'-------------------------------------------------------------
Imports System
Imports System.Drawing
Imports System.Globalization
Imports System.Windows.Forms

Class SevenSegmentClock
    Inherits Form

    Private dt As DateTime

    Shared Sub Main()
        Application.Run(new SevenSegmentClock())
    End Sub

    Sub New()
        Text = "Seven-Segment Clock"
        BackColor = Color.White
        ResizeRedraw = True
        MinimumSize = Size.op_Addition( _
                            SystemInformation.MinimumWindowSize, _
                            New Size(0, 1))
        Dim tmr As New Timer()
        AddHandler tmr.Tick, AddressOf TimerOnTick
        tmr.Interval = 100
        tmr.Enabled = True
    End Sub

    Private Sub TimerOnTick(ByVal obj As Object, ByVal ea As EventArgs)
        Dim dtNow As DateTime = DateTime.Now
        dtNow = new DateTime(dtNow.Year, dtNow.Month, dtNow.Day, _
```

*(continued)*

**SevenSegmentClock.vb**  *(continued)*

```
                        dtNow.Hour, dtNow.Minute, dtNow.Second)
        If dtNow <> dt Then
            dt = dtNow
            Invalidate()
        End If
    End Sub

    Protected Overrides Sub OnPaint(ByVal pea As PaintEventArgs)
        Dim ssd As New SevenSegmentDisplay(pea.Graphics)
        Dim strTime As String = _
                        dt.ToString("T", DateTimeFormatInfo.InvariantInfo)
        Dim szf As SizeF = ssd.MeasureString(strTime, Font)
        Dim fScale As Single = Math.Min(ClientSize.Width / szf.Width, _
                                        ClientSize.Height / szf.Height)

        Dim fnt As New Font(Font.FontFamily, fScale * Font.SizeInPoints)
        szf = ssd.MeasureString(strTime, fnt)
        ssd.DrawString(strTime, fnt, Brushes.Red, _
                    (ClientSize.Width - szf.Width) / 2, _
                    (ClientSize.Height - szf.Height) / 2)
    End Sub
End Class
```

However, notice that I've used a culture-invariant *ToString* method of *DateTime*. This is an excellent example of a program that works best with a culture-invariant string because it needs to know exactly what characters it's getting and doesn't want to encounter a.m. or p.m. indicators:

# An Analog Clock

Digital clocks were popular when they were new, but the pendulum has swung back (so to speak) to analog clocks. An analog clock needn't concern itself with different date and time formats, but the complexity of the graphics more than outweighs that convenience. Users have come to expect analog clocks to dynamically change size with the size of the window.

For greatest versatility, I decided to write the clock display logic as a child window control like the *CheckerChild* class in the CheckerWithChildren program in Chapter 8. That would make it easier to embed a clock display in another application or to write an application that displayed multiple clocks. Here's the code for the *ClockControl* class.

```vb
ClockControl.vb
'-------------------------------------------------
' ClockControl.vb (c) 2002 by Charles Petzold
'-------------------------------------------------
Imports System
Imports System.Drawing
Imports System.Drawing.Drawing2D
Imports System.Windows.Forms

Class ClockControl
    Inherits UserControl

    Private dt As DateTime

    Sub New()
        ResizeRedraw = True
        Enabled = False
    End Sub

    Property Time() As DateTime
        Set(ByVal Value As DateTime)
            Dim grfx As Graphics = CreateGraphics()
            Dim pn As New Pen(BackColor)

            InitializeCoordinates(grfx)

            If dt.Hour <> Value.Hour Then
                DrawHourHand(grfx, pn)
            End If

            If dt.Minute <> Value.Minute Then
                DrawHourHand(grfx, pn)
                DrawMinuteHand(grfx, pn)
            End If
```

*(continued)*

**ClockControl.vb**   *(continued)*

```
        If dt.Second <> Value.Second Then
            DrawMinuteHand(grfx, pn)
            DrawSecondHand(grfx, pn)
        End If

        If dt.Millisecond <> Value.Millisecond Then
            DrawSecondHand(grfx, pn)
        End If

        dt = Value
        pn = New Pen(ForeColor)
        DrawHourHand(grfx, pn)
        DrawMinuteHand(grfx, pn)
        DrawSecondHand(grfx, pn)
        grfx.Dispose()
    End Set
    Get
        Return dt
    End Get
End Property

Protected Overrides Sub OnPaint(ByVal pea As PaintEventArgs)
    Dim grfx As Graphics = pea.Graphics
    Dim pn As New Pen(ForeColor)
    Dim br As New SolidBrush(ForeColor)

    InitializeCoordinates(grfx)
    DrawDots(grfx, br)
    DrawHourHand(grfx, pn)
    DrawMinuteHand(grfx, pn)
    DrawSecondHand(grfx, pn)
End Sub

Private Sub InitializeCoordinates(ByVal grfx As Graphics)
    If Width = 0 OrElse Height = 0 Then Return

    grfx.TranslateTransform(Width \ 2, Height \ 2)
    Dim fInches As Single = Math.Min(Width / grfx.DpiX, _
                                     Height / grfx.DpiY)
    grfx.ScaleTransform(fInches * grfx.DpiX / 2000, _
                        fInches * grfx.DpiY / 2000)
End Sub

Private Sub DrawDots(ByVal grfx As Graphics, ByVal br As Brush)
    Dim i, iSize As Integer

    For i = 0 To 59
        If i Mod 5 = 0 Then iSize = 100 Else iSize = 30

        grfx.FillEllipse(br, 0 - iSize \ 2, -900 - iSize \ 2, _
                         iSize, iSize)
        grfx.RotateTransform(6)
    Next i
```

```
    End Sub

    Protected Overridable Sub DrawHourHand(ByVal grfx As Graphics, _
                                           ByVal pn As Pen)
        Dim gs As GraphicsState = grfx.Save()
        grfx.RotateTransform(360.0F * Time.Hour / 12 + _
                        30.0F * Time.Minute / 60)
        grfx.DrawPolygon(pn, New Point() { _
                    New Point(0, 150), New Point(100, 0), _
                    New Point(0, -600), New Point(-100, 0)})
        grfx.Restore(gs)
    End Sub

    Protected Overridable Sub DrawMinuteHand(ByVal grfx As Graphics, _
                                             ByVal pn As Pen)
        Dim gs As GraphicsState = grfx.Save()
        grfx.RotateTransform(360.0F * Time.Minute / 60 + _
                        6.0F * Time.Second / 60)
        grfx.DrawPolygon(pn, New Point() { _
                    New Point(0, 200), New Point(50, 0), _
                    New Point(0, -800), New Point(-50, 0)})
        grfx.Restore(gs)
    End Sub

    Protected Overridable Sub DrawSecondHand(ByVal grfx As Graphics, _
                                             ByVal pn As Pen)
        Dim gs As GraphicsState = grfx.Save()
        grfx.RotateTransform(360.0F * Time.Second / 60 + _
                        6.0F * Time.Millisecond / 1000)
        grfx.DrawLine(pn, 0, 0, 0, -800)
        grfx.Restore(gs)
    End Sub
End Class
```

*ClockControl* inherits from *UserControl* and overrides the *OnPaint* method. The *ClockControl* constructor sets the *ResizeRedraw* control style to *True* and also sets its *Enabled* property to *False*. *ClockControl* doesn't have any need for keyboard or mouse input, so any such input will pass through to the control's parent.

Notice the private *DateTime* field I've named *dt* and the read/write public property named *Time* that gives other objects access to this field. The control doesn't implement its own timer and doesn't set this property itself; the control simply displays the time indicated by the current value of its *Time* property. Keeping that *Time* property up to date is the responsibility of whatever class creates an instance of *ClockControl*.

The code implementing the *Set* accessor of the *Time* property seems inordinately lengthy. The temptation, of course, is to simplify the *Set* accessor like so:

```
dt = Value
Invalidate()
```

That *Invalidate* call would cause the control to get an *OnPaint* call, at which time it would redraw the clock. Visually, however, this simplification is a disaster. The *Invalidate* call causes the background of the control to be erased and the entire clock must be redrawn. That causes an annoying flickering of the image. Instead, I've taken a more attractive approach. Let me come back to the *Set* accessor of *Time* after I've discussed the *OnPaint* processing.

*OnPaint* creates a pen and a brush based on the control's foreground color and then calls five other methods. First, *InitializeCoordinates* sets up a coordinate system with an origin at the center of the control and isotropic coordinates that extend to 1000 units in all four directions.

Second, *DrawDots* draws the dots that indicate the minutes and hours. This method uses the *Graphics* class methods *FillEllipse* to draw a dot at 12:00 and *RotateTransform* to rotate 6° for the next dot. The *DrawHourHand*, *DrawMinuteHand*, and *DrawSecondHand* methods also use *RotateTransform*. I've made these three methods *Overridable* so that they can be overridden at some point (by a program in Chapter 13, to be precise).

The actual drawing code (*DrawPolygon* for the hour and minute hands and *DrawLine* for the second hand) assumes that the hands are pointing straight up. The call to *RotateTransform* before the drawing code rotates the hand to its proper position. Each of the hand-drawing routines makes a call to the *Save* method of the *Graphics* class to save the current graphics state before calling *RotateTransform*, and *Restore* after it's finished.

Notice that the position of the hour hand is based on both the *Hour* and *Minute* properties of the *DateTime* structure, the position of the minute hand is based on both *Minute* and *Second*, and the position of the second hand is based on the *Second* and *Millisecond* properties. Thus, the hands sweep continuously rather than jump in discrete steps.

Now we're ready to look at the *Set* accessor code of the *DateTime* property. After calling *CreateGraphics* to obtain a *Graphics* object for the control, a call to *InitializeCoordinates* sets up the proper coordinate system. Then the code creates a pen based on the control's background color. What it needs to do is effectively erase any hand that is changing position. The problem, however, is that drawing a particular hand in a background color might also affect one of the other two hands. For that reason, all three hands must be redrawn using the foreground color. Even though there's still a lot of drawing whenever the time changes, this process reduces flickering considerably.

Now that we have a control, implementing a form that uses this control is fairly easy.

**AnalogClock.vb**

```
'-------------------------------------------------
' AnalogClock.vb (c) 2002 by Charles Petzold
'-------------------------------------------------
Imports System
Imports System.Drawing
Imports System.Windows.Forms

Class AnalogClock
    Inherits Form

    Private clkctrl As ClockControl

    Shared Sub Main()
        Application.Run(new AnalogClock())
    End Sub

    Sub New()
        Text = "Analog Clock"
        BackColor = SystemColors.Window
        ForeColor = SystemColors.WindowText

        clkctrl = New ClockControl()
        clkctrl.Parent = Me
        clkctrl.Time = DateTime.Now
        clkctrl.Dock = DockStyle.Fill
        clkctrl.BackColor = Color.Black
        clkctrl.ForeColor = Color.White

        Dim tmr As New Timer()
        tmr.Interval = 100
        AddHandler tmr.Tick, AddressOf TimerOnTick
        tmr.Start()
    End Sub

    Private Sub TimerOnTick(ByVal obj As Object, ByVal ea As EventArgs)
        clkctrl.Time = DateTime.Now
    End Sub
End Class
```

In the constructor, the program creates an object of type *ClockControl*, sets the *Parent* property of the control to the form, and also initializes the control's *Time* property to the current date and time.

Next, the form sets a control property I haven't mentioned yet, which is named *Dock*. This property is implemented in *Control*, and I'll discuss it in much more detail in Chapter 12. For now, be aware that setting the *Dock* style of a control to *DockStyle.Fill* causes the control to fill up the entire display surface of its parent. The clock control will be automatically sized and resized to fit in the form's client area.

The last two properties of the clock control that I set are *BackColor* to black and *ForeColor* to white just to make a point that the control isn't controlling its color. The parent has control over that. Of course, it doesn't hurt that a white-on-black clock looks pretty cool:

The constructor processing concludes with setting the timer to an interval of 100 milliseconds (1/10 second). Clocks normally need just a 1-second update, but with this one, the second hand wouldn't give the appearance of sweeping continuously if it weren't updated more frequently. The *TimerOnTick* event handler simply sets the *Time* property of the clock control to the current date and time.

A program that didn't want a continuously sweeping second hand would set the timer to 1000 milliseconds and set the *Time* property of the clock control with a *DateTime* object that had a *Millisecond* property of 0. Because the *Millisecond* property is read-only, this job requires re-creating the *DateTime* object. The *TimerOnTick* code would look like this:

```
Dim dt As DateTime  = DateTime.Now
dt = New DateTime(dt.Year, dt.Month, dt.Day, dt.Hour, dt.Minute, dt.Second)
clkctrl.Time = dt
```

There are other ways to demonstrate that the time displayed by the clock control is entirely governed by the parent. Try replacing the *TimerOnTick* code with this:

```
clkctrl.Time = DateTime.op_Addition(clkctrl.Time, New TimeSpan(10000000))
```

The clock begins at the correct time but then moves at 10 times the normal speed. Or try this one:

```
clkctrl.Time = DateTime.op_Subtraction(clkctrl.Time, New TimeSpan(1000000))
```

The clock moves at normal speed but backward.

# A Little Puzzle Called Jeu de Taquin

It's now time to program a game. Well, more like a puzzle. This particular puzzle was invented in the 1870s, probably by the famous American puzzle-maker Sam Loyd (1841–1911). For a while, this puzzle was all the rage, particularly in Europe, and was known under various names, including the 15-puzzle, the 14-15 puzzle, and (in France) *Jeu de Taquin*, the "teasing game."

In its classic form, the puzzle consists of 15 square blocks numbered 1 through 15. The squares are arranged in a 4-by-4 grid, leaving one blank space. You can move the squares around the grid by shifting a square horizontally or vertically into the blank space, which in turn opens a different blank space.

As Sam Loyd presented it, the numbered squares were arranged in consecutive order except with the 14 and 15 reversed. He offered $1000 to anyone who could find a way to shift the squares around to correct the order of the 14 and 15. No one collected the reward because, from that starting point, the puzzle is insolvable.[4]

In computer form, this puzzle was one of the first game programs created for the Apple Macintosh, where it was called PUZZLE. It also appeared in early versions of the Microsoft Windows Software Development Kit (SDK) under the name MUZZLE, where it was the only sample program in the SDK coded in Microsoft Pascal rather than C. Both these programs initially displayed the 15 squares in consecutive order and presented a menu option to scramble the squares. You then attempted to restore the order of the squares or put them into different orders, such as going down the columns rather than across the rows. Because we haven't covered menus yet, my version of the program scrambles the squares when it first starts up. (That's where the timer comes into play.)

The tiles are child windows, but they set their *Enabled* property to *False* to let the parent process all keyboard and mouse input. Normally, controls indicate that they're disabled by graying their text, but they don't have to use this approach. In this case, they don't. The *OnPaint* method uses normal control colors to draw a 3D-like edge.

---

4. A mathematical analysis of the 14-15 puzzle first appeared in an 1879 article in the *American Journal of Mathematics*. The underlying math is summarized in James R. Newman, *The World of Mathematics* (New York: Simon and Schuster, 1956), 4: 2429–2432. The four-volume *World of Mathematics* was republished in 1988 by Tempus Books (a defunct imprint of Microsoft Press) and in 2000 by Dover Books. The section on the 14-15 puzzle appears on pages 2405 to 2408 in the Tempus edition.

**JeuDeTaquinTile.vb**

```vb
'------------------------------------------------
' JeuDeTaquinTile.vb (c) 2002 by Charles Petzold
'------------------------------------------------
Imports System
Imports System.Drawing
Imports System.Windows.Forms

Class JeuDeTaquinTile
    Inherits UserControl

    Private iNum As Integer

    Sub New(ByVal iNum As Integer)
        Me.iNum = iNum
        Enabled = False
    End Sub

    Protected Overrides Sub OnPaint(ByVal pea As PaintEventArgs)
        Dim grfx As Graphics = pea.Graphics
        grfx.Clear(SystemColors.Control)

        Dim cx As Integer = Size.Width
        Dim cy As Integer = Size.Height
        Dim wx As Integer = SystemInformation.FrameBorderSize.Width
        Dim wy As Integer = SystemInformation.FrameBorderSize.Height

        grfx.FillPolygon(SystemBrushes.ControlLightLight, _
            New Point() {New Point(0, cy), New Point(0, 0), _
                        New Point(cx, 0), New Point(cx - wx, wy), _
                        New Point(wx, wy), New Point(wx, cy - wy)})

        grfx.FillPolygon(SystemBrushes.ControlDark, _
            New Point() {New Point(cx, 0), New Point(cx, cy), _
                        New Point(0, cy), New Point(wx, cy - wy), _
                        New Point(cx - wx, cy - wy), _
                        New Point(cx - wx, wy)})

        Dim fnt As New Font("Arial", 24)
        Dim strfmt As New StringFormat()
        strfmt.Alignment = StringAlignment.Center
        strfmt.LineAlignment = StringAlignment.Center

        grfx.DrawString(iNum.ToString(), fnt, SystemBrushes.ControlText, _
                        RectangleF.op_Implicit(ClientRectangle), strfmt)
    End Sub
End Class
```

The program that creates these tiles and moves them around the grid is a bit more complicated. It creates the tile controls (and sizes the client area based on those controls) in an override of the *OnLoad* method implemented in the *Form* class. The *OnLoad* method is called soon before the form is first displayed; my experience indicates that obtaining *Graphics* objects and setting the size of a client area usually works better when done during *OnLoad* rather than during the constructor. *OnLoad* processing concludes with a call to the protected method *Randomize*, which uses a timer to scramble the tiles.

## JeuDeTaquin.vb

```
'------------------------------------------------
' JeuDeTaquin.vb (c) 2002 by Charles Petzold
'------------------------------------------------
Imports System
Imports System.Drawing
Imports System.Windows.Forms

Class JeuDeTaquin
    Inherits Form

    Const nRows As Integer = 4
    Const nCols As Integer = 4

    Private szTile As Size
    Private atile(nRows, nCols) As JeuDeTaquinTile
    Private rand As Random
    Private ptBlank As Point
    Private iTimerCountdown As Integer

    Shared Sub Main()
        Application.Run(new JeuDeTaquin())
    End Sub

    Sub New()
        Text = "Jeu de Taquin"
        FormBorderStyle = FormBorderStyle.Fixed3D
    End Sub

    Protected Overrides Sub OnLoad(ByVal ea As EventArgs)
        ' Calculate the size of the tiles and the form.
        Dim grfx As Graphics = CreateGraphics()
        szTile = New Size(CInt(2 * grfx.DpiX / 3), _
                          CInt(2 * grfx.DpiY / 3))
        ClientSize = New Size(nCols * szTile.Width, nRows * szTile.Height)
        grfx.Dispose()

        ' Create the tiles.
        Dim iRow, iCol, iNum As Integer
```

*(continued)*

**JeuDeTaquin.vb**    *(continued)*

```vbnet
        For iRow = 0 To nRows - 1
            For iCol = 0 To nCols - 1
                iNum = iRow * nCols + iCol + 1
                If iNum <> nRows * nCols Then
                    Dim tile As New JeuDeTaquinTile(iNum)
                    tile.Parent = Me
                    tile.Location = New Point(iCol * szTile.Width, _
                                                 iRow * szTile.Height)
                    tile.Size = szTile
                    atile(iRow, iCol) = tile
                End If
            Next iCol
        Next iRow
        ptBlank = New Point(nCols - 1, nRows - 1)
        Randomize()
    End Sub

    Protected Sub Randomize()
        rand = new Random()
        iTimerCountdown = 64 * nRows * nCols

        Dim tmr As New Timer()
        AddHandler tmr.Tick, AddressOf TimerOnTick
        tmr.Interval = 1
        tmr.Enabled = True
    End Sub

    Private Sub TimerOnTick(ByVal obj As Object, ByVal ea As EventArgs)
        Dim x As Integer = ptBlank.X
        Dim y As Integer = ptBlank.Y

        Select Case rand.Next(4)
            Case 0 : x += 1
            Case 1 : x -= 1
            Case 2 : y += 1
            Case 3 : y -= 1
        End Select

        If x >= 0 AndAlso x < nCols AndAlso y >= 0 AndAlso y < nRows Then
            MoveTile(x, y)
        End If

        iTimerCountdown -= 1

        If iTimerCountdown = 0 Then
            Dim tmr As Timer = DirectCast(obj, Timer)
            tmr.Stop()
            RemoveHandler tmr.Tick, AddressOf TimerOnTick
        End If
    End Sub
```

```
    Protected Overrides Sub OnKeyDown(ByVal kea As KeyEventArgs)
        If kea.KeyCode = Keys.Left AndAlso ptBlank.X < nCols - 1 Then
            MoveTile(ptBlank.X + 1, ptBlank.Y)

        ElseIf kea.KeyCode = Keys.Right AndAlso ptBlank.X > 0 Then
            MoveTile(ptBlank.X - 1, ptBlank.Y)

        ElseIf kea.KeyCode = Keys.Up AndAlso ptBlank.Y < nRows - 1 Then
            MoveTile(ptBlank.X, ptBlank.Y + 1)

        ElseIf kea.KeyCode = Keys.Down AndAlso ptBlank.Y > 0 Then
            MoveTile(ptBlank.X, ptBlank.Y - 1)
        End If
        kea.Handled = True
    End Sub

    Protected Overrides Sub OnMouseDown(ByVal mea As MouseEventArgs)
        Dim x As Integer = mea.X \ szTile.Width
        Dim y As Integer = mea.Y \ szTile.Height
        Dim x2, y2 As Integer

        If x = ptBlank.X Then
            If y < ptBlank.Y Then
                For y2 = ptBlank.Y - 1 To y Step -1
                    MoveTile(x, y2)
                Next y2
            ElseIf y > ptBlank.Y Then
                For y2 = ptBlank.Y + 1 To y
                    MoveTile(x, y2)
                Next y2
            End If
        ElseIf y = ptBlank.Y Then
            If x < ptBlank.X Then
                For x2 = ptBlank.X - 1 To x Step -1
                    MoveTile(x2, y)
                Next x2
            ElseIf x > ptBlank.X Then
                For x2 = ptBlank.X + 1 To x
                    MoveTile(x2, y)
                Next x2
            End If
        End If
    End Sub

    Private Sub MoveTile(ByVal x As Integer, ByVal y As Integer)
        atile(y, x).Location = New Point(ptBlank.X * szTile.Width, _
                                         ptBlank.Y * szTile.Height)
        atile(ptBlank.Y, ptBlank.X) = atile(y, x)
        atile(y, x) = Nothing
        ptBlank = New Point(x, y)
    End Sub
End Class
```

Everything else in the program just involves processing keyboard and mouse input leading up to a call to the *MoveTile* method at the bottom of the listing.

The two-dimensional *atile* array stores the tile objects. For example, the tile object stored at *atile(3,1)* is the tile currently in the fourth row and second column of the grid. One element of the *atile* array is always *Nothing*. That *Nothing* element corresponds to the coordinate currently not occupied by any tile. The *ptBlank* field also stores that coordinate. The *blank*—as I'll call it—governs the user interface; likewise, *ptBlank* plays a major role in the user interface code. Any tile that the program moves must be adjacent to the blank, and it must move into the blank.

When you use the mouse, you don't have to click a tile adjacent to the blank, however. If you click a tile in the same row or column as the blank, the program moves multiple tiles with one shot, which means it makes multiple calls to *MoveTile*. The *MoveTile* method both physically moves the tile (by setting the *Location* property of the tile being moved to the location of the blank) and adjusts the *atile* and *ptBlank* fields accordingly.

The keyboard interface involves the arrow keys. If you think about it, pressing any of the four arrow keys has an unambiguous meaning. For example, pressing the down key always moves the tile immediately above the blank (if any) into the location of the blank.

Here's a sample view of the program as I'm about halfway through solving it:

This is now the third program in this book in which creating a custom control has been found useful. As you undoubtedly know, Windows and the Windows Forms .NET Framework implement a multitude of ready-made controls in the form of buttons, labels, text-entry fields, list boxes, scroll bars, and much more. We'll begin exploring that world in Chapter 12.

# Images and Bitmaps

The world of computer graphics is generally divided into two distinct areas: *vector* graphics and *raster* graphics. In mathematics, a *vector* is a combination of a magnitude and a direction, and it can also refer to a line in a coordinate space. Vector graphics is the application of analytical geometry to draw lines, curves, and filled areas. With the use of outline fonts, text can also be considered part of vector graphics. Collections of vector drawing commands are sometimes stored in files or memory blocks called *metafiles*.

The term *raster* comes from video display technology and refers to the use of multiple scan lines to form a composite image. In raster graphics, images are described by rectangular arrays of pixels known as *bitmaps*.

Both vector and raster graphics have their origins in graphical display devices. Most display devices in use today are raster devices. In laser or ink jet printers, the image on the page is a rectangular array of pixels that are colored with dots. Cathode ray tubes (CRTs) display images as a collection of horizontal scan lines, each of which is made up of a series of pixels. The bits that define the CRT image are stored in a block of memory on the video display board.

Although raster output devices certainly seem normal today, in the early days of computer graphics (the 1950s), memory was too expensive for raster displays. Video displays attached to a computer worked much like an oscilloscope: the cathode ray didn't draw horizontal scan lines but was instead deflected directly to draw lines and curves under computer control. Vector printing devices were also more common in days gone by and still exist today in the form of plotters.

Vectors and rasters both have their place in the world of graphics. An architectural drawing is obviously a job for vector graphics, whereas a realistic-looking image of what the completed building will look like is a job for raster graphics. Vector and raster graphics are generally the provinces of different types of applications: *draw* programs do vector graphics, and *paint* programs do raster graphics. *Photo* programs are variations of paint programs that work with real-world raster images captured from digital cameras or scanned photographs.

As we've seen, vector images can be subjected to transforms that change their size and orientation. This transformation happens without any loss of resolution. A 10-point font scaled in size by a factor of 10 doesn't accumulate any jaggies at that new size because the vector outlines are being scaled. Raster images, however, usually have device dependencies that can't easily be ignored. Bitmaps have specific pixel sizes. Attempting to display a bitmap in a larger size can result in jaggies; in a smaller size, information can be lost. (GDI+ attempts to minimize these problems by using smoothing algorithms.) Bitmap images also contain specific color information that can't always be rendered on a specific output device.

Converting a vector image to a raster image is very easy. All that's necessary is to draw the various lines, curves, filled areas, and text on the surface of a bitmap. (We'll do this later in the chapter.) Converting a raster image to a vector image can be quite difficult, however, and is feasible only with simple images.

Many older or traditional books on computer graphics focus almost entirely on vector graphics. Today's dominance of raster graphics is a more recent phenomenon brought about by low-cost memory, scanners, and digital cameras. Also helping this trend are bitmap compression technologies, such as JPEG, that help cut down on the memory bulk normally associated with bitmaps.

Almost all the graphics found on the World Wide Web are stored as bitmaps; to many Web users, computer graphics is synonymous with JPEG and GIF files. This is not necessarily a good thing. Many Web graphics would be more efficiently stored and transmitted as vector images, particularly considering that such images often originate as lines, curves, and filled areas in paint programs. However, recent attempts at promoting vector graphics standards for the Web have not caught on much.[1]

---

1. You can learn about the proposed Scalable Vector Graphics (SVG) standard on the Web site of the World Wide Web consortium (*www.w3.org/Graphics/SVG*), and you can learn about the Vector Markup Language (VML), which is supported by recent versions of Internet Explorer, on the Microsoft Web site at *msdn.microsoft.com/workshop/author/vml*. Both are XML based. Finding Web sites that display images using SVG or VML is a much bigger challenge.

# Bitmap Support Overview

The *System.Drawing* namespace has two classes, named *Image* and *Bitmap*, that provide much of the raster graphics support in .NET. The *Bitmap* class as well as the *Metafile* class (to be covered in Chapter 23) are derived from *Image*, as shown in the following class hierarchy:

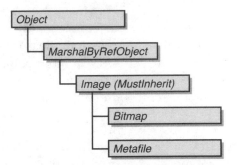

*Image* is a *MustInherit* class that can't be instantiated using a constructor. However, *Image* has two shared methods (four if you count overloads) that return objects of type *Image*. These methods are extremely powerful, for they can load a bitmap or a metafile from a file or a stream. You probably expect these methods to work with BMP files because that's the native Windows bitmap format. What you'll undoubtedly be pleased to learn is that these methods can also load files in several other popular bitmap formats, including GIF, JPEG, PNG, and TIFF. *Image* also has another shared method, which lets you create a *Bitmap* object from a Win32 bitmap handle.

Once you have an *Image* object, you can do a couple things with it. You can display it on the screen or a printer by using one of the *DrawImage* methods in the *Graphics* class. Or you can use the shared *FromImage* method of *Graphics* to return a *Graphics* object that applies to the image. This facility lets a program draw on a bitmap. Additional methods of the *Image* class allow you to save an image object in one of the supported formats. Thus, *Image* has a built-in format-conversion facility.

If you just need to load and display bitmap images, the *Image* class is probably all you need. The *Bitmap* class extends *Image* by providing a number of constructors that let you create a new bitmap of a particular size and color format. The *Bitmap* class also allows you to directly read and write individual pixels and to access the bitmap data as a block of memory.

The *Bitmap* class also includes a constructor that lets you load a bitmap that's been embedded in the .exe file as a *resource*. You can also use this technique for loading icons and custom cursors. I'll discuss binary resources later in this chapter.

Sometimes programmers will wonder whether they should use the *Image* or *Bitmap* class for a particular task. If everything you need to do can be done with *Image*, then use *Image*. The bonus is that your code (with some exceptions) will also work with metafiles.

# Bitmap File Formats

A bitmap is a rectangular array of bits that correspond to the pixels of a graphics output device. A bitmap has a particular height and width measured in pixels. A bitmap also has a particular *color depth*, which is the number of bits per pixel (commonly abbreviated *bpp*). Each pixel in the bitmap has the same number of bits, which determines how many unique colors are in the image:

Number of colors = 2 $^{\text{Number of bits per pixel}}$

The number of bits per pixel can generally range from 1 to 32 (and even beyond), although some formats are more common than others.

In graphical environments such as Windows, colors are usually represented as RGB (red-green-blue) values, where each primary is 1 byte and a full RGB color value is 3 bytes, or 24 bits. Such a color resolution seems to be fairly close to the ability of the human eye to differentiate between colors. It also approximates the ability of today's monitors to render distinct colors. An additional byte can represent levels of transparency, ranging from complete opacity to complete transparency. But 32 bits per pixel is not the ultimate limit. Some applications—such as medical imaging—require more bits per pixel for increased color resolution.

A bitmap with 1 bit per pixel stores a *bilevel*, or *monochrome*, image. Only two colors are possible; these are often black and white, but not always. Generally, such a bitmap contains a small color table (or color palette) that indicates the two colors associated with the two bit values.

In the early days of Windows, 4-bit-per-pixel images were popular, and these can still be found. For example, icons are often 16-color images. The 16 colors are generally combinations of the red, green, and blue primaries in regular and dark versions. Such a bitmap contains a color table indicating the exact colors corresponding to the 16 different possible combinations of pixels.

A very common bitmap format has 8 bits per pixel. Often, the image is *gray scale* and the 8 bits correspond to 256 (or fewer) gray shades from black to white. However, color images can also be stored in 8-bit-per-pixel bitmaps, in which case the 256 (or fewer) colors are usually specifically chosen for the particular image. This color choice is sometimes known as the *optimized palette* for the image.

A bitmap with 16 bits per pixel generally uses 5 bits each for the red, green, and blue levels, with 1 bit unused. Thus, each primary can have 32 different values, for a total of 32,768 unique colors. Sometimes green gets an extra bit because it's the color human eyes are most sensitive to. Such a bitmap is sometimes referred to as a *5-6-5*, referring to the number of bits used for each primary. The use of 15 or 16 bits per pixel is sometimes referred to as *high color* and is insufficient to represent color gradations in some real-world images.

A *full-color*, or *true-color*, bitmap has 24 bits per pixel. Each pixel is a 24-bit RGB color value. The use of exactly 3 bytes per pixel in a bitmap can result in a performance problem: generally, 32-bit processors are most efficient if they access 32-bit values on 32-bit memory boundaries.

A 32-bit-per-pixel bitmap can actually be a 24 bit-per-pixel image with 1 byte per pixel unused for performance purposes. Or the additional byte could provide transparency information, known as an *alpha* channel. For each pixel, the alpha value indicates a level of transparency for the pixel.

Bitmaps can be very large. For example, if you run your video adapter in 1600 × 1200 pixel mode, a 24-bit-per-pixel bitmap that occupies the entire screen is over 5 megabytes in size. For this reason, a great deal of research has gone into the development of image *compression* techniques.

One simple method that occurs to just about everyone who thinks about image compression is called *run-length encoding* (RLE). If there are 12 consecutive blue pixels, for example, it makes sense to store the number of repeated pixels rather than all 12 pixels. RLE generally works well for images that have a limited number of colors, such as cartoon like images.

To go beyond RLE, it's necessary for a compression program to analyze the data for recurring patterns. A major advance in data compression occurred in the late 1970s when Jacob Zif and Abraham Lempel published compression techniques now known as LZ77 and LZ78. These algorithms find patterns in the data on the fly and efficiently indicate when the patterns are reused. A 1984 article by Terry Welch of the Sperry Research Center (now part of Unisys) built on LZ78 to form a technique now called LZW. LZW is the basis of several popular compression formats.[2] In recent years, however, Unisys has restricted the unlicensed use of LZW. Given that LZW was already used in several entrenched standards (including GIF), much of the programming community has responded with disdain at the claims of Unisys, and LZW has been deliberately and conspicuously avoided in new compression formats.

---

2. *The Data Compression Book*, 2nd ed. (New York: M&T Books, 1985) by Mark Nelson and Jean-Loup Gailly is a good source for the history, technology, and programming of data compression techniques.

RLE and all the LZ techniques are known as *lossless* compression techniques because the original data can be entirely recovered from the compressed data. (It's fairly simple to prove that a particular lossless compression algorithm can't work for every possible file. For some files, application of the compression algorithm increases the file size!) Lossless compression is essential if you're dealing with spreadsheets or word processing documents. Lossless compression is much less of a concern for real-world images such as digitized photographs.

For that reason, *lossy* compression techniques have become popular in recent years when photographic images must be compressed. Lossy compression works best when it eliminates data that is imperceptible (or less perceptible) to human vision. Extreme levels of lossy compression can result in noticeable degradation of the image, however.

The bitmap file formats supported by the *Image* class are indicated by shared properties in *ImageFormat*, a class defined in the *System.Drawing.Imaging* namespace:

## *ImageFormat* Shared Properties

| Property | Type | Accessibility | Description |
|----------|------|---------------|-------------|
| *Bmp* | *ImageFormat* | Get | Windows device-independent bitmap (DIB) |
| *MemoryBmp* | *ImageFormat* | Get | Memory-based DIB (no file header) |
| *Icon* | *ImageFormat* | Get | Windows icon format |
| *Gif* | *ImageFormat* | Get | CompuServe Graphics Interchange Format |
| *Jpeg* | *ImageFormat* | Get | Joint Photographic Experts Group |
| *Png* | *ImageFormat* | Get | Portable Network Graphics |
| *Tiff* | *ImageFormat* | Get | Tag Image File Format |
| *Exif* | *ImageFormat* | Get | Exchangeable image format |
| *Wmf* | *ImageFormat* | Get | Windows metafile (original) |
| *Emf* | *ImageFormat* | Get | Windows enhanced metafile |

You may be familiar with many of these formats. For the sake of completeness, here's a brief description of each:

- **Bmp**   The native Windows bitmap file format, also known as the device-independent bitmap (DIB). The DIB was adapted from the OS/2 1.1 bitmap format and was introduced in Windows 3.0. (Prior to that time, the format of bitmaps in Windows was based on specific output devices. Although some applications also used the old format for file interchange, it wasn't intended for that purpose.)

  The DIB format is mostly defined in the documentation of certain structures used in the Win32 API, specifically *BITMAPFILE-HEADER*, *BITMAPINFO*, *BITMAPINFOHEADER*, and their variants. Chapter 15 of my book *Programming Windows*, 5th ed. (Microsoft Press, 1999) has an extensive discussion of the DIB format. DIB files are generally stored without any compression. A little-used RLE compression scheme is defined for some color formats.

- **MemoryBmp**   A memory-based DIB, which is a DIB that is not preceded by a *BITMAPFILEHEADER*.

- **Icon**   The Windows icon file format, an extension of the Windows DIB format.

- **Gif**   Pronounced with a soft *G* (like "jif"), the Graphics Interchange Format was developed in the late 1980s for use on CompuServe (an early online information service) and remains one of the two most popular graphics formats on the World Wide Web. The GIF file format uses LZW compression. The Gif87a.txt and Gif98a.txt documents that describe the file format can be found in many different locations on the Web. The GIF specification includes a rudimentary (but popular) animation facility.

- **Jpeg**   Pronounced "jay peg," JPEG stands for Joint Photographic Experts Group, which is a collection of industry representatives who developed a family of compression techniques—some lossy, some lossless—specifically for continuous-tone still images. The official JPEG Web site is *http://www.jpeg.org*. The actual JPEG specification is available as an ISO standard. The book *JPEG: Still Image Data Compression Standard* by William B. Pennebaker and Joan L. Mitchell (New York: Van Nostrand Reinhold, 1993) contains a very usable draft version and much useful background information as well.

As defined in the standard, however, JPEG is *not* a file format. What is commonly referred to as the JPEG file format is more correctly called the JPEG File Interchange Format (JFIF) and is described in the document *http://www.jpeg.org/public/jfif.pdf*. JFIF incorporates a lossy JPEG compression technique and has become (with GIF) one of the two most popular graphics formats on the Web. (Neither GIF nor JPEG is specifically referred to in the HTML specification, however, so they're really de facto Web standards.)

- **Png**   Pronounced "ping," Portable Network Graphics is a lossless format that was developed under the auspices of the World Wide Web Consortium (W3C) as a license-free alternative to GIF. Most modern Web browsers support PNG as well as GIF and JPEG. A good place to begin exploring PNG is *http://www.w3c.org/Graphics/ PNG*. If you want to compress nonphotographic images and you'd prefer to avoid GIF, PNG is the best alternative.

- **Tiff**   The Tag Image File Format was originally developed by Aldus (creators of the popular PageMaker application) and Microsoft, and the specification is now owned by Adobe. The 121-page TIFF 6.0 specification in PDF format is available at *http://partners.adobe.com/ asn/developer/pdfs/tn/TIFF6.pdf*.

- **Exif**   The Exchangeable image format was developed by the organization now known as Japan Electronic Industry Development Association (JEIDA) for use in digital cameras. The specification is published on the Web site of the International Imaging Industry Association (I3A), formerly the Photographic and Imaging Association, Inc. (PIMA) at *http://www.pima.net/standards/it10/PIMA15740/ Exif_2-1.PDF*.

- **Wmf**   This is not a bitmap file format! It is a format for a metafile, which is a collection of drawing functions (generally *vector* drawing functions) stored in binary form. WMF refers to the *old* Windows metafile format used prior to the 32-bit versions of Windows.

- **Emf**   The Windows enhanced metafile format, inaugurated in the 32-bit versions of Windows. Although you can treat metafiles like other images, they're really in a class of their own. I'll cover metafiles in more detail in Chapter 23.

# Loading and Drawing

The *Image* class is *MustInherit*, which means that you can't instantiate it using a constructor. However, as mentioned previously, the class includes four shared methods that let you obtain an *Image* object, and two that let you obtain a *Bitmap* object:

### *Image* Shared Methods (selection)

```
Function FromFile(ByVal strFilename As String) As Image

Function FromFile(ByVal strFilename As String,
                ByVal bUseICM As Boolean) As Image

Function FromStream(ByVal strm As Stream) As Image

Function FromStream(ByVal strm As Stream,
                ByVal bUseICM As Boolean) As Image

Function FromHbitmap(ByVal hBitmap As IntPtr) As Bitmap

Function FromHbitmap(Byval hBitmap As IntPtr,
                ByVal hPalette As IntPtr) As Bitmap
```

You probably won't use the last two methods in this table unless you're interfacing with Win32 code. The first two methods, however, are quite powerful and very simple, as you can see here:

```
Dim img As Image = Image.FromFile("CuteCat.jpg")
```

One nice feature of this method is that it uses the file's contents rather than the filename extension to determine the file's format. For example, even if Cute-Cat.jpg were actually a PNG file that you had perversely named, *FromFile* would still work. If the file can't be found or can't be opened, or if it's not a supported image file, or if something is wrong with the file's contents, *FromFile* throws an exception.

The second two methods use an object of type *Stream* rather than a filename, but files and streams are closely related. *Stream* is a *MustInherit* class in the *System.IO* namespace that implements methods such as *Read*, *Write*, and *Seek*. In many cases, a stream is simply an open file. However, a *Stream* object can also represent sequential data that is stored in a block of memory or that travels on a network connection. Appendix A focuses on files and streams.

The optional *Boolean* arguments for *FromFile* and *FromStream* deal with image color management (ICM), a subject that I'm afraid is beyond the scope of this book.

Although these first four shared methods are documented as returning an object of type *Image*, if you call *GetType* on the return value, you'll find the return value to be either of type *System.Drawing.Bitmap* or *System.Drawing.Imaging.Metafile*, depending on the type of file (or stream) you've loaded. That's why *Image* is a *MustInherit* class with no constructors: There is really no such thing as an object of type *Image*.

For many of the programs in this chapter, I'll be using a file named Apollo11FullColor.jpg that is stored with this book's source code in the Images And Bitmaps directory that contains the projects for this chapter. This image is the famous portrait of astronaut Buzz Aldrin taken by crewmate Neil Armstrong with a Hasselblad camera on the surface of the moon. As the filename implies, the bitmap is a full-color 24-bit-per-pixel image. Also included in the same directory for your experimentation are Apollo11GrayScale.jpg and Apollo11Palette.png, both of which store 8 bits per pixel. The images in all three files are 220 pixels wide and 240 pixels high. The resolution encoded in the JPEG files is 72 dpi.

Just to get started, here's a small program that uses *Image.FromFile* to obtain an *Image* object and the *Graphics* method *DrawImage* to display it.

**ImageFromFile.vb**

```
'-------------------------------------------------
' ImageFromFile.vb (c) 2002 by Charles Petzold
'-------------------------------------------------
Imports System
Imports System.Drawing
Imports System.Windows.Forms

Class ImageFromFile
    Inherits PrintableForm

    Shared Shadows Sub Main()
        Application.Run(new ImageFromFile())
    End Sub

    Sub New()
        Text = "Image From File"
    End Sub

    Protected Overrides Sub DoPage(ByVal grfx As Graphics, _
            ByVal clr As Color, ByVal cx As Integer, ByVal cy As Integer)
        Dim img As Image = _
                    Image.FromFile("..\..\Apollo11FullColor.jpg")
        grfx.DrawImage(img, 0, 0)
    End Sub
End Class
```

The argument to *FromFile* indicates the location of the JPEG file relative to the location of the ImageFromFile.exe file. If you've moved things around, the *FromFile* method won't find the file and will throw an exception. The arguments to *DrawImage* indicate the position of the upper left corner of the image relative to the client area. Using the point (0, 0) positions the image on the left and top edges:

You can also click on the client area to print the image. (Notice that I derived this class from the *PrintableForm* class we created in Chapter 5.) You'll probably be pleased to see that the printed image appears to be normal size and isn't shrunk to the size of a postage stamp, as so often happens when bitmap images are naively printed.

For comparison, you might want to load this same JPEG file into another application (for example, the Paint program that comes with Windows XP) and use the application's display options to display the photo at normal size. You'll probably find that the ImageFromFile program displays the image somewhat larger than other applications. Why this is so I'll explain soon.

Meanwhile, however, I want to call your attention to two flaws in Image-FromFile that I ignored just so you could see how easy it is to load and display a bitmap file. It's really not as easy as ImageFromFile implies! The first problem I already mentioned: if the image file isn't where *FromFile* expects it to be, the method will throw an exception. The program should be prepared to catch that exception. The second flaw involves the location of the *FromFile* call. In such a program, the call really needs to be executed only once, most conveniently in the program's constructor. The program can save the *Image* object in a field and access it from the *OnPaint* method. Here's a better version of the program.

```
BetterImageFromFile.vb
'-----------------------------------------------------
' BetterImageFromFile.vb (c) 2002 by Charles Petzold
'-----------------------------------------------------
Imports System
Imports System.Drawing
Imports System.Windows.Forms

Class BetterImageFromFile
    Inherits PrintableForm

    Private img As image

    Shared Shadows Sub Main()
        Application.Run(new BetterImageFromFile())
    End Sub

    Sub New()
        Text = "Better Image From File"
        Dim strFileName As String = "..\..\Apollo11FullColor.jpg"

        Try
            img = Image.FromFile(strFileName)
        Catch
            MessageBox.Show("Cannot find file " & strFileName & "!", _
                        Text, MessageBoxButtons.OK, _
                        MessageBoxIcon.Hand)
        End Try
    End Sub

    Protected Overrides Sub DoPage(ByVal grfx As Graphics, _
            ByVal clr As Color, ByVal cx As Integer, ByVal cy As Integer)
        If Not img Is Nothing Then grfx.DrawImage(img, 0, 0)
    End Sub
End Class
```

For purposes of clarity, however, I generally won't be checking for the existence of the file in the remaining programs in this chapter.

The shared *Image.FromStream* method, demonstrated in this next program, is useful if you have access to an open file or if you obtain a stream from a source other than a file system. For example, you can use the *FromStream* method to load an image from the Internet. Here's a program that accesses the

NASA Web site to load the original file that I cropped (and made a couple other changes to) to create the Apollo11 files included with this chapter.

## ImageFromWeb.vb

```
'--------------------------------------------
' ImageFromWeb.vb (c) 2002 by Charles Petzold
'--------------------------------------------
Imports System
Imports System.Drawing
Imports System.IO
Imports System.Net
Imports System.Windows.Forms

Class ImageFromWeb
    Inherits PrintableForm

    Private img As image

    Shared Shadows Sub Main()
        Application.Run(new ImageFromWeb())
    End Sub

    Sub New()
        Text = "Image From Web"

        Dim strUrl As String = _
            "http://images.jsc.nasa.gov/images/pao/AS11/10075267.jpg"

        Dim webreq As WebRequest = WebRequest.Create(strUrl)
        Dim webres As WebResponse = webreq.GetResponse()
        Dim strm As Stream = webres.GetResponseStream()

        img = Image.FromStream(strm)
        strm.Close()
    End Sub

    Protected Overrides Sub DoPage(ByVal grfx As Graphics, _
            ByVal clr As Color, ByVal cx As Integer, ByVal cy As Integer)
        grfx.DrawImage(img, 0, 0)
    End Sub
End Class
```

The statements using the *WebRequest* and *WebResponse* classes represent the standard approach to downloading Web files. In this program, the *GetResponseStream* method of *WebResponse* obtains a readable stream of the JPEG file. At that point, you can just pass that stream to the *Image.FromStream* method:

```
img = Image.FromStream(strm)
```

The ImageFromWeb program is missing a few features that should be standard in any program that downloads files from the Web. It probably should include a progress bar (easily implemented as an object of type *ProgressBar*), and the stream-reading code should probably be in a second thread of execution.

## Image Information

The *Image* class contains several properties that provide information about the object. First are three properties that indicate the size of the image in pixels:

### *Image* Properties (selection)

| Property | Type | Accessibility |
|----------|------|---------------|
| *Size* | *Size* | Get |
| *Width* | *Integer* | Get |
| *Height* | *Integer* | Get |

The *Width* and *Height* properties are consistent with the *Size* property. Use whichever is convenient.

Most modern bitmap formats include some indication of the resolution of the image in dots per inch or an equivalent. Such a resolution might not make much sense for some images, including the image I just displayed. You can display such an image larger or smaller and it's still the same. But for some bitmaps—perhaps ones in which the image is supposed to match the size of the object it portrays—some indication of the physical size of the image is helpful.

Where does the resolution come from? Usually from the program that originally creates the bitmap. For example, if you scan an image on a scanner at 300 dpi, the scanning software usually sets the resolution of the resultant image at 300 dpi. When you create an image in a paint application, it usually sets the resolution to the screen resolution under the assumption that you've made the image the appropriate size for your screen.

Additional properties of *Image* let you obtain the horizontal and vertical resolution of the *Image* object and the resultant metrical size:

## *Image* Properties (selection)

| Property | Type | Accessibility | Description |
|---|---|---|---|
| *HorizontalResolution* | *Single* | Get | In dots per inch |
| *VerticalResolution* | *Single* | Get | In dots per inch |
| *PhysicalDimension* | *SizeF* | Get | In hundredths of millimeters |

If the image doesn't have any resolution information, the *HorizontalResolution* and *VerticalResolution* properties return the resolution of the video display. You might want to ignore *PhysicalDimension* (because it doesn't work right for bitmaps) and calculate a metrical size of the image yourself. For example, the following statements calculate the size of the image in inches:

```
Dim cxInches As Single = img.Width / img.HorizontalResolution
Dim cyInches As Single = img.Height / img.VerticalResolution
```

The programs shown so far in this chapter used the following version of the *DrawImage* function to display the image:

```
grfx.DrawImage(img, x, y)
```

This method sizes the image based on its metrical dimension! That's why the programs shown earlier in this chapter display the image at a different size than most other Windows applications. We'll examine the image rendering methods in more detail later in this chapter.

Another property of the *Image* class indicates the image's pixel format. The pixel format indicates the color depth and how the pixels correspond to colors:

### *Image* Properties (selection)

| Property | Type | Accessibility |
|----------|------|---------------|
| *PixelFormat* | *PixelFormat* | Get |

This property will return one of the following members of the *PixelFormat* enumeration, defined in the *System.Drawing.Imaging* namespace:

### *PixelFormat* Enumeration (selection)

| Member | Value |
|--------|-------|
| *Undefined* or *DontCare* | &H00000000 |
| *Format1bppIndexed* | &H00030101 |
| *Format4bppIndexed* | &H00030402 |
| *Format8bppIndexed* | &H00030803 |
| *Format16bppGrayScale* | &H00101004 |
| *Format16bppRgb555* | &H00021005 |
| *Format16bppRgb565* | &H00021006 |
| *Format16bppArgb1555* | &H00061007 |
| *Format24bppRgb* | &H00021808 |
| *Format32bppRgb* | &H00022009 |
| *Format32bppArgb* | &H0026200A |
| *Format32bppPArgb* | &H000E200B |
| *Format48bppRgb* | &H0010300C |
| *Format64bppArgb* | &H0034400D |
| *Format64bppPArgb* | &H001C400E |

The number after the word *Format* indicates the number of bits per pixel: 1, 4, 8, 16, 32, 48, or 64. Those formats that have 1, 4, or 8 bits per pixel are indexed, which means that the pixel values are indices into a color palette. The formats containing the letters *Rgb* store red, green, and blue values for each pixel. The *Argb* formats also include an alpha channel for transparency. The *PArgb* formats contain red, green, and blue values that have been premultiplied by the alpha value. Just off hand, the numerical values of the enumeration members might appear to be random, but if you look more closely, you'll find some definite patterns. Take a look at the rightmost two hexadecimal digits. Each value is unique, ranging from &H00 (the ominous *Undefined* or *DontCare* value) to &H0E.

The next two rightmost digits indicate the number of bits per pixel: &H01, &H04, &H08, &H10, &H18, &H20, &H30, or &H40. The other bits are flags. The following *PixelFormat* enumeration values include *Max*, which indicates that the number of formats (including *Undefined*) is 15, plus the values that explain the meaning of the flags:

### *PixelFormat* Enumeration (selection)

| Member | Value | Description |
| --- | --- | --- |
| *Max* | &H0000000F | Number of formats |
| *Indexed* | &H00010000 | Pixel bits are palette indices |
| *Gdi* | &H00020000 | Windows GDI format |
| *Alpha* | &H00040000 | Contains transparency bit or byte |
| *PAlpha* | &H00080000 | Contains premultiplied transparency byte |
| *Extended* | &H00100000 | Uses more than 1 byte per primary or gray shade |
| *Canonical* | &H00200000 | Standard format |

The *Image* class also contains several shared methods that let you extract most of this information without digging into the bits:

### *Image* Shared Methods (selection)

```
Function GetPixelFormatSize(ByVal pf As PixelFormat) As Integer

Function IsAlphaPixelFormat(ByVal pf As PixelFormat) As Boolean

Function IsCanonicalPixelFormat(ByVal pf As PixelFormat) As Boolean

Function IsExtendedPixelFormat(ByVal pf As PixelFormat) As Boolean
```

The first of these methods returns the number of bits per pixel.

If the image is indexed, which you can determine by performing a bitwise *And* with the *PixelFormat* property and *PixelFormat.Indexed*, the image has a color palette. You can obtain that palette from the *Palette* property:

### *Image* Properties (selection)

| Property | Type | Accessibility |
|----------|------|---------------|
| *Palette* | *ColorPalette* | Get/Set |

This property is quite peculiar. You'll notice that it's both readable and writable. However, the *ColorPalette* class itself (which is defined in the *System.Drawing.Imaging* namespace) is *NonInheritable*, which means that you can't subclass it, and it has no public constructors, which means that you can't instantiate it. There is no way in all of .NET to obtain a *ColorPalette* object except through the *ColorPalette* property of an *Image* object.

*ColorPalette* itself has just two, read-only properties:

### *ColorPalette* Properties

| Property | Type | Accessibility |
|----------|------|---------------|
| *Entries* | *Color()* | Get |
| *Flags* | *Integer* | Get |

The *Entries* property returns the array of colors in the image's color palette.

Another property of the *Image* class indicates the file format:

### *Image* Properties (selection)

| Property | Type | Accessibility |
|----------|------|---------------|
| *RawFormat* | *ImageFormat* | Get |

I've already mentioned the *ImageFormat* class. That's the class that contains a shared property for each of the supported bitmap file formats as shown in the table earlier in this chapter (page 474).

The *RawFormat* property of the *Image* class is a bit difficult to use, however. You have to use it in conjunction with the only instance property (that is, the only nonshared property) of the *ImageFormat* class, which returns a globally unique identifier (GUID) for an *ImageFormat* object:

### *ImageFormat* **Instance Property**

| Property | Type | Accessibility |
|----------|------|---------------|
| *Guid* | *Guid* | Get |

Your program can test only whether a particular *Image* object is a particular *ImageFormat* type. For example, if you have an *Image* object named *img* that was loaded from a JPEG file, the expression

```
img.RawFormat.Guid.Equals(ImageFormat.Png.Guid)
```

returns *False* and

```
img.RawFormat.Guid.Equals(ImageFormat.Jpeg.Guid)
```

returns *True*. The expression

```
img.RawFormat.ToString()
```

returns the string

```
[ImageFormat: b96b3cae-0728-11d3-9d7b-0000f81ef32e]
```

while the expression

```
ImageFormat.Jpeg.ToString()
```

returns the string

```
Jpeg
```

You know which one to display to a user, right?

I'll cover some other *Image* properties and methods later in this chapter.

# Rendering the Image

As the sample programs shown so far in this chapter illustrate, the method of the *Graphics* class that displays images is called *DrawImage*, a method that comes in a whopping 30 versions for much flexibility. Another image-drawing method, named *DrawImageUnscaled*, is also available, but it provides no additional functionality over *DrawImage*.

As with the display of text, the display of images involves dealing with an object that already has a specific size. Just as a text string associated with a certain font has a size, a bitmap image also has a size, or rather *two* sizes: a pixel size and a metrical size. Displaying images in their metrical size (which the simplest versions of *DrawImage* do) is helpful when you're attempting to treat images in a device-independent manner. However, if you're otherwise drawing in units of pixels, you need to use a bit of math to anticipate the pixel size of such a rendered image. (I'll show you that math shortly.) At times—particularly when integrating images with controls—you'll want to display an image in its pixel size. *DrawImage* doesn't use the image's pixel size automatically, but it's easy to persuade the method to draw an image in its pixel size.

Traditionally, bitmaps have been resistant to transforms such as rotation. In Windows Forms and GDI+, the display of bitmaps is always affected by the world transform in much the same way as text.

The first argument to all the versions of *DrawImage* is an object of type *Image*. At the very least, the method also always includes a coordinate point. This point is in the form of two integers, two singles, a *Point*, a *PointF*, a *Rectangle*, or a *RectangleF* and indicates in world coordinates where the upper left corner of the image appears.

These four *DrawImage* methods size the image based on its metrical dimensions:

### *Graphics DrawImage* Methods (selection)

```
Sub DrawImage(ByVal img As Image,
              ByVal x As Integer, ByVal y As Integer)

Sub DrawImage(ByVal img As Image,
              ByVal x As Single, ByVal y As Single)

Sub DrawImage(ByVal img As Image, ByVal pt As Point)

Sub DrawImage(ByVal img As Image, ByVal ptf As PointF)
```

The size of the image is unaffected by any page transform but *is* affected by the world transform. Using these four methods of *DrawImage* is analogous to calling *DrawString* with a *Font* object created with a metrical size. The resultant image is the same metrical size on both the video display and the printer.

For example, the Apollo11 images are 220 pixels wide and 240 pixels high, and they have a resolution of 72 dpi. Thus, when displayed by the versions of *DrawImage* I've talked about so far, the width of the images is about 3 inches and the height is 3-1/3 inches.

The JPEG from the NASA Web site that the ImageFromWeb program accesses is 640 × 480 pixels in size but has no embedded resolution information. In such a case, the resolution of the image is assumed to be your screen resolution, which is probably 96 or 120 dpi.

At times, you need to anticipate how large an image will be when it's displayed. For example, you might need to center an image within a rectangle.

Because the four versions of *DrawImage* we've seen so far draw the image in its metrical size, centering that image within the client area requires a bit of work, as illustrated in the following program.

### CenterImage.vb

```
'-----------------------------------------------------
' CenterImage.vb (c) 2002 by Charles Petzold
'-----------------------------------------------------
Imports System
Imports System.Drawing
Imports System.Windows.Forms

Class CenterImage
    Inherits PrintableForm

    Private img As image

    Shared Shadows Sub Main()
        Application.Run(new CenterImage())
    End Sub

    Sub New()
        Text = "Center Image"
        img = Image.FromFile("..\..\Apollo11FullColor.jpg")
    End Sub

    Protected Overrides Sub DoPage(ByVal grfx As Graphics, _
            ByVal clr As Color, ByVal cx As Integer, ByVal cy As Integer)
        grfx.PageUnit = GraphicsUnit.Pixel
        grfx.PageScale = 1
        Dim rectf As RectangleF = grfx.VisibleClipBounds
        Dim cxImage As Single = grfx.DpiX * img.Width / _
                                img.HorizontalResolution
        Dim cyImage As Single = grfx.DpiY * img.Height / _
                                img.VerticalResolution
        grfx.DrawImage(img, (rectf.Width - cxImage) / 2, _
                        (rectf.Height - cyImage) / 2)
    End Sub
End Class
```

The *cxImage* and *cyImage* values are in units of pixels: dividing the pixel width and height of the image by the horizontal and vertical resolution provides the dimension of the image in inches, and then multiplying that by the *DpiX* and *DpiY* properties yields the dimension in device pixels of the displayed image.

If you were dealing only with the video display, you could then subtract *cxImage* and *cyImage* from the width and height of the client area and divide by 2. However, that method won't work on the printer. Instead, at the beginning of the *DoPage* method, I switch to pixel coordinates and use *VisibleClip-Bounds* to obtain the dimension of the output device in pixels. The *cxImage* and *cyImage* values are then subtracted from the pixel width and height of the device and divided by 2.

# Fitting to a Rectangle

The following four *DrawImage* methods specify a rectangular destination for the image. The rectangle is in world coordinates:

### *Graphics DrawImage* Methods (selection)

```
Sub DrawImage(ByVal img As Image,
            ByVal x As Integer, ByVal y As Integer,
            ByVal cx As Integer, ByVal cy As Integer)

Sub DrawImage(ByVal img As Image,
            ByVal x As Single, ByVal y As Single,
            ByVal cx As Single, ByVal cy As Single)

Sub DrawImage(ByVal img As Image, ByVal rect As Rectangle)

Sub DrawImage(ByVal img As Image, ByVal rectf As RectangleF)
```

These methods scale the image to the size of the rectangle, either stretching or compressing it to fit. One common use of these methods is to display an image in its pixel size rather than its metrical size. If page units are pixels, simply call

```
grfx.DrawImage(img, x, y, img.Width, img.Height)
```

The following program displays an image in its pixel dimensions centered within the client area (or printer page).

### CenterPixelSizeImage.vb

```
'-------------------------------------------------------
' CenterPixelSizeImage.vb (c) 2002 by Charles Petzold
'-------------------------------------------------------
Imports System
Imports System.Drawing
Imports System.Windows.Forms

Class CenterPixelSizeImage
    Inherits PrintableForm
```

```
    Private img As image

    Shared Shadows Sub Main()
        Application.Run(new CenterPixelSizeImage())
    End Sub

    Sub New()
        Text = "Center Pixel-Size Image"
        img = Image.FromFile("..\..\Apollo11FullColor.jpg")
    End Sub

    Protected Overrides Sub DoPage(ByVal grfx As Graphics, _
            ByVal clr As Color, ByVal cx As Integer, ByVal cy As Integer)
        grfx.DrawImage(img, (cx - img.Width) \ 2, _
                            (cy - img.Height) \ 2, _
                            img.Width, img.Height)
    End Sub
End Class
```

Because your video resolution is most likely greater than 72 dpi, this image is smaller than the one drawn by *DrawImage*:

On the printer, which has a default page transform that makes it appear to be a 100-dpi device, this version of the *DrawImage* method will render the 220 × 240 pixel bitmap as 2.2 × 2.4 inches. If you set page units to pixels in the *DoPage* method, the printed image will be much smaller, probably resulting in the postage stamp effect commonly encountered in less sophisticated graphics programming environments.

The following program loads an image and scales it to the entire size of the client area (or printable area of the printer page).

```
ImageScaleToRectangle.vb
'-------------------------------------------------------------
' ImageScaleToRectangle.vb (c) 2002 by Charles Petzold
'--------------------- ---------------------------------------
Imports System
Imports System.Drawing
Imports System.Windows.Forms

Class ImageScaleToRectangle
    Inherits PrintableForm

    Private img As image

    Shared Shadows Sub Main()
        Application.Run(new ImageScaleToRectangle())
    End Sub

    Sub New()
        Text = "Image Scale To Rectangle"
        img = Image.FromFile("..\..\Apollo11FullColor.jpg")
    End Sub

    Protected Overrides Sub DoPage(ByVal grfx As Graphics, _
            ByVal clr As Color, ByVal cx As Integer, ByVal cy As Integer)
        grfx.DrawImage(img, 0, 0, cx, cy)
    End Sub
End Class
```

As you make the client area much wider than it is tall, or much taller than it is wide, the image is distorted accordingly:

If you really do need to scale an image to the size of a rectangle, this effect is probably not what you had in mind. You probably want to scale the image *iso-tropically*, which means equally in both directions. Here's a program that scales a rectangle more intelligently.

## ImageScaleIsotropic.vb

```
'-------------------------------------------------------------
' ImageScaleIsotropic.vb (c) 2002 by Charles Petzold
'-------------------------------------------------------------
Imports System
Imports System.Drawing
Imports System.Windows.Forms

Class ImageScaleIsotropic
    Inherits PrintableForm

    Private img As image

    Shared Shadows Sub Main()
        Application.Run(new ImageScaleIsotropic())
    End Sub

    Sub New()
        Text = "Image Scale Isotropic"
        img = Image.FromFile("..\..\Apollo11FullColor.jpg")
    End Sub

    Protected Overrides Sub DoPage(ByVal grfx As Graphics, _
            ByVal clr As Color, ByVal cx As Integer, ByVal cy As Integer)
        ScaleImageIsotropically(grfx, img, New Rectangle(0, 0, cx, cy))
    End Sub

    Private Sub ScaleImageIsotropically(ByVal grfx As Graphics, _
            ByVal img As Image, ByVal rect As Rectangle)
        Dim szf As New SizeF(img.Width / img.HorizontalResolution, _
                            img.Height / img.VerticalResolution)
        Dim fScale As Single = Math.Min(rect.Width / szf.Width, _
                            rect.Height / szf.Height)

        szf.Width *= fScale
        szf.Height *= fScale
        grfx.DrawImage(img, rect.X + (rect.Width - szf.Width) / 2, _
                            rect.Y + (rect.Height - szf.Height) / 2, _
                            szf.Width, szf.Height)
    End Sub
End Class
```

The *ScaleImageIsotropically* method will work in all cases except when the horizontal and vertical resolutions of the device are different (as is the case with some printers) and when the *PageUnit* is *GraphicsUnit.Pixel* (which is *not* the default case for printers).

The method begins by calculating a *SizeF* structure that indicates the size of the *Image* object in inches. (This step wouldn't be necessary if the horizontal and vertical resolution of the image were the same.) Then a factor is calculated that is the minimum of the destination rectangle width and height divided by the image width and height. This *fScale* number is the factor that must be applied to the image size to isotropically scale it to the size of the destination rectangle. The method then calculates the origin of this rectangle and passes all the information to *DrawImage*. Here's the image:

The rectangle-destination versions of the *DrawImage* method can do additional tricks beyond just stretching an image. If you specify a negative width, the image is flipped around the vertical axis—it's a mirror image. A negative height flips the image around the horizontal axis and shows it upside down. In all cases, the upper left corner of the original unflipped image is always positioned at the *Point* or *PointF* portion of the rectangle you specify in the drawing method.

Let's look at a program that draws four images, some with negative widths and heights. In all four cases, the second and third arguments to *DrawImage* indicate the center of the client area.

**ImageReflection.vb**

```
'-------------------------------------------------
' ImageReflection.vb (c) 2002 by Charles Petzold
'-------------------------------------------------
Imports System
Imports System.Drawing
Imports System.Windows.Forms

Class ImageReflection
    Inherits PrintableForm

    Private img As Image

    Shared Shadows Sub Main()
        Application.Run(New ImageReflection())
    End Sub
```

```
    Sub New()
        Text = "Image Reflection"
        img = Image.FromFile("..\..\Apollo11FullColor.jpg")
    End Sub

    Protected Overrides Sub DoPage(ByVal grfx As Graphics, _
            ByVal clr As Color, ByVal cx As Integer, ByVal cy As Integer)
        grfx.DrawImage(img, cx \ 2, cy \ 2, img.Width, img.Height)
        grfx.DrawImage(img, cx \ 2, cy \ 2, -img.Width, img.Height)
        grfx.DrawImage(img, cx \ 2, cy \ 2, img.Width, -img.Height)
        grfx.DrawImage(img, cx \ 2, cy \ 2, -img.Width, -img.Height)
    End Sub
End Class
```

And here's the result showing the four images:

Notice that the program sizes the image based on its pixel dimension.

# Rotate and Shear

You can distort the image even more using the following two methods. These methods effectively translate, scale, shear, or rotate an image into a parallelogram.

### *Graphics DrawImage* Methods (selection)

```
Sub DrawImage(ByVal img As Image, ByVal apt As Point())
Sub DrawImage(ByVal img As Image, ByVal aptf As PointF())
```

The array argument must contain exactly three points. These points indicate the destination in world coordinates of three corners of the image:

*apt(0)* = destination of upper left corner of image
*apt(1)* = destination of upper right corner of image
*apt(2)* = destination of lower left corner of image

Because the resulting image is a parallelogram, the destination of the lower right corner of the image is implied.

Here's a program that sets these three points to the center of the top side of the client area, the center of the right side of the client area, and the center of the left side of the client area.

```
ImageAtPoints.vb
'------------------------------------------------
' ImageAtPoints.vb (c) 2002 by Charles Petzold
'------------------------------------------------
Imports System
Imports System.Drawing
Imports System.Windows.Forms

Class ImageAtPoints
    Inherits PrintableForm

    Private img As image

    Shared Shadows Sub Main()
        Application.Run(new ImageAtPoints())
    End Sub

    Sub New()
        Text = "Image At Points"
        img = image.FromFile("..\..\Apollo11FullColor.jpg")
    End Sub

    Protected Overrides Sub DoPage(ByVal grfx As Graphics, _
            ByVal clr As Color, ByVal cx As Integer, ByVal cy As Integer)
        grfx.DrawImage(img, New Point() {New Point(cx \ 2, 0), _
                                    New Point(cx, cy \ 2), _
                                    New Point(0, cy \ 2)})

    End Sub
End Class
```

And here's the image:

This isn't the only way to rotate or shear bitmap images. You can also use the normal world transform.

# Displaying Part of the Image

If you've kept count, you'll know that so far I've covered only 10 of the 30 versions of the *DrawImage* method. All the remaining methods let you specify a rectangular subsection of the bitmap to display. You specify this subsection in pixels relative to the upper left corner of the image. For an *Image* object named *image*, the rectangle

```
New Rectangle(0, 0, img.Width, img.Height)
```

indicates the entire image; the rectangle

```
New Rectangle(img.Width - 10, img.Height - 10, 10, 10)
```

indicates the 10-pixel-square rectangle at the lower right corner of the image.

Here are two versions of *DrawImage* that specify the destination as a point in world coordinates, a rectangular source specifying a subset of the image, and a *GraphicsUnit* argument:

### *Graphics DrawImage* **Methods (selection)**

```
Sub DrawImage(ByVal img As Image,
            ByVal xDst As Ingeger, ByVal yDst As Integer,
            ByVal rectSrc As Rectangle, ByVal gu As GraphicsUnit)

Sub DrawImage(ByVal img As Image,
            ByVal xDst As Single, ByVal yDst As Single,
            ByVal rectfSrc As RectangleF, ByVal gu As GraphicsUnit)
```

The concept here is simpler than the bizarre definitions of these methods would seem to imply. First, you always specify the source rectangle in units of pixels. (Thus, the version of *DrawImage* defined with a *RectangleF* structure rather than a *Rectangle* structure makes no sense.) Second, the *GraphicsUnit* argument must be *GraphicsUnit.Pixel*.

I happen to know that the coordinates of Buzz Aldrin's helmet in the image I've been using can be expressed approximately by the rectangle

```
New Rectangle(95, 0, 50, 55)
```

Let's take a look at a program that displays just this portion of the image.

**PartialImage.vb**

```
'---------------------------------------------------
' PartialImage.vb (c) 2002 by Charles Petzold
'---------------------------------------------------
Imports System
Imports System.Drawing
Imports System.Windows.Forms

Class PartialImage
    Inherits PrintableForm

    Private img As Image

    Shared Shadows Sub Main()
        Application.Run(new PartialImage())
    End Sub

    Sub New()
        Text = "Partial Image"
        img = Image.FromFile("..\..\Apollo11FullColor.jpg")
    End Sub

    Protected Overrides Sub DoPage(ByVal grfx As Graphics, _
            ByVal clr As Color, ByVal cx As Integer, ByVal cy As Integer)
        Dim rect As New Rectangle(95, 5, 50, 55)
        grfx.DrawImage(img, 0, 0, rect, GraphicsUnit.Pixel)
    End Sub
End Class
```

How large is the rendered image? Because the resolution of the file is 72 dpi, the image is drawn 50/72 inch wide and 55/72 inch high:

There are also four methods that let you specify both a source rectangle and a destination rectangle:

### Graphics DrawImage Methods (selection)

```
Sub DrawImage(ByVal image As Image, ByVal rectDst As Rectangle,
          ByVal xSrc As Integer, ByVal ySrc As Integer,
          ByVal cxSrc As Integer, ByVal cySrc As Integer,
          ByVal gu As GraphicsUnit, *)

Sub DrawImage(ByVal image As Image, ByVal rectDst As Rectangle,
          ByVal rectSrc As Rectangle, ByVal gu As GraphicsUnit)

Sub DrawImage(ByVal image As Image, ByVal rectDst As Rectangle,
          ByVal x As Single, ByVal y As Single,
          ByVal cx As Single, ByVal cy As Single,
          ByVal gu As GraphicsUnit, *)

Sub DrawImage(ByVal image As Image, ByVal rectfDst As RectangleF,
          ByVal rectfSrc As RectangleF, ByVal gu As GraphicsUnit)
```

In these methods, the source rectangle is in pixels and the destination rectangle is in world coordinates. The *GraphicsUnit* argument must be *GraphicsUnit.Pixel*.

Notice in this table that I've put an asterisk at the end of the argument list for two of the methods. The asterisk means that these methods can also have three optional arguments: an *ImageAttribute* object, a callback function to abort drawing an image, and data to pass to the callback function; thus, each of the two methods with the asterisks has three additional versions. (Unfortunately, I won't be able to discuss these additional versions of *DrawImage* in this book.)

Here's a program that displays Aldrin's helmet (the source rectangle) the size of the client area or the printer page (the destination rectangle).

**PartialImageStretch.vb**

```
'-------------------------------------------------------
' PartialImageStretch.vb (c) 2002 by Charles Petzold
'-------------------------------------------------------
Imports System
Imports System.Drawing
Imports System.Windows.Forms

Class PartialImageStretch
    Inherits PrintableForm

    Private img As image

    Shared Shadows Sub Main()
        Application.Run(new PartialImageStretch())
    End Sub

    Sub New()
        Text = "Partial Image Stretch"
        img = Image.FromFile("..\..\Apollo11FullColor.jpg")
    End Sub

    Protected Overrides Sub DoPage(ByVal grfx As Graphics, _
            ByVal clr As Color, ByVal cx As Integer, ByVal cy As Integer)
        Dim rectSrc As New Rectangle(95, 5, 50, 55)
        Dim rectDst As New Rectangle(0, 0, cx, cy)

        grfx.DrawImage(img, rectDst, rectSrc, GraphicsUnit.Pixel)
    End Sub
End Class
```

Here's the image stretched to the client area:

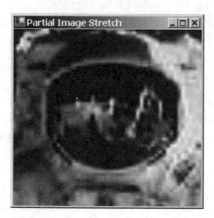

If the destination rectangle isn't the same aspect ratio as the source rectangle, the image will be distorted. But you can easily adapt the *ScaleImageIsotropically* method I showed earlier (on page 493) to partial images. To display the image in its pixel size, use the same width and height in the destination rectangle as specified in the source rectangle.

When you blow up smaller images like this and print them, you might expect to see jaggies. However, GDI+ performs an interpolation of the image pixels to smooth out the image.

To complete the collection of *DrawImage* methods, you can also display the partial image using an array of three points. The asterisk indicates that each of these methods is actually four methods.

### *Graphics DrawImage* Methods (selection)

```
Sub DrawImage(ByVal img As Image, ByVal aptDst As Point(),
          ByVal rectSrc As Rectangle,
          ByVal gu As GraphicsUnit, *)

Sub DrawImage(ByVal img As Image, ByVal aptfDst As PointF(),
          ByVal rectfSrc As RectangleF,
          ByVal gu As GraphicsUnit, *)
```

Again, the source rectangle is in pixels, the destination points are in world coordinates, and the *GraphicsUnit* argument must be *GraphicsUnit.Pixel*. Here's a sample program.

### PartialImageRotate.vb

```
'----------------------------------------------------
' PartialImageRotate.vb (c) 2002 by Charles Petzold
'----------------------------------------------------
Imports System
Imports System.Drawing
Imports System.Windows.Forms

Class PartialImageRotate
    Inherits PrintableForm

    Private img As image

    Shared Shadows Sub Main()
        Application.Run(new PartialImageRotate())
    End Sub

    Sub New()
        Text = "Partial Image Rotate"
        img = Image.FromFile("..\..\Apollo11FullColor.jpg")
    End Sub
```

*(continued)*

**PartialImageRotate.vb** *(continued)*

```
    Protected Overrides Sub DoPage(ByVal grfx As Graphics, _
            ByVal clr As Color, ByVal cx As Integer, ByVal cy As Integer)
        Dim aptDst() As Point = {New Point(0, cy \ 2), _
                                 New Point(cx \ 2, 0), _
                                 New Point(cx \ 2, cy)}
        Dim rectSrc As New Rectangle(95, 5, 50, 55)

        grfx.DrawImage(img, aptDst, rectSrc, GraphicsUnit.Pixel)
    End Sub
End Class
```

And now, if you've been keeping count, we're finished with the 30 *DrawImage* methods.

# Drawing on the Image

We've been drawing a bitmapped image on the video display and the printer. It's also possible to draw *on* an image. If you think about it, when Windows draws on the video display, it's really drawing on a big bitmap stored in memory on the video display adapter. Many printers, also, base their output on the contents of memory organized like a bitmap. So it makes sense that a Windows program should be able to draw on *any* bitmap by using the same graphics output functions you use on the video display and the printer.

To draw on an image, you need to obtain a *Graphics* object that refers to the image. You get that *Graphics* object from a shared method of the *Graphics* class:

### *Graphics* Shared Methods (selection)

```
Function FromImage(ByVal img As Image) As Graphics
```

For example, here's a statement that obtains a *Graphics* object named *grfxImage* based on an *Image* object named *img*:

```
Dim grfxImage As Graphics = Graphics.FromImage(img)
```

When you're finished with this *Graphics* object, call the *Dispose* method to get rid of it.

The *Graphics.FromImage* method won't work with every image format. The method will *not* work and will throw an exception if the *PixelFormat* property of the image is one of the following *PixelFormat* members:

*Format1bppIndexed*, *Format4bppIndexed*, *Format8bppIndexed*, *Format16bpp-GrayScale*, or *Format16Argb1555*. This restriction may make sense to you. Suppose you obtain a *Graphics* object based on an indexed image and then try to draw on the image with a color that's not in the image's palette table. The problem is similar if you could obtain a *Graphics* object for a gray-scaled image format or the 1-bit transparency format.

Neither can you obtain a *Graphics* object for an image loaded from an old Windows metafile (WMF) or a Windows enhanced metafile (EMF). In Chapter 23, I'll discuss some other ways to draw on metafiles.

You can use the *Graphics* object you obtain from *Graphics.FromImage* in the same way you use a *Graphics* object for the video display or the printer. If you check the *DpiX* and *DpiY* properties for the image-based *Graphics* object, you'll find that they are equal to the *HorizontalResolution* and *VerticalResolution* properties of the *Image* object. The default page transform is a *PageUnit* of *GraphicsUnit.Display* and a *PageScale* of 1, which for images is the same as *GraphicsUnit.Pixels*. By default, the *VisibleClipBounds* property of this *Graphics* object is equal to the width and height of the image in pixels.

You can set a different page transform for the *Graphics* object. If you change the *PageUnit* and *PageScale* properties, the *VisibleClipBounds* property indicates the dimensions of the image in page units. For example, if you set

```
grfxImage.PageUnit = GraphicsUnit.Inch
grfxImage.PageScale = 1
```

*VisibleClipBounds* indicates the size of the image in inches, which you could also calculate by dividing the pixel size of the image by the *HorizontalResolution* and *VerticalResolution* properties.

In a few moments, I'll be drawing text on the surface of a bitmap. So the questions naturally arise, What font should I use? Is the default *Font* property of the form satisfactory?

The default *Font* property for a form is an 8-point font. If you draw text on a bitmap using this font and then display the image in its metrical size (rather than pixel size), the text will be the same size as if you drew the text directly on the client area. However, if the resolution of the image is less than the resolution of the video display, the text certainly won't look exactly the same. The text on the image will be coarser than the text displayed directly on the window.

Consider this example. The sample bitmaps I've been using in this chapter are 72 dpi—1 pixel per point. That means that an 8-point font at this resolution is about 8 pixels in height. Using the form's default *Font* property, if you call

```
Font.GetHeight(72)
```

or, using the *Graphics* object created from one of the bitmaps I've been using in this chapter, if you call

```
Font.GetHeight(grfxImage)
```

you'll get 8.83 pixels for line spacing, confirming a character height of about 8 pixels.

Now, 8 pixels isn't a whole lot of space to draw well-rounded font characters. But that will be the font height *DrawString* will be limited to if you use the form's default *Font* property on a 72-dpi image. If the resolution of your video display is higher than 72 dpi and you display that image in its pixel size, the text on the image will appear very small. If you display the image in its metrical size, the image and the text will be larger. On a 96-dpi display, the image (and hence the text in the image) will be increased by a factor of 1-1/3. On a 120-dpi display, the image will be increased by a factor of 1-2/3. So, those 8 pixels are stretched to the normal size of the default *Font*.

Let's take a look. Here's the program.

```
DrawOnImage.vb
'------------------------------------------------
' DrawOnImage.vb (c) 2002 by Charles Petzold
'------------------------------------------------
Imports System
Imports System.Drawing
Imports System.Windows.Forms

Class DrawOnImage
    Inherits PrintableForm

    Private img As image
    Private str As String = "Apollo11"

    Shared Shadows Sub Main()
        Application.Run(new DrawOnImage())
    End Sub

    Sub New()
        Text  = "Draw on Image"
        img = Image.FromFile("..\..\Apollo11FullColor.jpg")

        Dim grfxImage As Graphics = Graphics.FromImage(img)
        grfxImage.PageUnit = GraphicsUnit.Inch
        grfxImage.PageScale = 1

        Dim szf As SizeF = grfxImage.MeasureString(str, Font)
        grfxImage.DrawString(str, Font, Brushes.White, _
                    grfxImage.VisibleClipBounds.Width - szf.Width, 0)
        grfxImage.Dispose()
    End Sub
```

```
      Protected Overrides Sub DoPage(ByVal grfx As Graphics, _
            ByVal clr As Color, ByVal cx As Integer, ByVal cy As Integer)
         grfx.PageUnit = GraphicsUnit.Pixel
         grfx.DrawImage(img, 0, 0)
         grfx.DrawString(str, Font, New SolidBrush(clr), _
                          grfx.DpiX * img.Width _
                          / img.HorizontalResolution, 0)
      End Sub
   End Class
```

Just for fun, I changed the page transform of the *Graphics* object associated with the image to draw in units of inches. I call *MeasureString* to obtain the dimensions of the string, and I set the coordinates of *DrawString* so that the string appears in the upper right corner of the image. The *DoPage* method calls *DrawImage* to draw the image and then—for comparison—the method also calls *DrawString* to display the same text string on the right side of the image. (Setting page units to pixels is necessary so that the text is positioned correctly on the printer.) You'll notice that the text on the image is considerably coarser and somewhat distorted because the image has been stretched on the display:

Is there anything you can do about this distortion problem? The problem arises from using a font that has only a 9-pixel height. You can solve the problem only if you use a font with a larger pixel size. That means using images with resolutions greater than the screen resolution or inflating the font size so that it's at least 12 pixels or so. The latter approach will make the text look larger, but at least it will be readable.

If you'll be displaying the image in its pixel size, you need to take a different approach. To make text on the image the same size as normal text displayed on the client area, you need to scale the font based on the ratio of the screen resolution to the image resolution. Here's an example.

**DrawOnPixelSizeImage.vb**

```
'-----------------------------------------------------
' DrawOnPixelSizeImage.vb (c) 2002 by Charles Petzold
'-----------------------------------------------------
Imports System
Imports System.Drawing
Imports System.Windows.Forms

Class DrawOnPixelSizeImage
    Inherits PrintableForm

    Private img As Image
    Private str As String = "Apollo11"

    Shared Shadows Sub Main()
        Application.Run(New DrawOnPixelSizeImage())
    End Sub

    Sub New()
        Text = "Draw on Pixel-Size Image"
        img = Image.FromFile("..\..\Apollo11FullColor.jpg")

        Dim grfxImage As Graphics = Graphics.FromImage(img)
        Dim grfxScreen As Graphics = CreateGraphics()
        Dim fnt As New Font(Font.FontFamily, _
                            grfxScreen.DpiY / grfxImage.DpiY _
                            * Font.SizeInPoints)
        Dim szf As SizeF = grfxImage.MeasureString(str, fnt)

        grfxImage.DrawString(str, fnt, Brushes.White, _
                             img.Width - szf.Width, 0)
        grfxImage.Dispose()
        grfxScreen.Dispose()
    End Sub

    Protected Overrides Sub DoPage(ByVal grfx As Graphics, _
            ByVal clr As Color, ByVal cx As Integer, ByVal cy As Integer)
        grfx.DrawImage(img, 0, 0, img.Width, img.Height)
        grfx.DrawString(str, Font, New SolidBrush(clr), img.Width, 0)
    End Sub
End Class
```

The constructor creates a new *Font* object (named *fnt*) that is the same as the default font but with a size in points scaled by the ratio of the screen resolution to the image resolution. This is the font I use in the calls to *MeasureString* and *DrawString*. Because I haven't set a nondefault page transform, I can use the pixel width of the image in the *DrawString* call to position the string. The font displayed on the image is visually the same size as the font displayed on the client area:

The two fonts now look identical, even though they are different point sizes. They appear to be the same size because they're displayed on two different surfaces (the image and the client area) with different display resolutions. Because I sized the font used on the image based on the screen resolution, the two fonts will differ on the printer by the extent to which the 100-dpi virtual resolution of the printer differs from the screen resolution.

I didn't mention my use of *Brushes.White* in the *DrawString* call to draw on the image. It's exactly what's appropriate, of course, given the black background, but suggests also that you really need to know what's on an existing image before you start drawing on it!

You can also draw on blank bitmaps that you create specifically for that purpose. I'll show you how to do that shortly.

## More on the *Image* Class

The *Image* class has several additional methods that let you save or manipulate the image in limited ways. Here are the three versions of the *Save* method:

### *Image Save* Methods (selection)

```
Sub Save(ByVal strFilename As String)

Sub Save(ByVal strFilename As String, ByVal if As ImageFormat)

Sub Save(ByVal strm As Stream, ByVal if As ImageFormat)
```

You can't use *Save* on any *Image* object loaded from a metafile or a memory bitmap. Nor can you save an image in a metafile or a memory bitmap format.

A warning: The first of these three methods does *not* use the specified filename extension to determine the format in which to save the file. That *Save* method will use the same format as the original file regardless of the filename extension. Use the second version of *Save* to specify a particular file format:

```
img.Save(strFilename, ImageFormat.Jpeg)
```

The ImageIO program in Chapter 16 shows how to use this version of *Save* in conjunction with a common File Save dialog box.

The following two methods can resize an image and rotate and flip it in certain fixed ways, respectively:

### *Image* Methods (selection)

```
Function GetThumbnailImage(ByVal cx As Integer, ByVal cy As Integer,
                           ByVal gtia As Image.GetThumbnailImageAbort,
                           ByVal pData As IntPtr) As Image

Sub RotateFlip(ByVal rft As RotateFlipType)
```

The *GetThumbnailImage* method is intended to be used to create a thumbnail of an image, which is a smaller version of the image that an application can use to convey the contents of the image while saving time and space. However, *GetThumbnailImage* is actually a general-purpose image-resizing function. You can make the image larger as well as smaller. The last two arguments are used to specify a callback function, but you can set them to *Nothing* and *IntPtr.Zero*, respectively, and the method will work just fine without them. Here's a program that creates a thumbnail designed to fit in a 64-pixel-square space.

**Thumbnail.vb**
```
'-----------------------------------------------
' Thumbnail.vb (c) 2002 by Charles Petzold
'-----------------------------------------------
Imports System
Imports System.Drawing
Imports System.Windows.Forms

Class Thumbnail
    Inherits PrintableForm

    Const iSquare As Integer = 64
    Private imgThumbnail As Image

    Shared Shadows Sub Main()
        Application.Run(new Thumbnail())
    End Sub

    Sub New()
        Text = "Thumbnail"
        Dim img As Image = _
```

```
                    Image.FromFile("..\..\Apollo11FullColor.jpg")
        Dim cxThumbnail, cyThumbnail As Integer

        If img.Width > img.Height Then
            cxThumbnail = iSquare
            cyThumbnail = iSquare * img.Height \ img.Width
        Else
            cyThumbnail = iSquare
            cxThumbnail = iSquare * img.Width \ img.Height
        End If
        imgThumbnail = img.GetThumbnailImage(cxThumbnail, _
                                             cyThumbnail, _
                                             Nothing, IntPtr.Zero)
    End Sub

    Protected Overrides Sub DoPage(ByVal grfx As Graphics, _
            ByVal clr As Color, ByVal cx As Integer, ByVal cy As Integer)
        Dim x, y As Integer

        For y = 0 To cy Step iSquare
            For x = 0 To cx Step iSquare
                grfx.DrawImage(imgThumbnail, _
                        x + (iSquare - imgThumbnail.Width) \ 2, _
                        y + (iSquare - imgThumbnail.Height) \ 2, _
                        imgThumbnail.Width, imgThumbnail.Height)
            Next x
        Next y
    End Sub
End Class
```

The program handles the *DoPage* method by filling up its client area (or the printer page) with the thumbnail image:

While the *GetThumbnailImage* method creates a new image, the *Rotate-Flip* method alters the existing image. The single argument is a member of the *RotateFlipType* enumeration:

## *RotateFlipType* Enumeration

| Member | Value | Result |
|---|---|---|
| *RotateNoneFlipNone*<br>*Rotate180FlipXY* | 0 | Hello |
| *Rotate90FlipNone*<br>*Rotate270FlipXY* | 1 | |
| *Rotate180FlipNone*<br>*RotateNoneFlipXY* | 2 | |
| *Rotate270FlipNone*<br>*Rotate90FlipXY* | 3 | |
| *RotateNoneFlipX*<br>*Rotate180FlipY* | 4 | |
| *Rotate90FlipX*<br>*Rotate270FlipY* | 5 | |
| *Rotate180FlipX*<br>*RotateNoneFlipY* | 6 | |
| *Rotate270FlipX*<br>*Rotate90FlipY* | 7 | |

Although the enumeration has 16 members, there are only 8 unique effects on the image. For 4 of these effects, the *Image* object gets its *Width* and *Height* properties switched around.

If you need to rotate or flip an image but you still want to retain the original unflipped unrotated image, you can first make a copy of the original *Image* object by using the *Clone* method:

```
Dim imgCopy As Image  = DirectCast(img.Clone(), Image)
```

# The *Bitmap* Class

So far, everything I've been discussing involves the *Image class*. As I mentioned at the beginning of this chapter, the *System.Drawing* namespace also includes a class named *Bitmap* that inherits from *Image*. All the *Image* properties apply to *Bitmap* as well. Anything you can do with an *Image* object you can also do with a *Bitmap* object. Plus more, of course. The *Bitmap* class allows you to get down and dirty with the bitmap bits.

The *Image* class has no constructors; the *Bitmap* class has 12 constructors. These first constructors load a *Bitmap* object from a file, a stream, or a resource:

### *Bitmap* Constructors (selection)

```
Bitmap(ByVal strFilename As String)

Bitmap(ByVal strFilename As String, ByVal bUseICM As Boolean)

Bitmap(ByVal strm As Stream)

Bitmap(ByVal strm As Stream, ByVal bUseICM As Boolean)

Bitmap(ByVal typ As Type, ByVal strResource As String)
```

The first four constructors basically duplicate the shared *FromFile* and *From-Stream* methods implemented in *Image*. The last loads a *Bitmap* object as a resource, which is usually embedded in the .exe file of the application. I'll explain resources later in this chapter.

Next is a collection of constructors that create new *Bitmap* objects based on an existing *Image* object:

### *Bitmap* Constructors (selection)

```
Bitmap(ByVal img As Image)

Bitmap(ByVal img As Image, ByVal sz As Size)

Bitmap(ByVal img As Image, ByVal cx As Integer, ByVal cy As Integer)
```

Although the first argument of these constructors is defined as an *Image*, it can also be another *Bitmap* object. The first constructor is similar to the *Clone* method of the *Image* class; it creates a new *Bitmap* object that is identical to the first. The second and third constructors are similar to the *GetThumbnailImage* method; the image is resized. In all cases, the new bitmap inherits the pixel format of the existing bitmap. In all cases, the resolution of the bitmap is set to the resolution of the video display.

The final four constructors have no equivalents in the *Image* class. These constructors let you create brand new *Bitmap* objects with blank images:

### *Bitmap* Constructors (selection)

```
Bitmap(ByVal cx As Integer, ByVal cy As Integer)

Bitmap(ByVal cx As Integer, ByVal cy As Integer,
     ByVal pf As PixelFormat)

Bitmap(ByVal cx As Integer, ByVal cy As Integer,
     ByVal grfx As Graphics)

Bitmap(ByVal cx As Integer, ByVal cy As Integer,
     ByVal cxRowBytes As Integer, ByVal pf As PixelFormat,
     ByVal pBytes As IntPtr)
```

The first three constructors initialize the pixels to 0. A pixel value of 0 has a different meaning for different types of bitmaps. For RGB bitmaps, 0 means black. For ARGB bitmaps, 0 means transparent. The fourth constructor also allows you to pass a pointer to an array of bytes that initializes the bitmap image.

The first constructor in the table creates a *Bitmap* object of the specified size with a pixel format of *PixelFormat.Format32bppArgb*. That's 32 bits per pixel with an alpha channel for transparency. The horizontal and vertical resolution are set to the resolution of the video display. The second constructor lets you specify a *PixelFormat* member if you want something other than *Format32bppArgb*.

The third constructor lets you specify a *Graphics* object. Regardless of whether you specify a *Graphics* object associated with the video display or the printer, and regardless of whether or not your printer is capable of color, the constructor always creates a *Bitmap* with a pixel format of *PixelFormat.Format32bppPArgb*. Notice that this pixel format implies a *premultiplied* alpha channel. The really important implication of creating a bitmap based on a *Graphics* object is that the *HorizontalResolution* and *VerticalResolution* properties of the *Bitmap* object are set to the *DpiX* and *DpiY* properties of the *Graphics* object. And that doesn't mean 100 dpi for the printer! That means 300, 600, 720, or something higher.

For example, suppose your printer has a resolution of 600 dpi. You want to create a bitmap based on the printer resolution. And why do you want to do this? Because if you'll eventually be printing the bitmap, you want anything you draw on this bitmap (including text) to be as fine and as rounded as the printer resolution will allow. But keep in mind that the bitmap size must be compatible with the resolution. A 2-inch-square 600-dpi bitmap will require widths and heights of 1200 pixels and will consume over 5 megabytes of memory. And be sure to use the metrical size when you display such a bitmap on the screen and the printer! (Don't worry: I'll have an example shortly.)

At any rate, if you prefer to create a bitmap with a resolution that matches neither the screen nor the printer, the *Bitmap* class provides a method that allows you to change the resolution of a bitmap you've loaded or created:

### *Bitmap* Methods (selection)

```
Sub SetResolution(ByVal xDpi As Single, ByVal yDpi As Single)
```

How do you get stuff on the surface of the bitmap? There are three approaches:

- You can create a *Graphics* object for the bitmap and draw on the bitmap as if it were any other graphics device. I demonstrated this approach earlier in the chapter. Remember that you can't create a *Graphics* object for every possible pixel format!

■ You can use the *SetPixel* and *GetPixel* methods of the *Bitmap* class to set (or get) the color of individual pixels in the bitmap.

■ You can use the *Bitmap* class methods *LockBits* and *UnlockBits* to get access to the actual bitmap data.

I won't be able to demonstrate the second and third approaches in this book.

## Hello World with a Bitmap

This HelloWorldBitmap program creates a bitmap and draws on the bitmap a 72-point version of the programmer's universal mantra. It then displays that bitmap on the client area and (optionally) on your printer page.

```vb
HelloWorldBitmap.vb
'-------------------------------------------------
' HelloWorldBitmap.vb (c) 2002 by Charles Petzold
'-------------------------------------------------
Imports System
Imports System.Drawing
Imports System.Windows.Forms

Class HelloWorldBitmap
    Inherits PrintableForm

    Const fResolution As Single = 300
    Private bm As bitmap

    Shared Shadows Sub Main()
        Application.Run(new HelloWorldBitmap())
    End Sub

    Sub New()
        Text = "Hello, World!"

        bm = New Bitmap(1, 1)
        bm.SetResolution(fResolution, fResolution)

        Dim grfx As Graphics = Graphics.FromImage(bm)
        Dim fnt As New Font("Times New Roman", 72)
        Dim sz As Size = grfx.MeasureString(Text, fnt).ToSize()

        bm = New Bitmap(bm, sz)
        bm.SetResolution(fResolution, fResolution)

        grfx = Graphics.FromImage(bm)
        grfx.Clear(Color.White)
```

*(continued)*

**HelloWorldBitmap.vb**  *(continued)*

```
        grfx.DrawString(Text, fnt, Brushes.Black, 0, 0)
        grfx.Dispose()
    End Sub

    Protected Overrides Sub DoPage(ByVal grfx As Graphics, _
            ByVal clr As Color, ByVal cx As Integer, ByVal cy As Integer)
        grfx.DrawImage(bm, 0, 0)
    End Sub
End Class
```

The bitmap is created in the program's constructor and, as you can see, the code is rather involved. The problem is that I wanted the bitmap to be the exact size of the text string it displays, but I didn't necessarily want to use a bitmap resolution associated with a real display device. Do you see the problem? You need *MeasureString* to get the dimensions of a text string, and you need a *Graphics* object to use *MeasureString*. But if you want that *Graphics* object to be based on a bitmap with an arbitrary device resolution, you need a *Bitmap* object or an *Image* object to get that *Graphics* object!

For that reason, the constructor creates two bitmaps. The first one is tiny, just 1 pixel square, but that's enough. The program assigns this tiny bitmap a 300-dpi resolution by using the *fResolution* constant. It obtains a *Graphics* object, creates a 72-point Times New Roman font, and then calls *MeasureString*.

The *MeasureString* dimensions are used to create a new bitmap. The bitmap must have the same 300-dpi resolution. The program then obtains a *Graphics* object for this bitmap, clears the background to white, and draws the text in black.

The program uses *DrawImage* to display the same bitmap on both the video display and the printer. The resulting image looks like a normal 72-point font. But the real proof that something interesting is happening here is the printer output: the font characters appear as round and unjaggy as any other 300-dpi output. Try changing the *fResolution* constant to something much smaller (say, 30 dpi), and witness the dramatic difference on both the video display and the printer.

# The Shadow Bitmap

Occasionally, implementing an *OnPaint* method can be costly in terms of processing time or memory. The client area could contain a complex image that has been assembled over a long period of time, for example. For such applications, implementing a *shadow bitmap* is usually an excellent solution. A shadow bitmap is a bitmap that your program draws on whenever it also draws on its client area outside the *OnPaint* method. Then the *OnPaint* method reduces to a simple call to *DrawImage*.

In Chapter 8, I presented a progam named Scribble that let you do free-form drawing on your client area with the mouse. At the time, I was able to show only one solution to saving the drawing for refreshing during the *OnPaint* method. That was the ScribbleWithSave program (on page 348), which saved every coordinate point in *ArrayList* objects. There's nothing wrong with this approach! In fact, if you wanted to give the user the option to edit the drawing by manipulating individual lines, saving every one of those coordinate points would be necessary. ScribbleWithSave is the first step to creating a drawing program that saves the drawing in a metafile format.

The following new version of the Scribble program is called ScribbleWith-Bitmap and maintains the entire image in a large bitmap. This program might be the first step in creating a paint program.

**ScribbleWithBitmap.vb**

```
'-------------------------------------------------------
' ScribbleWithBitmap.vb (c) 2002 by Charles Petzold
'-------------------------------------------------------
Imports System
Imports System.Drawing
Imports System.Windows.Forms

Class ScribbleWithBitmap
    Inherits Form

    Private bTracking As Boolean
    Private ptLast As Point
    Private bm As bitmap
    Private grfxBm As Graphics

    Shared Sub Main()
        Application.Run(new ScribbleWithBitmap())
    End Sub

    Sub New()
        Text = "Scribble with Bitmap"
        BackColor = SystemColors.Window
        ForeColor = SystemColors.WindowText

        ' Create bitmap
        Dim sz As Size = SystemInformation.PrimaryMonitorMaximizedWindowSize
        bm = New Bitmap(sz.Width, sz.Height)
```

*(continued)*

**ScribbleWithBitmap.vb**    *(continued)*

```
            ' Create Graphics object from bitmap
            grfxBm = Graphics.FromImage(bm)
            grfxBm.Clear(BackColor)
        End Sub

        Protected Overrides Sub OnMouseDown(ByVal mea As MouseEventArgs)
            If mea.Button <> MouseButtons.Left Then Return

            ptLast = New Point(mea.X, mea.Y)
            bTracking = True
        End Sub

        Protected Overrides Sub OnMouseMove(ByVal mea As MouseEventArgs)
            If Not bTracking Then Return

            Dim ptNew As New Point(mea.X, mea.Y)
            Dim pn As New Pen(ForeColor)
            Dim grfx As Graphics = CreateGraphics()

            grfx.DrawLine(pn, ptLast, ptNew)
            grfx.Dispose()

            ' Draw on bitmap
            grfxBm.DrawLine(pn, ptLast, ptNew)
            ptLast = ptNew
        End Sub

        Protected Overrides Sub OnMouseUp(ByVal mea As MouseEventArgs)
            bTracking = False
        End Sub

        Protected Overrides Sub OnPaint(ByVal pea As PaintEventArgs)
            Dim grfx As Graphics = pea.Graphics

            ' Display bitmap
            grfx.DrawImage(bm, 0, 0, bm.Width, bm.Height)
        End Sub
    End Class
```

The statements that I've added to the basic Scribble program are highlighted with comments: there aren't many of them. In the constructor, I create a bitmap with a size obtained from *SystemInformation.PrimaryMonitorMaximizedWindowSize*. The *FromImage* method of the *Graphics* class obtains a *Graphics* object, and the bitmap image is initialized with a call to *Clear*. During the *OnMouseMove* method, the *DrawLine* method draws on the bitmap as well as the client area. During *OnPaint*, the bitmap is displayed with a call to *DrawImage*.

The ScribbleWithBitmap version of the program is considerably shorter and sweeter than ScribbleWithSave. But this simplicity comes at a cost: In a very real sense, the coordinate points of the polylines have been lost. They can't easily be extracted again from the bitmap.

And here's another difference: The efficiency of the *OnPaint* method in ScribbleWithSave depends on how complex the drawing is. As more and more polylines are added to the total drawing, *OnPaint* will require longer to redraw them. The speed of the *OnPaint* method in ScribbleWithBitmap is independent of the complexity of the image.

As I mentioned, the ScribbleWithBitmap program creates a bitmap the size of a maximized window in its constructor. This is a fairly good approximation of how large such a shadow bitmap should be. However, if the user changes the display size while ScribbleWithBitmap is running, the bitmap could become inadequate. To deal with this eventuality, you need to install a handler for the *DisplaySettingsChanged* event in the *SystemEvents* class defined in the *Microsoft.Win32* namespace. But how do you respond to the event? If the display is getting larger, you could create a new bitmap with the new size and copy the old bitmap to the new one. But what happens if the display gets smaller? Do you create a smaller bitmap and potentially throw away part of the existing image? It's not an easy problem to solve!

# Binary Resources

If your application needs to display a particular bitmap, I've demonstrated numerous times in this chapter how you can load the bitmap from a file.

But as you know, storing bitmaps in separate files isn't always a good solution for an application that is distributed to other users. What happens if the program file and the bitmap file are separated? An overzealous user might be cleaning up the hard drive by erasing "unnecessary" files and suddenly, Bam! No more bitmap.

For this reason, it's often advantageous to store small binary files—particularly bitmaps, icons, and custom cursors—right in the application's .exe file. That way, they can never be lost. Files stored in the executable in this way are known as *resources*.

Visual Basic .NET lets you create binary resources by using an interactive image editor. To add a binary resource to a program, choose the Add New Item option from the Project menu. In the Add New Item dialog box, pick Local Project Items from the Categories list on the left. On the right, choose Bitmap File, Cursor File, or Icon File. Give the file whatever name you want. For bitmap files, the Properties window allows you to specify the dimensions and the color format. For cursor files, the default format is 32 pixels square and 16 colors. But you can also paint in two colors known as Screen and Reverse Screen. The Screen color is transparent. You use it to make a cursor nonrectangular (as most cursors are). The Reverse Screen color reverses the color of the background behind the cursor; Reverse Screen is rarely used. You also need to specify a hot spot for cursors.

For icon files, you have 16 colors available plus Screen and Reverse Screen by default. The Screen color is often used in icons to make them nonrectangular. The Reverse Screen color was popular in the early days of Windows but is much less used nowadays.

Normally, you create an icon that is 32 pixels square and has 16 colors. But icons are often also displayed in a smaller size, which are 16 pixels square. Windows will display the 32-pixel icon as a 16-pixel icon by eliminating every other row and column of pixels. If your icon doesn't look quite right after 75 percent of its content has been ripped out, you can also create a custom 16-pixel-square version that is stored in the same icon file. In the image editor, you can switch between these two formats by using the New Image Type option on the Image menu.

Now here's the most important rule whenever you create a bitmap, a cursor, or an icon file you want to use as a resource. Listen up.

In Visual Basic .NET, when you select any bitmap, icon, or cursor file in Solution Explorer that is part of a project, you'll see (or you can invoke) a Properties window for the file. Change the Build Action property to Embedded Resource. That property instructs Visual Basic .NET to embed the resource file in the .exe file for the project. In the program, you load such a resource by using a *Bitmap* constructor, a *Cursor* constructor, or an *Icon* constructor.

Let's look at an example with an icon resource. The project is called ProgramWithIcon, which means that the program file is ProgramWithIcon.vb, which means that it contains a class named *ProgramWithIcon*. Just to keep the rhythm going, I also named the icon file ProgramWithIcon.ico. The icon image is a simple file cabinet. The program doesn't do much except load the icon and set the form's *Icon* property.

---

**ProgramWithIcon.vb**

```
'-------------------------------------------------
' ProgramWithIcon.vb  2001 by Charles Petzold
'-------------------------------------------------
Imports System
Imports System.Drawing
Imports System.Windows.Forms
```

```
Class ProgramWithIcon
    Inherits Form

    Shared Sub Main()
        Application.Run(new ProgramWithIcon())
    End Sub

    Sub New()
        Text = "Program with Icon"
        Icon = New Icon(GetType(ProgramWithIcon), "ProgramWithIcon.ico")
    End Sub
End Class
```

**ProgramWithIcon.ico**

Again, if you're re-creating this program yourself in Visual Basic .NET, be sure to specify the Build Action for the icon file as Embedded Resource.

To load the icon, use the following constructor of the *Icon* class:

### *Icon* Constructors (selection)

```
Icon(ByVal typ As Type, ByVal strResource As String)
```

Other *Icon* constructors let you load icons from files or streams. If an icon file or resource contains multiple images, you can attempt to obtain an icon of a specific size based on an existing icon:

### *Icon* Constructors (selection)

```
Icon(ByVal icn As Icon, ByVal sz As Size)
Icon(ByVal icn As Icon, ByVal cx As Integer, ByVal cy As Integer)
```

These constructors try to match the available icons with the size you specify. They won't stretch or compress icons. You use the following properties of the *Icon* class to determine an icon's size:

### *Icon* Properties (selection)

| Property | Type | Accessibility |
|----------|------|---------------|
| *Size* | *Size* | Get |
| *Width* | *Integer* | Get |
| *Height* | *Integer* | Get |

You can also use these methods of the *Graphics* class to draw the icon on your client area:

### *Graphics* Methods (selection)

```
Sub DrawIcon(ByVal icn As Icon,
             ByVal x As Integer, ByVal y As Integer)

Sub DrawIcon(ByVal icn As Icon, ByVal rect As Rectangle)

Sub DrawIconUnstretched(ByVal icn As Icon, ByVal rect As Rectangle)
```

What ProgramWithIcon does, however, is simply assign the return value of the *Icon* constructor to the *Icon* property of the form. Notice the icon in the upper left corner of the form:

Now take a look at the *Icon* constructor in the program:

```
Icon = New Icon(GetType(ProgramWithIcon), "ProgramWithIcon.ico")
```

The first argument of the constructor refers to the *ProgramWithIcon* class. Within that *GetType* operator, you can use the name of any class that your program defines. Or you can use the name of any structure, enumeration, interface, or delegate that your program defines.

In any code in the *ProgramWithIcon* class, the expression

```
GetType(ProgramWithIcon)
```

is equivalent to:

```
Me.GetType()
```

This equivalence means that you can use the somewhat shorter constructor

```
Icon = New Icon(Me.GetType(), "ProgramWithIcon.ico")
```

and the program still works the same.

The second argument to the *Icon* constructor is the filename of the icon resource. If you're running the Visual Basic compiler from the command line, you use the */resource* (or, abbreviated, */res*) switch for each resource. For this program, for example, you need the compiler switch:

```
/res:ProgramWithIcon.ico
```

Loading a cursor is exactly the same as loading an icon. The *Cursor* constructor looks like this:

### *Cursor* Constructors (selection)

```
Cursor(ByVal typ As Type, ByVal strResource As String)
```

And I've already shown you this constructor for the *Bitmap* class:

### *Bitmap* Constructors (selection)

```
Bitmap(ByVal typ As Type, ByVal strResource As String)
```

And now we'll put the *Bitmap* constructor to use.

# Animation

Windows Forms and GDI+ are missing a couple features that are usually considered important for animation. In Chapter 8, I discussed how GDI+ doesn't support exclusive-OR (XOR) drawing. XOR drawing lets you draw an image and then draw it again to erase what you drew. Another problem is that Windows Forms doesn't allow any way to read pixels from the screen. When doing animation, it's often useful to read a block of pixels from the screen as a bitmap, draw on it, and then write it back to the screen.

Still, however, you can perform some rudimentary animation in a Windows Forms program. One approach to animation is called *frame animation* and involves the successive display of identically sized bitmaps, much like a movie. Here's a program that loads in four bitmaps as resources and then uses a *Timer* event to display a winking eye.

**Wink.vb**

```
'----------------------------------------
' Wink.vb (c) 2002 by Charles Petzold
'----------------------------------------
Imports System
Imports System.Drawing
Imports System.Windows.Forms

Class Wink
    Inherits Form

    Protected aimg(3) As Image
    Protected iImage As Integer = 0
    Protected iIncr As Integer = 1

    Shared Sub Main()
        Application.Run(New Wink())
    End Sub

    Sub New()
        Text = "Wink"
        ResizeRedraw = True
        BackColor = Color.White

        Dim i As Integer
        For i = 0 To 3
            aimg(i) = New Bitmap(Me.GetType(), "Eye" & (i + 1) & ".png")
        Next i

        Dim tmr As New Timer()
        tmr.Interval = 100
        AddHandler tmr.Tick, AddressOf TimerOnTick
        tmr.Enabled = True
    End Sub

    Protected Overridable Sub TimerOnTick(ByVal obj As Object, _
                                          ByVal ea As EventArgs)
        Dim grfx As Graphics = CreateGraphics()
        grfx.DrawImage(aimg(iImage), _
                    (ClientSize.Width - aimg(iImage).Width) \ 2, _
                    (ClientSize.Height - aimg(iImage).Height) \ 2, _
```

```
                        aimg(iImage).Width, aimg(iImage).Height)
        grfx.Dispose()
        iImage += iIncr

        If iImage = 3 Then
            iIncr = -1
        ElseIf iImage = 0 Then
            iIncr = 1
        End If
    End Sub
End Class
```

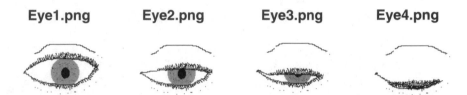

**Eye1.png**     **Eye2.png**     **Eye3.png**     **Eye4.png**

Notice that the constructor uses string concatenation to construct four file-names that refer to the image files: Eye1.png, Eye2.png, and so forth. The *Timer-OnTick* method uses *DrawImage* to display each image in the center of the client area. Here's the program caught in action:

When doing animation, you should try to display images in their pixel size to avoid stretching or compressing the image, which tends to sap the CPU.

Just for fun, I subclassed the *Wink* class in this program and used the *RotateFlip* method to make a set of right eyes out of the left eyes.

## DualWink.vb

```vb
'-----------------------------------------------
' DualWink.vb (c) 2002 by Charles Petzold
'-----------------------------------------------
Imports System
Imports System.Drawing
Imports System.Windows.Forms

Class DualWink
    Inherits Wink

    Private aimgRev(3) As Image

    Shared Shadows Sub Main()
        Application.Run(New DualWink())
    End Sub

    Sub New()
        Text = "Dual " & Text

        Dim i As Integer
        For i = 0 To 3
            aimgRev(i) = DirectCast(aimg(i).Clone(), Image)
            aimgRev(i).RotateFlip(RotateFlipType.RotateNoneFlipX)
        Next i
    End Sub

    Protected Overrides Sub TimerOnTick(ByVal obj As Object, _
                                        ByVal ea As EventArgs)
        Dim grfx As Graphics = CreateGraphics()

        grfx.DrawImage(aimg(iImage), _
                ClientSize.Width \ 2, _
                (ClientSize.Height - aimg(iImage).Height) \ 2, _
                aimg(iImage).Width, aimg(iImage).Height)

        grfx.DrawImage(aimgRev(3 - iImage), _
                ClientSize.Width \ 2 - aimgRev(3 - iImage).Width, _
                (ClientSize.Height - aimgRev(3 - iImage).Height) \ 2, _
                aimgRev(3 - iImage).Width, _
                aimgRev(3 - iImage).Height)
        grfx.Dispose()

        iImage += iIncr
        If iImage = 3 Then
            iIncr = -1
        ElseIf iImage = 0 Then
            iIncr = 1
        End If
    End Sub
End Class
```

This project also requires links to the four PNG files associated with the Wink program.

And now, what you've all been waiting for: the bouncing ball program. The Bounce program basically creates a square bitmap, draws a red ball on it, and then draws the bitmap in different places on the client area, simulating a ball that bounces off the walls.

## Bounce.vb

```
'-----------------------------------------
' Bounce.vb (c) 2002 by Charles Petzold
'-----------------------------------------
Imports System
Imports System.Drawing
Imports System.Windows.Forms

Class Bounce
    Inherits Form

    Const iTimerInterval As Integer = 25    ' In milliseconds
    Const iBallSize As Integer = 16         ' As fraction of client area
    Const iMoveSize As Integer = 4          ' As fraction of ball size

    Private bm As Bitmap
    Private xCenter, yCenter As Integer
    Private cxRadius, cyRadius, cxMove, cyMove, cxTotal, cyTotal As Integer

    Shared Sub Main()
        Application.Run(New Bounce())
    End Sub

    Sub New()
        Text = "Bounce"
```

*(continued)*

**Bounce.vb**    *(continued)*

```vb
        ResizeRedraw = True
        BackColor = Color.White

        Dim tmr As New Timer()
        tmr.Interval = iTimerInterval
        AddHandler tmr.Tick, AddressOf TimerOnTick
        tmr.Start()

        OnResize(EventArgs.Empty)
    End Sub

    Protected Overrides Sub OnResize(ByVal ea As EventArgs)
        Dim grfx As Graphics = CreateGraphics()
        grfx.Clear(BackColor)

        Dim fRadius As Single = _
                        Math.Min(ClientSize.Width / grfx.DpiX, _
                                 ClientSize.Height / grfx.DpiY) _
                                                     / iBallSize
        cxRadius = CInt(fRadius * grfx.DpiX)
        cyRadius = CInt(fRadius * grfx.DpiY)
        grfx.Dispose()

        cxMove = Math.Max(1, cxRadius \ iMoveSize)
        cyMove = Math.Max(1, cyRadius \ iMoveSize)
        cxTotal = 2 * (cxRadius + cxMove)
        cyTotal = 2 * (cyRadius + cyMove)

        bm = New Bitmap(cxTotal, cyTotal)
        grfx = Graphics.FromImage(bm)
        grfx.Clear(BackColor)
        DrawBall(grfx, New Rectangle(cxMove, cyMove, _
                                2 * cxRadius, 2 * cyRadius))
        grfx.Dispose()
        xCenter = ClientSize.Width \ 2
        yCenter = ClientSize.Height \ 2
    End Sub

    Protected Overridable Sub DrawBall(ByVal grfx As Graphics, _
            ByVal rect As Rectangle)
        grfx.FillEllipse(Brushes.Red, rect)
    End Sub

    Private Sub TimerOnTick(ByVal obj As Object, ByVal ea As EventArgs)
        Dim grfx As Graphics = CreateGraphics()
        grfx.DrawImage(bm, xCenter - cxTotal \ 2, _
                        yCenter - cyTotal \ 2, cxTotal, cyTotal)
        grfx.Dispose()

        xCenter += cxMove
        yCenter += cyMove
```

```
        If (xCenter + cxRadius >= ClientSize.Width) OrElse _
           (xCenter - cxRadius <= 0) Then
            cxMove = -cxMove
        End If
        If (yCenter + cyRadius >= ClientSize.Height) OrElse _
           (yCenter - cyRadius <= 0) Then
            cyMove = -cyMove
        End If
    End Sub
End Class
```

The big question, of course, is not how the ball is drawn on the client area but how the previous image of the ball is erased—and whether the program manages to accomplish that feat without an inordinate amount of flickering. The trick here is that the bitmap is actually larger than the ball, and the extra margin around the ball is sufficient to erase the previous ball.

Bounce reconstructs the bitmap whenever the form gets a call to *OnResize*. The radius of the ball is set to 1/16 of the width or height of the client area, whichever is less. But the program constructs a bitmap that is larger than the ball. On each of its four sides, the bitmap extends beyond the ball's dimensions by 1/4 of the radius. (You can change both these factors fairly easily.) The entire bitmap is colored white, and then the ball is drawn. (I put the ball-drawing code in a protected virtual method in hope that a future chapter, perhaps Chapter 17, will provide an override to draw a better-looking ball.)

The margins around the ball are stored as *cxMove* and *cyMove*. Not coincidentally, these two values are precisely the amount of space that the bitmap is moved on every call to *TimerOnTick*.

Such a simple approach to animation can't work in the general case. Change the background of the client area to anything but a solid color, and the whole technique falls apart.

# The Image List

In Chapter 12, we'll begin working with controls, specifically buttons, labels, and scroll bars, and soon after that, menus, list boxes, edit boxes, and others. You'll find that you can often use bitmaps on the surface of controls instead of (or in addition to) text. At the furthest extreme, a toolbar control that often appears below application menus is usually just a string of small bitmaps.

To help you deal with collections of images, the *System.Windows.Forms* namespace defines the *ImageList* class. An image list is essentially just a flexible array of *Image* objects with the same size and color format. You put images into an *ImageList* object (in a process I'll explain shortly) and access them as if you were dealing with an array. The images that you put into the image list don't have to be the same size when you put them in—but they will be scaled to the same size when you extract them.

These are the crucial *ImageList* properties:

### *ImageList* Properties (selection)

| Property | Type | Accessibility |
|---|---|---|
| *ImageSize* | *Size* | Get/Set |
| *ColorDepth* | *ColorDepth* | Get/Set |
| *TransparentColor* | *Color* | Get/Set |
| *Images* | *ImageList.ImageCollection* | Get |

The default *ImageSize* property value is 16 pixels square, and it doesn't get changed automatically when you start adding images to the image list. You'll probably need to set it yourself based on the size of the *Image* objects you're dealing with, and possibly also based on the resolution of the video display on which the program is running.

The *ColorDepth* property is a member of the *ColorDepth* enumeration:

### *ColorDepth* Enumeration

| Member | Value |
|---|---|
| *Depth4Bit* | 4 |
| *Depth8Bit* | 8 |
| *Depth16Bit* | 16 |
| *Depth24Bit* | 24 |
| *Depth32Bit* | 32 |

The default property is *Depth8Bit*, and you'll want to manually change this property based on the images you're using. Fortunately, the *ColorDepth* enumeration is defined in a very rational manner, so if you have an *Image* object (named *img*, for example) that you want to store in the image list, you can obtain the pixel format, obtain the number of bits per pixel by using the shared *Image.GetPixelFormatSize* method, and cast that to a value of type *ColorDepth*:

```
imglst.ColorDepth = _
    CType(Image.GetPixelFormatSize(img.PixelFormat), ColorDepth)
```

I know that fourth property named *Images* looks scary because the type of this property is defined as *ImageList.ImageCollection*. That long name only means that it's a class named *ImageCollection* that's defined in the *ImageList* class.

In an application, you'll never have to refer to the *ImageCollection* class: you need only refer to the *Images* property to use properties and methods of the *ImageCollection* class. The *Images* property is what stores all the images in the image list.

The functionality of the *Images* property shows up in a number of other classes in *System.Windows.Forms*. In Chapter 12, you'll encounter a property of the *Control* class named *Controls* that is of type *Control.ControlCollection*. In Chapter 14, you'll see a property of the *Menu* class named *MenuItems* that is of type *Menu.MenuItemCollection*. All these properties work pretty much the same. The types of the properties all implement the *IList*, *ICollection*, and *IEnumerable* interfaces (defined in the *System.Collections* namespace), which allow these properties to work like expandable arrays.

To create an object of type *ImageList*, you call the default constructor:

```
Dim imglst As New ImageList()
```

You'll then want to set the *ImageSize* and *ColorDepth* properties. You add *Image* objects to the image list by using one of the following methods:

### *ImageList.ImageCollection* Methods (selection)

```
Sub Add(ByVal img As Image)

Sub Add(ByVal img As Image, ByVal clrTransparent As Color)

Sub Add(ByVal icn As Icon)

Sub AddStrip(ByVal img As Image)
```

Because these methods are defined in the *ImageList.ImageCollection* class, you call them by using the *Images* property of the *ImageList* object. It's actually a lot simpler than it sounds:

```
imglist.Images.Add(img)
```

As you add each image, it is assigned an index beginning at 0. The *AddStrip* method adds multiple images, the number of which depends on the width of the image you pass to the method and the width of the *ImageSize* property.

The *ImageListCollection* class has the following four properties:

### ImageList.ImageCollection Properties

| Property | Type | Accessibility |
|---|---|---|
| *Empty* | *Boolean* | Get |
| *IsReadOnly* | *Boolean* | Get |
| *Count* | *Integer* | Get |
| *O* | *Image* | Get |

Use *Count* in an expression like this:

```
imglst.Images.Count
```

Most important, you can index the *Images* property as if it were an array. The expression

```
imglst.Images(2)
```

returns the third *Image* object in the image list. If the image list has fewer than three images, the expression throws an exception. The *IsReadOnly* property returns *False*, which means that you can also replace an image in the image list by using indexing:

```
imglst.Images(3) = img
```

However, if the image list doesn't already contain four images, the statement throws an exception.

You can also remove images from the image list, either individually or entirely:

### ImageList.ImageCollection Methods (selection)

```
Sub RemoveAt(ByVal index As Integer)
Sub Clear()
```

As you'll see in later chapters, you can use an *ImageList* object in conjunction with various controls, most importantly with the *ToolBar* control. Used by itself, *ImageList* is also a convenient way to store a number of images of the same size. The *ImageList* class provides the *Draw* method to draw these images:

### *ImageList Draw* **Methods**

```
Sub Draw(ByVal grfx As Graphics, ByVal pt As Point,
        ByVal index As Integer)

Sub Draw(ByVal grfx As Graphics, ByVal x As Integer,
        ByVal y As Integer, ByVal index As Integer)

Sub Draw(ByVal grfx As Graphics, ByVal x As Integer,
        ByVal y As Integer, ByVal cx As Integer,
        ByVal cy As Integer, ByVal index As Integer)
```

Notice that the index of the image in the image list is given in the last argument. For example,

```
imglst.Draw(grfx, x, y, 1)
```

draws the second image in the image list.

Watch out for the coordinates you pass to the *Draw* methods: The coordinate point passed to the first two *Draw* methods is in device units (pixels). The size of the image is based on the *ImageSize* property of the *ImageList* object, again in device units. Neither the page transform nor the world transform will affect these two methods! The use of device coordinates is intended to maximize performance but results in the postage-stamp effect on the printer. In the third *Draw* method, both the coordinate point and the width and height are in world coordinates.

# The Picture Box

Another image-related control class is *PictureBox*. The *PictureBox* class is descended from *Control* (and hence can process keyboard and mouse input), but usually the control does little more than display an image. Here are the crucial *PictureBox* properties:

### *PictureBox* **Properties (selection)**

| Property | Type | Accessibility |
| --- | --- | --- |
| *Image* | *Image* | Get/Set |
| *BorderStyle* | *BorderStyle* | Get/Get |
| *SizeMode* | *PictureBoxSizeMode* | Get/Set |

The members of the *BorderStyle* enumeration govern the border displayed around the image:

### *BorderStyle* Enumeration

| Member | Value |
| --- | --- |
| *None* | 0 |
| *FixedSingle* | 1 |
| *Fixed3D* | 2 |

The default is *None*. *PictureBoxSizeMode* is an enumeration that indicates how the image is displayed in the control:

### *PictureBoxSizeMode* Enumeration

| Member | Value |
| --- | --- |
| *Normal* | 0 |
| *StretchImage* | 1 |
| *AutoSize* | 2 |
| *CenterImage* | 3 |

The default is *Normal*. With *PictureBox*, as with other controls, you normally use the *Location* property to set the location of the control relative to its parent and the *Size* property to set the width and height of the control. If you specify a *SizeMode* of *PictureBoxSizeMode.Normal* or *PictureBoxSizeMode.CenterImage*, the image is displayed in its pixel size (not metrical size) within the picture box.

For *PictureBoxSizeMode.Normal*, the image is aligned with the top left of the control. If the control is larger than the pixel size of the image, you'll see the control *BackColor* around the right and bottom of the image. If the control is smaller than the image, part of the right and bottom of the image is hidden.

For *PictureBoxSizeMode.Centered*, the image is centered within the control. But the image is still displayed in its pixel size, so the image may be surrounded by the control background color, or the sides of the image may be hidden, depending on the size of the image and the size of the control.

If you set the *ClientSize* property of the *PictureBox* control equal to the *Size* property of the *Image* object, the control will be perfectly sized for the image. (The *ClientSize* property of the control indicates the size within the border.) Or you can use *PictureBoxSizeMode.AutoSize* to make the control size dependent on the *Image* size.

The *PictureBoxSizeMode.StretchImage* mode stretches the image to fit the size of the control. As you may fear, however, the image will be distorted if the aspect ratio of the control doesn't match that of the image.

So where's the *PictureBoxSizeMode* member that stretches the image iso-tropically? Alas, there isn't one. I'm forced to correct that deficiency with a *PictureBoxPlus* control that overrides *PictureBox* and adds a *NoDistort* property.

## PictureBoxPlus.vb

```
'------------------------------------------------
' PictureBoxPlus.vb (c) 2002 by Charles Petzold
'------------------------------------------------
Imports System
Imports System.Drawing
Imports System.Windows.Forms

Class PictureBoxPlus
    Inherits PictureBox

    Private bNoDistort As Boolean = False

    Property NoDistort() As Boolean
        Set(ByVal Value As Boolean)
            bNoDistort = Value
            Invalidate()
        End Set
        Get
            Return bNoDistort
        End Get
    End Property

    Protected Overrides Sub OnPaint(ByVal pea As PaintEventArgs)
        If (Not Image Is Nothing) AndAlso NoDistort AndAlso _
                SizeMode = PictureBoxSizeMode.StretchImage Then
            ScaleImageIsotropically(pea.Graphics, Image, ClientRectangle)
        Else
            MyBase.OnPaint(pea)
        End If
    End Sub

    Private Sub ScaleImageIsotropically(ByVal grfx As Graphics, _
            ByVal img As Image, ByVal rect As Rectangle)
        Dim szf As New SizeF(img.Width / img.HorizontalResolution, _
                            img.Height / img.VerticalResolution)
        Dim fScale As Single = Math.Min(rect.Width / szf.Width, _
                                        rect.Height / szf.Height)
        szf.Width *= fScale
        szf.Height *= fScale
        grfx.DrawImage(img, rect.X + (rect.Width - szf.Width) / 2, _
                        rect.Y + (rect.Height - szf.Height) / 2, _
                        szf.Width, szf.Height)
    End Sub
End Class
```

Only if *SizeMode* is *PictureBoxSizeMode.StretchImage* and the *NoDistort* property is *True* will this control display the image using the trusty *ScaleImage-Isotropically* method. Otherwise, the control calls the *OnPaint* method in the base class. Here's a program that tests the *PictureBoxPlus* control by using the control's *Dock* property to make the control fill the form's client area. The program is functionally similar to the ImageScaleIsotropic program.

**PictureBoxPlusDemo.vb**

```
'-----------------------------------------------------
' PictureBoxPlusDemo.vb (c) 2002 by Charles Petzold
'-----------------------------------------------------
Imports System
Imports System.Drawing
Imports System.Windows.Forms

Class PictureBoxPlusDemo
    Inherits Form

    Shared Sub Main()
        Application.Run(new PictureBoxPlusDemo())
    End Sub

    Sub New()
        Text = "PictureBoxPlus Demo"

        Dim picbox As New PictureBoxPlus()
        picbox.Parent = Me
        picbox.Dock = DockStyle.Fill
        picbox.Image = Image.FromFile("..\..\Apollo11FullColor.jpg")
        picbox.SizeMode = PictureBoxSizeMode.StretchImage
        picbox.NoDistort = True
    End Sub
End Class
```

# 12

# Buttons and Labels and Scrolls (Oh My!)

Much of the ease of use of Microsoft Windows and other graphical user interfaces results from the employment of familiar and consistent visual objects. Scroll bars, menus, push buttons, radio buttons, check boxes, text-entry fields, list boxes—these are all examples of *controls*. Controls are to the graphical user interface what subroutines are to programming languages. Controls let you structure and modularize your applications by off-loading low-level keyboard and mouse processing.

In the early days of Windows, controls were often referred to as *child windows*. With the exception of menus and scroll bars, controls appeared mostly in dialog boxes. Although it was possible to put controls on an application's main window, doing so was considered unusual and was rarely done. It wasn't until the 1991 introduction of Microsoft Visual Basic for Windows that a different Windows programming paradigm was introduced. Using Visual Basic, programmers could interactively assemble a collection of controls on the main window of an application and then write code associated with these controls. This style of programming has proved useful for developing front ends for distributed applications and is also a natural for many other "front panel" types of applications (such as the Windows CD Player).

I've already shown several examples of controls in this book. I used a *Panel* control in Chapter 4, a *Label* control in Chapter 8, and—what was once considered a relatively advanced topic in Windows programming—custom

controls in Chapter 8 andChapter 10. It's now time to begin more systemati-
cally exploring the numerous predefined controls available in the Microsoft
.NET Framework.

# Buttons and Clicks

Perhaps the archetypal control is the push button—that ubiquitous rectangular
object often labeled OK, Cancel, Open, or Save. Push buttons (also referred to
as *command* buttons) are intended to trigger an immediate action without
retaining any sort of on/off indication. You press a push button by clicking it
with the mouse or—if it has the input focus—by pressing the spacebar. Even if
a button doesn't have the input focus, you can sometimes trigger it by pressing
Enter or Esc. I'll discuss the use of the Enter key later in this chapter and talk
more about both Enter and Esc in Chapter 16.

The push button is implemented by the *Button* class, which is one of three
classes that are descended from the *MustInherit* class *ButtonBase*:

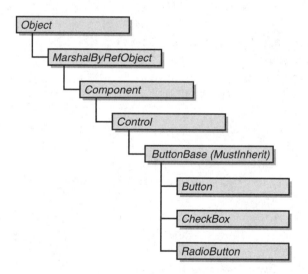

We'll examine the *CheckBox* and *RadioButton* classes later in this chapter.

In a Windows Forms program, you create a push button control by creating an object of type *Button*. By installing an event handler for the button's
*Click* event, you can have the button notify a form when the button has been
pressed. Here's a program that creates a single button. When you click the button, the form briefly displays some text.

## SimpleButton.vb

```
'----------------------------------------------------
' SimpleButton.vb (c) 2002 by Charles Petzold
'----------------------------------------------------
Imports System
Imports System.Drawing
Imports System.Windows.Forms

Class SimpleButton
    Inherits Form

    Shared Sub Main()
        Application.Run(New SimpleButton())
    End Sub

    Sub New()
        Text = "Simple Button"

        Dim btn As New Button()
        btn.Parent = Me
        btn.Text = "Click Me!"
        btn.Location = New Point(100, 100)
        AddHandler btn.Click, AddressOf ButtonOnClick
    End Sub

    Private Sub ButtonOnClick(ByVal obj As Object, ByVal ea As EventArgs)
        Dim grfx As Graphics = CreateGraphics()
        Dim ptfText As PointF = PointF.Empty
        Dim str As String = "Button clicked!"

        grfx.DrawString(str, Font, New SolidBrush(ForeColor), ptfText)
        System.Threading.Thread.Sleep(250)
        grfx.FillRectangle(New SolidBrush(BackColor), _
                    New RectangleF(ptfText, grfx.MeasureString(str, Font)))
        grfx.Dispose()
    End Sub
End Class
```

After setting its own caption bar text, the form's constructor begins by creating an object of type *Button*:

```
Dim btn As New Button()
```

The *Button* class has only a default constructor.

The next task is something I frequently forget to do, so I've tried to train myself to do it as quickly as possible after creating the control. You must assign the control a parent, and one way to do that is to set the *Parent* property of the control:

```
btn.Parent = Me
```

The keyword *Me* refers to the current object, which in this case is the form—the object of type *SimpleButton* that was created in the *Main* method. The button is made a child of the form.

Parents and children seem to abound in programming. There are parent and child processes, parent and child directories, and parent and child classes, to name a few examples. You might even conclude that the parent-child relationship is the primary metaphor of operating systems and programming languages. Controls must have parents too! A control without a parent isn't visible. When you set the *Parent* property of a control, you are actually mandating the following relationship between the parent and the control:

- The child control appears on the surface of its parent. Furthermore, the control is *clipped* to the surface of its parent, meaning that no part of the control can appear outside the surface of its parent.

- The child's location is specified relative to the upper left corner of the parent's client area.

- The child initially inherits some properties of its parent, specifically the *Font*, *ForeColor*, and *BackColor* properties.

Back to the SimpleButton program. The next statement in the constructor assigns some text to the button's *Text* property:

```
btn.Text = "Click Me!"
```

That is the text that will appear on the surface of the button. The next statement,

```
btn.Location = New Point(100, 100)
```

indicates where the upper left corner of the button is to appear relative to the upper left corner of the parent's client area. For the SimpleButton program, I just guessed at a coordinate point that I figured would be close to the center of the client area when the program started up. I'll get more precise with coordinates later on. All the location and size properties listed in Chapter 3 (page 98) are implemented in *Control*. For any descendant of *Control* other than *Form*, *ClientSize* is usually the same as *Size*.

Speaking of size, you might have noticed that I haven't specified a size for the button. That's because I'm hoping that the button will be created with a default size that will be suitable for our purposes. And if it isn't, getting a button with an inappropriate size will be an important lesson for us.

Finally, the form installs an event handler for the button's *Click* event:

```
AddHandler btn.Click, AddressOf ButtonOnClick
```

The button generates a *Click* event when it is clicked with the mouse or—if it has the input focus—when the spacebar is pressed. Because we'll be installing many event handlers in the chapters ahead, I'll be using a standard naming scheme. The name of the event handler will consist of the object type (in this case *Button*), perhaps another descriptive word if the class has more than one handler of a particular event of a particular object type, the word *On*, and the name of the event, in this case *Click*.

The *ButtonOnClick* method must be defined in accordance with the *EventHandler* delegate. The method has two arguments:

```
Sub ButtonOnClick(ByVal obj As Object, ByVal ea As EventArgs)
    ⋮
End Sub
```

In the SimpleButton program, the *ButtonOnClick* event simply displays a line of text in the upper left corner of the client area and then erases it 1/4 second later.

Keep in mind that despite the fact that *ButtonOnClick* handles *Click* events from the button, the event handler is still a method of the *SimpleButton* class. For example, when the *ButtonOnClick* method calls *CreateGraphics*, it's obtaining a *Graphics* object that pertains to the form, not to the button. If the *ButtonOnClick* method wants to access a property or method of the button, it can cast the *Object* argument like so:

```
Dim btn As Button = DirectCast(obj, Button)
```

Or, the constructor could simply store the *Button* object as a field in the *SimpleButton* class so it's accessible throughout the class. In this book I generally don't use fields unless I need them.

It's also important not to confuse the method I've called *ButtonOnClick* with the normal *OnClick* method in the *Form* class. If the SimpleButton program overrides the *OnClick* method, that method will get click events for the form, not for the button. When you click the button, the *ButtonOnClick* method is called. When you click anywhere else in the client area, the *OnClick* method is called.

Here's how the SimpleButton program comes up:

You can trigger the push button (and cause the *ButtonOnClick* method to display the text) by using the mouse or by pressing the spacebar or the Enter key.

# Keyboard and Mouse

I've already alluded to how the *SimpleButton* form and the push button respond to mouse input: When the mouse cursor is positioned over the push button, the button gets the mouse events. When the mouse cursor is otherwise positioned over the client area of the form, the form gets the mouse events. (But don't forget about mouse capturing: if you press the mouse button over the push button, the push button captures the mouse and continues to receive *all* mouse events until the mouse button is released or the push button loses the mouse capture.)

With regard to keyboard input, the difference between SimpleButton and most of the previous programs in this book is much more extreme: whenever the SimpleButton program is the active window, the button has the input focus. That means that the form gets *no* keyboard input.

You may want to verify this fact for yourself. If you were to include *OnKeyDown*, *OnKeyUp*, and *OnKeyPress* overrides in the *SimpleControl* class, they would reveal that the form itself gets no keystroke events. You could also install *KeyDown*, *KeyUp*, and *KeyPress* event handlers for the button. You'd need to add methods to the *SimpleButton* class that look like this:

```
Sub ButtonOnKeyDown(ByVal obj As Object, ByVal kea As KeyEventArgs)
    ⋮
End Sub
```

You'd also need to install event handlers for the button, like so:

```
AddHandler btn.KeyDown, AddressOf ButtonOnKeyDown
```

If you were to install keyboard event handlers for the button, you'd find that when SimpleButton is the active program, *most* of the keystrokes go to the button. The button itself ignores most of these events except when the spacebar is pressed.

I said that the button gets *most* of the keystrokes. There are a few keystrokes that neither the form nor the button control see at all. The missing keyboard events are the *KeyDown* events for the Enter key, the Tab key, and the arrow keys (up, down, left, and right), and the *KeyPress* events for the Enter and Tab keys.

It's no coincidence that the Tab key and the arrow keys constitute the normal keyboard interface for navigating among controls in Windows dialog boxes and that the Enter key is normally used for triggering the default push button.

These missing keystrokes are consumed in code implemented in the *Container-Control* class. You might recall that *ContainerControl* is one of the ancestors of *Form*. *ContainerControl* is the class responsible for implementing focus management among child controls. For this reason, a class such as *Form* that is responsible for maintaining a collection of controls is often called a *container* of the controls.

A control gets keyboard and mouse input only if it is both visible and enabled, which means that both the *Visible* and *Enabled* properties are set to *True*:

| Property | Type | Accessibility |
|----------|------|---------------|
| *Visible* | *Boolean* | Get/Set |
| *Enabled* | *Boolean* | Get/Set |

Both properties are *True* by default. If you set the *Visible* property to *False*, the control disappears from view and doesn't receive keyboard or mouse input. If the control is on a form, the mouse input that would have gone to the control goes to the form instead, just as if the control weren't there. If the non-visible control is the only control on the form, keyboard input goes to the form as usual.

If you set the *Enabled* property of a control to *False*, the control is still visible but it doesn't respond to keyboard or mouse input. Often a control indicates that it's disabled by displaying text in a faint gray color.

# Control Issues

Although SimpleButton may appear to be quite a simple program, I'm actually doing something very controversial in it. In fact, some people might look at such a program and shake their heads in exasperation. Can you believe that? What is it I'm doing that could possibly be so bad?

I'm coding.

As you may know, Visual Basic .NET includes the Windows Forms Designer, which lets you interactively design your form by selecting and positioning controls, and then writing code associated with each control. The Windows Forms Designer generates code in your .vb file that creates these controls and sets their properties. The advantage of the Windows Forms Designer is obvious: you get to move the controls around to an aesthetically pleasing configuration without getting involved in the actual numbers that specify their location and size. This is the feature that made Visual Basic 1.0 for Windows such a revolutionary product in 1991.

In this book, however, for the most part I'm going to pretend that the Windows Forms Designer doesn't exist. All my controls will be manually coded. There are some definite advantages to manually coding the locations and sizes of controls: You can use *Const* values. You can use variables. You can use arrays. You can use *For* loops. In the pages ahead, I'll demonstrate these options.

More important, however, is that the Windows Forms Designer will take you only so far. At some point, you'll need to write code, and you'll probably also need to understand the code that the Windows Forms Designer is generating.

Don't misunderstand me. There's nothing wrong with using the Windows Forms Designer. But there *is* something wrong with not being able to code the controls yourself.

# Deeper into Buttons

I didn't set the *Size* property of the *Button* object I created in the SimpleButton program, and nothing bad seemed to happen. On my machine, and probably on yours too, the button came out approximately the correct size. However, if your display is set for a resolution much larger than 120 dpi (also known as Large Fonts), it's possible that some of the button text was clipped. And that's no good.

When you decorate a form with controls, your primary design criteria must be to make it usable. Usability involves a number of factors. The controls shouldn't be too crowded, for example. They should be logically ordered. It helps if the form is aesthetically attractive in some way. But above all, control text can't be clipped! A user might figure out that "Cance" is really "Cancel," but it doesn't reflect well on you, the programmer.

You can size controls in a couple ways, which I'll be explaining in this chapter. Your experience with creating device-independent graphics involving text will certainly help in this regard. But sizing controls involves some intangibles as well. For example, if you set the height of a push button to the font height, the text will be clipped anyway because of the button border. The border of a push button is 4 pixels wide, but this information isn't available anywhere, and the size might be different in extreme device resolutions.

So how tall should a push button be? Traditionally, a height of 7/4 (or 175 percent) of the font height has been recommended. The next program in this chapter uses twice the font height, and those buttons certainly don't look too large. Testing your programs with different display resolutions is essential.

You'll have additional problems if you decide to translate your application to other languages. Translation affects the width of text strings, and some languages tend to be a little wordier than others.

The following program has two push buttons to demonstrate button sizing. One button makes the form 10 percent larger; the other makes it 10 percent smaller (within limits imposed by Windows). The buttons remain positioned in the center of the client area.

### TwoButtons.vb

```
'------------------------------------------------
' TwoButtons.vb (c) 2002 by Charles Petzold
'------------------------------------------------
Imports System
Imports System.Drawing
Imports System.Windows.Forms

Class TwoButtons
    Inherits Form

    ReadOnly btnLarger, btnSmaller As Button
    ReadOnly cxBtn, cyBtn, dxBtn As Integer

    Shared Sub Main()
        Application.Run(New TwoButtons())
    End Sub

    Sub New()
        Text = "Two Buttons"
        ResizeRedraw = True

        cxBtn = 5 * Font.Height
        cyBtn = 2 * Font.Height
        dxBtn = Font.Height

        btnLarger = New Button()
        btnLarger.Parent = Me
        btnLarger.Text = "&Larger"
        btnLarger.Size = New Size(cxBtn, cyBtn)
        AddHandler btnLarger.Click, AddressOf ButtonOnClick

        btnSmaller = New Button()
        btnSmaller.Parent = Me
        btnSmaller.Text = "&Smaller"
        btnSmaller.Size = New Size(cxBtn, cyBtn)
        AddHandler btnSmaller.Click, AddressOf ButtonOnClick
```

*(continued)*

**TwoButtons.vb**  *(continued)*

```vb
        OnResize(EventArgs.Empty)
    End Sub

    Protected Overrides Sub OnResize(ByVal ea As EventArgs)
        MyBase.OnResize(ea)
        btnLarger.Location = _
                New Point(ClientSize.Width \ 2 - cxBtn - dxBtn \ 2, _
                        (ClientSize.Height - cyBtn) \ 2)
        btnSmaller.Location = _
                New Point(ClientSize.Width \ 2 + dxBtn \ 2, _
                        (ClientSize.Height - cyBtn) \ 2)
    End Sub

    Private Sub ButtonOnClick(ByVal obj As Object, _
                            ByVal ea As EventArgs)
        Dim btn As Button = DirectCast(obj, Button)

        If btn Is btnLarger Then
            Left -= CInt(0.05 * Width)
            Top -= CInt(0.05 * Height)
            Width += CInt(0.1 * Width)
            Height += CInt(0.1 * Height)
        Else
            Left += CInt(Width / 22)
            Top += CInt(Height / 22)
            Width -= CInt(Width / 11)
            Height -= CInt(Height / 11)
        End If
    End Sub
End Class
```

The constructor calculates three values that it stores in fields: *cxBtn* and *cyBtn* indicate the width and height of each button, and *dxBtn* is the distance between the two buttons. All three values are based on the *Height* property of the form's *Font* property. Because controls inherit the *Font* property of their parents, the size of the font is applicable to the buttons as well. The buttons are made twice as high as the font height, and five times as wide. (I chose five times because it seemed to work right for this program; I'll discuss other approaches later in this chapter.) The constructor sets only the size of each button, not its location.

Because the location of each button depends on the size of the client area in this program, the button location isn't set until the *OnResize* method, which is called for the first time from the last statement of the constructor. The text of each button begins with an ampersand to indicate that the following letter should be underlined. The underlined letter functions as a keyboard accelerator. When the program runs, you'll have to momentarily press the Alt key to bring the underlines into view:

You can navigate between the buttons by using the Tab key or any of the four arrow keys. As you switch between the buttons, the dotted line just inside the button indicates the button that has the input focus. When a button has the input focus, all keystrokes (except the navigational keystrokes) go to that button. The button with the input focus generates a *Click* event when you press the spacebar.

The heavy outline indicates which button is the *default button*. The default button is the one that responds to pressing the Enter key. The difference between the button with the input focus and the default button may be a bit confusing. In this program, they are always the same button. As we begin working with other controls, however, the difference will become more apparent. Yes, the push button with the input focus is always the default button. However, if another type of control has the input focus, there can also be a default push button that will respond to the Enter key. In a dialog box, the button labeled OK or Open or Save is usually the default button. That button is triggered when a nonbutton control has the input focus and Enter is pressed. In addition, the button labeled Cancel is usually the *cancel button*, which is triggered when the Esc key is pressed. I'll explore these issues more in Chapter 16.

You can also trigger a button by pressing the underlined letter: *L* for Larger or *S* for Smaller. The button responds with a *Click* event, but the input focus doesn't change.

The *ButtonOnClick* method begins by casting the *Object* argument to an object of type *Button*. The method can then determine what to do by comparing that object with the *btnLarger* and *btnSmaller* objects that the constructor saved as fields. Depending on which button was pressed, the method responds by increasing or decreasing the size of the window by 10 percent and also by moving the window 5 percent so that it stays in the same location on the screen.

Changing the size of the window generates a call to the *OnResize* method, which responds by moving the buttons to the new center of the client area. I could have set the location during the *Click* event after recalculating the client size, but that would prevent the program from relocating the buttons when the user manually resizes the window.

Is it normal for a program to reposition controls based on the size of the client area? No, it's not. But it's an option that becomes apparent only when you break out of the walls in which the Windows Forms Designer imprisons you. This is why we write code to begin with: to be flexible.

## Appearance and Alignment

By default, buttons (and other controls) inherit their *Font*, *ForeColor*, and *Back-Color* properties from their parent. If your program creates some child controls and then changes the font, foreground color, or background color of the form, the child controls will also reflect these changes. For example, in the TwoButtons program, you could insert the statement

```
BackColor = Color.Blue
```

anywhere in the form's constructor, or even in the *ButtonOnClick* method. This statement will turn the form's background blue, and the buttons will also inherit a blue background.

But you can also set the *Font*, *ForeColor*, or *BackColor* property of one of the buttons, for example,

```
btnSmaller.BackColor = Color.Red
```

Once that statement is executed, the background color of the *btnSmaller* button will be set to red. (You can set either the *ForeColor* or the *BackColor* property to *Color.Transparent* or another transparent or partially transparent color.) Now what happens if the statement

```
BackColor = Color.Magenta
```

is executed? The form's background changes to magenta and the *btnLarger* button background changes to magenta, but the *btnSmaller* button background remains red.

How does that work? The control actually keeps track of which property the program has set and won't override that property when the corresponding property of the parent changes. The following methods restore the control to its default state, that is, inheriting these properties from its parent:

### *Control* Methods (selection)

```
Sub ResetFont( )
Sub ResetForeColor( )
Sub ResetBackColor( )
```

The *TextAlign* property defined in the *ButtonBase* class determines how the text is oriented within the button:

### *ButtonBase* Properties (selection)

| Property | Type | Accessibility |
|----------|------|---------------|
| *TextAlign* | *ContentAlignment* | Get/Set |

You set the property to one of the *ContentAlignment* enumeration values. Oddly enough, *ContentAlignment* is defined in the *System.Drawing* namespace but isn't used in conjunction with any class in that namespace.

### ContentAlignment Enumeration

| Member | Value |
|--------|-------|
| *TopLeft* | &H0001 |
| *TopCenter* | &H0002 |
| *TopRight* | &H0004 |
| *MiddleLeft* | &H0010 |
| *MiddleCenter* | &H0020 |
| *MiddleRight* | &H0040 |
| *BottomLeft* | &H0100 |
| *BottomCenter* | &H0200 |
| *BottomRight* | &H0400 |

Although these values appear to be bit flags, that idiosyncrasy is a legacy from a prerelease version of Windows Forms. Do not combine *ContentAlignment* values! The default *TextAlign* value for push buttons is *MiddleCenter*, which doesn't become apparent unless the button is somewhat larger than the text inside.

The *ButtonBase* class includes another property that affects the button's appearance:

### *ButtonBase* Properties (selection)

| Property | Type | Accessibility |
|----------|------|---------------|
| *FlatStyle* | *FlatStyle* | Get/Set |

*FlatStyle* is an enumeration defined in the *System.Windows.Forms* namespace:

### *FlatStyle* Enumeration

| Member | Value | Description |
|--------|-------|-------------|
| *Flat* | 0 | Flat rather than 3D |
| *Popup* | 1 | 3D effect on mouse hovering |
| *Standard* | 2 | Normal 3D appearance |
| *System* | 3 | Operating system standard |

The default is *FlatStyle.Standard*.

Here's a program that displays push buttons in all four styles. Notice how the program uses the shared *Enum.GetValues* method for obtaining an array of all the *FlatStyle* values. The program uses each enumeration value to assign both the *FlatStyle* and *Text* properties of the buttons.

**ButtonStyles.vb**

```
'-------------------------------------------------
' ButtonStyles.vb (c) 2002 by Charles Petzold
'-------------------------------------------------
Imports System
Imports System.Drawing
Imports System.Windows.Forms

Class ButtonStyles
    Inherits Form

    Shared Sub Main()
        Application.Run(New ButtonStyles())
    End Sub

    Sub New()
        Text = "Button Styles"

        Dim y As Integer = 50
        Dim fs As FlatStyle

        For Each fs In System.Enum.GetValues(GetType(FlatStyle))
            Dim btn As New Button()
```

```
            btn.Parent = Me
            btn.FlatStyle = fs
            btn.Text = fs.ToString()
            btn.Location = New Point(50, y)
            y += 50
        Next fs
    End Sub
End Class
```

Here's what the four styles look like:

The Standard style is the same as System, but in this screen shot, the button labeled Standard has the input focus and is thus the default button.

## Buttons with Bitmaps

Although you can set custom fonts and colors in your buttons, you may want to go to greater extremes in presenting a unique visual interface to your users. You can put a graphical image on your buttons in two ways. The first involves four properties of the *ButtonBase* class:

### *ButtonBase* Properties (selection)

| Property | Type | Accessibility |
| --- | --- | --- |
| *Image* | *Image* | Get/Set |
| *ImageList* | *ImageList* | Get/Set |
| *ImageIndex* | *Integer* | Get/Set |
| *ImageAlign* | *ContentAlignment* | Get/Set |

These properties let you specify a bitmap image to be displayed in the background of the button. Either you set the *Image* property to a specific *Image* or *Bitmap* object, or you set *ImageList* to an *ImageList* object and *ImageIndex* to an index within that list. The default *ImageAlign* property is *ContentAlignment.MiddleCenter*.

You can obtain these images in whatever manner is convenient—resources, files, or fabricated right in the program. You should set the width and height of the button equal to the width and height of the bitmap plus 8 (4 pixels for each border).

Although it's most common for a program to use a bitmap as an *alternative* to text, the two aren't mutually exclusive. If you also set the *Text* property, the text is displayed on top of the image.

Here's a version of the TwoButtons program that loads a couple 64-pixel-square images stored as resources for symbolizing the functionality of the buttons.

## BitmapButtons.vb

```
'-----------------------------------------------
' BitmapButtons.vb (c) 2002 by Charles Petzold
'-----------------------------------------------
Imports System
Imports System.Drawing
Imports System.Windows.Forms

Class BitmapButtons
    Inherits Form

    ReadOnly cxBtn, cyBtn, dxBtn As Integer
    ReadOnly btnLarger, btnSmaller As Button

    Shared Sub Main()
        Application.Run(New BitmapButtons())
    End Sub

    Sub New()
        Text = "Bitmap Buttons"
        ResizeRedraw = True

        dxBtn = Font.Height

        ' Create first button.
        btnLarger = New Button()
        btnLarger.Parent = Me
        btnLarger.Image = New Bitmap(Me.GetType(), "LargerButton.bmp")

        ' Calculate button dimensions based on image dimensions.
        cxBtn = btnLarger.Image.Width + 8
```

```
        cyBtn = btnLarger.Image.Height + 8
        btnLarger.Size = New Size(cxBtn, cyBtn)
        AddHandler btnLarger.Click, AddressOf ButtonLargerOnClick

        ' Create second button.
        btnSmaller = New Button()
        btnSmaller.Parent = Me
        btnSmaller.Image = New Bitmap(Me.GetType(), "SmallerButton.bmp")
        btnSmaller.Size = New Size(cxBtn, cyBtn)
        AddHandler btnSmaller.Click, AddressOf ButtonSmallerOnClick
        OnResize(EventArgs.Empty)
    End Sub

    Protected Overrides Sub OnResize(ByVal ea As EventArgs)
        MyBase.OnResize(ea)
        btnLarger.Location = _
                New Point(ClientSize.Width \ 2 - cxBtn - dxBtn \ 2, _
                        (ClientSize.Height - cyBtn) \ 2)
        btnSmaller.Location = _
                New Point(ClientSize.Width \ 2 + dxBtn \ 2, _
                        (ClientSize.Height - cyBtn) \ 2)
    End Sub

    Private Sub ButtonLargerOnClick(ByVal obj As Object, _
                                    ByVal ea As EventArgs)
        Left -= CInt(0.05 * Width)
        Top -= CInt(0.05 * Height)
        Width += CInt(0.1 * Width)
        Height += CInt(0.1 * Height)
    End Sub

    Private Sub ButtonSmallerOnClick(ByVal obj As Object, _
                                     ByVal ea As EventArgs)
        Left += CInt(Width / 22)
        Top += CInt(Height / 22)
        Width -= CInt(Width / 11)
        Height -= CInt(Height / 11)
    End Sub
End Class
```

**LargerButton.bmp**         **LargerButton.bmp**

Don't forget to indicate that the bitmaps are Embedded Resources in Visual Basic .NET!

The program calculates the *cxBtn* and *cyBtn* dimensions based on the size of the bitmap image plus 8. After creating each button, the constructor loads bitmap resources and sets the *Image* property of the button. Here's what the buttons look like:

## Multiple Handlers or One?

In the TwoButtons program, I have a single method that handles the *Click* events from both buttons. In the BitmapButtons program, I use two separate event handlers. As you begin developing forms and dialog boxes with many controls, you'll undoubtedly ponder which approach is best: to have one event handler for a collection of controls or to separate event handlers for each control.

Neither approach is entirely right or wrong. You'll probably write neater and more maintainable code if you have separate handlers for each control. However, if event handlers for several controls must share some code, it's probably best to consolidate those handlers into one.

## Drawing Your Own Buttons

Specifying a bitmap image in a button isn't the only approach to displaying custom buttons. You can also take over button painting entirely by installing an event handler for the button's *Paint* event. This approach is sometimes called *owner-draw*: your program is the owner of the button and it—rather than the buttons—does the drawing.

Owner-draw isn't quite as easy as using a bitmap, but it's probably a better approach if you're using simple vector drawing for the image, merely because vector drawing scales better.

What helps in creating owner-draw buttons is that you don't have to draw every single little thing. The *System.Windows.Forms* namespace contains a class named *ControlPaint* that includes a bunch of shared methods for drawing various pieces of common controls. For drawing push buttons, for example, the following two overloaded methods are useful:

### *ControlPaint* Shared Methods (selection)

```
Sub DrawButton(ByVal grfx As Graphics,
              ByVal x As Integer, ByVal y As Integer,
              ByVal cx As Integer, ByVal cy As Integer,
              ByVal bs As ButtonState)

Sub DrawButton(ByVal grfx As Graphics, ByVal rect As Rectangle,
              ByVal bs As ButtonState)

Sub DrawFocusRectangle(ByVal grfx As Graphics, ByVal rect As Rectangle)

Sub DrawFocusRectangle(ByVal grfx As Graphics, ByVal rect As Rectangle,
                    ByVal clrForeground As Color,
                    ByVal clrBackground As Color)
```

The *DrawButton* method really just draws the border around the button. The *ButtonState* enumeration is a collection of bit flags that governs the appearance of the button:

### *ButtonState* Enumeration

| Member | Value |
|--------|-------|
| *Normal* | &H0000 |
| *Inactive* | &H0100 |
| *Pushed* | &H0200 |
| *Checked* | &H0400 |
| *Flat* | &H4000 |
| *All* | &H4700 |

I use both these methods in the OwnerDrawButtons program.

**OwnerDrawButtons.vb**

```vb
'-------------------------------------------------
' OwnerDrawButtons.vb (c) 2002 by Charles Petzold
'-------------------------------------------------
Imports System
Imports System.Drawing
Imports System.Drawing.Drawing2D
Imports System.Windows.Forms

Class OwnerDrawButtons
    Inherits Form

    ReadOnly cxImage, cyImage As Integer
    ReadOnly cxBtn, cyBtn, dxBtn As Integer
    ReadOnly btnLarger, btnSmaller As Button

    Shared Sub Main()
        Application.Run(New OwnerDrawButtons())
    End Sub

    Sub New()
        Text = "Owner-Draw Buttons"
        ResizeRedraw = True

        cxImage = 4 * Font.Height
        cyImage = 4 * Font.Height
        cxBtn = cxImage + 8
        cyBtn = cyImage + 8
        dxBtn = Font.Height

        btnLarger = New Button()
        btnLarger.Parent = Me
        btnLarger.Size = New Size(cxBtn, cyBtn)
        AddHandler btnLarger.Click, AddressOf ButtonLargerOnClick
        AddHandler btnLarger.Paint, AddressOf ButtonOnPaint

        btnSmaller = New Button()
        btnSmaller.Parent = Me
        btnSmaller.Size = New Size(cxBtn, cyBtn)
        AddHandler btnSmaller.Click, AddressOf ButtonSmallerOnClick
        AddHandler btnSmaller.Paint, AddressOf ButtonOnPaint

        OnResize(EventArgs.Empty)
    End Sub

    Protected Overrides Sub OnResize(ByVal ea As EventArgs)
        MyBase.OnResize(ea)
        btnLarger.Location = _
                New Point(ClientSize.Width \ 2 - cxBtn - dxBtn \ 2, _
                        (ClientSize.Height - cyBtn) \ 2)
        btnSmaller.Location = _
                New Point(ClientSize.Width \ 2 + dxBtn \ 2, _
                        (ClientSize.Height - cyBtn) \ 2)
    End Sub
```

```
Private Sub ButtonLargerOnClick(ByVal obj As Object, _
                                ByVal ea As EventArgs)
    Left -= CInt(0.05 * Width)
    Top -= CInt(0.05 * Height)
    Width += CInt(0.1 * Width)
    Height += CInt(0.1 * Height)
End Sub

Private Sub ButtonSmallerOnClick(ByVal obj As Object, _
                                 ByVal ea As EventArgs)
    Left += CInt(Width / 22)
    Top += CInt(Height / 22)
    Width -= CInt(Width / 11)
    Height -= CInt(Height / 11)
End Sub

Private Sub ButtonOnPaint(ByVal obj As Object, _
                          ByVal pea As PaintEventArgs)
    Dim btn As Button = DirectCast(obj, Button)
    Dim grfx As Graphics = pea.Graphics
    Dim bs As ButtonState

    If btn Is DirectCast(GetChildAtPoint( _
                PointToClient(MousePosition)), Button) AndAlso _
                btn.Capture Then
        bs = ButtonState.Pushed
    Else
        bs = ButtonState.Normal
    End If

    ControlPaint.DrawButton(grfx, 0, 0, cxBtn, cyBtn, bs)

    Dim grfxstate As GraphicsState = grfx.Save()
    grfx.TranslateTransform((cxBtn - cxImage) \ 2, _
                            (cyBtn - cyImage) \ 2)

    If btn Is btnLarger Then
        DrawLargerButton(grfx, cxImage, cyImage)
    Else
        DrawSmallerButton(grfx, cxImage, cyImage)
    End If
    grfx.Restore(grfxstate)

    If btn.Focused Then
        ControlPaint.DrawFocusRectangle(grfx, _
            New Rectangle((cxBtn - cxImage) \ 2 + cxImage \ 16, _
                          (cyBtn - cyImage) \ 2 + cyImage \ 16, _
                          7 * cxImage \ 8, 7 * cyImage \ 8))
    End If
End Sub
```

*(continued)*

**OwnerDrawButtons.vb** *(continued)*

```
    Private Sub DrawLargerButton(ByVal grfx As Graphics, _
                         ByVal cx As Integer, ByVal cy As Integer)
        Dim br As New SolidBrush(btnLarger.ForeColor)
        Dim pn As New Pen(btnLarger.ForeColor)
        Dim i As Integer

        grfx.TranslateTransform(cx \ 2, cy \ 2)

        For i = 0 To 3
            grfx.DrawLine(pn, 0, 0, cx \ 4, 0)
            grfx.FillPolygon(br, New Point() { _
                             New Point(cx \ 4, -cy \ 8), _
                             New Point(cx \ 2, 0), _
                             New Point(cx \ 4, cy \ 8)})
            grfx.RotateTransform(90)
        Next i
    End Sub

    Private Sub DrawSmallerButton(ByVal grfx As Graphics, _
                         ByVal cx As Integer, ByVal cy As Integer)
        Dim br As New SolidBrush(btnSmaller.ForeColor)
        Dim pn As New Pen(btnSmaller.ForeColor)
        Dim i As Integer

        grfx.TranslateTransform(cx \ 2, cy \ 2)

        For i = 0 To 3
            grfx.DrawLine(pn, 3 * cx \ 8, 0, cx \ 2, 0)
            grfx.FillPolygon(br, New Point() { _
                             New Point(3 * cx \ 8, -cy \ 8), _
                             New Point(cx \ 8, 0), _
                             New Point(3 * cx \ 8, cy \ 8)})
            grfx.RotateTransform(90)
        Next i
    End Sub
End Class
```

For both buttons, I install a *Paint* event handler named *ButtonOnPaint*. The event handler begins drawing by calling *DrawButton*. That long *If* statement preceding the method call determines whether the flag passed as the last argument to the method should be *ButtonState.Normal* or *ButtonState.Pushed*. If you examine a normal push button, you'll find that the button switches to a pushed appearance when you press the mouse button over the button. The push button retains that appearance until you release the mouse button or you move the mouse cursor away from the button. If you move the mouse cursor back over the push button with the mouse button still pressed, the push button changes back to the pressed state. The logic I chose checks that the button's

*Capture* property is *True* and that the mouse cursor position is over the control. It works!

That takes care of the border around the button. The program next makes use of the *DrawLargerButton* and *DrawSmallerButton* methods to draw the interiors. Before calling these methods, however, the program calls *Translate-Transform* to shift the graphics origin to the area inside the border. I bracket the graphics transform calls with calls to the *Graphics* object's *Save* and *Restore* methods so that they won't interfere with the call to *DrawFocusRectangle*.

The *DrawLargerButton* and *DrawSmallerButton* methods draw the interiors. Notice that these methods begin by setting the origin to the center of the image and then draw the same image four times, each time rotating 90 degrees. (I actually used these same two methods to create the bitmaps I used in the Bit-mapButtons program.)

The *ButtonOnPaint* processing concludes with a call to *DrawFocusRect-angle* if the button has the keyboard input focus. This method draws the standard rectangular dotted line.

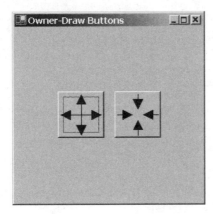

# Dropping Anchor

All the variations of the TwoButtons program shown so far have moved the two buttons to the center of the client area whenever the client area is resized. There are times when it would surely be convenient for controls to be dynamically positioned or resized depending on the size of the client area, but you'd prefer not to handle the *OnResize* code yourself. You're in luck, for Windows Forms supports two control properties that dynamically move (and even resize) controls. These properties are called *Anchor* and *Dock*:

### *Control* Properties (selection)

| Property | Type | Accessibility |
|----------|------|---------------|
| *Anchor* | *AnchorStyles* | Get/Set |
| *Dock* | *DockStyle* | Get/Set |

It's very easy to confuse these two properties! They are similar in some respects, and the *AnchorStyles* and *DockStyle* enumerations are just about identical. But the effects of the two properties are quite different. (Except when they're the same.)

Here's the *AnchorStyles* enumeration:

### *AnchorStyles* Enumeration

| Member | Value |
|--------|-------|
| *None* | &H00 |
| *Top* | &H01 |
| *Bottom* | &H02 |
| *Left* | &H04 |
| *Right* | &H08 |

Notice that the values are single bits. You can combine the *AnchorStyles* enumeration values with the Visual Basic bitwise *Or* operator.

You set the *Anchor* style for a control, not for a form. When you resize the form, the *Anchor* property determines which side or sides of the form the control remains the same distance from.

The default *Anchor* property is not *AnchorStyle.None*! The default is the value 5, which can be expressed as

```
AnchorStyles.Left Or AnchorStyles.Top
```

The default *Anchor* property means that when you resize a form, the controls remain the same distance from the left and top sides of the form, which is, of course, the behavior we normally expect.

Let's see if we can rewrite the TwoButtons program to take advantage of the *Anchor* property.

### TwoButtonsAnchor.vb

```
'-----------------------------------------------------
' TwoButtonsAnchor.vb (c) 2002 by Charles Petzold
'-----------------------------------------------------
```

```
Imports System
Imports System.Drawing
Imports System.Windows.Forms

Class TwoButtonsAnchor
    Inherits Form

    Shared Sub Main()
        Application.Run(New TwoButtonsAnchor())
    End Sub

    Sub New()
        Text = "Two Buttons with Anchor"
        ResizeRedraw = True

        Dim cxBtn As Integer = 5 * Font.Height
        Dim cyBtn As Integer = 2 * Font.Height
        Dim dxBtn As Integer = Font.Height

        Dim btn As New Button()
        btn.Parent = Me
        btn.Text = "&Larger"
        btn.Location = New Point(dxBtn, dxBtn)
        btn.Size = New Size(cxBtn, cyBtn)
        AddHandler btn.Click, AddressOf ButtonLargerOnClick

        btn = New Button()
        btn.Parent = Me
        btn.Text = "&Smaller"
        btn.Location = New Point(ClientSize.Width - cxBtn - dxBtn, _
                                 ClientSize.Height - cyBtn - dxBtn)
        btn.Size = New Size(cxBtn, cyBtn)
        btn.Anchor = AnchorStyles.Right Or AnchorStyles.Bottom
        AddHandler btn.Click, AddressOf ButtonSmallerOnClick
    End Sub

    Private Sub ButtonLargerOnClick(ByVal obj As Object, _
                                    ByVal ea As EventArgs)
        Left -= CInt(0.05 * Width)
        Top -= CInt(0.05 * Height)
        Width += CInt(0.1 * Width)
        Height += CInt(0.1 * Height)
    End Sub

    Private Sub ButtonSmallerOnClick(ByVal obj As Object, _
                                     ByVal ea As EventArgs)
        Left += CInt(Width / 22)
        Top += CInt(Height / 22)
        Width -= CInt(Width / 11)
        Height -= CInt(Height / 11)
    End Sub
End Class
```

The biggest change is that the *OnResize* method is gone. But if you ever need an *OnResize* method in a program that makes use of the *Anchor* property, be sure to call

```
MyBase.OnResize(ea)
```

or else anchoring won't work. By eliminating the *OnResize* method, I was able to make the *cxBtn*, *cyBtn*, and *dxBtn* variables local to the constructor. Also, because I use two different *Click* event handlers for the two buttons, the button objects don't have to be stored as fields either. I use the same *btn* variable for creating both buttons.

The Larger button is positioned in the upper left corner of the form, and the Smaller button is in the lower right corner of the form:

The buttons aren't flush against the edges. I use the *dxBtn* variable (equal to the font height) to specify the distance between the buttons and the side of the client area. The Larger button retains the default *Anchor* property, but the Smaller button is assigned a nondefault property:

```
btn.Anchor = AnchorStyles.Right Or AnchorStyles.Bottom
```

This means that the Smaller button will remain *dxBtn* pixels from the right and bottom sides of the client area regardless of any changes in the size of the client area. As you make the client area very small, the buttons will overlap.

I encourage you to experiment with the anchor styles. Here's what you'll find.

If the *Anchor* property contains *AnchorStyles* values indicating a pair of opposite sides, the control changes size when the form is resized. For example, if the *Anchor* property is *AnchorStyle.Top Or AnchorStyle.Bottom*, the width of the control stays the same but the height changes as you change the height of the form. That's because the same distance is maintained from the top and bottom of the control to the top and bottom of the form. If you make the form too small, it's possible for the control to be resized into nothingness.

If you set the *Anchor* property to a combination of *AnchorStyles* values for all four sides, both the width and height of the control change size as you change the size of the form.

If the *Anchor* property is set to just one *AnchorStyle* value indicating a side, for instance, *AnchorStyle.Right*, the distance between the control and the right side of the client area remains the same. As you change the height of the form, however, the control retains its approximate vertical position relative to the client area.

If you set the *Anchor* property to *AnchorStyle.None*, the control retains its approximate position in the client area relative to the size of the client area. For example, if you position a control in the center of the client area and set the *Anchor* property to *AnchorStyle.None*, as you resize the client area the control will remain the same size but will stay in the approximate center of the client area.

# Dock Around the Clock

Now for docking. Here are the *DockStyle* enumeration values:

### *DockStyle* Enumeration

| Member | Value |
|--------|-------|
| *None* | 0 |
| *Top* | 1 |
| *Bottom* | 2 |
| *Left* | 3 |
| *Right* | 4 |
| *Fill* | 5 |

The first thing you should notice is that these are not bit flags. You can't combine two or more styles. The default is *DockStyle.None*. When you set the *Dock* property to one of the four *DockStyle* values indicating a side, the control is positioned flush against the entire length of that side and will touch the two adjacent sides. For example, if you specify *DockStyle.Top*, the control will be positioned against the top of the client area and extend the full width of the client area. As you make the form wider, the control becomes wider as well.

In contrast, the process of anchoring usually doesn't cause the control to be resized. The control is resized only if the control is anchored to opposite edges and the form is resized. However, if you position a control on a particular side and make it extend the full width or height of that side, and then set the *Anchor* property with *AnchorStyles* values that combine those three sides, the effect is pretty similar to docking the control on that side.

Let's look at another version of the TwoButtons program that docks the two buttons on the top and bottom sides.

**TwoButtonsDock.vb**

```vb
'-----------------------------------------------
' TwoButtonsDock.vb (c) 2002 by Charles Petzold
'-----------------------------------------------
Imports System
Imports System.Drawing
Imports System.Windows.Forms

Class TwoButtonsDock
    Inherits Form

    Shared Sub Main()
        Application.Run(New TwoButtonsDock())
    End Sub

    Sub New()
        Text = "Two Buttons with Dock"
        ResizeRedraw = True

        Dim btn As New Button()
        btn.Parent = Me
        btn.Text = "&Larger"
        btn.Height = 2 * Font.Height
        btn.Dock = DockStyle.Top
        AddHandler btn.Click, AddressOf ButtonLargerOnClick

        btn = New Button()
        btn.Parent = Me
        btn.Text = "&Smaller"
        btn.Height = 2 * Font.Height
        btn.Dock = DockStyle.Bottom
        AddHandler btn.Click, AddressOf ButtonSmallerOnClick
    End Sub

    Private Sub ButtonLargerOnClick(ByVal obj As Object, _
                                    ByVal ea As EventArgs)
        Left -= CInt(0.05 * Width)
        Top  -= CInt(0.05 * Height)
```

```
        Width += CInt(0.1 * Width)
        Height += CInt(0.1 * Height)
    End Sub

    Private Sub ButtonSmallerOnClick(ByVal obj As Object, _
                                     ByVal ea As EventArgs)
        Left += CInt(Width / 22)
        Top += CInt(Height / 22)
        Width -= CInt(Width / 11)
        Height -= CInt(Height / 11)
    End Sub
End Class
```

This program dispenses with *cxBtn*, *cyBtn*, and *dxBtn* entirely and just sets the *Height* property of each button equal to twice the height of the default font. The *Dock* property positions the button against the specified side and makes it the width of the side:

Docking isn't often used with buttons! Docking makes much more sense with toolbars (docked at the top of the client area) and status bars (docked on the bottom of the client area), as I'll be demonstrating in Chapter 20. Docking also makes much more sense in a program visually structured like Windows Explorer, with a tree view control docked at the left of the client area, a list view control docked at the right of the client area, and a splitter control in between, as I'll demonstrate in Chapter 22.

What happens when you dock two controls on the same side? You'll probably be pleased to know that docking controls on the same side *doesn't* cause the controls to overlap one another. The controls are stacked on the edge. For example, if you use a *Dock* property of *DockStyle.Top* with both buttons in the TwoButtonsDock program, the buttons look like this:

Just offhand, it appears as if the most recently created control takes priority for actually touching the edge. In reality, the positioning is based on the *z-order*, a concept I'll explain shortly.

Then there's *DockStyle.Fill*. I used *DockStyle.Fill* in the AnalogClock program in Chapter 10 to make the clock control fill up the form's entire client area, and in the PictureBoxPlusDemo program in Chapter 11. Only one control should have its *Dock* property set to *DockStyle.Fill*. The control fills up the client area but won't overlap any other controls that have nondefault *Dock* properties set.

Keep in mind that nothing magical is happening with the *Anchor* and *Dock* properties that you couldn't do yourself during the *OnResize* method.

# Children of the Form

The *Control* class includes an important and very handy read-only property named *Controls*:

### *Control* Properties (selection)

| Property | Type | Accessibility |
|---|---|---|
| *Controls* | *Control.ControlCollection* | Get |

Although the *Controls* property is defined in the *Control* class, it is useful only in classes descended from *Control* that are parent to other controls, such as *Form*. The *Control.ControlCollection* type defined for this property might look a little peculiar, but it's only a public class named *ControlCollection* that's defined inside the *Control* class. In your programs, you don't need to refer to the name of this class. You only need to refer to the *Controls* property.

You've already seen something like this toward the end of Chapter 11. The *ImageList* class has a property named *Images* that is of type *ImageList.Image-Collection*. And in Chapter 14, you'll see that the *Menu* class has a property named *MenuItems* that is of type *Menu.MenuItemCollection*.

The *Control.ControlCollection* class implements the *IList*, *ICollection*, and *IEnumerable* interfaces (defined in the *System.Collections* namespace). The total effect is to make the *Controls* property appear to be a flexible array (similar to the *ArrayList* class I discussed toward the end of Chapter 8) to which you can add and delete members. The *Controls* property is essentially an array of all the controls that are children of the form. Here are all the properties of the *Con-trolCollection* class:

## *Control.ControlCollection* **Properties**

| Property | Type | Accessibility |
|----------|------|---------------|
| *IsReadOnly* | *Boolean* | Get |
| *Count* | *Integer* | Get |
| *()* | *Control* | Get |

Let's assume your form creates three buttons, named *btn1*, *btn2*, and *btn3*. You make these three buttons children of your form in the usual way:

```
btn1.Parent = Me
btn2.Parent = Me
btn3.Parent = Me
```

After these three statements are executed, you can obtain the number of controls that are children of the form by using the *Count* property of the form's *Controls* property. If those three buttons are the only children of the form, the expression

```
Controls.Count
```

returns 3. As the last line of the *Control.ControlCollection* properties table indicates, you can also index the *Controls* property as if it were an array. An object of type *Control* is returned. For example, the statement

```
Dim ctrl As Control = Controls(1)
```

sets the *ctrl* variable equal to the *btn2* object. If you know that the element is a push button, you can cast the return value to an object of type *Button*:

```
Dim btn As Button = DirectCast(Controls(1), Button)
```

That indexer is read-only. (The *ReadOnly* property returns *True* to indicate that fact.) You can't do something like this:

```
Controls(1) = New Button()    ' Won't work!
```

You can loop through all the child controls using *For*:

```
Dim i As Integer
For i = 0 to Controls.Count - 1
    Dim ctrl As Control = Controls(i)
    ...
Next i
```

In some cases you may find it more convenient to loop through the child controls using *For Each*:

```
Dim ctrl As Control
For Each ctrl In Controls
    ...
Next
```

Child controls get into the *Control.ControlCollection* class automatically when they are made children of the form. But you can also put controls into the collection by using one of the following two methods:

### Control.ControlCollection Methods (selection)

```
Sub Add(ByVal ctrl As Control)

Sub AddRange(ByVal() actrl As Control)
```

Just offhand, the statement

```
Controls.Add(btn1)
```

looks like we're calling a shared method named *Add* in the *Controls* class. Not so! *Controls* is a property of *Form* inherited from *Control*. The type of the property is *Control.ControlCollection*, a class that defines a method named *Add*. Calling that *Add* method is equivalent to

```
btn1.Parent = Me
```

The statement

```
Controls.AddRange(New Control() { btn1, btn2, btn3 })
```

is equivalent to the three statements earlier where I assigned the *Parent* property of the buttons. Of course, the *AddRange* statement would be a lot shorter if the three buttons were an array to begin with.

You can also remove controls from the collection:

### *Control.ControlCollection* Methods (selection)

```
Sub Remove(ByVal ctrl As Control)

Sub RemoveAt(ByVal iIndex As Integer)

Sub Clear()
```

Removing a control from the collection doesn't destroy the control. Removing a control is merely the equivalent of setting the *Parent* property of the control to *Nothing*. The *Clear* method removes all the controls from the collection.

When you remove a control from the collection, the remaining controls are reindexed to close up the indices. There won't be any skipped indices; the indices always range from 0 to 1 less than the *Count* property.

You can also obtain the index of a particular control:

### *Control.ControlCollection* Methods (selection)

```
Function Contains(ByVal ctrl As Control) As Boolean

Function GetChildIndex(ByVal ctrl As Control) As Integer

Function GetChildIndex(ByVal ctrl As Control,
               ByVal bThrowException As Boolean) As Integer
```

You may want to use the *Contains* method first to check whether the collection contains the control before calling *GetChildIndex*. If the collection doesn't contain the control, the first version of *GetChildIndex* will throw an exception. The second version won't throw an exception if *bThrowException* is set to *False*. Instead, if the control isn't part of the collection, the method returns −1.

You can also assign a control a new index:

### *Control.ControlCollection* Methods (selection)

```
Sub SetChildIndex(ByVal ctrl As Control, ByVal iNewIndex As Integer)
```

Again, the other controls are reindexed, so the indices are still consecutive, ranging from 0 to 1 less than the number of controls. If you want to give a particular control the highest index, you can specify *iNewIndex* as −1.

Why would you want to change indices in the control collection? Because the control collection indices aren't simply ways of accessing the individual controls. The indexing of the control collection is also the z-order of the controls.

# Z-Order

I've alluded before to the z-order of a group of controls that are children of the same form. The term *z-order* comes from the concept of a three-dimensional coordinate space: The *x* and *y* axes are the normal horizontal and vertical coordinates. The *z* axis is at right angles to the screen.

Most obviously, the z-order affects the appearance of overlapping controls that have the same parent. You can see z-order at work in the TwoButtons-Anchor program when you make the window small enough for the buttons to overlap. The button labeled Larger appears visually on top of the button labeled Smaller. The z-order also affects how controls are stacked when they are docked against the same edge of the form.

The z-order is established by the order in which you assign the *Parent* property of a control to the form or the order in which you add the control to the control collection. The z-order is established programmatically and can only be changed programmatically. The z-order does *not* change by the user clicking on the controls.

I often get confused about what constitutes the top and bottom of the z-order, so let me spell it out clearly here. A control at the *top* or *front* of the z-order has the following characteristics:

- It is the *first* control to be assigned its *Parent* property or to be added to the control collection.

- It is referenced by an index of 0 in the *Controls* property.

- It is visually on top of all other sibling controls. It's the control that gets the mouse events when the mouse cursor is positioned over the control, regardless of other controls that might occupy the same space.

- It is the control closest to the center of the client area when multiple controls are docked against the same edge of the container.

A control at the *bottom* or *back* of the z-order has the following characteristics:

- It is the *last* control to be assigned its *Parent* property or to be added to the control collection.

- It is referenced by an index of (*Controls.Count–1*) in the control collection.

- It is visually underneath all other sibling controls.

- If multiple controls are docked against the same edge of the container, it's the control on the edge.

Aside from the *SetChildIndex* method implemented in the *Control.ControlCollection* class, a container can also change the z-ordering of its children by calling either of the following two methods:

### *Control* Methods (selection)

| Method | Description |
| --- | --- |
| Sub BringToFront() | Elevates control to top of z-order |
| Sub SendToBack() | Puts control at bottom of z-order |

For example, if a form has three child controls, *btn1*, *btn2*, and *btn3*, and *btn1* is at the top of the z-order and *btn3* is at the bottom of the z-order, then

```
btn3.BringToFront()
```

puts *btn3* at the top of the z-order and *btn2* at the bottom. That's not the same as

```
btn1.SendToBack()
```

which puts *btn2* at the top of the z-order and *btn1* at the bottom.

## The Check Box

A second type of button is the check box. A check box consists of a small box followed by a text string. When you click the control (or press the spacebar when the control has the input focus), a check mark appears in the box. When you click the control again, the check mark disappears. Unlike the push button, the check box retains an on/off state.

These are the two crucial *CheckBox* properties:

### *CheckBox* Properties (selection)

| Property | Type | Accessibility | Description |
| --- | --- | --- | --- |
| *Checked* | *Boolean* | Get/Set | Default is *False* |
| *AutoCheck* | *Boolean* | Get/Set | Default is *True* |

The *Checked* property indicates whether or not the control is checked. You can use this property to initialize the state of the control or to obtain the state. You'll probably want to leave the *AutoCheck* property set to *True* so that the *CheckBox* control itself will toggle the state of the control as the user clicks it with the mouse.

Whenever the *Checked* property changes, the control triggers a *Checked-Changed* event.

### *CheckBox* Events (selection)

| Event | Method | Delegate | Argument |
| --- | --- | --- | --- |
| *CheckedChanged* | *OnCheckedChanged* | *EventHandler* | *EventArgs* |

The *CheckedChanged* event occurs under two conditions: when *AutoCheck* is *True* and the user clicks the *CheckBox* control, and when the program changes the *Checked* property itself, perhaps in initializing the control.

If you set *AutoCheck* to *False*, your program needs to install handlers for the control's *Click* event. The *Click* event processing will probably include the following statements to toggle the check mark:

```
Dim chkbox As CheckBox = DirectCast(obj, CheckBox)
chkbox.Checked = Not chkbox.Checked
```

Do not toggle the *Checked* property in the *CheckedChanged* event handler! Doing so will generate another *CheckedChanged* event, and another, and another... Here's a program that creates four *CheckBox* controls that let you set the bold, italic, underline, and strikeout attributes of a font.

**CheckBoxDemo.vb**

```
'-----------------------------------------------
' CheckBoxDemo.vb (c) 2002 by Charles Petzold
'-----------------------------------------------
Imports System
Imports System.Drawing
Imports System.Windows.Forms

Class CheckBoxDemo
    Inherits Form

    Shared Sub Main()
        Application.Run(New CheckBoxDemo())
    End Sub

    Sub New()
        Text = "CheckBox Demo"

        Dim achkbox(3) As CheckBox
        Dim cyText As Integer = Font.Height
        Dim cxText As Integer = cyText \ 2
        Dim astrText() As String = {"Bold", "Italic", _
                                    "Underline", "Strikeout"}
        Dim i As Integer

        For i = 0 To 3
            achkbox(i) = New CheckBox()
            achkbox(i).Text = astrText(i)
            achkbox(i).Location = New Point(2 * cxText, _
                                   (4 + 3 * i) * cyText \ 2)
            achkbox(i).Size = New Size(12 * cxText, cyText)
            AddHandler achkbox(i).CheckedChanged, _
                              AddressOf CheckBoxOnCheckedChanged
        Next i
        Controls.AddRange(achkbox)
    End Sub
```

```
        Private Sub CheckBoxOnCheckedChanged(ByVal obj As Object, _
                                    ByVal ea As EventArgs)
            Invalidate(False)
        End Sub

        Protected Overrides Sub OnPaint(ByVal pea As PaintEventArgs)
            Dim grfx As Graphics = pea.Graphics
            Dim fs As FontStyle = 0
            Dim afs() As FontStyle = {FontStyle.Bold, FontStyle.Italic, _
                               FontStyle.Underline, FontStyle.Strikeout}

            Dim i As Integer

            For i = 0 To 3
                If DirectCast(Controls(i), CheckBox).Checked Then
                    fs = fs Or afs(i)
                End If
            Next i

            Dim fnt As New Font(Font, fs)
            grfx.DrawString(Text, fnt, New SolidBrush(ForeColor), 0, 0)
        End Sub
    End Class
```

I defined an array of *CheckBox* controls just so I could have the opportunity to use the *AddRange* method of the *Controls* property! The *cyText* variable is the height of the form's (and hence the control's) *Font* property. I set the *cxText* variable to half that size to roughly approximate the average width of lowercase characters. These variables are used to set the *Location* and *Size* of each control. Although I set the height of each control to *cyText*, I use 150 percent of that value to space the controls. The width of 12 times *cxText* is sufficient for the text and the check box. Here's what the program looks like:

The processing of the *CheckedChanged* event simply invalidates the form, which generates a call to *OnPaint*. The *OnPaint* method indexes the form's

*Controls* property to obtain the *Checked* property of each of the four controls and assembles a *FontStyle* variable using that information. From there, it's a simple matter to create a new *Font* object and display some text.

Because *CheckBox* inherits from *ButtonBase*, it shares some properties with the *Button* class. The *TextAlign* property for check boxes indicates how the text is aligned within the rectangle defined by the *Size* property. The default is *ContentAlignment.MiddleLeft*, which means that the text is vertically positioned in the center of the rectangle and horizontally positioned at the left (but no farther left than the check box itself, obviously). In addition, the *CheckBox* class also has a *CheckAlign* property:

### *CheckBox* Properties (selection)

| Property | Type | Accessibility |
| --- | --- | --- |
| *CheckAlign* | *ContentAlignment* | Get/Set |

This property indicates the position of the check box within the rectangle. The default is also *ContentAlignment.MiddleLeft*.

If you'd like to put the check boxes at the right of the text, it makes sense to set both the *TextAlign* and *CheckAlign* properties to *ContentAlignment.MiddleRight* so that the text is right-justified as well. Another interesting variation is to make the height of the control about twice the font height and to set *CheckAlign* to *ContentAlignment.TopCenter* and *TextAlign* to *ContentAlignment.BottomCenter*. That horizontally centers the box above the horizontally centered text.

The *CheckBox* class includes another property that affects the appearance of the control:

### *CheckBox* Properties (selection)

| Property | Type | Accessibility |
| --- | --- | --- |
| *Appearance* | *Appearance* | Get/Set |

The *Appearance* enumeration is defined like so:

### *Appearance* Enumeration

| Member | Value |
| --- | --- |
| *Normal* | 0 |
| *Button* | 1 |

The *Button* option causes the *CheckBox* control to look like a push button, but one that retains a checked state. You'll need to increase the height of the control to accommodate the button border.

# The Three-State Alternative

Most of the time, a *CheckBox* object is an on/off, yes/no, 1/0 type control that George Boole would have approved of. But sometimes 1 bit isn't quite enough and 2 bits are way too many. For such cases, you can put the check box into a third state.

When might you need this option? Suppose you were writing a word processor, and somewhere (perhaps in a dialog box for font selection), you have a *CheckBox* control labeled Italic. If the user selects some text that isn't italic, the program should initialize the *CheckBox* control to its unchecked state. If the text *is* italic, the program initializes the *CheckBox* to its checked state. And if the text is partially italic and partially not italic? That's a good candidate for the third state. The check is drawn in the box, but it's a light gray color.

You shouldn't confuse this third state with a disabled *CheckBox* control. You would disable the *CheckBox* control if the selected text was displayed in a font that wasn't capable of the italic style.

To use a three-state *CheckBox*, you need to use the following two properties:

### *CheckBox* Properties (selection)

| Property | Type | Accessibility | Description |
| --- | --- | --- | --- |
| *ThreeState* | *Boolean* | Get/Set | Default is *False* |
| *CheckState* | *CheckState* | Get/Set | Use instead of *Checked* |

First, you set the *ThreeState* property to *True*. Then, instead of using the *Checked* property to initialize the control and to determine its current state, you use the *CheckState* property. The *CheckState* enumeration has three values:

### *CheckState* Enumeration

| Member | Value |
| --- | --- |
| *Unchecked* | 0 |
| *Checked* | 1 |
| *Indeterminate* | 2 |

If your program needs to be informed when the *CheckState* changes, don't install a handler for the *CheckedChanged* event. Install a handler for the *Check-StateChanged* event:

**CheckBox Events**

| Event | Method | Handler | Argument |
|---|---|---|---|
| *CheckStateChanged* | *OnCheckStateChanged* | *EventHandler* | *EventArgs* |

As the user clicks on a three-state *CheckBox*, the control cycles through the three states.

# The Label Control

Sometimes programmers wonder, Can I mix controls and graphics output on the same form? Yes, you can, and the CheckBoxDemo program proves it. Notice in CheckBoxDemo that the *CheckBoxOnCheckedChanged* method contains the single statement

```
Invalidate(False)
```

The *False* argument indicates that the method won't invalidate any part of the form occupied by child controls. Using the *False* argument to *Invalidate* prevents the controls from being unnecessarily redrawn.

Although you can mix controls and graphics on the same form, it's more common for programs to use additional controls to display text and other graphics.

You saw back in Chapter 4 how you can display text on a *Panel* control. A control specifically designed for the display of text is the *Label* control. The *Label* control has a fairly light ancestry:

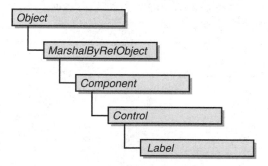

Here's another version of the CheckBoxDemo program that creates a *Label* control for displaying the sample line of text. Rather than invalidating the form in the *CheckBoxOnCheckedChanged* method and using the information to display the text in the *OnPaint* method, this version creates a new font during *CheckBoxOnCheckedChanged* and just sets the *Font* property of the *Label* control.

**CheckBoxWithLabel.vb**

```
'----------------------------------------------------
' CheckBoxWithLabel.vb (c) 2002 by Charles Petzold
'----------------------------------------------------
Imports System
Imports System.Drawing
Imports System.Windows.Forms

Class CheckBoxWithLabel
    Inherits Form

    Private lbl As Label

    Shared Sub Main()
        Application.Run(New CheckBoxWithLabel())
    End Sub

    Sub New()
        Text = "CheckBox Demo with Label"

        Dim cyText As Integer = Font.Height
        Dim cxText As Integer = cyText \ 2
        Dim astrText() As String = {"Bold", "Italic", _
                                "Underline", "Strikeout"}

        lbl = New Label()
        lbl.Parent = Me
        lbl.Text = Text & ": Sample Text"
        lbl.AutoSize = True

        Dim i As Integer
        For i = 0 To 3
            Dim chkbox As New CheckBox()
            chkbox.Parent = Me
            chkbox.Text = astrText(i)
            chkbox.Location = New Point(2 * cxText, _
                                (4 + 3 * i) * cyText \ 2)
            chkbox.Size = New Size(12 * cxText, cyText)
            AddHandler chkbox.CheckedChanged, _
                            AddressOf CheckBoxOnCheckedChanged

        Next i
    End Sub
```

**CheckBoxWithLabel.vb** *(continued)*

```
    Private Sub CheckBoxOnCheckedChanged(ByVal obj As Object, _
                                         ByVal ea As EventArgs)
        Dim fs As FontStyle = 0
        Dim afs() As FontStyle = {FontStyle.Bold, FontStyle.Italic, _
                                  FontStyle.Underline, FontStyle.Strikeout}
        Dim i As Integer

        For i = 0 To 3
            If DirectCast(Controls(i + 1), CheckBox).Checked Then
                fs = fs Or afs(i)
            End If
        Next i
        lbl.Font = New Font(lbl.Font, fs)
    End Sub
End Class
```

A *Label* control will wrap text into multiple lines if the text is longer than the width of the control. No scroll bars are provided, however. If you prefer that a *Label* control display only a single line of text, you have a few properties that help facilitate that:

### *Label* Properties (selection)

| Property | Type | Accessibility |
| --- | --- | --- |
| *PreferredWidth* | *Integer* | Get |
| *PreferredHeight* | *Integer* | Get |
| *AutoSize* | *Boolean* | Get/Set |

The *PreferredWidth* and *PreferredHeight* properties are consistent with the information returned from *MeasureString* rounded to the next highest integer. Use the *AutoSize* property (which by default is *False*) to make the label's size the same as the *PreferredWidth* and *PreferredHeight* values.

The *Label* control supports the same four properties as the *ButtonBase* control for displaying bitmaps: *Image*, *ImageList*, *ImageIndex*, and *ImageAlign*. The *AutoSize* property does *not* adjust the size of the control based on the size of the image.

Two additional properties affect the appearance of *Label* controls:

### *Label* Properties (selection)

| Property | Type | Accessibility |
|----------|------|---------------|
| BorderStyle | BorderStyle | Get/Set |
| UseMnemonic | Boolean | Get/Set |

The *BorderStyle* property causes a border to be drawn around the label. Set the property to one of the following enumeration values:

### *BorderStyle* Enumeration

| Member | Value |
|--------|-------|
| None | 0 |
| FixedSingle | 1 |
| Fixed3D | 2 |

The default is *BorderStyle.None.*

The *UseMnemonic* property (which by default is *True*) causes the *Label* control to suppress ampersands and underline the letter following the ampersand. But this raises a question: If a *Label* is used just to display some text or an image, why does it need a mnemonic? The purpose—as you'll find out later in this chapter—is to navigate to controls such as scroll bars and track bars (which have no text), and text boxes that have no fixed text.

## Tab Stops and Tab Order

As you've discovered, you can navigate among child controls by using the Tab key or the arrow keys. However, if you use Tab or the arrow keys with Check-BoxWithLabel, you'll find that the navigation skips the *Label* control. This makes sense: the *Label* control isn't intended to get input from the keyboard, so there's no reason why it should get keyboard focus.

Whether you can navigate to a control with the Tab key is governed by the *TabStop* property:

### *Control* Properties (selection)

| Property | Type | Accessibility |
|----------|------|---------------|
| TabStop | Boolean | Get/Set |
| TabIndex | Integer | Get/Set |

Buttons have a *TabStop* property of *True*; labels have a *TabStop* property of *False*.

If *TabStop* is *True*, the *TabIndex* property determines the order in which the Tab key causes focus to shift from control to control. *TabIndex* is set when you assign a parent to the control, so the *TabIndex* values initially are the same as the z-order indices. If you change the z-order, however, the *TabIndex* property doesn't change. Your program can also change the *TabIndex* independently of the z-order.

If two controls have the same *TabIndex*, the control with the lowest z-order index gets the focus first.

# Identifying the Controls

In the CheckBoxWithLabel program, I defined two arrays: one with the text strings for the four check boxes and the second containing the corresponding *FontStyle* enumeration values. Unfortunately, these arrays were defined in two different areas of the program. And if you change the order of the elements in one array without changing the other, the program will no longer work right.

Moreover, take a look at how the *Controls* property is indexed in the *OnPaint* method in the CheckBoxDemo program as compared to the *CheckBoxOnCheckedChanged* method in the CheckBoxWithLabel program. In the first program, the indices are 0 through 3. In the second program, however, the *Label* control is the first control made a child of the form, so it has an index of 0. The *CheckBox* controls are indices 1 through 4.

If I were to change the constructor in CheckBoxWithLabel so that the *Label* control is made a child of the form after the *CheckBox* controls, the program wouldn't work right. I don't have to tell you that making the *Controls* array indexing dependent on the ordering of control creation is a bad programming practice! For a few controls, it might not be so awful. But for many controls, it could easily turn into a nightmare.

There are several ways for your program to keep track of all the controls it creates. You can always save the control objects as fields, such as the TwoButtons program did. Or you could install different event handlers for each control. Another approach is to use a property (or something else) of the control to uniquely identify it. The *Text* property, of course, usually identifies the control, and in an event handler, you can even use the control text as a *Select* variable to test which control is generating the event. However, if you ever wanted to change the control text, you'd have to change both the code that assigned the control *Text* property and the *Select* and *Case* construction in the event handler.

If the *Text* property isn't quite what you want for identifying the controls, what *would* you prefer? The *Control* class includes the following two properties that you can set to help you identify the control:

### *Control* Properties (selection)

| Property | Type | Accessibility |
|----------|------|---------------|
| *Name* | *String* | Get/Set |
| *Tag* | *Object* | Get/Set |

When creating a control, you can assign the *Name* property to any convenient text that is not necessariliy related to the text displayed by the control. The *Tag* property is even more versatile because you can set it to any object. For example, here's a partial definition of a *CheckBox* control that's intended to select a color:

```
chkbox.Text = "Magenta"
chkbox.Tag = Color.Magenta
```

In the event handler, you first obtain the *CheckBox* control sending the event

```
Dim chkbox As CheckBox = DirectCast(obj, CheckBox)
```

and then cast the *Tag* property to a *Color* object:

```
Dim clr As Color = DirectCast(chkbox.Tag, Color)
```

If the *Tag* property is not a *Color* object, an exception will be raised. I'll have an example of the *Tag* property in the AutoScaleDemo program coming up shortly.

What's also nice about object-oriented programming in general (and Windows Forms in particular) is that you can easily add anything you want to the control to identify it. It's simply a matter of inheritance.

The following program creates a new class based on *CheckBox* that is specifically intended for displaying font styles. This new class adds just one field to the *CheckBox* class: a field named *fntstyle* of type *FontStyle*. As you can see, the definition of this new class (down at the bottom of the listing) requires a minimum amount of code.

### CustomCheckBox.vb

```
'-------------------------------------------------
' CustomCheckBox.vb (c) 2002 by Charles Petzold
'-------------------------------------------------
Imports System
Imports System.Drawing
Imports System.Windows.Forms
```

*(continued)*

**CustomCheckBox.vb** *(continued)*

```
Class CustomCheckBox
    Inherits Form

    Shared Sub Main()
        Application.Run(New CustomCheckBox())
    End Sub

    Sub New()
        Text = "Custom CheckBox Demo"

        Dim cyText As Integer = Font.Height
        Dim cxText As Integer = cyText \ 2
        Dim afs As FontStyle() = {FontStyle.Bold, FontStyle.Italic, _
                                  FontStyle.Underline, FontStyle.Strikeout}

        Dim lbl As New Label()
        lbl.Parent = Me
        lbl.Text = Text & ": Sample Text"
        lbl.AutoSize = True

        Dim i As Integer
        For i = 0 To 3
            Dim chkbox As New FontStyleCheckBox()
            chkbox.Parent = Me
            chkbox.Text = afs(i).ToString()
            chkbox.fntstyle = afs(i)
            chkbox.Location = New Point(2 * cxText, _
                                       (4 + 3 * i) * cyText \ 2)
            chkbox.Size = New Size(12 * cxText, cyText)
            AddHandler chkbox.CheckedChanged, _
                               AddressOf CheckBoxOnCheckedChanged
        Next i
    End Sub

    Private Sub CheckBoxOnCheckedChanged(ByVal obj As Object, _
                                         ByVal ea As EventArgs)
        Dim fs As FontStyle = 0
        Dim lbl As Label = Nothing
        Dim ctrl As Control

        For Each ctrl In Controls
            If ctrl.GetType() Is GetType(Label) Then
                lbl = DirectCast(ctrl, Label)
            ElseIf ctrl.GetType() Is GetType(FontStyleCheckBox) Then
                If DirectCast(ctrl, FontStyleCheckBox).Checked Then
                    fs = fs Or DirectCast(ctrl, FontStyleCheckBox).fntstyle
                End If
            End If
        Next
```

```
        lbl.Font = New Font(lbl.Font, fs)
    End Sub
End Class

Class FontStyleCheckBox
    Inherits CheckBox

    Public fntstyle As FontStyle
End Class
```

This program now defines the array of *FontStyle* values in the constructor. As each *FontStyleCheckBox* object is created, the program assigns the *FontStyle* value to the *fntstyle* field of the object. The program also dispenses with the *String* array. Instead, it converts the *FontStyle* value to a string for the *Text* property. And even if an array of strings were needed, at least the two arrays would be defined side by side and could be changed (if necessary) at the same time.

Now take a look at the *CheckBoxOnCheckedChanged* method. The method uses *For Each* to loop through all the controls in the *Controls* array and determines what type of control each one is. You can use the *GetType* method with any object to obtain its type, and you can use the Visual Basic *GetType* operator with any class name to obtain its type. If the control is a *FontStyle-CheckBox*, the program casts the control to an object of that type, and if the *Checked* property is *True*, accesses its *fntstyle* field. If the control is a *Label*, the program saves the *Label* object and concludes event handling by setting its *Font* property to the new font. This is code that can withstand changes in the array of *FontStyle* values and any changes in the order in which controls are created and made children of the form.

# The Auto-Scale Option

The programs shown in this chapter have used the *Font.Height* property of the form to scale the sizes of controls that display text. For horizontal sizing, I've used one-half the font height as a generous approximation of the average character width of lowercase letters. (It's even generous for the Courier font.) Because controls inherit their parent's font, this is a perfectly acceptable method of scaling controls. If you ever want to set a different font for the form (and hence its controls), do so early in the form's constructor before obtaining the font height.

The .NET Framework offers an alternative method of scaling controls that is referred to as *auto-scale*. In support of auto-scale are the following two properties of the *Form* class:

### *Form* Properties (selection)

| Property | Type | Accessibility | Description |
|---|---|---|---|
| *AutoScale* | *Boolean* | Get/Set | Default is *True* |
| *AutoScaleBaseSize* | *Size* | Get/Set | Width and height of form's font |

The only shared method of *Form* is also connected with the auto-scale feature:

### *Form* Shared Method

```
Function GetAutoScaleSize(ByVal fnt As Font) As SizeF
```

The *AutoScaleBaseSize* property and the *GetAutoScaleSize* method are useful in themselves even if you don't use the auto-scale feature. They are the only source in Windows Forms of the average character width associated with a particular font. By default, *AutoScaleBaseSize* returns the width and height of the form's *Font* property; *GetAutoScaleSize* returns the width and height of any *Font* object. The width is an average based on lowercase letters of the Latin alphabet. The height is the same as the *Height* property of the *Font* object.

If you set your display for 96 dpi (Small Fonts), *AutoScaleBaseSize* reports that the 8-point default Windows Forms font has an average width of 5 pixels and a height of 13 pixels. For 120 dpi (Large Fonts), *AutoScaleBaseSize* reports an average width of 6 pixels and a height of 15. So if you want to be more accurate about positioning controls, use

```
cxText = AutoScaleBaseSize.Width
cyText = AutoScaleBaseSize.Height
```

I just said that *AutoScaleBaseSize* returns the width and height of the form's *Font* property. That's true. And if you set a new *Font* property for the form, *AutoScaleBaseSize* reports the width and height of the new font. That's true as well. *However*, it's true only if the form doesn't set *AutoScaleBaseSize* itself. If the form sets *AutoScaleBaseSize* (by which I mean that you the programmer write code that sets *AutoScaleBaseSize*), the property returns whatever the form set it to.

And here's the secret of auto-scale: If the form sets *AutoScaleBaseSize* itself, the width and height of all the form's child controls are scaled based on the ratio of the height and width of the form's *Font* property to the height and width of the new *AutoScaleBaseSize* property. If the form doesn't set *AutoScale-BaseSize*, these two ratios are simply equal to 1 and no scaling takes place.

Basically, the form can use whatever coordinate system and sizes it wants when setting the *Location* and *Size* properties of its child controls. The form then uses *AutoScaleBaseSize* to indicate that coordinate system. All the scaling takes place after the form's constructor has completed based on the *Font* and *AutoScaleBaseSize* properties at that time.

The auto-scale process is confusing at first, so let's take a look at some examples.

## How the Windows Forms Designer Uses Auto-Scale

I mentioned that you'll someday have to look at the code that the Visual Basic .NET Windows Forms Designer generates, and you may need to understand certain aspects of it. Well, auto-scale is a primary example.

Let me assume that your display settings are set to 96 dpi (Small Fonts). When you use the Windows Forms Designer to design a form, it generates code that contains the pixel dimensions you've used. For example, a *Button* control might have its *Size* property set like so:

```
Me.button1.Size = New System.Drawing.Size(104, 26)
```

Yes, the Windows Forms Designer is a little verbose. But that's not the point. Normally, hard-coding pixel positions and sizes of controls is just begging for trouble. You're practically guaranteeing that somebody is going to run this program on a machine set for 120 dpi (Large Fonts) or an even higher resolution, and the text in the button will be truncated. But the Windows Forms Designer also adds the following statement to the constructor:

```
Me.AutoScaleBaseSize = New System.Drawing.Size(5, 13)
```

That size is the font width and height associated with 96 dpi. What the Windows Forms Designer is essentially doing here is embedding into the code the underlying display resolution upon which all the control locations and sizes are based.

If such a program runs on another machine that has a display setting of 96 dpi, the ratios of the font width and height to the *AutoScaleBaseSize* property width and height are 1, and the control locations and sizes are used directly.

However, if the program runs on a machine with a 120 dpi (Large Fonts) setting, the font width and height are 6 and 15, respectively. When your form's constructor concludes its processing, Windows Forms scales the horizontal locations and sizes of all the controls by a factor of 6/5 (that's the average width associated with the form's *Font* property divided by *AutoScaleBaseSize.Width*). The vertical locations and sizes are scaled by a factor of 15/13, which is the height of the form's font divided by *AutoScaleBaseSize.Height*.

And that's how the Windows Forms Designer gets away with hard-coding pixel coordinates and sizes.

You can do something like this yourself. You can code all the locations and sizes of controls using values that work right for your machine and then insert a statement that sets the *AutoScaleBaseSize* property to a *Size* also appropriate for your machine. Then you'll want to check out the program with a different font size, either by changing your display settings or by setting a new *Font* property in the constructor.

However, you can also use *AutoScaleBaseSize* in more interesting ways.

## Creative *AutoScaleBaseSize* Settings

Traditionally, Windows programmers coding in C and C++ using the Win32 API or the Microsoft Foundation Class (MFC) Library define their dialog boxes in a text format known as a *dialog box template* using a special device-independent coordinate system known as *dialog box coordinates*. All $x$ coordinates are 1/4 of the average character width; $y$ coordinates are expressed in units of 1/8 of the character height. If a control's location is specified as (40, 32), for example, the control is positioned 10 average character widths from the left of the dialog box and 4 character heights from the top.

A Windows Forms program can use this same traditional dialog box coordinate system. All that's necessary to make it work is the following statement in the constructor:

```
AutoScaleBaseSize = New Size(4, 8)
```

Here's another alternative: you can even specify locations and sizes entirely in units of integral character heights and character widths. Then you only need the statement

```
AutoScaleBaseSize = New Size(1, 1)
```

You may find such a coordinate system just a bit too coarse, however. Usually at least half a character height resolution is necessary for attractively spacing controls vertically.

## Inside Auto-Scale

After the code in your form's constructor is executed, the form and all children in the form are scaled based on the form's *Font* and *AutoScaleBaseSize* properties. The actual scaling is performed by a protected method of the *Control* class named *ScaleCore*, which is called first for the form and then for all the controls that are children of the form.

You can accomplish the same scaling as auto-scale by calling one of the *Scale* methods for the form:

### *Control* Methods (selection)

```
Sub Scale(ByVal fScale As Single)
Sub Scale(ByVal xScale As Single, ByVal yScale As Single)
```

For example, if you set the *AutoScale* property to *False*, you can mimic auto-scaling by inserting the following statement at the end of the form's constructor:

```
Scale(GetAutoScaleSize(Font).Width  / AutoScaleBaseSize.Width, _
    GetAutoScaleSize(Font).Height / AutoScaleBaseSize.Height)
```

That's the width and height of the form's *Font* divided by the width and height you've specified in the *AutoScaleBaseSize* property.

If you need to rescale existing controls later on—probably because you change the *Font* property someplace other than in the constructor—you can't rely on auto-scale to do it for you. You need to call *Scale* directly. But be aware that the form and controls don't retain any previous scaling history. Once the controls are scaled following the constructor code, they have simple pixel locations and sizes. You can't call *Scale* again based on the form's *Font* and *AutoScaleBaseSize*. You'll need to calculate the scaling factors based on the size of the old font and the size of the new font.

Here's a program that creates five push buttons that let you select five different font sizes. The program's constructor uses locations and sizes based on the traditional dialog box coordinates. Auto-scaling handles the initial scaling. When you press a button, the *Click* event handler scales everything again based on the existing font and the new font.

### AutoScaleDemo.vb

```
'-------------------------------------------------
' AutoScaleDemo.vb (c) 2002 by Charles Petzold
'-------------------------------------------------
Imports System
Imports System.Drawing
Imports System.Windows.Forms

Class AutoScaleDemo
    Inherits Form

    Shared Sub Main()
        Application.Run(new AutoScaleDemo())
    End Sub
```

*(continued)*

**AutoScaleDemo.vb** *(continued)*

```
Sub New()
    Text = "Auto-Scale Demo"
    Font = new Font("Arial", 12)
    FormBorderStyle = FormBorderStyle.FixedSingle

    Dim aiPointSize() As Integer = {8, 12, 16, 24, 32}
    Dim i As Integer
    For i = 0 To aiPointSize.GetUpperBound(0)
        Dim btn As New Button()
        btn.Parent = Me
        btn.Text = "Use " & aiPointSize(i).ToString() & "-point font"
        btn.Tag = aiPointSize(i)
        btn.Location = New Point(4, 16 + 24 * i)
        btn.Size = New Size(80, 16)
        AddHandler btn.Click, AddressOf ButtonOnClick
    Next i

    ClientSize = New Size(88, 16 + 24 * aiPointSize.Length)
    AutoScaleBaseSize = New Size(4, 8)
End Sub

Protected Overrides Sub OnPaint(ByVal pea As PaintEventArgs)
    pea.Graphics.DrawString(Text, Font, new SolidBrush(ForeColor), 0, 0)
End Sub

Private Sub ButtonOnClick(ByVal obj As Object, ByVal ea As EventArgs)
    Dim btn As Button = DirectCast(obj, Button)

    Dim szfOld As SizeF = GetAutoScaleSize(Font)
    Font = New Font(Font.FontFamily, DirectCast(btn.Tag, Integer))
    Dim szfNew As SizeF = GetAutoScaleSize(Font)

    Scale(szfNew.Width / szfOld.Width, szfNew.Height / szfOld.Height)
End Sub
End Class
```

This program uses the *Tag* property of the *Button* control to store the integer point size associated with each button. During the *ButtonOnClick* method, the *Tag* property is cast to an integer for creating the font. Here's what the program looks like with the 12-point font set for the form:

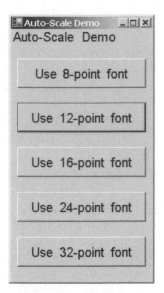

As you press each button, the entire form is resized to reflect the new font size.

If you create a control somewhere other than in your form's constructor, you may need to use *Scale*. Call the new control's *Scale* method with the sizes of the current font and the *AutoScaleBaseSize* property.

## A Hexadecimal Calculator

Here's a program that creates 29 *Button* controls to implement an infix notation hexadecimal calculator. The HexCalc program works with 64-bit *Long* integers and does addition, subtraction, multiplication, division, and remainders; bitwise *And*, *Or*, and exclusive *Or* operations; and left and right bit shifts. Here's what the program looks like:

You can use either the mouse or the keyboard with HexCalc. You begin by "clicking in" or typing the number (up to 16 hexadecimal digits), then the operation, and then the second number. You can then show the result by clicking the Equals button or by pressing either the equals (=) or the Enter key. To correct your entries, click the button labeled Back or press the Backspace key. Click the display box, or press the Esc key to clear the current entry. When you use the keyboard, some operations require typing the character associated with bit operations in the C programming language: & for *And*, | for *Or*, ^ for *Xor*, % for *Mod*, < for left shift, and > for right shift.

This is not a program I would care to put together in the Visual Basic .NET Windows Forms Designer! This many buttons of identical coordinates and sizes cry out for a more methodical approach. After a couple false starts, I decided to subclass *Button* in a class named *CalcButton*. In the *CalcButton* class, I implemented a constructor that has arguments for the button's parent, its text, its location and size, and an additional public field named *chKey* that contains the keyboard character that invokes the button. The *HexCalc* constructor contains 29 *New CalcButton* statements that create all the buttons. I use traditional dialog box coordinates for the buttons, but I call the short version of *Scale* directly to scale equally in all directions. That preserves the square appearance of most of the buttons.

## HexCalc.vb

```
'-------------------------------------------
' HexCalc.vb (c) 2002 by Charles Petzold
'-------------------------------------------
Imports System
Imports System.Drawing
Imports System.Windows.Forms

Class HexCalc
    Inherits Form

    Private btnResult As Button
    Private lNum As Long = 0
    Private lFirstNum As Long = 0
    Private bNewNumber As Boolean = True
    Private chOperation As Char = "="c

    Shared Sub Main()
        Application.Run(New HexCalc())
    End Sub

    Sub New()
        Text = "Hex Calc"
        Icon = New Icon(Me.GetType(), "HexCalc.ico")
        FormBorderStyle = FormBorderStyle.FixedSingle
        MaximizeBox = False
```

```
        Dim btn As Button
        btn = New CalcButton(Me, "D", "D"c, 8, 24, 14, 14)
        btn = New CalcButton(Me, "A", "A"c, 8, 40, 14, 14)
        btn = New CalcButton(Me, "7", "7"c, 8, 56, 14, 14)
        btn = New CalcButton(Me, "4", "4"c, 8, 72, 14, 14)
        btn = New CalcButton(Me, "1", "1"c, 8, 88, 14, 14)
        btn = New CalcButton(Me, "0", "0"c, 8, 104, 14, 14)
        btn = New CalcButton(Me, "E", "E"c, 26, 24, 14, 14)
        btn = New CalcButton(Me, "B", "B"c, 26, 40, 14, 14)
        btn = New CalcButton(Me, "8", "8"c, 26, 56, 14, 14)
        btn = New CalcButton(Me, "5", "5"c, 26, 72, 14, 14)
        btn = New CalcButton(Me, "2", "2"c, 26, 88, 14, 14)
        btn = New CalcButton(Me, "Back", Chr(8), 26, 104, 32, 14)
        btn = New CalcButton(Me, "C", "C"c, 44, 40, 14, 14)
        btn = New CalcButton(Me, "F", "F"c, 44, 24, 14, 14)
        btn = New CalcButton(Me, "9", "9"c, 44, 56, 14, 14)
        btn = New CalcButton(Me, "6", "6"c, 44, 72, 14, 14)
        btn = New CalcButton(Me, "3", "3"c, 44, 88, 14, 14)
        btn = New CalcButton(Me, "+", "+"c, 62, 24, 14, 14)
        btn = New CalcButton(Me, "-", "-"c, 62, 40, 14, 14)
        btn = New CalcButton(Me, "*", "*"c, 62, 56, 14, 14)
        btn = New CalcButton(Me, "/", "/"c, 62, 72, 14, 14)
        btn = New CalcButton(Me, "Equals", "="c, 62, 104, 46, 14)
        btn = New CalcButton(Me, "And", "&"c, 80, 24, 28, 14)
        btn = New CalcButton(Me, "Or", "|"c, 80, 40, 28, 14)
        btn = New CalcButton(Me, "Xor", "^"c, 80, 56, 28, 14)
        btn = New CalcButton(Me, "Mod", "%"c, 80, 72, 28, 14)
        btn = New CalcButton(Me, "Left", "<"c, 62, 88, 21, 14)
        btn = New CalcButton(Me, "Rt", ">"c, 87, 88, 21, 14)
        btnResult = New CalcButton(Me, "0", Chr(27), 8, 4, 100, 14)

        For Each btn In Controls
            AddHandler btn.Click, AddressOf ButtonOnClick
        Next btn

        ClientSize = New Size(116, 126)
        Scale(Font.Height / 8.0F)
    End Sub

    Protected Overrides Sub OnKeyPress(ByVal kpea As KeyPressEventArgs)
        Dim chKey As Char = Char.ToUpper(kpea.KeyChar)
        If chKey = vbCr Then chKey = "="c

        Dim ctrl As Control
        For Each ctrl In Controls
            Dim btn As CalcButton = DirectCast(ctrl, CalcButton)
            If chKey = btn.chKey Then
                InvokeOnClick(btn, EventArgs.Empty)
                Exit For
            End If
        Next
    End Sub
```

*(continued)*

**HexCalc.vb** *(continued)*

```vb
Private Sub ButtonOnClick(ByVal obj As Object, _
                          ByVal ea As EventArgs)
    Dim btn As CalcButton = DirectCast(obj, CalcButton)

    If btn.chKey = vbBack Then
        lNum \= 16

    ElseIf btn.chKey = Chr(27) Then
        lNum = 0

    ElseIf Char.IsLetterOrDigit(btn.chKey) Then
        If bNewNumber Then
            lFirstNum = lNum
            lNum = 0
            bNewNumber = False
        End If
        If lNum <= Long.MaxValue \ 16 Then
            If Char.IsDigit(btn.chKey) Then
                lNum = 16 * lNum + AscW(btn.chKey) - AscW("0")
            Else
                lNum = 16 * lNum + AscW(btn.chKey) + 10 - AscW("A")
            End If
        End If

    Else
        If Not bNewNumber Then
            Select Case chOperation
                Case "="c
                    lNum = lNum
                Case "+"c
                    lNum = lFirstNum + lNum
                Case "-"c
                    lNum = lFirstNum - lNum
                Case "*"c
                    lNum = lFirstNum * lNum
                Case "&"c
                    lNum = lFirstNum And lNum
                Case "|"c
                    lNum = lFirstNum Or lNum
                Case "^"c
                    lNum = lFirstNum Xor lNum
                Case "<"c
                    lNum = lFirstNum * CLng(2 ^ lNum)
                Case ">"c
                    lNum = lFirstNum \ CLng(2 ^ lNum)
                Case "/"c
                    If lNum <> 0 Then
                        lNum = lFirstNum \ lNum
                    Else
                        lNum = Long.MaxValue
                    End If
```

```
                    Case "%"c
                        If lNum <> 0 Then
                            lNum = lFirstNum Mod lNum
                        Else
                            lNum = Long.MaxValue
                        End If
                    Case Else
                        lNum = 0
                End Select
            End If
            bNewNumber = True
            chOperation = btn.chKey
        End If
        btnResult.Text = String.Format("{0:X}", lNum)
    End Sub
End Class

Class CalcButton
    Inherits Button

    Public chKey As Char

    Sub New(ByVal ctrlParent As Control, _
            ByVal str As String, ByVal chkey As Char, _
            ByVal x As Integer, ByVal y As Integer, _
            ByVal cx As Integer, ByVal cy As Integer)
        Parent = ctrlParent
        Text = str
        Me.chKey = chkey
        Location = New Point(x, y)
        Size = New Size(cx, cy)
        SetStyle(ControlStyles.Selectable, False)
    End Sub
End Class
```

## HexCalc.ico

The tricky part of this program was the keyboard interface. I didn't want the keys themselves to get the input focus. The dotted outline that the button draws to indicate input focus just didn't look right in this program. Shifting focus among the buttons by using the Tab key didn't make much sense either. And I had more keyboard equivalents than buttons.

To force keyboard events to the form, each button sets its *Selectable* style to *False*. This style prevents the button from obtaining the input focus.

The *OnKeyPress* method loops through the *Controls* array and finds the button corresponding to the keystroke. It then calls *InvokeOnClick* to mimic a *Click* event for the button. The *ButtonOnClick* method thus handles both button mouse clicks and keyboard equivalents.

# Radio Buttons and Group Boxes

Someday, no one will know why they're called radio buttons. You see, car radios once came equipped with a row of tall buttons that could be set to favorite radio stations. To select a station, you pushed in a button, which caused the previously pushed-in button to pop out. Because only one button could be pressed at a time, a group of radio button controls always reflects a group of mutually exclusive options.

What makes radio buttons different from other controls is that they always exist in a group. Because one (and only one) button in a group can be checked at any time, the states of the radio buttons affect each other. Turning one radio button on turns another off. The keyboard navigation is also somewhat different. Within a group of radio buttons, the arrow keys are supposed to move the input focus from button to button. As the input focus changes, the checked radio button also changes. The Tab key is supposed to move from the group of radio buttons to the next control. When you use the Tab key to move into a group of radio buttons, the checked radio button receives the input focus.

Fortunately, much of this user interface is taken care of for you. For each group of radio buttons, all you need to do is create a control of type *GroupBox* and make the *GroupBox* a child of your form. Then you make all the *RadioButton* objects in the group children of the *GroupBox*.

Let's look at the *RadioButton* class first. Like *CheckBox*, the *RadioButton* class includes properties named *Checked* and *AutoCheck*:

### *RadioButton* Properties (selection)

| Property | Type | Accessibility | Description |
|----------|------|---------------|-------------|
| Checked | Boolean | Get/Set | Default is *False* |
| AutoCheck | Boolean | Get/Set | Default is *True* |

The *Checked* property indicates whether the radio button is checked (which it visually illustrates by displaying a solid dot in a circle). Keeping the *AutoCheck* property set to *True* automates the process of using radio buttons. As the user clicks the radio buttons (or moves the input focus among the group), the radio buttons are automatically checked and unchecked. If you set *AutoCheck* to *False*, you'll have to install *Click* event handlers and do all the checking and unchecking yourself.

The only other public properties that *RadioButton* defines are *Appearance* and *CheckAlign*, which work just as they do in the *CheckBox* class.

The *CheckedChanged* event occurs whenever a radio button is checked or unchecked, either by the user or by the program:

### *RadioButton* Events (selection)

| Event | Method | Delegate | Argument |
|-------|--------|----------|----------|
| *CheckedChanged* | *OnCheckedChanged* | *EventHandler* | *EventArgs* |

You'll get two *CheckedChanged* events in a row, one for the radio button being unchecked and then one for the radio button being checked. You can tell these two events apart by looking at the *Checked* property of the button. During the *CheckedChanged* event, the *Checked* property reflects the new state.

The *GroupBox* class is a descendent of *Control* but implements only one public property (*FlatStyle*) and no additional methods or events beyond what *Control* defines.

Let's look at an example. The following program draws an ellipse based on the setting of eight radio buttons and one check box.

---

**RadioButtons.vb**

```
'------------------------------------------------
' RadioButtons.vb (c) 2002 by Charles Petzold
'------------------------------------------------
Imports System
Imports System.Drawing
Imports System.Windows.Forms

Class RadioButtons
    Inherits Form

    Private bFillEllipse As Boolean
    Private clrEllipse As Color

    Shared Sub Main()
        Application.Run(New RadioButtons())
    End Sub
```

*(continued)*

**RadioButtons.vb** *(continued)*

```vb
Sub New()
    Text = "Radio Buttons Demo"
    ResizeRedraw = True

    Dim astrColor() As String = {"Black", "Blue", "Green", "Cyan", _
                                 "Red", "Magenta", "Yellow", "White"}
    Dim grpbox As New GroupBox()
    grpbox.Parent = Me
    grpbox.Text = "Color"
    grpbox.Location = New Point(Font.Height \ 2, Font.Height \ 2)
    grpbox.Size = New Size(9 * Font.Height, _
                        (3 * astrColor.Length + 4) * Font.Height \ 2)
    Dim i As Integer
    For i = 0 To astrColor.GetUpperBound(0)
        Dim radbtn As New RadioButton()
        radbtn.Parent = grpbox
        radbtn.Text = astrColor(i)
        radbtn.Location = New Point(Font.Height, _
                                 3 * (i + 1) * Font.Height \ 2)
        radbtn.Size = New Size(7 * Font.Height, _
                            3 * Font.Height \ 2)
        AddHandler radbtn.CheckedChanged, _
                            AddressOf RadioButtonOnCheckedChanged

        If i = 0 Then
            radbtn.Checked = True
        End If
    Next i

    Dim chkbox As New CheckBox()
    chkbox.Parent = Me
    chkbox.Text = "Fill Ellipse"
    chkbox.Location = New Point(Font.Height, _
                    3 * (astrColor.Length + 2) * Font.Height \ 2)
    chkbox.Size = New Size(Font.Height * 7, 3 * Font.Height \ 2)
    AddHandler chkbox.CheckedChanged, AddressOf CheckBoxOnCheckedChanged
End Sub

Private Sub RadioButtonOnCheckedChanged(ByVal obj As Object, _
                                    ByVal ea As EventArgs)
    Dim radbtn As RadioButton = DirectCast(obj, RadioButton)

    If radbtn.Checked Then
        clrEllipse = Color.FromName(radbtn.Text)
        Invalidate(False)
    End If
End Sub

Private Sub CheckBoxOnCheckedChanged(ByVal obj As Object, _
                                ByVal ea As EventArgs)
    bFillEllipse = DirectCast(obj, CheckBox).Checked
```

```
        Invalidate(False)
    End Sub

    Protected Overrides Sub OnPaint(ByVal pea As PaintEventArgs)
        Dim grfx As Graphics = pea.Graphics
        Dim rect As New Rectangle(10 * Font.Height, 0, _
                            ClientSize.Width - 10 * Font.Height - 1, _
                            ClientSize.Height - 1)
        If bFillEllipse Then
            grfx.FillEllipse(New SolidBrush(clrEllipse), rect)
        Else
            grfx.DrawEllipse(New Pen(clrEllipse), rect)
        End If
    End Sub
End Class
```

An array of eight colors is defined toward the beginning of the constructor. All the vertical coordinates and sizes the program calculates are generalized enough to accommodate additional colors in this array, just as long as you make sure they're actual .NET Framework color names. (The width of the controls isn't sufficient to accommodate some of the longer color names, however.)

The constructor first creates a *GroupBox* control. The parent of the group box is the form. Next, the constructor creates eight radio buttons that are children of the group box. Notice at the bottom of the *For* loop that the program sets the *Checked* property of the first radio button. That statement generates a call to *RadioButtonOnCheckedChanged*, which initializes the *clrEllipse* field. The constructor concludes by creating a *CheckBox* control as a child of the form.

You can test that the keyboard interface works as I described. As you use the arrow keys to move the focus among the radio buttons, the buttons make calls to *RadioButtonOnCheckedChanged*. That method uses the shared *Color.FromName* method to convert the button text to a *Color* object. Both this method and *CheckBoxOnCheckedChanged* invalidate the client area to generate a call to *OnPaint*, which paints the ellipse:

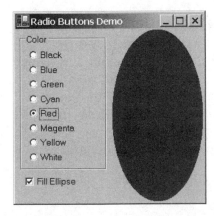

# Scroll Bars

When the subject of scroll bars first came up in Chapter 4, I discussed some of the differences between scroll bar controls and the scroll bars created as part of the auto-scroll feature in any class descended from *ScrollableControl* (including *Form* and *Panel*). With the auto-scroll feature, you specify the size of the client area you want, and the scroll bars appear automatically at the bottom and right of the client area. The auto-scroll scroll bars have no events associated with them—at least none that an application can get access to.

The *ScrollBar* class is a *MustInherit* class descended from *Control*:

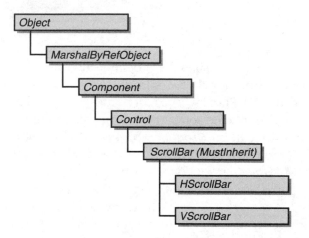

Descended from *ScrollBar* are the horizontal scroll bar (*HScrollBar*) and the vertical scroll bar (*VScrollBar*). You can position these scroll bar controls anywhere in your client area, and even make them whatever size you want. Although horizontal scroll bars have a default height and vertical scroll bars have a default width, you can indeed make very thin scroll bars or very pudgy ones. However, you can't set the background color or foreground color of scroll bars.

To keep the terminology consistent between horizontal and vertical scroll bars, let me refer to *thickness* and *length*. Thickness is the height of horizontal scroll bars and the width of vertical scroll bars. Length is the width of horizontal scroll bars and the height of vertical scroll bars. By default, newly created scroll bars have their thickness set to standard values—the same values you can obtain from *SystemInformation.VerticalScrollBarWidth* and *SystemInformation.HorizontalScrollBarHeight*.

Here are the five main properties that the *ScrollBar* class adds to *Control*:

### *ScrollBar* Properties (selection)

| Property | Type | Accessibility | Description |
|----------|------|---------------|-------------|
| *Value* | *Integer* | Get/Set | Ranges from *Minimum* to (*Maximum* + 1 - *LargeChange*) |
| *Minimum* | *Integer* | Get/Set | Default is 0 |
| *Maximum* | *Integer* | Get/Set | Default is 100 |
| *SmallChange* | *Integer* | Get/Set | Default is 1 |
| *LargeChange* | *Integer* | Get/Set | Default is 10 |

The *Value* property indicates the position of the scroll box on the scroll bar. It ranges from the *Minimum* setting to the, well, not quite *Maximum* setting. If you click the arrows at the ends of the scroll bar, the *Value* property changes by *SmallChange*. If you click on either side of the scroll box, the *Value* property changes by *LargeChange*.

Why does the *Value* range from *Minimum* to (*Maximum* + 1 − *LargeChange*)? Think of a document, perhaps a word processing document, that contains 500 lines of text. You set *Minimum* to 0 and *Maximum* to 499. Your client area is large enough to display 25 lines of text. Set *SmallChange* to 1 (that is, one line of text) and *LargeChange* to 25.

The size of the scroll box relative to the length of the scroll bar is based on the ratio of *LargeChange* to *Maximum*. That's the proportion of the document you can view.

When *Value* is 0, you view the top of the document, which comprises—assuming you're using zero-based indexing of the lines of the document—lines 0 through 24. When *Value* is 1, you view lines 1 through 25. And when *Value* is 475, you view lines 475 through 499. That's the bottom of the document, which means that *Value* doesn't need to get any higher. And that's why *Value* doesn't get higher than (*Maximum* + 1 − *LargeChange*), which in this example equals 475.

If you're not dealing with a document, you need to set *Maximum* so that you get the correct range for *Value*. I'll have an example soon.

Two events are implemented by *ScrollBar*:

### *ScrollBar* Events

| Event | Method | Handler | Argument |
|-------|--------|---------|----------|
| *ValueChanged* | *OnValueChanged* | *EventHandler* | *EventArgs* |
| *Scroll* | *OnScroll* | *ScrollEventHandler* | *ScrollEventArgs* |

The *ValueChanged* event occurs only when the *Value* property really truly changes. If the cat lies down on your keyboard, *ValueChanged* won't waste your time with a bunch of superfluous events. The *ValueChanged* event occurs not only when the user manipulates the scroll bar but also when the program sets the *Value* property. The *Scroll* event doesn't occur when the *Value* property is programmatically changed.

Moreover, the *Scroll* event gives you much more information about how the scroll bar is being manipulated. It's possible you might never need to use the *Scroll* event, but it's there if you find *ValueChanged* insufficient. The event handler for the *Scroll* event gets an object of type *ScrollEventArgs*, which has the following properties:

### *ScrollEventArgs* Properties

| Property | Type | Accessibility |
| --- | --- | --- |
| *NewValue* | *Integer* | Get/Set |
| *Type* | *ScrollEventType* | Get |

The *NewValue* property is what the scroll bar *Value* property will be set to after the event handler returns control back to the scroll bar. You can override that property by setting *NewValue* to something else. The *Type* property is of type *ScrollEventType*.

### *ScrollEventType* Enumeration

| Member | Value | Description |
| --- | --- | --- |
| *SmallDecrement* | 0 | Mouse: Left or top arrow |
| | | Keyboard: Left or Up arrow |
| *SmallIncrement* | 1 | Mouse: Right or bottom arrow |
| | | Keyboard: Right or Down arrow |
| *LargeDecrement* | 2 | Mouse: Left or top area |
| | | Keyboard: Page Up |
| *LargeIncrement* | 3 | Mouse: Right or bottom area |
| | | Keyboard: Page Down |
| *ThumbPosition* | 4 | Mouse: Button up on scroll box (thumb) |
| *ThumbTrack* | 5 | Mouse: Button down on scroll box (thumb) or move |
| *First* | 6 | Keyboard: Home |
| *Last* | 7 | Keyboard: End |
| *EndScroll* | 8 | Scrolling operation completed |

For example, suppose a scroll bar has the input focus and you press and release one of the keyboard arrow keys. Or you click with the mouse on the scroll bar arrow. You'll first get a *Scroll* event with the *Type* field set to *ScrollEventType.SmallIncrement* or *ScrollEventType.SmallDecrement*. Then you'll receive a *ValueChanged* event, followed by another *Scroll* event with the *Type* field equal to *ScrollEventType.EndScroll*. If *sb* is an object of type *ScrollBar* (with its *SmallChange* property set at the default value of 1) and *sea* is an object of type *ScrollEventArgs*, here's the sequence of events:

| Event | sb.Value | sea.Type | sea.NewValue |
| --- | --- | --- | --- |
| *Scroll* | $N$ | *SmallIncrement* | $N + 1$ |
| *ValueChanged* | $N + 1$ | | |
| *Scroll* | $N + 1$ | *EndScroll* | $N + 1$ |

If you keep the mouse button (or the arrow key) pressed, you'll get a series of events, finally terminated with an *EndScroll*:

| Event | sb.Value | sea.Type | sea.NewValue |
| --- | --- | --- | --- |
| *Scroll* | $N$ | *SmallIncrement* | $N + 1$ |
| *ValueChanged* | $N + 1$ | | |
| *Scroll* | $N + 1$ | *SmallIncrement* | $N + 2$ |
| *ValueChanged* | $N + 2$ | | |
| *Scroll* | $N + 2$ | *SmallIncrement* | $N + 3$ |
| *ValueChanged* | $N + 3$ | | |
| *Scroll* | $N + 3$ | *SmallIncrement* | $N + 4$ |
| *ValueChanged* | $N + 4$ | | |
| *Scroll* | $N + 4$ | *EndScroll* | $N + 4$ |

You won't get a *ValueChanged* event if the *Value* has reached its minimum or maximum. If you press the End key, generally you'll get the following:

| Event | sb.Value | sea.Type | sea.NewValue |
| --- | --- | --- | --- |
| *Scroll* | $N$ | *Last* | *Max* |
| *ValueChanged* | *Max* | | |
| *Scroll* | *Max* | *EndScroll* | *Max* |

The value *Max* refers to the maximum possible value, which is *sb.Maximum* $+1$ $-$*sb.LargeChange*.

However, if the scroll box is already at the end of the scroll bar, when you press the End key, you'll get the following:

| Event | sb.Value | sea.Type | sea.NewValue |
|---|---|---|---|
| Scroll | Max | Last | Max |
| Scroll | Max | EndScroll | Max |

If you grab the scroll box with the mouse and move it, you get the following sequence of events:

| Event | sb.Value | sea.Type | sea.NewValue |
|---|---|---|---|
| Scroll | N | ThumbTrack | N |
| Scroll | N | ThumbTrack | N + 1 |
| ValueChanged | N + 1 | | |
| Scroll | N + 1 | ThumbTrack | N + 2 |
| ValueChanged | N + 2 | | |
| Scroll | N + 2 | ThumbTrack | N + 3 |
| ValueChanged | N + 3 | | |
| Scroll | N + 3 | ThumbTrack | N + 4 |
| ValueChanged | N + 4 | | |
| Scroll | N + 4 | ThumbPosition | N + 4 |
| Scroll | N + 4 | EndScroll | N + 4 |

Depending on how fast you move the scroll bar, you might not get events for every possible value. And it's really how your program reacts to quick movement of the scroll box that determines whether you should install a *Scroll* handler rather than a *ValueChanged* handler. Try grabbing the scroll box with the mouse and shaking it violently. If your program can't keep up, consider the possibility of processing the *Scroll* event rather than *ValueChanged*. You can then ignore all values of *Type* except *EndScroll*, for example.

The ColorScroll program uses three scroll bars, labeled Red, Green, and Blue, that let you select a color mix. The program sets the form's background color to the resultant color you select. To keep all the scroll bars and labels visible, a white *Panel* control covers half the client area of the form. All the other controls—three scroll bars and six labels—are children of *Panel*.

## ColorScroll.vb

```
'-------------------------------------------------
' ColorScroll.vb (c) 2002 by Charles Petzold
'-------------------------------------------------
Imports System
Imports System.Drawing
Imports System.Windows.Forms

Class ColorScroll
    Inherits Form

    Private pnl As Panel
    Private alblName(2) As Label
    Private alblValue(2) As Label
    Private ascrbar(2) As VScrollBar

    Shared Sub Main()
        Application.Run(New ColorScroll())
    End Sub

    Sub New()
        Text = "Color Scroll"
        Dim aclr() As Color = {Color.Red, Color.Green, Color.Blue}

        ' Create the panel.
        pnl = New Panel()
        pnl.Parent = Me
        pnl.Location = New Point(0, 0)
        pnl.BackColor = Color.White

        ' Loop through the three colors.
        Dim i As Integer
        For i = 0 To 2
            alblName(i) = New Label()
            alblName(i).Parent = pnl
            alblName(i).ForeColor = aclr(i)
            alblName(i).Text = "&" & aclr(i).ToKnownColor().ToString()
            alblName(i).TextAlign = ContentAlignment.MiddleCenter

            ascrbar(i) = New VScrollBar()
            ascrbar(i).Parent = pnl
            ascrbar(i).SmallChange = 1
            ascrbar(i).LargeChange = 16
            ascrbar(i).Minimum = 0
            ascrbar(i).Maximum = 255 + ascrbar(i).LargeChange - 1
            AddHandler ascrbar(i).ValueChanged, _
                        AddressOf ScrollOnValueChanged
            ascrbar(i).TabStop = True
```

*(continued)*

**ColorScroll.vb**   *(continued)*

```
                alblValue(i) = New Label()
                alblValue(i).Parent = pnl
                alblValue(i).TextAlign = ContentAlignment.MiddleCenter
            Next i

            Dim clr As Color = BackColor
            ascrbar(0).Value = clr.R            ' Generates ValueChanged event.
            ascrbar(1).Value = clr.G
            ascrbar(2).Value = clr.B

            OnResize(EventArgs.Empty)
        End Sub

        Protected Overrides Sub OnResize(ByVal ea As EventArgs)
            MyBase.OnResize(ea)
            Dim cx As Integer = ClientSize.Width
            Dim cy As Integer = ClientSize.Height
            Dim cyFont As Integer = Font.Height
            Dim i As Integer

            pnl.Size = New Size(cx \ 2, cy)

            For i = 0 To 2
                alblName(i).Location = New Point(i * cx \ 6, cyFont \ 2)
                alblName(i).Size = New Size(cx \ 6, cyFont)
                ascrbar(i).Location = New Point((4 * i + 1) * cx \ 24, _
                                            2 * cyFont)
                ascrbar(i).Size = New Size(cx \ 12, cy - 4 * cyFont)
                alblValue(i).Location = New Point(i * cx \ 6, _
                                            cy - 3 * cyFont \ 2)
                alblValue(i).Size = New Size(cx \ 6, cyFont)
            Next i
        End Sub

        Private Sub ScrollOnValueChanged(ByVal obj As Object, _
                                    ByVal ea As EventArgs)
            Dim i As Integer

            For i = 0 To 2
                If obj Is ascrbar(i) Then
                    alblValue(i).Text = ascrbar(i).Value.ToString()
                End If
            Next i
            BackColor = Color.FromArgb(ascrbar(0).Value, _
                                    ascrbar(1).Value, _
                                    ascrbar(2).Value)
        End Sub
    End Class
```

The constructor creates all the controls and stores them as fields. The scroll bars must provide values from 0 through 255. Notice how I set *LargeChange* to 16 and then set the *Maximum* property to 255 plus *LargeChange* minus 1, which equals 270. The constructor doesn't position or size the controls, however. That brutal job is the responsibility of the *OnResize* method. The location and sizes are based on the size of the client area and the font height. The vertical scroll bars change width as you resize the form. (I tried to use anchoring for the effect I wanted, but I just couldn't get it to work right.) Here's a normal-size view of the program:

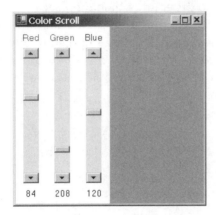

There are two sets of labels: the three Label controls stored in the *alblName* array are assigned the *Text* properties *Red*, *Green*, and *Blue*, and get their *ForeColor* properties set to the same color. I use the *aclr* array for both jobs. If you use the *ToString* method with a *Color* object, you get something like *Color [Red]*. But if the *Color* object is part of the *KnownColor* enumeration, you can convert the *Color* object to a *KnownColor* value by using the method *ToKnownColor*. The enumeration value converts to a string like *Red*.

The *TabStop* property inherited from *Control* is normally set to *False* for scroll bars. ColorScroll sets it to *True*. In addition, the Red, Green, and Blue labels are prefaced with an ampersand. Because labels are not tab stops, if they contain a letter preceded by an ampersand, the letter functions as an accelerator in setting the input to the next tab stop control. So not only can you shift the input focus among the scroll bars using the Tab key, you can also shift input focus by pressing R, G, or B.

When you move one of the scroll bars, it generates a *ValueChanged* event and a call to the program's *ScrollOnValueChanged* method. This method casts the *obj* argument to a *VScrollBar* object and then searches through the *ascrbar* array to find the match. The resultant index is used to set the corresponding *Label* control below the scroll bar that displays the value (*alblValue*). The method concludes by using the values from all three scroll bars to recompute a background color for the form.

Watch out when setting the scroll bar *Value* property from your program! The constructor for ColorScroll originally concluded with the following three statements to initialize the three scroll bars with the background color of the form:

```
ascrbar(0).Value = BackColor.R
ascrbar(1).Value = BackColor.G
ascrbar(2).Value = BackColor.B
```

However, the first statement caused a *ValueChanged* event, which performed a call to *ScrollOnValueChanged* in the program, which then set the background color based on the three scroll bar *Value* properties. But because the Green and Blue scroll bars hadn't been initialized yet, the background color effectively had its green and blue components—*BackColor.G* and *BackColor.B*—set to 0. Saving the background color first in another *Color* variable and using that variable to set the *Value* properties fixed the problem:

```
Dim clr As Color = BackColor
ascrbar(0).Value = clr.R
ascrbar(1).Value = clr.G
ascrbar(2).Value = clr.B
```

# The Track Bar Alternative

Very similar in functionality to scroll bars are track bars. From the programmer's perspective, one difference between scroll bars and track bars is that the horizontal or vertical orientation of a track bar is a property:

### *TrackBar* Properties (selection)

| Property | Type | Accessibility |
|---|---|---|
| *Orientation* | *Orientation* | Get/Set |

The *Orientation* enumeration is short and simple:

### *Orientation* Enumeration

| Member | Value |
|---|---|
| *Horizontal* | 0 |
| *Vertical* | 1 |

As you know from experimenting with the ColorScroll program, you can change the thickness of scroll bars. By default, you can't change the thickness of track bars, and the track bar is less amenable to such changes. The track bar usually needs a minimum thickness to display the tick marks, and it doesn't really use any extra thickness. If you want to experiment with changing the thickness of track bars, you must set the *AutoSize* property to *False*:

### *TrackBar* Properties (selection)

| Property | Type | Accessibility | Description |
| --- | --- | --- | --- |
| *AutoSize* | *Boolean* | Get/Set | Default is *True* |

By default, the *AutoSize* property is *True*, which means that the track bar will have a constant width (for vertical track bars) or height (for horizontal track bars) regardless of the *Size* property. The default *TabStop* property for track bars is also set to *True* (unlike scroll bars).

The *TrackBar* class has the following same properties as *ScrollBar* but with different *Maximum* and *LargeChange* defaults:

### *TrackBar* Properties (selection)

| Property | Type | Accessibility | Description |
| --- | --- | --- | --- |
| *Value* | *Integer* | Get/Set | Ranges from *Minimum* to *Maximum* |
| *Minimum* | *Integer* | Get/Set | Default is 0 |
| *Maximum* | *Integer* | Get/Set | Default is 10 |
| *SmallChange* | *Integer* | Get/Set | Default is 1 |
| *LargeChange* | *Integer* | Get/Set | Default is 5 |

The *Value* property of track bars ranges from *Minimum* to *Maximum* without any trickiness involving the *LargeChange* property. This actually makes track bars easier to use for applications like ColorScroll but harder to use for applications in which a document is scrolled.

Although vertical scroll bars have increasing values as you scroll the scroll box down, vertical track bars have increasing values as you scroll the scroll box up. Again, it's the difference between scrolling a document and selecting a value.

Two additional properties let you control tick marks on the track bar:

### *TrackBar* Properties (selection)

| Property | Type | Accessibility | Description |
| --- | --- | --- | --- |
| *TickStyle* | *TickStyle* | Get/Set | Default is *BottomRight* |
| *TickFrequency* | *Integer* | Get/Set | Default is 1 |

The *TickStyle* property lets you specify which side of the track bar contains the tick marks based on the following enumeration:

### *TickStyle* Enumeration

| Member | Value | Description |
|--------|-------|-------------|
| *None* | 0 | No tick marks |
| *TopLeft* | 1 | Tick marks on top for horizontal track bars and on left for vertical track bars |
| *BottomRight* | 2 | Tick marks on bottom for horizontal track bars and on right for vertical track bars |
| *Both* | 3 | Tick marks on both sides |

The default is *BottomRight*. If your *TickFrequency* is 1 (the default) and you set a wide range for the track bar, the tick marks may end up looking like a solid block of black.

You also have a bit more flexibility with track bars in specifying a background color or image:

### *TrackBar* Properties (selection)

| Property | Type | Accessibility |
|----------|------|---------------|
| *BackColor* | *Color* | Get/Set |
| *BackgroundImage* | *Image* | Get/Set |

The two crucial *TrackBar* events have the same names as those implemented in *ScrollBar*:

### *TrackBar* Events

| Event | Method | Delegate | Argument |
|-------|--------|----------|----------|
| *ValueChanged* | *OnValueChanged* | *EventHandler* | *EventArgs* |
| *Scroll* | *OnScroll* | *EventHandler* | *EventArgs* |

Both events are associated with normal *EventHandler* delegates. For track bars, the *Scroll* events and *ValueChanged* events always come in pairs (*Scroll* first, then *ValueChanged*) except when the *Value* property is programmatically set to a different value. In that case, a *ValueChanged* event occurs without a corresponding *Scroll* event.

Here's the ColorScroll program rewritten to use track bars.

**ColorTrackBar.vb**

```
'-----------------------------------------------
' ColorTrackBar.vb (c) 2002 by Charles Petzold
'-----------------------------------------------
Imports System
Imports System.Drawing
Imports System.Windows.Forms

Class ColorTrackBar
    Inherits Form

    Private pnl As Panel
    Private alblName(2) As Label
    Private alblValue(2) As Label
    Private atrkbar(2) As TrackBar

    Shared Sub Main()
        Application.Run(New ColorTrackBar())
    End Sub

    Sub New()
        Text = "Color Track Bar"
        Dim aclr As Color() = {Color.Red, Color.Green, Color.Blue}

        ' Create the panel.
        pnl = New Panel()
        pnl.Parent = Me
        pnl.Location = New Point(0, 0)
        pnl.BackColor = Color.White

        ' Loop through the three colors.
        Dim i As Integer
        For i = 0 To 2
            alblName(i) = New Label()
            alblName(i).Parent = pnl
            alblName(i).ForeColor = aclr(i)
            alblName(i).Text = "&" & aclr(i).ToKnownColor().ToString()
            alblName(i).TextAlign = ContentAlignment.MiddleCenter

            atrkbar(i) = New TrackBar()
            atrkbar(i).Parent = pnl
            atrkbar(i).Orientation = Orientation.Vertical
            atrkbar(i).BackColor = aclr(i)
            atrkbar(i).SmallChange = 1
            atrkbar(i).LargeChange = 16
            atrkbar(i).Minimum = 0
            atrkbar(i).Maximum = 255
            atrkbar(i).TickFrequency = 16
```

*(continued)*

**ColorTrackBar.vb**  *(continued)*

```
            AddHandler atrkbar(i).ValueChanged, _
                                AddressOf TrackBarOnValueChanged

            alblValue(i) = New Label()
            alblValue(i).Parent = pnl
            alblValue(i).TextAlign = ContentAlignment.MiddleCenter
        Next i

        Dim clr As Color = BackColor
        atrkbar(0).Value = clr.R          ' Generates ValueChanged event.
        atrkbar(1).Value = clr.G
        atrkbar(2).Value = clr.B

        OnResize(EventArgs.Empty)
    End Sub

    Protected Overrides Sub OnResize(ByVal ea As EventArgs)
        MyBase.OnResize(ea)

        Dim cx As Integer = ClientSize.Width
        Dim cy As Integer = ClientSize.Height
        Dim cyFont As Integer = Font.Height
        Dim i As Integer

        pnl.Size = New Size(cx \ 2, cy)

        For i = 0 To 2
            alblName(i).Location = New Point(i * cx \ 6, cyFont \ 2)
            alblName(i).Size = New Size(cx \ 6, cyFont)
            atrkbar(i).Height = cy - 4 * cyFont
            atrkbar(i).Location = _
                New Point( (1 + 2 * i) * cx \ 12 - atrkbar(i).Width \ 2, _
                2 * cyFont)
            alblValue(i).Location = New Point(i * cx \ 6, _
                                        cy - 3 * cyFont \ 2)
            alblValue(i).Size = New Size(cx \ 6, cyFont)
        Next i
    End Sub

    Private Sub TrackBarOnValueChanged(ByVal obj As Object, _
                                ByVal ea As EventArgs)
        Dim i As Integer
        For i = 0 To 2
            If obj Is atrkbar(i) Then
                alblValue(i).Text = atrkbar(i).Value.ToString()
            End If
        Next i
        BackColor = Color.FromArgb(atrkbar(0).Value, _
                                atrkbar(1).Value, _
                                atrkbar(2).Value)
    End Sub
End Class
```

As you can see, there aren't many differences between the two programs. The code that sets the *TrackBar* properties mostly reflects the difference between scroll bars and track bars. The ColorTrackBar program doesn't need to set the *TabStop* property, but it does need to set the *Orientation* and *TickFrequency* properties. In addition, the program takes advantage of the fact that track bars color their backgrounds by setting the *BackColor* property to red, green, or blue. The *OnResize* method is a little different as well because I decided to let the track bars retain their default width.

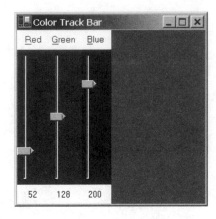

# 13

# Béziers and Other Splines

What is a spline? Even recent dictionaries define *spline* as "a flexible piece of wood, hard rubber, or metal used in drawing curves."[1] The definition conjures up a quaint image of an engineer wielding an awkward bendable contraption while hunched over a spread of graph paper attempting to fit a curve through a scattering of data points. These days a spline is more accurately described as "a curve calculated by a mathematical function that connects separate points with a high degree of smoothness.... *See also* Bézier curve."[2]

Pierre Etienne Bézier was born in Paris in 1910 into a family of engineers. He received a degree in mechanical engineering in 1930 and a second degree in electrical engineering the following year. In 1933, he began working at the French automotive company Renault, where he remained until 1975. During the 1950s, Bézier was responsible for implementing some of the first drilling and milling machines that operated under *NC*, that is, *numerical control* (a term rarely used these days).

Beginning in 1960, much of Bézier's work was centered around the UNI-SURF program, an early CAD/CAM system used at Renault for interactively designing automobile parts. What was required in such a system were mathematical definitions of complex curves that designers could manipulate without knowing about the underlying mathematics, which could then be used in manufacturing processes. From this work came the curve that now bears Bézier's name. Pierre Bézier died in 1999.[3]

---

1. *American Heritage Dictionary of the English Language*, 4th ed. (Boston: Houghton Mifflin, 2000).

2. *Microsoft Computer Dictionary*, 4th ed. (Redmond, WA: Microsoft Press, 1999).

3. Much of the biographical information is from Pierre Bézier, "Style, Mathematics and NC," *Computer-Aided Design 22*, no. 9 (November 1990): 523. Two of Bézier's books have been translated into English: Pierre Bézier, *Numerical Control: Mathematics and Applications* (London: John Wiley & Sons, 1972) and Pierre Bézier, *The Mathematical Basis of the UNISURF CAD System* (London: Butterworths, 1986). See also Pierre Bézier, "How a Simple System Was Born" in Gerald Farin, *Curves and Surfaces for Computer-Aided Geometric Design: A Practical Guide*, 4th ed. (San Diego: Academic Press, 1997).

The Bézier spline has come to assume a high degree of importance in computer graphics, ranking just under the straight line and the elliptical arc. In PostScript, the Bézier spline is used to render *all* curves—even elliptical arcs are approximated from Béziers. Bézier splines are also used to define the outlines of PostScript fonts. (TrueType uses a simpler and faster form of spline.)

# The Bézier Spline in Practice

A single Bézier spline is uniquely defined by four points, which we can call $p_0$, $p_1$, $p_2$, and $p_3$. The curve begins at $p0$ and ends at $p3$; thus, $p0$ is referred to as the *begin* point and $p3$ as the *end* point. (Collectively, $p_0$ and $p_3$ are often referred to as end points.) The points $p_1$ and $p_2$ are called *control* points. The control points function like magnets to pull the curve toward them. Here's a sample Bézier curve showing the two end points and two control points:

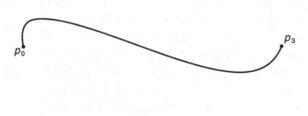

Notice how the curve begins at $p_0$ by heading toward $p_1$ but then abandons that trip and heads toward $p_2$. Not touching $p_2$ either, the curve ends at $p_3$. Here's another Bézier curve:

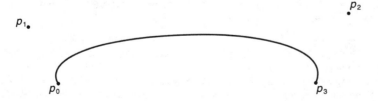

Only rarely does the Bézier curve pass through the two control points. However, if you position both control points between the end points, the Bézier curve becomes a straight line and passes through them:

At the other extreme, it's even possible to choose points that make the Bézier spline do a loop:

To draw a Bézier curve in a Windows Forms program, you need to specify the four points, either as four *Point* or *PointF* structures or as eight *Single* values:

### Graphics DrawBezier Methods

```
Sub DrawBezier(ByVal pn As Pen,
            ByVal pt0 As Point, ByVal pt1 As Point,
            ByVal pt2 As Point, ByVal pt3 As Point)

Sub DrawBezier(ByVal pn As Pen,
            ByVal ptf0 As PointF, ByVal ptf1 As PointF,
            ByVal ptf2 As PointF, ByVal ptf3 As PointF)

Sub DrawBezier(ByVal pn As Pen,
            ByVal x0 As Single, ByVal y0 As Single,
            ByVal x1 As Single, ByVal y1 As Single,
            ByVal x2 As Single, ByVal y2 As Single,
            ByVal x3 As Single, ByVal y3 As Single)
```

It's sometimes more convenient to specify these four points as an array of *Point* or *PointF* structures. The two *DrawBeziers* methods let you do that. (Notice the plural.) You can pass an array of four *Point* or *PointF* structures to the *DrawBeziers* method to draw one Bézier spline, or you can use the method to draw multiple connected Bézier splines:

### Graphics DrawBeziers Methods

```
Sub DrawBeziers(ByVal pn As Pen, ByVal apt() As Point)
Sub DrawBeziers(ByVal pn As Pen, ByVal aptf() As PointF)
```

When you draw multiple Bézier splines, the end point of each connected spline is the same as the begin point of the next spline, which means that each additional spline requires three more points. To draw $N$ Bézier curves, the number of points in the array must be equal to $3N + 1$. If the size of the array doesn't equal $3N + 1$, for $N \geq 1$, the method throws an exception.

There are no *FillBezier* or *FillBeziers* methods. If you want to use Bézier curves to fill enclosed areas, you need to use graphics paths, which I cover in Chapter 15.

You can get a good feel for the Bézier curve by experimenting with the following program.

**Bezier.vb**

```
'----------------------------------------------
' Bezier.vb (c) 2002 by Charles Petzold
'----------------------------------------------
Imports System
Imports System.Drawing
Imports System.Windows.Forms

Class Bezier
    Inherits Form

    Protected apt(3) As Point

    Shared Sub Main()
        Application.Run(New Bezier())
    End Sub

    Sub New()
        Text = "Bezier (Mouse Defines Control Points)"
        BackColor = SystemColors.Window
        ForeColor = SystemColors.WindowText
        ResizeRedraw = True

        OnResize(EventArgs.Empty)
    End Sub

    Protected Overrides Sub OnResize(ByVal ea As EventArgs)
        MyBase.OnResize(ea)

        Dim cx As Integer = ClientSize.Width
        Dim cy As Integer = ClientSize.Height

        apt(0) = New Point(cx \ 4, cy \ 2)
        apt(1) = New Point(cx \ 2, cy \ 4)
```

```
            apt(2) = New Point(cx \ 2, 3 * cy \ 4)
            apt(3) = New Point(3 * cx \ 4, cy \ 2)
        End Sub

        Protected Overrides Sub OnMouseDown(ByVal mea As MouseEventArgs)
            Dim pt As Point

            If mea.Button = MouseButtons.Left Then
                pt = apt(1)
            ElseIf mea.Button = MouseButtons.Right Then
                pt = apt(2)
            Else
                Return
            End If

            Cursor.Position = PointToScreen(pt)
        End Sub

        Protected Overrides Sub OnMouseMove(ByVal mea As MouseEventArgs)
            If mea.Button = MouseButtons.Left Then
                apt(1) = New Point(mea.X, mea.Y)
                Invalidate()
            ElseIf mea.Button = MouseButtons.Right Then
                apt(2) = New Point(mea.X, mea.Y)
                Invalidate()
            End If
        End Sub

        Protected Overrides Sub OnPaint(ByVal pea As PaintEventArgs)
            Dim grfx As Graphics = pea.Graphics
            grfx.DrawBeziers(New Pen(ForeColor), apt)

            Dim pn As New Pen(Color.FromArgb(128, ForeColor))
            grfx.DrawLine(pn, apt(0), apt(1))
            grfx.DrawLine(pn, apt(2), apt(3))
        End Sub
    End Class
```

The program fixes the two end points and lets you manipulate the two control points with the mouse. Use the left mouse button for $p_1$ and the right mouse button for $p_2$. I implemented a "snap to" feature in this program: when you press the left or right mouse button, the program uses the shared *Cursor.Position* property to move the position of the mouse cursor to the appropriate control point.

The program also draws gray lines from the end points to the control points. Here's a typical display:

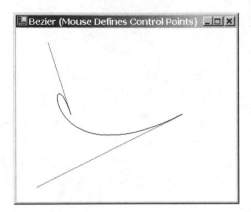

Bézier splines are useful in computer-assisted graphics design work because of several characteristics. First, with a little practice, you can usually manipulate the curve into something close to the shape you desire.

Second, the Bézier spline is very well controlled. Some splines don't pass through any of the points that define them. The Bézier spline is always anchored at the two end points. (As we'll see, this is one of the assumptions that is used to derive the Bézier formulas.) Also, some forms of splines have singularities where the curve veers off into infinity (an effect rarely desired in computer-design work). The Bézier spline is much better behaved. In fact, the Bézier spline is always bounded by a four-sided polygon (called a *convex hull*) that is formed by connecting the end points and the control points. (The way in which you connect the end points and the control points to form this convex hull depends on the particular curve.)

The third characteristic of the Bézier spline involves the relationship between the end points and the control points. At the begin point, the curve is always tangential to and in the same direction as a straight line drawn from the begin point to the first control point. (This relationship is visually illustrated in the Bezier program.) At the end point, the curve is always tangential to and in the same direction as a straight line drawn from the second control point to the end point. These are two other assumptions used to derive the Bézier formulas.

Fourth, the Bézier spline is often aesthetically pleasing. I know this is a subjective criterion, but I'm not the only person who finds the Bézier curve quite graceful.

# A More Stylish Clock

In the two decades since the dawn of analog clock programs, such programs have looked pretty much the same. Almost always the programmer uses a fairly simple polygon to draw the hands of the clock. It is now time to explore new vistas by drawing the clock hands using Bézier splines.

You'll recall that the AnalogClock program in Chapter 10 made use of a control that I implemented in a class named *ClockControl*. Fortunately, I had the foresight to isolate the clock hand-drawing code in *Protected Overridable* methods in that class. Here's a *BezierClockControl* class that makes calls to *DrawBeziers* in new *DrawHourHand* and *DrawMinuteHand* methods.

**BezierClockControl.vb**

```
'-----------------------------------------------------------
' BezierClockControl.vb (c) 2002 by Charles Petzold
'-----------------------------------------------------------
Imports System
Imports System.Drawing
Imports System.Drawing.Drawing2D
Imports System.Windows.Forms

Class BezierClockControl
    Inherits ClockControl

    Protected Overrides Sub DrawHourHand(ByVal grfx As Graphics, _
                                         ByVal pn As Pen)
        Dim gs As GraphicsState = grfx.Save()
        grfx.RotateTransform(360.0F * Time.Hour / 12 + _
                             30.0F * Time.Minute / 60)
        grfx.DrawBeziers(pn, New Point() _
            { _
            New Point(0, -600), New Point(0, -300), _
            New Point(200, -300), New Point(50, -200), _
            New Point(50, -200), New Point(50, 0), _
            New Point(50, 0), New Point(50, 75), _
            New Point(-50, 75), New Point(-50, 0), _
            New Point(-50, 0), New Point(-50, -200), _
            New Point(-50, -200), New Point(-200, -300), _
            New Point(0, -300), New Point(0, -600) _
            })
        grfx.Restore(gs)
    End Sub

    Protected Overrides Sub DrawMinuteHand(ByVal grfx As Graphics, _
                                           ByVal pn As Pen)
```

*(continued)*

**BezierClockControl.vb** *(continued)*

```
        Dim gs As GraphicsState = grfx.Save()
        grfx.RotateTransform(360.0F * Time.Minute / 60 + _
                            6.0F * Time.Second / 60)
        grfx.DrawBeziers(pn, New Point() _
            { _
            New Point(0, -800), New Point(0, -750), _
            New Point(0, -700), New Point(25, -600), _
            New Point(25, -600), New Point(25, 0), _
            New Point(25, 0), New Point(25, 50), _
            New Point(-25, 50), New Point(-25, 0), _
            New Point(-25, 0), New Point(-25, -600), _
            New Point(-25, -600), New Point(0, -700), _
            New Point(0, -750), New Point(0, -800) _
            })
        grfx.Restore(gs)
    End Sub
End Class
```

Each of the two calls to *DrawBeziers* passes an array of 16 *Point* structures to draw 5 Bézier curves. (Remember that the first Bézier curve drawn by *DrawBeziers* requires 4 points; each subsequent curve requires 3 more.)

The original AnalogClock program was so small that I decided it didn't make sense trying to subclass it. Instead, here's a brand new BezierClock program that takes advantage of the *BezierClockControl* class.

**BezierClock.vb**

```
'-------------------------------------------
' BezierClock.vb (c) 2002 by Charles Petzold
'-------------------------------------------
Imports System
Imports System.Drawing
Imports System.Windows.Forms

Class BezierClock
    Inherits Form

    Private clkctrl As BezierClockControl

    Shared Sub Main()
        Application.Run(New BezierClock())
    End Sub

    Sub New()
        Text = "Bezier Clock"

        clkctrl = New BezierClockControl()
        clkctrl.Parent = Me
        clkctrl.Time = DateTime.Now
```

```
        clkctrl.Dock = DockStyle.Fill
        clkctrl.BackColor = Color.Black
        clkctrl.ForeColor = Color.White

        Dim tmr As New Timer()
        tmr.Interval = 100
        AddHandler tmr.Tick, AddressOf OnTimerTick
        tmr.Start()
    End Sub

    Private Sub OnTimerTick(ByVal obj As Object, ByVal ea As EventArgs)
        clkctrl.Time = DateTime.Now
    End Sub
End Class
```

And here it is:

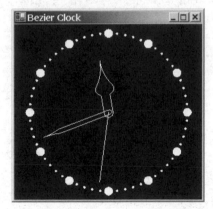

The curved tip of each hand is defined by two Bézier curves, one on each side. The straight-line portions are another pair of Bézier curves, and the rounded part at the center of the clock is another curve, for a total of five.

# Collinear Béziers

Although connected Bézier curves share end points, it's possible that the point at which one curve ends and the other begins won't be smooth. Mathematically speaking, the composite curve is considered to be smooth only if the first derivative of the curve is continuous—that is, it doesn't make any sudden changes.

When you draw multiple Bézier curves, you may want the resultant composite curve to be smooth where one curve ends and the next one begins. Then again, you may not. The hands of the clock have a combination of smoothness and discontinuity. The point at which the two Bézier curves meet at the tip of the clock hand has a discontinuous first derivative. Likewise, there's a discontinuity where the Bézier curve defining the curved part of the tip meets the straight line. However, the straight lines smoothly join the rounded part at the center of the clock.

If you want connected Bézier curves to join each other smoothly, the following three points must be collinear (that is, lie on the same line):

■ The second control point of the first Bézier

■ The end point of the first Bézier (which is the same as the begin point of the second Bézier)

■ The first control point of the second Bézier

Here's a program that draws four connected Bézier curves that are smooth at each connection. The end of the fourth Bézier curve meets the beginning of the first curve to create a closed curve.

**Infinity.vb**

```
'-------------------------------------------
' Infinity.vb (c) 2002 by Charles Petzold
'-------------------------------------------
Imports System
Imports System.Drawing
Imports System.Windows.Forms

Class Infinity
    Inherits PrintableForm

    Shared Shadows Sub Main()
        Application.Run(New Infinity())
    End Sub

    Sub New()
        Text = "Infinity Sign Using Bezier Splines"
    End Sub

    Protected Overrides Sub DoPage(ByVal grfx As Graphics, _
            ByVal clr As Color, ByVal cx As Integer, ByVal cy As Integer)
        cx -= 1
        cy -= 1

        Dim apt() As Point = _
        { _
            New Point(0, cy \ 2), _
            New Point(0, 0), _
            New Point(cx \ 3, 0), _
            New Point(cx \ 2, cy \ 2), _
```

```
            New Point(2 * cx \ 3, cy), _
            New Point(cx, cy), _
            New Point(cx, cy \ 2), _
            New Point(cx, 0), _
            New Point(2 * cx \ 3, 0), _
            New Point(cx \ 2, cy \ 2), _
            New Point(cx \ 3, cy), _
            New Point(0, cy), _
            New Point(0, cy \ 2) _
        }
        grfx.DrawBeziers(New Pen(clr), apt)
    End Sub
End Class
```

In the array, the first, fourth, seventh, tenth, and last points are end points. Each of those points is collinear with the two control points on either side. The result of these four Bézier splines is a design that somewhat resembles an infinity sign:

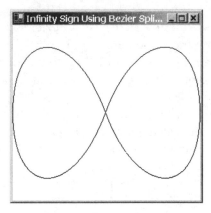

# Circles and Arcs with Béziers

Earlier in this chapter, I mentioned that PostScript uses Bézier splines to draw elliptical arcs. As you'll discover in Chapter 15, Windows Forms does so as well, at least when it comes time to store arcs and ellipses to a graphics path.

A couple of articles that describe the approximation of elliptical arcs using Bézier splines are available.[4] The first of these articles describes a fairly simple technique that you can use to draw segments of a circle. Suppose you want to

---

4. Tor Dokken, et al., "Good Approximation of Circles by Curvature-Continuous Bézier Curves," *Computer Aided Geometric Design* 7 (1990), 33–41. Michael Goldapp, "Approximation of Circular Arcs by Cubic Polynomials," *Computer Aided Geometric Design* 8 (1991), 227–238.

use a Bézier spline to draw a circular arc with a particular radius and an angular width of $\alpha$. You know that you must set $p0$ and $p3$ to the points at the beginning and the end of the arc, but how do you set $p_1$ and $p_2$? As this diagram illustrates, the problem reduces to finding the distance between the end points and control points—a single length labeled $L$:

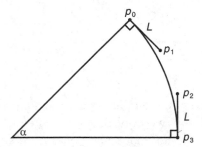

I've indicated that the lines connecting the end points with the control points are at right angles to the radii. How do we know this? Because of the collinearity requirement for smoothness. If you were to use a Bézier spline to draw another arc adjacent to this one with the same center and radius, the common end point and the two adjacent control points would need to be collinear. That means that the line from the end point to the control point is at right angles to the circle's radius.

If you know $L$, calculating the coordinates of $p_1$ and $p_2$ involves just basic trigonometry. But look how simple the calculations of $p1$ and $p2$ are when you use an angle of 90 degrees oriented with the horizontal and vertical coordinates:

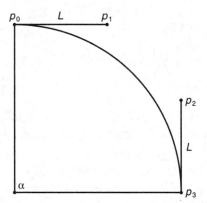

The calculation of $p_1$ and $p_2$ is also trivial when you use an angle of 180 degrees.

The first paper I cited demonstrates that a fairly good approximation results from

$$L = \frac{4}{3} \tan\left(\frac{1}{4}\alpha\right)$$

times the radius.

The BezierCircles program draws two complete circles using this approximation, first using two Bézier splines and then (more accurately) using four Bézier splines.

**BezierCircles.vb**

```
'--------------------------------------------------
' BezierCircles.vb (c) 2002 by Charles Petzold
'--------------------------------------------------
Imports System
Imports System.Drawing
Imports System.Windows.Forms

Class BezierCircles
    Inherits PrintableForm

    Shared Shadows Sub Main()
        Application.Run(New BezierCircles())
    End Sub

    Sub New()
        Text = "Bezier Circles"
    End Sub

    Protected Overrides Sub DoPage(ByVal grfx As Graphics, _
            ByVal clr As Color, ByVal cx As Integer, ByVal cy As Integer)
        Dim iRadius As Integer = Math.Min(cx - 1, cy - 1) \ 2

        ' Circle drawn normally
        grfx.DrawEllipse(New Pen(clr), _
                    cx \ 2 - iRadius, cy \ 2 - iRadius, _
                    2 * iRadius, 2 * iRadius)

        ' Two-segment (180-degree) approximation
        Dim L As Integer = CInt(iRadius * 4.0F / 3 * Math.Tan(Math.PI / 4))
        Dim apt() As Point = { _
                    New Point(cx \ 2, cy \ 2 - iRadius), _
                    New Point(cx \ 2 + L, cy \ 2 - iRadius), _
                    New Point(cx \ 2 + L, cy \ 2 + iRadius), _
                    New Point(cx \ 2, cy \ 2 + iRadius), _
```

*(continued)*

**BezierCircles.vb**  *(continued)*

```
                    New Point(cx \ 2 - L, cy \ 2 + iRadius), _
                    New Point(cx \ 2 - L, cy \ 2 - iRadius), _
                    New Point(cx \ 2, cy \ 2 - iRadius) _
                    }
        grfx.DrawBeziers(Pens.Blue, apt)

        ' Four-segment (90-degree) approximation
        L = CInt(iRadius * 4.0F / 3 * Math.Tan(Math.PI / 8))
        apt = New Point() { _
                    New Point(cx \ 2, cy \ 2 - iRadius), _
                    New Point(cx \ 2 + L, cy \ 2 - iRadius), _
                    New Point(cx \ 2 + iRadius, cy \ 2 - L), _
                    New Point(cx \ 2 + iRadius, cy \ 2), _
                    New Point(cx \ 2 + iRadius, cy \ 2 + L), _
                    New Point(cx \ 2 + L, cy \ 2 + iRadius), _
                    New Point(cx \ 2, cy \ 2 + iRadius), _
                    New Point(cx \ 2 - L, cy \ 2 + iRadius), _
                    New Point(cx \ 2 - iRadius, cy \ 2 + L), _
                    New Point(cx \ 2 - iRadius, cy \ 2), _
                    New Point(cx \ 2 - iRadius, cy \ 2 - L), _
                    New Point(cx \ 2 - L, cy \ 2 - iRadius), _
                    New Point(cx \ 2, cy \ 2 - iRadius) _
                    }
        grfx.DrawBeziers(Pens.Red, apt)
    End Sub
End Class
```

This program also visually demonstrates how the Bézier approximation differs from the *DrawEllipse* method. The program begins its *DoPage* processing by calling *DrawEllipse* to draw an ellipse in black. The two-Bézier approximation is drawn in blue, and the four-Bézier version in red. Remember that the arguments to the *Math* class trigonometric functions are in units of radians, so instead of dividing the angle by 4 as the formula for *L* indicates, I use an expression based on the *Math.PI* constant.

# Bézier Art

Many people—including Pierre Bézier[5] himself—have used Bézier splines to create interesting designs and patterns. These are generally lumped under the category of "Bézier art." There are no rules here except that a *For* loop is generally involved. Here's an example.

---

5. A sample of Pierre Bézier's artwork appears on Professor Brian Barsky's Web site at *http://www.cs.berkeley.edu/~barsky/gifs/bezier.html*.

## BezierArt.vb

```
'---------------------------------------------
' BezierArt.vb (c) 2002 by Charles Petzold
'---------------------------------------------
Imports System
Imports System.Drawing
Imports System.Windows.Forms

Class BezierArt
    Inherits PrintableForm

    Const iNum As Integer = 100

    Shared Shadows Sub Main()
        Application.Run(New BezierArt())
    End Sub

    Sub New()
        Text = "Bezier Art"
    End Sub

    Protected Overrides Sub DoPage(ByVal grfx As Graphics, _
            ByVal clr As Color, ByVal cx As Integer, ByVal cy As Integer)
        Dim pn As New Pen(clr)
        Dim aptf(3) As PointF
        Dim i As Integer

        For i = 0 To iNum - 1
            Dim rAngle As Double = 2 * i * Math.PI / iNum

            aptf(0).X = CSng(cx / 2 + cx / 2 * Math.Cos(rAngle))
            aptf(0).Y = CSng(5 * cy / 8 + cy / 16 * Math.Sin(rAngle))

            aptf(1) = New PointF(CSng(cx / 2), -cy)
            aptf(2) = New PointF(CSng(cx / 2), 2 * cy)

            rAngle += Math.PI

            aptf(3).X = CSng(cx / 2 + cx / 4 * Math.Cos(rAngle))
            aptf(3).Y = CSng(cy / 2 + cy / 16 * Math.Sin(rAngle))

            grfx.DrawBeziers(pn, aptf)
        Next i
    End Sub
End Class
```

Images that involve a lot of line or curve drawing usually look better when printed, but here's the video version of this one:

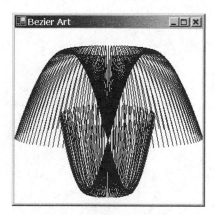

Although I'm stuck with black and white for images in this book, don't forget about color when you do your own Bézier art.

# The Mathematical Derivation

It's sometimes helpful to know the underlying formulas that a graphics system uses to render particular curves. For example, you may need to orient other graphics figures (text characters, perhaps) in relationship to a curve that the system has drawn. It's also a good exercise to *derive* the curves, if only so you don't think the formulas fell out of the sky one day.

A Bézier spline is a cubic polynomial. Like all cubic polynomials, a Bézier spline is uniquely defined by four points, which we have called $p_0$ (the begin point), $p_1$ and $p_2$ (the two control points), and $p_3$ (the end point). These four points can also be denoted as $(x_0, y_0)$, $(x_1, y_1)$, $(x_2, y_2)$, and $(x_3, y_3)$.

The general parametric form of a cubic polynomial in two dimensions is

$$x(t) = a_x \cdot t^3 + b_x \cdot t^2 + c_x \cdot t + d_x$$
$$y(t) = a_y \cdot t^3 + b_y \cdot t^2 + c_y \cdot t + d_y$$

where $a_x$, $b_x$, $c_x$, $d_x$, $a_y$, $b_y$, $c_y$, and $d_y$ are constants, and $t$ ranges from 0 to 1. Every Bézier spline is uniquely defined by these eight constants. The constants are dependent on the four points that define the spline. The object of this exercise is to develop equations for the eight constants in terms of the four points.

The first assumption is that the Bézier spline begins at the point $(x_0, y_0)$ when $t$ equals 0:

$$x(0) = x_0$$
$$y(0) = y_0$$

Even with this simple assumption we can make some headway in deriving the constants. If you put a 0 value for $t$ in the parametric equations, you get

$$x(0) = d_x$$
$$y(0) = d_y$$

This means that two of the constants are simply the coordinates of the begin point:

$$d_x = x_0 \qquad\qquad\qquad\qquad\qquad\qquad\qquad\text{(1a)}$$
$$d_y = y_0 \qquad\qquad\qquad\qquad\qquad\qquad\qquad\text{(1b)}$$

The second assumption regarding the Bézier spline is that it ends at the point $(x_3, y_3)$ when $t$ equals 1:

$$x(1) = x_3$$
$$y(1) = y_3$$

Substituting a value of 1 for $t$ in the parametric formulas yields the following:

$$x(1) = a_x + b_x + c_x + d_x$$
$$y(1) = a_y + b_y + c_y + d_y$$

This means that the constants relate to the coordinate of the end point like so:

$$a_x + b_x + c_x + d_x = x_3 \qquad\qquad\qquad\qquad\text{(2a)}$$
$$a_y + b_y + c_y + d_y = y_3 \qquad\qquad\qquad\qquad\text{(2b)}$$

The remaining two assumptions involve the first derivatives of the parametric equations, which describe the slope of the curve. The first derivatives of the generalized parametric equations of a cubic polynomial with respect to $t$ are

$$x'(t) = 3a_x t^2 + 2b_x t + c_x$$
$$y'(t) = 3a_y t^2 + 2b_y t + c_y$$

In particular, we're interested in the slope of the curve at the two end points. At the begin point, the Bézier spline is tangential to and in the same direction as a straight line drawn from the first begin point to the first control point. That straight line would normally be defined by the parametric equations

$$x(t) = (x_1 - x_0)\, t + x_0$$
$$y(t) = (y_1 - y_0)\, t + y_0$$

for $t$ ranging from 0 to 1. However, another way of expressing this straight line would be the parametric equations

$$x(t) = 3 (x_1 - x_0) t + x_0$$
$$y(t) = 3 (y_1 - y_0) t + y_0$$

where $t$ ranges from 0 to 1/3. Why 1/3? Because the section of the Bézier spline that is tangential to and in the same direction as the straight line from $p0$ to $p1$ is roughly 1/3 of the total Bézier spline. Here are the first derivatives of these revised parametric equations:

$$x' (t) = 3 (x1 - x0)$$
$$y' (t) = 3 (y1 - y0)$$

We want these equations to represent the slope of the Bézier spline when $t$ equals 0, so

$$x' (0) = 3 (x_1 - x_0)$$
$$y' (0) = 3 (y_1 - y_0)$$

Substitute $t$ in the generalized cubic first derivatives, and you get

$$x' (0) = c_x$$
$$y' (0) = c_y$$

That means

$$c_x = 3 (x_1 - x_0) \tag{3a}$$
$$c_y = 3 (y_1 - y_0) \tag{3b}$$

The last assumption is that at the end point, the Bézier spline is tangential to and in the same direction as a straight line drawn from the second control point to the end point. In other words,

$$x' (1) = 3 (x_3 - x_2)$$
$$y' (1) = 3 (y_3 - y_2)$$

Since we know from the generalized formulas that

$$x' (1) = 3a_x + 2b_x + c_x$$
$$y' (1) = 3a_y + 2b_y + c_y$$

then

$$3a_x + 2b_x + c_x = 3 (x_3 - x_2) \tag{4a}$$
$$3a_y + 2b_y + c_y = 3 (y_3 - y_2) \tag{4b}$$

Equations 1a, 2a, 3a, and 4a provide four equations and four unknowns that let us solve for $a_x$, $b_x$, $c_x$, and $d_x$ in terms of $x_0$, $x_1$, $x_2$, and $x_3$. Go through the algebra, and you find

$$a_x = -x_0 + 3x_1 - 3x_2 + x_3$$
$$b_x = 3x_0 - 6x_1 + 3x_2$$
$$c_x = 3x_0 + 3x_1$$
$$d_x = x_0$$

Equations 1b, 2b, 3b, and 4b let us do the same for the $y$ coefficients. We can then put the constants back into the generalized cubic parametric equations:

$$x(t) = (-x_0 + 3x_1 - 3x_2 + x_3)\, t^3 + (3x_0 - 6x_1 + 3x_2)\, t^2 + (3x_0 + 3x_1)\, t + x_0$$
$$y(t) = (-y_0 + 3y_1 - 3y_2 + y_3)\, t^3 + (3y_0 - 6y_1 + 3y_2)\, t^2 + (3y_0 + 3y_1)\, t + y_0$$

We're basically done. However, it's much more common for the terms to be rearranged to yield the more elegant and easier-to-use parametric equations:

$$x(t) = (1 - t)^3\, x_0 + 3t\, (1 - t)^2\, x_1 + 3t^2\, (1 - t)\, x_2 + t^3\, x_3$$
$$y(t) = (1 - t)^3\, y_0 + 3t\, (1 - t)^2\, y_1 + 3t^2\, (1 - t)\, y_2 + t^3\, y_3$$

These equations are the customary form in which the Bézier spline is expressed.

The *BezierManual* class in the following program overrides the *Bezier* class from the Bezier program earlier in this chapter and draws a second Bézier spline—this time calculated "manually" using the parametric equations I just derived.

### BezierManual.vb

```
'------------------------------------------------
' BezierManual.vb (c) 2002 by Charles Petzold
'------------------------------------------------
Imports System
Imports System.Drawing
Imports System.Windows.Forms

Class BezierManual
    Inherits Bezier

    Shared Shadows Sub Main()
        Application.Run(New BezierManual())
    End Sub

    Sub New()
        Text = "Bezier Curve ""Manually"" Drawn"
    End Sub

    Protected Overrides Sub OnPaint(ByVal pea As PaintEventArgs)
        MyBase.OnPaint(pea)
        BezierSpline(pea.Graphics, Pens.Red, apt)
    End Sub
```

*(continued)*

**BezierManual.vb** *(continued)*

```
    Private Sub BezierSpline(ByVal grfx As Graphics, _
                        ByVal pn As Pen, ByVal apt4Pts() As Point)
        Dim apt(99) As Point
        Dim i As Integer

        For i = 0 To apt.GetUpperBound(0)
            Dim t As Single = CSng(i / apt.GetUpperBound(0))
            Dim x As Single = (1 - t) * (1 - t) * (1 - t) * apt4Pts(0).X + _
                        3 * t * (1 - t) * (1 - t) * apt4Pts(1).X + _
                        3 * t * t * (1 - t) * apt4Pts(2).X + _
                        t * t * t * apt4Pts(3).X
            Dim y As Single = (1 - t) * (1 - t) * (1 - t) * apt4Pts(0).Y + _
                        3 * t * (1 - t) * (1 - t) * apt4Pts(1).Y + _
                        3 * t * t * (1 - t) * apt4Pts(2).Y + _
                        t * t * t * apt4Pts(3).Y
            apt(i) = New Point(CInt(x), CInt(y))
        Next i
        grfx.DrawLines(pn, apt)
    End Sub
End Class
```

The *OnPaint* method in BezierManual calls the *OnPaint* method in the base class (that's the *Bezier* class) and then calls the *BezierSpline* method in its own class. The *BezierSpline* method is defined much the same way as *Draw-Beziers* except that it has a *Graphics* object as a first argument and is equipped to handle only a single Bézier spline. This method uses an array of 100 *Point* structures, calculates each *Point* based on the parametric equations I derived above, and then draws the spline as a polyline. The program draws the manually calculated Bézier spline in red, so you can compare it with the version that Windows Forms draws. It's not exact, but it never differs by more than 1 pixel.

# The Canonical Spline

The *Graphics* class includes a second type of spline called the *canonical* spline, meaning a *standard* or *normal* spline. You draw a canonical spline by using one of the *DrawCurve* methods. *DrawCurve* comes in seven different versions, but you'll probably use the following four methods most frequently:

### *Graphics DrawCurve* Methods (selection)

```
Sub DrawCurve(ByVal pn As Pen, ByVal apt() As Point)

Sub DrawCurve(ByVal pn As Pen, ByVal aptf() As PointF)
```

## *Graphics DrawCurve* **Methods (selection)**   *(continued)*

```
Sub DrawCurve(ByVal pn As Pen, ByVal apt() As Point),
        ByVal fTension As Single)

Sub DrawCurve(ByVal pn As Pen, ByVal aptf() As PointF),
        ByVal fTension As Single)
```

At least two points are required. If the array contains only two points, the *DrawCurve* method draws a straight line from the first point to the second. For three points or more, the method draws a curved line that connects all the points.

The big difference between the Bézier spline and the canonical spline is that the canonical spline passes through every point in the array. The curve between each adjacent pair of points is sometimes called a *segment* of the total curve. The shape of each segment of the curve is governed by the two points at the beginning and the end of the segment (of course) but also the other two adjacent points. For example, for an array of *Point* structures named *apt*, the shape of the segment between *apt(3)* and *apt(4)* is also affected by the points *apt(2)* and *apt(5)*. The first and last segments are affected by only three points.

The spline is also affected by the *tension*, which is an explicit argument in some of the *DrawCurve* overloads. If you think of traditional wooden or metal splines, the tension is equivalent to the stiffness of the spline. The default is 0.5. A tension of 0 results in straight lines: *DrawCurve* becomes *DrawLines*. With tensions greater than 0.5, the curve gets curvier. You can set tensions less than 0, but they often result in loops. Tensions much higher than 1 can also create loops.

Let's experiment. The following program is much like the Bezier program except that it also includes a scroll bar for setting the tension and it gives you more flexibility in moving the points around.

### CanonicalSpline.vb

```
'-----------------------------------------------------
' CanonicalSpline.vb (c) 2002 by Charles Petzold
'-----------------------------------------------------
Imports System
Imports System.Drawing
Imports System.Windows.Forms

Class CanonicalSpline
    Inherits Form

    Protected apt(3) As Point
    Protected fTension As Single = 0.5

    Shared Sub Main()
        Application.Run(New CanonicalSpline())
    End Sub
```

*(continued)*

**CanonicalSpline.vb** *(continued)*

```vb
Sub New()
    Text = "Canonical Spline"
    BackColor = SystemColors.Window
    ForeColor = SystemColors.WindowText
    ResizeRedraw = True

    Dim scrbar As New VScrollBar()
    scrbar.Parent = Me
    scrbar.Dock = DockStyle.Right
    scrbar.Minimum = -100
    scrbar.Maximum = 109
    scrbar.SmallChange = 1
    scrbar.LargeChange = 10
    scrbar.Value = CInt(10 * fTension)
    AddHandler scrbar.ValueChanged, AddressOf ScrollOnValueChanged

    OnResize(EventArgs.Empty)
End Sub

Private Sub ScrollOnValueChanged(ByVal obj As Object, _
                                 ByVal ea As EventArgs)
    Dim scrbar As ScrollBar = DirectCast(obj, ScrollBar)
    fTension = scrbar.Value / 10.0F
    Invalidate(False)
End Sub

Protected Overrides Sub OnResize(ByVal ea As EventArgs)
    MyBase.OnResize(ea)

    Dim cx As Integer = ClientSize.Width
    Dim cy As Integer = ClientSize.Height

    apt(0) = New Point(cx \ 4, cy \ 2)
    apt(1) = New Point(cx \ 2, cy \ 4)
    apt(2) = New Point(cx \ 2, 3 * cy \ 4)
    apt(3) = New Point(3 * cx \ 4, cy \ 2)
End Sub

Protected Overrides Sub OnMouseDown(ByVal mea As MouseEventArgs)
    Dim pt As Point

    If mea.Button = MouseButtons.Left Then
        If ModifierKeys = Keys.Shift Then
            pt = apt(0)
        ElseIf ModifierKeys = Keys.None Then
            pt = apt(1)
        Else
            Return
        End If
    ElseIf mea.Button = MouseButtons.Right Then
        If ModifierKeys = Keys.None Then
            pt = apt(2)
```

```
                ElseIf ModifierKeys = Keys.Shift Then
                    pt = apt(3)
                Else
                    Return
                End If
            Else
                Return
            End If

            Cursor.Position = PointToScreen(pt)
    End Sub

    Protected Overrides Sub OnMouseMove(ByVal mea As MouseEventArgs)
        Dim pt As New Point(mea.X, mea.Y)

        If mea.Button = MouseButtons.Left Then
            If ModifierKeys = Keys.Shift Then
                apt(0) = pt
            ElseIf ModifierKeys = Keys.None Then
                apt(1) = pt
            Else
                Return
            End If
        ElseIf mea.Button = MouseButtons.Right Then
            If ModifierKeys = Keys.None Then
                apt(2) = pt
            ElseIf ModifierKeys = Keys.Shift Then
                apt(3) = pt
            Else
                Return
            End If
        Else
            Return
        End If

        Invalidate()
    End Sub

    Protected Overrides Sub OnPaint(ByVal pea As PaintEventArgs)
        Dim grfx As Graphics = pea.Graphics
        Dim br As New SolidBrush(ForeColor)
        Dim i As Integer

        grfx.DrawCurve(New Pen(ForeColor), apt, fTension)
        grfx.DrawString("Tension = " & fTension.ToString(), Font, br, 0, 0)

        For i = 0 To 3
            grfx.FillEllipse(br, apt(i).X - 3, apt(i).Y - 3, 7, 7)
        Next i
    End Sub
End Class
```

As with the Bezier program, you use the left mouse button and the right mouse button to change the locations of $p1$ and $p2$. In addition, the Canonical-Spline program lets you change the locations of $p0$ and $p3$ by using the left and right mouse buttons in conjunction with the Shift key. Here's a typical display:

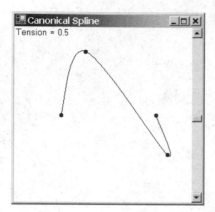

You adjust the tension with the scroll bar; the value is displayed in the upper left corner of the window. I've allowed the tension to range between –10 and 10, just so you can see for yourself how extreme values make the curve go crazy. Here's one of my favorites using the program's default setting of the *Point* array:

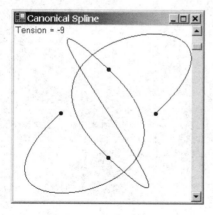

It's also possible to use a subset of the point array in the following *DrawCurve* methods:

### *Graphics DrawCurve* **Methods (selection)**

```
Sub DrawCurve(ByVal pn As Pen, ByVal aptf() As PointF),
            ByVal iOffset As Integer, ByVal iSegments As Integer)

Sub DrawCurve(ByVal pn As Pen, ByVal apt() As Point),
            ByVal iOffset As Integer, ByVal iSegments As Integer,
            ByVal fTension As Single)

Sub DrawCurve(ByVal pn As Pen, ByVal aptf() As PointF),
            ByVal iOffset As Integer, ByVal iSegments As Integer,
            ByVal fTension As Single)
```

Think of the *iOffset* argument as an index into the *Point* or *PointF* array. That's where the curve begins. The *iSegments* argument indicates the number of segments drawn and also the number of additional *Point* or *PointF* structures the method will use. For example, suppose *aptf* is an array of *PointF* structures. The call

```
grfx.DrawCurve(pen, aptf, 2, 3)
```

draws three segments, from *aptf(2)* to *aptf(3)*, from *aptf(3)* to *aptf(4)*, and from *aptf(4)* to *aptf(5)*. The visual results aren't the same as calling the simpler version of *DrawCurve* with just these four points. The versions with *iOffset* and *iSegments* use the *aptf(1)* point in determining the shape of the curve from *aptf(2)* to *apf(3)*, and the *aptf(6)* point for the curve between *aptf(4)* and *aptf(5)*.

The *DrawClosedCurve* methods connect the last point in the array to the first point in the array with an additional curve:

### *Graphics DrawClosedCurve* **Methods**

```
Sub DrawClosedCurve(ByVal pn As Pen, ByVal apt() As Point)

Sub DrawClosedCurve(ByVal pn As Pen, ByVal aptf() As PointF)

Sub DrawClosedCurve(ByVal pn As Pen, ByVal apt() As Point),
            ByVal fTension As Single, ByVal fm As FillMode)

Sub DrawClosedCurve(ByVal pn As Pen, ByVal aptf() As PointF),
            ByVal fTension As Single, ByVal fm As FillMode)
```

*DrawClosedCurve* does more than simply draw an additional segment. The first segment drawn by *DrawClosedCurve* is a little different than the segment drawn by *DrawCurve* because it is influenced by the last point in the array; similarly, the penultimate curve is influenced by the first point in the array.

Two of the *DrawClosedCurve* overloads have a *FillMode* argument. Of course you remember *FillMode*, an enumeration defined in the namespace *System.Drawing.Drawing2D* that is used in the *DrawPolygon* method to govern which enclosed areas are filled:

### *FillMode* Enumeration

| Member | Value | Comments |
|--------|-------|----------|
| *Alternate* | 0 | Default; alternates filled and unfilled areas |
| *Winding* | 1 | Most interior areas are filled |

But why—you ask—is a fill mode required in a method that simply draws lines and doesn't fill? It's a mystery, and the methods seem to work the same regardless of the *FillMode* setting.

The *FillMode* argument makes a lot more sense in the *FillClosedCurve* methods:

### Graphics *FillClosedCurve* Methods

```
Sub FillClosedCurve(ByVal br As Brush, ByVal apt As Point())

Sub FillClosedCurve(ByVal br As Brush, ByVal aptf As PointF())

Sub FillClosedCurve(ByVal br As Brush, ByVal apt As Point(),
            ByVal fm As FillMode)

Sub FillClosedCurve(ByVal br As Brush, ByVal aptf As PointF(),
            ByVal fm As FillMode)

Sub FillClosedCurve(ByVal br As Brush, ByVal apt As Point(),
            ByVal fm As FillMode, ByVal fTension As Single)

Sub FillClosedCurve(ByVal br As Brush, ByVal aptf As PointF(),
            ByVal fm As FillMode, ByVal fTension As Single)
```

The ClosedCurveFillModes program shown next is almost identical to the FillModesClassical program from Chapter 5. The program draws two five-pointed stars to illustrate the difference between *FillMode.Alternate* and *FillMode.Winding*.

### ClosedCurveFillModes.vb

```
'-----------------------------------------------------------
' ClosedCurveFillModes.vb (c) 2002 by Charles Petzold
'-----------------------------------------------------------
Imports System
Imports System.Drawing
Imports System.Drawing.Drawing2D
Imports System.Windows.Forms
```

```
Class ClosedCurveFillModes
    Inherits PrintableForm

    Shared Shadows Sub Main()
        Application.Run(New ClosedCurveFillModes())
    End Sub

    Private Sub New()
        Text = "FillClosedCurve Fill Modes"
        ClientSize = New Size(2 * ClientSize.Height, ClientSize.Height)
    End Sub

    Protected Overrides Sub DoPage(ByVal grfx As Graphics, _
            ByVal clr As Color, ByVal cx As Integer, ByVal cy As Integer)
        Dim br As New SolidBrush(clr)
        Dim apt(4) As Point
        Dim i As Integer

        For i = 0 To apt.GetUpperBound(0)
            Dim rAngle As Double = (i * 0.8 - 0.5) * Math.PI
            apt(i) = New Point( _
                        CInt(cx * (0.25 + 0.24 * Math.Cos(rAngle))), _
                        CInt(cy * (0.5 + 0.48 * Math.Sin(rAngle))))
        Next i

        grfx.FillClosedCurve(br, apt, FillMode.Alternate)

        For i = 0 To apt.GetUpperBound(0)
            apt(i).X += cx \ 2
        Next i

        grfx.FillClosedCurve(br, apt, FillMode.Winding)
    End Sub
End Class
```

While still recognizable as stars, these figures have a softer look:

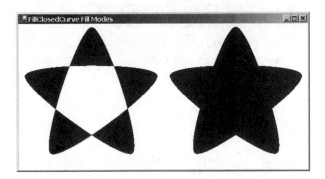

They look more like star-shaped cookies that came out of the cookie cutter with straight sides but then plumped up a little when baking.

# Canonical Curve Derivation

Like the Bézier spline, the canonical spline is a cubic, so it has the general parametric formulas

$$x(t) = a_x t^3 + b_x t^2 + c_x t + d_x$$
$$y(t) = a_y t^3 + b_y t^2 + c_y t + d_y$$

for $t$ ranging from 0 to 1. The first derivatives are

$$x'(t) = 3a_x t^2 + 2b_x t + c_x$$
$$y'(t) = 3a_y t^2 + 2b_y t + c_y$$

Let's look at four points, labeled $p_0$, $p_1$, $p_2$, and $p_3$. I'm going to develop the formulas for the segment between $p_1$ and $p_2$. That curve is based on those two points as well as the two adjoining points, $p_0$ and $p_3$. The first assumptions are that the curve begins at $p_1$ and ends at $p_2$:

$$x(0) = x_1$$
$$y(0) = y_1$$
$$x(1) = x_2$$
$$y(1) = y_2$$

From the generalized parametric formulas, we can then derive the equations

$$d_x = x_1$$
$$d_y = y_1$$
$$a_x + b_x + c_x + d_x = x_2$$
$$a_y + b_y + c_y + d_y = y_2$$

The other two assumptions govern the slope of the line at $p_1$ and $p_2$. The slope at $p_1$ is assumed to be the product of the tension (which I'll represent as $T$) and the slope of the straight line between $p_0$ and $p_2$. Similarly, the slope at $p_2$ is assumed to be the tension times the straight-line slope between $p_1$ and $p_3$:

$$x'(0) = T(x_2 - x_0)$$
$$y'(0) = T(y_2 - y_0)$$
$$x'(1) = T(x_3 - x_1)$$
$$y'(1) = T(y_3 - y_1)$$

From the first derivatives of the general parametric formulas, we find that

$$c_x = T(x_2 - x_0)$$
$$c_y = T(y_2 - y_0)$$

$$3a_x + 2b_x + c_x = T(x_3 - x_1)$$
$$3a_y + 2b_y + c_y = T(y_3 - y_1)$$

With a bit of algebra, solving the simultaneous equations yields

$$a_x = T(x_2 - x_0) + T(x_3 - x_1) + 2x_1 - 2x_2$$
$$a_y = T(y_2 - y_0) + T(y_3 - y_1) + 2y_1 - 2y_2$$
$$b_x = -2T(x_2 - x_0) - T(x_3 - x_1) - 3x_1 + 3x_2$$
$$b_y = -2T(y_2 - y_0) - T(y_3 - y_1) - 3y_1 + 3y_2$$
$$c_x = T(x_2 - x_0)$$
$$c_y = T(y_2 - y_0)$$
$$d_x = x_1$$
$$d_y = y_1$$

The CanonicalSplineManual program demonstrates that these constants are correct.

### CanonicalSplineManual.vb

```vb
'----------------------------------------------------
' CanonicalSplineManual.vb (c) 2002 by Charles Petzold
'----------------------------------------------------
Imports System
Imports System.Drawing
Imports System.Windows.Forms

Class CanonicalSplineManual
    Inherits CanonicalSpline

    Shared Shadows Sub Main()
        Application.Run(new CanonicalSplineManual())
    End Sub

    Sub New()
        Text = "Canonical Spline ""Manually"" Drawn"
    End Sub

    Protected Overrides Sub OnPaint(ByVal pea As PaintEventArgs)
        MyBase.OnPaint(pea)
        CanonicalSpline(pea.Graphics, Pens.Red, apt, fTension)
    End Sub

    Private Sub CanonicalSpline(ByVal grfx As Graphics, ByVal pn As Pen, _
            ByVal apt() As Point, ByVal fTension As Single)
        CanonicalSegment(grfx, pn, apt(0), apt(0), apt(1), apt(2), fTension)
        CanonicalSegment(grfx, pn, apt(0), apt(1), apt(2), apt(3), fTension)
```

*(continued)*

**CanonicalSplineManual.vb** *(continued)*

```
            CanonicalSegment(grfx, pn, apt(1), apt(2), apt(3), apt(3), fTension)
        End Sub

        Private Sub CanonicalSegment(ByVal grfx As Graphics, ByVal pn As Pen, _
                                ByVal pt0 As Point, ByVal pt1 As Point, _
                                ByVal pt2 As Point, ByVal pt3 As Point, _
                                ByVal fTension As Single)
            Dim apt(9) As Point

            Dim SX1 As Single = fTension * (pt2.X - pt0.X)
            Dim SY1 As Single = fTension * (pt2.Y - pt0.Y)
            Dim SX2 As Single = fTension * (pt3.X - pt1.X)
            Dim SY2 As Single = fTension * (pt3.Y - pt1.Y)
            Dim AX As Single = SX1 + SX2 + 2 * pt1.X - 2 * pt2.X
            Dim AY As Single = SY1 + SY2 + 2 * pt1.Y - 2 * pt2.Y
            Dim BX As Single = -2 * SX1 - SX2 - 3 * pt1.X + 3 * pt2.X
            Dim BY As Single = -2 * SY1 - SY2 - 3 * pt1.Y + 3 * pt2.Y
            Dim CX As Single = SX1
            Dim CY As Single = SY1
            Dim DX As Single = pt1.X
            Dim DY As Single = pt1.Y
            Dim i As Integer

            For i = 0 To apt.GetUpperBound(0)
                Dim t As Single = CSng(i / apt.GetUpperBound(0))
                apt(i).X = CInt(AX * t * t * t + BX * t * t + CX * t + DX)
                apt(i).Y = CInt(AY * t * t * t + BY * t * t + CY * t + DY)
            Next i

            grfx.DrawLines(pn, apt)
        End Sub
End Class
```

I want to point out a couple things here. The *CanonicalSpline* method only handles a four-element array and calls *CanonicalSegment* three times, each time displaying one of the three segments. The first segment and the last segment require special treatment because the curve is based on only three points rather than four.

The *CanonicalSegment* method uses an array of only 10 *Point* structures for each of the segments. That's not quite enough for a smooth curve, but it's enough to demonstrate that the method does indeed mimic the *DrawCurve* method implemented in the *Graphics* class.

I'll have some more sample programs using Bézier splines and canonical splines in Chapter 15 and Chapter 19.

# 14

# Menus

The menu is the focal point of most traditional Microsoft Windows applications. Residing just under the form's title bar, the menu essentially lists everything that the program is capable of doing—from simple operations like cut and paste to complex jobs like spelling checks. Even if an application supports a large number of function-key shortcuts, these shortcuts generally duplicate menu items.

The menus of many Windows applications look roughly similar. This consistency is an important aspect of the Windows user interface. Users learn a new program more quickly if the menu works like the menus in other Windows programs. When designing your programs' menus, you should look at existing Windows applications for hints about structure and content. This is not necessarily to say that you should perpetuate any inelegant design choices, but sometimes even an imperfect user interface can be good merely because it's consistent with other applications.

Microsoft Visual Basic .NET includes a Menu Designer that lets you interactively piece together the hierarchy of your program's menu. The Menu Designer is fairly easy to use, and it's adequate for creating simple menus. However, I can almost guarantee that someday soon you'll need to go beyond the capabilities of this Menu Designer, and you won't much like the code that it generates. For this reason, I'm going to approach menu design in this chapter strictly with code.

# Menus and Menu Items

The menu that sits between a form's title bar and the client area is referred to in Windows Forms as the form's *main menu*. Many applications also support *shortcut menus*, or *context menus*, which are menus that appear at the mouse cursor position when you right-click the mouse. A main menu is associated with a form, while a context menu is usually associated with a particular control; that is, clicking different controls often causes different context menus to be invoked.

A menu—either a main menu or a context menu—contains *menu items*. A menu item is generally associated with a word or a short phrase, such as File, Open, Save, Save As, Edit, Cut, Copy, Paste, or Select All. These are all menu items. I'll often refer to a menu item simply by the text associated with that item.

As you're undoubtedly aware, however, the File and Edit items seem quite different from Open, Save, Save As, Cut, Copy, and Select All. The File and Edit items are located on the visible part of the program's main menu; the others I mentioned are not. The items that run across the visible length of the main menu are known as *top-level* items. Selecting File or another top-level item from the main menu invokes the display of a rectangular area traditionally called a *pop-up* menu or a *drop-down* menu, but nowadays more commonly called a *submenu* or a *child* menu. (Yes, here's another parent-children relationship in Windows Forms!) The submenu invoked from the File item contains the additional menu items Open, Save, Save As, and so forth.

From the perspective of your Windows Forms program, the File menu item contains an *array* of other menu items; this array includes Open, Save, and Save As. The Edit menu item contains an array of menu items that includes Cut, Copy, and Select All.

In fact, if we step backward a moment, we can see that the main menu itself is an array of menu items—an array including File and Edit and everything else in the visible part of the main menu, probably ending with Help. Each menu item in the main menu is associated with its own array of menu items; each of these arrays represents a submenu of the main menu. Some of the menu items in these submenus also include their own arrays of menu items to invoke further nested submenus. Similarly, a context menu is an array of menu items, each of which can include additional arrays of menu items.

The *MainMenu*, *ContextMenu*, and *MenuItem* classes are all derived from the *Menu* class (defined as *MustInherit*) in the *System.Windows.Forms* namespace. Here's the class hierarchy:

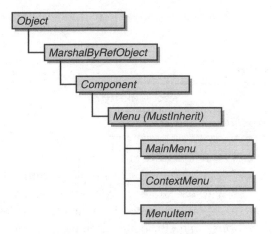

The first thing you should notice is that *Menu* isn't derived from *Control*, so such familiar properties as *BackColor*, *ForeColor*, and *Font* aren't available. Users can change the color and font of menus, but programs can't. If you want to display menus in nonstandard colors and fonts, you'll have to use the owner-draw facility I describe toward the end of this chapter.

I said that a form's main menu is an array of menu items. Here are the two constructors for *MainMenu*, the second of which clearly indicates this fact:

### *MainMenu* Constructors

```
MainMenu()

MainMenu(ByVal ami() As MenuItem)
```

To attach a particular *MainMenu* object to a form, you assign it to the form's *Menu* property:

### *Form* Properties (selection)

| Property | Type | Accessibility |
|----------|------|---------------|
| *Menu* | *MainMenu* | Get/Set |

Similarly, *ContextMenu* also has two constructors, the second of which also indicates that a context menu is an array of menu items:

### *ContextMenu* Constructors

```
ContextMenu()

ContextMenu(ByVal ami() As MenuItem)
```

The *ContextMenu* property of *Control* lets you attach a particular *ContextMenu* object to any control:

### *Control* Properties (selection)

| Property | Type | Accessibility |
|----------|------|---------------|
| *ContextMenu* | *ContextMenu* | Get/Set |

If you have a bunch of controls—or if you've divided your form into different functional areas using panels—each control can invoke a different context menu. However, it's not necessary to use the *ContextMenu* property of the control to implement context menus. You can instead "manually" invoke different context menus during the *OnMouseUp* method based on the current mouse cursor position.

Although the constructors for *MainMenu* and *ContextMenu* indicate that these objects are associated with arrays of menu items, I haven't shown you the constructors for *MenuItem* yet. Here are five of the six *MenuItem* constructors:

### *MenuItem* Constructors (selection)

```
MenuItem()

MenuItem(ByVal strText As String)

MenuItem(ByVal strText As String, ByVal ehClick As EventHandler)

MenuItem(ByVal strText As String, ByVal ehClick As EventHandler,
         ByVal sc As Shortcut)

MenuItem(ByVal strText As String, ByVal ami() As MenuItem)
```

*MenuItem* has one additional—and quite complex—constructor that merges menus.

We'll be looking at the *MenuItem* class in much detail throughout this chapter, but it won't hurt to see a couple quick examples now. For creating a top-level menu item like File, you might use the last constructor in the table:

```
New MenuItem("&File", amiFile)
```

Notice the ampersand that appears before the F in File. The ampersand indicates that the F is to be underlined and that it will be part of the built-in keyboard interface that Windows provides for menus. When the user presses the Alt key and then F, the submenu for File is displayed. Use two ampersands in a row if you want to display an ampersand in the menu text.

The *amiFile* argument to the constructor I've just shown would be an array of menu items for Open, Save, Save As, and so forth. One of the elements of this array is the menu item for Open, which could have been created using the constructor:

```
New MenuItem("&Open...", _
             AddressOf MenuFileOpenOnClick, _
             Shortcut.CtrlO)
```

Again, the ampersand indicates that the O is to be underlined. Pressing Alt, F, and then O causes the Open item to be invoked. The ellipsis indicates to the user that the menu item invokes a dialog box.

Every menu item that does *not* invoke a submenu is usually associated with a *Click* event handler that is called when the user clicks the item with the mouse or triggers it with the keyboard. I'll be using a standard naming scheme for such event handlers. In a real-life program, the *MenuFileOpenOnClick* method would be responsible for displaying the dialog box that lets the user select a file to open. (I'll be discussing dialog boxes in depth in Chapter 16.)

## Menu Shortcut Keys

I've mentioned the menu keyboard interface involving underlined letters. When the user presses the Alt key, the form goes into a special menu-selection mode. Pressing the F key displays the File submenu, and pressing O is equivalent to clicking the Open item.

Windows has an additional keyboard interface to the menu, traditionally known as *accelerators* but in Windows Forms known as *shortcuts*. You specify a shortcut by using values of the *Shortcut* enumeration. In the previous example, the value *Shortcut.CtrlO* indicates that the CTRL+O key combination is a shortcut to display a dialog box to open a file. When you use shortcuts with menu items, the text "CTRL+O" is also automatically inserted in the text of the menu item that is displayed to the user. When the user presses CTRL+O, the *MenuFileOpenOnClick* event handler is called directly, seemingly without the menu being involved. *Shortcut* is an enumeration of 150 key combinations recommended for use in menus. (It's the fourth largest enumeration in the .NET Framework.) The set shown in this first table involves the function keys, Insert, Delete, and Backspace:

### *Shortcut* Enumeration (selection)

| | | | | |
|---|---|---|---|---|
| *F1* | *ShiftF1* | *CtrlF1* | *CtrlShiftF1* | *AltF1* |
| *F2* | *ShiftF2* | *CtrlF2* | *CtrlShiftF2* | *AltF2* |
| *F3* | *ShiftF3* | *CtrlF3* | *CtrlShiftF3* | *AltF3* |
| *F4* | *ShiftF4* | *CtrlF4* | *CtrlShiftF4* | *AltF4* |

*(continued)*

### *Shortcut* Enumeration (selection)   *(continued)*

| | | | | |
|---|---|---|---|---|
| F5 | ShiftF5 | CtrlF5 | CtrlShiftF5 | AltF5 |
| F6 | ShiftF6 | CtrlF6 | CtrlShiftF6 | AltF6 |
| F7 | ShiftF7 | CtrlF7 | CtrlShiftF7 | AltF7 |
| F8 | ShiftF8 | CtrlF8 | CtrlShiftF8 | AltF8 |
| F9 | ShiftF9 | CtrlF9 | CtrlShiftF9 | AltF9 |
| F10 | ShiftF10 | CtrlF10 | CtrlShiftF10 | AlfF10 |
| F11 | ShiftF11 | CtrlF11 | CtrlShiftF11 | AltF11 |
| F12 | ShiftF12 | CtrlF12 | CtrlShiftF12 | AltF12 |
| Ins | ShiftIns | CtrlIns | | |
| Del | ShiftDel | CtrlDel | | |
| None | | | | AltBksp |

The default is *Shortcut.None*. The following table shows all the letters in combination with the Shift and Ctrl keys:

### *Shortcut* Enumeration (selection)

| | | | |
|---|---|---|---|
| CtrlA | CtrlN | CtrlShiftA | CtrlShiftN |
| CtrlB | CtrlO | CtrlShiftB | CtrlShiftO |
| CtrlC | CtrlP | CtrlShiftC | CtrlShiftP |
| CtrlD | CtrlQ | CtrlShiftD | CtrlShiftQ |
| CtrlE | CtrlR | CtrlShiftE | CtrlShiftR |
| CtrlF | CtrlS | CtrlShiftF | CtrlShiftS |
| CtrlG | CtrlT | CtrlShiftG | CtrlShiftT |
| CtrlH | CtrlU | CtrlShiftH | CtrlShiftU |
| CtrlI | CtrlV | CtrlShiftI | CtrlShiftV |
| CtrlJ | CtrlW | CtrlShiftJ | CtrlShiftW |
| CtrlK | CtrlX | CtrlShiftK | CtrlShiftX |
| CtrlL | CtrlY | CtrlShiftL | CtrlShiftY |
| CtrlM | CtrlZ | CtrlShiftM | CtrlShiftZ |

The values of these enumeration members are equal to the *Keys* enumeration values (covered in Chapter 6) as they are combined in the *KeyData* property of the *KevEventArgs* class. The following table shows shortcuts that consist of the number keys in combination with the Ctrl or Alt key:

### *Shortcut* Enumeration (selection)

| | | |
|---|---|---|
| *Ctrl0* | *CtrlShift0* | *Alt0* |
| *Ctrl1* | *CtrlShift1* | *Alt1* |
| *Ctrl2* | *CtrlShift2* | *Alt2* |
| *Ctrl3* | *CtrlShift3* | *Alt3* |
| *Ctrl4* | *CtrlShift4* | *Alt4* |
| *Ctrl5* | *CtrlShift5* | *Alt5* |
| *Ctrl6* | *CtrlShift6* | *Alt6* |
| *Ctrl7* | *CtrlShift7* | *Alt7* |
| *Ctrl8* | *CtrlShift8* | *Alt8* |
| *Ctrl9* | *CtrlShift9* | *Alt9* |

It's not possible to use a menu shortcut value that isn't defined in the *Shortcut* enumeration.

In Win32 programming, accelerator keys aren't restricted to menu items. In Windows Forms programming, however, shortcuts are always associated with menu items. If you want to define a shortcut that isn't associated with a menu item, you can define a menu item with that shortcut, include that menu item in your menu, and simply set the *Visible* property of the menu item to *False*. The item won't be displayed, but the shortcut will still be active.

## Your First Menu

We now know enough to create our first menu. Unfortunately, we don't know quite enough to make the menu items very useful, such as displaying dialog boxes or using the clipboard, but it's a start. The *Click* event handlers in this program mostly just display message boxes to indicate that the menu item has been clicked.

**FirstMainMenu.vb**

```
'-------------------------------------------------
' FirstMainMenu.vb (c) 2002 by Charles Petzold
'-------------------------------------------------
Imports System
Imports System.Drawing
Imports System.Windows.Forms
```

*(continued)*

**FirstMainMenu.vb**    *(continued)*

```
Class FirstMainMenu
    Inherits Form

    Shared Sub Main()
        Application.Run(new FirstMainMenu())
    End Sub

    Sub New()
        Text = "First Main Menu"

        ' Items on File submenu
        Dim miOpen As New MenuItem("&Open...", _
                        AddressOf MenuFileOpenOnClick, _
                        Shortcut.CtrlO)

        Dim miSave As New MenuItem("&Save", _
                        AddressOf MenuFileSaveOnClick, _
                        Shortcut.CtrlS)

        Dim miSaveAs As New MenuItem("Save &As...", _
                        AddressOf MenuFileSaveAsOnClick)

        Dim miDash As New MenuItem("-")
        Dim miExit As New MenuItem("E&xit", _
                        AddressOf MenuFileExitOnClick)

        ' File menu item
        Dim miFile As New MenuItem("&File", _
                        New MenuItem() {miOpen, miSave, miSaveAs, _
                                    miDash, miExit})
        ' Items on Edit submenu
        Dim miCut As New MenuItem("Cu&t", _
                        AddressOf MenuEditCutOnClick, _
                        Shortcut.CtrlX)

        Dim miCopy As New MenuItem("&Copy", _
                        AddressOf MenuEditCopyOnClick, _
                        Shortcut.CtrlC)

        Dim miPaste As New MenuItem("&Paste", _
                        AddressOf MenuEditPasteOnClick, _
                        Shortcut.CtrlV)

        ' Edit menu item
        Dim miEdit As New MenuItem("&Edit", _
                        New MenuItem() {miCut, miCopy, miPaste})

        ' Item on Help submenu
        Dim miAbout As New MenuItem("&About FirstMainMenu...", _
                        AddressOf MenuHelpAboutOnClick)

        ' Help menu item
        Dim miHelp As New MenuItem("&Help", New MenuItem() {miAbout})
```

```
        ' Main menu
        Menu = new MainMenu(new MenuItem() {miFile, miEdit, miHelp})
    End Sub

    Private Sub MenuFileOpenOnClick(ByVal obj As Object, _
                                ByVal ea As EventArgs)
        MessageBox.Show("File Open item clicked!", Text)
    End Sub

    Private Sub MenuFileSaveOnClick(ByVal obj As Object, _
                                ByVal ea As EventArgs)
        MessageBox.Show("File Save item clicked!", Text)
    End Sub

    Private Sub MenuFileSaveAsOnClick(ByVal obj As Object, _
                                ByVal ea As EventArgs)
        MessageBox.Show("File Save As item clicked!", Text)
    End Sub

    Private Sub MenuFileExitOnClick(ByVal obj As Object, _
                                ByVal ea As EventArgs)
        Close()
    End Sub

    Private Sub MenuEditCutOnClick(ByVal obj As Object, _
                                ByVal ea As EventArgs)
        MessageBox.Show("Edit Cut item clicked!", Text)
    End Sub

    Private Sub MenuEditCopyOnClick(ByVal obj As Object, _
                                ByVal ea As EventArgs)
        MessageBox.Show("Edit Copy item clicked!", Text)
    End Sub

    Private Sub MenuEditPasteOnClick(ByVal obj As Object, _
                                ByVal ea As EventArgs)
        MessageBox.Show("Edit Paste item clicked! ", Text)
    End Sub

    Private Sub MenuHelpAboutOnClick(ByVal obj As Object, _
                                ByVal ea As EventArgs)
        MessageBox.Show(Text & " " & Chr(169) & " 2002 by Charles Petzold")
    End Sub
End Class
```

That this is a lot of code for a program that displays only a few message boxes I won't deny. But considering the overall importance of a menu to most applications, the amount of code isn't unreasonable. Much of what your program does it will do in response to menu *Click* events.

The program demonstrates the use of four different *MenuItem* constructors. For the Open menu item on the File menu, the program uses the constructor with three arguments:

```
Dim miOpen As New MenuItem("&Open...",
                    AddressOf MenuFileOpenOnClick, _
                    Shortcut.CtrlO)
```

The Save As item on the File menu usually doesn't have a shortcut, so that constructor has only two arguments:

```
Dim miSaveAs As New MenuItem("Save &As...", _
                    AddressOf MenuFileSaveAsOnClick)
```

And here's a constructor that has only a text argument:

```
Dim miDash As New MenuItem("-")
```

When you specify a dash as the menu item in a submenu, a horizontal line is drawn in the submenu. This is the way you separate groups of items on a submenu.

When all the menu items on the File submenu have been created, the program creates a top-level menu item using yet another form of the *MenuItem* constructor:

```
Dim miFile As New MenuItem("&File", _
                    New MenuItem() {miOpen, miSave, miSaveAs, _
                                    miDash, miExit})
```

This constructor indicates the text of the item ("File") and an array of items that appear in the submenu invoked by that item.

The program continues with the Edit item (which invokes a submenu containing Cut, Copy, and Paste) and a Help item (containing just an About item). Finally, the form's constructor sets the *Menu* property of the form to an object of type *MainMenu*. The *MainMenu* constructor specifies an array of *MenuItem* objects that appear on the top level of the menu:

```
Menu = New MainMenu(New MenuItem() {miFile, miEdit, miHelp})
```

All the *Click* event handlers in FirstMainMenu display message boxes except the event handler for the Exit item on the File menu. That event handler calls the *Close* method of *Form* to close the form and terminate the program.

You don't need to have separate event handlers for each *Click* event. You could handle every menu item in the same event handler. But using separate event handlers is cleaner and probably easier to maintain. The only time it makes sense to handle multiple items in the same *Click* event handler is when they form part of a related group, usually referring to mutually exclusive options.

# Unconventional Menus

Although designing your menu to look like the menus of other Windows programs is helpful to your user, it's not mandatory. Sometimes—perhaps in a quickie program you're writing for yourself—you need only one menu item. If a top-level menu item doesn't invoke a submenu but instead carries out some action itself, it's customary to use an exclamation point to indicate that fact.

Here's a program that subclasses the JeuDeTaquin program from Chapter 10 to add a one-item menu with the command "Scramble!"

```
JeuDeTaquinWithScramble.vb
'-------------------------------------------------------------
' JeuDeTaquinWithScramble.vb (c) 2002 by Charles Petzold
'-------------------------------------------------------------
Imports System
Imports System.Drawing
Imports System.Windows.Forms

Class JeuDeTaquinWithScramble
    Inherits JeuDeTaquin

    Shared Shadows Sub Main()
        Application.Run(New JeuDeTaquinWithScramble())
    End Sub

    Sub New()
        Menu = New MainMenu(New MenuItem() { _
                    New MenuItem("&Scramble!", _
                             AddressOf MenuScrambleOnClick)})
    End Sub

    Private Sub MenuScrambleOnClick(ByVal obj As Object, _
                                    ByVal ea As EventArgs)
        Randomize()
    End Sub
End Class
```

Now you don't have to end the program to rescramble the tiles.

One of the first popular programs to use a visual hierarchical menu in the character-mode MS-DOS environment was Lotus 1-2-3. The 1-2-3 menus didn't have pop-up menus, however. The menu display was restricted to a single line, and each level of menu replaced the one above it.

You can simulate an arrangement like that in Windows Forms by defining multiple *MainMenu* objects and then dynamically setting them to the *Menu* property of your form. Here's a program that demonstrates this technique.

**OldFashionedMenu.vb**

```vb
'----------------------------------------------------
' OldFashionedMenu.vb (c) 2002 by Charles Petzold
'----------------------------------------------------
Imports System
Imports System.Drawing
Imports System.Windows.Forms

Class OldFashionedMenu
    Inherits Form

    Private mmMain, mmFile, mmEdit As MainMenu

    Shared Sub Main()
        Application.Run(New OldFashionedMenu())
    End Sub

    Sub New()
        Text = "Old-Fashioned Menu"

        Dim eh As EventHandler = AddressOf MenuOnClick

        mmMain = New MainMenu(New MenuItem() _
        { _
            New MenuItem("MAIN:"), _
            New MenuItem("&File", AddressOf MenuFileOnClick), _
            New MenuItem("&Edit", AddressOf MenuEditOnClick) _
        })
        mmFile = New MainMenu(New MenuItem() _
        { _
            New MenuItem("FILE:"), _
            New MenuItem("&New", eh), _
            New MenuItem("&Open...", eh), _
            New MenuItem("&Save", eh), _
            New MenuItem("Save &As...", eh), _
            New MenuItem("(&Main)", AddressOf MenuMainOnClick) _
        })
        mmEdit = New MainMenu(New MenuItem() _
        { _
            New MenuItem("EDIT:"), _
            New MenuItem("Cu&t", eh), _
            New MenuItem("&Copy", eh), _
            New MenuItem("&Paste", eh), _
            New MenuItem("De&lete", eh), _
            New MenuItem("(&Main)", AddressOf MenuMainOnClick) _
        })

        Menu = mmMain
    End Sub
```

```
        Private Sub MenuMainOnClick(ByVal obj As Object, _
                                    ByVal ea As EventArgs)
            Menu = mmMain
        End Sub

        Private Sub MenuFileOnClick(ByVal obj As Object, _
                                    ByVal ea As EventArgs)
            Menu = mmFile
        End Sub

        Private Sub MenuEditOnClick(ByVal obj As Object, _
                                    ByVal ea As EventArgs)
            Menu = mmEdit
        End Sub

        Private Sub MenuOnClick(ByVal obj As Object, _
                                ByVal ea As EventArgs)
            MessageBox.Show("Menu item clicked!", Text)
        End Sub
    End Class
```

# *MenuItem* Properties and Events

The one *MenuItem* constructor (of the five I originally listed) that I haven't demonstrated is the default constructor:

```
New MenuItem()
```

If you use this constructor, you must then have statements that set properties of the *MenuItem* object. The properties connected with the menu item text and shortcut are listed in this table:

### *MenuItem* Properties (selection)

| Property | Type | Accessibility |
| --- | --- | --- |
| *Text* | *String* | Get/Set |
| *Mnemonic* | *Char* | Get |
| *Shortcut* | *Shortcut* | Get/Set |
| *ShowShortcut* | *Boolean* | Get/Set |

The *Mnemonic* property is the character that follows the ampersand in the *Text* property (or 0 if there is no mnemonic character). You can set the *ShowShortcut* property to *False* to inhibit the display of the shortcut to the right of the menu item text.

The following list shows most of the read/write *Boolean* properties of *MenuItem*:

### *MenuItem* Properties (selection)

| Property | Type | Accessibility |
| --- | --- | --- |
| *Visible* | *Boolean* | Get/Set |
| *Enabled* | *Boolean* | Get/Set |
| *DefaultItem* | *Boolean* | Get/Set |
| *Break* | *Boolean* | Get/Set |
| *BarBreak* | *Boolean* | Get/Set |

Setting the *Visible* property to *False* causes the menu item to not appear in the menu. However, the shortcut (if any) still invokes the *Click* event handler. You can use this property to set shortcuts that aren't associated with any menu items. You can also make a number of menu items optionally invisible to implement a simplified-menu system that won't overwhelm beginners.

The *Enabled* property is probably the most commonly used of these five properties. It is often set to *False* to disable menu items that aren't currently applicable. When an item is disabled, the text is displayed in a weak font that indicates the item is unavailable. You can't trigger the *Click* event handler for a disabled item, either by clicking the item or by typing the keyboard shortcut.

Items on the File and Edit menus are often enabled and disabled based on certain conditions. The Save and Save As options are typically disabled if the program currently has no document loaded. A program disables the Cut and Copy options if a document has been loaded but nothing is currently selected in the document. A program disables Paste if the clipboard currently has nothing the program can use. I'll explain how to handle the disabling of menu items later in this chapter.

When you set the *DefaultItem* property to *True*, the menu item is displayed in boldface. For a program's main menu, the *DefaultItem* property makes sense only for items on submenus. When you double-click the item that invokes the submenu, the default item is triggered. For example, if you insert the statement

```
miExit.DefaultItem = True
```

in the constructor of FirstMainMenu, double-clicking the File item causes the program to terminate. Default items are more common on context menus.

Setting the *Break* property to *True* causes the menu item (and subsequent menu items) to be displayed in a new column. Setting the *BarBreak* property to

*True* has the same effect as *Break* but also draws a vertical line between the columns. Although it's not common, you can use *Break* and *BarBreak* with items on the top level of a main menu. Both properties have the same effect of displaying the menu item (and subsequent menu items) in a new row.

These are not all the properties of *MenuItem*. I'll get to the *Checked* and *RadioCheck* properties shortly. In addition, the *MenuItem* class—as well as *MainMenu* and *ContextMenu*—inherits from *Menu* an extremely important property named *MenuItems* (notice the plural) that I'll also talk about later in this chapter.

The *MenuItem* class defines five events, of which *Click* is obviously the most crucial. Two of the five events refer to the owner-draw facility of menus, which I'll discuss toward the end of this chapter. The other three events (including *Click*) are shown here:

**MenuItem Events (selection)**

| Event | Method | Delegate | Argument |
| --- | --- | --- | --- |
| *Click* | *OnClick* | *EventHandler* | *EventArgs* |
| *Popup* | *OnPopup* | *EventHandler* | *EventArgs* |
| *Select* | *OnSelect* | *EventHandler* | *EventArgs* |

Programs often install *Popup* event handlers for top-level items such as File or Edit. The *Popup* event tells you when the submenu associated with that top-level item is about to be displayed. As I mentioned earlier, some menu items, such as Cut, Copy, and Paste, must be enabled or disabled based on whether something has been selected in the document or whether the clipboard contains data the application can use. The *Popup* event handler is the perfect opportunity to perform this enabling and disabling of items.

The *Select* event occurs when the mouse cursor passes over a menu item or the user presses the arrow keys to move among menu items. The selected menu item is usually displayed in a different color. As you may know, some applications use a status bar to display a simple text description of each menu item as it's being selected. I'll demonstrate how to do this in Chapter 20.

# Checking the Items

If you look at the View menu of the Windows Calculator (and particularly if you switch to the Scientific format), you'll see several examples of menu items that are checked. Menu items that represent Boolean choices—such as the Digit Grouping item—can be checked or unchecked just like a *CheckBox* control.

Other groups of menu items, such as the Hex, Decimal, Octal, and Binary items in Calculator, represent mutually exclusive options. The currently selected item is indicated by a filled circle, called a *radio check*. (Some Windows programs use the regular menu check mark for mutually exclusive menu items as well as on-off items. The check mark is allowed but no longer encouraged for mutually exclusive items.)

You control the check mark and radio check with the following two properties of *MenuItem*:

### *MenuItem* Properties (selection)

| Property | Type | Accessibility |
|----------|------|---------------|
| *Checked* | *Boolean* | Get/Set |
| *RadioCheck* | *Boolean* | Get/Set |

Set the *Checked* property to *True* if the mark (regardless whether it's a check or a circle) is to be displayed. Set *RadioCheck* to *True* to display a circle (indicating mutually exclusive options) or *False* for check marks (for on-off items).

Here's a program similar to the RadioButtons program of Chapter 12. The main menu contains a single item named Format that contains ten items—eight items are used like radio buttons to select a color; the ninth item is a horizontal bar; and the tenth is an item with the text *Fill* that can be checked to indicate that the ellipse should be filled.

```
CheckAndRadioCheck.vb
'-------------------------------------------------
' CheckAndRadioCheck.vb (c) 2002 by Charles Petzold
'-------------------------------------------------
Imports System
Imports System.Drawing
Imports System.Windows.Forms

Class CheckAndRadioCheck
    Inherits Form

    Private miColor, miFill As MenuItem

    Shared Sub Main()
        Application.Run(New CheckAndRadioCheck())
    End Sub

    Sub New()
        Text = "Check and Radio Check"
        ResizeRedraw = True
```

```
        Dim astrColor() As String = {"Black", "Blue", "Green","Cyan", _
                                     "Red", "Magenta", "Yellow", "White"}

        Dim ami(astrColor.Length + 1) As MenuItem
        Dim ehColor As EventHandler = AddressOf MenuFormatColorOnClick
        Dim i As Integer

        For i = 0 To astrColor.GetUpperBound(0)
            ami(i) = New MenuItem(astrColor(i), ehColor)
            ami(i).RadioCheck = True
        Next i
        miColor = ami(0)
        miColor.Checked = True

        ami(astrColor.Length) = New MenuItem("-")
        miFill = New MenuItem("&Fill", _
                           AddressOf MenuFormatFillOnClick)
        ami(astrColor.Length + 1) = miFill

        Dim mi As New MenuItem("&Format", ami)
        Menu = New MainMenu(New MenuItem() {mi})
    End Sub

    Private Sub MenuFormatColorOnClick(ByVal obj As Object, _
                                    ByVal ea As EventArgs)
        miColor.Checked = False
        miColor = DirectCast(obj, MenuItem)
        miColor.Checked = True
        Invalidate()
    End Sub

    Private Sub MenuFormatFillOnClick(ByVal obj As Object, _
                                    ByVal ea As EventArgs)
        Dim mi As MenuItem = DirectCast(obj, MenuItem)
        mi.Checked = Not mi.Checked
        Invalidate()
    End Sub

    Protected Overrides Sub OnPaint(ByVal pea As PaintEventArgs)
        Dim grfx As Graphics = pea.Graphics

        If miFill.Checked Then
            Dim br As New SolidBrush(Color.FromName(miColor.Text))
            grfx.FillEllipse(br, 0, 0, ClientSize.Width - 1, _
                                    ClientSize.Height - 1)
        Else
            Dim pn As New Pen(Color.FromName(miColor.Text))
            grfx.DrawEllipse(pn, 0, 0, ClientSize.Width - 1, _
                                    ClientSize.Height - 1)
        End If
    End Sub
End Class
```

The constructor defines an array of eight text strings representing colors and then an array of *MenuItem* structures sufficient to accommodate those eight colors and two more menu items:

```
Dim ami(astrColor.Length + 1) As MenuItem
```

A group of mutually exclusive menu items are generally associated with the same *Click* event handler. For that reason, the event handler is defined before any of the menu items are created:

```
Dim ehColor As EventHandler = AddressOf MenuFormatColorOnClick
```

A *For* loop creates the eight menu items based on the eight color names and the *ehColor* event handler. The *RadioCheck* property is set to *True* so that a circle is displayed rather than a check mark when the *Checked* property is set to *True*.

The *miColor* variable stored as a field is the *MenuItem* object that is currently checked. The constructor sets this field to the first *MenuItem* in the array and then sets the *Checked* property to *True*.

```
miColor = ami(0)
miColor.Checked = True
```

Let me go over the *MenuFormatColorOnClick* handler now and then come back to the program's constructor. The *Click* event handler begins by unchecking the currently checked menu item:

```
miColor.Checked = False
```

The *miColor* field is then set to the first argument of the event handler, which is the item the user has clicked:

```
miColor = DirectCast(obj, MenuItem)
```

The event handler then checks the menu item

```
miColor.Checked = True
```

and invalidates the form to repaint the ellipse. This block of code demonstrates the customary way to check and uncheck mutually exclusive menu items.

Let's return to the constructor. After creating the eight menu items for the eight colors, it creates a ninth menu item that is a horizontal dividing line and then a tenth menu item for the Fill item:

```
miFill = New MenuItem("&Fill", AddressOf MenuFormatFillOnClick)

ami(astrColor.Length + 1) = miFill
```

The *miFill* variable is also stored as a field. The *OnPaint* method uses both *miColor* and *miFill* to draw (or fill) the ellipse.

The *MenuFormatFillOnClick* method doesn't need to access *miFill*, however. The event handler obtains the *MenuItem* object being clicked by casting the first argument,

```
Dim mi As MenuItem = DirectCast(obj, MenuItem)
```

and then toggles the state of that item:

```
mi.Checked = Not mi.Checked
```

You could replace these two statements with the single statement

```
miFill.Checked = Not miFill.Checked
```

but the event handler is more generalized if it doesn't refer to a specific menu item. If you added other on-off menu items that affected *OnPaint* processing, you could use the same general-purpose checking-and-unchecking method.

The *OnPaint* method in CheckAndRadioCheck converts the text color name from the menu item into a *Color* object by using the shared method *Color.FromName* in preparation for creating a brush or pen:

```
Color.FromName(miColor.Text)
```

Obviously, not every menu item has a *Text* property that can be directly converted into a usable object. Using menu text in this way isn't a good idea for a couple reasons. First, if the menu needs to be translated into another language, the new text might not convert to *Color* objects so readily. Second, it's awkward to put ampersands in the color names because they would have to be stripped out before passing the text to the *Color.FromName* method.

I'll demonstrate a more generalized approach to differentiating mutually exclusive menu items shortly. (Does it involve deriving a class from *MenuItem*? you ask. What do you think?)

# Working with Context Menus

Context menus are in some ways simpler than main menus, mostly because they are smaller, sometimes containing only a list of menu items without any submenus. The following program creates a context menu that lets you select the background color of the form.

**ContextMenuDemo.vb**

```vb
'------------------------------------------------
' ContextMenuDemo.vb (c) 2002 by Charles Petzold
'------------------------------------------------
Imports System
Imports System.Drawing
Imports System.Windows.Forms

Class ContextMenuDemo
    Inherits Form

    Private miColor As MenuItem

    Shared Sub Main()
        Application.Run(New ContextMenuDemo())
    End Sub

    Sub New()
        Text = "Context Menu Demo"

        Dim eh As EventHandler = AddressOf MenuColorOnClick
        Dim ami() As MenuItem = {New MenuItem("Black", eh), _
                                 New MenuItem("Blue", eh), _
                                 New MenuItem("Green", eh), _
                                 New MenuItem("Cyan", eh), _
                                 New MenuItem("Red", eh), _
                                 New MenuItem("Magenta", eh), _
                                 New MenuItem("Yellow", eh), _
                                 New MenuItem("White", eh)}

        Dim mi As MenuItem

        For Each mi In ami
            mi.RadioCheck = True
        Next mi

        miColor = ami(3)
        miColor.Checked = True
        BackColor = Color.FromName(miColor.Text)

        ContextMenu = New ContextMenu(ami)
    End Sub

    Private Sub MenuColorOnClick(ByVal obj As Object, _
                                 ByVal ea As EventArgs)
        miColor.Checked = False
        miColor = DirectCast(obj, MenuItem)
        miColor.Checked = True
        BackColor = Color.FromName(miColor.Text)
    End Sub
End Class
```

In this program, the eight menu items are defined right in the initialization of the *MenuItem* array named *ami*. As in the previous program, all the menu items use the same *Click* event handler. A *For* loop sets the *RadioCheck* property of each menu item to *True*. The constructor then sets the field variable *miColor* to the fourth menu item in the array, checks that item, and sets the background color to the checked item.

The constructor concludes by making a new *ContextMenu* object from the array of *MenuItem* objects and then assigning that to the *ContextMenu* property of the form:

```
ContextMenu = New ContextMenu(ami)
```

You can invoke the context menu by right-clicking anywhere within the client area. Alternatively, the *ContextMenu* class also has a method that lets you display a context menu without setting the *ContextMenu* property of a control:

### *ContextMenu* Methods (selection)

```
Sub Show(ByVal ctrl As Control, ByVal ptLocation As Point)
```

You can use this method if you need to display different context menus for a single control (or form) depending on where the mouse is clicked.

By converting the menu item text to a color, the ContextMenuDemo program has the same flaws as CheckAndRadioCheck. When implementing mutually exclusive menu items that use the same *Click* event handler, a much better (and more generalized) approach is to derive a class from *MenuItem* and use that class in your menu instead. The class derived from *MenuItem* includes a new field or property that stores an object to identify the item.

Here's a program that derives a class named *MenuItemColor* from *MenuItem*. The class includes a private field named *clr* to store a *Color* object. The public property named *Color* gives other classes access to that color. In addition, the new class also includes a new constructor that lets a *MenuItemColor* object be created with a specified color. The following program is very similar to ContextMenuDemo except that it uses *MenuItemColor* rather than *MenuItem*.

### BetterContextMenu.vb

```
'-------------------------------------------------
' BetterContextMenu.vb (c) 2002 by Charles Petzold
'-------------------------------------------------
Imports System
Imports System.Drawing
Imports System.Windows.Forms
```

*(continued)*

**BetterContextMenu.vb** *(continued)*

```
Class BetterContextMenu
    Inherits Form

    Private micColor As MenuItemColor

    Shared Sub Main()
        Application.Run(New BetterContextMenu())
    End Sub

    Sub New()
        Text = "Better Context Menu Demo"

        Dim eh As EventHandler = AddressOf MenuColorOnClick
        Dim amic As MenuItemColor() = _
        { _
            New MenuItemColor(Color.Black, "&Black", eh), _
            New MenuItemColor(Color.Blue, "B&lue", eh), _
            New MenuItemColor(Color.Green, "&Green", eh), _
            New MenuItemColor(Color.Cyan, "&Cyan", eh), _
            New MenuItemColor(Color.Red, "&Red", eh), _
            New MenuItemColor(Color.Magenta, "&Magenta", eh), _
            New MenuItemColor(Color.Yellow, "&Yellow", eh), _
            New MenuItemColor(Color.White, "&White", eh) _
        }
        Dim mic As MenuItemColor

        For Each mic In amic
            mic.RadioCheck = True
        Next mic

        micColor = amic(3)
        micColor.Checked = True
        BackColor = micColor.Color

        ContextMenu = New ContextMenu(amic)
    End Sub

    Private Sub MenuColorOnClick(ByVal obj As Object, _
                                 ByVal ea As EventArgs)
        micColor.Checked = False
        micColor = DirectCast(obj, MenuItemColor)
        micColor.Checked = True
        BackColor = micColor.Color
    End Sub
End Class

Class MenuItemColor
    Inherits MenuItem

    Private clr As Color

    Sub New(ByVal clr As Color, ByVal str As String, _
                        ByVal eh As EventHandler)
```

```
        MyBase.New(str, eh)
        Color = clr
    End Sub

    Property Color() As Color
        Set(ByVal Value As Color)
            clr = Value
        End Set
        Get
            Return clr
        End Get
    End Property
End Class
```

Now the program can set the *BackColor* property of the form directly from the *Color* property of the currently checked *MenuItemColor* object.

# The Menu Item Collection

If you look back at the FirstMainMenu program, you'll see that the menu was built from the inside out. It began by creating *MenuItem* objects for the innermost items (such as Open, Save, and so on). These were assembled into arrays to create top-level items (File, Edit, and so forth). Then the top-level menu items were gathered together into a *MainMenu* object.

A program might be more coherent and maintainable if the menu were created from the top down, beginning by creating a *MainMenu* object, adding *MenuItem* objects to the main menu to create top-level items (File, Edit, and so forth), and then adding other items in the submenus (Open, Save, and so forth).

This second approach is made possible by a couple important properties defined in the *Menu* class. As I mentioned early in this chapter, the *MenuItem*, *MainMenu*, and *ContextMenu* classes are all derived from *Menu*, so they all inherit these properties:

### *Menu* Properties (selection)

| Property | Type | Accessibility |
|----------|------|---------------|
| *IsParent* | *Boolean* | Get |
| *MenuItems* | *Menu.MenuItemCollection* | Get |

Does that *Menu.MenuItemCollection* type look like a familiar friend yet? It's quite similar to the *ImageList.ImageCollection* class in Chapter 11 and the *Control.ControlCollection* class in Chapter 12. Like those other classes, *Menu.MenuItemCollection* implements the *IList*, *ICollection*, and *IEnumerable* interfaces.

You can index the *MenuItems* property as if it were an array of *MenuItem* objects. You can also call methods named *Add*, *Remove*, and *Clear*.

The *IsParent* property indicates that a menu item is parent to other menu items and hence the *MenuItems* property is valid.

In addition, the *MenuItem* class has the following two related properties:

### *MenuItem* Properties (selection)

| Property | Type | Accessibility |
| --- | --- | --- |
| *Parent* | *Menu* | Get |
| *Index* | *Integer* | Get/Set |

The *Parent* property indicates the parent menu of a particular menu item; the *Index* property (which is also writable) indicates the zero-based index of a *MenuItem* object within a particular submenu.

The *Menu.MenuItemCollection* class implements the following methods that let you add child menu items to a main menu, a context menu, or another menu item:

### *Menu.MenuItemCollection* Methods (selection)

```
Function Add(ByVal strText As String) As MenuItem

Function Add(ByVal strText As String, _
            ByVal ehClick As EventHandler) As MenuItem

Function Add(ByVal strText As String, _
            ByVal ami() As MenuItem) As MenuItem

Function Add(ByVal mi As MenuItem) As Integer

Function Add(ByVal index As Integer, _
            ByVal mi As MenuItem) As Integer

Sub AddRange(ByVal ami() As MenuItem)
```

A program can use the following properties (the last of which is an indexer) to determine how many menu items the collection contains and to obtain them:

### *Menu.MenuItemCollection* Properties

| Property | Type | Accessibility |
| --- | --- | --- |
| *IsReadOnly* | *Boolean* | Get |
| *Count* | *Integer* | Get |
| *()* | *MenuItem* | Get |

Menu items can also be located and removed:

## *Menu.MenuItemCollection* Methods (selection)

```
Function Contains(ByVal mi As MenuItem) As Boolean

Function IndexOf(ByVal mi As MenuItem) As Integer

Sub Remove(ByVal mi As MenuItem)

Sub RemoveAt(ByVal index As Integer)

Sub Clear()
```

Here's a version of the ContextMenuDemo program, named ContextMenu-Add, that uses the *Add* and indexing facility of the *MenuItem* property to create the menu. The *ContextMenu* object is created first, and then the menu items are added to it.

### ContextMenuAdd.vb

```
'-------------------------------------------------
' ContextMenuAdd.vb (c) 2002 by Charles Petzold
'-------------------------------------------------
Imports System
Imports System.Drawing
Imports System.Windows.Forms

Class ContextMenuAdd
    Inherits Form

    Private miColor As MenuItem

    Shared Sub Main()
        Application.Run(New ContextMenuAdd())
    End Sub

    Sub New()
        Text = "Context Menu Using Add"

        Dim cm As New ContextMenu()
        Dim eh As EventHandler = AddressOf MenuColorOnClick
        Dim mi As MenuItem

        cm.MenuItems.Add("Black", eh)
        cm.MenuItems.Add("Blue", eh)
        cm.MenuItems.Add("Green", eh)
        cm.MenuItems.Add("Cyan", eh)
        cm.MenuItems.Add("Red", eh)
        cm.MenuItems.Add("Magenta", eh)
        cm.MenuItems.Add("Yellow", eh)
        cm.MenuItems.Add("White", eh)
```

*(continued)*

**ContextMenuAdd.vb** *(continued)*

```
        For Each mi In cm.MenuItems
            mi.RadioCheck = True
        Next mi

        miColor = cm.MenuItems(3)
        miColor.Checked = True
        BackColor = Color.FromName(miColor.Text)

        ContextMenu = cm
    End Sub

    Private Sub MenuColorOnClick(ByVal obj As Object, _
                                 ByVal ea As EventArgs)
        miColor.Checked = False
        miColor = DirectCast(obj, MenuItem)
        miColor.Checked = True
        BackColor = Color.FromName(miColor.Text)
    End Sub
End Class
```

This program could have saved a statement by assigning the new *Context-Menu* object to the *ContextMenu* property of the form:

```
ContextMenu = New ContextMenu()
```

The statements adding the items would then look like this:

```
ContextMenu.MenuItems.Add("Black", eh)
```

Earlier in this chapter, I transformed the ContextMenuDemo program into the BetterContextMenu program by defining a class named *MenuItemColor* that inherits from *MenuItem* but also stores a *Color* object. What would I need to do to convert the ContextMenuAdd program to use *MenuItemColor* objects?

What's most obvious is that I couldn't use the same *Add* method I used in ContextMenuAdd. The method call

```
cm.MenuItems.Add("Black", eh)
```

implicitly creates an object of type *MenuItem* and then adds it to the menu item collection. The following statement does the same job more explicitly:

```
cm.MenuItems.Add(New MenuItem("Black", eh))
```

To convert the program to use the *MenuItemColor* class, you'd need to make calls like so:

```
cm.MenuItems.Add(New MenuItemColor(Color.Black,  "Black", eh))
```

The next program has a single top-level menu item named Facename and uses the *Popup* event as an opportunity to add all the available font facenames to the menu. In theory, this approach is better than building the menu when the program starts up because the program can display fonts that are added after the program starts running.

**FontMenu.vb**

```
'------------------------------------------
' FontMenu.vb (c) 2002 by Charles Petzold
'------------------------------------------
Imports System
Imports System.Drawing
Imports System.Windows.Forms

Class FontMenu
    Inherits Form

    Const iPointSize As Integer = 24
    Private strFacename As String

    Shared Sub Main()
        Application.Run(New FontMenu())
    End Sub

    Sub New()
        Text = "Font Menu"
        strFacename = Font.Name
        Menu = New MainMenu()

        Dim mi As New MenuItem("&Facename")
        AddHandler mi.Popup, AddressOf MenuFacenameOnPopup
        mi.MenuItems.Add(" ")          ' Necessary for pop-up call
        Menu.MenuItems.Add(mi)
    End Sub

    Private Sub MenuFacenameOnPopup(ByVal obj As Object, _
                                    ByVal ea As EventArgs)
        Dim miFacename As MenuItem = DirectCast(obj, MenuItem)
        Dim aff() As FontFamily = FontFamily.Families
        Dim ehClick As EventHandler = AddressOf MenuFacenameOnClick
        Dim ami(aff.GetUpperBound(0)) As MenuItem
        Dim i As Integer

        For i = 0 To aff.GetUpperBound(0)
            ami(i) = New MenuItem(aff(i).Name)
            AddHandler ami(i).Click, ehClick

            If aff(i).Name = strFacename Then
                ami(i).Checked = True
            End If
        Next i
        miFacename.MenuItems.Clear()
        miFacename.MenuItems.AddRange(ami)
    End Sub
```

*(continued)*

**FontMenu.vb**   *(continued)*

```
    Private Sub MenuFacenameOnClick(ByVal obj As Object, _
                                    ByVal ea As EventArgs)
        Dim mi As MenuItem = DirectCast(obj, MenuItem)
        strFacename = mi.Text
        Invalidate()
    End Sub

    Protected Overrides Sub OnPaint(ByVal pea As PaintEventArgs)
        Dim grfx As Graphics = pea.Graphics
        Dim fnt As New Font(strFacename, iPointSize)
        Dim strfmt As New StringFormat()

        strfmt.Alignment = StringAlignment.Center
        strfmt.LineAlignment = StringAlignment.Center

        grfx.DrawString("Sample Text", fnt, _
                        New SolidBrush(ForeColor), _
                        RectangleF.op_Implicit(ClientRectangle), strfmt)
    End Sub
End Class
```

When the constructor defines the menu, it adds a single blank item to the submenu. At least one item in the submenu seems to be necessary to generate a *Popup* event.

The *MenuFacenameOnPopup* event handler begins by obtaining the top-level menu item:

```
Dim miFacename As MenuItem = DirectCast(obj, MenuItem)
```

The method then obtains an array of all the available font facenames by calling the shared *FontFamily.Families* method. It defines a *MenuItem* array of that size and then initializes all the entries, in the process setting the *Check* property of the item corresponding to the font facename currently stored in the *strFacename* field.

After the *MenuItem* array has been initialized, the method concludes by clearing all the existing entries from the pop-up menu and adding the new array of items:

```
miFacename.MenuItems.Clear()
miFacename.MenuItems.AddRange(ami)
```

To keep the code bulk down, this program doesn't have a fix for the problem that results when you pick a font facename that isn't capable of the *FontStyle.Regular* style (such as Aharoni). If you pick such a font, the *Font* constructor in the *OnPaint* method will throw an exception and terminate the program. (See Chapter 9 for more details on this issue and on working with fonts.)

But the real problem with this program is the size of the submenu. It's very likely that the list will exceed the height of your display. Picking a font facename is obviously a job for a dialog box, as I'll demonstrate in Chapter 16.

# The Standard Menu (A Proposal)

To make your program easy to read and maintain, it seems logical that the flow of the menu-creation code should mimic the hierarchy of the menu. Thus, the constructor should probably build the menu starting with the first top-level item (typically File), then all the items in the File submenu (typically New, Open, Save, and so forth), then the next top-level item (typically Edit), then the items in the Edit submenu, and ending with the About item on the Help menu.

As you begin experimenting with top-down menu construction using the *Add* method of the *Menu.MenuItemCollection* class, you'll find that not all *Add* methods are created equal. Some are more useful than others. You may want to adopt a standard style for the creation of your main menu that makes use of just a small subset of the *MenuItem* constructors and the *Add* methods. The proposal I've outlined here uses just one form of *MenuItem* constructor and one form of the *Add* method. You're free to disregard this proposal. I disregard it myself in later chapters. But I'd like to explore some of the issues involved in menu construction code.

Let's first look at some top-down menu creation statements for nonfunctional items without any event handlers or shortcuts. The code would look something like this:

```
Menu = New MainMenu()
Menu.MenuItems.Add("&File")
Menu.MenuItems(0).MenuItems.Add("&Open...")
Menu.MenuItems(0).MenuItems.Add("&Save...")
⋮
Menu.MenuItems.Add("&Edit")
Menu.MenuItems(1).MenuItems.Add("Cu&t")
Menu.MenuItems(1).MenuItems.Add("&Copy")
⋮
```

This code is all very orderly (if not exactly pretty): The top-level items (File and Edit) are added to the *MainMenu* object using the *Add* method of its *MenuItems* property. The expression *Menu.MenuItems(0)* refers to the File menu item, and *Menu.MenuItems(1)* refers to the Edit menu item. Each of those menu items has its own *MenuItems* property that is the collection of menu items on the submenu. You use the *Add* method of that *MenuItems* property to add items Open, Save, Cut, Copy, and so forth.

Except for groups of mutually exclusive menu items, most menu items should be associated with their own *Click* event handlers. To make the menu functional, you need to convert the previous statements into statements like this:

```
Menu.MenuItems(0).MenuItems.Add("&Open...", _
                          AddressOf MenuFileOpenOnClick)
```

But the Open item also commonly includes a CTRL+O shortcut, and there's no *Add* method that includes a shortcut argument. You'd need an additional statement like

```
Menu.MenuItems(0).MenuItems(0).Shortcut = Shortcut.CtrlO
```

to reference the *Shortcut* property of the Open menu item. But if you then modify your code to put a New item before the Open item, you need to change the statement so the indexing is different:

```
Menu.MenuItems(0).MenuItems(1).Shortcut = Shortcut.CtrlO
```

We're headed down a wrong path with this approach. I think you'll agree that setting the property of a menu item shouldn't require going through two levels of *MenuItems* properties.

Probably a better approach is to define the *MenuItem* first, as here,

```
miFileOpen = New MenuItem("&Open", _
                AddressOf MenuFileOpenOnClick), _
                Shortcut.CtrlO)
```

and then add this menu item to the *MenuItems* collection:

```
Menu.MenuItems(0).MenuItems.Add(miFileOpen)
```

Since the creation of the *miFileOpen* object spills over beyond one line of code, it may be clearer if we go with a simple constructor and a more explicit assignment of the *MenuItem* properties:

```
miFileOpen = New MenuItem("&Open")
AddHandler miFileOpen.Click, AddressOf MenuFileOpenOnClick
miFileOpen.Shortcut = Shortcut.CtrlO
Menu.MenuItems(0).MenuItems.Add(miFileOpen)
```

Does it ever make sense to use the version of *Add* that has a single *String* argument? It's a good choice when you want to add a horizontal separation line to the menu:

```
Menu.MenuItems(0).MenuItems.Add("-")
```

And this version of *Add* might make sense when adding a top-level item:

```
Menu.MenuItems.Add("F&ormat")
```

But many top-level items should have *Popup* event handlers installed to enable or disable menu items on the submenu. So here also, it makes more sense to create the *MenuItem* first, set its properties, and then add the menu item to the menu:

```
Dim mi As New MenuItem("&File")
AddHandler mi.Popup, AddressOf MenuFileOnPopup
Menu.MenuItems.Add(mi)
```

If you want to be totally consistent throughout your menu creation, all you need to use is one form of the *MenuItem* constructor (the one with just a *string* argument) and one form of the *Add* method (the one with a *MenuItem* argument).

As you may have gathered from much of this book, I prefer to keep the number of field variables in a class to a minimum. The Menu Designer in Microsoft Visual Basic .NET makes every *MenuItem* object a field. That's clearly unnecessary! Because most menu items have their own *Click* event handlers, it isn't necessary for the program to retain all the *MenuItem* objects. An exception is when items must be enabled or disabled during a *Popup* event. Those items should probably be stored as fields.

Finally, I want to justify one more little tiny variable—just a little *Integer* that I call *index*. Every time you add an item to the top level of the menu with a statement like

```
Menu.MenuItems.Add(mi)
```

you can also calculate a new *index* value:

```
index = Menu.MenuItems.Count - 1
```

Very conveniently, the *Add* method used to add a *MenuItem* object to the menu returns such an index value, so *index* can be obtained like this when the item is added:

```
index = Menu.MenuItems.Add(mi)
```

Use this *index* value to add items to each of the submenus, as here:

```
Menu.MenuItems(index).MenuItems.Add(miFileOpen)
```

For the File menu, the use of a variable rather than an explicit 0 is hardly necessary: File will always be the first item on the main menu, from now until the end of time. But the *index* variable makes loads of sense for later submenus, particularly if you someday revise your constructor code to insert a new submenu.

Here's a program that demonstrates my suggested approach to creating a standard menu from the top down consistently using one form of the *MenuItem* constructor and one form of the *Add* method.

### StandardMenu.vb

```
'-----------------------------------------------
' StandardMenu.vb (c) 2002 by Charles Petzold
'-----------------------------------------------
Imports System
Imports System.Drawing
Imports System.Windows.Forms

Class StandardMenu
    Inherits Form

    Private miFileOpen, miFileSave As MenuItem
    Private miEditCut, miEditCopy, miEditPaste As MenuItem

    ' Experimental variables for Popup code
    Private bDocumentPresent As Boolean = True
    Private bValidSelection As Boolean = True
    Private bStuffInClipboard As Boolean = False

    Shared Sub Main()
        Application.Run(New StandardMenu())
    End Sub

    Sub New()
        Text = "Standard Menu"
        Menu = New MainMenu()

        ' File
        Dim mi As New MenuItem("&File")
        AddHandler mi.Popup, AddressOf MenuFileOnPopup
        Dim index As Integer = Menu.MenuItems.Add(mi)

        ' File Open
        miFileOpen = New MenuItem("&Open...")
        AddHandler miFileOpen.Click, AddressOf MenuFileOpenOnClick
        miFileOpen.Shortcut = Shortcut.CtrlO
        Menu.MenuItems(index).MenuItems.Add(miFileOpen)

        ' File Save
        miFileSave = New MenuItem("&Save")
        AddHandler miFileSave.Click, AddressOf MenuFileSaveOnClick
        miFileSave.Shortcut = Shortcut.CtrlS
        Menu.MenuItems(index).MenuItems.Add(miFileSave)

        ' Horizontal line
        mi = New MenuItem("-")
        Menu.MenuItems(index).MenuItems.Add(mi)

        ' File Exit
        mi = New MenuItem("E&xit")
        AddHandler mi.Click, AddressOf MenuFileExitOnClick
        Menu.MenuItems(index).MenuItems.Add(mi)
```

```
        ' Edit
        mi = New MenuItem("&Edit")
        AddHandler mi.Popup, AddressOf MenuEditOnPopup
        index = Menu.MenuItems.Add(mi)

        ' Edit Cut
        miEditCut = New MenuItem("Cu&t")
        AddHandler miEditCut.Click, AddressOf MenuEditCutOnClick
        miEditCut.Shortcut = Shortcut.CtrlX
        Menu.MenuItems(index).MenuItems.Add(miEditCut)

        ' Edit Copy
        miEditCopy = New MenuItem("&Copy")
        AddHandler miEditCopy.Click, AddressOf MenuEditCopyOnClick
        miEditCopy.Shortcut = Shortcut.CtrlC
        Menu.MenuItems(index).MenuItems.Add(miEditCopy)

        ' Edit Paste
        miEditPaste = New MenuItem("&Paste")
        AddHandler miEditPaste.Click, AddressOf MenuEditCopyOnClick
        miEditPaste.Shortcut = Shortcut.CtrlV
        Menu.MenuItems(index).MenuItems.Add(miEditPaste)

        ' Help
        mi = New MenuItem("&Help")
        index = Menu.MenuItems.Add(mi)

        ' Help About
        mi = New MenuItem("&About StandardMenu...")
        AddHandler mi.Click, AddressOf MenuHelpAboutOnClick
        Menu.MenuItems(index).MenuItems.Add(mi)
End Sub

Private Sub MenuFileOnPopup(ByVal obj As Object, ByVal ea As EventArgs)
    miFileSave.Enabled = bDocumentPresent
End Sub

Private Sub MenuEditOnPopup(ByVal obj As Object, ByVal ea As EventArgs)
    miEditCut.Enabled = bValidSelection
    miEditCopy.Enabled = bValidSelection
    miEditPaste.Enabled = bStuffInClipboard
End Sub

Private Sub MenuFileOpenOnClick(ByVal obj As Object, _
                                ByVal ea As EventArgs)
    MessageBox.Show("This should be a File Open dialog box!", Text)
End Sub

Private Sub MenuFileSaveOnClick(ByVal obj As Object, _
                                ByVal ea As EventArgs)
```

*(continued)*

**StandardMenu.vb**    *(continued)*

```
        MessageBox.Show("This should be a File Save dialog box!", Text)
    End Sub

    Private Sub MenuFileExitOnClick(ByVal obj As Object, _
                                    ByVal ea As EventArgs)
        Close()
    End Sub

    Private Sub MenuEditCutOnClick(ByVal obj As Object, _
                                   ByVal ea As EventArgs)
        ' Copy selection to Clipboard; delete from document.
    End Sub

    Private Sub MenuEditCopyOnClick(ByVal obj As Object, _
                                    ByVal ea As EventArgs)
        ' Copy selection to Clipboard.
    End Sub

    Private Sub MenuEditPasteOnClick(ByVal obj As Object, _
                                     ByVal ea As EventArgs)
        ' Copy Clipboard data to document.
    End Sub

    Private Sub MenuHelpAboutOnClick(ByVal obj As Object, _
                                     ByVal ea As EventArgs)
        MessageBox.Show("StandardMenu " & Chr(169) & _
                        " 2002 by Charles Petzold", Text)
    End Sub
End Class
```

Although this is certainly not the tersest code imaginable, I think the program achieves a significant degree of clarity and maintainability.

# The Owner-Draw Option

We're nearing the end of this chapter and I still haven't shown you how to put little pictures in your menu items or how to use a different font or different colors.

Any menu feature beyond what I've covered so far requires that you use a facility called *owner-draw*. For every *MenuItem* object that you want to draw yourself, you must set the following property to *True*:

### *MenuItem* Properties (selection)

| Property | Type | Accessibility |
|----------|------|---------------|
| *OwnerDraw* | *Boolean* | Get/Set |

Usually you'd set this property only for items on pop-up menus. If you set *OwnerDraw* to *True*, you must also install event handlers for the following two events:

### *MenuItem* Events (selection)

| Event | Method | Delegate | Argument |
| --- | --- | --- | --- |
| *MeasureItem* | *OnMeasureItem* | *MeasureItemEventHandler* | *MeasureItemEventArgs* |
| *DrawItem* | *OnDrawItem* | *DrawItemEventHandler* | *DrawItemEventArgs* |

Whenever Windows is preparing to draw a menu item (which is usually when it's preparing to display a pop-up menu), it calls the handler for the *MeasureItem* event. The event is accompanied by an object of type *MeasureItemEventArgs*.

### *MeasureItemEventArgs* Properties

| Property | Type | Accessibility |
| --- | --- | --- |
| *Index* | *Integer* | Get |
| *Graphics* | *Graphics* | Get |
| *ItemWidth* | *Integer* | Get/Set |
| *ItemHeight* | *Integer* | Get/Set |

On entry to the *MeasureItem* event handler, the *ItemWidth* and *ItemHeight* properties are set to 0. Your responsibility is to set them to the total width and height of the menu item you intend to draw. The *Index* property is there to help your event handler figure out which item requires measurement. (As usual, the first argument to the event handler will also identify the *MenuItem* object in question.) If necessary, the *Graphics* property lets you obtain the device resolution in dots per inch, or the size of text items by calling *MeasureString*.

A short time later, Windows calls the *DrawItem* event handler, accompanied by an object of *DrawItemEventArgs*:

### *DrawItemEventArgs* Properties

| Property | Type | Accessibility |
| --- | --- | --- |
| *Index* | *Integer* | Get |
| *Graphics* | *Graphics* | Get |
| *Bounds* | *Rectangle* | Get |

*(continued)*

## *DrawItemEventArgs* Properties  *(continued)*

| Property | Type | Accessibility |
|----------|------|---------------|
| *State* | *DrawItemState* | Get |
| *Font* | *Font* | Get |
| *BackColor* | *Color* | Get |
| *ForeColor* | *Color* | Get |

Your program's responsibility is to draw the item using the *Graphics* object within the rectangle defined by the *Bounds* property. Don't assume that the *Bounds* property has an upper left corner at point (0, 0)! In fact, the *Bounds* rectangle is a rectangle within the entire pop-up menu.

The width of the *Bounds* rectangle will be greater than the amount you specified while handling the *MeasureItem* event to allow for a check mark of standard size at the left of the item.

The *DrawItemState* enumeration tells you whether the item is selected, disabled, or checked:

## *DrawItemState* Enumeration

| Member | Value |
|--------|-------|
| *None* | &H0000 |
| *Selected* | &H0001 |
| *Grayed* | &H0002 |
| *Disabled* | &H0004 |
| *Checked* | &H0008 |
| *Focus* | &H0010 |
| *Default* | &H0020 |
| *HotLight* | &H0040 |
| *Inactive* | &H0080 |
| *NoAccelerator* | &H0100 |
| *NoFocusRect* | &H0200 |
| *ComboBoxEdit* | &H1000 |

Some of these members apply to other types of controls that have owner-draw facilities.

Normally, the *BackColor* property of the *DrawItemEventArgs* object will be *SystemColors.Window* and the *ForeColor* property will be *SystemColors.Win-*

*dowText*. To be consistent with normal menu items, these are not the colors you should be using! Use *SystemColors.Menu* and *SystemColors.MenuText* instead. If the item is selected, *BackColor* will be *SystemColors.Highlight* and *ForeColor* will be *SystemColors.HighlightText*. These *are* the correct colors for selected menu items.

The *Font* property of the *DrawItemEventArgs* property will be the same as *SystemInformation.MenuFont*.

In addition, *DrawItemEventArgs* has two methods that assist you in drawing the item:

### *DrawItemEventArgs* Methods

```
Sub DrawBackground()

Sub DrawFocusRectangle()
```

The *DrawFocusRectangle* method isn't used with menu items.

You'll also find the following shared method of the *ControlPaint* class to be useful for drawing arrows, check marks, and radio buttons on menus:

### *ControlPaint* Shared *DrawMenuGlyph* Methods

```
Sub DrawMenuGlyph(ByVal grfx As Graphics, ByVal rect As Rectangle,
                ByVal mg As MenuGlyph)

Sub DrawMenuGlyph(ByVal grfx As Graphics, ByVal x As Integer,
                ByVal y As Integer, ByVal cx As Integer,
                ByVal cy As Integer, ByVal mg As MenuGlyph)
```

*MenuGlyph* is another enumeration:

### *MenuGlyph* Enumeration

| Member | Value |
| --- | --- |
| *Min* | 0 |
| *Arrow* | 0 |
| *Checkmark* | 1 |
| *Bullet* | 2 |
| *Max* | 2 |

You can size your menu items in a couple ways. The normal font used for menu items is (as I mentioned) available from *SystemInformation.MenuFont*. Another important measure is *SystemInformation.MenuCheckSize*, which is the default width and height of the check mark. As you can see in the shared *ControlPaint.DrawMenuGlyph* method, you specify the width and height of the glyph (such as the check mark) as you draw it. If you make your items taller than the normal menu items and you want to use check marks, you should probably scale the check mark glyph when you draw it. This implies that you should also take account of the scaled-up width of the check mark when you calculate the size of the item while handling the *MeasureItem* event.

Here's a program that has a single top-level item named Facename. The pop-up menu has three items showing the three most common font faces. The owner-draw logic displays these facename items in fonts based on the facenames.

**OwnerDrawMenu.vb**

```vb
'---------------------------------------------
' OwnerDrawMenu.vb (c) 2002 by Charles Petzold
'---------------------------------------------
Imports System
Imports System.Drawing
Imports System.Drawing.Text          ' For HotkeyPrefix enumeration
Imports System.Windows.Forms

Class OwnerDrawMenu
    Inherits Form

    Const iFontPointSize As Integer = 18     ' For menu items
    Private miFacename As MenuItem

    Shared Sub Main()
        Application.Run(New OwnerDrawMenu())
    End Sub

    Sub New()
        Text = "Owner-Draw Menu"

        ' Top-level items
        Menu = New MainMenu()
        Menu.MenuItems.Add("&Facename")

        ' Array of items on submenu
        Dim astrText() As String = {"&Times New Roman", _
                                    "&Arial", "&Courier New"}
        Dim ami(astrText.Length - 1) As MenuItem
        Dim ehOnClick As EventHandler = AddressOf MenuFacenameOnClick
        Dim ehOnMeasureItem As MeasureItemEventHandler = _
            New MeasureItemEventHandler(AddressOf MenuFacenameOnMeasureItem)
        Dim ehOnDrawItem As DrawItemEventHandler = _
            New DrawItemEventHandler(AddressOf MenuFacenameOnDrawItem)
        Dim i As Integer
```

```
        For i = 0 To ami.GetUpperBound(0)
            ami(i) = New MenuItem(astrText(i))
            ami(i).OwnerDraw = True
            ami(i).RadioCheck = True
            AddHandler ami(i).Click, ehOnClick
            AddHandler ami(i).MeasureItem, ehOnMeasureItem
            AddHandler ami(i).DrawItem, ehOnDrawItem
        Next i

        miFacename = ami(0)
        miFacename.Checked = True
        Menu.MenuItems(0).MenuItems.AddRange(ami)
    End Sub

    Private Sub MenuFacenameOnClick(ByVal obj As Object, _
                                    ByVal ea As EventArgs)
        miFacename.Checked = False
        miFacename = DirectCast(obj, MenuItem)
        miFacename.Checked = True
        Invalidate()
    End Sub

    Private Sub MenuFacenameOnMeasureItem(ByVal obj As Object, _
                                    ByVal miea As MeasureItemEventArgs)
        Dim mi As MenuItem = DirectCast(obj, MenuItem)
        Dim fnt As New Font(mi.Text.Substring(1), iFontPointSize)
        Dim strfmt As New StringFormat()
        strfmt.HotkeyPrefix = HotkeyPrefix.Show
        Dim szf As SizeF = miea.Graphics.MeasureString(mi.Text, fnt, _
                                                       1000, strfmt)

        miea.ItemWidth = CInt(Math.Ceiling(szf.Width))
        miea.ItemHeight = CInt(Math.Ceiling(szf.Height))
        miea.ItemWidth += SystemInformation.MenuCheckSize.Width * _
                        miea.ItemHeight \ _
                            SystemInformation.MenuCheckSize.Height
        miea.ItemWidth -= SystemInformation.MenuCheckSize.Width
    End Sub

    Private Sub MenuFacenameOnDrawItem(ByVal obj As Object, _
                                    ByVal diea As DrawItemEventArgs)
        Dim mi As MenuItem = DirectCast(obj, MenuItem)
        Dim grfx As Graphics = diea.Graphics
        Dim br As Brush

        ' Create the Font and StringFormat.
        Dim fnt As New Font(mi.Text.Substring(1), iFontPointSize)
        Dim strfmt As New StringFormat()
        strfmt.HotkeyPrefix = HotkeyPrefix.Show

        ' Calculate check mark and text rectangles.
        Dim rectCheck As Rectangle = diea.Bounds
```

*(continued)*

**OwnerDrawMenu.vb**   *(continued)*

```
            rectCheck.Width = SystemInformation.MenuCheckSize.Width * _
                            rectCheck.Height \ _
                                SystemInformation.MenuCheckSize.Height
            Dim rectText As Rectangle = diea.Bounds
            rectText.X += rectCheck.Width

            ' Do all the drawing.
            diea.DrawBackground()
            If (diea.State And DrawItemState.Checked) <> 0 Then
                ControlPaint.DrawMenuGlyph(grfx, rectCheck, MenuGlyph.Bullet)
            End If
            If (diea.State And DrawItemState.Selected) <> 0 Then
                br = SystemBrushes.HighlightText
            Else
                br = SystemBrushes.FromSystemColor(SystemColors.MenuText)
            End If
            grfx.DrawString(mi.Text, fnt, br, _
                            RectangleF.op_Implicit(rectText), strfmt)
        End Sub

        Protected Overrides Sub OnPaint(ByVal pea As PaintEventArgs)
            Dim grfx As Graphics = pea.Graphics
            Dim fnt As New Font(miFacename.Text.Substring(1), 12)
            Dim strfmt As New StringFormat()

            strfmt.Alignment = StringAlignment.Center
            strfmt.LineAlignment = StringAlignment.Center
            grfx.DrawString(Text, fnt, New SolidBrush(ForeColor), 0, 0)
        End Sub
End Class
```

I've set the *iFontPointSize* field to 18 just to have a jumbo font in the menu to ensure that the measuring and drawing logic is working correctly.

The *MenuFacenameOnMeasureItem* method begins by obtaining the *MenuItem* to be measured and constructing a font based on the *Text* property of that item:

```
Dim mi As MenuItem = DirectCast(obj, MenuItem)
Dim fnt As New Font(mi.Text.Substring(1), iFontPointSize)
```

The *Substring* method on the *Text* property skips past the ampersand. Next, the method creates a *StringFormat* object indicating that the letter following the ampersand will be underlined when the facename is displayed:

```
Dim strfmt As New StringFormat()
strfmt.HotkeyPrefix = HotkeyPrefix.Show
```

The *Text* property of the menu item is then measured based on the new *Font* and *StringFormat* objects:

```
Dim szf As SizeF = miea.Graphics.MeasureString(mi.Text, font, _
                                            1000, strfmt)
```

Without a check mark, the *szf* structure would provide the size of the menu item:

```
miea.ItemWidth = CInt(Math.Ceiling(sizef.Width))
miea.ItemHeight = CInt(Math.Ceiling(sizef.Height))
```

But the width must be increased by the width of the check mark when the height of the check mark is scaled to the height of the text

```
miea.ItemWidth += SystemInformation.MenuCheckSize.Width * _
                    miea.ItemHeight \ _
                        SystemInformation.MenuCheckSize.Height
```

and then decreased by the normal width of the check mark:

```
miea.ItemWidth -= SystemInformation.MenuCheckSize.Width
```

The *MenuFacenameOnDrawItem* method creates *Font* and *StringFormat* objects similarly and then calculates two *Rectangle* structures based on the *Bounds* property of the *DrawItemEventArgs* object. The first rectangle is the location and size of the check mark:

```
Dim rectCheck As Rectangle = diea.Bounds
rectCheck.Width = SystemInformation.MenuCheckSize.Width * _
                    rectCheck.Height \ _
                        SystemInformation.MenuCheckSize.Height
```

The second is the location and size of the text string:

```
Dim rectText As Rectangle = diea.Bounds
rectText.X += rectCheck.Width
```

From that point, it's simple. The *DrawBackground* method draws the background, *DrawMenuGlyph* draws the check mark, and *DrawString* draws the text, the color of which is based on whether or not the item is selected. And here's the result:

For some simple applications, such extensive processing of the *Measure-Item* and *DrawItem* events isn't required. For example, the following program loads a 64-pixel-square bitmap resource and uses this image as a menu item.

**HelpMenu.vb**

```
'-----------------------------------------------
' HelpMenu.vb (c) 2002 by Charles Petzold
'-----------------------------------------------
Imports System
Imports System.Drawing
Imports System.Windows.Forms

Class HelpMenu
    Inherits Form

    Private bmHelp As Bitmap

    Shared Sub Main()
        Application.Run(New HelpMenu())
    End Sub

    Sub New()
        Text = "Help Menu"

        bmHelp = New Bitmap(Me.GetType(), "Bighelp.bmp")

        Menu = New MainMenu()
        Menu.MenuItems.Add("&Help")

        Dim mi As New MenuItem("&Help")
        mi.OwnerDraw = True
        AddHandler mi.Click, AddressOf MenuHelpOnClick
        AddHandler mi.DrawItem, AddressOf MenuHelpOnDrawItem
        AddHandler mi.MeasureItem, AddressOf MenuHelpOnMeasureItem
        Menu.MenuItems(0).MenuItems.Add(mi)
    End Sub

    Private Sub MenuHelpOnMeasureItem(ByVal obj As Object, _
                            ByVal miea As MeasureItemEventArgs)
        miea.ItemWidth = bmHelp.Width
        miea.ItemHeight = bmHelp.Height
    End Sub

    Private Sub MenuHelpOnDrawItem(ByVal obj As Object, _
                            ByVal diea As DrawItemEventArgs)
        Dim rect As Rectangle = diea.Bounds
        rect.X += diea.Bounds.Width - bmHelp.Width
        rect.Width = bmHelp.Width

        diea.DrawBackground()
        diea.Graphics.DrawImage(bmHelp, rect)
    End Sub
```

```
      Private Sub MenuHelpOnClick(ByVal obj As Object, ByVal ea As EventArgs)
          MessageBox.Show("Help not yet implemented!", Text)
      End Sub
End Class
```

### Bighelp.bmp

The *MeasureItem* and *DrawItem* processing here is very modest. The *MeasureItem* handler needs only set *ItemWidth* and *ItemHeight* to the height and width of the bitmap, and *DrawItem* draws it, essentially right-justifying the image within the rectangle indicated by the *Bounds* property. The resulting effect perhaps mirrors the desperation of a new user:

# 15

# Paths, Regions, and Clipping

If you've ever done any graphics programming in PostScript, you probably already know what a graphics *path* is. In PostScript, you can't get to first base without using paths. While other graphics programming environments haven't gone to quite the extremes of PostScript in elevating the path to the role of central drawing object, the path has come to be recognized as a valuable graphics programming tool.

Very simply, the graphics path provides a way to connect straight lines and curves. As you know, you can draw connected straight lines using *Draw-Lines* and connected Bézier curves using *DrawBeziers*, but I haven't yet discussed any way to connect straight lines and Bézier curves to each other. That's what the path does. It sounds simple, but it opens up a variety of drawing techniques that I'll explore in this chapter and in Chapter 17 and Chapter 19.

You can also use paths for *clipping*. Clipping is the restriction of graphics output to a particular area of the screen or printer page. When you specify a path for clipping, the path is actually converted to a *region* first. A region describes an area of the output device in device coordinates.

## A Problem and Its Solution

Let's begin our exploration of graphics paths with a graphics programming problem. Suppose you want to draw a figure that's composed of a line, a semicircle, and another line, all connected to each other, and you want to use a pen that is considerably thicker than 1 pixel. Here's a possible first stab at drawing such a figure.

### LineArcCombo.vb

```
'-------------------------------------------------
' LineArcCombo.vb (c) 2002 by Charles Petzold
'-------------------------------------------------
Imports System
Imports System.Drawing
Imports System.Windows.Forms

Class LineArcCombo
    Inherits PrintableForm

    Shared Shadows Sub Main()
        Application.Run(New LineArcCombo())
    End Sub

    Sub New()
        Text = "Line & Arc Combo"
    End Sub

    Protected Overrides Sub DoPage(ByVal grfx As Graphics, _
            ByVal clr As Color, ByVal cx As Integer, ByVal cy As Integer)
        Dim pn As New Pen(clr, 25)
        grfx.DrawLine(pn, 25, 100, 125, 100)
        grfx.DrawArc(pn, 125, 50, 100, 100, -180, 180)
        grfx.DrawLine(pn, 225, 100, 325, 100)
    End Sub
End Class
```

The two lines are 100 units in length (that's 100 pixels on the video display and 1 inch on the printer), and the circle that forms the basis of the arc is 100 units in diameter. The pen is 25 units wide. And the result looks like this:

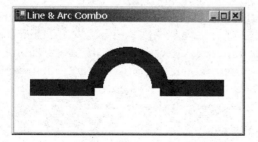

Perhaps this is exactly what you wanted. But it's not what I wanted. I wanted the lines and arc to be connected. Sure, they're touching each other, but they are definitely not visually connected. I don't want those notches on the bottom inside of the arc.

If you alter the LineArcCombo program to draw the figure twice, once with a thick gray pen and then with a 1-pixel-wide black pen, you might more clearly see what's going on here:

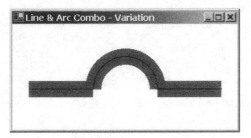

The 25-pixel-wide lines simply extend 12 pixels to each side of the 1-pixel-wide lines. Because the lines and arc are drawn with separate method calls, each figure is a distinct entity. At the two points at which the lines and arc meet, the wide lines intersect but do not form a composite whole.

You could perhaps finagle the coordinates to make this figure look right. You could, for example, lower the arc by 12 units or so. But deep in your heart of hearts, you know that you haven't solved the problem, only temporarily disguised it.

What we need here is some way of letting the graphics system know that the lines and arc are supposed to be connected. If you were dealing only with straight lines, drawing connected lines would be a snap: you'd use *DrawLines* to draw a polyline rather than *DrawLine* to draw discrete lines. For example, here's a program that draws something similar to what we want.

```
WidePolyline.vb
'-------------------------------------------
' WidePolyline.vb (c) 2002 by Charles Petzold
'-------------------------------------------
Imports System
Imports System.Drawing
Imports System.Windows.Forms

Class WidePolyline
    Inherits PrintableForm

    Shared Shadows Sub Main()
        Application.Run(New WidePolyline())
    End Sub

    Sub New()
        Text = "Wide Polyline"
    End Sub
```

*(continued)*

**WidePolyline.vb**   *(continued)*

```
    Protected Overrides Sub DoPage(ByVal grfx As Graphics, _
            ByVal clr As Color, ByVal cx As Integer, ByVal cy As Integer)
        Dim pn As New Pen(clr, 25)
        grfx.DrawLines(pn, New Point() { _
                            New Point(25, 100), New Point(125, 100), _
                            New Point(125, 50), New Point(225, 50), _
                            New Point(225, 100), New Point(325, 100)})
    End Sub
End Class
```

The *DrawLines* call includes an array of six *Point* structures to render a polyline that's composed of five lines:

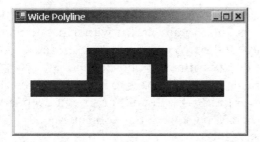

The graphics system knows that these lines are supposed to be connected because they're all included in one function call. The wide line is correctly drawn where the lines meet.

The use of a polyline in the WidePolyline program suggests another solution to the line-and-arc figure. You could look back in Chapter 5 to see how to draw an ellipse using a polyline, and then implement the arc in that way. Or you could convert the straight lines to Bézier splines (by specifying control points that are between and collinear to the end points), convert the arc to one or more Bézier splines (using formulas shown in Chapter 13), and then draw the whole thing using *DrawBeziers*.

But surely there's a more direct approach to letting the graphics system know that the lines and arc are connected. What we need is something like *DrawLines* that works with a combination of straight lines and arcs. And while we're at it, we may as well request that this magical function work with Bézier splines and cardinal splines as well.

That magical function (more precisely, a magical class) is *GraphicsPath*. Here's a program named LineArcPath that correctly draws the figure using only three more statements than LineArcCombo.

**LineArcPath.vb**

```
'-------------------------------------------------
' LineArcPath.vb (c) 2002 by Charles Petzold
'-------------------------------------------------
Imports System
Imports System.Drawing
Imports System.Drawing.Drawing2D
Imports System.Windows.Forms

Class LineArcPath
    Inherits PrintableForm

    Shared Shadows Sub Main()
        Application.Run(New LineArcPath())
    End Sub

    Sub New()
        Text = "Line & Arc in Path"
    End Sub

    Protected Overrides Sub DoPage(ByVal grfx As Graphics, _
            ByVal clr As Color, ByVal cx As Integer, ByVal cy As Integer)
        Dim path As New GraphicsPath()
        Dim pn As New Pen(clr, 25)

        path.AddLine(25, 100, 125, 100)
        path.AddArc(125, 50, 100, 100, -180, 180)
        path.AddLine(225, 100, 325, 100)

        grfx.DrawPath(pn, path)
    End Sub
End Class
```

One of these three additional statements creates the path at the beginning of the *DoPage* method:

```
Dim path As New GraphicsPath()
```

Although the class that implements the path is named *GraphicsPath*, I'll be using just the simple variable name *path* for instances of this class. *Graphics-Path* is defined in the *System.Drawing.Drawing2D* namespace, and an additional *Imports* statement accounts for another of the three additional statements in this program.

The LineArcCombo program drew the first line using the *DrawLine* method of the *Graphics* class:

```
grfx.DrawLine(pn, 25, 100, 125, 100)
```

The LineArcPath program replaces this statement with the *AddLine* method of the *GraphicsPath* class:

```
path.AddLine(25, 100, 125, 100)
```

The *AddLine* method doesn't have a *Pen* argument, but otherwise the arguments are identical to *DrawLine*. The same is true for *AddArc* as compared to *DrawArc*. The *AddLine* and *AddArc* calls don't draw anything. The coordinates specified in the method calls are simply accumulated in the path.

Finally (in the third of the three additional statements in this program), the path is actually drawn on the display device:

```
grfx.DrawPath(pn, path)
```

Notice that *DrawPath* is a method of our old friend the *Graphics* class. The result of the *DrawPath* call is exactly the figure we were hoping for:

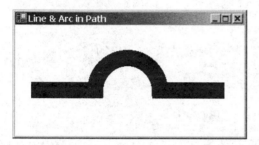

Programmers with experience in Win32 API or MFC programming will notice that the implementation of the graphics path in Windows Forms is conceptually different. In the Win32 API, the *BeginPath* function puts the device context into a special mode where all calls to the normal drawing functions (*LineTo*, *BezierTo*, and so forth) are not rendered but instead become part of the path. The path is ended with a call to *EndPath* and then drawn with a call to *StrokePath* (or something else is done with the path).

The Windows Forms approach is much more flexible. The Win32 API allows only one path to be in existence for a particular device context, but with Windows Forms, you can create and store as many paths as you want. And you don't need a *Graphics* object to create a path. The path exists independently of any *Graphics* object until it is rendered using *DrawPath* (or you do something else with the path).

You could, in fact, alter LineArcPath to store the *GraphicsPath* object as a field. You could create the path and make the calls to *AddLine* and *AddArc* in the form's constructor. The *DoPage* method would then just create the pen and call *DrawPath*. If you really wanted to get everything out of the way in the form's constructor, you could also make the pen-creation statement a field of the form.

## The Path, More Formally

Let's begin a more formal look at paths with a few definitions and a quick overview:

A *path* is a collection of device-independent coordinate points that describe straight lines and curves. These lines and curves might or might not be connected to each other. Any set of connected lines and curves within the path is known as a *figure* or a *subpath*. (Both terms are used in the Windows Forms interface. The terms are synonymous.) Thus, a path is composed of zero or more subpaths. Each subpath is a collection of connected lines and curves. The path created in the LineArcPath program has just one subpath.

A subpath can be either *open* or *closed*. A subpath is closed if the end of the last line in the subpath is connected to the beginning of the first line. (A special method in the *GraphicsPath* class—*CloseFigure*—is available to close a subpath.) Otherwise, the subpath is open. The single subpath created in the LineArcPath program is open.

I've already demonstrated the *DrawPath* method that draws the lines and curves that comprise a path on an output device. The *Graphics* class also includes a *FillPath* method that uses a brush to fill the interior of all closed subpaths in the path. For the purpose of the *FillPath* method, *all* open subpaths in the path are closed so that all the subpaths define enclosed areas.

As I'll demonstrate later in this chapter, you can also convert a path into a *region*. In contrast to a path (which is a collection of lines and curves), a region describes an area of the display surface. This area may be simple (a rectangle) or quite complex. You can fill the area defined by a region with a brush. Or you can use the region for clipping. Clipping restricts drawing to a particular area of the display surface.

Programmers approaching paths for the first time sometimes tend to think that a path is something much more than just a collection of lines and curve definitions. Let's disabuse ourselves of this notion by looking at the *Graphics-Path* properties. The path contains no other persistent data than what's accessible through its properties:

### *GraphicsPath* Properties

| Property | Type | Accessibility | Description |
|----------|------|---------------|-------------|
| *FillMode* | *FillMode* | Get/Set | *FillMode.Alternate* or *Fill-Mode.Winding* |
| *PointCount* | *Integer* | Get | Number of points in path |
| *PathPoints* | *PointF()* | Get | Array of coordinate points |
| *PathTypes* | *Byte()* | Get | Array of point types |
| *PathData* | *PathData* | Get | Duplicates *PathPoints* and *PathTypes* |

The *FillMode* enumeration is also used with the *DrawPolygon* method described in Chapter 5 and the *DrawClosedCurve* method featured in Chapter 13. For paths, the *FillMode* property determines how the path is filled (or how it's converted to a region) when the path contains overlapping lines.

The other four properties redundantly define nothing more than two arrays of identical size:

■ An array of *PointF* structures named *PathPoints*

■ An array of *Byte* values named *PathTypes*

The number of elements in these arrays (which you could obtain from *Path-Points.Length* or *PathTypes.Length*) is also provided by the *PointCount* property.

An additional layer of redundancy is provided by the *PathData* property. This property is an object of type *PathData*, defined in the *System.Drawing.Drawing2D* namespace. The *PathData* class has the following two properties:

### *PathData* Properties

| Property | Type | Accessibility | Description |
|----------|------|---------------|-------------|
| *Points* | *PointF()* | Get/Set | Array of coordinate points |
| *Types* | *Byte()* | Get/Set | Array of point types |

For any *GraphicsPath* object, the *Points* array of the *PathData* property is identical to the *PathPoints* property; the *Types* array of the *PathData* property is identical to the *PathTypes* property.

The values in the array of bytes that makes up the *PathTypes* property are actually values of the *PathPointType* enumeration, also defined in *System.Drawing.Drawing2D*:

### *PathPointType* Enumeration

| Member | Value |
| --- | --- |
| *Start* | &H0000 |
| *Line* | &H0001 |
| *Bezier* or *Bezier3* | &H0003 |
| *PathTypeMask* | &H0007 |
| *DashMode* | &H0010 |
| *PathMarker* | &H0020 |
| *CloseSubpath* | &H0080 |

Each *PointF* structure in the *PathPoints* array has an associated *PathPointType* of *Start*, *Line*, or *Bezier*. The *Start* type identifies the first point of a figure; the *Line* type indicates a point that defines a straight line; the *Bezier* type indicates a point that is part of a Bézier spline. Any arcs or canonical splines are converted into Bézier splines as they are added to the path. After my demonstration in Chapter 13 about how circles can be closely approximated using Bézier splines, such conversions should be plausible.

The last three values in the *PathPointType* enumeration table are flags that can be combined with the values of *Start*, *Line*, or *Bezier*. As you'll see, both the *PathMarker* and *CloseSubpath* flags are generated by *GraphicsPath* method calls.

The *PathTypeMask* enumeration member is a bit mask that lets you separate the values into point types (*Start*, *Line*, or *Bezier*) and flags (*DashMode*, *PathMarker*, or *CloseSubpath*).

What a path does *not* contain is anything that relates these coordinate points to real-world measurements. It is meaningless to ask if the coordinate points in a path are pixels or inches or millimeters or anything else. They're just points. They are converted to pixels, inches, or millimeters only when the path is rendered on an output device.

# Creating the Path

The *GraphicsPath* class has six constructors:

### *GraphicsPath* Constructors

```
GraphicsPath()

GraphicsPath(ByVal apt() As Point, ByVal abyPointType() As Byte)

GraphicsPath(ByVal aptf() As PointF, ByVal abyPointType() As Byte)

GraphicsPath(ByVal fm As FillMode)

GraphicsPath(ByVal apt() As Point, ByVal abyPointType() As Byte,
             ByVal fm As FillMode)

GraphicsPath(ByVal aptf() As PointF, ByVal abyPointType() As Byte,
             ByVal fm As FillMode)
```

If you don't specify a *FillMode* argument, the default is *FillMode.Alternate*.

As four of the constructors indicate, you can create a path using an array of *Point* or *PointF* structures and an array of corresponding *PathPointType* enumeration values, expressed as an array of *Byte* values. But it's unlikely that a program will start off creating a path in that way. Instead, these constructors are most profitably used to alter the *PathPoints* values of an existing path.

Normally, you create a new path using the default constructor:

```
Dim path As New GraphicsPath()
```

You then call methods of the *GraphicsPath* class that add straight lines and curves to the path. These methods are similar to corresponding methods in the *Graphics* class except that they begin with the word *Add* instead of *Draw* and they have no *Pen* argument.

Here are the methods of *GraphicsPath* that add straight lines, Bézier splines, arcs, and canonical splines to the current subpath. I'm not showing the arguments in the following table because for the most part they are the same as corresponding *Draw* methods defined in the *Graphics* class (except with no *Pen* arguments):

### *GraphicsPath* Methods (selection)

```
Sub AddLine(...)

Sub AddLines(...)

Sub AddArc(...)

Sub AddBezier(...)

Sub AddBeziers(...)

Sub AddCurve(...)
```

Arcs and canonical splines are converted to Bézier splines as they are added to the path.

If *path* is an object of type *GraphicsPath*, the following three calls add three connected lines to the path:

```
path.AddLine(0, 0, 0, 100)
path.AddLine(0, 100, 100, 100)
path.AddLine(100, 100, 100, 0)
```

The resultant figure looks like the left, bottom, and right sides of a square. I chose the coordinates so that the end point of each line is the same as the starting point of the next line, just as if I were drawing such a figure.

When defining a path, however, it's not necessary to be quite this meticulous. Until you specify otherwise (as I'll demonstrate shortly), the lines, arcs, Bézier splines, and canonical splines you add to the path all end up being part of the same figure. If the coordinates don't match up exactly, the path automatically generates a straight line to connect the pieces. You can achieve the same results as the three statements just shown by eliminating the second statement entirely:

```
path.AddLine(0, 0, 0, 100)
path.AddLine(100, 100, 100, 0)
```

Because the first line ends at (0, 100) and the second line begins at (100, 100), the path adds a line between those two points.

You can also make calls to the following three methods:

### *GraphicsPath* Methods (selection)

```
Sub StartFigure()

Sub CloseFigure()

Sub CloseAllFigures()
```

All three of these calls end the current subpath and begin a new subpath. In addition, *CloseFigure* closes the current subpath. If necessary, a straight line is automatically added to the path from the last point of the subpath to the first point of the subpath. *CloseAllFigures* closes all the subpaths that are part of the path so far.

The calls

```
path.AddLine(0, 0, 0, 100)
path.AddLine(0, 100, 100, 100)
path.AddLine(100, 100, 100, 0)
path.AddLine(100, 0, 0, 0)
path.CloseFigure()
```

explicitly create a square closed figure. The calls

```
path.AddLine(0, 0, 0, 100)
path.AddLine(100, 100, 100, 0)
path.CloseFigure()
```

create the same closed figure by forcing the path to automatically add lines for the bottom and top sides. The calls

```
path.AddLine(0, 0, 0, 100)
path.AddLine(0, 100, 100, 100)
path.AddLine(100, 100, 100, 0)
path.AddLine(100, 0, 0, 0)
path.StartFigure()
```

create a figure that consists of four sides of a square, but the figure isn't considered closed because it doesn't end with a call to *CloseFigure*.

The following methods start a new figure, which is then closed:

### *GraphicsPath* Methods (selection)

```
Sub AddRectangle(...)

Sub AddRectangles(...)

Sub AddPolygon(...)

Sub AddEllipse(...)

Sub AddPie(...)

Sub AddClosedCurve(...)
```

For example, the calls

```
path.AddLine(0, 0, 100, 0)
path.AddRectangle(New Rectangle(50, 50, 100, 100))
path.AddLine(200, 0, 0, 0)
```

create three subpaths:

- One line, unclosed

- Four lines, closed

- One line, unclosed

You can also add one path to another path:

### *GraphicsPath AddPath* Method

```
Sub AddPath(ByVal path As GraphicsPath, ByVal bConnect As Boolean)
```

The second argument indicates whether the path that is added should be connected to the current subpath.

The *AddString* methods add a text string to the path. The syntax of these methods is quite different from the syntax of the *DrawString* methods:

### *GraphicsPath AddString* Methods

```
Sub AddString(ByVal str As String, ByVal ff As FontFamily,
              ByVal iStyle As Integer, ByVal fSize As Single,
              ByVal pt As Point, ByVal sf As StringFormat)

Sub AddString(ByVal str As String, ByVal ff As FontFamily,
              ByVal iStyle As Integer, ByVal fSize As Single,
              ByVal ptf As PointF, ByVal sf As StringFormat)

Sub AddString(ByVal str As String, ByVal ff As FontFamily,
              ByVal iStyle As Integer, ByVal fSize As Single,
              ByVal rect As Rectangle, ByVal sf As StringFormat)

Sub AddString(ByVal str As String, ByVal ff As FontFamily,
              ByVal iStyle As Integer, ByVal fSize As Single,
              ByVal rectf As RectangleF, ByVal sf As StringFormat)
```

Despite the presence of arguments that don't look a bit like coordinate points, these methods do nothing more than add a series of straight lines and Bézier curves to the path. The lines and curves are the outlines of the font characters.

The arguments to *AddString* are actually not as odd as the method definitions initially suggest. The third argument is defined as an *Integer* but is really a member of the *FontStyle* enumeration (*Regular*, *Bold*, *Italic*, *Underline*, or *Strikeout*). The second, third, and fourth arguments are thus the same as three arguments used in a constructor to *Font*.

But why don't the *AddString* methods use *Font* arguments in the same way that *DrawString* does? Because a *Font* is most commonly a specific point size, and a path doesn't retain any metrical information. The *fSize* argument to *AddString* is not a point size. Specifying the *fSize* argument to *AddString* is similar to creating a *Font* with a pixel size and an argument of *GraphicsUnit.Pixel* or *GraphicsUnit.World*, as I discussed in Chapter 9 (on page 371). The text doesn't assume a metrical size until it's rendered.

Putting text into a path opens up such a wide variety of effects that Chapter 19 is entitled "Font Fun."

You can also insert nonfunctional markers into the path:

### *GraphicsPath* Methods (selection)

```
Sub SetMarkers()

Sub ClearMarkers()
```

You can then use the *GraphicsPathIterator* class to search for these markers. Such a facility possibly lets you edit a path with more ease.

# Rendering the Path

Most often, you call one of the following two methods of the *Graphics* class to render a path:

### *Graphics* Methods (selection)

```
Sub DrawPath(ByVal pn As Pen, ByVal path As GraphicsPath)

Sub FillPath(ByVal br As Brush, ByVal path As GraphicsPath)
```

The *DrawPath* method draws the lines and curves that comprise the path using the specified pen. *FillPath* fills the interiors of all closed subpaths using the specified brush. The method closes all unclosed subpaths for purposes of this function but doesn't permanently affect the path. If any lines of the path overlap, interiors are filled based on the current *FillPath* property of the *GraphicsPath* object. At the time of rendering, the points in the path are subject to any transforms that are in effect in the *Graphics* object.

Let's see how this stuff works in practice. The Flower program draws a flower using a path and a transform.

**Flower.vb**

```
'-------------------------------------------
' Flower.vb (c) 2002 by Charles Petzold
'-------------------------------------------
Imports System
Imports System.Drawing
Imports System.Drawing.Drawing2D
Imports System.Windows.Forms

Class Flower
    Inherits PrintableForm

    Shared Shadows Sub Main()
        Application.Run(New Flower())
    End Sub

    Sub New()
        Text = "Flower"
    End Sub
```

```
    Protected Overrides Sub DoPage(ByVal grfx As Graphics, _
            ByVal clr As Color, ByVal cx As Integer, ByVal cy As Integer)

        ' Draw green stem from lower left corner to center.
        grfx.DrawBezier(New Pen(Color.Green, 10), _
                New Point(0, cy), New Point(0, 3 * cy \ 4), _
                New Point(cx \ 4, cy \ 4), New Point(cx \ 2, cy \ 2))

        ' Set up transform for remainder of flower.
        Dim fScale As Single = Math.Min(cx, cy) / 2000.0F
        grfx.TranslateTransform(cx \ 2, cy \ 2)
        grfx.ScaleTransform(fScale, fScale)

        ' Draw red petals.
        Dim path As New GraphicsPath()
        path.AddBezier(New Point(0, 0), New Point(125, 125), _
                    New Point(475, 125), New Point(600, 0))
        path.AddBezier(New Point(600, 0), New Point(475, -125), _
                    New Point(125, -125), New Point(0, 0))

        Dim i As Integer
        For i = 0 To 7
            grfx.FillPath(Brushes.Red, path)
            grfx.DrawPath(Pens.Black, path)
            grfx.RotateTransform(360 \ 8)
        Next i

        ' Draw yellow circle in center.
        Dim rect As New Rectangle(-150, -150, 300, 300)
        grfx.FillEllipse(Brushes.Yellow, rect)
        grfx.DrawEllipse(Pens.Black, rect)
    End Sub
End Class
```

The *DoPage* method begins by drawing a Bézier spline from the lower left corner of the client area (or printer page) to the center to create the stem. Next, it sets up a world transform that creates a four-quadrant isotropic drawing area with the origin in the center and coordinates ranging from − 1000 to 1000.

The program needs to draw some petals next, and that's where the path comes into play. If petals looked like ellipses, I could just use *FillEllipse*. But petals are more accurately defined with a pair of Bézier splines, and filling such a figure requires a path. After the program creates the path, it calls *FillPath* and *DrawPath* eight times. After each pair of calls, the *RotateTransform* call changes the world transform of the *Graphics* object so that the eight petals are rotated around the center. *DoPage* finishes by drawing a yellow circle in the center of the client area.

I'm sure you remember the Scribble program from Chapter 8. At the time, I demonstrated how to save all the lines the user draws using the *ArrayList* class, which is an array-like object that can dynamically resize itself. The use of the *ArrayList* class is actually quite similar to saving coordinates in a path. And using a *GraphicsPath* object instead of an *ArrayList* object simplifies the program considerably. It's even simpler than the version in Chapter 11 (Scribble-WithBitmap) that saved the image using a shadow bitmap.

**ScribbleWithPath.vb**

```
'-------------------------------------------------
' ScribbleWithPath.vb (c) 2002 by Charles Petzold
'-------------------------------------------------
Imports System
Imports System.Drawing
Imports System.Drawing.Drawing2D
Imports System.Windows.Forms

Class ScribbleWithPath
    Inherits Form

    Private path As GraphicsPath
    Private bTracking As Boolean
    Private ptLast As Point

    Shared Sub Main()
        Application.Run(New ScribbleWithPath())
    End Sub

    Sub New()
        Text = "Scribble with Path"
        BackColor = SystemColors.Window
        ForeColor = SystemColors.WindowText
```

```
       ' Create the path.
       path = New GraphicsPath()
    End Sub

    Protected Overrides Sub OnMouseDown(ByVal mea As MouseEventArgs)
       If mea.Button <> MouseButtons.Left Then Return

       ptLast = New Point(mea.X, mea.Y)
       bTracking = True

       ' Start a figure.
       path.StartFigure()
    End Sub

    Protected Overrides Sub OnMouseMove(ByVal mea As MouseEventArgs)
       If Not bTracking Then Return

       Dim ptNew As New Point(mea.X, mea.Y)
       Dim grfx As Graphics = CreateGraphics()
       grfx.DrawLine(New Pen(ForeColor), ptLast, ptNew)
       grfx.Dispose()

       ' Add a line.
       path.AddLine(ptLast, ptNew)
       ptLast = ptNew
    End Sub

    Protected Overrides Sub OnMouseUp(ByVal mea As MouseEventArgs)
       bTracking = False
    End Sub

    Protected Overrides Sub OnPaint(ByVal pea As PaintEventArgs)
       ' Draw the path.
       pea.Graphics.DrawPath(New Pen(ForeColor), path)
    End Sub
End Class
```

Aside from the additional *Imports* statement, transforming the no-save version of Scribble to ScribbleWithPath requires defining a path as a field variable and then adding just four statements, all identified with comments.

The path is created in the form's constructor. Whenever the left mouse button is pressed when the cursor is positioned in the form's client area, a call to the *StartFigure* method begins a new subpath. An *AddLine* call during the *OnMouseMove* method adds a new line to the path. The *OnPaint* method is simply a call to *DrawPath*.

# Path Transforms

The *GraphicsPath* class contains several methods that let a program modify a path. The first of these is likely to be very confusing. (At least it was for me when I first encountered it.)

### *GraphicsPath* Transform Method

```
Sub Transform(ByVal matx As Matrix)
```

As you know from Chapter 7, the *Graphics* class has a property named *Transform* that is of type *Matrix*. The *Transform* property of the *Graphics* class affects the display of all subsequent graphics output. But the *Transform* in *GraphicsPath* is different. *Transform* is not a property of *GraphicsPath*; *Transform* is a method. And that's an important distinction. A property is usually a characteristic of an object; a method usually carries out an operation. A property is an adjective; a method is a verb.

The *Transform* method of the *GraphicsPath* class permanently alters the coordinates of the path by applying the specified transform to those coordinates. The *Transform* method doesn't affect coordinates subsequently added to the path. Nor does the *GraphicsPath* object retain the transform in any way.

For example, if you have a *Matrix* object named *matx* that describes a doubling of coordinate points, and you call

```
path.Transform(matx)
```

the result is equivalent to obtaining the array of coordinate points in the path using the *PathPoints* property, doubling all the numbers in the array, and then creating a new path based on those modified points.

The *Transform* method is the only method in the *GraphicsPath* class concerned with matrix transforms. To use it, you'll need to make use of the *Matrix* class, which is defined in the *System.Drawing.Drawing2D* namespace and which I touched on briefly toward the end of Chapter 7. The easiest way to use the *Matrix* class is first to create an identity matrix using the default constructor:

```
Dim matx As New Matrix()
```

You can then use various methods of the *Matrix* class to alter this transform. The *Translate* method is just like the *TranslateTransform* method of the *Graphics* class. (In fact, I wouldn't be surprised if the *Graphics* class implemented its *TranslateTransform* methods by simply calling the corresponding *Translate* method of its *Transform* property.)

### *Matrix Translate* **Methods**

```
Sub Translate(ByVal dx As Single, ByVal dy As Single)

Sub Translate(ByVal dx As Single, ByVal dy As Single,
          ByVal mo As MatrixOrder)
```

The *MatrixOrder* enumeration has two members, *Append* and *Prepend*.

The *Scale* method is just like the *ScaleTransform* method of the *Graphics* class:

### *Matrix Scale* **Methods**

```
Sub Scale(ByVal sx As Single, ByVal sy As Single)

Sub Scale(ByVal sx As Single, ByVal xy As Single,
          ByVal mo As MatrixOrder)
```

Earlier I mentioned doubling all the coordinates in a path. You can do that with the following three lines of code:

```
Dim matx As New Matrix()
matx.Scale(2, 2)
path.Transform(matx)
```

The *Matrix* class also includes a *Rotate* method:

### *Matrix* **Rotate Methods**

```
Sub Rotate(ByVal fAngle As Single)

Sub Rotate(ByVal fAngle As Single, ByVal mo As MatrixOrder)
```

You can alter the Flower program to use the *Rotate* method of the *Matrix* class rather than the *RotateTransform* method of the *Graphics* class. After creating the path, create a *Matrix* object that describes a rotation of 45 degrees:

```
Dim matx As New Matrix()
matx.Rotate(45)
```

Then in the *For* loop, rather than call *RotateTransform*, call the *Transform* method of the path:

```
path.Transform(matx)
```

In the original version of Flower, the path remains the same and the *Rotate-Transform* call affects how the coordinates are transformed as the path is rendered by the *Graphics* class. In the altered version, the coordinates stored in the path are rotated. By the end of the *For* loop, after eight rotations of 45 degrees, the coordinates of the path have been restored to their original values.

Here's an interesting method of the *Matrix* class that isn't duplicated by a method in the *Graphics* class:

### Matrix RotateAt Methods

```
Sub RotateAt(ByVal fAngle As Single, ByVal ptf As PointF)

Sub RotateAt(ByVal fAngle As Single, ByVal ptf As PointF,
          ByVal mo As MatrixOrder)
```

Normally the matrix transform rotates an image around the point (0, 0). This method lets you specify the point around which the rotation occurs. For example, suppose you create a path like this:

```
Dim path As New GraphicsPath()
path.AddRectangle(New Rectangle(0, 0, 100, 100))
```

The path contains the points (0, 0), (100, 0), (100, 100), and (0, 100). If you then create a *Matrix* object, call the *Rotate* method for 45 degrees, and apply it to the path like so:

```
Dim matx As New Matrix()
matx.Rotate(45)
path.Transform(matx)
```

the points in the path are, with some rounding, (0, 0), (70.7, 70.7), (0, 141.4), and (– 70.7, 70.7). If instead you use the *RotateAt* method specifying the center of the rectangle

```
Dim matx As New Matrix()
matx.RotateAt(45, New PointF(50, 50))
path.Transform(matx);
```

the path contains the points (50, −20.7), (120.7, 50), (50, 120.7), and (−20.7, 50). The *Matrix* class also includes a method for shearing:

### Matrix Shear Methods

```
Sub Shear(ByVal xShear As Single, ByVal yShear As Single)

Sub Shear(ByVal xShear As Single, ByVal yShear As Single,
          ByVal mo As MatrixOrder)
```

Applied to a default transform, this method results in the following transformation formulas:

$$x' = x + xShear \cdot y$$
$$y' = yShear \cdot x + y$$

# Other Path Modifications

*Transform* is not the only method of the *GraphicsPath* class that modifies all the coordinates of a path. The *Flatten* method is intended to convert all the Bézier splines in a path into straight-line segments:

### *GraphicsPath Flatten* Methods

```
Sub Flatten()

Sub Flatten(ByVal matx As Matrix)

Sub Flatten(ByVal matx As Matrix, ByVal fFlatness As Single)
```

You can optionally apply a *Matrix* to transform the points before flattening them.

The number of line segments decreases as the *fFlatness* argument gets higher. The default *fFlatness* argument is equivalent to an argument of 0.25. The method is not defined for values of 0.

The *Widen* method has a much more profound effect on the path than the *Flatten* method does. The first argument is always a *Pen* object:

### *GraphicsPath Widen* Methods

```
Sub Widen(ByVal pn As Pen)

Sub Widen(ByVal pn As Pen, ByVal matx As Matrix)

Sub Widen(ByVal pn As Pen, ByVal matx As Matrix,
        ByVal fFlatness As Single)
```

The method ignores the color of the pen and uses only the pen width, generally a width of at least a couple units or so. Imagine the path being drawn using a thick pen. The new path is the outline of that thick line. Every open path is converted into a closed path, and every closed path is converted into two closed paths. Before widening the path, the method converts all Bézier splines to polylines. You can optionally specify a flatness factor for this conversion; you can also optionally use a *Matrix* to transform the coordinates in the path before the widening process.

The results of the *Widen* method are sometimes a bit strange, so it helps to look at an example. The following program creates a path in the constructor containing one open subpath shaped like a V, and one closed subpath shaped like a triangle.

**WidenPath.vb**

```
'-------------------------------------------
' WidenPath.vb (c) 2002 by Charles Petzold
'-------------------------------------------
Imports System
Imports System.Drawing
Imports System.Drawing.Drawing2D
Imports System.Windows.Forms

Class WidenPath
    Inherits PrintableForm

    Private path As GraphicsPath

    Shared Shadows Sub Main()
        Application.Run(New WidenPath())
    End Sub

    Sub New()
        Text = "Widen Path"

        path = New GraphicsPath()
        ' Create open subpath.
        path.AddLines(New Point() {New Point(20, 10), _
                                   New Point(50, 50), _
                                   New Point(80, 10)})
        ' Create closed subpath.
        path.AddPolygon(New Point() {New Point(20, 30), _
                                     New Point(50, 70), _
                                     New Point(80, 30)})
    End Sub

    Protected Overrides Sub DoPage(ByVal grfx As Graphics, _
            ByVal clr As Color, ByVal cx As Integer, ByVal cy As Integer)
        grfx.ScaleTransform(cx / 300.0F, cy / 200.0F)
        Dim i As Integer

        For i = 0 To 5
            Dim pathClone As GraphicsPath = _
                               DirectCast(path.Clone(), GraphicsPath)
            Dim matx As New Matrix()
            Dim pnThin As New Pen(clr, 1)
            Dim pnThick As New Pen(clr, 5)
            Dim pnWiden As New Pen(clr, 7.5F)
            Dim br As New SolidBrush(clr)

            matx.Translate((i Mod 3) * 100, (i \ 3) * 100)

            If i < 3 Then
                pathClone.Transform(matx)
```

```
            Else
                pathClone.Widen(pnWiden, matx)
            End If

            Select Case i Mod 3
                Case 0
                    grfx.DrawPath(pnThin, pathClone)
                Case 1
                    grfx.DrawPath(pnThick, pathClone)
                Case 2
                    grfx.FillPath(br, pathClone)
            End Select
        Next i
    End Sub
End Class
```

The *DoPage* method makes six copies of this path using the *Clone* method and uses the *Transform* method to position each copy in a particular area of the display. It then draws the path six different ways. The results look like this:

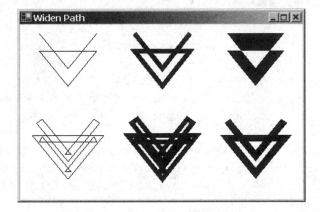

The top row shows the path drawn with a 1-unit-wide pen, drawn with a 5-unit-wide pen, and filled. The bottom row shows the same three drawing operations following a call to *Widen* using a 7.5-unit-wide pen.

The two renditions on the left side of the display show most clearly the effects of the *Widen* method. The open V-shaped subpath is converted into a closed subpath that outlines the path as if it had been drawn with a wide pen. The closed triangle subpath is converted into two paths, one on the outside and one on the inside of the line that would result from drawing the path with a wide pen. Of course, the little interior loops at the apexes look rather odd, but those are the results of the algorithm that the *Widen* method uses.

The two renditions in the center column look just like the ones in the left column except drawn with a thicker pen.

The filled path in the upper right corner has an unfilled interior area as a result of the default filling mode of the path, which is *FillMode.Alternating*. Change the fill mode to *FillMode.Winding* and all interior areas will be filled. The most interesting version is the figure in the lower right corner. That's the effect of *FillPath* on the widened path. It looks very much like *DrawPath* on the original path using a wide pen.

You can determine the smallest rectangle in which the path can fit by using the *GetBounds* method, either with or without taking into account the effect of a matrix transform and a wide pen:

### *GraphicsPath GetBounds* Methods

```
Function GetBounds() As RectangleF

Function GetBounds(ByVal matx As Matrix) As RectangleF

Function GetBounds(ByVal matx As Matrix,
                   ByVal pn As Pen) As RectangleF
```

Neither argument has any effect on the coordinates stored in the path. You should be aware that the calculated rectangle reflects the minimum and maximum $x$ and $y$ coordinates of all the points in the path. If the path contains Bézier splines, the rectangle reflects the coordinates of the control points, not the actual curve. To get a more accurate measurement of the figure, call *Flatten* before *GetBounds*.

In Chapter 7, I spoke of the matrix transform as being a *linear* transform. The linearity of the transform imposes certain restrictions on what you can do with the transform. Parallelograms will always be transformed into other parallelograms, for example.

The *GraphicsPath* class introduces another transform in the *Warp* method. Like the *Transform* method, the *Warp* method modifies all the coordinates of the path. But the *Warp* transform is nonlinear, the only nonlinear transform in GDI+.

To use *Warp*, you specify four source coordinates and four destination coordinates. The method maps the four source coordinates to the four corresponding destination coordinates. The source coordinates are specified as a *RectangleF* structure. Conveniently (but not necessarily), you can set the *RectangleF* argument to the *RectangleF* structure returned from *GetBounds*. The destination coordinates are specified as an array of *PointF* structures:

### *GraphicsPath Warp* Methods

```
Sub Warp(ByVal aptfDst() As PointF, ByVal rectfSrc As RectangleF)

Sub Warp(ByVal aptfDst() As PointF, ByVal rectfSrc As RectangleF,
        ByVal matx As Matrix )

Sub Warp(ByVal aptfDst() As PointF, ByVal rectfSrc As RectangleF,
        ByVal matx As Matrix, ByVal wm As WarpMode)

Sub Warp(ByVal aptfDst() As PointF, ByVal rectfSrc As RectangleF,
        ByVal matx As Matrix, ByVal wm As WarpMode,
        ByVal fFlatness As Single)
```

You can optionally also supply a *Matrix* object and a flatness value. The source points are transformed to the destination points like this:

- *aptfDst(0)* is the destination of the upper left corner of the rectangle.

- *aptfDst(1)* is the destination of the upper right corner of the rectangle.

- *aptfDst(2)* is the destination of the lower left corner of the rectangle.

- *aptfDst(3)* is the destination of the lower right corner of the rectangle.

An optional argument determines how intermediary points are calculated:

### *WarpMode* Enumeration

| Member | Value |
|---|---|
| *Perspective* | 0 |
| *Bilinear* | 1 |

The PathWarping program lets you experiment with the *Warp* function. The form's constructor creates a path with a square 8-by-8 checkerboard pattern. You then use the mouse to indicate the destination of this path.

**PathWarping.vb**

```
'-------------------------------------------
' PathWarping.vb (c) 2002 by Charles Petzold
'-------------------------------------------
Imports System
Imports System.Drawing
Imports System.Drawing.Drawing2D
Imports System.Windows.Forms

Class PathWarping
    Inherits Form
```

*(continued)*

**PathWarping.vb**   *(continued)*

```vb
Private miWarpMode As MenuItem
Private path As GraphicsPath
Private aptfDest(3) As PointF

Shared Sub Main()
    Application.Run(New PathWarping())
End Sub

Sub New()
    Text = "Path Warping"

    ' Create menu.
    Menu = New MainMenu()
    Menu.MenuItems.Add("&Warp Mode")
    Dim ehClick As EventHandler = AddressOf MenuWarpModeOnClick
    miWarpMode = New MenuItem("&" & CType(0, WarpMode).ToString(), _
                              ehClick)
    miWarpMode.RadioCheck = True
    miWarpMode.Checked = True
    Menu.MenuItems(0).MenuItems.Add(miWarpMode)
    Dim mi As New MenuItem("&" & CType(1, WarpMode).ToString(), ehClick)
    mi.RadioCheck = True
    Menu.MenuItems(0).MenuItems.Add(mi)

    ' Create path.
    path = New GraphicsPath()
    Dim i As Integer
    For i = 0 To 8
        path.StartFigure()
        path.AddLine(0, 100 * i, 800, 100 * i)
        path.StartFigure()
        path.AddLine(100 * i, 0, 100 * i, 800)
    Next i

    ' Initialize PointF array.
    aptfDest(0) = New PointF(50, 50)
    aptfDest(1) = New PointF(200, 50)
    aptfDest(2) = New PointF(50, 200)
    aptfDest(3) = New PointF(200, 200)
End Sub

Private Sub MenuWarpModeOnClick(ByVal obj As Object, _
                                ByVal ea As EventArgs)
    miWarpMode.Checked = False
    miWarpMode = DirectCast(obj, MenuItem)
    miWarpMode.Checked = True
    Invalidate()
End Sub

Protected Overrides Sub OnMouseDown(ByVal mea As MouseEventArgs)
    Dim pt As Point
```

```
        If mea.Button = MouseButtons.Left Then
            If ModifierKeys = Keys.None Then
                pt = Point.Round(aptfDest(0))
            ElseIf ModifierKeys = Keys.Shift Then
                pt = Point.Round(aptfDest(2))
            Else
                Return
            End If
        ElseIf mea.Button = MouseButtons.Right Then
            If ModifierKeys = Keys.None Then
                pt = Point.Round(aptfDest(1))
            ElseIf ModifierKeys = Keys.Shift Then
                pt = Point.Round(aptfDest(3))
            Else
                Return
            End If
        Else
            Return
        End If

        Cursor.Position = PointToScreen(pt)
    End Sub

    Protected Overrides Sub OnMouseMove(ByVal mea As MouseEventArgs)
        Dim pt As New Point(mea.X, mea.Y)

        If mea.Button = MouseButtons.Left Then
            If ModifierKeys = Keys.None Then
                aptfDest(0) = Point.op_Implicit(pt)
            ElseIf ModifierKeys = Keys.Shift Then
                aptfDest(2) = Point.op_Implicit(pt)
            Else
                Return
            End If
        ElseIf mea.Button = MouseButtons.Right Then
            If ModifierKeys = Keys.None Then
                aptfDest(1) = Point.op_Implicit(pt)
            ElseIf ModifierKeys = Keys.Shift Then
                aptfDest(3) = Point.op_Implicit(pt)
            Else
                Return
            End If
        Else
            Return
        End If

        Invalidate()
    End Sub

    Protected Overrides Sub OnPaint(ByVal pea As PaintEventArgs)
        Dim grfx As Graphics = pea.Graphics
```

*(continued)*

**PathWarping.vb**    *(continued)*

```
        Dim pathWarped As GraphicsPath = _
                            DirectCast(path.Clone(), GraphicsPath)
        Dim wm As WarpMode = CType(miWarpMode.Index, WarpMode)

        pathWarped.Warp(aptfDest, path.GetBounds(), New Matrix(), wm)
        grfx.DrawPath(New Pen(ForeColor), pathWarped)
    End Sub
End Class
```

Use the left and right mouse buttons to set the upper left and upper right destination coordinates. Use the left and right mouse buttons with the Shift key pressed to set the lower left and lower right destination coordinates. Use the menu to select between *Perspective* and *Bilinear* modes. (And notice the clever way in which the *OnPaint* method casts the *Index* property of the clicked menu item to a member of type *WarpMode*.) Here's an example of a *Perspective* warp:

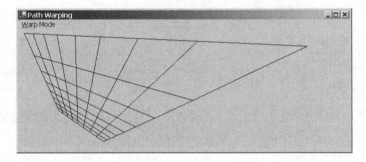

The *Bilinear* warp doesn't work, at least for this image.

The path provides a convenient way for you to implement your own non-linear transforms. You first store the figure you want to display in a path. You then access the *PathPoints* and *PathTypes* properties of the path to obtain all the coordinate points. Modify these points in whatever way you want, and then use one of the nondefault *GraphicsPath* constructors to create a new path based on the modified arrays. I have two examples of this technique in Chapter 19.

# Clipping with Paths

Besides drawing and filling paths, you can also use paths to set a clipping region for the *Graphics* object:

### *Graphics SetClip* Methods (selection)

```
Sub SetClip(ByVal path As GraphicsPath)
```

```
Sub SetClip(ByVal path As GraphicsPath, ByVal cm As CombineMode)
```

Suppose the path contains an ellipse. When you call the first version of *SetClip*, all subsequent drawing is restricted to that ellipse. I'll talk about the second version of *SetClip* shortly. But first, let's jump right into a demonstration program. The Clover program defines a path containing four overlapping ellipses and uses that for the clipping region.

## Clover.vb

```vb
'-------------------------------------------
' Clover.vb (c) 2002 by Charles Petzold
'-------------------------------------------
Imports System
Imports System.Drawing
Imports System.Drawing.Drawing2D
Imports System.Windows.Forms

Class Clover
    Inherits PrintableForm

    Shared Shadows Sub Main()
        Application.Run(New Clover())
    End Sub

    Sub New()
        Text = "Clover"
    End Sub

    Protected Overrides Sub DoPage(ByVal grfx As Graphics, _
            ByVal clr As Color, ByVal cx As Integer, ByVal cy As Integer)
        Dim path As New GraphicsPath()

        path.AddEllipse(0, cy \ 3, cx \ 2, cy \ 3)          ' Left
        path.AddEllipse(cx \ 2, cy \ 3, cx \ 2, cy \ 3)     ' Right
        path.AddEllipse(cx \ 3, 0, cx \ 3, cy \ 2)          ' Top
        path.AddEllipse(cx \ 3, cy \ 2, cx \ 3, cy \ 2)     ' Bottom

        grfx.SetClip(path)
        grfx.TranslateTransform(cx \ 2, cy \ 2)

        Dim pn As New Pen(clr)
        Dim fRadius As Single = CSng(Math.Sqrt(Math.Pow(cx \ 2, 2) + _
                                         Math.Pow(cy \ 2, 2)))
        Dim fAngle As Single

        For fAngle = Math.PI / 180 To Math.PI * 2 Step Math.PI / 180
            grfx.DrawLine(pn, 0, 0, fRadius * CSng(Math.Cos(fAngle)), _
                                -fRadius * CSng(Math.Sin(fAngle)))
        Next fAngle
    End Sub
End Class
```

The *GraphicsPath* is created in the *DoPage* method. The path consists of four ellipses based on the size of the client area or the printer page. The *SetClip* method sets the clipping region for the *Graphics* object based on the path.

The *DoPage* method next sets an origin in the center of the drawing space and draws 360 lines radiating from the center. These lines are clipped to the interior of the ellipses:

Such an image would be difficult to draw in any other way. You'll notice that the clipping region doesn't include the area where the ellipses overlap. That's a result of using the default path-filling mode of *FillMode.Alternate*. If you change the filling mode to

```
path.FillMode = FillMode.Winding
```

before calling *SetClip*, those overlapping areas become part of the clipping region as well.

Clipping is often an algorithmically slow process. I've derived the *Clover* class from *PrintableForm* so that you can click on the client area and print the image, but be forewarned that it could take an hour or more for the program to print.

The question naturally arises, How do the page transform and the world transform affect the clipping region?

When you call *SetClip*, the path coordinates are assumed to be world coordinates. The world coordinates are converted to device coordinates just as if you were drawing or filling the path. The clipping region is saved in device coordinates and remains in device coordinates. For example, after the *SetClip* call in Clover, you can change the page transform and the world transform to anything, and drawing will still be restricted to the same area of the window. In fact, I've used *TranslateTransform* in Clover without affecting the location of the clipping region.

The second version of *SetClip* I showed lets you combine the existing clipping region with the new clipping region specified in the *SetClip* method:

### *CombineMode* Enumeration

| Member | Value | Description |
|--------|-------|-------------|
| *Replace* | 0 | Clip = New |
| *Intersect* | 1 | Clip = New ∩ Existing |
| *Union* | 2 | Clip = New ∪ Existing |
| *Xor* | 3 | Clip = Union − Intersection |
| *Exclude* | 4 | Clip = Existing − New |
| *Complement* | 5 | Clip = New − Existing |

The following program creates a clipping region based on two overlapping ellipses. A menu item lets you select which *CombineMode* value is used to combine the two ellipses. The program then colors its entire client area. As in the PathWarping program, I've used the submenu indices (which range from 0 through 5) as the *CombineMode* value.

### ClippingCombinations.vb

```
'-----------------------------------------------------
' ClippingCombinations.vb (c) 2002 by Charles Petzold
'-----------------------------------------------------
Imports System
Imports System.Drawing
Imports System.Drawing.Drawing2D
Imports System.Windows.Forms

Class ClippingCombinations
    Inherits PrintableForm

    Private strCaption As String = "CombineMode = "
    Private miCombineMode As MenuItem

    Shared Shadows Sub Main()
        Application.Run(New ClippingCombinations())
    End Sub

    Sub New()
        Text = strCaption & CType(0, CombineMode).ToString()

        Menu = New MainMenu()
        Menu.MenuItems.Add("&CombineMode")
        Dim ehClick As EventHandler = AddressOf MenuCombineModeOnClick
        Dim i As Integer
```

*(continued)*

**ClippingCombinations.vb**  *(continued)*

```
        For i = 0 To 5
            Dim mi As New MenuItem("&" & CType(i, CombineMode).ToString())
            AddHandler mi.Click, ehClick
            mi.RadioCheck = True
            Menu.MenuItems(0).MenuItems.Add(mi)
        Next i
        miCombineMode = Menu.MenuItems(0).MenuItems(0)
        miCombineMode.Checked = True
    End Sub

    Private Sub MenuCombineModeOnClick(ByVal obj As Object, _
                                       ByVal ea As EventArgs)
        miCombineMode.Checked = False
        miCombineMode = DirectCast(obj, MenuItem)
        miCombineMode.Checked = True
        Text = strCaption & _
                    CType(miCombineMode.Index, CombineMode).ToString()
        Invalidate()
    End Sub

    Protected Overrides Sub DoPage(ByVal grfx As Graphics, _
            ByVal clr As Color, ByVal cx As Integer, ByVal cy As Integer)
        Dim path As New GraphicsPath()
        path.AddEllipse(0, 0, 2 * cx \ 3, cy)
        grfx.SetClip(path)
        path.Reset()
        path.AddEllipse(cx \ 3, 0, 2 * cx \ 3, cy)
        grfx.SetClip(path, CType(miCombineMode.Index, CombineMode))
        grfx.FillRectangle(Brushes.Red, 0, 0, cx, cy)
    End Sub
End Class
```

Here's the result when the two ellipses are combined with *CombineMode.Xor*:

Additional versions of the *SetClip* method let you set the clipping region (or combine the clipping region) with a rectangle:

### Graphics SetClip Methods (selection)

```
Sub SetClip(ByVal rect As Rectangle)

Sub SetClip(ByVal rect As Rectangle, ByVal cm As CombineMode)

Sub SetClip(ByVal rectf As RectangleF)

Sub SetClip(ByVal rectf As RectangleF, ByVal cm As CombineMode)
```

The *Graphics* class also includes methods named *IntersectClip* and *ExcludeClip* to modify the existing clipping region. To return the clipping region to normal (that is, an infinitely large region) call the following method:

### Graphics ResetClip Method

```
Sub ResetClip()
```

# Clipping Bitmaps

Clipping lets you draw nonrectangular areas of a bitmap. Here's a program that loads an image and defines a path in its constructor. In the *DoPage* method, the program sets a clipping region based on the path and draws the bitmap.

```vb
' KeyholeClip.vb
'-------------------------------------------
' KeyholeClip.vb (c) 2002 by Charles Petzold
'-------------------------------------------
Imports System
Imports System.Drawing
Imports System.Drawing.Drawing2D
Imports System.Windows.Forms

Class KeyholeClip
    Inherits PrintableForm

    Protected img As Image
    Protected path As GraphicsPath

    Shared Shadows Sub Main()
        Application.Run(New KeyholeClip())
    End Sub

    Sub New()
        Text = "Keyhole Clip"
```

*(continued)*

**KeyholeClip.vb** *(continued)*

```
        img = Image.FromFile( _
                "..\..\..\Images and Bitmaps\Apollo11FullColor.jpg")

        path = New GraphicsPath()
        path.AddArc(80, 0, 80, 80, 45, -270)
        path.AddLine(70, 180, 170, 180)
    End Sub

    Protected Overrides Sub DoPage(ByVal grfx As Graphics, _
            ByVal clr As Color, ByVal cx As Integer, ByVal cy As Integer)
        grfx.SetClip(path)
        grfx.DrawImage(img, 0, 0, img.Width, img.Height)
    End Sub
End Class
```

The result looks a bit incongruous (a keyhole on the moon?), but it works:

Obviously, I defined the path in this program based on this specific image, and under the assumption that the image would be drawn using its pixel dimension with the upper left corner at the point (0, 0).

But suppose you wanted to draw the clipped image in the center of the client area. It's easy to draw the image in the center, but how do you get the path in the center also? One solution is to re-create the path based on the size of the client area. Another solution is to translate the path or to use the following methods that translate the clipping region:

### Graphics *TranslateClip* Methods

```
Sub TranslateClip(ByVal cx As Integer, ByVal cy As Integer)
Sub TranslateClip(ByVal cx As Single, ByVal cy As Single)
```

The KeyholeClipCentered program overrides the KeyholeClip program and centers both the clipping region and the path in the client area.

**KeyholeClipCentered.vb**

```
'----------------------------------------------------
' KeyholeClipCentered.vb (c) 2002 by Charles Petzold
'----------------------------------------------------
Imports System
Imports System.Drawing
Imports System.Windows.Forms

Class KeyholeClipCentered
    Inherits KeyholeClip

    Shared Shadows Sub Main()
        Application.Run(new KeyholeClipCentered())
    End Sub

    Sub New()
        Text &= " Centered"
    End Sub

    Protected Overrides Sub DoPage(ByVal grfx As Graphics, _
            ByVal clr As Color, ByVal cx As Integer, ByVal cy As Integer)
        grfx.SetClip(path)

        Dim rectf As RectangleF = path.GetBounds()
        Dim xOffset As Integer = CInt((cx - rectf.Width) / 2 - rectf.X)
        Dim yOffset As Integer = CInt((cy - rectf.Height) / 2 - rectf.Y)

        grfx.TranslateClip(xOffset, yOffset)
        grfx.DrawImage(img, xOffset, yOffset, img.Width, img.Height)
    End Sub
End Class
```

It's also possible to create a new bitmap based on the size of the clipped image and to use transparency to get the same effect. The KeyholeBitmap program demonstrates this technique.

**KeyholeBitmap.vb**

```
'----------------------------------------------------
' KeyholeBitmap.vb (c) 2002 by Charles Petzold
'----------------------------------------------------
Imports System
Imports System.Drawing
Imports System.Drawing.Drawing2D
Imports System.Drawing.Imaging
Imports System.Windows.Forms

Class KeyholeBitmap
    Inherits PrintableForm

    Private bm As Bitmap
```

*(continued)*

**KeyholeBitmap.vb**   *(continued)*

```
    Shared Shadows Sub Main()
        Application.Run(New KeyholeBitmap())
    End Sub

    Sub New()
        Text = "Keyhole Bitmap"

        ' Load image.
        Dim img As Image = Image.FromFile( _
                    "..\..\..\Images and Bitmaps\Apollo11FullColor.jpg")

        ' Create clipping path.
        Dim path As New GraphicsPath()
        path.AddArc(80, 0, 80, 80, 45, -270)
        path.AddLine(70, 180, 170, 180)

        ' Get size of clipping path.
        Dim rectf As RectangleF = path.GetBounds()

        ' Create new bitmap initialized to transparent.
        bm = New Bitmap(CInt(rectf.Width), CInt(rectf.Height), _
                    PixelFormat.Format32bppArgb)

        ' Create Graphics Object based on new bitmap.
        Dim grfx As Graphics = Graphics.FromImage(bm)

        ' Draw original image on bitmap with clipping.
        grfx.SetClip(path)
        grfx.TranslateClip(-rectf.X, -rectf.Y)
        grfx.DrawImage(img, CInt(-rectf.X), CInt(-rectf.Y), _
                        img.Width, img.Height)
        grfx.Dispose()
    End Sub

    Protected Overrides Sub DoPage(ByVal grfx As Graphics, _
            ByVal clr As Color, ByVal cx As Integer, ByVal cy As Integer)
        grfx.DrawImage(bm, (cx - bm.Width) \ 2, _
                        (cy - bm.Height) \ 2, _
                        bm.Width, bm.Height)
    End Sub
End Class
```

The loading of the image and the creation of the path in the constructor are the same as in the KeyholeClip program. This program then obtains the size of the path and uses that size to create a new *Bitmap* object. The pixel format of the bitmap is specified as *Format32bppArgb* (which is the default anyway), and the bitmap is initialized to all zeros, which means that the entire bitmap image is initially transparent. Anything drawn on the bitmap won't be transparent.

The constructor then obtains a *Graphics* object for the bitmap and uses the path to set a clipping region. The problem, however, is that the new bitmap is smaller than the loaded bitmap, so the path isn't oriented correctly. The *TranslateClip* method moves the clipping region into place, and *DrawImage* (with the same offset factors as *TranslateClip*) renders the image on the new bitmap.

The *DoPage* method simply centers the bitmap in the display area. The program could save the new bitmap as a file as well.

# Regions and Clipping

Historically, regions predate the path support in Windows by many years. Regions were available in Windows 1.0 (which was released in 1985), while paths didn't become available in Windows until they were introduced in the 32-bit versions, beginning with Windows NT 3.1 in 1993 and Windows 95 in 1995.

With the introduction of paths, regions have become much less important in Windows graphics programming. They might even be ignored altogether if not for the role they play in clipping. Basically, when you define a path for clipping, the path is converted into a region. So the deeper you get into clipping, the more you'll have to learn about regions.

As you know, a graphics path is a collection of lines and curves. A region describes an area of the output device. It's fairly straightforward to convert a path to a region. In fact, one of the constructors of the *Region* class (which is defined in *System.Drawing*) creates a region directly from a path:

### *Region* Constructors (selection)

```
Region(ByVal path As GraphicsPath)
```

For the purpose of this constructor, all open subpaths are closed. The region encompasses the interiors of all the subpaths in the path. If the subpaths have overlapping areas, the filling mode of the path determines which interior areas become part of the region and which ones do not. Only one method of the *Graphics* class uses a region for drawing:

### Graphics *FillRegion* Method

```
Sub FillRegion(ByVal br As Brush, ByVal rgn As Region)
```

If the region was created from a path, this method is equivalent to calling *Fill-Path* on the original path.

Only one version of the *SetClip* method uses a region directly:

### Graphics SetClip Methods (selection)

```
Sub SetClip(ByVal rgn As Region, ByVal cm As CombineMode)
```

It may seem odd that there's no version of *SetClip* that has a region argument without any *CombineMode* argument. That's because the *Clip* property of the *Graphics* object is itself defined as a *Region*. Here are three clipping-related properties of *Graphics*.

### Graphics Properties (selection)

| Property | Type | Accessibility |
|----------|------|---------------|
| *Clip* | *Region* | Get/Set |
| *ClipBounds* | *RectangleF* | Get |
| *IsClipEmpty* | *Boolean* | Get |

So instead of using a method call to set the clipping region from a *Region* object,

```
grfx.SetClip(rgn)    ' Doesn't exist!
```

you just set the property:

```
grfx.Clip = rgn
```

The *ClipBounds* property indicates the smallest rectangle that encompasses the clipping region; *IsClipEmpty* indicates whether the clipping region defines a nonexistent area.

Two additional properties of the *Graphics* path relate to clipping:

### Graphics Properties (selection)

| Property | Type | Accessibility |
|----------|------|---------------|
| *VisibleClipBounds* | *RectangleF* | Get |
| *IsVisibleClipEmpty* | *Boolean* | Get |

With a new *Graphics* object, the *VisibleClipBounds* property indicates the size of the drawing surface. For a form, that's the size of the client area; for the printer, it's the size of the printable area of the page. The *ClipBounds* property indicates an "infinite" boundary rectangle. (Actually, it's not really infinite. It's just extremely large.)

When you set a clipping region for the *Graphics* object, *VisibleClipBounds* will be equal to the intersection of the original *VisibleClipBounds* and the *Clip-Bounds* property. If the clipping region is entirely within the display area, *VisibleClipBounds* and *ClipBounds* will be equal.

If *IsClipEmpty* is *True*, *IsVisibleClipEmpty* will also be *True*. However, it could be that *IsClipEmpty* is *False* but the clipping region is outside the boundaries of the client area (or printable area of the printer page). In that case, *IsVisibleClipEmpty* will be *True* because no part of the clipping region is within the display area.

# 16

# Dialog Boxes

Given that you can decorate an application's main form with buttons and other controls in the same way that you can design a dialog box, what makes a form different from a dialog box? In terms of managing events from the dialog box and its child controls, the difference is slight. Dialog boxes once represented a big conceptual leap in Microsoft Windows programming. In the Windows Forms library, however, there's not even a separate class for dialog boxes. You simply create another instance (or in most cases, an instance of another subclass) of *Form*.

Dialog boxes are either *modal* or *modeless*. Modal dialog boxes are the most common. As the name suggests, a modal dialog box changes the mode of input from the main application form to the dialog box. When your program displays a modal dialog box, the user can't switch between the dialog box and another form in your program. The user must explicitly end the dialog box, usually by clicking a push button marked OK (or Open or Save) or a button marked Cancel. The user can, however, switch to another program while the dialog box is still displayed. Some dialog boxes (called *system modal*) don't even allow switching to other programs: system modal dialog boxes report serious problems and must be ended before the user can do anything else in Windows. (It's not possible to create a system modal dialog box using the Windows Forms library.)

Modeless dialog boxes are much like additional forms the program creates. (The TwoForms and PaintTwoForms programs in Chapter 2 create two forms.) You can switch among the modeless dialog boxes a program creates and the program's main application form.

Programmers often use modal dialog boxes when a program needs to obtain information from a user beyond what can be easily managed in a menu.

(Remember the FontMenu program in Chapter 14?) The dialog box often defines fields or properties that allow the program to initialize the dialog box and (ultimately) obtain information from it.

Very often, programmers working with object-oriented languages find it difficult to decide what should be an object. One approach is to design your dialog boxes so that they have a single field (or property) that an application uses to get all the information from the dialog box. That means that the dialog box is associated with a specific object. There are worse ways to structure your programs!

Toward the end of this chapter, I discuss what are known as the *common* dialog boxes. These are the predefined dialog boxes that you can present to a user for the selection of files, fonts, or colors. As you'll see, each of these dialog boxes often returns a single object.

# Your First Modal Dialog Box

Dialog boxes differ from application forms mostly in the way in which they are invoked and (just as important) terminated. This SimpleDialog program demonstrates both of these jobs.

**SimpleDialog.vb**

```
'-------------------------------------------------
' SimpleDialog.vb (c) 2002 by Charles Petzold
'-------------------------------------------------
Imports System
Imports System.Drawing
Imports System.Windows.Forms

Class SimpleDialog
    Inherits Form

    Private strDisplay As String = ""

    Shared Sub Main()
        Application.Run(New SimpleDialog())
    End Sub

    Sub New()
        Text = "Simple Dialog"

        Menu = New MainMenu()
        Menu.MenuItems.Add("&Dialog!", AddressOf MenuOnClick)
    End Sub

    Sub MenuOnClick(ByVal obj As Object, ByVal ea As EventArgs)
        Dim dlg As New SimpleDialogBox()
```

```
        dlg.ShowDialog()     ' Returns when dialog box terminated.

        strDisplay = "Dialog box terminated with " & _
                        dlg.DialogResult.ToString() & "!"
        Invalidate()
    End Sub

    Protected Overrides Sub OnPaint(ByVal pea As PaintEventArgs)
        Dim grfx As Graphics = pea.Graphics
        grfx.DrawString(strDisplay, Font, New SolidBrush(ForeColor), 0, 0)
    End Sub
End Class

Class SimpleDialogBox
    Inherits Form

    Sub New()
        Text = "Simple Dialog Box"

        ' Standard stuff for dialog boxes
        FormBorderStyle = FormBorderStyle.FixedDialog
        ControlBox = False
        MaximizeBox = False
        MinimizeBox = False
        ShowInTaskbar = False

        ' Create OK button.
        Dim btn As New Button()
        btn.Parent = Me
        btn.Text = "OK"
        btn.Location = New Point(50, 50)
        btn.Size = New Size(10 * Font.Height, 2 * Font.Height)
        AddHandler btn.Click, AddressOf ButtonOkOnClick

        ' Create Cancel button.
        btn = New Button()
        btn.Parent = Me
        btn.Text = "Cancel"
        btn.Location = New Point(50, 100)
        btn.Size = New Size(10 * Font.Height, 2 * Font.Height)
        AddHandler btn.Click, AddressOf ButtonCancelOnClick
    End Sub

    Sub ButtonOkOnClick(ByVal obj As Object, ByVal ea As EventArgs)
        DialogResult = DialogResult.OK
    End Sub

    Sub ButtonCancelOnClick(ByVal obj As Object, ByVal ea As EventArgs)
        DialogResult = DialogResult.Cancel
    End Sub
End Class
```

The program contains two classes; both are derived from *Form*. The first class, named *SimpleDialog*, is the class for the program's main window. The *SimpleDialogBox* class is the class for the program's dialog box. In a real application, you'd probably put the two classes in two different files.

The *Main* method creates only an instance of the *SimpleDialog* class. The constructor of this class creates a very small menu containing just one item labeled "Dialog!" When you click this menu item, the *MenuOnClick* method invokes the dialog box. It begins this job by creating an instance of *SimpleDialogBox*:

```
Dim dlg As New SimpleDialogBox()
```

Although my dialog boxes will tend to be based on classes with long names such as SimpleDialogBox, I'll generally use a variable named *dlg* or something similar to refer to the dialog box.

When the program creates an object of type *SimpleDialogBox*, the default constructor defined in the *SimpleDialogBox* class is executed. That constructor begins by setting the text that will appear in the dialog box caption:

```
Text = "Simple Dialog Box"
```

It then sets five additional properties:

```
FormBorderStyle = FormBorderStyle.FixedDialog
ControlBox = False
MaximizeBox = False
MinimizeBox = False
ShowInTaskbar = False
```

Setting these five properties is common with dialog boxes. The *FixedDialog* border style doesn't allow resizing the dialog box, and the next three properties eliminate the control box (also known as the system menu), the maximize box, and the minimize box from the caption bar. Setting *ControlBox* to *False* also eliminates the close box. The caption bar contains only the dialog box text (in this case, "Simple Dialog Box"). Although some dialog boxes in Windows have no caption bar, it's best to use a caption bar so that the user has the option to move the dialog box to another location of the screen. Finally, you set the fifth property because you don't want the dialog box showing up in the Windows taskbar. The taskbar should be reserved for applications.

The constructor continues by creating two push buttons with the *Text* properties "OK" and "Cancel." Each button is associated with its own handler for the button's *Click* events.

The dialog box isn't visible yet! After the constructor in *SimpleDialogBox* finishes up, the code in the *MenuOnClick* method of *SimpleDialog* calls the *ShowDialog* method of the dialog box:

```
dlg.ShowDialog()
```

*ShowDialog* causes the dialog box to become visible. The *ShowDialog* method doesn't return until the dialog box is terminated.

*ShowDialog* is the method you must use to invoke a modal dialog box. During the time a modal dialog box is displayed, the user can't switch back to the program's main form. That's what it means to be modal. (As I said earlier, you can, however, switch to other applications running under Windows.) While the modal dialog box is displayed, the application form can't receive any keyboard or mouse input. However, the form can continue to receive *Tick* events from a *Timer* object and calls to *OnPaint*.

The two buttons in the dialog box have *Click* event handlers named *ButtonOkOnClick* and *ButtonCancelOnClick*. Both methods have just a single line that sets a property of the dialog box form, named *DialogResult*:

## *Form* Properties (selection)

| Property | Type | Accessibility |
| --- | --- | --- |
| *DialogResult* | *DialogResult* | Get/Set |

The *DialogResult* property must be set to one of the following enumeration values:

## *DialogResult* Enumeration

| Member | Value |
| --- | --- |
| *None* | 0 |
| *OK* | 1 |
| *Cancel* | 2 |
| *Abort* | 3 |
| *Retry* | 4 |
| *Ignore* | 5 |
| *Yes* | 6 |
| *No* | 7 |

You'll notice that these members correspond to text strings commonly displayed on buttons within a dialog box. If this table looks familiar, it's because you first encountered it in Chapter 2. The *Show* method of the *MessageBox* class returns a member of the *DialogResult* enumeration.

In the program at hand, the button labeled "OK" sets *DialogResult* to *DialogResult.OK*, and the button labeled "Cancel" sets the property to *DialogResult.Cancel*. What happens in either case is quite dramatic: the dialog box is closed. It disappears from the screen. The *ShowDialog* method that originally invoked the dialog box now returns control to the *MenuOnClick* method.

Although the dialog box has been terminated and is no longer visible, the dialog box object named *dlg* in the application form is still valid. That means that the *MenuOnClick* method can access the dialog box's *DialogResult* property to determine how the dialog box was terminated. In this particular case, the *MenuOnClick* method simply sets the *strDisplay* field variable and invalidates the form. The *OnPaint* method displays this string.

Now let's look at a couple shortcuts. First, the *ShowDialog* method is defined like so:

### *Form* Methods (selection)

```
Function ShowDialog() As DialogResult
```

The return value is the same as the *DialogResult* property of the dialog box when the dialog box was terminated. So, a program that invokes a dialog box can save the *DialogResult* when *ShowDialog* returns:

```
Dim dr As DialogResult = dlg.ShowDialog()
```

Or the *ShowDialog* call can go right into an *If* statement:

```
If dlg.ShowDialog() = DialogResult.OK Then
    ⋮
Else
    ⋮
End If
```

or a *Select* statement:

```
Select dlg.ShowDialog()
    Case DialogResult.OK
        ⋮
    Case DialogResult.Cancel
        ⋮
    Case Else
        ⋮
End Select
```

Generally, a program gets information from a dialog box if *DialogResult* is *OK* and just continues on its merry way if *DialogResult* is *Cancel*.

# Modal Dialog Box Termination

You're probably fairly happy with the code I showed in the SimpleDialogBox program. How much easier could it be to terminate a dialog box than just setting a *DialogResult* property in a button's *Click* event handler?

Well, keep reading.

As you probably know from experience, modal dialog boxes are almost always terminated when the user presses a push button. For that reason, the *Button* class—or more precisely, the *IButtonControl* interface that *Button* and *LinkLabel* implement—also includes a property named *DialogResult*:

### *IButtonControl* Property

| Property | Type | Accessibility |
|----------|------|---------------|
| *DialogResult* | *DialogResult* | Get/Set |

We've already seen that *Form* has a property named *DialogResult*, and now you see that *Button* has a property named *DialogResult* as well. Usually when you see the same property implemented in both the *Form* and *Button* classes, you'd naturally assume that both classes inherit the property from *Control*. But that's not the case with *DialogResult*, although the two implementations of the property are related.

When you set the *DialogResult* property of a button, you are essentially instructing the button to set the same *DialogResult* of its parent (the dialog box itself) when the button is clicked. The result is that you don't have to install event handlers for the dialog box buttons, as the SimplerDialog program demonstrates.

## SimplerDialog.vb

```
'-------------------------------------------------
' SimplerDialog.vb (c) 2002 by Charles Petzold
'-------------------------------------------------
Imports System
Imports System.Drawing
Imports System.Windows.Forms

Class SimplerDialog
    Inherits Form

    Private strDisplay As String = ""

    Shared Sub Main()
        Application.Run(New SimplerDialog())
    End Sub
```

*(continued)*

**SimplerDialog.vb**   *(continued)*

```vb
    Sub New()
        Text = "Simpler Dialog"

        Menu = New MainMenu()
        Menu.MenuItems.Add("&Dialog!", AddressOf MenuOnClick)
    End Sub

    Sub MenuOnClick(ByVal obj As Object, ByVal ea As EventArgs)
        Dim dlg As New SimplerDialogBox()
        Dim dr As DialogResult = dlg.ShowDialog()

        strDisplay = "Dialog box terminated with " & dr.ToString() & "!"
        Invalidate()
    End Sub

    Protected Overrides Sub OnPaint(ByVal pea As PaintEventArgs)
        Dim grfx As Graphics = pea.Graphics
        grfx.DrawString(strDisplay, Font, New SolidBrush(ForeColor), 0, 0)
    End Sub
End Class

Class SimplerDialogBox
    Inherits Form

    Sub New()
        Text = "Simpler Dialog Box"

        ' Standard stuff for dialog boxes
        FormBorderStyle = FormBorderStyle.FixedDialog
        ControlBox = False
        MaximizeBox = False
        MinimizeBox = False
        ShowInTaskbar = False

        ' Create OK button.
        Dim btn As New Button()
        btn.Parent = Me
        btn.Text = "OK"
        btn.Location = New Point(50, 50)
        btn.Size = New Size(10 * Font.Height, 2 * Font.Height)
        btn.DialogResult = DialogResult.OK

        ' Create Cancel button.
        btn = New Button()
        btn.Parent = Me
        btn.Text = "Cancel"
        btn.Location = New Point(50, 100)
        btn.Size = New Size(10 * Font.Height, 2 * Font.Height)
        btn.DialogResult = DialogResult.Cancel
    End Sub
End Class
```

This version of the program behaves the same way as SimpleButton when you press the OK or Cancel button. The dialog box doesn't need to explicitly set the form's *DialogResult* property unless you want to terminate the dialog box by means other than a button.

If you still need to do a little processing when the user presses the OK or Cancel button, you can always install *Click* event handlers as well. But for purposes of terminating the dialog box, you certainly don't have to.

# Accept and Cancel

The dialog boxes created so far are missing a small piece of the normal keyboard interface for dialog boxes. What's there works fine: using the keyboard Tab or arrow keys, you can move input focus between the OK and Cancel buttons. As you move the input focus, the button with the input focus also becomes the default button. You can trigger the button with the input focus by using the spacebar; you can also trigger the default button by using the Enter key.

What you can't do is terminate the dialog box with the Esc key. The Esc key is supposed to be the equivalent of pressing the Cancel button.

Moreover, if you put another type of control in the dialog box (a *Check-Box*, perhaps), you'll find that whenever the *CheckBox* has the input focus, there is no default push button. Pressing Enter does nothing in that case. If any non-*Button* control has the input focus, the OK button (or the equivalent of the OK button, labeled Open or Save or something else) is supposed to be the default push button, which means that it should respond to the Enter key.

You can take care of this aspect of the user interface by using the following two properties of *Form*:

### *Form* Properties (selection)

| Property | Type | Accessibility |
|----------|------|---------------|
| *AcceptButton* | *IButtonControl* | Get/Set |
| *CancelButton* | *IButtonControl* | Get/Set |

You can set these two properties to an object of any class that implements *IButtonControl*, which is currently either a *Button* or *LinkLabel* object.

The *AcceptButton* property indicates which *Button* control should be triggered whenever a non-*Button* control has the input focus and the Enter key is pressed. Regardless of how you set *AcceptButton*, any control that implements the *IButtonControl* interface will become the default button and respond to Enter if it has the input focus.

The *CancelButton* property indicates the *Button* control that should be triggered whenever the Esc key is pressed.

You may be curious about *IButtonControl*. You've already seen a third of what it means to implement the *IButtonControl* interface, which is to implement a property named *DialogResult*. The other two-thirds of *IButtonControl* are these two methods:

### *IButtonControl* Methods

```
Sub NotifyDefault(ByVal bDefault As Boolean)
Sub PerformClick()
```

When a control implementing *IButtonControl* gets a call to *NotifyDefault* with an argument of *True*, it is responsible for visually indicating that it is the default control (and hence will respond to the Enter key). A button indicates that it's the default control with a bold outline. The *PerformClick* method simulates a button click. That's the method of the default *Button* control that the form calls when the Enter key is pressed.

Generally, the *DialogResult* property of the *Button* control and the *AcceptButton* and *CancelButton* properties of the dialog box form go together. For example, when a form creates a button labeled OK or Load or Save, it sets the *DialogResult* property like so:

```
btn.DialogResult = DialogResult.OK
```

It also sets the *AcceptButton* property of the dialog box form to the *Button* object:

```
AcceptButton = btn
```

Similarly, when a form creates a Cancel button, it sets the *DialogResult* like this:

```
btn.DialogResult = DialogResult.Cancel
```

And it sets the *CancelButton* property of the form like so:

```
CancelButton = btn
```

I'll show you a program that sets these properties shortly.

# Screen Location

You've probably noticed that newly launched Windows applications often appear in different locations of the screen. When a Windows session first begins, Windows positions the first application in the upper left corner of the screen. Each successive application is then positioned somewhat to the right of and below the previous one in a cascaded pattern using an offset equal to *SystemInformation.CaptionButtonSize* plus *SystemInformation.FrameBorderSize*. While this behavior is fine for applications, the same rules also apply to dialog boxes, with less than optimal results. The result is that a dialog box could appear some distance from the application that invokes it. The problem may not be so evident in the SimpleDialog and SimplerDialog programs because you're probably running the programs, invoking the dialog box, closing the dialog box, and then closing the program. In that chain of events, the dialog box often appears suitably offset from the application form. But if you were to run a couple other programs before you invoke the dialog box, the results would be different.

You can override the default behavior governing the location of forms by using the *StartPosition* property:

### *Form* Properties (selection)

| Property | Type | Accessibility |
| --- | --- | --- |
| *StartPosition* | *FormStartPosition* | Get/Set |

*FormStartPosition* is an enumeration:

### *FormStartPosition* Enumeration

| Member | Value |
| --- | --- |
| *Manual* | 0 |
| *CenterScreen* | 1 |
| *WindowsDefaultLocation* | 2 |
| *WindowsDefaultBounds* | 3 |
| *CenterParent* | 4 |

The default for Windows Forms applications is *WindowsDefaultLocation*, which means that Windows positions the form as I described but the application itself sizes the form. Actually, the constructor for *Form* sets the size of the form, but the constructor in any class that inherits from *Form* can override that size. That's why all Windows Forms applications have the same default size, and this size is different from regular (non–Windows Forms) Windows programs that use a default size.

You can get the regular Windows default position *and* size by specifying *WindowsDefaultBounds*, which means that Windows sets both the location and size of the form. When you use *WindowsDefaultBounds*, any attempt to set the location or size of the form in your program's constructor will be ignored; when you use *WindowsDefaultLocation*, your constructor can set a size but not a location.

The *CenterParent* option allows a program to position a dialog box in the center of the program's form without doing any calculations. This placement might not be optimum, however. So far in this chapter, I haven't been resizing application client areas or dialog boxes, so *CenterParent* results in a dialog box that exactly overlays (and completely hides) the application that invoked it. *CenterScreen* positions a dialog box in the center of the screen and is useful for modeless dialog boxes that sometimes appear on the screen while an application is loading. Both *CenterParent* and *CenterScreen* allow a dialog box constructor to set its own size.

The *Manual* option lets a dialog box have complete freedom in setting its position and size. Generally, a dialog box will want to use this option to position itself relative to the form that invoked it. The best way for a dialog box to obtain the form that invoked it is the *ActiveForm* property.

Here's a program named BetterDialog with a dialog box that sets its location properly offset from the application form. The program also demonstrates the use of the *AcceptButton* and *CancelButton* properties I talked about earlier.

**BetterDialog.vb**

```
'-------------------------------------------------
' BetterDialog.vb (c) 2002 by Charles Petzold
'-------------------------------------------------
Imports System
Imports System.Drawing
Imports System.Windows.Forms

Class BetterDialog
    Inherits Form

    Private strDisplay As String = ""

    Shared Sub Main()
        Application.Run(New BetterDialog())
    End Sub

    Sub New()
        Text = "Better Dialog"

        Menu = New MainMenu()
        Menu.MenuItems.Add("&Dialog!", AddressOf MenuOnClick)
    End Sub
```

```
    Sub MenuOnClick(ByVal obj As Object, ByVal ea As EventArgs)
        Dim dlg As New BetterDialogBox()
        Dim dr As DialogResult = dlg.ShowDialog()

        strDisplay = "Dialog box terminated with " & dr.ToString() & "!"
        Invalidate()
    End Sub

    Protected Overrides Sub OnPaint(ByVal pea As PaintEventArgs)
        Dim grfx As Graphics = pea.Graphics
        grfx.DrawString(strDisplay, Font, New SolidBrush(ForeColor), 0, 0)
    End Sub
End Class

Class BetterDialogBox
    Inherits Form

    Sub New()
        Text = "Better Dialog Box"

        ' Standard stuff for dialog boxes
        FormBorderStyle = FormBorderStyle.FixedDialog
        ControlBox = False
        MaximizeBox = False
        MinimizeBox = False
        ShowInTaskbar = False
        StartPosition = FormStartPosition.Manual
        Location = Point.op_Addition(ActiveForm.Location, _
                    Size.op_Addition(SystemInformation.CaptionButtonSize, _
                                    SystemInformation.FrameBorderSize))
        ' Create OK button.
        Dim btn As New Button()
        btn.Parent = Me
        btn.Text = "OK"
        btn.Location = New Point(50, 50)
        btn.Size = New Size(10 * Font.Height, 2 * Font.Height)
        btn.DialogResult = DialogResult.OK
        AcceptButton = btn

        ' Create Cancel button.
        btn = New Button()
        btn.Parent = Me
        btn.Text = "Cancel"
        btn.Location = New Point(50, 100)
        btn.Size = New Size(10 * Font.Height, 2 * Font.Height)
        btn.DialogResult = DialogResult.Cancel
        CancelButton = btn
    End Sub
End Class
```

Now as part of the standard housekeeping at the beginning of the dialog box constructor, the *StartPosition* property is set to *FormStartPosition.Manual*. The dialog box also sets its *Location* property equal to the *Location* property of the active form (the form that invoked the dialog box) plus those two *System-Information* properties I mentioned earlier.

Also take note that as the dialog box creates each of the two buttons, it also sets the *AcceptButton* and *CancelButton* properties of the dialog box form. The dialog box now has a full and proper keyboard interface.

# The About Box

One common dialog box found in nearly all nontrivial applications is called an *about* box. The about box can be as simple as a copyright notice or as complex as a display of system resources and perhaps a toll-free telephone number and a Web site for tech support.

Here's a program that displays an about box containing an icon, two label controls, and one button.

```
AboutBox.vb
'-----------------------------------------------
' AboutBox.vb (c) 2002 by Charles Petzold
'-----------------------------------------------
Imports System
Imports System.Drawing
Imports System.Windows.Forms

Class AboutBox
    Inherits Form

    Shared Sub Main()
        Application.Run(New AboutBox())
    End Sub

    Sub New()
        Text = "About Box"
        Icon = New Icon(Me.GetType(), "AforAbout.ico")

        Menu = New MainMenu()
        Menu.MenuItems.Add("&Help")
        Menu.MenuItems(0).MenuItems.Add("&About AboutBox...", _
                                AddressOf MenuAboutOnClick)
    End Sub
```

```
    Sub MenuAboutOnClick(ByVal obj As Object, ByVal ea As EventArgs)
        Dim dlg As New AboutDialogBox()
        dlg.ShowDialog()
    End Sub
End Class

Class AboutDialogBox
    Inherits Form

    Sub New()
        Text = "About AboutBox"

        StartPosition = FormStartPosition.CenterParent
        FormBorderStyle = FormBorderStyle.FixedDialog
        ControlBox = False
        MaximizeBox = False
        MinimizeBox = False
        ShowInTaskbar = False

        ' Create first label with program name.
        Dim lbl1 As New Label()
        lbl1.Parent = Me
        lbl1.Text = " AboutBox Version 1.0 "
        lbl1.Font = New Font(FontFamily.GenericSerif, 24, _
                             FontStyle.Italic)
        lbl1.AutoSize = True
        lbl1.TextAlign = ContentAlignment.MiddleCenter

        ' Create picture box containing icon.
        Dim icon As New Icon(Me.GetType(), "AforAbout.ico")
        Dim picbox As New PictureBox()
        picbox.Parent = Me
        picbox.Image = icon.ToBitmap()
        picbox.SizeMode = PictureBoxSizeMode.AutoSize
        picbox.Location = New Point(lbl1.Font.Height \ 2, _
                                    lbl1.Font.Height \ 2)

        lbl1.Location = New Point(picbox.Right, lbl1.Font.Height \ 2)

        Dim iClientWidth As Integer = lbl1.Right

        ' Create second label with copyright and link.
        Dim lnklbl2 As New LinkLabel()
        lnklbl2.Parent = Me
        lnklbl2.Text = Chr(169) & " 2002 by Charles Petzold"
        lnklbl2.Font = New Font(FontFamily.GenericSerif, 16)
        lnklbl2.Location = New Point(0, lbl1.Bottom + lnklbl2.Font.Height)
        lnklbl2.Size = New Size(iClientWidth, lnklbl2.Font.Height)
        lnklbl2.TextAlign = ContentAlignment.MiddleCenter
```

*(continued)*

**AboutBox.vb**  *(continued)*

```
        ' Set link area and event handler.
        lnklbl2.LinkArea = New LinkArea(10, 15)
        AddHandler lnklbl2.LinkClicked, AddressOf LinkLabelOnLinkClicked

        ' Create OK button.
        Dim btn As New Button()
        btn.Parent = Me
        btn.Text = "OK"
        btn.Size = New Size(4 * btn.Font.Height, _
                            2 * btn.Font.Height)
        btn.Location = New Point((iClientWidth - btn.Size.Width) \ 2, _
                            lnklbl2.Bottom + 2 * btn.Font.Height)
        btn.DialogResult = DialogResult.OK
        btn.TabIndex = 0

        CancelButton = btn
        AcceptButton = btn
        ClientSize = New Size(iClientWidth, _
                            btn.Bottom + 2 * btn.Font.Height)
    End Sub

    Private Sub LinkLabelOnLinkClicked(ByVal obj As Object, _
            ByVal lllcea As LinkLabelLinkClickedEventArgs)
        System.Diagnostics.Process.Start("http://www.charlespetzold.com")
    End Sub
End Class
```

## AforAbout.ico

The constructors of both the *AboutBox* class and the *AboutDialogBox* class load the icon resource. The *AboutBox* class sets the resource as the form icon by using the *Icon* property. The *AboutDialogBox* class creates a *Picture-Box* control for displaying the icon in the dialog box.

The constructor of the *AboutDialogBox* class is a bit involved because of the positioning of the controls. For the first *Label* control (which contains the name of the program in a 24-point italic font), the *AutoSize* property is set to

*True*. For the *PictureBox* control, the *SizeMode* property is set to *PictureBox-SizeMode.AutoSize*. The picture box is positioned based on the resultant size of the label, and the label is positioned based on the resultant size of the picture box.

The second label is actually a *LinkLabel* control, for which a *LinkClicked* event handler is installed. Click on my name in the copyright notice and the event handler calls the shared *Process.Start* method in the *System.Diagnostics* namespace using my Web site address as an argument. *Process.Start* starts up your Web browser to take you to my Web site.

For a dialog box with one button, the *DialogResult* property of the button is usually assigned *DialogResult.OK*. You should also assign both the *Accept-Button* and *CancelButton* properties of the form to that button. Notice that I've also set the button *TabIndex* property to 0, making it the control with the input focus when the dialog box is displayed. Otherwise the *LinkLabel* would have the input focus.

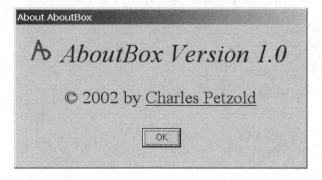

Aside from a button, you don't need to use controls in a dialog box like this. Instead of using *Label* and *PictureBox* controls, you can call *DrawString* and *DrawIcon* from the *OnPaint* method in the *AboutDialogBox* class.

Actually, for very simple dialog boxes, you don't even need to derive a class from *Form* to use for the dialog box. You'll recall in Chapter 2 how forms could be created by making an instance of *Form* rather than a class derived from *Form*. You can do the same thing with dialog boxes. In fact, the problem of sharing data between an application form and a dialog box becomes much simpler when the dialog box isn't in a separate form.

Much simpler, yes, but also not quite as structured. Wouldn't it be nice to write dialog boxes that could be reused in other applications? It might not always be possible, but it should always be a goal.

# Defining Properties in Dialog Boxes

The RadioButtons program in Chapter 12 shows how you can define a group of radio buttons and a check box to indicate the color of an ellipse and whether the ellipse is outlined or filled. Let's implement the same controls (plus a couple buttons) in a dialog box instead. The dialog box must have some provision that lets a program initialize the controls and also some way for an application to obtain the user's selections. You generally provide this interface through public properties of the dialog box form or, in some cases—particularly if you're in a hurry—through public fields.

This dialog box implements two public properties, named *Color* and *Fill*, that give another class access to the two items that the user sets using the dialog box.

```
ColorFillDialogBox.vb
'----------------------------------------------------
' ColorFillDialogBox.vb (c) 2002 by Charles Petzold
'----------------------------------------------------
Imports System
Imports System.Drawing
Imports System.Windows.Forms

Class ColorFillDialogBox
    Inherits Form

    Protected grpbox As GroupBox
    Protected chkbox As CheckBox

    Sub New()
        Text = "Color/Fill Select"

        FormBorderStyle = FormBorderStyle.FixedDialog
        ControlBox = False
        MinimizeBox = False
        MaximizeBox = False
        ShowInTaskbar = False
        Location = Point.op_Addition(ActiveForm.Location, _
                        Size.op_Addition(SystemInformation.CaptionButtonSize, _
                                         SystemInformation.FrameBorderSize))

        Dim astrColor() As String = {"Black", "Blue", "Green", "Cyan", _
                                     "Red", "Magenta", "Yellow", "White"}
        grpbox = New GroupBox()
        grpbox.Parent = Me
        grpbox.Text = "Color"
        grpbox.Location = New Point(8, 8)
        grpbox.Size = New Size(96, 12 * (astrColor.Length + 1))
```

```
        Dim i As Integer
        For i = 0 To astrColor.GetUpperBound(0)
            Dim radiobtn As New RadioButton()
            radiobtn.Parent = grpbox
            radiobtn.Text = astrColor(i)
            radiobtn.Location = New Point(8, 12 * (i + 1))
            radiobtn.Size = New Size(80, 10)
        Next i

        chkbox = New CheckBox()
        chkbox.Parent = Me
        chkbox.Text = "Fill Ellipse"
        chkbox.Location = New Point(8, grpbox.Bottom + 4)
        chkbox.Size = New Size(80, 10)

        Dim btn As New Button()
        btn.Parent = Me
        btn.Text = "OK"
        btn.Location = New Point(8, chkbox.Bottom + 4)
        btn.Size = New Size(40, 16)
        btn.DialogResult = DialogResult.OK

        AcceptButton = btn

        btn = New Button()
        btn.Parent = Me
        btn.Text = "Cancel"
        btn.Location = New Point(64, chkbox.Bottom + 4)
        btn.Size = New Size(40, 16)
        btn.DialogResult = DialogResult.Cancel

        CancelButton = btn

        ClientSize = New Size(112, btn.Bottom + 8)
        AutoScaleBaseSize = New Size(4, 8)
    End Sub

    Property Color() As Color
        Set(ByVal Value As Color)
            Dim i As Integer
            For i = 0 To grpbox.Controls.Count - 1
                Dim radiobtn As RadioButton = _
                    DirectCast(grpbox.Controls(i), RadioButton)
                If Value.Equals(Color.FromName(radiobtn.Text)) Then
                    radiobtn.Checked = True
                    Exit For
                End If
            Next i
        End Set
        Get
            Dim i As Integer
            For i = 0 To grpbox.Controls.Count - 1
                Dim radiobtn As RadioButton = _
```

*(continued)*

**ColorFillDialogBox.vb** *(continued)*

```
                    DirectCast(grpbox.Controls(i), RadioButton)
                If radiobtn.Checked Then
                    Return Color.FromName(radiobtn.Text)
                End If
            Next i
            Return Color.Black
        End Get
    End Property

    Property Fill() As Boolean
        Set(ByVal Value As Boolean)
            chkbox.Checked = Value
        End Set
        Get
            Return chkbox.Checked
        End Get
    End Property
End Class
```

The constructor uses a classical dialog box coordinate system to create, position, and size all the controls. The code is flexible enough to let you put additional colors in the *astrColor* array.

The class stores the *GroupBox* and *CheckBox* objects as protected fields, but it doesn't keep track of the current state of the radio buttons or check boxes. The class relies on the auto-check facility of these two controls to keep the check state consistent with the user's selections. But it's still necessary for the class to provide an interface to the state of the controls.

That interface is provided in the public *Color* and *Fill* properties defined toward the bottom of the program. The *Fill* property is quite simple. The *Get* accessor returns the *Checked* property of the check box; the *Set* accessor sets that property. The *Color* property, however, requires a search through all the radio buttons, which is equivalent to a search through all the children of the group box control, which is also equivalent to looping through the *Controls* property of the group box. The *Get* accessor returns a *Color* object represented by the currently checked radio button; the *Set* accessor checks the radio button corresponding to a particular *Color* object. (Another approach for determining the checked radio button is to install an event handler for the radio buttons and keep track of the last checked button in a field.)

Here's what the dialog box looks like (although we haven't yet encountered a program that invokes it):

Now this is not a dialog box that a whole lot of different applications require, but it's written to allow reuse. That's the goal.

The DrawOrFillEllipse program implements a menu item to invoke this dialog box and then uses the results to update its client area with a colored (and possibly filled) ellipse.

**DrawOrFillEllipse.vb**

```
'--------------------------------------------------
' DrawOrFillEllipse.vb (c) 2002 by Charles Petzold
'--------------------------------------------------
Imports System
Imports System.Drawing
Imports System.Windows.Forms

Class DrawOrFillEllipse
    Inherits Form

    Private clrEllipse As Color = Color.Red
    Private bFillEllipse As Boolean = False

    Shared Sub Main()
        Application.Run(New DrawOrFillEllipse())
    End Sub

    Sub New()
        Text = "Draw or Fill Ellipse"
        ResizeRedraw = True

        Menu = New MainMenu()
        Menu.MenuItems.Add("&Options")
```

*(continued)*

**DrawOrFillEllipse.vb** *(continued)*

```
            Menu.MenuItems(0).MenuItems.Add("&Color...", _
                                AddressOf MenuColorOnClick)
    End Sub

    Sub MenuColorOnClick(ByVal obj As Object, ByVal ea As EventArgs)
        Dim dlg As New ColorFillDialogBox()
        dlg.Color = clrEllipse
        dlg.Fill = bFillEllipse

        If dlg.ShowDialog() = DialogResult.OK Then
            clrEllipse = dlg.Color
            bFillEllipse = dlg.Fill
            Invalidate()
        End If
    End Sub

    Protected Overrides Sub OnPaint(ByVal pea As PaintEventArgs)
        Dim grfx As Graphics = pea.Graphics
        Dim rect As New Rectangle(0, 0, ClientSize.Width - 1, _
                                    ClientSize.Height - 1)
        If bFillEllipse Then
            grfx.FillEllipse(New SolidBrush(clrEllipse), rect)
        Else
            grfx.DrawEllipse(New Pen(clrEllipse), rect)
        End If
    End Sub
End Class
```

I want to draw your attention to the *MenuColorOnClick* method, which is the event handler associated with the menu item to invoke the dialog box. The method creates an object of type *ColorFillDialogBox*. Keep in mind that you can set just about any property of the dialog box form at this time. You may want to change the *Text* property, for example. A dialog box designed for reuse could specifically implement other properties that let an application program alter its appearance and functionality.

The *MenuColorOnClick* method continues with dialog box initialization by setting the two custom properties implemented in *ColorFillDialogBox* from fields in the *DrawOrFillEllipse* class:

```
dlg.Color = clrEllipse
dlg.Fill = bFillEllipse
```

The next statement calls the *ShowDialog* method of the dialog box form, which won't return until the dialog box is closed. At that time, the program compares the return value of *ShowDialog* with *DialogResult.OK*. If the dialog box was terminated with the OK button, the program stores the new values of the properties and invalidates the client area:

```
If dlg.ShowDialog() = DialogResult.OK Then
    clrEllipse = dlg.Color
    bFillEllipse = dlg.Fill
    Invalidate()
End If
```

The *MenuColorOnClick* method represents very standard code for creating, initializing, invoking, and obtaining information from dialog boxes.

# Implementing an Apply Button

In recent years, some dialog boxes have sprouted buttons labeled Apply. The Apply button doesn't make the dialog box go away, but it causes the application to use the new settings specified in the dialog box.

The Apply button upsets the normal orderly relationship between an application and a modal dialog box. It requires that the application be informed when the Apply button has been pressed before the *ShowDialog* method returns control to the application.

It is very tempting to implement an Apply button by defining a public method in your application form that the dialog box form calls when the Apply button is pressed. In fact, you may wonder why this isn't the right way to go. It isn't a good idea because the class implementing the dialog box would then require an application using that class to implement a particular method with a particular name. Do you know of any .NET class that forces an application to define a particular method to use the class?

No you don't. But you're *very* familiar with the facility by which the .NET classes communicate to applications, and that is by events.

Let's rewrite the *ColorFillDialogBox* class so that it includes, first, an Apply button; second, a property to enable and disable that button; and third, an event. This job is going to be easier than you probably fear!

Here's a *ColorFillDialogBoxWithApply* class that inherits from *ColorFillDialogBox*. Besides implementing an Apply button, this class must also move the controls around a bit and set a new client size to accommodate the new button.

**ColorFillDialogBoxWithApply.vb**

```
'------------------------------------------------------------
' ColorFillDialogBoxWithApply.vb (c) 2002 by Charles Petzold
'------------------------------------------------------------
Imports System
Imports System.Drawing
Imports System.Windows.Forms
```

*(continued)*

**ColorFillDialogBoxWithApply.vb** *(continued)*

```
Class ColorFillDialogBoxWithApply
    Inherits ColorFillDialogBox

    Private btnApply As Button

    Event Apply As EventHandler

    Sub New()
        grpbox.Location = New Point(36, 8)
        chkbox.Location = New Point(36, grpbox.Bottom + 4)

        btnApply = New Button()
        btnApply.Parent = Me
        btnApply.Enabled = False
        btnApply.Text = "Apply"
        btnApply.Location = New Point(120, chkbox.Bottom + 4)
        btnApply.Size = New Size(40, 16)
        AddHandler btnApply.Click, AddressOf ButtonApplyOnClick

        ClientSize = New Size(168, btnApply.Bottom + 8)
        AutoScaleBaseSize = New Size(4, 8)
    End Sub

    Property ShowApply() As Boolean
        Set(ByVal Value As Boolean)
            btnApply.Enabled = Value
        End Set
        Get
            Return btnApply.Enabled
        End Get
    End Property

    Sub ButtonApplyOnClick(ByVal obj As Object, ByVal ea As EventArgs)
        RaiseEvent Apply(Me, EventArgs.Empty)
    End Sub
End Class
```

Toward the top of this class, you'll see the statement

```
Event Apply As EventHandler
```

This statement defines a public event named *Apply* that is based on the *EventHandler* delegate.

The class also has a new private field named *btnApply*. Obviously, this is the *Button* object labeled *Apply*, which is created in the new constructor. Notice that the constructor sets the *Enabled* property for this button to *False*. A program using this dialog box may not want to deal with an Apply button. But then how is the button enabled? By a public property, of course! This class implements a new property named *ShowApply* that lets a program using the dialog box enable or disable the Apply button at will.

The Apply button isn't associated with any *DialogResult* because the Apply button doesn't terminate the dialog box. Instead, I install an event handler named *ButtonApplyOnClick* for the button's *Click* event. This method contains the magic code required to implement an event in a class. Here's what's executed whenever the user triggers the Apply button:

```
RaiseEvent Apply(Me, EventArgs.Empty)
```

If any event handlers are installed, *RaiseEvent* causes all of them to be called with the *EventHandler* arguments: the first argument indicates the origin of the event (the dialog box form), and the second argument is an object of type *EventArgs*.

To be even more consistent with the .NET classes, the *ButtonApplyOn-Click* method would call a protected overrideable method named *OnApply* with a single *EventArgs* argument. *OnApply* would then contain the code to call the *Apply* event handlers.

And here's the program that uses the new version of the dialog box.

**DrawOrFillEllipseWithApply.vb**

```
'-------------------------------------------------------------
' DrawOrFillEllipseWithApply.vb (c) 2002 by Charles Petzold
'-------------------------------------------------------------
Imports System
Imports System.Drawing
Imports System.Windows.Forms

Class DrawOrFillEllipseWithApply
    Inherits Form

    Private clrEllipse As Color = Color.Red
    Private bFillEllipse As Boolean = False

    Shared Sub Main()
        Application.Run(New DrawOrFillEllipseWithApply())
    End Sub

    Sub New()
        Text = "Draw or Fill Ellipse with Apply"
        ResizeRedraw = True

        Menu = New MainMenu()
        Menu.MenuItems.Add("&Options")
        Menu.MenuItems(0).MenuItems.Add("&Color...", _
                        AddressOf MenuColorOnClick)
    End Sub

    Sub MenuColorOnClick(ByVal obj As Object, ByVal ea As EventArgs)
        Dim dlg As ColorFillDialogBoxWithApply = _
```

*(continued)*

**DrawOrFillEllipseWithApply.vb** *(continued)*

```
                              New ColorFillDialogBoxWithApply()
        dlg.ShowApply = True
        AddHandler dlg.Apply, AddressOf ColorFillDialogOnApply

        dlg.Color = clrEllipse
        dlg.Fill = bFillEllipse

        If dlg.ShowDialog() = DialogResult.OK Then
            clrEllipse = dlg.Color
            bFillEllipse = dlg.Fill
            Invalidate()
        End If
    End Sub

    Sub ColorFillDialogOnApply(ByVal obj As Object, ByVal ea As EventArgs)
        Dim dlg As ColorFillDialogBoxWithApply = _
                  DirectCast(obj, ColorFillDialogBoxWithApply)
        clrEllipse = dlg.Color
        bFillEllipse = dlg.Fill
        Invalidate()
    End Sub

    Protected Overrides Sub OnPaint(ByVal pea As PaintEventArgs)
        Dim grfx As Graphics = pea.Graphics
        Dim rect As New Rectangle(0, 0, ClientSize.Width - 1, _
                                        ClientSize.Height - 1)
        If bFillEllipse Then
            grfx.FillEllipse(New SolidBrush(clrEllipse), rect)
        Else
            grfx.DrawEllipse(New Pen(clrEllipse), rect)
        End If
    End Sub
End Class
```

During the *MenuColorOnClick* method, the program enables the Apply button and installs an event handler for the button:

```
dlg.ShowApply = True
AddHandler dlg.Apply, AddressOf ColorFillDialogOnApply
```

The *ColorFillDialogOnApply* event handler casts the object argument to an object of type *ColorFillDialogBoxWithApply* in order to get access to the *Color* and *Fill* properties. The program then sets its fields from the properties and invalidates the client area. As I mentioned earlier, even if a modal dialog box is active, an application form can still get *Paint* events. So, the client area is able to update itself based on the new dialog box settings.

# The Modeless Dialog Box

At the beginning of this chapter, I mentioned that dialog boxes can be either *modal* or *modeless*. So far we've been looking at modal dialog boxes, certainly the more common of the two types. Modeless dialog boxes allow the user to switch between the dialog box and the form that created it.

Modeless dialog boxes are preferred when the user would find it convenient to keep the dialog box displayed for a while. Perhaps the most common modeless dialog boxes are the Find and Replace dialog boxes displayed by word processing programs. As a user, you probably want to keep such a dialog box active for a while so that you can do multiple find or replace actions. Yet while the dialog box is active, you also want to be able to edit the document on which you're running the find or replace.

The modeless dialog box implemented in this next class is based on the ColorScroll program in Chapter 12. The form contains three scroll bars and six labels that resize themselves based on the form's size. The dialog box is intended to remain active during the entire duration of the program that displays it; thus, it has no buttons or a close box on its caption bar. A property named *Color* provides public access to the scroll bar values.

```
ColorScrollDialogBox.vb
'-------------------------------------------------------
' ColorScrollDialogBox.vb (c) 2002 by Charles Petzold
'-------------------------------------------------------
Imports System
Imports System.Drawing
Imports System.Windows.Forms

Class ColorScrollDialogBox
    Inherits Form

    Private alblName(2) As Label
    Private alblValue(2) As Label
    Private ascrbar(2) As VScrollBar

    Event Changed As EventHandler

    Sub New()
        Text = "Color Scroll Dialog Box"

        ControlBox = False
        MinimizeBox = False
        MaximizeBox = False
        ShowInTaskbar = False
```

*(continued)*

**ColorScrollDialogBox.vb**   *(continued)*

```
        Dim aclr() As Color = {Color.Red, Color.Green, Color.Blue}
        Dim i As Integer

        For i = 0 To 2
            alblName(i) = New Label()
            alblName(i).Parent = Me
            alblName(i).ForeColor = aclr(i)
            alblName(i).Text = "&" & aclr(i).ToKnownColor().ToString()
            alblName(i).TextAlign = ContentAlignment.MiddleCenter

            ascrbar(i) = New VScrollBar()
            ascrbar(i).Parent = Me
            ascrbar(i).SmallChange = 1
            ascrbar(i).LargeChange = 16
            ascrbar(i).Minimum = 0
            ascrbar(i).Maximum = 255 + ascrbar(i).LargeChange - 1
            AddHandler ascrbar(i).ValueChanged, _
                                        AddressOf ScrollOnValueChanged
            ascrbar(i).TabStop = True

            alblValue(i) = New Label()
            alblValue(i).Parent = Me
            alblValue(i).TextAlign = ContentAlignment.MiddleCenter
        Next i

        OnResize(EventArgs.Empty)
    End Sub

    Property Color() As Color
        Set(ByVal Value As Color)
            ascrbar(0).Value = Value.R
            ascrbar(1).Value = Value.G
            ascrbar(2).Value = Value.B
        End Set
        Get
            Return Color.FromArgb(ascrbar(0).Value, _
                                  ascrbar(1).Value, _
                                  ascrbar(2).Value)
        End Get
    End Property

    Protected Overrides Sub OnResize(ByVal ea As EventArgs)
        MyBase.OnResize(ea)

        Dim cx As Integer = ClientSize.Width
        Dim cy As Integer = ClientSize.Height
        Dim cyFont As Integer = Font.Height
        Dim i As Integer

        For i = 0 To 2
            alblName(i).Location = New Point(i * cx \ 3, cyFont \ 2)
```

```
            alblName(i).Size = New Size(cx \ 3, cyFont)
            ascrbar(i).Location = New Point((4 * i + 1) * cx \ 12, _
                                            2 * cyFont)
            ascrbar(i).Size = New Size(cx \ 6, cy - 4 * cyFont)
            alblValue(i).Location = New Point(i * cx \ 3, _
                                                cy - 3 * cyFont \ 2)
            alblValue(i).Size = New Size(cx \ 3, cyFont)
        Next i
    End Sub

    Private Sub ScrollOnValueChanged(ByVal obj As Object, _
                                      ByVal ea As EventArgs)
        Dim i As Integer
        For i = 0 To 2
            If obj Is ascrbar(i) Then
                alblValue(i).Text = ascrbar(i).Value.ToString()
            End If
        Next i

        RaiseEvent Changed(Me, EventArgs.Empty)
    End Sub
End Class
```

As we've seen, modal dialog boxes don't usually need to implement their own public events unless they include an Apply button. However, modeless dialog boxes almost always need to actively communicate with the application that invokes them, and the best way to do this is through events.

The *ColorScrollDialogBox* class implements an event named *Changed* that is triggered whenever one of the scroll bars has a *ValueChanged* event. If I wanted to imitate the Microsoft .NET Framework more, I'd also include a protected virtual *OnChanged* method in the class. The *OnChanged* method would be called by *ScrollOnValueChanged*, and *OnChanged* would then call the *Changed* event.

You don't use *ShowDialog* with a modeless dialog box. *ShowDialog* doesn't return until the dialog box is closed, and that's not what you want. Instead, you use *Show*, a method of *Form* we encountered in Chapter 2 and haven't seen since.

Another crucial part of implementing modeless dialog boxes involves this property:

### *Form* Properties (selection)

| Property | Type | Accessibility |
|----------|------|---------------|
| Owner | Form | Get/Set |

You set the *Owner* property of the modeless dialog box to the application form. Doing so causes the form to own the dialog box. Being owned by an application form means that the modeless dialog box will always appear *in front of* the application form. Also, whenever the application form is minimized, the modeless dialog box disappears from the screen.

The following program creates an object of type *ColorScrollDialogBox*, sets the *Owner* property to itself (the application form), initializes the *Color* property of the dialog box with the application form's *BackColor* property, sets an event handler for the dialog box's *Changed* event, and then calls the dialog box's *Show* method. The dialog box stays active (and lets you change the application form's background color) until the application is terminated.

### ModelessColorScroll.vb

```
'---------------------------------------------------
' ModelessColorScroll.vb (c) 2002 by Charles Petzold
'---------------------------------------------------
Imports System
Imports System.Drawing
Imports System.Windows.Forms

Class ModelessColorScroll
    Inherits Form

    Shared Sub Main()
        Application.Run(New ModelessColorScroll())
    End Sub

    Sub New()
        Text = "Modeless Color Scroll"

        Dim dlg As New ColorScrollDialogBox()
        dlg.Owner = Me
        dlg.Color = BackColor
        AddHandler dlg.Changed, AddressOf ColorScrollOnChanged
        dlg.Show()
    End Sub

    Sub ColorScrollOnChanged(ByVal obj As Object, ByVal ea As EventArgs)
        Dim dlg As ColorScrollDialogBox = _
                        DirectCast(obj, ColorScrollDialogBox)
        BackColor = dlg.Color
    End Sub
End Class
```

The Transform program in Chapter 18 demonstrates another modeless dialog box (which itself invokes a modal dialog box) that lets you interactively set the six elements of a matrix transform.

# The Common Dialog Boxes

One of the primary goals of Windows has always been to promote a standardized user interface. In the early days of Windows, some user interface conventions were established fairly quickly. Almost every software manufacturer adopted the ALT+FILE+OPEN selection to open a file, for example. However, the actual file-open dialog boxes were often quite dissimilar.

It wasn't until Windows 3.1 that the *common dialog box library* became part of the Windows API. Much of this library is exposed in the .NET Framework and consists of dialog boxes to open and close files, select colors and fonts, and aid in printing. The class hierarchy is as follows:

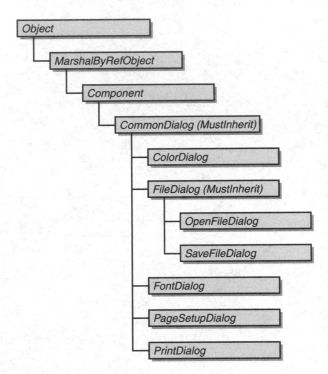

Both *CommonDialog* and *FileDialog* are *MustInherit* classes and can't be instantiated. That leaves six classes that you can use in applications. I'll cover *ColorDialog*, *FontDialog*, *OpenFileDialog*, and *SaveFileDialog* in this chapter, and *PageSetupDialog* and *PrintDialog* when I go deeper into printing in Chapter 21.

# Choosing Fonts and Colors

Let's take a look at both *FontDialog* and *ColorDialog* in a single program that lets you set the *BackColor*, *ForeColor*, and *Font* properties of a form.

**FontAndColorDialogs.vb**

```
'-----------------------------------------------------
' FontAndColorDialogs.vb (c) 2002 by Charles Petzold
'-----------------------------------------------------
Imports System
Imports System.Drawing
Imports System.Windows.Forms

Class FontAndColorDialogs
    Inherits Form

    Shared Sub Main()
        Application.Run(New FontAndColorDialogs())
    End Sub

    Sub New()
        Text = "Font and Color Dialogs"
        ResizeRedraw = True

        Menu = New MainMenu()
        Menu.MenuItems.Add("&Format")
        Menu.MenuItems(0).MenuItems.Add("&Font...", _
                                AddressOf MenuFontOnClick)
        Menu.MenuItems(0).MenuItems.Add("&Background Color...", _
                                AddressOf MenuColorOnClick)
    End Sub

    Sub MenuFontOnClick(ByVal obj As Object, ByVal ea As EventArgs)
        Dim fntdlg As New FontDialog()
        fntdlg.Font = Font
        fntdlg.Color = ForeColor
        fntdlg.ShowColor = True

        If fntdlg.ShowDialog() = DialogResult.OK Then
            Font = fntdlg.Font
            ForeColor = fntdlg.Color
            Invalidate()
        End If
    End Sub

    Sub MenuColorOnClick(ByVal obj As Object, ByVal ea As EventArgs)
        Dim clrdlg As New ColorDialog()
        clrdlg.Color = BackColor

        If clrdlg.ShowDialog() = DialogResult.OK Then
            BackColor = clrdlg.Color
```

```
        End If
    End Sub

    Protected Overrides Sub OnPaint(ByVal pea As PaintEventArgs)
        Dim grfx As Graphics = pea.Graphics
        Dim strfmt As New StringFormat()
        strfmt.Alignment = StringAlignment.Center
        strfmt.LineAlignment = StringAlignment.Center

        grfx.DrawString("Hello common dialog boxes!", Font, _
                    New SolidBrush(ForeColor), _
                    RectangleF.op_Implicit(ClientRectangle), strfmt)
    End Sub
End Class
```

The program creates a Format menu containing two items: Font and Background Color. Although this program uses prewritten common dialog boxes rather than dialog boxes that we've written ourselves, the structure of the two menu *Click* event handlers should look very familiar. Look at *MenuColorOnClick*, for example. The dialog box is first created:

```
Dim clrdlg As New ColorDialog()
```

It's then initialized by setting a property:

```
clrdlg.Color = BackColor
```

And then the *ShowDialog* method is called:

```
If clrdlg.ShowDialog() = DialogResult.OK Then
    BackColor = clrdlg.Color
End If
```

If *ShowDialog* returns *DialogResult.OK*, the program uses information from the dialog box.

Although this program uses the form's *Font*, *ForeColor*, and *BackColor* properties to initialize the two dialog boxes and then sets these properties based on what the user sets in the dialog boxes, you could instead define fields in your form that are associated with the dialog box settings.

The *FontDialog* class lets the user choose both a font and a font color identified by the following two properties:

### *FontDialog* Properties (selection)

| Property | Type | Accessibility |
|----------|------|---------------|
| *Font* | *Font* | Get/Set |
| *Color* | *Color* | Get/Set |

The FontAndColorDialogs program simply initializes these two properties from the *Font* and *ForeColor* properties of the form and then sets these two form properties if the dialog box is terminated with the OK button.

The FontAndColorDialogs program sets the *ShowColor* property to enable the color option on the dialog box, which by default is disabled. The following properties let you control the appearance of the color option and other parts of the font dialog box:

### *FontDialog* Properties (selection)

| Property | Type | Accessibility | Default |
|----------|------|---------------|---------|
| *ShowEffects* | *Boolean* | Get/Set | *True* |
| *ShowColor* | *Boolean* | Get/Set | *False* |
| *ShowApply* | *Boolean* | Get/Set | *False* |
| *ShowHelp* | *Boolean* | Get/Set | *False* |

If you set the *ShowEffects* property to *False*, the dialog box won't let you select underline or strikeout. Here's what the dialog box looks like when both *Show-Effects* and *ShowColor* are set to *True*:

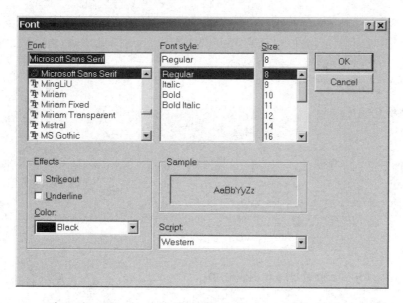

The *ShowApply* and *ShowHelp* options control the appearance of buttons labeled *Apply* and *Help*. If you enable these buttons, you'll want to handle the following events.

### *FontDialog* Events (selection)

| Event | Method | Delegate | Argument |
|---|---|---|---|
| *Apply* | *OnApply* | *EventHandler* | *EventArgs* |
| *HelpRequest* | *OnHelpRequest* | *EventHandler* | *EventArgs* |

We've already had experience in using an Apply button, but I'll also demonstrate using the Apply button in *FontDialog* in the next version of the program.

The *FontDialog* class has several other properties that control the appearance of fonts in the dialog box, but the defaults are usually sufficient. However, later on in this chapter (in the HeadDump program), I'll use the following property:

### *FontDialog* Properties (selection)

| Property | Type | Accessibility | Default |
|---|---|---|---|
| *FixedPitchOnly* | *Boolean* | Get/Set | *False* |

Set this property to *True* if you want to limit the display of fonts to those that have a uniform character width.

The *ColorDialog* dialog box lets you choose a color, which is represented by a property named *Color* of type *Color*:

### *ColorDialog* Properties (selection)

| Property | Type | Accessibility |
|---|---|---|
| *Color* | *Color* | Get/Set |

Several other *Boolean* properties control various aspects of the dialog box:

### *ColorDialog* Properties (selection)

| Property | Type | Accessibility | Default |
|---|---|---|---|
| *FullOpen* | *Boolean* | Get/Set | *False* |
| *AllowFullOpen* | *Boolean* | Get/Set | *True* |
| *SolidColorOnly* | *Boolean* | Get/Set | *False* |
| *AnyColor* | *Boolean* | Get/Set | *False* |
| *ShowHelp* | *Boolean* | Get/Set | *False* |

The *ColorDialog* class doesn't support an Apply button. Here's the default color dialog box:

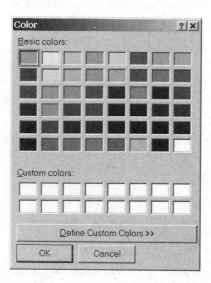

Normally, you just click one of the displayed colors and press OK. If none of those colors is satisfactory, you can click the button labeled Define Custom Colors. The dialog box expands like so:

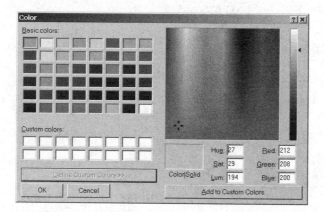

What you can do now is define custom colors over at the right and then add them to the collection labeled Custom Colors at the left. You can't make the dialog box return to its original appearance unless you end it by pressing OK or Cancel. If you set the *FullOpen* property to *True* before calling *ShowDialog*, the dialog box opens in the wide version. If you set the *AllowFullOpen* property to

*False* (regardless of the setting of *FullOpen*), the small version of the dialog box comes up and the Define Custom Colors button is disabled.

An application using the *ColorDialog* class has access to the custom colors through this property:

### *ColorDialog* Properties (selection)

| Property | Type | Accessibility |
|----------|------|---------------|
| *CustomColors* | *Integer()* | Get/Set |

The custom colors are stored as an array of sixteen 32-bit integers, where red is the least significant byte, green the next byte, blue the next, and the most significant byte is 0. (*Do not* use these integers in the shared *Color.FromArgb* method that returns a *Color* object based on an integer. That method interprets blue as the least significant byte, and then green, red, and an alpha value where 0 is transparent.)

Suppose a user invokes the color dialog box from the FontAndColorDialogs program, clicks the Define Custom Colors button, and then carefully defines 16 custom colors. The user then selects one of them and presses OK. Then the user invokes the dialog box again and…. The custom colors are gone!

What happened? It's very simple. Look at the *MenuColorOnClick* method. The program re-creates the dialog box every time it's invoked. At the end of the *MenuColorOnClick* method, there are no more references to the *ColorDialog* object named *clrdlg*, so it becomes eligible for garbage collection.

If you leave the *AllowFullOpen* property set to *True*, it is very impolite not to save the custom colors between various invocations of the dialog box. You can do this in a couple ways. You can define an array of integers as a field:

```
Private aiCustomColors() As Integer
```

Before invoking the dialog box with *ShowDialog*, you set the property from the field, like so:

```
clrdlg.CustomColors = aiCustomColors
```

After *ShowDialog* returns, regardless of how the user ended the dialog box, the custom colors are saved back in the field:

```
aiCustomColors = clrdlg.CustomColors
```

There's an even easier approach. Simply remove the statement

```
Dim clrdlg As New ColorDialog()
```

from the *MenuColorOnClick* method and make it a field. Now the program uses only one instance of *ColorDialog* during the entire time the application is running.

Here's a better version of the FontAndColorDialogs program that also implements the Apply button in the font dialog box.

### BetterFontAndColorDialogs.vb

```vb
'-------------------------------------------------------------
' BetterFontAndColorDialogs.vb (c) 2002 by Charles Petzold
'-------------------------------------------------------------
Imports System
Imports System.Drawing
Imports System.Windows.Forms

Class BetterFontAndColorDialogs
    Inherits Form

    Protected clrdlg As ColorDialog = New ColorDialog()

    Shared Sub Main()
        Application.Run(New BetterFontAndColorDialogs())
    End Sub

    Sub New()
        Text = "Better Font and Color Dialogs"

        Menu = New MainMenu()
        Menu.MenuItems.Add("&Format")
        Menu.MenuItems(0).MenuItems.Add("&Font...", _
                                AddressOf MenuFontOnClick)
        Menu.MenuItems(0).MenuItems.Add("&Background Color...", _
                                AddressOf MenuColorOnClick)
    End Sub

    Sub MenuFontOnClick(ByVal obj As Object, ByVal ea As EventArgs)
        Dim fntdlg As New FontDialog()
        fntdlg.Font = Font
        fntdlg.Color = ForeColor
        fntdlg.ShowColor = True
        fntdlg.ShowApply = True
        AddHandler fntdlg.Apply, AddressOf FontDialogOnApply

        If fntdlg.ShowDialog() = DialogResult.OK Then
            Font = fntdlg.Font
            ForeColor = fntdlg.Color
            Invalidate()
        End If
    End Sub
```

```
    Sub MenuColorOnClick(ByVal obj As Object, ByVal ea As EventArgs)
        clrdlg.Color = BackColor

        If clrdlg.ShowDialog() = DialogResult.OK Then
            BackColor = clrdlg.Color
        End If
    End Sub

    Sub FontDialogOnApply(ByVal obj As Object, ByVal ea As EventArgs)
        Dim fntdlg As FontDialog = DirectCast(obj, FontDialog)
        Font = fntdlg.Font
        ForeColor = fntdlg.Color
        Invalidate()
    End Sub

    Protected Overrides Sub OnPaint(ByVal pea As PaintEventArgs)
        Dim grfx As Graphics = pea.Graphics
        grfx.DrawString("Hello common dialog boxes!", Font, _
                    New SolidBrush(ForeColor), 0, 0)
    End Sub
End Class
```

Now the custom colors are preserved when the dialog box is terminated and reshown.

Unfortunately, saving the dialog box settings from one invocation to another raises an additional question: How do you preserve settings when you terminate and rerun the *program*?

For that job, you probably want to take advantage of the Windows registry.

# Using the Windows Registry

The Windows registry is a general-purpose mechanism that applications (and Windows itself) use to store program information that must be retained when an application terminates. The information is stored in a hierarchical format. You can use the Registry Editor program (Regedit.exe) that comes with Windows to examine (and, if you're very brave, even modify) the contents of the registry on your machine.

The information in the registry is organized by *keys*, which are often written in the syntax of directory paths. For example, in the Registry Editor, you can find the key HKEY_CURRENT_USER\Software\Microsoft\Notepad to examine all the information stored in the registry by the Microsoft Notepad program. Each piece of information has a name (for example, iPointSize and iWindowPosX), a type (in both these cases, a REG_DWORD, which is a 32-bit unsigned integer), and a value.

The Windows registry is supported with two classes in the *Microsoft.Win32* namespace. The *Registry* class consists solely of seven shared read-only fields for the seven possible root keys in the registry. The Description column shows how these root keys are defined in the Win32 header files and displayed in the Registry Editor:

### *Registry* Shared Fields

| Field | Type | Accessibility | Description |
|---|---|---|---|
| *ClassesRoot* | *RegistryKey* | read-only | HKEY_CLASSES_ROOT |
| *CurrentUser* | *RegistryKey* | read-only | HKEY_CURRENT_USER |
| *LocalMachine* | *RegistryKey* | read-only | HKEY_LOCAL_MACHINE |
| *Users* | *RegistryKey* | read-only | HKEY_USERS |
| *PerformanceData* | *RegistryKey* | read-only | HKEY_PERFORMANCE_DATA |
| *CurrentConfig* | *RegistryKey* | read-only | HKEY_CURRENT_CONFIG |
| *DynData* | *RegistryKey* | read-only | HKEY_DYN_DATA |

Most applications will probably restrict themselves to the *CurrentUser* key to store user-specific information such as favorite fonts, colors, and other settings.

The second class is *RegistryKey*. The following methods are probably the most common:

### *RegistryKey* Methods (selection)

```
Function CreateSubKey(ByVal strSubKey As String) As RegistryKey

Function OpenSubKey(ByVal strSubKey As String) As RegistryKey

Function OpenSubKey(ByVal strSubKey As String,
                    ByVal bWritable As Boolean) As RegistryKey

Sub SetValue(ByVal strName As String, ByVal obj As Object)

Function GetValue(ByVal strName As String) As Object

Sub Close()
```

Notice that the *CreateSubKey* and *OpenSubKey* methods are members of the *RegistryKey* class and also return *RegistryKey* objects. The first *RegistryKey* object you obtain is from one of the fields of the *Registry* class, for example:

```
Dim regkey As RegistryKey = Registry.CurrentUser
```

You then obtain another *RegistryKey* object by combining that registry key with a subkey argument passed to *CreateSubKey* or *OpenSubKey*. For example, if *regkey* has been obtained from *Registry.CurrentUser*, the call

```
regkey = regkey.OpenSubKey("Software\Microsoft\Notepad")
```

returns a registry key suitable for reading the information stored by Notepad. Or you can do both calls in one shot:

```
Dim regkey As RegistryKey = _
    Registry.CurrentUser.OpenSubKey("Software\Microsoft\Notepad")
```

But that call obtains the key for Notepad. That's not the key you want to use for your application. You'll want to make your own key using the *CreateSubKey* method, for example:

```
Dim regkey As RegistryKey = _
    Registry.CurrentUser.CreateSubKey("Software\MyCompany\MyApp")
```

You'll probably use *CreateSubKey* when your program is first installed or the first time it runs. Subsequently, you can use *OpenSubKey* to open the key for reading:

```
Dim regkey As RegistryKey  = _
    Registry.CurrentUser.OpenSubKey("Software\MyCompany\MyApp")
```

You can also use *OpenSubKey* to open the key for writing:

```
Dim regkey As RegistryKey = _
    Registry.CurrentUser.OpenSubKey("Software\MyCompany\MyApp", True)
```

After you're finished accessing the registry, close it like so:

```
regkey.Close()
```

The *SetValue* and *GetValue* methods let you read and write values associated with names. But watch out: the syntax of the *SetValue* call makes it appear as if you can use an object of any type as the second argument, for example, an object of type *Font*:

```
regkey.SetValue("MyFont", fnt)
```

This call will work (kind of), but the problem arises when you try to retrieve that same object with a call to *GetValue*:

```
fnt = DirectCast(regkey.GetValue("MyFont"), Font)   ' Won't work!
```

If the registry had been originally designed with an object-oriented interface in mind, these two calls might work. But it wasn't, and they won't. Basically, you're limited to storing strings, 32-bit integers, and byte arrays. (A byte array lets you store generalized binary information, though probably not as conveniently as you'd like.)

The *SetValue* call just shown actually stores *fnt.ToString()*, which is a string that describes the *Font* object. When you call *GetValue*, however, that string can't be cast into an object of type *Font*, and the invalid cast will cause a run-time exception. If you need to store an object of type *Font* in the registry, you must store everything you need to re-create the font in the form of strings, 32-bit integers, and byte arrays.

Let's look at an example. The *DialogsWithRegistry* class in the following program subclasses *BetterFontAndColorDialogs* and adds registry support. The seven *Const* fields define the registry key and all the registry names I use in the program.

**DialogsWithRegistry.vb**

```
'-----------------------------------------------------
' DialogsWithRegistry.vb (c) 2002 by Charles Petzold
'-----------------------------------------------------
Imports Microsoft.Win32
Imports System
Imports System.Drawing
Imports System.Windows.Forms

Class DialogsWithRegistry
    Inherits BetterFontAndColorDialogs

    Const strRegKey As String = _
            "Software\ProgrammingWindowsWithVBdotNet\DialogsWithRegistry"
    Const strFontFace As String = "FontFace"
    Const strFontSize As String = "FontSize"
    Const strFontStyle As String = "FontStyle"
    Const strForeColor As String = "ForeColor"
    Const strBackColor As String = "BackColor"
    Const strCustomClr As String = "CustomColor"

    Shared Shadows Sub Main()
        Application.Run(New DialogsWithRegistry())
    End Sub

    Sub New()
        Text = "Font and Color Dialogs with Registry"

        Dim regkey As RegistryKey = _
                        Registry.CurrentUser.OpenSubKey(strRegKey)

        If Not regkey Is Nothing Then
            Font = New Font( _
                    DirectCast(regkey.GetValue(strFontFace), String), _
                    Single.Parse( _
                        DirectCast(regkey.GetValue(strFontSize), String)), _
                    CType(regkey.GetValue(strFontStyle), FontStyle))
            ForeColor = Color.FromArgb(CInt(regkey.GetValue(strForeColor)))
            BackColor = Color.FromArgb(CInt(regkey.GetValue(strBackColor)))

            Dim i, aiColors(16) As Integer
```

```
            For i = 0 To 15
                aiColors(i) = CInt(regkey.GetValue(strCustomClr & i))
            Next i
            clrdlg.CustomColors = aiColors
            regkey.Close()
        End If
    End Sub

    Protected Overrides Sub OnClosed(ByVal ea As EventArgs)
        Dim i As Integer
        Dim regkey As RegistryKey = _
                    Registry.CurrentUser.OpenSubKey(strRegKey, True)

        If regkey Is Nothing Then
            regkey = Registry.CurrentUser.CreateSubKey(strRegKey)
        End If

        regkey.SetValue(strFontFace, Font.Name)
        regkey.SetValue(strFontSize, Font.SizeInPoints.ToString())
        regkey.SetValue(strFontStyle, CInt(Font.Style))
        regkey.SetValue(strForeColor, ForeColor.ToArgb())
        regkey.SetValue(strBackColor, BackColor.ToArgb())

        For i = 0 To 15
            regkey.SetValue(strCustomClr & i, clrdlg.CustomColors(i))
        Next i
        regkey.Close()
    End Sub
End Class
```

Let's look at the override of the *OnClosed* method first. *OnClosed* is called when the form has been closed. That's a good time for the program to write information to the registry. If the *OpenSubKey* call returns *Nothing*, the program must be running for the first time, so it calls *CreateSubKey* to create the registry key. Each *SetValue* call stores either an integer or a string in the registry. For the form's *Font* property, three values must be stored: the *Name*, *SizeInPoints*, and *Style* properties. The *SizeInPoints* property of *Font* is a *Single*, so that value is converted to a string representation with *ToString*. The *ToArgb* method of the *Color* class converts *Color* objects into integers.

Also take note of the *SetValue* call in the *For* loop that's used to store the custom colors. The value name is

```
strCustomClr & i
```

which creates names of CustomColor0, CustomColor1, through CustomColor15.

The values are loaded from the registry in the program's constructor. The form's font is re-created using the face name, point size, and style values. The point size has to be converted from a string back to a *Single* using the shared

*Parse* method of the *Single* structure. The shared *Color.FromArgb* method converts the stored integers back into *Color* objects.

Because implementing registry support requires working with two blocks of code, registry read and write code can be difficult to debug. The best approach is to get all the *SetValue* calls working first. Monitor your progress with the Registry Editor. (F5 refreshes the display.) The Registry Editor also lets you delete an entire key, so you can test how well your program re-creates the registry entries from scratch. When you get all the *SetValue* calls working, then code the *GetValue* calls.

# The Open File Dialog Box

Both *OpenFileDialog* and *SaveFileDialog* inherit from the *MustInherit* class *FileDialog*, which implements a number of properties common to both classes. Both *OpenFileDialog* and *SaveFileDialog* are *NonInheritable*, meaning (of course) that you can't inherit from them.

Both *OpenFileDialog* and *SaveFileDialog* are primarily responsible for returning to your program a fully qualified filename that the user specifies either by selecting from a list box or by manually typing. Considering that this is file I/O we're speaking of here, however, using these dialog boxes can be more complex than using those involved with fonts or color.

Let's look at *OpenFileDialog* first. Three properties are connected with the retrieval of a filename or filenames from the dialog box:

### *OpenFileDialog* Properties (selection)

| Property | Type | Accessibility |
|----------|------|---------------|
| *Multiselect* | *Boolean* | Get/Set |
| *FileName* | *String* | Get/Set |
| *FileNames* | *String()* | Get |

By default, *Multiselect* is *False*, indicating that the user can select only one file from the dialog box, in which case *FileName* indicates the selected file.

Armed with only this information, let's take a look at HeadDump, a hexadecimal dump program that displays only as much of the selected file as can fit in the client area. This program makes use of the *ComposeLine* function from the HexDump module in Appendix A (which you should consult for information about files and streams as implemented in .NET).

## HeadDump.vb

```
'-------------------------------------------
' HeadDump.vb (c) 2002 by Charles Petzold
'-------------------------------------------
Imports System
Imports System.Drawing
Imports System.IO
Imports System.Windows.Forms

Class HeadDump
    Inherits Form

    Const strProgName As String = "Head Dump"
    Private strFileName As String = ""

    Shared Sub Main()
        Application.Run(New HeadDump())
    End Sub

    Sub New()
        Text = strProgName
        Font = New Font(FontFamily.GenericMonospace, Font.SizeInPoints)

        Menu = New MainMenu()
        Menu.MenuItems.Add("&File")
        Menu.MenuItems(0).MenuItems.Add("&Open...", _
                            AddressOf MenuFileOpenOnClick)
        Menu.MenuItems.Add("F&ormat")
        Menu.MenuItems(1).MenuItems.Add("&Font...", _
                            AddressOf MenuFormatFontOnClick)
    End Sub

    Sub MenuFileOpenOnClick(ByVal obj As Object, ByVal ea As EventArgs)
        Dim dlg As New OpenFileDialog()

        If dlg.ShowDialog() = DialogResult.OK Then
            strFileName = dlg.FileName
            Text = strProgName & " - " & Path.GetFileName(strFileName)
            Invalidate()
        End If
    End Sub

    Sub MenuFormatFontOnClick(ByVal obj As Object, ByVal ea As EventArgs)
        Dim dlg As New FontDialog()

        dlg.Font = Font
        dlg.FixedPitchOnly = True

        If dlg.ShowDialog() = DialogResult.OK Then
            Font = dlg.Font
```

*(continued)*

**HeadDump.vb**  *(continued)*

```
            Invalidate()
        End If
    End Sub

    Protected Overrides Sub OnPaint(ByVal pea As PaintEventArgs)
        Dim grfx As Graphics = pea.Graphics
        Dim br As New SolidBrush(ForeColor)
        Dim fs As FileStream
        Dim iLine As Integer

        Try
            fs = New FileStream(strFileName, FileMode.Open, _
                            FileAccess.Read, FileShare.Read)
        Catch
            Return
        End Try

        For iLine = 0 To ClientSize.Height \ Font.Height
            Dim abyBuffer(16) As Byte
            Dim iCount As Integer = fs.Read(abyBuffer, 0, 16)

            If iCount = 0 Then Exit For

            Dim str As String = HexDump.ComposeLine(16 * iLine, _
                                            abyBuffer, iCount)
            grfx.DrawString(str, Font, br, 0, iLine * Font.Height)
        Next iLine

        fs.Close()
    End Sub
End Class
```

Because hexadecimal dumps become a chaotic jumble when displayed with proportional fonts, this form sets its *Font* property to the *GenericMonospace* font. The menu the program creates allows changing this font to another fixed-pitch font as well as selecting a file.

The *MenuFileOpenOnClick* method shows how to create and display an *OpenFileDialog* object. If *ShowDialog* returns *DialogResult.OK*, the program saves the *FileName* property in a field named *strFileName* and then sets a new *Text* property for the form, using the shared *Path.GetFileName* method to extract the filename from the fully qualified path and filename. The *OnPaint* method is responsible for opening the file, reading bytes, and formatting them. Here's the program displaying its own source code file:

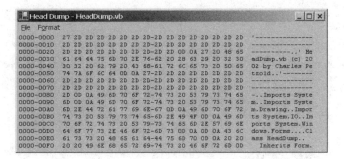

What you'll find when experimenting with HeadDump is that the initial directory that opens in the open file dialog box is the one known as My Documents. You can then navigate to other directories. *OpenFileDialog* automatically saves the directory you finally select in the Windows registry. The next time you run the program, the open file dialog box will display the files in the last directory you navigated to using that dialog box.

By default, *OpenFileDialog* changes the current directory associated with the application as you're navigating through the directories. If you want to set an initial directory for the dialog box or you want it to restore the current directory when the dialog box terminates, you can use the following two properties:

### *FileDialog* Properties (selection)

| Property | Type | Accessibility |
| --- | --- | --- |
| *InitialDirectory* | *String* | Get/Set |
| *RestoreDirectory* | *Boolean* | Get/Set |

Although most users navigate through directories and select files by picking the directories and files from lists, a user can also manually type a directory name or a filename. The following two properties are set to *True* by default so that the dialog box itself checks for valid path names and filenames before closing the dialog box:

### *FileDialog* Properties (selection)

| Property | Type | Accessibility |
| --- | --- | --- |
| *CheckPathExists* | *Boolean* | Get/Set |
| *CheckFileExists* | *Boolean* | Get/Set |

If you want to let the user create a new file using *OpenFileDialog*, set *CheckFileExists* to *False*.

The following two properties let you enable a check box labeled Open As Read-Only on the dialog box and determine whether the user checked it:

### *OpenFileDialog* Properties (selection)

| Property | Type | Accessibility |
|----------|------|---------------|
| *ShowReadOnly* | *Boolean* | Get/Set |
| *ReadOnlyChecked* | *Boolean* | Get/Set |

If you enable this check box and the user checks it, your program shouldn't save any changes to the file back to disk.

The other remaining properties I want to discuss involve the messy area of file types and filename extensions. You may have noticed that the *OpenFileDialog* in HeadDump has a combo box labeled Files Of Type that is blank:

For the HeadDump program, that's not so bad because the program can open and display any type of file. But for most programs, you want to force *OpenFileDialog* to display files of only specific types. You do this by using a text string called a *filter*. For the HeadDump program, I could have defined the filter like this:

```
"All Files (*.*)|*.*"
```

or like this:

```
"All Files|*.*"
```

The portion of the string up to the vertical bar is what the dialog box displays in the Files Of Type combo box. The string to the right of the vertical bar indicates the types of files the dialog box is to display, in this case, all files.

It's up to you whether or not the portion of the text string to the left of the vertical bar includes a file specification. That's the part the user sees, and it doesn't determine which files the dialog box displays.

If you were writing a clone of the Notepad program (which I'll actually be doing in Chapter 18), you would define the filter like so:

```
"Text Documents (*.txt)|*.txt|" & _
"All Files|*.*"
```

In this case, the Files Of Type combo box has two lines. When the user selects the first line in the combo box, the dialog box displays all files that have a *txt* extension; when the user selects the second line, the dialog box displays all files. Although I've written the string in two lines with a concatenation symbol (&) for clarity, it's really just one long string with the pieces separated by vertical bars:

```
"Text Documents (*.txt)|*.txt|All Files|*.*"
```

There are always twice as many pieces of the string as there are lines in the combo box.

If you were writing a program that was able to load a variety of image files, you'd define a filter something like this:

```
"All Image Files|*.bmp;*.gif;*.jpeg;*.jpg;*.jfif;*.png;*.tif;*.tiff|" & _
"Windows Bitmap (*.bmp)|*.bmp|" + _
"Graphics Interchange Format (*.gif)|*.gif|" + _
"JPEG File Interchange Format (*.jpg)|*.jpg;*.jpeg;*.jfif|" + _
"Portable Network Graphics (*.png)|*.png|" + _
"Tag Image File Format (*.tif)|*.tif;*.tiff|" + _
"All Files (*.*)|*.*"
```

The Files Of Type combo box would have seven lines in this case. As you'll notice, some of the file types are associated with multiple filename specifications. These are separated by semicolons. For example, if the user selects the line in the combo box that reads

```
JPEG File Interchange Format (*.jpg)
```

the dialog box displays files with extensions jpg, jpeg, and jfif. The part that's displayed in the combo box could alternatively be

```
JPEG File Interchange Format
```

or

```
JPEG/JFIF
```

or

```
JPEG File Interchange Format (*.jpg, *.jpeg, *.jfif)
```

Use whatever you think is best for the user.

You use the following two properties to specify the filter to be used for the Files Of Type combo type and the line number of the filter that is to be initially displayed:

### *FileDialog* Properties (selection)

| Property | Type | Accessibility |
| --- | --- | --- |
| *Filter* | *String* | Get/Set |
| *FilterIndex* | *Integer* | Get/Set |

On return from *ShowDialog*, *FilterIndex* indicates the index of the line selected by the user in the Files Of Type combo box. These line numbers begin at 1.

Here's a program that implements an *OpenFileDialog* that has a filter to specify every type of file supported by the shared *Image.FromFile* method.

**ImageOpen.vb**

```
'-----------------------------------------
' ImageOpen.vb (c) 2002 by Charles Petzold
'-----------------------------------------
Imports System
Imports System.Drawing
Imports System.IO
Imports System.Windows.Forms

Class ImageOpen
    Inherits Form

    Protected strProgName As String
    Protected strFileName As String
    Protected img As Image

    Shared Sub Main()
        Application.Run(New ImageOpen())
    End Sub

    Sub New()
        strProgName = "Image Open"
        Text = strProgName
        ResizeRedraw = True
```

```
        Menu = New MainMenu()
        Menu.MenuItems.Add("&File")
        Menu.MenuItems(0).MenuItems.Add(New MenuItem("&Open...", _
                            AddressOf MenuFileOpenOnClick, _
                            Shortcut.CtrlO))
    End Sub

    Sub MenuFileOpenOnClick(ByVal obj As Object, ByVal ea As EventArgs)
        Dim dlg As New OpenFileDialog()

        dlg.Filter = "All Image Files|*.bmp;*.ico;*.gif;*.jpeg;*.jpg;" & _
                    "*.jfif;*.png;*.tif;*.tiff;*.wmf;*.emf|" & _
                    "Windows Bitmap (*.bmp)|*.bmp|" & _
                    "Windows Icon (*.ico)|*.ico|" & _
                    "Graphics Interchange Format (*.gif)|*.gif|" & _
                    "JPEG File Interchange Format (*.jpg)|" & _
                                    "*.jpg;*.jpeg;*.jfif|" & _
                    "Portable Network Graphics (*.png)|*.png|" & _
                    "Tag Image File Format (*.tif)|*.tif;*.tiff|" & _
                    "Windows Metafile (*.wmf)|*.wmf|" & _
                    "Enhanced Metafile (*.emf)|*.emf|" & _
                    "All Files (*.*)|*.*"

        If dlg.ShowDialog() = DialogResult.OK Then
            Try
                img = Image.FromFile(dlg.FileName)
            Catch exc As Exception
                MessageBox.Show(exc.Message, strProgName)
                Return
            End Try

            strFileName = dlg.FileName
            Text = strProgName & " - " & Path.GetFileName(strFileName)
            Invalidate()
        End If
    End Sub

    Protected Overrides Sub OnPaint(ByVal pea As PaintEventArgs)
        Dim grfx As Graphics = pea.Graphics

        If Not img Is Nothing Then
            grfx.DrawImage(img, 0, 0)
        End If
    End Sub
End Class
```

This program is structurally similar to the HeadDump program except that it attempts to load the image immediately after *ShowDialog* returns. Although the dialog box itself checks to make sure that the file exists, nothing prevents the user from specifying an existing file that's not an image file. If the file is not an image file (or the file is corrupted in some way), *Image.FromFile* throws an exception and the program displays a message box reporting the problem. The *OnPaint* method simply uses *DrawImage* to display the loaded image.

# The Save File Dialog Box

Has it occurred to you yet that we're on the verge of writing a program that can convert between various bitmap file formats using the standard Open and Save dialog boxes? It's a little tricky to carry it off—and the implementation isn't quite optimum—but that's my goal in the remainder of the chapter.

The *SaveFileDialog* class adds just two properties to the properties defined by *FileDialog*:

### *SaveFileDialog* Properties

| Property | Type | Accessibility | Default |
|----------|------|---------------|---------|
| *CreatePrompt* | *Boolean* | Get/Set | *False* |
| *OverwritePrompt* | *Boolean* | Get/Set | *True* |

These two properties affect the display of message boxes that can be displayed while *SaveFileDialog* is still displayed. If you set *CreatePrompt* to *True* and the user specifies a file that doesn't exist, the dialog box will display a message box asking whether the user really wants to create that file. If you leave *OverwritePrompt* set to *True*, the dialog box asks for confirmation if the user selects a file that already exists.

Usually when an application invokes a dialog box to save a document, the application suggests a filename, and very often a default filename extension. For example, Notepad displays a filename of *.txt in the save file dialog box.

For a program that can convert between image formats, however, it's more proper for the save file dialog box to suggest a filename *without* an extension. The filename is the same as the filename of the loaded file. But the filename extension should be based on whatever format the user wants to save the file in, and that's not known when the dialog box is displayed.

Here's a way to do it. First, before displaying the dialog box, set the *FileName* property of *SaveFileDialog* to the opened filename without the extension. You can use the shared *Path.GetFileNameWithoutExtension* method to strip an extension from a filename. Second, specify that the dialog box itself appends an extension to the selected file by setting the following property to *True*:

### *FileDialog* Properties (selection)

| Property | Type | Accessibility | Default |
|---|---|---|---|
| *AddExtension* | *Boolean* | Get/Set | *False* |

The extension that *SaveFileDialog* appends to the filename is the first filename extension listed in the line of the filter that the user selects in the Save As Type combo box.

Here's one possible implementation. The *ImageIO* class overrides the *ImageOpen* class and adds a Save As item to the menu.

## ImageIO.vb

```
'---------------------------------------
' ImageIO.vb (c) 2002 by Charles Petzold
'---------------------------------------
Imports System
Imports System.Drawing
Imports System.Drawing.Imaging
Imports System.IO
Imports System.Windows.Forms

Class ImageIO
    Inherits ImageOpen

    Private miSaveAs As MenuItem

    Shared Shadows Sub Main()
        Application.Run(new ImageIO())
    End Sub

    Sub New()
        strProgName = "Image I/O"
        Text = strProgName

        AddHandler Menu.MenuItems(0).Popup, AddressOf MenuFileOnPopup
        miSaveAs = new MenuItem("Save &As...")
        AddHandler miSaveAs.Click, AddressOf MenuFileSaveAsOnClick
        Menu.MenuItems(0).MenuItems.Add(miSaveAs)
    End Sub

    Sub MenuFileOnPopup(ByVal obj As Object, ByVal ea As EventArgs)
        miSaveAs.Enabled = Not img Is Nothing
    End Sub

    Sub MenuFileSaveAsOnClick(ByVal obj As Object, ByVal ea As EventArgs)
        Dim savedlg As New SaveFileDialog()
```

*(continued)*

**ImageIO.vb**   *(continued)*

```
        savedlg.InitialDirectory = Path.GetDirectoryName(strFileName)
        savedlg.FileName = Path.GetFileNameWithoutExtension(strFileName)
        savedlg.AddExtension = True
        savedlg.Filter = "Windows Bitmap (*.bmp)|*.bmp|" & _
                         "Graphics Interchange Format (*.gif)|*.gif|" & _
                         "JPEG File Interchange Format (*.jpg)|" & _
                                          "*.jpg;* .jpeg;*.jfif|" & _
                         "Portable Network Graphics (*.png)|*.png|" & _
                         "Tagged Imaged File Format (*.tif)|*.tif;*.tiff"

        Dim aif() As ImageFormat = {ImageFormat.Bmp, ImageFormat.Gif, _
                             ImageFormat.Jpeg, ImageFormat.Png, _
                             ImageFormat.Tiff}

        If savedlg.ShowDialog() = DialogResult.OK Then
            Try
                img.Save(savedlg.FileName, aif(savedlg.FilterIndex - 1))
            Catch exc As Exception
                MessageBox.Show(exc.Message, Text)
                Return
            End Try

            strFileName = savedlg.FileName
            Text = strProgName & " - " & Path.GetFileName(strFileName)
        End If
    End Sub
End Class
```

Notice that the filter for the *SaveFileDialog* object doesn't include an All Files or All Image Files line and includes only those formats that work with the *Save* method of the *Image* class. The idea here is that the user accepts the filename (without the extension) displayed in the dialog box and selects the format using the Save As Type combo box. If the user selects "JPEG File Interchange Format," for example, the dialog box appends a .jpg filename extension to the base filename.

As I mentioned in Chapter 11, however, the *Save* method of the *Image* class doesn't actually use the filename extension to determine the format in which to save the file. For that reason the program also defines an array of *ImageFormat* values that correspond to the listed image types. In the *Save* method, the *FilterIndex* property accesses the proper *ImageFormat* value. (Recall that *FilterIndex* values start at one rather than zero.)

I mentioned at the beginning of this discussion that the implementation isn't optimum. That's because I think the absence of a displayed filename extension may be confusing to the more sophisticated user. It's not clear whether or not the program will append a filename extension. Fortunately, if the user types an extension, the dialog box won't append another one.

What's the best approach? I like an approach in which the filename is always displayed *with* an extension, and as the user selects different lines in the Save As Type combo box, the displayed filename extension changes accordingly. When you're programming using the Win32 API, it's possible to get access to the various controls in the common dialog boxes and perform little tricks like this. In the Windows Forms interface, however, access to those controls is hidden away.

Another approach to implementing format conversions is to force the user to make a decision before the save file dialog box is even displayed. You do this by making a submenu of the Save As menu item that lists the various formats: Windows Bitmap, Graphics Interchange Format, JPEG, and so forth. Each of these items invokes a *SaveFileDialog* that has a single-line filter for a specific file type.

# 17

# Brushes and Pens

Pens and brushes are fundamental to the Windows Forms graphics system. You use pens to draw straight lines and curves, and you use brushes to fill areas enclosed by straight lines and curves, and to draw text. It's hard to get started at all in Windows Forms without knowing something about pens and brushes. You can't even display text without knowing what a brush is.

Yet brushes are also one of the most all-encompassing objects in Windows Forms because you can create brushes based on paths and bitmaps, neither of which is an elementary graphics topic. Moreover, if brushes encompass almost everything we've learned about Windows Forms graphics so far, then pens are even more encompassing because pens can be based on brushes.

Here's the class hierarchy of the classes I'll be discussing in this chapter:

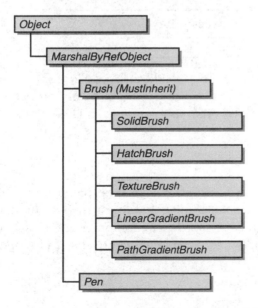

Both *Brush* and *Pen* are defined in the *System.Drawing* namespace, but *Brush* is a *MustInherit* class and hence can't be instantiated. Of the five classes derived from *Brush*, *SolidBrush* and *TextureBrush* are defined in the *System.Drawing* namespace, and *HatchBrush*, *LinearGradientBrush*, and *PathGradientBrush* are defined in the *System.Drawing.Drawing2D* namespace.

Because the five brush classes are derived from *Brush*, it's sometimes convenient to store an instance of one of these classes in a variable of type *Brush*:

```
Dim br As Brush = new SolidBrush(ForeColor)
```

However, the classes derived from *Brush* define their own read/write properties, and it's easier to read and write these properties if you save the object in a variable of its own type.

## Filling in Solid Colors

*SolidBrush* is by far the simplest of the five classes derived from *Brush*. The class has just one constructor, which we've been using since Chapter 3:

### *SolidBrush* Constructor

```
SolidBrush(ByVal clr As Color)
```

And the class has just one property:

### *SolidBrush* Property

| Property | Type | Accessibility |
|----------|------|---------------|
| *Color* | *Color* | Get/Set |

In many cases, when you need a solid brush, you'll probably take advantage of the *Brushes* class, which has 141 shared read-only properties, each of which returns a *Brush* object based on one of the standard colors.

## Hatch Brushes

The hatch brush fills an area with a small repeating pattern, most commonly consisting of horizontal, vertical, or diagonal lines. At first, the hatch brush seems like one of the quainter approaches to computer graphics, conjuring up an ancient age of black-and-white bar graphs, pie charts, and other staples of business graphics.

While the use of color has certainly made hatch brushes less necessary, hatch brushes can continue to play a role in graphics output. Many users (myself included) still prefer noncolor laser printers to color ink jet printers. In some cases—when you're printing color photographs on a black-and-white printer, for example—different colors are mapped to gray shades and the results are often satisfactory. But sometimes different colors are used to represent data, for example, to indicate varying population levels on a map. Such colored graphics suffer greatly when the colors are blindly rendered as gray shades. Using hatch brushes instead allows an easier interpretation of the patterns on the map.

In Windows Forms, hatch patterns are based on monochrome 8-pixel-square bitmaps. Here's such a bitmap for a brick pattern:

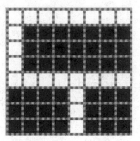

This pattern doesn't begin looking like a brick until it's repeated horizontally and vertically:

The *HatchBrush* class is defined in the *System.Drawing.Drawing2D* namespace. There are only two constructors:

### HatchBrush Constructors

```
HatchBrush(ByVal hs As HatchStyle, ByVal clrForeground As Color)
HatchBrush(ByVal hs As HatchStyle, ByVal clrForeground As Color,
                                    ByVal clrBackground As Color)
```

Although the bitmaps used for hatch brushes are monochrome, the 0's and 1's of the bitmap can be mapped to any two colors you want. In the simpler hatch brushes with line patterns, the foreground color is the color of the lines themselves; the background color is the color between the lines.

Watch out: The first time you use the first constructor, you'll probably choose black for the foreground color, like this:

```
New HatchBrush(hs, Color.Black)    ' Won't work right!
```

or this:

```
New HatchBrush(hs, ForeColor)      ' Probably won't work right!
```

The problem is that the default *background* color for hatch brushes is black, and you should choose white for maximum brush contrast:

```
New HatchBrush(hs, Color.White)    ' Correct!
```

The more explicit equivalent is

```
New HatchBrush(hs, Color.White, Color.Black)    ' Correct!
```

Many hatch brushes will look fine with the foreground and background colors swapped like so:

```
New HatchBrush(hs, Color.Black, Color.White)    ' Satisfactory
```

However, with swapped colors, the brick pattern is rendered as white bricks and black mortar, which looks a bit peculiar.

A *HatchBrush* object is defined entirely by three properties, which are the same as the three arguments specified in the second constructor:

### *HatchBrush* Properties

| Property | Type | Accessibility |
| --- | --- | --- |
| *HatchStyle* | *HatchStyle* | Get |
| *ForegroundColor* | *Color* | Get |
| *BackgroundColor* | *Color* | Get |

The *HatchStyle* property is a member of the *HatchStyle* enumeration. What makes Windows Forms GDI+ different from Windows GDI in the implementation of hatch brushes is the sheer number of hatch styles. GDI has 6 hatch styles (horizontal, vertical, two diagonal, and two cross hatches); GDI+ has 53 of them.

The *HatchStyle* enumeration provides members for all 53 styles. (You'll see 54 in the documentation, but *Cross* and *LargeGrid* are identical.) It also has two members named *Min* and *Max* that unfortunately are set equal to 0 and 4 respectively. If *HatchStyle.Max* were correctly set to 52, it could be useful in generalizing code that presents all the possible hatch styles to the user. In the meantime, the two sample programs coming up contain hard-coded values for the minimum and maximum *HatchStyle* values.

The following program displays 32-pixel-square rectangles showing all the hatch styles.

**HatchBrushArray.vb**

```
'-------------------------------------------------
' HatchBrushArray.vb (c) 2002 by Charles Petzold
'-------------------------------------------------
Imports System
Imports System.Drawing
Imports System.Drawing.Drawing2D
Imports System.Windows.Forms

Class HatchBrushArray
    Inherits PrintableForm

    Const iSize As Integer = 32
    Const iMargin As Integer = 8

    ' HatchStyle minimum and maximum values
    Const hsMin As HatchStyle = CType(0, HatchStyle)
    Const hsMax As HatchStyle = CType(52, HatchStyle)

    Shared Shadows Sub Main()
        Application.Run(New HatchBrushArray())
    End Sub

    Sub New()
        Text = "Hatch Brush Array"
        ClientSize = New Size(8 * iSize + 9 * iMargin, _
                              7 * iSize + 8 * iMargin)
    End Sub

    Protected Overrides Sub DoPage(ByVal grfx As Graphics, _
            ByVal clr As Color, ByVal cx As Integer, ByVal cy As Integer)
        Dim hbr As HatchBrush
        Dim hs As HatchStyle
        Dim x, y As Integer

        For hs = hsMin To hsMax
            hbr = New HatchBrush(hs, Color.White, Color.Black)
            y = hs \ 8
            x = hs Mod 8

            grfx.FillRectangle(hbr, iMargin + x * (iMargin + iSize), _
                                    iMargin + y * (iMargin + iSize), _
                                    iSize, iSize)

        Next hs
    End Sub
End Class
```

The screen output looks like this:

Because the rectangles are 32 pixels square, each rectangle shows the 8-pixel-square hatch pattern repeated 16 times—4 times horizontally times 4 times vertically.

You can also print the hatch patterns by clicking the client area. Different printers might render the hatch patterns a little differently. For example, on a laser printer I have, each 8-pixel-square hatch pattern is displayed as a 1/15-inch square. Because the default page transform of the printer makes it appear to be a 100-dpi device, the 32-pixel-square rectangles displayed by HatchBrush-Array are 0.32 inch square, a dimension that allows almost 25 repetitions of the pattern—5 times horizontally times 5 times vertically. When I direct the printer output to my fax machine, however, each rectangle shows 64 repetitions of the pattern.

Hatch patterns are not affected by transforms! If you insert statements in HatchBrushArray that set a nondefault page transform or world transform, you'll find that the transforms affect the location and size of the displayed rectangles (of course), but they don't affect the appearance of the pattern. The hatch lines don't spread wider or become closer; nor are they rotated or sheared.

In a drawing program, you may want to include a convenient way for a user to select a hatch style. Here's a program that puts all the hatch styles on a menu.

## HatchBrushMenu.vb

```
'-------------------------------------------------
' HatchBrushMenu.vb (c) 2002 by Charles Petzold
'-------------------------------------------------
Imports System
Imports System.Drawing
```

```
Imports System.Drawing.Drawing2D
Imports System.Windows.Forms

Class HatchBrushMenu
    Inherits Form

    Private hsmiChecked As HatchStyleMenuItem

    ' HatchStyle minimum and maximum values
    Const hsMin As HatchStyle = CType(0, HatchStyle)
    Const hsMax As HatchStyle = CType(52, HatchStyle)

    Shared Sub Main()
        Application.Run(New HatchBrushMenu())
    End Sub

    Sub New()
        Text = "Hatch Brush Menu"
        ResizeRedraw = True

        Menu = New MainMenu()
        Menu.MenuItems.Add("&Hatch-Style")

        Dim hs As HatchStyle
        For hs = hsMin To hsMax
            Dim hsmi As New HatchStyleMenuItem()
            hsmi.HatchStyle = hs
            AddHandler hsmi.Click, AddressOf MenuHatchStyleOnClick
            If hs Mod 8 = 0 Then hsmi.BarBreak = True
            Menu.MenuItems(0).MenuItems.Add(hsmi)
        Next hs
        hsmiChecked = DirectCast(Menu.MenuItems(0).MenuItems(0), _
                                 HatchStyleMenuItem)
        hsmiChecked.Checked = True
    End Sub

    Sub MenuHatchStyleOnClick(ByVal obj As Object, ByVal ea As EventArgs)
        hsmiChecked.Checked = False
        hsmiChecked = DirectCast(obj, HatchStyleMenuItem)
        hsmiChecked.Checked = True
        Invalidate()
    End Sub

    Protected Overrides Sub OnPaint(ByVal pea As PaintEventArgs)
        Dim grfx As Graphics = pea.Graphics
        Dim hbr As New HatchBrush(hsmiChecked.HatchStyle, _
                                  Color.White, Color.Black)
        grfx.FillEllipse(hbr, ClientRectangle)
    End Sub
End Class
```

*(continued)*

**HatchBrushMenu.vb**    *(continued)*

```
Class HatchStyleMenuItem
    Inherits MenuItem

    Const cxImage As Integer = 32
    Const cyImage As Integer = 32
    Const iMargin As Integer = 2
    ReadOnly cxCheck, cyCheck As Integer
    Public HatchStyle As HatchStyle

    Sub New()
        OwnerDraw = True
        cxCheck = SystemInformation.MenuCheckSize.Width
        cyCheck = SystemInformation.MenuCheckSize.Height
    End Sub

    Protected Overrides Sub OnMeasureItem( _
            ByVal miea As MeasureItemEventArgs)
        miea.ItemWidth = 2 * cxImage + 3 * iMargin - cxCheck
        miea.ItemHeight = cyImage + 2 * iMargin
    End Sub

    Protected Overrides Sub OnDrawItem(ByVal diea As DrawItemEventArgs)
        diea.DrawBackground()
        If (diea.State And DrawItemState.Checked) <> 0 Then
            ControlPaint.DrawMenuGlyph(diea.Graphics, _
                            diea.Bounds.Location.X + iMargin, _
                            diea.Bounds.Location.Y + iMargin, _
                            cxImage, cyImage, MenuGlyph.Checkmark)
        End If
        Dim hbr As New HatchBrush(HatchStyle, Color.White, Color.Black)
        diea.Graphics.FillRectangle(hbr, _
                        diea.Bounds.X + 2 * iMargin + cxImage, _
                        diea.Bounds.Y + iMargin, cxImage, cyImage)
    End Sub
End Class
```

The program defines a *HatchStyleMenuItem* class that subclasses *Menu-Item* to provide a public *HatchStyle* field, but it also implements support for owner-draw items. When the application creates this menu, it inserts bar breaks every eight items. The resultant submenu is large, but not unwieldy, and provides a reasonable way for a user to select a hatch style:

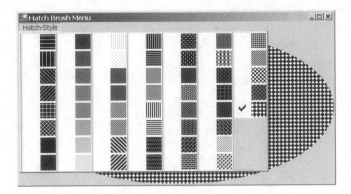

It's about time we look at the actual names of these hatch styles. In the following tables, the images have a default background color of black and a foreground color of white. Each rectangle has 16 repetitions of the pattern (4 horizontally and 4 vertically).

The following six *HatchStyle* values are consistent with the Windows GDI:

## *HatchStyle* Enumeration (selection)

| Member | Value | Image |
|---|---|---|
| *Horizontal* | 0 | |
| *Vertical* | 1 | |
| *ForwardDiagonal* | 2 | |
| *BackwardDiagonal* | 3 | |
| *Cross or LargeGrid* | 4 | |
| *DiagonalCross* | 5 | |

The following styles simulate gray shades. The member names indicate an approximate percentage of foreground color in the pattern:

## *HatchStyle* Enumeration (selection)

| Member | Value | Image |
|---|---|---|
| *Percent05* | 6 | |
| *Percent10* | 7 | |

*(continued)*

## *HatchStyle* Enumeration (selection) *(continued)*

| Member | Value | Image |
| --- | --- | --- |
| *Percent20* | 8 | |
| *Percent25* | 9 | |
| *Percent30* | 10 | |
| *Percent40* | 11 | |
| *Percent50* | 12 | |
| *Percent60* | 13 | |
| *Percent70* | 14 | |
| *Percent75* | 15 | |
| *Percent80* | 16 | |
| *Percent90* | 17 | |

Next are some variations of the standard horizontal, vertical, and diagonal hatch styles:

## HatchStyle Enumeration (selection)

| Member | Value | Image |
| --- | --- | --- |
| *LightDownwardDiagonal* | 18 | |
| *LightUpwardDiagonal* | 19 | |
| *DarkDownwardDiagonal* | 20 | |
| *DarkUpwardDiagonal* | 21 | |
| *WideDownwardDiagonal* | 22 | |
| *WideUpwardDiagonal* | 23 | |
| *LightVertical* | 24 | |
| *LightHorizontal* | 25 | |

**HatchStyle Enumeration (selection)**  *(continued)*

| Member | Value | Image |
|---|---|---|
| *NarrowVertical* | 26 | |
| *NarrowHorizontal* | 27 | |
| *DarkVertical* | 28 | |
| *DarkHorizontal* | 29 | |
| *DashedDownwardDiagonal* | 30 | |
| *DashedUpwardDiagonal* | 31 | |
| *DashedHorizontal* | 32 | |
| *DashedVertical* | 33 | |

Finally, here's a group of miscellaneous patterns:

*HatchStyle* **Enumeration (selection)**

| Member | Value | Image |
|---|---|---|
| *SmallConfetti* | 34 | |
| *LargeConfetti* | 35 | |
| *ZigZag* | 36 | |
| *Wave* | 37 | |
| *DiagonalBrick* | 38 | |
| *HorizontalBrick* | 39 | |
| *Weave* | 40 | |
| *Plaid* | 41 | |
| *Divot* | 42 | |
| *DottedGrid* | 43 | |
| *DottedDiamond* | 44 | |

*(continued)*

## *HatchStyle* Enumeration (selection) *(continued)*

| Member | Value | Image |
|---|---|---|
| *Shingle* | 45 | |
| *Trellis* | 46 | |
| *Sphere* | 47 | |
| *SmallGrid* | 48 | |
| *SmallCheckerBoard* | 49 | |
| *LargeCheckerBoard* | 50 | |
| *OutlinedDiamond* | 51 | |
| *SolidDiamond* | 52 | |

# The Rendering Origin

There's something you should know about the hatch brush, and it's something that affects more sophisticated brushes as well. In fact, it's part of the model under which the Windows Forms graphics system was developed. To illustrate what I'm talking about, consider the following program.

### OverlappingHatchBrushes.vb

```
'-------------------------------------------------------------
' OverlappingHatchBrushes.vb (c) 2002 by Charles Petzold
'-------------------------------------------------------------
Imports System
Imports System.Drawing
Imports System.Drawing.Drawing2D
Imports System.Windows.Forms

Class OverlappingHatchBrushes
    Inherits PrintableForm

    Shared Shadows Sub Main()
        Application.Run(New OverlappingHatchBrushes())
    End Sub
```

```
    Sub New()
        Text = "Overlapping Hatch Brushes"
    End Sub

    Protected Overrides Sub DoPage(ByVal grfx As Graphics, _
            ByVal clr As Color, ByVal cx As Integer, ByVal cy As Integer)
        Dim hbr As New HatchBrush(HatchStyle.HorizontalBrick, Color.White)
        Dim i As Integer

        For i = 0 To 9
            grfx.FillRectangle(hbr, i * cx \ 10, i * cy \ 10, _
                               cx \ 8, cy \ 8)
        Next i
    End Sub
End Class
```

This program uses the same hatch brush to draw 10 overlapping rectangles. But the rectangles don't seem to be distinct because the hatches in each rectangle coincide:

When you fill an area with a hatch pattern, the pattern is simply repeated horizontally and vertically. But that doesn't tell the whole story. The pattern has to be initially oriented at a particular pixel position. You might have suspected that the pattern is oriented with the graphics object being drawn, for example, with the upper left corner of a rectangle. But this program pretty much demonstrates that's *not* the case. In fact, the hatch pattern bitmap is oriented with the upper left corner of the drawing area, which is the upper left corner of the client area or the printable area of the printer page.

A good way to think about this is that the brush blankets the entire display surface that your *Graphics* object refers to. When you draw a filled area with a particular brush, you're actually making a hole or a stencil that looks into that patterned surface.

You can override the default behavior of hatch-brush orientation by using a property of the *Graphics* class.

### *Graphics* Properties (selection)

| Property | Type | Accessibility |
|---|---|---|
| *RenderingOrigin* | *Point* | Get/Set |

The *RenderingOrigin* property affects only the display of hatch brushes. (Other types of brushes have other approaches to changing brush orientation.) By default, the *RenderingOrigin* property is the point (0, 0). If you set a new point in device coordinates, subsequent hatch brushes will be oriented with that point.

Here's a program that draws 10 staggered rectangles, using a different *RenderingOrigin* value for each.

```
HatchBrushRenderingOrigin.vb
'-------------------------------------------------------
' HatchBrushRenderingOrigin.vb (c) 2002 by Charles Petzold
'-------------------------------------------------------
Imports System
Imports System.Drawing
Imports System.Drawing.Drawing2D
Imports System.Windows.Forms

Class HatchBrushRenderingOrigin
    Inherits PrintableForm

    Shared Shadows Sub Main()
        Application.Run(new HatchBrushRenderingOrigin())
    End Sub

    Sub New()
        Text = "Hatch Brush Rendering Origin"
    End Sub

    Protected Overrides Sub DoPage(ByVal grfx As Graphics, _
            ByVal clr As Color, ByVal cx As Integer, ByVal cy As Integer)
        Dim hbr As New HatchBrush(HatchStyle.HorizontalBrick, Color.White)
        Dim i As Integer

        For i = 0 To 9
            grfx.RenderingOrigin = New Point(i * cx \ 10, i * cy \ 10)
```

```
            grfx.FillRectangle(hbr, i * cx \ 10, i * cy \ 10, _
                               cx \ 8, cy \ 8)
        Next i
    End Sub
End Class
```

The result shows that the hatch pattern begins anew at the upper left corner of each rectangle:

There are a couple situations in which you'll want to change the rendering origin. If you're using hatch patterns for bar graphs, all the patterns will normally be oriented with the upper left corner of the drawing area. Even if you're using a different pattern for each bar, the patterns can connect with each other in distracting ways. In such a case, you'll want to set a new rendering origin for each bar based on the upper left corner of the bar.

You can also experience the opposite problem. Say you're coloring a parent window and one or more child windows with the same hatch pattern. You probably want the child window to blend in with the parent. But the hatch pattern the child draws is oriented with the child's upper left corner. The child will want to set the rendering origin to the upper left corner of its parent.

# Texture Brushes

If you've gone through the list of hatch brushes and not discovered one you like, or if you need more than two colors in your brush, or if you want a brush that's subject to transforms, you'll want to explore the *TextureBrush* class.

A texture brush is based on an object of type *Image*—or a rectangular subset of an *Image* object—that repeats horizontally and vertically.

### *TextureBrush* Constructors

```
TextureBrush(ByVal img As Image)

TextureBrush(ByVal img As Image, ByVal rectSrc As Rectangle)

TextureBrush(ByVal img As Image, ByVal rectfSrc As RectangleF)

TextureBrush(ByVal img As Image, ByVal wm As WrapMode)

TextureBrush(ByVal img As Image, ByVal wm As WrapMode,
        ByVal rectSrc As Rectangle)

TextureBrush(ByVal img As Image, ByVal wm As WrapMode,
        ByVal rectfSrc As RectangleF)

TextureBrush(ByVal img As Image, ByVal rectSrc As Rectangle,
        ByVal ia As ImageAttributes )

TextureBrush(ByVal img As Image, ByVal rectSrc As RectangleF,
        ByVal ia As ImageAttributes)
```

The *WrapMode* enumeration is defined in the *System.Drawing.Drawing2D* namespace:

### *WrapMode* Enumeration

| Member | Value |
|--------|-------|
| *Tile* | 0 |
| *TileFlipX* | 1 |
| *TileFlipY* | 2 |
| *TileFlipXY* | 3 |
| *Clamp* | 4 |

As we'll see shortly, the enumeration determines how the image repeats horizontally and vertically. The two versions of the constructor with an *ImageAttributes* argument don't require a *WrapMode* argument because *ImageAttributes* has its own method to set the wrap mode.

Here's a program that constructs a texture brush from a subset of the Apollo 11 image from Chapter 11. A menu option lets you select the wrap mode. The *OnPaint* method displays two overlapping ellipses using the brush.

### TextureBrushDemo.vb

```
'-------------------------------------------------
' TextureBrushDemo.vb (c) 2002 by Charles Petzold
'-------------------------------------------------
Imports System
Imports System.Drawing
```

```vb
Imports System.Drawing.Drawing2D
Imports System.Windows.Forms

Class TextureBrushDemo
    Inherits PrintableForm

    Private miChecked As MenuItem
    Private tbr As TextureBrush

    Shared Shadows Sub Main()
        Application.Run(New TextureBrushDemo())
    End Sub

    Sub New()
        Text = "Texture Brush Demo"

        Dim img As Image = Image.FromFile( _
                "..\..\..\Images and Bitmaps\Apollo11FullColor.jpg")
        tbr = New TextureBrush(img, New Rectangle(95, 0, 50, 55))

        Menu = New MainMenu()
        Menu.MenuItems.Add("&Wrap-Mode")

        Dim wm As WrapMode
        For Each wm In System.Enum.GetValues(GetType(WrapMode))
            Dim mi As New MenuItem()
            mi.Text = wm.ToString()
            AddHandler mi.Click, AddressOf MenuWrapModeOnClick
            Menu.MenuItems(0).MenuItems.Add(mi)
        Next wm

        miChecked = Menu.MenuItems(0).MenuItems(0)
        miChecked.Checked = True
    End Sub

    Sub MenuWrapModeOnClick(ByVal obj As Object, ByVal ea As EventArgs)
        miChecked.Checked = False
        miChecked = DirectCast(obj, MenuItem)
        miChecked.Checked = True

        tbr.WrapMode = CType(miChecked.Index, WrapMode)
        Invalidate()
    End Sub

    Protected Overrides Sub DoPage(ByVal grfx As Graphics, _
            ByVal clr As Color, ByVal cx As Integer, ByVal cy As Integer)
        grfx.FillEllipse(tbr, 0, 0, 2 * cx \ 3, 2 * cy \ 3)
        grfx.FillEllipse(tbr, cx \ 3, cy \ 3, 2 * cx \ 3, 2 * cy \ 3)
    End Sub
End Class
```

What this program does as well is demonstrate the see-through stencil effect of Windows Forms graphics. As long as the *OnPaint* method is using the same unaltered brush, the patterns will coincide exactly:

By default, *WrapMode* is *Tile*, which repeats the identical image horizontally and vertically. If you use the menu to change *WrapMode* to *TileFlipX*, the images in every other column are flipped left-to-right:

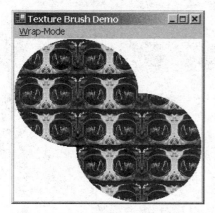

A *WrapMode* of *TileFlipY* turns the images in every other row upside down. The *TileFlipXY* option combines both effects.

The *Clamp* option results in the most extreme effect. The entire brush consists of only one rendition of the image in the upper left corner of the client area. The rest of the brush is transparent. You can see the bottom right part of the single image inside the ellipse:

As I mentioned earlier, the page transform and world transform do not affect hatch brushes. The transforms do affect texture brushes, however.

Suppose you modify the *DoPage* method of the TextureBrushDemo program so that it doesn't display an ellipse but instead displays a rectangle sized to fit exactly 9 repetitions of the 50 × 55 pixel image, for example:

```
grfx.FillRectangle(tbr, 0, 0, 150, 165)
```

No matter what you do with the page transform or the world transform—regardless of any scaling, shearing, or rotation—the resultant parallelogram (for that, in general, is what the rectangle will be drawn as) will always be filled with exactly nine repetitions of the pattern, scaled, sheared, or rotated accordingly.

I also mentioned earlier that the *RenderingOrigin* property of the *Graphics* object affects only the *HatchBrush* object. The *TextureBrush* class itself has an alternative property that allows you to do something similar—plus lots more. Here's a complete list of the *TextureBrush* properties:

### *TextureBrush* Properties

| Property | Type | Accessibility |
|----------|------|---------------|
| *Image* | *Image* | Get |
| *WrapMode* | *WrapMode* | Get/Set |
| *Transform* | *Matrix* | Get/Set |

Yes, that third property is a matrix transform that affects the brush itself. For example, if you add the statement

```
tbr.Transform = New Matrix(2, 0, 0, 2, 0, 0)
```

to the *DoPage* method of TextureBrushDemo, the ellipses (or rectangle or whatever you're drawing in that method) will be the same size and position, but the repeating image that makes up the pattern will be twice as large: 100 × 110 pixels. You can rotate or shear the pattern if you want. The *TextureBrush* class also includes the methods *TranslateTransform*, *ScaleTransform*, *Rotate-Transform*, *MultiplyTransform*, and *ResetTransform*, which are quite similar to the same-named methods in the *Graphics* class. (These are the only methods in *TextureBrush* that aren't in *Brush*.) Use translation to simulate a different rendering origin.

As with the similarly named methods in the *Graphics* class, the various transform methods in the *TextureBrush* class are cumulative. For example, if you put the statement

```
tbr.RotateTransform(45)
```

in the *DoPage* method, the brush pattern will be rotated an additional 45 degrees whenever *DoPage* is called. To prevent unpredictable results, preface the *RotateTransform* call with a call to *ResetTransform*. Or better yet, put the *RotateTransform* call in the program's constructor. Here's what you'll get:

The *Transform* property of the *TextureBrush* class affects only the size and orientation of the brush pattern—not any objects you draw using the brush. The *Transform* property of the *Graphics* class affects both the size and orientation of the texture brush pattern and any objects you draw. If you use both, the pattern is affected by the composite transform.

# Linear Gradient Brushes

The remaining two brush classes are *LinearGradientBrush* and *PathGradientBrush*; the word *gradient* here refers to a transition between colors. *LinearGradientBrush* involves a transition between two colors, sometimes called a *fountain*. At first, it may seem complicated to define a way in which one color merges with another, and that's probably why there are a couple different ways of specifying such a brush.

A gradient between two colors can be defined by a pair of parallel lines. Each line is a pure color. The color makes a transition between the two lines. Here's an example with the first color being *Color.LightGray* and the second *Color.DarkGray*:

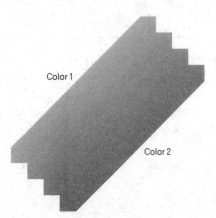

The linear-gradient brush is thus an infinitely long stripe with two parallel borders of two colors.

To define such a brush, you don't need to specify two parallel lines. It's much easier to specify two points. The two parallel borders are at right angles to the line connecting the two points:

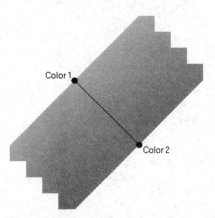

Note that there are an infinite number of pairs of points that result in the same linear gradient. I'm going to refer to the line connecting those two points as the *gradient line*. I also want to define the term *mix line* as the line at right angles to the gradient line and parallel to the two border lines, midway between them.

The *LinearGradientBrush* class has eight constructors. Two of these let you specify two points and two colors:

### *LinearGradientBrush* Constructors (selection)

```
LinearGradientBrush(ByVal pt1 As Point, ByVal pt2 As Point,
                    ByVal clr1 As Color, ByVal clr2 As Color)

LinearGradientBrush(ByVal ptf1 As PointF, ByVal ptf2 As PointF,
                    ByVal clr1 As Color, ByVal clr2 As Color)
```

The only difference between these two constructors is the use of either *Point* or *PointF* structures. The points are in world coordinates. The color at the first point (*pt1* or *ptf1*) is *clr1*, and the color at the second point (*pt2* or *ptf2*) is *clr2*.

Let's take a look at a program that creates a *LinearGradientBrush* object in its *DoPage* method, defining the first point as (*cx*\4, *cy*\4) and the second as (3\**cx*\4, 3\**cy*\4). The two colors are *Color.White* and *Color.Black*. The program then colors a rectangle the size of its display area with this brush.

### TwoPointLinearGradientBrush.vb

```
'---------------------------------------------------------------
' TwoPointLinearGradientBrush.vb (c) 2002 by Charles Petzold
'---------------------------------------------------------------
Imports System
Imports System.Drawing
Imports System.Drawing.Drawing2D
Imports System.Windows.Forms

Class TwoPointLinearGradientBrush
    Inherits PrintableForm

    Shared Shadows Sub Main()
        Application.Run(New TwoPointLinearGradientBrush())
    End Sub

    Sub New()
        Text = "Two-Point Linear Gradient Brush"
    End Sub

    Protected Overrides Sub DoPage(ByVal grfx As Graphics, _
            ByVal clr As Color, ByVal cx As Integer, ByVal cy As Integer)
        Dim lgbr As New LinearGradientBrush( _
                        New Point(cx \ 4, cy \ 4), _
                        New Point(3 * cx \ 4, 3 * cy \ 4), _
                        Color.White, Color.Black)
        grfx.FillRectangle(lgbr, 0, 0, cx, cy)
    End Sub
End Class
```

I haven't yet mentioned what happens outside the stripe that the *Linear-GradientBrush* object defines. As you can see, by default the brush is tiled:

The wide continuous stripe from the lower left to the upper right is defined by the two brush coordinates. On either side of the stripe (in this case, the upper left and lower right of the client area), the stripe is repeated. This behavior is controlled by the *WrapMode* property of the brush. *WrapMode.Tile* (the default) is the same as *WrapMode.TileFlipY*, and it causes the brush to be tiled with no flipping, as shown previously.

*WrapMode.TileFlipX* is the same as *Wrapmode.TileFlipXY* and causes the brush to be flipped so that there are no discontinuities, like so:

*WrapMode.Clamp* is not allowed for linear-gradient brushes.

Let me emphasize again that any *Fill* method you call with a particular brush essentially provides only a window through which you view the brush. When using texture brushes or gradient brushes, the appearance of any filled area depends to some degree on *where* the area is drawn. If you draw a small rectangle using the brush defined by the TwoPointLinearGradientBrush program, it might not even seem like much of a gradient.

In many cases, you'll define a particular linear-gradient brush based on the actual coordinates of the object you're filling. For example, if you want to fill a rectangle with a linear-gradient brush, you'll define the brush with the same coordinates you use to draw the rectangle. In such cases, you might find it convenient to use the following constructors for *LinearGradientBrush* that have a rectangle argument:

### *LinearGradientBrush* Constructors (selection)

```
LinearGradientBrush(ByVal rect As Rectangle,
                ByVal clr1 As Color, ByVal clr2 As Color,
                ByVal lgm As LinearGradientMode)

LinearGradientBrush(ByVal rectf As RectangleF,
                ByVal clr1 As Color, ByVal clr2 As Color,
                ByVal lgm As LinearGradientMode)
```

The *LinearGradientMode* enumeration defines how the gradient line is formed from the sides or corners of the rectangle:

### *LinearGradientMode* Enumeration

| Member | Value | Description |
| --- | --- | --- |
| *Horizontal* | 0 | Gradient line is horizontal, *clr1* at left side, *clr2* at right |
| *Vertical* | 1 | Gradient line is vertical, *clr1* at top side, *clr2* at bottom |
| *ForwardDiagonal* | 2 | Mix line passes through upper right and lower left corners; upper left corner is *clr1* and lower right is *clr2* |
| *BackwardDiagonal* | 3 | Mix line passes through upper left and lower right corners; upper right corner is *clr1* and lower left is *clr2* |

Notice that for the last two enumeration values, two opposite corners of the rectangle define the mix line rather than the gradient line. Although the two other corners of the rectangle are pure colors and the border lines pass through those two corners, those two corners do *not* define the gradient line unless the rectangle is a square. Let's take a closer look.

The following program defines a linear-gradient brush based on a rectangle that is half the width and height of the display area, and centered within the display area. You can use the menu to set the constructor's *LinearGradient-Mode* argument. After filling the display area with that brush, the *DoPage* method also draws the rectangle used in creating the brush.

**RectangleLinearGradientBrush.vb**

```
'-----------------------------------------------------------------
' RectangleLinearGradientBrush.vb (c) 2002 by Charles Petzold
'-----------------------------------------------------------------
Imports System
Imports System.Drawing
Imports System.Drawing.Drawing2D
Imports System.Windows.Forms

Class RectangleLinearGradientBrush
    Inherits PrintableForm

    Private miChecked As MenuItem

    Shared Shadows Sub Main()
        Application.Run(new RectangleLinearGradientBrush())
    End Sub

    Sub New()
        Text = "Rectangle Linear-Gradient Brush"

        Menu = new MainMenu()
        Menu.MenuItems.Add("&Gradient-Mode")

        Dim gm As LinearGradientMode
        For Each gm In System.Enum.GetValues(GetType(LinearGradientMode))
            Dim mi As New MenuItem()
            mi.Text = gm.ToString()
            AddHandler mi.Click, AddressOf MenuGradientModeOnClick
            Menu.MenuItems(0).MenuItems.Add(mi)
        Next gm

        miChecked = Menu.MenuItems(0).MenuItems(0)
        miChecked.Checked = True
    End Sub

    Sub MenuGradientModeOnClick(ByVal obj As Object, ByVal ea As EventArgs)
        miChecked.Checked = False
        miChecked = DirectCast(obj, MenuItem)
        miChecked.Checked = True
        Invalidate()
    End Sub

    Protected Overrides Sub DoPage(ByVal grfx As Graphics, _
            ByVal clr As Color, ByVal cx As Integer, ByVal cy As Integer)
        Dim rectBrush As New Rectangle(cx \ 4, cy \ 4, cx \ 2, cy \ 2)
```

*(continued)*

**RectangleLinearGradientBrush.vb**  *(continued)*

```
        Dim lgbr As New LinearGradientBrush( _
                            rectBrush, Color.White, Color.Black, _
                            CType(miChecked.Index, LinearGradientMode))
        grfx.FillRectangle(lgbr, 0, 0, cx, cy)
        grfx.DrawRectangle(Pens.Black, rectBrush)
    End Sub
End Class
```

Here's an example when you've used the menu to select *LinearGradient-Mode.ForwardDiagonal* and the window has been widened somewhat:

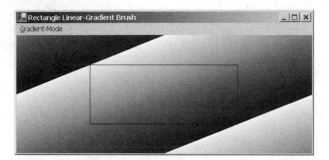

Although the upper left corner of the brush rectangle is colored with the first color and the lower right corner with the second color, the gradient line is obviously not the line from the upper left corner to the lower right corner because the gradient line is always at right angles to the border lines. Instead, the mix line (parallel to the border lines and midway between them) passes through the upper right and lower left corners of the rectangle.

The four final constructors for *LinearGradientBrush* let you specify a rectangle and an angle:

## *LinearGradientBrush* Constructors (selection)

```
LinearGradientBrush(ByVal rect As Rectangle,
                ByVal clr1 As Color, ByVal clr2 As Color,
                ByVal fAngle As Single)

LinearGradientBrush(ByVal rect As Rectangle,
                ByVal clr1 As Color, ByVal clr2 As Color,
                ByVal fAngle As Single, ByVal bScale As Boolean)

LinearGradientBrush(ByVal rectf As RectangleF,
                ByVal clr1 As Color, ByVal clr2 As Color,
                ByVal fAngle As Single)

LinearGradientBrush(ByVal rectf As RectangleF,
                ByVal clr1 As Color, ByVal clr2 As Color,
                ByVal fAngle As Single, ByVal bScale As Boolean)
```

If *fAngle* is 0, the effect is identical to *LinearGradientMode.Horizontal*: the gradient line is horizontal from the left side of the rectangle to right side.

As *fAngle* increases, the gradient line rotates clockwise that number of degrees. The upper left corner of the rectangle is the first color, and the lower right corner is the second color. When *fAngle* reaches 90 degrees, the effect is identical to *LinearGradientMode.Vertical*: the gradient line is vertical from the top of the rectangle to the bottom. As *fAngle* increases beyond 90 degrees, the gradient line continues to rotate clockwise. But now the upper right corner of the rectangle is the first color, and the lower left corner of the rectangle is the second color.

The optional *bScale* argument indicates whether the rotation angle is scaled by any transform associated with the brush.

I've already alluded to the *WrapMode* and *Transform* properties of *Linear-GradientBrush*. This table of four properties also includes the rectangle specified (or implied) by the constructor and an array of two colors used in the brush:

### *LinearGradientBrush* Properties (selection)

| Property | Type | Accessibility |
| --- | --- | --- |
| *Rectangle* | *RectangleF* | Get |
| *LinearColors* | *Color()* | Get/Set |
| *WrapMode* | *WrapMode* | Get/Set |
| *Transform* | *Matrix* | Get/Set |

In addition to duplicating the *TranslateTransform*, *ScaleTransform*, *RotateTransform*, *MultiplyTransform*, and *ResetTransform* methods defined in the *TextureBrush* class, the *LinearGradientBrush* class also includes these two methods:

### *LinearGradientBrush* Methods (selection)

```
Sub SetBlendTriangularShape(ByVal fFocus As Single)

Sub SetBlendTriangularShape(ByVal fFocus As Single,
                            ByVal fScale As Single)

Sub SetSigmaBellShape(ByVal fFocus As Single)

Sub SetSigmaBellShape(ByVal fFocus As Single,
                      ByVal fScale As Single)
```

Normally, the gradient is from the first color to the second color. These two methods change the gradient so that it goes from the first color to the second color and then back to the first. Both arguments (which I'll describe shortly) can range from 0 to 1.

Let's take a look. Here's the unaltered RectangleLinearGradientBrush program running with the default *LinearGradientMode* of *Horizontal*:

The gradient is white at the left side of the rectangle and makes a transition to black at the right side of the rectangle. If you insert the statement

```
lgbr.SetBlendTriangularShape(0.33)
```

right after the brush creation statement, the output looks like this:

The gradient goes from white at the left side of the rectangle to black and then back to white at the right side of the rectangle. The *fFocus* argument of 0.33 indicates that the black peaks at 1/3 of the way between the two sides of the rectangle.

When you replace that method call with

```
lgbr.SetSigmaBellShape(0.33)
```

the window looks like this:

The transition is more of a bell shape, again peaking 1/3 of the way between the left and right sides of the rectangle.

In both methods, the *fScale* argument indicates to what extent the gradient goes to the second color. The default is 1. Anything less then 1 causes the transition to go only partially to the second color. An *fScale* of 0 causes the brush to consist of only the first color, with no gradient.

To get even deeper into the control of the gradient colors, you can use the following three properties:

### *LinearGradientBrush* Properties (selection)

| Property | Type | Accessibility |
| --- | --- | --- |
| *Blend* | *Blend* | Get/Set |
| *InterpolationColors* | *ColorBlend* | Get/Set |
| *GammaCorrection* | *Boolean* | Get/Set |

Both *Blend* and *ColorBlend* are fairly simple classes. Both classes have just two read/write properties, which are both equally sized arrays. The two *Blend* properties are *Single* arrays named *Positions* and *Factors*, which indicate the factors (0 through 1) used to scale the two colors at relative positions (ranging from 0 to 1) along the gradient line. The two *ColorBlend* properties are arrays named *Positions* and *Colors*, which indicate the colors at relative positions along the gradient line.

# Path Gradient Brushes

The final type of brush is named *PathGradientBrush*. In the constructor, you define a polygon (which, as you know, is simply an array of points) and the brush is defined for the interior of the polygon. Alternatively, you can simply specify a *GraphicsPath* object:

### *PathGradientBrush* Constructors

```
PathGradientBrush(ByVal apt() As Point)

PathGradientBrush(ByVal aptf() As PointF)

PathGradientBrush(ByVal apt() As Point, ByVal wm As WrapMode)

PathGradientBrush(ByVal aptf() As PointF, ByVal wm As WrapMode)

PathGradientBrush(ByVal path As GraphicsPath)
```

Let's leap right into this subject by specifying a triangle in the *PathGradientBrush* constructor and seeing what happens.

```
TriangleGradientBrush.vb
'-------------------------------------------------
' TriangleGradientBrush.vb (c) 2002 by Charles Petzold
'-------------------------------------------------
Imports System
Imports System.Drawing
Imports System.Drawing.Drawing2D
Imports System.Windows.Forms

Class TriangleGradientBrush
    Inherits PrintableForm

    Shared Shadows Sub Main()
        Application.Run(New TriangleGradientBrush())
    End Sub

    Sub New()
        Text = "Triangle Gradient Brush"
    End Sub

    Protected Overrides Sub DoPage(ByVal grfx As Graphics, _
            ByVal clr As Color, ByVal cx As Integer, ByVal cy As Integer)
        Dim apt() As Point = {New Point(cx, 0), _
                              New Point(cx, cy), _
                              New Point(0, cy)}
        Dim pgbr As New PathGradientBrush(apt)
        grfx.FillRectangle(pgbr, 0, 0, cx, cy)
    End Sub
End Class
```

This program doesn't seem to do too much. An array of three points is defined (the upper right, lower right, and lower left corners of the display area), and then a *PathGradientBrush* is created from those points. The result, however, is quite cool:

Obviously, some default behavior was wisely defined!

Notice that I'm filling the entire client rectangle with this brush, yet the resultant object looks like a triangle. That's because I used a triangle to define the brush. Outside of the triangle, the brush is transparent. Whatever was on the display surface before the *FillRectangle* call will be unaffected.

In the generalized *PathGradientBrush*, gradients occur between each pair of points along the sides of the polygon and from the sides of the polygon to the center. The location of the center point and the colors are defined by the following three properties:

### *PathGradientBrush* Properties (selection)

| Property | Type | Accessibility |
|----------|------|---------------|
| *CenterPoint* | *PointF* | Get/Set |
| *CenterColor* | *Color* | Get/Set |
| *SurroundColors* | *Color()* | Get/Set |

The *CenterPoint* property is initially set to the average of the points in the polygon, which could actually be outside the polygon if the polygon has some concavity. The *CenterColor* property is initially set to *Color.Black*. The *SurroundColors* property is initialized as an array with one element equal to *Color.White*. You can set *SurroundColors* to an array of any size up to the number of points you used to create the brush.

For example, if you insert the line

```
pgbr.SurroundColors = New Color() {Color.Red, Color.Green, Color.Blue}
```

in the program right before the *FillRectangle* call, the point (*cx*, 0) will be red, (*cx*, *cy*) will be green, and (0, *cy*) will be blue. Try it! Here's a program that creates a polygon describing a five-pointed star. It sets the center color to white and the surround color to black.

**StarGradientBrush.vb**

```
'-------------------------------------------------
' StarGradientBrush.vb (c) 2002 by Charles Petzold
'-------------------------------------------------
Imports System
Imports System.Drawing
Imports System.Drawing.Drawing2D
Imports System.Windows.Forms

Class StarGradientBrush
    Inherits PrintableForm

    Shared Shadows Sub Main()
        Application.Run(New StarGradientBrush())
    End Sub

    Sub New()
        Text = "Star Gradient Brush"
    End Sub

    Protected Overrides Sub DoPage(ByVal grfx As Graphics, _
            ByVal clr As Color, ByVal cx As Integer, ByVal cy As Integer)
        Dim apt(4) As Point
        Dim i As Integer

        For i = 0 To apt.GetUpperBound(0)
            Dim rAngle As Double = (i * 0.8 - 0.5) * Math.PI
            apt(i).X = CInt(cx * (0.5 + 0.48 * Math.Cos(rAngle)))
            apt(i).Y = CInt(cy * (0.5 + 0.48 * Math.Sin(rAngle)))
        Next i

        Dim pgbr As New PathGradientBrush(apt)
        pgbr.CenterColor = Color.White
        pgbr.SurroundColors = New Color() {Color.Black}
        grfx.FillRectangle(pgbr, 0, 0, cx, cy)
    End Sub
End Class
```

You can almost see how GDI+ draws the gradients as it circles around the points of the polygon. The latter gradients draw over the earlier ones and cause an effect that makes it look like part of the star goes through itself:

You can also use a path for defining a *PathGradientBrush* object. Here's a program that overrides the Bounce program from Chapter 11 to provide a new *DrawBall* method.

### BouncingGradientBrushBall.vb

```
'-------------------------------------------------------------
' BouncingGradientBrushBall.vb (c) 2002 by Charles Petzold
'-------------------------------------------------------------
Imports System
Imports System.Drawing
Imports System.Drawing.Drawing2D
Imports System.Windows.Forms

Class BouncingGradientBrushBall
    Inherits Bounce

    Shared Shadows Sub Main()
        Application.Run(New BouncingGradientBrushBall())
    End Sub

    Sub New()
        Text = "Bouncing Gradient Brush Ball"
    End Sub

    Protected Overrides Sub DrawBall(ByVal grfx As Graphics, _
                                     ByVal rect As Rectangle)
        Dim path As New GraphicsPath()
        path.AddEllipse(rect)

        Dim pgbr As New PathGradientBrush(path)
        pgbr.CenterPoint = New PointF((rect.Left + rect.Right) \ 3, _
                                      (rect.Top + rect.Bottom) \ 3)

        pgbr.CenterColor = Color.White
        pgbr.SurroundColors = New Color() {Color.Red}
        grfx.FillRectangle(pgbr, rect)
    End Sub
End Class
```

As you'll recall, the *DrawBall* method is responsible for drawing a ball on a bitmap. The earlier version just drew a red *Ellipse* object using the *Rectangle* argument to the method. This version defines a path based on that ellipse and then creates a *PathGradientBrush* object based on that path. Normally, the gradient center would be the center of the ellipse, but this method moves the center a bit to the upper left. The center color is set to white, and the surround color is set to red. The method concludes by drawing a rectangle using this brush. (The brush is transparent outside the boundaries of the ellipse.) The resultant ball looks more realistic than the earlier one because the white spot gives the appearance of reflected light.

# Tiling the Brush

Here are two other useful properties of *PathGradientBrush*:

### *PathGradientBrush* Properties (selection)

| Property | Type | Accessibility |
| --- | --- | --- |
| *Rectangle* | *RectangleF* | Get |
| *WrapMode* | *WrapMode* | Get/Set |

*Rectangle* is a read-only property calculated by the brush when the brush is created. It is the smallest rectangle that encloses the polygon. This rectangle is not affected by the *CenterPoint* property; that is, *CenterPoint* is not necessarily inside this rectangle.

For a path-gradient brush, the *WrapMode* property is *WrapMode.Clamp* by default. Besides setting the *WrapMode* property, you can also optionally specify a nondefault value in the constructor. The reason I mention both the *Rectangle* and *WrapMode* properties together is because the effect of *WrapMode* is highly dependent on the rectangle.

Let's make another triangle, this one of a fixed size and occupying the upper left half of a square. A two-argument version of the constructor is used to set the wrap mode, which is based on a menu selection.

**TriangleTile.vb**

```
'-----------------------------------------------
' TriangleTile.vb (c) 2002 by Charles Petzold
'-----------------------------------------------
Imports System
Imports System.Drawing
Imports System.Drawing.Drawing2D
Imports System.Windows.Forms

Class TriangleTile
    Inherits PrintableForm

    Const iSide As Integer = 50    ' Side of square for triangle
    Private miChecked As MenuItem

    Shared Shadows Sub Main()
        Application.Run(New TriangleTile())
    End Sub

    Sub New()
        Text = "Triangle Tile"

        Menu = New MainMenu()
        Menu.MenuItems.Add("&Wrap-Mode")

        Dim wm As WrapMode
        For Each wm In System.Enum.GetValues(GetType(WrapMode))
            Dim mi As New MenuItem()
            mi.Text = wm.ToString()
            AddHandler mi.Click, AddressOf MenuWrapModeOnClick
            Menu.MenuItems(0).MenuItems.Add(mi)
        Next wm

        miChecked = Menu.MenuItems(0).MenuItems(0)
        miChecked.Checked = True
    End Sub
```

*(continued)*

**TriangleTile.vb** *(continued)*

```
    Sub MenuWrapModeOnClick(ByVal obj As Object, ByVal ea As EventArgs)
        miChecked.Checked = False
        miChecked = DirectCast(obj, MenuItem)
        miChecked.Checked = True
        Invalidate()
    End Sub

    Protected Overrides Sub DoPage(ByVal grfx As Graphics, _
            ByVal clr As Color, ByVal cx As Integer, ByVal cy As Integer)
        Dim apt() As Point = {New Point(0, 0), _
                              New Point(iSide, 0), _
                              New Point(0, iSide)}
        Dim pgbr As New PathGradientBrush(apt, _
                                    CType(miChecked.Index, WrapMode))
        grfx.FillRectangle(pgbr, 0, 0, cx, cy)
    End Sub
End Class
```

Without the second argument to the constructor, the default *WrapMode* is *WrapMode.Clamp*, which means that the polygon isn't repeated at all. With *WrapMode.Tile*, which we've set as the initial wrap mode, the polygon is repeated horizontally and vertically over the entire filled area (in this case, the client rectangle).

You can, of course, achieve different kinds of effects by using different wrap modes. If you use *WrapMode.TileFlipX*, every other polygon is flipped around the vertical axis:

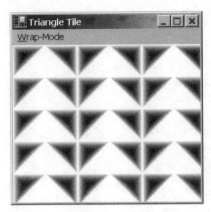

Similarly, *WrapMode.TileFlipY* causes every other polygon to be flipped around the horizontal axis:

Finally, the *WrapMode.TileFlipXY* option is a combination of the two effects:

And this is now beginning to look like an interesting pattern.

The uncolored white areas in that last screen shot are the background of the window showing through the transparent areas of the brush. The brush is only a triangle, so it can't entirely fill an area with tiling. Only a brush composed of a rectangle can fill an area with horizontal and vertical tiling, as in this program.

```
SquareTile.vb
'-----------------------------------------------
' SquareTile.vb (c) 2002 by Charles Petzold
'-----------------------------------------------
Imports System
Imports System.Drawing
Imports System.Drawing.Drawing2D
Imports System.Windows.Forms

Class SquareTile
    Inherits PrintableForm

    Const iSide As Integer = 50    ' Side of square

    Shared Shadows Sub Main()
        Application.Run(new SquareTile())
    End Sub

    Sub New()
        Text = "Square Tile"
    End Sub

    Protected Overrides Sub DoPage(ByVal grfx As Graphics, _
            ByVal clr As Color, ByVal cx As Integer, ByVal cy As Integer)
        Dim apt() As Point = {New Point(0, 0), New Point(iSide, 0), _
                            New Point(iSide, iSide), New Point(0, iSide)}
        Dim pgbr As New PathGradientBrush(apt, WrapMode.TileFlipXY)
        pgbr.SurroundColors = New Color() {Color.Red, Color.Lime, _
                                            Color.Blue, Color.White}
        grfx.FillRectangle(pgbr, 0, 0, cx, cy)
    End Sub
End Class
```

This program looks pretty cool in color, even though this monochrome rendition doesn't capture the full effect:

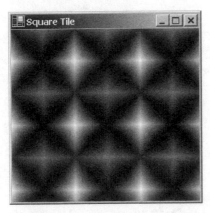

But if you remove the *SurroundColors* assignment, the gray-shaded version also looks like an interesting pattern—or at least more interesting than the few statements of code would seem to imply:

Although a rectangular brush is the only brush shape capable of filling an entire area with tiling, it's also possible to fill an entire area by using two (or more) nonrectangular brushes. Here's a program that creates two interlocking triangular brushes and fills the client area twice.

```
TwoTriangleTile.vb
'-------------------------------------------------
' TwoTriangleTile.vb (c) 2002 by Charles Petzold
'-------------------------------------------------
Imports System
Imports System.Drawing
Imports System.Drawing.Drawing2D
Imports System.Windows.Forms
```

*(continued)*

**TwoTriangleTile.vb** *(continued)*

```
Class TwoTriangleTile
    Inherits PrintableForm
    Const iSide As Integer = 50    ' Side of square for triangle

    Shared Shadows Sub Main()
        Application.Run(New TwoTriangleTile())
    End Sub

    Sub New()
        Text = "Two-Triangle Tile"
    End Sub

    Protected Overrides Sub DoPage(ByVal grfx As Graphics, _
            ByVal clr As Color, ByVal cx As Integer, ByVal cy As Integer)
        ' Define the triangle and create the first brush.
        Dim apt() As Point = _
            {New Point(0, 0), New Point(iSide, 0), New Point(0, iSide)}
        Dim pgbr1 As New PathGradientBrush(apt, WrapMode.TileFlipXY)

        ' Define another triangle and create the second brush.
        apt = New Point() {New Point(iSide, 0), New Point(iSide, iSide), _
                        New Point(0, iSide)}
        Dim pgbr2 As New PathGradientBrush(apt, WrapMode.TileFlipXY)

        grfx.FillRectangle(pgbr1, 0, 0, cx, cy)
        grfx.FillRectangle(pgbr2, 0, 0, cx, cy)
    End Sub
End Class
```

Notice that the second polygon simply defines a triangle in the lower right corner of the square. The combination of the two triangle brushes fills the entire area:

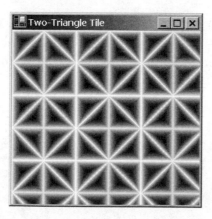

Because the overall effect appears to be tiled squares, you might ask, Isn't it possible to do this pattern with one *PathGradientBrush*? No, it's not, because a *PathGradientBrush* has only one center. Each square in this pattern has two centers. (Of course, you could simulate this effect with a *TextureBrush* because then you're defining a tiled bitmap.)

Using *PathGradientBrush* is so much fun, it's hard to stop. Let's consider the following honeycomb-like pattern:

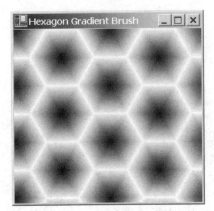

The black centers indicate that the polygon used in the *PathGradientBrush* object is a hexagon. Yet the tiling doesn't look possible. Each column of hexagons might be vertically tiled, but they certainly aren't horizontally tiled. The trick here, again, is to use two brushes. One brush does all the even columns of hexagons, and the other does the odd columns. Both brushes are tiled both horizontally and vertically.

**HexagonGradientBrush.vb**

```
'-------------------------------------------------------
' HexagonGradientBrush.vb (c) 2002 by Charles Petzold
'-------------------------------------------------------
Imports System
Imports System.Drawing
Imports System.Drawing.Drawing2D
Imports System.Windows.Forms

Class HexagonGradientBrush
    Inherits PrintableForm

    Const fSide As Single = 50     ' Side (also radius) of hexagon

    Shared Shadows Sub Main()
        Application.Run(New HexagonGradientBrush())
    End Sub
```

*(continued)*

**HexagonGradientBrush.vb**   *(continued)*

```
Sub New()
    Text = "Hexagon Gradient Brush"
End Sub

Protected Overrides Sub DoPage(ByVal grfx As Graphics, _
        ByVal clr As Color, ByVal cx As Integer, ByVal cy As Integer)
    ' Calculate half the hexagon height.
    Dim fHalf As Single = CSng(fSide * Math.Sin(Math.PI / 3))

    ' Define a hexagon including some extra width.
    Dim aptf() As PointF = {New PointF(fSide, 0), _
                            New PointF(fSide * 1.5, 0), _
                            New PointF(fSide, 0), _
                            New PointF(fSide / 2, -fHalf), _
                            New PointF(-fSide / 2, -fHalf), _
                            New PointF(-fSide, 0), _
                            New PointF(-fSide * 1.5, 0), _
                            New PointF(-fSide, 0), _
                            New PointF(-fSide / 2, fHalf), _
                            New PointF(fSide / 2, fHalf)}

    ' Create the first brush.
    Dim pgbr1 As PathGradientBrush = _
                    New PathGradientBrush(aptf, WrapMode.Tile)

    ' Offset the hexagon and define the second brush.
    Dim i As Integer
    For i = 0 To aptf.GetUpperBound(0)
        aptf(i).X += fSide * 1.5F
        aptf(i).Y += fHalf
    Next i
    Dim pgbr2 As PathGradientBrush = _
                    New PathGradientBrush(aptf, WrapMode.Tile)

    grfx.FillRectangle(pgbr1, 0, 0, cx, cy)
    grfx.FillRectangle(pgbr2, 0, 0, cx, cy)
    End Sub
End Class
```

# Pens Can Be Brushes Too

So far in this chapter I've been discussing brushes, but I've also been talking about pens, and that's because pens can be created from brushes. Here's the complete list of *Pen* constructors:

## *Pen* Constructors

```
Pen(ByVal clr As Color)

Pen(ByVal clr As Color, ByVal fWidth As Single)

Pen(ByVal br As Brush)

Pen(ByVal br As Brush, ByVal fWidth As Single)
```

Creating a *Pen* from a *SolidBrush* object is equivalent to creating a *Pen* from the *Color* object that the *SolidBrush* object is based on.

With pens, it's very helpful to remember the stenciling effect that I mentioned earlier. When you draw with a pen created from a brush, you are effectively creating a slit through which you can view the brush. For example, here's a program that creates a *Pen* object based on a *LinearGradientBrush*.

### GradientPen.vb

```vb
'---------------------------------------------------
' GradientPen.vb (c) 2002 by Charles Petzold
'---------------------------------------------------
Imports System
Imports System.Drawing
Imports System.Drawing.Drawing2D
Imports System.Windows.Forms

Class GradientPen
    Inherits PrintableForm

    Shared Shadows Sub Main()
        Application.Run(New GradientPen())
    End Sub

    Sub New()
        Text = "Gradient Pen"
    End Sub

    Protected Overrides Sub DoPage(ByVal grfx As Graphics, _
            ByVal clr As Color, ByVal cx As Integer, ByVal cy As Integer)
        Dim lgbr As New LinearGradientBrush( _
                            New Rectangle(0, 0, cx, cy), _
                            Color.White, Color.Black, _
                            LinearGradientMode.BackwardDiagonal)
        Dim pn As New Pen(lgbr, Math.Min(cx, cy) \ 25)
        pn.Alignment = PenAlignment.Inset

        grfx.DrawRectangle(pn, 0, 0, cx, cy)
        grfx.DrawLine(pn, 0, 0, cx, cy)
        grfx.DrawLine(pn, 0, cy, cx, 0)
    End Sub
End Class
```

The brush is based on a rectangle that encompasses the entire drawing area. The *LinearGradientMode* is set as *BackwardDiagonal*, which means that the mix line is from the upper left corner of the rectangle to the lower right corner. When you draw a line coinciding with (or parallel to) the mix line using a pen created with this brush, it has a constant color, not a gradient.

Although all the lines drawn by this program use the same pen, they have different gradients. The diagonal line from the lower left to the upper right goes from black to white. The horizontal and vertical lines go from black to gray, or gray to white.

In this program, I use a pen width that is a minimum of 1/25 of the width and height of the display area. The following table shows some width-related properties of the *Pen* class:

### *Pen* Properties (selection)

| Property | Type | Accessibility |
|---|---|---|
| *Width* | *Single* | Get/Set |
| *Transform* | *Matrix* | Get/Set |
| *Alignment* | *PenAlignment* | Get/Set |

The *Width* property is in world coordinates, but it's never smaller than 1 pixel. If you specifically want a 1-pixel pen, specify a width of 0.

Along with the *Transform* property, the *Pen* class has the customary array of transform-setting methods: *TranslateTransform*, *ScaleTransform*, *Rotate-Transform*, *MultiplyTransform*, and *ResetTransform*. However, the transform does *not* affect the location and orientation of lines you draw with a pen, nor the brush that the pen may be based on. The transform affects only the pen width. The type of transform that makes most sense for pens is scaling. With *ScaleTransform* (or setting the *Transform* property manually), you can make pens that have different horizontal and vertical widths. For example, suppose you have a pen that is 10 units wide. If you call

```
pn.ScaleTransform(2, 4)
```

the pen will have a horizontal width of 20 and a vertical width of 40, which means that vertical lines with this pen will have a width of 20 units, horizontal lines will have a width of 40 units, and diagonal lines will have a width somewhere in between. *RotateTransform* will rotate that effect.

I set the pen's *Alignment* property in the GradientPen program. The *Alignment* property can have one of the values of the *PenAlignment* enumeration defined in *System.Drawing.Drawing2D*:

### *PenAlignment* Enumeration

| Member | Value |
|--------|-------|
| Center | 0 |
| Inset | 1 |
| Outset | 2 |
| Left | 3 |
| Right | 4 |

The *Alignment* property governs how wide pens appear when you draw rectangles or ellipses. By default, the property is *PenAlignment.Center*, which means that the wide pen is centered over the specified coordinates. In the GradientPen program, the lines drawn by *DrawRectangle* would be half outside the client area. Switching to *PenAlignment.Inset* causes the whole pen to appear inside the rectangle.

The following three properties concern the *Brush* or *Color* object used in the *Pen*:

### *Pen* Properties (selection)

| Property | Type | Accessibility |
|----------|------|---------------|
| PenType | PenType | Get |
| Color | Color | Get/Set |
| Brush | Brush | Get/Set |

The *PenType* enumeration is defined in *System.Drawing.Drawing2D*:

### *PenType* Enumeration

| Member | Value |
| --- | --- |
| SolidColor | 0 |
| HatchFill | 1 |
| TextureFill | 2 |
| PathGradient | 3 |
| LinearGradient | 4 |

If you've created a pen with a color or with *SolidBrush*, the *Color* property of *Pen* is valid; otherwise, the *Brush* property is valid. However, you can change either the *Color* or *Brush* property of an existing pen and effectively change the pen type.

# A Dash of Style

Pens needn't be solid lines. They can instead consist of patterns of dots and dashes. This style is specified with the pen property named *DashStyle*:

### *Pen* Properties (selection)

| Property | Type | Accessibility |
| --- | --- | --- |
| DashStyle | DashStyle | Get/Set |
| DashOffset | Single | Get/Set |
| DashPattern | Single() | Get/Set |

The *DashStyle* enumeration is defined in *System.Drawing.Drawing2D*:

### *DashStyle* Enumeration

| Member | Value |
| --- | --- |
| Solid | 0 |
| Dash | 1 |
| Dot | 2 |

### *DashStyle* **Enumeration**   *(continued)*

| Member | Value |
|--------|-------|
| *DashDot* | 3 |
| *DashDotDot* | 4 |
| *Custom* | 5 |

The appearance of the dots and dashes is affected by the pen width and any transforms that are in effect. The following program demonstrates this.

**PenDashStyles.vb**

```
'-------------------------------------------------
' PenDashStyles.vb (c) 2002 by Charles Petzold
'-------------------------------------------------
Imports System
Imports System.Drawing
Imports System.Drawing.Drawing2D
Imports System.Windows.Forms

Class PenDashStyles
    Inherits PrintableForm

    Private miChecked As MenuItem

    Shared Shadows Sub Main()
        Application.Run(New PenDashStyles())
    End Sub

    Sub New()
        Text = "Pen Dash Styles"

        Menu = New MainMenu()
        Menu.MenuItems.Add("&Width")

        Dim aiWidth() As Integer = {1, 2, 5, 10, 15, 20, 25}
        Dim iWidth As Integer
        For Each iWidth In aiWidth
            Menu.MenuItems(0).MenuItems.Add(iWidth.ToString(), _
                                    AddressOf MenuWidthOnClick)
        Next iWidth
        miChecked = Menu.MenuItems(0).MenuItems(0)
        miChecked.Checked = True
    End Sub

    Sub MenuWidthOnClick(ByVal obj As Object, ByVal ea As EventArgs)
        miChecked.Checked = False
        miChecked = DirectCast(obj, MenuItem)
        miChecked.Checked = True
```

*(continued)*

**PenDashStyles.vb**   *(continued)*

```
        Invalidate()
    End Sub

    Protected Overrides Sub DoPage(ByVal grfx As Graphics, _
            ByVal clr As Color, ByVal cx As Integer, ByVal cy As Integer)
        Dim pn As New Pen(clr)
        pn.Width = Convert.ToInt32(miChecked.Text)
        Dim i As Integer

        For i = 0 To 4
            pn.DashStyle = CType(i, DashStyle)
            Dim y As Integer = (i + 1) * cy \ 6
            grfx.DrawLine(pn, cx \ 8, y, 7 * cx \ 8, y)
        Next i
    End Sub
End Class
```

The program constructs a menu that lets you select various widths from 1 through 25. The program displays five lines using the first five dash styles equally spaced in the client area. Here's the Morse code effect when you select a width of 25:

As I'll demonstrate in the next section, you have some control over the appearance of large dashes and dots.

If you need to draw a dashed or dotted polyline, use *DrawLines* or a path. Don't use multiple calls to *DrawLine* because the dash pattern starts anew with each line.

You can control how the dash begins in each line by using the *DashOffset* property. The property indicates an offset into the dash style where the pattern of dots and dashes begins. The offset is in increments of the dot size and is independent of the pen width. For example, if you insert the line

```
pn.DashOffset = 1
```

into the PenDashStyles program, the patterns begin one dot size later and look like this:

The *DashOffset* value is a *Single*, so it can take on nonintegral values. If you want the *DashDot* or *DashDotDot* styles to begin with dots rather than dashes, set *DashOffset* equal to 4:

```
pn.DashOffset = 4
```

You can also set your own pattern of dots and dashes using the *DashPattern* property. The array of *Single* values you specify indicates an alternating series of dash lengths and space lengths, all in increments of the dot size. Here's an example:

```
pn.DashPattern = New Single() {2, 1, 4, 3}
```

After setting *DashPattern*, *DashStyle* is *Custom* and the line drawn with *pn* will contain a two-dot dash, one space, a four-dot dash, and three spaces.

# Caps and Joins

As the PenDashStyle program indicates, when lines start to get wide, they assume a graphical form of their own. You may like the square and rectangular appearance of the dots and dashes in styled lines, but you may prefer a more rounded appearance instead.

This is the realm of line *caps* (also known as *ends*) and *joins*. The cap governs the appearance of the lines at their beginning and end, or the appearance of the dots and dashes. The join governs what happens at the meeting of two connected lines. Here are the four basic caps and joins properties:

### *Pen* Properties (selection)

| Property | Type | Accessibility |
|----------|------|---------------|
| *StartCap* | *LineCap* | Get/Set |
| *EndCap* | *LineCap* | Get/Set |

### *Pen* Properties (selection)   *(continued)*

| Property | Type | Accessibility |
|----------|------|---------------|
| *DashCap* | *DashCap* | Get/Set |
| *LineJoin* | *LineJoin* | Get/Set |

I want to begin with the *LineJoin* property because that's probably the simplest. The property can take on one of the following enumeration values:

### *LineJoin* Enumeration

| Member | Value | Description |
|--------|-------|-------------|
| *Miter* | 0 | Default, pointed |
| *Bevel* | 1 | Leveled off |
| *Round* | 2 | Rounded |
| *MiterClipped* | 3 | Pointed with limitations |

The *LineJoin* property affects only lines that are connected, that is, polylines drawn with *DrawLines* or connected lines in a path. Here's a program that draws simple V-shaped polylines with the four different *LineJoin* values.

**LineJoins.vb**

```
'-------------------------------------------
' LineJoins.vb (c) 2002 by Charles Petzold
'-------------------------------------------
Imports System
Imports System.Drawing
Imports System.Drawing.Drawing2D
Imports System.Windows.Forms

Class LineJoins
    Inherits PrintableForm

    Shared Shadows Sub Main()
        Application.Run(New LineJoins())
    End Sub

    Sub New()
        Text = "Line Joins: Miter, Bevel, Round, MiterClipped"
    End Sub

    Protected Overrides Sub DoPage(ByVal grfx As Graphics, _
            ByVal clr As Color, ByVal cx As Integer, ByVal cy As Integer)
        Dim pnNarrow As New Pen(clr)
```

```
        Dim pnWide As New Pen(Color.Gray, cx \ 16)
        Dim apt() As Point = {New Point(1 * cx \ 32, 1 * cy \ 8), _
                              New Point(4 * cx \ 32, 6 * cy \ 8), _
                              New Point(7 * cx \ 32, 1 * cy \ 8)}
        Dim i As Integer

        For i = 0 To 3
            pnWide.LineJoin = CType(i, LineJoin)
            grfx.DrawLines(pnWide, apt)
            grfx.DrawLines(pnNarrow, apt)
            grfx.TranslateTransform(cx \ 4, 0)
        Next i
    End Sub
End Class
```

And here's what it looks like:

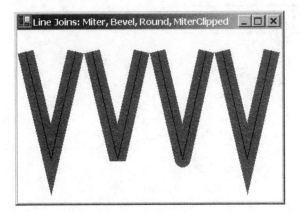

The wide gray pen is the one whose *LineJoin* property is set. The thin black line shows the actual geometric line. You'll notice that the *MiterClipped* join looks just like *Miter*, but try making the form very tall: the *Miter* join continues to get longer and pointier, but at some point the *MiterClipped* join is truncated to look the same as a *Bevel* join. There's a reason to limit the length of miter joins: as the angle between two joined lines increases, the miter join can become very long. For example, a 1-inch-thick polyline joined at an angle of 1 degree would have a miter join that extended over 4½ feet![*] The *Pen* class has a special property to limit this extent when the *LineJoin* property is *MiterClipped*:

---

[*] Let $w$ be the width of the line and $\alpha$ the join angle. It's easy to show that the extension of the miter tip past the actual join point is $(w/2)/\sin(\alpha/2)$.

### *Pen* Properties (selection)

| Property | Type | Accessibility |
| --- | --- | --- |
| *MiterLimit* | *Single* | Get/Set |

The property truncates the miter join at a distance of *pn.MiterLimit* × *pn.Width* / 2. The default *MiterLimit* is 10. If the *Width* property of the pen is 20, the miter extends only 100 units past the theoretical end of the line.

Let's now take a look at the *DashCap* property that affects the appearance of dots and dashes in styled lines. The property can take on one of the following enumeration values.

### *DashCap* Enumeration

| Member | Value |
| --- | --- |
| *Flat* | 0 |
| *Round* | 2 |
| *Triangle* | 3 |

Here's a variation of the PenDashStyles program that displays a *DashDotDot* line using the three different *DashCap* values.

### PenDashCaps.vb

```
'--------------------------------------------
' PenDashCaps.vb (c) 2002 by Charles Petzold
'--------------------------------------------
Imports System
Imports System.Drawing
Imports System.Drawing.Drawing2D
Imports System.Windows.Forms

Class PenDashCaps
    Inherits PrintableForm

    Private miChecked As MenuItem

    Shared Shadows Sub Main()
        Application.Run(new PenDashCaps())
    End Sub

    Sub New()
        Text = "Pen Dash Caps: Flat, Round, Triangle"
```

```
        Menu = new MainMenu()
        Menu.MenuItems.Add("&Width")

        Dim aiWidth() As Integer = {1, 2, 5, 10, 15, 20, 25}
        Dim iWidth As Integer
        For Each iWidth In aiWidth
            Menu.MenuItems(0).MenuItems.Add(iWidth.ToString(), _
                                            AddressOf MenuWidthOnClick)
        Next iWidth
        miChecked = Menu.MenuItems(0).MenuItems(0)
        miChecked.Checked = True
    End Sub

    Sub MenuWidthOnClick(ByVal obj As Object, ByVal ea As EventArgs)
        miChecked.Checked = False
        miChecked = DirectCast(obj, MenuItem)
        miChecked.Checked = True
        Invalidate()
    End Sub

    Protected Overrides Sub DoPage(ByVal grfx As Graphics, _
            ByVal clr As Color, ByVal cx As Integer, ByVal cy As Integer)
        Dim pn As New Pen(clr, Convert.ToInt32(miChecked.Text))
        pn.DashStyle = DashStyle.DashDotDot
        Dim dc As DashCap

        For Each dc In System.Enum.GetValues(GetType(DashCap))
            pn.DashCap = dc
            grfx.DrawLine(pn, cx \ 8, cy \ 4, 7 * cx \ 8, cy \ 4)
            grfx.TranslateTransform(0, cy \ 4)
        Next dc
    End Sub
End Class
```

Here's the display when you select a width of 25:

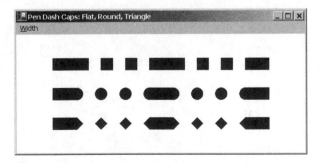

These look a little odd because the beginning and end of the actual line is still squared off. The appearance of the beginning and end of the line is affected by the *StartCap* and *EndCap* properties, both of which are of type *LineCap*. You can insert the following statement into the PenDashCaps program to make these two properties consistent with the *DashCap* property:

```
pn.StartCap = CType(dc, LineCap)
pn.EndCap = pn.StartCap
```

The display then looks like this:

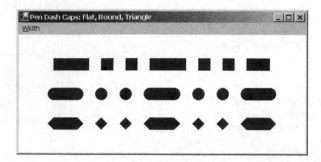

The two lines with the round and triangle caps aren't quite aligned with the flat caps. The reason they're not is that (as we'll see) the round and triangle caps go beyond the geometric point marking the beginning and end of the line. But the full width of the dashes and dots is kept consistent regardless of the cap style.

Here's the complete *LineCap* enumeration:

### *LineCap* Enumeration

| Member | Value |
| --- | --- |
| *Flat* | &H00 |
| *Square* | &H01 |
| *Round* | &H02 |
| *Triangle* | &H03 |
| *NoAnchor* | &H10 |
| *SquareAnchor* | &H11 |
| *RoundAnchor* | &H12 |
| *DiamondAnchor* | &H13 |
| *ArrowAnchor* | &H14 |
| *AnchorMask* | &HF0 |
| *Custom* | &HFF |

And here's a program that draws wide lines using all these values. The width of the line is fixed at the *Font.Height* property. In addition, the program draws thin lines showing the geometric beginning and end of each line.

### LineCaps.vb

```
'----------------------------------------------
' LineCaps.vb (c) 2002 by Charles Petzold
'----------------------------------------------
Imports System
Imports System.Drawing
Imports System.Drawing.Drawing2D
Imports System.Windows.Forms

Class LineCaps
    Inherits PrintableForm

    Shared Shadows Sub Main()
        Application.Run(New LineCaps())
    End Sub

    Sub New()
        Text = "Line Caps"
    End Sub

    Protected Overrides Sub DoPage(ByVal grfx As Graphics, _
            ByVal clr As Color, ByVal cx As Integer, ByVal cy As Integer)
        Dim pnWide As New Pen(Color.Gray, Font.Height)
        Dim pnNarrow As New Pen(clr)
        Dim br As New SolidBrush(clr)
        Dim lc As LineCap

        For Each lc In System.Enum.GetValues(GetType(LineCap))
            grfx.DrawString(lc.ToString(), Font, br, _
                            Font.Height, Font.Height \ 2)
            pnWide.StartCap = lc
            pnWide.EndCap = lc
            grfx.DrawLine(pnWide, 2 * cx \ 4, Font.Height, _
                            3 * cx \ 4, Font.Height)
            grfx.DrawLine(pnNarrow, 2 * cx \ 4, Font.Height, _
                            3 * cx \ 4, Font.Height)
            grfx.TranslateTransform(0, 2 * Font.Height)
        Next lc
    End Sub
End Class
```

Here's the result:

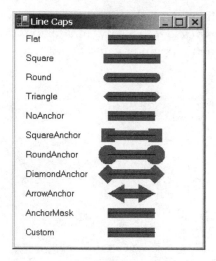

Keep in mind that I'm using the same enumeration value for the beginning and end of the line. You can use different values if you want.

The *NoAnchor* value produces the same result as *Flat*. The *SquareAnchor*, *RoundAnchor*, and *DiamondAnchor* line ends are similar to *Square*, *Round*, and *Triangle*, respectively (as their enumeration values indicate), except that they are larger.

If the various line caps provided by the *LineCap* enumeration aren't enough for you, you can set the *StartCap* and/or *EndCap* properties of the pen equal to *LineCap.Custom* and then make use of the following properties:

### *Pen* Properties (selection)

| Property | Type | Accessibility |
|----------|------|---------------|
| *CustomStartCap* | *CustomLineCap* | Get/Set |
| *CustomEndCap* | *CustomLineCap* | Get/Set |

The *CustomLineCap* class (in *System.Drawing.Drawing2D*) lets you use a path to define the outline of your custom caps. In addition, the *AdjustableArrowCap* class derives from *CustomLineCap* to let you draw arrow caps with more control over the arrow size and filled interior.

# 18

# Edit, List, and Spin

Just about every Microsoft Windows program requires a little text input from the user every now and then. Back in Chapter 6, I discussed how your program can install handlers for the *KeyDown*, *KeyUp*, and *KeyPress* events to obtain keyboard input and echo the input back to the user. For many simple purposes, however, you can make use of a type of control traditionally called an *edit control*, but in the Microsoft .NET Framework referred to as a *text box*.

A text box can range from a small, single-line entry field to a multiline control with word wrap, such as that used in the Microsoft Notepad program. Writing a clone of Notepad is a traditional exercise for a book like this, and we'll accomplish most of that job in this chapter. (I'll add printing support in Appendix 21 and drag-and-drop in Appendix 24.)

In this chapter, I'll also discuss several other important types of controls. The *list box* presents a scrollable list of options to the user; the *combo box* combines the text box and the list box. When numbers are involved, you'll probably want to use the up-down control, more commonly called a *spin button*.

## Single-Line Text Boxes

The simplest text box control is named *TextBox*, which is derived from the *TextBoxBase* class (defined as *MustInherit*), as shown in the class hierarchy on the top of the following page.

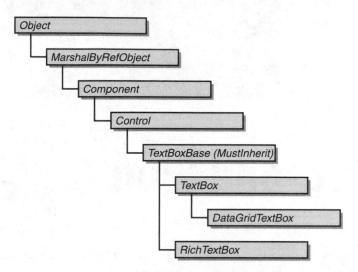

Also deriving from *TextBoxBase* is *RichTextBox*. The *RichTextBox* control provides additional functionality over *TextBox* in the same way that the Microsoft WordPad program provides additional features over Notepad. In *TextBox* (as in Notepad), you can define a font, but the font applies to the entire document. In *RichTextBox* (as in WordPad), you can define different fonts as well as other formatting for different parts of the document.

The most important property for text boxes is *Text* because it contains the text that the user enters into the text box. A program can also initialize the text of the text box and limit the length of the text:

### *TextBoxBase* Properties (selection)

| Property | Type | Accessibility |
|----------|------|---------------|
| *Text* | *String* | Get/Set |
| *MaxLength* | *Integer* | Get/Set |
| *TextLength* | *Integer* | Get |
| *Lines* | *String( )* | Get/Set |

The *TextLength* property is the same as *Text.Length*.

The *Lines* property might also be called *Paragraphs* since it divides the document into text blocks terminated by end-of-line characters. These blocks show up as lines of text if word wrap is off but as paragraphs if word wrap is on.

When you use a text box in a dialog box, in many cases you need to fish the text out of the text box only when the user presses OK. But some dialog boxes like to keep closer track of what the user is entering. Perhaps the dialog box enables the OK button only when the text box contains some valid information. The most useful event for text boxes is actually defined in *Control*:

### *Control* Events (selection)

| Event | Method | Delegate | Argument |
|-------|--------|----------|----------|
| *TextChanged* | *OnTextChanged* | *EventHandler* | *EventArgs* |

Here's a program that creates a text box and a label control. By installing a handler for the text box's *TextChanged* event, the program can track the text that the user enters in the text box and replicate it in the label control.

**TextBoxDemo.vb**

```
'-----------------------------------------------
' TextBoxDemo.vb (c) 2002 by Charles Petzold
'-----------------------------------------------
Imports System
Imports System.Drawing
Imports System.Windows.Forms

Class TextBoxDemo
    Inherits Form

    Private lbl As Label

    Shared Sub Main()
        Application.Run(New TextBoxDemo())
    End Sub

    Sub New()
        Text = "TextBox Demo"

        ' Create text box control.
        Dim txtbox As New TextBox()
        txtbox.Parent = Me
        txtbox.Location = New Point(Font.Height, Font.Height)
        txtbox.Size = New Size(ClientSize.Width - 2 * Font.Height, _
                               Font.Height)
        txtbox.Anchor = txtbox.Anchor Or AnchorStyles.Right
        AddHandler txtbox.TextChanged, AddressOf TextBoxOnTextChanged

        ' Create label control.
        lbl = New Label()
        lbl.Parent = Me
        lbl.Location = New Point(Font.Height, 3 * Font.Height)
        lbl.AutoSize = True
    End Sub
```

*(continued)*

**TextBoxDemo.vb**   *(continued)*

```
    Sub TextBoxOnTextChanged(ByVal obj As Object, ByVal ea As EventArgs)
        Dim txtbox As TextBox = DirectCast(obj, TextBox)
        lbl.Text = txtbox.Text
    End Sub
End Class
```

Because I've set the *Anchor* property of the text box, the control will stretch wider when you resize the form. However, the actual size of the text box doesn't limit the amount of text you can enter. As you enter text beyond the width of the text box, the text will automatically scroll to the left. When that happens, the label control may not be able to display all the text even though it has its *AutoSize* property set:

The default background and foreground colors of the text box are *System-Colors.Window* and *SystemColors.WindowText*, as opposed to the *SystemColors.Control* and *SystemColors.ControlText* colors that the form uses. The text box inherits its default *Font* property from its parent. The default *BorderStyle* property is *BorderStyle.Fixed3D*, which gives the control a sunken appearance. You can also use *None* or *FixedSingle*.

I want you to take a moment to experiment with the TextBoxDemo program or the Notepad program or any other text box anywhere in Windows. As you undoubtedly know, the caret in the text box indicates the insertion point—where text will be inserted when you type. You can move the caret anywhere you want within the entire block of text by using the cursor arrow keys. You can also change the location of the caret by clicking with the mouse.

If you hold down the Shift key and move the cursor arrow keys, you define a *selection*, which is a block of text that the text box highlights using a reverse-video effect. You can also use the mouse to define a selection in the text box by dragging the mouse with the button pressed.

Here's the important point: If there's text selected in the text box, the caret is always at the beginning or the end of the selection. It's important to realize this because the properties that provide information about the selection also provide information about the caret position. Four properties of *TextBoxBase* are concerned with the selection and hence also the caret position:

### *TextBoxBase* Properties (selection)

| Property | Type | Accessibility |
| --- | --- | --- |
| *SelectionStart* | *Integer* | Get/Set |
| *SelectionLength* | *Integer* | Get/Set |
| *SelectedText* | *String* | Get/Set |
| *HideSelection* | *Boolean* | Get/Set |

The *SelectionStart* property is a zero-based index indicating the character position of the beginning of the selection. If *SelectionStart* is 0, the selection begins at the very beginning of the text in the text box.

The *SelectionLength* property indicates the number of characters in the selection. If *SelectionLength* is 0, no text is selected and *SelectionStart* indicates the caret position. If both *SelectionStart* and *SelectionLength* are 0, the caret is located at the very beginning of the text box contents.

If *SelectionLength* is greater than 0, the precise caret position isn't available. Depending on how you've selected the text (that is, whether you used the left arrow or the right arrow, or you swept the mouse in a particular direction), the caret could be at either the beginning or the end of the selection. The caret position is either *SelectionStart* or (*SelectionStart* + *SelectionLength*).

If there's no selection, *SelectedText* is the empty string. Otherwise, it's a text string of the selected text. The *SelectionLength* property is really just a shortcut for *SelectedText.Length*.

Notice that the *SelectedText* property is writable. If a program wants to delete the selected text from the text box (without deleting the unselected text), it can simply set the property to an empty string:

```
txtbox.SelectedText = ""
```

If a program wants to insert text at the caret position, it can call

```
txtbox.SelectedText = "insert text"
```

If there's currently a selection, the inserted text will replace the selection. If there's no selection, the text will be inserted at the caret position.

The *HideSelection* property is normally *True*. That means that when the text box loses the input focus, it no longer highlights the selection. This is normal behavior. Later on in this chapter, I use a nondefault setting of *HideSelection* in connection with a find-and-replace modeless dialog box.

The *TextBox* control doesn't have an event that allows a program to determine when the selection changes. However, the *RichTextBox* control does have an event named *SelectionChanged*.

The *Select* and *SelectAll* methods allow a program to set a selection in a text box:

### *TextBoxBase* Methods (selection)

```
Sub Select(ByVal iStart As Integer, ByVal iLength As Integer)
Sub SelectAll()
Sub Clear()
```

The *Select* method is equivalent to setting the *SelectionStart* and *SelectionLength* properties. The *SelectAll* method is equivalent to setting *SelectionStart* to 0 and *SelectionLength* to *TextLength*. The *Clear* method is equivalent to setting *Text* to an empty string.

By experimenting with TextBoxDemo, you may have noticed that the text box automatically works with the clipboard. You can type CTRL+X to delete the selected text and copy it to the clipboard, CTRL+C to copy selected text to the clipboard without deleting it, and CTRL+V to paste text from the clipboard. We'll see how to do this programmatically later in the chapter. The standard *TextBox* also includes an undo facility. If you select some text and delete it using the Delete key, you can bring it back by typing CTRL+Z. It's only a one-level undo: pressing CTRL+Z again makes the deleted text go away, and pressing CTRL+Z again restores the text.

# Multiline Text Boxes

It's fairly easy to convert a single-line text box to a multiline text box. Basically, you set the *Multiline* property to *True* and (most likely) make the text box large enough to display more than one line. However, a number of other properties are involved with multiline text boxes, so let's begin by getting familiar with them.

Here's *Multiline* and two other related properties:

### *TextBox* Properties (selection)

| Property | Type | Accessibility | Default |
|---|---|---|---|
| Multiline | Boolean | Get/Set | False |
| WordWrap | Boolean | Get/Set | True |
| ScrollBars | ScrollBars | Get/Set | ScrollBars.None |

The *Multiline* and *WordWrap* properties are implemented in *TextBoxBase* and are also inherited by *RichTextBox*. The *ScrollBars* property is implemented in *TextBox* and can have one of the following values:

### *ScrollBars* Enumeration

| Member | Value |
|---|---|
| None | 0 |
| Horizontal | 1 |
| Vertical | 2 |
| Both | 3 |

Setting the property to *Horizontal*, *Vertical*, or *Both* makes the scroll bars appear even if they're not needed, which is the case when there's not enough text to make them useful. However, if the scroll bars aren't currently needed, they are disabled. Regardless of the setting of the *ScrollBars* property, the horizontal scroll bar won't be displayed if *WordWrap* is set to *True*.

The *RichTextBox* control also has a *ScrollBars* property, but the property is a different type—*RichTextBoxScrollBars*—and it lets you get more specific about when you want the scroll bars to appear:

### *RichTextBoxScrollBars* Enumeration

| Member | Value |
|---|---|
| None | 0 |
| Horizontal | 1 |
| Vertical | 2 |
| Both | 3 |
| ForcedHorizontal | 17 |
| ForcedVertical | 18 |
| ForcedBoth | 19 |

The *Horizontal*, *Vertical*, and *Both* members cause the scroll bars to be displayed only when they're needed. The members beginning with the word *Forced* cause the scroll bars to be displayed regardless.

You can't center text vertically in multiline text boxes. The most control you have is with the *TextAlign* property:

### *TextBox* Properties (selection)

| Property | Type | Accessibility |
|----------|------|---------------|
| *TextAlign* | *HorizontalAlignment* | Get/Set |

*HorizontalAlignment* is an enumeration:

### *HorizontalAlignment* Enumeration

| Member | Value |
|--------|-------|
| *Left* | 0 |
| *Right* | 1 |
| *Center* | 2 |

As you know, the Tab and Enter keys have special meaning in dialog boxes or in any form that has child controls. The Tab key causes the focus to shift among controls; Enter usually activates the OK button. For single-line text boxes implemented in dialog boxes, you probably want the Tab and Enter keys to function normally. For multiline text boxes, however, you probably want the text box itself to capture the Tab and Enter keys. If so, set these two properties to *True*:

### *TextBox* Properties (selection)

| Property | Type | Accessibility | Default |
|----------|------|---------------|---------|
| *AcceptsReturn* | *Boolean* | Get/Set | *True* |
| *AcceptsTab* | *Boolean* | Get/Set | *False* |

*AcceptsReturn* is implemented in *TextBox*; *AcceptsTab* is implemented in *TextBoxBase*. If the *AcceptButton* property of the parent form isn't set, the text box will capture the Enter key regardless of the *AcceptsReturn* property.

# Cloning Notepad

We're now ready to begin building a clone of Notepad. To present the code in manageable chunks, I'm going to build this program up through several levels of inheritance.

Here's the first module, which creates the text box and uses *DockStyle.Fill* to make it fill the form's client area. The constructor concludes by setting several properties appropriate for multiline text boxes.

**NotepadCloneNoMenu.vb**

```
'-------------------------------------------------------
' NotepadCloneNoMenu.vb (c) 2002 by Charles Petzold
'-------------------------------------------------------
Imports System
Imports System.Drawing
Imports System.Windows.Forms

Class NotepadCloneNoMenu
    Inherits Form

    Protected txtbox As TextBox

    Shared Sub Main()
        Application.Run(New NotepadCloneNoMenu())
    End Sub

    Sub New()
        Text = "Notepad Clone No Menu"

        txtbox = New TextBox()
        txtbox.Parent = Me
        txtbox.Dock = DockStyle.Fill
        txtbox.BorderStyle = BorderStyle.None
        txtbox.Multiline = True
        txtbox.ScrollBars = ScrollBars.Both
        txtbox.AcceptsTab = True
    End Sub
End Class
```

Considering the length of this program, it has a high level of functionality and works much like the Notepad program when the Word Wrap menu item is checked. Here's what it looks like with some text typed in.

Before beginning to implement a menu in Notepad Clone, I want to implement some code that accesses the Windows registry. As you may know, whenever you change the Word Wrap menu item in Notepad or the font that it uses, the new settings are used when you next run Notepad. You can view all the Notepad registry settings in the Registry Editor (Regedit.exe) under HKEY_CURRENT_USER with the key Software\Microsoft\Notepad.

Besides saving the Word Wrap setting and the font, Notepad also uses the registry to save its window size and position on the desktop. If you move or resize Notepad, terminate the program, and then run it again, it will appear in the saved location and with the saved size.

At first, implementing a feature to save the location and size seems to involve merely saving the form's *DesktopBounds* property in the registry when the program terminates and setting the property from the registry when the program next runs. Such a scheme would indeed work fine were it not for those window-display options known as *minimize* and *maximize*.

Let's examine these cases: When you maximize any Windows program and then restore it, the program returns to the same location and size as before it was maximized. Similarly, when you minimize and then restore the program, it goes back to the same location and size. Windows obviously saves the location and size of the program's window before the window becomes minimized or maximized. A program using the Win32 API has access to this information in the *WINDOWPLACEMENT* structure (where it is referred to as the *normal position*). The *WINDOWPLACEMENT* structure is used in the API functions *GetWindowPlacement* and *SetWindowPlacement*.

A Windows Forms program doesn't always have direct access to the normal position. When a form is maximized, the *DesktopBounds* property reflects the *maximized* location and size. If the form has a sizing border, the location of the maximized form has negative coordinates because the form is positioned with the sizing border outside the area of the desktop. When a form is minimized, the *DesktopBounds* property has special *X* and *Y* values of –32000, and the *Height* and *Width* values represent the size of the minimized button on the Windows taskbar. Only when the form is not minimized or maximized does *DesktopBounds* reflect the normal position of the form.

Do you see the problem yet? It manifests itself if the program is terminated when it happens to be minimized or maximized. Because *DesktopBounds* doesn't reflect the normal position of the form, that's not what the program should save in the registry.

For this reason, a Windows Forms program that wants to save its normal position in the registry should maintain a field specifically for that purpose. (In the program coming up shortly, I call this field *rectNormal*.) The program can set this field from *DesktopBounds* in its constructor, and it can also reset the field from *DesktopBounds* during any call to *OnMove* or *OnResize* when the form isn't minimized or maximized. Use the *WindowState* property to determine whether the window is minimized or maximized:

### *Form* Properties (selection)

| Property | Type | Accessibility |
|----------|------|---------------|
| *WindowState* | *FormWindowState* | Get/Set |

The *FormWindowState* enumeration has the following members:

### *FormWindowState* Enumeration

| Member | Value |
|--------|-------|
| *Normal* | 0 |
| *Minimized* | 1 |
| *Maximized* | 2 |

Here's the next installment in the Notepad Clone series, which derives from NotepadCloneNoMenu and implements the overhead required to access the registry. It also uses the registry to save and restore the location and size of the window. As I mentioned, the *rectNormal* field is set during the constructor (a time during which the *WindowState* property is always *FormWindowState.Normal*) and in the *OnMove* and *OnResize* methods whenever *WindowState* equals *FormWindowState.Normal*.

## NotepadCloneWithRegistry.vb

```vb
'------------------------------------------------------------
' NotepadCloneWithRegistry.vb (c) 2002 by Charles Petzold
'------------------------------------------------------------
Imports Microsoft.Win32
Imports System
Imports System.Drawing
Imports System.Windows.Forms

Class NotepadCloneWithRegistry
    Inherits NotepadCloneNoMenu

    Protected strProgName As String
    Private rectNormal As Rectangle
    Private strRegKey As String = "Software\ProgrammingWindowsWithVBdotNet\"
    Const strWinState As String = "WindowState"
    Const strLocationX As String = "LocationX"
    Const strLocationY As String = "LocationY"
    Const strWidth As String = "Width"
    Const strHeight As String = "Height"

    Shared Shadows Sub Main()
        Application.Run(New NotepadCloneWithRegistry())
    End Sub

    Sub New()
        strProgName = "Notepad Clone with Registry"
        Text = strProgName
        rectNormal = DesktopBounds
    End Sub

    Protected Overrides Sub OnMove(ByVal ea As EventArgs)
        MyBase.OnMove(ea)
        If WindowState = FormWindowState.Normal Then
            rectNormal = DesktopBounds
        End If
    End Sub

    Protected Overrides Sub OnResize(ByVal ea As EventArgs)
        MyBase.OnResize(ea)
        If WindowState = FormWindowState.Normal Then
            rectNormal = DesktopBounds
        End If
    End Sub

    Protected Overrides Sub OnLoad(ByVal ea As EventArgs)
        MyBase.OnLoad(ea)

        ' Construct complete registry key.
        strRegKey = strRegKey & strProgName

        ' Load registry information.
        Dim regkey As RegistryKey = _
```

```
                        Registry.CurrentUser.OpenSubKey(strRegKey)
        If Not regkey Is Nothing Then
            LoadRegistryInfo(regkey)
            regkey.Close()
        End If
    End Sub

    Protected Overrides Sub OnClosed(ByVal ea As EventArgs)
        MyBase.OnClosed(ea)

        ' Save registry information.
        Dim regkey As RegistryKey = _
                        Registry.CurrentUser.OpenSubKey(strRegKey, True)
        If regkey Is Nothing Then
            regkey = Registry.CurrentUser.CreateSubKey(strRegKey)
        End If
        SaveRegistryInfo(regkey)
        regkey.Close()
    End Sub

    Protected Overridable Sub SaveRegistryInfo(ByVal regkey As RegistryKey)
        regkey.SetValue(strWinState, CInt(WindowState))
        regkey.SetValue(strLocationX, rectNormal.X)
        regkey.SetValue(strLocationY, rectNormal.Y)
        regkey.SetValue(strWidth, rectNormal.Width)
        regkey.SetValue(strHeight, rectNormal.Height)
    End Sub

    Protected Overridable Sub LoadRegistryInfo(ByVal regkey As RegistryKey)
        Dim x As Integer = DirectCast(regkey.GetValue(strLocationX, 100), _
                                    Integer)
        Dim y As Integer = DirectCast(regkey.GetValue(strLocationY, 100), _
                                    Integer)
        Dim cx As Integer = DirectCast(regkey.GetValue(strWidth, 300), _
                                    Integer)
        Dim cy As Integer = DirectCast(regkey.GetValue(strHeight, 300), _
                                    Integer)
        rectNormal = New Rectangle(x, y, cx, cy)

        ' Adjust rectangle for any change in desktop size.
        Dim rectDesk As Rectangle = SystemInformation.WorkingArea
        rectNormal.Width = Math.Min(rectNormal.Width, rectDesk.Width)
        rectNormal.Height = Math.Min(rectNormal.Height, rectDesk.Height)
        rectNormal.X -= Math.Max(rectNormal.Right - rectDesk.Right, 0)
        rectNormal.Y -= Math.Max(rectNormal.Bottom - rectDesk.Bottom, 0)

        ' Set form properties.
        DesktopBounds = rectNormal
        WindowState = CType(DirectCast(regkey.GetValue(strWinState, 0), _
                                    Integer), _
                            FormWindowState)
    End Sub
End Class
```

An earlier program in this book that used the registry (DialogsWithRegistry in Chapter 16) loaded information during the form's constructor and saved information during the *OnClosed* method. The NotepadCloneWithRegistry program, however, loads information during the *OnLoad* method, which is associated with the *Load* event and is called after the constructor code executes but before the program is made visible.

I chose this alternative because I wanted each installment in the Notepad Clone series to use its own area of the registry based on its own program name. The constructor in NotepadCloneWithRegistry sets both the *strProgName* field and the *Text* property to the string "Notepad Clone with Registry". The next program in the series (coming up soon) derives from NotepadCloneWithRegistry and is called NotepadCloneWithFile. Its constructor sets the *strProgName* field to "Notepad Clone with File" and initially sets the *Text* property to "Notepad Clone with File – Untitled".

When NotepadCloneWithFile runs, all the default constructors in all the ancestral classes are executed beginning with *Object* and ending with the constructor in the *NotepadCloneWithFile* class. If the *NotepadCloneWithRegistry* constructor were to load information from the registry, it would use a key based on the program name "Notepad Clone With Registry" rather than the appropriate "Notepad Clone With File."

By the time the *OnLoad* method in NotepadCloneWithRegistry is called, however, all the default constructors have been executed. If the NotepadCloneWithRegistry program is running, *strProgName* will equal "Notepad Clone with Registry". If the NotepadCloneWithFile program is running, *strProgName* will equal "Notepad Clone with File". The *OnLoad* method uses *strProgName* to form a registry key that is also later used in the *OnClosed* method.

The *OnLoad* method in NotepadCloneWithRegistry calls the *Overridable* method I've named *LoadRegistryInfo*, and the *OnClosed* method calls another *Overridable* method named *SaveRegistryInfo*. Both these virtual methods have *RegistryKey* arguments. Thus, any subsequent program in the Notepad Clone series can simply override these two *Overridable* methods to load and save registry information. The overrides must also call the base methods. We'll see how this works shortly.

*SaveRegistryInfo* saves the *WindowState* property and the four components of the *rectNormal* field. *LoadRegistryInfo* first sets the *rectNormal* field from these four components. However, it could be that the user changed the desktop size after closing the earlier instance of the program. If so, *rectNormal* is adjusted to fit within the desktop. The method sets the *DesktopBounds* property from the adjusted *rectNormal* field and then sets the *WindowState* property from the value saved in the registry. Thus, if you close the program in a minimized or maximized state, that state will be reflected the next time the program is run. However, if you then restore the program to its normal size, the location and size will be the same as the previous instance, before it was minimized or maximized. (This behavior is a little different from the Windows Notepad program. Notepad always comes up in its normal state regardless of how the previous instance was closed.)

# The Notepad Clone with File I/O

The next step for the Notepad Clone series is implementing a File menu in the program. We've seen file I/O code before, but because I'm trying to write a "real-life" program here, Notepad Clone must do what other programs dealing with documents do, which is sometimes display a message box saying, "The text in the file has changed. Do you want to save the changes?"

The following property of *TextBoxBase* is useful for implementing such a facility:

### *TextBoxBase* Properties (selection)

| Property | Type | Accessibility |
| --- | --- | --- |
| *Modified* | *Boolean* | Get/Set |

When you create a new *TextBox* or *RichTextBox*, the *Modified* property is initialized to *False*. Thereafter, whenever the user does something to change the contents of the text box (such as typing), the text box sets its *Modified* property to *True*. Your program uses this property to determine whether the contents of the text box must be saved to a file. Whenever your program saves the contents of the text box to a file, it must reset the property to *False*. (An indicator that the text has changed is sometimes called a *dirty bit*.)

On several occasions, a program dealing with documents should display a message box asking whether the document should be saved: when the user selects New from the File menu, essentially deleting the existing file from the application; when the user selects Open from the File menu, replacing the existing file; and when the user wants to exit the program. In the NotepadCloneWithFile program (coming up soon), the method that checks whether it's OK to delete the existing document is called *OkToTrash*.

If the user chooses to save the existing document to a file, the program normally must perform the same operation as if the user had selected Save from the File menu. However, if the document has no name, the Save As dialog box must be displayed. If the user then clicks the Cancel button in the dialog box, the file isn't saved, but neither does the program perform the New, Open, or Exit operation.

To handle the last case, the program must override the *OnClosing* method, which occurs before the form is closed, after which the *OnClosed* method is called. The *OnClosing* method is accompanied by a *CancelEventArgs* object, which has a single *Boolean* property (named *Cancel*) that the *OnClosing* method can set to *True* to prevent the program from being closed.

NotepadCloneWithFile also requires a method of *TextBoxBase* that I haven't mentioned yet:

### *TextBoxBase* Methods (selection)

```
Sub ClearUndo()
```

Some background is required here. As I mentioned, the *TextBoxBase* class implements a single-level undo feature. When a change is made to the contents of the text box, the previous version is often saved. As we'll see in the next section, *TextBoxBase* also includes a *Boolean* property named *CanUndo* that returns *True* to indicate the existence of a previous version and a method named *Undo* that reverts to the previous version.

However, at times you don't want the user to be able to revert to the previous contents of the text box, for example, when the program loads the text box from a file. It doesn't make much sense for the Undo command to revert to the text box state before the file was loaded. In such cases, the program calls *ClearUndo* to delete the previous version of the text box contents.

Here's the version of Notepad Clone that implements a File menu. Currently, three options involving printing are left unimplemented. I'll be supplying code for those items in Appendix 21, in the NotepadCloneWithPrinting program.

**NotepadCloneWithFile.vb**

```
'-------------------------------------------------------
' NotepadCloneWithFile.vb (c) 2002 by Charles Petzold
'-------------------------------------------------------
Imports Microsoft.Win32        ' For registry classes
Imports System
Imports System.ComponentModel  ' For CancelEventArgs class
Imports System.Drawing
Imports System.IO
Imports System.Text            ' For Encoding class
Imports System.Windows.Forms

Class NotepadCloneWithFile
    Inherits NotepadCloneWithRegistry
```

```
' Fields
Protected strFileName As String
Const strEncoding As String = "Encoding"      ' For registry
Const strFilter As String = _
                    "Text Documents(*.txt)|*.txt|All Files(*.*)|*.*"
Private miEncoding As MenuItem
Private mieChecked As MenuItemEncoding


' Entry point
Shared Shadows Sub Main()
    Application.Run(New NotepadCloneWithFile())
End Sub


' Constructor
Sub New()
    strProgName = "Notepad Clone with File"
    MakeCaption()

    Menu = New MainMenu()

    ' File menu
    Dim mi As New MenuItem("&File")
    Menu.MenuItems.Add(mi)
    Dim index As Integer = Menu.MenuItems.Count - 1

    ' File New
    mi = New MenuItem("&New")
    AddHandler mi.Click, AddressOf MenuFileNewOnClick
    mi.Shortcut = Shortcut.CtrlN
    Menu.MenuItems(index).MenuItems.Add(mi)

    ' File Open
    Dim miFileOpen As New MenuItem("&Open...")
    AddHandler miFileOpen.Click, AddressOf MenuFileOpenOnClick
    miFileOpen.Shortcut = Shortcut.CtrlO
    Menu.MenuItems(index).MenuItems.Add(miFileOpen)

    ' File Save
    Dim miFileSave As New MenuItem("&Save")
    AddHandler miFileSave.Click, AddressOf MenuFileSaveOnClick
    miFileSave.Shortcut = Shortcut.CtrlS
    Menu.MenuItems(index).MenuItems.Add(miFileSave)

    ' File Save As
    mi = New MenuItem("Save &As...")
    AddHandler mi.Click, AddressOf MenuFileSaveAsOnClick
    Menu.MenuItems(index).MenuItems.Add(mi)

    ' File Encoding
    miEncoding = New MenuItem("&Encoding")
    Menu.MenuItems(index).MenuItems.Add(miEncoding)
    Menu.MenuItems(index).MenuItems.Add("-")
```

*(continued)*

**NotepadCloneWithFile.vb** *(continued)*

```vb
        ' File Encoding submenu
        Dim eh As EventHandler = AddressOf MenuFileEncodingOnClick
        Dim astrEncodings() As String = {"&ASCII", "&Unicode", _
                                         "&Big-Endian Unicode", _
                                         "UTF-&7", "&UTF-&8"}
        Dim aenc() As Encoding = {Encoding.ASCII, Encoding.Unicode, _
                                  Encoding.BigEndianUnicode, _
                                  Encoding.UTF7, Encoding.UTF8}
        Dim i As Integer

        For i = 0 To astrEncodings.GetUpperBound(0)
            Dim mie As New MenuItemEncoding()
            mie.Text = astrEncodings(i)
            mie.encode = aenc(i)
            mie.RadioCheck = True
            AddHandler mie.Click, eh
            miEncoding.MenuItems.Add(mie)
        Next i
        ' Set default to UTF-8
        mieChecked = DirectCast(miEncoding.MenuItems(4), MenuItemEncoding)
        mieChecked.Checked = True

        ' File Page Setup
        mi = New MenuItem("Page Set&up...")
        AddHandler mi.Click, AddressOf MenuFileSetupOnClick
        Menu.MenuItems(index).MenuItems.Add(mi)

        ' File Print Preview
        mi = New MenuItem("Print Pre&view...")
        AddHandler mi.Click, AddressOf MenuFilePreviewOnClick
        Menu.MenuItems(index).MenuItems.Add(mi)

        ' File Print
        mi = New MenuItem("&Print...")
        AddHandler mi.Click, AddressOf MenuFilePrintOnClick
        mi.Shortcut = Shortcut.CtrlP
        Menu.MenuItems(index).MenuItems.Add(mi)
        Menu.MenuItems(index).MenuItems.Add("-")

        ' File Exit
        mi = New MenuItem("E&xit")
        AddHandler mi.Click, AddressOf MenuFileExitOnClick
        Menu.MenuItems(index).MenuItems.Add(mi)

        ' Set system event.
        AddHandler SystemEvents.SessionEnding, AddressOf OnSessionEnding
    End Sub

    ' Event overrides
    Protected Overrides Sub OnLoad(ByVal ea As EventArgs)
        MyBase.OnLoad(ea)
```

```
        ' Deal with the command-line argument.
        Dim astrArgs As String() = Environment.GetCommandLineArgs()
        If astrArgs.Length > 1 Then
            If File.Exists(astrArgs(1)) Then
                LoadFile(astrArgs(1))
            Else
                Dim dr As DialogResult = _
                    MessageBox.Show("Cannot find the " & _
                                    Path.GetFileName(astrArgs(1)) & _
                                    " file." & vbLf & vbLf & _
                                    "Do you want to create a new file?", _
                                    strProgName, _
                                    MessageBoxButtons.YesNoCancel, _
                                    MessageBoxIcon.Question)

                Select Case dr
                    Case DialogResult.Yes    ' Create and close file.
                        strFileName = astrArgs(1)
                        File.Create(strFileName).Close()
                        MakeCaption()

                    Case DialogResult.No     ' Don't do anything.

                    Case DialogResult.Cancel ' Close program
                        Close()
                End Select
            End If
        End If
End Sub

Protected Overrides Sub OnClosing(ByVal cea As CancelEventArgs)
    MyBase.OnClosing(cea)
    cea.Cancel = Not OkToTrash()
End Sub

' Event handlers
Private Sub OnSessionEnding(ByVal obj As Object, _
                           ByVal seea As SessionEndingEventArgs)
    seea.Cancel = Not OkToTrash()
End Sub

' Menu items
Sub MenuFileNewOnClick(ByVal obj As Object, ByVal ea As EventArgs)
    If Not OkToTrash() Then Return

    txtbox.Clear()
    txtbox.ClearUndo()
    txtbox.Modified = False
    strFileName = Nothing
    MakeCaption()
End Sub

Sub MenuFileOpenOnClick(ByVal obj As Object, ByVal ea As EventArgs)
    If Not OkToTrash() Then Return
```

*(continued)*

**NotepadCloneWithFile.vb**  *(continued)*

```
        Dim ofd As New OpenFileDialog()
        ofd.Filter = strFilter
        ofd.FileName = "*.txt"
        If ofd.ShowDialog() = DialogResult.OK Then LoadFile(ofd.FileName)
    End Sub

    Sub MenuFileEncodingOnClick(ByVal obj As Object, ByVal ea As EventArgs)
        mieChecked.Checked = False
        mieChecked = DirectCast(obj, MenuItemEncoding)
        mieChecked.Checked = True
    End Sub

    Sub MenuFileSaveOnClick(ByVal obj As Object, ByVal ea As EventArgs)
        If strFileName Is Nothing OrElse strFileName.Length = 0 Then
            SaveFileDlg()
        Else
            SaveFile()
        End If
    End Sub

    Sub MenuFileSaveAsOnClick(ByVal obj As Object, ByVal ea As EventArgs)
        SaveFileDlg()
    End Sub

    Protected Overridable Sub MenuFileSetupOnClick(ByVal obj As Object, _
                                                ByVal ea As EventArgs)
        MessageBox.Show("Page Setup not yet implemented!", strProgName)
    End Sub

    Protected Overridable Sub MenuFilePreviewOnClick(ByVal obj As Object, _
                                                ByVal ea As EventArgs)
        MessageBox.Show("Print Preview not yet implemented!", strProgName)
    End Sub

    Protected Overridable Sub MenuFilePrintOnClick(ByVal obj As Object, _
                                                ByVal ea As EventArgs)
        MessageBox.Show("Print not yet implemented!", strProgName)
    End Sub

    Sub MenuFileExitOnClick(ByVal obj As Object, ByVal ea As EventArgs)
        If OkToTrash() Then Application.Exit()
    End Sub

    ' Method overrides
    Protected Overrides Sub LoadRegistryInfo(ByVal regkey As RegistryKey)
        MyBase.LoadRegistryInfo(regkey)

        ' Set encoding setting.
        Dim index As Integer = DirectCast(regkey.GetValue(strEncoding, 4), _
                                    Integer)
        mieChecked.Checked = False
```

```
        mieChecked = DirectCast(miEncoding.MenuItems(index), _
                                MenuItemEncoding)
        mieChecked.Checked = True
End Sub

Protected Overrides Sub SaveRegistryInfo(ByVal regkey As RegistryKey)
    MyBase.SaveRegistryInfo(regkey)
    regkey.SetValue(strEncoding, mieChecked.Index)
End Sub

' Utility routines
Protected Sub LoadFile(ByVal strFileName As String)
    Dim sr As StreamReader
    Try
        sr = New StreamReader(strFileName)
    Catch exc As Exception
        MessageBox.Show(exc.Message, strProgName, _
                        MessageBoxButtons.OK, _
                        MessageBoxIcon.Asterisk)
        Return
    End Try

    txtbox.Text = sr.ReadToEnd()
    sr.Close()
    Me.strFileName = strFileName
    MakeCaption()

    txtbox.SelectionStart = 0
    txtbox.SelectionLength = 0
    txtbox.Modified = False
    txtbox.ClearUndo()
End Sub

Private Sub SaveFile()
    Try
        Dim sw As New StreamWriter(strFileName, False, _
                                   mieChecked.encode)
        sw.Write(txtbox.Text)
        sw.Close()
    Catch exc As Exception
        MessageBox.Show(exc.Message, strProgName, _
                        MessageBoxButtons.OK, _
                        MessageBoxIcon.Asterisk)
        Return
    End Try
    txtbox.Modified = False
End Sub

Private Function SaveFileDlg() As Boolean
    Dim sfd As New SaveFileDialog()

    If Not strFileName Is Nothing AndAlso strFileName.Length > 1 Then
        sfd.FileName = strFileName
```

*(continued)*

**NotepadCloneWithFile.vb**    *(continued)*

```
        Else
            sfd.FileName = "*.txt"
        End If

        sfd.Filter = strFilter

        If sfd.ShowDialog() = DialogResult.OK Then
            strFileName = sfd.FileName
            SaveFile()
            MakeCaption()
            Return True
        Else
            Return False    ' Return values are for OkToTrash.
        End If
    End Function

    Protected Sub MakeCaption()
        Text = strProgName & " - " & FileTitle()
    End Sub

    Protected Function FileTitle() As String
        If Not strFileName = Nothing AndAlso strFileName.Length > 1 Then
            Return Path.GetFileName(strFileName)
        Else
            Return "Untitled"
        End If
    End Function

    Protected Function OkToTrash() As Boolean
        If Not txtbox.Modified Then
            Return True
        End If
        Dim dr As DialogResult = _
                MessageBox.Show("The text in the " & FileTitle() & _
                                " file has changed." & vbLf & vbLf & _
                                "Do you want to save the changes?", _
                                strProgName, _
                                MessageBoxButtons.YesNoCancel, _
                                MessageBoxIcon.Exclamation)
        Select Case dr
            Case DialogResult.Yes : Return SaveFileDlg()
            Case DialogResult.No : Return True
            Case DialogResult.Cancel : Return False
        End Select
        Return False
    End Function
End Class

Class MenuItemEncoding
    Inherits MenuItem

    Public encode As Encoding
End Class
```

Although using the File Open menu option is the most common way of loading a file into Windows Notepad, you can also run Notepad from a command line and specify a file as an argument. NotepadCloneWithFile likewise overrides the *OnLoad* method and attempts to load a file specified as a command-line argument.

The Notepad program includes a special combo box in the Save As dialog box that lets you specify a file encoding.

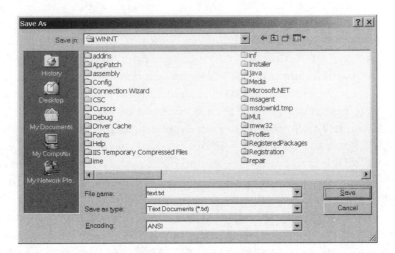

See it at the bottom? The options are ANSI, Unicode, Unicode Big Endian, and UTF-8. (If you're unfamiliar with these terms and the encoding of text files under Windows, you'll probably want to read the section on "Reading and Writing Text" in *Appendix A*.)

Unfortunately, Windows Forms programs don't have quite the same flexibility as Windows API programs in enhancing the common dialog boxes. For this reason, I've added an Encoding item to the File menu. This item invokes another submenu that lists five encoding options: ASCII, Unicode, Big-Endian Unicode, UTF-7, and UTF-8. A small *MenuItemEncoding* class overrides *MenuItem* so that the appropriate object of the *Encoding* class can be stored along with each of these five items.

NotepadCloneWithFile overrides the *SaveRegistryInfo* and *LoadRegistryInfo* methods in NotepadCloneWithRegistry to save and later reload the character encoding the user selects. Notice that these methods call the methods in the base class so that the program continues to save and load the location and size of the window.

# Notepad Clone Continued

The next program we're going to look at is NotepadCloneWithEdit. This program derives from NotepadCloneWithFile and implements an Edit menu. The Edit menu would be more difficult than it is (and would require material I won't cover until Appendix 24) were it not for the built-in support that *TextBoxBase* has for the clipboard. Even with the earliest program in the Notepad Clone series, you can type CTRL+Z, CTRL+X, CTRL+C, and CTRL+V to perform undo, cut, copy, and paste operations.

As I mentioned earlier, the undo operation restores the text of the text box to a previous version. Both the cut and copy operations copy the selected text to the clipboard. In addition, the cut operation deletes the text. The paste operation copies text from the clipboard to the text box. If text is selected at the time of the paste operation, the selection is replaced by the pasted text.

Although *TextBoxBase* supports these operations directly, Undo, Cut, Copy, and Paste should also be options on the Edit menu. In addition, a Delete item (with a Delete key shortcut) should delete selected text without copying it to the clipboard. (In some applications, a Clear menu item does the work of Delete.) Interestingly enough, if you simply create an Edit menu with these items—and you specify the appropriate *Shortcut* properties—you effectively disable the ability of the text box to respond to these keystrokes! The reason for this behavior is that the menu gets priority over keystrokes, and if (for example) CTRL+C is a shortcut in a menu item, that keystroke is consumed by the menu and never reaches the text box.

You can get the shortcuts to work in the text box again by installing *Click* event handlers for the Undo, Cut, Copy, Paste, and Delete menu items and by calling the following five methods in response to the events:

### *TextBoxBase* Methods (selection)

```
Sub Undo()
Sub Cut()
Sub Copy()
Sub Paste()
Sub Clear()
```

You'll also want to install a *Popup* event handler for the Edit menu to enable and disable these five items appropriately. You can enable the Undo item based on the return value of the following property:

## *TextBoxBase* Properties (selection)

| Property | Type | Accessibility |
|----------|------|---------------|
| *CanUndo* | *Boolean* | Get |

Enable the Cut, Copy, and Delete (or Clear) menu items only if the *Selection-Length* property is greater than 0. Otherwise, there's no selected text to delete or copy to the clipboard.

The tough one is Paste. The Paste menu item should be enabled only if there's text in the clipboard. Until Appendix 24, I'm afraid you'll just have to take my word for it that you should enable the Paste item if the following expression returns *True*:

```
Clipboard.GetDataObject().GetDataPresent(GetType(String))
```

*GetDataObject* is a shared method of *Clipboard* that returns an object of type *IDataObject*. *GetDataPresent* is a method of that interface that returns *True* if the clipboard contains data of the type specified by its argument, which in this case is a *String*.

If the Edit menu contained only Undo, Cut, Copy, Paste, and Delete, it would be a snap. Even a Select All option can be implemented by a call to *SelectAll*, and the Time/Date item found on Notepad's Edit menu is also easy using the *ToString* method of the *DateTime* class. But Notepad's Edit menu also includes Find, Find Next, Replace, and Go To, the latter of which lets the user jump to a particular line of the document. I decided not to implement the Go To item, primarily because the text box controls are missing a method that indicates the character offset of a specified line. (In Win32 API programming, this facility is provided by the *EM_LINEINDEX* message.) I'll make up for this omission in the Format menu, when I allow you to do something Notepad doesn't: select a text color and a background color.

The following file supports dialog boxes for Find and Replace. Both *Find-Dialog* and *ReplaceDialog* are descended from the *MustInherit* class *FindReplace-Dialog*. The *FindReplaceDialog* class creates all the controls common to both dialog boxes. The two classes descended from *FindReplaceDialog* disable certain of these controls and (in one case) move a button to a more appropriate location.

```
FindReplaceDialog.vb
'---------------------------------------------------------
' FindReplaceDialog.vb (c) 2002 by Charles Petzold
'---------------------------------------------------------
Imports System
Imports System.Drawing
Imports System.Windows.Forms
```

*(continued)*

**FindReplaceDialog.vb** *(continued)*

```
Class FindDialog
    Inherits FindReplaceDialog

    Sub New()
        Text = "Find"
        lblReplace.Visible = False
        txtboxReplace.Visible = False
        btnReplace.Visible = False
        btnReplaceAll.Visible = False
        btnCancel.Location = btnReplace.Location
    End Sub
End Class

Class ReplaceDialog
    Inherits FindReplaceDialog

    Sub New()
        Text = "Replace"
        grpboxDirection.Visible = False
    End Sub
End Class

MustInherit Class FindReplaceDialog
    Inherits Form

    ' Fields
    Protected lblFind, lblReplace As Label
    Protected txtboxFind, txtboxReplace As TextBox
    Protected chkboxMatchCase As CheckBox
    Protected grpboxDirection As GroupBox
    Protected radbtnUp, radbtnDown As RadioButton
    Protected btnFindNext, btnReplace, btnReplaceAll, btnCancel As Button

    ' Public events
    Event FindNext As EventHandler
    Event Replace As EventHandler
    Event ReplaceAll As EventHandler
    Event CloseDlg As EventHandler

    ' Constructor
    Sub New()
        FormBorderStyle = FormBorderStyle.FixedDialog
        ControlBox = False
        MinimizeBox = False
        MaximizeBox = False
        ShowInTaskbar = False
        StartPosition = FormStartPosition.Manual
        Location = Point.op_Addition(ActiveForm.Location, _
                    Size.op_Addition(SystemInformation.CaptionButtonSize, _
                                SystemInformation.FrameBorderSize))
```

```
lblFind = New Label()
lblFind.Parent = Me
lblFind.Text = "Fi&nd what:"
lblFind.Location = New Point(8, 8)
lblFind.Size = New Size(64, 8)

txtboxFind = New TextBox()
txtboxFind.Parent = Me
txtboxFind.Location = New Point(72, 8)
txtboxFind.Size = New Size(136, 8)
AddHandler txtboxFind.TextChanged, _
                        AddressOf TextBoxFindOnTextChanged

lblReplace = New Label()
lblReplace.Parent = Me
lblReplace.Text = "Re&place with:"
lblReplace.Location = New Point(8, 24)
lblReplace.Size = New Size(64, 8)

txtboxReplace = New TextBox()
txtboxReplace.Parent = Me
txtboxReplace.Location = New Point(72, 24)
txtboxReplace.Size = New Size(136, 8)

chkboxMatchCase = New CheckBox()
chkboxMatchCase.Parent = Me
chkboxMatchCase.Text = "Match &case"
chkboxMatchCase.Location = New Point(8, 50)
chkboxMatchCase.Size = New Size(64, 8)

grpboxDirection = New GroupBox()
grpboxDirection.Parent = Me
grpboxDirection.Text = "Direction"
grpboxDirection.Location = New Point(100, 40)
grpboxDirection.Size = New Size(96, 24)

radbtnUp = New RadioButton()
radbtnUp.Parent = grpboxDirection
radbtnUp.Text = "&Up"
radbtnUp.Location = New Point(8, 8)
radbtnUp.Size = New Size(32, 12)

radbtnDown = New RadioButton()
radbtnDown.Parent = grpboxDirection
radbtnDown.Text = "&Down"
radbtnDown.Location = New Point(40, 8)
radbtnDown.Size = New Size(40, 12)

btnFindNext = New Button()
btnFindNext.Parent = Me
btnFindNext.Text = "&Find Next"
```

*(continued)*

**FindReplaceDialog.vb**   *(continued)*

```
        btnFindNext.Enabled = False
        btnFindNext.Location = New Point(216, 4)
        btnFindNext.Size = New Size(64, 16)
        AddHandler btnFindNext.Click, AddressOf ButtonFindNextOnClick

        btnReplace = New Button()
        btnReplace.Parent = Me
        btnReplace.Text = "&Replace"
        btnReplace.Enabled = False
        btnReplace.Location = New Point(216, 24)
        btnReplace.Size = New Size(64, 16)
        AddHandler btnReplace.Click, AddressOf ButtonReplaceOnClick

        btnReplaceAll = New Button()
        btnReplaceAll.Parent = Me
        btnReplaceAll.Text = "Replace &All"
        btnReplaceAll.Enabled = False
        btnReplaceAll.Location = New Point(216, 44)
        btnReplaceAll.Size = New Size(64, 16)
        AddHandler btnReplaceAll.Click, AddressOf ButtonReplaceAllOnClick

        btnCancel = New Button()
        btnCancel.Parent = Me
        btnCancel.Text = "Cancel"
        btnCancel.Location = New Point(216, 64)
        btnCancel.Size = New Size(64, 16)
        AddHandler btnCancel.Click, AddressOf ButtonCancelOnClick
        CancelButton = btnCancel

        ClientSize = New Size(288, 84)
        AutoScaleBaseSize = New Size(4, 8)
    End Sub

    ' Properties
    Property FindText() As String
        Set(ByVal Value As String)
            txtboxFind.Text = Value
        End Set
        Get
            Return txtboxFind.Text
        End Get
    End Property

    Property ReplaceText() As String
        Set(ByVal Value As String)
            txtboxReplace.Text = Value
        End Set
        Get
            Return txtboxReplace.Text
        End Get
    End Property
```

```
        Property MatchCase() As Boolean
            Set(ByVal Value As Boolean)
                chkboxMatchCase.Checked = Value
            End Set
            Get
                Return chkboxMatchCase.Checked
            End Get
        End Property

        Property FindDown() As Boolean
            Set(ByVal Value As Boolean)
                If Value Then
                    radbtnDown.Checked = True
                Else
                    radbtnUp.Checked = True
                End If
            End Set
            Get
                Return radbtnDown.Checked
            End Get
        End Property

        ' Event handlers
        Sub TextBoxFindOnTextChanged(ByVal obj As Object, ByVal ea As EventArgs)
            btnReplace.Enabled = txtboxFind.Text.Length > 0
            btnFindNext.Enabled = btnReplace.Enabled
            btnReplaceAll.Enabled = btnReplace.Enabled
        End Sub

        Sub ButtonFindNextOnClick(ByVal obj As Object, ByVal ea As EventArgs)
            RaiseEvent FindNext(Me, EventArgs.Empty)
        End Sub

        Sub ButtonReplaceOnClick(ByVal obj As Object, ByVal ea As EventArgs)
            RaiseEvent Replace(Me, EventArgs.Empty)
        End Sub

        Sub ButtonReplaceAllOnClick(ByVal obj As Object, ByVal ea As EventArgs)
            RaiseEvent ReplaceAll(Me, EventArgs.Empty)
        End Sub

        Sub ButtonCancelOnClick(ByVal obj As Object, ByVal ea As EventArgs)
            RaiseEvent CloseDlg(Me, EventArgs.Empty)
            Close()
        End Sub
End Class
```

*FindReplaceDialog* has four properties that give the main program access to the text of two text boxes (the "find" text and the "replace" text), the Match Case check box, and the pair of radio buttons for specifying a search up or down in the document.

*FindDialog* and *ReplaceDialog* are both intended to be modeless dialog boxes. Indeed, these are classic examples of dialog boxes that work best by being modeless. You want the dialog box to be up and visible as you perform a repetitive search or replace operation. As you know from Chapter 16, modeless dialog boxes usually communicate to the underlying program through events. FindReplaceDialog defines four public events:

```
Event FindNext As EventHandler
Event Replace As EventHandler
Event ReplaceAll As EventHandler
Event CloseDlg As EventHandler
```

These events are triggered when the user presses the dialog box buttons labeled Find Next, Replace, Replace All, and Cancel.

Here's NotepadCloneWithEdit, which adds an Edit menu and implements all the items on that menu.

**NotepadCloneWithEdit.vb**
```
'-------------------------------------------------------
' NotepadCloneWithEdit.vb (c) 2002 by Charles Petzold
'-------------------------------------------------------
Imports System
Imports System.Drawing
Imports System.Windows.Forms

Class NotepadCloneWithEdit
    Inherits NotepadCloneWithFile

    Private miEditUndo, miEditCut, miEditCopy As MenuItem
    Private miEditPaste, miEditDelete As MenuItem
    Private strFind As String = ""
    Private strReplace As String = ""
    Private bMatchCase As Boolean = False
    Private bFindDown As Boolean = True

    Shared Shadows Sub Main()
        Application.Run(New NotepadCloneWithEdit())
    End Sub

    Sub New()
        strProgName = "Notepad Clone with Edit"
        MakeCaption()

        ' Edit menu
        Dim mi As New MenuItem("&Edit")
        AddHandler mi.Popup, AddressOf MenuEditOnPopup
        Menu.MenuItems.Add(mi)
        Dim index As Integer = Menu.MenuItems.Count - 1
```

```
' Edit Undo menu item
miEditUndo = New MenuItem("&Undo")
AddHandler miEditUndo.Click, AddressOf MenuEditUndoOnClick
miEditUndo.Shortcut = Shortcut.CtrlZ
Menu.MenuItems(index).MenuItems.Add(miEditUndo)
Menu.MenuItems(index).MenuItems.Add("-")

' Edit Cut menu item
miEditCut = New MenuItem("Cu&t")
AddHandler miEditCut.Click, AddressOf MenuEditCutOnClick
miEditCut.Shortcut = Shortcut.CtrlX
Menu.MenuItems(index).MenuItems.Add(miEditCut)

' Edit Copy menu item
miEditCopy = New MenuItem("&Copy")
AddHandler miEditCopy.Click, AddressOf MenuEditCopyOnClick
miEditCopy.Shortcut = Shortcut.CtrlC
Menu.MenuItems(index).MenuItems.Add(miEditCopy)

' Edit Paste menu item
miEditPaste = New MenuItem("&Paste")
AddHandler miEditPaste.Click, AddressOf MenuEditPasteOnClick
miEditPaste.Shortcut = Shortcut.CtrlV
Menu.MenuItems(index).MenuItems.Add(miEditPaste)

' Edit Delete menu item
miEditDelete = New MenuItem("De&lete")
AddHandler miEditDelete.Click, AddressOf MenuEditDeleteOnClick
miEditDelete.Shortcut = Shortcut.Del
Menu.MenuItems(index).MenuItems.Add(miEditDelete)
Menu.MenuItems(index).MenuItems.Add("-")

' Edit Find menu item
mi = New MenuItem("&Find...")
AddHandler mi.Click, AddressOf MenuEditFindOnClick
mi.Shortcut = Shortcut.CtrlF
Menu.MenuItems(index).MenuItems.Add(mi)

' Edit Find Next menu item
mi = New MenuItem("Find &Next")
AddHandler mi.Click, AddressOf MenuEditFindNextOnClick
mi.Shortcut = Shortcut.F3
Menu.MenuItems(index).MenuItems.Add(mi)

' Edit Replace menu item
mi = New MenuItem("&Replace...")
AddHandler mi.Click, AddressOf MenuEditReplaceOnClick
mi.Shortcut = Shortcut.CtrlH
Menu.MenuItems(index).MenuItems.Add(mi)
Menu.MenuItems(index).MenuItems.Add("-")
```

*(continued)*

**NotepadCloneWithEdit.vb** *(continued)*

```vb
    ' Edit Select All menu item
    mi = New MenuItem("Select &All")
    AddHandler mi.Click, AddressOf MenuEditSelectAllOnClick
    mi.Shortcut = Shortcut.CtrlA
    Menu.MenuItems(index).MenuItems.Add(mi)

    ' Edit Time/Date menu item
    mi = New MenuItem("Time/&Date")
    AddHandler mi.Click, AddressOf MenuEditTimeDateOnClick
    mi.Shortcut = Shortcut.F5
    Menu.MenuItems(index).MenuItems.Add(mi)
End Sub

Sub MenuEditOnPopup(ByVal obj As Object, ByVal ea As EventArgs)
    miEditUndo.Enabled = txtbox.CanUndo

    miEditCopy.Enabled = txtbox.SelectionLength > 0
    miEditCut.Enabled = miEditCopy.Enabled
    miEditDelete.Enabled = miEditCopy.Enabled

    miEditPaste.Enabled = _
        Clipboard.GetDataObject().GetDataPresent(GetType(String))
End Sub

Sub MenuEditUndoOnClick(ByVal obj As Object, ByVal ea As EventArgs)
    txtbox.Undo()
    txtbox.ClearUndo()
End Sub

Sub MenuEditCutOnClick(ByVal obj As Object, ByVal ea As EventArgs)
    txtbox.Cut()
End Sub

Sub MenuEditCopyOnClick(ByVal obj As Object, ByVal ea As EventArgs)
    txtbox.Copy()
End Sub

Sub MenuEditPasteOnClick(ByVal obj As Object, ByVal ea As EventArgs)
    txtbox.Paste()
End Sub

Sub MenuEditDeleteOnClick(ByVal obj As Object, ByVal ea As EventArgs)
    txtbox.Clear()
End Sub

Sub MenuEditFindOnClick(ByVal obj As Object, ByVal ea As EventArgs)
    If OwnedForms.Length > 0 Then Return

    txtbox.HideSelection = False
    Dim dlg As New FindDialog()
    dlg.Owner = Me
```

```
        dlg.FindText = strFind
        dlg.MatchCase = bMatchCase
        dlg.FindDown = bFindDown
        AddHandler dlg.FindNext, AddressOf FindDialogOnFindNext
        AddHandler dlg.CloseDlg, AddressOf FindReplaceDialogOnCloseDlg
        dlg.Show()
    End Sub

    Sub MenuEditFindNextOnClick(ByVal obj As Object, ByVal ea As EventArgs)
        If strFind.Length = 0 Then
            If OwnedForms.Length > 0 Then Return
            MenuEditFindOnClick(obj, ea)
        Else
            FindNext()
        End If
    End Sub

    Sub MenuEditReplaceOnClick(ByVal obj As Object, ByVal ea As EventArgs)
        If OwnedForms.Length > 0 Then Return

        txtbox.HideSelection = False
        Dim dlg As New ReplaceDialog()
        dlg.Owner = Me
        dlg.FindText = strFind
        dlg.ReplaceText = strReplace
        dlg.MatchCase = bMatchCase
        dlg.FindDown = bFindDown
        AddHandler dlg.FindNext, AddressOf FindDialogOnFindNext
        AddHandler dlg.Replace, AddressOf ReplaceDialogOnReplace
        AddHandler dlg.ReplaceAll, AddressOf ReplaceDialogOnReplaceAll
        AddHandler dlg.CloseDlg, AddressOf FindReplaceDialogOnCloseDlg
        dlg.Show()
    End Sub

    Sub MenuEditSelectAllOnClick(ByVal obj As Object, ByVal ea As EventArgs)
        txtbox.SelectAll()
    End Sub

    Sub MenuEditTimeDateOnClick(ByVal obj As Object, ByVal ea As EventArgs)
        Dim dt As DateTime = DateTime.Now
        txtbox.SelectedText = dt.ToString("t") & " " & dt.ToString("d")
    End Sub

    Sub FindDialogOnFindNext(ByVal obj As Object, ByVal ea As EventArgs)
        Dim dlg As FindReplaceDialog = DirectCast(obj, FindReplaceDialog)
        strFind = dlg.FindText
        bMatchCase = dlg.MatchCase
        bFindDown = dlg.FindDown
        FindNext()
    End Sub
```

*(continued)*

**NotepadCloneWithEdit.vb**   *(continued)*

```
Private Function FindNext() As Boolean
    If bFindDown Then
        Dim iStart As Integer = txtbox.SelectionStart + _
                                txtbox.SelectionLength
        While iStart + strFind.Length <= txtbox.TextLength
            If String.Compare(strFind, 0, txtbox.Text, iStart, _
                              strFind.Length, Not bMatchCase) = 0 Then
                txtbox.SelectionStart = iStart
                txtbox.SelectionLength = strFind.Length
                Return True
            End If
            iStart += 1
        End While
    Else
        Dim iStart As Integer = txtbox.SelectionStart - strFind.Length
        While iStart >= 0
            If String.Compare(strFind, 0, txtbox.Text, iStart, _
                              strFind.Length, Not bMatchCase) = 0 Then
                txtbox.SelectionStart = iStart
                txtbox.SelectionLength = strFind.Length
                Return True
            End If
            iStart -= 1
        End While
    End If
    MessageBox.Show("Cannot find """ & strFind & """", strProgName, _
                    MessageBoxButtons.OK, MessageBoxIcon.Exclamation)
    Return False
End Function

Sub ReplaceDialogOnReplace(ByVal obj As Object, ByVal ea As EventArgs)
    Dim dlg As FindReplaceDialog = DirectCast(obj, FindReplaceDialog)
    strFind = dlg.FindText
    strReplace = dlg.ReplaceText
    bMatchCase = dlg.MatchCase
    If String.Compare(strFind, txtbox.SelectedText, _
                      Not bMatchCase) = 0 Then
        txtbox.SelectedText = strReplace
    End If
    FindNext()
End Sub

Sub ReplaceDialogOnReplaceAll(ByVal obj As Object, _
                              ByVal ea As EventArgs)
    Dim dlg As FindReplaceDialog = DirectCast(obj, FindReplaceDialog)
    Dim str As String = txtbox.Text
    strFind = dlg.FindText
    strReplace = dlg.ReplaceText
    bMatchCase = dlg.MatchCase
    If bMatchCase Then
        str = str.Replace(strFind, strReplace)
```

```
        Else
            Dim i As Integer
            For i = 0 To str.Length - strFind.Length - 1 Step 0
                If String.Compare(str, i, strFind, 0, _
                                  strFind.Length, True) = 0 Then
                    str = str.Remove(i, strFind.Length)
                    str = str.Insert(i, strReplace)
                    i += strReplace.Length
                Else
                    i += 1
                End If
            Next i
        End If
        If str <> txtbox.Text Then
            txtbox.Text = str
            txtbox.SelectionStart = 0
            txtbox.SelectionLength = 0
            txtbox.Modified = True
        End If
    End Sub

    Sub FindReplaceDialogOnCloseDlg(ByVal obj As Object, _
                                    ByVal ea As EventArgs)
        txtbox.HideSelection = True
    End Sub
End Class
```

When a menu item invokes a modeless dialog box, you usually don't want the item to invoke multiple copies of the dialog box. For that reason, the Find and Replace menu items check whether the *OwnedForms* property (which returns an array of *Form* objects) has a *Length* property greater than 0. If it does, one of the modeless dialog boxes is up and another shouldn't be displayed. As usual, the *Owner* property of the modeless dialog box is assigned *Me*, referring to the program itself. When the program creates either of the two modeless dialog boxes, it also installs event handlers for the events implemented by the dialog boxes. It's in response to these events that the program does most of its work. For the actual search logic, the program uses the *Compare* method of the *String* class. For replacing text, it uses *Remove* and *Insert*. These methods are described in Appendix C.

The next installment in the Notepad Clone series is comparatively simple. It implements the Format menu, which expands on the Notepad functionality by including Background Color along with the standard Word Wrap and Font options. Word Wrap is simply a checked menu item, while the Font and Background Color items make use of *FontDialog* and *ColorDialog*.

**NotepadCloneWithFormat.vb**

```vb
'--------------------------------------------------------
' NotepadCloneWithFormat.vb (c) 2002 by Charles Petzold
'--------------------------------------------------------
Imports Microsoft.Win32
Imports System
Imports System.Drawing
Imports System.Windows.Forms

Class NotepadCloneWithFormat
    Inherits NotepadCloneWithEdit

    ' Strings for registry
    Const strWordWrap As String = "WordWrap"
    Const strFontFace As String = "FontFace"
    Const strFontSize As String = "FontSize"
    Const strFontStyle As String = "FontStyle"
    Const strForeColor As String = "ForeColor"
    Const strBackColor As String = "BackColor"
    Const strCustomClr As String = "CustomColor"

    Private clrdlg As New ColorDialog()
    Private miFormatWrap As MenuItem

    Shared Shadows Sub Main()
        Application.Run(New NotepadCloneWithFormat())
    End Sub

    Sub New()
        strProgName = "Notepad Clone with Format"
        MakeCaption()

        ' Format
        Dim mi As New MenuItem("F&ormat")
        AddHandler mi.Popup, AddressOf MenuFormatOnPopup
        Menu.MenuItems.Add(mi)
        Dim index As Integer = Menu.MenuItems.Count - 1

        ' Format Word Wrap
        miFormatWrap = New MenuItem("&Word Wrap")
        AddHandler miFormatWrap.Click, AddressOf MenuFormatWrapOnClick
        Menu.MenuItems(index).MenuItems.Add(miFormatWrap)

        ' Format Font
        mi = New MenuItem("&Font...")
        AddHandler mi.Click, AddressOf MenuFormatFontOnClick
        Menu.MenuItems(index).MenuItems.Add(mi)

        ' Format Background Color
        mi = New MenuItem("Background &Color...")
        AddHandler mi.Click, AddressOf MenuFormatColorOnClick
        Menu.MenuItems(index).MenuItems.Add(mi)
    End Sub
```

```vbnet
Protected Overrides Sub OnLoad(ByVal ea As EventArgs)
    MyBase.OnLoad(ea)

    ' Help
    Dim mi As New MenuItem("&Help")
    Menu.MenuItems.Add(mi)
    Dim index As Integer = Menu.MenuItems.Count - 1

    ' Help About
    mi = New MenuItem("&About " & strProgName & "...")
    AddHandler mi.Click, AddressOf MenuHelpAboutOnClick
    Menu.MenuItems(index).MenuItems.Add(mi)
End Sub

Sub MenuFormatOnPopup(ByVal obj As Object, ByVal ea As EventArgs)
    miFormatWrap.Checked = txtbox.WordWrap
End Sub

Sub MenuFormatWrapOnClick(ByVal obj As Object, ByVal ea As EventArgs)
    Dim mi As MenuItem = DirectCast(obj, MenuItem)
    mi.Checked = mi.Checked Xor True
    txtbox.WordWrap = mi.Checked
End Sub

Sub MenuFormatFontOnClick(ByVal obj As Object, ByVal ea As EventArgs)
    Dim fntdlg As New FontDialog()
    fntdlg.ShowColor = True
    fntdlg.Font = txtbox.Font
    fntdlg.Color = txtbox.ForeColor
    If fntdlg.ShowDialog() = DialogResult.OK Then
        txtbox.Font = fntdlg.Font
        txtbox.ForeColor = fntdlg.Color
    End If
End Sub

Sub MenuFormatColorOnClick(ByVal obj As Object, ByVal ea As EventArgs)
    clrdlg.Color = txtbox.BackColor
    If clrdlg.ShowDialog() = DialogResult.OK Then
        txtbox.BackColor = clrdlg.Color
    End If
End Sub

Sub MenuHelpAboutOnClick(ByVal obj As Object, ByVal ea As EventArgs)
    MessageBox.Show(strProgName & " " & Chr(169) & _
                    " 2002 by Charles Petzold", strProgName)
End Sub

Protected Overrides Sub LoadRegistryInfo(ByVal regkey As RegistryKey)
    MyBase.LoadRegistryInfo(regkey)
    txtbox.WordWrap = CBool(regkey.GetValue(strWordWrap))
    txtbox.Font = New Font( _
        DirectCast(regkey.GetValue(strFontFace), String), _
```

*(continued)*

**NotepadCloneWithFormat.vb** *(continued)*

```
            Single.Parse(DirectCast(regkey.GetValue(strFontSize), _
                                    String)), _
            CType(regkey.GetValue(strFontStyle), FontStyle))
        txtbox.ForeColor = Color.FromArgb( _
                            CInt(regkey.GetValue(strForeColor)))
        txtbox.BackColor = Color.FromArgb( _
                            CInt(regkey.GetValue(strBackColor)))

        Dim i, aiColors(16) As Integer

        For i = 0 To 15
            aiColors(i) = CInt(regkey.GetValue(strCustomClr & i))
        Next i
        clrdlg.CustomColors = aiColors
    End Sub

    Protected Overrides Sub SaveRegistryInfo(ByVal regkey As RegistryKey)
        MyBase.SaveRegistryInfo(regkey)
        regkey.SetValue(strWordWrap, CInt(txtbox.WordWrap))
        regkey.SetValue(strFontFace, txtbox.Font.Name)
        regkey.SetValue(strFontSize, txtbox.Font.SizeInPoints.ToString())
        regkey.SetValue(strFontStyle, CInt(txtbox.Font.Style))
        regkey.SetValue(strForeColor, txtbox.ForeColor.ToArgb())
        regkey.SetValue(strBackColor, txtbox.BackColor.ToArgb())

        Dim i As Integer
        For i = 0 To 15
            regkey.SetValue(strCustomClr & i, clrdlg.CustomColors(i))
        Next i
    End Sub
End Class
```

This version of the program also implements a Help menu that includes an About item. I moved the creation of this item to yet another override of the *OnLoad* method. Doing so allows the About item to include the *strProgName* field indicating the name of the program. If the About item were created in the constructor, any program that derived from this one would have the wrong program name in the menu item.

All the options you specify on the Format menu are saved in the registry, so this program again overrides the *LoadRegistryInfo* and *SaveRegistryInfo* methods.

In Appendix 21, I'll enhance the Notepad Clone program by implementing the three items on the File menu involved with printing (in NotepadCloneWith-Printing). In Appendix 24, I'll complete the program (finally named simply *NotepadClone*) by adding drag-and-drop functionality. You'll be able to drag a file or selected text from another application into the program.

# Special-Purpose Text Boxes

Although text boxes are used most often to allow a user to enter and edit text, they have a couple special-purpose uses as well, which are indicated by the following properties:

### *TextBox* Properties (selection)

| Property | Type | Accessibility |
|---|---|---|
| *PasswordChar* | *Char* | Get/Set |
| *CharacterCasing* | *CharacterCasing* | Get/Set |
| *ReadOnly* | *Boolean* | Get/Set |

You can use a text box in situations where the user must enter a password or other information that should be hidden from others. Normally, *Password-Char* is 0, but if you set it to something else, everything the user types in the text box will appear as that character. Generally, password boxes use an asterisk for this purpose. The *Multiline* property must be *False* for *PasswordChar* to work.

Sometimes in connection with password entry, text must be converted to uppercase or lowercase. That's the purpose of the *CharacterCasing* property. Set it to one of the following values:

### *CharacterCasing* Enumeration

| Member | Value |
|---|---|
| *Normal* | 0 |
| *Upper* | 1 |
| *Lower* | 2 |

The *ReadOnly* property is defined in *TextBoxBase* and also applies to *RichTextBox* controls. If this property is set to *True*, the user can't type anything into the text box. However, the text box still has a caret, and text can still be selected and copied to the clipboard. A read-only text box is an excellent choice for programs that must display textual information to the user, particularly when the length of the information can't be anticipated. While a *Label* control might work fine for short strings, the *TextBox* lets the user scroll longer blocks of text. The ability to copy text from the text box to the clipboard is an added bonus. The next program in this chapter (EnumerateEnumeration) uses a read-only text box.

# The Rich Text Box

I haven't gone into many details about *RichTextBox* because, I'm afraid, the topic is just too big for this book. The class is so named for two reasons. First, it supports *rich text*, which means formatted text—text that can have a variety of fonts, paragraph indents, and tabs. The second reason is that *RichTextBox* imports and exports text according to the specification known as the Rich Text Format (RTF). RTF was developed at Microsoft around 1986 for the purpose of exchanging formatted text among Windows applications. RTF version 1.6 is documented at *http://msdn.microsoft.com/library/specs/rtfspec.htm.*

An RTF document is a text file that defines the back slash (\) for formatting tags (such as \i to begin a block of italic text) and the curly braces { and } for enclosing groups of tags. Although RTF has a long history and is supported as an exchange format by many word processors, at this time in the evolution of formatted text, perhaps the biggest problem with RTF is that it's not HTML.

While Windows Notepad is built around the Win32 equivalent of the *Text-Box* control, Windows WordPad is built around the Win32 equivalent of the *RichTextBox* control. In a *TextBox* control, you can specify a color or a font for the entire contents of the control; in a *RichTextBox* control, you can specify multiple fonts, colors, paragraph alignments, indents, and so forth. You specify this formatting based on the current selection by using a number of properties, such as *SelectionFont*, *SelectionColor*, *SelectionAlignment*, *SelectionIndent*, and so on.

To get access to the RTF data, use these two properties:

**RichTextBox Properties (selection)**

| Property | Type | Accessibility |
|----------|------|---------------|
| *Rtf* | *String* | Get/Set |
| *SelectedRtf* | *String* | Get/Set |

The *RichTextBox* class also includes two methods (with three overloads each) that let you load a file directly into the control (*LoadFile*) and save the document directly to a file (*SaveFile*).

# ToolTips

A *ToolTip* is a small rectangular window that displays some helpful explanatory text, usually when the mouse pointer hovers over a particular control. ToolTips are implemented in Windows Forms in the *ToolTip* class. Although ToolTips in Windows Forms are more limited than those defined in the Win32 API, they are also much easier to use.

You need to define only one *ToolTip* object to provide ToolTips for a collection of controls:

```
Dim tip As New ToolTip()
```

Generally, you'll define a *ToolTip* object for your form (if your form contains controls) and in the constructor of each dialog box your program creates. If your form contains no controls other than a toolbar and a status bar, you don't need a *ToolTip* object in your form because those controls have their own ToolTip facility. (Appendix 20 covers toolbars and status bars.)

*ToolTip* is one of those rare classes in which a couple of methods are much more important than its properties and events:

### *ToolTip* Methods (selection)

```
Sub SetToolTip(ByVal ctrl As Control, ByVal strTip As String)

Function GetToolTip(ByVal ctrl As Control) As String

Sub RemoveAll()
```

For the single *ToolTip* object you create for a particular dialog box, you call *SetToolTip* once for each control to associate ToolTip text with the control, as here:

```
Dim tip As New ToolTip()
tip.SetToolTip(btnBigger, "This button increases the font size")
tip.SetToolTip(btnSmaller, "This button decreases the font size")
```

To make the ToolTip text appear in multiple lines, use line feed characters (*vbLf*). For lengthy ToolTip text, I usually insert line feed characters every 32 characters or so.

If you want to remove a ToolTip for a particular control, set the text to *Nothing*:

```
tip.SetToolTip(btn, Nothing)
```

To remove all the ToolTips, call

```
tip.RemoveAll()
```

There's no way to get a list of all the controls for which ToolTips have been defined.

The following two *ToolTip* properties affect the visibility of the ToolTip text:

### *ToolTip* Properties (selection)

| Property | Type | Accessibility | Default |
|----------|------|---------------|---------|
| *Active* | *Boolean* | Get/Set | *True* |
| *ShowAlways* | *Boolean* | Get/Set | *False* |

Set *Active* to *False* to disable the display of ToolTip text for all the controls associated with the *ToolTip* object. Set *ShowAlways* to *True* to display the ToolTip text even if the parent form of the control isn't currently active.

To prevent hectic pop-up activity on the screen, ToolTips usually aren't displayed immediately. A period of time elapses (by default, 0.5 second) after the mouse pointer has stopped moving before the ToolTip is displayed. After another period of time (5 seconds by default), the ToolTip is removed from the screen. The following properties control the timing associated with a particular *ToolTip* object:

### *ToolTip* Properties (selection)

| Property | Type | Accessibility | Default |
|----------|------|---------------|---------|
| *AutomaticDelay* | *Integer* | Get/Set | 500 (milliseconds) |
| *InitialDelay* | *Integer* | Get/Set | *AutomaticDelay* |
| *ReshowDelay* | *Integer* | Get/Set | *AutomaticDelay* / 5 |
| *AutoPopDelay* | *Integer* | Get/Set | 10 × *AutomaticDelay* |

When you set the *AutomaticDelay* property, the other three properties are automatically set to the values indicated in the "Default" column of the table. The idea here is that you can change all timings proportionally just by changing the one property. However, you can then change the other three properties independently. The other three properties are the ones that directly affect the Tool-Tip display:

- *InitialDelay* indicates the period of time from when the mouse cursor stops moving to when the ToolTip text is displayed.

- The *ReshowDelay* property is the period of time before a new Tool-Tip is displayed when you move the mouse cursor from one control to another.

- *AutoPopDelay* indicates the time that a ToolTip remains displayed.

Let's take a look at a program that has three single-line text boxes, a multiline read-only text box, and ToolTips to make life easier for the user. Although this program is one of only two examples of ToolTips in this book, you should probably implement them everywhere you use controls.

Throughout this book, I've shown tables of the various enumerations defined in the .NET Framework class library, usually with the numeric values associated with the enumeration members. You may have wondered where these tables came from, since the .NET documentation doesn't include the numeric values. I constructed those tables from a program I wrote early on in my .NET exploration and which I've polished into the following piece of code I call EnumerateEnumeration.

**EnumerateEnumeration.vb**

```
'-----------------------------------------------------
' EnumerateEnumeration.vb (c) 2002 by Charles Petzold
'-----------------------------------------------------
Imports System
Imports System.Drawing
Imports System.Text                    ' For the StringBuilder class
Imports System.Windows.Forms

Class EnumerateEnumeration
    Inherits Form

    Private btn As Button
    Private txtboxLibrary, txtboxNamespace, _
            txtboxEnumeration, txtboxOutput As TextBox
    Private chkboxHex As CheckBox

    Shared Sub Main()
        Application.Run(New EnumerateEnumeration())
    End Sub

    Sub New()
        Text = "Enumerate Enumeration"
        ClientSize = New Size(242, 164)

        Dim lbl As New Label()
        lbl.Parent = Me
        lbl.Text = "Library:"
        lbl.Location = New Point(8, 8)
        lbl.Size = New Size(56, 8)

        txtboxLibrary = New TextBox()
        txtboxLibrary.Parent = Me
        txtboxLibrary.Text = "system.windows.forms"
        txtboxLibrary.Location = New Point(64, 8)
        txtboxLibrary.Size = New Size(120, 12)
        txtboxLibrary.Anchor = txtboxLibrary.Anchor Or AnchorStyles.Right

        Dim tip As New ToolTip()
        tip.SetToolTip(txtboxLibrary, _
                    "Enter the name of a .NET dynamic" & vbLf & _
                    "link libary, such as 'mscorlib'," & vbLf & _
                    "'system.windows.forms', or" & vbLf & _
                    "'system.drawing'.")
```

*(continued)*

**EnumerateEnumeration.vb** *(continued)*

```
        lbl = New Label()
        lbl.Parent = Me
        lbl.Text = "Namespace:"
        lbl.Location = New Point(8, 24)
        lbl.Size = New Size(56, 8)

        txtboxNamespace = New TextBox()
        txtboxNamespace.Parent = Me
        txtboxNamespace.Text = "System.Windows.Forms"
        txtboxNamespace.Location = New Point(64, 24)
        txtboxNamespace.Size = New Size(120, 12)
        txtboxNamespace.Anchor = txtboxNamespace.Anchor _
                            Or AnchorStyles.Right

        tip.SetToolTip(txtboxNamespace, _
                       "Enter the name of a namespace" & vbLf & _
                       "within the library, such as" & vbLf & _
                       "'System', 'System.IO'," & vbLf & _
                       "'System.Drawing'," & vbLf & _
                       "'System.Drawing.Drawing2D'," & vbLf & _
                       "or 'System.Windows.Forms'.")

        lbl = New Label()
        lbl.Parent = Me
        lbl.Text = "Enumeration:"
        lbl.Location = New Point(8, 40)
        lbl.Size = New Size(56, 8)

        txtboxEnumeration = New TextBox()
        txtboxEnumeration.Parent = Me
        txtboxEnumeration.Text = "ScrollBars"
        txtboxEnumeration.Location = New Point(64, 40)
        txtboxEnumeration.Size = New Size(120, 12)
        txtboxEnumeration.Anchor = txtboxEnumeration.Anchor Or _
                                            AnchorStyles.Right

        tip.SetToolTip(txtboxEnumeration, _
                       "Enter the name of an enumeration" & vbLf & _
                       "defined in the namespace.")

        chkboxHex = New CheckBox()
        chkboxHex.Parent = Me
        chkboxHex.Text = "Hex"
        chkboxHex.Location = New Point(192, 16)
        chkboxHex.Size = New Size(40, 8)
        chkboxHex.Anchor = AnchorStyles.Top Or AnchorStyles.Right
        AddHandler chkboxHex.CheckedChanged, _
                            AddressOf CheckBoxOnCheckedChanged

        tip.SetToolTip(chkboxHex, "Check this box to display the" & vbLf & _
                            "enumeration values in hexadecimal.")
```

```
        btn = New Button()
        btn.Parent = Me
        btn.Text = "OK"
        btn.Location = New Point(192, 32)
        btn.Size = New Size(40, 16)
        btn.Anchor = AnchorStyles.Top Or AnchorStyles.Right
        AddHandler btn.Click, AddressOf ButtonOkOnClick
        AcceptButton = btn

        tip.SetToolTip(btn, "Click this button to display results.")

        txtboxOutput = New TextBox()
        txtboxOutput.Parent = Me
        txtboxOutput.ReadOnly = True
        txtboxOutput.Multiline = True
        txtboxOutput.ScrollBars = ScrollBars.Vertical
        txtboxOutput.Location = New Point(8, 56)
        txtboxOutput.Size = New Size(226, 100)
        txtboxOutput.Anchor = AnchorStyles.Left Or AnchorStyles.Top Or _
                              AnchorStyles.Right Or AnchorStyles.Bottom

        AutoScaleBaseSize = New Size(4, 8)

        ' Initialize the display.
        ButtonOkOnClick(btn, EventArgs.Empty)
    End Sub

    Private Sub CheckBoxOnCheckedChanged(ByVal sender As Object, _
                                         ByVal ea As EventArgs)
        btn.PerformClick()
    End Sub

    Private Sub ButtonOkOnClick(ByVal sender As Object, _
                          ByVal ea As EventArgs)
        FillTextBox(txtboxOutput, txtboxLibrary.Text, _
                 txtboxNamespace.Text, txtboxEnumeration.Text, _
                 chkboxHex.Checked)
    End Sub

    Shared Function FillTextBox(ByVal txtboxOutput As TextBox, _
                          ByVal strLibrary As String, _
                          ByVal strNamespace As String, _
                          ByVal strEnumeration As String, _
                          ByVal bHexadecimal As Boolean) As Boolean
        Dim strEnumText As String = strNamespace & "." & strEnumeration
        Dim strAssembly As String
        Try
            strAssembly = System.Reflection.Assembly. _
                          LoadWithPartialName(strLibrary).FullName
        Catch
            Return False
        End Try
```

*(continued)*

**EnumerateEnumeration.vb** *(continued)*

```vb
        Dim strFullText As String = strEnumText & "," & strAssembly

        ' Get the type of the enum.
        Dim typ As Type = Type.GetType(strFullText, False, True)
        If typ Is Nothing Then
            txtboxOutput.Text = """" & strFullText & _
                               """ is not a valid type."
            Return False
        ElseIf Not typ.IsEnum Then
            txtboxOutput.Text = """" & strEnumText & _
                               """ is a valid type but not an enum."
            Return False
        End If

        ' Get all the members in that enum.
        Dim astrMembers() As String = System.Enum.GetNames(typ)
        Dim arr As Array = System.Enum.GetValues(typ)
        Dim aobjMembers(arr.GetUpperBound(0)) As Object
        arr.CopyTo(aobjMembers, 0)

        ' Create a StringBuilder for the text.
        Dim sb As New StringBuilder()

        ' Append the enumeration name and headings.
        sb.Append(strEnumeration)
        sb.Append(" Enumeration" & vbCrLf & _
                "Member" & vbTab & "Value" & vbCrLf)

        ' Append the text rendition and the actual numeric values.
        Dim i As Integer
        For i = 0 To astrMembers.GetUpperBound(0)
            sb.Append(astrMembers(i))
            sb.Append(vbTab)
            If bHexadecimal Then
                sb.Append("&H" & System.Enum.Format(typ, aobjMembers(i), _
                                                "X"))
            Else
                sb.Append(System.Enum.Format(typ, aobjMembers(i), "D"))
            End If
            sb.Append(vbCrLf)
        Next i

        ' Append some other information.
        sb.Append(vbCrLf & "Total = " & _
                astrMembers.Length.ToString() & vbCrLf)
        sb.Append(vbCrLf & typ.AssemblyQualifiedName & vbCrLf)

        ' Set the text box Text property from the StringBuilder.
        txtboxOutput.Text = sb.ToString()
        txtboxOutput.SelectionLength = 0
        Return True
    End Function
End Class
```

The constructor creates three pairs of labels and single-line text boxes to let the user type in a DLL name, a namespace in that library, and an enumeration in that namespace. A check box lets you indicate that the results should be displayed in hexadecimal. A push button lets you indicate when everything is finished and the results should be displayed. Each of these controls is associated with some ToolTip text.

The results are displayed in a read-only text box. Notice the use of the *Anchor* property to make all the text boxes flexible in size. As you make the form wider, all three single-line text boxes increase in width. As you make the form shorter or taller, the read-only text box changes height.

Here's a view of the program from the last time I used it:

Notice that the read-only text box has a different default background color than the normal text boxes. Because read-only text boxes still implement a caret and clipboard interface, I've been able to select the text I want from the text box and type CTRL+C to copy it to the clipboard. I then paste the text into my Microsoft Word document for the chapter and convert the text to a Word table.

After a little while working with this program, you may begin to be annoyed at having to retype various commonly used libraries and namespaces. Later on in this chapter, I'll present another version of this program, named EnumerateEnumerationCombo, that has combo boxes that use the Windows registry to save all valid combinations of library names, namespaces, and enumerations.

To accommodate this second program is the reason that all the display code is isolated in the *FillTextBox* method, which I've also defined as shared. It's shared because EnumerateEnumerationCombo needs to make use of the *FillTextBox* method but doesn't derive from EnumerateEnumeration. *FillTextBox* returns *True* if the combination of three text strings was valid and *False* otherwise. EnumerateEnumeration doesn't use this information; EnumerateEnumerationCombo does.

*FillTextBox* uses the *GetType* method of the *Type* class to obtain a *Type* object for the enumeration. The argument to *GetType* is a text string that takes the following form:

```
namespace.enumeration,library
```

Notice the normal period separating the namespace and the enumeration name, and also the comma preceding the library name. The library name must include version information, which is the reason for the *Assembly.LoadWithPartialName* call. In a Visual Basic program this method call needs to be fully qualified with the *System.Reflection* namespace because *Assembly* is also a Visual Basic keyword.

The program obtains the enumeration member names and values from the shared *GetNames* and *GetValues* methods of the *Enum* class.

The relationship between the library name and the namespace can be a bit tricky: The system.drawing.dll library contains everything in the namespace *System.Drawing*. However, everything in the namespace *System.Drawing.Drawing2D* is also located in system.drawing.dll. Many of the basic namespaces (such as *System* and *System.IO*) are located in mscorlib.dll, which stands for "Microsoft Core Library."

Notice the use of the *StringBuilder* class to build the string that's displayed in the read-only text box. (I discuss *StringBuilder* in Appendix C.) The original version put everything into the text box line-by-line using string appending with the &= operator. I was beginning to suspect a problem with that approach when the *EmfPlusRecordType* enumeration required 30 seconds to display using a pre-release version of Microsoft Visual Studio .NET and my pokey machine. Switching to the *StringBuilder* class made the update instantaneous.

# The List Box

The *ListBox* control is often used in a manner similar to a group of radio buttons—to provide a way for a user to pick one item from a list of several items. However, list boxes generally take up less space on the screen and also let the user select multiple items. The *ComboBox* control (which I'll talk about later in this chapter) usually takes up even less space and often includes an area for the user to type information, much like a *TextBox* control.

Both *ListBox* and *ComboBox* are derived from *ListControl*, as shown in the following class hierarchy:

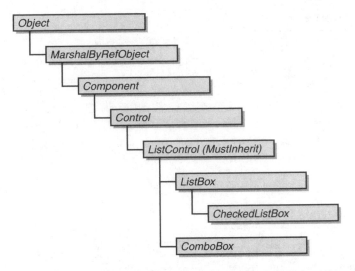

Usually after creating a list box, you want to fill it with items. You do that using the *Items* property:

### *ListBox* Properties (selection)

| Property | Type | Accessibility |
|----------|------|---------------|
| *Items* | *ListBox.ObjectCollection* | Get |

The *ObjectCollection* class is by now a familiar implementation of the *IList*, *ICollection*, and *IEnumerable* interfaces. You can index *Items* as an array, use the *Add* and *AddRange* methods to add items to the list box, and search for items with the *Contains* and *IndexOf* methods.

The items in a *ListBox* control are defined to be of type *Object*, not necessarily strings. Each object in *ListBox* is displayed using the object's *ToString* method. Of course, when the program retrieves items from the list box, it is responsible for casting the object to its proper type.

It's possible for the list box to contain multiple identical items. For example, if you add an item to a list box that's already in the collection, the collection will contain two copies of the item. Because such a situation confuses the user, it's probably undesirable.

As you add items to a list box, each item is assigned an index beginning at 0. The index determines the item's position in the list box. Generally, the indices are consecutive as the items are added. However, if you've set the *Sorted* property to *True*, the indices will be consecutive based on the alphabetical order of the items.

### *ListBox* Properties (selection)

| Property | Type | Accessibility |
|---|---|---|
| *Sorted* | *Boolean* | Get/Set |
| *TopIndex* | *Integer* | Get/Set |

The *TopIndex* property indicates the index of the item displayed at the top of the list box. By default, *TopIndex* is 0.

The *PreferredHeight* property indicates the height of the list box required to fit all the items:

### *ListBox* Properties (selection)

| Property | Type | Accessibility |
|---|---|---|
| *PreferredHeight* | *Integer* | Get |
| *IntegralHeight* | *Boolean* | Get/Set |

Generally, you don't set the height of the list box to *PreferredHeight*. The *IntegralHeight* property is *True* by default to adjust the height you set so that partial items aren't displayed.

If the height of the list box doesn't accommodate the full number of items, a vertical scroll bar will be displayed. Optionally, you can display the scroll bar regardless of the number of items. You can also optionally display a horizontal scroll bar for items that exceed the width of the list box:

### *ListBox* Properties (selection)

| Property | Type | Accessibility |
|---|---|---|
| *ScrollAlwaysVisible* | *Boolean* | Get/Set |
| *HorizontalScrollbar* | *Boolean* | Get/Set |

The following properties of *ListBox* involve the selection of items:

### *ListBox* Properties (selection)

| Property | Type | Accessibility |
|---|---|---|
| *SelectionMode* | *SelectionMode* | Get/Set |
| *SelectedIndex* | *Integer* | Get/Set |
| *SelectedItem* | *Object* | Get/Set |

### *ListBox* Properties (selection)    *(continued)*

| Property | Type | Accessibility |
|---|---|---|
| *SelectedIndices* | *ListBox.Selected-IndexCollection* | Get |
| *SelectedItems* | *ListBox.Selected-ObjectCollection* | Get |

The *SelectionMode* property is one of the following members of the *Selection-Mode* enumeration:

### *SelectionMode* Enumeration

| Member | Value |
|---|---|
| *None* | 0 |
| *One* | 1 |
| *MultiSimple* | 2 |
| *MultiExtended* | 3 |

The default is *One*. At any time, only one item in the list box is highlighted, which is indicated by a reverse-video display. Whenever the list box has the input focus, the same item is also surrounded by a dotted line—a focus rectangle similar to that on push buttons—but the focus rectangle might be a bit difficult to see because it's the same size as the reverse-video rectangle. You can also select an item with the mouse.

By default, a newly created and filled list box has no selection, in which case *SelectedIndex* returns –1 and *SelectedItem* returns *Nothing*. You'll probably want to use one of these two properties to initialize the list box to a particular index or item.

With the *MultiSimple* option, the user can select multiple items in the list box. Each selected item is indicated by reverse-video. The focus rectangle is independent of any selection rectangle. You can move the dotted-line focus rectangle among the items using the cursor-movement keys. Pressing the spacebar selects (or deselects) the item indicated by the focus rectangle. In addition, you can select (or deselect) an item with the mouse, in which case that item also gets the focus rectangle.

A list box with the *MultiExtended* option at first looks much like a single-selection list box. Using the cursor-movement keys, you change both the reverse-video selection rectangle and the dotted-line focus rectangle. However, you can extend a selection by holding down the Shift key while pressing the cursor-movement keys. But if you then release the Shift key and press a cursor-movement key—or click an item with the mouse—the selection again becomes just one item. In a *MultiExtended* list box, you can also select (or deselect) individual items by clicking them with the mouse while the Ctrl key is pressed.

The *MultiExtended* list box probably makes most sense when the user is likely to select a *range* of items. Use *MultiSimple* when the items the user is likely to select are not consecutive.

In a single-selection list box, use *SelectedIndex* or *SelectedItem* to obtain the selected index or item. If *lstbox* is an object of type *ListBox*,

```
lstbox.SelectedItem
```

is equivalent to

```
lstbox.Items(lstbox.SelectedIndex)
```

You can also use the *Text* property to obtain the text representation of the selected item. The expression

```
lstbox.Text
```

is equivalent to

```
lstbox.SelectedItem.ToString()
```

In a multiselection list box, the properties *SelectedIndices* and *SelectedItems* give you access to the selected items. The *SelectedIndexCollection* and *SelectedObjectCollection* classes both have *Count* properties and indexers. The *Count* property indicates the number of selected items, and—as usual—the indexer can range from 0 to (*Count* –1). The indexer for the *SelectedIndices* object returns the index of the selected item within the list box. For example, if *index* is a number between 0 and (*Count* –1),

```
lstbox.SelectedItems(index)
```

is equivalent to

```
lstbox.Items(lstbox.SelectedIndices(index))
```

To initialize a multiselection list box, you can call the *SetSelected* method for each item you want to select:

### *ListBox* Methods (selection)

```
Sub SetSelected(ByVal index As Integer, ByVal bSelect As Boolean)
Function GetSelected(ByVal index As Integer) As Boolean
Sub ClearSelected()
```

In addition, the *GetSelected* method returns *True* for each index that corresponds to a selected item. *ClearSelected* deselects all items in the list box.

Often when you use list boxes in a dialog box, you need only obtain the selected item or items when the user presses the OK button. However, at times, you'll want to react whenever the selected item changes. For that purpose there are two events:

### *ListBox* Events (selection)

| Event | Method | Delegate | Argument |
|---|---|---|---|
| *SelectedIndexChanged* | *OnSelectedIndexChanged* | *EventHandler* | *EventArgs* |
| *SelectedValueChanged* | *OnSelectedValueChanged* | *EventHandler* | *EventArgs* |

*SelectedValueChanged* is implemented in *ListControl* and is also available in *ComboBox*. These two events are basically equivalent and occur whether the selection changes programmatically or by the user. In a *MultiSimple* list box, these two events are fired even when the focus rectangle changes and not the selection.

Here's a simple program that lists the current MS-DOS environment variable names in a list box and displays the value of the currently selected item.

### EnvironmentVars.vb

```
'-------------------------------------------------
' EnvironmentVars.vb (c) 2002 by Charles Petzold
'-------------------------------------------------
Imports System
Imports System.Collections
Imports System.Drawing
Imports System.Windows.Forms

Class EnvironmentVars
    Inherits Form

    Private lbl As Label

    Shared Sub Main()
        Application.Run(New EnvironmentVars())
    End Sub

    Sub New()
        Text = "Environment Variables"

        ' Create Label control.
        lbl = New Label()
        lbl.Parent = Me
        lbl.Anchor = lbl.Anchor Or AnchorStyles.Right
        lbl.Location = New Point(Font.Height, Font.Height)
        lbl.Size = New Size(ClientSize.Width - 2 * Font.Height, Font.Height)
```

*(continued)*

**EnvironmentVars.vb** *(continued)*

```
            ' Create ListBox control.
            Dim lstbox As New ListBox()
            lstbox.Parent = Me
            lstbox.Location = New Point(Font.Height, 3 * Font.Height)
            lstbox.Size = New Size(12 * Font.Height, 8 * Font.Height)
            lstbox.Sorted = True
            AddHandler lstbox.SelectedIndexChanged, _
                                    AddressOf ListBoxOnSelectedIndexChanged

            ' Set environment strings in ListBox control.
            Dim dict As IDictionary = Environment.GetEnvironmentVariables()
            Dim astr(dict.Keys.Count - 1) As String

            dict.Keys.CopyTo(astr, 0)
            lstbox.Items.AddRange(astr)
            lstbox.SelectedIndex = 0
        End Sub

        Private Sub ListBoxOnSelectedIndexChanged(ByVal obj As Object, _
                                        ByVal ea As EventArgs)
            Dim lstbox As ListBox = DirectCast(obj, ListBox)
            Dim strItem As String = DirectCast(lstbox.SelectedItem, String)

            lbl.Text = Environment.GetEnvironmentVariable(strItem)
        End Sub
End Class
```

Notice that the environment names are an array of strings added to the list box using the *AddRange* method. The constructor concludes by setting the *SelectedIndex* property to 0. Doing so generates a call to the *SelectedIndexChanged* event handler, which retrieves the selected item and sets the *Label* text with it. Here's a sample view of the program:

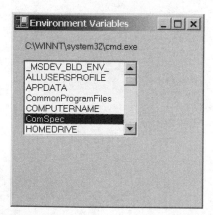

List boxes have an owner-draw option that you can enable by setting the *DrawMode* property. You set the property to one of the members of the *Draw-*

*Mode* enumeration, which specifies whether all the items have the same height or are different heights:

### DrawMode Enumeration

| Member | Value |
|---|---|
| *Normal* | 0 |
| *OwnerDrawFixed* | 1 |
| *OwnerDrawVariable* | 2 |

As usual, you must also install handlers for the *MeasureItem* and *DrawItem* events.

# List Box + Text Box = Combo Box

In its classical form, the combo box looks like a text box with an arrow at the right. Click the arrow and a list box drops down. But this traditional usage is not the only way in which you can use combo boxes. The critical property is *DropDownStyle*:

### ComboBox Properties (selection)

| Property | Type | Accessibility |
|---|---|---|
| *DropDownStyle* | *ComboBoxStyle* | Get/Set |
| *DroppedDown* | *Boolean* | Get/Set |

The *DropDownStyle* property is set to a member of the *ComboBoxStyle* enumeration:

### ComboBoxStyle Enumeration

| Member | Value | Description |
|---|---|---|
| *Simple* | 0 | Editable field, list always present |
| *DropDown* | 1 | Editable field, list drops down (default) |
| *DropDownList* | 2 | Noneditable field, list drops down |

What I referred to as the *classical* combo box has the default style of *DropDown*. The user can type something into the edit field or select something from the list. The style of *DropDownList* is most like a regular list box except it takes up less space. The *DroppedDown* property is *True* if the list part of the combo box is visible.

Like a list box, a combo box has an *Items* property that contains all the items in the list:

### *ComboBox* Properties (selection)

| Property | Type | Accessibility |
|----------|------|---------------|
| *Items* | *ComboBox.ObjectCollection* | Get |

The *ObjectCollection* class has a *Count* property, an indexer, and familiar methods such as *Add*, *AddRange*, *Insert*, and *Remove*.

The following properties indicate the index of the selected item and the selected item itself:

### *ComboBox* Properties (selection)

| Property | Type | Accessibility |
|----------|------|---------------|
| *SelectedIndex* | *Integer* | Get/Set |
| *SelectedItem* | *Object* | Get/Set |

In a *ListBox* object, *SelectedIndex* and *SelectedItem* are usually valid, except possibly after a list box is first created and the properties aren't initialized. In a *ComboBox*, however, if the user is currently typing something into the edit field, *SelectedIndex* returns −1 and *SelectedItem* returns *Nothing*.

The *Text* property always indicates the text that appears in the edit field. Thus, the *Text* property changes as the user selects different items from the list part of the combo box and as the user types something into the edit field.

The following table shows the most useful events implemented by *ComboBox*:

### *ComboBox* Events (selection)

| Event | Method | Delegate | Argument |
|-------|--------|----------|----------|
| *TextChanged* | *OnTextChanged* | *EventHandler* | *EventArgs* |
| *SelectedIndex-Changed* | *OnSelectedIndex-Changed* | *EventHandler* | *EventArgs* |
| *SelectionChange-Committed* | *OnSelectionChange-Committed* | *EventHandler* | *EventArgs* |

The *TextChanged* event occurs when the user scrolls through the items in the list box or types something into the edit field. The *SelectedIndexChanged* event occurs only when the user scrolls through the items in the list box. For *Drop-Down* and *DropDownList* combo boxes, if the list part is dropped down and the user scrolls through the items, both *TextChanged* and *SelectedIndexChanged* events occur; only when the drop-down list is retracted does the *Selection-ChangeCommitted* event occur. However, if the user scrolls through items using the cursor keys without causing the drop-down list to drop down, *Selection-ChangeCommitted* events occur with each change in the selection. For *Simple* combo boxes, *SelectionChangedCommitted* events occur whenever the selection changes.

In the following enhancement of the EnumerateEnumeration program, I replaced all three list boxes with combo boxes and installed *TextChanged* event handlers for all three. By handling *TextChanged* events, the program can test for valid combinations with every keystroke that the user types into the edit field. The push button is eliminated because it is no longer necessary.

**EnumerateEnumerationCombo.vb**

```
'-------------------------------------------------------------
' EnumerateEnumerationCombo.vb (c) 2002 by Charles Petzold
'-------------------------------------------------------------
Imports Microsoft.Win32
Imports System
Imports System.Drawing
Imports System.Windows.Forms

Class EnumerateEnumerationCombo
    Inherits Form

    Private comboHex As CheckBox
    Private comboLibrary, comboNamespace, comboEnumeration As ComboBox
    Private txtboxOutput As TextBox

    Const strRegKeyBase As String = _
        "Software\ProgrammingWindowsWithVBdotNet\EnumerateEnumerationCombo"

    Shared Sub Main()
        Application.Run(New EnumerateEnumerationCombo())
    End Sub

    Sub New()
        Text = "Enumerate Enumeration (Combo)"
        ClientSize = New Size(242, 164)

        Dim lbl As New Label()
        lbl.Parent = Me
        lbl.Text = "Library:"
```

*(continued)*

**EnumerateEnumerationCombo.vb** *(continued)*

```
        lbl.Location = New Point(8, 8)
        lbl.Size = New Size(56, 8)

        comboLibrary = New ComboBox()
        comboLibrary.Parent = Me
        comboLibrary.DropDownStyle = ComboBoxStyle.DropDown
        comboLibrary.Sorted = True
        comboLibrary.Location = New Point(64, 8)
        comboLibrary.Size = New Size(120, 12)
        comboLibrary.Anchor = comboLibrary.Anchor Or AnchorStyles.Right
        AddHandler comboLibrary.TextChanged, _
                            AddressOf ComboBoxLibraryOnTextChanged

        lbl = New Label()
        lbl.Parent = Me
        lbl.Text = "Namespace:"
        lbl.Location = New Point(8, 24)
        lbl.Size = New Size(56, 8)

        comboNamespace = New ComboBox()
        comboNamespace.Parent = Me
        comboNamespace.DropDownStyle = ComboBoxStyle.DropDown
        comboNamespace.Sorted = True
        comboNamespace.Location = New Point(64, 24)
        comboNamespace.Size = New Size(120, 12)
        comboNamespace.Anchor = comboNamespace.Anchor Or AnchorStyles.Right
        AddHandler comboNamespace.TextChanged, _
                            AddressOf ComboBoxNamespaceOnTextChanged

        lbl = New Label()
        lbl.Parent = Me
        lbl.Text = "Enumeration:"
        lbl.Location = New Point(8, 40)
        lbl.Size = New Size(56, 8)

        comboEnumeration = New ComboBox()
        comboEnumeration.Parent = Me
        comboEnumeration.DropDownStyle = ComboBoxStyle.DropDown
        comboEnumeration.Sorted = True
        comboEnumeration.Location = New Point(64, 40)
        comboEnumeration.Size = New Size(120, 12)
        comboEnumeration.Anchor = comboEnumeration.Anchor Or _
                                AnchorStyles.Right
        AddHandler comboEnumeration.TextChanged, _
                            AddressOf ComboBoxEnumerationOnTextChanged

        comboHex = New CheckBox()
        comboHex.Parent = Me
        comboHex.Text = "Hex"
        comboHex.Location = New Point(192, 25)
        comboHex.Size = New Size(40, 8)
        comboHex.Anchor = AnchorStyles.Top Or AnchorStyles.Right
```

```
        AddHandler comboHex.CheckedChanged, _
                         AddressOf CheckBoxOnCheckedChanged

    txtboxOutput = New TextBox()
    txtboxOutput.Parent = Me
    txtboxOutput.ReadOnly = True
    txtboxOutput.Multiline = True
    txtboxOutput.ScrollBars = ScrollBars.Vertical
    txtboxOutput.Location = New Point(8, 56)
    txtboxOutput.Size = New Size(226, 100)
    txtboxOutput.Anchor = AnchorStyles.Left Or AnchorStyles.Top Or _
                         AnchorStyles.Right Or AnchorStyles.Bottom

    AutoScaleBaseSize = New Size(4, 8)

    ' Initialize display.
    FillComboBox(comboLibrary, strRegKeyBase)
    UpdateTextBox()
End Sub

Private Sub ComboBoxLibraryOnTextChanged(ByVal obj As Object, _
                                    ByVal ea As EventArgs)
    FillComboBox(comboNamespace, strRegKeyBase & "\" & _
                         comboLibrary.Text)
    ComboBoxNamespaceOnTextChanged(obj, ea)
End Sub

Private Sub ComboBoxNamespaceOnTextChanged(ByVal obj As Object, _
                                    ByVal ea As EventArgs)
    FillComboBox(comboEnumeration, strRegKeyBase & "\" & _
                         comboLibrary.Text & "\" & _
                         comboNamespace.Text)
    ComboBoxEnumerationOnTextChanged(obj, ea)
End Sub

Private Sub ComboBoxEnumerationOnTextChanged(ByVal obj As Object, _
                                    ByVal ea As EventArgs)
    UpdateTextBox()
End Sub

Private Sub CheckBoxOnCheckedChanged(ByVal obj As Object, _
                                    ByVal ea As EventArgs)
    UpdateTextBox()
End Sub

Private Sub UpdateTextBox()
    If EnumerateEnumeration.FillTextBox(txtboxOutput, _
            comboLibrary.Text, comboNamespace.Text, _
            comboEnumeration.Text, comboHex.Checked) Then
        If Not comboLibrary.Items.Contains(comboLibrary.Text) Then
            comboLibrary.Items.Add(comboLibrary.Text)
        End If
```

*(continued)*

**EnumerateEnumerationCombo.vb** *(continued)*

```
            If Not comboNamespace.Items.Contains(comboNamespace.Text) Then
                comboNamespace.Items.Add(comboNamespace.Text)
            End If
            If Not comboEnumeration.Items.Contains( _
                                        comboEnumeration.Text) Then
                comboEnumeration.Items.Add(comboEnumeration.Text)
            End If
            Dim strRegKey As String = strRegKeyBase & "\" & _
                                comboLibrary.Text & "\" & _
                                comboNamespace.Text & "\" & _
                                comboEnumeration.Text
            Dim regkey As RegistryKey = _
                    Registry.CurrentUser.OpenSubKey(strRegKey)
            If regkey Is Nothing Then
                regkey = Registry.CurrentUser.CreateSubKey(strRegKey)
            End If
            regkey.Close()
        End If
    End Sub

    Private Function FillComboBox(ByVal combo As ComboBox, _
                                ByVal strRegKey As String) As Boolean
        combo.Items.Clear()
        Dim regkey As RegistryKey = _
                        Registry.CurrentUser.OpenSubKey(strRegKey)
        If Not regkey Is Nothing Then
            Dim astrSubKeys() As String = regkey.GetSubKeyNames()
            regkey.Close()
            If astrSubKeys.Length > 0 Then
                combo.Items.AddRange(astrSubKeys)
                combo.SelectedIndex = 0
                Return True
            End If
        End If
        combo.Text = ""
        Return False
    End Function
End Class
```

When you first run the program, all three combo boxes are empty. It is your responsibility to type a valid library, namespace, and enumeration name. Like I said, the program checks for a valid combination with every keystroke. When a valid combination is encountered, the enumeration information is displayed by the shared *FillTextBox* method in the original EnumerateEnumeration program.

The program also stores the valid combination in the registry, and each valid combination is then added to the combo boxes. The tree structure of the registry is perfect for an application like this. If you look in the Registry Editor after entering a few valid combinations of libraries, namespaces, and enumerations, you'll see that no actual data is stored in the registry! Each valid combination becomes a key. You'll see entries with keys like this:

```
Software\ProgrammingWindowsWithVBdotNet\EnumerateEnumerationCombo
 \system.drawing\System.Drawing.Drawing2D\DashStyle
```

And this:

```
Software\ProgrammingWindowsWithVBdotNet\EnumerateEnumerationCombo
 \system.windows.forms\System.Windows.Forms\DockStyle
```

As you change the selection or text in the first combo box (where you enter the library name), the *FillComboBox* method in the program obtains the list of registry subkeys of the particular library name. Those subkeys are used to fill the second combo box (the one for the namespace names). Similarly, as you change the selection or text in the namespace combo box, *FillComboBox* obtains the list of valid enumerations for the third combo box. The more you use the program, the more useful it becomes.

## Up-Down Controls

The Windows Forms up-down control is more traditionally known as a *spin* button. There are two types of up-down controls, as shown in the following class hierarchy:

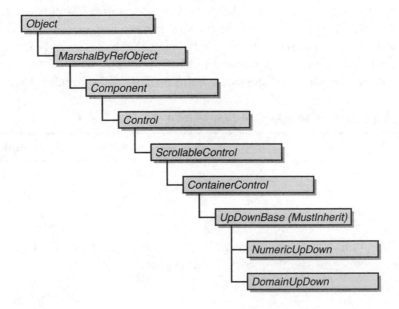

The controls consist of an edit field with a pair of arrow buttons at the right. The *NumericUpDown* control lets the user select from a range of numbers while the *DomainUpDown* control lets the user select from a collection of objects that are identified by strings. I'll be focusing on the *NumericUpDown* control in this section.

You generally set the following properties to initialize the control:

### *NumericUpDown* Properties (selection)

| Property | Type | Accessibility |
| --- | --- | --- |
| *Value* | *Decimal* | Get/Set |
| *Minimum* | *Decimal* | Get/Set |
| *Maximum* | *Decimal* | Get/Set |
| *Increment* | *Decimal* | Get/Set |

Notice the *Decimal* type. For more information on *Decimal*, see Appendix B. The *Increment* property indicates the change in the *Value* when the up and down arrows are clicked. The defaults let *Value* range from 0 through 100 with an increment of 1. You can set the *Minimum* and *Maximum* properties to *Decimal.MinValue* and *Decimal.MaxValue* to effectively remove any limitations.

The *Minimum* and *Maximum* properties are very strict: if the user manually enters a number outside the *Minimum* and *Maximum* range, the spin control changes the number to either *Minimum* or *Maximum*. (Watch out for this in modal dialog boxes. It's possible the OK button will dismiss the dialog box before the user has a chance to notice that the value has changed.) If the program sets the *Value* property to a number outside the range, an exception is raised.

The following properties control the display of the number in the control:

### *NumericUpDown* Properties (selection)

| Property | Type | Accessibility | Default |
| --- | --- | --- | --- |
| *DecimalPlaces* | *Integer* | Get/Set | 0 |
| *ThousandsSeparator* | *Boolean* | Get/Set | *False* |
| *Hexadecimal* | *Boolean* | Get/Set | *False* |

The *ValueChanged* event indicates when the value of the control has changed, either by the user or by the program:

### *NumericUpDown* Events (selection)

| Event | Method | Delegate | Argument |
|-------|--------|----------|----------|
| *ValueChanged* | *OnValueChanged* | *EventHandler* | *EventArgs* |

To demonstrate *NumericUpDown* controls, I've written a program that uses nine of them. The Transform program lets you experiment with matrix transforms, either by altering the six elements of the matrix or by effectively making calls to the various methods implemented by the *Matrix* class, such as *Scale* or *Shear*. I've divided the program into three files, one for the form and the other two for the two dialog boxes.

The bulk of the main form consists of two methods called during the *Paint* event: *DrawAxes* draws a coordinate system, and *DrawHouse* draws a little house. The house is drawn based on a *Matrix* object stored as a field.

### Transform.vb

```vb
'-------------------------------------------------
' Transform.vb (c) 2002 by Charles Petzold
'-------------------------------------------------
Imports System
Imports System.Drawing
Imports System.Drawing.Drawing2D
Imports System.Drawing.Imaging      ' For bitmap
Imports System.Windows.Forms

Class Transform
    Inherits Form

    Private matx As New Matrix()

    Shared Sub Main()
        Application.Run(New Transform())
    End Sub

    Sub New()
        Text = "Transform"
        ResizeRedraw = True
        BackColor = Color.White
        Size = Size.op_Addition(Size, Size)

        ' Create modal dialog box.
        Dim dlg As New MatrixElements()
        dlg.Owner = Me
        dlg.Matrix = matx
        AddHandler dlg.Changed, AddressOf MatrixDialogOnChanged
        dlg.Show()
    End Sub
```

*(continued)*

**Transform.vb** *(continued)*

```vb
Protected Overrides Sub OnPaint(ByVal pea As PaintEventArgs)
    Dim grfx As Graphics = pea.Graphics
    DrawAxes(grfx)
    grfx.Transform = matx
    DrawHouse(grfx)
End Sub

Private Sub DrawAxes(ByVal grfx As Graphics)
    Dim br As Brush = Brushes.Black
    Dim pn As Pen = Pens.Black
    Dim strfmt As New StringFormat()
    Dim i As Integer

    ' Horizontal axis
    strfmt.Alignment = StringAlignment.Center
    For i = 1 To 10
        grfx.DrawLine(pn, 100 * i, 0, 100 * i, 10)
        grfx.DrawString((i * 100).ToString(), Font, br, _
                        100 * i, 10, strfmt)
        grfx.DrawLine(pn, 100 * i, 10 + Font.Height, _
                        100 * i, ClientSize.Height)
    Next i

    ' Vertical axis
    strfmt.Alignment = StringAlignment.Near
    strfmt.LineAlignment = StringAlignment.Center

    For i = 1 To 10
        grfx.DrawLine(pn, 0, 100 * i, 10, 100 * i)
        grfx.DrawString((i * 100).ToString(), Font, br, _
                        10, 100 * i, strfmt)
        Dim cxText As Single = grfx.MeasureString( _
                                (i * 100).ToString(), Font).Width
        grfx.DrawLine(pn, 10 + cxText, 100 * i, _
                        ClientSize.Width, 100 * i)
    Next i
End Sub

Private Sub DrawHouse(ByVal grfx As Graphics)
    Dim rectFacade As New Rectangle(0, 40, 100, 60)
    Dim rectDoor As New Rectangle(10, 50, 25, 50)
    Dim rectWindows() As Rectangle = {New Rectangle(50, 50, 10, 10), _
                                        New Rectangle(60, 50, 10, 10), _
                                        New Rectangle(70, 50, 10, 10), _
                                        New Rectangle(50, 60, 10, 10), _
                                        New Rectangle(60, 60, 10, 10), _
                                        New Rectangle(70, 60, 10, 10), _
                                        New Rectangle(15, 60, 5, 7), _
                                        New Rectangle(20, 60, 5, 7), _
                                        New Rectangle(25, 60, 5, 7)}
```

```
        Dim rectChimney As New Rectangle(80, 5, 10, 35)
        Dim ptRoof() As Point = {New Point(50, 0), _
                                 New Point(0, 40), _
                                 New Point(100, 40)}

        ' Create bitmap and br for chimney.
        Dim bm As New Bitmap(8, 6)
        Dim bits() As Byte = {0, 0, 0, 0, 0, 0, 0, 0, _
                              1, 1, 1, 0, 1, 1, 1, 0, _
                              1, 1, 1, 0, 1, 1, 1, 0, _
                              0, 0, 0, 0, 0, 0, 0, 0, _
                              1, 0, 1, 1, 1, 0, 1, 1, _
                              1, 0, 1, 1, 1, 0, 1, 1}
        Dim i As Integer

        For i = 0 To 47
            If (bits(i) = 1) Then
                bm.SetPixel(i Mod 8, i \ 8, Color.DarkGray)
            Else
                bm.SetPixel(i Mod 8, i \ 8, Color.LightGray)
            End If
        Next i
        Dim br As New TextureBrush(bm)

        ' Draw entire house.
        grfx.FillRectangle(Brushes.LightGray, rectFacade)
        grfx.DrawRectangle(Pens.Black, rectFacade)
        grfx.FillRectangle(Brushes.DarkGray, rectDoor)
        grfx.DrawRectangle(Pens.Black, rectDoor)
        grfx.FillRectangles(Brushes.White, rectWindows)
        grfx.DrawRectangles(Pens.Black, rectWindows)
        grfx.FillRectangle(br, rectChimney)
        grfx.DrawRectangle(Pens.Black, rectChimney)
        grfx.FillPolygon(Brushes.DarkGray, ptRoof)
        grfx.DrawPolygon(Pens.Black, ptRoof)
    End Sub

    Private Sub MatrixDialogOnChanged(ByVal obj As Object, _
                                      ByVal ea As EventArgs)
        Dim dlg As MatrixElements = DirectCast(obj, MatrixElements)
        matx = dlg.Matrix
        Invalidate()
    End Sub
End Class
```

The program also displays a modeless dialog box titled Matrix Elements, which is implemented in the following source code file. The dialog box has six *NumericUpDown* controls that let you select the six elements of the matrix and also implements an event named *Changed*. When you click the Update button, the *Changed* event is triggered to let the main program know that a new matrix is available. (The main program processes this event in the *MatrixDialogOn-Changed* event handler.) The *Matrix* object is accessed as a property.

**MatrixElements.vb**

```vb
'-----------------------------------------------
' MatrixElements.vb (c) 2002 by Charles Petzold
'-----------------------------------------------
Imports System
Imports System.Drawing
Imports System.Drawing.Drawing2D
Imports System.Windows.Forms

Class MatrixElements
    Inherits Form

    Private matx As Matrix
    Private btnUpdate As Button
    Private updown(5) As NumericUpDown

    Event Changed As EventHandler

    Sub New()
        Text = "Matrix Elements"
        FormBorderStyle = FormBorderStyle.FixedDialog
        ControlBox = False
        MinimizeBox = False
        MaximizeBox = False
        ShowInTaskbar = False

        Dim strLabel() As String = {"X Scale:", "Y Shear:", _
                                    "X Shear:", "Y Scale:", _
                                    "X Translate:", "Y Translate:"}
        Dim i As Integer

        For i = 0 To 5
            Dim lbl As New Label()
            lbl.Parent = Me
            lbl.Text = strLabel(i)
            lbl.Location = New Point(8, 8 + 16 * i)
            lbl.Size = New Size(64, 8)

            updown(i) = New NumericUpDown()
            updown(i).Parent = Me
            updown(i).Location = New Point(76, 8 + 16 * i)
            updown(i).Size = New Size(48, 12)
            updown(i).TextAlign = HorizontalAlignment.Right
            AddHandler updown(i).ValueChanged, _
                    AddressOf UpDownOnValueChanged
            updown(i).DecimalPlaces = 2
            updown(i).Increment = 0.1D
            updown(i).Minimum = Decimal.MinValue
            updown(i).Maximum = Decimal.MaxValue
        Next i
```

```
        btnUpdate = New Button()
        btnUpdate.Parent = Me
        btnUpdate.Text = "Update"
        btnUpdate.Location = New Point(8, 108)
        btnUpdate.Size = New Size(50, 16)
        AddHandler btnUpdate.Click, AddressOf ButtonUpdateOnClick
        AcceptButton = btnUpdate

        Dim btn As New Button()
        btn.Parent = Me
        btn.Text = "Methods..."
        btn.Location = New Point(76, 108)
        btn.Size = New Size(50, 16)
        AddHandler btn.Click, AddressOf ButtonMethodsOnClick

        ClientSize = New Size(134, 132)
        AutoScaleBaseSize = New Size(4, 8)
End Sub

Property Matrix() As Matrix
    Set(ByVal Value As Matrix)
        matx = Value
        Dim i As Integer
        For i = 0 To 5
            updown(i).Value = CDec(Value.Elements(i))
        Next i
    End Set
    Get
        matx = New Matrix(CSng(updown(0).Value), _
                          CSng(updown(1).Value), _
                          CSng(updown(2).Value), _
                          CSng(updown(3).Value), _
                          CSng(updown(4).Value), _
                          CSng(updown(5).Value))

        Return matx
    End Get
End Property

Private Sub UpDownOnValueChanged(ByVal obj As Object, _
                                 ByVal ea As EventArgs)
    Dim grfx As Graphics = CreateGraphics()
    Dim boolEnableButton As Boolean = True

    Try
        grfx.Transform = Matrix
    Catch
        boolEnableButton = False
    End Try

    btnUpdate.Enabled = boolEnableButton
    grfx.Dispose()
End Sub
```

*(continued)*

**MatrixElements.vb** *(continued)*

```
    Private Sub ButtonUpdateOnClick(ByVal obj As Object, _
                                    ByVal ea As EventArgs)
        RaiseEvent Changed(Me, EventArgs.Empty)
    End Sub

    Private Sub ButtonMethodsOnClick(ByVal obj As Object, _
                                     ByVal ea As EventArgs)
        Dim dlg As New MatrixMethods()
        dlg.Matrix = Matrix
        If dlg.ShowDialog() = DialogResult.OK Then
            Matrix = dlg.Matrix
            btnUpdate.PerformClick()
        End If
    End Sub
End Class
```

The MatrixElements dialog box also contains a second button, labeled Methods. That button invokes a modal dialog box titled Matrix Methods, which is implemented in the following source code file. MatrixMethods contains another three *NumericUpDown* controls that provide arguments to the various methods of the *Matrix* class that alter the matrix elements. Each method is implemented by a button that also dismisses the dialog box.

**MatrixMethods.vb**

```
'-------------------------------------------------
' MatrixMethods.vb (c) 2002 by Charles Petzold
'-------------------------------------------------
Imports System
Imports System.Drawing
Imports System.Drawing.Drawing2D
Imports System.Windows.Forms

Class MatrixMethods
    Inherits Form

    Private matx As Matrix
    Private btnInvert As Button
    Private updown(2) As NumericUpDown
    Private radbtn(1) As RadioButton

    Sub New()
        Text = "Matrix Methods"
        FormBorderStyle = FormBorderStyle.FixedDialog
        ControlBox = False
        MinimizeBox = False
        MaximizeBox = False
        ShowInTaskbar = False
        Location = Point.op_Addition(ActiveForm.Location, _
                   Size.op_Addition(SystemInformation.CaptionButtonSize, _
                                    SystemInformation.FrameBorderSize))
```

```
Dim astrLabel() As String = {"X / DX:", "Y / DY:", "Angle:"}
Dim i As Integer

For i = 0 To 2
    Dim lbl As New Label()
    lbl.Parent = Me
    lbl.Text = astrLabel(i)
    lbl.Location = New Point(8, 8 + 16 * i)
    lbl.Size = New Size(32, 8)

    updown(i) = New NumericUpDown()
    updown(i).Parent = Me
    updown(i).Location = New Point(40, 8 + 16 * i)
    updown(i).Size = New Size(48, 12)
    updown(i).TextAlign = HorizontalAlignment.Right
    updown(i).DecimalPlaces = 2
    updown(i).Increment = 0.1D
    updown(i).Minimum = Decimal.MinValue
    updown(i).Maximum = Decimal.MaxValue
Next i

' Create group box and radio buttons.
Dim grpbox As New GroupBox()
grpbox.Parent = Me
grpbox.Text = "Order"
grpbox.Location = New Point(8, 60)
grpbox.Size = New Size(80, 32)

For i = 0 To 1
    radbtn(i) = New RadioButton()
    radbtn(i).Parent = grpbox
    radbtn(i).Text = New String() {"Prepend", "Append"}(i)
    radbtn(i).Location = New Point(8, 8 + 12 * i)
    radbtn(i).Size = New Size(50, 10)
    radbtn(i).Checked = (i = 0)
Next i

' Create 8 buttons for terminating dialog.
Dim astrButton() As String = {"Reset", "Invert", "Translate", _
                              "Scale", "Rotate", "RotateAt", _
                              "Shear", "Cancel"}
Dim aeh() As EventHandler = {AddressOf ButtonResetOnClick, _
                             AddressOf ButtonInvertOnClick, _
                             AddressOf ButtonTranslateOnClick, _
                             AddressOf ButtonScaleOnClick, _
                             AddressOf ButtonRotateOnClick, _
                             AddressOf ButtonRotateAtOnClick, _
                             AddressOf ButtonShearOnClick}
For i = 0 To 7
    Dim btn As New Button()
    btn.Parent = Me
    btn.Text = astrButton(i)
```

*(continued)*

**MatrixMethods.vb** *(continued)*

```
            btn.Location = New Point(100 + 72 * (i \ 4),8 + 24 * (i Mod 4))
            btn.Size = New Size(64, 14)

            If i = 0 Then AcceptButton = btn
            If i = 1 Then btnInvert = btn

            If i < 7 Then
                AddHandler btn.Click, aeh(i)
                btn.DialogResult = DialogResult.OK
            Else
                btn.DialogResult = DialogResult.Cancel
                CancelButton = btn
            End If
        Next i

        ClientSize = New Size(240, 106)
        AutoScaleBaseSize = New Size(4, 8)
    End Sub

    Property Matrix() As Matrix
        Set(ByVal Value As Matrix)
            matx = Value
            btnInvert.Enabled = Matrix.IsInvertible
        End Set
        Get
            Return matx
        End Get
    End Property

    Private Sub ButtonResetOnClick(ByVal obj As Object, _
                                   ByVal ea As EventArgs)
        Matrix.Reset()
    End Sub

    Private Sub ButtonInvertOnClick(ByVal obj As Object, _
                                    ByVal ea As EventArgs)
        Matrix.Invert()
    End Sub

    Private Sub ButtonTranslateOnClick(ByVal obj As Object, _
                                       ByVal ea As EventArgs)
        Matrix.Translate(CSng(updown(0).Value), _
                         CSng(updown(1).Value), PrependOrAppend)
    End Sub

    Private Sub ButtonScaleOnClick(ByVal obj As Object, _
                                   ByVal ea As EventArgs)
        Matrix.Scale(CSng(updown(0).Value), _
                     CSng(updown(1).Value), PrependOrAppend)
    End Sub
```

```
    Private Sub ButtonRotateOnClick(ByVal obj As Object, _
                                ByVal ea As EventArgs)
        Matrix.Rotate(CSng(updown(2).Value), PrependOrAppend)
    End Sub

    Private Sub ButtonRotateAtOnClick(ByVal obj As Object, _
                                ByVal ea As EventArgs)
        Matrix.RotateAt(CSng(updown(2).Value), _
                    New PointF(CSng(updown(0).Value), _
                            CSng(updown(1).Value)), PrependOrAppend)
    End Sub

    Private Sub ButtonShearOnClick(ByVal obj As Object, _
                                ByVal ea As EventArgs)
        Matrix.Shear(CSng(updown(0).Value), _
                    CSng(updown(1).Value), PrependOrAppend)
    End Sub

    Private Function PrependOrAppend() As MatrixOrder
        If radbtn(0).Checked Then
            Return MatrixOrder.Prepend
        Else
            Return MatrixOrder.Append
        End If
    End Function
End Class
```

Here's a view of the program with both dialog boxes displayed:

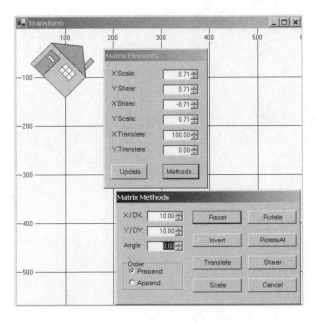

The chimney of the house is a *TextureBrush* based on a *Bitmap* image that looks like bricks. I could have used a *HatchBrush* here with *Hatch-Style.HorizontalBrick*. But, as you'll recall from Chapter 11, the *HatchBrush* isn't subject to transforms; the *TextureBrush* is. As you make the house larger, the bricks of the chimney also get larger. The bricks can also be sheared and rotated. You'll also notice that GDI+ uses a smoothing algorithm to avoid a giant-pixel effect.

# 19

# Font Fun

The TrueType and OpenType fonts available to Windows Forms programs are outline fonts, which means that each character is defined by a series of straight lines and splines. As we saw in Chapter 9 and subsequent chapters, outline fonts are continuously scalable. The font definitions also contain built-in hints that help avoid distortions that result when scaled floating-point coordinates must be rounded to a particular pixel grid.

Because font characters are defined by a series of straight lines and curves, they integrate well with the rest of the Windows Forms graphics system. Font characters are subject to transforms, they can be colored with any brush, and the character outlines can become part of a graphics path.

With the use of these various graphics programming techniques, singly and in combination, text can transcend its customary role—that of being read—and aspire to become something like art.

## Getting Started

Since Chapter 5, I've been deriving from a class named *PrintableForm* (implemented in PrintableForm.vb) whenever I've wanted to demonstrate some graphics technique on both the video display and the printer. A class derived from *PrintableForm* overrides the *DoPage* method to draw its graphics. *DoPage* is called during the form's *OnPaint* method to paint the client area. When you click the client area, the *DoPage* method is also called to display graphics on the printer.

For this chapter, I want to define a new class, named *FontMenuForm*, that derives from *PrintableForm* and also includes a single menu item labeled "Font!". The item invokes a standard Font dialog box that lets you change a protected field named *fnt*. The *FontMenuForm* class also contains a couple methods that are handy for displaying text.

**FontMenuForm.vb**

```vb
'-----------------------------------------------
' FontMenuForm.vb (c) 2002 by Charles Petzold
'-----------------------------------------------
Imports System
Imports System.Drawing
Imports System.Windows.Forms

Class FontMenuForm
    Inherits PrintableForm

    Protected strText As String = "Sample Text"
    Protected fnt As New Font("Times New Roman", 24, FontStyle.Italic)

    Shared Shadows Sub Main()
        Application.Run(New FontMenuForm())
    End Sub

    Sub New()
        Text = "Font Menu Form"

        Menu = New MainMenu()
        Menu.MenuItems.Add("&Font!", AddressOf MenuFontOnClick)
    End Sub

    Private Sub MenuFontOnClick(ByVal obj As Object, ByVal ea As EventArgs)
        Dim dlg As New FontDialog()
        dlg.Font = fnt

        If dlg.ShowDialog() = DialogResult.OK Then
            fnt = dlg.Font
            Invalidate()
        End If
    End Sub

    Protected Overrides Sub DoPage(ByVal grfx As Graphics, _
            ByVal clr As Color, ByVal cx As Integer, ByVal cy As Integer)
        Dim szf As SizeF = grfx.MeasureString(strText, fnt)
        Dim br As New SolidBrush(clr)

        grfx.DrawString(strText, fnt, br, (cx - szf.Width) / 2, _
                                          (cy - szf.Height) / 2)
    End Sub
```

```
    Function GetAscent(ByVal grfx As Graphics, ByVal fnt As Font) As Single
        Return fnt.GetHeight(grfx) * _
                fnt.FontFamily.GetCellAscent(fnt.Style) / _
                    fnt.FontFamily.GetLineSpacing(fnt.Style)
    End Function

    Function GetDescent(ByVal grfx As Graphics, ByVal fnt As Font) As Single
        Return fnt.GetHeight(grfx) * _
                fnt.FontFamily.GetCellDescent(fnt.Style) / _
                    fnt.FontFamily.GetLineSpacing(fnt.Style)
    End Function

    Function PointsToPageUnits(ByVal grfx As Graphics, _
                            ByVal fnt As Font) As Single
        Dim fFontSize As Single

        If grfx.PageUnit = GraphicsUnit.Display Then
            fFontSize = 100 * fnt.SizeInPoints / 72
        Else
            fFontSize = grfx.DpiX * fnt.SizeInPoints / 72
        End If

        Return fFontSize
    End Function
End Class
```

A program that derives from the *FontMenuForm* class should override the *DoPage* method (as when deriving from the *PrintableForm* class) and also make use of the *fnt* and *strText* fields. Optionally, the program can set those two fields in its constructor to different initial values.

The *GetAscent* and *GetDescent* methods calculate the ascent and descent of a particular font by using a technique I discussed in Chapter 9. The *Point-ToPageUnits* method calculates the point size of a font in page units. The method assumes that the default page units are in effect for the *Graphics* object argument. Printers have default page units of *GraphicsUnit.Display*, and the video display has default page units of *GraphicsUnit.Pixel*.

# Brushed Text

Throughout Chapter 17, I resisted demonstrating how you can use the whole variety of available brushes with text because I was saving them for this chapter. Here, for example, is a program that displays text using a *HatchBrush* created with *HatchStyle.HorizontalBrick*.

**Bricks.vb**

```
'------------------------------------------
' Bricks.vb (c) 2002 by Charles Petzold
'------------------------------------------
Imports System
Imports System.Drawing
Imports System.Drawing.Drawing2D
Imports System.Windows.Forms

Class Bricks
    Inherits FontMenuForm

    Shared Shadows Sub Main()
        Application.Run(New Bricks())
    End Sub

    Sub New()
        Text = "Bricks"

        strText = "Bricks"
        fnt = New Font("Times New Roman", 144)
    End Sub

    Protected Overrides Sub DoPage(ByVal grfx As Graphics, _
            ByVal clr As Color, ByVal cx As Integer, ByVal cy As Integer)
        Dim szf As SizeF = grfx.MeasureString(strText, fnt)
        Dim hbr As New HatchBrush(HatchStyle.HorizontalBrick, _
                                  Color.White, Color.Black)

        grfx.DrawString(strText, fnt, hbr, (cx - szf.Width) / 2, _
                                           (cy - szf.Height) / 2)
    End Sub
End Class
```

When you enlarge the client area sufficiently, the output looks like this:

Hatch brushes work best with larger font styles. With some of the skimpier hatch brushes, the appearance can be improved by outlining the characters, a technique I'll demonstrate later in the chapter.

Here's a program that displays text with a gradient brush.

**GradientText.vb**

```
'-------------------------------------------------
' GradientText.vb (c) 2002 by Charles Petzold
'-------------------------------------------------
Imports System
Imports System.Drawing
Imports System.Drawing.Drawing2D
Imports System.Windows.Forms

Class GradientText
    Inherits FontMenuForm

    Shared Shadows Sub Main()
        Application.Run(New GradientText())
    End Sub

    Sub New()
        Text = "Gradient Text"
        Width *= 3
        strText = "Gradient"
        fnt = New Font("Times New Roman", 144, FontStyle.Italic)
    End Sub

    Protected Overrides Sub DoPage(ByVal grfx As Graphics, _
            ByVal clr As Color, ByVal cx As Integer, ByVal cy As Integer)
        Dim szf As SizeF = grfx.MeasureString(strText, fnt)
        Dim ptf As New PointF((cx - szf.Width) / 2, _
                              (cy - szf.Height) / 2)

        Dim rectf As New RectangleF(ptf, szf)
        Dim lgbr As New LinearGradientBrush(rectf, _
                              Color.White, Color.Black, _
                              LinearGradientMode.ForwardDiagonal)
        grfx.Clear(Color.Gray)
        grfx.DrawString(strText, fnt, lgbr, ptf)
    End Sub
End Class
```

The text is white at the upper left corner and black at the lower right corner, displayed against a gray background:

If you insert the lines

```
szf.Width /= 8
szf.Height /= 8
```

before the *RectangleF* creation and the line

```
lgbr.WrapMode = WrapMode.TileFlipXY
```

after the brush creation, you get a smaller tiled brush that looks like this:

It's also possible to achieve some interesting effects using plain old solid brushes, as illustrated in the DropShadow program.

**DropShadow.vb**
```
'--------------------------------------------
' DropShadow.vb (c) 2002 by Charles Petzold
'--------------------------------------------
Imports System
Imports System.Drawing
Imports System.Windows.Forms

Class DropShadow
    Inherits FontMenuForm

    Const iOffset As Integer = 10 ' About 1/10 inch (exactly on printer)
```

```
    Shared Shadows Sub Main()
        Application.Run(new DropShadow())
    End Sub

    Sub New()
        Text = "Drop Shadow"
        Width *= 2
        strText = "Shadow"
        fnt = New Font("Times New Roman", 108)
    End Sub

    Protected Overrides Sub DoPage(ByVal grfx As Graphics, _
            ByVal clr As Color, ByVal cx As Integer, ByVal cy As Integer)
        Dim szf As SizeF = grfx.MeasureString(strText, fnt)
        Dim x As Single = (cx - szf.Width) / 2
        Dim y As Single = (cy - szf.Height) / 2

        grfx.Clear(Color.White)
        grfx.DrawString(strText, fnt, Brushes.Gray, x, y)
        grfx.DrawString(strText, fnt, Brushes.Black, x - iOffset, _
                                                     y - iOffset)
    End Sub
End Class
```

This program does a drop-shadow effect by displaying the same text with two different brushes offset by 10 units:

If the offset is very small and you choose the colors right, you can achieve an embossed or an engraved effect, as shown in the EmbossedText program.

### EmbossedText.vb

```
'---------------------------------------------
' EmbossedText.vb (c) 2002 by Charles Petzold
'---------------------------------------------
Imports System
Imports System.Drawing
Imports System.Windows.Forms
```

*(continued)*

**EmbossedText.vb** *(continued)*

```
Class EmbossedText
    Inherits FontMenuForm

    Private iOffset As Integer = 2

    Shared Shadows Sub Main()
        Application.Run(New EmbossedText())
    End Sub

    Sub New()
        Text = "Embossed Text"
        Width *= 2
        Menu.MenuItems.Add("&Toggle!", AddressOf MenuToggleOnClick)
        strText = "Emboss"
        fnt = New Font("Times New Roman", 108)
    End Sub

    Private Sub MenuToggleOnClick(ByVal obj As Object, _
                                  ByVal ea As EventArgs)
        iOffset = -iOffset

        If (iOffset > 0) Then
            Text = "Embossed Text"
            strText = "Emboss"
        Else
            Text = "Engraved Text"
            strText = "Engrave"
        End If

        Invalidate()
    End Sub

    Protected Overrides Sub DoPage(ByVal grfx As Graphics, _
            ByVal clr As Color, ByVal cx As Integer, ByVal cy As Integer)
        Dim szf As SizeF = grfx.MeasureString(strText, fnt)
        Dim x As Single = (cx - szf.Width) / 2
        Dim y As Single = (cy - szf.Height) / 2

        grfx.Clear(Color.White)
        grfx.DrawString(strText, fnt, Brushes.Gray, x, y)
        grfx.DrawString(strText, fnt, Brushes.White, x - iOffset, _
                                                     y - iOffset)
    End Sub
End Class
```

The program draws gray text and then white text against a white background. By default, the program comes up like this:

The program includes a menu option labeled "Toggle!" that lets you switch to the engraved effect:

These two effects are fundamentally the same. The only difference is the choice of a positive or negative offset between the two text displays. Because we are accustomed to light sources that come from above, we interpret an apparent shadow that appears on the bottom and right of the characters to be the result of raised text, and a shadow on the top and left to result from sunken text. Turn this book (or your monitor) upside down to swap the effects.

As demonstrated in the BlockFont program, you can draw the same text string multiple times with the same color to achieve a block effect.

### BlockFont.vb

```
'-------------------------------------------
' BlockFont.vb (c) 2002 by Charles Petzold
'-------------------------------------------
Imports System
Imports System.Drawing
Imports System.Windows.Forms

Class BlockFont
    Inherits FontMenuForm
```

*(continued)*

**BlockFont.vb** *(continued)*

```vb
    Const iReps As Integer = 50 ' About 1/2 inch (exactly on printer)

    Shared Shadows Sub Main()
        Application.Run(New BlockFont())
    End Sub

    Sub New()
        Text = "Block Font"
        Width *= 2
        strText = "Block"
        fnt = New Font("Times New Roman", 108)
    End Sub

    Protected Overrides Sub DoPage(ByVal grfx As Graphics, _
            ByVal clr As Color, ByVal cx As Integer, ByVal cy As Integer)
        Dim szf As SizeF = grfx.MeasureString(strText, fnt)
        Dim x As Single = (cx - szf.Width - iReps) / 2
        Dim y As Single = (cy - szf.Height + iReps) / 2
        Dim i As Integer

        grfx.Clear(Color.LightGray)

        For i = 0 To iReps
            grfx.DrawString(strText, fnt, Brushes.Black, x + i, y - i)
        Next i
        grfx.DrawString(strText, fnt, Brushes.White, x + iReps, y - iReps)
    End Sub
End Class
```

After drawing multiple black text strings, the *DoPage* method finishes with a white one. Here's the result:

You might also want to use an outlined font on top, which will give a stronger look against a white background.

# Font Transforms

It became clear from the first investigations into the world transform in Chapter 7 that text is subject to the same scaling, rotation, and shearing effects as any other graphics object. The RotatedFont program derives from *FontMenuForm* to draw a series of identical text strings circling the center of the display area.

**RotatedFont.vb**

```
'------------------------------------------------
' RotatedFont.vb (c) 2002 by Charles Petzold
'------------------------------------------------
Imports System
Imports System.Drawing
Imports System.Windows.Forms

Class RotatedFont
    Inherits FontMenuForm

    Const iDegrees As Integer = 20      ' Should be divisor of 360

    Shared Shadows Sub Main()
        Application.Run(New RotatedFont())
    End Sub

    Sub New()
        Text = "Rotated Font"
        strText = "   Rotated Font"
        fnt = New Font("Arial", 18)
    End Sub

    Protected Overrides Sub DoPage(ByVal grfx As Graphics, _
            ByVal clr As Color, ByVal cx As Integer, ByVal cy As Integer)
        Dim br As New SolidBrush(clr)
        Dim strfmt As New StringFormat()
        Dim i As Integer

        strfmt.LineAlignment = StringAlignment.Center
        grfx.TranslateTransform(cx \ 2, cy \ 2)

        For i = 0 To 359 Step iDegrees
            grfx.DrawString(strText, fnt, br, 0, 0, strfmt)
            grfx.RotateTransform(iDegrees)
        Next i
    End Sub
End Class
```

The *DoPage* method calls *TranslateTransform* to set the origin in the middle of the display area. It then draws 18 versions of the text string, each rotated an additional 20 degrees around the origin. The *DrawString* call uses a *StringFormat* object that vertically centers the text string with respect to the origin, and the text string begins with three blank characters so that there won't be a mess in the center. Here's the result with the 18-point Arial font set by the program:

Feel free to use the program's Font! menu item to change the font to something other than Arial.

Here's a program that uses the *GetAscent* method in FontMenuForm. In Chapter 7, I demonstrated that negative scaling factors cause graphics objects to be flipped around either the horizontal or the vertical axis, or both. The ReflectedText program displays the text string "Reflect" using four combinations of positive and negative scaling.

**ReflectedText.vb**

```
'-------------------------------------------------
' ReflectedText.vb (c) 2002 by Charles Petzold
'-------------------------------------------------
Imports System
Imports System.Drawing
Imports System.Drawing.Drawing2D
Imports System.Windows.Forms

Class ReflectedText
    Inherits FontMenuForm

    Shared Shadows Sub Main()
        Application.Run(new ReflectedText())
    End Sub
```

```
    Sub New()
        Text = "Reflected Text"
        Width *= 2
        strText = "Reflect"
        fnt = New Font("Times New Roman", 54)
    End Sub

    Protected Overrides Sub DoPage(ByVal grfx As Graphics, _
            ByVal clr As Color, ByVal cx As Integer, ByVal cy As Integer)
        Dim br As New SolidBrush(clr)
        Dim fAscent As Single = GetAscent(grfx, fnt)
        Dim strfmt As StringFormat = StringFormat.GenericTypographic
        Dim i As Integer

        grfx.TranslateTransform(cx \ 2, cy \ 2)

        For i = 0 To 3
            Dim grfxstate As GraphicsState = grfx.Save()

            Select Case (i)
                Case 0 : grfx.ScaleTransform(1, 1)
                Case 1 : grfx.ScaleTransform(1, -1)
                Case 2 : grfx.ScaleTransform(-1, 1)
                Case 3 : grfx.ScaleTransform(-1, -1)
            End Select

            grfx.DrawString(strText, fnt, br, 0, -fAscent, strfmt)
            grfx.Restore(grfxstate)
        Next i
    End Sub
End Class
```

The *TranslateTransform* call sets the origin in the center of the client area. The particular *ScaleTransform* call used for each of the four text displays has different combinations of 1 and –1 for scaling. The *–fAscent* argument in *Draw-String* positions the text with the left end of its baseline at the origin:

You can also combine effects. Here's the same program with a *Rotate-Transform* call between *TranslateTransform* and *ScaleTransform*.

## RotateAndReflect.vb

```
'-----------------------------------------------------
' RotateAndReflect.vb (c) 2002 by Charles Petzold
'-----------------------------------------------------
Imports System
Imports System.Drawing
Imports System.Drawing.Drawing2D
Imports System.Windows.Forms

Class RotateAndReflect
    Inherits FontMenuForm

    Shared Shadows Sub Main()
        Application.Run(New RotateAndReflect())
    End Sub

    Sub New()
        Text = "Rotated and Reflected Text"
        strText = "Reflect"
        fnt = New Font("Times New Roman", 36)
    End Sub

    Protected Overrides Sub DoPage(ByVal grfx As Graphics, _
            ByVal clr As Color, ByVal cx As Integer, ByVal cy As Integer)
        Dim br As New SolidBrush(clr)
        Dim fAscent As Single = GetAscent(grfx, fnt)
        Dim strfmt As StringFormat = StringFormat.GenericTypographic
        Dim i As Integer

        grfx.TranslateTransform(cx \ 2, cy \ 2)

        For i = 0 To 3
            Dim grfxstate As GraphicsState = grfx.Save()
            grfx.RotateTransform(-45)

            Select Case (i)
                Case 0 : grfx.ScaleTransform(1, 1)
                Case 1 : grfx.ScaleTransform(1, -1)
                Case 2 : grfx.ScaleTransform(-1, 1)
                Case 3 : grfx.ScaleTransform(-1, -1)
            End Select

            grfx.DrawString(strText, fnt, br, 0, -fAscent, strfmt)
            grfx.Restore(grfxstate)
        Next i
    End Sub
End Class
```

I've also made the font a little smaller so that the screen shot isn't inordinately huge:

Rotation doesn't distort the individual characters. If you tilt this book side to side, you'll see that each text string displayed so far is entirely normal except that it's oriented in a different direction. When you shear a text string, however, the individual characters *are* distorted. The horizontal and vertical strokes will no longer be at right angles to each other.

Here's a program that uses the *Shear* method of the *Matrix* class to set a horizontal shear of 0.5.

```
SimpleShear.vb
'----------------------------------------------------------
' SimpleShear.vb (c) 2002 by Charles Petzold
'----------------------------------------------------------
Imports System
Imports System.Drawing
Imports System.Drawing.Drawing2D
Imports System.Windows.Forms

Class SimpleShear
    Inherits FontMenuForm

    Shared Shadows Sub Main()
        Application.Run(New SimpleShear())
    End Sub

    Sub New()
        Text = "Simple Shear"
```

*(continued)*

**SimpleShear.vb** *(continued)*

```
        strText = "Shear"
        fnt = New Font("Times New Roman", 72)
    End Sub

    Protected Overrides Sub DoPage(ByVal grfx As Graphics, _
            ByVal clr As Color, ByVal cx As Integer, ByVal cy As Integer)
        Dim br As New SolidBrush(clr)
        Dim matx As New Matrix()

        matx.Shear(0.5, 0)
        grfx.Transform = matx
        grfx.DrawString(strText, fnt, br, 0, 0)
    End Sub
End Class
```

The particular call to *Shear* in this program changes the default transformation matrix from

$$\begin{vmatrix} 1 & 0 & 0 \\ 0 & 1 & 0 \\ 0 & 0 & 1 \end{vmatrix}$$

to

$$\begin{vmatrix} 1 & 0 & 0 \\ 0.5 & 1 & 0 \\ 0 & 0 & 1 \end{vmatrix}$$

and the transformation formulas from

$$x' = x$$
$$y' = y$$

to

$$x' = x + 0.5 \cdot y$$
$$y' = y$$

At the very top of the client area (or printer page), $y$ equals 0 and the shear has no effect. But as you move down the client area, $y$ gets larger and hence $x'$ is shifted more to the right. Here's the resultant text string:

Although the characters bend to the left, notice that they still sit on a horizontal baseline; that is, the characters are not simply rotated but definitely distorted. This is a reverse oblique (or italic) effect. As you increase the first argument to *Shear*, the effect becomes more pronounced; if you make the argument negative, you'll get more normal-looking oblique text.

If you switch around the coordinates to the *Shear* method like so,

```
matx.Shear(0, 0.5)
```

you'll get vertical shear:

Here you can see that the vertical strokes on the *h* and *r* are still vertical, but the baseline is now at an angle to the horizontal axis.

Using shear with text can be a bit tricky. For example, suppose you want to draw some text on a baseline, as does the TextOnBaseline program in Chapter 9 (on page 383):

Now suppose you want to give the text an artificial oblique look using shear. You probably want the text to sit on the same baseline in the same location, but just tilted forward a bit. Because shear is always relative to the graphical origin, you need to use translation to move the origin to the baseline.

The BaselineTilt program is much like TextOnBaseline but has been modified to derive from FontMenuForm. The BaselineTilt program is also a little different in that it sets the baseline three-quarters of the distance down the client area rather than one-half (to take better advantage of client area real estate) and makes use of the *GetAscent* method in FontMenuForm.

**BaselineTilt.vb**

```
'------------------------------------------------
' BaselineTilt.vb (c) 2002 by Charles Petzold
'------------------------------------------------
Imports System
Imports System.Drawing
Imports System.Drawing.Drawing2D
Imports System.Windows.Forms

Class BaselineTilt
    Inherits FontMenuForm

    Shared Shadows Sub Main()
        Application.Run(New BaselineTilt())
    End Sub

    Sub New()
        Text = "Baseline Tilt"
        strText = "Baseline"
```

```
        fnt = New Font("Times New Roman", 144)
    End Sub

    Protected Overrides Sub DoPage(ByVal grfx As Graphics, _
            ByVal clr As Color, ByVal cx As Integer, ByVal cy As Integer)
        Dim yBaseline As Single = 3 * cy \ 4
        Dim cyAscent As Single = GetAscent(grfx, fnt)

        grfx.DrawLine(New Pen(clr), 0, yBaseline, cx, yBaseline)
        grfx.TranslateTransform(0, yBaseline)

        Dim matx As Matrix = grfx.Transform
        matx.Shear(-0.5, 0)
        grfx.Transform = matx

        grfx.DrawString(strText, fnt, New SolidBrush(clr), 0, -cyAscent)
    End Sub
End Class
```

This new program also shears the text string. The *TranslateTransform* call sets the origin at the designated baseline on the left side of the client area:

```
grfx.TranslateTransform(0, yBaseline)
```

The following three calls set a negative horizontal shear:

```
Dim matx As Matrix = grfx.Transform
matx.Shear(-0.5, 0)
grfx.Transform = matx
```

However, because of the previous *TranslateTransform* call, the shear is relative to the new origin. Here are the transformation formulas:

$$x' = x - 0.5 \cdot y$$
$$y' = y + yBaseline$$

The point (0, 0) in world coordinates maps to the point (0, *yBaseline*) in client area coordinates, which is the designated baseline. Points above the baseline (world coordinates with negative $y$ values) are sheared to the right. Points below the baseline (positive $y$ values) are sheared to the left.

The program displays the text at the world coordinate (0, *−cyAscent*), where *cyAscent* is the height of the characters above the baseline. I'm using a *DrawString* call with no *StringFormat* argument, so the specified world coordinates indicate the point that corresponds to the upper left corner of the text string. The transformation formulas map the coordinate (0, *−cyClient*) to the point (0.5 × *cyAscent, yBaseline − cyAscent*). The left side of the baseline of the text string is displayed at the point (0, 0) in world coordinates, which (as I mentioned) is mapped to the point (0, *yBaseline*), exactly where we want it:

Although that certainly looks like an italic text string, it's not: the lowercase a is roman style, not italic.

Now that we know how to display normal text and sheared text on the same baseline, a very interesting technique suddenly becomes available. Here's a program that demonstrates the technique, exaggerating the shear and making the sheared text taller as well.

**TiltedShadow.vb**

```
'-------------------------------------------------
' TiltedShadow.vb (c) 2002 by Charles Petzold
'-------------------------------------------------
Imports System
Imports System.Drawing
Imports System.Drawing.Drawing2D
Imports System.Windows.Forms

Class TiltedShadow
    Inherits FontMenuForm

    Shared Shadows Sub Main()
        Application.Run(New TiltedShadow())
    End Sub

    Sub New()
        Text = "Tilted Shadow"
        strText = "Shadow"
        fnt = New Font("Times New Roman", 54)
    End Sub

    Protected Overrides Sub DoPage(ByVal grfx As Graphics, _
            ByVal clr As Color, ByVal cx As Integer, ByVal cy As Integer)
        Dim fAscent As Single = GetAscent(grfx, fnt)

        ' Set baseline 3/4 down client area.
        grfx.TranslateTransform(0, 3 * cy \ 4)

        ' Save the graphics state.
        Dim grfxstate As GraphicsState = grfx.Save()
```

```
        ' Set scaling and shear, and draw shadow.
        grfx.MultiplyTransform(New Matrix(1, 0, -3, 3, 0, 0))
        grfx.DrawString(strText, fnt, Brushes.DarkGray, 0, -fAscent)

        ' Draw text without scaling or shear.
        grfx.Restore(grfxstate)
        grfx.DrawString(strText, fnt, Brushes.Black, 0, -fAscent)
    End Sub
End Class
```

Like the BaselineTilt program, the TiltedShadow program calls *TranslateTransform* to set the origin at the client-area coordinate *(0, 3 \* cy / 4)*. The *MultiplyTransform* call then multiplies the transform by the matrix:

$$\begin{vmatrix} 1 & 0 & 0 \\ -3 & 3 & 0 \\ 0 & 0 & 1 \end{vmatrix}$$

The resultant composite transform is

$$x' = x - 3 \cdot y$$
$$y' = 3 \cdot y + (3 * cy / 4)$$

The shear is more extreme than in the earlier program, and the $y$ coordinates are tripled as well. Combined with text displayed normally on the baseline, the result is a shadow effect:

This effect doesn't work well when some of the text characters have descenders: the shadow then appears in front of the text. To make the shadow seem to fall back from the bottom of the descenders, change the variable I've called *fAscent* to be the sum of the ascent and the descent:

```
Dim fAscent As Single = GetAscent(grfx, fnt) + GetDescent(grfx, fnt)
```

Of course, you'll want to change the *strText* variable to use an appropriate text string:

Notice that the shadow falls back from the bottom of the *q* and the *y*.

# Text and Paths

The *GraphicsPath* class includes a method named *AddString* that lets you add a text string to a path. The straight lines and curves that make up the character outlines become part of the path. As usual, however, text is a little different from other graphics objects, and adding text to a path requires some special considerations.

The first problem involves the *AddString* method itself. As you'll recall from Chapter 15, most of the *Add* methods in *GraphicsPath* are very similar to the corresponding *Draw* methods in the *Graphics* class. For example, using the *Graphics* class, you can draw a line by calling

```
grfx.DrawLine(pn, x1, y1, x2, y2)
```

You can add a line to a path by calling

```
path.AddLine(x1, y1, x2, y2)
```

The *AddLine* method doesn't require a *Pen* argument because the path retains only the coordinates of the lines.

In contrast, the *AddString* methods of *GraphicsPath* are considerably different from the *DrawString* methods of the *Graphics* class. Instead of specifying a font (as in *DrawString*), you specify the three basic components that go into making a font (a font family, a style, and a size) plus a destination (either a point or a rectangle) and a *StringFormat* object:

### *GraphicsPath AddString* Methods

```
Sub AddString(ByVal str As String, ByVal ff As FontFamily,
            ByVal iStyle As Integer, ByVal fSize As Single,
            ByVal pt As Point, ByVal sf As StringFormat)

Sub AddString(ByVal str As String, ByVal ff As FontFamily,
            ByVal iStyle As Integer, ByVal fSize As Single,
            ByVal ptf As PointF , ByVal sf As StringFormat)

Sub AddString(ByVal str As String, ByVal ff As FontFamily,
            ByVal iStyle As Integer, ByVal fSize As Single,
            ByVal rect As Rectangle , ByVal sf As StringFormat)

Sub AddString(ByVal str As String, ByVal ff As FontFamily,
            ByVal iStyle As Integer, ByVal fSize As Single,
            ByVal rectf As RectangleF, ByVal sf As StringFormat)
```

Notice that the third argument is defined as an *Integer*, but it's really a member of the *FontStyle* enumeration cast to an *Integer*.

When you create a font for drawing, you generally base the font on a specific metrical size. Very often, you specify the font size in points, but you can also use inches or millimeters. As I showed in Chapter 9, it's also possible to create a font that is *not* a specific metrical size by using the *GraphicsUnit.Pixel* or *GraphicsUnit.World* value in the *Font* constructor. The size of such a font is just a number. When you render text using that font, the size is interpreted at that time in terms of the current page coordinates of the output device.

A path doesn't retain metrical information. The path is only a collection of coordinates. For that reason, the *AddString* method can't be defined in terms of a *Font*. (And if there were an *AddString* method that *did* include a *Font* argument, it would undoubtedly be restricted to a *Font* object created with *GraphicsUnit.Pixel* or *GraphicsUnit.World*.)

Let's assume you add a text string to a path by calling *AddString* with a fourth argument of 72. What does that number mean? How large will the font be? It all depends on the page transform in effect when you eventually render that path by calling *DrawPath* or *FillPath*. If the page unit is *GraphicsUnit.Point*, the text will be rendered in the same size as a 72-point font drawn using *DrawString*. But if you render the path on the printer using the default *GraphicsUnit.Display* page units, the 72 units will be interpreted as 0.72 inch, and the text will be rendered in the same size as a 52-point font. (That's 0.72

inch times 72 points to an inch.) If you render the path on the screen using the default *GraphicsUnit.Pixel* page units, the size of the font will depend on the video resolution. If the video resolution is 120 dpi, for example, the 72-unit size of the font will be interpreted as 72/120 inch and will appear about the size of a 43-point font. (That's 72/120 inch times 72 points to the inch.)

It's likely that you want text in a path to be compatible with text displayed normally. Perhaps the simplest approach is to call *AddString* with the desired point size of the font. Then, before rendering the path, you simply set page units to points:

```
grfx.PageUnit = GraphicsUnit.Point
```

Another approach (one that I'll be using in the sample programs in the remainder of this chapter) lets you use the default page units when rendering the font. But you need to calculate an *fSize* argument to *AddString* based on the desired point size of the font and the resolution of the device. (That means you can't use the same path on both the screen and the printer.) Suppose you already have a *Font* object named *fnt*, and you want to add text to a path based on that font. The second argument of *AddString* is just *fnt.FontFamily*. The third argument is *fnt.FontStyle* cast to an *Integer*. The fourth argument is calculated like so:

```
If grfx.PageUnit = GraphicsUnit.Display Then
    fFontSize = 100 * fnt.SizeInPoints / 72
Else
    fFontSize = grfx.DpiX * fnt.SizeInPoints / 72
End If
```

The first calculation is for the printer; the second is for the video display. If you look back at the FontMenuForm program, you'll see that I've implemented this calculation in the *PointsToPageUnits* method.

Regardless of what precautions you take to calculate font sizes, text displayed using *DrawString* and text displayed by rendering a path on which *AddString* was earlier called won't be identical, particularly on the video display. When you call *DrawString*, some adjustments are made to the text to make it more readable. If you need two chunks of text to be rendered in exactly the same size (for example, if one overlays the other), don't use a path for one and *DrawString* for the other. Use a path for both.

I've mentioned *hints* in connection with outline fonts. When you add a text string to a path, all that's saved in the path are floating-point coordinates. The hints are gone. When that path is eventually rendered, the floating-point coordinates must be converted to pixels. Some rounding will be involved, and the rounding isn't likely to be entirely consistent. For example, the widths of the two vertical strokes of the *H* might differ by a pixel. For large font sizes, you won't notice the problem. On high-resolution devices like the printer, you won't notice the problem either. But for normal font sizes on the video display, the appearance of the text will be intolerable.

For that reason, text added to paths looks best in larger font sizes or on high-resolution output devices like the printer. *Use a path only for special text effects; avoid using paths for normal text.*

Let's look at an example. Some graphics systems let you create an *outline*, or *hollow*, font that consists of just an outline with an unfilled interior. Windows Forms doesn't include such a style in the *FontStyle* enumeration. To display outlined font characters, however, you can use a path, as I've done in the Hollow-Font program.

**HollowFont.vb**

```
'-----------------------------------------------
' HollowFont.vb (c) 2002 by Charles Petzold
'-----------------------------------------------
Imports System
Imports System.Drawing
Imports System.Drawing.Drawing2D
Imports System.Windows.Forms

Class HollowFont
    Inherits FontMenuForm

    Shared Shadows Sub Main()
        Application.Run(New HollowFont())
    End Sub

    Sub New()
        Text = "Hollow Font"
        Width *= 2
        strText = "Hollow"
        fnt = New Font("Times New Roman", 108)
    End Sub

    Protected Overrides Sub DoPage(ByVal grfx As Graphics, _
            ByVal clr As Color, ByVal cx As Integer, ByVal cy As Integer)
        Dim path As New GraphicsPath()
        Dim fFontSize As Single = PointsToPageUnits(grfx, fnt)

        ' Get coordinates for a centered string.
        Dim szf As SizeF = grfx.MeasureString(strText, fnt)
        Dim ptf As New PointF((cx - szf.Width) / 2, _
                              (cy - szf.Height) / 2)

        ' Add text to the path.
        path.AddString(strText, fnt.FontFamily, fnt.Style, _
                fFontSize, ptf, New StringFormat())
```

*(continued)*

**HollowFont.vb** *(continued)*

```
        ' Draw the path.
        grfx.DrawPath(New Pen(clr), path)
    End Sub
End Class
```

Before calling *AddString*, the program calculates a font size—here stored in a variable named *fFontSize*—using the technique I described earlier. The program also calculates a *PointF* argument to *AddString* that has the effect of centering the string in the client area when the path is drawn (which happens at the end of the *DoPage* method).

The HollowFont program calculates the *PointF* destination of the text before adding the text to the path because the *DrawPath* method itself has no argument to indicate where the path is drawn. All the coordinates in the path are simply interpreted as world coordinates when *DrawPath* is called. However, the *PointF* argument to *AddString* indicates the upper left coordinate of the text string. All the coordinates of the text characters are relative to that point, and those are the coordinates stored in the path. The HollowFont program calculates this point using *MeasureString* with the original *Font* object as if it were preparing to display text using *DrawString*. Here's the result:

Try clicking the Font! menu item to specify a 12-point font. You'll see that the text doesn't look very readable on the video display. It's a rounding problem.

There's another approach to centering text stored in a path. This alternative approach is more generalized because it's based on the coordinates stored within the path itself. The *GraphicsPath* method *GetBounds* returns a *RectangleF* that is the smallest rectangle encompassing all the coordinates of the path.

You can use that rectangle to center the contents of the path, perhaps most easily by calling *TranslateTransform* on the destination *Graphics* object.

Don't assume that the rectangle returned from *GetBounds* will have an upper left corner of (0, 0), even if you call *AddString* with a *PointF* argument of (0, 0). The *Left* property of the rectangle will probably be a bit greater than 0 because there's normally a little margin before the first text character. The *Top* property of the rectangle will likewise often be larger than 0.

Here's a program that calls *AddString* with a *PointF* argument of (0, 0) and then centers the path in the client area using the bounding rectangle of the path.

**HollowFontCenteredPath.vb**

```
'------------------------------------------------------------
' HollowFontCenteredPath.vb (c) 2002 by Charles Petzold
'------------------------------------------------------------
Imports System
Imports System.Drawing
Imports System.Drawing.Drawing2D
Imports System.Windows.Forms

Class HollowFontCenteredPath
    Inherits FontMenuForm

    Shared Shadows Sub Main()
        Application.Run(New HollowFontCenteredPath())
    End Sub

    Sub New()
        Text = "Hollow Font (Centered Path)"
        Width *= 2
        strText = "Hollow"
        fnt = New Font("Times New Roman", 108)
    End Sub

    Protected Overrides Sub DoPage(ByVal grfx As Graphics, _
            ByVal clr As Color, ByVal cx As Integer, ByVal cy As Integer)
        Dim path As New GraphicsPath()
        Dim fFontSize As Single = PointsToPageUnits(grfx, fnt)

        ' Add text to the path.
        path.AddString(strText, fnt.FontFamily, fnt.Style, _
                fFontSize, New PointF(0, 0), New StringFormat())

        ' Get the path bounds for centering.
        Dim rectfBounds As RectangleF = path.GetBounds()
        grfx.TranslateTransform( _
                (cx - rectfBounds.Width) / 2 - rectfBounds.Left, _
                (cy - rectfBounds.Height) / 2 - rectfBounds.Top)
```

*(continued)*

**HollowFontCenteredPath.vb**   *(continued)*

```
        ' Draw the path.
        Dim pn As New Pen(clr, fFontSize / 50)
        pn.DashStyle = DashStyle.Dot
        grfx.DrawPath(pn, path)
    End Sub
End Class
```

Notice the call to *TranslateTransform* based on the width and height of the display area, and the dimensions and upper left corner of the bounding rectangle.

I've also defined the pen a little differently, this time making the width equal to 1/50 of *fFontSize* and setting a *DashStyle* of *Dot*:

If you compare this screen shot with the one from HollowFont, you'll see that it's centered a little differently. The vertical centering of the HollowFont text is based on the height returned from *MeasureString*, which is a height associated with the font and includes descenders and diacritical marks, even if they're not present in the particular text string being measured. For example, *MeasureString* returns the same height for the strings "Ã", "a", and "y".

The text displayed by HollowFontCenteredPath, however, is vertically centered based solely on the coordinates in the path. The centering of the text is more visually accurate.

Do you remember the HowdyWorldFullFit program in Chapter 9 that attempted to expand a string by using *MeasureString* and *ScaleTransform* to fit a rectangle? It didn't quite manage to fill the destination rectangle because *MeasureString* includes margins for descenders and diacritical marks. Here's a program that uses the path bounding rectangle and *ScaleTransform* to tightly fill the client area with a short text string.

**FullFit.vb**

```
'-------------------------------------------------
' FullFit.vb (c) 2002 by Charles Petzold
'-------------------------------------------------
Imports System
Imports System.Drawing
Imports System.Drawing.Drawing2D
Imports System.Windows.Forms

Class FullFit
    Inherits FontMenuForm

    Shared Shadows Sub Main()
        Application.Run(New FullFit())
    End Sub

    Sub New()
        Text = "Full Fit"
        strText = "Full Fit"
        fnt = New Font("Times New Roman", 108)
    End Sub

    Protected Overrides Sub DoPage(ByVal grfx As Graphics, _
            ByVal clr As Color, ByVal cx As Integer, ByVal cy As Integer)
        Dim path As New GraphicsPath()

        ' Add text to the path.
        path.AddString(strText, fnt.FontFamily, fnt.Style, _
                        100, New Point(0, 0), New StringFormat())

        ' Set the world transform.
        Dim rectfBounds As RectangleF = path.GetBounds()
        Dim aptfDest() As PointF = {New PointF(0, 0), New PointF(cx, 0), _
                                                    New PointF(0, cy)}
        grfx.Transform = New Matrix(rectfBounds, aptfDest)

        ' Fill the path.
        grfx.FillPath(New SolidBrush(clr), path)
    End Sub
End Class
```

The program sets a world transform using the powerful *Matrix* constructor that has two arguments, a *RectangleF* structure and an array of three *PointF* structures:

```
grfx.Transform = New Matrix(rectfBounds, aptfDest)
```

This constructor calculates a transform that maps three corners of the *RectangleF* structure to the three *PointF* structures. Simply set the *RectangleF* structure to the path bounding rectangle, and the three *PointF* structures to three corners of the display area, and the path fills the space.

You'll definitely want to print this one as well. You can change the font, but you'll see that the initial font size doesn't matter. The text is always scaled to the size of the client area. That's why the *AddString* call in this program has an arbitrary hard-coded font size value of 100.

I mentioned earlier that when you need to use a path for displaying text, you should also use it for any other text that must match in size, even if the other text doesn't require a path. Here's a program that uses the same path for two *FillPath* calls and one *DrawPath* call. The two *FillPath* calls could have been done with a call to *DrawString* except the text wouldn't have aligned correctly on the screen.

**DropShadowWithPath.vb**

```
'---------------------------------------------------
' DropShadowWithPath.vb (c) 2002 by Charles Petzold
'---------------------------------------------------
Imports System
Imports System.Drawing
Imports System.Drawing.Drawing2D
Imports System.Windows.Forms

Class DropShadowWithPath
    Inherits FontMenuForm

    Const iOffset As Integer = 10 ' About 1/10 inch (exactly on printer)

    Shared Shadows Sub Main()
        Application.Run(New DropShadowWithPath())
    End Sub
```

```
    Sub New()
        Text = "Drop Shadow with Path"
        Width *= 2
        strText = "Shadow"
        fnt = New Font("Times New Roman", 108)
    End Sub

    Protected Overrides Sub DoPage(ByVal grfx As Graphics, _
            ByVal clr As Color, ByVal cx As Integer, ByVal cy As Integer)
        Dim path As New GraphicsPath()
        Dim fFontSize As Single = PointsToPageUnits(grfx, fnt)

        ' Get coordinates for a centered string.
        Dim szf As SizeF = grfx.MeasureString(strText, fnt)
        Dim ptf As New PointF((cx - szf.Width) / 2, _
                              (cy - szf.Height) / 2)

        ' Add the text to the path.
        path.AddString(strText, fnt.FontFamily, fnt.Style, _
                       fFontSize, ptf, New StringFormat())

        ' Clear, fill, translate, fill, and draw.
        grfx.Clear(Color.White)
        grfx.FillPath(Brushes.Black, path)
        path.Transform(New Matrix(1, 0, 0, 1, -10, -10))
        grfx.FillPath(Brushes.White, path)
        grfx.DrawPath(Pens.Black, path)
    End Sub
End Class
```

When you outline font characters, you can color them in the same color as the background. I prefer this drop-shadow effect to the earlier one:

You can use a similar technique for a block effect on a white background.

Here's a program that draws the outline of the font characters using a pen created from a hatch brush with a width that's 1/20 of the *fFontSize* value.

**HollowFontWidePen.vb**

```
'---------------------------------------------------
' HollowFontWidePen.vb (c) 2002 by Charles Petzold
'---------------------------------------------------
Imports System
Imports System.Drawing
Imports System.Drawing.Drawing2D
Imports System.Windows.Forms

Class HollowFontWidePen
    Inherits FontMenuForm

    Shared Shadows Sub Main()
        Application.Run(New HollowFontWidePen())
    End Sub

    Sub New()
        Text = "Hollow Font (Wide Pen)"
        Width *= 2
        strText = "Wide Pen"
        fnt = New Font("Times New Roman", 108, _
                    FontStyle.Bold Or FontStyle.Italic)
    End Sub

    Protected Overrides Sub DoPage(ByVal grfx As Graphics, _
            ByVal clr As Color, ByVal cx As Integer, ByVal cy As Integer)
        Dim path As New GraphicsPath()
        Dim fFontSize As Single = PointsToPageUnits(grfx, fnt)

        ' Add text to the path.
        path.AddString(strText, fnt.FontFamily, fnt.Style, _
                    fFontSize, New PointF(0, 0), New StringFormat())

        ' Get the path bounds for centering.
        Dim rectfBounds As RectangleF = path.GetBounds()
        grfx.TranslateTransform( _
                (cx - rectfBounds.Width) / 2 - rectfBounds.Left, _
                (cy - rectfBounds.Height) / 2 - rectfBounds.Top)

        ' Draw the path.
        Dim br As New HatchBrush(HatchStyle.Trellis, _
                                Color.White, Color.Black)
        Dim pn As New Pen(br, fFontSize / 20)
        grfx.DrawPath(pn, path)
    End Sub
End Class
```

The effect isn't quite satisfactory to my eyes:

What's needed here, I think, is a border around the brush pattern. In other words, the character outlines themselves need to be outlined. Is such a thing possible? Yes, it's what happens when you call the *Widen* method of the *GraphicsPath* class. A new path is created based on the existing path as if it had been drawn with a pen of a specific width. Here's a demonstration program.

```vb
HollowFontWidened.vb
'-------------------------------------------------
' HollowFontWidened.vb (c) 2002 by Charles Petzold
'-------------------------------------------------
Imports System
Imports System.Drawing
Imports System.Drawing.Drawing2D
Imports System.Windows.Forms

Class HollowFontWidened
    Inherits FontMenuForm

    Shared Shadows Sub Main()
        Application.Run(new HollowFontWidened())
    End Sub

    Sub New()
        Text = "Hollow Font (Widened)"
        Width *= 2
        strText = "Widened"
        fnt = New Font("Times New Roman", 108, _
                    FontStyle.Bold Or FontStyle.Italic)
    End Sub

    Protected Overrides Sub DoPage(ByVal grfx As Graphics, _
            ByVal clr As Color, ByVal cx As Integer, ByVal cy As Integer)
        Dim path As New GraphicsPath()
        Dim fFontSize As Single = PointsToPageUnits(grfx, fnt)

        ' Add text to the path.
        path.AddString(strText, fnt.FontFamily, fnt.Style, _
                    fFontSize, New PointF(0, 0), New StringFormat())
```

*(continued)*

**HollowFontWidened.vb** *(continued)*

```
        ' Get the path bounds for centering.
        Dim rectfBounds As RectangleF = path.GetBounds()
        grfx.TranslateTransform( _
                    (cx - rectfBounds.Width) / 2 - rectfBounds.Left, _
                    (cy - rectfBounds.Height) / 2 - rectfBounds.Top)

        ' Widen, fill, and draw the path.
        path.Widen(New Pen(Color.Black, fFontSize / 20))
        Dim br As New HatchBrush(HatchStyle.Trellis, _
                                Color.White, Color.Black)
        grfx.DrawPath(New Pen(Color.Black, 2), path)
        grfx.FillPath(br, path)
    End Sub
End Class
```

All the new code appears at the bottom of the *DoPage* method. The previous program called *DrawPath* used a wide pen based on a hatch brush. This new program draws basically the same thing by calling *Widen* based on a wide pen and then calling *FillPath* using the hatch brush.

You can verify that the results are the same by commenting out the *Draw-Path* call in the HollowFontWidened program. But the *DrawPath* call is the one that provides the effect I was after. It outlines the outlines:

I arrived at some of the coding decisions in HollowBrushWidened through experimentation. I originally called *DrawPath* after *FillPath*, but *DrawPath* drew a bunch of little squiggles and loops that are a result of the algorithm used in widening the path. (Try leaving out the *FillPath* call to see what I'm talking about. You may actually like the effect—like a mechanical drawing machine a bit out of alignment.) I moved *FillPath* after *DrawPath* to cover up the squiggles and then needed to use a pen width of 2 in *DrawPath* because the brush was obscuring much of the pen.

You can also set a clipping region from a path, which means that you can clip graphics output to the interior of a text string. Here's a program that sets a clipping region and then draws a bunch of Bézier splines in random colors.

## ClipText.vb

```
'-----------------------------------------
' ClipText.vb (c) 2002 by Charles Petzold
'-----------------------------------------
Imports System
Imports System.Drawing
Imports System.Drawing.Drawing2D
Imports System.Windows.Forms

Class ClipText
    Inherits FontMenuForm

    Shared Shadows Sub Main()
        Application.Run(New ClipText())
    End Sub

    Sub New()
        Text = "Clip Text"
        Width *= 2
        strText = "Clip Text"
        fnt = New Font("Times New Roman", 108, FontStyle.Bold)
    End Sub

    Protected Overrides Sub DoPage(ByVal grfx As Graphics, _
            ByVal clr As Color, ByVal cx As Integer, ByVal cy As Integer)
        Dim path As New GraphicsPath()
        Dim fFontSize As Single = PointsToPageUnits(grfx, fnt)

        ' Add text to the path.
        path.AddString(strText, fnt.FontFamily, fnt.Style, _
                    fFontSize, New PointF(0, 0), New StringFormat())

        ' Set the clipping region.
        grfx.SetClip(path)

        ' Get the path bounds and center the clipping region.
        Dim rectfBounds As RectangleF = path.GetBounds()
        grfx.TranslateClip( _
                (cx - rectfBounds.Width) / 2 - rectfBounds.Left, _
                (cy - rectfBounds.Height) / 2 - rectfBounds.Top)

        ' Draw clipped lines.
        Dim rand As New Random()
        Dim y As Integer
        For y = 0 To cy - 1
            Dim pn As New Pen(Color.FromArgb(rand.Next(255), _
                                             rand.Next(255), _
                                             rand.Next(255)))
            grfx.DrawBezier(pn, New Point(0, y), _
                                New Point(cx \ 3, y + cy \ 3), _
```

*(continued)*

**ClipText.vb**    *(continued)*

```
                                 New Point(2 * cx \ 3, y - cy \ 3), _
                                 New Point(cx, y))
        Next y
    End Sub
End Class
```

Here's the result:

## Nonlinear Transforms

The matrix transform is widely available throughout the Windows Forms graphics system. You can apply it to a *Graphics* object, to a path, and to brushes and pens. But the matrix transform is always a *linear* transform. Parallel lines are always mapped to other parallel lines, and after awhile, you might begin to see those consistently parallel lines as bars on a jail cell.

The *GraphicsPath* class has one nonlinear transform available through a method named *Warp*. Here's a program that stores some text in a path and then uses *Warp* to scrunch together the top of the path.

**WarpText.vb**

```
'------------------------------------------
' WarpText.vb (c) 2002 by Charles Petzold
'------------------------------------------
Imports System
Imports System.Drawing
Imports System.Drawing.Drawing2D
Imports System.Windows.Forms

Class WarpText
    Inherits FontMenuForm

    Private iWarpMode As Integer = 0
```

```
    Shared Shadows Sub Main()
        Application.Run(New WarpText())
    End Sub

    Sub New()
        Text = "Warp Text - " & CType(iWarpMode, WarpMode).ToString()
        Menu.MenuItems.Add("&Toggle!", AddressOf MenuToggleOnClick)
        strText = "WARP"
        fnt = New Font("Arial Black", 24)
    End Sub

    Private Sub MenuToggleOnClick(ByVal obj As Object, _
            ByVal ea As EventArgs)
        iWarpMode = iWarpMode Xor 1
        Text = "Warp Text - " & CType(iWarpMode, WarpMode).ToString()
        Invalidate()
    End Sub

    Protected Overrides Sub DoPage(ByVal grfx As Graphics, _
            ByVal clr As Color, ByVal cx As Integer, ByVal cy As Integer)
        Dim path As New GraphicsPath()

        ' Add text to the path.
        path.AddString(strText, fnt.FontFamily, fnt.Style, _
                    100, New PointF(0, 0), New StringFormat())

        ' Warp the path.
        Dim rectfBounds As RectangleF = path.GetBounds()
        Dim aptfDest() As PointF = {New PointF(cx \ 3, 0), _
                                    New PointF(2 * cx \ 3, 0), _
                                    New PointF(0, cy), _
                                    New PointF(cx, cy)}
        path.Warp(aptfDest, rectfBounds, New Matrix(), _
                CType(iWarpMode, WarpMode))

        ' Fill the path.
        grfx.FillPath(New SolidBrush(clr), path)
    End Sub
End Class
```

Earlier, in the FullFit program, I used a constructor of *Matrix* that calculated a transform that mapped three corners of a rectangle into three points in an array. The *Warp* method is similar, but it maps four corners of a rectangle (again, I use the bounding rectangle of the path) into four points of an array. For the destination array, I used the two bottom corners of the client area and two points at the top of the client area closer to the center than the top corners.

The menu item labeled "Toggle!" lets you switch between perspective and bilinear warp modes. The bilinear mode doesn't work well with this image.

Although the *Warp* method is the only nonlinear transform directly available to Windows Forms programmers, the graphics path actually gives you the ability to perform *any* nonlinear transform that you can conceive and describe mathematically. Here's how you do it:

- Get the array of coordinates in the path by using the *PathPoints* property.

- Modify those coordinates by using custom transformation formulas.

- Create a new path based on the modified coordinates.

The hard part, of course, is devising the transformation formulas.

Here's a program that displays a string of text that gets progressively taller toward the center.

**TallInTheCenter.vb**

```
'-------------------------------------------------
' TallInTheCenter.vb (c) 2002 by Charles Petzold
'-------------------------------------------------
Imports System
Imports System.Drawing
Imports System.Drawing.Drawing2D
Imports System.Windows.Forms

Class TallInTheCenter
    Inherits FontMenuForm

    Shared Shadows Sub Main()
        Application.Run(New TallInTheCenter())
    End Sub
```

```
   Sub New()
       Text = "Tall in the Center"
       Width *= 2
       strText = Text
       fnt = New Font("Times New Roman", 48)
   End Sub

   Protected Overrides Sub DoPage(ByVal grfx As Graphics, _
           ByVal clr As Color, ByVal cx As Integer, ByVal cy As Integer)
       Dim path As New GraphicsPath()
       Dim fFontSize As Single = PointsToPageUnits(grfx, fnt)

       ' Add text to the path.
       path.AddString(strText, fnt.FontFamily, fnt.Style, _
                       fFontSize, New PointF(0, 0), New StringFormat())

       ' Shift the origin to the center of the path.
       Dim rectf As RectangleF = path.GetBounds()
       path.Transform(New Matrix(1, 0, 0, 1, _
                           -(rectf.Left + rectf.Right) / 2, _
                           -(rectf.Top + rectf.Bottom) / 2))
       rectf = path.GetBounds()

       ' Modify the path.
       Dim aptf() As PointF = path.PathPoints
       Dim i As Integer
       For i = 0 To aptf.GetUpperBound(0)
           aptf(i).Y *= 4 * (rectf.Width - Math.Abs(aptf(i).X)) / _
                                               rectf.Width

       Next i
       path = New GraphicsPath(aptf, path.PathTypes)

       ' Fill the path.
       grfx.TranslateTransform(cx \ 2, cy \ 2)
       grfx.FillPath(New SolidBrush(clr), path)
   End Sub
End Class
```

One helpful technique in programs like this is to prepare the path for a nonlinear transform by first performing a linear transform. After obtaining the path bounds (stored in the *rectf* variable), the program shifts the origin to the center of the path:

```
path.Transform(New Matrix(1, 0, 0, 1, _
                   -(rectf.Left + rectf.Right) / 2, _
                   -(rectf.Top + rectf.Bottom) / 2))
```

The program then calls *GetBounds* again to store the new bounds in *rectf*.

To begin the nonlinear transform, the program obtains the array of *PointF* structures that make up the path:

```
Dim aptf() As PointF = path.PathPoints
```

It then modifies the points, making the *Y* coordinates larger depending on how close the points are to the center:

```
For i = 0 To aptf.GetUpperBound(0)
    aptf(i).Y *= 4 * (rectf.Width - Math.Abs(aptf(i).X)) / rectf.Width
Next i
```

Then it creates a new path:

```
path = New GraphicsPath(aptf, path.PathTypes)
```

Here's what it looks like:

As in the FullFit program, the initial size of the font doesn't matter.

Here's another example. This one is called WrapText (not WarpText), and it wraps a text string around the circumference of a circle. The initial size of the font doesn't matter in this program either, but the program needs to know the character ascent, so it bases the *AddString* call on an actual font.

```
WrapText.vb
'-------------------------------------------
' WrapText.vb (c) 2002 by Charles Petzold
'-------------------------------------------
Imports System
Imports System.Drawing
Imports System.Drawing.Drawing2D
Imports System.Windows.Forms

Class WrapText
    Inherits FontMenuForm

    Const fRadius As Single = 100

    Shared Shadows Sub Main()
        Application.Run(New WrapText())
```

```
    End Sub

    Sub New()
        Text = "Wrap Text"
        strText = "e snake ate the tail of th"
        fnt = New Font("Times New Roman", 48)
    End Sub

    Protected Overrides Sub DoPage(ByVal grfx As Graphics, _
            ByVal clr As Color, ByVal cx As Integer, ByVal cy As Integer)
        Dim path As New GraphicsPath()
        Dim fFontSize As Single = PointsToPageUnits(grfx, fnt)

        ' Add text to the path.
        path.AddString(strText, fnt.FontFamily, fnt.Style, _
                    fFontSize, New PointF(0, 0), New StringFormat())

        ' Shift the origin to left baseline, y increasing up.
        Dim rectf As RectangleF = path.GetBounds()
        path.Transform(New Matrix(1, 0, 0, -1, -rectf.Left, _
                                    GetAscent(grfx, fnt)))

        ' Scale so width equals 2*PI.
        Dim fScale As Single = CSng(2 * Math.PI / rectf.Width)
        path.Transform(New Matrix(fScale, 0, 0, fScale, 0, 0))

        ' Modify the path.
        Dim aptf() As PointF = path.PathPoints
        Dim i As Integer
        For i = 0 To aptf.GetUpperBound(0)
            aptf(i) = New PointF( _
                CSng(fRadius * (1 + aptf(i).Y) * Math.Cos(aptf(i).X)), _
                CSng(fRadius * (1 + aptf(i).Y) * Math.Sin(aptf(i).X)))
        Next i
        path = New GraphicsPath(aptf, path.PathTypes)

        ' Fill the path.
        grfx.TranslateTransform(cx \ 2, cy \ 2)
        grfx.FillPath(New SolidBrush(clr), path)
    End Sub
End Class
```

Notice that the text string is intended to loop from the end to the beginning. It's written without blanks at the beginning and end because blanks wouldn't become part of the path, and the last nonblank character would run into the first one.

In this program, initially performing matrix transforms on the path was crucial to making the transformation formulas as simple as they are. The path is given an origin at the left side of the text baseline and is scaled so that it has a width of $2\pi$. The $X$ coordinates of the path are thus simply an angle in radians and can be passed directly to the *Cos* and *Sin* methods. The results of the *Cos* and *Sin* methods are scaled by the *Y* coordinates in combination with the desired radius of the circle:

Look closely and you'll see that the baselines of each character are arched and that each character is wider at the top than at the bottom. Use a shorter text string to exaggerate the effect.

# 20

# Toolbars and Status Bars

In providing a modern user interface for your programs, toolbars and status bars are the next step beyond the standard menu and dialog boxes. Although quite different in functionality—a toolbar usually contains pictorial buttons that often duplicate menu items, whereas a status bar usually conveys textual information to the user—these two types of controls have several similarities in the Microsoft .NET Framework. Both the *ToolBar* class and the *StatusBar* class are descended from *Control*, and both controls are customarily docked on an edge of the client area, the toolbar traditionally at the top and the status bar at the bottom. Both controls are usually host to smaller items. A toolbar is made up of multiple *ToolBarButton* items, and a status bar usually has multiple panels that are instances of the *StatusBarPanel* class. Both *ToolBarButton* and *StatusBar-Panel* are descended from *Component*.

As you'll recall, when you add a menu to a form, the menu doesn't lie on top of the form's client area. Instead, the client area is reduced in size to accommodate the menu. Similarly, when you enable the auto-scroll feature of your form, the client area is reduced in size to accommodate the scroll bars.

Toolbars and status bars are not like menus and scroll bars, however. They may seem architecturally similar, but toolbars and status bars are controls just like buttons and text boxes. They have a *Parent* property and sit on top of their parent. When the parent of a toolbar or status bar is a form, the control sits on top of the client area. The client area is *not* reduced in size to accommodate the control. (This difference is mostly an historical legacy. Menus and scroll bars existed from the early days of Windows and hence were considered part of the standard application window. Toolbars and status bars were introduced later and weren't integrated into the architecture of the standard window.)

The implications are simple: When you include a toolbar or status bar in your form, you can't draw over the entire height of your client area. The toolbar hides the top of your client area, and the status bar hides the bottom. The problem is also fairly simple to solve. Instead of drawing on your client area, you'll want to draw on a *Panel* control that fills the space between the toolbar and the status bar.

Real-world applications that implement a toolbar or a status bar should give the user an option to hide these items. The user can decide whether these items are worth the space they take away from the client area. You can implement a View menu to provide such options. Showing or hiding the toolbar or the status bar is just a matter of toggling the control's *Visible* property.

The status bar is the simpler of the two controls, so let's begin with that.

## The Basic Status Bar

If you need a status bar to display only one item—a description of menu items, for example—you can create a status bar and give it some text with three lines of code, as the SimpleStatusBar program illustrates.

```
SimpleStatusBar.vb
'-------------------------------------------------------
' SimpleStatusBar.vb (c) 2002 by Charles Petzold
'-------------------------------------------------------
Imports System
Imports System.Drawing
Imports System.Windows.Forms

Class SimpleStatusBar
    Inherits Form

    Shared Sub Main()
        Application.Run(New SimpleStatusBar())
    End Sub

    Sub New()
        Text = "Simple Status Bar"
        ResizeRedraw = True

        ' Create status bar.
        Dim sbar As New StatusBar()
        sbar.Parent = Me
        sbar.Text = "My initial status bar text"
    End Sub
```

```
     Protected Overrides Sub OnPaint(ByVal pea As PaintEventArgs)
         Dim grfx As Graphics = pea.Graphics
         Dim pn As New Pen(ForeColor)

         grfx.DrawLine(pn, 0, 0, ClientSize.Width, ClientSize.Height)
         grfx.DrawLine(pn, ClientSize.Width, 0, 0, ClientSize.Height)
     End Sub
 End Class
```

Of course, in a real program, you wouldn't store the *StatusBar* object as a local variable of the constructor because you need access to it while processing events. I added an *OnPaint* method just to drive home the fact that the status bar hides the bottom of the client area:

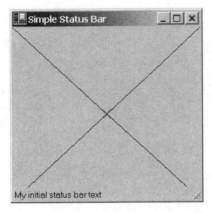

Notice that the diagonal lines seem to stop before reaching the corners of the form. The lines actually go all the way to the corners, but they're covered by the status bar.

The *StatusBar* control doesn't need to be explicitly positioned or sized; it extends across the full width of the form at the bottom. As you resize the form, the status bar also changes size. This behavior is a result of the *Dock* property of *StatusBar* being initialized to *DockStyle.Bottom* by default. A sizing grip appears at the right side of the status bar. This gives the user a larger target for grabbing the lower left corner of the form to resize it. You can remove the sizing grip by setting the *SizingGrip* property to *False*:

### *StatusBar* Properties (selection)

| Property | Type | Accessibility |
| --- | --- | --- |
| *SizingGrip* | *Boolean* | Get/Set |

*SizingGrip* is one of the few properties that *StatusBar* implements itself; most of the *StatusBar* properties are inherited from *Control*.

The *BackColor* and *ForeColor* properties of the status bar are initialized to *SystemColors.Control* and *SystemColors.ControlText*, and they can't be changed. (You could, however, change the form's *BackColor* property to make the status bar stand out.) The *BackgroundImage* property has no effect on the status bar. The status bar has no border style.

The *TabStop* property of the status bar is initialized to *False*, and you'll probably not want to change it. If you have other controls in your client area, you probably don't want the Tab key to give the status bar input focus.

If you want to display multiple items in a status bar, you need to make use of status bar *panels*. These panels have a much wider variety of options than the status bar itself. I'll be discussing status bar panels shortly.

# The Status Bar and Auto-Scroll

I've already warned you how the status bar affects the visibility of your client area. Here's another warning: You definitely don't want to enable the auto-scroll feature of your form when using a status bar. The status bar is treated just like any other control that is docked to the bottom. It becomes part of the display area that is scrolled by the scroll bars.

Here's a program that sets its *AutoScroll* property to *True* to demonstrate the problem.

```
StatusBarAndAutoScroll.vb
'-------------------------------------------------------
' StatusBarAndAutoScroll.vb (c) 2002 by Charles Petzold
'-------------------------------------------------------
Imports System
Imports System.Drawing
Imports System.Windows.Forms

Class StatusBarAndAutoScroll
    Inherits Form

    Shared Sub Main()
        Application.Run(New StatusBarAndAutoScroll())
    End Sub

    Sub New()
        Text = "Status Bar and Auto-Scroll"
        AutoScroll = True

        ' Create status bar.
        Dim sbar As New StatusBar()
```

```
        sbar.Parent = Me
        sbar.Text = "My initial status bar text"

        ' Create labels as children of the form.
        Dim lbl As New Label()
        lbl.Parent = Me
        lbl.Text = "Upper left"
        lbl.Location = New Point(0, 0)
        lbl.AutoSize = True

        lbl = New Label()
        lbl.Parent = Me
        lbl.Text = "Lower right"
        lbl.Location = New Point(250, 250)
        lbl.AutoSize = True
    End Sub
End Class
```

When you run this program, you need to scroll to the bottom of the client area to see the status bar! Here's what the program looks like when you scroll to the bottom right corner of the client area:

This doesn't look right at all. The status bar shouldn't be affected by the scroll bars. In fact, the status bar shouldn't even be within the area surrounded by the scroll bars. It should appear *below* the horizontal scroll bar.

To get this program looking and working right—and to solve the painting problem that results from the reduction of the client area—you can use the *Panel* control. A program that uses toolbars or status bars should almost always begin with the creation of a *Panel* control (or other control) that initially fills the client area.

You can persuade the *Panel* control to fill the client area by setting its *Dock* property to *DockStyle.Fill*. Then just about anything you'd normally do with the client area (decorate it with controls or paint on it) you would do to the *Panel* control. The only controls that remain children of the *Form* aside from the *Panel* are the toolbar and the status bar.

Here's an example.

**SimpleStatusBarWithPanel.vb**

```
'-------------------------------------------------------------
' SimpleStatusBarWithPanel.vb (c) 2002 by Charles Petzold
'-------------------------------------------------------------
Imports System
Imports System.Drawing
Imports System.Windows.Forms

Class SimpleStatusBarWithPanel
    Inherits Form

    Shared Sub Main()
        Application.Run(New SimpleStatusBarWithPanel())
    End Sub

    Sub New()
        Text = "Simple Status Bar with Panel"

        ' Create panel.
        Dim pnl As New Panel()
        pnl.Parent = Me
        pnl.BackColor = SystemColors.Window
        pnl.ForeColor = SystemColors.WindowText
        pnl.AutoScroll = True
        pnl.Dock = DockStyle.Fill
        pnl.BorderStyle = BorderStyle.Fixed3D

        ' Create status bar as child of form.
        Dim sbar As New StatusBar()
        sbar.Parent = Me
        sbar.Text = "My initial status bar text"

        ' Create labels as children of panel.
        Dim lbl As New Label()
        lbl.Parent = pnl
        lbl.Text = "Upper left"
        lbl.Location = New Point(0, 0)
        lbl.AutoSize = True

        lbl = New Label()
        lbl.Parent = pnl
        lbl.Text = "Lower right"
        lbl.Location = New Point(250, 250)
        lbl.AutoSize = True
    End Sub
End Class
```

Notice that this program sets the *AutoScroll* property of the *Panel* object to *True* and creates two *Label* objects as children of the panel.

The *Panel* is given a *Dock* property of *DockStyle.Fill* so that it initially fills the client area. When the *StatusBar* is then created, it assigns itself a *Dock* property of *DockStyle.Bottom*. The *Panel* and the *StatusBar* then essentially divide the client area into two nonoverlapping parts. With the panel's *AutoScroll* property set to *True*, the status bar appears below the scroll bars:

# Status Bar Panels

In the examples shown so far, the status bar is barely more functional than a label control that's docked to the bottom of the form. If you hide the sizing grip, you'd be hard pressed to tell them apart.

The status bar becomes more versatile when you make use of *StatusBar-Panel* objects. A status bar can contain zero or more status bar panels. *Status-Bar* has two properties that involve the *StatusBarPanel* objects:

### *StatusBar* Properties (selection)

| Property | Type | Accessibility |
|---|---|---|
| *ShowPanels* | *Boolean* | Get/Set |
| *Panels* | *StatusBar.StatusBarPanelCollection* | Get |

The *ShowPanels* property is initially *False*, and any panels that the status bar contains are ignored. Only one text string is displayed, which is the *Text* property of the *StatusBar* object itself. When you set the *ShowPanels* property to

*True*, the *Text* property of *StatusBar* is ignored, and instead the text strings associated with the *StatusBarPanel* objects are displayed. Each status bar panel is associated with a text string and an optional icon. Or you can use the owner-draw facility of the *StatusBar* class.

The *Panels* property of *StatusBar* is yet another collection class that provides an indexer and implements methods such as *Add*, *AddRange*, *Insert*, and *Remove* to maintain a collection of *StatusBarPanel* objects.

Here's a simple program that creates a status bar with two panels.

**TwoStatusBarPanels.vb**

```
'-------------------------------------------------
' TwoStatusBarPanels.vb (c) 2002 by Charles Petzold
'-------------------------------------------------
Imports System
Imports System.Drawing
Imports System.Windows.Forms

Class TwoStatusBarPanels
    Inherits Form

    Shared Sub Main()
        Application.Run(new TwoStatusBarPanels())
    End Sub

    Sub New()
        Text = "Two Status Bar Panels"
        BackColor = SystemColors.Window
        ForeColor = SystemColors.WindowText

        Dim sbar As New StatusBar()
        sbar.Parent = Me
        sbar.ShowPanels = True

        Dim sbp1 As New StatusBarPanel()
        sbp1.Text = "Panel 1"

        Dim sbp2 As New StatusBarPanel()
        sbp2.Text = "Panel 2"

        sbar.Panels.Add(sbp1)
        sbar.Panels.Add(sbp2)
    End Sub
End Class
```

This program creates one *StatusBar* object and two *StatusBarPanel* objects. Here's what it looks like:

*StatusBarPanel* doesn't derive from *Control*. The class has no *BackColor*, *ForeColor*, or *Font* property, no *Location* or *Size* property. (There is, however, a *Width* property, and that's initialized to 100 pixels.) *StatusBarPanel* has a *Parent* property, but it's read-only.

The only way to associate a *StatusBarPanel* object with a *StatusBar* object is through the *Panels* property of *StatusBar*. The TwoStatusBarPanels program shows the most common means of making this association, which is to use the *Add* method of *StatusBar.StatusBarPanelCollection*. Another approach is to make an array of *StatusBarPanel* objects and use the *AddRange* method:

```
sbar.Panels.AddRange(New StatusBarPanel() {sbp1, sbp2})
```

It's also possible to skip the explicit creation of the *StatusBarPanel* objects and use an overload of the *Add* method that requires just a string:

```
sbar.Panels.Add("Panel 1")
sbar.Panels.Add("Panel 2")
```

If you need to get access to the particular *StatusBarPanel* to set the *Text* property (for example), you can simply index the *Panels* property like an array:

```
sbar.Panels(1).Text = "New panel 2 text"
```

## *StatusBarPanel* Properties

*StatusBarPanel* has 10 noninherited properties. The only read-only property indicates the *StatusBar* control that the particular *StatusBarPanel* is associated with:

### *StatusBarPanel* Properties (selection)

| Property | Type | Accessibility |
|----------|------|---------------|
| *Parent* | *StatusBar* | Get |

The following properties of *StatusBarPanel* involve the panel's display of text:

### *StatusBarPanel* Properties (selection)

| Property | Type | Accessibility |
| --- | --- | --- |
| Style | StatusBarPanelStyle | Get/Set |
| Text | String | Get/Set |
| Icon | Icon | Get/Set |
| ToolTipText | String | Get/Set |

*StatusBarPanelStyle* is an enumeration that basically indicates whether the panel should be flagged as owner-draw:

### *StatusBarPanelStyle* Enumeration

| Member | Value |
| --- | --- |
| Text | 1 |
| OwnerDraw | 2 |

*StatusBarPanel* doesn't implement any events of its own. The *StatusBar* class has a *DrawItem* event, and the event arguments contain the *StatusBarPanel* object that should be drawn.

The *Text* property is undoubtedly the most commonly used property of *StatusBarPanel*. The panel can also contain an icon that appears left of the text. You'll want to experiment with sizing the icon so that it fits correctly in the status bar.

The *ToolTipText* property is handy. Set it to a short descriptive text string that's displayed when the mouse cursor hovers over the panel. I'll demonstrate the *ToolTipText* property in the next program, DateAndTimeStatus.

The following properties affect the size and appearance of each panel:

### *StatusBarPanel* Properties (selection)

| Property | Type | Accessibility |
| --- | --- | --- |
| BorderStyle | StatusBarPanelBorderStyle | Get/Set |
| Alignment | HorizontalAlignment | Get/Set |
| AutoSize | StatusBarPanelAutoSize | Get/Set |
| Width | Integer | Get/Set |
| MinWidth | Integer | Get/Set |

Each panel can have a different border style based on members of this enumeration:

### *StatusBarPanelBorderStyle* Enumeration

| Member | Value |
|--------|-------|
| *None* | 1 |
| *Raised* | 2 |
| *Sunken* | 3 |

The default is *Sunken*.

The *Alignment* property affects text within the panel, not the orientation of the panel itself. It uses the *HorizontalAlignment* enumeration that other controls also use:

### *HorizontalAlignment* Enumeration

| Member | Value |
|--------|-------|
| *Left* | 0 |
| *Right* | 1 |
| *Center* | 2 |

By default, the size of each panel is based on its *Width* property, which by default is 100 pixels. You can use the *AutoSize* property to size panels based on their text contents or to use the space left over:

### *StatusBarPanelAutoSize* Enumeration

| Member | Value | Comments |
|--------|-------|----------|
| *None* | 1 | Default; size based on *Width* property |
| *Spring* | 2 | Uses remaining space |
| *Contents* | 3 | Size based on text width |

The *MinWidth* property affects only status bar panels with an *AutoSize* setting of *StatusBarPanelAutoSize.Spring*. The default is 10 pixels.

One conventional strategy is to make the first status bar panel (the leftmost one) have a border style of *StatusBarPanelBorderStyle.None* with an *AutoSize* setting of *StatusBarPanelAutoSize.Spring*. You'd probably use this panel for menu help strings. The remaining panels can have a border style of

*StatusBarPanelBorderStyle.Sunken* with an *AutoSize* property of *StatusBar-PanelAutoSize.None* or *StatusBarPanelAutoSize.Contents.*

Here's a program that creates a status bar with three panels just as I described. The two panels at the right of the status bar display the current date and time.

```
DateAndTimeStatus.vb
'-------------------------------------------------------
' DateAndTimeStatus.vb (c) 2002 by Charles Petzold
'-------------------------------------------------------
Imports System
Imports System.Drawing
Imports System.Windows.Forms

Class DateAndTimeStatus
    Inherits Form

    Private sbpMenu, sbpDate, sbpTime As StatusBarPanel

    Shared Sub Main()
        Application.Run(New DateAndTimeStatus())
    End Sub

    Sub New()
        Text = "Date and Time Status"
        BackColor = SystemColors.Window
        ForeColor = SystemColors.WindowText

        ' Create status bar.
        Dim sbar As New StatusBar()
        sbar.Parent = Me
        sbar.ShowPanels = True

        ' Create status bar panels.
        sbpMenu = New StatusBarPanel()
        sbpMenu.Text = "Reserved for menu help"
        sbpMenu.BorderStyle = StatusBarPanelBorderStyle.None
        sbpMenu.AutoSize = StatusBarPanelAutoSize.Spring

        sbpDate = New StatusBarPanel()
        sbpDate.AutoSize = StatusBarPanelAutoSize.Contents
        sbpDate.ToolTipText = "The current date"

        sbpTime = New StatusBarPanel()
        sbpTime.AutoSize = StatusBarPanelAutoSize.Contents
        sbpTime.ToolTipText = "The current time"

        ' Attach status bar panels to status bar.
        sbar.Panels.AddRange(New StatusBarPanel() _
                                    {sbpMenu, sbpDate, sbpTime})
```

```
        ' Set the timer for 1 second.
        Dim tmr As New Timer()
        AddHandler tmr.Tick, AddressOf TimerOnTick
        tmr.Interval = 1000
        tmr.Start()
    End Sub

    Private Sub TimerOnTick(ByVal obj As Object, ByVal ea As EventArgs)
        Dim dt As DateTime = DateTime.Now

        sbpDate.Text = dt.ToShortDateString()
        sbpTime.Text = dt.ToShortTimeString()
    End Sub
End Class
```

This program also adds *ToolTipText* properties to two of the status bar panels. Here's what the status bar looks like:

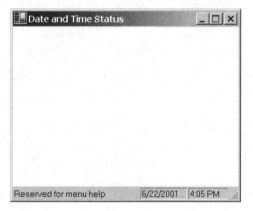

## Menu Help

One of the primary uses of a status bar is to provide *menu help*, which involves the display of short text strings that describe each menu item as the user moves the mouse or cursor over the items.

Providing menu help takes advantage of a couple features of menus and forms that don't show up in more conventional uses of the menu. As you may recall, the *MenuItem* class implements five events. So far in this book, I've made use of the *Popup* event when a pop-up menu is first displayed and the *Click* event when the user picks an item from the menu. I've also demonstrated how to use the *MeasureItem* and *DrawItem* events for implementing owner-draw menu items.

The fifth *MenuItem* event is named *Select*, and it occurs whenever the mouse cursor passes over a menu item or the user presses the arrow keys to move among menu items. *Select* is the event you must handle to display menu help. As the cursor moves among menu items, you display a text string in the status bar for each item.

When you first try implementing menu help in a *Select* event handler, you'll encounter an annoying problem: the last menu help string remains in the status bar after the user finally clicks a menu item! At that point, you might seek a solution by resetting the status bar text during every *Click* event handler installed for the *MenuItem* objects. But then what happens when the user dismisses a menu by pressing the Esc key? Again, the last menu help string remains in the status bar.

There *is* a solution to this problem. To provide you with a way to initialize and clean up a session of menu help, the *Form* class has the following two events:

### *Form* Events (selection)

| Event | Method | Delegate | Argument |
| --- | --- | --- | --- |
| *MenuStart* | *OnMenuStart* | *EventHandler* | *EventArgs* |
| *MenuComplete* | *OnMenuComplete* | *EventHandler* | *EventArgs* |

These events signal the beginning and end of a menu operation. The crucial one is *MenuComplete*. When that event occurs, you want to reset the menu help text. Perhaps you want to set it to the text string that was displayed in the status bar at the time you received a *MenuStart* event.

That's the strategy the following program uses. It creates a status bar with a single status bar panel and uses that panel to display the menu help text. The status bar panel text is initialized to the string "Ready". The *OnMenuStart* method saves that text, and the *OnMenuComplete* method restores it.

The program installs the same *Select* event handler for all the menu items. That handler is the method *MenuOnSelect*. But because MenuHelpFirstTry is a simple demonstration program, it doesn't install any *Click* event handlers for the menu items.

```
MenuHelpFirstTry.vb
'-------------------------------------------------
' MenuHelpFirstTry.vb (c) 2002 by Charles Petzold
'-------------------------------------------------
Imports System
Imports System.Drawing
Imports System.Windows.Forms
```

```
Class MenuHelpFirstTry
    Inherits Form

    Private sbpMenuHelp As StatusBarPanel
    Private strSavePanelText As String

    Shared Sub Main()
        Application.Run(New MenuHelpFirstTry())
    End Sub

    Sub New()
        Text = "Menu Help (First Try)"
        BackColor = SystemColors.Window
        ForeColor = SystemColors.WindowText

        ' Create a status bar with one panel.
        Dim sbar As New StatusBar()
        sbar.Parent = Me
        sbar.ShowPanels = True
        sbpMenuHelp = New StatusBarPanel()
        sbpMenuHelp.Text = "Ready"
        sbpMenuHelp.AutoSize = StatusBarPanelAutoSize.Spring
        sbar.Panels.Add(sbpMenuHelp)

        ' Construct a simple menu.
        ' For this demo, we can ignore the Click handlers
        '    but what we really need are Select handlers.
        Menu = New MainMenu()
        Dim ehSelect As EventHandler = AddressOf MenuOnSelect

        ' Create File menu items.
        Dim mi As New MenuItem("File")
        AddHandler mi.Select, ehSelect
        Menu.MenuItems.Add(mi)

        mi = New MenuItem("Open")
        AddHandler mi.Select, ehSelect
        Menu.MenuItems(0).MenuItems.Add(mi)

        mi = New MenuItem("Close")
        AddHandler mi.Select, ehSelect
        Menu.MenuItems(0).MenuItems.Add(mi)

        mi = New MenuItem("Save")
        AddHandler mi.Select, ehSelect
        Menu.MenuItems(0).MenuItems.Add(mi)

        ' Create Edit menu items.
        mi = New MenuItem("Edit")
        AddHandler mi.Select, ehSelect
        Menu.MenuItems.Add(mi)
```

*(continued)*

**MenuHelpFirstTry.vb** *(continued)*

```
        mi = New MenuItem("Cut")
        AddHandler mi.Select, ehSelect
        Menu.MenuItems(1).MenuItems.Add(mi)

        mi = New MenuItem("Copy")
        AddHandler mi.Select, ehSelect
        Menu.MenuItems(1).MenuItems.Add(mi)

        mi = New MenuItem("Paste")
        AddHandler mi.Select, ehSelect
        Menu.MenuItems(1).MenuItems.Add(mi)
    End Sub

    Protected Overrides Sub OnMenuStart(ByVal ea As EventArgs)
        strSavePanelText = sbpMenuHelp.Text
    End Sub

    Protected Overrides Sub OnMenuComplete(ByVal ea As EventArgs)
        sbpMenuHelp.Text = strSavePanelText
    End Sub

    Private Sub MenuOnSelect(ByVal obj As Object, ByVal ea As EventArgs)
        Dim mi As MenuItem = DirectCast(obj, MenuItem)
        Dim str As String

        Select Case mi.Text
            Case "File" : str = "Commands for working with files"
            Case "Open" : str = "Opens an existing document"
            Case "Close" : str = "Closes the current document"
            Case "Save" : str = "Saves the current document"
            Case "Edit" : str = "Commands for editing the document"
            Case "Cut" : str = "Deletes the selection and " & _
                               "copies it to the clipboard"
            Case "Copy" : str = "Copies the selection to the " & _
                               "clipboard"
            Case "Paste" : str = "Replaces the current selection " & _
                               "with the clipboard contents"
            Case Else : str = ""
        End Select

        sbpMenuHelp.Text = str
    End Sub
End Class
```

The *MenuOnSelect* method determines the text of the selected menu item and uses that to select a menu help string, which it then uses to set the *Text* property of the *StatusBarPanel* object. Here's the program in action:

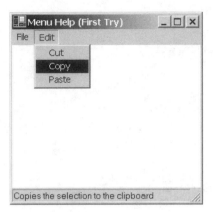

The *Select* events are generated regardless of whether the menu item is enabled, so the program displays the same text strings even if the menu items aren't currently available. Sometimes users are confused when certain items are disabled. (I know I am.) The menu help text might clarify why an item isn't currently available.

As is, the MenuHelpFirstTry program works fine, and you may like the idea of consolidating all the menu-help text in one place, such as the *MenuOnSelect* method. I'm not real wild about it myself, though. I'd rather bind each menu-help string with the actual menu item. Regardless, the *MenuOnSelect* method definitely needs a better means of determining which item has been selected. The *Select* and *Case* construction using the *Text* property of the *Menu-Item* object needs to duplicate the text strings exactly, and that can be a hassle.

One approach that I find appealing is to define a new class (named *Menu-ItemHelp*, for example) that subclasses *MenuItem*. *MenuItemHelp* simply adds a new property named *HelpText* that stores an additional text string. You can set the *HelpText* property when creating each object of *MenuItemHelp*:

```
mi.Text = "&Open..."
mi.HelpText = "Opens an existing document"
```

The *MenuOnSelect* method then becomes much simpler:

```
Sub MenuOnSelect(Dim obj As Object, Dim ea As EventArgs)
    sbpMenuHelp.Text = DirectCast(obj, MenuItemHelp).HelpText
End Sub
```

You can go a step further by providing another property in *MenuItemHelp* that stores the status bar panel where the help text is to be displayed. The class itself can override the *OnSelect* methods to set the help text in the status bar panel. The MenuItemHelp.vb file defines such a class that derives from *MenuItem*.

## MenuItemHelp.vb

```
'------------------------------------------------
' MenuItemHelp.vb (c) 2002 by Charles Petzold
'------------------------------------------------
Imports System
Imports System.Drawing
Imports System.Windows.Forms

Class MenuItemHelp
    Inherits MenuItem

    ' Private fields
    Private sbpHelpPanel As StatusBarPanel
    Private strHelpText As String

    ' Constructors
    Sub New()
    End Sub

    Sub New(ByVal strText As String)
        MyBase.New(strText)
    End Sub

    ' Properties
    Property HelpPanel() As StatusBarPanel
        Set(ByVal Value As StatusBarPanel)
            sbpHelpPanel = Value
        End Set
        Get
            Return sbpHelpPanel
        End Get
    End Property

    Property HelpText() As String
        Set(ByVal Value As String)
            strHelpText = Value
        End Set
        Get
            Return strHelpText
        End Get
    End Property

    ' Method override
    Protected Overrides Sub OnSelect(ByVal ea As EventArgs)
        MyBase.OnSelect(ea)
        If Not HelpPanel Is Nothing Then
            HelpPanel.Text = HelpText
        End If
    End Sub
End Class
```

Here's a revised version of the MenuHelpFirstTry program that creates *MenuItemHelp* objects rather than *MenuItem* objects. Each *MenuItemHelp* object is assigned its *HelpPanel* and *HelpText* properties as it's being created.

**MenuHelpSubclass.vb**

```vb
'-------------------------------------------------
' MenuHelpSubclass.vb (c) 2002 by Charles Petzold
'-------------------------------------------------
Imports System
Imports System.Drawing
Imports System.Windows.Forms

Class MenuHelpSubclass
    Inherits Form

    Private sbpMenuHelp As StatusBarPanel
    Private strSavePanelText As String

    Shared Sub Main()
        Application.Run(New MenuHelpSubclass())
    End Sub

    Sub New()
        Text = "Menu Help"
        BackColor = SystemColors.Window
        ForeColor = SystemColors.WindowText

        ' Create a status bar with one panel.
        Dim sbar As New StatusBar()
        sbar.Parent = Me
        sbar.ShowPanels = True

        sbpMenuHelp = New StatusBarPanel()
        sbpMenuHelp.Text = "Ready"
        sbpMenuHelp.AutoSize = StatusBarPanelAutoSize.Spring
        sbar.Panels.Add(sbpMenuHelp)

        ' Construct a simple menu with MenuItemHelp items.
        Menu = New MainMenu()

        ' Create File menu items.
        Dim mih As New MenuItemHelp("&File")
        mih.HelpPanel = sbpMenuHelp
        mih.HelpText = "Commands for working with files"
        Menu.MenuItems.Add(mih)

        mih = New MenuItemHelp("&Open...")
        mih.HelpPanel = sbpMenuHelp
        mih.HelpText = "Opens an existing document"
        Menu.MenuItems(0).MenuItems.Add(mih)
```

*(continued)*

**MenuHelpSubclass.vb** *(continued)*

```
            mih = New MenuItemHelp("&Close")
            mih.HelpPanel = sbpMenuHelp
            mih.HelpText = "Closes the current document"
            Menu.MenuItems(0).MenuItems.Add(mih)

            mih = New MenuItemHelp("&Save")
            mih.HelpPanel = sbpMenuHelp
            mih.HelpText = "Saves the current document"
            Menu.MenuItems(0).MenuItems.Add(mih)

            ' Create Edit menu items.
            mih = New MenuItemHelp("&Edit")
            mih.HelpPanel = sbpMenuHelp
            mih.HelpText = "Commands for editing the document"
            Menu.MenuItems.Add(mih)

            mih = New MenuItemHelp("Cu&t")
            mih.HelpPanel = sbpMenuHelp
            mih.HelpText = "Deletes the selection and " & _
                          "copies it to the clipboard"
            Menu.MenuItems(1).MenuItems.Add(mih)

            mih = New MenuItemHelp("&Copy")
            mih.HelpPanel = sbpMenuHelp
            mih.HelpText = "Copies the selection to the clipboard"
            Menu.MenuItems(1).MenuItems.Add(mih)

            mih = New MenuItemHelp("&Paste")
            mih.HelpPanel = sbpMenuHelp
            mih.HelpText = "Replaces the current selection " & _
                          "with the clipboard contents"
            Menu.MenuItems(1).MenuItems.Add(mih)
        End Sub

        Protected Overrides Sub OnMenuStart(ByVal ea As EventArgs)
            strSavePanelText = sbpMenuHelp.Text
        End Sub

        Protected Overrides Sub OnMenuComplete(ByVal ea As EventArgs)
            sbpMenuHelp.Text = strSavePanelText
        End Sub
End Class
```

# The Basic Toolbar

Near the end of Chapter 11, I discussed the *ImageList* class, which is a collection of images of the same size and color depth. A *ToolBar* control is basically an *ImageList* object and a collection of *ToolBarButton* objects. Each button displays one of the images in the *ImageList*.

Most applications use toolbar images that are 16 pixels square. That's the default size for *ImageList* and that's what I use throughout this chapter. If you want to use a smaller or larger button—even nonrectangular buttons—you must first create bitmaps of the desired size. (That's the obvious part.) Before adding the images to *ImageList*, set the *ImageSize* property to the size of the images. That image size will trickle through all the rest of the *ToolBar* and *ToolBarButton* objects.

These are the most essential properties of *ToolBar*:

### *ToolBar* Properties (selection)

| Property | Type | Accessibility |
|---|---|---|
| *ImageList* | *ImageList* | Get/Set |
| *Buttons* | *ToolBar.ToolBarButtonCollection* | Get |
| *ShowToolTips* | *Boolean* | Get/Set |

Each *ToolBar* is associated with one *ImageList*, which, of course, usually contains multiple images.

The *Buttons* property is a collection of the sort we've seen several times now. You can index *Buttons* like an array; each element is an object of type *ToolBarButton*. The *ToolBarButtonCollection* class has several methods, including *Add*, *AddRange*, *Insert*, and *Remove*, that let you manage the buttons associated with a toolbar.

I've included the *ShowToolTips* property with this group of essential properties because it's fairly easy to assign ToolTips to your toolbar buttons, but you won't see them unless you set this *ShowToolTips* property to *True*.

Here are the most essential *ToolBarButton* properties:

### *ToolBarButton* Properties (selection)

| Property | Type | Accessibility |
|---|---|---|
| *ImageIndex* | *Integer* | Get/Set |
| *ToolTipText* | *String* | Get/Set |

*ImageIndex* is an index that indicates which image of the *ImageList* object is displayed on the button. *ToolTipText* is the text displayed when the mouse hovers over the button. The images on toolbar buttons can be fairly obscure, so ToolTips can be a big help.

I'll be talking about *ToolBar* events shortly, but let's first take a look at a simple do-nothing program that has a do-nothing menu and a do-nothing toolbar based on an image list based on a bitmap named StandardButtons.bmp.

**SimpleToolBar.vb**

```
'--------------------------------------------------
' SimpleToolBar.vb (c) 2002 by Charles Petzold
'--------------------------------------------------
Imports System
Imports System.Drawing
Imports System.Windows.Forms

Class SimpleToolBar
    Inherits Form

    Shared Sub Main()
        Application.Run(New SimpleToolBar())
    End Sub

    Sub New()
        Text = "Simple Toolbar"

        ' Create a simple menu (just for show).
        Menu = New MainMenu()
        Menu.MenuItems.Add("File")
        Menu.MenuItems.Add("Edit")
        Menu.MenuItems.Add("View")
        Menu.MenuItems.Add("Help")

        ' Create ImageList.
        Dim bm As New Bitmap(Me.GetType(), "StandardButtons.bmp")

        Dim imglst As New ImageList()
        imglst.Images.AddStrip(bm)
        imglst.TransparentColor = Color.Cyan

        ' Create ToolBar.
        Dim tbar As New ToolBar()
        tbar.Parent = Me
        tbar.ImageList = imglst
        tbar.ShowToolTips = True

        ' Create ToolBarButtons.
        Dim astr() As String = {"New", "Open", "Save", "Print", _
                                "Cut", "Copy", "Paste"}
        Dim i As Integer

        For i = 0 To astr.GetUpperBound(0)
            Dim tbb As New ToolBarButton()
            tbb.ImageIndex = i
            tbb.ToolTipText = astr(i)
```

```
        tbar.Buttons.Add(tbb)
    Next i
  End Sub
End Class
```

## StandardButtons.bmp

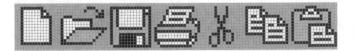

You can create individual bitmaps for each button, or you can create images for a bunch of buttons in one bitmap. In the SimpleToolBar program, I've used the default *ImageList* bitmap size of 16 pixels square. The StandardButtons.bmp file contains seven images for seven toolbar buttons, so the total size of the bitmap is 112 by 16 pixels. If you're creating a bitmap for an *ImageList*, the width must be an integral multiple of its height. Also, as I discussed in Chapter 11, when you include a bitmap with a project in Microsoft Visual Basic .NET, you must set the Build Action property to Embedded Resource.

If you don't want to experience the fun of creating your own buttons, you can use the standard buttons included with Microsoft Visual Studio .NET (but not, unfortunately, with Visual Basic .NET). These are stored by default in subdirectories of the directory \Program Files\Microsoft Visual Studio .NET\Common7\Graphics\Bitmaps. The subdirectories OffCtlBr and Assorted contain bitmaps appropriate for toolbar buttons.

The SimpleToolBar program begins by creating a few top-level menu items. I added those only so that you can see how a menu and a toolbar look together. Next, the StandardButtons.bmp image is loaded as a resource. (See Chapter 11 for details on loading resources.) The program creates an *ImageList* object and uses the *AddStrip* method of the *Images* property to include the whole bitmap in the image list. Because the default *ImageSize* property indicates that the images are 16 pixels square, the *ImageList* object can easily figure out that there are seven images in the strip.

It's not evident from the monochrome reproduction in this book, but the background of StandardButtons.bmp is cyan, which is specified in the SimpleToolBar program as the transparent color for the *ImageList*.

The next step is to create the toolbar. Three properties are assigned: the *Parent* property indicates that the toolbar is a child of the form, the *ImageList* property associates the toolbar with a collection of images, and the *ShowToolTips* property enables ToolTips.

Next, the program creates seven *ToolBarButton* objects, setting the *ImageIndex* property to the numbers 0 through 6, corresponding to the seven images.

(If the original images are not in the same order as the buttons you want to create, setting the proper *ImageIndex* value essentially reorders the images.) Each button also gets a short ToolTip. The program adds each button to the toolbar by using the *Add* method of the *Buttons* property:

```
tbar.Buttons.Add(tbb)
```

And here's the result:

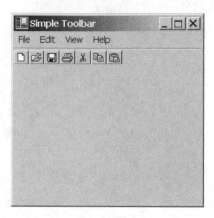

If you experiment with this program, you'll find that the buttons work much like push button controls. As you'll see later in this chapter, you can also create buttons that toggle or invoke a menu.

You'll probably want the toolbar to be distinct from the client area in some way, but you'll likely be using a *Panel* control for display purposes anyway, and you can give that a background color of *SystemColors.Window* (which is usually white).

# Toolbar Variations

Before we get into handling events from the toolbar, let's take a look at a few properties that affect the toolbar's appearance:

### *ToolBar* Properties (selection)

| Property | Type | Accessibility | Default |
|---|---|---|---|
| *Wrappable* | *Boolean* | Get/Set | *True* |
| *Divider* | *Boolean* | Get/Set | *True* |
| *BorderStyle* | *BorderStyle* | Get/Set | *BorderStyle.None* |

### *ToolBar* Properties (selection)   *(continued)*

| Property | Type | Accessibility | Default |
|---|---|---|---|
| *Appearance* | *ToolBarAppearance* | Get/Set | *ToolBarAppearance.Normal* |
| *TextAlign* | *ToolBarTextAlign* | Get/Set | *ToolBarTextAlign.Underneath* |

When you make the form narrower than the toolbar, the *Wrappable* property indicates whether the toolbar wraps to two lines or is truncated at the right. By default, it wraps.

The *Divider* property is responsible for the line that separates the toolbar and the menu. If you set the property to *False*, the line disappears:

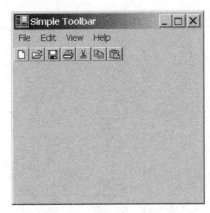

You'll probably want to keep the divider for aesthetic reasons.

The *BorderStyle* property (which you can also set to *FixedSingle* or *Fixed3D*) affects the display of a border that extends the width of the form. Here's an example without a divider but with a *BorderStyle* of *FixedSingle*.

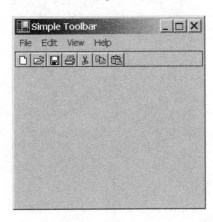

I don't think the border works as well as the divider does.

The *Appearance* property can take on one of the following properties of the *ToolBarAppearance* enumeration:

### *ToolBarAppearance* Enumeration

| Member | Value |
|--------|-------|
| *Normal* | 0 |
| *Flat* | 1 |

Applications these days seem to prefer a *Flat* appearance. Here are flat buttons with *Divider* set to *True* and no border:

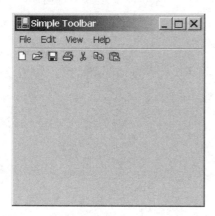

The *Flat* appearance looks better when the area below the toolbar is a different color.

The *TextAlign* property can take on one of the members of the *ToolBar-TextAlign* enumeration:

### *ToolBarTextAlign* Enumeration

| Member | Value |
|--------|-------|
| *Underneath* | 0 |
| *Right* | 1 |

This property involves a feature we haven't examined yet, which is that buttons can also include a text string:

### *ToolBarButton* Properties (selection)

| Property | Type | Accessibility |
|----------|------|---------------|
| *Text* | *String* | Get/Set |

For example, if you include the statement

```
tbb.Text = astr(i)
```

in the *For* loop in SimpleToolBar, the buttons look like this:

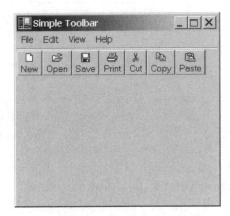

Notice that the buttons have different sizes based on the width of the text string. If you set the *TextAlign* property of the toolbar to *ToolBarTextAlign.Right*, the buttons become wider but shorter:

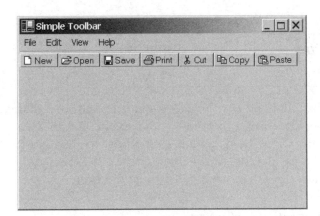

# Toolbar Events

The SimpleToolBar program doesn't handle any events, so it can't do anything in response to button clicks. In addition to the events that *ToolBar* inherits from *Control*, *ToolBar* implements two of its own events:

### *ToolBar* Events

| Event | Method | Delegate | Argument |
|-------|--------|----------|----------|
| *ButtonClick* | *OnButtonClick* | *ToolBarButtonClick-EventHandler* | *ToolBarButton-ClickEventArgs* |
| *ButtonDropDown* | *OnButtonDropDown* | *ToolBarButtonClick-EventHandler* | *ToolBarButton-ClickEventArgs* |

The *ButtonClick* event is the more important event and occurs when the user clicks one of the buttons on the toolbar. The *ButtonDropDown* event applies only to buttons that have a certain style that is intended to invoke a menu. (I'll discuss button styles shortly.)

Notice that these two events are associated with the toolbar and not with the individual buttons. The *ToolBarButton* class doesn't define any events. Therefore, all button clicks on a toolbar go to a single event handler. The event handler must determine which button has been clicked. The *ToolBarButton-ClickEventArgs* argument to the event handler has a single property that provides precisely this information:

### *ToolBarButtonClickEventArgs* Property

| Property | Type | Accessibility |
|----------|------|---------------|
| *Button* | *ToolBarButton* | Get/Set |

One approach to handling the *ButtonClick* event is to first save all the *ToolBarButton* objects as fields. During the *ButtonClick* event, you then compare this *Button* property with those fields to determine how to respond to the click. Another approach is to use the *Tag* property of the *ToolBarButton* object to store something (anything) that helps you handle the event:

### *ToolBarButton* Properties (selection)

| Property | Type | Accessibility |
|----------|------|---------------|
| *Tag* | *Object* | Get/Set |

In many cases, toolbar buttons duplicate menu items. For this reason, it makes a whole lot of sense to set the *Tag* property of the button equal to the *MenuItem* object of the menu item that the button duplicates.

Let's look at an example that's both simple and functional. The TextBoxWithToolBar program is a stripped-down version of the Notepad clone programs from Chapter 18. It's so stripped down that it contains only an Edit menu with Cut, Copy, and Paste items. But this program also includes a toolbar that duplicates those three items. The *ToolBar* object uses an *ImageList* based on the StandardButtons.bmp bitmap from the SimpleToolBar program. But only indices 4, 5, and 6 are used for the Cut, Copy, and Paste images.

## TextBoxWithToolBar.vb

```
'---------------------------------------------------------
' TextBoxWithToolBar.vb (c) 2002 by Charles Petzold
'---------------------------------------------------------
Imports System
Imports System.Drawing
Imports System.Windows.Forms

Class TextBoxWithToolBar
    Inherits Form

    Private txtbox As TextBox
    Private miEditCut, miEditCopy, miEditPaste As MenuItem
    Private tbbCut, tbbCopy, tbbPaste As ToolBarButton

    Shared Sub Main()
        Application.Run(New TextBoxWithToolBar())
    End Sub

    Sub New()
        Text = "Text Box with Toolbar"

        ' Create TextBox.
        txtbox = New TextBox()
        txtbox.Parent = Me
        txtbox.Dock = DockStyle.Fill
        txtbox.Multiline = True
        txtbox.ScrollBars = ScrollBars.Both
        txtbox.AcceptsTab = True

        ' Create ImageList.
        Dim bm As New Bitmap(Me.GetType(), "StandardButtons.bmp")
        Dim imglst As New ImageList()
        imglst.Images.AddStrip(bm)
        imglst.TransparentColor = Color.Cyan

        ' Create ToolBar with ButtonClick event handler.
        Dim tbar As New ToolBar()
```

**TextBoxWithToolBar.vb** *(continued)*

```
tbar.Parent = Me
tbar.ImageList = imglst
tbar.ShowToolTips = True
AddHandler tbar.ButtonClick, AddressOf ToolBarOnClick

' Create the Edit menu.
Menu = New MainMenu()
Dim mi As New MenuItem("&Edit")
AddHandler mi.Popup, AddressOf MenuEditOnPopup
Menu.MenuItems.Add(mi)

' Create the Edit Cut menu item.
miEditCut = New MenuItem("Cu&t")
AddHandler miEditCut.Click, AddressOf MenuEditCutOnClick
miEditCut.Shortcut = Shortcut.CtrlX
Menu.MenuItems(0).MenuItems.Add(miEditCut)

' And create the Cut toolbar button.
tbbCut = New ToolBarButton()
tbbCut.ImageIndex = 4
tbbCut.ToolTipText = "Cut"
tbbCut.Tag = miEditCut
tbar.Buttons.Add(tbbCut)

' Create the Edit Copy menu item.
miEditCopy = New MenuItem("&Copy")
AddHandler miEditCopy.Click, AddressOf MenuEditCopyOnClick
miEditCopy.Shortcut = Shortcut.CtrlC
Menu.MenuItems(0).MenuItems.Add(miEditCopy)

' And create the Copy toolbar button.
tbbCopy = New ToolBarButton()
tbbCopy.ImageIndex = 5
tbbCopy.ToolTipText = "Copy"
tbbCopy.Tag = miEditCopy
tbar.Buttons.Add(tbbCopy)

' Create the Edit Paste menu item.
miEditPaste = New MenuItem("&Paste")
AddHandler miEditPaste.Click, AddressOf MenuEditPasteOnClick
miEditPaste.Shortcut = Shortcut.CtrlV
Menu.MenuItems(0).MenuItems.Add(miEditPaste)

' And create the Paste toolbar button.
tbbPaste = New ToolBarButton()
tbbPaste.ImageIndex = 6
tbbPaste.ToolTipText = "Paste"
tbbPaste.Tag = miEditPaste
tbar.Buttons.Add(tbbPaste)

' Set Timer for enabling buttons.
Dim tmr As New Timer()
```

```
        tmr.Interval = 250
        AddHandler tmr.Tick, AddressOf TimerOnTick
        tmr.Start()
    End Sub

    Private Sub MenuEditOnPopup(ByVal obj As Object, ByVal ea As EventArgs)
        miEditCopy.Enabled = txtbox.SelectionLength > 0
        miEditCut.Enabled = miEditCopy.Enabled

        miEditPaste.Enabled = _
            Clipboard.GetDataObject().GetDataPresent(GetType(String))
    End Sub

    Private Sub TimerOnTick(ByVal obj As Object, ByVal ea As EventArgs)
        tbbCopy.Enabled = txtbox.SelectionLength > 0
        tbbCut.Enabled = tbbCopy.Enabled

        tbbPaste.Enabled = _
            Clipboard.GetDataObject().GetDataPresent(GetType(String))
    End Sub

    Private Sub ToolBarOnClick(ByVal obj As Object, _
                            ByVal tbbcea As ToolBarButtonClickEventArgs)
        Dim tbb As ToolBarButton = tbbcea.Button
        Dim mi As MenuItem = DirectCast(tbb.Tag, MenuItem)
        mi.PerformClick()
    End Sub

    Private Sub MenuEditCutOnClick(ByVal obj As Object, _
                            ByVal ea As EventArgs)
        txtbox.Cut()
    End Sub

    Private Sub MenuEditCopyOnClick(ByVal obj As Object, _
                            ByVal ea As EventArgs)
        txtbox.Copy()
    End Sub

    Private Sub MenuEditPasteOnClick(ByVal obj As Object, _
                            ByVal ea As EventArgs)
        txtbox.Paste()
    End Sub
End Class
```

When the constructor creates the *ToolBar* object, it assigns the *ToolBar-OnClick* method as the handler for the *ButtonClick* event:

```
AddHandler tbar.ButtonClick, AddressOf ToolBarOnClick
```

The *ToolBarButton* objects are created after each corresponding *MenuItem* object. The *Tag* property of each *ToolBarButton* is assigned the corresponding *MenuItem* object. Here's the assignment for the Cut button:

```
tbbCut.Tag = miEditCut
```

The big payoff comes in the relative simplicity of the *ToolBarOnClick* method:

```
Sub ToolBarOnClick(Dim obj As Object, _
                   Dim tbbcea As ToolBarButtonClickEventArgs)
    Dim tbb As ToolBarButton = tbbcea.Button
    Dim mi As MenuItem = DirectCast(tbb.Tag, MenuItem)
    mi.PerformClick()
End Sub
```

The method obtains the *ToolBarButton* object being clicked, casts the *Tag* property to a *MenuItem*, and simulates a click. This approach is so elegant that you could even reduce the body of the method to a single statement:

```
DirectCast(tbbcea.Button.Tag, MenuItem).PerformClick()
```

The only messy part involves enabling and disabling the buttons based on the validity of the Cut, Copy, and Paste operations. As usual, the Cut, Copy, and Paste menu items are enabled and disabled during the *Popup* event for the Edit menu. However, the buttons are always in view, and they must be enabled and disabled using another technique.

If the edit control in the program were a *RichTextBox* rather than a *TextBox*, you could install an event handler for the *SelectionChanged* event. (*TextBox* doesn't define a *SelectionChanged* event.) Whenever the selection changes, the event handler could then enable the Cut and Copy buttons only if some text has been selected, much like the *Popup* event handler for the Edit menu.

That doesn't solve the problem for the Paste button, however. The Paste button must be enabled whenever there's text on the clipboard. Short of attempting to intercept Win32 messages that indicate clipboard changes, perhaps the only real solution is to create a *Timer* and enable the Paste button during the *Tick* event if text is on the clipboard. Because the *Timer* had to be created anyway, I decided to enable all three buttons during that *Tick* event.

Along with the *Enabled* property, the *ToolBarButton* class also includes a *Visible* property:

### *ToolBarButton* Properties (selection)

| Property | Type | Accessibility |
|----------|------|---------------|
| *Visible* | *Boolean* | Get/Set |
| *Enabled* | *Boolean* | Get/Set |

# Toolbar Styles

So far, the toolbar buttons we've created have functioned much like push buttons. You can also make a toolbar button function like a check box that can be toggled on or off. Or, a toolbar button can invoke a menu. These options are available through the following properties:

### *ToolBarButton* Properties (selection)

| Property | Type | Accessibility |
|----------|------|---------------|
| *Style* | *ToolBarButtonStyle* | Get/Set |
| *Pushed* | *Boolean* | Get/Set |
| *PartialPush* | *Boolean* | Get/Set |
| *DropDownMenu* | *Menu* | Get/Set |

Despite its definition, the *DropDownMenu* property must actually be of type *ContextMenu*. Set the *Style* property to one of the following enumeration values:

### *ToolBarButtonStyle* Enumeration

| Member | Value |
|--------|-------|
| *PushButton* | 1 |
| *ToggleButton* | 2 |
| *Separator* | 3 |
| *DropDownButton* | 4 |

*ToolBarButtonStyle.PushButton* is the default.

The *Pushed* and *PartialPush* properties apply only to buttons that have their *Style* set to *ToolBarButtonStyle.ToggleButton*. Such buttons maintain an on/off state. Each time the button is clicked, it generates a *ButtonClick* event and the value of the *Pushed* property is toggled. Your program can also initialize the state of the button by setting the *Pushed* property itself. Set the *PartialPush* property to *True* to give the button a special appearance that indicates a halfway state (much like the *ThreeState* property of the *CheckBox* control described in Chapter 12).

When you use the *ToolBarButtonStyle.Separator* style, the button ignores any image or text that may be associated with it and displays a separator instead. For toolbars that have their *Appearance* property set to *ToolBarAppearance.Flat*, the separator is a vertical line that looks much like the horizontal divider line that separates the toolbar from the menu. When the *Appearance* property is set to *ToolBarAppearance.Normal*, the separator manifests itself as a small gap between the buttons.

The *ToolBarButtonStyle.DropDownButton* option invokes a menu when the button is pressed. You specify the menu in the *DropDownMenu* property of the button. You can handle the *ButtonDropDown* event if you need to initialize the menu in some way before it's displayed.

Let's look at toggle buttons first. Here's a program that displays a four-button toolbar based on a bitmap named FontStyleButtons.bmp. The buttons allow you to indicate bold, italic, underline, or strikeout styles for a string of displayed text.

**ToggleButtons.vb**

```
'-----------------------------------------------
' ToggleButtons.vb (c) 2002 by Charles Petzold
'-----------------------------------------------
Imports System
Imports System.Drawing
Imports System.Windows.Forms

Class ToggleButtons
    Inherits Form

    Protected pnl As Panel
    Protected tbar As ToolBar
    Protected strText As String = "Toggle"
    Protected clrText As Color = SystemColors.WindowText
    Private fntstyle As FontStyle = FontStyle.Regular

    Shared Sub Main()
        Application.Run(New ToggleButtons())
    End Sub

    Sub New()
        Text = "Toggle Buttons"

        ' Create panel to fill interior.
        pnl = New Panel()
        pnl.Parent = Me
        pnl.Dock = DockStyle.Fill
        pnl.BackColor = SystemColors.Window
        pnl.ForeColor = SystemColors.WindowText
        AddHandler pnl.Resize, AddressOf PanelOnResize
        AddHandler pnl.Paint, AddressOf PanelOnPaint

        ' Create ImageList.
        Dim bm As New Bitmap(Me.GetType(), "FontStyleButtons.bmp")
        Dim imglst As New ImageList()
        imglst.ImageSize = New Size(bm.Width \ 4, bm.Height)
```

```
        imglst.Images.AddStrip(bm)
        imglst.TransparentColor = Color.White

        ' Create ToolBar.
        tbar = New ToolBar()
        tbar.ImageList = imglst
        tbar.Parent = Me
        tbar.ShowToolTips = True
        AddHandler tbar.ButtonClick, AddressOf ToolBarOnClick

        ' Create ToolBarButtons.
        Dim afs() As FontStyle = {FontStyle.Bold, FontStyle.Italic, _
                            FontStyle.Underline, FontStyle.Strikeout}
        Dim i As Integer
        For i = 0 To 3
            Dim tbarbtn As New ToolBarButton()
            tbarbtn.ImageIndex = i
            tbarbtn.Style = ToolBarButtonStyle.ToggleButton
            tbarbtn.ToolTipText = afs(i).ToString()
            tbarbtn.Tag = afs(i)
            tbar.Buttons.Add(tbarbtn)
        Next i
End Sub

Private Sub ToolBarOnClick(ByVal obj As Object, _
                        ByVal tbbcea As ToolBarButtonClickEventArgs)
        Dim tbb As ToolBarButton = tbbcea.Button

        ' If the Tag isn't a FontStyle, don't do anything.
        If tbb.Tag Is Nothing Then Return
        If Not tbb.Tag.GetType() Is GetType(FontStyle) Then Return

        ' Set or clear the bit in the fntstyle field.
        If tbb.Pushed Then
            fntstyle = fntstyle Or CType(tbb.Tag, FontStyle)
        Else
            fntstyle = fntstyle And Not CType(tbb.Tag, FontStyle)
        End If
        pnl.Invalidate()
End Sub

Private Sub PanelOnResize(ByVal obj As Object, ByVal ea As EventArgs)
        Dim pnl As Panel = DirectCast(obj, Panel)
        pnl.Invalidate()
End Sub

Private Sub PanelOnPaint(ByVal obj As Object, _
                        ByVal pea As PaintEventArgs)
        Dim pnl As Panel = DirectCast(obj, Panel)
        Dim grfx As Graphics = pea.Graphics
        Dim fnt As New Font("Times New Roman", 72, fntstyle)
        Dim szf As SizeF = grfx.MeasureString(strText, fnt)
```

*(continued)*

**ToggleButtons.vb**  *(continued)*

```
        grfx.DrawString(strText, fnt, New SolidBrush(clrText), _
                    (pnl.Width - szf.Width) / 2, _
                    (pnl.Height - szf.Height) / 2)
    End Sub
End Class
```

## FontStyleButtons.bmp

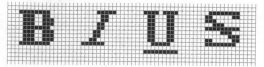

This program creates a *Panel* control that fills the client area (at least before the toolbar is created) and displays any output that would normally go in the client area. The *PanelOnPaint* event handler displays a string of centered text. Because it's displaying centered text, the panel must be repainted whenever it's resized. However, the handy *ResizeRedraw* property is protected. One possibility is to subclass *Panel*; another (which is what this program does) is to install an event handler for the panel's *Resize* event and invalidate the panel there.

Notice that the *Font* object created in the *PanelOnPaint* method uses a *FontStyle* argument stored as a field named *fntstyle*. This is the field that the buttons will alter.

As in the TextBoxWithToolBar program, the ToggleButtons program installs its *ToolBarOnClick* method as the event handler for the toolbar's *ButtonClick* event. The *Style* property for each button is set to *ToolBarButtonStyle.ToggleButton* in the constructor, and the *ToolBarOnClick* method assigns the *Tag* property for each button the *FontStyle* enumeration member associated with the button.

Once again, the use of an appropriate *Tag* property makes the *ToolBarOnClick* method relatively straightforward. After obtaining the *ToolBarButton* object from the event argument and checking that the *Tag* type is a *FontStyle* object, *ToolBarOnClick* sets or clears a bit in the *fntstyle* field.

```
If tbb.Pushed
    fntstyle = fntstyle Or CType(tbb.Tag, FontStyle)
Else
    fntstyle = fntstyle And Not CType(tbb.Tag, FontStyle)
End If
```

The method then concludes by invalidating the panel, which generates a call to *PanelOnPaint*.

Although I've demonstrated the *PushButton* and *ToggleButton* styles separately, keep in mind that any toolbar can contain a mix of buttons with different styles. The third style is *ToolBarButtonStyle.DropDownButton*, which invokes a menu indicated by the *DropDownMenu* property.

Although *DropDownMenu* is defined as an object of type *Menu*, it's really an object of type *ContextMenu* (which derives from *Menu*). You can define an appropriate object for the *DropDownMenu* property like so:

```
Dim menu As New ContextMenu()
menu.MenuItems.Add("First Item")
menu.MenuItems.Add("Second Item")
menu.MenuItems.Add("Third Item")
```

Of course, you'd also define event handlers for the items. Then assign these properties of the *ToolBarButton* object:

```
tbb.Style = ToolBarButtonStyle.DropDownMenu
tbb.DropDownMenu = menu
```

A property of *ToolBar* indicates whether the drop-down buttons in the toolbar are displayed with little arrows that visually indicate that they invoke menus:

### *ToolBar* Properties (selection)

| Property | Type | Accessibility |
|----------|------|---------------|
| *DropDownArrows* | *Boolean* | Get/Set |

The default is *True*.

There's a catch to *DropDownMenu* buttons that I haven't mentioned yet. It's more of a convention than an actual requirement, but if you're familiar with applications that use such toolbar buttons, you know they don't invoke normal text-based menus. The menus instead usually contain little pictures. Thus, implementing a *DropDownMenu* button almost always involves an owner-draw menu.

Here's a program named DropDownMenuButton that derives from ToggleButtons and adds a fifth button to set the text color. The button invokes an owner-draw menu that displays 16 common colors and also re-creates the button image itself to indicate the selected color.

## DropDownMenuButton.vb

```
'----------------------------------------------------------
' DropDownMenuButton.vb (c) 2002 by Charles Petzold
'----------------------------------------------------------
Imports System
Imports System.Drawing
Imports System.Windows.Forms

Class DropDownMenuButton
    Inherits ToggleButtons

    Shared Shadows Sub Main()
        Application.Run(New DropDownMenuButton())
    End Sub

    Sub New()
        Text = "Drop-Down Menu Button"
        strText = "Drop-Down"

        ' Create bitmap for new button and add it to ImageList.
        tbar.ImageList.Images.Add(CreateBitmapButton(clrText))

        ' Create the menu for the button.
        Dim menu As New ContextMenu()
        Dim ehOnClick As EventHandler = AddressOf MenuColorOnClick
        Dim ehOnMeasureItem As MeasureItemEventHandler = _
                            AddressOf MenuColorOnMeasureItem
        Dim ehOnDrawItem As DrawItemEventHandler = _
                            AddressOf MenuColorOnDrawItem
        Dim aclr() As Color = _
        { _
        Color.FromArgb(&H0, &H0, &H0), Color.FromArgb(&H0, &H0, &H80), _
        Color.FromArgb(&H0, &H80, &H0), Color.FromArgb(&H0, &H80, &H80), _
        Color.FromArgb(&H80, &H0, &H0), Color.FromArgb(&H80, &H0, &H80), _
        Color.FromArgb(&H80, &H80, &H0), Color.FromArgb(&H80, &H80, &H80), _
        Color.FromArgb(&HC0, &HC0, &HC0), Color.FromArgb(&H0, &H0, &HFF), _
        Color.FromArgb(&H0, &HFF, &H0), Color.FromArgb(&H0, &HFF, &HFF), _
        Color.FromArgb(&HFF, &H0, &H0), Color.FromArgb(&HFF, &H0, &HFF), _
        Color.FromArgb(&HFF, &HFF, &H0), Color.FromArgb(&HFF, &HFF, &HFF) _
        }
```

```
        Dim i As Integer
        For i = 0 To aclr.GetUpperBound(0)
            Dim mic As New MenuItemColor()
            mic.OwnerDraw = True
            mic.Color = aclr(i)
            AddHandler mic.Click, ehOnClick
            AddHandler mic.MeasureItem, ehOnMeasureItem
            AddHandler mic.DrawItem, ehOnDrawItem
            mic.Break = (i Mod 4 = 0)
            menu.MenuItems.Add(mic)
        Next i

        ' Finally, make the button itself.
        Dim tbb As New ToolBarButton()
        tbb.ImageIndex = 4
        tbb.Style = ToolBarButtonStyle.DropDownButton
        tbb.DropDownMenu = menu
        tbb.ToolTipText = "Color"
        tbar.Buttons.Add(tbb)
    End Sub

    Private Sub MenuColorOnClick(ByVal obj As Object, ByVal ea As EventArgs)
        ' Set the new text color.
        Dim mic As MenuItemColor = DirectCast(obj, MenuItemColor)
        clrText = mic.Color
        pnl.Invalidate()

        ' Make a new button bitmap.
        tbar.ImageList.Images(4) = CreateBitmapButton(clrText)
        tbar.Invalidate()
    End Sub

    Private Sub MenuColorOnMeasureItem(ByVal obj As Object, _
                                       ByVal miea As MeasureItemEventArgs)

        miea.ItemHeight = 18
        miea.ItemWidth = 18
    End Sub

    Private Sub MenuColorOnDrawItem(ByVal obj As Object, _
                                    ByVal diea As DrawItemEventArgs)
        Dim mic As MenuItemColor = DirectCast(obj, MenuItemColor)
        Dim br As New SolidBrush(mic.Color)
        Dim rect As Rectangle = diea.Bounds

        rect.X += 1
        rect.Y += 1
        rect.Width -= 2
        rect.Height -= 2
        diea.Graphics.FillRectangle(br, rect)
    End Sub
```

*(continued)*

**DropDownMenuButton.vb** *(continued)*

```
        Private Function CreateBitmapButton(ByVal clr As Color) As Bitmap
            Dim bm As New Bitmap(16, 16)
            Dim grfx As Graphics = Graphics.FromImage(bm)
            Dim fnt As New Font("Arial", 10, FontStyle.Bold)
            Dim szf As SizeF = grfx.MeasureString("A", fnt)
            Dim fScale As Single = Math.Min(bm.Width / szf.Width, _
                                            bm.Height / szf.Height)

            fnt = New Font(fnt.Name, fScale * fnt.SizeInPoints, fnt.Style)

            Dim strfmt As New StringFormat()
            strfmt.Alignment = StringAlignment.Center
            strfmt.LineAlignment = StringAlignment.Center

            grfx.Clear(Color.White)
            grfx.DrawString("A", fnt, New SolidBrush(clr), _
                            bm.Width \ 2, bm.Height \ 2, strfmt)
            grfx.Dispose()
            Return bm
        End Function
    End Class

Class MenuItemColor
    Inherits MenuItem

    Private clr As Color

    Property Color() As Color
        Set(ByVal Value As Color)
            clr = Value
        End Set
        Get
            Return clr
        End Get
    End Property
End Class
```

This file also contains an override of the *MenuItem* class that stores a property named *Color*.

The *CreateBitmapButton* method toward the bottom of the program creates a 16-pixel-square bitmap containing a single "A" displayed with the Arial font and colored with the indicated argument to the method. The program's constructor begins by creating an initial bitmap and adding it to the *ImageList* object created by the ToggleButtons program.

The constructor then creates a context menu based on the *MenuItemColor* class defined at the bottom of the program. Event handlers for the *Click*, *MeasureItem*, and *DrawItem* events are installed. The button itself has a *Style* property of *ToolBarButtonStyle.DropDownButton*. The *DropDownMenu* property is set to the menu just created.

The *MeasureItem* event handler sets the size of the menu item to 18 pixels square, and the *DrawItem* handler draws a rectangle 1 pixel within the item bounds. Here's the resultant menu:

The images in the menu aren't square because the *MeasureItem* event handler doesn't take account of the additional space added to the width for a possible check box.

The *MenuColorOnClick* event handler sets the *clrText* field that the *PanelOnPaint* method uses for coloring the text and then invalidates the *Panel*. It concludes by creating a new bitmap for the button.

The standard toolbar allows push buttons, toggle buttons, and drop-down menus. If you'd like something more elaborate—a combo box, for example—you must take a slightly different approach. You'll want to create a *Panel* control that is a child of your *Form* and parent to one or more *ToolBar* controls and whatever *ComboBox* or other controls you need.

# 21

# Printing

Printing in a Windows Forms application is relatively painless, but the key word here is *relatively*. It seems easy only when you've had experience grappling with the Win32 printer API. Printing will never be quite as easy as displaying text and graphics on the screen, mostly because of the wide variety of printer types, their relatively slow speed, printer options (such as trays, bins, and paper sizes), and common problems such as paper jams.

Part of the difficulty in learning about printing in Windows Forms is the existence of several interlocking classes, all of which seem to refer to each other. For example, the *PrinterSettings* class has a property of type *PageSettings*, and the *PageSettings* class has a property of type *PrinterSettings*, and that's just the beginning. After awhile, the *System.Drawing.Printing* namespace starts to look like a hall of mirrors. Much of the process of learning about printing involves sorting out the various classes.

Although I'll be giving you enough information in the early pages of this chapter to handle printing entirely on your own, you'll probably want to take advantage of the common dialog box library (discussed toward the end of the chapter) to help out and make your application consistent with others. The *System.Windows.Forms* namespace contains classes to display standard print and page-setup dialog boxes, and a print preview window.

Let's begin this journey with the printers themselves.

# Printers and Their Settings

Windows allows a user to install multiple printers. (More accurately, the user can install *device drivers* for multiple printers. The printers don't actually have to be attached to the machine.) The installed printers are listed in the Printers dialog box that you can invoke from the Settings item on the Start menu. At any time, only one of these printers is the *default* printer. The user can change which printer is the default in this Printers dialog box.

From the perspective of a Windows Forms program, a particular printer is described by an object of type *PrinterSettings*, which like most of the classes I'll discuss in this chapter (except for the common dialog boxes) is defined in the *System.Drawing.Printing* namespace. The *PrinterSettings* class has only a default constructor, which creates an object for the default printer:

### *PrinterSettings* Constructor

```
PrinterSettings()
```

For example, the statement

```
Dim prnset As New PrinterSettings()
```

creates a new instance of *PrinterSettings* that refers to the default printer.

The following three properties indicate some basic information about the printer:

### *PrinterSettings* Properties (selection)

| Property | Type | Accessibility |
|---|---|---|
| *PrinterName* | *String* | Get/Set |
| *IsValid* | *Boolean* | Get |
| *IsDefaultPrinter* | *Boolean* | Get |

*PrinterName* is a string that usually indicates the make and model of the printer. It's the same string you'll see in the Printers dialog box. Here are some examples:

```
HP LaserJet 1100 (MS)
NEC Silentwriter LC890 v47.0
Hewlett-Packard HP-GL/2 Plotter
Fax
```

During the installation of a printer, the user can change the name that refers to the printer, so the printer name you encounter in a *PrinterSettings* object might not be standard.

The *IsValid* and *IsDefaultPrinter* properties will usually be set to *True* when you create a new *PrinterSettings* object. However, if no printers are installed, *PrinterName* returns the string "<no default printer>" and *IsValid* equals *False*.

Notice that *PrinterName* is writable, which means that you can set it to a string that identifies another installed printer. When you set the *PrinterName* property, all the other properties of *PrinterSettings* also change to reflect that printer. Obviously, the string you set *PrinterName* to must match the name of an installed printer. If the string doesn't match, no exception is thrown but the *IsValid* property will be set to *False*.

To intelligently set the *PrinterName* property to the name of another installed printer, you can first obtain a list of all installed printers by using the only shared property of *PrinterSettings*:

### *PrinterSettings* Shared Property

| Property | Type | Accessibility |
| --- | --- | --- |
| *InstalledPrinters* | *PrinterSettings.StringCollection* | Get |

The *StringCollection* class is defined within *PrinterSettings*. It's really just an array of read-only strings. Suppose you make use of the *InstalledPrinters* property like so:

```
Dim sc As PrinterSettings.StringCollection = PrinterSettings.InstalledPrinters()
```

You can then use the following two properties with the *sc* object:

### *PrinterSettings.StringCollection* Properties

| Property | Type | Accessibility |
| --- | --- | --- |
| *Count* | *Integer* | Get |
| *()* | *String* | Get |

The quantity *sc.Count* is the number of installed printers (or 0 if no printers are installed), *sc(0)* is the name of the first printer, *sc(1)* is the name of the second, and so forth. You don't need to save the value of *InstalledPrinters* in a variable. You can access the property itself. For example,

```
PrinterSettings.InstalledPrinters.Count
```

is the number of installed printers, and

```
PrinterSettings.InstalledPrinters(1)
```

is the name of the second printer. Here's some code that puts all the installed printers in a *ComboBox* named *combo*:

```
Dim str As String
For Each str In PrinterSettings.InstalledPrinters
    combo.Items.Add(str)
Next
```

You can change the printer that the *PrinterSettings* object refers to by setting the *PrinterName* property to one of the strings in the collection. If you've defined the *StringCollection* variable *sc*, you do it like this:

```
prnset.PrinterName = sc(2)
```

You can also assign the *PrinterName* property directly by indexing the *InstalledPrinters* property:

```
prnset.PrinterName = PrinterSettings.InstalledPrinters(2)
```

Unless something is seriously wrong, the *IsValid* property of *prnset* should then be *True*, and *IsDefaultPrinter* will be *False*, even if you set *PrinterName* to the name of the default printer.

Let me repeat: When you set the *PrinterName* property to the name of an installed printer, all the properties of the *PrinterSettings* object change to reflect that printer.

Here are a couple properties that indicate very basic capabilities of the printer:

### *PrinterSettings* Properties (selection)

| Property | Type | Accessibility |
|----------|------|---------------|
| *IsPlotter* | *Boolean* | Get |
| *SupportsColor* | *Boolean* | Get |
| *LandscapeAngle* | *Integer* | Get |

If the *IsPlotter* property is *True*, you probably shouldn't rely on the printer to display bitmaps. If the printer doesn't support color, you may want to use alternatives to color in some graphics. (For example, if you're using color for bar graphs or maps, you may want to substitute hatch brushes when printing, as I discussed in Chapter 17.) The *LandscapeAngle* property usually indicates either 90 degrees or 270 degrees. However, if the printer isn't capable of landscape mode, the property will be equal to 0.

No further information is available from *PrinterSettings* about the technology of the printer (that is, whether it works by laser or ink jets or something else).

*PrinterSettings* also has three properties that return collections of items. These properties indicate the available paper sources on the printer (that is, bins and trays), the various paper sizes supported by the printer (including envelopes), and the display resolutions available on the printer:

### *PrinterSettings* Properties (selection)

| Property | Type | Accessibility | Items |
|---|---|---|---|
| *PaperSources* | *PrinterSettings.-PaperSourceCollection* | Get | *PaperSource* |
| *PaperSizes* | *PrinterSettings.-PaperSizeCollection* | Get | *PaperSize* |
| *PrinterResolutions* | *PrinterSettings.Printer-ResolutionCollection* | Get | *PrinterResolution* |

These properties are all quite similar in how they work. The three classes in the second column of the table (headed Type) are all defined within the *PrinterSettings* class, and each of them has just two, read-only properties: *Count*, which is the number of items in the collection, and an indexer, which returns an object of the type indicated in the last column of the table, labeled Items.

For example, the *PaperSources* property is essentially a collection of *PaperSource* objects. The quantity

```
prnset.PaperSources.Count
```

indicates the number of these *PaperSource* objects. You can reference each one by indexing the property, so that

```
prnset.PaperSources(2)
```

is an object of type *PaperSource*, the third in the collection. If the number of items in the collection is less than 3, then attempting to reference the third item in the array will cause an exception to be thrown.

Let's take a look at the *PaperSource*, *PaperSize*, and *PrinterResolution* classes. The *PaperSource* class has two, read-only properties:

### *PaperSource* Properties

| Property | Type | Accessibility |
| --- | --- | --- |
| *SourceName* | *String* | Get |
| *Kind* | *PaperSourceKind* | Get |

The *SourceName* property is a text description that should be meaningful to a user (such as "Manual Paper Feed"). *PaperSourceKind* is an enumeration:

### *PaperSourceKind* Enumeration

| Member | Value | Member | Value |
| --- | --- | --- | --- |
| *Upper* | 1 | *TractorFeed* | 8 |
| *Lower* | 2 | *SmallFormat* | 9 |
| *Middle* | 3 | *LargeFormat* | 10 |
| *Manual* | 4 | *LargeCapacity* | 11 |
| *Envelope* | 5 | *Cassette* | 14 |
| *ManualFeed* | 6 | *FormSource* | 15 |
| *AutomaticFeed* | 7 | *Custom* | 257 |

Keep in mind that the *PaperSources* property of *PrinterSettings* is a collection of *all* the possible paper sources on the printer. The property does *not* indicate the currently default paper source. (That's coming later.)

The *PaperSizes* property of *PrinterSettings* is a collection of all the paper sizes supported by the printer. Each item is an object of type *PaperSize*, which has the following four properties:

### *PaperSize* Properties

| Property | Type | Accessibility |
| --- | --- | --- |
| *PaperName* | *String* | Get/Set |
| *Width* | *Integer* | Get/Set |
| *Height* | *Integer* | Get/Set |
| *Kind* | *PaperKind* | Get |

*PaperName* is a text string that should be meaningful to the user, such as "Envelope #10". The *Width* and *Height* properties indicate the size of the paper (or envelope) in hundredths of an inch. *PaperKind* is an enumeration that has more members (117 at last count) than is convenient to list here. Here are some sample values that might be encountered in the United States and Europe:

### *PaperKind* Enumeration (selection)

| Member | Value | Description |
| --- | --- | --- |
| *Letter* | 1 | 8.5 in. by 11 in. |
| *Legal* | 5 | 8.5 in. by 14 in. |
| *Executive* | 7 | 7.25 in. by 10.5 in. |
| *A4* | 9 | 210 mm by 297 mm |
| *A5* | 11 | 148 mm by 210 mm |

The *PrinterResolutions* property of *PrinterSettings* is a collection of *PrinterResolution* objects. The *PrinterResolution* class has three properties:

### *PrinterResolution* Properties

| Property | Type | Accessibility |
| --- | --- | --- |
| *X* | *Integer* | Get |
| *Y* | *Integer* | Get |
| *Kind* | *PrinterResolutionKind* | Get |

*PrinterResolutionKind* is another enumeration:

### *PrinterResolutionKind* Enumeration

| Member | Value |
| --- | --- |
| *Custom* | 0 |
| *Draft* | −1 |
| *Low* | −2 |
| *Medium* | −3 |
| *High* | −4 |

Every printer has at least five items in the *PrinterResolutions* collection. Four of these items have *PrinterResolutionKind* values of *Draft*, *Low*, *Medium*, and *High*, with *X* and *Y* properties set equal to –1. These four enumeration values are not necessarily associated with unique printer resolutions. If the printer is capable of only one resolution, all these options result in the same resolution.

The remaining one or more items in the *PrinterResolutions* collection indicate the actual device resolutions available on the printer. These remaining items all have *PrinterResolutionKind* values of *Custom*. The *X* and *Y* properties indicate the actual resolution in dots per inch.

For example, a printer may be capable of two resolutions: 600 × 600 and 1200 × 1200. The *PrinterResolutions* collection will have six items. Two of the items will have *PrinterResolutionKind* values of *Custom*; one will have *X* and *Y* values of 600; the other will have *X* and *Y* values of 1200. The other four items are *Draft*, *Low*, *Medium*, and *High* with *X* and *Y* values of –1.

The following properties of *PrinterSettings* involve printing a multipage document:

### *PrinterSettings* Properties (selection)

| Property | Type | Accessibility |
| --- | --- | --- |
| *CanDuplex* | *Boolean* | Get |
| *Duplex* | *Duplex* | Get/Set |
| *MaximumCopies* | *Integer* | Get |
| *Copies* | *Short* | Get/Set |
| *Collate* | *Boolean* | Get/Set |

The *CanDuplex* property is *True* if the printer is capable of printing on both sides of the page. If the property is *True*, you can set the *Duplex* property to one of the following values:

### *Duplex* Enumeration

| Member | Value |
| --- | --- |
| *Simplex* | 1 |
| *Vertical* | 2 |
| *Horizontal* | 3 |
| *Default* | –1 |

The *Simplex* member indicates one-side printing. The *Vertical* and *Horizontal* options refer to the two different ways that double-sided pages can be printed. *Vertical* indicates that the pages are intended to be joined vertically, just like a regular book. The *Horizontal* option is for pages that are joined horizontally, usually at the top.

The *Copies* property is 1 by default. You can set it to any value up to *MaximumCopies* to force the printer driver to print multiple copies. *Collate* indicates the order of the copies. If you print two copies of three pages and *Collate* equals *False*, the pages will be printed in the order 1, 1, 2, 2, 3, 3. When *Collate* is *True*, the order is 1, 2, 3, 1, 2, 3. The default value of *Collate* depends on the printer.

If you programmatically set the following properties, nothing will happen. These properties are intended to be used in conjunction with the *PrintDialog* class that I'll discuss later in this chapter:

### *PrinterSettings* Properties (selection)

| Property | Type | Accessibility |
|----------|------|---------------|
| *PrintRange* | *PrintRange* | Get/Set |
| *MinimumPage* | *Integer* | Get/Set |
| *MaximumPage* | *Integer* | Get/Set |
| *FromPage* | *Integer* | Get/Set |
| *ToPage* | *Integer* | Get/Set |
| *PrintToFile* | *Boolean* | Get/Set |

The final property of the *PrinterSettings* class is an object of type *PageSettings*, another important class in *System.Drawing.Printing*:

### *PrinterSettings* Properties (selection)

| Property | Type | Accessibility |
|----------|------|---------------|
| *DefaultPageSettings* | *PageSettings* | Get |

I'll discuss the *PageSettings* class in detail shortly. The class describes the characteristics of a printed page. For example, *PrinterSettings* has a *PaperSources* property that is a collection of all the paper sources available on the printer. *PageSettings* has a *PaperSource* property that indicates a paper source for a particular page.

The *DefaultPageSettings* property in *PrinterSettings* indicates—as the name implies—the default page settings. As you'll see, you can change the page settings for an entire document or for each page as a document is being printed.

*PrinterSettings* has several methods that allow you to interface with Win32 code. In particular, you can copy the information from *PrinterSettings* into Win32 *DEVMODE* or *DEVNAMES* structures, or you can copy from a *DEVMODE* or *DEVNAMES* structure into *PrinterSettings*.

In addition, there is one method of *PrinterSettings* that might be of interest even for a Windows Forms program that isn't interfacing with Win32 code:

### *PrinterSettings* Methods (selection)

```
Function CreateMeasurementGraphics() As Graphics
```

This method returns something that in Win32 is called an *information device context*. You can use the *Graphics* object from *CreateMeasurementGraphics* to obtain information about the printer, but not to draw on a printer page. This method allows you to obtain additional information about any installed printer at any time, for example, during a program's constructor. The ability to obtain such information is much less vital in Windows Forms, primarily because Windows Forms fonts are handled in a more device-independent manner than fonts in Win32 API programs.

Let's now move from *PrinterSettings* to *PageSettings*, and then we'll have conquered two of the basic classes of *System.Drawing.Printing*.

# Page Settings

The *PageSettings* class describes those printer characteristics that can change with each page. It's tempting to consider a *PageSettings* object in a vacuum. However, a particular *PageSettings* object is always associated with a particular printer. A little thought will convince you why this is so: if the *PageSettings* object indicates that a page is to be printed on ledger paper (that's 17 inches by 11 inches), the printer better support that size.

Programs commonly get access to precreated *PageSettings* objects, such as the *DefaultPageSettings* property in *PrinterSettings*. But you can also create a *PageSettings* object using the class's constructor:

### *PageSettings* Constructors

```
PageSettings()

PageSettings(ByVal prnset As PrinterSettings)
```

The first constructor creates a *PageSettings* object for the default printer; the second creates a *PageSettings* object based on a particular installed printer indicated by the *PrinterSettings* argument. In either case, the *PageSettings* object contains default page settings for the printer.

Default page settings for installed printers are defined by the user in Printing Preferences dialog boxes that the user invokes from the Printers dialog box. A Windows Forms program can change those default settings when printing a document, but any changes made by the Windows Forms program do *not* affect other applications. For example, if the user has selected landscape mode in the Printing Preferences dialog box, a Windows Forms program can print in portrait mode, but nothing the program does will change the landscape selection in the Printing Preferences dialog box.

The *PageSettings* class has eight properties, seven of which are writable as well as readable:

### *PageSettings* Properties

| Property | Type | Accessibility |
| --- | --- | --- |
| *PrinterSettings* | *PrinterSettings* | Get/Set |
| *Landscape* | *Boolean* | Get/Set |
| *Bounds* | *Rectangle* | Get |
| *Margins* | *Margins* | Get/Set |
| *Color* | *Boolean* | Get/Set |
| *PaperSource* | *PaperSource* | Get/Set |
| *PaperSize* | *PaperSize* | Get/Set |
| *PrinterResolution* | *PrinterResolution* | Get/Set |

Notice that the first property in this table is the *PrinterSettings* property that indicates the printer these page settings are associated with. When you obtain a *PageSettings* object from the *DefaultPageSettings* property of a *PrinterSettings* object, the *PrinterSettings* property of the *PageSettings* object is the same object as the original *PrinterSettings* object.

In other words, if you create a *PrinterSettings* object named *prnset*, then the expression

```
prnset.Equals(prnset.DefaultPageSettings.PrinterSettings)
```

returns *True*. Remember that objects are actually references, so any change you make to any property in *prnset* will be reflected in *prnset.DefaultPageSettings.PrinterSettings*.

However, if you create a *PageSettings* object named *pageset*, then the expression

```
pageset.Equals(pageset.PrinterSettings.DefaultPageSettings)
```

returns *False*, even though all the corresponding properties of the two objects will initially be equal. An object of type *PageSettings* refers to the settings of a particular page. You may want to change the settings for a particular page without changing the default page settings for the document.

In most cases, you'll use the remaining properties in *PageSettings* just to obtain information. However, your program can also (within limits) set the properties to change the way in which a page is printed.

For example, the *Landscape* property is *False* to indicate portrait mode and *True* for landscape mode. That's informational. Your application can use that information to print somewhat differently depending on how the page is oriented. But your program can also change that property itself without any intervention by the user.

The read-only *Bounds* property is a *Rectangle* object that indicates the size of the page in units of hundredths of an inch, taking into account the paper size and the *Landscape* setting. For example, letter-size paper in portrait mode will have a *Bounds* property of (0, 0, 850, 1100). In landscape mode, the *Bounds* property is (0, 0, 1100, 850).

The *Margins* property indicates default margins for the page, which are initially set to 1 inch on all four sides. You can construct a new *Margins* object using the following constructors:

### *Margins* Constructors

```
Margins()

Margins(ByVal Left As Integer, ByVal Right As Integer,
        ByVal Top As Integer, ByVal Bottom As Integer)
```

The class has four properties, which indicate the margins in hundredths of an inch:

### *Margins* Properties

| Property | Type | Accessibility |
|----------|------|---------------|
| *Left* | *Integer* | Get/Set |
| *Right* | *Integer* | Get/Set |
| *Top* | *Integer* | Get/Set |
| *Bottom* | *Integer* | Get/Set |

Sometimes a user will specify that pages should not be printed in color even if the printer is capable of color. Perhaps the color ink-jet cartridge is empty. The *Color* property of the *PageSettings* object indicates whether the user wants color to be used on the page.

The next three properties in the table are *PaperSource*, *PaperSize*, and *PrinterResolution*. You'll recall that the *PrinterSettings* class has three properties named *PaperSources*, *PaperSizes*, and *PrinterResolutions* (all plurals) that correspond to these three properties of *PageSettings*. The *PaperSource* property in *PageSettings*, for example, is one of the items from the *PaperSources* collection in *PrinterSettings*.

If you want to change one of these three properties from your program, be sure to set the property from a member of the corresponding collection. For example, if you have an object of type *PageSettings* named *pageset* and you want to change the printer resolution to *Draft*, the code can look something like this:

```
Dim prnres As PrinterResolution
For Each prnres In pageset.PrinterSettings.PrinterResolutions
    If prnres.Kind = PrinterResolutionKind.Draft Then
        pageset.PrinterResolution = prnres
        Exit For
    End If
Next
```

The *For Each* statement loops through all the items of the *PrinterResolutions* collection in the *PrinterSettings* object associated with the *PageSettings* object. When there's a match, the code sets the *PrinterResolution* property and bails out. You need to set the *PrinterResolution* property of *PageSettings* from pre-created *PrinterResolution* objects because the *PrinterResolution* class has no public constructor.

There aren't many occasions when your program will want to change the *PaperSource* or *PaperSize* property. However, suppose you implement a mail-merge facility and you want to alternately print letters and envelopes in one print job. You would need to change the *PaperSource* and *PaperSize* properties accordingly, based on specifications the user made in the application.

The *PaperSize* property is not affected by the *Landscape* property. If the *Landscape* property is *False*, the *Bounds* property *Width* and *Height* will equal the *Width* and *Height* properties of the *PaperSize* property. If *Landscape* is *True*, the *Bounds*, *Width*, and *Height* properties will be swapped. The *Paper-Size* properties will not.

So far, we haven't gotten to the point where we can actually print something. That job requires defining an object of type *PrintDocument*.

# Defining a Document

A print job consists of one or more pages printed on a particular printer and is represented by the *PrintDocument* class. *PrintDocument* has only a default constructor:

### *PrintDocument* Constructor

```
PrintDocument()
```

Generally, a program begins the process of printing by creating an object of type *PrintDocument*:

```
Dim prndoc As New PrintDocument()
```

You could create this object anew for each print job. However, if you're using the standard print dialog boxes—or some other means of allowing the user to select printers and printer options—you probably want to retain those settings in the *PrintDocument* object and use the same instance for the duration of the program. In that case, you'd define *prndoc* as a field and create it only once.

*PrintDocument* has only four properties, but two of them are objects of type *PrinterSettings* and *PageSettings*, so there's much more information packed into the *PrintDocument* object than you'd expect at first glance:

### *PrintDocument* Properties

| Property | Type | Accessibility |
|---|---|---|
| *PrinterSettings* | *PrinterSettings* | Get/Set |
| *DefaultPageSettings* | *PageSettings* | Get/Set |
| *DocumentName* | *String* | Get/Set |
| *PrintController* | *PrintController* | Get/Set |

When you create a new *PrintDocument* object, the *PrinterSettings* property indicates the default printer. If you want, you can change the *PrinterSettings* property or individual properties of the *PrinterSettings* property. For example,

```
prndoc.PrinterSettings.Copies = 2
```

The *DefaultPageSettings* property is initially set from the *DefaultPageSettings* property of the *PrinterSettings* object. You can change that as well, or properties of that property, for example, as shown here:

```
prndoc.DefaultPageSettings.Landscape = True
```

For a new *PrintDocument* object, the expression

```
prndoc.PrinterSettings.Equals(prndoc.DefaultPageSettings.PrinterSettings)
```

returns *True,* but

```
prndoc.DefaultPageSettings.Equals(prndoc.PrinterSettings.DefaultPageSettings)
```

returns *False.* That's because you may want to change the *DefaultPageSettings* for the document without changing the default page settings for the printer.

The *DocumentName* property is initialized to the text string "document". You'll probably want to change that. The name shows up whenever the print job is identified, such as in the window that lists outstanding print jobs as they're being printed. I'll discuss the *PrintController* property shortly.

The *PrintDocument* class has four public events:

### *PrintDocument* Events

| Event | Method | Delegate | Argument |
|-------|--------|----------|----------|
| *BeginPrint* | *OnBeginPrint* | *PrintEventHandler* | *PrintEventArgs* |
| *QueryPageSettings* | *OnQueryPageSettings* | *QueryPageSettingsEventHandler* | *QueryPageSettingsEventArgs* |
| *PrintPage* | *OnPrintPage* | *PrintPageEventHandler* | *PrintPageEventArgs* |
| *EndPrint* | *OnEndPrint* | *PrintEventHandler* | *PrintEventArgs* |

The *BeginPrint* and *EndPrint* events are triggered once for every print job. The *QueryPageSettings* and *PrintPage* events are triggered for every page in the print job. The *PrintPage* event handler indicates whether there are more pages to be printed.

At the very least, you'll set a handler for the *PrintPage* event. If you want to use different page settings for each page (for example, to alternate the printing of letters and envelopes in a single print job), you'll also install a handler for the *QueryPageSettings* event. Install handlers for *BeginPrint* and *EndPrint* if you need to perform lengthy initialization or cleanup. I'll go over the arguments to these event handlers shortly.

Finally, you initiate printing by calling the following method, which is the only method in *PrintDocument* that isn't associated with an event:

### *PrintDocument* Method

```
Sub Print()
```

The *Print* method doesn't return until the program is finished printing the document. The application can't respond to any user input during this time. In the interim, the *PrintDocument* event handlers installed by the program will be called, beginning with the *BeginPrint* handler, then the *QueryPageSettings* and *PrintPage* handlers for each page, and finally the *EndPrint* handler.

# Handling *PrintDocument* Events

The following class hierarchy shows the descendents of *EventArgs* that are involved with the *PrintDocument* event handlers:

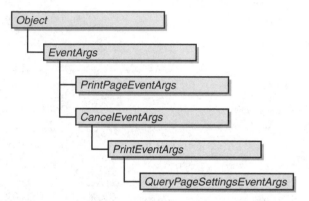

*CancelEventArgs* is defined in the *System.ComponentModel* namespace. The *PrintEventArgs* object associated with the *BeginPrint* and *EndPrint* events has a single property that it inherits from *CancelEventArgs*:

### *PrintEventArgs* Property

| Property | Type | Accessibility |
|----------|------|---------------|
| Cancel | Boolean | Get/Set |

The *BeginPrint* event handler can set *Cancel* to *True* to abort the print job (for example, when the print job needs more memory than is available).

The *QueryPageSettingsEventArgs* class adds another property to *Cancel*:

### *QueryPageSettingsEventArgs* Property

| Property | Type | Accessibility |
|----------|------|---------------|
| PageSettings | PageSettings | Get/Set |

The handler for the *QueryPageSettings* event can change *PageSettings* properties in preparation for the corresponding *PrintPage* event.

The *PrintPageEventArgs* class has four read-only properties and two read-write properties:

### *PrintPageEventArgs* Properties

| Property | Type | Access |
|----------|------|--------|
| *Graphics* | *Graphics* | Get |
| *HasMorePages* | *Boolean* | Get/Set |
| *Cancel* | *Boolean* | Get/Set |
| *PageSettings* | *PageSettings* | Get |
| *PageBounds* | *Rectangle* | Get |
| *MarginBounds* | *Rectangle* | Get |

The *Graphics* object is created anew for each page. If you set properties of the *Graphics* object—such as *PageUnit* or *PageScale*—for one page, don't expect the properties to be in effect for subsequent pages. The default *PageUnit* is *GraphicsUnit.Display*, which makes the printer seem like a 100-dpi device. The *DpiX* and *DpiY* properties of the *Graphics* object reflect the *PrinterResolution* property of *PageSettings*.

On entry to the print-page event handler, *HasMorePages* is always set to *False*. For printing multiple pages, you must set it to *True* on return from the event handler for the handler to be invoked again. On the last page, leave the property set to *False*.

The *Cancel* property is also usually set to *False*. Set it to *True* if your program needs to abort the print job. Setting *Cancel* to *True* is different from not setting *HasMorePages* to *True* in that the operating system will attempt to cease the printing of pages already in the queue.

The *PageSettings* property is for informational purposes while printing. The property will reflect any changes made in the *QueryPageSettings* event handler.

For your convenience, the *PrintPageEventArgs* object also includes a *PageBounds* rectangle, which is the same as the *Bounds* property of *PageSettings*, and a *MarginBounds* rectangle, which is the dimensions of the page less the margins indicated by the *Margins* property of *PageSettings*. I'll cover these properties in more detail shortly.

Let's take a look at some code. First, here's a simple dialog box that lets the user pick one of the installed printers from a combo box.

**PrinterSelectionDialog.vb**

```
'-------------------------------------------------------------
' PrinterSelectionDialog.vb (c) 2002 by Charles Petzold
'-------------------------------------------------------------
Imports System
Imports System.Drawing
Imports System.Drawing.Printing
Imports System.Windows.Forms

Class PrinterSelectionDialog
    Inherits Form

    Private combo As ComboBox

    Sub New()
        Text = "Select Printer"
        FormBorderStyle = FormBorderStyle.FixedDialog
        ControlBox = False
        MaximizeBox = False
        MinimizeBox = False
        ShowInTaskbar = False
        StartPosition = FormStartPosition.Manual
        Location = Point.op_Addition(ActiveForm.Location, _
                    Size.op_Addition(SystemInformation.CaptionButtonSize, _
                                    SystemInformation.FrameBorderSize))
        Dim lbl As New Label()
        lbl.Parent = Me
        lbl.Text = "Printer:"
        lbl.Location = New Point(8, 8)
        lbl.Size = New Size(40, 8)

        combo = New ComboBox()
        combo.Parent = Me
        combo.DropDownStyle = ComboBoxStyle.DropDownList
        combo.Location = New Point(48, 8)
        combo.Size = New Size(144, 8)

        ' Add the installed printers to the combo box.
        Dim str As String
        For Each str In PrinterSettings.InstalledPrinters
            combo.Items.Add(str)
        Next str

        Dim btn As New Button()
        btn.Parent = Me
        btn.Text = "OK"
        btn.Location = New Point(40, 32)
        btn.Size = New Size(40, 16)
        btn.DialogResult = DialogResult.OK
        AcceptButton = btn
```

```
        btn = New Button()
        btn.Parent = Me
        btn.Text = "Cancel"
        btn.Location = New Point(120, 32)
        btn.Size = New Size(40, 16)
        btn.DialogResult = DialogResult.Cancel
        CancelButton = btn

        ClientSize = New Size(200, 56)
        AutoScaleBaseSize = New Size(4, 8)
    End Sub

    Property PrinterName() As String
        Set(ByVal Value As String)
            combo.SelectedItem = Value
        End Set
        Get
            Return combo.SelectedItem.ToString()
        End Get
    End Property
End Class
```

The combo box is of type *DropDownList*, so the user is prohibited from typing anything in the edit field. A read/write property named *PrinterName* allows a program to initialize the selected item in the combo box to the default printer and to obtain the item the user selects.

The PrintThreePages program makes use of this dialog box. To let the user initiate printing, the program creates a menu containing a File submenu with a Print item. The handler for the Print menu item displays the dialog box to let the user choose a printer. The program installs both *QueryPageSettings* and *Print-Page* event handlers to print three pages, each of which contains the page number in a big font centered on the page. Just for kicks, the program sets the resolution settings to "draft" mode for the entire document and alternates between portrait and landscape for each page.

**PrintThreePages.vb**

```
'-------------------------------------------------
' PrintThreePages.vb (c) 2002 by Charles Petzold
'-------------------------------------------------
Imports System
Imports System.Drawing
Imports System.Drawing.Printing
Imports System.Windows.Forms

Class PrintThreePages
    Inherits Form
```

*(continued)*

**PrintThreePages.vb**    *(continued)*

```vb
    Const iNumberPages As Integer = 3
    Private iPageNumber As Integer

    Shared Sub Main()
        Application.Run(New PrintThreePages())
    End Sub

    Sub New()
        Text = "Print Three Pages"

        Menu = New MainMenu()
        Menu.MenuItems.Add("&File")
        Menu.MenuItems(0).MenuItems.Add("&Print...", _
                                        AddressOf MenuFilePrintOnClick)
    End Sub

    Private Sub MenuFilePrintOnClick(ByVal obj As Object, _
                                     ByVal ea As EventArgs)
        ' Create PrintDocument.
        Dim prndoc As New PrintDocument()

        ' Create dialog box and set PrinterName property.
        Dim dlg As New PrinterSelectionDialog()
        dlg.PrinterName = prndoc.PrinterSettings.PrinterName

        ' Show dialog box and bail out if not OK.
        If dlg.ShowDialog() <> DialogResult.OK Then Return

        ' Set PrintDocument to selected printer.
        prndoc.PrinterSettings.PrinterName = dlg.PrinterName

        ' Set printer resolution to "draft".
        Dim prnres As PrinterResolution
        For Each prnres In prndoc.PrinterSettings.PrinterResolutions
            If prnres.Kind = PrinterResolutionKind.Draft Then
                prndoc.DefaultPageSettings.PrinterResolution = prnres
                Exit For
            End If
        Next

        ' Set remainder of PrintDocument properties.
        prndoc.DocumentName = Text
        AddHandler prndoc.PrintPage, AddressOf OnPrintPage
        AddHandler prndoc.QueryPageSettings, AddressOf OnQueryPageSettings

        ' Commence printing.
        iPageNumber = 1
        prndoc.Print()
    End Sub
```

```
    Private Sub OnQueryPageSettings(ByVal obj As Object, _
                                 ByVal qpsea As QueryPageSettingsEventArgs)
        If qpsea.PageSettings.PrinterSettings.LandscapeAngle <> 0 Then
            qpsea.PageSettings.Landscape = Not qpsea.PageSettings.Landscape
        End If
    End Sub

    Private Sub OnPrintPage(ByVal obj As Object, _
                         ByVal ppea As PrintPageEventArgs)
        Dim grfx As Graphics = ppea.Graphics
        Dim fnt As New Font("Times New Roman", 360)
        Dim str As String = iPageNumber.ToString()
        Dim szf As SizeF = grfx.MeasureString(str, fnt)

        grfx.DrawString(str, fnt, Brushes.Black, _
                    (grfx.VisibleClipBounds.Width - szf.Width) / 2, _
                    (grfx.VisibleClipBounds.Height - szf.Height) / 2)
        ppea.HasMorePages = iPageNumber < iNumberPages
        iPageNumber += 1
    End Sub
End Class
```

Let's take a look at the *MenuFilePrintOnClick* method first. That's the method that's executed when the user selects Print from the File menu. It begins by creating a new *PrintDocument* object and a new *PrinterSelectionDialog* object. The constructor in *PrinterSelectionDialog* fills a combo box with installed printers. The method then sets the *PrinterName* property of the dialog box to the default printer:

```
dlg.PrinterName = prndoc.PrinterSettings.PrinterName
```

That becomes the selected item in the combo box.

If the user returns from the dialog box by pressing OK, the *PrinterName* property of the *PrinterSettings* property of the *PrintDocument* object is set to the selected printer:

```
prndoc.PrinterSettings.PrinterName = dlg.PrinterName
```

The method then sets the *PrinterResolution* property of the *DefaultPageSettings* property of *PrintDocument* to draft mode using code similar to what I showed earlier for doing such jobs. All pages of the document will now be printed with the resolution associated with draft mode. (You can determine what that resolution is by examining the *DpiX* and *DpiY* properties of the *Graphics* object during the *PrintPage* method.)

The *MenuFilePrintOnClick* method concludes by setting the *Document-Name* property of the *PrintDocument* object, installing event handlers for the

*PrintPage* and *QueryPageSettings* events, initializing the page number, and calling the *Print* method in *PrintDocument* to begin printing.

The next code executed in the program will be the *OnQueryPageSettings* event handler for the first page. If the printer supports landscape mode, the method toggles the *Landscape* property of the *PageSettings* object passed as a property of *QueryPageSettingsEventArgs*:

```
qpsea.PageSettings.Landscape = Not qpsea.PageSettings.Landscape
```

After the *OnQueryPageSettings* method returns, the *OnPrintPage* event handler is called for the first page. That handler displays a large number centered on the page.

If the printer is set up to print in portrait mode by default, the first page will be in landscape mode, the second in portrait, and the third in landscape. Notice that *PrintPage* doesn't have to do anything special except use the current *VisibleClipBounds* property of the *Graphics* object to center the text. *VisibleClipBounds* reflects the current orientation for the printer.

Whenever you print from PrintThreePages, the *PrintDocument* object is created anew. That means your default printer always shows up as the selected printer in the dialog box, even if you switched to another printer in a previous print job. You might want to consider storing the *PrintDocument* object as a field. Just move this entire statement outside the *MenuFilePrintOnClick* method:

```
Dim prndoc As New PrintDocument()
```

Now the object will retain any changes made while the program is running. As I mentioned earlier, no changes are made that affect any other application or the same application when run later.

# The Page Dimensions

To intelligently draw text and graphics on a printer page, you need to know some details about the size of the area in which you can draw. From Chapter 5 until now, I've been assuming that you can draw anywhere on the printable area of the printer page. But you really should be drawing only within certain margins that the user has specified.

Unfortunately, taking into account the user's selection of margins is a problematic area of printing in a Windows Forms application. You may think you have all the information you need, but you really don't.

Let's take a look at what you *do* have. A *PrintPage* event handler is passed an object of type *PrintPageEventArgs*. One property of that class is a *Rectangle* object named *PageBounds*. *PageBounds* is equal to the *Bounds* property of the *PageSettings* class, and it indicates the dimension of the physical page, taking portrait or landscape orientation into account, in units of hundredths of an inch. For example, for 8.5-by-11-inch letter-size paper in portrait mode, *PageBounds* is equal to (0, 0, 850, 1100).

The *PageSettings* class also includes an object named *Margins*, which indicates the margins the user desires on all four sides of the page in units of hundredths of an inch. By default, all four margins are initially equal to 100.

The *MarginBounds* property of *PrintPageEventArgs* is a *Rectangle* object based on *PageBounds* but taking margins into account. For letter-size paper with default margins, *MarginBounds* is the rectangle (100, 100, 650, 900).

So far, so good. The problem, however, is that the *Graphics* object you obtain from *PrintPageEventArgs* is set up to print on the *printable area* of the page. Printers usually can't print to the very edge of the paper because of the presence of rollers and paper guides and whatnot in the printer. The origin of this *Graphics* object—that is, the location where graphics appear when you specify the point (0, 0) in drawing methods—is the upper left corner of the printable area of the page. The origin is consistent with the *VisibleClipBounds* property of the *Graphics* object.

When my printer is loaded with standard 8.5-by-11-inch paper and printing is set for portrait mode, *VisibleClipBounds* reports a rectangle of (0, 0, 800, 1060). By default, these units are 1/100 inch, so the printable area of the page is 8 inches wide and 10.6 inches high. The unprintable area is 0.5 inch total on the left and right, and 0.4 inch total on the top and bottom.

However, you can't assume that the unprintable area on my printer is 0.25 inch on the left and right, and 0.20 inch on the top and bottom. Depending on the printer, the unprintable area might be unequally distributed between the left and right, and the top and bottom of the page.

What we need is a rectangle describing the printable area of the page relative to the total page. Unfortunately, we've now run out of information. No more information exists in *PrinterSettings*, *PageSettings*, *PrintDocument*, or *PrintPageEventArgs* that reveals how the unprintable area is distributed along the edges of the page.

If you're content to live with approximations, you can calculate a rectangle relative to *VisibleClipBounds* (and hence usable with *Graphics* drawing methods) that describes the area of the page within the user-selected margins.

If the *PrintPageEventArgs* object is named *ppea* and the *Graphics* object is named *grfx*, the expression

```
(ppea.PageBounds.Width - grfx.VisibleClipBounds.Width) / 2
```

is the approximate unprintable margin on the left side of the page, and

```
(ppea.PageBounds.Height - grfx.VisibleClipBounds.Height) / 2
```

is the approximate unprintable margin on the top side of the page. Subtract these two values from *ppea.MarginBounds.Left* and *ppea.MarginBounds.Top*, respectively, and you get the point in drawing coordinates that is approximately the upper left corner of the area of the page in which you should print to respect the user's margins.

Here's a calculation of a display rectangle that takes the user's margins into account:

```
Dim rectf As New RectangleF( _
    ppea.MarginBounds.Left - _
    (ppea.PageBounds.Width - grfx.VisibleClipBounds.Width) / 2, _
    ppea.MarginBounds.Top - _
    (ppea.PageBounds.Height - grfx.VisibleClipBounds.Height) / 2, _
    ppea.MarginBounds.Width, ppea.MarginBounds.Height)
```

Again, let me emphasize that this is an approximate calculation because it assumes the unprintable margins are distributed equally between the left and right sides, and the top and bottom. But it's the best you can do within the Windows Forms interface.

I use this rectangle calculation in the following program, which simply draws the rectangle and two lines connecting its corners.

**PrintWithMargins.vb**

```
'------------------------------------------------
' PrintWithMargins.vb (c) 2002 by Charles Petzold
'------------------------------------------------
Imports System
Imports System.Drawing
Imports System.Drawing.Printing
Imports System.Windows.Forms

Class PrintWithMargins
    Inherits Form

    Shared Sub Main()
        Application.Run(New PrintWithMargins())
    End Sub
```

```
    Sub New()
        Text = "Print with Margins"

        Menu = New MainMenu()
        Menu.MenuItems.Add("&File")
        Menu.MenuItems(0).MenuItems.Add("&Print...", _
                                        AddressOf MenuFilePrintOnClick)
    End Sub

    Private Sub MenuFilePrintOnClick(ByVal obj As Object, _
                                     ByVal ea As EventArgs)
        ' Create PrintDocument.
        Dim prndoc As New PrintDocument()

        ' Create dialog box and set PrinterName property.
        Dim dlg As New PrinterSelectionDialog()
        dlg.PrinterName = prndoc.PrinterSettings.PrinterName

        ' Show dialog box and bail out if not OK.
        If dlg.ShowDialog() <> DialogResult.OK Then Return

        ' Set PrintDocument to selected printer.
        prndoc.PrinterSettings.PrinterName = dlg.PrinterName

        ' Set remainder of PrintDocument properties and commence.
        prndoc.DocumentName = Text
        AddHandler prndoc.PrintPage, AddressOf OnPrintPage
        prndoc.Print()
    End Sub

    Private Sub OnPrintPage(ByVal obj As Object, _
                            ByVal ppea As PrintPageEventArgs)
        Dim grfx As Graphics = ppea.Graphics
        Dim rectf As New RectangleF( _
            ppea.MarginBounds.Left - _
            (ppea.PageBounds.Width - grfx.VisibleClipBounds.Width) / 2, _
            ppea.MarginBounds.Top - _
            (ppea.PageBounds.Height - grfx.VisibleClipBounds.Height) / 2, _
            ppea.MarginBounds.Width, ppea.MarginBounds.Height)

        grfx.DrawRectangle(Pens.Black, rectf.X, rectf.Y, _
                                       rectf.Width, rectf.Height)
        grfx.DrawLine(Pens.Black, rectf.Left, rectf.Top, _
                                  rectf.Right, rectf.Bottom)
        grfx.DrawLine(Pens.Black, rectf.Right, rectf.Top, _
                                  rectf.Left, rectf.Bottom)
    End Sub
End Class
```

If you're not satisfied with this approximation, you'll have to access the Win32 *GetDeviceCaps* function with the arguments *PHYSICALOFFSETX* and *PHYSICALOFFSETY*.

If you're more comfortable with units other than 1/100 inch, you can convert the *PageBounds* and *MarginBounds* values to something else using the *PrinterUnitConvert* class. This class has one shared method, named *Convert*, that's defined in six versions:

### *PrinterUnitConvert* Shared Convert Method

```
Function Convert(ByVal iValue As Integer, ByVal puFrom As PrinterUnit,
          ByVal puTo As PrinterUnit) As Integer

Function Convert(ByVal dValue As Double, ByVal puFrom As PrinterUnit,
          ByVal puTo As PrinterUnit) As Double

Function Convert(ByVal pt As Point, ByVal puFrom As PrinterUnit,
          ByVal puTo As PrinterUnit) As Point

Function Convert(ByVal sz As Size, ByVal puFrom As PrinterUnit,
          ByVal puTo As PrinterUnit) As Size

Function Convert(ByVal rect As Rectangle, ByVal puFrom As PrinterUnit,
          ByVal puTo As PrinterUnit) As Rectangle

Function Convert(ByVal marg As Margins, ByVal puFrom As PrinterUnit,
          ByVal puTo As PrinterUnit) As Margins
```

*PrinterUnit* is an enumeration:

### *PrinterUnit* Enumeration

| Member | Value |
| --- | --- |
| *Display* | 0 |
| *ThousandthsOfAnInch* | 1 |
| *HundredthsOfAMillimeter* | 2 |
| *TenthsOfAMillimeter* | 3 |

The member *Display* indicates hundredths of an inch.

## The Print Controller

Earlier, when discussing the *PrintDocument* class, I skipped over the *PrintController* property. By default, you can set that property to an instance of a class descended from the *PrintController* class. Here's the class hierarchy:

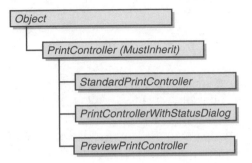

The *PrintController* class defines four methods:

## *PrintController* Methods

```
Sub OnStartPrint(ByVal prndoc As PrintDocument,
                 ByVal pea As PrintEventArgs)

Function OnStartPage(ByVal prndoc As PrintDocument,
                     ByVal ppea As PrintPageEventArgs) As Graphics

Sub OnEndPage(ByVal prndoc As PrintDocument,
              ByVal ppea As PrintPageEventArgs)

Sub OnEndPrint(ByVal prndoc As PrintDocument,
               ByVal pea As PrintEventArgs)
```

As you've seen, when a program initiates printing by calling the *Print* method of the *PrintDocument* class, the *PrintDocument* object responds by triggering the four events defined by the class. These events are *BeginPrint*, *QueryPageSettings*, *PrintPage*, and *EndPrint*.

But *PrintDocument* also makes calls to the four methods of the particular *PrintController* object that is indicated by its *PrintController* property. *Print-Document* calls the *OnStartPrint* method of *PrintController* after triggering its own *BeginPrint* event. *PrintDocument* calls *OnStartPage* and *OnEndPage* before and after triggering each *PrintPage* event. And finally, *PrintDocument* calls *OnEndPrint* in the *PrintController* after triggering its own *EndPrint* event.

In particular, the *OnStartPage* method in the *PrintController* object is responsible for obtaining the *Graphics* object that is eventually passed to the *PrintPage* event handler. (Notice the return value from the *OnStartPage* method.) This *Graphics* object essentially determines where the graphics output in *PrintPage* goes.

Normally, the graphics output goes to the printer, of course, and that's the responsibility of the *PrintController* object. However, the *PreviewPrintController* object has something else in mind. This particular controller creates a *Graphics* object based on a bitmap that represents the printer page. And that (as we shall see toward the end of this chapter) is how print preview is implemented in Windows Forms.

The default *PrintController* property of *PrintDocument* is an object of type *PrintControllerWithStatusDialog*, and that very name discloses another responsibility of the print controller: it displays the dialog box that shows the name of the print document and the page currently printing.

If you don't want that dialog box to be displayed, set the *PrintController* property of *PrintDocument* to an object of type *StandardPrintController*. *StandardPrintController* does everything *PrintControllerWithStatusDialog* does but without the dialog box.

If you'd prefer to display printing progress with something other than the dialog box, you can derive a class from *StandardPrintController*. Here, for example, is a print controller that displays the printing status in a panel of a status bar.

**StatusBarPrintController.vb**

```
'-----------------------------------------------------------
' StatusBarPrintController.vb (c) 2002 by Charles Petzold
'-----------------------------------------------------------
Imports System
Imports System.Drawing
Imports System.Drawing.Printing
Imports System.Windows.Forms

Class StatusBarPrintController
    Inherits StandardPrintController

    Private sbp As StatusBarPanel
    Private iPageNumber As Integer
    Private strSaveText As String

    Sub New(ByVal sbp As StatusBarPanel)
        Me.sbp = sbp
    End Sub

    Overrides Sub OnStartPrint(ByVal prndoc As PrintDocument, _
                        ByVal pea As PrintEventArgs)
        strSaveText = sbp.Text        ' Probably "Ready" or similar.
        sbp.Text = "Starting printing"
        iPageNumber = 1
        MyBase.OnStartPrint(prndoc, pea)
    End Sub

    Overrides Function OnStartPage(ByVal prndoc As PrintDocument, _
                        ByVal ppea As PrintPageEventArgs) As Graphics
        sbp.Text = "Printing page " & iPageNumber
        iPageNumber += 1
        Return MyBase.OnStartPage(prndoc, ppea)
    End Function
```

```
    Overrides Sub OnEndPage(ByVal prndoc As PrintDocument, _
                            ByVal ppea As PrintPageEventArgs)
        MyBase.OnEndPage(prndoc, ppea)
    End Sub

    Overrides Sub OnEndPrint(ByVal prndoc As PrintDocument, _
                             ByVal pea As PrintEventArgs)
        sbp.Text = strSaveText
        MyBase.OnEndPrint(prndoc, pea)
    End Sub
End Class
```

Notice first that the class overrides all four methods of *StandardPrintController* but also makes sure to call the corresponding methods in the base class. Doing so assures that all the normal activity of the print controller still takes place. The only enhancement this version adds is to keep a status bar panel updated. The panel object is required in the class's constructor.

Here's a version of PrintThreePages that forgoes the dialog box to select a printer but instead creates a status bar with one panel.

### PrintWithStatusBar.vb

```
'-----------------------------------------------------
' PrintWithStatusBar.vb (c) 2002 by Charles Petzold
'-----------------------------------------------------
Imports System
Imports System.Drawing
Imports System.Drawing.Printing
Imports System.Windows.Forms

Class PrintWithStatusBar
    Inherits Form

    Private sbar As StatusBar
    Private sbp As StatusBarPanel
    Const iNumberPages As Integer = 3
    Private iPageNumber As Integer

    Shared Sub Main()
        Application.Run(New PrintWithStatusBar())
    End Sub

    Sub New()
        Text = "Print with Status Bar"

        Menu = New MainMenu()
        Menu.MenuItems.Add("&File")
        Menu.MenuItems(0).MenuItems.Add("&Print", _
                                      AddressOf MenuFilePrintOnClick)
        sbar = New StatusBar()
```

*(continued)*

**PrintWithStatusBar.vb** *(continued)*

```
        sbar.Parent = Me
        sbar.ShowPanels = True
        sbp = New StatusBarPanel()
        sbp.Text = "Ready"
        sbp.Width = Width \ 2
        sbar.Panels.Add(sbp)
    End Sub

    Private Sub MenuFilePrintOnClick(ByVal obj As Object, _
                                     ByVal ea As EventArgs)
        Dim prndoc As New PrintDocument()
        prndoc.DocumentName = Text
        prndoc.PrintController = New StatusBarPrintController(sbp)
        AddHandler prndoc.PrintPage, AddressOf OnPrintPage
        iPageNumber = 1
        prndoc.Print()
    End Sub

    Private Sub OnPrintPage(ByVal obj As Object, _
                            ByVal ppea As PrintPageEventArgs)
        Dim grfx As Graphics = ppea.Graphics
        Dim fnt As New Font("Times New Roman", 360)
        Dim str As String = iPageNumber.ToString()
        Dim szf As SizeF = grfx.MeasureString(str, fnt)

        grfx.DrawString(str, fnt, Brushes.Black, _
                        (grfx.VisibleClipBounds.Width - szf.Width) / 2, _
                        (grfx.VisibleClipBounds.Height - szf.Height) / 2)
        System.Threading.Thread.Sleep(1000)
        ppea.HasMorePages = iPageNumber < iNumberPages
        iPageNumber += 1
    End Sub
End Class
```

When setting up the *PrintDocument* in response to the menu click, this version also sets the *PrintController* property:

```
prndoc.PrintController = new StatusBarPrintController(sbp)
```

Because the three pages went by a little too fast for me to confirm that the program was working right, I inserted a call to the *Sleep* method of the *Thread* class in the *OnPrintPage* method.

The only problem with this approach to displaying printer status is that it's deceptive. The absence of the modal dialog box indicates to the user that the application is ready to continue responding to user input. It's not. The application can't respond to user input until the *Print* method of *PrintDocument* returns. When a program reports printing status in a status bar, it should also implement background printing, which requires a second thread of execution.

# Using the Standard Print Dialog Box

Part of the collection of common dialog boxes in *System.Windows.Forms* is *PrintDialog*, a dialog box that lets users select a printer and change the settings for that printer. *PrintDialog* also includes a facility for users to specify whether to print an entire document, a range of pages, or a selection (that is, the part of the document that has been highlighted).

You create a new *PrintDialog* object with the default constructor:

### *PrintDialog* Constructor

```
PrintDialog()
```

You must initialize one (but not both) of the following properties:

### *PrintDialog* Properties (selection)

| Property | Type | Accessibility |
| --- | --- | --- |
| *Document* | *PrintDocument* | Get/Set |
| *PrinterSettings* | *PrinterSettings* | Get/Set |

Setting the *Document* property is preferred; the *PrintDialog* object then uses the *PrinterSettings* property from that *PrintDocument* object to set its own *PrinterSettings* property.

The bulk of the additional options available with *PrintDialog* involve letting the user print an entire document, a range of pages, or the current selection. The *PrintDialog* dialog box displays these three options (labeled All, Pages, and Selection) as radio buttons. By default, only the All option is enabled and, of course, it's checked.

You can optionally enable the Pages and Selection buttons as well. You do so (and select a few other options on the dialog box) using the following properties:

### *PrintDialog* Properties (selection)

| Property | Type | Accessibility | Default |
| --- | --- | --- | --- |
| *AllowSelection* | *Boolean* | Get/Set | *False* |
| *AllowSomePages* | *Boolean* | Get/Set | *False* |
| *AllowPrintToFile* | *Boolean* | Get/Set | *True* |
| *PrintToFile* | *Boolean* | Get/Set | *False* |

*(continued)*

### *PrintDialog* Properties (selection)   *(continued)*

| Property | Type | Accessibility | Default |
|----------|------|---------------|---------|
| *ShowNetwork* | *Boolean* | Get/Set | *True* |
| *ShowHelp* | *Boolean* | Get/Set | *False* |

If you set *ShowHelp* to *True*, you must install a handler for the *HelpRequest* event (inherited from *CommonDialog*). The *AllowPrintToFile* property enables the check box for printing to a file. The *PrintToFile* property indicates whether or not the check box is checked.

When you enable the Pages radio button, the user has the option to type in a From page and a To page. You can specify initial values and minimum and maximum values for these two fields, but not as properties in *PrintDialog*. The properties are defined instead in *PrinterSettings*. After you set the *Document* property of *PrintDialog*, you can use the *PrinterSettings* property of *PrintDialog* to reference these properties:

### *PrinterSettings* Properties (selection)

| Property | Type | Accessibility |
|----------|------|---------------|
| *PrintRange* | *PrintRange* | Get/Set |
| *MinimumPage* | *Integer* | Get/Set |
| *MaximumPage* | *Integer* | Get/Set |
| *FromPage* | *Integer* | Get/Set |
| *ToPage* | *Integer* | Get/Set |
| *PrintToFile* | *Boolean* | Get/Set |

The *PrintRange* property is an enumeration of type *PrintRange*, which has the following values:

### *PrintRange* Enumeration

| Member | Value |
|--------|-------|
| *AllPages* | 0 |
| *Selection* | 1 |
| *SomePages* | 2 |

You're probably tempted to set *MinimumPage* to 1 and *MaximumPage* to the total number of pages in the document. You can also initialize *FromPage* and *ToPage* to those same values. That's actually not such a hot idea for some applications (for example, a Notepad clone). When the *PrintDialog* dialog box is displayed, the user has the option to change the printer, orientation, page size, and so forth, and any of these items could affect the total number of pages in the printed document.

As with any common dialog box, after initializing the *PrintDialog* object, you call its *ShowDialog* method. *ShowDialog* returns a *DialogResult* enumeration value. On return from *PrintDialog*, the *PrintRange* property indicates which option the user has selected. For a range of pages, *FromPage* and *ToPage* indicate the page range.

Let's start off simple. The following program is another version of PrintThreePages that uses a *PrintDialog* object.

```
SimplePrintDialog.vb
'-----------------------------------------------------
' SimplePrintDialog.vb (c) 2002 by Charles Petzold
'-----------------------------------------------------
Imports System
Imports System.Drawing
Imports System.Drawing.Printing
Imports System.Windows.Forms

Class SimplePrintDialog
    Inherits Form

    Const iNumberPages As Integer = 3
    Private iPagesToPrint, iPageNumber As Integer

    Shared Sub Main()
        Application.Run(New SimplePrintDialog())
    End Sub

    Sub New()
        Text = "Simple PrintDialog"

        Menu = New MainMenu()
        Menu.MenuItems.Add("&File")
        Menu.MenuItems(0).MenuItems.Add("&Print...", _
                                    AddressOf MenuFilePrintOnClick)
    End Sub

    Private Sub MenuFilePrintOnClick(ByVal obj As Object, _
                            ByVal ea As EventArgs)
        ' Create the PrintDocument and PrintDialog.
        Dim prndoc As New PrintDocument()
        Dim prndlg As New PrintDialog()
        prndlg.Document = prndoc
```

*(continued)*

**SimplePrintDialog.vb**  *(continued)*

```
        ' Allow a page range.
        prndlg.AllowSomePages = True
        prndlg.PrinterSettings.MinimumPage = 1
        prndlg.PrinterSettings.MaximumPage = iNumberPages
        prndlg.PrinterSettings.FromPage = 1
        prndlg.PrinterSettings.ToPage = iNumberPages

        ' If the dialog box returns OK, print.
        If prndlg.ShowDialog() = DialogResult.OK Then
            prndoc.DocumentName = Text
            AddHandler prndoc.PrintPage, AddressOf OnPrintPage

            ' Determine which pages to print.
            Select Case prndlg.PrinterSettings.PrintRange
                Case PrintRange.AllPages
                    iPagesToPrint = iNumberPages
                    iPageNumber = 1

                Case PrintRange.SomePages
                    iPagesToPrint = 1 + prndlg.PrinterSettings.ToPage - _
                                    prndlg.PrinterSettings.FromPage()
                    iPageNumber = prndlg.PrinterSettings.FromPage
            End Select
            prndoc.Print()
        End If
    End Sub

    Private Sub OnPrintPage(ByVal obj As Object, _
                            ByVal ppea As PrintPageEventArgs)
        Dim grfx As Graphics = ppea.Graphics
        Dim fnt As New Font("Times New Roman", 360)
        Dim str As String = iPageNumber.ToString()
        Dim szf As SizeF = grfx.MeasureString(str, fnt)

        grfx.DrawString(str, fnt, Brushes.Black, _
                        (grfx.VisibleClipBounds.Width - szf.Width) / 2, _
                        (grfx.VisibleClipBounds.Height - szf.Height) / 2)
        iPageNumber += 1
        iPagesToPrint -= 1
        ppea.HasMorePages = iPagesToPrint > 0
    End Sub
End Class
```

The hard part of this program is allowing the user to select a range of pages to print. The *iNumberPages* field is hard-coded as 3. But along with the *iPageNumber* field, I also include a new field, named *iPagesToPrint*, which can take on a value from 1 to *iNumberPages*.

Before invoking *PrintDialog*, the program sets all the properties of *Print-Dialog* (including the properties in *PrinterSettings* rather than *PrintDialog* itself) that involve the page range. On returning from *PrintDialog*, the program checks the value of *PrintRange* and initializes *iPagesToPrint* and *iPageNumber* (the first page to print) accordingly.

Some features of *PrintDialog* are handled for you automatically. If you select Print To File, a dialog box appears asking you for a filename, and the graphics output for the printer is saved in that file.

As you can see by experimentation, every time *PrintDialog* is invoked, all the settings revert to their default values. As you probably know by experience, some Windows applications also work like that, and they can be quite annoying. If you have multiple printers, for example, you may want to print on a non-default printer from a particular application. If you select that nondefault printer once in *PrintDialog*, the dialog box should probably display that printer on subsequent evocations. The same goes for other settings you specify in the dialog box.

To make settings persistent, store both the *PrintDialog* and *PrintDocument* objects as fields. You can simply move both these statements outside the *MenuFilePrintOnClick* method:

```
Dim prndoc As New PrintDocument()
Dim prndlg As New PrintDialog()
```

Then move this statement to the form's constructor:

```
prndlg.Document = prndoc
```

I'll be using this approach in the remaining programs in this chapter.

# Setting Up the Page

The second common dialog box connected with printing is *PageSetupDialog*. This dialog box usually lets the user specify margins, page orientation, page sources, and paper sizes. But the dialog box can also be used to select a default printer and printer options. *PageSetupDialog* has a single constructor:

### *PageSetupDialog* Constructor

```
PageSetupDialog()
```

You then set one (and only one) of the following properties:

### *PageSetupDialog* Properties (selection)

| Property | Type | Accessibility |
| --- | --- | --- |
| *Document* | *PrintDocument* | Get/Set |
| *PrinterSettings* | *PrinterSettings* | Get/Set |
| *PageSettings* | *PageSettings* | Get/Set |

Setting the *Document* property is recommended. *PageSetupDialog* then sets the *PrinterSettings* and *PageSettings* properties from that *PrintDocument* object. To make everything work right, you must use the same *PrintDocument* object with both *PageSetupDialog* and *PrintDialog*.

Here are the remaining *PageSetupDialog* properties:

### *PageSetupDialog* Properties (selection)

| Property | Type | Accessibility |
| --- | --- | --- |
| *AllowMargins* | *Boolean* | Get/Set |
| *AllowOrientation* | *Boolean* | Get/Set |
| *AllowPaper* | *Boolean* | Get/Set |
| *AllowPrinter* | *Boolean* | Get/Set |
| *ShowNetwork* | *Boolean* | Get/Set |
| *ShowHelp* | *Boolean* | Get/Set |
| *MinMargins* | *Margins* | Get/Set |

All the *Boolean* properties are *True* by default except *ShowHelp*. Setting them to *False* disables certain aspects of the dialog box. The Network button is on the additional dialog box invoked when you press the Printer button. The *MinMargins* property is set to all zeros by default.

Changes the user makes in the *PageSetupDialog* dialog box are reflected in the *PageSettings* object that the dialog box obtains from the *PrintDocument* object.

The ImagePrint program derives from ImageIO in Chapter 16 (which itself derived from ImageOpen) to add Page Setup and Print options to the File menu. You can now use the program to load, save, and print bitmaps.

## ImagePrint.vb

```
'------------------------------------------------
' ImagePrint.vb (c) 2002 by Charles Petzold
'------------------------------------------------
Imports System
Imports System.Drawing
Imports System.Drawing.Printing
Imports System.Windows.Forms

Class ImagePrint
    Inherits ImageIO

    Private prndoc As PrintDocument = New PrintDocument()
    Private setdlg As PageSetupDialog = New PageSetupDialog()
    Private prndlg As PrintDialog = New PrintDialog()
    Private miFileSet, miFilePrint, miFileProps As MenuItem

    Shared Shadows Sub Main()
        Application.Run(New ImagePrint())
    End Sub

    Sub New()
        strProgName = "Image Print"
        Text = strProgName

        ' Initialize PrintDocument and common dialog boxes.
        AddHandler prndoc.PrintPage, AddressOf OnPrintPage
        setdlg.Document = prndoc
        prndlg.Document = prndoc

        ' Add menu items.
        AddHandler Menu.MenuItems(0).Popup, AddressOf MenuFileOnPopup
        Menu.MenuItems(0).MenuItems.Add("-")

        ' File Page Setup item
        miFileSet = New MenuItem("Page Set&up...")
        AddHandler miFileSet.Click, AddressOf MenuFileSetupOnClick
        Menu.MenuItems(0).MenuItems.Add(miFileSet)

        ' File Print item
        miFilePrint = New MenuItem("&Print...")
        AddHandler miFilePrint.Click, AddressOf MenuFilePrintOnClick
        miFilePrint.Shortcut = Shortcut.CtrlP
        Menu.MenuItems(0).MenuItems.Add(miFilePrint)
        Menu.MenuItems(0).MenuItems.Add("-")

        ' File Properties item
        miFileProps = New MenuItem("Propert&ies...")
```

*(continued)*

**ImagePrint.vb** *(continued)*

```
        AddHandler miFileProps.Click, AddressOf MenuFilePropsOnClick
        Menu.MenuItems(0).MenuItems.Add(miFileProps)
    End Sub

    Protected Overrides Sub OnPaint(ByVal pea As PaintEventArgs)
        If Not img Is Nothing Then
            ScaleImageIsotropically(pea.Graphics, img, _
                    RectangleF.op_Implicit(ClientRectangle))
        End If
    End Sub

    Private Sub MenuFileOnPopup(ByVal obj As Object, ByVal ea As EventArgs)
        Dim bEnable As Boolean = Not img Is Nothing
        miFilePrint.Enabled = bEnable
        miFileSet.Enabled = bEnable
        miFileProps.Enabled = bEnable
    End Sub

    Private Sub MenuFileSetupOnClick(ByVal obj As Object, _
                                     ByVal ea As EventArgs)
        setdlg.ShowDialog()
    End Sub

    Private Sub MenuFilePrintOnClick(ByVal obj As Object, _
                                     ByVal ea As EventArgs)
        If prndlg.ShowDialog() = DialogResult.OK Then
            prndoc.DocumentName = Text
            prndoc.Print()
        End If
    End Sub

    Private Sub MenuFilePropsOnClick(ByVal obj As Object, _
                                     ByVal ea As EventArgs)
        Dim str As String = _
            "Size = " & img.Size.ToString() & vbLf & _
            "Horizontal Resolution = " & img.HorizontalResolution & _
            vbLf & _
            "Vertical Resolution = " & img.VerticalResolution & vbLf & _
            "Physical Dimension = " & img.PhysicalDimension.ToString() & _
            vbLf & _
            "Pixel Format = " & img.PixelFormat
        MessageBox.Show(str, "Image Properties")
    End Sub

    Private Sub OnPrintPage(ByVal obj As Object, _
                            ByVal ppea As PrintPageEventArgs)
        Dim grfx As Graphics = ppea.Graphics
        Dim rectf As New RectangleF( _
            ppea.MarginBounds.Left - _
            (ppea.PageBounds.Width - grfx.VisibleClipBounds.Width) / 2, _
            ppea.MarginBounds.Top - _
            (ppea.PageBounds.Height - grfx.VisibleClipBounds.Height) / 2, _
```

```
                 ppea.MarginBounds.Width, ppea.MarginBounds.Height)
        ScaleImageIsotropically(grfx, img, rectf)
    End Sub

    Private Sub ScaleImageIsotropically(ByVal grfx As Graphics, _
                        ByVal img As Image, ByVal rectf As RectangleF)
        Dim szf As New SizeF(img.Width / img.HorizontalResolution, _
                        img.Height / img.VerticalResolution)
        Dim fScale As Single = Math.Min(rectf.Width / szf.Width, _
                                    rectf.Height / szf.Height)

        szf.Width *= fScale
        szf.Height *= fScale
        grfx.DrawImage(img, rectf.X + (rectf.Width - szf.Width) / 2, _
                        rectf.Y + (rectf.Height - szf.Height) / 2, _
                        szf.Width, szf.Height)
    End Sub
End Class
```

*PrintDocument* and both dialog boxes (*PageSetupDialog* and *PrintDialog*) are defined as fields and initialized in the program's constructor. The constructor also adds Page Setup and Print items to the menu as well as a Properties item that displays information about the image.

Processing the Page Setup menu item is a snap. The *MenuFileSetupOn-Click* method simply calls the *ShowDialog* method of *PageSetupDialog*. It doesn't even have to check the return value. The Print menu item is also fairly simple: The *MenuFilePrintOnClick* method begins by invoking *PrintDialog*. If *PrintDialog* returns *DialogResult.OK*, the method sets the *DocumentName* property of the *PrintDocument* object and calls *Print*. (The handler for the *PrintPage* event is set during the constructor.)

The *OnPrintPage* method first calculates a display rectangle with margins using the formulas I showed in the PrintWithMargins program. The method then displays the bitmap as large as possible within these margins while maintaining the correct aspect ratio. It makes use of a slightly modified version of the *ScaleImageIsotropically* method in the ImageScaleIsotropic program from Chapter 11. (I changed the *Rectangle* argument in the original version to a *RectangleF* to be consistent with the calculated display rectangle.) The program also overrides the previous *OnPaint* method to use the same display logic.

# Print Preview

Once your application supports printing, it's fairly easy to implement a print preview feature. Basically, your normal *PrintPage* event handler is used to display printer output on the surfaces of bitmaps rather than to the printer. These bitmaps are then presented to the user. But before I show you how easy it is, let's examine what goes on behind the scenes. You may want to know these details if you prefer to take a different approach to handling the print preview bitmaps.

The key to print preview is the *PrintController* property of *PrintDocument*. By default, *PrintController* is set to *PrintControllerWithStatusDialog*, but I've already demonstrated how you can change this property to something else to allow you to display an alternative to the status dialog box.

For a more extreme effect, you can set the *PrintController* property of *PrintDocument* to an object of type *PreviewPrintController*:

```
Dim ppc As New PreviewPrintController()
prndoc.PrintController = ppc
```

The *PreviewPrintController* class has a single property:

### *PreviewPrintController* Property

| Property | Type | Accessibility |
| --- | --- | --- |
| *UseAntiAlias* | *Boolean* | Get/Set |

Set the other properties of the *PrintDocument* object as usual, just as if you were going to print. Then initiate printing normally by calling the *Print* method of *PrintDocument*:

```
prndoc.Print()
```

Recall that the print controller is responsible for obtaining the *Graphics* object that the *PrintDocument* passes to the *PrintPage* event handler. *PreviewPrintController* doesn't obtain a *Graphics* object for the printer. Instead, it creates a bitmap for each page and obtains a *Graphics* object for drawing on that bitmap. That's actually the *Graphics* object passed to the *PrintPage* event handler.

When the *Print* method returns, you can get access to these bitmaps. The only noninherited method of *PreviewPrintController* returns an array of *PreviewPageInfo* classes:

### *PreviewPrintController* Method

```
Function GetPreviewPageInfo() As PreviewPageInfo()
```

The *PreviewPageInfo* class has two properties:

### *PreviewPageInfo* Properties

| Property | Type | Accessibility |
| --- | --- | --- |
| *Image* | *Image* | Get |
| *PhysicalSize* | *Size* | Get |

The pixel size of the *Image* property is the pixel size of your printer page. The *PhysicalSize* property indicates the dimensions in hundredths of an inch. Now you have a collection of bitmaps, each of which corresponds to a page of the printed document. You can display these bitmaps however you want.

Is there an even easier approach? Yes, there is. You begin by creating an object of type *PrintPreviewDialog*:

```
Dim predlg As New PrintPreviewDialog()
```

*PrintPreviewDialog* is descended from *Form*, so it has lots of properties, methods, and events. But you really don't have to bother with many of them. Here are a few that *PrintPreviewDialog* implements itself:

### *PrintPreviewDialog* Properties (selection)

| Property | Type | Accessibility |
| --- | --- | --- |
| *Document* | *PrintDocument* | Get/Set |
| *PrintPreviewControl* | *PrintPreviewControl* | Get |
| *UseAntiAlias* | *Boolean* | Get/Set |
| *HelpButton* | *Boolean* | Get/Set |

The essential property you must set is *Document*, and you set it to the same *PrintDocument* object you use for printing and page setup. *PrintPreviewControl* is another class defined in *System.Windows.Forms* and represents the controls that ultimately appear on the form that displays the bitmaps with your page images.

Here's the usual code to initialize and initiate print preview:

```
predlg.Document = prndoc
predlg.ShowDialog()
```

The *ShowDialog* method does all the work. It takes the *PrintDocument* object stored as its *Document* property, sets the *PrintController* to *PreviewPrintController*, calls the *Print* method of *PrintDocument*, and then shows a form displaying those bitmaps with a series of controls. You can also print from print preview, in which case the print preview dialog box just uses the same *PrintDocument* object with the same event handlers. For that eventuality, you should set the *DocumentName* property of *PrintDocument* before calling *ShowDialog*.

Let's implement printing with page setup and print preview in our Notepad clone. The NotepadCloneWithPrinting program inherits from the NotepadCloneWithFormat program in Chapter 18.

## NotepadCloneWithPrinting.vb

```vb
'-----------------------------------------------------------
' NotepadCloneWithPrinting.vb (c) 2002 by Charles Petzold
'-----------------------------------------------------------
Imports System
Imports System.Drawing
Imports System.Drawing.Printing
Imports System.IO
Imports System.Windows.Forms

Class NotepadCloneWithPrinting
    Inherits NotepadCloneWithFormat

    Private prndoc As New PrintDocument()
    Private setdlg As New PageSetupDialog()
    Private predlg As New PrintPreviewDialog()
    Private prndlg As New PrintDialog()
    Private strPrintText As String
    Private iStartPage, iNumPages, iPageNumber As Integer

    Shared Shadows Sub Main()
        Application.Run(New NotepadCloneWithPrinting())
    End Sub

    Sub New()
        strProgName = "Notepad Clone with Printing"
        MakeCaption()

        ' Initialize printer-related objects and dialogs
        AddHandler prndoc.PrintPage, AddressOf OnPrintPage
        setdlg.Document = prndoc
        predlg.Document = prndoc
        prndlg.Document = prndoc
        prndlg.AllowSomePages = True
        prndlg.PrinterSettings.FromPage = 1
        prndlg.PrinterSettings.ToPage = prndlg.PrinterSettings.MaximumPage
    End Sub

    Protected Overrides Sub MenuFileSetupOnClick(ByVal obj As Object, _
                                               ByVal ea As EventArgs)
        setdlg.ShowDialog()
    End Sub

    Protected Overrides Sub MenuFilePreviewOnClick(ByVal obj As Object, _
                                                ByVal ea As EventArgs)
        prndoc.DocumentName = Text     ' Just in case it's printed
        strPrintText = txtbox.Text
        iStartPage = 1
        iNumPages = prndlg.PrinterSettings.MaximumPage
        iPageNumber = 1
        predlg.ShowDialog()
    End Sub
```

```
Protected Overrides Sub MenuFilePrintOnClick(ByVal obj As Object, _
                                        ByVal ea As EventArgs)
    prndlg.AllowSelection = txtbox.SelectionLength > 0
    If prndlg.ShowDialog() = DialogResult.OK Then
        prndoc.DocumentName = Text

        ' Initialize some important fields.
        Select Case prndlg.PrinterSettings.PrintRange
            Case PrintRange.AllPages
                strPrintText = txtbox.Text
                iStartPage = 1
                iNumPages = prndlg.PrinterSettings.MaximumPage

            Case PrintRange.Selection
                strPrintText = txtbox.SelectedText
                iStartPage = 1
                iNumPages = prndlg.PrinterSettings.MaximumPage

            Case PrintRange.SomePages
                strPrintText = txtbox.Text
                iStartPage = prndlg.PrinterSettings.FromPage
                iNumPages = prndlg.PrinterSettings.ToPage - _
                                        iStartPage + 1

        End Select

        ' And commence printing.
        iPageNumber = 1
        prndoc.Print()
    End If
End Sub

Private Sub OnPrintPage(ByVal obj As Object, _
                    ByVal ppea As PrintPageEventArgs)
    Dim grfx As Graphics = ppea.Graphics
    Dim fnt As Font = txtbox.Font
    Dim cyFont As Single = fnt.GetHeight(grfx)
    Dim strfmt As New StringFormat()
    Dim rectfFull, rectfText As RectangleF
    Dim iChars, iLines As Integer

    ' Calculate RectangleF for header and footer.
    If grfx.VisibleClipBounds.X < 0 Then
        rectfFull = RectangleF.op_Implicit(ppea.MarginBounds)
    Else
        rectfFull = New RectangleF( _
            ppea.MarginBounds.Left - (ppea.PageBounds.Width - _
                    grfx.VisibleClipBounds.Width) / 2, _
            ppea.MarginBounds.Top - (ppea.PageBounds.Height - _
                    grfx.VisibleClipBounds.Height) / 2, _
            ppea.MarginBounds.Width, ppea.MarginBounds.Height)
    End If
```

*(continued)*

```
        ' Calculate RectangleF for text.
        rectfText = RectangleF.Inflate(rectfFull, 0, -2 * cyFont)
        Dim iDisplayLines As Integer = _
                                CInt(Math.Floor(rectfText.Height / cyFont))
        rectfText.Height = iDisplayLines * cyFont

        ' Set up StringFormat Object for rectanglar display of text.
        If txtbox.WordWrap Then
            strfmt.Trimming = StringTrimming.Word
        Else
            strfmt.Trimming = StringTrimming.EllipsisCharacter
            strfmt.FormatFlags = strfmt.FormatFlags Or _
                                                StringFormatFlags.NoWrap
        End If

        ' For "some pages" get to the first page.
        While iPageNumber < iStartPage AndAlso strPrintText.Length > 0
            If txtbox.WordWrap Then
                grfx.MeasureString(strPrintText, fnt, rectfText.Size, _
                                    strfmt, iChars, iLines)
            Else
                iChars = CharsInLines(strPrintText, iDisplayLines)
            End If
            strPrintText = strPrintText.Substring(iChars)
            iPageNumber += 1
        End While

        ' If we've prematurely run out of text, cancel the print job.
        If strPrintText.Length = 0 Then
            ppea.Cancel = True
            Return
        End If

        ' Display text for this page
        grfx.DrawString(strPrintText, fnt, Brushes.Black, rectfText, strfmt)

        ' Get text for next page.
        If txtbox.WordWrap Then
            grfx.MeasureString(strPrintText, fnt, rectfText.Size, _
                                strfmt, iChars, iLines)
        Else
            iChars = CharsInLines(strPrintText, iDisplayLines)
        End If
        strPrintText = strPrintText.Substring(iChars)

        ' Reset StringFormat to display header and footer.
        strfmt = New StringFormat()

        ' Display filename at top.
        strfmt.Alignment = StringAlignment.Center
        grfx.DrawString(FileTitle(), fnt, Brushes.Black, rectfFull, strfmt)
```

```
            ' Display page number at bottom.
            strfmt.LineAlignment = StringAlignment.Far
            grfx.DrawString("Page " & iPageNumber, fnt, Brushes.Black, _
                        rectfFull, strfmt)

            ' Decide whether to print another page.
            iPageNumber += 1
            ppea.HasMorePages = (strPrintText.Length > 0) AndAlso _
                            (iPageNumber < iStartPage + iNumPages)

            ' Reinitialize variables for printing from preview form.
            If Not ppea.HasMorePages Then
                strPrintText = txtbox.Text
                iStartPage = 1
                iNumPages = prndlg.PrinterSettings.MaximumPage
                iPageNumber = 1
            End If
        End Sub

    Private Function CharsInLines(ByVal strPrintText As String, _
                            ByVal iNumLines As Integer) As Integer
        Dim index As Integer = 0
        Dim i As Integer
        For i = 0 To iNumLines - 1
            index = 1 + strPrintText.IndexOf(vbLf, index)
            If index = 0 Then
                Return strPrintText.Length
            End If
        Next i
        Return index
    End Function
End Class
```

To make my program just a little better than Notepad, I decided to implement the two options in the *PrintDialog* dialog box that let you print a selection or a range of pages.

In this program, the *PrintDocument* object and all *three* print dialog boxes are defined as fields. These are initialized during the program's constructor. Also stored as fields are four variables that assist the program in printing a document.

The *MenuFilePrintOnClick* method is more extensive than anything we've seen so far, and it's primarily a result of implementing the options to print a selection or a range of pages as well as the entire document. For example, the *strPrintText* variable must equal the text to be printed. Normally, this variable is obtained from the *Text* property of the text box, but if a selection is to be printed, the variable must be obtained from *SelectedText*. To put it simply, the purpose of all this code is to set *iStartPage* (the first page to be printed) and *iNumPages* (the number of pages to be printed) to different values depending on which of the three printing options has been chosen.

The *MenuFilePreviewOnClick* method (which is invoked when the Print Preview menu item is clicked) sets *strPrintText*, *iStartPage*, *iNumPages*, and *iPageNumber* as if it were printing the whole document.

The *PrintPage* event handler begins by calculating a display rectangle. If printing normally, that involves the formula I showed earlier using *MarginBounds*, *PageBounds*, and *VisibleClipBounds*. However, if the *PrintPage* event handler is called as a result of a print preview, *VisibleClipBounds* indicates a drawing space larger than the bitmap, and the graphics origin is the upper left corner of the bitmap. In that case, the display rectangle is simply set to the *MarginBounds* property. When the word-wrap option is selected, the *PrintPage* event handler can rely on the word-wrapping abilities of *DrawString*. Notice how the method adjusts the calculated text display rectangle (*rectfText*) so that only an integral number of lines are displayed. That adjustment avoids clipping problems. Similarly, setting the *Trimming* property of the *StringFormat* object to *StringTrimming.Word* assures that the last word on the page isn't truncated. The *MeasureString* overload that returns the number of characters displayed is ideal for adjusting the *strPrintText* variable in preparation for the next page.

Non-word-wrapped text actually proved a little more difficult. The *OnPrintPage* method sets the *Trimming* property of the *StringFormat* object to *StringTrimming.EllipsisCharacter* and the *FormatFlags* property to *StringFormatFlags.NoWrap* to get the display of each page right. However, *MeasureString* insisted on returning the number of characters actually displayed, not the number that would have been displayed if each line weren't truncated. I was forced to write a little routine, *CharsInLines*, that searches for end-of-line characters and adjust *strPrintText* in that way.

Another approach to printing non-word-wrapped text would be to use the *Lines* property to obtain a *String* array containing all the individual lines of text. The *OnPrintPage* method could then simply call *DrawString* for each line. However, this approach would have worked only for printing the whole document or a range of pages. The *TextBoxBase* class doesn't have a property that returns the *selected* text broken down into lines.

The Print Preview dialog box contains a button to print the document before returning to the application. To handle that eventuality, when *OnPrintPage* has reached the last page, it also reinitializes the *strPrintText*, *iStartPage*, *iNumPages*, and *iPageNumber* fields in preparation for the regular print job.

# 22

# Tree View and List View

I take it you're familiar with the Microsoft Windows Explorer program. The client area of Windows Explorer is dominated by two large and sophisticated controls. The *tree-view* control on the left displays a hierarchical list of the user's disk drives and directories. The *list-view* control on the right displays the subdirectories and files in the selected directory in one of four formats: a simple list, a table with multiple columns, names with small icons, or names with large icons. (Recent versions of Windows Explorer also include a Thumbnail view.)

In this chapter, I'll discuss the Windows Forms implementation of the tree-view and list-view controls. The sophistication and versatility of these controls makes an exhaustive discussion impossible. But I'll certainly cover them in enough detail to get you started.

Before we begin, however, I'd like to direct your attention to a third control in Windows Explorer: that thin vertical bar that looks like a sizing border but appears *between* the tree-view and list-view controls. You move it sideways with the mouse to adjust how the client area of Windows Explorer is divided between the two controls. As one control gets larger, the other gets smaller. That's called a *splitter* control.

## Splitsville

You've probably seen splitters in other applications besides Windows Explorer. In Microsoft Word, for example, you can choose Split from the Window menu and divide your document into two regions with a horizontal splitter. This feature allows you to work on one section of a document while keeping another section in view. Again, the splitter adjusts the relative sizes of the two views. By default, Microsoft Basic Studio .NET uses splitters to separate its client area into four areas.

Splitters are also used to display Web pages that make use of *frames*, a feature introduced in HTML 4.0. The *HTML 4.0 Specification* (Section 16.1) has a good explanation of the rationale behind frame-based architecture:

> HTML frames allow authors to present documents in multiple views, which may be independent windows or subwindows. Multiple views offer designers a way to keep certain information visible, while other views are scrolled or replaced. For example, within the same window, one frame might display a static banner, a second a navigation menu, and a third the main document that can be scrolled through or replaced by navigating in the second frame.

Although the size of these frames can be fixed, by default they are adjustable with splitters. Both horizontal and vertical splitters often appear on the same Web page.

The Windows Forms splitter control is implemented in the *Splitter* class, which is based on *Control*. Once you've correctly created and positioned a splitter, you can generally ignore it. Only rarely will you need to process splitter events. A splitter affects the size of other controls in much the same way as a sizing border. If your controls react well to being resized, they will adapt just fine to being resized with splitters.

A splitter is always associated with a *target* control, which is the control that the splitter directly alters the size of, though other controls can also be affected by the splitter's movement. A splitter is attached to a target control through the mechanism of docking, which I introduced in Chapter 12. As you'll recall, the *Control* class implements a property named *Dock* that can be assigned one of the following members of the *DockStyle* enumeration:

### *DockStyle* Enumeration

| Member | Value |
| --- | --- |
| *None* | 0 |
| *Top* | 1 |
| *Bottom* | 2 |
| *Left* | 3 |
| *Right* | 4 |
| *Fill* | 5 |

The default is *DockStyle.None*. When you specify one of the next four members in the table, the control is positioned flush against that side of its parent and extended to the two adjacent sides. For example, if *ctrl* is an instance of any class descended from *Control* and you set the *Dock* property as

```
ctrl.Dock = DockStyle.Left
```

then *ctrl* will be moved to the far left side of its parent and will be resized to occupy the full space between the top and the bottom of the parent. Whenever the parent is resized, *ctrl* will also be resized accordingly. The *Control* class performs this magic during the *OnResize* method. For that reason (and others), whenever you override *OnResize*, you should call the base class version of the method.

The *DockStyle.Fill* option causes the control to fill up the surface of its parent. I used *DockStyle.Fill* in the AnalogClock program in Chapter 10, the PictureBoxPlusDemo program of Chapter 11, and in the various Notepad clone programs beginning in Chapter 18.

What happens when you dock two or more controls against the same side? Or you use *DockStyle.Fill* with two or more controls? Or you use *DockStyle.Fill* with one control and one of the other nondefault *DockStyle* members with another control? In all these cases, the behavior is determined by the z-order of the controls.

I discussed z-order in Chapter 12, but here's a brief review. As you add controls to a parent, they are assigned a *child index* beginning with 0. A control with a child index of 0 is said to be at the *top* or the *front* of the z-order. When controls overlap, the child control on the top of the z-order appears on top of the other controls and receives mouse events when the cursor passes over the control. The child control with the highest child index is said to be at the bottom of the z-order.

Programs can reorder controls by calling the *BringToFront* and *SendToBack* methods implemented by *Control* or by calling the *SetChildIndex* method implemented by *Control.ControlCollection*. It's usually easiest just to create the controls in the desired order in the first place.

So, what happens when two or more child controls have a *Dock* property equal to *DockStyle.Fill*? The child control at the top of the z-order—that is, the child control added to the parent earliest and therefore having the lowest child index—appears on top of the others. For example, consider the following code, which could appear in the constructor of a class derived from *Form*:

```
Dim pnl1 As New Panel()
pnl1.Parent = Me
pnl1.Dock = DockStyle.Fill

Dim pnl2 As New Panel()
pnl2.Parent = Me
pnl2.Dock = DockStyle.Fill
```

The control named *pnl1* will be visible; *pnl2* will not. The general rule is that only one child control should have a *Dock* property of *DockStyle.Fill*. (I violate this rule in the ImageDirectory program later in this chapter. That program has two controls with *DockStyle.Fill* but at any time only one of them has a *Visible* property of *True*.)

It's possible to add other controls to the parent before the control that has a *Dock* property of *DockStyle.Fill*, for example,

```
Dim btn As New Button()
btn.Parent = Me

Dim pnl As New Panel()
pnl.Parent = Me
pnl.Dock = DockStyle.Fill
```

The *Button* control is at the top of the z-order and appears on top of the *Panel* control. The *Panel* control fills the client area of the parent. It might look as if the *Button* control is a child of the *Panel* control, but it's not. The controls are simply overlapping, and the one at the top of the z-order gets priority of visibility.

The following case is similar:

```
Dim pnl1 As New Panel()
pnl1.Parent = Me
pnl1.Dock = DockStyle.Left

Dim pnl2 As New Panel()
pnl2.Parent = Me
pnl2.Dock = DockStyle.Fill
```

Notice that the first *Panel* control has a *Dock* property of *DockStyle.Left*. It's on the top of the z-order, so it gets priority. The second panel will still fill the client area of its parent, but the left part will be obscured by *pnl1*. That's probably not a desirable situation.

This case is much more useful and (with the addition of a splitter control) quite common:

```
Dim pnl1 As New Panel()
pnl1.Parent = Me
pnl1.Dock = DockStyle.Fill

Dim pnl2 As New Panel()
pnl2.Parent = Me
pnl2.Dock = DockStyle.Left
```

All I've done here is switch around the two *Dock* properties. Now both panels are fully visible. The first panel appears at the right side of the client area and the second panel appears at the left. As you make the client area wider and narrower, *pnl1* at the right changes size because that's the one with *DockStyle.Fill*; *pnl2* on the left side of the client area doesn't change size in that case.

I've already demonstrated this technique in the SimpleStatusBarWithPanel program toward the beginning of Chapter 20. That program begins by creating a *Panel* with a *Dock* property of *DockStyle.Fill* and then the *StatusBar* control, which has a default setting of *DockStyle.Bottom*.

If you change the last line of the preceding code to be

```
pnl2.Dock = DockStyle.Right
```

then *pnl1* appears at the left of the client area and *pnl2* at the right. As you change the size of the client area, *pnl1* (now at the left) changes size accordingly; *pnl2* remains the same size. A splitter control between these two panels would be ideal.

What happens when you use the same *Dock* property with two controls? Here's an example:

```
Dim pnl1 As New Panel()
pnl1.Parent = Me
pnl1.Dock = DockStyle.Left

Dim pnl2 As New Panel()
pnl2.Parent = Me
pnl2.Dock = DockStyle.Left
```

As the second control is added to the parent, the control at the top of the z-order (*pnl1*) gets pushed toward the center of the client area. The control at the bottom of the z-order is positioned at the left edge of the parent.

Here's an example of two controls that don't have the same *Dock* property but do have *Dock* properties that seem to conflict:

```
Dim pnl1 As New Panel()
pnl1.Parent = Me
pnl1.Dock = DockStyle.Left

Dim pnl2 As New Panel()
pnl2.Parent = Me
pnl2.Dock = DockStyle.Top
```

The first panel has a *Dock* property of *DockStyle.Left*, and the second has *DockStyle.Top*. Initially, the first panel is positioned to hug the left of the client area and extend from the top of the parent to the bottom. The second panel essentially pushes the first panel down. The second panel is positioned at the top of the client area and extends to the client's full width. The first panel ends up below the second panel. Both panels are fully visible.

And now we're ready to add splitters to the mix. To keep the discussion general, I'll continue to use *Panel* controls in these examples. These panels could, of course, contain other controls, and they could also be scrollable.

It's important to know what happens when multiple controls are docked against the same edge of a parent because—if you're not careful—you could very easily end up with splitters at the edge of the window, where they do no good. The target control of a splitter is the control that's docked to the same edge as the splitter but with a lower z-order. For this reason, you generally create the splitter *before* the target control.

Most commonly, splitter controls are placed between two controls so that moving the splitter causes one control to increase in size and the other control to get smaller. However, you can use splitters in an even simpler way to change the size of a single control. Here's a program that uses a splitter to resize a single panel control.

```
OnePanelWithSplitter.vb
'-------------------------------------------------------------
' OnePanelWithSplitter.vb (c) 2002 by Charles Petzold
'-------------------------------------------------------------
Imports System
Imports System.Drawing
Imports System.Windows.Forms

Class OnePanelWithSplitter
    Inherits Form

    Shared Sub Main()
        Application.Run(New OnePanelWithSplitter())
    End Sub

    Sub New()
        Text = "One Panel with Splitter"

        Dim split As New Splitter()
        split.Parent = Me
        split.Dock = DockStyle.Left

        Dim pnl As New Panel()
        pnl.Parent = Me
        pnl.Dock = DockStyle.Left
        pnl.BackColor = Color.Lime
        AddHandler pnl.Resize, AddressOf PanelOnResize
        AddHandler pnl.Paint, AddressOf PanelOnPaint
    End Sub

    Private Sub PanelOnResize(ByVal obj As Object, ByVal ea As EventArgs)
        Dim pnl As Panel = DirectCast(obj, Panel)
        pnl.Invalidate()
    End Sub

    Private Sub PanelOnPaint(ByVal obj As Object, _
```

```
                              ByVal pea As PaintEventArgs)
        Dim pnl As Panel = DirectCast(obj, Panel)
        Dim grfx As Graphics = pea.Graphics

        grfx.DrawEllipse(Pens.Black, 0, 0, _
                         pnl.Width - 1, pnl.Height - 1)
    End Sub
End Class
```

Both the splitter and the panel have a *Dock* property of *DockStyle.Left*. But remember that controls at the bottom of the z-order are closest to the docking edge. That's why the splitter is created first. The panel essentially pushes the splitter away from the left edge of the parent, so the splitter ends up on the right edge of the panel.

Normally, a panel is the same color as its parent, so I've deliberately changed the *BackColor* property of the panel control so that you won't have to rely on faith that the splitter control is actually changing its size. Throughout this section, I'll be using colors to indicate positioning: in this case, *lime* stands for *left*. I've also installed handlers for the panel's *Resize* and *Paint* events, so you're additionally assured that you're seeing the entire panel control. Here's what the program looks like:

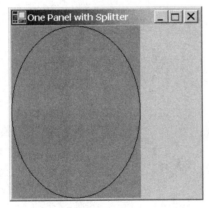

You can't actually see the splitter in this example because its *BackColor* property is the same as its parent's. But if you move the mouse to the right side of the panel, the cursor changes to small parallel vertical lines. You can then adjust the size of the panel. Splitters don't have a keyboard interface. The cursor used by splitters is *Cursors.VSplit* for vertical splitters (like this one) or *Cursors.HSplit* for horizontal splitters.

Here's a program that shows you how to make a splitter affect two panels that together fill the client area. The first panel has a *Dock* property of

*DockStyle.Fill*, and both the splitter and the second panel get *DockStyle.Right* properties.

### TwoPanelsWithSplitter.vb

```
'-------------------------------------------------------------
' TwoPanelsWithSplitter.vb (c) 2002 by Charles Petzold
'-------------------------------------------------------------
Imports System
Imports System.Drawing
Imports System.Windows.Forms

Class TwoPanelsWithSplitter
    Inherits Form

    Shared Sub Main()
        Application.Run(new TwoPanelsWithSplitter())
    End Sub

    Sub New()
        Text = "Two Panels with Splitter"

        Dim pnl1 As New Panel()
        pnl1.Parent = Me
        pnl1.Dock = DockStyle.Fill
        pnl1.BackColor = Color.Lime
        AddHandler pnl1.Resize, AddressOf PanelOnResize
        AddHandler pnl1.Paint, AddressOf PanelOnPaint

        Dim split As New Splitter()
        split.Parent = Me
        split.Dock = DockStyle.Right

        Dim pnl2 As New Panel()
        pnl2.Parent = Me
        pnl2.Dock = DockStyle.Right
        pnl2.BackColor = Color.Red
        AddHandler pnl2.Resize, AddressOf PanelOnResize
        AddHandler pnl2.Paint, AddressOf PanelOnPaint
    End Sub

    Private Sub PanelOnResize(ByVal obj As Object, ByVal ea As EventArgs)
        DirectCast(obj, Panel).Invalidate()
    End Sub

    Private Sub PanelOnPaint(ByVal obj As Object, _
                             ByVal pea As PaintEventArgs)
        Dim pnl As Panel = DirectCast(obj, Panel)
        Dim grfx As Graphics = pea.Graphics
        grfx.DrawEllipse(Pens.Black, 0, 0, _
                         pnl.Width - 1, pnl.Height - 1)
    End Sub
End Class
```

As you're experimenting with this program, you'll see the lime panel on the left and the red panel on the right. (Notice the mnemonics.) The splitter is more visible now because it's gray. Here's how the program starts up:

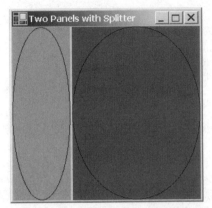

The target of the splitter is the panel on the right because they both have *Dock* properties of *DockStyle.Right*, but the splitter actually affects the size of both panels. But what happens when you make the parent form wider or narrower? The first panel—the one on the left—changes size because that's the one with *DockStyle.Fill*. This behavior has an additional implication, however: if you make the client area too narrow, the panel on the left will disappear from view and the panel on the right will be clipped as well.

When you create a program with two controls (such as panels) separated by a splitter, give some thought to which control should be affected by changes in the parent's size. Create that one first with *DockStyle.Fill*.

Here's a program that uses that rule to create a form with three panels. The center one (colored *cyan* for *center*) has the *DockStyle.Fill* property, so that's the one that changes size as you change the client area size.

**SplitThreeAcross.vb**

```
'-------------------------------------------------
' SplitThreeAcross.vb (c) 2002 by Charles Petzold
'-------------------------------------------------
Imports System
Imports System.Drawing
Imports System.Windows.Forms

Class SplitThreeAcross
    Inherits Form

    Shared Sub Main()
        Application.Run(new SplitThreeAcross())
    End Sub
```

*(continued)*

**SplitThreeAcross.vb** *(continued)*

```vb
Sub New()
    Text = "Split Three Across"

    Dim pnl1 As New Panel()
    pnl1.Parent = Me
    pnl1.Dock = DockStyle.Fill
    pnl1.BackColor = Color.Cyan
    AddHandler pnl1.Resize, AddressOf PanelOnResize
    AddHandler pnl1.Paint, AddressOf PanelOnPaint

    Dim split1 As New Splitter()
    split1.Parent = Me
    split1.Dock = DockStyle.Left

    Dim pnl2 As New Panel()
    pnl2.Parent = Me
    pnl2.Dock = DockStyle.Left
    pnl2.BackColor = Color.Lime
    AddHandler pnl2.Resize, AddressOf PanelOnResize
    AddHandler pnl2.Paint, AddressOf PanelOnPaint

    Dim split2 As New Splitter()
    split2.Parent = Me
    split2.Dock = DockStyle.Right

    Dim pnl3 As New Panel()
    pnl3.Parent = Me
    pnl3.Dock = DockStyle.Right
    pnl3.BackColor = Color.Red
    AddHandler pnl3.Resize, AddressOf PanelOnResize
    AddHandler pnl3.Paint, AddressOf PanelOnPaint

    pnl1.Width = ClientSize.Width \ 3
    pnl2.Width = ClientSize.Width \ 3
    pnl3.Width = ClientSize.Width \ 3
End Sub

Private Sub PanelOnResize(ByVal obj As Object, ByVal ea As EventArgs)
    DirectCast(obj, Panel).Invalidate()
End Sub

Private Sub PanelOnPaint(ByVal obj As Object, _
                         ByVal pea As PaintEventArgs)
    Dim pnl As Panel = DirectCast(obj, Panel)
    Dim grfx As Graphics = pea.Graphics

    grfx.DrawEllipse(Pens.Black, 0, 0, _
                     pnl.Width - 1, pnl.Height - 1)
End Sub
End Class
```

Again, because the center panel changes size when you resize the form, the center panel can also disappear from view if you make the client area too narrow. As you make the client area even narrower, the right panel slides under the left panel because the left panel is at the top of the z-order. To make sure that all panels are visible when the program starts up, at the end of the constructor, I give them each a width equal to 1/3 the client area.

In an arrangement like this, you don't need to make the center panel the one that changes size with the client area. The requirements of a particular application will determine which approach seems most natural.

Perhaps a better approach when designing dual-splitter forms is to begin with a single splitter controlling the size of two controls and then make two more controls and a splitter as children of one of those existing controls. You use this approach when you're mixing horizontal and vertical splitters in a form that resembles an HTML frame, as in the following program.

**SplitThreeFrames.vb**

```
'-------------------------------------------------
' SplitThreeFrames.vb (c) 2002 by Charles Petzold
'-------------------------------------------------
Imports System
Imports System.Drawing
Imports System.Windows.Forms

Class SplitThreeFrames
    Inherits Form

    Shared Sub Main()
        Application.Run(new SplitThreeFrames())
    End Sub

    Sub New()
```

*(continued)*

**SplitThreeFrames.vb** *(continued)*

```
        Text = "Split Three Frames"

        Dim pnl As New Panel()
        pnl.Parent = Me
        pnl.Dock = DockStyle.Fill

        Dim split1 As New Splitter()
        split1.Parent = Me
        split1.Dock = DockStyle.Left

        Dim pnl1 As New Panel()
        pnl1.Parent = Me
        pnl1.Dock = DockStyle.Left
        pnl1.BackColor = Color.Lime
        AddHandler pnl1.Resize, AddressOf PanelOnResize
        AddHandler pnl1.Paint, AddressOf PanelOnPaint

        Dim pnl2 As New Panel()
        pnl2.Parent = pnl
        pnl2.Dock = DockStyle.Fill
        pnl2.BackColor = Color.Blue
        AddHandler pnl2.Resize, AddressOf PanelOnResize
        AddHandler pnl2.Paint, AddressOf PanelOnPaint

        Dim split2 As New Splitter()
        split2.Parent = pnl
        split2.Dock = DockStyle.Top

        Dim pnl3 As New Panel()
        pnl3.Parent = pnl
        pnl3.Dock = DockStyle.Top
        pnl3.BackColor = Color.Tan
        AddHandler pnl3.Resize, AddressOf PanelOnResize
        AddHandler pnl3.Paint, AddressOf PanelOnPaint

        pnl1.Width = ClientSize.Width \ 3
        pnl3.Height = ClientSize.Height \ 3
    End Sub

    Private Sub PanelOnResize(ByVal obj As Object, ByVal ea As EventArgs)
        DirectCast(obj, Panel).Invalidate()
    End Sub

    Private Sub PanelOnPaint(ByVal obj As Object, _
                             ByVal pea As PaintEventArgs)
        Dim pnl As Panel = DirectCast(obj, Panel)
        Dim grfx As Graphics = pea.Graphics

        grfx.DrawEllipse(Pens.Black, 0, 0, _
                         pnl.Width - 1, pnl.Height - 1)
    End Sub
End Class
```

The SplitThreeFrames program begins by creating two panels (on the right and the left) with a vertical splitter between them. The first panel (named simply *pnl*) gets the *DockStyle.Fill* property. I don't give it a color because this panel will be a parent to other panels that will entirely cover its surface. The second panel (named *pnl1* and colored lime) is created with *DockStyle.Left*. The result consists of two panels with a vertical splitter between them.

But wait, there's more! The first panel (named *pnl*) becomes a parent to two more panels and a splitter. The first child (*pnl2*) of that panel gets the *DockStyle.Fill* property and a color of *blue* (for *bottom*). The program then creates another splitter and a panel (*pnl3*) colored *tan* (for *top*) with *DockStyle.Top* properties.

The constructor concludes by setting the initial size of the left and top panels.

As you change the size of the client area, the panel on the bottom right changes size, but that's only because it has a *DockStyle.Fill* property and is a child of another panel that has a *DockStyle.Fill* property.

The only properties of the *Splitter* class I've been using so far are *Parent* and *Dock*. The following properties of the *Splitter* class (with a couple inherited from *Control*) are probably the most useful:

### *Splitter* Properties (selection)

| Property | Type | Accessibility |
| --- | --- | --- |
| *SplitPosition* | *Integer* | Get/Set |
| *MinSize* | *Integer* | Get/Set |
| *MinExtra* | *Integer* | Get/Set |
| *Width* | *Integer* | Get/Set |

*(continued)*

**Splitter Properties (selection)**    *(continued)*

| Property | Type | Accessibility |
| --- | --- | --- |
| *Height* | *Integer* | Get/Set |
| *BorderStyle* | *BorderStyle* | Get/Set |
| *BackColor* | *Color* | Get/Set |

The *SplitPosition* property indicates the width of the target control, if the splitter is vertical, or the height of the target control, if the splitter is horizontal. If the splitter is not yet bound to a target control, however, the property will equal –1. When you create splitters in a constructor (such as we've been doing), the splitters aren't assigned target controls until after the constructor concludes. For that reason, don't use *SplitPosition* in the constructor. If you need to initialize the relative sizes of controls that use splitters, do it by sizing the controls, as the Split-ThreeAcross and SplitThreeFrames programs demonstrate.

The *MinSize* property indicates the minimum width (or height) to which you can resize the target control using the splitter. The *MinExtra* property indicates the minimum width (or height) of the control on the other side of the splitter. By default, these properties are set to 25 pixels. (You can easily see the effect of these properties by using any of the programs shown so far in this chapter.) I wouldn't recommend that you set these properties to 0 because a user might get confused if a control shrinks down to nothing. But you can set them very low if you want to give the user the opportunity to move the control almost completely out of the way.

The thickness of a vertical splitter is controlled by the *Width* property; for a horizontal splitter, the thickness is controlled by the *Height* property. By default that thickness is 3 pixels. The default *BorderStyle* property of the splitter is *BorderStyle.None*, which makes the splitter a simple strip of unadorned *Back-Color. BorderStyle.Fixed3D* is the same as *BorderStyle.None* for splitters of a default thickness. For splitters greater than 3 pixels in thickness, *Border-Style.Fixed3D* gives the splitter a 3D look. *BorderStyle.FixedSingle* makes the splitter stand out more by coloring the outer edges black. The *ForeColor* property has no effect on splitters.

The *Splitter* class adds two events to those implemented in *Control*:

### *Splitter* Events

| Event | Method | Delegate | Argument |
|-------|--------|----------|----------|
| *SplitterMoving* | *OnSplitterMoving* | *SplitterEventHandler* | *SplitterEventArgs* |
| *SplitterMoved* | *OnSplitterMoved* | *SplitterEventHandler* | *SplitterEventArgs* |

Both events are delivered with an object of type *SplitterEventArgs*, which has the following properties:

### *SplitterEventArgs* Properties

| Property | Type | Accessibility | Description |
|----------|------|---------------|-------------|
| *X* | *Integer* | Get | Mouse cursor position |
| *Y* | *Integer* | Get | Mouse cursor position |
| *SplitX* | *Integer* | Get/Set | Splitter position |
| *SplitY* | *Integer* | Get/Set | Splitter position |

All positions are relative to the parent window of the splitter. The *SplitX* and *SplitY* properties indicate the position of the upper left corner of the splitter relative to the client area. For vertical splitters, *SplitY* equals 0, and for horizontal splitters, *SplitX* equals 0. I haven't had much luck with the *SplitterMoved* event. It does not seem to be working right in the initial release of the Microsoft .NET Framework.

Here's a program that creates two panels with a splitter. Initially, each panel occupies about half the client area, which, as you know, you can change with the splitter. However, when you resize the form, the two panels change size proportionally.

**SplitTwoProportional.vb**

```
'-------------------------------------------------------------
' SplitTwoProportional.vb (c) 2002 by Charles Petzold
'-------------------------------------------------------------
Imports System
Imports System.Drawing
Imports System.Windows.Forms

Class SplitTwoProportional
    Inherits Form

    Private pnl2 As Panel
    Private fProportion As Single = 0.5F

    Shared Sub Main()
        Application.Run(New SplitTwoProportional())
```

*(continued)*

**SplitTwoProportional.vb** *(continued)*

```
    End Sub

    Sub New()
        Text = "Split Two Proportional"

        Dim pnl1 As New Panel()
        pnl1.Parent = Me
        pnl1.Dock = DockStyle.Fill
        pnl1.BackColor = Color.Red
        AddHandler pnl1.Resize, AddressOf PanelOnResize
        AddHandler pnl1.Paint, AddressOf PanelOnPaint

        Dim split As New Splitter()
        split.Parent = Me
        split.Dock = DockStyle.Left
        AddHandler split.SplitterMoving, AddressOf SplitterOnMoving

        pnl2 = New Panel()
        pnl2.Parent = Me
        pnl2.Dock = DockStyle.Left
        pnl2.BackColor = Color.Lime
        AddHandler pnl2.Resize, AddressOf PanelOnResize
        AddHandler pnl2.Paint, AddressOf PanelOnPaint

        OnResize(EventArgs.Empty)
    End Sub

    Protected Overrides Sub OnResize(ByVal ea As EventArgs)
        MyBase.OnResize(ea)
        pnl2.Width = CInt(fProportion * ClientSize.Width)
    End Sub

    Private Sub SplitterOnMoving(ByVal obj As Object, _
                            ByVal sea As SplitterEventArgs)
        fProportion = CSng(sea.SplitX) / ClientSize.Width
    End Sub

    Private Sub PanelOnResize(ByVal obj As Object, ByVal ea As EventArgs)
        DirectCast(obj, Panel).Invalidate()
    End Sub

    Private Sub PanelOnPaint(ByVal obj As Object, _
                            ByVal pea As PaintEventArgs)
        Dim pnl As Panel = DirectCast(obj, Panel)
        Dim grfx As Graphics = pea.Graphics

        grfx.DrawEllipse(Pens.Black, 0, 0, _
                        pnl.Width - 1, pnl.Height - 1)
    End Sub
End Class
```

This program retains an instance variable named *fProportion* equal to the ratio of the panel on the left to the width of the client area. It's initialized to 0.5 and altered whenever the user moves the splitter. That's the *SplitterOnMoving* event. When the user resizes the program's client area, the *OnResize* method sets the size of the left panel based on the *fProportion* value and the new width of the client.

Now that we know what kind of control goes *between* a tree view and a list view, we're ready to look at these two controls in detail.

# Tree Views and Tree Nodes

The *TreeView* control is most commonly used to display a list of disk drives and directories like the one at the left side of Windows Explorer. However, you can use *TreeView* controls for displaying any hierarchical information. Microsoft Visual Basic .NET uses a tree view for displaying projects and files, and the Microsoft Document Explorer (the program that displays the .NET programming documentation) also uses a tree view for displaying namespaces, classes, members, and so forth.

The bulk of the tree view implementation in Windows Forms consists of the *TreeView*, *TreeNode*, and *TreeNodeCollection* classes. An object of type *TreeNode* is a single entry in the tree view. A *TreeNode* object is associated with a string and an optional image. In Windows Explorer, the string is a drive or directory name, and the images resemble disk drives and folders.

The *TreeNode* class contains a property named *Nodes* that is a collection of other *TreeNode* objects:

### *TreeNode* Properties (selection)

| Property | Type | Accessibility |
|----------|------|---------------|
| *Nodes* | *TreeNodeCollection* | Get |

The *Nodes* property contains all the subnodes (or child nodes) of the node. *TreeNodeCollection* is a familiar sort of class. It implements the *IList*, *ICollection*, and *IEnumerable* interfaces, and it lets you index the collection like an array:

### *TreeNodeCollection* Properties

| Property | Type | Accessibility |
|----------|------|---------------|
| *()* | *TreeNode* | Get/Set |
| *Count* | *Integer* | Get |
| *IsReadOnly* | *Boolean* | Get |

The customary way to add child nodes to an existing node is through the *Add* and *AddRange* methods of *TreeNodeCollection*:

### *TreeNodeCollection* Methods (selection)

```
Function Add(ByVal strNode As String) As TreeNode
Function Add(ByVal node As TreeNode) As Integer
Sub AddRange(ByVal anode() As TreeNode)
```

*TreeNodeCollection* also contains familiar methods named *Insert*, *Remove*, *Clear*, and others. All the nodes in the same *TreeNodeCollection* object are sometimes referred to collectively as *siblings*. The *TreeNode* object to which the collection belongs is the parent.

I haven't yet said anything about *TreeView*. Basically, *TreeView* is a collection of top-level (or root) *TreeNode* objects. Like *TreeNode*, *TreeView* contains a *Nodes* property:

### *TreeView* Properties (selection)

| Property | Type | Accessibility |
| --- | --- | --- |
| *Nodes* | *TreeNodeCollection* | Get |

This *Nodes* property is a collection of all the root *TreeNode* objects.

Conceptually, *TreeView* is similar to *MainMenu* or *ContextMenu*, while *TreeNode* is similar to *MenuItem*. (See Chapter 14 for information on menu objects.) That is, just as *MainMenu* or *ContextMenu* is a collection of nested *MenuItem* objects, *TreeView* is a collection of nested *TreeNode* items. However, as you'll recall, all three of these menu-related classes are derived from the *Menu* class. *TreeView* and *TreeNode* are not related in that way: *TreeView* derives from *Control*, while *TreeNode* derives from *MarshalByRefObject*.

And with this information, we're ready to construct our first tree. Here's a program that has the beginnings of an animal/mineral/vegetable hierarchy.

**SimpleTreeView.vb**

```
'-------------------------------------------------
' SimpleTreeView.vb (c) 2002 by Charles Petzold
'-------------------------------------------------
Imports System
Imports System.Drawing
Imports System.Windows.Forms

Class SimpleTreeView
    Inherits Form
```

```
    Shared Sub Main()
        Application.Run(New SimpleTreeView())
    End Sub

    Sub New()
        Text = "Simple Tree View"

        Dim treevu As New TreeView()
        treevu.Parent = Me
        treevu.Dock = DockStyle.Fill

        treevu.Nodes.Add("Animal")
        treevu.Nodes(0).Nodes.Add("Dog")
        treevu.Nodes(0).Nodes(0).Nodes.Add("Poodle")
        treevu.Nodes(0).Nodes(0).Nodes.Add("Irish Setter")
        treevu.Nodes(0).Nodes(0).Nodes.Add("German Shepherd")
        treevu.Nodes(0).Nodes.Add("Cat")
        treevu.Nodes(0).Nodes(1).Nodes.Add("Calico")
        treevu.Nodes(0).Nodes(1).Nodes.Add("Siamese")
        treevu.Nodes(0).Nodes.Add("Primate")
        treevu.Nodes(0).Nodes(2).Nodes.Add("Chimpanzee")
        treevu.Nodes(0).Nodes(2).Nodes.Add("Ape")
        treevu.Nodes(0).Nodes(2).Nodes.Add("Human")
        treevu.Nodes.Add("Mineral")
        treevu.Nodes(1).Nodes.Add("Calcium")
        treevu.Nodes(1).Nodes.Add("Zinc")
        treevu.Nodes(1).Nodes.Add("Iron")
        treevu.Nodes.Add("Vegetable")
        treevu.Nodes(2).Nodes.Add("Carrot")
        treevu.Nodes(2).Nodes.Add("Asparagus")
        treevu.Nodes(2).Nodes.Add("Broccoli")
    End Sub
End Class
```

The constructor creates the entire *TreeView* control through the use of 20 calls to the *Add* method in *TreeNodeCollection*. Three of these calls involve the *Nodes* property of the *TreeView* object and hence create top-level nodes:

```
treevu.Nodes.Add("Animal")
⋮
treevu.Nodes.Add("Mineral")
⋮
treevu.Nodes.Add("Vegetable")
```

Although the program doesn't refer explicitly to any *TreeNode* objects, they are certainly there. Each of the *Add* methods creates a *TreeNode* object. The second *Add* call is this one:

```
treevu.Nodes(0).Nodes.Add("Dog")
```

The first part of that statement (*treevu.Nodes(0)*) refers to the first *TreeNode* object in the *TreeView* object's collection, that is, "Animal". The second *Nodes* property is the collection of child *TreeNode* objects of "Animal", to which the node "Dog" is added. Similarly, the following statement adds a child node under "Dog":

```
treevu.Nodes(0).Nodes(0).Nodes.Add("Poodle")
```

Here's the program with some of the nodes expanded:

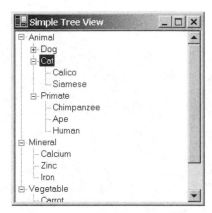

You'll want to experiment with this program a bit to get the hang of the default user interface implemented in *TreeView* controls. Using the up and down cursor-movement keys, you can change the selected item (indicated by reverse video). If the item has a plus sign to its left, you can use the right arrow key to view the child nodes. The left arrow key has two functions. When the selected node doesn't have any children, it causes the selection to jump to the parent node. When the selected node is already expanded (that is, has a minus sign next to it), the left arrow key collapses the node. Of course, you can also click with the mouse on the pluses and minuses to expand and collapse nodes.

Scroll bars are displayed by default when they are needed. If you don't want them, you can set the *Scrollable* property of *TreeView* to *False*.

Although the SimpleTreeView program creates the entire *TreeView* control right in its constructor, a program must often modify the contents of a *TreeView* control later on, at runtime. You can cause items to be sorted by setting the following property to *True*:

## *TreeView* Properties (selection)

| Property | Type | Accessibility |
|----------|------|---------------|
| *Sorted* | *Boolean* | Get/Set |

Regardless of whether or not the items are sorted, to prevent performance problems when modifying a *TreeView* control, call the following methods before and after any sequence of statements that affect multiple nodes:

### *TreeView* Methods (selection)

```
Sub BeginUpdate()
Sub EndUpdate()
```

# Images in Tree Views

As you can see from the SimpleTreeView program, you get the plus signs and minus signs for free. However, you can suppress them if you want to. The following properties are all *True* by default:

### *TreeView* Properties (selection)

| Property | Type | Accessibility |
|---|---|---|
| *ShowPlusMinus* | *Boolean* | Get/Set |
| *ShowLines* | *Boolean* | Get/Set |
| *ShowRootLines* | *Boolean* | Get/Set |

If *ShowLines* is *False*, all the lines that normally connect the nodes are not displayed. If *ShowRootLines* is *False*, the root items are displayed without any lines or pluses and minuses. The other items are displayed normally.

*TreeView* controls often display little pictures to the left of each node. Often these images change when the node is expanded. For example, Windows Explorer shows a closed folder for a collapsed directory node and an open folder for an expanded directory node.

Images in a *TreeView* control are based on a single *ImageList* object that applies to the entire control:

### *TreeView* Properties (selection)

| Property | Type | Accessibility |
|---|---|---|
| *ImageList* | *ImageList* | Get/Set |
| *ImageIndex* | *Integer* | Get/Set |
| *SelectedImageIndex* | *Integer* | Get/Set |

The *ImageIndex* property indicates the default image displayed for a node that is not selected. *SelectedImageIndex* indicates the default image for a selected node.

More commonly, you'll want to specify indices for each *TreeNode* object:

### *TreeNode* Properties (selection)

| Property | Type | Accessibility |
|----------|------|---------------|
| *ImageIndex* | *Integer* | Get/Set |
| *SelectedImageIndex* | *Integer* | Get/Set |

However, *TreeNode* doesn't have its own *ImageList* property. The indices refer to the *ImageList* property in the *TreeView* control to which the *TreeNode* object belongs.

You can also specify these image indices when you create a *TreeNode* object. Here's a complete list of the *TreeNode* constructors:

### *TreeNode* Constructors

```
TreeNode()

TreeNode(ByVal strNode As String)

TreeNode(ByVal strNode As String, ByVal anodes() As TreeNode)

TreeNode(ByVal strNode As String, ByVal indexImage As Integer,
         ByVal indexImageSelected As Integer)

TreeNode(ByVal strNode As String, ByVal indexImage As Integer,
         ByVal indexImageSelected As Integer, ByVal anodes() As TreeNode)
```

In the SimpleTreeView program, I used the *Add* method of *TreeNodeCollection* that has a string argument. Another version of *Add* has a *TreeNode* argument. Thus, it's possible to create a *TreeNode* object first and then add it to a *TreeNodeCollection* object. Two of the *TreeNode* constructors let you specify arrays of child *TreeNode* objects. These constructors let you build up a *TreeView* hierarchy from the lowest descendents up to the root.

# Tree View Events

The *TreeNode* class doesn't define any events on its own. However, *TreeView* implements 11 events in addition to the ones it inherits from *Control*. Here are the 6 crucial ones:

### *TreeView* Events (selection)

| Event | Method | Delegate | Argument |
|-------|--------|----------|----------|
| *BeforeExpand* | *OnBeforeExpand* | *TreeViewCancel-EventHandler* | *TreeViewCancel-EventArgs* |
| *BeforeCollapse* | *OnBeforeCollapse* | *TreeViewCancel-EventHandler* | *TreeViewCancel-EventArgs* |
| *BeforeSelect* | *OnBeforeSelect* | *TreeViewCancel-EventHandler* | *TreeViewCancel-EventArgs* |
| *AfterExpand* | *OnAfterExpand* | *TreeViewEventHandler* | *TreeView-EventArgs* |
| *AfterCollapse* | *OnAfterCollapse* | *TreeViewEventHandler* | *TreeView-EventArgs* |
| *AfterSelect* | *OnAfterSelect* | *TreeViewEventHandler* | *TreeView-EventArgs* |

These events occur when the user (or the program) expands, collapses, or selects a node. As you can see, the events come in pairs. The events that begin with the word *Before* occur before the *TreeView* carries out the operation. The *TreeViewCancelEventArgs* object that accompanies these events has the following properties:

### *TreeViewCancelEventArgs* Properties

| Property | Type | Accessibility |
|----------|------|---------------|
| *Node* | *TreeNode* | Get |
| *Action* | *TreeViewAction* | Get |
| *Cancel* | *Boolean* | Get/Set |

The *Node* property indicates the *TreeNode* object that the user is attempting to expand, collapse, or select. The *Action* property is a member of the following enumeration:

### *TreeViewAction* Enumeration

| Member | Value |
|--------|-------|
| *Unknown* | 0 |
| *ByKeyboard* | 1 |
| *ByMouse* | 2 |

*(continued)*

### *TreeViewAction* Enumeration *(continued)*

| Member | Value |
|--------|-------|
| *Collapse* | 3 |
| *Expand* | 4 |

If, for one reason or another, the program decides that it can't let the operation proceed, the event handler can set the *Cancel* property (inherited from *CancelEventArgs*) to *True*.

Otherwise, the expand, collapse, or select will be carried out by the *Tree-View* control and the events beginning with the word *After* will occur. The accompanying *TreeViewEventArgs* object has the following properties:

### *TreeViewEventArgs* Properties

| Property | Type | Accessibility |
|----------|------|---------------|
| *Node* | *TreeNode* | Get |
| *Action* | *TreeViewAction* | Get |

I won't be demonstrating any of the other events implemented by *Tree-View*. The *BeforeLabelEdit* and *AfterLabelEdit* events occur only if the *LabelEdit* property is set to *True*. This facility lets users edit the text of a tree node. The *BeforeCheck* and *AfterCheck* events occur only if the *CheckBoxes* property is *True*, indicating that check boxes the user can check are placed next to the nodes on the tree. *TreeNode* has a property named *Checked* that indicates whether the node is checked. The *ItemDrag* event occurs when something is dragged to the *TreeView* control.

Keep in mind that *TreeView* inherits many methods, properties, and events from *Control*. For example, if you want to implement a context menu with items based on what node was right-clicked, you can install a handler for the *MouseDown* event and pass the mouse coordinates to the *GetNodeAt* method of *TreeView*.

## Node Navigation

When a *TreeView* event handler gets called, it usually must carry out some activity depending on the particular *TreeNode* object being expanded, collapsed, or selected. The nodes can be identified in several ways. Here are some useful basic properties:

## *TreeNode* Properties (selection)

| Property | Type | Accessibility |
| --- | --- | --- |
| *TreeView* | *TreeView* | Get |
| *Index* | *Integer* | Get |
| *Text* | *String* | Get/Set |
| *Tag* | *Object* | Get/Set |

The *TreeView* property indicates the *TreeView* control that the *TreeNode* object is part of. The *Index* is the index of the node in the collection of its siblings. The *Text* property is the text displayed by the node, obviously, and the *Tag* property allows the attachment of arbitrary information to the node for identification (or other) purposes.

The *TreeNode* class also includes several read-only properties that let a program navigate through the nodes:

## *TreeNode* Properties (selection)

| Property | Type | Accessibility |
| --- | --- | --- |
| *Parent* | *TreeNode* | Get |
| *FirstNode* | *TreeNode* | Get |
| *LastNode* | *TreeNode* | Get |
| *NextNode* | *TreeNode* | Get |
| *PrevNode* | *TreeNode* | Get |
| *NextVisibleNode* | *TreeNode* | Get |
| *PrevVisibleNode* | *TreeNode* | Get |

The *Parent* property indicates the parent node. The *FirstNode* and *LastNode* properties refer to child nodes. (These are also available from the node's *Nodes* property.) The *NextNode* and *PrevNode* properties refer to sibling nodes. The *NextVisibleNode* and *PrevVisibleNode* properties could refer to siblings, children, or parents. These are the next (or previous) nodes that would be selected using the up and down arrow keys.

The *TreeNode* class has two properties that let a program determine whether a node is expanded, collapsed, or selected:

### *TreeNode* Properties (selection)

| Property | Type | Accessibility |
|----------|------|---------------|
| *IsExpanded* | *Boolean* | Get |
| *IsSelected* | *Boolean* | Get |

A program can expand or collapse a *TreeNode* without any help from the user:

### *TreeNode* Methods (selection)

```
Sub Expand()
Sub ExpandAll()
Sub Collapse()
Sub Toggle()
```

The *ExpandAll* method expands all child nodes of the node for which the method is called. To expand or collapse the entire tree, you use these methods in *TreeView*:

### *TreeView* Methods (selection)

```
Sub ExpandAll()
Sub CollapseAll()
```

You can use this property of *TreeView* to obtain or set the selected node:

### *TreeView* Properties (selection)

| Property | Type | Accessibility |
|----------|------|---------------|
| *SelectedNode* | *TreeNode* | Get/Set |

There is one remaining—and sometimes quite convenient—technique for identifying a particular node, available from the *FullPath* property of *TreeNode*:

### *TreeNode* Properties (selection)

| Property | Type | Accsessibility |
|----------|------|---------------|
| *FullPath* | *String* | Get |
| *PathSeparator* | *String* | Get/Set |

For any node, *FullPath* returns a text string that is formed by concatenating the text of the node with all its parent nodes going back to the root. The text strings are separated by the string indicated by the *PathSeparator* property. By default, *PathSeparator* is the backslash. In the SimpleTreeView program, the *FullPath* property for the "Siamese" node is "Animal\Cats\Siamese".

This *FullPath* property is ideal when you're working with a *TreeView* control that displays disks and directories, which (not coincidentally) is the next task we're going to tackle.

## The Directory Tree

As we all know, displaying disks and directories is the most common job of a *TreeView* control. One might even expect the Windows Forms library to contain a class descended from *TreeView* that implements a standard directory tree. But even if there were, using it surely wouldn't be as much fun as making our own!

The following *DirectoryTreeView* class derives from *TreeView* and is used in the next two programs in this chapter and in another program (ExplorerLike) at the end of this chapter. The class makes use of some file I/O classes that I go over in more detail in Appendix A.

```
DirectoryTreeView.vb
'---------------------------------------------------
' DirectoryTreeView.vb (c) 2002 by Charles Petzold
'---------------------------------------------------
Imports System
Imports System.Drawing
Imports System.IO
Imports System.Windows.Forms

Class DirectoryTreeView
    Inherits TreeView

    Sub New()
        ' Make a little more room for long directory names.
        Width *= 2

        ' Get images for tree.
        ImageList = New ImageList()
        ImageList.Images.Add(New Bitmap(Me.GetType(), "35FLOPPY.BMP"))
        ImageList.Images.Add(New Bitmap(Me.GetType(), "CLSDFOLD.BMP"))
        ImageList.Images.Add(New Bitmap(Me.GetType(), "OPENFOLD.BMP"))

        ' Construct tree.
        RefreshTree()
    End Sub
```

*(continued)*

**DirectoryTreeView.vb** *(continued)*

```vb
Sub RefreshTree()
    ' Turn off visual updating and clear tree.
    BeginUpdate()
    Nodes.Clear()

    ' Make disk drives the root nodes.
    Dim astrDrives() As String = Directory.GetLogicalDrives()
    Dim str As String
    For Each str In astrDrives
        Dim tnDrive As New TreeNode(str, 0, 0)
        Nodes.Add(tnDrive)
        AddDirectories(tnDrive)
        If str = "C:\" Then
            SelectedNode = tnDrive
        End If
    Next str
    EndUpdate()
End Sub

Private Sub AddDirectories(ByVal tn As TreeNode)
    tn.Nodes.Clear()
    Dim strPath As String = tn.FullPath
    Dim dirinfo As New DirectoryInfo(strPath)
    Dim adirinfo() As DirectoryInfo

    ' Avoid message box reporting drive A has no diskette!
    If Not dirinfo.Exists Then Return

    Try
        adirinfo = dirinfo.GetDirectories()
    Catch
        Return
    End Try

    Dim di As DirectoryInfo
    For Each di In adirinfo
        Dim tnDir As New TreeNode(di.Name, 1, 2)
        tn.Nodes.Add(tnDir)

        ' We could now fill up the whole tree with this statement:
        '         AddDirectories(tnDir)
        ' But it would be too slow. Try it!

    Next di
End Sub

Protected Overrides Sub OnBeforeExpand( _
        ByVal tvcea As TreeViewCancelEventArgs)
    MyBase.OnBeforeExpand(tvcea)
    BeginUpdate()

    Dim tn As TreeNode
    For Each tn In tvcea.Node.Nodes
```

```
         AddDirectories(tn)
      Next tn
      EndUpdate()
   End Sub
End Class
```

35Floppy.bmp    Clsdfold.bmp    Openfold.bmp

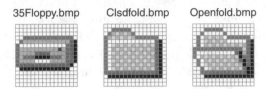

DirectoryTreeView requires three small bitmaps that I copied from the collection provided with Visual Studio .NET. The directory, by default, is Program Files\Microsoft Visual Studio .NET\Common7\Graphics\Bitmaps\Outline\NoMask. (These bitmaps are not included in Visual Basic .NET.) Although I would have preferred displaying different images depending on the type of drive (floppy, hard disk, CD-ROM, and so forth), it's not possible using the Windows Forms classes to obtain the drive type.

The *DirectoryTreeView* class implements one public method, named *RefreshTree*, that programs using the class can call to refresh the entire directory structure. (As you probably know, programs that use tree views displaying directories generally have a menu item named *Refresh*.) The constructor also calls *RefreshTree* to construct the tree.

*RefreshTree* obtains string representations of the system's disk drives by calling the shared *Directory.GetLogicalDrives* method. This method returns an array of strings generally beginning with "A:\", "C:\", and so on. These strings become the root nodes. For each drive, *RefreshTree* calls *AddDirectories*.

*AddDirectories* has a *TreeNode* argument and is responsible for creating child nodes consisting of subdirectory names. The method uses the wonderful *FullPath* property of *TreeNode* to create a *DirectoryInfo* object. The *GetDirectories* method of *DirectoryInfo* then obtains an array of *DirectoryInfo* objects that are used to make child nodes.

It's possible that *GetDirectories* will raise an exception. This happens for a floppy disk drive if no diskette is present, for example, and even for some directories to which access is denied. For that reason, the method is called in a *Try* block. Unfortunately, if a disk drive is empty (as is so often the case for drive A), *GetDirectories* also displays an annoying message box reporting the problem to the user *before* raising the exception. (Press Cancel or Continue to make the message box go away.) The message box is even displayed when console applications call *GetDirectories*! It's obviously a design flaw or a bug in *GetDirectories*, but until it's fixed, you probably want to prevent the message box from being displayed by checking the *Exists* property before calling *GetDirectories*, as is shown in the *AddDirectories* method of *DirectoryTreeView*.

I am well aware that every programmer faced with the job of constructing a directory tree immediately thinks *recursive function*. In fact, *AddDirectories* can indeed be called recursively to construct the entire directory tree. I've even included a statement (commented out, however) that calls *AddDirectories* recursively. You're welcome to remove the comment mark and see for yourself why I rejected this approach: it just takes too much time. It's much more efficient to call *AddDirectories* only when it's needed.

So why, you ask, does the *RefreshTree* method call *AddDirectories* at all? Initially, the tree needs to display only the disk drives. Calling *AddDirectories* for each disk drive seems unnecessary. However, disk drives that contain directories must be displayed with a plus sign that allows the user to expand the node. The only way to get the plus signs displayed is to add child nodes. So, even though only the disk drives are displayed initially, the subdirectories of the root of each drive are also added to the tree.

The *DirectoryTreeView* class also overrides the *OnBeforeExpand* method of *TreeView*. The first time this method will be called is when the user expands one of the disk drive nodes. However, *OnBeforeExpand* doesn't need to build the child nodes of the disk drive. Those already exist. Instead, the method needs to build child nodes for each of the newly displayed nodes—again, for the sole purpose of forcing *TreeView* to display a plus sign if the directory contains subdirectories.

Here's a program that makes use of DirectoryTreeView in a very simple way. This program creates a *Panel* control on the right, a *DirectoryTreeView* control on the left, and a *Splitter* in between. It installs an event handler for the *AfterSelect* event that *DirectoryTreeView* inherits from *TreeView* and displays a list of files in that directory in the panel.

**DirectoriesAndFiles.vb**

```
'-------------------------------------------------------
' DirectoriesAndFiles.vb (c) 2002 by Charles Petzold
'-------------------------------------------------------
Imports System
Imports System.Drawing
Imports System.IO
Imports System.Windows.Forms

Class DirectoriesAndFiles
    Inherits Form
```

```
Private dirtree As DirectoryTreeView
Private pnl As Panel
Private tnSelect As TreeNode

Shared Sub Main()
    Application.Run(New DirectoriesAndFiles())
End Sub

Sub New()
    Text = "Directories and Files"
    BackColor = SystemColors.Window
    ForeColor = SystemColors.WindowText

    pnl = New Panel()
    pnl.Parent = Me
    pnl.Dock = DockStyle.Fill
    AddHandler pnl.Paint, AddressOf PanelOnPaint

    Dim split As New Splitter()
    split.Parent = Me
    split.Dock = DockStyle.Left
    split.BackColor = SystemColors.Control

    dirtree = New DirectoryTreeView()
    dirtree.Parent = Me
    dirtree.Dock = DockStyle.Left
    AddHandler dirtree.AfterSelect, _
                        AddressOf DirectoryTreeViewOnAfterSelect

    ' Create menu with one item.
    Menu = New MainMenu()
    Menu.MenuItems.Add("View")
    Dim mi As New MenuItem("Refresh", _
                    AddressOf MenuOnRefresh, Shortcut.F5)
    Menu.MenuItems(0).MenuItems.Add(mi)
End Sub

Private Sub DirectoryTreeViewOnAfterSelect(ByVal obj As Object, _
                            ByVal tvea As TreeViewEventArgs)

    tnSelect = tvea.Node
    pnl.Invalidate()
End Sub

Private Sub PanelOnPaint(ByVal obj As Object, _
                    ByVal pea As PaintEventArgs)
    If tnSelect Is Nothing Then Return

    Dim pnl As Panel = DirectCast(obj, Panel)
    Dim grfx As Graphics = pea.Graphics
    Dim dirinfo As New DirectoryInfo(tnSelect.FullPath)
    Dim fi, afi() As FileInfo
    Dim br As New SolidBrush(pnl.ForeColor)
    Dim y As Integer = 0
```

*(continued)*

**DirectoriesAndFiles.vb**   *(continued)*

```
        Try
            afi = dirinfo.GetFiles()
        Catch
            Return
        End Try

        For Each fi In afi
            grfx.DrawString(fi.Name, Font, br, 0, y)
            y += Font.Height
        Next fi
    End Sub

    Private Sub MenuOnRefresh(ByVal obj As Object, ByVal ea As EventArgs)
        dirtree.RefreshTree()
    End Sub
End Class
```

Because this is only a demonstration program, the list of files is only one column long, so the list might be truncated. Here's a view of one of the subdirectories of my WINNT directory (a directory that in some versions of Windows is named WINDOWS):

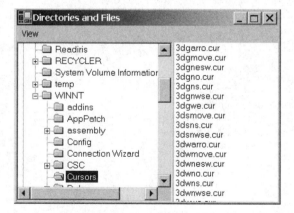

This program also has a View menu with one item: Refresh. The menu item rebuilds the directory tree by calling the *RefreshTree* method in the *DirectoryTreeView* class.

# Displaying Images

In Chapter 23, I'll be delving into metafiles, which are binary collections of graphics drawing commands that describe an image. In preparation for that chapter, I wanted to look at some metafile clip art that I had. Generally, when I want to look at a directory full of images, I use a particular freeware program. The program displays a tree view on the left and thumbnails on the right. You click on a thumbnail to see the full-size image. But while the program works fine with many different bitmap formats, it doesn't read metafiles at all. Recent versions of Windows Explorer display thumbnails of bitmaps and metafiles, but Windows Explorer requires an external program for displaying the full-size images.

In Windows Forms, both the *Bitmap* and *Metafile* classes are descended from *Image*. Metafiles can be read from the disk using the shared *Image.From-File* method just as easily as bitmaps, and metafiles can also be displayed as easily with *DrawImage*. In a Windows Forms program that loads and displays bitmaps, metafile support is free.

Let's set some simple goals. A program named ImageDirectory will display a *TreeView* control on the left listing directories. On the right, the program will display a collection of thumbnails showing all the image files (bitmaps *and* metafiles) in the selected directory. Click on a thumbnail to see the image enlarged to the size of the form.

We've already written a good chunk of this program. That's the *DirectoryTreeView* control. The other half of the program's client area will consist of a *Panel* control. Each thumbnail is a *Button* control that displays the image scaled down to the size of a button. Here's an *ImagePanel* control that descends from *Panel* to do this job.

**ImagePanel.vb**

```
'-------------------------------------------------
' ImagePanel.vb (c) 2002 by Charles Petzold
'-------------------------------------------------
Imports System
Imports System.Drawing
Imports System.IO
Imports System.Windows.Forms

Class ImagePanel
    Inherits Panel

    ' Image button size
    Const cxButton As Integer = 100
    Const cyButton As Integer = 100
```

*(continued)*

**ImagePanel.vb** *(continued)*

```vb
    Private btnClicked As Button
    Private tip As New ToolTip()
    Private tmr As New Timer()

    ' Fields for Timer Tick event
    Private astrFileNames() As String
    Private i, x, y As Integer

    ' Public event
    Event ImageClicked As EventHandler

    ' Constructor
    Sub New()
        AutoScroll = True
        tmr.Interval = 1
        AddHandler tmr.Tick, AddressOf TimerOnTick
    End Sub

    ' Public properties
    ReadOnly Property ClickedControl() As Control
        Get
            Return btnClicked
        End Get
    End Property

    ReadOnly Property ClickedImage() As Image
        Get
            Try
                Return Image.FromFile(btnClicked.Tag.ToString())
            Catch
                Return Nothing
            End Try
        End Get
    End Property

    ' Public method
    Sub ShowImages(ByVal strDirectory As String)
        Controls.Clear()
        tip.RemoveAll()
        Try
            astrFileNames = Directory.GetFiles(strDirectory)
        Catch
            Return
        End Try

        i = 0
        x = 0
        y = 0
        tmr.Start()
    End Sub
```

```vb
' Event handlers
Private Sub TimerOnTick(ByVal obj As Object, ByVal ea As EventArgs)
    Dim img As Image

    If i = astrFileNames.Length Then
        tmr.Stop()
        Return
    End If

    Try
        img = Image.FromFile(astrFileNames(i))
    Catch
        i += 1
        Return
    End Try

    Dim cxImage As Integer = img.Width
    Dim cyImage As Integer = img.Height

    ' Convert image to small size for button.
    Dim szf As New SizeF(cxImage / img.HorizontalResolution, _
                         cyImage / img.VerticalResolution)
    Dim fScale As Single = Math.Min(cxButton / szf.Width, _
                                    cyButton / szf.Height)

    szf.Width *= fScale
    szf.Height *= fScale

    Dim sz As Size = Size.Ceiling(szf)
    Dim bitmap As New bitmap(img, sz)
    img.Dispose()

    ' Create button and add to pnl.
    Dim btn As New Button()
    btn.Image = bitmap
    btn.Location = Point.op_Addition(New Point(x, y), _
                   Point.op_Explicit(AutoScrollPosition))
    btn.Size = New Size(cxButton, cyButton)
    btn.Tag = astrFileNames(i)
    AddHandler btn.Click, AddressOf ButtonOnClick
    Controls.Add(btn)

    ' Give button a ToolTip.
    tip.SetToolTip(btn, String.Format("{0}" & vbLf & "{1}x{2}", _
                        Path.GetFileName(astrFileNames(i)), _
                        cxImage, cyImage))

    ' Adjust i, x, and y for next image.
    AdjustXY(x, y)
    i += 1
End Sub
```

*(continued)*

**ImagePanel.vb** *(continued)*

```
    Private Sub ButtonOnClick(ByVal obj As Object, ByVal ea As EventArgs)
        btnClicked = DirectCast(obj, Button)
        RaiseEvent ImageClicked(Me, EventArgs.Empty)
    End Sub

    Protected Overrides Sub OnResize(ByVal ea As EventArgs)
        MyBase.OnResize(ea)
        AutoScrollPosition = Point.Empty

        Dim x As Integer = 0
        Dim y As Integer = 0
        Dim ctrl As Control

        For Each ctrl In Controls
            ctrl.Location = Point.op_Addition(New Point(x, y), _
                            Point.op_Explicit(AutoScrollPosition))
            AdjustXY(x, y)
        Next ctrl
    End Sub

    Private Sub AdjustXY(ByRef x As Integer, ByRef y As Integer)
        y += cyButton
        If y + cyButton > _
                Height - SystemInformation.HorizontalScrollBarHeight Then
            y = 0
            x += cxButton
        End If
    End Sub
End Class
```

The *ImagePanel* constructor sets its *AutoScroll* property to *True*. If there are more buttons than can fit in the allotted space for the panel, the scroll bars need to be displayed so that the user can scroll to the other buttons.

*ImagePanel* implements a public method named *ShowImages* that has a single argument specifying a directory name. *ShowImages* is responsible for obtaining an array of all the files in that directory, loading an *Image* object for each file in the directory that doesn't raise an exception when *Image.FromFile* is called, creating a bitmap that contains the image scaled down to the size of the button, creating the button, and also creating a ToolTip that has the name of the image and its pixel dimensions.

Actually, that was the first version of the program. It turned out that this job took much too long for directories containing many large bitmaps. My solution was to spread out the job using a *Timer* object. (It's a simple form of multitasking that doesn't require using multiple threads.) The *Timer* object is created as a field of the *ImagePanel* object and given a tick interval of 1 millisecond during the *ImagePanel* constructor. After the *ShowImages* method gets the array of filenames, it initializes a few variables (an index of the filename array and *x* and *y* coordinates for the buttons) and starts the timer.

The *Tick* event handler is responsible for calling *Image.FromFile* and creating a button based on that image. Notice that *Image.FromFile* is called for every file in the directory! If *Image.FromFile* returns properly, it successfully loaded an image. If it throws an exception, either the file wasn't an image file supported by the method or the file was corrupted in some way.

You should also notice that this job can be interrupted before the entire directory has been read. Whenever *ShowImages* is called, it clears all the buttons and ToolTips and starts over again with the new directory.

The *ImagePanel* class also implements a public event named *Image-Clicked*. This event is triggered whenever one of the buttons is clicked. The two read-only properties *ClickedControl* and *ClickedImage* return the button that was clicked and the image displayed on that button.

Here's the program itself. ImageDirectory makes use of *ImagePanel* as well as *DirectoryTreeView*, with a *Splitter* control to separate them on the client area. The constructor also creates an object of type *PictureBoxPlus*, which is a class I created in Chapter 11 that enhances *PictureBox* to provide a *NoDistort* property that maintains the correct aspect ratio when an image is stretched to the size of the control. This *PictureBoxPlus* control is used to display the clicked image stretched to the size of the client area. The control has its *Visible* property initially set to *False*.

**ImageDirectory.vb**

```
'-------------------------------------------------
' ImageDirectory.vb (c) 2002 by Charles Petzold
'-------------------------------------------------
Imports System
Imports System.Drawing
Imports System.Windows.Forms

Class ImageDirectory
    Inherits Form

    Private picbox As PictureBoxPlus
    Private dirtree As DirectoryTreeView
    Private imgpnl As ImagePanel
    Private split As Splitter
    Private tnSelect As TreeNode
    Private ctrlClicked As Control
    Private ptPanelAutoScroll As Point

    Shared Sub Main()
        Application.Run(New ImageDirectory())
    End Sub
```

*(continued)*

**ImageDirectory.vb** *(continued)*

```vb
Sub New()
    Text = "Image Directory"
    BackColor = SystemColors.Window
    ForeColor = SystemColors.WindowText

    ' Create (invisible) control for displaying large image.
    picbox = New PictureBoxPlus()
    picbox.Parent = Me
    picbox.Visible = False
    picbox.Dock = DockStyle.Fill
    picbox.SizeMode = PictureBoxSizeMode.StretchImage
    picbox.NoDistort = True
    AddHandler picbox.MouseDown, AddressOf PictureBoxOnMouseDown

    ' Create controls for displaying thumbnails.
    imgpnl = New ImagePanel()
    imgpnl.Parent = Me
    imgpnl.Dock = DockStyle.Fill
    AddHandler imgpnl.ImageClicked, AddressOf ImagePanelOnImageClicked

    split = New Splitter()
    split.Parent = Me
    split.Dock = DockStyle.Left
    split.BackColor = SystemColors.Control

    dirtree = New DirectoryTreeView()
    dirtree.Parent = Me
    dirtree.Dock = DockStyle.Left
    AddHandler dirtree.AfterSelect, _
                               AddressOf DirectoryTreeViewOnAfterSelect

    ' Create menu with one item (Refresh).
    Menu = New MainMenu()
    Menu.MenuItems.Add("&View")
    Dim mi As New MenuItem("&Refresh", _
                           AddressOf MenuOnRefresh, Shortcut.F5)
    Menu.MenuItems(0).MenuItems.Add(mi)
End Sub

Private Sub DirectoryTreeViewOnAfterSelect(ByVal obj As Object, _
                                ByVal tvea As TreeViewEventArgs)
    tnSelect = tvea.Node
    imgpnl.ShowImages(tnSelect.FullPath)
End Sub

Private Sub MenuOnRefresh(ByVal obj As Object, ByVal ea As EventArgs)
    dirtree.RefreshTree()
End Sub
```

```
    Private Sub ImagePanelOnImageClicked(ByVal obj As Object, _
                                  ByVal ea As EventArgs)
        ' Get clicked control and image.
        ctrlClicked = imgpnl.ClickedControl
        picbox.Image = imgpnl.ClickedImage

        ' Save auto-scroll position.
        ptPanelAutoScroll = imgpnl.AutoScrollPosition
        ptPanelAutoScroll.X *= -1
        ptPanelAutoScroll.Y *= -1

        ' Hide and disable the normal controls.
        imgpnl.Visible = False
        imgpnl.Enabled = False
        imgpnl.AutoScrollPosition = Point.Empty
        split.Visible = False
        split.Enabled = False
        dirtree.Visible = False
        dirtree.Enabled = False

        ' Make the picture box visible.
        picbox.Visible = True
    End Sub

    ' Event handlers and method involved with restoring controls
    Private Sub PictureBoxOnMouseDown(ByVal obj As Object, _
                                  ByVal mea As MouseEventArgs)
        RestoreControls()
    End Sub

    Protected Overrides Sub OnKeyDown(ByVal kea As KeyEventArgs)
        If kea.KeyCode = Keys.Escape Then
            RestoreControls()
        End If
    End Sub

    Private Sub RestoreControls()
        picbox.Visible = False
        dirtree.Visible = True
        dirtree.Enabled = True
        split.Enabled = True
        split.Visible = True
        imgpnl.AutoScrollPosition = ptPanelAutoScroll
        imgpnl.Visible = True
        imgpnl.Enabled = True
        ctrlClicked.Focus()
    End Sub
End Class
```

Whenever the selection in the *DirectoryTreeView* control changes (indicated by a call to the *DirectoryTreeViewOnAfterSelect* event handler), the program calls the *ShowImages* method of the *ImagePanel*. Here's the program displaying metafiles from one of the directories of Visual Studio .NET (a directory not included with Visual Basic .NET).

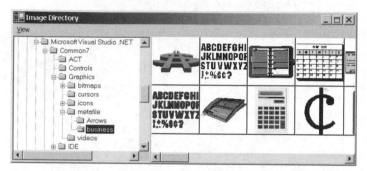

Whenever one of the buttons is clicked, the program is notified by a call to its *ImagePanelOnImageClicked* event handler. The event handler responds by making the three visible controls invisible and the invisible control (*Picture-BoxPlus*) visible. The image is stretched to the size of the client area with its aspect ratio maintained:

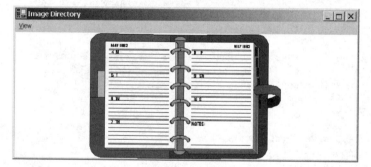

The client area can be returned to normal by clicking the client area or pressing the Esc key.

## List View Basics

In its most sophisticated form, the *ListView* control displays textual information in rows and columns with column headings. The first column of information contains the list view *items*, and the other columns contain *subitems* associated with each item. For example, in Windows Explorer, the filename is the item, and the file size, modified date, and attributes are all subitems. The *ListView* control can also display the simple list of items themselves (without subitems), the items in multiple columns with small icons, and items in multiple columns with large icons.

A number of different classes are involved in creating a *ListView* object, but let's begin our tour with the *ListView* class itself. *ListView* has several essential properties:

### *ListView* Properties (selection)

| Property | Type | Accessibility |
|---|---|---|
| *View* | *View* | Get/Set |
| *SmallImageList* | *ImageList* | Get/Set |
| *LargeImageList* | *ImageList* | Get/Set |
| *Columns* | *ListView.ColumnHeaderCollection* | Get |
| *Items* | *ListView.ListViewItemCollection* | Get |

The *View* enumeration contains members for the four different formats in which a *ListView* control can display its data. You're probably familiar with the four options from what you've seen in various menus, including a toolbar button in the standard *OpenFileDialog* and *SaveFileDialog* dialog boxes:

### *View* Enumeration

| Member | Value |
|---|---|
| *LargeIcon* | 0 |
| *Details* | 1 |
| *SmallIcon* | 2 |
| *List* | 3 |

For the *LargeIcon* option, each item is displayed with a large bitmap (generally 48 pixels square) that is one of the images stored in the *LargeImageList* property. For the other *View* options, the item is displayed with a small bitmap (generally 16 pixels square) from the *SmallImageList* property. The images in these two *ImageList* objects must coincide; for example, the third image in *LargeImageList* should be a larger version of the third image in *SmallImageList*.

The *Columns* property is an object of type *ListView.ColumnHeaderCollection*, which is yet another implementation of the *ICollection*, *IEnumerable*, and *IList* interfaces. (There are more to come in this chapter.) Here's a complete list of its properties:

### *ListView.ColumnHeaderCollection* Properties

| Property | Type | Accessibility |
|----------|------|---------------|
| *0* | *ColumnHeader* | Get |
| *Count* | *Integer* | Get |
| *IsReadOnly* | *Boolean* | Get |

As you can see, an object of type *ListView.ColumnHeaderCollection* is basically a collection of read-only *ColumnHeader* objects. The class implements the customary *Clear*, *Insert*, *Remove*, *Add*, and *AddRange* methods. Here are those last two methods as implemented in this class:

### *ListView.ColumnHeaderCollection* Methods (selection)

```
Function Add(ByVal colhead As ColumnHeader) As Integer

Function Add(ByVal strText As String, ByVal iWidth As Integer,
             ByVal ha As HorizontalAlignment) As ColumnHeader

Sub AddRange(ByVal acolheads() As ColumnHeader)
```

As you can deduce from the second *Add* implementation, a *ColumnHeader* object is basically some text, an initial width of the column in pixels, and an alignment. You've seen the *HorizontalAlignment* enumeration before:

### *HorizontalAlignment* Enumeration

| Member | Value |
|--------|-------|
| *Left* | 0 |
| *Right* | 1 |
| *Center* | 2 |

The alignment is considered an important element of the column header because it affects not only the text in the column header but also the items or subitems listed in that column as well.

*ColumnHeader* itself has a default constructor and only three read/write properties, which are the same as the arguments to the *Add* method just shown:

### *ColumnHeader* Properties (selection)

| Property | Type | Accessibility |
|----------|------|---------------|
| *Text* | *String* | Get/Set |
| *Width* | *Integer* | Get/Set |
| *TextAlign* | *HorizontalAlignments* | Get/Set |

The only other properties of *ColumnHeader* are read-only, and they indicate the *ListView* object to which the *ColumnHeader* object belongs and the index of that column header among the collection of column headers.

Let's go back to the table of essential *ListView* properties. The last item in the table was a property named *Items*, which is an object of type *ListView.ListViewItemCollection*. Here are its properties:

### *ListView.ListViewItemCollection* Properties

| Property | Type | Accessibility |
|----------|------|---------------|
| *()* | *ListViewItem* | Get/Set |
| *Count* | *Integer* | Get |
| *IsReadOnly* | *Boolean* | Get |

The *Items* property of *ListView* is basically a collection of *ListViewItem* objects. As usual, we can get a hint of what a *ListViewItem* is by looking at the *Add* and *AddRange* methods of *ListView.ListViewItemCollection*:

### *ListView.ListViewItemCollection* Methods (selection)

```
Function Add(ByVal lvitem As ListViewItem) As ListViewItem

Function Add(ByVal strItem As String) As ListViewItem

Function Add(ByVal strItem As String,
             ByVal indexImage As Integer) As ListViewItem

Sub AddRange(ByVal alvitems() As ListViewItem)
```

The *strItem* argument is the text string associated with the item. Regardless of what view is selected, this text string is always displayed. The *View.Details* option also displays subitems, which we haven't encountered just yet. The *indexImage* argument is an index into both the *LargeImageList* and *SmallImageList* properties of the *ListView* control.

*ListViewItem* has seven different constructors:

### *ListViewItem* Constructors

```
ListViewItem()

ListViewItem(ByVal strItem As String)

ListViewItem(ByVal strItem As String, ByVal indexImage As Integer)

ListViewItem(ByVal astrItems() As String)

ListViewItem(ByVal astrItems() As String, ByVal indexImage As Integer)

ListViewItem(ByVal astrItems() As String, ByVal indexImage As Integer,
             ByVal clrFore As Color, ByVal clrBack As Color,
             ByVal fnt As Font)

ListViewItem(ByVal aSubItems() As ListViewItem.ListViewSubItem,
             ByVal indexImage As Integer)
```

When you specify an array of strings in the constructor, you're actually specifying an item and one or more subitems associated with that item.

The following properties of the *ListViewItem* class are essential:

### *ListViewItem* Properties (selection)

| Property | Type | Accessibility |
| --- | --- | --- |
| *Text* | *String* | Get/Set |
| *ImageIndex* | *Integer* | Get/Set |
| *Tag* | *Object* | Get/Set |
| *SubItems* | *ListViewItem.ListViewSubItemCollection* | Get |

The *ListViewItem* object contains text and an image index as well as a *Tag* property that lets you attach arbitrary data to the item. *ListViewItem* also contains a collection of subitems, which are objects of *ListViewItem.ListViewSubItemCollection*. Here's a complete list of properties of that class:

### *ListViewItem.ListViewSubItemCollection* Properties

| Property | Type | Accessibility |
| --- | --- | --- |
| *()* | *ListViewItem.ListViewSubItem* | Get/Set |
| *Count* | *Integer* | Get |
| *IsReadOnly* | *Boolean* | Get |

As usual, we can get an insight into what constitutes a subitem by looking at the arguments of the *Add* and *AddRange* methods of the class:

### *ListViewItem.ListViewSubItemCollection* Methods (selection)

```
Function Add(ByVal strText As String) As ListViewSubItem

Function Add(ByVal strText As String,
            ByVal clrFore As Color, ByVal clrBack As Color,
            ByVal fnt As Font) As ListViewSubItem

Function Add(ByVal lvsi As ListViewItem.ListViewSubItem) As ListViewSubItem

Sub AddRange(ByVal astrText() As String)

Sub AddRange(ByVal astrText() As string, ByVal clrFore As Color,
            ByVal clrBack As Color, ByVal fnt As Font)

Sub AddRange(ByVal alvsi() As ListViewItem.ListViewSubItem)
```

The *ListViewItem.ListViewSubItem* constructors have similar arguments:

### *ListViewItem.ListViewSubItem* Constructors

```
ListViewItem.ListViewSubItem()

ListViewItem.ListViewSubItem(ByVal lviOwner As ListViewItem,
                            ByVal strText As String)

ListViewItem.ListViewSubItem(ByVal lviOwner As ListViewItem,
                            ByVal strText As String,
                            ByVal clrForeground As Color,
                            ByVal clrBackground As Color,
                            ByVal fnt As Font)
```

The class has only four properties:

### *ListViewItem.ListViewSubItem* Properties

| Property | Type | Accessibility |
| --- | --- | --- |
| *Text* | *String* | Get/Set |
| *Font* | *Font* | Get/Set |
| *BackColor* | *Color* | Get/Set |
| *ForeColor* | *Color* | Get/Set |

It's now time to put all this information into service. I trust you'll recall the series of SysInfo (system information) programs that were the highlight of Chapter 4 and also showed up in some subsequent chapters. I'd now like to show a version that uses a *ListView* control. This program also makes use of the

SysInfoReflectionStrings.vb file that provides several public shared properties and methods, the *Labels* and *Values* properties being the most important. Both properties return arrays of strings that indicate (respectively) the names of the shared properties in the *SystemInformation* class and their current values. The *Count* property returns the number of strings in the arrays. The *MaxLabelWidth* and *MaxValueWidth* methods return the maximum width of the string in each array. I use those methods in this program to set the initial column widths.

### SysInfoListView.vb

```
'-------------------------------------------------------
' SysInfoListView.vb (c) 2002 by Charles Petzold
'-------------------------------------------------------
Imports System
Imports System.Drawing
Imports System.Windows.Forms

Class SysInfoListView
    Inherits Form

    Shared Sub Main()
        Application.Run(New SysInfoListView())
    End Sub

    Sub New()
        Text = "System Information (List View)"

        ' Create ListView control.
        Dim listvu As New ListView()
        listvu.Parent = Me
        listvu.Dock = DockStyle.Fill
        listvu.View = View.Details

        ' Define columns based on maximum string widths.
        Dim grfx As Graphics = CreateGraphics()
        listvu.Columns.Add("Property", _
                CInt(SysInfoReflectionStrings.MaxLabelWidth(grfx, Font)), _
                HorizontalAlignment.Left)
        listvu.Columns.Add("Value", _
                CInt(SysInfoReflectionStrings.MaxValueWidth(grfx, Font)), _
                HorizontalAlignment.Left)
        grfx.Dispose()

        ' Get the data that will be displayed.
        Dim iNumItems As Integer = SysInfoReflectionStrings.Count
        Dim astrLabels() As String = SysInfoReflectionStrings.Labels
        Dim astrValues() As String = SysInfoReflectionStrings.Values
```

```
        ' Define the items and subitems.
        Dim i As Integer
        For i = 0 To iNumItems - 1
            Dim lvi As New ListViewItem(astrLabels(i))
            lvi.SubItems.Add(astrValues(i))
            listvu.Items.Add(lvi)
        Next i
    End Sub
End Class
```

As you can see, despite the tongue-twistingly long class names involved with the various *ListView* collections, the actual code is rather terse. The constructor begins by creating the *ListView* object, assigning the form as its parent, giving the object a *Dock* property of *DockStyle.Fill*, and then setting the *View* property to *View.Details*. (Anything else would be meaningless for this program.) This particular *ListView* object doesn't use any image lists.

Next, the constructor defines the two column headers by calling the three-argument *Add* method of the *Columns* property. The items and subitems are added in the *For* loop at the bottom. In that *For* loop, the program creates a *ListViewItem* object based on an element of the *astrLabels* array. It then uses the *Add* method of the *SubItems* property to add a single subitem, which is an element of the *astrValues* array. The *ListViewItem* object is then added to the *ListView* object using the *Add* method of the *Items* property.

And here's the result:

The scroll bars are provided by default. You'll probably want to experiment with this program a bit to examine the other features that the default *ListView* provides and also to try out some properties I haven't talked about here.

# List View Events

When experimenting with the SysInfoListView program, you'll find that you can select an item in the first column using the mouse or the up and down arrow keys. With the Shift key pressed, you can extend the selection to multiple items. You can also select and deselect individual items (without affecting other selected items) by clicking with the mouse while holding down the Ctrl key. (To turn off the default multiselection feature in a *ListView* object, set the *MultiSelect* property to *False*.)

A program may or may not be interested that the user is changing the selection. However, most programs that use a *ListView* object for something other than simple display purposes will almost definitely be interested in something called item *activation*. Windows Explorer, for example, launches applications when the user activates an item. By default, activation occurs when the user double-clicks an item or a group of items, or presses the Enter key when one or more items have been selected. However, you can change that behavior by using the following property:

### *ListView* Properties (selection)

| Property | Type | Accessibility |
| --- | --- | --- |
| *Activation* | *ItemActivation* | Get/Set |

The *ItemActivation* enumeration has the following members:

### *ItemActivation* Enumeration

| Member | Value |
| --- | --- |
| *Standard* | 0 |
| *OneClick* | 1 |
| *TwoClick* | 2 |

*Standard* is default. Both the *OneClick* and *TwoClick* options cause items to change color as the mouse cursor moves over them. The *OneClick* option requires one click for activation; the *TwoClick* option requires two clicks.

Here are the three most important events implemented by the *ListView* class:

### *ListView* Events (selection)

| Event | Method | Delegate | Argument |
|-------|--------|----------|----------|
| *SelectedIndex-Changed* | *OnSelectedIndex-Changed* | *EventHandler* | *EventArgs* |
| *ItemActivate* | *OnItemActivate* | *EventHandler* | *EventArgs* |
| *ColumnClick* | *OnColumnClick* | *ColumnClickEventHandler* | *ColumnClick-EventArgs* |

None of the other classes associated with the *ListView* control implement any events. The other *ListView* events involve editing, checking, and dragging items.

*ListView* also supports all the events implemented in *Control*. If, for example, a program wants to customize and display a context menu depending on what item the user is clicking with the right mouse button, it can install a *MouseDown* event handler and determine what item the user is clicking by calling the *GetItemAt* method of *ListView*.

When the user clicks a column heading, the *ColumnClick* event is accompanied by the following information:

### *ColumnClickEventArgs* Property

| Property | Type | Accessibility |
|----------|------|---------------|
| *Column* | *Integer* | Get |

The *SelectedIndexChanged* and *ItemActivate* events aren't accompanied by any information. The program handling these events will want to use the following two properties of *ListView* to obtain the currently selected items:

### *ListView* Properties (selection)

| Property | Type | Accessibility |
|----------|------|---------------|
| *SelectedIndices* | *ListView.Selected-IndexCollection* | Get |
| *SelectedItems* | *ListView.SelectedList-ViewItemCollection* | Get |

Yes, these are yet two more collections! The first is just a read-only collection of integers:

### *ListView.SelectedIndexCollection* Properties

| Property | Type | Accessibility |
|----------|------|---------------|
| *()* | *Integer* | Get |
| *Count* | *Integer* | Get |
| *IsReadOnly* | *Boolean* | Get |

The *Add* and *AddRange* methods of this class are not public. The second collection has the following properties:

### *ListView.SelectedListViewItemCollection* Properties

| Property | Type | Accessibility |
|----------|------|---------------|
| *()* | *ListViewItem* | Get |
| *Count* | *Integer* | Get |
| *IsReadOnly* | *Boolean* | Get |

Again, the *Add* and *AddRange* methods are not public. To initialize the selection of items programmatically, use the following property of *ListViewItem*:

### *ListViewItem* Properties (selection)

| Property | Type | Accessibility |
|----------|------|---------------|
| *Selected* | *Boolean* | Get/Set |

You can also use this property instead of *SelectedIndices* or *SelectedItems* to obtain the selected items. You'll need to loop through all the items of the *ListView* object and check which ones have the *Selected* property set.

The following class, *FileListView*, derives from *ListView* to display a list of files stored in a given directory. Unlike the list view in Windows Explorer, *FileListView* doesn't display subdirectories along with files.

**FileListView.vb**

```
'----------------------------------------------
' FileListView.vb (c) 2002 by Charles Petzold
'----------------------------------------------
Imports System
Imports System.Diagnostics        ' For Process.Start
Imports System.Drawing
Imports System.IO
Imports System.Windows.Forms
```

```
Class FileListView
    Inherits ListView

    Private strDirectory As String

    Sub New()
        View = View.Details

        ' Get images for file icons.
        Dim imglst As New ImageList()
        imglst.Images.Add(New Bitmap(Me.GetType(), "DOC.BMP"))
        imglst.Images.Add(New Bitmap(Me.GetType(), "EXE.BMP"))
        SmallImageList = imglst
        LargeImageList = imglst

        ' Create columns.
        Columns.Add("Name", 100, HorizontalAlignment.Left)
        Columns.Add("Size", 100, HorizontalAlignment.Right)
        Columns.Add("Modified", 100, HorizontalAlignment.Left)
        Columns.Add("Attribute", 100, HorizontalAlignment.Left)
    End Sub

    Sub ShowFiles(ByVal strDirectory As String)
        ' Save directory name as field.
        Me.strDirectory = strDirectory
        Items.Clear()

        Dim dirinfo As New DirectoryInfo(strDirectory)
        Dim fi, afi() As FileInfo
        Try
            afi = dirinfo.GetFiles()
        Catch
            Return
        End Try

        For Each fi In afi
            ' Create ListViewItem.
            Dim lvi As New ListViewItem(fi.Name)

            ' Assign ImageIndex based on filename extension.
            If Path.GetExtension(fi.Name).ToUpper() = ".EXE" Then
                lvi.ImageIndex = 1
            Else
                lvi.ImageIndex = 0
            End If

            ' Add file length and modified time sub-items.
            lvi.SubItems.Add(fi.Length.ToString("N0"))
            lvi.SubItems.Add(fi.LastWriteTime.ToString())

            ' Add attribute subitem.
            Dim strAttr As String = ""
```

*(continued)*

**FileListView.vb** *(continued)*

```
            If (fi.Attributes And FileAttributes.Archive) <> 0 Then
                strAttr &= "A"
            End If
            If (fi.Attributes And FileAttributes.Hidden) <> 0 Then
                strAttr &= "H"
            End If
            If (fi.Attributes And FileAttributes.ReadOnly) <> 0 Then
                strAttr &= "R"
            End If
            If (fi.Attributes And FileAttributes.System) <> 0 Then
                strAttr &= "S"
            End If
            lvi.SubItems.Add(strAttr)

            ' Add completed ListViewItem to FileListView.
            Items.Add(lvi)
        Next fi
    End Sub

    Protected Overrides Sub OnItemActivate(ByVal ea As EventArgs)
        MyBase.OnItemActivate(ea)
        Dim lvi As ListViewItem
        For Each lvi In SelectedItems
            Try
                Process.Start(Path.Combine(strDirectory, lvi.Text))
            Catch

            End Try
        Next lvi
    End Sub
End Class
```

Doc.bmp     Exe.bmp

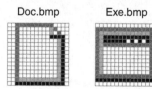

Windows Explorer probably uses the API function *ExtractAssociatedIcon* to obtain an image for each file it displays. However, that facility isn't exposed in the Windows Forms classes. To provide some sample images anyway, FileList-View loads two bitmaps that I copied from the Program Files\Microsoft Visual Studio .NET\Common7\Graphics\Bitmaps\Outline\NoMask directory. Both the *SmallImageList* and *LargeImageList* properties get the same pair of small images. The constructor concludes by creating four columns.

The *FileListView* class implements a public *ShowFiles* method that does most of the work of the class. The method creates an object of type *Directory-Info* based on the specified directory and then gets an array of *FileInfo* structures by calling the *GetFiles* method. Each member of the array becomes an item and three subitems. Much of the code is devoted to formatting the items. If the filename extension is .exe, the *ImageIndex* property is set to 1 for the Exe.bmp image; otherwise, it's set to 0 for the Doc.bmp image. (I know: What about .dll files? What about .com files? You're welcome to enhance the image logic if you wish.)

*FileListView* also overrides the *OnItemActivate* method. For each selected item, the program calls the shared *Process.Start* method. If the file is an executable, the file will be launched directly. If the file is a document with a known association, the associated file will be launched with the document.

To see what this custom *ListView* control looks like, we need a Windows Explorer–like program that combines both *DirectoryTreeView* and *FileListView*. ExplorerLike is such a program.

### ExplorerLike.vb

```
'-------------------------------------------------
' ExplorerLike.vb (c) 2002 by Charles Petzold
'-------------------------------------------------
Imports System
Imports System.Drawing
Imports System.Windows.Forms

Class ExplorerLike
    Inherits Form

    Private filelist As FileListView
    Private dirtree As DirectoryTreeView
    Private mivChecked As MenuItemView

    Shared Sub Main()
        Application.Run(New ExplorerLike())
    End Sub

    Sub New()
        Text = "Windows Explorer-Like Program"
        BackColor = SystemColors.Window
        ForeColor = SystemColors.WindowText

        ' Create controls.
        filelist = New FileListView()
        filelist.Parent = Me
        filelist.Dock = DockStyle.Fill

        Dim split As New Splitter()
```

*(continued)*

**ExplorerLike.vb** *(continued)*

```vb
        split.Parent = Me
        split.Dock = DockStyle.Left
        split.BackColor = SystemColors.Control

        dirtree = New DirectoryTreeView()
        dirtree.Parent = Me
        dirtree.Dock = DockStyle.Left
        AddHandler dirtree.AfterSelect, _
                AddressOf DirectoryTreeViewOnAfterSelect

        ' Create View menu.
        Menu = New MainMenu()
        Menu.MenuItems.Add("&View")

        Dim astrView() As String = {"Lar&ge Icons", "S&mall Icons", _
                                "&List", "&Details"}
        Dim aview() As View = {View.LargeIcon, View.SmallIcon, _
                                View.List, View.Details}
        Dim eh As EventHandler = AddressOf MenuOnView
        Dim i As Integer

        For i = 0 To 3
            Dim miv As New MenuItemView()
            miv.Text = astrView(i)
            miv.vu = aview(i)
            miv.RadioCheck = True
            AddHandler miv.Click, eh
            If i = 3 Then
                mivChecked = miv
                mivChecked.Checked = True
                filelist.View = mivChecked.vu
            End If
            Menu.MenuItems(0).MenuItems.Add(miv)
        Next i

        Menu.MenuItems(0).MenuItems.Add("-")

        ' View Refresh menu item
        Dim mi As New MenuItem("&Refresh", _
                        AddressOf MenuOnRefresh, Shortcut.F5)
        Menu.MenuItems(0).MenuItems.Add(mi)
    End Sub

    Private Sub DirectoryTreeViewOnAfterSelect(ByVal obj As Object, _
                                            ByVal tvea As TreeViewEventArgs)
        filelist.ShowFiles(tvea.Node.FullPath)
    End Sub

    Private Sub MenuOnView(ByVal obj As Object, ByVal ea As EventArgs)
```

```
        mivChecked.Checked = False
        mivChecked = DirectCast(obj, MenuItemView)
        mivChecked.Checked = True
        filelist.View = mivChecked.vu
    End Sub

    Private Sub MenuOnRefresh(ByVal obj As Object, ByVal ea As EventArgs)
        dirtree.RefreshTree()
    End Sub
End Class

Class MenuItemView
    Inherits MenuItem

    Public vu As View
End Class
```

Most of this program is devoted to processing menu commands that let you change the *View* property of the *FileListView* control and refresh the *DirectoryTreeView* contents. The only connection between the two controls is implemented in the *DirectoryTreeViewOnAfterSelect* event handler, which calls the *ShowFiles* method of *FileListView* with the newly selected directory. Here's the program showing part of the Windows system directory:

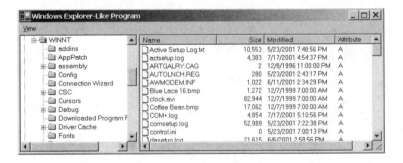

# 23

# Metafiles

Metafiles are to vector graphics as bitmaps are to raster graphics. While bitmaps generally originate from real-world images, metafiles are usually constructed by humans in collaboration with computer programs. A metafile consists of a series of binary records that correspond to graphics function calls—to draw lines, curves, filled areas, and text. Metafiles can also contain embedded bitmaps. A metafile can be stored in a disk file or can reside entirely in memory.

Paint programs create bitmaps; drawing programs create metafiles. In a well-designed drawing program, you can easily grab on-screen graphical objects with the mouse and move them somewhere else. That's because all the individual components of the picture are stored as separate records. In a paint program, such feats aren't possible without a lot of heavy image analysis. Paint programs generally restrict you to moving or inserting rectangular chunks of the bitmap.

Because a metafile describes an image in terms of graphical drawing commands, the metafile image can be scaled in size without loss of resolution. Bitmaps don't work that way; if you display a bitmap at twice the size, you don't get twice the resolution. The bits in the bitmap are simply replicated horizontally or vertically. Any smoothing that might be imposed on the display may eliminate jaggies, but at the cost of making the image fuzzier.

A metafile can be converted to a bitmap, but with some loss of information: the graphical objects that make up the metafile are no longer separate and become blended together in one big image. Converting bitmaps to metafiles is a much more difficult job, usually restricted to very simple images and requiring a lot of processing power to analyze edges and outlines. However, as I noted earlier, a metafile can contain an embedded bitmap.

Metafiles are used most often these days for sharing pictures among programs through the clipboard and for clip art. Because metafiles describe a picture as a collection of graphics function calls, they generally take up much less space and are more device independent than bitmaps.

However, rendering a metafile can be slower than rendering a bitmap containing the same image. A bitmap of a particular size and color format takes the same time to display regardless of the complexity of the image. The time it takes to display a metafile is directly related to the number of drawing commands it contains.

Don't confuse metafiles with graphics paths! A path is simply a collection of coordinates; a metafile includes specifications of pens and brushes as well. A path stores text as a series of character outlines; a metafile stores the arguments to the actual *DrawString* call. There are no standard formats for saving paths to files or passing them through the clipboard. Metafiles have been *designed* to be saved as files and passed through the clipboard. (I'll discuss using metafiles with the clipboard in Chapter 24.)

Metafiles have been supported under Windows since version 1.0 (1985). The original metafile format is now referred to as the Windows Metafile and is associated with a filename extension of .wmf. Metafiles were enhanced with the introduction of the 32-bit versions of Windows. The 32-bit versions of Windows continued to support the old metafile format and also introduced a new metafile format, called the Enhanced Metafile and associated with a filename extension of .emf.

The GDI+ graphics system in Windows Forms introduces a number of new drawing commands, and these commands affect metafiles as well. Enhanced metafiles that contain GDI+ drawing commands are referred to as EMF+ ("EMF plus") metafiles, but the filename extension is still .emf. It's also possible to create metafiles from a Windows Forms program that are compatible with the original EMF format and readable by regular old 32-bit Windows programs.

# Loading and Rendering Existing Metafiles

You already know from Chapter 11 how to load and display metafiles. You can use the same shared *FromFile* method of the *Image* class to load a metafile from disk just as you can load a bitmap image from disk:

```
Dim img As Image = Image.FromFile("PrettyPicture.emf")
```

You can also display this metafile in the same way you display a bitmap. Use one of the many *DrawImage* methods of the *Graphics* class:

```
grfx.DrawImage(img, x, y)
```

If you have any WMF or EMF files on your hard drive (and it's likely you do if you've installed any application that has a clip art library), you can use the ImageIO program from Chapter 16 to load and display those metafiles. Even Microsoft Visual Studio .NET (but not, alas, Microsoft Visual Basic .NET) comes with a collection of metafiles located by default in the C:\Program Files\Microsoft Visual Studio .NET\Common7\Graphics\Metafile directory.

Metafiles are considered to be images because—like the *Bitmap* class— the *Metafile* class is descended from *Image*:

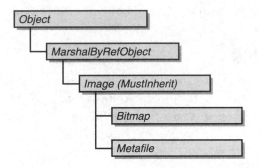

Also like *Bitmap*, the *Metafile* class is *NotInheritable*. Although the *Image* and *Bitmap* classes are defined in the *System.Drawing* namespace, *Metafile* and its related classes and enumerations are defined in the *System.Drawing.Imaging* namespace. If you call *GetType* on the return value of *Image.FromFile*, you'll get a type of either *System.Drawing.Bitmap* or *System.Drawing.Imaging.Metafile*.

Watch out for the terminology involving metafiles and *Metafile* objects. A metafile is a collection of drawing commands that can exist in a disk file or in memory. A *Metafile* object is an instance of the *Metafile* class. The shared *From-File* method of the *Image* class creates a *Metafile* object based on an existing metafile.

The bulk of the *Metafile* class is its 39 constructors, but some constructors are much simpler than others. To create a *Metafile* object from an existing metafile referenced by either a filename or a *Stream* object, you can use the following two constructors:

### *Metafile* Constructors (selection)

```
Metafile(ByVal strFileName As String)
Metafile(ByVal strm As Stream)
```

These two constructors are essentially equivalent to the corresponding shared *FromFile* methods of the *Image* class except (of course) the constructors explicitly return an object of type *Metafile*:

```
Dim mf As New Metafile("PrettyPicture.emf")
```

Because *Metafile* is descended from *Image*, you use the same methods for displaying the metafile:

```
grfx.DrawImage(mf, x, y)
```

Indeed, you can do just about anything with the metafile that is supported by the *Image* class. If you've loaded an existing metafile from a file or stream, however, you can't use the shared *FromImage* method of the *Graphics* class to obtain a *Graphics* object for drawing on the metafile. That method is reserved for metafiles that you create anew in your programs.

# Metafile Sizes and Rendering

As you'll recall from Chapter 11, the *Image* class has several properties that describe the image. Because *Metafile* is descended from *Image*, these properties also apply to metafiles. In particular, you'll find the following properties useful when working with metafiles:

### *Image* Properties (selection)

| Property | Type | Accessibility |
|---|---|---|
| *Size* | *Size* | Get |
| *Width* | *Integer* | Get |
| *Height* | *Integer* | Get |
| *HorizontalResolution* | *Single* | Get |
| *VerticalResolution* | *Single* | Get |
| *PhysicalDimension* | *SizeF* | Get |

As you'll recall, for *Bitmap* objects, the *Size*, *Width*, and *Height* properties indicate the pixel dimension of the bitmap—the number of rows and columns of bits. The *HorizontalResolution* and *VerticalResolution* properties report information that's probably encoded in the bitmap: the number of pixels per inch horizontally and vertically. You can easily calculate a metrical size of the bitmap in inches by dividing the *Width* by the *HorizontalResolution* and the *Height* by the *VerticalResolution*. If you convert those dimensions to millimeters and multiply by 100, you should get numbers equal to the *PhysicalDimension* property, which should be the size of the bitmap in units of hundredths of millimeters. *PhysicalDimension* doesn't work right for bitmaps, however.

For *Metafile* objects, the *Size*, *Width*, and *Height* properties are a little different. In many cases, these properties reflect the extents of the coordinates and sizes of all the objects in the metafile. For example, if the metafile consisted of a single *DrawLine* call with endpoint coordinates of (–50, 25) and (100, 250), the *Width* would probably be 150 (or thereabouts) and the *Height* would be 225 (or so). However, as we'll see shortly, the creator of the metafile can set the *Width* and *Height* properties to something different. Also, wide lines could affect the size of the image and hence the *Width* and *Height* properties. So, even though metafiles don't have pixels, they have something equivalent to a pixel size.

*Metafile* objects also have valid *HorizontalResolution* and *VerticalResolution* properties that indicate how the coordinates of the metafile relate to inches. That hypothetical metafile with a single *DrawLine* call might have *Horizontal-Resolution* and *VerticalResolution* values of 75, so the image would be 2 inches wide and 3 inches high. The *PhysicalDimension* property (which seems to work better for metafiles than for bitmaps) would be (5080, 7620) in this case—the size in hundredths of millimeters.

To display a metafile in its metrical size with the upper left corner at the point (*x*, *y*), use

```
grfx.DrawImage(mf, x, y)
```

or one of the *DrawImage* variants that uses *Point* or *PointF* arguments. The displayed size of the image is not affected by the page transform but is affected by the world transform.

The following *DrawImage* method—and its variants using *Rectangle* and *RectangleF* arguments—displays a metafile stretched to the rectangle:

```
grfx.DrawImage(mf, x, y, cx, cy)
```

Both the page transform and the world transform affect the interpretation of the *x*, *y*, *cx*, and *cy* arguments. To display a metafile in its pixel size, set page units to pixels and use

```
grfx.DrawImage(mf, x, y, mf.Width, mf.Height)
```

The *Metafile* class has no additional public properties beyond what it inherits from the *Image* class. However, the metafile itself has a header that provides additional information about the metafile. The metafile header is encapsulated in the *MetafileHeader* class. You can obtain an object of *Metafile-Header* using the following instance method:

### *Metafile* Nonshared *GetMetafileHeader* Method

```
Function GetMetafileHeader() As MetafileHeader
```

Or, for a metafile for which you don't have a *Metafile* object, you can use one of the following shared methods:

### *Metafile* Shared *GetMetafileHeader* Methods (selection)

```
Function GetMetafileHeader(ByVal strFileName As String) As MetafileHeader
Function GetMetafileHeader(ByVal strm As Stream) As MetafileHeader
```

There are two additional shared *GetMetafileHeader* methods for use with Win32 handles to a metafile or an enhanced metafile.

The *MetafileHeader* class has 10 read-only properties. Here are 5 of them:

### *MetafileHeader* Properties (selection)

| Property | Type | Accessibility |
| --- | --- | --- |
| *Type* | *MetafileType* | Get |
| *Version* | *Integer* | Get |
| *MetafileSize* | *Integer* | Get |
| *EmfPlusHeaderSize* | *Integer* | Get |
| *WmfHeader* | *MetaHeader* | Get |

The *Type* property indicates the type of the metafile based on the *MetafileType* enumeration:

### *MetafileType* Enumeration

| Member | Value |
| --- | --- |
| *Invalid* | 0 |
| *Wmf* | 1 |
| *WmfPlaceable* | 2 |
| *Emf* | 3 |
| *EmfPlusOnly* | 4 |
| *EmfPlusDual* | 5 |

The *Wmf* members identify the old 16-bit metafiles. An *Emf* metafile was created by a 32-bit Windows program using the Windows API or MFC. By default (as we'll see), the metafiles created by a Windows Forms program are of type *Emf-PlusDual*, which means that they contain both GDI and GDI+ records. Such metafiles are usable by Win32 and Windows Forms programs. An *EmfPlusOnly* metafile contains only GDI+ records and is usable only by Windows Forms programs.

The *MetafileSize* property indicates the actual storage size of the entire metafile. For metafiles stored on disk, it's equal to the file size. For WMF types, the *WmfHeader* property has additional information about the metafile.

The following are all the methods of *MetafileHeader*, which mostly provide a *Boolean* interface to the *Type* property:

### *MetafileHeader* Methods

```
Function IsWmf() As Boolean

Function IsWmfPlaceable() As Boolean

Function IsEmf() As Boolean

Function IsEmfPlus() As Boolean

Function IsEmfPlusOnly() As Boolean

Function IsEmfPlusDual() As Boolean

Function IsEmfOrEmfPlus() As Boolean

Function IsDisplay() As Boolean
```

For *MetafileType.Emf* metafiles, the *IsEmf* and *IsEmfOrEmfPlus* methods return *True*. For *MetafileType.EmfPlusOnly* metafiles, *IsEmfPlus*, *IsEmfPlusOnly*, and *IsEmfOrEmfPlus* return *True*. For *MetafileType.EmfPlusDual* metafiles, *IsEmfPlus*, *IsEmfPlusDual*, and *IsEmfOrEmfPlus* return *True*.

As we'll see, a metafile is always created based on a particular graphics output device. The *IsDisplay* method returns *True* for a metafile based on the video display and *False* for a metafile based on a printer.

These are the remaining *MetafileHeader* properties:

### *MetafileHeader* Properties (selection)

| Property | Type | Accessibility |
| --- | --- | --- |
| *Bounds* | *Rectangle* | Get |
| *DpiX* | *Single* | Get |
| *DpiY* | *Single* | Get |
| *LogicalDpiX* | *Integer* | Get |
| *LogicalDpiY* | *Integer* | Get |

The *Width* and *Height* of the *Bounds* property should agree with the *Width* and *Height* properties that the *Metafile* object inherits from *Image*. The *DpiX* and *DpiY* properties should agree with the *HorizontalResolution* and *VerticalResolution* properties of the *Image* class. The *LogicalDpiX* and *LogicalDpiY* properties don't have any relevance for Windows Forms programs, and you should ignore them.

The *X* and *Y* properties of the *Bounds* property aren't necessarily 0. For example, earlier I discussed a hypothetical metafile that consisted of a sole *DrawLine* call with coordinates of (–50, 25) and (100, 250). The *Bounds* property of the metafile header is generally the smallest rectangle that encloses all the graphical objects in the metafile. A simple calculation predicts that the *Bounds* property will be the rectangle (–50, 25, 150, 225).

Actually, in this case, you're more likely to see a *Bounds* property of (–51, 24, 153, 228). Because GDI+ draws lines up to and including the second point, the line is actually a pixel longer than simple arithmetic would dictate. Also, the line has a finite width, which increases the total dimension by another pixel on either end. Moreover, the program creating the metafile can set a *Bounds* property other than what the contents of the metafile would imply.

The origin of the *Bounds* rectangle—that is, its *X* and *Y* properties—doesn't affect the positioning of the metafile when you render it. For example, if you draw the hypothetical simple metafile I've been discussing using the call

```
grfx.DrawImage(mf, 0, 0)
```

you'll see the whole metafile. The upper left corner of the *Bounds* rectangle is displayed at the point specified in the *DrawImage* call, in this example, the point (0, 0).

Here's a program that has an *OpenFileDialog* object configured to load disk-based metafiles and display them.

**MetafileViewer.vb**

```
'-------------------------------------------------
' MetafileViewer.vb (c) 2002 by Charles Petzold
'-------------------------------------------------
Imports System
Imports System.Drawing
Imports System.Drawing.Imaging
Imports System.Drawing.Printing
Imports System.IO                    ' For Path class
Imports System.Windows.Forms

Class MetafileViewer
    Inherits Form

    Protected mf As Metafile
    Protected strProgName As String
    Protected strFileName As String
    Private miFileSaveAs, miFilePrint, _
            miFileProps, miViewChecked As MenuItem
```

```
Shared Sub Main()
    Application.Run(New MetafileViewer())
End Sub

Sub New()
    strProgName = "Metafile Viewer"
    Text = strProgName
    ResizeRedraw = True

    Menu = New MainMenu()

    ' File menu
    Dim mi As New MenuItem("&File")
    AddHandler mi.Popup, AddressOf MenuFileOnPopup
    Menu.MenuItems.Add(mi)

    ' File Open menu item
    mi = New MenuItem("&Open...")
    AddHandler mi.Click, AddressOf MenuFileOpenOnClick
    mi.Shortcut = Shortcut.CtrlO
    Menu.MenuItems(0).MenuItems.Add(mi)

    ' File Save As Bitmap menu item
    miFileSaveAs = New MenuItem("Save &As Bitmap...")
    AddHandler miFileSaveAs.Click, AddressOf MenuFileSaveAsOnClick
    Menu.MenuItems(0).MenuItems.Add(miFileSaveAs)
    Menu.MenuItems(0).MenuItems.Add("-")

    ' File Print menu item
    miFilePrint = New MenuItem("&Print...")
    AddHandler miFilePrint.Click, AddressOf MenuFilePrintOnClick
    Menu.MenuItems(0).MenuItems.Add(miFilePrint)
    Menu.MenuItems(0).MenuItems.Add("-")

    ' File Properties menu item
    miFileProps = New MenuItem("Propert&ies...")
    AddHandler miFileProps.Click, AddressOf MenuFilePropsOnClick
    Menu.MenuItems(0).MenuItems.Add(miFileProps)

    ' Edit menu (temporary until Chapter 24)
    Menu.MenuItems.Add("&Edit")

    ' View menu
    Menu.MenuItems.Add("&View")
    Dim astr As String() = {"&Stretched to Window", _
                            "&Metrical Size", "&Pixel Size"}
    Dim eh As EventHandler = AddressOf MenuViewOnClick
    Dim str As String
    For Each str In astr
        Menu.MenuItems(2).MenuItems.Add(str, eh)
    Next str
    miViewChecked = Menu.MenuItems(2).MenuItems(0)
```

*(continued)*

**MetafileViewer.vb** *(continued)*

```
        miViewChecked.Checked = True
    End Sub

    Private Sub MenuFileOnPopup(ByVal obj As Object, ByVal ea As EventArgs)
        Dim bEnabled As Boolean = Not mf Is Nothing

        miFilePrint.Enabled = bEnabled
        miFileSaveAs.Enabled = bEnabled
        miFileProps.Enabled = bEnabled
    End Sub

    Private Sub MenuFileOpenOnClick(ByVal obj As Object, _
                                    ByVal ea As EventArgs)
        Dim dlg As New OpenFileDialog()
        dlg.Filter = "All Metafiles|*.wmf;.emf|" & _
                     "Windows Metafile (*.wmf)|*.wmf|" & _
                     "Enhanced Metafile (*.emf)|*.emf|" & _
                     "All files|*.*"
        If dlg.ShowDialog() = DialogResult.OK Then
            Try
                mf = New Metafile(dlg.FileName)
            Catch exc As Exception
                MessageBox.Show(exc.Message, strProgName)
                Return
            End Try
            strFileName = dlg.FileName
            Text = strProgName & " - " & Path.GetFileName(strFileName)
            Invalidate()
        End If
    End Sub

    Protected Overridable Sub MenuFileSaveAsOnClick(ByVal obj As Object, _
                                                    ByVal ea As EventArgs)
        MessageBox.Show("Not yet implemented!", strProgName)
    End Sub

    Private Sub MenuFilePrintOnClick(ByVal obj As Object, _
                                     ByVal ea As EventArgs)
        Dim prndoc As New PrintDocument()
        prndoc.DocumentName = Text
        AddHandler prndoc.PrintPage, AddressOf OnPrintPage
        prndoc.Print()
    End Sub

    Private Sub MenuFilePropsOnClick(ByVal obj As Object, _
                                     ByVal ea As EventArgs)
        Dim mh As MetafileHeader = mf.GetMetafileHeader()
        Dim str As String = _
            "Image Properties" & _
            vbLf & vbTab & "Size = " & mf.Size.ToString() & _
            vbLf & vbTab & "Horizontal Resolution = " & _
            mf.HorizontalResolution & _
```

```
                    vbLf & vbTab & "Vertical Resolution = " & _
            mf.VerticalResolution & _
            vbLf & vbTab & "Physical Dimension = " & _
            mf.PhysicalDimension.ToString() & _
            vbLf & vbLf & "Metafile Header Properties" & _
            vbLf & vbTab & "Bounds = " & mh.Bounds.ToString() & _
            vbLf & vbTab & "DpiX = " & mh.DpiX & _
            vbLf & vbTab & "DpiY = " & mh.DpiY & _
            vbLf & vbTab & "LogicalDpiX = " & mh.LogicalDpiX & _
            vbLf & vbTab & "LogicalDpiY = " & mh.LogicalDpiY & _
            vbLf & vbTab & "Type = " & mh.Type & _
            vbLf & vbTab & "Version = " & mh.Version & _
            vbLf & vbTab & "MetafileSize = " & mh.MetafileSize
        MessageBox.Show(str, Text)
    End Sub

    Private Sub MenuViewOnClick(ByVal obj As Object, ByVal ea As EventArgs)
        miViewChecked.Checked = False
        miViewChecked = DirectCast(obj, MenuItem)
        miViewChecked.Checked = True
        Invalidate()
    End Sub

    Private Sub OnPrintPage(ByVal obj As Object, _
                            ByVal ppea As PrintPageEventArgs)
        Dim grfx As Graphics = ppea.Graphics
        Dim rect As New Rectangle( _
            ppea.MarginBounds.Left - _
            (ppea.PageBounds.Width - _
                CInt(grfx.VisibleClipBounds.Width)) \ 2, _
            ppea.MarginBounds.Top - _
            (ppea.PageBounds.Height - _
                CInt(grfx.VisibleClipBounds.Height)) \ 2, _
            ppea.MarginBounds.Width, _
            ppea.MarginBounds.Height)
        DisplayMetafile(grfx, rect)
    End Sub

    Protected Overrides Sub OnPaint(ByVal pea As PaintEventArgs)
        If Not mf Is Nothing Then
            DisplayMetafile(pea.Graphics, ClientRectangle)
        End If
    End Sub

    Private Sub DisplayMetafile(ByVal grfx As Graphics, _
                                ByVal rect As Rectangle)
        Select Case miViewChecked.Index
            Case 0 : grfx.DrawImage(mf, rect)
            Case 1 : grfx.DrawImage(mf, rect.X, rect.Y)
            Case 2 : grfx.DrawImage(mf, rect.X, rect.Y, mf.Width, mf.Height)
        End Select
    End Sub
End Class
```

This program has a couple features that go beyond the ImageOpen program from Chapter 16 (which also can load and display metafiles). First, it has a Properties item on the File menu that displays the most important information about the metafile from the *Image* and *MetafileHeader* properties. It also has a menu item to select three different ways of displaying the metafile using *DrawImage*. The Print option lets you print the metafile based on that menu selection.

Several menu items are not yet implemented. The program has an entire Edit menu that I'll show code for in Chapter 24. The File menu also has an unimplemented Save As Bitmap item that I'll go over in the next section.

# Converting Metafiles to Bitmaps

I mentioned earlier that it's easy to convert a metafile into a bitmap. In fact, the facility is built into Windows Forms. If you use the ImageIO program to load a metafile, you can save it as a bitmap.

It's possible that you'll want to perform this conversion yourself, either to maintain more control over the process or when you don't want to save the bitmap to a disk file. Perhaps you're dealing with a metafile that contains lots of drawing commands and converting it to a bitmap would speed up the display.

The following program inherits from MetafileViewer and includes a method called *MetafileToBitmap* that converts a *Metafile* object to a *Bitmap* object. The program ends up saving the bitmap to a disk file anyway (just as ImageIO does), but you can use the method for other purposes as well.

```
MetafileConvert.vb
'------------------------------------------------
' MetafileConvert.vb (c) 2002 by Charles Petzold
'------------------------------------------------
Imports System
Imports System.Drawing
Imports System.Drawing.Imaging
Imports System.IO                    ' For Path class
Imports System.Windows.Forms

Class MetafileConvert
    Inherits MetafileViewer

    Shared Shadows Sub Main()
        Application.Run(new MetafileConvert())
    End Sub

    Sub New()
        strProgName = "Metafile Convert"
```

```
        Text = strProgName
    End Sub

    Protected Overrides Sub MenuFileSaveAsOnClick(ByVal obj As Object, _
                                      ByVal ea As EventArgs)
        Dim dlg As New SaveFileDialog()
        If Not strFileName Is Nothing AndAlso strFileName.Length > 0 Then
            dlg.InitialDirectory = Path.GetDirectoryName(strFileName)
        End If
        dlg.FileName = Path.GetFileNameWithoutExtension(strFileName)
        dlg.AddExtension = True
        dlg.Filter = "Windows Bitmap (*.bmp)|*.bmp|" & _
                     "Graphics Interchange Format (*.gif)|*.gif|" & _
                     "JPEG File Interchange Format (*.jpg)|" & _
                         "*.jpg;*.jpeg;*.jfif|" & _
                     "Portable Network Graphics (*.png)|*.png|" & _
                     "Tagged Image File Format (*.tif)|*.tif;*.tiff"

        Dim aif As ImageFormat() = {ImageFormat.Bmp, ImageFormat.Gif, _
                          ImageFormat.Jpeg, ImageFormat.Png, _
                          ImageFormat.Tiff}

        If dlg.ShowDialog() = DialogResult.OK Then
            Dim bm As Bitmap = MetafileToBitmap(mf)
            Try
                bm.Save(dlg.FileName, aif(dlg.FilterIndex - 1))
            Catch exc As Exception
                MessageBox.Show(exc.Message, Text)
            End Try
        End If
    End Sub

    Private Function MetafileToBitmap(ByVal mf As Metafile) As Bitmap
        Dim grfx As Graphics = CreateGraphics()
        Dim cx As Integer = CInt(grfx.DpiX * mf.Width / _
                                      mf.HorizontalResolution)
        Dim cy As Integer = CInt(grfx.DpiY * mf.Height / _
                                      mf.VerticalResolution)
        Dim bm As New Bitmap(cx, cy, grfx)
        grfx.Dispose()

        grfx = Graphics.FromImage(bm)
        grfx.DrawImage(mf, 0, 0, cx, cy)
        grfx.Dispose()
        Return bm
    End Function
End Class
```

To convert a metafile to a bitmap, you must first create a *Bitmap* object of a particular size. Then you obtain a *Graphics* object to draw on the bitmap:

```
grfx = Graphics.FromImage(bm)
```

If the size of the bitmap is stored in the variables *cx* and *cy*, you can cover the bitmap with the metafile by using the following code:

```
grfx.DrawImage(mf, 0, 0, cx, cy)
```

These two lines of code will work regardless of the size of the bitmap you create. If you need to display a metafile image on a button, for example, you'll want to make the bitmap the size of the button.

The *MetafileToBitmap* method in the MetafileConvert program creates a bitmap that's based on the metrical size of the metafile. The *Bitmap* constructor used in this method includes a *Graphics* object, in this case a *Graphics* object for the video display. The bitmap will thus have the same resolution as the video display. From that resolution—and the size and resolution of the metafile—it's easy to calculate the pixel size of the bitmap.

The bitmap that *MetafileToBitmap* creates is the same size as the bitmap the *Save* method of *Image* creates when it converts a metafile to a bitmap.

Another approach to converting a metafile to a bitmap is so simple and straightforward that it eluded me for a long time. As you'll recall, one of the *Bitmap* constructors takes a single *Image* argument. That argument can be a *Metafile* object:

```
Dim bm As New Bitmap(mf)
```

The resultant bitmap has the same pixel size as the original metafile but with the resolution of the video display.

# Creating New Metafiles

So far, I've discussed only 2 of the 39 *Metafile* constructors. Those two constructors are the only ones that directly load an existing metafile based on a filename or a *Stream*. Three of the *Metafile* constructors create a metafile object based on Win32 metafile handles and are useful for interfacing with existing code. The remaining 34 constructors to *Metafile* create a new metafile, which very often means that the constructors create a new disk file or delete the contents of an existing file in preparation for creating a new metafile. Here are the two simplest constructors that create a new metafile:

### *Metafile* Constructors (selection)

```
Metafile(ByVal strFileName As String, ByVal ipHdc As IntPtr)
Metafile(ByVal strm As Stream, ByVal ipHdc As IntPtr)
```

That second argument is quite an oddity. The metafile needs to be associated with a particular graphics output device in order to obtain resolution information. It would make more sense for the second argument to be a *Graphics* object, like so:

```
Dim mf As New Metafile("NewFile.emf", grfx)    ' Wrong, unfortunately!
```

This functionality would match that of the *Bitmap* constructor in the *Metafile-ToBitmap* method I just described.

Instead, the second argument to the *Metafile* constructor is defined as a Win32 device context handle. The *Graphics* object encapsulates the Win32 device context, so you need to use the *GetHdc* and *ReleaseHdc* methods of the *Graphics* class to obtain and release this handle:

```
Dim ipHdc As IntPtr = grfx.GetHdc()
Dim mf As New Metafile("NewFile.emf", ipHdc)
grfx.ReleaseHdc(ipHdc)
```

In most cases, you'll want to create a metafile that is based on the resolution of the video display, but you won't be creating a new metafile in your *OnPaint* method. Instead, as you know, in any class descended from *Control*, you can use the *CreateGraphics* method to obtain such a *Graphics* object. You should call *Dispose* on this *Graphics* object after you're finished using it, so your creation of a new metafile will look something like this:

```
Dim grfxVideo As Graphics = CreateGraphics()
Dim ipHdc As IntPtr = grfxVideo.GetHdc()
Dim mf As New Metafile("NewFile.emf", ipHdc)
grfxVideo.ReleaseHdc(ipHdc)
grfxVideo.Dispose()
```

This code is certainly wordier than equivalent Win32 code. One option of the Win32 metafile-creation function lets you specify a *Nothing* device to indicate the video display, but unfortunately, that option isn't allowed in the *Metafile* constructor.

After you've created the metafile, you must obtain another *Graphics* object to insert drawing commands in the metafile. You obtain this *Graphics* object by using the same shared method you use for drawing on a bitmap:

```
Dim grfxMetafile As Graphics = Graphics.FromImage(mf)
```

For purposes of clarity, I've given these two different *Graphics* objects different names. But because they don't overlap, you can use just one *Graphics* variable if that's convenient.

With the *Graphics* object obtained from the *FromImage* method, you can call any drawing method. A coded record of each method ends up in the metafile. The *Graphics* class also has a method that can be used only with metafiles:

### *Graphics* Methods (selection)

```
Sub AddMetafileComment(ByVal abyData() As Byte)
```

After drawing on the metafile, you'll also want to call *Dispose* on this second *Graphics* object:

```
grfxMetafile.Dispose()
```

Here's a small program that inherits from *PrintableForm* and creates a metafile in its constructor. In its *DoPage* method, the CreateMetafile program obtains the size of the metafile and uses that to display multiple copies in its client area or on the printer page.

**CreateMetafile.vb**

```
'----------------------------------------------------------
' CreateMetafile.vb (c) 2002 by Charles Petzold
'----------------------------------------------------------
Imports System
Imports System.Drawing
Imports System.Drawing.Imaging
Imports System.IO                       ' Not used for anything yet!
Imports System.Windows.Forms

Class CreateMetafile
    Inherits PrintableForm

    Private mf As Metafile

    Shared Shadows Sub Main()
        Application.Run(New CreateMetafile())
    End Sub

    Sub New()
        Text = "Create Metafile"

        ' Create the metafile.
        Dim grfx As Graphics = CreateGraphics()
        Dim ipHdc As IntPtr = grfx.GetHdc()
        mf = New Metafile("CreateMetafile.emf", ipHdc)
        grfx.ReleaseHdc(ipHdc)
        grfx.Dispose()

        ' Draw on the metafile.
        grfx = Graphics.FromImage(mf)

        grfx.FillEllipse(Brushes.Gray, 0, 0, 100, 100)
        grfx.DrawEllipse(Pens.Black, 0, 0, 100, 100)
        grfx.FillEllipse(Brushes.Blue, 20, 20, 20, 20)
        grfx.FillEllipse(Brushes.Blue, 60, 20, 20, 20)
```

```
        grfx.DrawArc(New Pen(Color.Red, 10), 20, 20, 60, 60, 30, 120)
        grfx.Dispose()
    End Sub

    Protected Overrides Sub DoPage(ByVal grfx As Graphics, _
            ByVal clr As Color, ByVal cx As Integer, ByVal cy As Integer)
        Dim x, y As Integer

        For y = 0 To cy Step mf.Height
            For x = 0 To cx Step mf.Width
                grfx.DrawImage(mf, x, y, mf.Width, mf.Height)
            Next x
        Next y
    End Sub
End Class
```

The image contained in the metafile consists of calls to *DrawEllipse*, *Fill-Ellipse*, and *DrawArc*. These calls—with the proper pens and brushes—are rendered on the client area by the program's *DoPage* method. The program uses *DrawImage* with width and height arguments to draw the image in its pixel dimension:

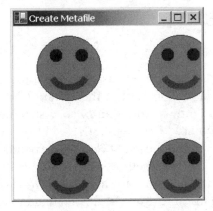

The only peculiarity you might observe is that these multiple images aren't pressed up against each other. The margin around each image is one of the side effects of the technique that the *Metafile* class uses to convert floating-point coordinates in GDI+ curves to integer coordinates in GDI metafile records. We'll see shortly how you can control the dimensions of this boundary so that the overindulgent margins go away.

The CreateMetafile program uses this form of the *DrawImage* method to render the metafile in its pixel (rather than metrical) size:

```
grfx.DrawImage(mf, x, y, mf.Width, mf.Height)
```

For the video display, I could just as easily display the metafile in its metrical size:

```
grfx.DrawImage(mf, x, y)
```

Because the metafile has the same resolution as the video display, the results would be the same. However, the two versions of *DrawImage* would probably render different-sized images on the printer. As with bitmaps, it's easier to accurately position metafiles when displaying them in their pixel size.

An alternative is replacing the entire body of *DoPage* with the following statement:

```
grfx.FillRectangle(New TextureBrush(mf), 0, 0, cx, cy)
```

This statement fills the client area with a *TextureBrush* object created from the metafile. And you probably thought texture brushes could only be created from bitmaps!

Every time you run the CreateMetafile program, it re-creates a file named CreateMetafile.emf. But re-creating that file each time is unnecessary. You might try inserting the following code in the *CreateMetafile* constructor right after the assignment of the *Text* property:

```
If File.Exists("CreateMetafile.emf") Then
    mf = New Metafile("CreateMetafile.emf")
    Return
End If
```

This code loads the metafile if it exists and then exits from the constructor. (The shared *Exists* method of the *File* class is defined in the *System.IO* namespace. The CreateMetafile program conveniently includes an *Imports* statement for this namespace, even though it's not required for anything else in the program.)

The CreateMetafile program retains the *Metafile* object (named *mf*) as a field. Doing so is necessary for the *DoPage* method to use the metafile that the constructor creates. But it isn't strictly necessary to save the *Metafile* object. The *DoPage* method itself can load the metafile. The CreateMetafileReload program is similar to CreateMetafile where the constructor creates the metafile only if it doesn't exist. But the *Metafile* object isn't saved as a field. Instead, the filename is stored as a field and the *DoPage* method loads the metafile itself.

### CreateMetafileReload.vb

```
'-----------------------------------------------------------
' CreateMetafileReload.vb (c) 2002 by Charles Petzold
'-----------------------------------------------------------
Imports System
Imports System.Drawing
Imports System.Drawing.Imaging
```

```
Imports System.IO
Imports System.Windows.Forms

Class CreateMetafileReload
    Inherits PrintableForm

    Const strMetafile As String = "CreateMetafileReload.emf"

    Shared Shadows Sub Main()
        Application.Run(New CreateMetafileReload())
    End Sub

    Sub New()
        Text = "Create Metafile (Reload)"
        If Not File.Exists(strMetafile) Then

            ' Create the metafile.
            Dim grfx As Graphics = CreateGraphics()
            Dim ipHdc As IntPtr = grfx.GetHdc()
            Dim mf As New Metafile(strMetafile, ipHdc)
            grfx.ReleaseHdc(ipHdc)
            grfx.Dispose()

            ' Draw on the metafile.
            grfx = Graphics.FromImage(mf)
            grfx.FillEllipse(Brushes.Gray, 0, 0, 100, 100)
            grfx.DrawEllipse(Pens.Black, 0, 0, 100, 100)
            grfx.FillEllipse(Brushes.Blue, 20, 20, 20, 20)
            grfx.FillEllipse(Brushes.Blue, 60, 20, 20, 20)
            grfx.DrawArc(New Pen(Color.Red, 10), 20, 20, 60, 60, 30, 120)
            grfx.Dispose()
        End If
    End Sub

    Protected Overrides Sub DoPage(ByVal grfx As Graphics, _
            ByVal clr As Color, ByVal cx As Integer, ByVal cy As Integer)
        Dim mf As New Metafile(strMetafile)
        Dim x, y As Integer

        For y = 0 To cy Step mf.Height
            For x = 0 To cx - 1 Step mf.Width
                grfx.DrawImage(mf, x, y, mf.Width, mf.Height)
            Next x
        Next y
    End Sub
End Class
```

I've been demonstrating the use of *Metafile* constructors with *String* arguments indicating filenames. You can also specify a *Stream* argument. For example, you can replace the constructor in the *DoPage* method with the following code and it will work the same:

```
Dim fs As New FileStream(strMetafile, FileMode.Open)
Dim mf As New Metafile(fs)
fs.Close()
```

What *won't* work is a *FileStream* constructor that opens the file for writing only or a *FileMode* argument that destroys the contents of the file.

Similarly, you can use a *FileStream* object in the program's constructor to create the *Metafile* object:

```
Dim fs As New FileStream(strMetafile, FileMode.Create)
Dim mf As New Metafile(fs, ipHdc)
```

Notice that this *FileMode* argument indicates that the file should be re-created. After all the *Graphics* calls have been made to insert commands into the metafile, close the stream:

```
fs.Close()
```

It's also possible to use a *MemoryStream* object to create the metafile in memory. Because *MemoryStream* objects don't have names, a program must retain either the *MemoryStream* object or the *Metafile* object as a field.

Let's go back to the original CreateMetafile program. If you earlier followed my suggestions by inserting a block of code that called *File.Exists*, remove it. Now replace the *Metafile* constructor

```
mf = New Metafile("CreateMetafile.emf", ipHdc)
```

with this one:

```
mf = New Metafile(New MemoryStream(), ipHdc)
```

*MemoryStream* is defined in the *System.IO* namespace. With this variation of the constructor, the metafile is created and accessed in memory. No file is left behind.

In the following program, the *MemoryStream* object (but not the *Metafile* object) is stored as a field.

**CreateMetafileMemory.vb**

```
'-------------------------------------------------------------
' CreateMetafileMemory.vb (c) 2002 by Charles Petzold
'-------------------------------------------------------------
Imports System
Imports System.Drawing
Imports System.Drawing.Imaging
Imports System.IO
Imports System.Windows.Forms
```

```
Class CreateMetafileMemory
    Inherits PrintableForm

    ReadOnly ms As MemoryStream = New MemoryStream()

    Shared Shadows Sub Main()
        Application.Run(New CreateMetafileMemory())
    End Sub

    Sub New()
        Text = "Create Metafile (Memory)"

        ' Create the metafile.
        Dim grfx As Graphics = CreateGraphics()
        Dim ipHdc As IntPtr = grfx.GetHdc()
        Dim mf As New Metafile(ms, ipHdc)
        grfx.ReleaseHdc(ipHdc)
        grfx.Dispose()

        ' Draw on the metafile.
        grfx = Graphics.FromImage(mf)
        grfx.FillEllipse(Brushes.Gray, 0, 0, 100, 100)
        grfx.DrawEllipse(Pens.Black, 0, 0, 100, 100)
        grfx.FillEllipse(Brushes.Blue, 20, 20, 20, 20)
        grfx.FillEllipse(Brushes.Blue, 60, 20, 20, 20)
        grfx.DrawArc(New Pen(Color.Red, 10), 20, 20, 60, 60, 30, 120)
        grfx.Dispose()
    End Sub

    Protected Overrides Sub DoPage(ByVal grfx As Graphics, _
            ByVal clr As Color, ByVal cx As Integer, ByVal cy As Integer)
        ms.Position = 0
        Dim mf As New Metafile(ms)
        Dim x, y As Integer

        For y = 0 To cy Step mf.Height
            For x = 0 To cx Step mf.Width
                grfx.DrawImage(mf, x, y, mf.Width, mf.Height)
            Next x
        Next y
    End Sub
End Class
```

Notice that the first statement of the *DoPage* method sets the position of the *MemoryStream* object back to 0. Otherwise, an exception is thrown that is very hard to diagnose.

Creating a metafile in memory is useful if you just need to pass a metafile through the clipboard. You'll see how to use the clipboard to copy and paste metafiles in Chapter 24.

# The Metafile Boundary Rectangle

When you insert *Graphics* drawing commands into a metafile, the metafile calculates a boundary rectangle. This is the smallest rectangle that encompasses all the objects stored in the metafile. You can obtain the width and height of this boundary rectangle by using the *Size*, *Width*, and *Height* properties that the *Metafile* class inherits from *Image*. Or you can obtain the complete boundary rectangle from the *Bounds* property of the *MetafileHeader* object associated with the metafile. The programs shown so far in this chapter demonstrate that the metafile often calculates a boundary rectangle that is larger than the contents would imply. If you want total control over the boundary, you can use alternative versions of the *Metafile* constructor. Here are four versions that let you specify a boundary rectangle when creating a metafile stored in a file:

### *Metafile* Constructors (selection)

```
Metafile(ByVal strFileName As String, ByVal ipHdc As IntPtr,
        ByVal rect As Rectangle)

Metafile(ByVal strFileName As String, ByVal ipHdc As IntPtr,
        ByVal rectf As RectangleF)

Metafile(ByVal strFileName As String, ByVal ipHdc As IntPtr,
        ByVal rect As Rectangle, ByVal mfu As MetafileFrameUnit)

Metafile(ByVal strFileName As String, ByVal ipHdc As IntPtr,
        ByVal rectf As RectangleF, ByVal mfu As MetafileFrameUnit)
```

*MetafileFrameUnit* is an enumeration defined in the *System.Drawing.Imaging* namespace. The enumeration indicates the units of the boundary rectangle specified in the constructor. *MetafileFrameUnit* plays no other role in the metafile, and the argument you specify is not retained:

### *MetafileFrameUnit* Enumeration

| Member | Value | Description |
|---|---|---|
| *Pixel* | 2 | Units of pixels |
| *Point* | 3 | Units of 1/72 inch |
| *Inch* | 4 | Units of inches |
| *Document* | 5 | Units of 1/300 inch |
| *Millimeter* | 6 | Units of millimeters |
| *GdiCompatible* | 7 | Units of 1/100 millimeter |

If you specify no *MetafileFrameUnit* argument, the default is *GdiCompatible*. This is probably not what you want!

For simple metafile creation, the easiest *MetafileFrameUnit* is definitely *Pixel*. For example, here's the metafile-creation statement in the original version of CreateMetafile:

```
mf = new Metafile("CreateMetafile.emf", ipHdc)
```

Try replacing it with this one:

```
mf = New Metafile("CreateMetafile.emf", ipHdc, _
            New Rectangle(0, 0, 101, 101), MetafileFrameUnit.Pixel)
```

That rectangle is defined in accordance with the coordinates later passed to the various *Graphics* methods. Now the *Width* and *Height* properties of the *Metafile* object obtained during the *DoPage* method are 101 and 101. Thus, the displayed images are 101 pixels apart:

"Why 101?" you ask. Because the largest object in the metafile was created using this call:

```
grfx.DrawEllipse(Pens.Black, 0, 0, 100, 100)
```

As you'll recall, when the pen is 1 pixel wide, the total width and height of such an object will be 101 pixels.

It isn't necessary for the boundary rectangle to have an origin at (0, 0), nor for the boundary rectangle to accurately describe the coordinates of the drawing methods in the metafile. For example, if you change the rectangle argument to

```
mf = New Metafile("CreateMetafile.emf", ipHdc, _
            New Rectangle(-25, -25, 75, 75), MetafileFrameUnit.Pixel)
```

the images are displayed like so:

The metafile image has a width and height of 75 pixels, but the origin is (–25, –25). Because no negative coordinates were used in the graphics objects inserted in the metafile, the top and left sides of the image are empty. When displaying the metafile, the image is clipped to the *Bounds* rectangle.

It's also possible to specify the rectangle in combination with a *Stream* argument:

### *Metafile* Constructors (selection)

```
Metafile(ByVal strm As Stream, ByVal ipHdc As IntPtr, _
        ByVal rect As Rectangle)

Metafile(ByVal strm As Stream, ByVal ipHdc As IntPtr, _
        ByVal rectf As RectangleF)

Metafile(ByVal strm As Stream, ByVal ipHdc As IntPtr, _
        ByVal rect As Rectangle, ByVal mfu As MetafileFrameUnit)

Metafile(ByVal strm As Stream, ByVal ipHdc As IntPtr, _
        ByVal rectf As RectangleF, ByVal mfu As MetafileFrameUnit)
```

For example, you can replace the metafile constructor in the original version of the CreateMetafile program with the following:

```
mf = New Metafile(New MemoryStream(), ipHdc, _
                New Rectangle(0, 0, 101, 101), MetafileFrameUnit.Pixel)
```

It's also possible to create a new metafile without specifying either a filename or a *Stream*:

### *Metafile* **Constructors (selection)**

```
Metafile(ByVal ipHdc As IntPtr, ByVal rect As Rectangle)

Metafile(ByVal ipHdc As IntPtr, ByVal rectf As RectangleF)

Metafile(ByVal ipHdc As IntPtr, ByVal rect As Rectangle,
        ByVal mfu As MetafileFrameUnit)

Metafile(ByVal ipHdc As IntPtr, ByVal rectf As RectangleF,
        ByVal mfu As MetafileFrameUnit)
```

When you specify neither a filename nor a *Stream*, the metafile is created in memory but you don't have access to the memory buffer as you do with a *MemoryStream* object. Here's another alternative metafile-creation statement for CreateMetafile:

```
mf = New Metafile(ipHdc, _
                New Rectangle(0, 0, 101, 101), MetafileFrameUnit.Pixel)
```

This last set of constructors would seem to imply that it should be possible to create a new metafile by specifying only a device context handle, but such a constructor doesn't exist.

You can use a *MetafileFrameUnit* other than *Pixel*, but doing so probably makes sense only if you're also drawing on the metafile in units other than pixels. Let's examine how the metafile and the page transform interact.

# Metafiles and the Page Transform

A metafile has a width and a height that are available from the *Size*, *Width*, and *Height* properties of the *Image* class and the *Bounds* property of the *MetafileHeader* class. It is convenient to think of the width and height of the metafile in terms of pixels, much like a bitmap. But the metafile's width and height are really more closely related to the extents of all the coordinates and sizes used in the graphics functions that went into the metafile.

A metafile also has a resolution in dots per inch that is available from the *HorizontalResolution* and *VerticalResolution* properties of the *Image* class and the *DpiX* and *DpiY* properties of the *MetafileHeader* class. These resolutions indicate how the coordinates and sizes encoded in the metafile correspond to inches.

In addition, a metafile has a metrical dimension, which you can calculate from the pixel dimension and the resolution. Or you can use the *PhysicalDimension* property of the *Image* class to obtain the size in hundredths of millimeters.

The resolution of a metafile is set when the metafile is created. The *Metafile* constructor requires a device context handle, and that output device provides a resolution for the metafile. All the coordinates and sizes in the graphics calls encoded within the metafile must be consistent with that resolution. As you add graphics calls to the metafile, coordinates and sizes are adjusted based on any page transform in effect.

Let's take a look at a program that creates a metafile containing four overlapping rectangles. Each rectangle is 1 inch square and is drawn with a 1-point-wide pen, but each rectangle is created with a different page transform in effect.

**MetafilePageUnits.vb**

```
'------------------------------------------------------
' MetafilePageUnits.vb (c) 2002 by Charles Petzold
'------------------------------------------------------
Imports System
Imports System.Drawing
Imports System.Drawing.Imaging
Imports System.Drawing.Printing      ' Not used for anything yet!
Imports System.Windows.Forms

Class MetafilePageUnits
    Inherits PrintableForm

    Private mf As Metafile

    Shared Shadows Sub Main()
        Application.Run(New MetafilePageUnits())
    End Sub

    Sub New()
        Text = "Metafile Page Units"

        ' Create metafile.
        Dim grfx As Graphics = CreateGraphics()
        Dim ipHdc As IntPtr = grfx.GetHdc()
        mf = New Metafile("MetafilePageUnits.emf", ipHdc)
        grfx.ReleaseHdc(ipHdc)
        grfx.Dispose()

        ' Get Graphics Object for drawing on metafile.
        grfx = Graphics.FromImage(mf)
        grfx.Clear(Color.White)

        ' Draw in units of pixels (1-point pen width).
        grfx.PageUnit = GraphicsUnit.Pixel
        Dim pn As New Pen(Color.Black, grfx.DpiX / 72)
        grfx.DrawRectangle(pn, 0, 0, grfx.DpiX, grfx.DpiY)
```

```
        ' Draw in units of 1/100 inch (1-point pen width).
        grfx.PageUnit = GraphicsUnit.Inch
        grfx.PageScale = 0.01F
        pn = New Pen(Color.Black, 100.0F / 72)
        grfx.DrawRectangle(pn, 25, 25, 100, 100)

        ' Draw in units of millimeters (1-point pen width).
        grfx.PageUnit = GraphicsUnit.Millimeter
        grfx.PageScale = 1
        pn = New Pen(Color.Black, 25.4F / 72)
        grfx.DrawRectangle(pn, 12.7F, 12.7F, 25.4F, 25.4F)

        ' Draw in units of pts (1-point pen width).
        grfx.PageUnit = GraphicsUnit.Point
        pn = New Pen(Color.Black, 1)
        grfx.DrawRectangle(pn, 54, 54, 72, 72)
        grfx.Dispose()
    End Sub

    Protected Overrides Sub DoPage(ByVal grfx As Graphics, _
            ByVal clr As Color, ByVal cx As Integer, ByVal cy As Integer)
        grfx.DrawImage(mf, 0, 0)
    End Sub
End Class
```

Despite the fact that the four rectangles are drawn in units of pixels, inches, millimeters, and points, it's comforting to see how these rectangles are stored and rendered in a consistent manner:

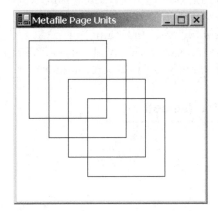

The first rectangle (the one at the top left) is drawn in units of pixels:

```
grfx.PageUnit = GraphicsUnit.Pixel
Dim pn As New Pen(Color.Black, grfx.DpiX / 72)
grfx.DrawRectangle(pn, 0, 0, grfx.DpiX, grfx.DpiY)
```

The default *PageUnit* property setting for a metafile based on the video display is *GraphicsUnit.Pixel*, so that first statement isn't strictly required. But it's necessary if you try the variation I'm going to describe next.

So far, all the metafiles we've created have been based on the video display resolution. You can also base a metafile on the printer. Simply replace the statement

```
Dim grfx As Graphics = CreateGraphics()
```

near the top of the constructor with these statements that obtain a *Printer-Settings* object for the default printer and then a *Graphics* object suitable for creating a metafile:

```
Dim prnset As New PrinterSettings()
Dim grfx As Graphics = prnset.CreateMeasurementGraphics()
```

As the resultant metafile is rendered on the screen and the printer, it appears to be the same as the original one based on the video display. However, a little exploration will reveal that the new metafile resolution is now consistent with your default printer. In addition, all the coordinates and sizes encoded in the metafile reflect this higher resolution.

# The Metafile Type

A metafile consists of a header and records. We'll examine how to view metafile records toward the end of this chapter, but for now you should know that each record is identified by a member of the *EmfPlusRecordType* enumeration, which is defined in the *System.Drawing.Imaging* namespace. At 253 members, *EmfPlusRecordType* is the largest enumeration in all of the Microsoft .NET Framework. Here are three related members of the enumeration:

### *EmfPlusRecordType* Enumeration (selection)

| Member | Value |
| --- | --- |
| *EmfPolyline* | 4 |
| *DrawLines* | 16397 |
| *WmfPolyline* | 66341 |

The third item in this little list has a prefix of *Wmf*, which stands for Windows Metafile and indicates the 16-bit metafile format. This particular record identifies a GDI function call of *Polyline* using points with 16-bit coordinates. You'll find *WmfPolyline* records in metafiles created before the advent of the 32-bit versions of Windows or in metafiles created by 32-bit programs to be backward compatible with earlier code. Such metafiles are still much-used in libraries of clip art.

The *EmfPolyline* member has a prefix of *Emf*, which stands for Enhanced Metafile and indicates the 32-bit metafile format. Again, the record identifies a function call of *Polyline*, but the points have 32-bit coordinates. You'll find such records in enhanced metafiles created by 32-bit versions of Windows.

The *DrawLines* record identifies the *DrawLines* method of the *Graphics* class. You'll find such records only in EMF+ metafiles created by Windows Forms programs.

For backward compatibility with 32-bit Windows programs, the default behavior of the *Metafile* class results in metafiles that actually have two sets of records: EMF records (such as *EmfPolyline*) and EMF+ records (such as *Draw-Lines*). The EMF records mimic the functionality of the EMF+ records.

However, you can create shorter metafiles if you're using the metafiles in a more restricted way. For example, if you intend the metafiles to be read only by Win32 programs, the metafiles don't need the EMF+ records. If the metafiles will be read only by other Windows Forms programs, the metafiles don't need EMF records.

Here are some simple *Metafile* constructors that have *EmfType* arguments in conjunction with an optional description string:

### *Metafile* Constructors (selection)

```
Metafile(ByVal strFileName As String, ByVal ipHdc As IntPtr,
        ByVal et As EmfType)

Metafile(ByVal strFileName As String, ByVal ipHdc As IntPtr,
        ByVal et As EmfType, ByVal strDescription As String)

Metafile(ByVal strm As Stream, ByVal ipHdc As IntPtr,
        ByVal et As EmfType)

Metafile(ByVal strm As Stream, ByVal ipHdc As IntPtr,
        ByVal et As EmfType, ByVal strDescription As String)

Metafile(ByVal ipHdc As IntPtr, ByVal et As EmfType)

Metafile(ByVal ipHdc As IntPtr, ByVal et As EmfType,
        ByVal strDescription As String)
```

The description string usually describes the image, possibly with a copyright notice. It's embedded in the metafile header. The *EmfType* enumeration is defined like so:

### *EmfType* Enumeration

| Member | Value |
| --- | --- |
| *EmfOnly* | 3 |
| *EmfPlusOnly* | 4 |
| *EmfPlusDual* | 5 |

When you specify an *EmfType* argument of *EmfOnly*, the metafile contains only EMF records. You should use this option if the metafiles your program creates will be used only by non–Windows Forms programs.

When you specify an *EmfType* argument of *EmfPlusOnly*, the metafile contains only EMF+ records. Such metafiles have the advantage of being comparatively small, but they are usable only by other Windows Forms programs.

The *EmfType* argument of *EmfPlusDual* is the default. The metafile contains both EMF and EMF+ records. Consequently, the metafile is just about equal to the size of a corresponding *EmfOnly* metafile plus an *EmfPlusOnly* metafile.

If you want to create a 16-bit WMF from a Windows Forms program, you must create a WMF handle using Win32 code and pass that handle to the appropriate *Metafile* constructor. You can also create a *Metafile* object based on an EMF handle obtained using Win32 code.

So far, I've shown you 22 of the 39 constructors and described the three that create *Metafile* objects from Win32 metafiles handles. The remaining 14 constructors let you specify both a boundary rectangle and a metafile type.

Ten of these constructors begin with a filename or *Stream* followed by an *IntPtr* to a device context handle. Next is either a *Rectangle* or *RectangleF* object with a *MetafileFrameUnit* member. The constructor concludes with an *EmfType* member, a description string, or both. But if the constructor begins with a *Stream*, it must have an *EmfType* member.

The other four constructors begin with an *IntPtr* to a device context handle. Next is a *Rectangle* or *RectangleF* object with a *MetafileFrameUnit* member. The constructor concludes with an *EmfType* member and an optional description string.

Here are the three most generalized, most inclusive, and longest *Metafile* constructors:

### *Metafile* Constructors (selection)

```
Metafile(ByVal strFileName As String, ByVal ipHdc As IntPtr,
         ByVal rectf As RectangleF, ByVal mfu As MetafileFrameUnit,
         ByVal et As EmfType, ByVal strDescription As String)

Metafile(ByVal strm As Stream, ByVal ipHdc As IntPtr,
         ByVal rectf As RectangleF, ByVal mfu As MetafileFrameUnit,
         ByVal et As EmfType, ByVal strDescription As String)

Metafile(ByVal ipHdc As IntPtr, ByVal rectf As RectangleF,
         ByVal mfu As MetafileFrameUnit, ByVal et As EmfType,
         ByVal strDescription As String)
```

# Enumerating the Metafile

Because metafiles are often stored on disk, the inquisitive programmer can be tempted to open them as regular files and go poking around inside. That sounds like fun to me, but there's also a method of the *Graphics* class that lets you examine metafile records in a more structured manner. Basically, you provide a method in your program that is called for each record in the metafile.

The *EnumerateMetafile* method comes in 36 versions, of which this is the simplest:

### Graphics *EnumerateMetafile* Methods (selection)

```
Sub EnumerateMetafile(ByVal mf As Metafile, ByVal pt As Point,
                      ByVal emp As Graphics.EnumerateMetafileProc)
```

It may seem odd that *EnumerateMetafile* is a method of our old friend the *Graphics* class. But you'll see shortly that the method not only enumerates a metafile but also provides a way to render it on a record-by-record basis. As your method gets access to every record of the metafile, it can decide to let the record be rendered, skip the record, or (if you're particularly brave) modify the record and render it. And that's also why there are so many versions of the *EnumerateMetafile* method. The methods are similar to the various overloads of *DrawImage*.

Rather than list all 36 versions of *EnumerateMetafile*, here's a summary of the required and optional arguments:

■   The first argument is always a *Metafile* object.

■   The second argument is always a destination. You can specify a *Point*, a *PointF*, an array of three *Point* or *PointF* structures, a *Rectangle*, or a *RectangleF*. Just as in *DrawImage*, when you specify an array of three *Point* or *PointF* structures, the points represent the destination of the top left, top right, and bottom left corners of the image.

- Next can be an optional argument that indicates a source rectangle within the metafile. If the destination argument is a *Point*, a *Point* array, or a *Rectangle*, the source rectangle must be a *Rectangle*. If the destination argument is a *PointF*, a *PointF* array, or a *RectangleF*, the source rectangle must be a *RectangleF*. The destination rectangle must be followed by a *GraphicsUnit* value indicating the units of the source rectangle.

- The next argument is required. It's a method in your program that you've defined in accordance with the *Graphics.EnumerateMetafileProc* delegate. This is the method that gets called for each record in the metafile.

- The next argument is optional. It's an *IntPtr* that is defined as a pointer to programmer-defined data that's supposed to be passed to the enumeration method defined in the previous argument. However, there is no argument in the *Graphics.EnumerateMetafileProc* delegate for this programmer-defined data.

- If the optional *IntPtr* argument is present, it can be followed by another optional argument, which is an *ImageAttributes* object that determines certain aspects of how the image is displayed.

Here's that simplest call to *EnumerateMetafile* as it might appear in an actual program:

```
grfx.EnumerateMetafile(mf, New Point(0, 0), _
                    AddressOf EnumMetafileProc)
```

The last argument makes reference to a method named *EnumMetafileProc* that is defined in accordance with *the Graphics.EnumerateMetafileProc* delegate. Such a method appears in your program looking something like this:

```
Function EnumMetafileProc(ByVal eprt As EmfPlusRecordType, _
        ByVal iFlags As Integer, ByVal iDataSize As Integer, _
        ByVal ipData As IntPtr, _
        ByVal prc As PlayRecordCallback) As Boolean
    ⋮
    Return bContinue
End Function
```

This metafile enumeration method returns *True* to continue enumerating the metafile and *False* otherwise.

The arguments to the enumeration method (which I'll identify briefly here and discuss in more detail shortly) begin with a member of the *EmfPlusRecordType* enumeration that identifies the record. The *iFlags* argument is undocumented.

The *iDataSize* argument indicates the number of bytes that the *ipData* argument points to. This data is unique for each record type. For example, a record type that indicates a polyline would store a point count and multiple points in *ipData*.

The last argument is of type *PlayRecordCallback*, which is a delegate defined in the *System.Drawing.Imaging* namespace. You recall that *EnumerateMetafileProc* is also a delegate. It's very unusual for an argument of a delegate to be another delegate. Here's how the *PlayRecordCallback* delegate is defined:

```
Public Delegate Sub PlayRecordCallback(ByVal eprt As EmfPlusRecordType, _
                                       ByVal iFlags As Integer, _
                                       ByVal iDataSize As Integer, _
                                       ByVal ipData As IntPtr)
```

Instead of defining a method in your program in accordance with the *PlayRecordCallback* delegate (which is what you usually do with a delegate), the last argument to your enumeration method indicates the method you're supposed to call to render that particular metafile record. The delegate indicates the arguments to that method. So you could define your enumeration method like so:

```
Function EnumMetafileProc(ByVal eprt As EmfPlusRecordType, _
         ByVal iFlags As Integer, ByVal iDataSize As Integer, _
         ByVal ipData As IntPtr, _
         ByVal prc As PlayRecordCallback) As Boolean
    ⋮
    prc(eprt, iFlags, iDataSize, ipData)
    Return True
End Function
```

Notice the call to the *PlayRecordCallback* delegate. When you call *EnumerateMetafile* with this *EnumMetafileProc* method, *EnumerateMetafile* should function just like *DrawImage*, except perhaps a bit slower because *EnumMetafileProc* is getting access to each metafile record.

Alas, *PlayRecordCallback* doesn't work, and you should probably ignore the last argument to the enumeration method. Instead, use this method of the *Metafile* class to render a metafile record in your enumeration method:

### Metafile *PlayRecord* Method

```
Sub PlayRecord(ByVal eprt As EmfPlusRecordType, ByVal iFlags As Integer,
               ByVal iDataSize As Integer, ByVal abyData() As Byte)
```

This method looks a lot like the *PlayRecordCallback* delegate except that the last argument is an array of bytes instead of an *IntPtr*. For converting between the *IntPtr* argument to the enumeration method and the array of bytes required by *PlayRecord*, you can use the shared *Copy* method in the *Marshal* class of the *System.Runtime.InteropServices* namespace.

Because you call *PlayRecord* in your enumeration method and *PlayRecord* is a method of the *Metafile* class, the *Metafile* object must be stored as a field in your program. Here's an enumeration method that simply renders the metafile:

```
Function EnumMetafileProc(ByVal eprt As EmfPlusRecordType, _
             ByVal iFlags As Integer, ByVal iDataSize As Integer, _
             ByVal ipData As IntPtr, _
             ByVal prc As PlayRecordCallback) As Boolean
    Dim abyData(iDataSize) As Byte
    Marshal.Copy(ipData, abyData, 0, iDataSize)
    mf.PlayRecord(eprt, iFlags, iDataSize, abyData)
    Return True
End Function
```

The following program creates a write-only text box and a panel control, with a splitter control between them. It also implements an *OpenFileDialog* dialog box to open a metafile. The metafile is displayed normally on the panel. When the metafile is first loaded, the program creates a *StringWriter* object and then calls *EnumerateMetafile* to enumerate the metafile using the *EnumMetafileProc* method defined in the program. *EnumMetafileProc* formats the information into the *StringWriter* object. On return from *EnumerateMetafile*, the program puts the resultant string into the text box.

**EnumMetafile.vb**

```
'-------------------------------------------------
' EnumMetafile.vb (c) 2002 by Charles Petzold
'-------------------------------------------------
Imports System
Imports System.Drawing
Imports System.Drawing.Imaging
Imports System.IO
Imports System.Runtime.InteropServices
Imports System.Windows.Forms

Class EnumMetafile
    Inherits Form

    Private mf As Metafile
    Private pnl As panel
    Private txtbox As TextBox
    Private strCaption As String
    Private strwrite As StringWriter

    Shared Sub Main()
        Application.Run(New EnumMetafile())
    End Sub
```

```
Sub New()
    strCaption = "Enumerate Metafile"
    Text = strCaption

    ' Create the text box for displaying records.
    txtbox = New TextBox()
    txtbox.Parent = Me
    txtbox.Dock = DockStyle.Fill
    txtbox.Multiline = True
    txtbox.WordWrap = False
    txtbox.ReadOnly = True
    txtbox.TabStop = False
    txtbox.ScrollBars = ScrollBars.Vertical

    ' Create the splitter between the panel and the text box.
    Dim split As New Splitter()
    split.Parent = Me
    split.Dock = DockStyle.Left

    ' Create the panel for displaying the metafile.
    pnl = New Panel()
    pnl.Parent = Me
    pnl.Dock = DockStyle.Left
    AddHandler pnl.Paint, AddressOf PanelOnPaint

    ' Create the menu.
    Menu = New MainMenu()
    Menu.MenuItems.Add("&Open!", AddressOf MenuOpenOnClick)
End Sub

Private Sub MenuOpenOnClick(ByVal obj As Object, ByVal ea As EventArgs)
    Dim dlg As New OpenFileDialog()
    dlg.Filter = "All Metafiles|*.wmf;*.emf|" & _
                 "Windows Metafile (*.wmf)|*.wmf|" & _
                 "Enhanced Metafile (*.emf)|*.emf"
    If dlg.ShowDialog() = DialogResult.OK Then
        Try
            mf = New Metafile(dlg.FileName)
        Catch exc As Exception
            MessageBox.Show(exc.Message, strCaption)
            Return
        End Try

        Text = strCaption & " - " & Path.GetFileName(dlg.FileName)
        pnl.Invalidate()

        ' Enumerate the metafile for the text box.
        strwrite = New StringWriter()
        Dim grfx As Graphics = CreateGraphics()
        grfx.EnumerateMetafile(mf, New Point(0, 0), _
                                 AddressOf EnumMetafileProc)
        grfx.Dispose()
```

*(continued)*

**EnumMetafile.vb**  *(continued)*

```
            txtbox.Text = strwrite.ToString()
            txtbox.SelectionLength = 0
        End If
    End Sub

    Private Function EnumMetafileProc(ByVal eprt As EmfPlusRecordType, _
             ByVal iFlags As Integer, ByVal iDataSize As Integer, _
             ByVal ipData As IntPtr, _
             ByVal prc As PlayRecordCallback) As Boolean
        strwrite.Write("{0} ({1}, {2})", eprt, iFlags, iDataSize)

        If iDataSize > 0 Then
            Dim abyData(iDataSize) As Byte
            Marshal.Copy(ipData, abyData, 0, iDataSize)
            Dim by As Byte
            For Each by In abyData
                strwrite.Write(" {0:X2}", by)
            Next by
        End If
        strwrite.WriteLine()
        Return True
    End Function

    Private Sub PanelOnPaint(ByVal obj As Object, _
                            ByVal pea As PaintEventArgs)
        Dim pnl As Panel = DirectCast(obj, Panel)
        Dim grfx As Graphics = pea.Graphics

        If Not mf Is Nothing Then
            grfx.DrawImage(mf, 0, 0)
        End If
    End Sub
End Class
```

Although this program mysteriously doesn't work with any of the metafiles created in this chapter (or with metafiles created by programs from my book *Programming Windows*), here's the program displaying one of the metafiles included with Visual Studio .NET:

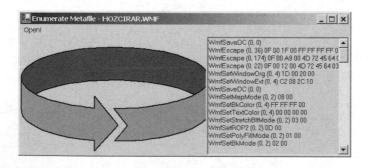

The metafile records are shown at the right. Following the record type, the flag and the number of bytes of data are in parentheses. The hexadecimal bytes follow. No attempt has been made in this program to convert the bytes into meaningful information.

As you can see, the metafile records are of variable size. Each record type corresponds to a particular GDI function call or a *Graphics* method call. The data that accompanies each record corresponds to the arguments of the call. Obviously, this data is dependent on the record type.

The new metafile records that correspond to methods of the *Graphics* class are currently undocumented (at the time I'm writing this) but will undoubtedly be documented sometime in the future. If you're interested in getting a head start on metafile enumeration, you can begin by exploring the format of the older WMF and EMF records. Each record type corresponds to a structure beginning with the letters *EMR* ("enhanced metafile record") defined in the Win32 header file wingdi.h.

The EMR structure is part of every record. It contains the record type and a size. Here's the structure in C syntax as it's defined in the header file:

```
typedef struct tagEMR
{
    DWORD iType;
    DWORD nSize;
}
EMR;
```

Here's the structure for a polyline. It begins with an EMR structure.

```
typedef struct tagEMRPOLYLINE
{
    EMR emr;
    RECTL rclBounds;
    DWORD cptl;
    POINTL aptl[1];
}
EMRPOLYLINE;
```

Everything following the EMR field corresponds to the data that accompanies the record in the Windows Forms enumeration.

If you're not familiar with Win32 structures, be aware that *RECTL* and *POINTL* have *long* fields (but those are 32-bit C *long* integers, not 64-bit Visual Basic *Long* integers), and *RECTS* and *POINTS* structures have *short* fields, which are 16-bits in length and equivalent to the Visual Basic .NET *Short*. Moreover, a rectangle is defined in terms of the upper left corner and lower right corner, not in terms of the upper left corner and the width and height.

# 24

# Clip, Drag, and Drop

The Windows clipboard allows data to be transferred from one application to another. The clipboard is a relatively simple mechanism that doesn't require much overhead in either the program that places data on it or the program that later gets access to it. Most applications use the Windows clipboard even when cut-and-paste operations involve the transfer of data solely within the application.

Programs that deal with documents or other data give the user access to the clipboard through the standard menu options Cut, Copy, and Paste, duplicated by the keyboard shortcuts (inherited from the Apple Macintosh) CTRL+X, CTRL+C, and CTRL+V. When a user selects Cut or Copy, the program transfers selected data from the application to the clipboard. The data is in a particular format or formats, usually text, bitmap, metafile, or binary. The Cut command has the additional effect of deleting the selection from the document. When a user selects Paste from the menu, the program determines whether the clipboard contains data in a format that the program can use. If it does, the program transfers the data from the clipboard to the program.

Programs should not transfer data to the clipboard without an explicit instruction from the user. For example, a user who performs a Cut or Copy (or a CTRL+X or CTRL+C) operation in one program should be able to assume that the data will remain on the clipboard until the next Cut or Copy operation.

As you may recall from Chapter 18, the *TextBox* and *RichTextBox* controls implement their own clipboard interfaces. A program using these controls need only call the appropriate methods implemented in *TextBoxBase*. In the general case, however, you don't have that convenience. You must instead access the clipboard yourself.

The drag-and-drop facility in Microsoft Windows is closely related to the clipboard, so I'll be discussing that in this chapter as well.

# Items and Formats

Only one item is stored on the clipboard at any time. Whenever a program copies an item to the clipboard, the new item replaces what was there before.

However, an application can copy a particular item to the clipboard in multiple formats. For example, consider a spreadsheet program in which the user selects an array of rows and columns, and then triggers the Copy command. The spreadsheet program will probably use a variety of formats for storing those rows and columns on the clipboard. Of most importance to the application is probably a binary format known only to the application itself; this private format allows the program to retrieve the exact data (with any formatting that is present) when the user triggers Paste.

The spreadsheet program can also copy the selected rows and columns into the clipboard in a text-based comma-separated format that other spreadsheet or database programs can use. It could also format the data into text using tabs between the columns; this format is suitable when you paste the data into a word processing program. Perhaps the spreadsheet application could even create a bitmap or a metafile containing an image of the rows and columns.

The application pasting data from the clipboard doesn't need to handle all these different formats. It can simply select the format it can use most efficiently.

As you might expect, the existence of clipboard items in multiple formats adds a layer of complexity to clipboard programming.

# The Tiny (But Powerful) *Clipboard* Class

The *Clipboard* class is part of the *System.Windows.Forms* namespace. The class is defined as *NotInheritable* and it has no public constructors. You can't instantiate it, and you can't inherit from it. The class has no properties and just two shared methods, one of which comes in two versions. You use these methods to set data to the clipboard or get data out:

### *Clipboard* Shared Methods

```
Sub SetDataObject(ByVal obj As Object)

Sub SetDataObject(ByVal obj As Object,
                  ByVal bRemainAfterExit As Boolean)

Function GetDataObject() As IDataObject
```

As long as you're using only one data format, putting data on the clipboard is the easier of the two operations. For example, if you have a *String* named *str* that you want to copy to the clipboard, simply call

```
Clipboard.SetDataObject(str, True)
```

Whatever was on the clipboard before is deleted and replaced with this item. Similarly, you can put a bitmap on the clipboard:

```
Clipboard.SetDataObject(bm, True)
```

You can also put a metafile on the clipboard:

```
Clipboard.SetDataObject(mf, True)
```

In all three of these cases, a copy is made of the object for the clipboard's purposes. It's OK if you change the object after the *SetDataObject* call. It won't change what's on the clipboard. This sequence of statements won't cause any problems:

```
Clipboard.SetDataObject(str, True)
str = Nothing
```

Once something is on the clipboard, the only way you can affect it is with another call to *SetDataObject*; that second call to *SetDataObject* replaces the clipboard item with a new one.

I've set the second argument of *SetDataObject* to *True* in these examples because that's probably what you'll want to use whenever you put a string, a bitmap, or a metafile on the clipboard. If you set the second argument to *False*,

```
Clipboard.SetDataObject(str, False)
```

or if you don't include the argument at all,

```
Clipboard.SetDataObject(str)
```

the item that you put on the clipboard disappears when your program terminates. It's probably best for the user if the item is still on the clipboard regardless of whether or not your program is still running.

However, the items you put on the clipboard are not limited to strings, bitmaps, and metafiles. You can put *any* object on the clipboard. Here's some code that creates a new *Button* object, sets the *Text* property, and then copies the object to the clipboard:

```
Dim btn As New Button()
btn.Text = "OK"
Clipboard.SetDataObject(btn)
```

In cases where the object passed to *SetDataObject* is not a string, a metafile, or a bitmap, you must use the short form of *SetDataObject* or specify *False* as the second argument. The reason for this restriction is that the clipboard can't be used for transferring arbitrary objects (such as *Button* objects) between applications. Only the application that put the *Button* object on the clipboard can retrieve it. Thus, it makes no sense for the object to be on the clipboard after the program terminates.

And that's about all that's involved in putting one data format on the clipboard. Later in this chapter, I'll demonstrate how you work with multiple data formats.

Getting data from the clipboard isn't quite as simple as putting data on the clipboard. The *GetDataObject* method is defined as returning an instance of a class that implements the *IDataObject* interface, which means that you call *Get-DataObject* like so:

```
Dim data As IDataObject = Clipboard.GetDataObject()
```

The object called *data* now contains everything you need to know about the contents of the clipboard, and our attention must now focus on the *IDataObject* interface.

## Getting Objects from the Clipboard

I'm first going to show you a fairly simple and straightforward way to get objects from the clipboard, a job you'll probably perform in response to the user selecting Paste from the menu.

The shared *GetDataObject* method of the *Clipboard* class isn't documented as returning an object of a particular class. It's documented only as returning an instance of a class that implements the *IDataObject* interface. That gives us enough information to use the methods defined in *IDataObject* using the object returned from *GetDataObject*. *IDataObject* defines four methods (12 if you count overloads). Here are two of them in their simplest forms:

### *IDataObject* Methods (selection)

```
Function GetDataPresent(ByVal typ As Type) As Boolean
Function GetData(ByVal typ As Type) As Object
```

The *GetDataPresent* method should probably be named *IsDataPresent* to be more consistent with the rest of the Windows Forms methods and properties. If you have an object named *data* returned from *Clipboard.GetDataObject*, the expression

```
data.GetDataPresent(GetType(String))
```

returns *True* if the clipboard contains a *String* object. Notice the use of the *Get-Type* operator to get the *Type* object that identifies the *String* class. Similarly,

```
data.GetDataPresent(GetType(Bitmap))
```

returns *True* if there's a *Bitmap* object on the clipboard, and

```
data.GetDataPresent(GetType(Metafile))
```

returns *True* if a *Metafile* object is available. If you're in the habit of putting nonstandard objects on the clipboard, you can also make calls like this:

```
data.GetDataPresent(GetType(Button))
```

It's possible to make these calls without actually saving the return value from the *Clipboard.GetDataObject* call. For example,

```
Clipboard.GetDataObject().GetDataPresent(GetType(Bitmap))
```

returns *True* if the clipboard contains a *Bitmap* object.

It's customary to use the *GetDataPresent* method during the *Popup* event of the Edit menu. You enable the Paste item only if *GetDataPresent* returns *True* for the data type you're interested in.

By the way, the fact that

```
data.GetDataPresent(GetType(String))
```

returns *True* doesn't imply that *GetDataPresent* will return *False* for other types. Like I said, the clipboard can contain multiple formats of the same clipboard item. The clipboard could contain a *String* object with some text, a *Metafile* object containing a *DrawString* call displaying that same text string, and a *Bitmap* rendition of the same text. The application getting data from the clipboard should check for the most useful format.

To get an object from the clipboard, you call the *GetData* method. For example,

```
Dim str As String = DirectCast(data.GetData(GetType(String)), String)
```

Because *GetData* returns an *Object*, the return value must be cast to the desired data type. Similarly,

```
Dim bm As Bitmap = DirectCast(data.GetData(GetType(Bitmap)), Bitmap)
```

If you compile with Option Strict Off, the cast can be implicit:

```
Dim bm As Bitmap = data.GetObject(GetType(Bitmap))
```

Getting an object from the clipboard doesn't affect the contents of the clipboard. The return value of *GetData* is a copy of the object stored on the clipboard.

It's time to see how this all works in actual code. The following program does little more than copy *String* objects to and from the clipboard.

**ClipText.vb**

```
'-----------------------------------------------------------
' ClipText.vb (c) 2002 by Charles Petzold
'-----------------------------------------------------------
Imports System
Imports System.Drawing
Imports System.Windows.Forms
```

*(continued)*

**ClipText.vb**   *(continued)*

```vb
Class ClipText
    Inherits Form

    Private strText As String = "Sample text for the clipboard"
    Private miCut, miCopy, miPaste As MenuItem

    Shared Sub Main()
        Application.Run(New ClipText())
    End Sub

    Sub New()
        Text = "Clip Text"
        ResizeRedraw = True

        Menu = New MainMenu()

        ' Edit menu
        Dim mi As New MenuItem("&Edit")
        AddHandler mi.Popup, AddressOf MenuEditOnPopup
        Menu.MenuItems.Add(mi)

        ' Edit Cut menu item
        miCut = New MenuItem("Cu&t")
        AddHandler miCut.Click, AddressOf MenuEditCutOnClick
        miCut.Shortcut = Shortcut.CtrlX
        Menu.MenuItems(0).MenuItems.Add(miCut)

        ' Edit Copy menu item
        miCopy = New MenuItem("&Copy")
        AddHandler miCopy.Click, AddressOf MenuEditCopyOnClick
        miCopy.Shortcut = Shortcut.CtrlC
        Menu.MenuItems(0).MenuItems.Add(miCopy)

        ' Edit Paste menu item
        miPaste = New MenuItem("&Paste")
        AddHandler miPaste.Click, AddressOf MenuEditPasteOnClick
        miPaste.Shortcut = Shortcut.CtrlV
        Menu.MenuItems(0).MenuItems.Add(miPaste)
    End Sub

    Private Sub MenuEditOnPopup(ByVal obj As Object, ByVal ea As EventArgs)
        miCopy.Enabled = strText.Length > 0
        miCut.Enabled = miCopy.Enabled
        miPaste.Enabled = _
                Clipboard.GetDataObject().GetDataPresent(GetType(String))
    End Sub

    Private Sub MenuEditCutOnClick(ByVal obj As Object, _
                                   ByVal ea As EventArgs)
        MenuEditCopyOnClick(obj, ea)
        strText = ""
```

```
        Invalidate()
    End Sub

    Private Sub MenuEditCopyOnClick(ByVal obj As Object, _
                               ByVal ea As EventArgs)
        Clipboard.SetDataObject(strText, True)
    End Sub

    Private Sub MenuEditPasteOnClick(ByVal obj As Object, _
                               ByVal ea As EventArgs)
        Dim data As IDataObject = Clipboard.GetDataObject()
        If data.GetDataPresent(GetType(String)) Then
            strText = DirectCast(data.GetData(GetType(String)), String)
        End If
        Invalidate()
    End Sub

    Protected Overrides Sub OnPaint(ByVal pea As PaintEventArgs)
        Dim grfx As Graphics = pea.Graphics
        Dim strfmt As New StringFormat()
        strfmt.LineAlignment = StringAlignment.Center
        strfmt.Alignment = StringAlignment.Center

        grfx.DrawString(strText, Font, New SolidBrush(ForeColor), _
                    RectangleF.op_Implicit(ClientRectangle), strfmt)
    End Sub
End Class
```

The ClipText program maintains a *String* variable named *strText* that it displays centered in its client area. The constructor creates an Edit menu with Cut, Copy, and Paste items. The *Popup* event handler enables the Cut and Copy items only if the string has a nonzero length. The Paste item is enabled only if the clipboard contains a *String* object.

The *Click* event handler for the Copy command uses the *SetDataObject* method of *Clipboard* to copy *strText* to the clipboard. The Cut event handler calls the Copy event handler and also deletes the string from the program by setting *strText* to the empty string.

The *Click* event handler for the Paste command first checks whether the clipboard still contains an object of type *String*. (You might find that check redundant considering that the Paste item isn't enabled if the clipboard isn't storing text. However, given that Windows is a multitasking environment, it's possible for the clipboard contents to change between the time a submenu is displayed and an item is clicked. Calling *GetData* for an object type that no longer exists on the clipboard won't cause an exception to be raised, but *GetData* will return a *Nothing* value, and ClipText isn't quite prepared for that eventuality.) If the clipboard contains text, the Paste event handler calls *GetData* to obtain the *String* object and then assigns that string to *strText*.

You can experiment with ClipText in conjunction with Microsoft Notepad, word processors, and Web browsers. As you'll see, when you copy text from a word processor or a Web browser and paste it into ClipText, the text loses any formatting it had. That result isn't unexpected: you know that *String* objects normally don't include any formatting, and you'd probably be startled to see ClipText display a block of text with rich text format (RTF) or HTML tags. I'll explain shortly how you can go beyond plain text with the clipboard.

In Chapter 23, I introduced the MetafileViewer program and the Metafile-Convert program, which inherited from MetafileViewer. The following program inherits from MetafileConvert and implements an Edit menu to transfer metafiles to and from the clipboard.

**MetafileClip.vb**

```
'-------------------------------------------------
' MetafileClip.vb (c) 2002 by Charles Petzold
'-------------------------------------------------
Imports System
Imports System.Drawing
Imports System.Drawing.Imaging
Imports System.Windows.Forms

Class MetafileClip
    Inherits MetafileConvert

    Private miCut, miCopy, miPaste, miDel As MenuItem

    Shared Shadows Sub Main()
        Application.Run(New MetafileClip())
    End Sub

    Sub New()
        strProgName = "Metafile Clip"
        Text = strProgName

        ' Edit menu
        AddHandler Menu.MenuItems(1).Popup, AddressOf MenuEditOnPopup

        ' Edit Cut menu item
        miCut = New MenuItem("Cu&t")
        AddHandler miCut.Click, AddressOf MenuEditCutOnClick
        miCut.Shortcut = Shortcut.CtrlX
        Menu.MenuItems(1).MenuItems.Add(miCut)

        ' Edit Copy menu item
        miCopy = New MenuItem("&Copy")
        AddHandler miCopy.Click, AddressOf MenuEditCopyOnClick
        miCopy.Shortcut = Shortcut.CtrlC
        Menu.MenuItems(1).MenuItems.Add(miCopy)

        ' Edit Paste menu item
```

```
        miPaste = New MenuItem("&Paste")
        AddHandler miPaste.Click, AddressOf MenuEditPasteOnClick
        miPaste.Shortcut = Shortcut.CtrlV
        Menu.MenuItems(1).MenuItems.Add(miPaste)


        ' Edit Delete menu item
        miDel = New MenuItem("De&lete")
        AddHandler miDel.Click, AddressOf MenuEditDelOnClick
        miDel.Shortcut = Shortcut.Del
        Menu.MenuItems(1).MenuItems.Add(miDel)
    End Sub

    Private Sub MenuEditOnPopup(ByVal obj As Object, ByVal ea As EventArgs)
        Dim bEnable As Boolean = Not mf Is Nothing

        miCopy.Enabled = bEnable
        miCut.Enabled = bEnable
        miDel.Enabled = bEnable
        miPaste.Enabled = _
            Clipboard.GetDataObject().GetDataPresent(GetType(Metafile))
    End Sub

    Private Sub MenuEditCutOnClick(ByVal obj As Object, _
                                   ByVal ea As EventArgs)
        MenuEditCopyOnClick(obj, ea)
        MenuEditDelOnClick(obj, ea)
    End Sub

    Private Sub MenuEditCopyOnClick(ByVal obj As Object, _
                                    ByVal ea As EventArgs)
        Clipboard.SetDataObject(mf, True)
    End Sub

    Private Sub MenuEditPasteOnClick(ByVal obj As Object, _
                                     ByVal ea As EventArgs)
        Dim data As IDataObject = Clipboard.GetDataObject()

        If data.GetDataPresent(GetType(Metafile)) Then
            mf = DirectCast(data.GetData(GetType(Metafile)), Metafile)
        End If

        strFileName = "clipboard"
        Text = strProgName & " - " & strFileName
        Invalidate()
    End Sub

    Private Sub MenuEditDelOnClick(ByVal obj As Object, _
                                   ByVal ea As EventArgs)
        mf = Nothing
        strFileName = Nothing
        Text = strProgName
        Invalidate()
    End Sub
End Class
```

Besides Cut, Copy, and Paste, this program also includes a Delete item on the Edit menu. (In some applications, an item named Clear is essentially the equivalent of Delete.) The Delete option doesn't actually involve the clipboard because (unlike Cut) it deletes without first copying to the clipboard. However, if you're already implementing Delete and Copy, adding Cut is usually trivial. In fact, you can think of a Cut operation as a Copy followed by a Delete. That's exactly how the *Click* event handler for the Cut option is written:

```
Private Sub MenuEditCutOnClick(ByVal obj As Object, _
                               ByVal ea As EventArgs)
    MenuEditCopyOnClick(obj, ea)
    MenuEditDelOnClick(obj, ea)
End Sub
```

Because the MetafileClip program deals with files as well as the clipboard, the other complication involves dealing with the form's caption bar. In the earlier versions of the program, I set the *Text* property of the form to the program name (separated into words) stored in the *strProgName* field along with the currently loaded filename stored in the *strFileName* field:

```
Metafile Viewer - Picture.emf
```

In the MetafileClip version, the *strProgName* text is "Metafile Clip".

When the Delete option is selected, the *strFileName* variable must be set to *Nothing* and *Text* set to just the *strProgName*. That much is obvious. The more difficult problem is what should be done when a metafile is loaded from the clipboard. I decided to set the *strFileName* field to "clipboard". Other possibilities are "untitled" or "metafile".

In Chapter 16, I introduced the ImageOpen program to load *Image* objects from files and the ImageIO program to save them. In Chapter 21, the Image-Print program added printing capabilities. Now the ImageClip program inherits from ImagePrint to add clipboard capability.

**ImageClip.vb**

```
'---------------------------------------------
' ImageClip.vb (c) 2002 by Charles Petzold
'---------------------------------------------
Imports System
Imports System.Drawing
Imports System.Drawing.Imaging
Imports System.Windows.Forms

Class ImageClip
    Inherits ImagePrint

    Private miCut, miCopy, miPaste, miDel As MenuItem

    Shared Shadows Sub Main()
```

```
        Application.Run(New ImageClip())
End Sub

Sub New()
    strProgName = "Image Clip"
    Text = strProgName

    ' Edit menu
    Dim mi As New MenuItem("&Edit")
    AddHandler mi.Popup, AddressOf MenuEditOnPopup
    Menu.MenuItems.Add(mi)
    Dim index As Integer = Menu.MenuItems.Count - 1

    ' Edit Cut menu item
    miCut = New MenuItem("Cu&t")
    AddHandler miCut.Click, AddressOf MenuEditCutOnClick
    miCut.Shortcut = Shortcut.CtrlX
    Menu.MenuItems(index).MenuItems.Add(miCut)

    ' Edit Copy menu item
    miCopy = New MenuItem("&Copy")
    AddHandler miCopy.Click, AddressOf MenuEditCopyOnClick
    miCopy.Shortcut = Shortcut.CtrlC
    Menu.MenuItems(index).MenuItems.Add(miCopy)

    ' Edit Paste menu item
    miPaste = New MenuItem("&Paste")
    AddHandler miPaste.Click, AddressOf MenuEditPasteOnClick
    miPaste.Shortcut = Shortcut.CtrlV
    Menu.MenuItems(index).MenuItems.Add(miPaste)

    ' Edit Delete menu item
    miDel = New MenuItem("De&lete")
    AddHandler miDel.Click, AddressOf MenuEditDelOnClick
    miDel.Shortcut = Shortcut.Del
    Menu.MenuItems(index).MenuItems.Add(miDel)
End Sub

Private Sub MenuEditOnPopup(ByVal obj As Object, ByVal ea As EventArgs)
    Dim bEnable As Boolean = Not img Is Nothing

    miCopy.Enabled = bEnable
    miCut.Enabled = bEnable
    miDel.Enabled = bEnable

    Dim data As IDataObject = Clipboard.GetDataObject()
    miPaste.Enabled = data.GetDataPresent(GetType(Bitmap)) OrElse _
                    data.GetDataPresent(GetType(Metafile))
End Sub
```

*(continued)*

**ImageClip.vb** *(continued)*

```
    Private Sub MenuEditCutOnClick(ByVal obj As Object, _
                                   ByVal ea As EventArgs)
        MenuEditCopyOnClick(obj, ea)
        MenuEditDelOnClick(obj, ea)
    End Sub

    Private Sub MenuEditCopyOnClick(ByVal obj As Object, _
                                    ByVal ea As EventArgs)
        Clipboard.SetDataObject(img, True)
    End Sub

    Private Sub MenuEditPasteOnClick(ByVal obj As Object, _
                                     ByVal ea As EventArgs)
        Dim data As IDataObject = Clipboard.GetDataObject()

        If data.GetDataPresent(GetType(Metafile)) Then
            img = DirectCast(data.GetData(GetType(Metafile)), Image)
        ElseIf data.GetDataPresent(GetType(Bitmap)) Then
            img = DirectCast(data.GetData(GetType(Bitmap)), Image)
        End If

        strFileName = "Clipboard"
        Text = strProgName & " - " & strFileName
        Invalidate()
    End Sub

    Private Sub MenuEditDelOnClick(ByVal obj As Object, _
                                   ByVal ea As EventArgs)
        img = Nothing
        strFileName = Nothing
        Text = strProgName
        Invalidate()
    End Sub
End Class
```

The enhancements here are similar to those in MetafileClip, but the Image-Clip program adds another complexity. The program is dealing with an object defined as *Image* (stored as the field *img*), but which is actually either a *Bitmap* or a *Metafile* object. There's no problem with using an *Image* object in the *Set-DataObject* method:

```
Clipboard.SetDataObject(img, True)
```

The *SetDataObject* method probably calls *GetType* on the first argument to determine the type of the object. Depending on what type the *img* object is, *GetType* will return *System.Drawing.Bitmap* or *System.Drawing.Imaging.Metafile*.

However, you can't use *GetType(Image)* in the *GetDataPresent* or *GetData* method of the *IDataObject* interface. If your program has the ability to paste either a bitmap or a metafile, you should enable the Paste menu item if the clipboard contains either a bitmap *or* a metafile:

```
miPaste.Enabled = data.GetDataPresent(GetType(Bitmap)) OrElse _
                data.GetDataPresent(GetType(Metafile))
```

It's possible that the clipboard contains both a *Bitmap* and a *Metafile* representing the same image. When the user selects Paste, the program has to decide which one to load.

I decided that the *Metafile* object should take priority:

```
If data.GetDataPresent(GetType(Metafile)) Then
    img = DirectCast(data.GetData(GetType(Metafile)), Image)
ElseIf data.GetDataPresent(GetType(Bitmap)) Then
    img = DirectCast(data.GetData(GetType(Bitmap)), Image)
End If
```

This was not an arbitrary choice! Ask yourself, What kind of program puts both a metafile and a bitmap on the clipboard? It's probably a drawing program—a program that essentially works with metafiles. When such an application copies an image to the clipboard, it also converts the image to a bitmap. That way the image is available to applications that can't handle metafiles.

It's highly unlikely that the metafile originated with a paint program. Paint programs don't usually have the ability to convert bitmaps to metafiles. Such conversions are rather specialized and work only with very simple images.

Thus, the metafile is the *real* image and the bitmap is only a conversion. A program that can deal with both metafiles and bitmaps should load metafiles from the clipboard in preference to bitmaps.

# Clipboard Data Formats

At first, it seems so simple: you put an object of type *String*, *Bitmap*, *Metafile*, or even *Button* on the clipboard, and you extract an object of type *String*, *Bitmap*, *Metafile*, or *Button* from the clipboard.

But not every application running under Windows is a Windows Forms program! Some Windows programs place objects on the clipboard that don't directly correspond to Windows Forms types. The problem goes both ways: Windows applications that make use of the Win32 API or MFC are not prepared to deal directly with Windows Forms objects.

Let's examine the seemingly simple data type known as *text*. Some existing Windows programs store text in Unicode, but most of them don't. If a Windows program passes 8-bit ANSI text strings to the clipboard, a Windows Forms program should be able to read the text as a normal *String* object. Likewise, when a Windows Forms program puts a *String* object on the clipboard, it should be readable by programs that know only the ANSI character set. There's even another text encoding known as OEM text that dates back to the character-mode environment of MS-DOS. OEM stands for "original equipment manufacturer," but in the United States, it really refers to the 8-bit character set IBM used in the original PC. (You may remember the line-drawing characters used by character-mode programs.) ANSI text and OEM text differ in the upper 128 characters.

These requirements suggest that the clipboard must perform conversions among multiple text encodings. Regardless of the encoding of the text that goes on the clipboard, the clipboard must make several additional encodings available to other applications.

It's already fairly clear that these conversions between different encodings are taking place. The ClipText program successfully transfers text to and from regular Windows programs that use either ANSI or Unicode text encoding.

However, the problems of text don't stop with character encodings. Consider a word processor that copies a block of text to the clipboard. What happens to the formatting of the text? If the user wants to paste such text back into the same word processing program (perhaps in the same document or in a different one), the text certainly shouldn't lose its formatting. On the other hand, if the user wants to paste the text into Notepad, all the formatting should be stripped from the text. What should happen if you paste the text into *another* word processing program? You probably want the formatting to be preserved, and that implies that the text on the clipboard should be stored in a way that includes formatting in an application-independent manner (RTF, for example, or possibly HTML).

Or suppose you copy text from a Web browser to the clipboard. The HTML formatting should be preserved for applications that understand HTML, but it shouldn't be imposed on applications that can't deal with it. Most users probably don't want to see HTML tags when they copy text from a Web browser to Notepad!

Some text is intended to be read by programs rather than people. For example, many database and spreadsheet programs can copy and paste information in a comma-separated value (CSV) text format. This format provides an application-independent way of sharing database records or numeric tables.

So, the simple statement that copies a text string to the clipboard,

```
Clipboard.SetDataObject(str)
```

probably doesn't quite do what you want if *str* is a text string that consists of RTF, HTML, or CSV text. Preferably there should be some way for an application to specify what type of text it's actually putting on the clipboard.

When a word processing application copies text to the clipboard, the application itself is probably in the best position to convert its internal format into RTF and plain, unformatted text. The implication is that applications should be able to set data on the clipboard in several different formats at once. (At first, that doesn't seem possible. When you call *SetDataObject*, the object passed as an argument replaces the current contents of the clipboard. You can't call *SetDataObject* multiple times to put multiple formats of the same text on the clipboard. However, as we'll soon see, the argument to *SetDataObject* can be an object that itself specifies several different objects.)

To a Windows Forms program, bitmaps and metafiles are objects of type *Bitmap* and *Metafile*. To a non–Windows Forms program, however, there are two types of bitmaps: the old-style, device-dependent bitmaps that were introduced in Windows 1.0 and the DIBs (device-independent bitmaps) introduced in Windows 3.0. And, as I discussed in Chapter 23, non–Windows Forms programs deal with the original metafile format (WMF) and the enhanced metafile format (EMF).

Here's the key to making all this work: the clipboard stores not only chunks of data but also identifications of the data formats. To a Windows Forms program, a particular clipboard format is usually identified by a text string, such as "DeviceIndependentBitmap" or "Text". These text strings are also associated with ID numbers, such as 8 for "DeviceIndependentBitmap" and 1 for "Text". The ID numbers are the same as the identifiers beginning with *CF* ("clipboard format") defined in the Win32 header files used by C programmers.

The *GetFormats* method defined in the *IDataObject* interface provides a list of all the data formats currently stored on the clipboard:

### *IDataObject GetFormats* Methods

```
Function GetFormats() As String()
Function GetFormats(ByVal bIncludeConversions As Boolean) As String()
```

The call

```
Dim astr() As String = data.GetFormats()
```

is equivalent to

```
Dim astr() As String = data.GetFormats(True)
```

Both calls return string identifications of all the clipboard formats currently available from the clipboard. Some of these formats represent conversions from the data currently stored on the clipboard. To restrict the list to just unconverted formats, use

```
Dim astr() As String = data.GetFormats(False)
```

Sometimes data is converted as it's put on the clipboard. Those formats will be returned regardless of the *GetFormats* argument. For example, if a Windows Forms program puts a *String* object on the clipboard, *GetFormats* (regardless of the argument) returns the strings

```
System.String
UnicodeText
Text
```

The "UnicodeText" and "Text" types allow a Win32 API or MFC program to obtain the clipboard text in either Unicode or an 8-bit ANSI encoding.

When Notepad puts text on the clipboard, *GetFormats* with a *False* argument returns these four strings:

```
UnicodeText
Locale
Text
OEMText
```

A call to *GetFormats* with no arguments or a *True* argument returns those four strings and this one as well:

```
System.String
```

When a Windows Forms program puts a *Bitmap* object on the clipboard, then regardless of the arguments, *GetFormats* returns the strings

```
System.Drawing.Bitmap
WindowsForms10PersistentObject
Bitmap
```

When a Windows Forms program puts a *Metafile* object on the clipboard, then regardless of the arguments, *GetFormats* returns the strings

```
System.Drawing.Imaging.Metafile
WindowsForms10PersistentObject
```

It's also possible to use the format strings in the *GetDataPresent* and *GetData* methods defined in the *IDataObject* interface:

### *IDataObject* Methods (selection)

```
Function GetDataPresent(ByVal strFormat As String) As Boolean

Function GetDataPresent(ByVal strFormat As String,
                        ByVal bAllowConversions As Boolean) As Boolean

Function GetData(ByVal strFormat As String) As Object

Function GetData(ByVal strFormat As String,
                 ByVal bAllowConversions As Boolean) As Object
```

The call

```
Dim str As String = DirectCast(data.GetData(GetType(String)), String)
```

is equivalent to

```
Dim str As String = DirectCast(data.GetData("System.String"), String)
```

That's pretty obvious. But those two calls are also equivalent to this one:

```
Dim str As String = DirectCast(data.GetData("UnicodeText"), String)
```

The *GetData* method always converts the clipboard data into a Microsoft .NET Framework data type, so in this case *GetData* returns a *String* object.

Consider the following call:

```
Dim str As String = DirectCast(data.GetData("Text"), String)
```

Is this one equivalent as well? Maybe, maybe not. If a Unicode-aware program put a string on the clipboard that contained Hebrew, Arabic, or Cyrillic characters, for example, the string identified with "Text" is an 8-bit ANSI version of the original Unicode text. The Unicode characters that have no equivalents in the ANSI character set are replaced by question marks.

In any event, if you set the second argument of *GetDataPresent* or *GetData* to *False*, you won't get a converted type. The expression

```
DirectCast(data.GetData("Text", False), String)
```

returns *Nothing* if Unicode text was put on the clipboard.

If you prefer not to hard-code those text strings in your program, you can make use of the *DataFormats* class. This class contains 21 shared read-only fields that return the text strings for those clipboard formats directly supported by the .NET Framework. Here are the clipboard formats that originated in the Win32 API. The column at the right shows the Win32 clipboard ID number associated with each format.

## *DataFormats* Shared Fields (selection)

| Field | Type | Value | ID |
|---|---|---|---|
| Text | String | "Text" | 1 |
| Bitmap | String | "Bitmap" | 2 |
| MetafilePict | String | "MetaFilePict" | 3 |
| SymbolicLink | String | "SymbolicLink" | 4 |
| Dif | String | "DataInterchangeFormat" | 5 |
| Tiff | String | "TaggedImageFileFormat" | 6 |
| OemText | String | "OEMText" | 7 |
| Dib | String | "DeviceIndependentBitmap" | 8 |
| Palette | String | "Palette" | 9 |
| PenData | String | "PenData" | 10 |
| Riff | String | "RiffAudio" | 11 |
| WaveAudio | String | "WaveAudio" | 12 |
| UnicodeText | String | "UnicodeText" | 13 |
| EnhancedMetafile | String | "EnhancedMetafile" | 14 |
| FileDrop | String | "FileDrop" | 15 |
| Locale | String | "Locale" | 16 |

For example, the expression

```
DataFormats.Text
```

returns the string "Text", and the expression

```
DataFormats.Dib
```

returns the string "DeviceIndependentBitmap". I'll be referring to these formats by their text names because the text versions most accurately reflect the manner in which the clipboard identifies the data format.

The "Text" and "OEMText" formats are both 8-bit encodings. The "Text" format is the ANSI encoding used by most Windows programs. The "OEMText" encoding is the character set used in character-mode MS-DOS programs. The "OEMText" format is provided so that you can copy, cut, and paste in the MS-DOS Command Prompt window. A clipboard item identified by the format "Locale" is a number that usually accompanies 8-bit character encodings to identify the character set. The "UnicodeText" format identifies Unicode text.

The "SymbolicLink" string identifies text in the Symbolic Link (SYLK) format created by Microsoft for the MultiPlan spreadsheet program, and the

"DataInterchangeFormat" string identifies text in the Data Interchange Format (DIF) devised by Software Arts for the VisiCalc spreadsheet program. Both these clipboard formats were introduced in Windows 1.0 and, as you might expect, aren't used much these days.

When a Windows Forms program specifies a clipboard format of "Text", "OEMText", "UnicodeText", "SymbolicLink", or "DataInterchangeFormat" in the *GetData* method, the method returns an object of type *String*.

The "Bitmap" and "DeviceIndependentBitmap" strings identify the device-dependent and the device-independent bitmaps, respectively. The "Palette" format identifies a color palette format used in conjunction with 256-color DIBs. The "TaggedImageFileFormat" string identifies the TIFF bitmap format.

The "MetaFilePict" and "EnhancedMetafile" strings represent the old and enhanced metafile formats, respectively.

When a Windows Forms program specifies a clipboard format of "Bitmap" or "DeviceIndepedentBitmap" in the *GetData* method, the method returns an object of type *Bitmap*. For "Enhanced Metafile", *GetData* returns an object of type *Metafile*. However, for "MetaFilePict", *GetData* returns an object of type *MemoryStream*. That's simply a block of memory that a program can access using *ReadByte* and *Read* methods defined by the *MemoryStream* class. *GetData* returns a *MemoryStream* object for "MetaFilePict" because old-style metafiles are not stored in the clipboard directly. Instead, the clipboard stores a small data structure that references a handle to the metafile.

The "PenData" string is used in conjunction with the (now abandoned) pen extensions to Windows. "RiffAudio" identifies multimedia data in the Resource Interchange File Format, and "WaveAudio" identifies waveform audio files. The first release of Windows Forms has no multimedia support. For these clipboard formats (and for "Palette"), *GetData* returns an object of type *MemoryStream*.

Finally, "FileDrop" identifies a list of files that probably originated in Windows Explorer. (Select one or more files, and then perform a Copy or Cut to place a "FileDrop" object on the clipboard.) To a Windows Forms program, a "FileDrop" item is an array of strings. Although you can use "FileDrop" items with the clipboard, the format is used more often in conjunction with drag-and-drop operations (which I'll discuss toward the end of this chapter).

So far, most of these additional formats are not very useful to the Windows Forms programmer. When a Windows Forms program puts a *String* object on the clipboard, the *String* object is automatically converted to the "Text" and "UnicodeText" formats for other applications. If another application puts text (of whatever type) on the clipboard, that text is automatically converted to a *String* object for a Windows Forms program.

Similarly, as we've seen, Windows Forms programs can transfer bitmaps and metafiles to and from the clipboard without getting involved with the conversions necessary for non–Windows Forms programs.

Five additional shared fields are defined in the *DataFormats* class that are of more use to Windows Forms programs:

### *DataFormats* Shared Fields (selection)

| Field | Type | Value |
| --- | --- | --- |
| *CommaSeparatedValue* | *String* | "Csv" |
| *Html* | *String* | "HTML Format" |
| *Rtf* | *String* | "Rich Text Format" |
| *Serializable* | *String* | "WindowsForms10PersistentObject" |
| *StringFormat* | *String* | "System.String" |

These formats are not currently defined in the Win32 clipboard interface, but some Win32 programs use the first three. "Csv" is a text format used by spreadsheet and database programs for exchanging data. In a block of spreadsheet rows and columns, columns are separated by commas and rows are separated by end-of-line characters. When a database uses "Csv", fields are separated by commas and records are separated by end-of-line characters. Numbers are stored in a readable ASCII format; text is delimited by quotation marks.

Although "Csv" is a text format, a call to *GetData* with a "Csv" argument does *not* return an object of type *String*. It returns a *MemoryStream* object that contains text terminated with a zero character. To extract the *String* object from this *MemoryStream* object, you can use the following code:

```
Dim ms As MemoryStream = DirectCast(data.GetData("Csv"), MemoryStream)
Dim sr As New StreamReader(ms)
Dim str As String = sr.ReadToEnd()
```

You'll also need an *Imports* statement for the *System.IO* namespace. (See Appendix A for more information about the *MemoryStream* and *StreamReader* classes.) The *String* object will probably end with a &H0000 character.

When a Windows Forms program specifies "HTML Format" or "Rich Text Format", the *GetData* method returns an object of type *String*. However, in the former case, the *String* object will contain HTML tags along with the text. In the latter case, the *String* object may or may not contain RTF tags. Because plain text is a subset of RTF, the *String* object could contain just plain text.

The "WindowsForms10PersistentObject" format shows up when a Windows Forms program has copied a *Bitmap* or *Metafile* object to the clipboard.

The return type of *GetData* is either *Bitmap* or *Metafile*. You don't generally need to use this format.

As I mentioned earlier, the "System.String" format causes *GetData* to return an object of type *String*. It's exactly like using an argument of *Get-Type(String)*.

Here's a program that expands its Paste menu to include options to paste plain text, RTF, HTML, or CSV.

### RichTextPaste.vb

```vb
'------------------------------------------------
' RichTextPaste.vb (c) 2002 by Charles Petzold
'------------------------------------------------
Imports System
Imports System.Drawing
Imports System.IO
Imports System.Windows.Forms

Class RichTextPaste
    Inherits Form

    Private strPastedText As String = ""
    Private miPastePlain, miPasteRTF, miPasteHTML, miPasteCSV As MenuItem

    Shared Sub Main()
        Application.Run(New RichTextPaste())
    End Sub

    Sub New()
        Text = "Rich-Text Paste"
        ResizeRedraw = True

        Menu = New MainMenu()

        ' Edit menu
        Dim mi As New MenuItem("&Edit")
        AddHandler mi.Popup, AddressOf MenuEditOnPopup
        Menu.MenuItems.Add(mi)

        ' Edit Paste Plain Text menu item
        miPastePlain = New MenuItem("Paste &Plain Text")
        AddHandler miPastePlain.Click, AddressOf MenuEditPastePlainOnClick
        Menu.MenuItems(0).MenuItems.Add(miPastePlain)

        ' Edit Paste RTF menu item
        miPasteRTF = New MenuItem("Paste &Rich Text Format")
        AddHandler miPasteRTF.Click, AddressOf MenuEditPasteRTFOnClick
        Menu.MenuItems(0).MenuItems.Add(miPasteRTF)
```

*(continued)*

**RichTextPaste.vb** *(continued)*

```vb
        ' Edit Paste HTML menu item
        miPasteHTML = New MenuItem("Paste &HTML")
        AddHandler miPasteHTML.Click, AddressOf MenuEditPasteHTMLOnClick
        Menu.MenuItems(0).MenuItems.Add(miPasteHTML)

        ' Edit Paste CSV menu item
        miPasteCSV = New MenuItem("Paste &Comma-Separated Values")
        AddHandler miPasteCSV.Click, AddressOf MenuEditPasteCSVOnClick
        Menu.MenuItems(0).MenuItems.Add(miPasteCSV)
    End Sub

    Private Sub MenuEditOnPopup(ByVal obj As Object, ByVal ea As EventArgs)
        miPastePlain.Enabled = _
            Clipboard.GetDataObject().GetDataPresent(GetType(String))
        miPasteRTF.Enabled = _
            Clipboard.GetDataObject().GetDataPresent(DataFormats.Rtf)
        miPasteHTML.Enabled = _
            Clipboard.GetDataObject().GetDataPresent(DataFormats.Html)
        miPasteCSV.Enabled = _
            Clipboard.GetDataObject().GetDataPresent _
                                    (DataFormats.CommaSeparatedValue)
    End Sub

    Private Sub MenuEditPastePlainOnClick(ByVal obj As Object, _
                                          ByVal ea As EventArgs)
        Dim data As IDataObject = Clipboard.GetDataObject()
        If data.GetDataPresent(GetType(String)) Then
            strPastedText = DirectCast(data.GetData(GetType(String)), _
                                String)
            Invalidate()
        End If
    End Sub

    Private Sub MenuEditPasteRTFOnClick(ByVal obj As Object, _
                                        ByVal ea As EventArgs)
        Dim data As IDataObject = Clipboard.GetDataObject()
        If data.GetDataPresent(DataFormats.Rtf) Then
            strPastedText = DirectCast(data.GetData(DataFormats.Rtf), _
                                String)
            Invalidate()
        End If
    End Sub

    Private Sub MenuEditPasteHTMLOnClick(ByVal obj As Object, _
                                         ByVal ea As EventArgs)
        Dim data As IDataObject = Clipboard.GetDataObject()
        If data.GetDataPresent(DataFormats.Html) Then
            strPastedText = _
                        DirectCast(data.GetData(DataFormats.Html), String)
            Invalidate()
        End If
    End Sub
```

```
        Private Sub MenuEditPasteCSVOnClick(ByVal obj As Object, _
                                            ByVal ea As EventArgs)
            Dim data As IDataObject = Clipboard.GetDataObject()
            If data.GetDataPresent(DataFormats.CommaSeparatedValue) Then
                Dim ms As MemoryStream = _
                                DirectCast(data.GetData("Csv"), MemoryStream)
                Dim sr As New StreamReader(ms)
                strPastedText = sr.ReadToEnd()
                Invalidate()
            End If
        End Sub

        Protected Overrides Sub OnPaint(ByVal pea As PaintEventArgs)
            Dim grfx As Graphics = pea.Graphics
            grfx.DrawString(strPastedText, Font, New SolidBrush(ForeColor), _
                        RectangleF.op_Implicit(ClientRectangle))
        End Sub
End Class
```

Try selecting some text in a Web browser, copying it to the clipboard, and then using this program to see what formats are available. For CSV, the code to convert the *MemoryStream* object to a *String* is similar to the code I showed earlier. For RTF and HTML, the program simply displays the text without attempting to parse the formatting tags.

# Clipboard Viewers

A *clipboard viewer* is a program that displays the current contents of the clipboard. Here's a clipboard viewer that contains 21 radio buttons corresponding to the 21 fields of the *DataFormats* class. The program sets a 1-second timer and checks the clipboard contents during the *Tick* event. (The Win32 messages that inform an application when the clipboard contents have changed are not directly available to a Windows Forms program.) The radio buttons are enabled according to what formats are available. When you click a button, the clipboard item in that format is rendered on the right side of the form.

```
ClipView.vb
'---------------------------------------------
' ClipView.vb (c) 2002 by Charles Petzold
'---------------------------------------------
Imports System
Imports System.Drawing
Imports System.Drawing.Imaging
Imports System.IO
Imports System.Windows.Forms
```

*(continued)*

**ClipView.vb** *(continued)*

```vb
Class ClipView
    Inherits Form

    Private astrFormats() As String = _
        {DataFormats.Bitmap, DataFormats.CommaSeparatedValue, _
        DataFormats.Dib, DataFormats.Dif, DataFormats.EnhancedMetafile, _
        DataFormats.FileDrop, DataFormats.Html, DataFormats.Locale, _
        DataFormats.MetafilePict, DataFormats.OemText, _
        DataFormats.Palette, DataFormats.PenData, DataFormats.Riff, _
        DataFormats.Rtf, DataFormats.Serializable, _
        DataFormats.StringFormat, DataFormats.SymbolicLink, _
        DataFormats.Text, DataFormats.Tiff, DataFormats.UnicodeText, _
        DataFormats.WaveAudio}

    Private pnlDisplay As Panel
    Private aradio() As RadioButton
    Private radioChecked As RadioButton

    Shared Sub Main()
        Application.Run(New ClipView())
    End Sub

    Sub New()
        Text = "Clipboard Viewer"

        ' Create variable-width panel for clipboard display.
        pnlDisplay = New Panel()
        pnlDisplay.Parent = Me
        pnlDisplay.Dock = DockStyle.Fill
        AddHandler pnlDisplay.Paint, AddressOf PanelOnPaint
        pnlDisplay.BorderStyle = BorderStyle.Fixed3D

        ' Create splitter.
        Dim split As New Splitter()
        split.Parent = Me
        split.Dock = DockStyle.Left

        ' Create panel for radio buttons.
        Dim pnl As New Panel()
        pnl.Parent = Me
        pnl.Dock = DockStyle.Left
        pnl.Width = 200

        ' Create radio buttons.
        ReDim aradio(astrFormats.Length - 1)
        Dim eh As EventHandler = AddressOf RadioButtonOnClick
        Dim i As Integer
        For i = 0 To astrFormats.GetUpperBound(0)
            aradio(i) = New RadioButton()
            aradio(i).Parent = pnl
            aradio(i).Location = New Point(4, 12 * i)
            aradio(i).Size = New Size(300, 12)
```

```
        AddHandler aradio(i).Click, eh
        aradio(i).Tag = astrFormats(i)
    Next i

    ' Set autoscale base size.
    AutoScaleBaseSize = New Size(4, 8)

    ' Set timer for 1 second.
    Dim tmr As New Timer()
    tmr.Interval = 1000
    AddHandler tmr.Tick, AddressOf TimerOnTick
    tmr.Enabled = True
End Sub

Private Sub TimerOnTick(ByVal obj As Object, ByVal ea As EventArgs)
    Dim data As IDataObject = Clipboard.GetDataObject()
    Dim i As Integer

    For i = 0 To astrFormats.Length - 1
        aradio(i).Text = astrFormats(i)
        aradio(i).Enabled = data.GetDataPresent(astrFormats(i))
        If aradio(i).Enabled Then
            If Not data.GetDataPresent(astrFormats(i), False) Then
                aradio(i).Text &= "*"
            End If
            Dim objClip As Object = data.GetData(astrFormats(i))
            Try
                aradio(i).Text &= " (" & _
                                objClip.GetType().ToString() & ")"
            Catch
                aradio(i).Text &= " (Exception on GetType!)"
            End Try
        End If
    Next i
    pnlDisplay.Invalidate()
End Sub

Private Sub RadioButtonOnClick(ByVal obj As Object, _
                            ByVal ea As EventArgs)
    radioChecked = DirectCast(obj, RadioButton)
    pnlDisplay.Invalidate()
End Sub

Private Sub PanelOnPaint(ByVal obj As Object, _
                        ByVal pea As PaintEventArgs)
    Dim panel As Panel = DirectCast(obj, Panel)
    Dim grfx As Graphics = pea.Graphics
    Dim br As New SolidBrush(panel.ForeColor)

    If radioChecked Is Nothing OrElse Not radioChecked.Enabled Then
        Return
    End If
```

*(continued)*

**ClipView.vb** *(continued)*

```
        Dim data As IDataObject = Clipboard.GetDataObject()
        Dim objClip As Object = _
                    data.GetData(DirectCast(radioChecked.Tag, String))

        If objClip Is Nothing Then
            Return
        ElseIf objClip.GetType() Is GetType(String) Then
            grfx.DrawString(DirectCast(objClip, String), Font, br, _
                        RectangleF.op_Implicit(panel.ClientRectangle))

        ElseIf objClip.GetType() Is GetType(String()) Then
            Dim str As String = String.Join(vbLf, _
                                        DirectCast(objClip, String()))
            grfx.DrawString(str, Font, br, _
                        RectangleF.op_Implicit(panel.ClientRectangle))

        ElseIf objClip.GetType() Is GetType(Bitmap) OrElse _
                objClip.GetType() Is GetType(Metafile) OrElse _
                objClip.GetType() Is GetType(Image) Then
            grfx.DrawImage(DirectCast(objClip, Image), 0, 0)

        ElseIf objClip.GetType() Is GetType(MemoryStream) Then
            Dim strm As Stream = DirectCast(objClip, Stream)
            Dim abyBuffer(16) As Byte
            Dim lAddress As Long = 0
            Dim fnt As New Font(FontFamily.GenericMonospace, _
                            Font.SizeInPoints)
            Dim y As Single = 0
            Dim iCount As Integer = strm.Read(abyBuffer, 0, 16)

            While iCount > 0
                Dim str As String = _
                        HexDump.ComposeLine(lAddress, abyBuffer, iCount)
                grfx.DrawString(str, fnt, br, 0, y)
                lAddress += 16
                y += fnt.GetHeight(grfx)

                If y > panel.Bottom Then Exit While

                iCount = strm.Read(abyBuffer, 0, 16)
            End While
        End If
    End Sub
End Class
```

During the *Tick* event handler, the button text is set to the text version of the clipboard format. If the format is available, the button text also includes an asterisk if the format has been converted from another clipboard format. The .NET data type of the clipboard format is enclosed in parentheses.

Here's what the program looks like after I've copied part of the program text from Microsoft Visual Basic .NET to the clipboard:

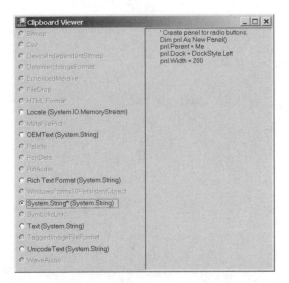

The *PanelOnPaint* method is responsible for updating the panel at the right. It can handle several .NET data types. For *String*, the text is simply displayed using *DrawText*. *DrawText* is also used for an array of *String* objects, which is the case for the "FileDrop" clipboard type. For data types of *Bitmap* and *Metafile*, the *PanelOnPaint* method uses *DrawImage*. And for the data type of *MemoryStream*, *PanelOnPaint* uses the shared *ComposeLine* method from the HexDump program in Appendix A.

The ClipView program doesn't list every format of data on the clipboard. It shows only those formats that are directly supported within Windows Forms by virtue of being represented by a field in the *DataFormats* class. As I mentioned earlier, it's possible to use the *GetFormats* method defined by the *IDataObject* interface to get a *String* array of all the formats of the current clipboard item. That's what the ClipViewAll program uses.

```
ClipViewAll.vb
'----------------------------------------------
' ClipViewAll.vb (c) 2002 by Charles Petzold
'----------------------------------------------
Imports System
Imports System.Drawing
Imports System.Drawing.Imaging
Imports System.IO
Imports System.Windows.Forms

Class ClipViewAll
    Inherits Form
```

*(continued)*

**ClipViewAll.vb** *(continued)*

```
    Private pnlDisplay, pnlButtons As Panel
    Private radioChecked As RadioButton
    Private astrFormatsSave(0) As String

    Shared Sub Main()
        Application.Run(New ClipViewAll())
    End Sub

    Sub New()
        Text = "Clipboard Viewer (All Formats)"

        ' Create variable-width panel for clipboard display.
        pnlDisplay = New Panel()
        pnlDisplay.Parent = Me
        pnlDisplay.Dock = DockStyle.Fill
        AddHandler pnlDisplay.Paint, AddressOf PanelOnPaint
        pnlDisplay.BorderStyle = BorderStyle.Fixed3D

        ' Create splitter.
        Dim split As New Splitter()
        split.Parent = Me
        split.Dock = DockStyle.Left

        ' Create panel for radio buttons.
        pnlButtons = New Panel()
        pnlButtons.Parent = Me
        pnlButtons.Dock = DockStyle.Left
        pnlButtons.AutoScroll = True
        pnlButtons.Width = Width \ 2

        ' Set timer for 1 second.
        Dim tmr As New Timer()
        tmr.Interval = 1000
        AddHandler tmr.Tick, AddressOf TimerOnTick
        tmr.Enabled = True
    End Sub

    Private Sub TimerOnTick(ByVal obj As Object, ByVal ea As EventArgs)
        Dim data As IDataObject = Clipboard.GetDataObject()
        Dim astrFormats() As String = data.GetFormats()
        Dim bUpdate As Boolean = False
        Dim i As Integer

        ' Determine whether clipboard formats have changed.
        If astrFormats.Length <> astrFormatsSave.Length Then
            bUpdate = True
        Else
            For i = 0 To astrFormats.GetUpperBound(0)
                If astrFormats(i) <> astrFormatsSave(i) Then
                    bUpdate = True
                    Exit For
                End If
        End If
```

```
            Next i
        End If

        ' Invalidate display regardless.
        pnlDisplay.Invalidate()

        ' Don't update buttons if formats haven't changed.
        If Not bUpdate Then
            Return
        End If

        ' Formats have changed, so re-create radio buttons.
        astrFormatsSave = astrFormats
        pnlButtons.Controls.Clear()

        Dim grfx As Graphics = CreateGraphics()
        Dim eh As EventHandler = AddressOf RadioButtonOnClick
        Dim cxText As Integer = AutoScaleBaseSize.Width
        Dim cyText As Integer = AutoScaleBaseSize.Height

        For i = 0 To astrFormats.GetUpperBound(0)
            Dim radio As New RadioButton()
            radio.Parent = pnlButtons
            radio.Text = astrFormats(i)

            If Not data.GetDataPresent(astrFormats(i), False) Then
                radio.Text &= "*"
            End If

            Try
                Dim objClip As Object = data.GetData(astrFormats(i))
                radio.Text &= " (" & objClip.GetType().ToString() & ")"
            Catch
                radio.Text &= " (Exception on GetData or GetType!)"
            End Try

            radio.Tag = astrFormats(i)
            radio.Location = New Point(cxText, i * 3 * cyText \ 2)
            radio.Size = New Size((radio.Text.Length + 20) * cxText, _
                                  3 * cyText \ 2)
            AddHandler radio.Click, eh
        Next i
        grfx.Dispose()
        radioChecked = Nothing
    End Sub

    Private Sub RadioButtonOnClick(ByVal obj As Object, _
                                   ByVal ea As EventArgs)
        radioChecked = DirectCast(obj, RadioButton)
        pnlDisplay.Invalidate()
    End Sub
```

*(continued)*

**ClipViewAll.vb** *(continued)*

```vb
    Private Sub PanelOnPaint(ByVal obj As Object, _
                            ByVal pea As PaintEventArgs)
        Dim pnl As Panel = DirectCast(obj, Panel)
        Dim grfx As Graphics = pea.Graphics
        Dim br As New SolidBrush(pnl.ForeColor)

        If radioChecked Is Nothing Then Return

        Dim data As IDataObject = Clipboard.GetDataObject()
        Dim objClip As Object = _
                    data.GetData(DirectCast(radioChecked.Tag, String))

        If objClip Is Nothing Then
            Return
        ElseIf objClip.GetType() Is GetType(String) Then
            grfx.DrawString(DirectCast(objClip, String), Font, br, _
                        RectangleF.op_Implicit(pnl.ClientRectangle))

        ElseIf objClip.GetType() Is GetType(String()) Then
            Dim str As String = _
                        String.Join(vbLf, DirectCast(objClip, String()))
            grfx.DrawString(str, Font, br, _
                        RectangleF.op_Implicit(pnl.ClientRectangle))

        ElseIf objClip.GetType() Is GetType(Bitmap) OrElse _
                objClip.GetType() Is GetType(Metafile) OrElse _
                objClip.GetType() Is GetType(Image) Then
            grfx.DrawImage(DirectCast(objClip, Image), 0, 0)

        ElseIf objClip.GetType() Is GetType(MemoryStream) Then
            Dim strm As Stream = DirectCast(objClip, Stream)
            Dim abyBuffer(16) As Byte
            Dim lAddress As Long = 0
            Dim fnt As New Font(FontFamily.GenericMonospace, _
                            Font.SizeInPoints)
            Dim y As Single = 0
            Dim iCount As Integer = strm.Read(abyBuffer, 0, 16)

            While iCount > 0
                Dim str As String = _
                        HexDump.ComposeLine(lAddress, abyBuffer, iCount)
                grfx.DrawString(str, fnt, br, 0, y)
                lAddress += 16
                y += fnt.GetHeight(grfx)

                If y > pnl.Bottom Then Exit While

                iCount = strm.Read(abyBuffer, 0, 16)
            End While
        End If
    End Sub
End Class
```

Every second, this program checks whether the clipboard formats have changed and, if they have, re-creates a collection of radio buttons, one for each format. Like the ClipView program, the text for each radio button also indicates whether the format is native and the .NET type of the data.

Here's what the program looks like after I've copied some text from Microsoft Word to the clipboard:

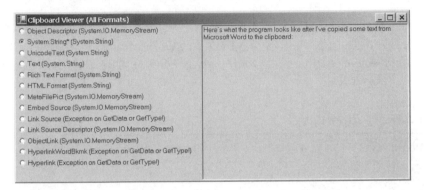

Yes, this display does indeed reveal that the clipboard contains 13 different formats of the same text item.

Because the clipboard provides a medium for applications to exchange data, it's essential that you test your clipboard code with other applications. You'll find the ClipView and ClipViewAll programs useful for exploring the clipboard from the perspective of a Windows Forms program, but the data your program copies to the clipboard must also make sense to non–Windows Forms programs.

If you begin exploring the various clipboard formats that some applications use (such as the list in the ClipViewAll display from Word), you'll find that some of them originated in the OLE (object linking and embedding) specification, while others (like "HyperlinkWordBkmk") are obviously private to the application.

Using a private clipboard format is simple. You just make up a name for the format, store it in a *String*, and use that *String* as the clipboard format. You'll want to avoid collisions with other applications using their own private formats, so give the format a name you're sure will be unique. It's pretty easy if you use the name of the application as part of the clipboard format name, for example, "WriteALot Version 2.1 Formatted Text".

Win32 programs generally refer to clipboard formats using ID numbers. (The first table of the *DataFormats* fields earlier in this chapter shows the ID numbers associated with the standard clipboard formats.) Windows also assigns identification numbers when applications use nonstandard formats. The *DataFormats* class has a shared method named *GetFormat* that essentially translates the format name and the format ID:

### *DataFormats* Shared Methods

```
Function GetFormat(ByVal id As Integer) As Format
Function GetFormat(ByVal strName As String) As Format
```

*Format* is another class defined within *DataFormats*, so it appears in the class library documentation as *DataFormats.Format*. The class has just two, read-only properties:

### *Format* Properties

| Property | Type | Accessibility |
|----------|------|---------------|
| *Id* | *Integer* | Get |
| *Name* | *String* | Get |

For example, the call

```
DataFormats.GetFormat("DeviceIndependentBitmap").Id
```

returns 8, and the call

```
DataFormats.GetFormat(8).Name
```

returns the string "DeviceIndependentBitmap". Nonstandard formats return numbers that can vary from session to session, so you shouldn't hard-code them in your programs.

If you use a private clipboard format, you should supplement it with standard formats. That requires that you use multiple clipboard formats for the same clipboard item.

# Setting Multiple Clipboard Formats

As you've seen, you use the shared *SetDataObject* method of the *Clipboard* class to put data on the clipboard. Here's a call that puts text on the clipboard:

```
Clipboard.SetDataObject(strText)
```

You use similar calls for putting objects of type *Bitmap* or *Metafile* on the clipboard.

But what if the *strText* variable contains a block of RTF or HTML text? How do you indicate that fact in the *SetDataObject* call? And what if you need to put multiple formats on the clipboard? Because each call to *SetDataObject* replaces the item already on the clipboard, that doesn't seem possible.

The solution to both these problems is the *DataObject* class. Recall that the shared *GetDataObject* method of *Clipboard* is documented as returning an object of a class that implements the *IDataObject* interface. *DataObject* is the only class in the .NET Framework that implements the *IDataObject* interface. (This doesn't necessarily mean that *Clipboard.GetDataObject* returns an object of type *DataObject*. It could create a new class dynamically. But you'll find that *Clipboard.GetDataObject* often does indeed return an object of type *DataObject*.)

*DataObject* has three constructors:

## *DataObject* Constructors

```
DataObject()

DataObject(ByVal objData As Object)

DataObject(ByVal strFormat As String, ByVal objData As Object)
```

For example, the call

```
Clipboard.SetDataObject(strText)
```

is equivalent to

```
Clipboard.SetDataObject(New DataObject(strText))
```

or

```
Clipboard.SetDataObject(New DataObject(DataFormats.StringFormat, strText))
```

If *strText* actually contains a block of HTML, you can use

```
Clipboard.SetDataObject(New DataObject(DataFormats.Html, strText))
```

if the item shouldn't remain on the clipboard after the program terminates, and

```
Clipboard.SetDataObject(New DataObject(DataFormats.Html, strText), True)
```

if it should remain.

*DataObject* implements the *IDataObject* interface, so it supports all the methods defined for *IDataObject*; the class doesn't support any other methods or properties. I've already discussed the *GetDataPresent*, *GetData*, and *GetFormats* methods. The only remaining method is *SetData*, and that's the one you'll use when you use *DataObject* for defining multiple formats:

### *DataObject SetData* **Method**

```
Sub SetData(ByVal objData As Object)

Sub SetData(ByVal typeFormat As Type, ByVal objData As Object)

Sub SetData(ByVal strFormat As String, ByVal objData As Object)

Sub SetData(ByVal strFormat As String, ByVal bConvert As Boolean,
          ByVal objData As Object)
```

You create an object of type *DataObject*, use calls to *SetData* to store multiple formats of a single item, and then pass the *DataObject* object to *Clipboard.Set-DataObject*. By default, items are converted to compatible formats unless you use the last overload in the table and set the *bConvert* argument to *False*.

For example, suppose *strText* is a string of plain text you want to copy to the clipboard, *strHtml* contains the same text with HTML formatting, and *strRtf* is the same string with RTF formatting. Here's a sequence for storing these multiple formats on the clipboard:

```
Dim data As New DataObject()
data.SetData(strText)
data.SetData(DataFormats.Html, strHtml)
data.SetData(DataFormats.Rtf, strRtf)
Clipboard.SetDataObject(data, True)
```

Watch out: Nobody's checking whether *strHtml* and *strRtf* are really blocks of HTML and RTF! Likewise, any data that your program obtains from the clipboard might not necessarily be what it's labeled. You'll want to parse HTML and RTF text strings from the clipboard very carefully.

Here's a program, MultiCopy, that copies a two-dimensional array of *Single* values (defined as a field named *afValues*) to the clipboard in three different formats: a private format, the CSV format, and a plain text format.

**MultiCopy.vb**

```
'-------------------------------------------
' MultiCopy.vb (c) 2002 by Charles Petzold
'-------------------------------------------
Imports System
Imports System.Drawing
Imports System.IO
Imports System.Windows.Forms

Class MultiCopy
    Inherits Form

    Const strFormat As String = "MultiCopy.InternalFormat"
    Private afValues(,) As Single = {{0.12F, 3.45F, 6.78F, 9.01F}, _
                                     {2.34F, 5.67F, 8.9F, 1.23F}, _
                                     {4.56F, 7.89F, 0.12F, 3.45F}}
```

```
Shared Sub Main()
    Application.Run(New MultiCopy())
End Sub

Sub New()
    Text = "Multi Copy"
    Menu = New MainMenu()

    ' Edit menu
    Dim mi As New MenuItem("&Edit")
    Menu.MenuItems.Add(mi)

    ' Edit Copy menu item
    mi = New MenuItem("&Copy")
    AddHandler mi.Click, AddressOf MenuEditCopyOnClick
    mi.Shortcut = Shortcut.CtrlC
    Menu.MenuItems(0).MenuItems.Add(mi)
End Sub

Private Sub MenuEditCopyOnClick(ByVal obj As Object, _
                                ByVal ea As EventArgs)
    Dim data As New DataObject()

    ' Define internal clipboard format.
    Dim ms As New MemoryStream()
    Dim bw As New BinaryWriter(ms)
    Dim iRow, iCol As Integer

    bw.Write(afValues.GetLength(0))
    bw.Write(afValues.GetLength(1))

    For iRow = 0 To afValues.GetUpperBound(0)
        For iCol = 0 To afValues.GetUpperBound(1)
            bw.Write(afValues(iRow, iCol))
        Next iCol
    Next iRow

    bw.Close()
    data.SetData(strFormat, ms)

    ' Define CSV clipboard format.
    ms = New MemoryStream()
    Dim sw As New StreamWriter(ms)

    For iRow = 0 To afValues.GetUpperBound(0)
        For iCol = 0 To afValues.GetUpperBound(1)
            sw.Write(afValues(iRow, iCol))

            If iCol < afValues.GetUpperBound(1) Then
                sw.Write(",")
            Else
                sw.WriteLine()
```

*(continued)*

**MultiCopy.vb** *(continued)*

```
            End If
        Next iCol
    Next iRow

    sw.Write(Chr(0))
    sw.Close()
    data.SetData(DataFormats.CommaSeparatedValue, ms)

    ' Define String clipboard format.
    Dim strw As New StringWriter()

    For iRow = 0 To afValues.GetUpperBound(0)
        For iCol = 0 To afValues.GetUpperBound(1)
            strw.Write(afValues(iRow, iCol))
            If iCol < afValues.GetLength(1) - 1 Then
                strw.Write(vbTab)
            Else
                strw.WriteLine()
            End If
        Next iCol
    Next iRow
    strw.Close()
    data.SetData(strw.ToString())

    Clipboard.SetDataObject(data, False)
    End Sub
End Class
```

Most of what this program does takes place during the *MenuEditCopyOn-Click* event handler. That method begins by defining an object of type *DataObject* and concludes by calling *Clipboard.SetDataObject* to copy the object to the clipboard. In between, the data is formatted in three different ways.

A private format is identified by the string "MultiCopy.InternalFormat". The array of *Single* values (preceded by the integer number of rows and columns) is stored in a binary format in a *MemoryStream* object. The method uses the *BinaryWriter* class (discussed in Appendix A) to facilitate the writing of binary objects to the stream. The method adds the memory stream to the *DataObject* object using the call

```
data.SetData(strFormat, ms)
```

where *strFormat* is the string "MultiCopy.InternalFormat".

Next the method formats the data in CSV. Again, it creates a *MemoryStream* object for storing the data, and this time it creates a *StreamWriter* object to facilitate the addition of formatted text strings to the stream. Values in the same row are separated by commas; lines are separated by carriage returns and line feeds. The method adds this memory stream to the *DataObject* object using the call

```
data.SetData(DataFormats.CommaSeparatedValue, ms)
```

Finally, the information is formatted into plain text. The process is much like CSV formatting except that tabs are used rather than commas to separate values in the same row. Another difference is that the text isn't put into a memory stream. Instead, the program uses a *StringWriter* object to construct a string containing formatted text. This format is added to the *DataObject* object using the call

```
data.SetData(sw.ToString())
```

# Drag and Drop

The drag-and-drop facility in Windows allows a user to grab something with the mouse and drag it to another part of the same application or a different application. Usually what the user grabs is one or more files or a block of text, although images and other types of data can also be dragged and dropped.

The application from which you drag an object is called the drag-and-drop *source*. The application that you drag the object to is the drag-and-drop *target*. Drag-and-drop usually requires that the left mouse button be pressed, although some applications allow dragging with the right button pressed.

The Windows Explorer application is very often a drag-and-drop source for a list of files (referred to as the clipboard type "FileDrop"). For example, if you select a file in Windows Explorer and then drag it to the client area of Notepad, Notepad will open the file and display it. The Microsoft WordPad program can be a drag-and-drop source and target for text. If you select some text in WordPad, you can drag it to another application that serves as a drag-and-drop target. Similarly, WordPad can be a target for dragged text.

Data dragged from one application to another is generally moved, copied, or linked, depending on the status of the Shift and Ctrl keys:

### Drag-and-Drop Actions

| Key Pressed | Action |
| --- | --- |
| None | Move |
| Ctrl | Copy |
| Shift+Ctrl | Link |

In a Move operation, the drag-and-drop source deletes the object. In a Copy, the target receives a copy of the object. In a Link, the source and target each get references to the same object.

If you use the mouse to grab a file list in Windows Explorer or a block of text in WordPad, and you drag that to the client area of any program shown in this book so far, the cursor will change to a circle with a slash—the international no-no sign. To become a drag-and-drop target, a control or form must first have its *AllowDrop* property set to *True*:

### *Control* Properties (selection)

| Property | Type | Accessibility |
| --- | --- | --- |
| *AllowDrop* | *Boolean* | Get/Set |

The following four events are associated with being a drag-and-drop target:

### *Control* Events (selection)

| Event | Method | Delegate | Arguments |
| --- | --- | --- | --- |
| *DragEnter* | *OnDragEnter* | *DragEventHandler* | *DragEventArgs* |
| *DragOver* | *OnDragOver* | *DragEventHandler* | *DragEventArgs* |
| *DragDrop* | *OnDragDrop* | *DragEventHandler* | *DragEventArgs* |
| *DragLeave* | *OnDragLeave* | *EventHandler* | *EventArgs* |

A *DragEnter* event occurs when a control or form has its *AllowDrop* property set to *True* and the mouse pointer dragging an object first enters the control or the form's client area. After that *DragEnter* event, as the mouse is moved within the control or the client area, *DragOver* events occur. If the mouse is then moved outside the control or the client area, a *DragLeave* event occurs.

A control or form can signal its receptiveness to being a target for the dragged data during the *DragEnter* event or during one of the subsequent *DragOver* events. (We'll see how shortly.) At that point, the cursor changes from a slashed circle to an arrow with a little box on its tail, possibly accompanied by a plus sign (for a Copy) or a curved arrow (for a Link). If the mouse is then released over the client area, a *DragDrop* event occurs.

If the control or form doesn't signal its receptiveness to the data, the cursor remains a slashed circle. If the mouse is released over the client area, a *DragLeave* event occurs, not a *DragDrop*.

Generally, you'll want to handle the *DragOver* and *DragDrop* events. During the *DragOver* event, you decide whether you can accept the data that's being dragged to your control or form. If only certain areas of the control or form are valid for a drop, you can signal when the drop is valid and when it's not. During the *DragDrop* event, you actually get access to the data. (It's just like a clipboard paste.)

The *DragEnter*, *DragOver*, and *DragDrop* events are all accompanied by an object of type *DragEventArgs*, which has the following properties:

### *DragEventArgs* Properties

| Property | Type | Accessibility |
|---|---|---|
| *KeyState* | *Integer* | Get |
| *X* | *Integer* | Get |
| *Y* | *Integer* | Get |
| *Data* | *IDataObject* | Get |
| *AllowedEffect* | *DragDropEffects* | Get |
| *Effect* | *DragDropEffects* | Get/Set |

The first three properties give you some information about the keyboard and mouse at the time of the event. The *KeyState* property uses a set of bit flags to indicate which mouse buttons and modifier keys are currently pressed:

### *KeyState* Bit Flags

| Key or Button | Bit Flag |
|---|---|
| Left mouse button | &H01 |
| Right mouse button | &H02 |
| Shift key | &H04 |
| Ctrl key | &H08 |
| Middle mouse button | &H10 |
| Alt key | &H20 |

The *X* and *Y* properties indicate the location of the mouse pointer in screen coordinates. (Use the *PointToClient* method of *Control* to convert to client area coordinates.)

The next property is named *Data*, and it's an object of a class that implements the *IDataObject* interface, just as in the *GetDataObject* method of the *Clipboard* class. During the *DragEnter* or *DragOver* event, you can use the *GetFormats* or *GetDataPresent* methods to determine whether the data is of a type your program can handle. During the *DragDrop* event, you use the *GetData* method to obtain a copy of the data.

The *AllowedEffect* property contains one or more members of the *Drag-DropEffects* enumeration:

### *DragDropEffects* Enumeration

| Member | Value |
| --- | --- |
| *None* | &H00000000 |
| *Copy* | &H00000001 |
| *Move* | &H00000002 |
| *Link* | &H00000004 |
| *Scroll* | &H80000000 |
| *All* | &H80000003 |

The *AllowedEffect* property is effectively set by the drag-and-drop source to indicate the options available to a drag-and-drop target. Most commonly, a drag-and-drop source will set *AllowedEffect* to

```
DragDropEffects.Copy Or DragDropEffects.Move Or DragDropEffects.Link
```

During the *DragEnter* and *DragOver* events, and based on the *KeyState*, *X*, *Y*, *Data*, and *AllowedEffect* properties of the *DragEventArgs* object, the potential drag-and-drop target decides whether it can accept the dropped data. If it can, it sets the *Effect* property to one of the members of the *DragDropEffects* enumeration, a member that is included in the *AllowedEffect* property. Generally, the target uses the *KeyState* property to determine whether *Effect* should be set to the *Copy*, *Move*, or *Link* member. (That's what controls the appearance of the cursor.) Setting the *Effect* property to *DragDropEffects.None* signals that the target can't accept the data. After the user drops the object, the drag-and-drop source is informed which member of the enumeration the target specified.

For any particular drag-and-drop operation, the potential drag-and-drop target needs to set the *Effect* property only once; that value will be reflected in the *DragEventArgs* argument of subsequent *DragOver* and *DragDrop* events. It's as if a single *DragEventArgs* object were used for the entire drag-and-drop operation. However, the *DragOver* event handler will probably want to change *Effect* based on the current status of the Ctrl and Shift keys.

In Chapter 18, I began a series of programs that progressively attempted to emulate Notepad. The adventure continued in Chapter 21, and is now about to come to a conclusion. The following file makes the program a drag-and-drop target for text or a "FileDrop" list. (The real Notepad is only a target for "File-Drop".) The file is called simply NotepadClone.vb because the program is as finished as it's going to get in this book.

## NotepadClone.vb

```vb
'------------------------------------------------
' NotepadClone.vb (c) 2002 by Charles Petzold
'------------------------------------------------
Imports System
Imports System.Drawing
Imports System.Windows.Forms

Class NotepadClone
    Inherits NotepadCloneWithPrinting

    Shared Shadows Sub Main()
        Application.Run(New NotepadClone())
    End Sub

    Sub New()
        strProgName = "NotepadClone"
        MakeCaption()

        txtbox.AllowDrop = True
        AddHandler txtbox.DragOver, AddressOf TextBoxOnDragOver
        AddHandler txtbox.DragDrop, AddressOf TextBoxOnDragDrop
    End Sub

    Private Sub TextBoxOnDragOver(ByVal obj As Object, _
                                  ByVal dea As DragEventArgs)
        If dea.Data.GetDataPresent(DataFormats.FileDrop) OrElse _
            dea.Data.GetDataPresent(DataFormats.StringFormat) Then
            If (dea.AllowedEffect And DragDropEffects.Move) <> 0 Then
                dea.Effect = DragDropEffects.Move
            End If
            If ((dea.AllowedEffect And DragDropEffects.Copy) <> 0) AndAlso _
                ((dea.KeyState And &H8) <> 0) Then
                dea.Effect = DragDropEffects.Copy
            End If
        End If
    End Sub

    Private Sub TextBoxOnDragDrop(ByVal obj As Object, _
                                  ByVal dea As DragEventArgs)
        If dea.Data.GetDataPresent(DataFormats.FileDrop) Then
            If Not OkToTrash() Then Return
            Dim astr() As String = _
                DirectCast(dea.Data.GetData(DataFormats.FileDrop), String())
            LoadFile(astr(0)) ' In NotepadCloneWithFile.cs
        ElseIf dea.Data.GetDataPresent(DataFormats.StringFormat) Then
            txtbox.SelectedText = _
                DirectCast(dea.Data.GetData(DataFormats.StringFormat), _
                        String)
        End If
    End Sub
End Class
```

During the constructor, the program sets the *AllowDrop* property of the *TextBox* control to *True* and sets handlers for the text box's *DragOver* and *DragDrop* events. During the *DragOver* event, the program checks for data formats of "FileDrop" or "System.String" and then sets the *Effect* property of the *DragEventArgs* object to either *DragDropEffects.Move* or *DragDropEffects.Copy*, depending on what the drag-and-drop source supports and the status of the Ctrl key.

During the *DragDrop* event, the program does something different, depending on the data format. A format of "FileDrop" causes the program to load the file. Although "FileDrop" usually indicates a *list* of files, NotepadClone can use only one file. For a format of "System.String", the program performs an operation similar to a Paste.

You can experiment with transferring text into NotepadClone by using the program in conjunction with a drag-and-drop source such as WordPad. As you drag something from WordPad to NotepadClone, you can control the appearance of the cursor by pressing and releasing the Ctrl key. When the *DragDrop* event finally occurs, WordPad is notified of the last setting of the *Effect* property. WordPad is responsible for deleting or not deleting the selected text.

Let's now examine what's involved in becoming a drag-and-drop source. Any class descended from *Control* can initiate a drag-and-drop operation by calling the following method, generally in response to a *MouseDown* event:

### *Control* Methods (selection)

```
Function DoDragDrop(ByVal objData As Object,
                 ByVal dde As DragDropEffects) As DragDropEffects
```

The first argument is the object that the drag-and-drop source has to offer. This argument could be an object of type *DataObject* if the drag-and-drop source can provide data in multiple formats or if it wants to be more explicit about the format of the data (for example, specifying "HTML Format" for a *String* type). The second argument is one or more members of the *DragDropEffects* enumeration.

The method doesn't return until the drag-and-drop operation has completed. At that point, *DoDragDrop* returns a member of the *DragDropEffects* enumeration specified by the drag-and-drop target or *DragDropEffects.None* if the target didn't accept the data or the operation was aborted in some way.

Although *DoDragDrop* doesn't return until the operation has completed, a control or form can be periodically notified during the process by handling the *QueryContinueDrag* event. In the following table, ellipses are used to indicate the event name in the method, delegate, and event argument names:

### *Control* Events (selection)

| Event | Method | Delegate | Argument |
|---|---|---|---|
| *QueryContinueDrag* | *On...* | *...EventHandler* | *...EventArgs* |

The *QueryContinueDragEventArgs* object that accompanies the event has the following properties:

### *QueryContinueDragEventArgs* Properties

| Property | Type | Accessibility |
|---|---|---|
| *KeyState* | *Integer* | Get |
| *EscapePressed* | *Boolean* | Get |
| *Action* | *DragAction* | Get/Set |

The drag-and-drop source can set the *Action* property to one of the following members of the *DragAction* enumeration:

### *DragAction* Enumeration

| Member | Value |
|---|---|
| *Continue* | 0 |
| *Drop* | 1 |
| *Cancel* | 2 |

Normally, the drag-and-drop operation will be cancelled if the user presses the Esc key. You can override that behavior—or cancel the operation for other reasons—by handling this event.

Here's a program that overrides and enhances ImageClip to become both a drag-and-drop source and target.

**ImageDrop.vb**

```
'-------------------------------------------------
' ImageDrop.vb (c) 2002 by Charles Petzold
'-------------------------------------------------
Imports System
Imports System.Drawing
Imports System.Drawing.Imaging
Imports System.IO
Imports System.Windows.Forms
```

*(continued)*

**ImageDrop.vb**  *(continued)*

```vb
Class ImageDrop
    Inherits ImageClip

    Private bIsTarget As Boolean

    Shared Shadows Sub Main()
        Application.Run(New ImageDrop())
    End Sub

    Sub New()
        strProgName = "Image Drop"
        Text = strProgName
        AllowDrop = True
    End Sub

    Protected Overrides Sub OnDragOver(ByVal dea As DragEventArgs)
        If dea.Data.GetDataPresent(DataFormats.FileDrop) OrElse _
            dea.Data.GetDataPresent(GetType(Metafile)) OrElse _
            dea.Data.GetDataPresent(GetType(Bitmap)) Then
            If (dea.AllowedEffect And DragDropEffects.Move) <> 0 Then
                dea.Effect = DragDropEffects.Move
            End If
            If ((dea.AllowedEffect And DragDropEffects.Copy) <> 0) AndAlso _
                ((dea.KeyState And &H8) <> 0) Then
                dea.Effect = DragDropEffects.Copy
            End If
        End If
    End Sub

    Protected Overrides Sub OnDragDrop(ByVal dea As DragEventArgs)
        If dea.Data.GetDataPresent(DataFormats.FileDrop) Then
            Dim astr() As String = _
                DirectCast(dea.Data.GetData(DataFormats.FileDrop), String())
            Try
                img = Image.FromFile(astr(0))
            Catch exc As Exception
                MessageBox.Show(exc.Message, Text)
                Return
            End Try

            strFileName = astr(0)
            Text = strProgName & " - " & Path.GetFileName(strFileName)
            Invalidate()
        Else
            If dea.Data.GetDataPresent(GetType(Metafile)) Then
                img = DirectCast(dea.Data.GetData(GetType(Metafile)), Image)
            ElseIf dea.Data.GetDataPresent(GetType(Bitmap)) Then
                img = DirectCast(dea.Data.GetData(GetType(Bitmap)), Image)
            End If

            bIsTarget = True
            strFileName = "DragAndDrop"
```

```
                    Text = strProgName & " - " & strFileName
                    Invalidate()
            End If
        End Sub

        Protected Overrides Sub OnMouseDown(ByVal mea As MouseEventArgs)
            If Not img Is Nothing Then
                bIsTarget = False
                Dim dde As DragDropEffects = DoDragDrop(img, _
                                DragDropEffects.Copy Or DragDropEffects.Move)
                If dde = DragDropEffects.Move AndAlso Not bIsTarget Then
                    img = Nothing
                    Invalidate()
                End If
            End If
        End Sub
    End Class
```

The *OnDragOver* and *OnDragDrop* methods are similar to the *DragOver* and *DragDrop* event handlers in NotepadClone. ImageDrop also becomes a drag-and-drop source by calling *DoDragDrop* during the *OnMouseDown* method. The program allows Copy and Move actions; if *DoDragDrop* returns *DragDropEffects.Move*, the program effectively deletes its copy of the *Image* object by setting the *image* variable to *Nothing*.

An earlier version of this program that I attempted didn't quite work right when I used the program to perform a Move operation on itself. That's because *DoDragDrop* returns after the *OnDragDrop* method returns, and the program would delete the image it had just obtained! I defined the *bIsTarget* variable for this one special case: the program no longer deletes an image moved from itself.

# Appendix A

# Files and Streams

Most file I/O support in the Microsoft .NET Framework is implemented in the *System.IO* namespace. On first exploration, however—and even during subsequent forays—*System.IO* can be a forbidding place. It doesn't help to be reassured that the .NET Framework offers a rich array of file I/O classes and tools. For a Microsoft Visual Basic 6.0 programmer whose main arsenal of file I/O consists of functions such as *Open*, *Input*, *Print*, and *Put*, the .NET file I/O support can seem excessively convoluted and complex.

This appendix provides a logical progression to guide you through *System.IO*. I want to identify the really important stuff and also let you know some of the rationale for the multitude of classes.

The .NET Framework distinguishes between files and streams. A *file* is a collection of data stored on a disk with a name and (often) a directory path. When you open a file for reading or writing, it becomes a *stream*. A stream is something on which you can perform read and write operations. But streams encompass more than just open disk files. Data coming over a network is a stream, and you can also create a stream in memory. In a console application, keyboard input and text output are also streams.

## The Most Essential File I/O Class

If you learn just one class in the *System.IO* namespace, let it be *FileStream*. You use this basic class to open, read from, write to, and close files. *FileStream* inherits from the class *Stream* (which is defined as *MustInherit*), and many of its properties and methods are derived from *Stream*.

To open an existing file or create a new file, you create an object of type *FileStream*. These five *FileStream* constructors have a nice orderly set of overloads:

### *FileStream* Constructors (selection)

```
FileStream(ByVal strFileName As String, ByVal fm As FileMode)

FileStream(ByVal strFileName As String, ByVal fm As FileMode,
           ByVal fa As FileAccess)

FileStream(ByVal strFileName As String, ByVal fm As FileMode,
           ByVal fa As FileAccess, ByVal fs As FileShare)

FileStream(ByVal strFileName As String, ByVal fm As FileMode,
           ByVal fa As FileAccess, ByVal fs As FileShare,
           ByVal iBufferSize As Integer)

FileStream(ByVal strFileName As String, ByVal fm As FileMode,
           ByVal fa As FileAccess, ByVal fs As FileShare,
           ByVal iBufferSize As Integer, ByVal bAsync As Boolean)
```

There are four additional *FileStream* constructors based on the operating system file handle. Those are useful for interfacing with existing code. *FileMode*, *FileAccess*, and *FileShare* are all enumerations defined in the *System.IO* namespace.

The *FileMode* enumeration indicates whether you want to open an existing file or create a new file and what should happen when the file you want to open doesn't exist or the file you want to create already exists:

### *FileMode* Enumeration

| Member | Value | Description |
|--------|-------|-------------|
| *CreateNew* | 1 | Fails if file exists |
| *Create* | 2 | Deletes file contents if file already exists |
| *Open* | 3 | Fails if file does not exist |
| *OpenOrCreate* | 4 | Creates new file if file does not exist |
| *Truncate* | 5 | Fails if file does not exist; deletes contents of file |
| *Append* | 6 | Fails if file is opened for reading; creates new file if file does not exist; seeks to end of file |

By *fail*, I mean that the *FileStream* constructor throws an exception such as *IOException* or *FileNotFoundException*. Almost always, you should call the *FileStream* constructor in a *Try* block to gracefully recover from any problems regarding the presumed existence or nonexistence of the file.

Unless you specify a *FileAccess* argument, the file is opened for both reading and writing. The *FileAccess* argument indicates whether you want to read from the file, write to it, or both:

### *FileAccess* Enumeration

| Member | Value | Description |
|--------|-------|-------------|
| *Read* | 1 | Fails for *FileMode.CreateNew, FileMode.Create, FileMode.Truncate*, or *FileMode.Append* |
| *Write* | 2 | Fails if file is read-only |
| *ReadWrite* | 3 | Fails for *FileMode.Append* or if file is read-only |

There's one case in which a *FileAccess* argument is required: when you open a file with *FileMode.Append*, the constructor fails if the file is opened for reading. Because files are opened for reading and writing by default, the following constructor always fails:

```
New FileStream(strFileName, FileMode.Append)
```

If you want to use *FileMode.Append*, you also need to include an argument of *FileAccess.Write*:

```
New FileStream(strFileName, FileMode.Append, FileAccess.Write)
```

Unless you specify a *FileShare* argument, the file is open for exclusive use by your process. No other process (or the same process) can open the same file. Moreover, if any other process already has the file open and you don't specify a *FileShare* argument, the *FileStream* constructor will fail. The *FileShare* argument lets you be more specific about file sharing:

### *FileShare* Enumeration (selection)

| Member | Value | Description |
|--------|-------|-------------|
| *None* | 0 | Allow other processes no access to the file; default |
| *Read* | 1 | Allow other processes to read the file |
| *Write* | 2 | Allow other processes to write to the file |
| *ReadWrite* | 3 | Allow other processes full access to the file |

When you only need to read from a file, it's common to allow other processes to read from it also; in other words, *FileAccess.Read* should usually be accompanied by *FileShare.Read*. This courtesy goes both ways: if another process has a file open with *FileAccess.Read* and *FileShare.Read*, your process won't be able to open it unless you specify both flags as well.

# *FileStream* Properties and Methods

Once you've opened a file by creating an object of type *FileStream*, you have access to the following five properties implemented in *Stream* that the *FileStream* class overrides:

### *Stream* Properties

| Property | Type | Accessibility |
|----------|------|---------------|
| *CanRead* | *Boolean* | Get |
| *CanWrite* | *Boolean* | Get |
| *CanSeek* | *Boolean* | Get |
| *Length* | *Long* | Get |
| *Position* | *Long* | Get/Set |

The first two properties depend on the *FileAccess* value you used to create the *FileStream* object. The *CanSeek* property is always *True* for open files. The property can return *False* for other types of streams (such as network streams).

The *Length* and *Position* properties are applicable only to seekable streams. Notice that both *Length* and *Position* are *Long* integers, and in theory allow file sizes up to $2^{63}$ bytes, approximately $9 \times 10^{18}$ bytes, or 9 exabytes, which should be a sufficient maximum file size for at least a couple years. Setting the *Position* property is a straightforward way of seeking in the file. (I'll discuss a more conventional *Seek* method shortly.) For example, if *fs* is an object of type *FileStream*, you can seek to the 100th byte in the file with the statement

```
fs.Position = 100
```

You can seek to the end of a file (for appending to the file) with the statement

```
fs.Position = fs.Length
```

All the following methods implemented by *Stream* are overridden by *FileStream*:

### *Stream* Methods (selection)

```
Function ReadByte() As Integer

Function Read(ByVal abyBuffer() As Byte,
              ByVal iBufferOffset As Integer,
              ByVal iCount As Integer) As Integer

Sub WriteByte(ByVal byValue As Byte)
```

### *Stream* Methods (selection)   *(continued)*

```
Sub Write(ByVal abyBuffer() As Byte,
         ByVal iBufferOffset As Integer, ByVal iCount As Integer)

Function Seek(ByVal lOffset As Long,
             ByVal so As SeekOrigin) As Long

Sub SetLength(ByVal lSize As Long)

Sub Flush()

Sub Close()
```

You can read either individual bytes with *ReadByte* or multiple bytes with *Read*. Both methods return an *Integer* value, but that value means different things to each of the methods. *ReadByte* normally returns the next byte from the file cast to an *Integer* without sign extension. For example, the byte &HFF becomes the integer &H000000FF, or 255. A return value of −1 indicates an attempt to read past the end of the file.

*Read* returns the number of bytes read into the buffer, up to *iCount*. For files, *Read* returns the same value as the *iCount* argument unless *iCount* is greater than the remaining number of bytes in the file. A return value of 0 indicates that there are no more bytes to be read in the file. For other types of streams (network streams, for example), *Read* can return a value less than *iCount* but always at least 1 unless the entire stream has been read. The second argument to *Read* and *Write* is an offset into the buffer, not an offset into the stream!

The *Seek* method is similar to traditional file-seeking functions. The *SeekOrigin* enumeration defines where the *lOffset* argument to the *Seek* method is measured from:

### *SeekOrigin* Enumeration

| Member | Value |
|--------|-------|
| *Begin* | 0 |
| *Current* | 1 |
| *End* | 2 |

If the stream is writable and seekable, the *SetLength* method sets a new length for the file, possibly truncating the contents if the new length is shorter than the existing length. *Flush* causes all data in memory buffers to be written to the file.

Despite what may or may not happen as a result of garbage collection on the *FileStream* object, you should always explicitly call the *Close* method for any files you open.

If you ignore exception handling, in most cases, you can read an entire file into memory—including allocating a memory buffer based on the size of the file—in just four statements:

```
Dim fs As New FileStream("MyFile", FileMode.Open, _
                         FileAccess.Read, FileShare.Read)
Dim abyBuffer(fs.Length) As Byte
fs.Read(abyBuffer, 0, CInt(fs.Length))
fs.Close()
```

I say "in most cases" because this code assumes the file is less than $2^{31}$ bytes (or 2 gigabytes). That assumption comes into play in the casting of the last argument of the *Read* method from a 64-bit *Long* to a 32-bit *Integer*. If the file is larger than 2 gigabytes, you'll have to read it in multiple calls to *Read*. (But you probably shouldn't even be *trying* to read a multigigabyte file entirely into memory!)

*FileStream* is an excellent choice for a traditional hex-dump program.

**HexDump.vb**

```
'-------------------------------------------
' HexDump.vb (c) 2002 by Charles Petzold
'-------------------------------------------
Imports System
Imports System.IO

Module HexDump
    Function Main(ByVal astrArgs() As String) As Integer
        ' If there's no argument, display syntax and ask for filenames.
        If astrArgs.Length = 0 Then
            Console.WriteLine("Syntax: HexDump file1 file2 ...")
            Console.Write("Enter file name(s): ")
            astrArgs = Console.ReadLine().Split(Nothing)
        End If

        ' If the user enters nothing, dive out.
        If astrArgs(0).Length = 0 Then
            Return 1
        End If

        ' Dump each file.
        Dim strFileName As String
        For Each strFileName In astrArgs
            DumpFile(strFileName)
        Next strFileName
        Return 0
    End Function
```

```
Sub DumpFile(ByVal strFileName As String)
    Dim fs As FileStream
    Try
        fs = New FileStream(strFileName, FileMode.Open, _
                            FileAccess.Read, FileShare.Read)
    Catch exc As Exception
        Console.WriteLine("HexDump: {0}", exc.Message)
        Return
    End Try
    Console.WriteLine(strFileName)
    DumpStream(fs)
    fs.Close()
End Sub

Private Sub DumpStream(ByVal strm As Stream)
    Dim abyBuffer(16) As Byte
    Dim lAddress As Long = 0
    Dim iCount As Integer = strm.Read(abyBuffer, 0, 16)

    While iCount > 0
        Console.WriteLine(ComposeLine(lAddress, abyBuffer, iCount))
        lAddress += 16
        iCount = strm.Read(abyBuffer, 0, 16)
    End While
End Sub

Function ComposeLine(ByVal lAddress As Long, _
                     ByVal abyBuffer() As Byte, _
                     ByVal iCount As Integer) As String
    Dim str As String = String.Format("{0:X4}-{1:X4}  ", _
                                      CInt(lAddress \ 65536), _
                                      CInt(lAddress Mod 65536))
    Dim i As Integer

    ' Format hexadecimal bytes.
    For i = 0 To 15
        If i < iCount Then
            str &= String.Format("{0:X2}", abyBuffer(i))
        Else
            str &= "  "
        End If

        If i = 7 AndAlso iCount > 7 Then
            str &= "-"
        Else
            str &= " "
        End If
    Next i

    str &= " "
```

*(continued)*

**HexDump.vb**   *(continued)*

```
        ' Format character display
        For i = 0 To 15
            Dim ch As Char = Chr(abyBuffer(i))

            If i >= iCount Then ch = " "c
            If Char.IsControl(ch) Then ch = " "c

            str += ch.ToString()
        Next i

        Return str
    End Function
End Module
```

This program uses the version of *Main* that has a single argument. The argument is an array of strings, each of which is a command-line argument to the program. If you run the program like so:

```
HexDump file1.vb file2.exe
```

then the argument to *Main* is a string array with two elements. Any wildcards in the arguments are *not* automatically expanded. (I'll get to wildcard expansion later in this appendix.) If you don't specify an argument, the program asks for one. If you're running the program from Visual Basic .NET, the easiest argument for testing the program is HexDump.exe itself.

Once HexDump successfully opens each file, the program uses the *Read* method to read 16-byte chunks from the file, and then HexDump's shared *ComposeLine* method displays them. I've reused the *ComposeLine* method in the HeadDump program in Chapter 16.

*FileStream* has a couple more features I want to mention briefly. For file sharing, you can lock and unlock sections of the file for exclusive use:

### *FileStream* Methods (selection)

```
Sub Lock(ByVal lPosition As Long, ByVal lLength As Long)
Sub Unlock(ByVal lPosition As Long, ByVal lLength As Long)
```

If the file system supports asynchronous reading and writing, and if you use the last constructor in the table shown earlier with a last argument of *True*, you can use the *BeginRead*, *EndRead*, *BeginWrite*, and *EndWrite* methods to read from and write to the file asynchronously.

## The Problem with *FileStream*

I asserted earlier that *FileStream* is the most essential class *in System.IO* because it opens files and lets you read and write bytes. But if you need to deal with other data types, you'd have to assemble the bytes into those data types (such as *Char* or *Integer*), and you'd have to disassemble basic types into bytes in preparation for writing. Would you like to do this yourself? I didn't think so.

So, unless reading and writing arrays of bytes is entirely satisfactory to you, you probably can't limit your knowledge of file I/O to the *FileStream* class. As I'll demonstrate shortly, you use the *StreamReader* and *StreamWriter* classes for reading and writing text files, and *BinaryReader* and *BinaryWriter* for reading and writing binary files of types other than byte arrays.

## Other Stream Classes

The *FileStream* class is one of several classes descended from the *MustInherit* class *Stream*. For a class that can't be instantiated, *Stream* plays a very important role in the .NET Framework. This hierarchy diagram shows six classes descended from *Stream*:

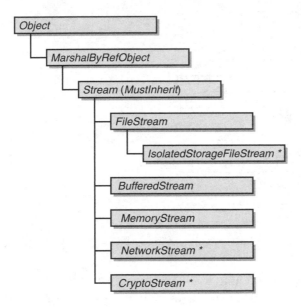

The stream classes with an asterisk are defined in namespaces other than *System.IO*.

In addition, a number of methods in other classes scattered throughout the .NET Framework return objects of type *Stream*. For example, as I'll show later in this appendix, a .NET program that reads files from the Web does so using a *Stream* object. A program in Chapter 11 demonstrates that you can also load image files (such as JPEGs) from streams.

For performance purposes, the *FileStream* class creates a buffered stream. An area of memory is maintained so that every call to *ReadByte*, *Read*, *Write-*

*Byte*, and *Write* doesn't necessarily result in a call to the operating system to read from or write to the file. If you have a *Stream* object that isn't a buffered stream, you can convert it to a buffered stream using the *BufferedStream* class.

The *MemoryStream* class lets you create an expandable area of memory that you can access using the *Stream* methods. I demonstrate how to use the *MemoryStream* class in the CreateMetafileMemory program in Chapter 23 and in several programs in Chapter 24.

# Reading and Writing Text

One important type of file is the text file, which consists entirely of lines of text separated by end-of-line markers. The *System.IO* class has specific classes to read and write text files. Here's the object hierarchy:

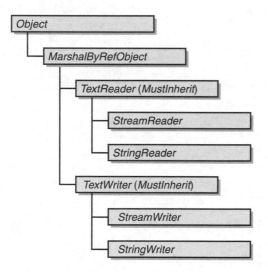

Although these classes are not descended from *Stream*, they almost certainly make use of the *Stream* class.

The two classes I'm going to focus on here are *StreamReader* and *Stream-Writer*, which are designed for reading and writing text files or text streams. The two other inheritable classes are *StringReader* and *StringWriter*, which are not strictly file I/O classes. They use similar methods to read to and write from strings. I discuss these classes briefly at the end of Appendix C and demonstrate the *StringWriter* class in the EnumMetafile program in Chapter 23.

Text may seem to be a very simple form of data storage, but in recent years, text has assumed a layer of complexity as a result of the increased use of Unicode. The *System.Char* data type in the .NET Framework—and the *Char* alias in Visual Basic .NET—is a 16-bit value representing a character in the Unicode character set. The .NET Framework *System.String* type (and the Visual Basic .NET *String* alias) represents a string of Unicode characters. But what happens when you write strings from a Visual Basic .NET program to a file? Do you want to write them as Unicode? That makes sense only if every application that reads the file you create expects to be reading Unicode! You probably want to avoid Unicode if you know that other applications reading the file are anticipating encountering 8-bit ASCII characters.

The first 256 characters in Unicode are the same as the 128 characters of ASCII and the 128 characters of the ISO Latin Alphabet No. 1 extension to ASCII. (The combination of these two character sets is often referred to in Windows API documentation as the *ANSI* character set.) For example, the capital *A* is &H41 in ASCII and &H0041 in Unicode. Unicode strings that contain exclusively (or mostly) ASCII contain a lot of zero bytes. In environments where files must be shared among various operating systems, these zeros cause problems for a lot of traditional C-based and UNIX-based programs because those programs interpret a zero byte as a string-termination character.

To alleviate these problems, the *StreamWriter* class lets you have control over how the Unicode strings in your Visual Basic .NET program are converted for storage in a file. You assert this control via classes defined in the *System.Text* namespace. Similarly, *StreamReader* lets your program read text files in various formats and convert the text from the files to Unicode strings in your program.

Let's look at *StreamWriter* first. You use this class to write to new or existing text files.

Four of the *StreamWriter* constructors let you create an object of type *StreamWriter* based on a filename:

### *StreamWriter* Constructors (selection)

```
StreamWriter(ByVal strFileName As String)

StreamWriter(ByVal strFileName As String, ByVal bAppend As Boolean)

StreamWriter(ByVal strFileName As String, ByVal bAppend As Boolean,
             ByVal enc As Encoding)

StreamWriter(ByVal strFileName As String, ByVal bAppend As Boolean,
             ByVal enc As Encoding, ByVal iBufferSize As Integer)
```

These constructors open the file for writing, probably using a *FileStream* constructor internally. By default, if the file exists, the contents will be destroyed. The *bAppend* argument allows you to override that default action. The remaining constructors create an object of type *StreamWriter* based on an existing *Stream* object:

### *StreamWriter* Constructors (selection)

```
StreamWriter(ByVal strm As Stream)

StreamWriter(ByVal strm As Stream, ByVal enc As Encoding)

StreamWriter(ByVal strm As Stream, ByVal enc As Encoding,
           ByVal iBufferSize As Integer)
```

If you use a constructor without an *Encoding* argument, the resultant *StreamWriter* object will *not* store strings to the file in a Unicode format with 2 bytes per character. Nor will it convert your strings to ASCII. Instead, the *StreamWriter* object will store strings in a format known as UTF-8, which I'll discuss shortly.

If you use one of the *StreamWriter* constructors with an *Encoding* argument, you need an object of type *Encoding*, which is a class defined in the *System.Text* namespace. It's easiest (and in many cases, sufficient) to use one of the shared properties of the *Encoding* class to obtain this object:

### *Encoding* Shared Properties

| Property | Type | Accessibility |
|---|---|---|
| *Default* | *Encoding* | Get |
| *Unicode* | *Encoding* | Get |
| *BigEndianUnicode* | *Encoding* | Get |
| *UTF8* | *Encoding* | Get |
| *UTF7* | *Encoding* | Get |
| *ASCII* | *Encoding* | Get |

The *Encoding* argument to the *StreamWriter* constructor can also be an instance of one of the classes in *System.Text* that derive from *Encoding*, which are *ASCIIEncoding*, *UnicodeEncoding*, *UTF7Encoding*, and *UTF8Encoding*. The constructors for these classes often have a few options, so you may want to check them out if the shared properties aren't doing precisely what you want.

When you specify an encoding of *Encoding.Unicode*, each character is written to the file in 2 bytes with the least significant byte first, in accordance with the so-called little-endian architecture of Intel microprocessors. The file or stream begins with the bytes &HFF and &HFE, which correspond to the Unicode character &HFEFF, which is defined in the Unicode standard as the byte order mark (BOM).

An encoding of *Encoding.BigEndianUnicode* stores the most significant byte of each character first. The file or stream begins with the bytes &HFE and

&HFF, which also correspond to the Unicode character &HFEFF. The Unicode character &HFFFE is intentionally undefined so that applications can determine the byte ordering of a Unicode file from its first two bytes.

If you want to store strings in Unicode but you don't want the byte order marks emitted, you can instead obtain an *Encoding* argument for the *StreamWriter* constructor by creating an object of type *UnicodeEncoding*:

```
New UnicodeEncoding(bBigEndian, bIncludeByteOrderMark)
```

Set the two Boolean arguments appropriately.

UTF-8 is a character encoding designed to represent Unicode characters without using any zero bytes (and hence, to be C and UNIX friendly). UTF stands for *UCS Transformation Format*. UCS stands for *Universal Character Set*, which is another name for ISO 10646, a character-encoding standard with which Unicode is compatible.

In UTF-8, each Unicode character is translated to a sequence of 1 to 6 non-zero bytes. Unicode characters in the ASCII range (&H0000 through &H007F) are translated directly to single-byte values. Thus, Unicode strings that contain only ASCII are translated to ASCII files. UTF-8 is documented in RFC 2279. (RFC stands for Request for Comments. RFCs are documentations of Internet standards. You can obtain RFCs from many sources, including the Web site of the Internet Engineering Task Force, *http://www.ietf.org.*)

When you specify *Encoding.UTF8*, the *StreamWriter* class converts the Unicode text strings to UTF-8. In addition, it writes the three bytes &HEF, &HBB, and &HBF to the beginning of the file or stream. These bytes are the Unicode BOM converted to UTF-8.

If you want to use UTF-8 encoding but you don't want those three bytes emitted, don't use *Encoding.UTF8*. Use *Encoding.Default* instead or one of the constructors that doesn't have an *Encoding* argument. These options also provide UTF-8 encoding, but the three identification bytes are not emitted.

Alternatively, you can create an object of type *UTF8Encoding* and pass that object as the argument to *StreamWriter*. Use

```
New UTF8Encoding()
```

or

```
New UTF8Encoding(False)
```

to suppress the three bytes, and use

```
New UTF8Encoding(True)
```

to emit the identification bytes.

UTF-7 is documented in RFC 2152. Unicode characters are translated to a sequence of bytes that has an upper bit of 0. UTF-7 is intended for environments in which only 7-bit values can be used, such as e-mail. Use *Encoding.UTF7* in the *StreamWriter* constructor for UTF-7 encoding. No identification bytes are involved with UTF-7.

When you specify an encoding of *Encoding.ASCII*, the resultant file or stream contains only ASCII characters, that is, characters in the range &H00 through &H7F. Any Unicode character not in this range is converted to a question mark (ASCII code &H3F). This is the only encoding in which data is actually lost.

So what do you do if you have character strings that contain only characters from the Windows ANSI character set (characters &H00 through &HFF) and you want to write these strings to a file in a one-byte-per-character format? You can't use *Encoding.ASCII* because characters &H80 through &HFF will be replaced by question marks. And you can't use *Encoding.UTF8* because characters &H80 through &HFF will be written to the file as a pair of bytes. In such a case you need to obtain an *Encoding* object using the shared *GetEncoding* method of the *Encoding* class with an argument of 1252 (the code page identifier for the Windows character set). This is the argument you pass to the *StreamWriter* constructor:

```
Encoding.GetEncoding(1252)
```

Once you've created a *StreamWriter* object, you can access a few handy properties:

### *StreamWriter* Properties (selection)

| Property | Type | Accessibility |
|----------|------|---------------|
| *BaseStream* | *Stream* | Get |
| *Encoding* | *Encoding* | Get |
| *AutoFlush* | *Boolean* | Get/Set |
| *NewLine* | *String* | Get/Set |

The *BaseStream* property returns either the *Stream* object you used to create the *StreamWriter* object or the *Stream* object that the *StreamWriter* class created based on the filename you supplied. If the base stream supports seeking, you can use that object to perform seeking operations on that stream.

The *Encoding* property returns the encoding you specified in the constructor or *UTF8Encoding* if you specified no encoding. Setting *AutoFlush* to *True* performs a flush of the buffer after every write.

The *NewLine* property is inherited from *TextWriter*. By default, it's the string *vbCrLf* (carriage return and line feed), but you can change it to *vbLf* (line feed). If you change it to anything else, the files won't be readable by *Stream-Reader* objects.

The versatility of the *StreamWriter* class involves the *Write* and *WriteLine* methods that the class inherits from *TextWriter*:

### *TextWriter* Methods (selection)

```
Sub Write(...)

Sub WriteLine(...)

Sub Flush()

Sub Close()
```

*TextWriter* supports (and *StreamWriter* inherits) 17 versions of *Write* and 18 versions of *WriteLine* that let you specify any object as an argument to the method. The object you specify is converted to a string by the use of its *ToString* method. The *WriteLine* method follows the string with an end-of-line marker. A version of *WriteLine* with no arguments writes just an end-of-line marker. The *Write* and *WriteLine* methods also include versions with formatting strings, just as the *Console.Write* and *Console.WriteLine* methods do.

Here's a tiny program that appends text to the same file every time you run the program.

### StreamWriterDemo.vb

```
'-----------------------------------------------------------
' StreamWriterDemo.vb (c) 2002 by Charles Petzold
'-----------------------------------------------------------
Imports System
Imports System.IO

Module StreamWriterDemo
    Sub Main()
        Dim sw As New StreamWriter("StreamWriterDemo.txt", True)
        sw.WriteLine("You ran the StreamWriterDemo program on {0}", _
                     DateTime.Now)
        sw.Close()
    End Sub
End Module
```

Notice the *True* argument to the constructor, indicating that the file will be appended to. The Unicode strings in the program are converted to UTF-8, but they will appear to be ASCII.

The *StreamReader* class is for reading text files or streams. There are five constructors for opening a text file for reading:

### *StreamReader* Constructors (selection)

```
StreamReader(ByVal strFileName As String)

StreamReader(ByVal strFileName As String, ByVal enc As Encoding)

StreamReader(ByVal strFileName As String, ByVal bDetect As Boolean)

StreamReader(ByVal strFileName As String, ByVal enc As Encoding,
        ByVal bDetect As Boolean)

StreamReader(ByVal strFileName As String, ByVal enc As Encoding,
        ByVal bDetect As Boolean, ByVal iBufferSize As Integer)
```

There is an additional set of five constructors for creating a *StreamReader* object based on an existing stream:

### *StreamReader* Constructors (selection)

```
StreamReader(ByVal strm As Stream)

StreamReader(ByVal strm As Stream, ByVal enc As Encoding)

StreamReader(ByVal strm As Stream, ByVal bDetect As Boolean)

StreamReader(ByVal strm As Stream, ByVal enc As Encoding,
        ByVal bDetect As Boolean)

StreamReader(ByVal strm As Stream, ByVal enc As Encoding,
        ByVal bDetect As Boolean, ByVal iBufferSize As Integer)
```

If you set *bDetect* to *True*, the constructor will attempt to determine the encoding of the file from the first two or three bytes. Or you can specify the encoding explicitly. If you set *bDetect* to *True* and also specify an encoding, the constructor will use the specified encoding only if it can't detect the encoding of the file. (For example, ASCII and UTF-7 can't be differentiated by inspection because they don't begin with a BOM and both contain only bytes in the range &H00 through &H7F.)

The *StreamReader* class has the following two, read-only properties:

### *StreamReader* Properties

| Property | Type | Accessibility |
|---|---|---|
| *BaseStream* | *Stream* | Get |
| *CurrentEncoding* | *Encoding* | Get |

The *CurrentEncoding* property may change between the time the object is constructed and the time the first read operation performed on the file or stream because the object has knowledge of identification bytes only after the first read operation.

Here are the methods to peek, read, and close text files:

### *StreamReader* Methods (selection)

```
Function Peek() As Integer

Function Read() As Integer

Function Read(ByVal achBuffer() As Char,
              ByVal iBufferOffset As Integer,
              ByVal iCount As Integer) As Integer

Function ReadLine() As String

Function ReadToEnd() As String

Sub Close()
```

The *Peek* and the first *Read* methods both return the next character in the stream or 1 if the end of the stream has been reached. You must explicitly cast the return value to a *Char* if the return value is not −1. The second *Read* method returns the number of characters read or 0 if the end of the stream has been reached.

The *ReadLine* method reads the next line up to the next end-of-line marker and strips the end-of-line characters from the resultant string. The method returns a zero-length character string if the line of text contains only an end-of-line marker; the method returns *Nothing* if the end of the stream has been reached.

*ReadToEnd* returns everything from the current position to the end of the file. The method returns *Nothing* if the end of the stream has been reached.

Here's a program that assumes the command-line argument is a URI (Universal Resource Identifier) of an HTML file (or other text file) on the Web. It obtains a *Stream* for that file using some boilerplate code involving the *WebRequest* and *WebResponse* classes. It then constructs a *StreamReader* object from that stream, uses *ReadLine* to read each line, and then displays each line using *Console.WriteLine* with a line number.

### HtmlDump.vb

```
'-----------------------------------------------
' HtmlDump.vb (c) 2002 by Charles Petzold
'-----------------------------------------------
Imports System
Imports System.IO
Imports System.Net
```

*(continued)*

**HtmlDump.vb**   *(continued)*

```
Module HtmlDump
    Function Main(ByVal astrArgs() As String) As Integer
        Dim strUri As String

        ' If there's no argument, display syntax and ask for URI.
        If astrArgs.Length = 0 Then
            Console.WriteLine("Syntax: HtmlDump URI")
            Console.Write("Enter URI: ")
            strUri = Console.ReadLine()
        Else
            strUri = astrArgs(0)
        End If

        ' If the user enters a blank string, dive out.
        If strUri.Length = 0 Then
            Return 1
        End If

        Dim webreq As WebRequest
        Dim webres As WebResponse

        Try
            webreq = WebRequest.Create(strUri)
            webres = webreq.GetResponse()
        Catch exc As Exception
            Console.WriteLine("HtmlDump: {0}", exc.Message)
            Return 1
        End Try

        If webres.ContentType.Substring(0, 4) <> "text" Then
            Console.WriteLine("HtmlDump: URI must be a text type.")
            Return 1
        End If

        Dim strm As Stream = webres.GetResponseStream()
        Dim sr As New StreamReader(strm)
        Dim strLine As String
        Dim iLine As Integer = 1

        strLine = sr.ReadLine()
        While Not strLine Is Nothing
            Console.WriteLine("{0:D5}: {1}", iLine, strLine)
            iLine += 1
            strLine = sr.ReadLine()
        End While

        strm.Close()
        Return 0
    End Function
End Module
```

Try it with the URL *http://www.charlespetzold.com.*

# Binary File I/O

By definition, any file that's not a text file is a binary file. I've already discussed the *FileStream* class, which lets you read and write bytes. But most binary files consist of data types that are stored as multiple bytes. Unless you want to write code that constructs and deconstructs integers and other types from their constituent bytes, you'll want to take advantage of the *BinaryReader* and *Binary-Writer* classes, both of which are derived solely from *Object*:

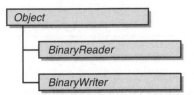

The constructors for these classes require a *Stream* object. If you want to use a file with these classes, create a new *FileStream* object (or obtain one from some other means) first. For the *BinaryWriter* class, the *Encoding* you optionally specify affects the storage of text in the stream:

### *BinaryWriter* Constructors

```
BinaryWriter(ByVal strm As Stream)

BinaryWriter(ByVal strm As Stream, ByVal enc As Encoding)
```

The constructors for *BinaryReader* are identical:

### *BinaryReader* Constructors

```
BinaryReader(ByVal strm As Stream)

BinaryReader(ByVal strm As Stream, ByVal enc As Encoding)
```

Both classes have a single read-only property named *BaseStream* that is the *Stream* object you specified in the constructor.

The *Write* methods in *BinaryWriter* are defined for all the basic types as well as for arrays of bytes and characters.

### *BinaryWriter* Public Methods

```
Sub Write(...)

Sub Write(ByVal abyBuffer() As Byte, ByVal iBufferOffset As Integer,
        ByVal iBytesToWrite As Integer)

Sub Write(ByVal achBuffer() As Char, ByVal iBufferOffset As Integer,
        ByVal iBytesToWrite As Integer)

Function Seek(ByVal iOffset As Integer,
            ByVal so As SeekOrigin) As Long

Sub Flush()

Sub Close()
```

You can use an object of any basic type (*Boolean*, *Byte*, *Byte()*, *Char*, *Char()*, *Double*, *Decimal*, *Integer*, *Long*, *Short*, *Single*, or *String*) as an argument to *Write*.

These methods do not store any information about the type of the data. Each type uses as many bytes as necessary. For example, a *Single* is stored in 4 bytes. A *Boolean* requires 1 byte. The sizes of arrays are not stored. A 256-element *Byte* array is stored in 256 bytes.

Strings stored in the file are preceded by the byte length stored as a 7-bit encoded integer. (The 7-bit integer encoding uses as many bytes as necessary to store an integer in 7-bit chunks. The first byte of storage is the lowest 7 bits of the integer, and so forth. The high bit of each byte is 1 if there are more bytes. The *BinaryWriter* class includes a protected method named *Write7Bit-EncodedInt* that performs this encoding.)

The *Close* method closes the underlying stream that the *BinaryWriter* object is based on.

The *BinaryReader* class has separate methods to read all the various types.

### *BinaryReader* Methods (selection)

```
Function ReadBoolean() As Boolean

Function ReadByte() As Byte

Function ReadBytes(ByVal iCount As Integer) As Byte()

Function ReadChar() As Char

Function ReadChars(ByVal iCount As Integer) As Char()

Function ReadInt16() As Short

Function ReadInt32() As Integer

Function ReadInt64() As Long

Function ReadSingle() As Single

Function ReadDouble() As Double

Function ReadDecimal() As Decimal
```

These methods throw an exception of type *EndOfStreamException* if the end of the stream has been reached. In most cases, your program will know the format of a binary file it's accessing and can avoid end-of-stream conditions. However, for maximum protection, you should put your read statements in *Try* blocks in case you encounter corrupted files.

You can also read individual characters, or arrays of bytes or characters:

### *BinaryReader* Methods (selection)

```
Function PeekChar() As Integer

Function Read() As Integer

Sub Read(ByVal abyBuffer() As Byte, ByVal iBufferOffset As Integer,
         ByVal iBytesToRead As Integer)

Sub Read(ByVal achBuffer() As Char, ByVal iBufferOffset As Integer,
         ByVal iBytesToRead As Integer)

Sub Close()
```

The *PeekChar* and the first *Read* method involve characters, not bytes, and will assume that the file is UTF-8 encoded if you don't explicitly indicate an encoding in the constructor. The methods return −1 if the end of the stream has been reached.

If you'll be using binary file I/O a lot, you may want to structure your classes for this purpose. When you save an instance of a class to a file, you want to save sufficient information to re-create that object when you read the file. In a well-designed class, you'll probably be saving all the properties of the class that are necessary to re-create the object.

Let's assume you have a class named *SampleClass* that has three properties necessary to re-create the object: a *Single* named *Value*, a *String* named *Text*, and an object of type *Fish* stored as a property named *BasicFish*. (*Fish* is another class you've created.) *SampleClass* also has a constructor defined to create a new object from these three items:

```
Public Sub New(ByVal fValue As Single, ByVal strText As String, _
          ByVal fsh As Fish)
    ⋮
End Sub
```

Let's also assume that you need to use a binary file to store information that consists of many objects, including objects of type *SampleClass*. Each class you create can implement both an instance method named *Write* and a shared method named *Read*. Here's the *Write* method for *SampleClass*. Notice the *BinaryWriter* argument.

```
Public Sub Write(ByVal bw As BinaryWriter)
    bw.Write(Value)
    bw.Write(Text)
    BasicFish.Write(bw)
End Sub
```

Because the *Value* and *Text* properties are basic types, this method can simply call the *Write* method of *BinaryWriter* for them. But for the *BasicFish* property, it must call the similar *Write* method you've also implemented in the *Fish* class, passing to it the *BinaryWriter* argument.

The *Read* method is shared because it must create an instance of *SampleClass* after reading binary data from the file:

```
Public Shared Function Read(ByVal br As BinaryReader) As SampleClass
    Dim fValue As Single = br.ReadSingle()
    Dim strText As String = br.ReadString()
    Dim fsh As Fish = Fish.Read(br)
    Return New SampleClass(fValue, strText, fsh)
End Function
```

Notice that the *Fish* class must also have a similar shared *Read* method.

# The *Environment* Class

Let's leave the *System.IO* namespace briefly to take a look at the *Environment* class, which is defined in the *System* namespace. *Environment* has a collection of miscellaneous properties and methods that are useful for obtaining information about the machine on which the program is running and the current user logged on to the machine. As its name suggests, the *Environment* class also allows a program to obtain environment strings. (I make use of this latter facility in the EnvironmentVars program in Chapter 18.)

Two methods in *Environment* provide information about the file system:

### *Environment* Shared Methods (selection)

```
Function GetLogicalDrives() As String()

Function GetFolderPath(ByVal sf As Environment.SpecialFolder) As String
```

I have a fairly normal system with a CD-ROM drive and an Iomega Zip drive, so on my machine, *GetLogicalDrives* returns the following four strings, in this order:

```
A:\
C:\
D:\
E:\
```

The argument to *GetFolderPath* is a member of the *Environment.Special-Folder* enumeration. The rightmost column in the following table indicates the return string from *GetFolderPath* on a machine running the default installation of Microsoft Windows XP, where I've used an ellipsis to indicate that the return string includes the user's name (which is the same as the value returned from the shared property *Environment.UserName*).

## *Environment.SpecialFolder* Enumeration

| Member | Value | Common Return Values |
|---|---|---|
| *Programs* | 2 | C:\Documents and Settings\...\Start Menu\ Programs |
| *Personal* | 5 | C:\Documents and Settings\...\My Documents |
| *Favorites* | 6 | C:\Documents and Settings\...\Favorites |
| *Startup* | 7 | C:\Documents and Settings\...\Start Menu\ Programs\Startup |
| *Recent* | 8 | C:\Documents and Settings\...\Recent |
| *SendTo* | 9 | C:\Documents and Settings\...\SendTo |
| *StartMenu* | 11 | C:\Documents and Settings\...\Start Menu |
| *DesktopDirectory* | 16 | C:\Documents and Settings\...\Desktop |
| *Templates* | 21 | C:\Documents and Settings\...\Templates |
| *ApplicationData* | 26 | C:\Documents and Settings\...\Application Data |
| *LocalApplicationData* | 28 | C:\Documents and Settings\...\Local Settings\Application Data |
| *InternetCache* | 32 | C:\Documents and Settings\...\Local Settings\Temporary Internet Files |
| *Cookies* | 33 | C:\Documents and Settings\...\Cookies |
| *History* | 34 | C:\Documents and Settings\...\Local Settings\History |
| *CommonApplicationData* | 35 | C:\Documents and Settings\All Users\ Application Data |
| *System* | 37 | C:\WINDOWS\System32 |
| *ProgramFiles* | 38 | C:\Program Files |
| *CommonProgramFiles* | 43 | C:\Program Files\Common Files |

Oddly enough, the *SpecialFolder* enumeration is defined within the *Environment* class. Instead of calling *GetFolderPath* as

```
Environment.GetFolderPath(SpecialFolder.Personal)    ' Won't work!
```

you need to preface *SpecialFolder* with the class in which it's defined:

```
Environment.GetFolderPath(Environment.SpecialFolder.Personal)
```

The *Environment* class also includes a couple properties that relate to the file system and file I/O:

### *Environment* Shared Properties (selection)

| Property | Type | Accessibility |
|----------|------|---------------|
| *SystemDirectory* | *String* | Get |
| *CurrentDirectory* | *String* | Get/Set |

The *SystemDirectory* property returns the same string as the *GetFolderPath* method with the *Environment.SpecialFolder.System* argument.

The *CurrentDirectory* property lets a program obtain or set the current drive and directory for the application. When setting the directory, you can use a relative directory path, including the ".." string to indicate the parent directory. To change to the root directory of another drive, use the drive letter like so:

```
Environment.CurrentDirectory = "D:\"
```

If the current drive and directory are on a drive other than C and you use

```
Environment.CurrentDirectory = "C:"
```

the current directory is set to the last current directory on drive C before the current drive was changed to something other than C. This technique doesn't seem to work with other drives. The call

```
Environment.CurrentDirectory = "D:"
```

always seems to set the current directory as the root directory of drive D.

As you'll see shortly, other classes defined in the *System.IO* namespace have equivalents to *GetLogicalDrives* and *CurrentDirectory*.

# File and Path Name Parsing

At times, you need to parse and scan filenames and path names. For example, your program may have a fully qualified filename and you may need just the directory or the drive. The *Path* class, defined in the *System.IO* namespace, consists solely of shared methods and shared read-only fields that ease jobs like these.

In the following table, the right two columns show sample return values from the methods when the *strFileName* argument is the indicated string at the top of the column. In these examples, I'm assuming the current directory is C:\Docs.

## *Path* Shared Methods (examples)

| Method | \DirA\MyFile | DirA\MyFile.txt |
|---|---|---|
| `Function IsPathRooted`<br>`   (ByVal strFileName As String) As Boolean` | True | False |
| `Function HasExtension`<br>`   (ByVal strFileName As String) As Boolean` | False | True |
| `Function GetFileName`<br>`   (ByVal strFileName As String) As String` | MyFile | MyFile.txt |
| `Function GetFileNameWithoutExtension`<br>`   (ByVal strFileName As String) As String` | MyFile | MyFile |
| `Function GetExtension`<br>`   (ByVal strFileName As String) As String` | | .txt |
| `Function GetDirectoryName`<br>`   (ByVal strFileName As String) As String` | \DirA | DirA |
| `Function GetFullPath`<br>`   (ByVal strFileName As String) As String` | C:\DirA\MyFile | C:\Docs\DirA\<br>MyFile.txt |
| `Function GetPathRoot`<br>`   (ByVal strFileName As String) As String` | \ | |

What's interesting here is that neither DirA nor MyFile has to exist for these methods to work. The methods are basically performing string manipulation, possibly in combination with the current directory.

The following two methods return a new path and filename:

## *Path* Shared Methods (selection)

```
Function Combine(ByVal strLeftPart As String,
                 ByVal strRightPart As String) As String

Function ChangeExtension(ByVal strFileName As String,
                         ByVal strNewExtension As String) As String
```

The *Combine* method joins together a path name (on the left) with a path and/ or filename (on the right). Use *Combine* rather than string concatenation for this job. Otherwise, you have to worry about whether a backslash is the end of the left part or the beginning of the right part. The *ChangeExtension* method simply changes the filename extension from one string to another. Include a period in the new extension. Set the *strNewExtension* argument to *Nothing* to remove the extension.

The following methods obtain an appropriate directory for storing temporary data and a fully qualified unique filename the program can use to store temporary data:

### *Path* Shared Methods (selection)

```
Function GetTempPath() As String
Function GetTempFileName() As String
```

If you must do your own file and path name parsing, don't hard-code characters that you think you'll encounter in the strings. Use the following shared read-only fields of *Path* instead:

### *Path* Shared Fields

| Field | Type | Accessibility | Windows Default |
|---|---|---|---|
| *PathSeparator* | *Char* | read-only | ; |
| *VolumeSeparatorChar* | *Char* | read-only | : |
| *DirectorySeparatorChar* | *Char* | read-only | \ |
| *AltDirectorySeparatorChar* | *Char* | read-only | / |
| *InvalidPathChars* | *Char()* | read-only | " < > \| |

# Parallel Classes

Another common file I/O job is obtaining a list of all files and subdirectories in a directory. Four classes provide you with information about files and directories: *Directory*, *File*, *DirectoryInfo*, and *FileInfo*. All four of these classes (as well as the *Path* class I just described) are *NotInheritable*. Here's the class hierarchy:

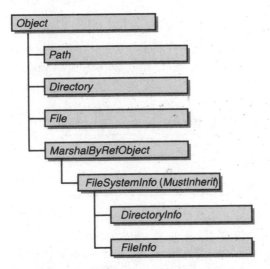

*Directory* and *File* can't be instantiated; the two classes consist solely of shared methods.

*DirectoryInfo* and *FileInfo* contain *no* shared methods or properties, and you must obtain an object of type *DirectoryInfo* or *FileInfo* to use these classes. Both classes derive from the *MustInherit* class *FileSystemInfo*, so they share some properties and methods.

As the names suggest, *Directory* and *DirectoryInfo* provide similar methods, except that the *Directory* methods are shared and require an argument that is a directory name. The *DirectoryInfo* properties and methods are not shared; the constructor argument indicates the directory name to which the properties and methods apply.

Similarly, *File* and *FileInfo* provide corresponding methods, except that you indicate a particular filename in the shared *File* method calls and you create an instance of *FileInfo* by specifying a filename in the constructor.

If you need information about a particular file, you may wonder whether it's best to use *File* or *FileInfo* (or similarly for directories, whether to use *Directory* or *DirectoryInfo*). If you need only one item of information, it's probably easiest to use the appropriate shared method in *File* or *Directory*. However, if you need multiple items, it makes more sense to create an object of type *FileInfo* or *DirectoryInfo* and then use the instance properties and methods. But don't feel pressured to use one class in preference to the other.

# Working with Directories

Let's begin with the *Directory* and *DirectoryInfo* classes. The following three shared methods of the *Directory* class have no equivalents in the *DirectoryInfo* class:

### *Directory* Shared Methods (selection)

```
Function GetLogicalDrives() As String()
Function GetCurrentDirectory() As String
Sub SetCurrentDirectory(ByVal strPath As String)
```

These methods essentially duplicate the shared *GetLogicalDrives* method and the *CurrentDirectory* property of the *Environment* class.

To use any of the properties or methods of the *DirectoryInfo* class, you need a *DirectoryInfo* object. One of the ways in which you can obtain such an object is by using the *DirectoryInfo* constructor:

### *DirectoryInfo* Constructor

```
DirectoryInfo(ByVal strPath As String)
```

The directory doesn't have to exist. Indeed, if you want to create a new directory, creating an object of type *DirectoryInfo* is a first step.

After creating an object of type *DirectoryInfo*, you can determine whether the directory exists. Even if the directory doesn't exist, you can obtain certain information about the directory as if it did exist. The two rightmost columns of the following table show examples. The column heading is the string passed to the *DirectoryInfo* constructor. The current directory is assumed to be C:\Docs.

### *DirectoryInfo* Properties (selection)

| Property | Type | Accessibility | DirA | DirA\DirB.txt |
|----------|------|---------------|------|---------------|
| *Exists* | *Boolean* | Get | | |
| *Name* | *String* | Get | DirA | DirB.txt |
| *FullName* | *String* | Get | C:\Docs\DirA | C:\Docs\DirA\ DirB.txt |
| *Extension* | *String* | Get | | .txt |
| *Parent* | *DirectoryInfo* | Get | C:\Docs | C:\Docs\DirA |
| *Root* | *DirectoryInfo* | Get | C:\ | C:\ |

*FullName* and *Extension* are inherited from the *FileSystemInfo* class.

A few of these properties are also duplicated as shared methods in the *Directory* class. Because they are shared methods, they require an argument indicating the path name you're interested in:

### *Directory* Shared Methods (selection)

```
Function Exists(ByVal strPath As String) As Boolean

Function GetParent(ByVal strPath As String) As DirectoryInfo

Function GetDirectoryRoot(ByVal strPath As String) As String
```

I mentioned earlier that you can create a *DirectoryInfo* object based on a directory that doesn't exist. You can then create that directory on the disk by calling the *Create* method, or you can create a subdirectory of the directory:

### *DirectoryInfo* Methods (selection)

```
Sub Create()

Function CreateSubdirectory(ByVal strPath As String) As DirectoryInfo

Sub Refresh()
```

Notice that the *CreateSubdirectory* call returns another *DirectoryInfo* object with information about the new directory. If the indicated directory already exists, *no* exception is thrown. The directory used to create the *DirectoryInfo* object or passed to *CreateSubdirectory* can contain multiple levels of directory names.

If the directory doesn't exist when you create the *DirectoryInfo* object and you then call *Create*, the *Exists* property won't suddenly become *True*. You must call the *Refresh* method (inherited from *FileSystemInfo*) to refresh the *DirectoryInfo* information.

The *Directory* class also has a shared method to create a new directory:

### *Directory* Shared Methods (selection)

```
Function CreateDirectory(ByVal strPath As String) As DirectoryInfo
```

You can delete directories using the *Delete* method of *DirectoryInfo*:

### *DirectoryInfo Delete* Methods

```
Sub Delete()

Sub Delete(ByVal bRecursive As Boolean)
```

The methods have corresponding shared versions in the *Directory* class:

### *Directory Delete* **Shared Methods**

```
Sub Delete(ByVal strPath As String)
Sub Delete(ByVal strPath As String, ByVal bRecursive As Boolean)
```

If you use the second version of *Delete* in either table and you set the *bRecursive* argument to *True*, the method also erases all files and subdirectories in the indicated directory. Otherwise, the directory must be empty or an exception will be thrown.

Although the following information is more useful in connection with files, this table of four properties completes our survey of the *DirectoryInfo* properties:

### *DirectoryInfo* **Properties (selection)**

| Property | Type | Accessibility |
|---|---|---|
| *Attributes* | *FileAttributes* | Get/Set |
| *CreationTime* | *DateTime* | Get/Set |
| *LastAccessTime* | *DateTime* | Get/Set |
| *LastWriteTime* | *DateTime* | Get/Set |

These properties are all inherited from the *FileSystemInfo* class, and except for *Attributes*, they are all duplicated by shared methods in the *Directory* class:

### *Directory* **Shared Methods (selection)**

```
Function GetCreationTime(ByVal strPath As String) As DateTime
Function GetLastAccessTime(ByVal strPath As String) As DateTime
Function GetLastWriteTime(ByVal strPath As String) As DateTime
Sub SetCreationTime(ByVal strPath As String, ByVal dt As DateTime)
Sub SetLastAccessTime(ByVal strPath As String, ByVal dt As DateTime)
Sub SetLastWriteTime(ByVal strPath As String, ByVal dt As DateTime)
```

The *DateTime* structure is defined in the *System* namespace. *FileAttributes* is a collection of bit flags defined as an enumeration:

## *FileAttributes* Enumeration

| Member | Value |
|--------|-------|
| ReadOnly | &H00000001 |
| Hidden | &H00000002 |
| System | &H00000004 |
| Directory | &H00000010 |
| Archive | &H00000020 |
| Device | &H00000040 |
| Normal | &H00000080 |
| Temporary | &H00000100 |
| SparseFile | &H00000200 |
| ReparsePoint | &H00000400 |
| Compressed | &H00000800 |
| Offline | &H00001000 |
| NotContentIndexed | &H00002000 |
| Encrypted | &H00004000 |

Directories always have the *Directory* bit (&H10) set.

To move a directory and all its contents to another directory on the same disk, you can use the *MoveTo* method:

## *DirectoryInfo* Methods (selection)

```
Sub MoveTo(ByVal strPathDestination As String)
```

Or you can use the shared *Move* method in the *Directory* class:

## *Directory* Shared Methods (selection)

```
Sub Move(ByVal strPathSource As String, _
        ByVal strPathDestination As String)
```

With either method call, the destination must not currently exist.

The remaining methods of *DirectoryInfo* and *Directory* obtain an array of all the files and subdirectories in a directory, or only those directories and files that match a specified pattern using wildcards (question marks and asterisks). Here are the six methods of *DirectoryInfo*:

### *DirectoryInfo* Methods (selection)

```
Function GetDirectories() As DirectoryInfo()
Function GetDirectories(ByVal strPattern As String) As DirectoryInfo()
Function GetFiles() As FileInfo()
Function GetFiles(ByVal strPattern As String) As FileInfo()
Function GetFileSystemInfos() As FileSystemInfo()
Function GetFileSystemInfos(ByVal strPattern As String) As FileSystemInfo()
```

The *GetDirectories* method returns a collection of directories as an array of *DirectoryInfo* objects. Likewise, the *GetFiles* method returns a collection of files as an array of *FileInfo* objects. The *GetFileSystemInfos* method returns both directories and files as an array of *FileSystemInfo* objects. You'll recall that *FileSystemInfo* is the parent class for both *DirectoryInfo* and *FileInfo*.

The *Directory* class has a similar set of six methods, but these all return arrays of strings:

### *Directory* Shared Methods (selections)

```
Function GetDirectories(ByVal strPath As String) As String()
Function GetDirectories(ByVal strPath As String,
                        ByVal strPattern As String) As String()
Function GetFiles(ByVal strPath As String) As String()
Function GetFiles(ByVal strPath As String,
                  ByVal strPattern As String) As String()
Function GetFileSystemEntries(ByVal strPath As String) As String()
Function GetFileSystemEntries(ByVal strPath As String,
                              ByVal strPattern As String) As String()
```

We're now fully equipped to enhance the HexDump program shown earlier so that it works with wildcard file specifications on the command line. Here's WildCardHexDump.

### WildCardHexDump.vb

```
'-----------------------------------------------------------
' WildCardHexDump.vb (c) 2002 by Charles Petzold
'-----------------------------------------------------------
Imports System
Imports System.IO
```

```
Module WildCardHexDump
    Function Main(ByVal astrArgs() As String) As Integer
        ' If there's no argument, display syntax and ask for filenames.
        If astrArgs.Length = 0 Then
            Console.WriteLine("Syntax: WildCardHexDump file1 file2 ...")
            Console.Write("Enter file specifications(s): ")
            astrArgs = Console.ReadLine().Split(Nothing)
        End If

        ' If the user enters nothing, dive out.
        If astrArgs(0).Length = 0 Then
            Return 1
        End If

        ' Dump each file or collection of files.
        Dim str As String
        For Each str In astrArgs
            ExpandWildCard(str)
        Next str

        Return 0
    End Function

    Private Sub ExpandWildCard(ByVal strWildCard As String)
        Dim strFile, astrFiles(), strDir As String

        Try
            astrFiles = Directory.GetFiles(strWildCard)
        Catch
            Try
                strFile = Path.GetFileName(strWildCard)
                If strDir Is Nothing OrElse strDir.Length = 0 Then
                    strDir = "."
                End If
                astrFiles = Directory.GetFiles(strDir, strFile)
            Catch
                Console.WriteLine(strWildCard & ": No Files found!")
                Return
            End Try
        End Try

        If astrFiles.Length = 0 Then
            Console.WriteLine(strWildCard & ": No files found!")
        End If

        For Each strFile In astrFiles
            HexDump.DumpFile(strFile)
        Next strFile
    End Sub
End Module
```

Besides normal wildcards, I wanted to be able to specify just a directory name as an argument. For example, I wanted

```
WildCardHexDump c:\
```

to be the equivalent of

```
WildCardHexDump c:\*.*
```

The *ExpandWildCard* method begins by attempting to obtain all the files in the particular command-line argument:

```
astrFiles = Directory.GetFiles(strWildCard)
```

This call will work if *strWildCard* specifies only a directory (such as "c:\"). Otherwise, it throws an exception. That's why it's in a *Try* block. The *Catch* block assumes that the command-line argument has path and filename components, and it obtains these components using the shared *GetDirectoryName* and *Get-FileName* methods of *Path*. However, the *GetFiles* method of *Directory* doesn't want a first argument that is *Nothing* or an empty string. Before calling *GetFiles*, the program avoids that problem by setting the path name to ".", which indicates the current directory.

# File Manipulation and Information

Like the *Directory* and *DirectoryInfo* classes, the *File* and *FileInfo* classes are very similar and share much functionality. Like the *Directory* class, all the methods in the *File* class are shared, and the first argument to every method is a string that indicates the path name of the file. The *FileInfo* class inherits from *FileSystemInfo*. You create an object of type *FileInfo* based on a filename that could include a full or a relative directory path.

### *FileInfo* Constructor

```
FileInfo(ByVal strFileName As String)
```

The file doesn't have to exist. You can determine whether the file exists, and also some information about it, with the following read-only properties:

### *FileInfo* Properties (selection)

| Property | Type | Accessibility |
|----------|------|---------------|
| *Exists* | *Boolean* | Get |
| *Name* | *String* | Get |
| *FullName* | *String* | Get |

### *FileInfo* Properties (selection)    *(continued)*

| Property | Type | Accessibility |
|----------|------|---------------|
| *Extension* | *String* | Get |
| *DirectoryName* | *String* | Get |
| *Directory* | *DirectoryInfo* | Get |
| *Length* | *Long* | Get |

Only one of these properties is duplicated in the *File* class:

### *File* Methods

```
Function Exists(ByVal strFileName As String) As Boolean
```

*FileInfo* has four additional properties that reveal the attributes of the file and the dates the file was created, last accessed, and last written to:

### *FileInfo* Properties (selection)

| Property | Type | Accessibility |
|----------|------|---------------|
| *Attributes* | *FileAttributes* | Get/Set |
| *CreationTime* | *DateTime* | Get/Set |
| *LastAccessTime* | *DateTime* | Get/Set |
| *LastWriteTime* | *DateTime* | Get/Set |

These properties, all of which are inherited from *FileSystemInfo*, are all duplicated by shared methods in the *File* class:

### *File* Shared Methods (selection)

```
Function GetAttributes(ByVal strFileName As String) As FileAttributes

Function GetCreationTime(ByVal strFileName As String) As DateTime

Function GetLastAccessTime(ByVal strFileName As String) As DateTime

Function GetLastWriteTime(ByVal strFileName As String) As DateTime

Sub SetAttributes(ByVal strFileName As String,
              ByVal fa As FileAttributes)

Sub SetCreationTime(ByVal strFileName As String,
              ByVal dt As DateTime)

Sub SetLastAccessTime(ByVal strFileName As String,
              ByVal dt As DateTime)

Sub SetLastWriteTime(ByVal strFileName As String,
              ByVal dt As DateTime)
```

The following methods let you copy, move, or delete the file. I've included the *Refresh* method here, which refreshes the object's properties after you've made a change to the file:

### *FileInfo* Methods (selection)

```
Function CopyTo(ByVal strFileName As String) As FileInfo
Function CopyTo(ByVal strFileName As String,
               ByVal bOverwrite As Boolean) As FileInfo
Sub MoveTo(ByVal strFileName As String)
Sub Delete()
Sub Refresh()
```

The copy, move, and delete facilities are duplicated in the *File* class:

### *File* Shared Methods (selection)

```
Sub Copy(ByVal strFileNameSrc As String, ByVal strFileNameDst As String)
Sub Copy(ByVal strFileNameSrc As String, ByVal strFileNameDst As String,
         ByVal bOverwrite As boolean)
Sub Move(ByVal strFileNameSrc As String, ByVal strFileNameDst As String)
Sub Delete(ByVal strFileName As String)
```

And finally, the *File* and *FileInfo* classes have several methods to open files:

### *FileInfo* Methods (selection)

```
Function Create() As FileStream
Function Open(ByVal fm As FileMode) As FileStream
Function Open(ByVal fm As FileMode,
             ByVal fa As FileAccess) As FileStream
Function Open(ByVal fm As FileMode, ByVal fa As FileAccess,
             ByVal fs As FileShare) As FileStream
Function OpenRead() As FileStream
Function OpenWrite() As FileStream
Function OpenText() As StreamReader
Function CreateText() As StreamWriter
Function AppendText() As StreamWriter
```

These are handy if you've just obtained an array of *FileInfo* objects from a *Get-Files* call on a *DirectoryInfo* object and you want to poke your nose into each and every file.

You can also use the corresponding shared methods implemented in the *File* class:

### *File* Shared Methods (selection)

```
Function Create(ByVal strFileName As String) As FileStream

Function Open(ByVal strFileName As String,
           ByVal fm As FileMode) As FileStream

Function Open(ByVal strFileName As String, ByVal fm As FileMode,
           ByVal fa As FileAccess) As FileStream

Function Open(ByVal strFileName As String,
           ByVal fm As FileMode, ByVal fa As FileAccess,
           ByVal fs As FileShare) As FileStream

Function OpenRead(ByVal strFileName As String) As FileStream

Function OpenWrite(ByVal strFileName As String) As FileStream

Function OpenText(ByVal strFileName As String) As StreamReader

Function CreateText(ByVal strFileName As String) As StreamWriter

Function AppendText(ByVal strFileName As String) As StreamWriter
```

However, these methods don't provide any real advantage over using the appropriate constructors of the *FileStream*, *StreamReader*, or *StreamWriter* class. Indeed, their very presence in the *File* class was initially one of the aspects of the entire *System.IO* namespace that I found most confusing. It doesn't make sense to use a class like *File* merely to obtain an object of type *FileStream* so that you can then use *FileStream* properties and methods. It's easier to use just a single class if that's sufficient for your purposes.

# Appendix B

# Math Class

Working with numbers is the most fundamental programming task. The Microsoft .NET Framework and Microsoft Visual Basic .NET add a few features to numbers that may be new even to veteran Visual Basic programmers. In this appendix, I'll discuss those features as well as the all-important *Math* class, which contains methods that replace the Visual Basic 6.0 math functions *Abs*, *Atn*, *Cos*, *Exp*, *Log*, *Round*, *Sgn*, *Sin*, *Sqr*, and *Tan*.

## Numeric Types

Visual Basic .NET supports 7 numeric types that fall into three categories: integral, floating point, and decimal:

### Visual Basic .NET Numeric Types

| Bits | Integer | | Floating Point | Decimal |
| | Signed | Unsigned | | |
| --- | --- | --- | --- | --- |
| 8 | | *Byte* | | |
| 16 | *Short* | | | |
| 32 | *Integer* | | *Single* | |
| 64 | *Long* | | *Double* | |
| 128 | | | | *Decimal* |

In a Visual Basic .NET program, an integer literal (that is, a number written without a decimal point) is assumed to be an *Integer* unless its value is larger than a maximum *Integer*, in which case the number is assumed to be a *Long*. A literal with a decimal point (or that includes an exponent indicated with an *E* or *e* followed by a number) is assumed to be a *Double*. You can use the following suffixes on numeric literals to clarify your intentions:

### Suffixes for Numeric Literals

| Type | Suffix |
|------|--------|
| Short | S |
| Integer | I |
| Long | L |
| Single | F |
| Double | R |
| Decimal | D |

The F suffix stands for "float" and the R suffix for "real," which is the mathematical term for floating-point numbers. To specify a *Byte* literal, use the Visual Basic *CByte* function.

The Visual Basic .NET type names are aliases for structures defined in the *System* class of the .NET Framework. These structures are all derived from *ValueType*, which itself derives from *Object*:

### .NET Framework Numeric Types

| Bits | Integer Signed | Integer Unsigned | Floating Point | Decimal |
|------|--------|----------|----------------|---------|
| 8 | SByte | Byte | | |
| 16 | Int16 | UInt16 | | |
| 32 | Int32 | UInt32 | Single | |
| 64 | Int64 | UInt64 | Double | |
| 128 | | | | Decimal |

The *SByte*, *UInt16*, *UInt32*, and *UInt64* types are not compliant with the Common Language Specification (CLS) and are not supported under Visual Basic .NET.

# Checking Integer Overflow

Consider the following code:

```
Dim x As Short = 32767
x += 1S
```

Here's another one:

```
Dim x As Short = -32768
x -= 1S
```

These are examples of integer overflow and underflow, and both the increment and decrement operations will raise an exception of type *OverflowException*. That's probably what you want to happen. But sometimes programmers take advantage of integer overflow and underflow. To separate clever techniques from nasty bugs, Visual Basic .NET allows you to optionally turn off integer overflow and underflow checking by using the following compiler switch:

```
/removeintchecks+
```

The following compiler switch results in the default option:

```
/removeintchecks-
```

In Visual Basic .NET, you can set this compiler switch by first invoking the Property Pages dialog box for the project. On the left side of the dialog box, select Optimizations from Configuration Properties. On the right side of the dialog box, check or uncheck the option Remove Integer Overflow Checks.

When you disable runtime checking of overflow and underflow, the increment and decrement operations shown earlier will result in the *Short* variable being set to −32768 and 32767, respectively.

Regardless of any compiler switches, integer division by zero always raises a *DivideByZeroException*.

# The Decimal Type

The Visual Basic 6.0 *Decimal* type has been elevated to a full-fledged numeric type under Visual Basic .NET. The *Decimal* type uses 16 bytes (128 bits) to store each value. The 128 bits break down into a 96-bit integral part, a 1-bit sign, and a scaling factor that can range from 0 through 28. Mathematically, the scaling factor is a negative power of 10 and indicates the number of decimal places in the number.

Don't confuse the *Decimal* type with a *binary-coded decimal* (BCD) type found in some programming languages. In a BCD type, each decimal digit is stored using 4 bits. The *Decimal* type stores the number as a binary integer. For example, if you define a *Decimal* equal to 12.34, the number is stored as the integer &H4D2 (or 1234) with a scaling factor of 2. A BCD encoding would store the number as &H1234.

As long as a decimal number has 28 significant digits (or fewer) and 28 decimal places (or fewer), the *Decimal* data type stores the number exactly. This is not true with floating point! If you define a *Single* equal to 12.34, it's essentially stored as the value &HC570A4 (or 12,939,428) divided by &H100000 (or 1,048,576), which is only *approximately* 12.34. Even if you define a *Double* equal to 12.34, it's stored as the value &H18AE147AE147AE (or

6,946,802,425,218,990) divided by &H2000000000000 (or 562,949,953,421,312), which again only approximately equals 12.34.

And that's why you should use *Decimal* when you're performing calculations where you don't want pennies to mysteriously crop up and disappear. The floating-point data type is great for scientific and engineering applications but often undesirable for financial ones.

If you want to explore the internals of the *Decimal*, you can make use of the following constructor:

### *Decimal* Constructors (selection)

```
Decimal(ByVal iLow As Integer, ByVal iMiddle As Integer,
        ByVal iHigh As Integer, ByVal bNegative As Boolean,
        ByVal byScale As Byte)
```

Although defined as signed integers, the first three arguments of the constructor are treated as unsigned integers to form a composite 96-bit unsigned integer. The *byScale* argument (which can range from 0 through 28) is the number of decimal places. For example, the expression

```
New Decimal(123456789, 0, 0, False, 5)
```

creates the *Decimal* number

1234.56789

The largest positive *Decimal* number is

```
New Decimal(-1, -1, -1, False, 0)
```

or

79,228,162,514,264,337,593,543,950,335

which you can also obtain from the *MaxValue* field of the *Decimal* structure:

```
Decimal.MaxValue
```

The smallest *Decimal* number closest to 0 is

```
New Decimal(1, 0, 0, False, 28)
```

which equals

0.0000000000000000000000000001

or

$1 \times 10^{-28}$

If you divide this number by 2 in a Visual Basic .NET program, the result is 0.

It's also possible to obtain the bits used to store a *Decimal* value:

### *Decimal* Shared Methods (selection)

```
Function GetBits(ByVal dValue As Decimal) As Integer()
```

This method returns an array of four integers. The first, second, and third elements of the array are the low, medium, and high components of the 96-bit unsigned integer. The fourth element contains the sign and the scaling factor: bits 0 through 15 are 0; bits 16 through 23 contain a scaling value between 0 and 28; bits 24 through 30 are 0; and bit 31 is 0 for positive and 1 for negative.

Given a *Decimal* number named *dValue*, you can execute the statement

```
Dim ai() As Integer = Decimal.GetBits(dValue)
```

If *ai(3)* is negative, the *Decimal* number is negative. The scaling factor is

```
(ai(3) \ &H10000) And &HFF
```

I already indicated how floating-point representation is often only approximate. When you start performing arithmetic operations on floating-point numbers, the approximations can get worse. Almost everyone who has used floating point is well aware that a number that should be 4.55 (for example) is often stored as 4.549999 or 4.550001.

The decimal representation is much better behaved. For example, suppose *d1* is defined like so:

```
Dim d1 As Decimal = 12.34D
```

Internally, *d1* has an integer part of 1234 and a scaling factor of 2. Also, suppose *d2* is defined like this:

```
Dim d2 As Decimal = 56.789D
```

The integer part is 56789, and the scaling factor is 3. Now add these two numbers:

```
Dim d3 As Decimal = d1 + d2
```

Internally, the integer part of *d1* is multiplied by 10 (to get 12340), and the scaling factor is set to 3. Now the integer parts can be added directly: 12340 plus 56789 equals 69129 with a scaling factor of 3. The actual number is 69.129. Everything is exact.

Now multiply the two numbers:

```
Dim d4 As Decimal = d1 * d2
```

Internally, the two integral parts are multiplied (1234 times 56789 equals 70,077,626), and the scaling factors are added (2 plus 3 equals 5). The actual numeric result is 700.77626. Again, the calculation is exact.

When dividing…well, division is messy no matter how you do it. But for the most part, when using *Decimal*, you have much better control over the precision and accuracy of your results.

# Floating-Point Infinity and NaNs

The two floating-point data types—*Single* and *Double*—are defined in accordance with the ANSI/IEEE Std 754-1985, the *IEEE Standard for Binary Floating-Point Arithmetic*.

A *Single* value consists of a 24-bit signed mantissa and an 8-bit signed exponent. The precision is approximately seven decimal digits. Values range from

$$-3.402823 \times 10^{38}$$

to

$$3.402823 \times 10^{38}$$

The smallest possible *Single* value greater than 0 is

$$1.401298 \times 10^{-45}$$

You can obtain these three values as fields in the *Single* structure:

**Single Structure Constant Fields (selection)**

| Field | Type |
|---|---|
| MinValue | Single |
| MaxValue | Single |
| Epsilon | Single |

A *Double* value consists of a 53-bit signed mantissa and an 11-bit signed exponent. The precision is approximately 15 to 16 decimal digits. Values range from

$$-1.79769313486232 \times 10^{308}$$

to

$$1.79769313486232 \times 10^{308}$$

The smallest possible *Double* value greater than 0 is

$$4.94065645841247 \times 10^{-324}$$

The *MinValue*, *MaxValue*, and *Epsilon* fields are also defined in the *Double* structure.

Here's some code that divides a floating-point number by 0:

```
Dim f1 As Single = 1
Dim f2 As Single = 0
Dim f3 As Single = f1 / f2
```

If these were integers and you used the integer divide (the backslash \), a *DivideByZeroException* would be raised. But these are IEEE floating-point numbers. An exception is *not* raised. Indeed, floating-point operations *never* raise exceptions. Instead, in this case, *f3* takes on a special value. If you use *Console.WriteLine* to display *f3*, it will display the word

```
Infinity
```

If you change the initialization of *f1* to −1, *Console.WriteLine* will display

```
-Infinity
```

In the IEEE standard, positive infinity and negative infinity are legitimate values of floating-point numbers. You can even perform arithmetic on infinite values. For example, the expression

```
1 / f3
```

equals 0.

If you change the initialization of *f1* in the preceding code to 0, then *f3* will equal a value known as *Not a Number*, which is universally abbreviated as *NaN* and pronounced "nan." Here's how *Console.WriteLine* displays a NaN:

```
NaN
```

You can also create a NaN by adding a positive infinity to a negative infinity or by a number of other calculations.

Both the *Single* and *Double* structures have shared methods to determine whether a *Single* or *Double* value is infinity or NaN. Here are the methods in the *Single* structure:

### *Single* Structure Shared Methods (selection)

```
Function IsInfinity(ByVal fValue As Single) As Boolean

Function IsPositiveInfinity(ByVal fValue As Single) As Boolean

Function IsNegativeInfinity(ByVal fValue As Single) As Boolean

Function IsNaN(ByVal fValue As Single) As Boolean
```

For example, the expression

```
Single.IsInfinity(fVal)
```

returns *True* if *fVal* is either positive infinity or negative infinity.

The *Single* structure also has constant fields that represent these values:

### *Single* Structure Constant Fields (selection)

| Field | Type |
| --- | --- |
| *PositiveInfinity* | *Single* |
| *NegativeInfinity* | *Single* |
| *NaN* | *Single* |

Identical fields are defined in the *Double* structure. These values correspond to specific bit patterns defined in the IEEE standard.

# The *Math* Class

The *Math* class in the *System* namespace consists solely of a collection of shared methods and the following two constant fields:

### *Math* Constant Fields

| Field | Type | Value |
| --- | --- | --- |
| *PI* | *Double* | 3.14159265358979 |
| *E* | *Double* | 2.71828182845905 |

*Math.PI*, of course, is the ratio of the circumference of a circle to its diameter, and *Math.E* is the limit of

$$\left(1 + \frac{1}{n}\right)^{n}$$

as *n* approaches infinity.

Most of the methods in the *Math* class are defined only for *Double* values. However, some methods are defined for integer and *Decimal* values as well. The following two methods are defined for every numeric type:

## *Math* Shared Methods (selection)

```
Function Max(ByVal n1 As numeric-type,
             ByVal n2 As numeric-type) As type

Function Min(ByVal n1 As numeric-type,
             ByVal n2 As numeric-type) As type
```

The two values must be the same type.

The following two methods are defined for *Single, Double, Decimal, Short* and *Integer*:

## *Math* Shared Methods (selection)

```
Function Sign(ByVal s As signed-type) As Integer

Function Abs(ByVal s As signed-type) As type
```

The *Sign* method returns 1 if the argument is positive, −1 if the argument is negative, and 0 if the argument is 0. The *Abs* method returns the negative value of the argument if the argument is negative, and the argument itself if the argument is 0 or positive.

The *Abs* method is the only method of the *Math* class that can throw an exception, and then only for integral arguments, and only for one particular value for each integral type. If the argument is the *MinValue* of the particular integral type (for example, −32768 for *Short*), then an *OverflowException* is raised because 32768 can't be represented by a *Short*.

The following methods perform various types of rounding on *Double* and *Decimal* values:

## *Math* Shared Methods (selection)

```
Function Floor(ByVal rValue As Double) As Double

Function Ceiling(ByVal rValue As Double) As Double

Function Round(ByVal rValue As Double) As Double

Function Round(ByVal rValue As Double,
              ByVal iDecimals As Integer) As Double

Function Round(ByVal dValue As Decimal) As Decimal

Function Round(ByVal dValue As Decimal,
              ByVal iDecimals As Integer) As Decimal
```

*Floor* returns the largest whole number less than or equal to the argument; *Ceiling* returns the smallest whole number greater than or equal to the argument. The call

```
Math.Floor(3.5)
```

returns 3, and

```
Math.Ceiling(3.5)
```

returns 4. The same rules apply to negative numbers. The call

```
Math.Floor(-3.5)
```

returns −4, and

```
Math.Ceiling(-3.5)
```

returns −3.

The *Floor* method returns the nearest whole number in the direction of negative infinity, and that's why it's sometimes also known as *rounding toward negative infinity*; likewise, *Ceiling* returns the nearest whole number in the direction of positive infinity and is sometimes called *rounding toward positive infinity*. It's also possible to round toward 0, which is to obtain the nearest whole number closest to 0. You round toward 0 using the Visual Basic .NET *Fix* function. The expression

```
Fix(3.5)
```

returns 3, and

```
Fix(-3.5)
```

returns −3. Rounding toward 0 is sometimes called *truncation*.

The Visual Basic *Int* function rounds towards negative infinity like *Floor*, but it returns an *Integer* value. *Floor* doesn't perform a type conversion.

The *Round* methods with a single argument return the whole number nearest to the argument. If the argument to *Round* is midway between two whole numbers, the return value is the nearest even number. For example, the call

```
Math.Round(4.5)
```

returns 4, and

```
Math.Round(5.5)
```

returns 6. The Visual Basic *CInt* and *CLong* functions also round numbers and covert to an integer type. With *Round* you can optionally supply an integer that indicates the number of decimal places in the return value. For example,

```
Math.Round(5.285, 2)
```

returns 5.28.

# Floating-Point Remainders

Much confusion surrounds functions that calculate floating-point remainders. The Visual Basic remainder or modulus operator (*Mod*) is defined for all numeric types. Here's a Visual Basic statement using *Single* numbers with the remainder operator:

```
fResult = fDividend Mod fDivisor
```

The sign of *fResult* is the same as the sign of *fDividend*, and *fResult* can be calculated with the formula

```
fResult = fDividend - n * fDivisor
```

where *n* is the largest possible integer less than or equal to *fDividend / fDivisor*. For example, the expression

```
4.5 Mod 1.25
```

equals 0.75. Let's run through the calculation. The expression 4.5 / 1.25 equals 3.6, so *n* equals 3. The quantity 4.5 minus (3 times 1.25) equals 0.75.

The IEEE standard defines a remainder a little differently, where *n* is the integer *closest* to *fDividend / fDivisor*. You can calculate a remainder in accordance with the IEEE standard using this method:

### *Math* Shared Methods (selection)

```
Function IEEERemainder(ByVal rDividend As Double,
                 ByVal rDivisor As Double) As Double
```

The expression

```
Math.IEEERemainder(4.5, 1.25)
```

returns −0.5. That's because 4.5 / 1.25 equals 3.6, and the closest integer to 3.6 is 4. When *n* equals 4, the quantity 4.5 minus (4 times 1.25) equals −0.5.

# Powers and Logarithms

Three methods of the *Math* class involve powers:

### *Math* Shared Methods (selection)

```
Function Pow(ByVal rBase As Double,
             ByVal rPower As Double) As Double

Function Exp(ByVal rPower As Double) As Double

Function Sqrt(ByVal rValue As Double) As Double
```

*Pow* calculates the value

rBase$^\text{rPower}$

The expression

```
Math.Exp(rPower)
```

is equivalent to

```
Math.Pow(Math.E, rPower)
```

and the square root function

```
Math.Sqrt(rValue)
```

is equivalent to

```
Math.Pow(rValue, 0.5)
```

The *Sqrt* method returns NaN if the argument is negative.

The *Math* class has three methods that calculate logarithms:

### *Math* Shared Methods (selection)

```
Function Log10(ByVal rValue As Double) As Double
Function Log(ByVal rValue As Double) As Double
Function Log(ByVal rValue As Double,
            ByVal rBase As Double) As Double
```

The expression

```
Math.Log10(rValue)
```

is equivalent to

```
Math.Log(rValue, 10)
```

and

```
Math.Log(rValue)
```

is equivalent to

```
Math.Log(rValue, Math.E)
```

The logarithm methods return *PositiveInfinity* for an argument of 0 and *NaN* for an argument less than 0.

# Trigonometric Functions

Trigonometric functions describe the relationship between the sides and angles of triangles. The trig functions are defined for right triangles:

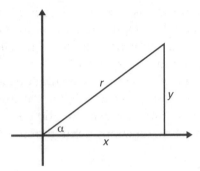

For angle α in a right triangle where $x$ is the adjacent leg, $y$ is the opposite leg, and $r$ is the hypotenuse, the three basic trigonometric functions are

$\sin(\alpha) = y \, / \, r$
$\cos(\alpha) = x \, / \, r$
$\tan(\alpha) = y \, / \, x$

Trigonometric functions can also be used to define circles and ellipses. For constant $r$ and a ranging from 0 degrees to 360 degrees, the set of coordinates ($x$, $y$) where

$x = r \cdot \sin(\alpha)$
$y = r \cdot \cos(\alpha)$

define a circle centered at the origin with radius $r$. Chapter 5 shows how to use trigonometric functions to draw circles and ellipses. Trig functions also show up in various graphics exercises in Chapters 13, 15, 17, and 19. The trigonometric functions in the *Math* class require angles specified in radians rather than degrees. There are $2\pi$ radians in 360 degrees. The rationale for using radians can be illustrated by considering the following arc $l$ subtended by angle α:

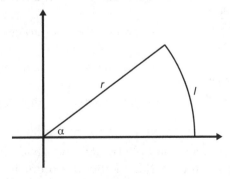

What is the length of arc $l$? Because the circumference of the entire circle equals $2\pi r$, the length of arc $l$ equals $(\alpha/360)2\pi r$, where α is measured in degrees. However, if $\alpha$ is measured in radians, then the length of arc *l* simply equals $\alpha$r. For a unit circle (radius equal to 1), the length of arc *l* equals the angle $\alpha$ in radians. And that's how the radian is defined: in a unit circle, an arc of length *l* is subtended by an angle in radians equal to *l*.

For example, an angle of 90 degrees in a unit circle subtends an arc with length $\pi/2$. Thus, 90 degrees is equivalent to $\pi/2$ radians. An angle of 180 degrees is equivalent to $\pi$ radians. There are $2\pi$ radians in 360 degrees.

Here are the three basic trigonometric functions defined in the *Math* class:

### *Math* Shared Methods (selection)

```
Function Sin(ByVal rAngle As Double) As Double

Function Cos(ByVal rAngle As Double) As Double

Function Tan(ByVal rAngle As Double) As Double
```

If you have an angle in degrees, multiply by $\pi$ and divide by 180 to convert to radians:

```
Math.Sin(Math.PI * rAngleInDegrees / 180)
```

The *Sin* and *Cos* methods return values ranging from −1 to 1. In theory, the *Tan* method should return infinity at $\pi/2$ (90 degrees) and $3\pi/2$ (270 degrees), but it returns very large values instead.

The following methods are inverses of the trigonometric functions. They return angles in radians:

### *Math* Shared Methods (selection)

| Method | Argument | Return Value |
|---|---|---|
| Function Asin<br>   (ByVal rValue As Double) As Double | −1 through 1 | $-\pi/2$ through $\pi/2$ |
| Function Acos<br>   (ByVal rValue As Double) As Double | −1 through 1 | $\pi$ through 0 |
| Function Atan<br>   (ByVal rValue As Double) As Double | $-\infty$ through $\infty$ | $-\pi/2$ through $\pi/2$ |
| Function Atan2(ByVal y As Double,<br>   ByVal x As Double) As Double | $-\infty$ through $\infty$ | $-\pi$ through $\pi$ |

To convert the return value to degrees, multiply by 180 and divide by $\pi$.

The *Asin* and *Acos* methods return NaN if the argument is not in the proper range. The *Atan2* method uses the signs of the two arguments to determine the quadrant of the angle:

## *Atan2* Return Values

| *y* Argument | *x* Argument | Return Value |
|---|---|---|
| Positive | Positive | 0 through $\pi/2$ |
| Positive | Negative | $\pi/2$ through $\pi$ |
| Negative | Negative | $\pi$ through $3\pi/2$ |
| Negative | Positive | $3\pi/2$ through $2\pi$ |

Less commonly used are the hyperbolic trigonometric functions. While the common trigonometric functions define circles and ellipses, the hyperbolic trig functions define hyperbolas:

## *Math* Shared Methods (selection)

```
Function Sinh(ByVal rAngle As Double) As Double

Function Cosh(ByVal rAngle As Double) As Double

Function Tanh(ByVal rAngle As Double) As Double
```

The angle is expressed in hyperbolic radians.

# Appendix C

# String Theory

Just about every programming language ever invented implements text strings a little differently. Unlike floating-point numbers, strings are not blessed (or cursed) with an industry standard.

Dating back from the days when it was called BASIC, Microsoft Visual Basic has always had strong support for the manipulation of character strings. Visual Basic .NET adds many string functions to the collection in Visual Basic 6.0. In this appendix, I'll be discussing the string functions implemented in the Microsoft .NET Framework.

In Visual Basic .NET, the data type for a text string is named *String*, which is an alias for the class *System.String*. The *String* data type is related to the *Char* data type: a *String* object can be constructed from an array of characters and also converted into an array of characters. Both string literals and character literals are defined with double quotation marks. When defining a character, follow the second quotation mark with a *c*:

```
Dim ch As Char = "x"c
```

A string has a specific length, and once a string is created, its length can't be changed. Nor can any of the individual characters that make up a string be changed. A Visual Basic .NET string is thus said to be *immutable*. Whenever you need to change a string in some way, you must create another string. Many methods of the *String* class create new strings based on existing strings. Many methods and properties throughout the .NET Framework create and return strings.

Here's a common pitfall: you might expect that there's a method of *String* named *ToUpper* that converts all the characters in a string to uppercase, and that's precisely the case. But for a *String* instance named *str*, you can't just call the method like so:

```
str.ToUpper()    ' Won't do anything!
```

Syntactically, this statement is valid, but it has no effect on the *str* variable. Strings are immutable, and hence the characters of *str* can't be altered. The

*ToUpper* method creates a new string. You need to assign the return value of *ToUpper* to another string variable:

```
Dim strUpper As String = str.ToUpper()
```

Or you could assign it to the same string variable:

```
str = str.ToUpper()
```

In the second case, the original string (the one containing lowercase letters) still exists, but since it's probably no longer referenced anywhere in the program, it becomes eligible for garbage collection.

Here's another example. Suppose you define a string like so:

```
Dim str As String = "abcdifg"
```

You can access a particular character of the string by indexing the string property *Chars* like it's an array:

```
Dim ch As Char = str.Chars(4)
```

In this case, *ch* is the character *i*. But the *Chars* property is read-only. You can't set a particular character of a string using *Chars*:

```
str.Chars(4) = "e"c    ' Won't work!
```

So, how *do* you replace characters in a Visual Basic .NET string? There are a couple ways. The method call

```
str = str.Replace("i"c, "e"c)
```

will replace *all* occurrences of *i* with *e*. Alternatively, you can first call *Remove* to create a new string with one or more characters removed at a specified index with a specified length. For example, the call

```
str = str.Remove(4, 1)
```

removes one character at the fourth position (the *i*). You can then call *Insert* to insert a new string, which in this case is a single character:

```
str = str.Insert(4, "e")
```

Or you can do both jobs in one statement:

```
str = str.Remove(4, 1).Insert(4, "e")
```

Despite the use of a single string variable named *str*, the two method calls in this last statement create two additional strings, and the quoted *e* is yet another string.

Another approach is also possible. You can convert the string into a character array, set the appropriate element of the array, and then construct a new string based on the character array:

```
Dim ach() As Char = str.ToCharArray()
ach(4) = "e"c
str = New String(ach)
```

Or you can patch together a new string from substrings:

```
str = str.Substring(0, 4) & "e" & str.Substring(5)
```

I'll discuss all these *String* class methods more formally in the course of this appendix.

# The *Char* Type

Each element of a string is a *Char*, which is an alias for the .NET structure *System.Char*. A program can specify a single literal character using double quotation marks and a *c*:

```
Dim ch As Char = "A"c
```

Although *Char* is derived from *ValueType*, a *Char* variable isn't directly usable as a number. To convert a *Char* variable named *ch* to an integer, for example, requires the Visual Basic *Asc* or *AscW* function:

```
Dim i As Integer = AscW(ch)
```

To go the other way and convert an integer to a character, use the Visual Basic *Chr* or *ChrW* function.

Character variables have numeric values from &H0000 through &HFFFF and refer to characters in the Unicode character set. The book *The Unicode Standard Version 3.0* (Addison-Wesley, 2000) is the essential reference to Unicode. The *W* in the names of the *AscW* and *ChrW* functions indicates that they work with *wide* (16-bit) characters. The *Asc* and *Chr* functions work only with 8-bit characters.

To determine whether a particular character is a letter, number, control character, or whatever, you use shared methods defined in the *Char* structure. The argument is either a character or a string with an index value.

### *Char* Shared Methods (selection)

```
Function IsControl(ByVal ch As Char) As Boolean

Function IsControl(ByVal str As String,
                ByVal index As Integer) As Boolean

Function IsSeparator(ByVal ch As Char) As Boolean

Function IsSeparator(ByVal str As String,
                ByVal index As Integer) As Boolean
```

*(continued)*

### *Char* Shared Methods (selection)  *(continued)*

```
Function IsWhiteSpace(ByVal ch As Char) As Boolean

Function IsWhiteSpace(ByVal str As String,
                      ByVal index As Integer) As Boolean

Function IsPunctuation(ByVal ch As Char) As Boolean

Function IsPunctuation(ByVal str As String,
                       ByVal index As Integer) As Boolean

Function IsSymbol(ByVal ch As Char) As Boolean

Function IsSymbol(ByVal str As String,
                  ByVal index As Integer) As Boolean

Function IsDigit(ByVal ch As Char) As Boolean

Function IsDigit(ByVal str As String,
                 ByVal index As Integer) As Boolean

Function IsNumber(ByVal ch As Char) As Boolean

Function IsNumber(ByVal str As String,
                  ByVal index As Integer) As Boolean

Function IsLetter(ByVal ch As Char) As Boolean

Function IsLetter(ByVal str As String,
                  ByVal index As Integer) As Boolean

Function IsUpper(ByVal ch As Char) As Boolean

Function IsUpper(ByVal str As String,
                 ByVal index As Integer) As Boolean

Function IsLower(ByVal ch As Char) As Boolean

Function IsLower(ByVal str As String,
                 ByVal index As Integer) As Boolean

Function IsLetterOrDigit(ByVal ch As Char) As Boolean

Function IsLetterOrDigit(ByVal str As String,
                         ByVal index As Integer) As Boolean

Function IsSurrogate(ByVal ch As Char) As Boolean

Function IsSurrogate(ByVal str As String,
                     ByVal index As Integer) As Boolean
```

The call

```
Char.IsControl(str.Chars(index))
```

is equivalent to

```
Char.IsControl(str, index)
```

You might be able to avoid using these methods for ASCII characters (character values &H0000 through &H007F), but these methods also apply to all Unicode characters. The *IsSurrogate* method refers to the area of Unicode with values &HD800 through &HDFFF that is reserved for expansion.

The *Char* structure also defines a couple other handy methods. One returns a member of the *UnicodeCategory* enumeration (defined in *System.Globalization*), and the other returns the numeric value of the character converted to a *Double*:

### *Char* Shared Methods (selection)

```
Function GetUnicodeCategory(ByVal ch As Char) As UnicodeCategory

Function GetUnicodeCategory(ByVal str As String,
                        ByVal index As Integer) As UnicodeCategory

Function GetNumericValue(ByVal ch As Char) As Double

Function GetNumericValue(ByVal str As String,
                        ByVal index As Integer) As Double
```

# String Constructors and Properties

In many cases, you'll define a string variable using a literal:

```
Dim str As String = "Hello, world!"
```

or a literal inserted right in a function call:

```
Console.WriteLine("Hello, world!")
```

or as the return value from one of the many methods that return string variables. One ubiquitous string-returning method is named *ToString* and converts an object to a string. For example, the expression

```
55.ToString()
```

returns the string "55".

To include a double quotation mark in a string, use two double quotation marks in succession.

One of the less common methods of creating a string is by using one of the eight *String* constructors. Five of the *String* constructors involve pointers and are not compliant with the Common Language Specification (CLS). The remaining three *String* constructors create a *String* object by repeating a single character or converting from an array of characters:

### *String* Constructors (selection)

```
String(ByVal ch As Char, ByVal iCount As Integer)
String(ByVal ach() As Char)
String(ByVal ach() As Char, ByVal iStartIndex As Integer,
                            ByVal iCount As Integer)
```

In the third constructor, *iStartIndex* is an index into the character array and *iCount* indicates a number of characters beginning at that index. The length of the resultant string will equal *iCount*.

The *String* class has just two properties, both of which are read-only:

### *String* Properties

| Property | Type | Accessibility |
|----------|------|---------------|
| *Length* | *Integer* | Get |
| *Chars()* | *Char* | Get |

The first indicates the number of characters in the string; the second is an indexer that lets you access the individual characters of the string.

*String* is a reference type. You can define a string variable without initializing it:

```
Dim str1 As String
```

But this is the same as assigning a string variable the value *Nothing*:

```
Dim str2 As String = Nothing
```

What the *Nothing* value means is that no memory has been allocated for the string. Having a *Nothing* value is different from having an empty string:

```
Dim str3 As String = ""
```

An empty string has memory allocated for the instance of the string, but the *str3.Length* property equals 0. Attempting to determine the length of a *Nothing* string—making reference to *str2.Length*, for example—causes an exception to be thrown.

You can also initialize a string variable to an empty string using the only public field of the *String* class:

### *String* Shared Field

| Field | Type | Accessibility |
|-------|------|---------------|
| *Empty* | *String* | read-only |

For example,

```
Dim str As String = String.Empty
```

You can define an array of strings like so:

```
Dim astr(5) As String
```

An array of six strings is created, each of which is *Nothing*. You can also create an array of initialized strings:

```
Dim astr() As String = {"abc", "defghi", "jkl"}
```

This statement creates an array with three elements; that is, *astr.Length* returns 3. Each string has a specific length; for example, *astr(1).Length* returns 6.

The *String* class implements the *IComparable*, *ICloneable*, *IConvertible*, and *IEnumerable* interfaces, which implies that the *String* class contains certain methods defined in these interfaces. Because *String* implements the *IEnumerable* interface, you can use *String* with the *For Each* statement to enumerate the characters in a string. The statements

```
Dim ch As Char
For Each ch in str
    ⋮
Next ch
```

are equivalent to (and quite a bit shorter than)

```
Dim i As Integer
For i = 0 To str.Length - 1
    Dim ch As Char = str.Chars(i)
    ⋮
Next i
```

In the *For Each* block, *ch* is read-only. In the *For* block, *ch* is not read-only but (as usual) the characters in the string can't be altered.

After *IEnumerable*, perhaps the next most important interface that *String* implements is *IComparable*, which means that the *String* class implements a method named *CompareTo* that lets you use arrays of strings with the *BinarySearch* and *Sort* methods defined in the *Array* class. I'll go over these methods later in this appendix.

# Copying Strings

There are several ways to copy a string. Perhaps the simplest is using the equals sign:

```
Dim strCopy As String = str
```

Like every class in the .NET Framework, the *String* class inherits the *ToString* method from *Object*. Because the *String* class implements *ICloneable*, it also implements the *Clone* method. These methods provide additional (if somewhat redundant) methods to copy strings:

### *String* Methods (selection)

```
Function ToString() As String
Function Clone() As Object
```

If you use *Clone*, you must cast the result to a *string*:

```
Dim strCopy As String = DirectCast(str.Clone(), String)
```

The *String* class also implements a shared method that copies a string:

### *String Copy* Shared Method

```
Function Copy(ByVal str As String) As String
```

Two of the *String* constructors convert a character array to a string. You can also convert a string back to a character array:

### *String* Methods (selection)

```
Function ToCharArray() As Char()
Function ToCharArray(ByVal iStartIndex As Integer,
                ByVal iCount As Integer) As Char()
Sub CopyTo(ByVal iStartIndexSrc As Integer, ByVal achDst() As Char,
                ByVal iStartIndexDst As Integer, ByVal iCount As Integer)
```

The *ToCharArray* methods create the character array. The *iStartIndex* argument refers to a starting index in the string. To use the *CopyTo* method, the *achDst* array must already exist. The first argument is a starting index for the string; the third argument is a starting index in the character array. The *CopyTo* method is the equivalent of

```
For i = 0 To iCount - 1
    achDst(iStartIndexDst + i) = str.Chars(iStartIndexSrc + i)
Next i
```

The *Substring* methods create a new string that is a section of an existing string:

### *String Substring* Method

```
Function Substring(ByVal iStartIndex As Integer) As String

Function Substring(ByVal iStartIndex As Integer,
                   ByVal iCount As Integer) As String
```

The first version returns a substring that begins at the index and continues to the end of the string.

# Converting Strings

Two methods, each with two versions, convert strings to lowercase or upper-case:

### *String* Methods (selection)

```
Function ToUpper() As String

Function ToUpper(ByVal ci As CultureInfo) As String

Function ToLower() As String

Function ToLower(ByVal ci As CultureInfo) As String
```

The *CultureInfo* class is defined in *System.Globalization* and in this case refers to a particular language as used in a particular country.

# Concatenating Strings

It's often necessary to tack together two or more strings, a process known as *string concatenation*. In Visual Basic .NET you can use the + operator or (if other objects must be converted to strings during the concatenation) the & operator. The concatenation operator is convenient for defining a string literal that's a little too long to fit on a single line:

```
Dim str As String = "Those who profess to favor freedom and yet " & _
                    "depreciate agitation. . .want crops without " & _
                    "plowing up the ground, they want rain without " & _
                    "thunder and lightning. They want the ocean " & _
                    "without the awful roar of its many waters. " & _
                    ChrW(&Hx2014) + " Frederick Douglass";
```

You can also use the += or &= operator to append a string to the end of an existing string:

```
str &= vbCrLf
```

The *String* class also defines a shared *Concat* method:

### String *Concat* Shared Method (selection)

```
Function Concat(ByVal str1 As String,
               ByVal str2 As String) As String

Function Concat(ByVal str1 As String, ByVal str2 As String,
               ByVal str3 As String) As String

Function Concat(ByVal str1 As String,
               ByVal str2 As String, ByVal str3 As String,
               ByVal str4 As String) As String

Function Concat(ByVal ParamArray astr() As String) As String
```

Notice the *ParamArray* keyword in the last version of *Concat*. What that keyword means in this case is that you can specify either an array of strings or any number of strings. For example, if you have an array of strings defined as

```
Dim astr() As String = {"abc", "def", "ghi", "jkl", "mno", "pqr"}
```

and you pass that array to the *Concat* method

```
Dim str As String = String.Concat(astr)
```

the result is the string "abcdefghijklmnopqr". Alternatively, you can pass the individual strings directly to the *Concat* method:

```
Dim str As String = String.Concat("abc", "def", "ghi", "jkl", "mno", "pqr")
```

Although the *String* class defines *Concat* versions with two, three, four, or a variable number of arguments, only the version with the *ParamArray* argument is necessary. That method actually encompasses the other three methods.

Another set of *Concat* methods are the same except with *Object* arguments:

### String *Concat* Shared Method (selection)

```
Function Concat(ByVal obj As Object) As String

Function Concat(ByVal obj1 As Object,
               ByVal obj2 As Object) As String

Function Concat(ByVal obj1 As Object, ByVal obj2 As Object,
               ByVal obj3 As Object) As String

Function Concat(ByVal ParamArray aobj() As Object) As String
```

The *Object* arguments are converted to strings by the objects' *ToString* methods. The call

```
String.Concat(55, "-", 33, "=", 55 - 33)
```

creates the string "55-33=22".

It's sometimes necessary to concatenate an array of strings but with some kind of separator between each array element. You can do that using the *Join* shared method:

### *String Join* **Shared Method**

```
Function Join(ByVal strSeparator As String,
         ByVal astr() As String) As String

Function Join(ByVal strSeparator As String,
         ByVal astr() As String, ByVal iStartIndex As Integer,
         ByVal iCount As Integer) As String
```

For example, if you have an array of strings defined as

```
Dim astr() As String = {"abc", "def", "ghi", "jkl", "mno", "pqr"}
```

you might want to create a composite string with end-of-line indicators between each pair. Call

```
Dim str As String = String.Join(vbCrLf, astr)
```

The separator is not appended following the last string.

The second version of *Join* lets you select a contiguous subset of strings from the array before joining them.

# Comparing Strings

*String* is a class (not a structure), and *string* is a reference type (not a value type). Normally that would imply that the comparison operators (= and <>) wouldn't work correctly for strings. You'd be comparing object references rather than characters. However, the = and <> operators have been redefined for strings and work as you'd expect. The expressions

```
(str = "New York")
```

and

```
(str <> "New Jersey")
```

return *Boolean* values based on a case-sensitive character-by-character comparison.

There are also several methods defined in the *String* class that return *Boolean* values indicating the result of a case-sensitive string comparison:

### *String* Methods (selection)

```
Function Equals(ByVal str As String) As Boolean
Function Equals(ByVal obj As Object) As Boolean
Function StartsWith(ByVal str As String) As Boolean
Function EndsWith(ByVal str As String) As Boolean
```

If a string is defined as

```
Dim str As String = "The end of time"
```

then

```
str.StartsWith("The")
```

returns *True* but

```
str.StartsWith("the")
```

returns *False*.

There's also a shared version of the *Equals* method:

### *String* Shared Methods (selection)

```
Function Equals(ByVal str1 As String,
                ByVal str2 As String) As Boolean
```

For example, instead of

```
If str = "New York" Then
```

you can use

```
If String.Equals(str, "New York") Then
```

Methods like this one are provided primarily for languages that don't have operators for comparison.

The remaining comparison methods implemented in *String*, which I'll discuss momentarily, return an integer value that indicates whether one string is less than, equal to, or greater than another string:

## *String* Comparison Method Return Values

| Return Value | Meaning |
| --- | --- |
| Negative | *str1 < str2* |
| Zero | *str1 = str2* |
| Positive | *str1 > str2* |

Watch out: the comparison methods are defined as returning negative, zero, or positive integers, *not* −1, 0, or 1.

Usually if you're interested in whether one string is less than or greater than another, it's because you're sorting the strings in some way. And that implies that you probably don't want to perform a comparison based on the strict numeric values of the character codes. For example, you probably want the characters *e* and *é* to be regarded as less than *F*, despite the higher values of their character codes. Such a comparison is known as a *lexical* comparison rather than a *numeric* comparison.

Here's the relationship among a few select characters when compared numerically:

D < E < F < d < e < f < È < É < Ê < Ë < è < é < ê < ë

And here's the lexical comparison:

d < D < e < E < é < É < è < È < ê < Ê < ë < Ë < f < F

Is a lexical comparison also case insensitive? Mostly it is. For example, the string "New Jersey" is considered less than "new York" despite the lowercase 'n' in the second string. But when two strings are identical except for case, lowercase letters are considered less than uppercase letters, that is, "the" is less than "The". However, "Them" is less than "then".

In other words, by default, a lexical comparison is case sensitive only when a method must decide whether or not to return 0. Otherwise, it's case insensitive.

The lexical comparison also implies a certain relationship among letters, numbers, and other characters. In general, control characters are considered to be less than single quotes and dashes, which are less than white-space characters. Next comes punctuation and other symbols, digits (0 through 9), and finally letters. A *Nothing* string is less than the empty string, which is less than any other character. For example,

```
"New" < "New York" < "Newark"
```

The nonshared method *CompareTo* performs a lexical comparison between a string instance and an argument:

### String *CompareTo* Method

```
Function CompareTo(ByVal str2 As String) As Integer
Function CompareTo(ByVal obj2 As Object) As Integer
```

The first string is the string object you're calling *CompareTo* on, for example,

```
str1.CompareTo(str2)
```

The *CompareTo* method with the object argument is necessary to implement the *IComparable* interface. The *CompareTo* method is used by the shared *Array.BinarySearch* and *Array.Sort* methods, as I'll discuss shortly.

All the other comparison methods are shared. The *CompareOrdinal* methods perform a strict numeric comparison based on the character value:

### String *CompareOrdinal* Shared Method

```
Function CompareOrdinal(ByVal str1 As String,
                        ByVal str2 As String) As Integer
Function CompareOrdinal(ByVal str1 As String,
                        ByVal iStartIndex1 As Integer,
                        ByVal str2 As String,
                        ByVal iStartIndex2 As Integer,
                        ByVal iCount As Integer) As Integer
```

The shared *Compare* methods perform a lexical comparison:

### String *Compare* Shared Method

```
Function Compare(ByVal str1 As String,
                 ByVal str2 As String) As Integer
Function Compare(ByVal str1 As String, ByVal str2 As String,
                 ByVal bIgnoreCase As Boolean) As Integer
Function Compare(ByVal str1 As String, ByVal str2 As String,
                 ByVal bIgnoreCase As Boolean,
                 ByVal ci As CultureInfo) As Integer
Function Compare(ByVal str1 As String,
                 ByVal iStartIndex1 As Integer,
                 ByVal str2 As String,
                 ByVal iStartIndex2 As Integer,
                 ByVal iCount As Integer) As Integer
```

### *String Compare* **Shared Method**   *(continued)*

```
Function Compare(ByVal str1 As String,
                 ByVal iStartIndex1 As Integer,
                 ByVal str2 As String,
                 ByVal iStartIndex2 As Integer,
                 ByVal iCount As Integer,
                 ByVal bIgnoreCase As Boolean) As Integer

Function Compare(ByVal str1 As String,
                 ByVal iStartIndex1 As Integer,
                 ByVal str2 As String,
                 ByVal iStartIndex2 As Integer,
                 ByVal iCount As Integer,
                 ByVal bIgnoreCase As Boolean,
                 ByVal ci As CultureInfo) As Integer
```

The *bIgnoreCase* argument affects the return value only when the two strings are the same except for case. Case-insensitive comparisons are much more useful for searching rather than sorting. The method calls

```
string.Compare("ë", "Ë")
```

and

```
string.Compare("ë", "Ë", False)
```

both return negative values, but

```
string.Compare("ë", "Ë", True)
```

returns 0. The calls

```
string.Compare("e", "ë", bIgnoreCase)
```

and

```
string.Compare("e", "Ë", bIgnoreCase)
```

always return negative values, regardless of the presence or value of the *bIgnore-Case* argument.

There is no comparison method implemented in the *String* class that reports that "André" equals "Andre".

## Searching the String

You can search for characters or strings within a string variable using versions of the *IndexOf* method. This method always returns an index referencing the source string.

### *String IndexOf* Methods

```
Function IndexOf(ByVal ch As Char) As Integer

Function IndexOf(ByVal ch As Char,
                 ByVal iStartIndex As Integer) As Integer

Function IndexOf(ByVal ch As Char, ByVal iStartIndex As Integer,
                 ByVal iCount As Integer) As Integer

Function IndexOf(ByVal str As String) As Integer

Function IndexOf(ByVal str As String,
                 ByVal iStartIndex As Integer) As Integer

Function IndexOf(ByVal str As String, ByVal iStartIndex As Integer,
                 ByVal iCount As Integer) As Integer
```

You can search for a specific character or another string. The search is case sensitive. The method returns −1 if the character or string isn't found. You can optionally include a starting index and a character count. The return value is measured from the beginning of the string, not from the starting index.

With a string defined as

```
Dim str As String = "hello world"
```

then

```
str.IndexOf("o"c)
```

returns 4, and

```
str.IndexOf("wo")
```

returns 6.

You can also perform the search starting at the end of the string:

### *String LastIndexOf* Methods

```
Function LastIndexOf(ByVal ch As Char) As Integer

Function LastIndexOf(ByVal ch As Char,
                     ByVal iStartIndex As Integer) As Integer

Function LastIndexOf(ByVal ch As Char,
                     ByVal iStartIndex As Integer,
                     ByVal iCount As Integer) As Integer

Function LastIndexOf(ByVal str As String) As Integer

Function LastIndexOf(ByVal str As String,
                     ByVal iStartIndex As Integer) As Integer

Function LastIndexOf(ByVal str As String,
                     ByVal iStartIndex As Integer,
                     ByVal iCount As Integer) As Integer
```

Although the methods search from the end of the string, the returned index is still measured from the beginning of the string. For the string shown above, the call

```
str.LastIndexOf("o"c)
```

returns 7, and

```
str.LastIndexOf("wo")
```

returns 6.

The following methods have a first argument that is an array of characters. The methods determine the first or last index in the string of a character that matches any character in the array:

### *String* Methods (selection)

```
Function IndexOfAny(ByVal ach() As Char) As Integer

Function IndexOfAny(ByVal ach() As Char,
                    ByVal iStartIndex As Integer) As Integer

Function IndexOfAny(ByVal ach() As Char,
                    ByVal iStartIndex As Integer,
                    ByVal iCount As Integer) As Integer

Function LastIndexOfAny(ByVal ach() As Char) As Integer

Function LastIndexOfAny(ByVal ach() As Char,
                        ByVal iStartIndex As Integer) As Integer

Function LastIndexOfAny(ByVal ach() As Char,
                        ByVal iStartIndex As Integer,
                        ByVal iCount As Integer) As Integer
```

If a character array and a string are defined like so:

```
Dim achVowel() As Char = {"a"c, "e"c, "i"c, "o"c, "u"c}
Dim str As String = "hello world"
```

then

```
str.IndexOfAny(achVowel)
```

returns 1, and

```
str.LastIndexOfAny(achVowel)
```

returns 7.

# Trimming and Padding

Sometimes when processing text files (such as program source code files), it's convenient to remove *white space*, which refers to the nonvisible characters that separate other elements in the string. The *String* class has methods to do so. For purposes of these methods, white-space characters are assumed to be the following Unicode characters:

## Unicode White-Space Characters

| | |
|---|---|
| &H0009 (tab) | &H2003 (em space) |
| &H000A (line feed) | &H2004 (three-per-em space) |
| &H000B (vertical tab) | &H2005 (four-per-em space) |
| &H000C (form feed) | &H2006 (six-per-em space) |
| &H000D (carriage return) | &H2007 (figure space) |
| &H0020 (space) | &H2008 (punctuation space) |
| &H00A0 (no-break space) | &H2009 (thin space) |
| &H2000 (en quad) | &H200A (hair space) |
| &H2001 (em quad) | &H200B (zero-width space) |
| &H2002 (en space) | &H3000 (ideographic space) |

You can either use the predefined white-space characters or define your own array of characters.

## *String* Methods (selection)

```
Function Trim() As String
Function Trim(ByVal ParamArray ach() As Char) As String
Function TrimStart(ByVal ParamArray ach() As Char) As String
Function TrimEnd(ByVal ParamArray ach() As Char) As String
```

To remove the predefined white-space characters from the beginning and end of a string named *str*, use

```
str.Trim()
```

or

```
str.Trim(Nothing)
```

You can also remove the predefined white-space characters from the beginning of a string, as here:

```
str.TrimStart(Nothing)
```

or the end, as here:

```
str.TrimEnd(Nothing)
```

Alternatively, you can specify the characters (not necessarily white-space characters) you want removed from the beginning or end of a string. You can either define a character array and pass that to the *Trim* (or *TrimStart* or *Trim-End*) method

```
Dim achTrim() As Char = {" "c, "-"c, "_"c}
str.Trim(achTrim)
```

or list the characters explicitly in the method call:

```
str.Trim(" "c, "-"c, "_"c)
```

Both method calls cause these three characters to be stripped from the beginning and end of the string.

You can also add spaces (or any other character) to the beginning or end of a string to achieve a specified total width:

### *String* Methods (selection)

```
Function PadLeft(ByVal iTotalLength As Integer) As String

Function PadLeft(ByVal iTotalLength As Integer,
          ByVal ch As Char) As String

Function PadRight(ByVal iTotalLength As Integer) As String

Function PadRight(ByVal iTotalLength As Integer,
          ByVal ch As Char) As String
```

# String Manipulation

Here are some miscellaneous methods that let you insert one string into another, remove a range of characters, and replace a particular character or string within a string. I showed examples of all these methods at the beginning of this appendix:

### *String* Methods (selection)

```
Function Insert(ByVal iIndex As Integer,
          ByVal strInsert As String) As String

Function Remove(ByVal iIndex As Integer,
          ByVal iCount As Integer) As String

Function Replace(ByVal chOld As Char,
          ByVal chNew As Char) As String

Function Replace(ByVal strOld As String,
          ByVal strNew As String) As String
```

Sometimes you need to break a string down into *tokens*, which are substrings delimited by certain fixed characters, usually white-space characters. Use the *Split* method:

### *String Split* Method

```
Function Split(ByVal ParamArray achSeparators() As Char) As String()

Function Split(ByVal ParamArray achSeparators() As Char,
               ByVal iReturnCount As Integer) As String()
```

If you set the first argument to *Nothing*, the method uses the set of white-space characters shown earlier.

# Formatting Strings

As you know from Chapter 1, the first argument of the *Console.Write* or *Console.WriteLine* method can be a string that describes the formatting of the remaining arguments. To perform the same type of formatting but save the results in a string, use the shared *Format* method of the *String* class:

### *String Format* Shared Method (selection)

```
Function Format(ByVal strFormat As String,
               ByVal obj As Object) As String

Function Format(ByVal strFormat As String, ByVal obj1 As Object,
               ByVal obj2 As Object) As String

Function Format(ByVal strFormat As String,
               ByVal obj1 As Object, ByVal obj2 As Object ,
               ByVal obj3 As Object) As String

Function Format(ByVal strFormat As String,
               ByVal ParamArray aobj() As Object) As String
```

For example, the following call to *Format*,

```
String.Format("The sum of {0} and {1} is {2}", 2, 3, 2 + 3)
```

creates the string "The sum of 2 and 3 is 5".

# Array Sorting and Searching

The *String* class implements the *IComparable* interface, which merely requires that it implement the following method:

### *IComparable* **Method**

```
Function CompareTo(ByVal obj As Object) As Integer
```

This method is called by two useful shared methods of *Array* named *Sort* and *BinarySearch*. You can use these two methods with arrays of objects of any class that implements *IComparable*.

Here are the two basic *Sort* methods:

### *Array Sort* **Shared Methods (selection)**

```
Sub Sort(ByVal arr As Array)

Sub Sort(ByVal arr As Array,
         ByVal iStartIndex As Integer, ByVal iCount As Integer)
```

The second version allows you to use a subset of the array. Suppose you define an array of strings like so:

```
Dim astr() As String = _
    {"New Jersey", "New York", "new Mexico", "New Hampshire"}
```

Notice the lowercase *n* in the third string. After calling

```
Array.Sort(astr)
```

the elements of the array are reordered to be "New Hampshire", "New Jersey", "new Mexico", and "New York". Because the *Sort* method uses the *CompareTo* method of *String*, the sorting is case insensitive. However, if the array also included "New Mexico" (with an uppercase *N*), "New Mexico" would be appear after "new Mexico" in the sorted array.

The next two versions of the *Sort* method require two corresponding arrays of equal size, optionally with a starting index and an element count:

### *Array Sort* **Shared Methods (selection)**

```
Sub Sort(ByVal arrKeys As Array, ByVal arrItems As Array)

Sub Sort(ByVal arrKeys As Array, ByVal arrItems As Array,
         ByVal iStartIndex As Integer, ByVal iCount As Integer)
```

The method sorts the first array and reorders the second array accordingly. I use this version of the *Sort* method in the SysInfoReflectionStrings program in Chapter 4 to sort an array of *SystemInformation* property names stored in *astrLabels*:

```
Array.Sort(astrLabels, astrValues)
```

The corresponding array of *SystemInformation* values stored in *astrValues* is also reordered so that the array elements still correspond to each other. If you want to perform a sort using a method other than *CompareTo*, you use one of the following *Sort* methods:

**Array Sort Shared Methods (selection)**

```
Sub Sort(ByVal arr As Array, ByVal comp As IComparer)

Sub Sort(ByVal arr As Array, ByVal iStartIndex As Integer,
         ByVal iCount As Integer, ByVal comp As IComparer)

Sub Sort(ByVal arrKeys As Array, ByVal arrItems As Array,
         ByVal comp As IComparer)

Sub Sort(ByVal arrKeys As Array, ByVal arrItems As Array,
         ByVal iStartIndex As Integer, ByVal iCount As Integer,
         ByVal comp As IComparer)
```

The argument of type *IComparer* can be an instance of any class that implements the *IComparer* interface. That's not the *String* class! *String* implements the *IComparable* interface, not *IComparer*.

The *IComparer* interface is defined in the *System.Collections* namespace. A class that implements *IComparer* must define the following method:

**IComparer Method**

```
Function Compare(ByVal obj1 As Object,
                 ByVal obj2 As Object) As Integer
```

This method is not shared, and hence, is not defined in the *String* class. (The only methods named *Compare* implemented in *String* are shared methods.)

The *System.Collections* namespace contains two classes that implement *IComparer*, which are *Comparer* (to perform a case-sensitive comparison just like the default) and *CaseInsensitiveComparer* (for a case-insensitive string comparison). Both these classes have a shared member named *Default* that returns an instance of the class.

For example, to perform a case-sensitive sort of the string array *astr*, call

```
Array.Sort(astr)
```

or

```
Array.Sort(astr, Comparer.Default)
```

To perform a case-insensitive sort, call

```
Array.Sort(astr, CaseInsensitiveComparer.Default)
```

The case-insensitive compare is much more useful in the *BinarySearch* method rather than the *Sort* method (or when sorting in preparation for a binary search):

### *Array BinarySearch* **Shared Method**

```
Function BinarySearch(ByVal arr As Array,
                      ByVal obj As Object) As Integer

Function BinarySearch(ByVal arr As Array,
                      ByVal iStartIndex As Integer,
                      ByVal iCount As Integer,
                      ByVal obj As Object) As Integer

Function BinarySearch(ByVal arr As Array, ByVal obj As Object,
                      ByVal comp As IComparer) As Integer

Function BinarySearch(ByVal arr As Array,
                      ByVal iStartIndex As Integer,
                      ByVal iCount As Integer, ByVal obj As Object,
                      ByVal comp As IComparer)
```

To perform a binary search, the array must be sorted. The sorted array of four state names contains the elements

```
"New Hampshire", "New Jersey", "new Mexico", "New York"
```

The call

```
Array.BinarySearch(astr, "New York")
```

returns 3 because the string is identical to *astr(3)*. The call

```
Array.BinarySearch(astr, "New Mexico")
```

returns −4. The negative number indicates that the string isn't in the array. (Remember, by default the search is case sensitive!) The complement of the return value is 3, which means that *astr(3)* is the next highest element of the array.

The call

```
Array.BinarySearch(astr, "new Mexico"))
```

returns 2 because the argument matches *astr(2)*. The call

```
Array.BinarySearch(astr, "New Mexico", CaseInsensitiveComparer.Default))
```

performs a case-insensitive search and also returns 2.

# The *StringBuilder* Class

You may wonder if there's a performance penalty associated with frequent re-creations of *String* objects. Sometimes there is. Consider the following program, which uses the &= operator in 10,000 string-appending operations to construct a large string.

**StringAppend.vb**

```
'----------------------------------------------
' StringAppend.vb (c) 2002 by Charles Petzold
'----------------------------------------------
Imports System

Module StringAppend
    Const iIterations As Integer = 10000

    Sub Main()
        Dim dt As DateTime = DateTime.Now
        Dim str As String = String.Empty
        Dim i As Integer

        For i = 1 To iIterations
            str &= "abcdefghijklmnopqrstuvwxyz" & vbCrLf
        Next i

        Console.WriteLine(DateTime.op_Subtraction(DateTime.Now, dt))
    End Sub
End Module
```

The program calls the *Now* method of the *DateTime* class at the beginning and end to calculate an elapsed time, which is displayed in hours, minutes, seconds, and units of 100 nanoseconds. (See Chapter 10 for information about *DateTime* and related classes.) Each string-appending operation causes a new *String* object to be created, which requires another memory allocation. Each previous string is marked for garbage collection.

Of course, how fast this program runs depends on how fast your machine is. But it could take about a minute or so.

A better solution in a case like this is the appropriately named *String-Builder* class, defined in the *System.Text* namespace. Unlike the string maintained by the *String* class, the string maintained by *StringBuilder* can be altered. *StringBuilder* dynamically reallocates the memory used for the string. Whenever the size of the string is about to exceed the size of the memory buffer, the buffer is doubled in size. To convert a *StringBuilder* object to a *String* object, call the *ToString* method.

Here's a revised version of the program, which uses *StringBuilder*.

**StringBuilderAppend.vb**

```
'----------------------------------------------
' StringBuilderAppend.vb (c) 2002 by Charles Petzold
'----------------------------------------------
Imports System
Imports System.Text
```

```
Module StringBuilderAppend
    Const iIterations As Integer = 10000

    Sub Main()
        Dim dt As DateTime = DateTime.Now
        Dim sb As New StringBuilder()
        Dim i As Integer

        For i = 1 To iIterations
            sb.Append("abcdefghijklmnopqrstuvwxyz" & vbCrLf)
        Next i
        Dim str As String = sb.ToString()

        Console.WriteLine(DateTime.op_Subtraction(DateTime.Now, dt))
    End Sub
End Module
```

You'll probably find that this program does its work in well under a second. It seems to run in under 1/1000 the time of the original version.

Another efficient approach is to use the *StringWriter* class defined in the *System.IO* namespace. As I mentioned in Appendix A, both *StringWriter* and *StreamWriter* (which you use for writing to text files) derive from the abstract *TextWriter* class. Like *StringBuilder*, *StringWriter* assembles a composite string. The big advantage with *StringWriter* is that you can use the whole array of *Write* and *WriteLine* methods defined in the *TextWriter* class. Here's a sample program that performs the same task as the previous two programs but using a *StringWriter* object.

### StringWriterAppend.vb

```
'---------------------------------------------------
' StringWriterAppend.vb (c) 2002 by Charles Petzold
'---------------------------------------------------
Imports System
Imports System.IO

Module StringWriterAppend
    Const iIterations As Integer = 10000

    Sub Main()
        Dim dt As DateTime = DateTime.Now
        Dim sw As New StringWriter()
        Dim i As Integer

        For i = 1 To iIterations
            sw.WriteLine("abcdefghijklmnopqrstuvwxyz" & vbCrLf)
        Next i
        Dim str As String = sw.ToString()
```

*(continued)*

```
        Console.WriteLine(DateTime.op_Subtraction(DateTime.Now, dt))
    End Sub
End Module
```

The speed of this program is comparable to StringBuilderAppend.

There's a lesson in all this. As operating systems, programming languages, class libraries, and frameworks provide an ever-increasing level of abstraction, we programmers can sometimes lose sight of all the mechanisms going on beneath the surface. What looks like a simple addition in code can actually involve many layers of low-level activity.

We may be insulated from this low-level activity, but we must train ourselves to still feel the heat. If a particular operation seems slow to you, or to require too much memory, or to involve inordinately convoluted code, try to determine why and then search for an alternative. It's likely that someone has already provided exactly what you need.

# Index

Send feedback about this index to *mspindex@microsoft.com*

## Symbols and Numbers

+, &, +=, and &= operators for concatenating strings, 10, 1241

14-15 (15-, Jeu de Taquin) puzzle, 463–68, 651

## A

about box, 738–41

AboutBox class, 740

AboutBox.vb program, 738–41

AboutDialogBox class, 740

accelerators, 645

AcceptButton property, 733–34, 738, 741, 844

AcceptsReturn property, 844

AcceptsTab property, 844

access modifiers, 20

Acos method, 1230

Action property, 1061, 1062, 1175

Activate method, 207

Activated event, 207

activation, 1086

Activation property, 1086

active form, 206–7

Active property, 877–78

ActiveBorder property, 109, 111

ActiveCaption property, 109, 111

ActiveCaptionText property, 109, 110, 111

ActiveForm property, 206–7

Add method, 347, 439, 529–30, 566, 664, 665, 666, 669, 885, 959, 974, 1056, 1057, 1080, 1081, 1083, 1085

AddArc method, 690, 694

AddBézier method, 694

AddBéziers method, 694

AddClosedCurve method, 696

AddCurve method, 694

AddDirectories method, 1067, 1068

AddEllipse method, 696

AddExtension property, 777

AddHandler statement, 63

AddingConstructors.vb program, 32–34

AddingMethods.vb program, 18–19

AddLine method, 690, 694–96, 701, 930

AddLines method, 694

AddMetafileComment method, 1110

AddPath method, 696–97

AddPie method, 696

AddPolygon method, 696

AddRange method, 566, 571, 664, 885, 890, 959, 1056, 1080, 1081, 1083

AddRectangle method, 696

AddRectangles method, 696

AddString method, 697, 930, 931, 932, 934, 935, 938, 948

AddStrip method, 529, 530, 973

AdjustableArrowCap class, 836

AfterCheck event, 1062

AfterCollapse event, 1061

AfterExpand event, 1061

AfterLabelEdit event, 1062

AfterSelect event, 1061

AgeOfInnocence.vb program, 420–21

AliceBlue property, 106, 107, 108

alignment of text, 403–8

Alignment property, 117, 119, 394, 403–4, 405, 406, 824, 960, 961

AllAboutFont.vb program, 373–74

AllowDrop property, 1170, 1174

AllowedEffect property, 1171, 1172

AllowFullOpen property, 759, 760–61

AllowMargins property, 1028

AllowOrientation property, 1028

AllowPaper property, 1028

AllowPrinter property, 1028

AllowPrintToFile property, 1023, 1024

AllowSelection property, 1023

AllowSomePages property, 1023

alpha channel, 473

Alt property, 210

American Standard Code for Information Interchange (ASCII), 235–36

AnalogClock.vb program, 461–62

Anchor property, 557–61, 562, 564, 840, 883

AnchorStyles enumeration, 558

animation, 521–27

animation programs

  Bounce.vb, 525–27

  DualWink.vb, 523–25

  Wink.vb, 522–23

anti-aliased text, 394–96

AntiAliasedText.vb program, 395–96

anti-aliasing, 174–77

AntiAlias.vb program, 175–76

AntiqueWhite property, 106, 107, 108

AnyColor property, 759

Appearance enumeration, 572–73
Appearance property, 572, 593, 975, 976, 983–84
AppendText method, 1214, 1215
Application class, 55
Apply button, 747–50
Apply event, 748, 759
AppStarting property, 326
AppWorkspace property, 109, 111
ArbitraryCoordinates.vb program, 273–75
arcs, 190–93
    drawn with Bézier splines, 621–24
ArgumentOutOfRangeException exception, 27
Arial fonts, 354
ArrangeStartingPosition property, 131
array sorting and searching, 1252–55
array variables, 14–15
ArrayList class, 346–47, 700
ArrayList object, 347–48, 349, 515, 700
arrays of points, 89–90
Arrow property, 326
art, from Bézier splines, 624–26
Asc function, 1235
ascenders of fonts, 382
Ascent metric, 381–82, 383
ASCII (American Standard Code for Information
        Interchange), 235–36
ASCII control keys, 214–15
ASCII property, 1190–92
AscW function, 1235
Asin method, 1230
Assembly keyword, 884
Assembly.LoadWithPartialName method, 884
Atan method, 1230
Atan2 method, 1230–31
Attributes property, 1208, 1213
Augmentation Research Center, 295
AutoScaleBaseSize property, 584–85, 587
AutoCheck property, 569–70, 592–93
AutoFlush property, 1192
AutomaticDelay property, 878
AutoPopDelay property, 878
auto-scale option for controls
    AuoScaleBaseSize property, 584–85, 587
    introduced, 581–83
    Scale method, 584–87
    Windows Forms Designer and, 583–84
AutoScale property, 582
AutoscaleBaseSize property, 582–83, 584
AutoScaleDemo.vb program, 585–87
auto-scroll approach, 141
AutoScroll property, 141, 142, 145, 146, 149, 954–57,
    1074
AutoScrollMargin property, 144, 145

AutoScrollMinSize property, 145, 146, 148, 149
AutoScrollPosition property, 145, 146, 148, 150, 154, 224
AutoSize property, 576, 605, 740–41, 840, 960, 961–62

## B

b prefix, 40
BackColor property, 59, 68, 106, 107, 113, 462, 532,
        538, 546, 609, 663, 676–77, 756, 757, 954, 1045,
        1052, 1083
BackgroundColor property, 784
BackgroundImage property, 954
BarBreak property, 654–55
baseline of fonts, 382, 383–84
BaselineTilt.vb program, 926–28
BaseStream property, 1192, 1194
BASIC (Beginner's All Purpose Symbolic Instruction
        Code), 1
BCD (binary-coded decimal) type, 1219
BeforeCheck event, 1062
BeforeCollapse event, 1061
BeforeExpanded event, 1061
BeforeLabelEdit event, 1062
BeforeSelect event, 1061
BeginContainer method, 268
Beginner's All Purpose Symbolic Instruction Code
        (BASIC), 1
BeginPath function, 690
BeginPrint event, 1007, 1008
BeginUpdate method, 1059
BetterBlockOut.vb program, 315–17
BetterContextMenu.vb program, 661–63
BetterDialog.vb program, 736–38
BetterFamiliesList.vb program, 387
BetterFontAndColorDialogs.vb program, 762–63
BetterImageFromFile.vb program, 480
BetterPieChart.vb program, 196–97
Bézier, Pierre Etienne, 611
Bézier splines
    arcs with, 621–24
    art, 624–26
    circles with, 621–24
    in clipped text, 942–44
    clock programs, 617–19
    collinear, 619–21
    introduced, 611–12
    mathematical derivation, 626–30
    in practice, 612–16
BézierArt.vb program, 624–26
BézierCircles.vb program, 623–24
BézierClockControl class, 617, 618
BézierClockControl.vb program, 617–18
BézierClock.vb program, 618–19

BézierManual class, 629
BézierManual.vb program, 629–30
BézierSpline method, 630
Bézier.vb program, 614–16
BigEndianUnicode property, 1190–92
bilevel (monochrome) images, 472
Bilinear warp, 712
binary file I/O, 1197–1200
binary resources, 517–21
binary-coded decimal (BCD) type, 1219
BinaryReader class, 1197
BinarySearch method, 1254–55
BinaryWriter class, 1168, 1197
Bitmap class, 471, 472, 510–13, 1071, 1097
bitmap (raster) fonts, 351, 352
Bitmap object, 471, 477, 510–13, 720, 1106, 1107, 1108,
    1109, 1144, 1145, 1147, 1148, 1151, 1152, 1153,
    1159
bitmap (Bmp) property, 474, 475
BitmapButtons.vb program, 550–52
bitmaps. *See also* images; raster graphics
    buttons with, 549–52
    clipping, 717–21
    converting metafiles to, 1106–8
    defined, 469
    file formats, 472–76
    Hello World with a bitmap, 513–14
    introduced, 469–70
    shadow, 514–17
    support overview, 471–72
bits per pixel (bpp), 472–73
Blend property, 809
BlockFont.vb program, 917–18
BlockOut.vb program, 312–15
Bmp (bitmap) property, 474, 475
Bold property, 371
BoldAndItalicBigger.vb program, 364
BoldAndItalicTighter.vb program, 401–3
BoldAndItalic.vb program, 358–59
Boolean type, 13, 40
BorderStyle enumeration, 531–32, 577
BorderStyle property, 333, 531, 577, 840, 960–61, 974,
    975, 1052
Bottom property, 95, 98, 1004
Bounce.vb program, 525–27
BouncingGradientBrushBall.vb program, 813–14
boundary rectangle, 116–19
Bounds property, 98, 333, 675, 676, 681, 1003, 1004,
    1005, 1015, 1101, 1102
BoxingTheClient.vb program, 178
bpp (bits per pixel), 472–73
Break property, 654–55
Bricks.vb program, 911–13

BringToFront method, 569, 1041
browser keys, 218
Brush class, 67, 781, 782
Brush object, 67, 107–8, 782
brush programs. *See also* pen programs
    BlockFont.vb, 917–18
    BouncingGradientBrushBall.vb, 813–14
    Bricks.vb, 911–13
    DropShadow.vb, 914–15
    EmbossedText.vb, 915–17
    GradientText.vb, 913–14
    HatchBrushArray.vb, 785–86
    HatchBrushMenu.vb, 786–89
    HatchBrushRenderingOrigin.vb, 794–95
    HexagonGradientBrush.vb, 821–22
    OverlappingHatchBrushes.vb, 792–94
    RectangleLinearGradientBrush.vb, 805–6
    SquareTile.vb, 818–19
    StarGradientBrush.vb, 812–13
    TextureBrushDemo.vb, 796–800
    TriangleGradientBrush.vb, 810–12
    TriangleTile.vb, 815–18
    TwoPointLinearGradientBrush.vb, 802–3
    TwoTriangleTile.vb, 819–21
Brush property, 825, 826
brushes. *See also* pens
    Brushes.Black, 68, 170
    gradient, 913–14
    hatch, 782–92, 911–13
        rendering origin, 792–95
    introduced, 67–68, 107–8, 781–82
    linear gradient, 800–809
    path gradient, 810–14
        tiling, 814–22
    solid, 782, 914–18
    for text, 911–18
    texture, 795–800
Brushes class, 67, 782
Brushes.Black, 68, 170
BufferedStream class, 1187, 1188
Button class, 536, 537, 572, 731, 733, 734
Button control, 1042, 1071
    Anchor property, 557–61, 562, 564
    appearance and alignment, 546–49
    with bitmaps, 549–52
    Dock property, 557–58, 561–64
    handlers, 552
    hexadecimal calculator, 587–92
    introduced, 536–40
    keyboard input and, 540–41
    mouse input and, 540–41
    owner-draw, 552–57
    sizing, 542–46, 583

Button object, 537, 542, 545, 565, 748, 1135, 1145
button programs
  BitmapButtons.vb, 550–52
  ButtonStyles.vb, 548–49
  HexCalc.vb, 587–92
  OwnerDrawButtons.vb, 554–57
  SimpleButton.vb, 537–40
  TwoButtonsAnchor.vb, 558–60
  TwoButtonsDock.vb, 562–64
  TwoButtons.vb, 543–46
Button property, 302, 303, 978
ButtonApplyOnClick method, 749
ButtonBase class, 536, 547–48, 549–50, 576
ButtonClick event, 978, 981, 983, 986
ButtonDropDown event, 978, 984
ButtonOnClick method, 539, 540, 545, 546, 586, 592
ButtonOnPaint method, 556, 557
Buttons property, 971, 974
ButtonState enumeration, 553
ButtonStyles.vb program, 548–49
by prefix, 40
ByRef keyword, 15
Byte type, 11, 13, 40
ByVal keyword, 15

## C

CalcButton class, 588
calculator program (HexCalc.vb), 587–92
Calendar object, 439–41
CalendarDate class, 20, 21, 22, 23, 26, 34, 35, 36
CalendarDate object, 23, 25
CalendarDate structure, 16, 17, 18, 19
calendars, 439–41
camel casing, 40
cancel button, 545
Cancel property, 237, 1008, 1009, 1061
CancelButton property, 733–34, 738, 741
CancelEventArgs class, 1008
CanDuplex property, 1000
CanFocus property, 237
canonical splines
  introduced, 630–38
  mathematical derivation, 638–40
CanonicalSegment method, 640
CanonicalSpline method, 640
CanonicalSplineManual.vb program, 639–40
CanonicalSpline.vb program, 631–34
CanRead property, 1182
CanSeek property, 1182
CanUndo property, 852, 861
CanWrite property, 1182
Capacity property, 347

caps (ends), 829–36
caption (title) bar, 51
CaptionHeight property, 103–4
Capture property, 312, 319, 556–57
CaptureLoss.vb program, 318–19
capturing the mouse, 301, 309, 311–12
caret, 238–42
Caret class, 238, 241, 242
Caret object, 245
Caret.vb program, 238–41
Cartesian coordinates, 68–69
Catch blocks, 24–25, 386–87
Ceiling method, 92, 94, 1225–26
CenterColor property, 811
CenterImage.vb program, 489–90
centering text, 116–20
CenterPixelSizeImage.vb program, 490–91
CenterPoint property, 811, 814
ch prefix, 40
Changed event, 753, 754, 901
ChangeExtension method, 1203–4
Char type, 13, 40, 1235–37
character keys, 208
CharacterCasing enumeration, 875
CharacterCasing property, 875
Chars property, 1234, 1238
Check property, 668
CheckAlign property, 572, 593
CheckAndRadioCheck.vb program, 656–59
CheckBox class, 572
CheckBox control, 569–73, 579, 595, 655, 733
  three-state alternative, 573–74
CheckBox object, 744
CheckBoxDemo.vb program, 570–72
CheckBoxOnCheckedChanged method, 574, 575, 578, 581, 595
CheckBoxWithLabel.vb program, 575–76
Checked property, 569–70, 571–72, 573, 581, 592–93, 656, 658, 744, 1062
CheckedChanged event, 569–70, 571, 574, 593
CheckedListBox class, 885
Checker class, 336
CheckerChild class, 457
CheckerChild.vb program, 338–39
CheckerChildWithFocus.vb program, 341–42
Checker.vb program, 334–36
CheckerWithChildrenAndFocus.vb program, 342–43
CheckerWithChildren.vb program, 339–41
CheckerWithKeyboard class, 336
CheckerWithKeyboard.vb program, 336–38
CheckFileExists property, 771, 772
CheckPathExists property, 771
CheckState enumeration, 573–74

CheckState property, 573
CheckStateChanged event, 574
child index, 1041
child menus (submenus), 642
child windows. *See* controls
children of controls, 301
Chr function, 1235
ChrW function, 1235
CInt function, 1226
circles
    drawn with Bézier splines, 621–24
    parametric equations, 182
classes. *See also* inside front cover
    AboutBox, 740
    AboutDialogBox, 740
    AdjustableArrowCap, 836
    Application, 55
    ArrayList, 346–47, 700
    BézierClockControl, 617, 618
    BézierManual, 629
    BinaryReader, 1197
    BinaryWriter, 1168, 1197
    Bitmap, 471, 472, 510–13, 1071, 1097
    Brush, 67, 781, 782
    Brushes, 67, 782
    BufferedStream, 1187, 1188
    Button, 536, 537, 572, 731, 733, 734
    ButtonBase, 536, 547–48, 549–50, 576
    CalcButton, 588
    CalendarDate, 20, 21, 22, 23, 26, 34, 35, 36
    CancelEventArgs, 1008
    Caret, 238, 241, 242
    CheckBox, 572
    CheckedListBox, 885
    Checker, 336
    CheckerChild, 457
    CheckerWithKeyboard, 336
    Clipboard, 1134–36
    ClockControl, 457, 459
    Clover, 714
    Color, 105
    ColorDialog, 755, 756–63, 871
    ColorFillDialogBoxWithApply, 747
    ColorPalette, 486
    ColorScrollDialogBox, 753, 754
    ComboBox, 884–85
    CommonDialog, 755
    Console, 7, 9, 43, 60
    ContainerControl, 52, 53, 341, 541
    ContextMenu, 661
    Control. *See* Control class
    ControlCollection, 564, 565, 566, 568
    ControlPaint, 369, 553, 677

Cursor, 325–26, 327, 331
Cursors, 326
CustomLineCap, 836
DataFormats, 1149–52, 1155, 1159
DataGridTextBox, 838
DataObject, 1165, 1166, 1168, 1169
DateTime, 861, 1256
DateTimeFormatInfo, 443
DaylightTime, 436
defined, 19
Directory, 1204–12
DirectoryInfo, 1204–12
DirectoryTree, 1065–70
DirectoryTreeView, 1065, 1067–68, 1070, 1078
DomainUpDown, 897–98
DoPage, 260, 261
DrawOrFillEllipse, 746
DropDownList, 1011
EnhancedDate, 34, 36, 37
Environment, 50, 1200–1202
EventArgs, 1008
Exception, 24
File, 1204–5, 1212–15
FileDialog, 755
    OpenFileDialog class, 755, 768–76
    SaveFileDialog class, 755, 776–79
FileInfo, 1204–5, 1212–15
FileListView, 1088, 1091, 1093
FileStream
    introduced, 1179–81
    problem with, 1186–87
    properties and methods, 1182–86
FileSystemInfo, 1207
FindDialog, 861, 866
Font, 66, 67, 129, 355, 357, 369, 372, 397
FontCollection, 391
FontDialog, 372, 755, 756–63, 871
FontFamily, 381, 391
FontMenuForm, 910, 911
Form, 52, 53, 58, 74, 75, 76, 128, 129, 206–7, 728, 731,
    741
Graphics. *See* Graphics class
GraphicsContainer, 268
GraphicsPath, 688, 689, 691, 694, 702, 708, 930, 931,
    941, 944
GraphicsPathIterator, 698
GraphicsState, 267–68
HatchBrush, 781, 782, 783, 908
HatchStyleMenuItem, 788
HelloWorld, 80, 81, 82
HScrollBar, 596
Icon, 519

classes, *continued*

Image, 471, 472, 474, 477, 482, 483, 484, 485, 486, 507–10, 778, 1096, 1097, 1098, 1099, 1119

ImageCollection, 529

ImageFormat, 474, 486, 487, 778

ImageIO, 777

ImageList, 528–31, 565

ImageListCollection, 530

ImagePanel, 1071, 1074–75

InheritAndConstruct, 76

InheritHelloWorld, 80, 81, 82

InheritTheForm, 75

InstalledFontCollection, 391

instances of, 21

introduced, 38

KeyEventArgs, 646

KeyExamine, 232

LinearGradientBrush, 781, 782

ListBox, 884–85

ListControl, 884–85

MarshalByRefObject, 76

Math, 181, 624. *See also* Math class

Matrix, 286–89, 702, 703, 904, 923

MemoryStream, 1187, 1188

Menu, 565, 642–43, 663, 664

MenuItem, 644, 655, 666, 788, 859, 963–64, 967, 969, 990

MenuItemCollection, 663–69

MenuItemColor, 661, 666, 990

MenuItemEncoding, 859

MenuItemHelp, 967, 969

MenuItems, 529

MessageBox, 45–51

Metafile, 471, 1071, 1097, 1098, 1099, 1123, 1124

MetafileHeader, 1099, 1119

MouseConnect, 327

MouseEventArgs, 302

MustInherit, 439, 471, 477, 478, 536, 596, 755, 768, 782, 861, 1187, 1188

NonInheritable, 162, 486, 768, 1097, 1134, 1204

NotepadCloneWithFile, 850

NumericUpDown, 897–98

Object, 36, 37, 52

ObjectCollection, 885, 892

objects as instances of, 21

OpenFileDialog, 755, 768–76

PageSettings, 993, 1002–5, 1015

PageSetupDialog, 1027–31

PaintEventArgs, 62–63, 64, 69, 153, 154, 162

Path, 1203

PathData, 692

PathGradientBrush, 781, 782, 810, 811

Pen, 107, 781, 782

Pens, 163

PictureBox, 531–34

PictureBoxPlus, 1075

PreviewPageInfo, 1032

PreviewPrintController, 1019–20

PrintableForm, 178, 258, 361, 479, 909–10

PrintController, 1018–22

PrintControllerWithStatusDialog, 1019, 1020

PrintDialogBox, 1023–27

PrintDocument, 1006–8, 1018–20, 1022

PrinterSettings, 163, 993, 994–1002

PrintEventArgs, 1008

PrintPageEventArgs, 169, 1008

PrivateFontCollection, 391, 392

ProgramWithIcon, 518, 520, 521

QueryPageSettingsEventArgs, 1008, 1014

RadioButton, 592, 593

Registry, 764

RegistryKey, 764

ReplaceDialog, 861, 866

RichTextBox, 838, 876

SampleClass, 1199–1200

ScrollableControl, 53, 145–46, 596

ScrollBar, 596–97

SelectedIndexCollection, 888

SelectedObjectCollection, 888

SevenSegmentDisplay, 452, 454

SimpleButton, 539, 540

SimpleControl, 540

SimpleDialog, 728

SimpleDialogBox, 728

SolidBrush, 781, 782

Splitter, 1040, 1051

StandardPrintController, 1019, 1020, 1021

StatusBar, 951, 958

StatusBarPanel, 951, 959

Stream, 477, 1187, 1188

StreamReader, 1188, 1189

StreamWriter, 1188, 1189, 1257

String, 1233, 1239

StringBuilder, 884, 1255–58

StringCollection, 995

StringFormat, 403, 412, 417–18

StringReader, 1188

StringWriter, 1188, 1257

StructLayoutAttribute, 232

structures vs., 86–87

SuperString, 7–8

SysInfoList, 144

SysInfoReflection, 223

SysInfoReflectionStrings, 1083–84

SysInfoStrings, 137, 153, 155–60

SystemBrushes, 111

SystemColors, 109–10
SystemEvents, 151, 513
SystemInformation, 127–28, 155, 1084
System.IO, 15, 1188
SystemPens, 110, 164
TenCentimeterRuler, 258
TextBox, 837–38
TextBoxBase, 837–38, 852, 860, 1133
TextReader, 1188
TextureBrush, 781, 782, 795, 799, 800, 908
TextWriter, 1188, 1257
Thread, 54, 1022
Timer, 425, 426–29
TimeZone, 434
ToolBar, 951
ToolBarButton, 951, 978
ToolBarButtonCollection, 971
ToolTip, 876, 877
TrackBar, 605
TreeNode, 1055–59, 1060
TreeNodeCollection, 1055, 1056, 1057, 1060
TreeView, 1055, 1056
Type, 884
TypeAway, 245
UpDownBase, 897
UserControl, 338, 459
VScrollBar, 596
WebRequest, 481
WebResponse, 481
Wink, 523
Clear method, 64–65, 106, 107, 113–14, 530, 566, 567,
  665, 842, 860
ClearMarkers method, 697
ClearSelected method, 888
ClearType fonts, 352, 395, 396
ClearUndo method, 852
Click event
  clipboard programs, 1139, 1142
  control programs, 536, 538, 539, 545, 570, 585, 593
  dialog box programs, 728, 729, 731, 733, 749, 757
  menu programs, 645, 647, 649, 650, 655, 658, 670, 671
  mouse programs, 322, 323, 341
  status bar and toolbar programs, 963, 964, 990
ClickedControl property, 1075
ClickedImage property, 1075
clicks, 298, 322–23
Clicks property, 302, 303
client area, 51, 69, 99–103, 149–53, 268–72
client area coordinates, 103
client area programs
  WhatSizeTransform.vb, 271–72
  WhatSize.vb, 269–70

ClientEllipse.vb program, 189–90
ClientRectangle property, 99, 103, 186–87
ClientSize property, 99–100, 149, 166, 169, 267, 268,
  532, 538
Clip property, 174, 326–27, 722
clipboard
  Clipboard class, 1134–36
  data formats, 1145–55
  drag-and-drop facility, 1169–77
  getting objects from, 1136–45
  introduced, 1133
  items and formats, 1134
  setting multiple formats, 1164–69
Clipboard class, 1134–36
clipboard programs
  ClipText.vb, 1137–40
  ClipViewAll.vb, 1159–63
  ClipView.vb, 1155–59
  ImageClip.vb, 1142–45
  ImageDrop.vb, 1175–77
  MetafileClip.vb, 1140–42
  MultiCopy.vb, 1166–69
  NotepadClone.vb, 1172–74
  RichTextPaste.vb, 1153–55
clipboard viewers, 1155–64
ClipBounds property, 722, 723
clipped controls, 538
clipping. *See also* path and clipping programs; paths
  bitmaps, 717–21
  defined, 685
  with paths, 712–17
  regions and, 685, 721–23
clipping region, 153–55
clipping text, 410–12
ClippingCombinations.vb program, 715–16
ClipRectangle property, 63, 64, 153–54
ClipText.vb program, 942–44, 1137–40
ClipViewAll.vb program, 1159–63
ClipView.vb program, 1155–59
clock programs
  AnalogClock.vb, 461–62
  BézierClockControl.vb, 617–18
  BézierClock.vb, 618–19
  ClockControl.vb, 457–60
  DateAndTimeStatus.vb, 962–63
  DigitalClock.vb, 449–50
  DigitalClockWithDate.vb, 450–52
  SevenSegmentClock.vb, 455–56
  SevenSegmentDisplay.vb, 452–55
  SimpleClock.vb, 447–48
ClockControl class, 457, 459
ClockControl object, 461

ClockControl.vb program, 457–60
clocks
　analog, 457–62
　seven-segment LCD, 452–56
　simple culture-specific, 447–52
Clone method, 510, 511, 707, 1240
CLong function, 1226
Close method, 306, 650, 764–65, 1183, 1193, 1195, 1198,
　1199
CloseAllFigures method, 695
closed subpaths, 691
ClosedCurveFillModes.vb program, 636–38
CloseFigure method, 691, 695
CloseInFive.vb program, 428–29
Clover class, 714
Clover.vb program, 713–14
code, managed, 6
coding controls, 541–42
Collapse method, 1064
CollapseAll method, 1064
Collate property, 1000
Collection, 347, 349
Colon method, 454
Color class, 105
Color object, 106, 107, 163, 579, 603, 659, 661, 666, 744,
　761
Color property, 663, 742, 744, 750, 751, 757, 759, 782,
　825, 826, 990, 1003, 1005
Color structure, 59, 65, 104–6
Color.Black, 170
ColorDepth enumeration, 528–29
ColorDepth property, 528, 529
ColorDialog class, 755, 756–63, 871
ColorDialog object, 761, 762
ColorFillDialogBox object, 746, 747
ColorFillDialogBox.vb program, 742–45
ColorFillDialogBoxWithApply class, 747
ColorFillDialogBoxWithApply object, 750
ColorFillDialogBoxWithApply.vb program, 747–49
ColorFillDialogOnApply event, 750
ColorPalette class, 486
ColorPalette object, 486
ColorPalette property, 486
colors
　defined, 105
　depth, 472–73
　known, 112
　list, inside back cover
　repainting, 113–16
　system, 108–11, 112–13
　user-preference, 109
ColorScrollDialogBox class, 753, 754
ColorScrollDialogBox.vb program, 751–53

ColorScroll.vb program, 600–604
ColorTrackBar.vb program, 607–9
Column property, 1087
ColumnClick event, 1087
Columns property, 1079, 1080, 1085
Combine method, 1203–4
CombineMode enumeration, 715
ComboBox class, 884–85
ComboBox control, 891–97
ComboBoxStyle enumeration, 891–92
command buttons. *See* Button control
command line. *See* console
common dialog boxes
　ColorDialog, 755, 756–63
　FontDialog, 755, 756–63
　introduced, 26, 726, 755
　OpenFileDialog, 755, 768–76
　SaveFileDialog class, 755, 776–79
CommonDialog class, 755
Compare method, 871, 1246–47, 1254
CompareOrdinal method, 1246
CompareTo method, 1246, 1253–54
comparing strings, 1243–47
compiler (vbc.exe), 3
compiler switches
　reference (r), 45
　target (t), 43–44
ComposeLine function, 768
ComposeLine method, 1159, 1186
compression techniques for images, 473–74
Concat method, 1242–43
concatenating strings, 10, 1241–43
console, 1–6
console applications vs. Windows applications, 43–44
Console class, 7, 9, 43, 60
console programs
　AddingConstructors.vb, 32–34
　AddingMethods.vb, 18–19
　ConsoleAdder.vb, 9–10
　ConsoleHelloWithImports.vb, 8
　ConsoleHelloWorld.vb, 6–7
　ConsolidatingData.vb, 17–18
　DefiningTheClass.vb, 19–21
　FirstBasicProgram.vb, 2–3, 5
　InheritingTheClass.vb, 34–36
　MinAndMax.vb, 12–13
　PropertiesAndExceptions.vb, 28–30
　SharingMethods.vb, 21–23
ConsoleAdder.vb program, 9–10
ConsoleHelloWithImports.vb program, 8
ConsoleHelloWorld.vb program, 6–7
ConsolidatingData.vb program, 17–18
Const fields, 181

constructors
   BinaryReader, 1197
   BinaryWriter, 1197
   Bitmap, 511–12, 518, 521
   CalendarDate, 31–32
   ContextMenu, 643
   Cursor, 518, 521
   DataObject, 1165
   DateTime, 430, 437, 439–41
   Decimal, 1220
   defined, 31
   DirectoryInfo, 1206
   FileInfo, 1212
   FileStream, 1180, 1181
   Font, 357, 359–60, 364–65, 367, 374, 376, 378, 386,
      668, 931
   FontFamily, 378–79, 392
   GraphicsPath, 694
   HatchBrush, 783
   HexCalc, 588
   Icon, 518, 519–21
   introduced, 31–34
   LinearGradientBrush, 802, 804, 806–7
   ListViewItem, 1082
   ListViewItem.ListViewSubItem, 1083
   MainMenu, 643, 650
   Margins, 1004
   Matrix, 286–87, 937, 945
   MenuItem, 644, 650, 653, 669, 671
   Metafile, 1108–9, 1116, 1118–19, 1123, 1125
   NotepadCloneWithRegistry, 850
   PageSettings, 1002–3
   PageSetupDialog, 1027
   PathGradientBrush, 810
   Pen, 164, 823
   Point, 91, 93
   PointF, 93
   PrintDialog, 1023
   PrintDocument, 1006
   PrinterSettings, 994
   Rectangle, 93–94
   RectangleF, 94
   Region, 721
   Size, 91, 93
   SizeF, 93
   SolidBrush, 782
   StreamReader, 1194
   StreamWriter, 1189–90
   String, 1237–38
   StringFormat, 398, 415–16
   SysInfoPanel, 142–43
   TextureBrush, 796
   TimeSpan, 437
   TreeNode, 1060

container of controls, 540
ContainerControl class, 52, 53, 341, 541
Contains method, 97, 567, 665, 885
ContainsFocus property, 237
ContentAlignment enumeration, 547
context (shortcut) menus, 299, 642, 659–63
ContextMenu class, 661
ContextMenu object, 661, 665, 666
ContextMenu property, 644, 661, 666
ContextMenuAdd.vb program, 665–66
ContextMenuDemo.vb program, 659–61
control characters, 225–26
Control class, 112–13, 139, 231, 300–301, 312, 317–18,
   323, 326, 338, 538, 564, 566, 579, 584, 596, 951,
   954, 959, 1040, 1041
Control object, 206, 565
control points, 612, 616
control programs. *See also* Notepad clone
   AutoScaleDemo.vb, 585–87
   BitmapButtons.vb, 550–52
   ButtonStyles.vb, 548–49
   CheckBoxDemo.vb, 570–72
   CheckBoxWithLabel.vb, 575–76
   ColorScroll.vb, 600–604
   ColorTrackBar.vb, 607–9
   CustomCheckBox.vb, 579–81
   EnumerateEnumerationCombo.vb, 893–97
   EnumerateEnumeration.vb, 879–84
   EnvironmentBars.vb, 889–90
   HexCalc.vb, 587–92
   MatrixElements.vb, 902–4
   MatrixMethods.vb, 904–8
   OwnerDrawButtons.vb, 554–57
   RadioButtons.vb, 593–95
   SimpleButton.vb, 537–40
   TextBoxDemo.vb, 839–40
   Transform.vb, 899–901
   TwoButtonsAnchor.vb, 558–60
   TwoButtonsDock.vb, 562–64
   TwoButtons.vb, 543–46
Control properties, 98, 99
Control property, 109, 110, 111, 210, 241
ControlCollection class, 564, 565, 566, 568
ControlDark property, 109, 110, 111
ControlDarkDark property, 109, 110, 111
ControlLight property, 109, 110, 111
ControlLightLight property, 109, 110, 111
ControlPaint class, 369, 553, 677
controls
   auto-scale option
      AuoScaleBaseSize property, 584–85, 587
      introduced, 581–83
      Scale method, 584–87
      Windows Forms Designer and, 583–84

controls, *continued*
  Button. *See* Button control
  CheckBox, 569–73, 579, 595, 655, 733
    three-state alternative, 573–74
  children of, 301
  as children on forms, 564–67
  clipped, 538
  coding, 541–42
  ComboBox, 891–97
  container of, 540
  defined, 53
  DialogBox. *See* dialog boxes
  edit. *See* TextBox control
  GroupBox, 592–95
  HScrollBar, 140, 596
  identifying, 578–81
  introduced, 535–36
  Label, 331–33, 574–77, 578, 603, 740–41
  LinkLabel, 741
  ListBox, 884–91
  ListView. *See* ListView control
  NumericUpDown, 897–908
  owner draw feature, 163
  Panel, 331, 600, 952, 955–57, 974, 986, 991, 1042,
    1043, 1068, 1071
    scrolling, 141–45
  parents of, 301
  PictureBox, 531–34, 740, 741
  RadioButton, 592–95
  ResizeRedraw, 459
  RichTextBox, 238, 394, 838, 876
  ScrollBar, 140, 596–604
  splitter
    examples, 1044–55
    introduced, 1039–44
  StatusBar. *See* status bars
  tab order, 577–78
  target, 1040, 1044
  TextBox. *See* TextBox control
  ToolBar. *See* toolbars
  TrackBar, 604–9
  TreeView. *See* TreeView control
  up-down, 897–908
  VScrollBar, 140, 596
  z-order, 567–69
Controls property, 564, 565, 568, 571–72, 578, 744
ControlText property, 109, 110, 111
Convert method, 1018
converting strings, 1241
convex hull, 616
coordinate points, 68–70, 87–89
coordinates
  arbitrary, 272–75

  arrays of points, 89–90
  Cartesian, 68–69
  client area, 103
  coordinate points, 87–89
  current position, 173, 177
  default, 69
  desktop, 103
  device, 266
  dialog box, 584
  form, 103
  manual conversions, 256–58
  page, 266
  point conversions, 103–4
  screen, 103
  world, 164, 281–82
CoordinateSpace enumeration, 270–71
Copies property, 1000
Copy method, 860, 1214, 1240
copying strings, 1239–41
CopyTo method, 1214, 1240
Cos method, 949–50, 1230
Cosh method, 1231
Count property, 137, 347, 530, 565, 567, 664, 892, 995,
    997, 1055, 1080, 1081, 1082, 1088
Courier fonts, 353
Create method, 1207, 1214, 1215
CreateBitmapButton method, 990
CreateChildren method, 342
CreateDirectory method, 1207
CreateGraphics method, 71, 139, 162, 346, 460, 539, 1109
CreateMeasurementGraphics method, 163, 1002
CreateMetafileMemory.vb program, 1114–15
CreateMetafileReload.vb program, 1112–14
CreateMetafile.vb program, 1110–12
CreatePrompt property, 776
CreateSampleFont method, 389
CreateSubdirectory method, 1207
CreateSubKey method, 764–65, 767
CreateText method, 1214, 1215
CreationTime property, 1208, 1213
Cross property, 326
culture-invariant formats, 442
culture-specific formats, 442
current position, 173, 177
Current property, 326–27, 330, 331
CurrentDirectory property, 1202
CurrentEncoding property, 1194–95
CurrentInfo property, 443–44
CurrentTimeZone property, 434
CurrentUser key, 764
cursor
  defined, 238
  movement, keypad, 214

Cursor class, 325–26, 327, 331
Cursor object, 333
Cursor property, 60, 331, 333, 344
Cursors class, 326
curves and parametric equations, 182–85
CustomCheckBox.vb program, 579–81
CustomColors property, 761
CustomEndCap property, 836
CustomLineCap class, 836
CustomStartCap property, 836
Cut method, 860
cx prefix, 40
cy prefix, 40

# D

d prefix, 40
DashCap enumeration, 832
DashCap property, 830, 832, 833–34
DashedEllipse.vb program, 191
DashOffset property, 826, 828, 829
DashPattern property, 826, 829
DashStyle enumeration, 826–27, 828–29
DashStyle property, 826, 936
Data property, 1171
data types, 11–15, 39, 40, 1217–18, 1219–22
DataFormats class, 1149–52, 1155, 1159
DataGridTextBox class, 838
DataObject class, 1165, 1166, 1168, 1169
Date property, 431
DateAdd function, 439
DateAndTimeStatus.vb program, 962–63
DatePlus object, 36
dates. *See also* clocks
    calendars, 439–41
    DateTime structure, 430–32, 434
    local time and universal time, 432–36
    readable renditions, 441–47
    tick count, 436–39
DateSerial function, 432
DateTime class, 861, 1256
DateTime object, 436, 437–47, 441, 442, 456
DateTime property, 460
DateTime structure, 430–32, 434
DateTimeFormatInfo class, 443
Day property, 431
DaylightName property, 435
DaylightTime class, 436
DayOfWeek property, 431
DayOfYear function, 16–17, 18, 19
DayOfYear method, 19, 20, 22, 23, 25, 26
DayOfYear property, 30, 431
Days property, 438

DaysSince1600 property, 36
Deactivate event, 207
dead keys, 234–35
Decimal type, 12, 40, 1217–18, 1219–22
DecimalPlaces property, 898
default button, 545
default printer, 994
Default property, 326, 1190–92
DefaultFont property, 356
DefaultItem property, 654
DefaultPageSettings property, 1001, 1002, 1003, 1006–7, 1013
DefiningTheClass.vb program, 19–21
delegates, 61
Delete method, 1207–8, 1214
Delta property, 302, 303, 436
depth of colors, 472–73
Descartes, René, 68–69
descenders of fonts, 382
Descent metric, 381–82, 383
desktop coordinates, 103
Desktop property, 109, 111
DesktopBounds property, 99, 846–47, 850
DesktopLocation property, 99, 103
detents, 300
device coordinates, 266
device drivers, 994
device independence through text, 249–50
device-independent bitmap (DIB), 475
DEVMODE structure, 1002
DEVNAMES structure, 1002
dialog box coordinates, 584
dialog box programs
    AboutBox.vb, 738–41
    BetterDialog.vb, 736–38
    BetterFontAndColorDialogs.vb, 762–63
    ColorFillDialogBox.vb, 742–45
    ColorFillDialogBoxWithApply.vb, 747–49
    ColorScrollDialogBox.vb, 751–53
    DialogsWithRegistry.vb, 766–68
    DrawOrFillEllipse.vb, 745–47
    DrawOrFillEllipseWithApply.vb, 749–50
    FontAndColorDialogs.vb, 756–58
    HeadDump.vb, 769–71
    ImageIO.vb, 777–79
    ImageOpen.vb, 774–76
    ModelessColorScroll.vb, 754
    SimpleDialog.vb, 726–30
    SimplerDialog.vb, 733
dialog box templates, 584
dialog boxes
    about box, 738–41
    accept and cancel, 733–34

dialog boxes, *continued*
Apply button, 747–50
common
ColorDialog, 755, 756–63
FontDialog, 755, 756–63
introduced, 26, 726, 755
OpenFileDialog, 755, 768–76
SaveFileDialog class, 755, 776–79
defining properties, 742–47
introduced, 725–26
modal
first, 726–30
introduced, 725
termination, 731–33
modeless, 725, 751–54
screen location, 734–38
system modal, 725
Windows registry and, 763–68
DialogResult enumeration, 49–50, 729
DialogResult property, 729, 730, 731, 733, 734, 741, 749
DialogsWithRegistry.vb program, 766–68
DIB (device-independent bitmap), 475
DigitalClock.vb program, 449–50
DigitalClockWithDate.vb program, 450–52
Dim keyword, 20
dimensions, metrical, 268–72
DirectCast keyword, 67
directories, working with, 1206–12
DirectoriesAndFiles.vb program, 1068–70
Directory class, 1204–12
Directory property, 1213
DirectoryInfo class, 1204–12
DirectoryInfo object, 1067, 1091
DirectoryName property, 1213
DirectoryTree class, 1065–70
DirectoryTreeView class, 1065, 1067–68, 1070, 1078
DirectoryTreeViewOnAfterSelect event, 1078, 1093
DirectoryTreeView.vb program, 1065–67
dirty bits, 851
disassembler (ildasm.exe), 5
displaying text, 66
DisplayKeyInfo method, 230
DisplayRectangle property, 103
DisplaySettingsChanged event, 151, 513
Dispose method, 139, 162, 241–42, 502, 1110
DivideByZeroException exception, 1219, 1223
Divider property, 974, 975, 976
Dock property, 461, 534, 557–58, 561–64, 953, 955, 1040–43, 1045–46, 1047, 1051, 1085
DockStyle enumeration, 561, 1040–43
Document property, 1023, 1028, 1033
DocumentName property, 167–68, 1006, 1007, 1013–14, 1031, 1033
documents, defining, 1006–8

DoDragDrop method, 1174, 1177
DoIt method, 270, 272
DomainUpDown class, 897–98
DoPage class, 260, 261
DoPage method
brush and pen programs, 799, 800
font and text programs, 375, 389, 909, 911, 918, 919, 942
image and bitmap programs, 490, 491, 505, 509
metafile programs, 1110, 1112, 1113, 1115
page-related programs, 262, 272, 274, 292–93
path and clipping programs, 689, 690–91, 699, 707, 714, 717, 721
spline programs, 624
vector graphics programs, 173, 195
dots per inch, 253–54
DotsPerInch.vb program, 254
double clicks, 298, 322–23
Double type, 12, 40, 1217–18, 1222–24
DoubleClick event, 322, 323
DoubleClickSize property, 298
DoubleClickTime property, 298
DpiX property, 253, 255, 256, 266, 367, 489, 503, 511, 1009, 1101–2, 1119
DpiY property, 253, 255, 256, 266, 360, 367, 489, 503, 511, 1009, 1101–2, 1119
DragAction enumeration, 1175
drag-and-drop facility, 1169–77
DragDrop event, 1170–72, 1174, 1177
DragDropEffects enumeration, 1172, 1174
DragEnter event, 1170–72
DragFullWindows property, 150–51
dragging, 298
DragLeave event, 1170–72
DragOver event, 1170–72, 1174, 1177
Draw method, 530–31
draw programs, 470
DrawArc method, 190–91, 193, 1111
DrawBackground method, 677, 681
DrawBall method, 813, 814
DrawBézier method, 613
DrawBéziers method, 613–14, 617, 618, 630, 685, 688
DrawButton method, 553, 556
DrawClosedCurve method, 635–36, 692
DrawCurve method, 630–31, 635, 640
DrawDots method, 460
DrawEllipse method, 184, 189–90, 198, 624, 1111
DrawFocusRectangle method, 553, 557, 677
DrawHourHand method, 460, 617
DrawHouse.vb program, 179
DrawIcon method, 520, 741
DrawIconUnstretched method, 520
DrawImage function, 483

DrawImage method
  clipboard programs, 1159
  dialog box programs, 776
  image and bitmap programs, 471, 478, 479, 487–89,
    490, 491, 494, 495–96, 497–98, 499, 501, 514, 515,
    516, 523
  metafile programs, 1097, 1099, 1102, 1106, 1111, 1112
  path and clipping programs, 721
  tree view and list view programs, 1071
DrawImageUnscaled method, 487
DrawItem event, 675, 682, 891, 960, 990, 991
DrawItemEventArgs object, 163, 681
DrawItemState enumeration, 676
DrawLargeButton method, 557
DrawLine method, 165, 166, 173, 193, 230, 259, 460,
    516, 687, 689, 690, 828
DrawLines method, 178, 179–80, 193, 346, 349, 631,
    685, 687, 688, 828, 830, 1123
DrawMenuGlyph enumeration, 677
DrawMenuGlyph method, 677, 678, 681
DrawMinuteHand method, 460, 617
DrawMode enumeration, 890–91
DrawMode property, 890–91
DrawOnImage.vb program, 504–5
DrawOnPixelSizeImage.vb program, 505–7
DrawOrFillEllipse class, 746
DrawOrFillEllipse.vb program, 745–47
DrawOrFillEllipseWithApply.vb program, 749–50
DrawPath method, 690–91, 698, 699, 701, 708, 931, 934,
    938, 942
DrawPie method, 193–96
DrawPolygon method, 188, 262, 460, 636, 692
DrawRectangle method, 185–87, 193, 262
DrawRectangles method, 187
DrawSecondHand method, 460
DrawSmallerButton method, 557
DrawString method
  clock, timer, and time programs, 451, 454
  dialog box programs, 741
  font and text programs, 356, 359, 361, 369, 370, 377,
    386, 392–94, 396, 397, 398, 401, 403–4, 405, 406,
    407, 409, 412, 415, 416, 417, 421, 423, 920, 921,
    927, 931, 932, 934, 938
  form-related programs, 66, 67, 68, 70, 73, 102, 108,
    113, 116–20, 122–25
  image and bitmap programs, 504, 505, 507
  keyboard programs, 245–46, 247
  menu programs, 681
  metafile programs, 1096
  page-related programs, 270, 277–78
  path and clipping programs, 697
  printing programs, 1038
    system information programs, 128, 131, 133, 148–49,
      153
    vector graphics programs, 171, 173
DrawStringDisabled method, 369
DrawText method, 1159
drop-down menus, 642
DropDownArrows property, 987
DropDownList class, 1011
DropDownMenu property, 983, 987, 988, 990
DropDownMenuButton.vb program, 988–91
DropDownStyle property, 891
DroppedDown property, 891, 892
DropShadow.vb program, 914–15
DropShadowWithPath.vb program, 938–39
DualWink.vb program, 523–25
Duplex enumeration, 1000–1001
Duplex property, 1000

**E**

E constant, 1224
echoing key characters, 242–46
edit control. *See* TextBox control
Effect property, 1171, 1172, 1174
Elements property, 287
ellipse programs
  ArbitraryCoordinates.vb, 273–75
  DrawOrFillEllipse.vb, 745–47
  DrawOrFillEllipseWithApply.vb, 749–50
  OnePanelWithSplitter.vb, 1044–45
  RadioButtons.vb, 593–95
  SplitThreeAcross.vb, 1047–49
  SplitThreeFrames.vb, 1049–51
  SplitTwoProportional.vb, 1053–55
  TryOneInchEllipse.vb, 255–56
  TwoPanelsWithSplitter.vb, 1045–47
ellipses
  drawing, 188–90
  filled, 198
  parametric equations, 182–84
em dash, 125
Em height metric, 381–82, 383
em size (height, point size) of fonts, 352, 354–55, 364–69,
    381–82, 383
EmbossedText.vb program, 915–17
Emf (enhanced metafile format) property, 474, 476
EmfPlusHeaderSize property, 1100
EmfPlusRecordType enumeration, 884, 1122–23
EmfType enumeration, 1124
EM_LINEINDEX message, 861
Empty field, 88
Empty property, 530
EMR structure, 1131

Enabled property, 301, 427, 459, 463, 541, 654, 748, 982
Encoding property, 1192
end points, 612, 616
End property, 436
EndCap property, 829, 833, 836
EndContainer method, 268
EndOfStreamException exception, 1199
EndPath method, 690
EndPrint event, 1007
ends (caps), 829–36
ends of lines, 179–81
EndsWith method, 1244
EndUpdate method, 1059
Engelbart, Douglas C., 295
enhanced metafile format (Emf) property, 474, 476
EnhancedDate class, 34, 36, 37
EnterLeave.vb program, 324–25
Entries property, 486
EnumerateEnumerationCombo.vb program, 893–97
EnumerateEnumeration.vb program, 879–84
EnumerateMetafile method, 1125–26, 1127, 1128
enumerating metafiles, 1125–31
EnumMetafileProc method, 1126, 1127, 1128
EnumMetafile.vb program, 1128–31
Environment class, 50, 1200–1202
EnvironmentBars.vb program, 889–90
Environment.SpecialFolder enumeration, 1201–2
Equals method, 88, 89, 1244
EscapePressed property, 1175
EvenBetterBlockOut.vb program, 320–22
event handlers, 61
EventArgs class, 1008
event-driven input, 60–62
events
    CheckBox, 569–70, 574
    ComboBox, 892–93
    Control, 79, 101, 209, 225, 238, 301–2, 322, 324, 839,
        1170–72, 1174–75
    FontDialog, 759
    Form, 207, 236–37, 964
    key-down and key-up, 209–10, 222
    ListBox, 889
    ListView, 1086–93
    MenuItem, 655, 675
    mouse, 300–303, 324–25
    NumericUpDown, 899
    On methods and, 79–83
    PrintDocument, 1007, 1008–14
    RadioButton, 593
    ScrollBar, 597–98
    ScrollEventArgs, 599–600
    Splitter, 1053
    Timer, 426–27

    toolbar, 978–82
    TrackBar, 606
    TreeView, 1060–62
Exception class, 24
exception handling
    introduced, 23–25
    throwing exceptions, 25–27
Exception object, 24
exceptions
    ArgumentOutOfRangeException, 27
    DivideByZeroException, 1219, 1223
    EndOfStreamException, 1199
    FileNotFoundException, 1180
    IOException, 1180
    OverflowException, 1219
Exchangeable image format (Exif) property, 474, 476
ExcludeClip method, 717
exclusive-OR (XOR) drawing, 314–15, 521
Exif (Exchangeable image format) property, 474, 476
Exists method, 1207, 1213
Exists property, 1206, 1212
Exit method, 58, 306
ExitOnX.vb program, 211–12
Exp method, 1227–28
Expand method, 1064
ExpandAll method, 1064
ExpandWildCard method, 1212
ExplorerLike.vb program, 1091–93
Extension property, 1206, 1207, 1213
ExtractAssociatedIcon function, 1090

**F**
f prefix, 40
face (typeface) name, 352
Families method, 668
Families property, 385, 390, 391, 392
FamiliesList.vb program, 388–90
family of type, 352
figures (subpaths), 691
file and stream programs
    HexDump.vb, 1184–86
    HtmlDump.vb, 1195–96
    StreamWriterDemo.vb, 1193
    WildCardHexDump.vb, 1210–12
File class, 1204–5, 1212–15
FileAccess enumeration, 15, 1181
FileAttributes enumeration, 1208–9
FileDialog class, 755
    OpenFileDialog class, 755, 768–76
    SaveFileDialog class, 755, 776–79
FileInfo class, 1204–5, 1212–15
FileListView class, 1088, 1091, 1093
FileListView.vb program, 1088–90

FileMode enumeration, 15, 1180, 1181
FileName property, 768, 770, 776
FileNames property, 768
FileNotFoundException exception, 1180
files, defined, 1179
files and streams
    binary file I/O, 1197–1200
    Environment class, 1200–1202
    file and path name parsing, 1202–4
    file manipulation and information, 1212–15
    FileStream class
        introduced, 1179–81
        problem with, 1186–87
        properties and methods, 1182–86
    introduced, 1179
    other stream classes, 1187–88
    parallel classes, 1204–5
    reading and writing text, 1188–96
    working with directories, 1206–12
FileShare enumeration, 1181
FileStream class
    introduced, 1179–81
    problem with, 1186–87
    properties and methods, 1182–86
FileStream object, 1114, 1179, 1182, 1184, 1197
FileSystemInfo class, 1207
Fill method, 455, 803
fill mode, 201–4
Fill property, 742, 744, 750
FillClosedCurve method, 636
FillComboBox method, 897
FillEllipse method, 198, 460, 699, 1111
FillMode enumeration, 201, 636
FillMode property, 692
FillModesClassical.vb program, 201–2
FillModesOddity.vb program, 203–4
FillPath method, 698, 699, 708, 721, 931, 938, 942
FillPie method, 198–99
FillPolygon method, 200–201, 455
FillRectangle method, 197–98, 245, 811, 812
FillRectangles method, 198
FillRegion method, 721
FillTextBox method, 883–84, 896
Filter property, 774
FilterIndex property, 774, 778
filters, 772–74
Finally blocks, 25
FindDialog class, 861, 866
FindReplaceDialog.vb program, 861–66
first programs, 2–3, 5–7. *See also* "Hello, world!"
    programs
FirstBasicProgram.vb, 2-3 program, 5
FirstMainMenu.vb program, 647–50
FirstNode property, 1063

FixedPitchOnly property, 759
Flags property, 486
FlatStyle enumeration, 548
Flatstyle property, 548
Flatten method, 705, 708
floating-point infinity, 1222–24
floating-point remainders, 1227
Floor method, 1225–26
Flower.vb program, 698–700
Flush method, 1183, 1193, 1198
Focus method, 237
Focused property, 237
Font class, 66, 67, 129, 355, 357, 369, 372, 397
font metrics, 380–84
Font object, 66, 356, 357, 369, 372, 375, 506, 582, 680,
    681, 765–66, 986
font programs. *See also* text programs
    AllAboutFont.vb, 373–74
    BetterFamiliesList.vb, 387
    BetterFontAndColorDialogs.vb, 762–63
    BlockFont.vb, 917–18
    BoldAndItalicBigger.vb, 364
    BoldAndItalic.vb, 358–59
    FamiliesList.vb, 388–90
    FontandColorDialogs.vb, 756–58
    FontMenuForm.vb, 910–11
    FontMenu.vb, 666–69
    FontNames.vb, 361–62
    FontSizes.vb, 362–63
    GetFamiliesList.vb, 390
    HollowFontCenteredPath.vb, 935–36
    HollowFont.vb, 933–35
    HollowFontWidened.vb, 941–42
    HollowFontWidePen.vb, 939–41
    HowdyWorldFullFit.vb, 376–77
    HowdyWorld.vb, 374–76
    InstalledFontsList.vb, 391–92
    NaiveFamiliesList.vb, 385–86
    RotatedFont.vb, 919–20
    TextOnBaseline.vb, 383–84
    TwentyFourPointPrinterFonts.vb, 367–69
    TwentyFourPointScreenFonts.vb, 365–67
Font property
    control programs, 538, 544, 546, 571, 575, 583, 584,
        585
    dialog box programs, 756, 757, 758, 767, 770
    font and text programs, 356, 358, 364, 374, 840
    form-related programs, 66–67, 71
    image and bitmap programs, 503–4
    menu programs, 676
    mouse programs, 306
    page-related programs, 249, 253, 260, 265–66
    system information programs, 129

Font property, *continued*
  tree view and list view programs, 1083
  vector graphics programs, 171
FontAndColorDialogs.vb program, 756–58
FontCollection class, 391
FontCollection property, 391–92
FontDialog class, 372, 755, 756–63, 871
FontFamily class, 381, 391
FontFamily object, 357, 378–80, 392
  arrays, 385–90
FontFamily property, 371, 378
FontHeight property, 129, 356
FontMenuForm class, 910, 911
FontMenuForm.vb program, 910–11
FontMenu.vb program, 666–69
FontNames.vb program, 361–62
fonts. *See also* text
  Arial, 354
  ascenders, 382
  baseline, 382, 383–84
  bitmap (raster), 351, 352
  ClearType, 352, 395, 396
  Courier, 353
  creating by name, 359–64
  default, 356
  defined, 354
  descenders, 382
  design metrics, 380–84
  DrawString method and, 392–94
  font metrics, 380–84
  FontCollection property, 391–92
  FontFamily object, 357, 378–80
    arrays, 385–90
  getting started, 909–11
  height (em size, point size), 352, 354–55, 364–69,
    381–82, 383
  Helvetica, 354
  introduced, 66–67, 351–52
  italic, 353
  line spacing, 355, 381–82, 383
  oblique, 353
  OpenType, 352
  outline, 352
  roman (serif), 354
  sans serif, 354
  serif (roman), 354
  stroke (plotter, vector), 351, 352
  Times New Roman, 354, 381–83
  transforms, 919–30
    nonlinear, 944–50
  TrueType, 352, 353
  typographical terminology, 352–54
  units, 369–71
  variations on, 357–59

FontSizes.vb program, 362–63
FontStyle enumeration, 357–58, 578, 579, 581, 931, 933,
    986
FontStyle object, 986
FontStyleCheckBox object, 581
ForeColor property, 107, 113, 164, 462, 538, 546, 603,
    676–77, 756, 757, 758, 954, 1083
ForegroundColor property, 784
foreign keyboards, 233–37
Form class, 52, 53, 58, 74, 75, 76, 128, 129, 206–7, 728,
    731, 741
form coordinates, 103
Form object, 56, 58, 67, 72, 86, 301
Format method, 11, 442, 1252
FormatFlags property, 245, 399
formatting strings, 9–11, 1252
FormBorderStyle enumeration, 59
FormProperties.vb program, 58–60
form-related programs
  FormProperties.vb, 58–60
  FormSize.vb, 100–101
  FourCorners.vb, 118–19
  HelloCenteredAlignment.vb, 119–20
  HelloCenteredMeasured.vb, 121–22
  HelloCenteredRectangle.vb, 123
  HelloWorld.vb, 78–79
  HuckleberryFinn.vb, 124–25
  InheritTheForm.vb, 74–75
  InheritWithConstructor.vb, 75–76
  InheritWithPaint.vb, 76–77
  InstantiateHelloWorld.vb, 81–83
  NewForm.vb, 51–52
  PaintEvent.vb, 64–65
  PaintHello.vb, 70
  PaintTwoForms.vb, 71–72
  RandomClearResizeRedraw.vb, 115–16
  RandomClear.vb, 114
  RunFormBadly.vb, 55–56
  RunFormBetter.vb, 56–57
  ShowFormAndSleep.vb, 54–55
  ShowForm.vb, 53
  TwoForms.vb, 57–58
  TwoPaintHandlers.vb, 73–74
forms
  active, 206–7
  client area, 51, 69, 99–103, 149–53, 268–72
  controls as children of, 564–67
  defined, 51
  inheriting, 74–76
  introduced, 51–53
  multiple, 71–72
  point conversions, 103–4
  presentation area, 127
  properties, 58–60

running, 55–58
showing, 53–55
size, 97–99
FormSize.vb program, 100–101
FormStartPosition enumeration, 735–36
FormStartPosition property, 60
FormWindowState enumeration, 847
fountain (transition between two colors), 800
FourByFours.vb program, 199–200
FourCorners.vb program, 118–19
frame animation, 522
FrameBorderSize property, 149
frames, 1040
FromArgb method, 106, 761, 768
FromFile method, 477, 478, 479, 511, 775–76, 1071, 1074, 1075, 1096, 1097, 1098
FromHbitmap method, 477
FromHdc method, 163, 372
FromHfont method, 372
FromHwnd method, 163
FromImage method, 163, 471, 502–3, 516, 1098
FromLogFont method, 372
FromLTRB method, 95, 333
FromName method, 659
FromPage property, 1001, 1024
FromStream method, 477, 480–81, 482, 511
FromSystemColor method, 111
full-color (true-color) bitmaps, 473
FullFit.vb program, 936–38
FullName property, 1206, 1207, 1212
FullOpen property, 759, 760
FullPath property, 1064–65, 1067
function keys, 213

**G**

GammaCorrection property, 809
garbage collection, 14
GDI+, 66, 173–74, 521, 1096
GdiCharSet property, 372
GdiVerticalFont property, 372
general linear transformation of the plane, 283
GenericFontFamilies enumeration, 380
GenericMonospace property, 380
GenericSansSerif property, 380
GenericSerif property, 380
GenericTypographic object, 403
Get accessors, 28, 744
GetAscent method, 920, 926
GetAttributes method, 1213
GetAutoScaleSize method, 582
GetBits method, 1221–22
GetBounds method, 708, 934, 935, 947

GetCellAscent method, 381
GetCellDescent method, 381
GetChildIndex method, 567
GetCreationTime method, 1208, 1213
GetCurrentDirectory method, 1206
GetData method, 1136, 1137, 1139, 1149, 1151, 1152, 1153
GetDataObject method, 861, 1134, 1136, 1165
GetDataPresent method, 861, 1136–37, 1149
GetDaylightChanges method, 435, 436
GetDayOfMonth method, 441
GetDeviceCaps function, 1018
GetDirectories method, 1067–68, 1210
GetDirectory method, 1203
GetDirectoryName method, 1212
GetDirectoryRoot method, 1207
GetEmHeight method, 381
GetExtension method, 1203
GetFamilies method, 390, 391
GetFamiliesList.vb program, 390
GetFileName method, 1203, 1212
GetFileName property, 770
GetFileNameWithoutExtension method, 776, 1203
GetFiles method, 1091, 1210, 1212
GetFileSystemEntries method, 1210
GetFileSystemInfos method, 1210
GetFolderPath method, 50, 414, 1200, 1201, 1202
GetFontFamilyArray method, 390
GetFormat method, 1164
GetFormats method, 1147–48, 1159
GetFullPath method, 1203
GetHashCode method, 88, 89
GetHdc method, 1109
GetHeight method, 128–29, 267, 270, 355, 362, 369, 370, 371, 372, 373, 374, 380–81, 382, 383, 386, 397
GetItemAt method, 1087
GetLastAccessTime method, 1208, 1213
GetLastWriteTime method, 1208, 1213
GetLineSpacing method, 381
GetLogicalDrives method, 1200, 1206
GetMetafileHeader method, 1099–1100
GetMonth method, 26, 28, 441
GetNames method, 884
GetNodeAt method, 1062
GetNumericValue method, 1237
GetParent property, 1207
GetPathRoot method, 1203
GetPixel method, 513
GetPixelFormatSize method, 485, 529
GetPreviewPageInfo method, 1032
GetProperties method, 158
GetResponseStream method, 481–82
GetSelected method, 888

GetSysInfo method, 158
GetTabStops method, 418
GetTempFileName method, 1204
GetTempPath method, 1204
GetThumbnailImage method, 508, 510
getting properties, 27–30
GetToolTip method, 877
GetType method, 37, 88, 89, 478, 581, 884, 1144
GetType operator, 158, 520
GetUnicodeCategory method, 1237
GetUpperBound method, 15
GetUtcOffset method, 435
GetValue method, 158, 764–65, 768
GetValues method, 884
GetWindowPlacement function, 846
GetYear method, 441
Gif (Graphics Interchange Format) property, 474, 475
GMT (Greenwich Mean Time), 432–33
GotFocus event, 238, 242
GoTo statement, 25
GOTO statements, 2
gradient brushes, 913–14
gradient line, 801
GradientPen.vb program, 823–24
GradientText.vb program, 913–14
graphics. *See* bitmaps; images; raster graphics; text;
    vector graphics
Graphics class
    brush and pen programs, 794, 800
    clock, timer, and time programs, 454, 460
    font and text programs, 355, 369, 371, 394, 930, 931
    form-related programs, 66
    image and bitmap programs, 471, 502, 520
    metafile programs, 1097, 1098, 1131
    page-related programs, 267, 287
    path and clipping programs, 689, 690, 691, 694, 702,
        703, 717
    vector graphics programs, 162, 165, 173–74
Graphics Interchange Format (Gif) property, 474, 475
Graphics object
    brush and pen programs, 794, 799
    clock, timer, and time programs, 454, 455, 465
    font and text programs, 360, 367, 369, 911, 935, 944
    form-related programs, 64, 69, 71
    image and bitmap programs, 471, 502, 503–4, 505, 514
    metafile programs, 1107, 1108, 1109, 1110, 1122
    mouse programs, 346
    page-related programs, 253, 255, 267, 268
    path and clipping programs, 690, 698, 699, 714, 721,
        722, 723
    printing programs, 1009, 1014, 1015, 1016, 1019–20,
        1032
    system information programs, 139
    vector graphics programs, 162–63

graphics programs. *See* image and bitmap programs;
    vector graphics programs
Graphics property, 63–64, 675, 676, 1009
GraphicsContainer class, 268
Graphics.FromHdc method, 163
Graphics.FromHwnd method, 163
Graphics.FromImage method, 163
GraphicsPath class, 688, 689, 691, 694, 702, 708, 930,
    931, 941, 944
GraphicsPath method, 934
GraphicsPath object, 690, 700, 714, 810
GraphicsPathIterator class, 698
GraphicsState class, 267–68
GraphicsUnit enumeration, 258–59, 365, 369
gray scale, 472
GrayText property, 109, 110
Greenwich Mean Time (GMT), 432–33
Gregorian calendar, 440
grid fitting and text fitting, 400–403
GroupBox control, 592–95
GroupBox object, 744
Guid property, 487

**H**

Hand property, 326
Handle property, 231
Handled property, 210, 225
HasExtension method, 1203
HasMorePages property, 168–69, 1009
hatch brushes, 782–92, 911–13
    rendering origin, 792–95
HatchBrush class, 781, 782, 783, 908
HatchBrush object, 784, 799
HatchBrushArray.vb program, 785–86
HatchBrushMenu.vb program, 786–89
HatchBrushRenderingOrigin.vb program, 794–95
HatchStyle enumeration, 784, 789–92
HatchStyle property, 784–85, 788, 789
HatchStyleMenuItem class, 788
HeadDump.vb program, 769–71
heap, 86
Hebrew alphabet, 246–47
Hebrew calendar, 441
HebrewCalendar object, 441
height (em size, point size) of fonts, 352, 354–55,
    364–69, 381–82, 383
Height property
    control programs, 544, 563, 581, 582
    font and text programs, 355, 356, 362, 372, 374, 380–
        81, 397–98, 401
    form-related programs, 59, 90, 95, 98, 121
    image and bitmap programs, 482, 483, 510, 520
    metafile programs, 1098–99, 1119

mouse programs, 306
page-related programs, 273
printing programs, 998–99
system information programs, 129, 133
tree view and list view programs, 1052
"Hello, world!" programs
ConsoleHelloWithImports.vb, 8
ConsoleHelloWorld.vb, 6–7
HELLO.C, 41
HelloCenteredAlignment.vb, 119–20
HelloCenteredMeasured.vb, 121–22
HelloCenteredRectangle.vb, 123
HelloWorldBitmap.vb, 513–14
HelloWorld.vb, 78–79
InheritHelloWorld.vb, 80–81
InstantiateHelloWorld.vb, 81–83
MessageBoxHellowWorld.vb, 45–46
PaintHello.vb, 70
HELLO.C program, 41
HelloCenteredAlignment.vb program, 119–20
HelloCenteredMeasured.vb program, 121–22
HelloCenteredRectangle.vb program, 123
HelloPrinter.vb program, 170–71
HELLO.RC resource script, 41
HelloWorld class, 80, 81, 82
HelloWorldBitmap.vb program, 513–14
HelloWorld.vb program, 78–79
help, menu, 963–70
Help property, 326, 330
HelpButton property, 1033
HelpMenu.vb program, 682–83
HelpPanel property, 969
HelpRequest event, 759, 1024
HelpText property, 967, 969
Helvetica fonts, 354
hexadecimal calculator, 587–92
Hexadecimal property, 898
HexagonGradientBrush.vb program, 821–22
HexCalc.vb program, 587–92
hex-dump programs
HexDump.vb, 1184–86
WildCardHexDump.vb, 1210–12
HexDump.vb program, 1184–86
Hide method, 53, 241, 327, 338
HideSelection property, 841, 842
high color, 473
Highlight property, 109, 110, 111
HighlightText property, 109, 110, 111
Hijri (Islamic) calendar, 440, 441
hit-testing, 334–44
HitTestText.vb program, 343–44
HollowFontCenteredPath.vb program, 935–36
HollowFont.vb program, 933–35

HollowFontWidened.vb program, 941–42
HollowFontWidePen.vb program, 939–41
horizontal alignment of text, 403–8
horizontal (x-) shear, 290
HorizontalAlignment enumeration, 844, 961, 1080
HorizontalResolution property, 483, 503, 512, 1098–99, 1119
HorizontalScrollbar property, 886
HorizontalScrollBarHeight property, 149
HotkeyPrefix enumeration, 408–9
HotkeyPrefix property, 408–10
HotTrack property, 109, 111
Hour property, 431, 460
Hours property, 438
HowdyWorldFullFit.vb program, 376–77
HowdyWorld.vb program, 374–76
HScroll property, 145, 146
HScrollBar class, 596
HScrollBar control, 140, 596
HSplit property, 326
HtmlDump.vb program, 1195–96
HuckleberryFinnHalfHeight.vb program, 410–12
HuckleberryFinn.vb program, 124–25
HundredPixelsSquare.vb program, 250
HWnd property, 318
hyperbolic trigonometric functions, 1231

**I**

i prefix, 40
Ibeam property, 326
IButtonControl interface, 731, 733, 734
ICloneable interface, 1239, 1240
ICollection interface, 663, 1055
IComparable interface, 1239, 1246, 1252
IComparer interface, 1254
Icon class, 519
Icon property, 474, 475, 518, 740, 960
IConvertible interface, 1239
Id property, 1164
IDataObject interface, 1136, 1159, 1165
identity matrix, 286
identity transform, 284
IEEERemainder method, 1227
IEnumerable interface, 663, 1055, 1239
IFormatProvider interface, 443, 445
ILDASM (Intermediate Language Disassembler), 5
ildasm.exe disassembler, 5
IList interface, 663, 1055
image and bitmap programs
BetterImageFromFile.vb, 480
CenterImage.vb, 489–90
CenterPixelSizeImage.vb, 490–91

image and bitmap programs, *continued*
   DrawOnImage.vb, 504–5
   DrawOnPixelSizeImage.vb, 505–7
   HelloWorldBitmap.vb, 513–14
   ImageAtPoints.vb, 496–97
   ImageFromFile.vb, 478–79
   ImageFromWeb.vb, 480–82
   ImageReflection.vb, 494–95
   ImageScaleIsotropic.vb, 492–94
   ImageScaleToRectangle.vb, 491–92
   PartialImageRotate.vb, 501–2
   PartialImageStretch.vb, 499–501
   PartialImage.vb, 498–99
   PictureBoxPlusDemo.vb, 534
   PictureBoxPlus.vb, 533–34
   ProgramWithIcon.vb, 518–19
   ScribbleWithBitmap.vb, 513–17
   Thumbnail.vb, 508–10
Image class, 471, 472, 474, 477, 482, 483, 484, 485, 486,
   507–10, 778, 1096, 1097, 1098, 1099, 1119
image compression techniques, 473–74
Image object, 477, 478, 483, 486, 487, 488, 493, 497,
   502, 507, 510, 511, 514, 528, 529, 530, 795, 1144
Image property, 531, 549, 550, 551–52, 576, 799, 1006,
   1032–33
ImageAlign property, 549, 550, 576
ImageAtPoints.vb program, 496–97
ImageAttribute object, 499
ImageClicked event, 1075
ImageClip.vb program, 1142–45
ImageCollection class, 529
ImageDirectory.vb program, 1074–78
ImageDrop.vb program, 1175–77
ImageFormat class, 474, 486, 487, 778
ImageFormat object, 486
ImageFromFile.vb program, 478–79
ImageFromWeb.vb program, 480–82
ImageIndex property, 549, 550, 576, 971, 974, 1059,
   1060, 1082
ImageIO class, 777
ImageIO.vb program, 777–79
ImageList class, 528–31, 565
ImageList object, 528–31, 970, 971, 973, 979, 990, 1059
ImageList property, 549, 550, 576, 971, 973, 1059, 1060
ImageListCollection class, 530
ImageOpen.vb program, 774–76
ImagePanel class, 1071, 1074–75
ImagePanelOnImageClicked event, 1078
ImagePanel.vb program, 1071–74
ImagePrint.vb program, 1028–31
ImageReflection.vb program, 494–95
images. *See also* bitmaps
   animation, 521–27
   binary resources, 517–21

displaying
   parts of, 497–502
   in tree views, 1071–78
drawing on, 502–7
fitting to rectangles, 490–95
formation, 482–87
introduced, 469–70
loading and drawing, 477–82
rendering, 487–90
rotating, 495–97
shearing, 495–97
in tree views, 1059–60
Images property, 528, 529, 530, 565, 973
ImageScaleIsotropic.vb program, 492–94
ImageScaleToRectangle.vb program, 491–92
ImageSize property, 528, 530, 531, 532, 973
IME (Input Method Editor), 218–19
immutable strings, 1233
Imports statement, 8, 52, 53, 65, 689, 701, 1152
InactiveBorder property, 109, 111
InactiveCaption property, 109, 111
InactiveCaptionText property, 109, 110
Increment property, 898
Index property, 664, 675, 1063
IndexOf method, 665, 885, 1247–48
IndexOfAny method, 1249
infinity, floating-point, 1222–24
Infinity.vb program, 620–21
Inflate method, 96
Info property, 109, 111
information device context, 1002
InfoText property, 110
inheritance, instances and, 34–37
InheritAndConstruct class, 76
InheritHelloWorld class, 80, 81, 82
InheritHelloWorld.vb program, 80–81
inheriting forms, 74–76
InheritingTheClass.vb program, 34–36
InheritTheForm class, 75
InheritTheForm.vb program, 74–75
InheritWithConstructor.vb program, 75–76
InheritWithPaint.vb program, 76–77
InitialDelay property, 878
InitialDirectory property, 771
InitializeCoordinates method, 460
input, event-driven, 60–62
input focus, 206–7, 237–38
Input Method Editor (IME), 218–19
InputLanguageChanged event, 236–37
InputLanguageChanging event, 236–37
Insert method, 871, 1234, 1251
InstalledFontCollection class, 391
InstalledFontsList.vb program, 391–92

InstalledPrinters property, 995, 996
instances and inheritance, 34–37
instances of classes, 21
InstantiateHelloWorld.vb program, 81–83
Int32 structure, 39
integer formatting, 10–11
integer overflow, 1218–19
Integer type, 10, 11, 15, 28, 39, 40, 1217–18
IntegralHeight property, 886
Intermediate Language Disassembler (ILDASM), 5
InterpolationColors property, 809
IntersectClip method, 717
IntersectsWith method, 97
Interval property, 427
Invalidate method, 71, 101–2, 114, 153, 314–15, 460, 574
InvariantInfo property, 443–44
inverse trigonometric functions, 1230
InvokeOnClick method, 592
IOException exception, 1180
IsAlphaPixelFormat method, 485
IsCanonicalPixelFormat method, 485
IsClipEmpty property, 722, 723
IsControl method, 1235, 1236
IsDaylightSavingTime method, 435
IsDefaultPrinter property, 994–95
IsDigit method, 1236
IsDisplay method, 1101
IsEmf method, 1101
IsEmfOrEmfPlus method, 1101
IsEmfPlus method, 1101
IsEmfPlusDual method, 1101
IsEmfPlusOnly method, 1101
IsEmpty property, 88, 90, 95
IsExpanded property, 1064
IsExtendedPixelFormat method, 485
IsIdentity property, 287
IsInfinity method, 1223, 1224
IsInvertible property, 287
Islamic (Hijri) calendar, 440, 441
IsLeapYear function, 18, 19
IsLeapYear method, 19, 20, 21, 22, 30
IsLetter method, 1236
IsLetterOrDigit method, 1236
IsLower method, 1236
IsNaN method, 1223
IsNegativeInfinity method, 1223
IsNumber method, 1236
ISO 8601 format, 446
isotropic scaling, 492
IsParent property, 663, 664
IsPathRooted method, 1203
IsPlotter property, 996, 997
IsPositiveInfinity method, 1223

IsPunctuation method, 1236
IsReadOnly property, 530, 565, 664, 1055, 1080, 1081, 1082, 1088
IsSelected property, 1064
IsSeparator method, 1235
IsStyleAvailable method, 379, 387, 389
IsSurrogate method, 1236, 1237
IsSymbol method, 1236
IsUpper method, 1236
IsValid property, 994–95, 996
IsVisibleClipEmpty property, 722, 723
IsWhiteSpace method, 1236
IsWmf method, 1101
IsWmfPlaceable method, 1101
italic fonts, 353
Italic property, 371
ItemActivate event, 1087
ItemActivation enumeration, 1086
ItemDrag event, 1062
ItemHeight property, 675, 683
Items property, 885, 892, 1079, 1081, 1085
ItemWidth property, 675, 683

**J**

jagged arrays, 15
Jeu de Taquin (14-15,15-) puzzle, 463–68, 651
JeuDeTaquinTile.vb program, 463–64
JeuDeTaquin.vb program, 465–68
JeuDeTaquinWithScamble.vb program, 651
Join method, 1243
joins, 179–80, 829–36
Joint Photographic Experts Group (Jpeg) property, 474, 475
Julian calendar, 440
JulianCalendar object, 440

**K**

Kemeny, John G., 1
keyboard. *See also* Keys enumeration
    alternatives to the mouse, 296–97
    Button control and keyboard input, 540–41
    caret and, 238–42
    control characters, 225–26
    echoing key characters, 242–46
    foreign, 233–37
    ignoring, 205–6
    input focus and, 206–7, 237–38
    interface
        mouse, 336–38
        SysInfo, 223–24
    introduced, 205

keyboard, *continued*
    invoking the Win32 API, 231–33
    key-down and key-up events, 209–10, 222
    KeyPress event, 225
    keys and characters, 207–8
    looking at the keys, 226–31
    menu shortcut keys, 645–47
    right-to-left problems, 246–47
    testing the modifier keys, 221
keyboard programs
    Caret.vb, 238–41
    CheckerWithKeyboard.vb, 336–38
    ExitOnX.vb, 211–12
    KeyExamine.vb, 227–31
    KeyExamineWithScroll.vb, 232–33
    SysInfoKeyboard.vb, 223–24
    TypeAway.vb, 242–46
KeyChar property, 225
KeyCode property, 210, 219, 222
KeyData bit masks, 220
KeyData property, 210, 220, 646
key-down and key-up events, 209–10, 222
KeyDown event, 209, 222, 225, 226, 230, 540
KeyEventArgs class, 646
KeyEventArgs object, 222, 230
KeyEventArgs properties, 210, 219–20
KeyExamine class, 232
KeyExamine.vb program, 227–31
KeyExamineWithScroll.vb program, 232–33
KeyholeBitmap.vb program, 719–21
KeyholeClipCentered.vb program, 718–19
KeyholeClip.vb program, 717–18
keypad, unused, 214
keypad cursor movement, 214
keypad numbers, 213–14
keypad operators, 213
KeyPress event, 225, 226, 230, 540
KeyPressEventArgs object, 230
KeyPressEventArgs properties, 225
keys
    characters and, 207–8
    dead, 234–35
Keys enumeration
    ASCII control keys, 214–15
    browser and player keys, 218
    function keys, 213
    Input Method Editor (IME), 218–19
    introduced, 210
    KeyData bit masks, 220
    keypad cursor movement, 214
    keypad numbers, 213–14
    keypad operators, 213
    keypad, unused, 214

letter keys, 211–12
    Microsoft keys, 215–16
    miscellaneous keys, 216
    modifier keys, 219–21
    mouse buttons, 216
    number keys, 212
    shift keys, 215
    Shortcut enumeration and, 646
    special keys, 216–17
    symbols keys, 217
KeyState property, 1171, 1175
KeyUp event, 209, 222, 225, 226, 230
KeyValue property, 210
Kind property, 998–99
KnownColor enumeration, 112, 603
Kurtz, Thomas E., 1

# L

l prefix, 40
Label control, 331–33, 574–77, 578, 603, 740–41
Label object, 333, 581, 957
LabelEdit property, 1062
Labels property, 137, 1083–84
Landscape property, 1003, 1004, 1005, 1014
LandscapeAngle property, 996, 997
LargeChange property, 597, 602–3, 605
LargeImageList property, 1079, 1081, 1090
LastAccessTime property, 1208, 1213
LastIndexOf method, 1248–49
LastIndexOfAny method, 1249
LastNode property, 1063
LastWriteTime property, 1208, 1213
Left property, 95, 98, 935, 1004
Lempel, Abraham, 473
Length property, 14, 871, 1182, 1213, 1238
LET keyword, 2
letter keys, 211–12
lexical string comparisons, 1245–47
Lib keyword, 232
Line Spacing metric, 381–82, 383
line spacing of fonts, 355, 381–82, 383
LineAlignment property, 117, 119, 403–4, 405, 406, 407
linear gradient brushes, 800–809
linear transforms, 282–85, 708, 944
LineArcCombo.vb program, 685–87
LinearColors property, 807
LineArcPath.vb program, 688–91
LinearGradientBrush class, 781, 782
LinearGradientBrush object, 802, 803, 823
LinearGradientMode enumeration, 804, 805, 806, 808, 824
LineCap enumeration, 834, 836
LineCaps.vb program, 835–36

LineJoin enumeration, 830
LineJoin property, 830, 831
LineJoins.vb program, 830–32
lines
    ends, 179–81
    joins, 179–80
    multiple connected lines (polylines), 177–81
    straight, 165–66
Lines property, 838, 1038
LineTo function, 173
LinkClicked event, 741
LinkLabel control, 741
ListBox class, 884–85
ListBox control, 884–91
ListBox object, 892
ListControl class, 884–85
ListView control. *See also* TreeView control
    basics, 1078–85
    events, 1086–93
    introduced, 1039
ListView control programs. *See also* TreeView control
        programs
    ExplorerLike.vb, 1091–93
    FileListView.vb, 1088–90
    SysInfoListView.vb, 1083–85
Load event, 306, 850
LoadRegistryInfo method, 850, 859, 874
local time, 432–36
location of the mouse cursor, 297–98
Location property, 94, 98, 103, 143, 146, 468, 532, 571,
        572, 582, 738
Lock method, 1186
LockBits method, 513
Log method, 1228
Log10 method, 1228
logarithms and powers, 1227–28
LogicalDpiX property, 1101, 1102
LogicalDpiY property, 1101, 1102
Long type, 11, 40, 1217–18
lossless compression techniques, 474
lossy compression techniques, 474
LostFocus event, 238, 242
Loyd, Sam, 463
LParam property, 318
LZ and LZW data compression techniques, 473–74

**M**

Main function, 6
main menu, 642
Main method, 35–36, 45–46, 57, 58, 72, 75, 77, 80–81,
        538, 728
MainMenu object, 643, 650, 651, 669
managed code, 6

manual menu coding, Menu Designer vs., 641
MarginBounds property, 169, 1009, 1015, 1016, 1018,
        1038
Margins property, 1003, 1004
MarshalByRefObject class, 76
Math class
    checking integer overflow, 1218–19
    constant fields, 1224
    Decimal type, 1217–18, 1219–22
    floating-point infinity, 1222–24
    floating-point remainders, 1227
    introduced, 181, 624, 1217
    Not a Number (NaN), 1223–24
    numeric types, 1217–18
    powers and logarithms, 1227–28
    shared methods, 1224–26
    trigonometric functions, 1228–31
Math.Abs method, 344
Math.Max method, 275, 307
Math.Min method, 307, 375
Math.PI constant, 624
Math.Sin method, 181
Matrix class, 286–89, 702, 703, 904, 923
Matrix object, 174, 286, 287, 703, 704, 709, 899
matrix transforms, 286
MatrixElements.vb program, 902–4
matrixes
    identity, 286
    introduced, 285–86
    shear and, 289–91
MatrixMethods.vb program, 904–8
MatrixOrder enumeration, 281, 703
MaximizeBox property, 59
Maximum property, 145, 597, 602–3, 605, 898
MaximumCopies property, 1000
MaximumRange property, 1001, 1024
MaxLabelWidth method, 137, 1084
MaxLength property, 838
MaxValueWidth method, 137, 143, 1084
MaxWidth method, 137
MaxWindowTrackSize property, 151
Me keyword, 27, 76, 143, 538
MeasureCharacterRanges method, 369
MeasureItem event, 163, 675, 678, 682, 891, 990, 991
MeasureItemEventArgs object, 163
MeasureString method
    clock, timer, and time programs, 451, 454
    font and text programs, 355, 359, 369, 370, 371, 374,
            375, 380–81, 396–98, 401, 423, 934, 936
    form-related programs, 120–22
    image and bitmap programs, 505, 506, 514
    keyboard programs, 245–46
    menu programs, 675
    mouse programs, 343

MeasureString method, *continued*
  page-related programs, 267
  printing programs, 1038
  system information programs, 128, 131, 138–39
  vector graphics programs, 171
measuring strings, 120–22
memory, heap, 86
memory-based DIB (MemoryBmp) property, 474, 475
MemoryStream class, 1187, 1188
MemoryStream object, 1114, 1115, 1151, 1152, 1155,
    1159, 1168
menu bar, 51
Menu class, 565, 642–43, 663, 664
Menu Designer, manual menu coding vs., 641
menu help, 963–70
menu items, 642
menu programs
  BetterContextMenu.vb, 661–63
  CheckAndRadioCheck.vb, 656–59
  ContextMenuAdd.vb, 665–66
  ContextMenuDemo.vb, 659–61
  FirstMainMenu.vb, 647–50
  FontMenu.vb, 666–69
  HelpMenu.vb, 682–83
  JeuDeTaquinWithScamble.vb, 651
  OldFashionedMenu.vb, 651–53
  OwnerDrawMenu.vb, 678–81
  StandardMenu.vb, 671–74
Menu property, 110, 111, 643, 650, 651
MenuColorOnClick event, 991
MenuColorOnClick method, 746, 747, 757, 761–62
MenuComplete event, 964
MenuFacenameOnMeasureItem method, 680, 681
MenuFacenameOnPopup event, 668
MenuFileOpenOnClick method, 645, 770
MenuFilePreviewOnClick method, 1038
MenuFilePrintOnClick method, 1013–14, 1027, 1037
MenuFileSetupOnClick method, 1031
MenuFormatColorOnClick method, 658
MenuFormatFillOnClick method, 659
MenuHelpFirstTry.vb program, 964–67
MenuHelpSubclass.vb program, 969–70
MenuItem class, 644, 655, 666, 788, 859, 967, 969, 990
MenuItem object, 653, 661, 664, 666, 668, 670, 671, 674,
    967, 981, 982
MenuItem property, 665
MenuItem structure, 658, 659
MenuItemCollection class, 663–69
MenuItemColor class, 661, 666, 990
MenuItemColor object, 661, 663
MenuItemEncoding class, 859
MenuItemHelp class, 967, 969
MenuItemHelp.vb program, 967–68

MenuItems class, 529
MenuItems collection, 670
MenuItems property, 565, 663, 664, 669
MenuOnClick method, 728, 730
MenuOnSelect method, 966, 967
menus
  checking items, 655–59
  child (submenus), 642
  context (shortcut), 299, 642, 659–63
  drop-down, 642
  first, 647–50
  introduced, 641
  main, 642
  manual coding vs. Menu Designer, 641
  menu items and, 642–45
  MenuItem properties and events, 653–55
  MenuItemCollection class, 663–69
  owner-draw, 674–83
  pop-up, 642
  shortcut (context), 299, 642, 659–63
  shortcut keys, 645–47
  standard, 669–74
  submenus (child), 642
  top-level items, 642
  unconventional, 651–53
MenuStart event, 964
MenuText property, 110
MenuItem class, 963–64
message box programs
  MessageBoxHellowWorld.vb, 45–46
  MyDocumentsFolder.vb, 50–51
MessageBox class, 45–51
MessageBoxButtons enumeration, 47–48
MessageBoxDefaultButton enumeration, 48–49
MessageBoxHellowWorld.vb program, 45–46
MessageBoxIcon enumeration, 48
MessageBoxOptions enumeration, 49
metadata, 155
Metafile class, 471, 1071, 1097, 1098, 1099, 1123, 1124
Metafile object, 1097, 1106, 1109, 1112, 1114, 1124,
    1128, 1144, 1145, 1147, 1148, 1151, 1152, 1153,
    1159
metafile programs
  CreateMetafileMemory.vb, 1114–15
  CreateMetafileReload.vb, 1112–14
  CreateMetafile.vb, 1110–12
  EnumMetafile.vb, 1128–31
  MetafileConvert.vb, 1106–8
  MetafilePageUnits.vb, 1120–22
  MetafileViewer.vb, 1102–6
MetafileClip.vb program, 1140–42
MetafileConvert.vb program, 1106–8
MetafileFrameUnit enumeration, 1116–17, 1119

MetafileHeader class, 1099, 1119
MetafileHeader property, 1106
MetafilePageUnits.vb program, 1120–22
metafiles. *See also* vector graphics
  boundary rectangle, 116–19
  converting to bitmaps, 1106–8
  creating, 1108–15
  enumerating, 1125–31
  introduced, 469, 1095–96
  loading and rendering, 1096–98
  page transform, 1119–22
  paths vs., 1096
  sizes and rendering, 1098–1106
  type, 1122–25
MetafileSize property, 1100, 1101
MetafileToBitmap method, 1106, 1108, 1109
MetafileType enumeration, 1100
MetafileViewer.vb program, 1102–6
methods
  Array
    BinarySearch shared, 1254–55
    Sort shared, 1253–54
  BinaryReader, 1198–1200
  BinaryWriter Public, 1198
  Bitmap, 512
  Calendar, 441
  Caret, 241–42
  Char, shared, 1235–37
  Clipboard, shared, 1134–36
  Color.FromArgb, shared, 106
  ContextMenu, 661
  Control, 53–54, 102, 139, 237, 317–18, 356, 547, 569,
    585, 1174
    Invalidate, 101–2
  Control.ControlCollection, 566–67
  ControlPaint
    shared, 553
    shared DrawMenuGlyph, 677, 678, 681
  Cursor, shared, 327
  DataFormats, shared, 1164
  DataObjectSetData, 1165–66
  DateTime, 434, 446
    ToString, 442–47
  Decimal, shared, 1221–22
  defined, 7, 27
  Directory
    Delete shared, 1208
    shared, 1206, 1207, 1208, 1209, 1210
  DirectoryInfo, 1207, 1209, 1210
    Delete, 1207
  DrawArc, 190–91, 193
  DrawEllipse, 189–90
  DrawItemEventArgs, 677
  DrawPolygon, 188

  DrawRectangles, 187
  Environment, shared, 1200–1201
  File, 1213
    shared, 1213, 1214, 1215
  FileInfo, 1214
  FileStream, 1186
  FillEllipse, 198
  FillPie, 198–99
  FillPolygon, 200–201
  FillRectangle, 197–98
  FillRectangles, 198
  Font, 371–78
  FontFamily, 379, 381
    shared, 390
  Form, 104, 207, 730
  Graphics, 64–65, 114, 139, 267, 281, 289, 520, 698,
    1110
    DrawBézier, 613
    DrawBéziers, 613–14, 617, 618
    DrawClosedCurve, 635–36
    DrawCurve, 630–31, 635
    DrawImage, 471, 478, 479, 487–89, 490, 491, 494,
      495–96, 497–98, 499, 501
    DrawString, 392–94
    EnumerateMetafile, 1125–26, 1127, 1128
    FillClosedCurve, 636
    FillRegion, 721
    MeasureString, 396–98
    ResetClip, 717
    SetClip, 712–13, 714, 715, 717, 722
    shared, 502–3
    TransformPoints, 270, 271
    TranslateClip, 718
  GraphicsPath, 694–98
    AddPath, 696–97
    AddString, 697, 930, 931
    Flatten, 705
    GetBounds, 708
    Transform, 702
    Warp, 708–9
    Widen, 705
  IButtonControl, 734
  IComparable, 1253–54
  IComparer, 1254
  IDataObject, 1136–37, 1149
    GetFormats, 1147–48
  Image, 508, 510
    Save, 507–8
    shared, 477, 485
  ImageListDraw, 530–31
  ImageList.ImageCollection, 529–30
  LinearGradientBrush, 807
  ListBox, 888
  ListView.ColumnHeaderCollection, 1080

methods, *continued*
ListViewItem.ListViewSubItemCollection, 1083
ListView.ListViewItemCollection, 1081
Math, shared, 1224–26, 1227–28, 1230–31
Matrix
  Rotate, 703, 704
  RotateAt, 704
  Scale, 703
  Shear, 704
  Translate, 702, 703
Menu.MenuItemCollection, 664, 665
MessageBoxShow, 46–47
Metafile
  nonshared GetMetafileHeader, 1099–1100
  PlayRecord, 1127–28
  shared GetMetafileHeader, 1100
MetafileHeader, 1101
On, 79–83
Overridable, 37, 850
Pathshared, 1203–4
Point
  instance, 88–89
  shared, 92
PreviewPrintController, 1032
PrintController, 1019
PrintDocument, 1007–8
PrinterSettings, 1002
PrinterUnitConvertshared Convert, 1018
PrivateFontCollection, 392
Protected Overridable, 617
Rectangle, 96–97
  shared, 94, 95
RegistryKey, 764–65
shared, 21–23, 77
Single structure, shared, 1223
SizeF, instance, 93
Sizeshared, 92
Stream, 1182–83
StreamReader, 1195
String, 1240, 1244, 1249, 1250–51
  Compare shared, 1246–47
  CompareOrdinal shared, 1246
  CompareTo, 1246
  comparison, 1245
  Concat shared, 1242–43
  Copy shared, 1240
  Format shared, 1252
  IndexOf, 1247–48
  Join shared, 1243
  LastIndexOf, 1248–49
  shared, 1244
  Split, 1252
  Substring, 1240–41
StringFormat, 418

TextBoxBase, 842, 852, 860
TextWriter, 1193
Timer, 427–28
TimeZone, 435–36
ToolTip, 877
TreeNode, 1064
TreeNodeCollection, 1056
TreeView, 1059, 1064
metrical dimensions, 268–72
Microsoft ClearType, 352, 395, 396
Microsoft Intermediate Language (MSIL), 5
Microsoft keys, 215–16
Microsoft.Win32 namespace, 517, 764
Millisecond property, 431, 460, 462
Milliseconds property, 438
MinAndMax.vb program, 12–13
MinExtra property, 1051, 1052
Minimum property, 145, 597, 605, 898
MinimumRange property, 1001, 1024
MinimumSize property, 275, 375
MinMargins property, 1028
MinSize property, 1051, 1052
Minute property, 431, 460
Minutes property, 438
MinWidth property, 960, 961
MiterLimit property, 832
mix line, 801
MMConv method, 258, 262
Mnemonic property, 653
MobyDick.vb program, 276–80
modal dialog boxes
  first, 726–30
  introduced, 725
  termination, 731–33
modeless dialog boxes, 725, 751–54
ModelessColorScroll.vb program, 754
Modified property, 851
modifier keys, 208, 219–21
ModifierKeys property, 221, 323–24
Modifiers property, 210, 220, 222
Module definition, 6
modules, 77–79
monochrome (bilevel) images, 472
Month property, 28, 431
mouse
  Button control and mouse input, 540–41
  capturing, 301, 309, 311–12
  clicks, 298, 322–23
  dark side, 296–97
  defined, 297
  definitions, 297–98
  double clicks, 298, 322–23
  dragging, 298

events, 300–303, 324–25
history, 295–96
hit-testing, 334–44
ignoring, 297
information about, 298–99
introduced, 295–96
keyboard alternatives, 296–97
keyboard interface and, 336–38
mouse cursor, 297–98, 325–33
mouse wheel, 299–300, 303–7
movement, 307–9
properties, 323–24
scribbling with, 345–49
tracking, 309–11, 312, 322
mouse buttons, 216
mouse cursor, 297–98, 325–33
mouse programs
  BetterBlockOut.vb, 315–17
  BlockOut.vb, 312–15
  CaptureLoss.vb, 318–19
  CheckerChild.vb, 338–39
  CheckerChildWithFocus.vb, 341–42
  Checker.vb, 334–36
  CheckerWithChildrenAndFocus.vb, 342–43
  CheckerWithChildren.vb, 339–41
  CheckerWithKeyboard.vb, 336–38
  EnterLeave.vb, 324–25
  EvenBetterBlockOut.vb, 320–22
  HitTestText.vb, 343–44
  MouseConnect.vb, 309–11
  MouseConnectWaitCursor.vb, 327–28
  MouseCursorsProperty.vb, 331–33
  MouseCursors.vb, 328–30
  MouseWeb.vb, 307–9
  PoePoem.vb, 304–7
  Scribble.vb, 345–46
  ScribbleWithSave.vb, 347–49
mouse wheel, 299–300, 303–7
MouseButtons enumeration, 302
MouseButtons property, 298, 299, 323
MouseButtonsSwapped property, 151, 298, 299
MouseConnect class, 327
MouseConnect.vb program, 309–11
MouseConnectWaitCursor.vb program, 327–28
MouseCursorsProperty.vb program, 331–33
MouseCursors.vb program, 328–30
MouseDown event, 301, 302, 303, 312, 330, 1062, 1087
MouseEnter event, 324
MouseEventArgs class, 302
MouseEventArgs object, 303, 311, 323, 343
MouseHover event, 324
MouseLeave event, 324
MouseMove event, 301, 302, 303, 307, 312, 330, 333

MousePosition property, 323, 326
MousePresent property, 298, 299
MouseUp event, 301, 302, 303, 312, 322
MouseWeb.vb program, 307–9
MouseWheel event, 301, 302, 303
MouseWheelPresent property, 300
MouseWheelScrollLines property, 300, 303
Move event, 101
Move method, 1209, 1214
MoveTile method, 468
MoveTo function, 173
MoveTo method, 1209, 1214
Msg property, 318
MsgBox function, 46
MSIL (Microsoft Intermediate Language), 5
MultiCopy.vb program, 1166–69
Multiline property, 842, 843, 875
multiple connected lines (polylines), 177–81
multiple forms, 71–72
MultiplyTransform method, 289, 800, 807, 824, 929
MultiSelect property, 768, 1086
MustInherit class, 439, 471, 477, 478, 536, 596, 755, 768,
    782, 861, 1187, 1188
MUZZLE program, 463
MyDocumentsFolder.vb program, 50–51
MyPaintHandler method, 64

## N

NaiveFamiliesList.vb program, 385–86
Name property, 158, 371, 378, 379, 579, 767, 1164,
    1206, 1212
namespaces. *See also* inside front cover
  introduced, 7–9, 38
  Microsoft.Win32, 517, 764
  System, 7, 9, 24, 37, 39, 50, 181, 430, 434, 435, 1224
  System.Collections, 346–47
  System.ComponentModel, 1008
  System.Diagnostics, 741
  System.Drawing, 59, 66, 67, 86, 105, 357, 471, 547,
    782, 884, 1097
  System.Drawing.Drawing2D, 176, 201, 270, 280, 286,
    636, 689, 692, 693, 702, 782, 783, 884
  System.Drawing.Imaging, 474, 484, 1097, 1116, 1122
  System.Drawing.Printing, 167, 993, 994
  System.Drawing.Text, 391, 408
  System.Globalization, 436, 439, 443
  System.IO, 15, 477, 1152, 1179, 1203, 1257
  System.Runtime.InteropServices, 232
  System.Text, 1189, 1256
  System.Threading, 54
  System.Windows.Forms, 46, 52, 55, 62–63, 127, 325,
    326, 425, 548, 553, 642, 993, 1023, 1134

naming conventions, 39–40
NaN (Not a Number), 1223–24
NativeMouseWheelSupport property, 300
NC (numerical control), 611
.NET Framework SDK, 3
New operator, 14, 31, 76, 87
NewForm.vb program, 51–52
NewLine property, 1192, 1193
NewValue property, 598
NextNode property, 1063
NextVisibleNode property, 1063
No property, 326
Node property, 1061, 1062
Nodes property, 1055, 1056, 1057–58
NoDistort property, 533, 534, 1075
NoMove2D property, 326
NoMoveHoriz property, 326
NoMoveVert property, 326
noncharacter keys, 208
NonInheritable class, 162, 486, 768, 1097, 1134, 1204
nonlinear transforms, 944–50
normal splines. *See* canonical splines
Not a Number (NaN), 1223–24
Notepad clone
    drag-and-drop facility, 1172–74
    Edit menu, 860–71
    file I/O, 851–59
    Format menu, 871–74
    introduced, 845–47
    page setup and print preview, 1033–38
    registry access, 847–51
NotepadCloneNoMenu.vb program, 845–46
NotepadClone.vb program, 1172–74
NotepadCloneWithEdit.vb program, 866–71
NotepadCloneWithFile class, 850
NotepadCloneWithFile.vb program, 852–59
NotepadCloneWithFormat.vb program, 871–74
NotepadCloneWithPrinting.vb program, 1033–38
NotepadCloneWithRegistry.vb program, 847–51
Nothing keyword, 20, 468, 508, 567, 1238, 1252
Nothing string, 1245
NotifyDefault method, 734
Now method, 1256
Now property, 431–32, 434
number keys, 212
Number method, 454–55
numeric string comparisons, 1245–47
numeric types, 1217–18
numerical control (NC), 611
NumericUpDown class, 897–908
NumericUpDown control, 897–908

**O**

obj prefix, 40
Object class, 36, 37, 52
Object type, 40
ObjectCollection class, 885, 892
objects
    ArrayList, 347–48, 349, 515, 700
    Bitmap, 471, 477, 510–13, 720, 1106, 1107, 1108, 1109,
        1144, 1145, 1147, 1148, 1151, 1152, 1153, 1159
    Brush, 67, 107–8, 782
    Button, 537, 542, 545, 565, 748, 1135, 1145
    Calendar, 439–41
    CalendarDate, 23, 25
    Caret, 245
    CheckBox, 744
    ClockControl, 461
    Color, 106, 107, 163, 579, 603, 659, 661, 666, 744, 761,
        767, 768
    ColorDialog, 761, 762
    ColorFillDialogBox, 746, 747
    ColorFillDialogBoxWithApply, 750
    ColorPalette, 486
    ContextMenu, 661, 665, 666
    Control, 206, 565
    Cursor, 333
    DatePlus, 36
    DateTime, 436, 437–47, 441, 442, 456
    DirectoryInfo, 1067, 1091
    for displaying text strings, 133–37
    DrawItemEventArgs, 163, 681
    Exception, 24
    FileStream, 1114, 1179, 1182, 1184, 1197
    Font, 66, 356, 357, 369, 372, 375, 506, 582, 680, 681,
        765–66, 986
    FontFamily, 357, 378–80, 392
        arrays, 385–90
    FontStyle, 986
    FontStyleCheckBox, 581
    Form, 56, 58, 67, 72, 86, 301
    GenericTypographic, 403
    Graphics. *See* Graphics object
    GraphicsPath, 690, 700, 714, 810
    GroupBox, 744
    HatchBrush, 784, 799
    HebrewCalendar, 441
    Image, 477, 478, 483, 486, 487, 488, 493, 497, 502,
        507, 510, 511, 514, 528, 529, 530, 795, 1144
    ImageAttribute, 499
    ImageFormat, 486
    ImageList, 528–31, 970, 971, 973, 979, 990, 1059
    as instances of classes, 21
    introduced, 16–21

JulianCalendar, 440
KeyEventArgs, 222
Label, 333, 581, 957
LinearGradientBrush, 802, 803, 823
ListBox, 892
MainMenu, 643, 650, 651, 669
Matrix, 174, 286, 287, 703, 704, 709, 899
MeasureItemEventArgs, 163
MemoryStream, 1114, 1115, 1151, 1152, 1155, 1159, 1168
MenuItem, 653, 661, 664, 666, 668, 670, 671, 674, 967, 981, 982
MenuItemColor, 661, 663
Metafile, 1097, 1106, 1109, 1112, 1114, 1124, 1128, 1144, 1145, 1147, 1148, 1151, 1152, 1153, 1159
MouseEventArgs, 303, 311, 323, 343
OpenFileDialog, 770, 1102, 1128
PageBounds, 1015
PageSettings, 1002, 1003, 1004, 1005, 1014
PaintEventArgs, 76
PaperSource, 997–98
PathGradientBrush, 813, 814, 821
Pen, 107, 163–64
Point, 347
PointF, 403, 405, 406
PreviewPrintController, 1032
PrintDialog, 1025, 1037
PrintDocument, 167, 168, 169, 1005, 1006, 1013–14, 1032, 1033
PrinterSelectionDialog, 1013
PrinterSettings, 994, 995, 996, 1003, 1005, 1122
PrintPageEventArgs, 162, 1015, 1016
PrintPreviewDialog, 1033
PropertyInfo, 158
Rectangle, 347, 1015
RectangleF, 403, 414
Region, 722
SaveFileDialog, 778, 779
ScrollEventArgs, 598, 599
SevenSegmentDisplay, 455
SimpleButton, 538
Size, 397–98
SolidBrush, 108, 823
StatusBar, 953
StatusBarPanel, 957–58, 959, 960, 966
Stream, 477, 1097, 1187, 1188, 1197
StreamWriter, 1168, 1189–90
String, 1136, 1137, 1139, 1140, 1145, 1146, 1151, 1152, 1155, 1159, 1233, 1255, 1256
StringFormat, 116–20, 246, 398–400, 401, 417, 451, 680, 681, 920, 931, 1038
StringWriter, 1169, 1257
TextureBrush, 1112

Timer, 427, 729, 1074
TimeSpan, 435, 436, 437–39
TimeZone, 435
ToolBar, 981
ToolBarButton, 970, 971, 973, 981, 982, 986, 987
ToolTip, 877, 878
TreeNode, 1055, 1056, 1057–58, 1060, 1061, 1062
Type, 37, 884
UnicodeEncoding, 1191
VScrollBar, 603
WaitCursor, 327
oblique fonts, 353
off-by-1 errors, 199–200
Offset method, 88, 89, 96
OffsetX property, 287
OffsetY property, 287
OkToTrash method, 851
OldFashionedMenu.vb program, 651–53
On methods, 79–83
OnActivated method, 207
OnAfterCollapse method, 1061
OnAfterExpand method, 1061
OnAfterSelect method, 1061
OnBeforeCollapse method, 1061
OnBeforeExpand method, 1061, 1068
OnBeforeSelect method, 1061
OnButtonClick method, 978
OnButtonDropDown method, 978
OnCaptureLost method, 322
OnChanged method, 753
OnCheckedChanged method, 569, 593
OnCheckStateChanged method, 574
OnClick method, 167, 322, 338, 339, 539, 655
OnClosed method, 767, 850, 852
OnClosing method, 852
OnColumnClick method, 1087
OnDeactivate method, 207
OnDoubleClick method, 322
OnDragDrop method, 1170, 1177
OnDragEnter method, 1170
OnDragLeave method, 1170
OnDragOver method, 1170, 1177
OnDrawItem method, 675
OnEndPage method, 1019
OnEndPrint method, 1019
OnePanelWithSplitter.vb program, 1044–45
one-shot timer, 428–29
OnGotFocus method, 238, 242, 338
OnInputLanguageChanged method, 236
OnInputLanguageChanging method, 236
OnItemActivate method, 1087, 1091
OnKeyDown method, 209, 223, 245, 338, 540
OnKeyPress method, 225, 245, 540, 592

OnKeyUp method, 209, 540
OnLoad method, 306, 465, 850, 859, 874
OnLostFocus method, 238, 242, 338
OnMeasureItem method, 675
OnMenuComplete method, 964
OnMenuStart method, 964
OnMouseDown method, 301, 314, 319, 324, 343, 344, 349, 1177
OnMouseEnter method, 324
OnMouseHover method, 324
OnMouseLeave method, 324
OnMouseMove method, 301, 307, 309, 311, 314–15, 328, 330, 331, 346, 349, 516, 701
OnMouseUp method, 301, 311, 314, 315, 322, 335, 338, 349, 644
OnMouseWheel method, 301, 307
OnMove method, 101, 847
OnPage method, 260
OnPaint method
    brush and pen programs, 796, 798
    clock, timer, and time programs, 450, 451, 452, 455, 459, 463
    control programs, 571–72, 578, 595
    dialog box programs, 729, 730, 741, 770, 776
    font and text programs, 909
    form-related programs, 79, 81, 82–83, 102, 113, 114
    image and bitmap programs, 479, 514–15, 516, 517, 534
    introduced, 76–77
    keyboard programs, 230, 231
    menu programs, 659, 668
    metafile programs, 1109
    mouse programs, 309, 311, 314, 319, 327, 328, 330, 338, 346, 349
    page-related programs, 268, 274
    path and clipping programs, 701
    spline programs, 630
    status bar and toolbar programs, 953
    system information programs, 138, 139, 144, 148, 150, 153
    vector graphics programs, 162, 171, 173
OnPopup method, 655
OnPrintPage event, 1014
OnPrintPage method, 1022, 1031, 1038
OnQueryPageSettings event, 1014
OnQueryPageSettings method, 1014
OnResize method, 101, 114, 115–16, 306, 307, 333, 339, 451, 452, 527, 544, 557, 560, 603, 609, 847, 1041
OnSelect method, 655, 967
OnSelectedIndexChanged method, 889, 892, 1087
OnSelectedValueChanged method, 889
OnSelectionChangeCommitted method, 892
OnSplitterMoved method, 1053

OnSplitterMoving method, 1053
OnStartPage method, 1019
OnStartPrint method, 1019
OnTextChanged method, 839, 892
OnTick event, 448
OnTick method, 426–27
OnValueChanged method, 899
op_Addition operator, 91, 438
Open method, 1214, 1215
open subpaths, 691
OpenFileDialog class, 755, 768–76
OpenFileDialog object, 770, 1102, 1128
OpenRead method, 1214, 1215
OpenSubKey method, 76, 764–65
OpenText method, 1214, 1215
OpenType fonts, 352
OpenWrite method, 1214, 1215
op_Equality operator, 89, 432
operators
    DateTime, 432
    GetType, 158, 520
    keypad, 213
    New, 14, 31, 76, 87
    op_Addition, 91, 438
    op_Equality, 89, 432
    op_Explicit, 91
    op_GreaterThan, 432
    op_GreaterThanOrEqual, 432
    op_Inequality, 432
    op_LessThan, 432
    op_LessThanOrEqual, 432
    op_Subtraction, 91, 439
op_Explicit operator, 91
op_GreaterThan operator, 432
op_GreaterThanOrEqual operator, 432
op_Inequality operator, 432
op_LessThan operator, 432
op_LessThanOrEqual operator, 432
op_Subtraction operator, 91, 439
optimized palettes, 472
Orientation enumeration, 604
Orientation property, 604, 609
outline fonts, 352
OutlineClientRectangle.vb program, 187
OverflowException exception, 1219
OverlappingHatchBrushes.vb program, 792–94
overloads, 9
Overridable method, 37, 850
Overrides modifier, 37
OverwritePrompt property, 776
OwnedForms property, 871
owner draw feature, 163
Owner property, 753, 871

owner-draw buttons, 552–57
owner-draw menus, 674–83
OwnerDraw property, 674–75
OwnerDrawButtons.vb program, 554–57
OwnerDrawMenu.vb program, 678–81

## P

padding strings, 1251
page coordinates, 266
page dimensions, 1014–18
page transforms, 266–67, 1119–22
    limitations, 275–76
page units and page scale, 258–62
PageBounds object, 1015
PageBounds property, 169, 1009, 1018
pages. *See also* ruler programs; transforms
    device independence through text, 249–50
    dots per inch, 253–54
    real-world measurements and, 250–53
    setting up, 1027–31
PageScale property, 174, 258, 261, 262, 264, 265–66,
        267, 268, 274, 275, 370, 503
PageSettings class, 993, 1002–5, 1015
PageSettings object, 1002, 1003, 1004, 1005, 1014
PageSettings property, 993, 1008–9, 1028
PageSetupDialog class, 1027–31
PageUnit property, 174, 258, 260, 261, 262, 264, 265–66,
        267, 268, 270, 273, 275, 369, 370, 382, 493, 503,
        1009, 1122
Paint event, 67, 69, 72, 73, 79, 143, 145, 148, 162, 168,
        314–15, 552, 556, 750, 899, 1045
    cautions for use, 71
    handling, 62–65
paint programs, 470
PaintEventArgs class, 62–63, 64, 69, 153, 154, 162
PaintEventArgs object, 76
PaintEventHandler delegate, 62–63, 79
PaintEvent.vb program, 64–65
PaintHello.vb program, 70
PaintTwoForms.vb program, 71–72
Palette property, 486
palettes, optimized, 472
PanEast property, 326
Panel control, 331, 600, 952, 955–57, 974, 986, 991,
        1042, 1043, 1068, 1071
    scrolling, 141–45
PanelOnPaint method, 143, 144, 986, 991, 1159
Panels property, 957, 958, 959
PanNE property, 326
PanNorth property, 326
PanNW property, 326
PanSE property, 326

PanSouth property, 326
PanSW property, 326
PanWest property, 326
PaperKind enumeration, 999
PaperName property, 998–99
PaperSize property, 1003, 1005
PaperSizes property, 997, 998
PaperSource property, 1003, 1005
PaperSourceKind enumeration, 998
PaperSources property, 997, 998
ParamArray keyword, 1242
parametric equations, curves and, 182–85
PARC (Xerox Palo Alto Research Center), 296
Parent property, 461, 537, 538, 567, 568, 664, 951, 959,
        973, 1051, 1063, 1206
parents of controls, 301
Parse method, 767–68
parsing file and path names, 1202–4
PartialImageRotate.vb program, 501–2
PartialImageStretch.vb program, 499–501
PartialImage.vb program, 498–99
PartialPush property, 983
Pascal casing, 39
PasswordChar property, 875
Paste method, 860
path and clipping programs
    ClippingCombinations.vb, 715–16
    Clover.vb, 713–14
    Flower.vb, 698–700
    KeyholeBitmap.vb, 719–21
    KeyholeClipCentered.vb, 718–19
    KeyholeClip.vb, 717–18
    LineArcCombo.vb, 685–87
    LineArcPath.vb, 688–91
    PathWarping.vb, 709–12
    ScribbleWithPath.vb, 700–701
    WidenPath.vb, 705–8
    WidePolyline.vb, 687–88
Path class, 1203
path gradient brushes, 810–14
    tiling, 814–22
PathData class, 692
PathData property, 692
PathGradientBrush class, 781, 782, 810, 811
PathGradientBrush object, 813, 814, 821
PathPoints property, 692, 702, 946
PathPointType enumeration, 693, 694
paths. *See also* clipping
    clipping with, 712–17
    creating, 694–98
    defined, 685, 691
    definitions, 691
    figures (subpaths), 691

paths, *continued*
  introduced, 193, 685–91
  metafiles vs., 1096
  other modifications, 705–12
  overview, 691–93
  rendering, 698–701
  text and, 930–44
  transforms, 702–4
PathSeparator property, 1064–65
PathTypes property, 692, 693
PathWarping.vb program, 709–12
Peek method, 1195
PeekChar method, 1199
Pen class, 107, 781, 782
Pen object, 107, 163–64
pen programs. *See also* brush programs
  GradientPen.vb, 823–24
  LineCaps.vb, 835–36
  LineJoins.vb, 830–32
  PenDashCaps.vb, 832–34
  PenDashStyles.vb, 827–29
  PenWidths.vb, 263–64
PenAlignment enumeration, 825
PenDashCaps.vb program, 832–34
PenDashStyles.vb program, 827–29
pens. *See also* brushes
  caps (ends) and, 829–36
  dashed, 826–29
  introduced, 107–8, 163–64, 781–82, 822–26
  joins and, 829–36
  Pens.Black, 170
  widths, 263–66
Pens class, 163
Pens.Black, 170
PenType enumeration, 826
PenType property, 825
PenWidths.vb program, 263–64
PerformClick method, 734
Perspective warp, 712
photo programs, 470
PhysicalDimension property, 483, 1098–99, 1119
PhysicalSize property, 1032–33
PI constant, 1224
PictureBox class, 531–34
PictureBox control, 531–34, 740, 741
PictureBoxPlus class, 1075
PictureBoxPlusDemo.vb program, 534
PictureBoxPlus.vb program, 533–34
PictureBoxSizeMode enumeration, 532–33
PieChart.vb program, 194–95
pies, 193–97
  filled, 198–99
PixelFormat enumeration, 484–85

PixelFormat property, 484, 486, 502–3
PixelOffsetMode enumeration, 176–77
PixelOffsetMode property, 174–75, 176, 177, 394
pixels
  printing and, 254–56
  real-world measurements and, 250–53
  square, 250
player keys, 218
PlayRecord method, 1127–28
PlayRecordCallback method, 1127
plotter (stroke, vector) fonts, 351, 352
Png (Portable Network Graphics) property, 474, 476
PoePoem.vb program, 304–7
point conversions, 103–4
Point object, 347
point size (em size, height) of fonts, 352, 354–55, 364–69, 381–82, 383
Point structure, 87–89, 90–91, 262, 272, 347, 349, 618, 635, 688
  arrays of, 89–90, 455
PointCount property, 692
pointer, 297
PointF object, 403, 405, 406
PointF structure, 91–93, 122, 393, 635, 708, 937–38
POINTL structure, 1131
Points property, 692
POINTS structure, 1131
PointsToPageUnits method, 932
PointToClient method, 104, 323
PointToScreen method, 104
PolyEllipse.vb program, 183–84
polygons, 188
  filled, 200–204
Polyline function, 1123
polylines (multiple connected lines), 177–81
Popup event, 655, 666, 668, 671, 860, 963, 982, 1139
pop-up menus, 642
Portable Network Graphics (Png) property, 474, 476
Position property, 241, 326–27, 338, 615, 1182
PositionCaret method, 245, 344
Pow method, 1227–28
powers and logarithms, 1227–28
PreferredHeight property, 576, 886
PreferredWidth property, 576
presentation area, 127
PreviewPageInfo class, 1032
PreviewPrintController class, 1019–20
PreviewPrintController object, 1032
PrevNode property, 1063
PrevVisibleNode property, 1063
PrimaryMonitorMaximizedWindowSize property, 151
PrimaryMonitorSize property, 151
Print method, 168, 1007–8, 1022, 1032

print preview, 1031–38
PRINT statement, 2
printable area, 169, 1015
PrintableForm class, 178, 258, 361, 479, 909–10
PrintableForm.vb program, 172–73
PrintableTenCentimeterRuler.vb program, 260–61
PrintController class, 1018–22
PrintController property, 1006, 1018, 1019, 1022, 1032
PrintControllerWithStatusDialog class, 1019, 1020
PrintDialog object, 1025, 1037
PrintDialogBox class, 1023–27
PrintDocument class, 1006–8, 1018–20, 1022
PrintDocument event, 1007, 1008–14
PrintDocument object, 167, 168, 169, 1005, 1006, 1013–
     14, 1032, 1033
PrintDocumentOnPrintPage method, 168–69, 171, 173
PrinterName property, 994–95, 996, 1011, 1013
PrinterResolution property, 1003, 1005, 1009, 1013
PrinterResolutionKind enumeration, 999–1000
PrinterResolutions collection, 1005
PrinterResolutions property, 997, 999, 1000
PrinterSelectionDialog object, 1013
PrinterSelectionDialog.vb program, 1009–11
PrinterSettings class, 163, 993, 994–1002
PrinterSettings object, 994, 995, 996, 1003, 1005, 1122
PrinterSettings property, 993, 1003, 1006, 1013, 1023,
     1028
PrinterUnit enumeration, 1018
PrintEventArgs class, 1008
printing
     Color.Black, 170
     defining documents, 1006–8
     handling PrintDocument events, 1008–14
     introduced, 167–73, 993
     page dimensions, 1014–18
     PageSettings class, 993, 1002–5
     pixels and, 254–56
     print preview, 1031–38
     PrintController class, 1018–22
     PrintDialogBox class, 1023–27
     PrinterSettings class, 163, 993, 994–1002
     setting up pages, 1027–31
printing programs
     ImagePrint.vb, 1028–31
     NotepadCloneWithPrinting.vb, 1033–38
     PrinterSelectionDialog.vb, 1009–11
     PrintThreePages.vb, 1011–14
     PrintWithMargins.vb, 1016–18
     PrintWithStatusBar.vb, 1021–22
     SimplePrintDialog.vb, 1025–27
     StatusBarPrintController.vb, 1020–21
PrintPage event, 162, 168, 1007, 1011, 1013–14, 1015,
     1031, 1032, 1038

PrintPageEventArgs class, 169, 1008
PrintPageEventArgs object, 162, 1015, 1016
PrintPageEventHandler delegate, 168
PrintPreviewControl property, 1033
PrintPreviewDialog object, 1033
PrintRange enumeration, 1024
PrintRange property, 1001, 1024, 1025
PrintThreePages.vb program, 1011–14
PrintToFile property, 1001, 1023, 1024
PrintWithMargins.vb program, 1016–18
PrintWithStatusBar.vb program, 1021–22
Private keyword, 20, 26, 37
PrivateFontCollection class, 391, 392
ProgramWithIcon.vb program, 518–19
projects, 4–5
properties
     AutoScroll, 954–57
     Brushes, shared, 108
     ButtonBase, 547, 548, 549–50
     Caret, 241
     CheckBox, 569–70, 572, 573
     Color, shared, 106
     ColorDialog, 759, 761
     ColorPalette, 486
     ColumnClickEventArgs, 1087
     ColumnHeader, 1081
     ComboBox, 891, 892
     Control, 54, 55, 66–67, 98, 99, 103, 237, 312, 331, 356,
          557–58, 564, 577–78, 579, 644, 1170
          shared, 221, 323–24, 356
     Control.ControlCollection, 565
     Cursor, shared, 326–27
     Cursors, shared read-only, 326
     DateTime, 430–31, 436–37
          shared, 431–32
     DateTimeFormatInfoshared, 443–44
     DaylightTime, 436
     defined, 27
     DirectoryInfo, 1206–7, 1208
     DragEventArgs, 1171
     DrawItemEventArgs, 675–76
     Encoding, shared, 1190–92
     Environment, shared, 1202
     FileDialog, 771, 774, 777
     FileInfo, 1212–13
     Font, 371–78
     FontCollection, 391
     FontDialog, 757–58, 759
     FontFamily
          nonshared, 379
          shared, 380, 385
     Form, 98–99, 582, 643, 729, 733, 735, 753, 847
          shared, 206–7

properties, *continued*
Format, 1164
forms, 58–60
getting, 27–30
Graphics, 174–75, 253, 258, 394–95, 396, 722–23, 794
GraphicsPath, 692
HatchBrush, 784
IButtonControl, 731
Icon, 520
Image, 482, 483, 484, 486, 1098–99
ImageFormat
instance, 487
shared, 474–76
ImageList, 528
ImageList.ImageCollection, 530
KeyEventArgs, 210, 219–20
KeyPressEventArgs, 225
Label, 576–77
LinearGradientBrush, 807, 809
ListBox, 885, 886–87
ListView, 1075, 1086, 1087
ListView.ColumnHeaderCollection, 1080
ListViewItem, 1082, 1088
ListViewItem.ListViewSubItem, 1083
ListViewItem.ListViewSubItemCollection, 1082
ListView.ListViewItemCollection, 1081
ListView.SelectedIndexCollection, 1088
ListView.SelectedListViewItemCollection, 1088
Margins, 1004
Matrix, 287
MeasureItemEventArgs, 675
Menu, 663, 664
MenuItem, 653–55, 656, 664, 674–75
Menu.MenuItemCollection, 664
Message, 318
MetafileHeader, 1100, 1101–2
mouse, 323–24
MouseEventArgs, 302
NumericUpDown, 898
OpenFileDialog, 768, 772
PageSettings, 1003–4
PageSetupDialog, 1028
PaintEventArgs, 63–64
PaperSize, 998–99
PaperSource, 998
PathData, 692
PathGradientBrush, 811, 814–15
Pen, 164, 824, 825, 826, 829–30, 832, 836
Pens, shared, 107
PictureBox, 531
Point, 88
PreviewPageInfo, 1032–33
PreviewPrintController, 1032
PrintDialog, 1023–24

PrintDocument, 1006–7
PrinterResolution, 999
PrinterSettings, 994–1002, 1024
shared, 995
PrinterSettings.StringCollection, 995
PrintEventArgs, 1008
PrintPageEventArgs, 1009
PrintPreviewDialog, 1033
QueryContinueDragEventArgs, 1175
QueryPageSettingsEventArgs, 1008–9
RadioButton, 592–93
Rectangle, 94–95
RichTextBox, 876
SaveFileDialog, 776
ScrollableControl, 145–46
ScrollBar, 597
ScrollEventArgs, 598
setting, 27–30
Size, 90
SolidBrush, 782
Splitter, 1051–52
SplitterEventArgs, 1053
state and, 173–74
StatusBar, 953–54, 957
StatusBarPanel, 959–63
Stream, 1182
StreamReader, 1194–95
StreamWriter, 1192–93
String, 1238
StringFormat, 117, 399, 403, 408–10, 412–17, 423
shared, 400
SystemBrushes, shared, 111
SystemColors, shared, 109–10
SystemInformation. *See* system information
SystemPens, shared, 110
TextBox, 843, 844, 875
TextBoxBase, 838, 841, 851, 861
TextureBrush, 799
Timer, 427
TimeSpan, 438
TimeZone, 435
shared, 434
ToolBar, 971, 974–75, 987
ToolBarButton, 971, 977, 978, 982, 983
ToolBarButtonClickEventArgs, 978
ToolTextTip, 963
ToolTip, 877–78
TrackBar, 604, 605–6
TreeNode, 1055, 1060, 1063–65
TreeNodeCollection, 1055
TreeView, 1056, 1058, 1059, 1064
TreeViewCancelEventArgs, 1061
TreeViewEventArgs, 1062

PropertiesAndExceptions.vb program, 28–30
PropertyInfo object, 158
Protected keyword, 20, 37, 76
Protected Overridable methods, 617
Public keyword, 20, 26, 37, 76
push buttons. *See* Button control
Pushed property, 983
PUZZLE program, 463
puzzle programs
    JeuDeTaquinTile.vb, 463–64
    JeuDeTaquin.vb, 465–68
    JeuDeTaquinWithScramble.vb, 651

**Q**

QueryContinueDrag event, 1174–75
QueryPageSettings event, 1007, 1011, 1013–14
QueryPageSettingsEventArgs class, 1008, 1014

**R**

r (reference) compiler switch, 45
r prefix, 40
radio checks, 656
RadioButton class, 592, 593
RadioButton control, 592–95
RadioButtonOnCheckedChanged method, 595
RadioButtons.vb program, 593–95
RadioCheck property, 656, 658, 661
RaiseEvent statement, 749
RandomClearResizeRedraw.vb program, 115–16
RandomClear.vb program, 114
Randomize method, 465
RandomRectangle.vb program, 429
raster (bitmap) fonts, 351, 352
raster graphics, 161, 469–70. *See also* bitmaps; images
RawFormat property, 486
Read method, 44, 60, 71, 1182, 1183, 1184, 1186, 1195,
    1199–1200
ReadBoolean method, 1198
ReadByte method, 1182, 1183, 1198
ReadBytes method, 1198
ReadChar method, 1198
ReadChars method, 1198
ReadDecimal method, 1198
ReadDouble method, 1198
ReadInt16 method, 1198
ReadInt32 method, 1198
ReadInt64 method, 1198
ReadLine method, 44, 60, 71, 1195
ReadOnly property, 875
ReadOnlyChecked property, 772
ReadSingle method, 1198

ReadToEnd method, 1195
RECT structure, 231–32
Rectangle object, 347, 1015
Rectangle property, 807, 814–15
Rectangle structure, 93–97, 393, 398, 498, 681
RectangleF object, 403, 414
RectangleF structure, 94, 123, 498, 708, 934–35, 937–38
RectangleLinearGradientBrush.vb program, 805–6
rectangles
    drawing, 185–87
    filled, 197–98
    text in, 122–25
RectangleToClient method, 104
RectangleToScreen method, 104
RECTL structure, 1131
RECTS structure, 1131
recursive functions, 1068
ReDim statement, 14
reference (r) compiler switch, 45
reference types, 38, 86
ReflectedText.vb program, 920–21
reflection, 155–60
Refresh method, 1207, 1214
RefreshTree method, 1067, 1068, 1070
Region object, 722
regions
    clipping and, 685, 721–23
    defined, 685, 691
registry, 763–68, 847–51
Registry class, 764
RegistryKey class, 764
ReleaseHdc method, 1109
Remove method, 530, 566, 665, 871, 1234, 1251
RemoveAll method, 877
RemoveAt method, 566, 665
RemoveHandler statement, 63
rendering origin, 792–95
RenderingOrigin property, 794, 799
repainting colors, 113–16
Replace method, 1251
ReplaceDialog class, 861, 866
ResetBackColor method, 547
ResetClip method, 717
ResetFont method, 356, 547
ResetForeColor method, 547
ResetTransform method, 281, 287, 800, 807, 824
ReshowDelay property, 878
Resize event, 101, 986, 1045
ResizeRedraw control, 459
ResizeRedraw property, 115, 116, 986
resolution
    dots per inch, 253–54
    video, 251

resources, 517–21
Restore method, 267, 268, 270, 557
RestoreDirectory property, 771
Result property, 318
RFC 1123 format, 446
Rich Text Format (RTF), 876
RichTextBox class, 838, 876
RichTextBox control, 238, 394, 838, 876
RichTextBoxScrollBars enumeration, 843–44
RichTextPaste.vb program, 1153–55
Right property, 95, 98, 1004
right-to-left problems, 246–47
RLE (run-length encoding), 473, 474
roman (serif) fonts, 354
Roosevelt, Alice, 105
Root property, 1206
Rotate method, 703, 704
RotateAndReflect.vb program, 922–23
RotateAt method, 704
RotatedFont.vb program, 919–20
RotatedRectangles.vb program, 292–93
RotateFlip enumeration, 510
RotateFlip method, 508, 510, 523
RotateTransform method, 278, 281, 284, 287, 293, 460,
    699, 703, 800, 807, 824, 825, 922
rotating images and bitmaps, 495–97
Round method, 1225–26
RoundedRectangle method, 193
RoundRect function, 192
RoundRect.vb program, 192–93
RTF (Rich Text Format), 876
Rtf property, 876
ruler programs
    PrintableTenCentimeterRuler.vb, 260–61
    SixInchRuler.vb, 264–66
    TenCentimeterRulerAuto.vb, 261–62
    TenCentimeterRuler.vb, 256–58
Run method, 55, 56, 57, 58, 60, 61, 75
RunFormBadly.vb program, 55–56
RunFormBetter.vb program, 56–57
run-length encoding (RLE), 473, 474

## S

s prefix, 40
SampleClass class, 1199–1200
sans serif fonts, 354
Save method, 267–68, 270, 507–8, 557, 778
SaveFileDialog object, 778, 779
SaveRegistryInfo method, 850, 859, 874
Scalable Vector Graphics (SVG), 470
Scale method, 584–87, 703
ScaleCore method, 584

ScaleImageIsotropically method, 493, 501, 534, 1031
ScaleTransform method, 279–80, 281, 282, 284, 287,
    288, 377, 800, 807, 824, 825, 921, 922, 936
screen area, 251
screen coordinates, 103
Scribble.vb program, 345–46
ScribbleWithBitmap.vb program, 513–17
ScribbleWithPath.vb program, 700–701
ScribbleWithSave.vb program, 347–49
scribbling with the mouse, 345–49
scroll bars
    introduced, 140–41
    scroll box (thumb), 140
    ScrollableControl class, 145–46
    scrolling panel controls, 141–45
    scrolling without controls, 146–49
scroll box (thumb), 140
Scroll event, 145, 597–98, 599–600, 606
Scrollable property, 1058
ScrollableControl class, 53, 145–46, 596
ScrollAlwaysVisible property, 886
ScrollBar class, 596–97
ScrollBar control, 140, 596–604
ScrollBar property, 110, 111
ScrollBars enumeration, 843
ScrollBars property, 843
ScrollEventArgs events, 599–600
ScrollEventArgs object, 598, 599
ScrollEventType enumeration, 598–99
ScrollLines method, 232
ScrollOnValueChanged method, 603, 604, 753
ScrollWindow function, 231–32
ScrollWindow method, 230–31
SDKs, .NET Framework, 3
searching, array, 1252–55
searching strings, 1247–49
Second property, 431, 460
Seconds property, 438
Seek method, 1183, 1198
SeekOrigin enumeration, 1183
segments of curves, 631
Select event, 655, 967
Select method, 842
SelectAll method, 842
Selected property, 1088
SelectedImageIndex property, 1059, 1060
SelectedIndex property, 886, 887, 888, 890, 892
SelectedIndexChanged event, 889, 890, 892–93, 1087
SelectedIndexCollection class, 888
SelectedIndices property, 887, 888, 1087, 1088
SelectedItem property, 886, 887, 888, 892
SelectedItems property, 887, 888, 1087, 1088
SelectedNode property, 1064

SelectedObjectCollection class, 888
SelectedRtf property, 876
SelectedText, 841
SelectedValueChanged event, 889
selection (block of text), 840
SelectionChangeCommitted property, 892–93
SelectionChanged event, 842, 982
SelectionLength property, 841, 842, 861
SelectionMode enumeration, 887
SelectionMode property, 886, 887
SelectionStart property, 841, 842
SendToBack method, 569, 1041
serial polling, 60
serif (roman) fonts, 354
Set accessors, 28, 744
SetAttributes method, 1213
SetBlendTriangularShape method, 807
SetChildIndex method, 567, 568, 1041
SetClip method, 712–13, 714, 715, 717, 722
SetCreationTime method, 1208, 1213
SetCurrentDirectory method, 1206
SetData method, 1165–66
SetDataObject method, 1134–36, 1139, 1144, 1147, 1164, 1165
SetLastAccessTime method, 1208, 1213
SetLastWriteTime method, 1208, 1213
SetLength method, 1183
SetMarkers method, 697
SetMonth method, 26–27, 28
SetPixel method, 513
SetResolution method, 512
SetSelected method, 888
SetSigmaBellShape method, 807
SetTabStops method, 418–20
setting properties, 27–30
SetToolTip method, 877
SetValue method, 764–65, 767, 768
SetWindowPlacement function, 846
SevenSegmentClock.vb program, 455–56
SevenSegmentDisplay class, 452, 454
SevenSegmentDisplay object, 455
SevenSegmentDisplay.vb program, 452–55
shadow bitmaps, 514–17
Shadows modifier, 37, 80
shared methods, 21–23, 77
Shared modifier, 21–23, 77
SharingMethods.vb program, 21–23
Shear method, 704, 923, 924, 925
shearing and matrixes, 289–91
shearing images and bitmaps, 495–97
shearing text, 923–30
shift keys, 208, 215
Shift property, 210

Short type, 11, 13, 40, 1217–18
Shortcut enumeration, 645–47
shortcut (context) menus, 299, 642, 659–63
Shortcut property, 653, 670
Show method, 46–47, 53–54, 58, 71, 241, 327, 338, 661, 753, 754
ShowAlways property, 877–78
ShowApply property, 748, 758
ShowColor property, 758
show-count variable, 327
ShowDialog method, 728–29, 730, 746, 747, 753, 757, 761, 770, 774, 775, 1025, 1031, 1033
ShowEffects property, 758
ShowFiles method, 1091
ShowFormAndSleep.vb program, 54–55
ShowForm.vb program, 53
ShowHelp property, 758, 759, 1024, 1028
ShowImages method, 1074–75
ShowLines property, 1059
ShowNetwork property, 1024, 1028
ShowPanels property, 957–58
ShowPlusMinus property, 1059
ShowReadOnly property, 772
ShowRootLines property, 1059
ShowShortcut property, 653
ShowSounds property, 151
ShowToolTips property, 971, 973
siblings, 1056
SimpleButton class, 539, 540
SimpleButton object, 538
SimpleButton.vb program, 537–40
SimpleClock.vb program, 447–48
SimpleControl class, 540
SimpleDialog class, 728
SimpleDialogBox class, 728
SimpleDialog.vb program, 726–30
SimplePrintDialog.vb program, 1025–27
SimplerDialog.vb program, 733
SimpleShear.vb program, 923–25
SimpleStatusBar.vb program, 952–53
SimpleStatusBarWithPanel.vb program, 955–57
SimpleToolBar.vb program, 972–74
SimpleTreeView.vb program, 1056–58
Sin method, 949–50, 1230
SineCurve.vb program, 180–81
Single type, 12, 40, 1217–18, 1222–24
Sinh method, 1231
SixInchRuler.vb program, 264–66
Size object, 397–98
Size property, 94, 98, 241, 372, 482, 520, 542, 571, 572, 582, 583, 1098–99, 1119
Size structure, 90–91
SizeAll property, 326

SizeF structure, 91–93, 121, 397–98, 493

SizeInPoints property, 372, 382, 767

SizeMode property, 531, 532, 533, 741

SizeNESW property, 326

SizeNS property, 326

SizeNWSE property, 326

SizeWE property, 326

SizingGrip property, 953–54

Sleep method, 54, 1022

SmallChange property, 597, 605

SmallImageList property, 1079, 1081, 1090

SmoothingMode enumeration, 176

SmoothingMode property, 174–75, 176, 394

Software Development Kits. *See* SDKs, .NET Framework

solid brushes, 782, 914–18

SolidBrush class, 781, 782

SolidBrush object, 108, 823

SolidColorOnly property, 759

solutions, 4–5

Sort method, 158, 1253–54

Sorted property, 885–86, 1058

sorting arrays, 1252–55

SourceName property, 998

SpecialFolder enumeration, 50

spin buttons, 897–908

Spiral.vb program, 184–85

spline programs

    BézierArt.vb, 624–26

    BézierCircles.vb, 623–24

    BézierClockControl.vb, 617–18

    BézierClock.vb, 618–19

    BézierManual.vb, 629–30

    Bézier.vb, 614–16

    CanonicalSplineManual.vb, 639–40

    CanonicalSpline.vb, 631–34

    ClosedCurveFillModes.vb, 636–38

    Infinity.vb, 620–21

splines

    Bézier

        arcs with, 621–24

        art, 624–26

        circles with, 621–24

        in clipped text, 942–44

        clock programs, 617–19

        collinear, 619–21

        introduced, 611–12

        mathematical derivation, 626–30

        in practice, 612–16

    canonical

        introduced, 630–38

        mathematical derivation, 638–40

    defined, 611

    introduced, 611–12

Split method, 1252

SplitPosition property, 1051, 1052

Splitter class, 1040, 1051

splitter control

    examples, 1044–55

    introduced, 1039–44

splitter control programs

    OnePanelWithSplitter.vb, 1044–45

    SplitThreeAcross.vb, 1047–49

    SplitThreeFrames.vb, 1049–51

    SplitTwoProportional.vb, 1053–55

    TwoPanelsWithSplitter.vb, 1045–47

SplitterMoved event, 1053

SplitterMoving event, 1053

SplitterOnMoving event, 1055

SplitThreeAcross.vb program, 1047–49

SplitThreeFrames.vb program, 1049–51

SplitTwoProportional.vb program, 1053–55

SplitX property, 1053

SplitY property, 1053

Sqrt method, 1227–28

square pixels, 250

SquareTile.vb program, 818–19

standard splines. *See* canonical splines

StandardMenu.vb program, 671–74

StandardName property, 435

StandardPrintController class, 1019, 1020, 1021

StarGradientBrush.vb program, 812–13

Start method, 427–28, 741, 1091

Start property, 436

StartCap property, 829, 833, 836

StartFigure method, 695, 701

StartPosition property, 60, 735, 738

StartsWith method, 1244

state, properties and, 173–74

state machines, 61

State property, 676

stateless graphics programming environment, 66, 174

status bar programs. *See also* toolbar programs

    DateAndTimeStatus.vb, 962–63

    MenuHelpFirstTry.vb, 964–67

    MenuHelpSubclass.vb, 969–70

    MenuItemHelp.vb, 967–68

    SimpleStatusBar.vb, 952–53

    SimpleStatusBarWithPanel.vb, 955–57

    StatusBarAndAutoScroll.vb, 954–55

    TwoStatusBarPanels.vb, 958–59

status bars. *See also* toolbars

    AutoScroll property and, 954–57

    basic, 952–54

    introduced, 951–52

    menu help, 963–70

    panels, 957–63

    StatusBarPanel properties, 959–63

StatusBar class, 951, 958

StatusBar object, 953
StatusBarAndAutoScroll.vb program, 954–55
StatusBarPanel class, 951, 959
StatusBarPanel object, 957–58, 959, 960, 966
StatusBarPanelAutoSize enumeration, 961
StatusBarPanelBorderStyle enumeration, 961
StatusBarPanelStyle enumeration, 960
StatusBarPrintController.vb program, 1020–21
Stop method, 427–28
str prefix, 40
straight lines, 165–66
Stream class, 477, 1187, 1188
Stream object, 477, 1097, 1187, 1188, 1197
StreamReader class, 1188, 1189
streams. *See* files and streams
StreamWriter class, 1188, 1189, 1257
StreamWriter object, 1168, 1189–90
StreamWriterDemo.vb program, 1193
Strikeout property, 371
String class, 1233, 1239
String object, 1136, 1137, 1139, 1140, 1145, 1146, 1151,
    1152, 1155, 1159, 1233, 1255, 1256
string programs. *See also* text programs
  StringAppend.vb, 1255–56
  StringBuilderAppend.vb, 1256–57
  StringWriterAppend.vb, 1257–58
String type, 13–14, 40
StringAlignment enumeration, 117, 403
StringAlignmentPoint.vb program, 405–8
StringAlignmentRectangle.vb program, 404–5
StringAppend.vb program, 1255–56
StringBuilder class, 884, 1255–58
StringBuilderAppend.vb program, 1256–57
StringCollection class, 995
StringFormat class, 403, 412, 417–18
StringFormat object, 116–20, 246, 398–400, 401, 417,
    451, 680, 681, 920, 931, 1038
StringFormatFlags enumeration, 398–99, 415
StringFormat.GenericTypographic property, 246
StringReader class, 1188
strings. *See also* text
  array sorting and searching, 1252–55
  Char type, 1235–37
  comparing, 1243–47
  concatenating, 10, 1241–43
  constructors and properties, 1237–39
  converting, 1241
  copying, 1239–41
  formatting, 9–11, 1252
  immutable, 1233
  introduced, 1233–35
  manipulating, 1251–52
  measuring, 120–22

padding, 1251
searching, 1247–49
StringBuilder class, 1255–58
trimming, 1249–51
white space in, 1249–51
StringTrimming enumeration, 412–17
StringWriter class, 1188, 1257
StringWriter object, 1169, 1257
StringWriterAppend.vb program, 1257–58
stroke (plotter, vector) fonts, 351, 352
StrokePath method, 690
StructLayoutAttribute class, 232
structured exception handling. *See* exception handling
structures
  CalendarDate, 16, 17, 18, 19
  classes vs., 86–87
  Color, 59, 65, 104–6
  DateTime, 430–32, 434
  DEVMODE, 1002
  DEVNAMES, 1002
  EMR, 1131
  Int32, 39
  introduced, 38, 85
  MenuItem, 658, 659
  Point, 87–89, 90–91, 262, 272, 347, 349, 618, 635, 688
    arrays of, 89–90, 455
  PointF, 91–93, 122, 393, 635, 708, 937–38
  POINTL, 1131
  POINTS, 1131
  RECT, 231–32
  Rectangle, 93–97, 393, 398, 498, 681
  RectangleF, 94, 123, 498, 708, 934–35, 937–38
  RECTL, 1131
  RECTS, 1131
  Size, 90–91
  SizeF, 91–93, 121, 397–98, 493
  WINDOWPLACEMENT, 846
Style property, 371, 767, 960, 983, 986
Sub keyword, 6
SubItems property, 1082
submenus (child menus), 642
subpaths (figures), 691
SubString method, 423
Substring methods, 680, 1240–41
SuperString class, 7–8
SupportsColor property, 996
SurroundColors property, 811
SVG (Scalable Vector Graphics), 470
symbols keys, 217
SysInfoColumns.vb program, 132–33
SysInfoEfficient.vb program, 154–55
SysInfoFirstTry.vb program, 129–31
SysInfoKeyboard.vb program, 223–24

SysInfoList class, 144
SysInfoList.vb program, 138–40
SysInfoListView.vb program, 1083–85
SysInfoPanel.vb program, 141–45
SysInfoReflection class, 223
SysInfoReflectionStrings class, 1083–84
SysInfoReflectionStrings.vb program, 156–58
SysInfoReflection.vb program, 158–60
SysInfoScroll.vb program, 147–49
SysInfoStrings class, 137, 153, 155–60
SysInfoStrings.vb program, 134–37
SysInfoUpdate.vb program, 151–53
system colors, 108–11, 112–13
system information
    client area size, 149–53
    clipping region updating, 153–55
    formatting into columns, 131–33
    introduced, 127–28
    listing, 137–40
    objects for displaying text strings, 133–37
    reflection and, 155–60
    scroll bars and
        introduced, 140–41
        scroll box (thumb), 140
        ScrollableControl class, 145–46
        scrolling panel controls, 141–45
        scrolling without controls, 146–49
    shared properties, 298–99, 300
    spacing lines of text, 128–29
system information programs
    SysInfoColumns.vb, 132–33
    SysInfoEfficient.vb, 154–55
    SysInfoFirstTry.vb, 129–31
    SysInfoKeyboard.vb, 223–24
    SysInfoList.vb, 138–40
    SysInfoListView.vb, 1083–85
    SysInfoPanel.vb, 141–45
    SysInfoReflectionStrings.vb, 156–58
    SysInfoReflection.vb, 158–60
    SysInfoScroll.vb, 147–49
    SysInfoStrings.vb, 134–37
    SysInfoUpdate.vb, 151–53
system modal dialog boxes, 725
System namespace, 7, 9, 24, 37, 39, 50, 181, 430, 434, 435, 1224
SystemBrushes class, 111
System.Collections namespace, 346–47
System.ComponentModel namespace, 1008
System.Diagnostics namespace, 741
SystemDirectory property, 1202
System.Drawing namespace, 59, 66, 67, 86, 105, 357, 471, 547, 782, 884, 1097

System.Drawing.Drawing2D namespace, 176, 201, 270, 280, 286, 636, 689, 692, 693, 702, 782, 783, 884
System.Drawing.Imaging namespace, 474, 484, 1097, 1116, 1122
System.Drawing.Printing namespace, 167, 993, 994
System.Drawing.Text namespace, 391, 408
SystemEvents class, 151, 513
System.Globalization namespace, 436, 439, 443
SystemInformation class, 127–28, 155, 1084
SystemInformation property, 1253
SystemInformationMinimumWindowSize property, 275
System.IO class, 15, 1188
System.IO namespace, 15, 477, 1152, 1179, 1203, 1257
SystemPens class, 110, 164
System.Runtime.InteropServices namespace, 232
SystemsColors class, 109–10
System.Text namespace, 1189, 1256
System.Threading namespace, 54
System.Windows.Forms namespace, 46, 52, 55, 62–63, 127, 325, 326, 425, 548, 553, 642, 993, 1023, 1134

# T

t (target) compiler switch, 43–44
tab order of controls, 577–78
tab stops, 417–23
TabIndex property, 577–78, 741
TabStop property, 577–78, 603, 605, 954
Tag Image File Format (Tiff) property, 474, 476
Tag property, 579, 586, 978, 979, 981, 986, 1063, 1082
TallInTheCenter.vb program, 946–48
Tan method, 1230
Tanh method, 1231
target (t) compiler switch, 43–44
target control, 1040, 1044
TenCentimeterRuler class, 258
TenCentimeterRulerAuto.vb program, 261–62
TenCentimeterRuler.vb program, 256–58
text. *See also* fonts; strings
    alignment, 403–8
    anti-aliased, 394–96
    brushes for, 911–18
    centering, 116–20
    clipping, 410–12
    device independence through, 249–50
    displaying, 66
    formatting into columns, 131–33
    grid fitting and text fitting, 400–403
    hit-testing, 343–44
    horizontal alignment, 403–8
    HotkeyPrefix property, 408–10
    MeasureString method and, 396–98
    objects for displaying text strings, 133–37

paths and, 930–44
reading and writing, 1188–96
in rectangles, 122–25
shearing, 923–30
spacing lines of, 128–29
StringFormat object and, 398–400
tab stops and, 417–23
trimming, 412–17
vertical alignment, 403–8
text fitting and grid fitting, 400–403
text programs. *See also* font programs; Notepad clone;
        string programs
AgeOfInnocence.vb, 420–21
AntiAliasedText.vb, 395–96
BaselineTilt.vb, 926–28
BoldAndItalicTighter.vb, 401–3
Bricks.vb, 911–13
ClipText.vb, 942–44
CloseInFive.vb, 428–29
DropShadow.vb, 914–15
DropShadowWithPath.vb, 938–39
EmbossedText.vb, 915–17
EnumerateEnumerationCombo.vb, 893–97
EnumerateEnumeration.vb, 879–84
FullFit.vb, 936–38
GradientText.vb, 913–14
HuckleberryFinnHalfHeight.vb, 410–12
RandomRectangle.vb, 429
ReflectedText.vb, 920–21
RotateAndReflect.vb, 922–23
SimpleShear.vb, 923–25
StringAlignmentPoint.vb, 405–8
StringAlignmentRectangle.vb, 404–5
TallInTheCenter.vb, 946–48
TextBoxDemo.vb, 839–40
TextColumns.vb, 421–23
TiltedShadow.vb, 928–30
TrimmingTheText.vb, 413–17
UnderlinedText.vb, 409–10
WarpText.vb, 944–46
WrapText.vb, 948–50
Text property
    clipboard programs, 1135
    control programs, 538, 548, 550, 578, 603
    dialog box programs, 770
    font and text programs, 838, 888, 892
    menu programs, 653, 659, 680
    mouse programs, 333
    status bar and toolbar programs, 957–58, 959, 960, 977
    tree view and list view programs, 1063, 1081, 1082,
        1083
TextAlign property, 547, 572, 844, 975, 976, 977, 1081

TextBox class, 837–38
TextBox control
    introduced, 246
    multiline, 842–45
    Notepad clone
        Edit menu, 860–71
        file I/O, 851–59
        Format menu, 871–74
        introduced, 845–47
        registry access, 847–51
    RichTextBox control, 238, 394, 838, 876
    single-line, 837–42
    special-purpose, 875
TextBoxBase class, 837–38, 852, 860, 1133
TextBoxDemo.vb program, 839–40
TextBoxWithToolBar.vb program, 978–82
TextChanged event, 839
TextChanged property, 892–93
TextColumns.vb program, 421–23
TextLength property, 838
TextOnBaseline.vb program, 383–84
TextReader class, 1188
TextRenderingHint enumeration, 394–95, 396
TextRenderingHint property, 246, 394–95, 396
texture brushes, 795–800
TextureBrush class, 781, 782, 795, 799, 800, 908
TextureBrush object, 1112
TextureBrushDemo.vb program, 796–800
TextWriter class, 1188, 1257
ThousandsSeparator property, 898
Thread class, 54, 1022
ThreeState property, 573
throwing exceptions, 25–27
thumb (scroll box), 140
Thumbnail.vb program, 508–10
tick count, 436–39
Tick event, 426–27, 729, 982, 1075, 1155, 1158
TickFrequency property, 605, 606, 609
Ticks property, 436, 437, 438
TickStyle enumeration, 606
TickStyle property, 605, 606
Tiff (Tag Image File Format) property, 474, 476
TiltedShadow.vb program, 928–30
time. *See also* clock programs; clocks; timer
    calendars, 439–41
    DateTime structure, 430–32, 434
    local, 432–36
    readable renditions, 441–47
    tick count, 436–39
    universal, 432–36
time designators, 446
Time property, 459, 461, 462

TimeOfDay property, 432, 436
timer. *See also* time
  defined, 425
  introduced, 425–26
  one-shot, 428–29
Timer class, 425, 426–29
Timer event, 522
Timer object, 427, 729, 1074
TimerOnTick method, 462, 523, 527
Times New Roman fonts, 354, 381–83
TimeSerial function, 432
TimeSpan object, 435, 436, 437–39
TimeZone class, 434
TimeZone object, 435
title (caption) bar, 51
ToArgb method, 767
ToArray method, 349
ToCharArray method, 1240
Today property, 431–32, 434
toggle keys, 208
Toggle method, 1064
ToggleButtons.vb program, 984–87
ToLocalTime method, 434, 435
ToLongDateString method, 446
ToLongTimeString method, 446
ToolBar class, 951
ToolBar object, 981
toolbar programs. *See also* status bar programs
  DropDownMenuButton.vb, 988–91
  SimpleToolBar.vb, 972–74
  TextBoxWithToolBar.vb, 978–82
  ToggleButtons.vb, 984–87
ToolBarAppearance enumeration, 976
ToolBarButton class, 951, 978
ToolBarButton object, 970, 971, 973, 981, 982, 986, 987
ToolBarButtonCollection class, 971
ToolBarButtonStyle enumeration, 983
ToolBarOnClick method, 981, 982, 986
toolbars. *See also* status bars
  basic, 970–74
  events, 978–82
  introduced, 951–52
  styles, 983–91
  variations, 974–77
ToolBarTextAlign enumeration, 976
ToolTip class, 876, 877
ToolTip object, 877, 878
ToolTips, 876–84
ToolTipText property, 960, 971
Top property, 95, 98, 935, 1004
ToPage property, 1001, 1024

TopIndex property, 886
ToPoint method, 93
ToShortDateString method, 446
ToShortTimeString method, 446
ToSize method, 93
ToString method, 36, 37, 88, 89, 102, 131, 133, 442–47, 456, 603, 767, 861, 885, 1240
TotalDays property, 438
TotalHours property, 438
TotalMilliseconds property, 438
TotalMinutes property, 438
TotalSeconds property, 438
ToUniversalTime method, 434, 435
ToUpper method, 1233–34
TrackBar class, 605
TrackBar control, 604–9
tracking the mouse, 309–11, 312, 322
Transform method, 702, 707
transform programs
  MobyDick.vb, 276–80
  RotatedRectangles.vb, 292–93
Transform property, 174, 287, 702, 799, 800, 807, 824
TransformPoints method, 270, 271, 272
transforms
  combining, 291–93
  font, 919–30
    nonlinear, 944–50
  general linear transformation of the plane, 283
  identity, 284
  linear, 282–85, 708, 944
  matrix, 286
  nonlinear, 944–50
  page, 266–67
    limitations, 275–76
  path, 702–4
  world, 276–81
Transform.vb program, 899–901
Translate method, 702, 703
TranslateClip method, 718, 721
TranslateTransform method
  brush and pen programs, 800, 807, 824
  control programs, 557
  font and text programs, 919, 921, 922, 927, 929, 935, 936
  page-related programs, 279, 280, 281, 282, 284, 287, 288, 292, 293
  path and clipping programs, 702, 714
Transparent property, 105, 106, 107, 108, 546
TransparentColor property, 528
TreeNode class, 1055–59, 1060
TreeNode object, 1055, 1056, 1057–58, 1060, 1061, 1062
TreeNodeCollection class, 1055, 1056, 1057, 1060

TreeView class, 1055, 1056

TreeView control. *See also* ListView control

    DirectoryTree class, 1065–70

    displaying images, 1071–78

    events, 1060–62

    images in, 1059–60

    introduced, 1039

    node navigation, 1062–65

    TreeNode class, 1055–59

TreeView control programs. *See also* ListView control

    programs

    DirectoriesAndFiles.vb, 1068–70

    DirectoryTreeView.vb, 1065–67

    ImageDirectory.vb, 1074–78

    ImagePanel.vb, 1071–74

    SimpleTreeView.vb, 1056–58

TreeView property, 1063

TreeViewAction enumeration, 1061–62

TriangleGradientBrush.vb program, 810–12

TriangleTile.vb program, 815–18

trigonometric functions, 1228–31

Trim method, 1250–51

TrimEnd method, 1250–51

Trimming property, 412–17, 1038

trimming strings, 1249–51

trimming text, 412–17

TrimmingTheText.vb program, 413–17

TrimStart method, 1250–51

true-color (full-color) bitmaps, 473

TrueType fonts, 352, 353

Truncate method, 92, 93, 94

Try blocks, 24–25, 386–87

TryOneInchEllipse.vb program, 255–56

TwentyFourPointPrinterFonts.vb program, 367–69

TwentyFourPointScreenFonts.vb program, 365–67

TwoButtonsAnchor.vb program, 558–60

TwoButtonsDock.vb program, 562–64

TwoButtons.vb program, 543–46

TwoForms.vb program, 57–58

TwoPaintHandlers.vb program, 73–74

TwoPanelsWithSplitter.vb program, 1045–47

TwoPointLinearGradientBrush.vb program, 802–3

TwoStatusBarPanels.vb program, 958–59

TwoTriangleTile.vb program, 819–21

Type class, 884

Type object, 37, 884

Type property, 598, 1100

TypeAway class, 245

TypeAway.vb program, 242–46

typeface (face) name, 352

Types property, 692

typographical terminology, 352–54

**U**

Underline property, 371

UnderlinedText.vb program, 409–10

Undo method, 852, 860

Unicode

    em dash, 125

    encoding, 1190–92

    Hebrew alphabet, 246–47

    introduced, 236

    white space characters, 1250

Unicode property, 1190–92

UnicodeCategory enumeration, 1237

UnicodeEncoding object, 1191

Union method, 97

Unit property, 372

universal time, 432–36

Unlock method, 1186

UnlockBits method, 513

UpArrow property, 326

Update method, 102

UpdateAllInfo method, 153

up-down controls, 897–908

UpDownBase class, 897

UseAntiAlias property, 1032, 1033

UseMnemonic property, 577

UserControl class, 338, 459

user-preference colors, 109

UserPreferenceChanged event, 151

UTC (Coordinated Universal Time), 433

UtcNow property, 431–32, 434

UTF7 property, 1190–92

UTF8 property, 1190–92

**V**

Value property, 597, 598, 604, 605, 898

value types, 38, 86

ValueChanged event, 597–98, 599–600, 603, 604, 606, 753, 898–99

Values property, 137, 1083–84

vbc.exe compiler, 3

vector (plotter, stroke) fonts, 351, 352

vector graphics. *See also* metafiles; pens

    anti-aliasing, 174–77

    arcs, 190–93

    circles, parametric equations, 182

    curves and parametric equations, 182–85

    ellipses

        drawing, 188–90

        filled, 198

        parametric equations, 182–84

    fill mode, 201–4

    getting Graphics objects, 162–63

vector graphics, *continued*
  introduced, 161–62, 469–70
  multiple connected lines (polylines), 177–81
  off-by-1 errors and, 199–200
  PieChart.vb, 194–95
  pies, 193–97
    filled, 198–99
  polygons, 188
    filled, 200–204
  printing, introduced, 167–73
  properties and state, 173–74
  rectangles, 185–87
    filled, 197–98
  straight lines, 165–66
vector graphics programs
  AntiAlias.vb, 175–76
  BetterPieChart.vb, 196–97
  BoxingTheClient.vb, 178
  ClientEllipse.vb, 189–90
  DashedEllipse.vb, 191
  DrawHouse.vb, 179
  FillModesClassical.vb, 201–2
  FillModesOddity.vb, 203–4
  FourByFours.vb, 199–200
  HelloPrinter.vb, 170–71
  OutlineClientRectangle.vb, 187
  PolyEllipse.vb, 183–84
  PrintableForm.vb, 172–73
  RoundRect.vb, 192–93
  SineCurve.vb, 180–81
  Spiral.vb, 184–85
  XMarksTheSpot.vb, 166
Vector Markup Language (VML), 470
Version property, 1100
vertical alignment of text, 403–8
vertical (y-) shear, 290
VerticalResolution property, 483, 503, 512, 1098–99, 1119
VerticalScrollBarWidth property, 149
video resolution, 251
View enumeration, 1079
View property, 1079, 1085, 1093
VirtualScreen property, 151
Visibility property, 241
visible light, 104–5
Visible property, 54, 55, 301, 541, 647, 654, 982, 1075
VisibleClipBounds property, 169, 171, 173, 268, 270,
    273, 292, 490, 503, 722, 723, 1014, 1015, 1038
Visual Basic .NET, 2–6
VML (Vector Markup Language), 470
VScroll property, 145, 146
VScrollBar class, 596
VScrollBar control, 140, 596
VScrollBar object, 603
VSplit property, 326

**W**
WaitCursor object, 327
WaitCursor property, 326
Warp method, 708–9, 944, 945, 946
WarpMode enumeration, 709
WarpText.vb program, 944–46
WebRequest class, 481
WebResponse class, 481
Welch, Terry, 473
WhatSizeTransform.vb program, 271–72
WhatSize.vb program, 269–70
white space in strings, 1249–51
Widen method, 705, 707, 941
WidenPath.vb program, 705–8
WidePolyline.vb program, 687–88
Width property
  brush and pen programs, 824
  font and text programs, 397–98, 401
  form-related programs, 59, 90, 95, 98, 121
  image and bitmap programs, 482, 483, 510, 520
  metafile programs, 1098–99, 1119
  page-related programs, 273
  printing programs, 998–99
  status bar and toolbar programs, 959, 960, 961
  tree view and list view programs, 1051, 1052, 1081
  vector graphics programs, 164
WildCardHexDump.vb program, 1210–12
Win32 API, 231–33
Window property, 110, 111
WindowFrame property, 110
WINDOWPLACEMENT structure, 846
windows, child. *See* controls
Windows applications vs. console applications, 43–44
Windows Forms, 51, 521–22. *See also* forms
Windows Forms Designer
  auto-scale option and, 583–84
  manual coding vs., 541–42
Windows metafile format (Wmf) property, 474, 476
Windows registry, 763–68, 847–51
WindowState property, 847, 850
WindowText property, 110, 111
Wink class, 523
Wink.vb program, 522–23
With statement, 65
WM_CAPTURECHANGED message, 317, 319, 322
Wmf (Windows metafile format) property, 474, 476
WmfHeader property, 1100, 1101
WndProc method, 317–18, 319, 322
WordWrap property, 843
WorkingArea property, 151
world coordinates, 164, 281–82
world transform, 276–81
WParam property, 318

WrapMode enumeration, 796, 798
WrapMode property, 799, 803, 807, 814–15, 816, 817
Wrappable property, 974
WrapText.vb program, 948–50
Write method, 9, 10, 44, 71, 1183, 1193, 1198, 1199–1200, 1252, 1257
WriteByte method, 1182
WriteLine method, 7, 9, 10, 22, 24, 37, 44, 71, 442, 1193, 1252, 1257

**X**

x prefix, 40
X property, 88, 94, 302, 999, 1053, 1171
x- (horizontal) shear, 290
Xerox Palo Alto Research Center (PARC), 296
XMarksTheSpot.vb program, 166
XOR (exclusive-OR) drawing, 314–15, 521

**Y**

y prefix, 40
Y property, 88, 95, 302, 999, 1053, 1171
y- (vertical) shear, 290
Year property, 30, 431
Yellow property, 106, 107, 108
YellowGreen property, 106, 107, 108

**Z**

Z (Zulu) time, 446
Zif, Jacob, 473
z-order of controls, 567–69
Zulu (Z) time, 446

# Charles Petzold

Charles Petzold (*www.charlespetzold.com*) is a full-time freelance writer who has been programming for Microsoft Windows since 1985 and writing about Windows programming for nearly as long. He wrote the very first magazine article about Windows programming for the December 1986 issue of *Microsoft Systems Journal*. His book *Programming Windows* (first published by Microsoft Press in 1988 and currently in its fifth edition) taught a generation of programmers how to write applications for Windows. In May 1994, Petzold was one of only seven people (and the only writer) to be given a Windows Pioneer Award from *Windows Magazine* and Microsoft Corporation for his contribution to the success of Microsoft Windows. He is also the author of a unique introduction to the inner workings of computers entitled *Code: The Hidden Language of Computer Hardware and Software*. Petzold is currently researching a book on the historical origins of software.

## Squangle

As its name implies, a *squangle* combines the features of a rafter square and an angle-measuring bevel. Often made of lightweight anodized aluminum with rule and square measurement lines scribed on the front, a squangle usually has thumbscrews for adjusting and measuring angles from 45° thru 90°. Some squangles even offer a level vial built into the bevel piece. Carpenters, plumbers, boat builders, steel workers, and general do-it-yourselfers use squangles to do the work of many tools at once, thereby saving money in the process—just like programming with a flexible, general-purpose language such as Visual Basic .NET!

At Microsoft Press, we use tools to illustrate our books for software developers and IT professionals. Tools very simply and powerfully symbolize human inventiveness. They're a metaphor for people extending their capabilities, precision, and reach. From simple calipers and pliers to digital micrometers and lasers, these stylized illustrations give each book a visual identity, and a personality to the series. With tools and knowledge, there's no limit to creativity and innovation. Our tagline says it all: *the tools you need to put technology to work.*

The manuscript for this book was prepared and galleyed using Microsoft Word. Pages were composed by Microsoft Press using Adobe FrameMaker+SGML for Windows, with text in Garamond and display type in Helvetica Condensed. Composed pages were delivered to the printer as electronic prepress files.

| | |
|---|---|
| Cover Designer: | Methodologie, Inc. |
| Interior Graphic Designer: | James D. Kramer |
| Principle Compositor: | Paula Gorelick |
| Interior Artists: | Michael Kloepfer |
| Principal Copy Editor: | Rebecca McKay |
| Indexer: | Hugh C. Maddocks |

# Get the expert guidance you need to succeed in .NET Framework development with Visual Basic .NET!

**Applied Microsoft® .NET Framework
Programming in Microsoft Visual Basic® .NET**

| | |
|---|---|
| U.S.A. | **$49.99** |
| Canada | $72.99 |

ISBN: 0-7356-1787-2

The Microsoft .NET Framework provides powerful technologies such as ASP.NET Web Forms, XML Web services, and Windows® Forms to simplify developing applications and components that work seamlessly on the Internet. This book shows how to make the most of the .NET Framework's common language runtime (CLR). Written by two highly respected developer/ writers, it's intended for anyone who understands OOP concepts such as data abstraction, inheritance, and polymorphism. The book clearly explains the extensible type system of the CLR, examines how the CLR manages the behavior of types, and explores how an application manipulates types. While focusing on Visual Basic .NET, its in-depth explanations and concepts apply equally to all programming languages that target the .NET Framework.

microsoft.com/mspress

# Learn how to *turn data into solutions* with SQL Server 2000, Visual Basic .NET, and XML Web services.

**Programming Microsoft® SQL Server™
2000 with Microsoft Visual Basic® .NET**

**U.S.A.     $59.99**
Canada     $86.99
ISBN: 0-7356-1535-7

Discover the fastest ways to transform data into potent business solutions with this definitive guide for professional developers. You'll get complete details about the programmatic features of SQL Server 2000, the language enhancements in Visual Basic .NET, the development advances in the Microsoft Visual Studio® .NET integrated development environment, and the state-of-the-art technologies of the .NET Framework, including ADO.NET, ASP.NET, and XML Web services. You'll also get in-depth coverage of SQL Server programming topics, including details about using T-SQL, and tips on creating user-defined objects such as tables, views, and stored procedures. If you're looking for expert insights on how to build powerful, secure solutions with SQL Server 2000 and Visual Basic .NET, this is the book for you.

microsoft.com/mspress

# Real-world developer training for results on the job—
## and on the exam.

**MCAD/MCSD Self-Paced Training Kit:
Developing Windows®-Based Applications with
Microsoft® Visual Basic® .NET and Microsoft
Visual C#™ .NET**

**U.S.A.** **$69.99**
Canada $99.99
ISBN: 0-7356-1533-0

Build real-world programming skills—and prepare for **MCP Exams 70-306** and **70-316**—with this official Microsoft study guide. Work at your own pace through the lessons and hands-on exercises to learn how to build Windows-based applications using Visual Basic .NET and Visual C# .NET. Then extend your expertise through additional skill-building exercises. As you gain practical experience with essential Windows development tasks, you're also preparing for MCAD or MCSD certification. It even includes a 60-day evaluation version of Microsoft Visual Studio® .NET Professional Edition development software on DVD.

*Microsoft*®
microsoft.com/mspress

Get a **Free**
e-mail newsletter, updates,
special offers, links to related books,
and more when you
## register on line!

Register your Microsoft Press® title on our Web site and you'll get a FREE subscription to our e-mail newsletter, *Microsoft Press Book Connections*. You'll find out about newly released and upcoming books and learning tools, online events, software downloads, special offers and coupons for Microsoft Press customers, and information about major Microsoft® product releases. You can also read useful additional information about all the titles we publish, such as detailed book descriptions, tables of contents and indexes, sample chapters, links to related books and book series, author biographies, and reviews by other customers.

## Registration is easy. Just visit this Web page and fill in your information:

*http://www.microsoft.com/mspress/register*

**Microsoft**®

--------------------------------------------------------------

## Proof of Purchase

Use this page as proof of purchase if participating in a promotion or rebate offer on this title. Proof of purchase must be used in conjunction with other proof(s) of payment such as your dated sales receipt—see offer details.

*Programming Microsoft® Windows®
with Visual Basic® .NET*
0-7356-1799-6

**CUSTOMER NAME**

Microsoft Press, PO Box 97017, Redmond, WA 98073-9830